1 MONTH OF FREE READING

at
www.ForgottenBooks.com

By purchasing this book you are eligible for one month membership to ForgottenBooks.com, giving you unlimited access to our entire collection of over 1,000,000 titles via our web site and mobile apps.

To claim your free month visit:
www.forgottenbooks.com/free950174

* Offer is valid for 45 days from date of purchase. Terms and conditions apply.

ISBN 978-0-260-46682-2
PIBN 10950174

This book is a reproduction of an important historical work. Forgotten Books uses state-of-the-art technology to digitally reconstruct the work, preserving the original format whilst repairing imperfections present in the aged copy. In rare cases, an imperfection in the original, such as a blemish or missing page, may be replicated in our edition. We do, however, repair the vast majority of imperfections successfully; any imperfections that remain are intentionally left to preserve the state of such historical works.

Forgotten Books is a registered trademark of FB &c Ltd.
Copyright © 2018 FB &c Ltd.
FB &c Ltd, Dalton House, 60 Windsor Avenue, London, SW19 2RR.
Company number 08720141. Registered in England and Wales.

For support please visit www.forgottenbooks.com

ACTS AND RESOLVES

OF THE

SEVENTY-FIRST LEGISLATURE

OF THE

STATE OF MAINE

1903.

Published by the Secretary of State, agreeably to Resolves of June 28, 1820, February 18, 1840, and March 16, 1842.

AUGUSTA
KENNEBEC JOURNAL PRINT
1903

STAMFORD LIBRARY
L 5870

CONTENTS OF PUBLIC LAWS.

SESSION OF 1903.

CHAP.		PAGE
1	An Act to amend Chapter one hundred and forty-three of the Revised Statutes, relating to Insane Persons..............	5
2	An Act to amend Section twenty-eight of Chapter seventy-three of the Revised Statutes, relating to Conveyances....	5
3	An Act to amend Chapter three hundred and seventy-two of the Public Laws of eighteen hundred and eighty-five, relating to the compensation of the County Commissioners for Oxford County	5
4	An Act to amend Section seventeen of Chapter forty of the Revised Statutes, as amended by Chapter two hundred and sixty-one of the Public Laws of eighteen hundred and eighty-five, and by Chapter sixty-one of the Public Laws of eighteen hundred and ninety-one, relating to Migratory Fish	6
5	An Act to amend Section fifteen of Chapter fifteen of the Revised Statutes, relating to Burying-Grounds...........	7
6	An Act to amend Section twenty-four of Chapter one hundred and two, Public Laws of eighteen hundred and ninety-one, as amended by Chapter two hundred and sixty-seven, Public Laws of eighteen hundred and ninety-three, relating to providing for the printing and distributing ballots at the public expense and regulating voting for State and City Elections,	8
7	An Act to fix the salary of the Judge of Probate for Hancock County	9
8	An Act to amend Section forty-seven of Chapter seventy-seven of the Revised Statutes, relating to the times of holding terms of the Supreme Judicial Court in Knox County..	10
9	An Act to amend Chapter two hundred fifty-eight of the Public Laws of eighteen hundred ninety-three as amended by Chapter one hundred thirty of the Public Laws of eighteen hundred and ninety-five, relating to the taxation of Savings Banks	11
10	An Act to amend Section thirty-five of Chapter one hundred twenty-four of the Revised Statutes as amended by Chapter twenty-five of the Public Laws of eighteen hundred ninety-one, relating to the Transportation of Animals..........	13
11	An Act to amend Section fifty-seven of Chapter thirty-eight of the Revised Statutes of Maine, relating to the weight of a bushel of Beans...	14
12	An Act to amend Section eighty-four of Chapter six of the Revised Statutes, relating to county Roads and Bridges in unincorporated townships	14

CONTENTS.

CHAP.		PAGE
13	An Act establishing the Salary of the County Treasurer of the County of York....................................	15
14	An Act in relation to the salaries of the Justices of the Supreme Judicial Court....................................	16
15	An Act to enlarge the powers of the Railroad Commissioners over Street Railroads....................................	16
16	An Act concerning Attorneys at Law.....................	17
17	An Act for the protection of Railroad Signals..............	18
18	An Act to amend Section forty-one of Chapter seventy-seven, of the Revised Statutes, relating to the Supreme Judicial Court	19
19	An Act extending sundry existing statutes to Street Railroads	19
20	An Act to amend Section three, Chapter two hundred two, Public Laws of eighteen hundred eighty-nine, entitled, "An Act to fix the salaries of the Judge and Register of Probate and County Commissioners of Waldo county"............	21
21	An Act to abolish Chapter five hundred and eighty-two, Public Laws of eighteen hundred and sixty-eight, relating to taking fish in Frenchman's Bay except by the ordinary process of fishing with hook and line......................	21
22	An Act amendatory of and additional to Chapter one hundred and forty-two of the Revised Statutes, relating to the State Reform School	22
23	An Act to amend Section fourteen of Chapter fifty-one of the Revised Statutes, relating to the width of the location of Railroads	27
24	An Act to amend Chapter ninety-seven, Section three of the Revised Statutes, relating to Bastard Children and their maintenance	27
25	An Act to enlarge the powers of Street Railroads in taking Lands	28
26	An Act to repeal Sections thirty-four, thirty-five, thirty-six, thirty-seven, and thirty-eight of Chapter twenty-six of the Revised Statutes, relating to inquests in cases of suspected Incendiarism	29
27	An Act to amend Chapter fifty-two of the Public Laws of eighteen hundred and ninety-five, relating to the salary of the Register of Probate for the county of Penobscot......	30
28	An Act to amend Chapter two hundred and thirty-six of the Public Laws of one thousand eight hundred and ninety-three, relating to the taking of lands or other property by Railroads	30
29	An Act to correct an error in Chapter seventy-nine of the Public Acts of eighteen hundred and ninety-nine, and to amend Section two of Chapter sixty of the Revised Statutes, allowing divorces in state, provided libelee resides therein..	31
30	An Act to repeal Section two hundred of Chapter six of the Revised Statutes as amended by Section ten, Chapter seventy, Public Laws of eighteen hundred ninety-five, relating to Tax Sales...	32
31	An Act to repeal Section two hundred one, Chapter six of the Revised Statutes, relating to Tax Sales..................	32
32	An Act to amend Chapter one hundred sixty-two of the Public Laws of eighteen hundred ninety-five, relating to Tax Sales,	32

CONTENTS.

CHAP.		PAGE
33	An Act to amend Section eighty-three of Chapter six of the Revised Statutes, relating to Tax Sales..................	33
34	An Act to set apart an annual Old Home Week............	33
35	An Act to amend Chapter two hundred and ninety-six of the Public Laws of eighteen hundred and ninety-seven, relating to the employment of Superintendent of Schools..........	34
36	An Act relating to Lost Goods and Stray Beasts............	35
37	An Act relating to Houses of Correction...................	37
39	An Act relating to Work Houses.........................	39
39	An Act relating to the dedication of Streets................	40
40	An Act to repeal Chapter twenty-three of the Revised Statutes, relating to Pounds and impounding Beasts............	41
41	An Act to repeal Sections one to thirty-five inclusive, of Chapter thirty-eight of the Revised Statutes, relating to the inspection of Pork and Beef............................	41
42	An Act to repeal Sections seven to twenty-two inclusive of Chapter thirty-nine of the Revised Statutes, relating to the inspection of Pot and Pearl Ashes and the inspection of Nails	41
43	An Act to repeal Sections fourteen and seventeen, Chapter eight of the Revised Statutes, relating to duties of County Treasurers	42
44	An Act to repeal Section nine of Chapter thirteen of the Revised Statutes, relating to the practice of Medicine and Surgery	42
45	An Act to amend Section twelve of Chapter three of the Revised Statutes as amended by Chapter three hundred and thirty-five of the Public Laws of eighteen hundred and eighty-five and to repeal conflicting statutes, relating to the election of Collectors of Taxes..........................	42
46	An Act to amend Paragraph one, Section six, of Chapter six of the Revised Statutes, relating to Property exempt from Taxation	43
47	An Act to repeal Sections forty, forty-two and one hundred twenty-eight of Chapter fifty-one of the Revised Statutes, relating to Railroads	43
48	An Act to amend Chapter ninety-seven of the Public Laws of eighteen hundred and eighty-seven, relating to assessment of damages resulting from the raising and lowering of Ways	43
49	An Act to repeal Chapter twenty-five of the Revised Statutes, except sections eleven and twelve, relating to Watch and Ward in towns	44
50	An Act to repeal Sections fifty-eight and fifty-nine of Chapter thirty-eight of the Revised Statutes, relating to bounties on Silk, and on Beet Sugar................................	44
51	An Act to repeal Section thirty and Section thirty-one of Chapter thirty-nine of the Revised Statutes, relating to Fire Arms	45
52	An Act to amend Section one hundred twenty-nine of Chapter forty-seven of the Revised Statutes, relating to officers and corporators of Savings Banks.............................	45
53	An Act to repeal Sections twenty-one, twenty-two, forty-six, sixty-six and seventy of Chapter two of the Revised Statutes, relating to the duties of Treasurer of State and Secretary of State	45

CONTENTS.

CHAP.		PAGE
54	An Act to repeal Section sixty-seven of Chapter two of the Revised Statutes and to amend Section eighty-seven of Chapter six of the Revised Statutes, relating to the duties of the Treasurer of State............	46
55	An Act to repeal Sections thirty-nine, forty, forty-one of Chapter three of the Revised Statutes, relating to the returns made by Assessors	46
56	An Act relating to the duties of Secretary of State.........	46
57	An Act to amend Chapter one hundred and fifty-two of the Public Laws of eighteen hundred ninety-five, relating to State Examination and certification of Teachers.........	47
58	An Act to amend Chapter two hundred and seventy-three of the Public Laws of eighteen hundred eighty-five, relating to the holding of County Teacher's Conventions...........	47
59	An Act establishing the salary of the County Attorney for the County of York............	48
60	An Act establishing the salary of the County Attorney for the County of Kennebec.........	48
61	An Act to authorize municipalities to make contracts for Water, Gas and Light............	49
62	An Act to prevent injury to Books and works of Art.........	49
63	An Act to amend Chapter two hundred and eighty-five of the Public Laws of nineteen hundred and one, entitled "An Act providing for State Roads and for the improvement thereof"............	49
64	An Act to amend Section three, Chapter eighty of the Public Laws of eighteen hundred ninety-nine, relating to the election of truant officers and the filling of vacancies occurring in the office of Truant Officer............	50
65	An Act to provide for the recording of Plans.............	51
66	An Act to amend Section three of Chapter two hundred and sixteen of the Public Laws of eighteen hundred and ninety-three, relating to the Conveyance of Scholars and to the maintenance of the public schools...........	51
67	An Act relating to the salary of the Sheriff of the county of Aroostook, and fixing the same at five hundred dollars a year	53
68	An Act for the better education of youth.............	53
69	An Act to amend Chapter one hundred and ninety-four of the Public Laws of nineteen hundred and one entitled, "An Act additional to Chapter twenty-nine of the Revised Statutes, relating to Bowling Alleys............	54
70	An Act to amend Chapter two hundred and eighty-four of the Public Laws of nineteen hundred one, relating to Sea and Shore Fisheries	55
71	An Act to repeal Section sixteen of Chapter seventy-eight of the Revised Statutes, relating to the duties of County Commissioners	56
72	An Act to repeal Sections seven, eight, nine and ten of Chapter sixty-one of the Revised Statutes, relating to the rights of Married Women	57
73	An Act to amend Chapter two hundred and sixty-six of the Public Laws of eighteen hundred and ninety-three, as amended by Chapter one hundred and twenty-eight of the	

CONTENTS.

CHAP.		PAGE
	Public Laws of eighteen hundred and ninety-nine and one hundred and sixty-seven of the Public Laws of nineteen hundred and one, relating to the Militia..................	57
74	An Act to repeal Sections eight, nine, ten, eleven and twelve of Chapter one hundred thirty-three of the Public Laws of eighteen hundred and ninety-seven, relating to Pardons.....	58
75	An Act relating to waiving of the Provisions of Wills by Widows	59
76	An Act to amend Chapter one hundred and fifty-nine of the Public Laws of nineteen hundred and one, providing for the retirement of commissioned officers of the militia or the National Guard of the State of Maine......................	59
77	An Act to amend Chapter ninety-four of the Public Laws of eighteen hundred eighty-seven, relating to Agricultural Societies	60
78	An Act to amend Section twenty-nine of Chapter eighteen of the Revised Statutes, relating to ways across station grounds of Railroads	61
79	An Act to amend Chapter sixty-one Public Laws of eighteen hundred eighty-seven, relating to Loan and Building Associations	61
80	An Act relating to the commitment of the Insane, and to abolish the right of appeal to Justices of the Peace and Quorum	63
81	An Act to amend Section four of Chapter eighty-six of the Revised Statutes as amended by Chapter one hundred fifty-seven, Public Laws of eighteen hundred and ninety-three, relating to trustee suits..................................	63
82	An Act to amend Paragraph five of Section sixty-two of Chapter eighty-one of the Revised Statutes, relating to property exempt from attachment and execution................	64
83	An Act relating to the attachment of Partnership Property...	65
84	An Act to authorize Executors and Administrators to provide for the perpetual care of Burial Lots......................	65
85	An Act relating to commitments by Trial Justices and Judges of Police and Municipal courts...........................	66
86	An Act relating to Street Railroad Locations................	66
87	An Act to amend Section one of Chapter one hundred fourteen of the Revised Statutes, relating to Duties payable by Public Officers	67
88	An Act relating to the Dissolution of Attachments by filing bond	67
89	An Act relating to the Acknowledgment of Deeds............	68
90	An Act relating to the authority of courts over Guardians ad litem or next friend..................................	69
91	An Act to amend Chapter sixty-seven of the Revised Statutes and Chapter one hundred forty-three of the Revised Statutes, relating to the appointment of Guardians for persons insane	69
92	An Act to amend Chapter forty-two of the Public Laws of eighteen hundred ninety-nine, relating to the taking of Black Bass in certain lakes in Kennebec and Somerset Counties, also Sabattus Pond in Androscoggin County, as amended by Chapter two hundred eighty-seven Public Laws of nineteen hundred one	70

CONTENTS.

CHAP.		PAGE
93	An Act to amend Section fifteen of Chapter fifty-one of the Revised Statutes, relating to recording Locations of Railroads	70
94	An Act to amend Section eleven of Chapter sixty-eight of the Revised Statutes, relating to Trust Estates	71
95	An Act to amend Chapter forty-three of the Public Laws of eighteen hundred ninety-one, relating to the practice of Dentistry	72
96	An Act to repeal Section thirty-six of Chapter sixty-three of the Revised Statutes, relating to Examination before Judges of Probate	72
97	An Act to amend Chapter forty-six of the Public Laws of eighteen hundred and ninety-nine, establishing a Naval Reserve as a part of the National Guard of the State of Maine	72
98	An Act to regulate the practice of Embalming and the transportation of the bodies of persons who have died of infectious diseases	74
99	An Act providing for a license for non-residents to hunt Moose and Deer	77
100	An Act to amend Chapter three hundred thirty-two of the Public Laws of eighteen hundred ninety-seven, relating to the powers and duties of School Committees and the manner of electing Town Superintendents	79
101	An Act to amend Section one of Chapter two hundred forty-nine of the Public Laws of nineteen hundred and one, in relation to compensation for clerk hire in Adjutant General's office	80
102	An Act to amend Section one of Chapter two hundred and forty-two of the Public Laws of eighteen hundred and eighty-nine, in relation to the salary of the Adjutant General	81
103	An Act amendatory of Section two of Chapter two hundred and eighty-seven of the Public Laws of eighteen hundred and ninety-three as amended by Chapter thirty-three of the Public Laws of eighteen hundred and ninety-nine, and Chapter one hundred and sixty-three of the Public Laws of nineteen hundred and one, relating to the better protection of Sheep	81
104	An Act establishing the jurisdiction and term of office of Women appointed to solemnize marriages, administer oaths and take acknowledgment of deeds	82
105	An Act to amend Seection two of Chapter twenty of the Revised Statutes, relating to Ferries	83
106	An Act to amend Section one hundred and six of Chapter forty-seven of the Revised Statutes, relating to the reserve fund of Savings Banks	83
107	An Act to amend Chapter one hundred and thirty-six, Public Laws of eighteen hundred and eighty-seven, relating to unclaimed Deposits in Savings Banks	84
108	An Act to amend Section eighty of Chapter eighteen of the Revised Statutes, relating to injuries on Highways	85
109	An Act to amend Section one of Chapter thirty of the Revised Statutes, as amended by Chapter one hundred fifteen of the Public Laws of eighteen hundred ninety-five, and Sections	

CONTENTS.

CHAP.		PAGE
	three and four of Chapter thirty of the Revised Statutes, in relation to Dogs....................................	86
110	An Act in regard to compensation of Town Officers........	87
111	An Act to amend Section ninety-eight of Chapter eighty-two of the Revised Statutes, relating to Evidence.............	88
112	An Act to provide for the protection of Trees and Shrubs from injurious insects and diseases.......................	88
113	An Act to regulate Costs in the taking of lands or other property for public uses.................................	89
114	An Act to amend Section six of Chapter three of the Public Laws of eighteen hundred ninety-nine entitled "An Act to amend Section six of Chapter one hundred fifty-six of the Public Laws of eighteen hundred ninety-five entitled "An Act to amend Section six of Chapter thirty-five of the Revised Statutes," relating to Intelligence Offices...........	90
115	An Act in relation to Judges of Municipal Courts...........	91
116	An Act to regulate the placing of Permanent Moorings in harbors	91
117	An Act to amend Chapter seventy-seven of the Public Laws of eighteen hundred and ninety-nine, relating to giving mortgagees a lien for costs of foreclosure under Section five of Chapter ninety of the Revised Statutes..................	92
118	An Act relating to proof of Attested Instruments............	93
119	An Act to correct an error, and repeal "An Act approved February eleven, nineteen hundred three," relating to Migratory Fish	93
120	An Act to amend Section two of Chapter ninety-three of the Public Laws of eighteen hundred and ninety-nine, fixing the salary of the County Commissioners of Kennebec County	94
121	An Act relating to the office of County Commissioners.......	94
122	An Act to enable cities and towns to establish permanent Fuel Yards	95
123	An Act to amend Section twenty-one of Chapter one hundred and sixteen of the Revised Statutes, and Chapter two hundred and twenty-five of the Public Laws of eighteen hundred and ninety-three, relating to fees of Registers of Deeds....	95
124	An Act to amend Section thirty-five of Chapter ninety-nine of the Revised Statutes, relating to Powers and Duties of Bail Commissioners	96
125	An Act to regulate the taking of Bail in Criminal Prosecutions	96
126	An Act in aid of the soldiers of the Aroostook War.........	97
127	An Act fixing the salary of the Judge of Probate of Sagadahoc County	98
128	An Act to amend Chapter eighty-nine of the Public Laws of eighteen hundred ninety-nine amendatory of Chapter one hundred and sixteen of the Public Laws of eighteen hundred ninety-five as amended by Chapter two hundred and eighty-six of the Public Laws of eighteen hundred ninety-seven and Chapter two hundred and six of the Public Laws of nineteen hundred one, entitled "An Act to provide for the Schooling of Children in unorganized Townships......	98

CONTENTS.

CHAP.		PAGE
129	An Act to repeal so much of Section five of Chapter forty-two of the Public Laws of eighteen hundred and ninety-nine, as prohibits fishing in the inlet stream of Squaw Pan Lake from Thibadeau's landing to the source of said stream.	100
130	An Act regulating the sale or exchange of Mortgaged Personal Property	101
131	An Act amending Section one of Chapter two hundred eighty-four of the Public Laws of eighteen hundred ninety-three, in relation to Ways.	101
132	An Act relating to claims against the estates of Deceased Persons	102
133	An Act to amend Chapter three hundred and seventy-eight of the Public Laws of eighteen hundred and eighty-five, relating to Electric Posts and Wires.	102
134	An Act in relation to the discharge of debtors in cases now pending in Insolvent Courts.	104
135	An Act to amend Chapter eighty-six of the Revised Statutes, relating to Trustee Process.	104
136	An Act to repeal so much of Chapter thirty of the Revised Statutes, as amended by Section five of Chapter forty-two of the Public Laws of eighteen hundred ninety-nine, as prohibits fishing through the ice in Dexter pond, in Dexter, Penobscot county	105
137	An Act to amend Chapter three, Section fifty-nine, Paragraph twelve of the Revised Statutes, relating to dealers in Old Junk	105
138	An Act additional to Chapter sixteen of the Revised Statutes, relating to Public Drains and Sewers.	106
139	An Act to prohibit Spitting upon the floors of street cars.	106
140	An Act to amend Section one of Chapter one hundred eighty-five of the Public Laws of nineteen hundred one, relating to Truants	107
141	An Act to amend Section three of Chapter one hundred and three of the Public Laws of eighteen hundred and ninety-five, relating to Telegraph and Telephone Companies.	108
142	An Act to amend Section fifty-seven of Chapter eleven of Revised Statutes, as amended by Chapter two hundred eleven of the Public Laws of nineteen hundred one, relating to school house Lots and Grounds.	108
143	An Act to repeal so much of Chapter thirty of the Revised Statutes as amended by Section five of Chapter forty-two of the Public Laws of eighteen hundred ninety-nine, as prohibits fishing through the ice in Indian pond, situated partly in Franklin and partly in Somerset County.	109
144	An Act to change the name of the State Reform School.	109
145	An Act to repeal so much of Chapter thirty of the Revised Statutes, as amended by Chapter forty-two of the Public Laws of one thousand eight hundred and ninety-nine, as prohibits fishing in Goodwin brook, and Higgins stream above the first dam, tributaries to Moose pond, in Somerset county	110
146	An Act to amend an act entitled "An Act to regulate the admission to practice of attorneys, solicitors and counsellors, to provide for a board of examiners, and to repeal conflict-	

CONTENTS. XI

CHAP.		PAGE
	ing acts," approved March seventeen, eighteen hundred ninety-nine	110
147	An Act to amend Section five of Chapter one hundred thirty-seven of the Revised Statutes as amended by Section one of Chapter two hundred ninety-five of the Public Laws of eighteen hundred ninety-three, relating to Insane Criminals	112
148	An Act to amend Chapter one hundred and one, Public Laws of eighteen hundred and eighty-seven, relating to Paupers,	114
149	An Act relating to suits in equity to quiet Title.............	115
150	An Act additional to Chapter seventy-three of the Revised Statutes, relating to Titles to property....................	117
151	An Act relating to Assaults upon officers and hindering or obstructing them while in the discharge of their duties,	117
152	An Act to amend Section forty-three of Chapter two hundred eighty-four, Public Acts of nineteen hundred one, relating to migratory fish in Mill river...........................	118
153	An Act to amend Section five of Chapter seventeen of the Revised Statutes as amended by Chapter one hundred eighty-eight of the Public Laws of eighteen hundred and ninety-three, relating to Nuisances........................	119
154	An Act to repeal so much of Chapter thirty of the Revised Statutes, as amended by Section five of Chapter forty-two of the Public Laws of eighteen hundred ninety-nine, and as amended by Chapter two hundred thirty of the Private and Special Laws of nineteen hundred one, as prohibits fishing through the ice in Large Greenwood pond in Elliottsville and Willimantic, in Piscataquis County..................	119
155	An Act relating to compensation of County Commissioners of Hancock County	120
156	An Act to exempt Religious Institutions from the Collateral Inheritance Tax	120
157	An Act relating to Trespassers............................	121
158	An Act to change time of holding sessions of County Commissioners in Aroostook County.........................	122
159	An Act to amend Section one of Chapter seventy-five of the Revised Statutes, as amended by Chapter one hundred and fifty-seven of the Public Laws of eighteen hundred and ninety-five, and by Chapters one hundred and ninety-three and one hundred and ninety-six of the Public Laws of eighteen hundred and ninety-seven, relating to Descent of real estate	122
160	An Act amendatory of Section one of Chapter two hundred and twenty-one of the Public Laws of eighteen hundred and ninety-seven, relating to waiving the provisions of a Will by a widow or widower, and to the Wills in which no provision is made for the widow or widower, and the interest which the widow or widower shall have in the personal estate of the testator or testatrix in such cases............	124
161	An Act relating to bonds to be given by Treasurers of towns and plantations	125
162	An Act to repeal so much of Chapter thirty of the Revised Statutes, as amended by Section five of Chapter forty-two of the Public Laws of eighteen hundred and ninety-nine,	

CHAP.		PAGE
	and as amended by Chapter three hundred seventy-nine of the Private and Special Laws of nineteen hundred and one, as prohibits fishing through the ice in Big Carry pond, or West Carry pond, so called, in Somerset County..........	126
163	An Act to repeal so much of Chapter thirty of the Revised Statutes, as amended by Section five of Chapter forty-two of the Public Laws of eighteen hundred and ninety-nine, and as amended by Chapter three hundred twenty-nine of the Private and Special Laws of nineteen hundred and one, as prohibits ice fishing in Black, Whittier and Perry ponds, in the towns of Vienna and Chesterville, in Kennebec and Franklin Counties	126
164	An Act to amend Section sixteen, Chapter fifty-one of the Revised Statutes, relating to Railroads...................	127
165	An Act to amend Section six of Chapter eleven of the Revised Statutes of Maine, relating to the raising and expending of Common School Funds	128
166	An Act to repeal Sections one to forty-seven, inclusive, and Sections forty-nine to eighty-two, inclusive, of Chapter forty-seven of the Revised Statutes, relating to Banks of Discount	129
167	An Act to amend Sections thirty-two, thirty-three, thirty-four, and thirty-five of Chapter eighteen of the Revised Statutes, relating to the assessment of damages upon abutters on city streets	129
168	An Act to amend Chapter one hundred of the Public Laws of eighteen hundred and ninety-one, entitled "An Act to create a Forest Commission and for the protection of forests"....	131
169	An Act to amend Section six of Chapter two hundred sixty-seven of the Public Laws of eighteen hundred and ninety-three, entitled "An Act to provide for the printing and distributing ballots at the public expense and to regulate voting for State and City Elections"..........................	132
170	An Act to amend Section thirty-eight of Chapter twenty-seven of the Revised Statutes and Section forty of Chapter twenty-seven of the Revised Statutes, as amended by Chapter one hundred forty of the Public Laws of eighteen hundred and eighty-seven and Chapter one hundred thirty-two of the Public Laws of eighteen hundred and ninety-one, relating to Intoxicating Liquors...........................	133
171	An Act to amend Section fifteen of Chapter one hundred and thirty-two of the Revised Statutes, relating to Appeals from magistrates in criminal cases...........................	135
172	An Act to amend Section forty-four of Chapter two of the Revised Statutes, relating to the publication of the Public Laws	135
173	An Act relating to defense of actions brought against Administrators and Executors	136
174	An Act relating to Bonds given by Collectors of Taxes.....	136
175	An Act to amend Chapter two hundred and eighty-six, Public Laws of nineteen hundred and one, relating to taxation of interest bearing deposits in Trust and Banking Companies,	137
176	An Act to amend Chapter fifty-one of the Revised Statutes, relating to the duties of Railroad Commissioners..........	138
177	An Act to provide for the assessment and expenditure of the	

CHAP.		PAGE
	income arising from the Permanent School Fund in certain towns	139
178	An Act to amend Chapter two hundred and seventy-nine of the Public Laws of eighteen hundred and ninety-seven, as amended by Chapter two hundred and forty of the Public Laws of nineteen hundred and one, relating to the packing of Sardines	139
179	An Act to repeal so much of Chapter thirty of the Revised Statutes, as amended by Section five of Chapter forty-two of the Public Laws of eighteen hundred and ninety-nine, and as amended by Chapter three hundred and seventy-nine of the Private and Special Laws of nineteen hundred and one, as closes Oaks pond, in Cornville, to ice fishing	141
180	An Act to amend Section four, Section eleven, Section nineteen, of Chapter eighteen of the Public Laws of eighteen hundred ninety-one as amended by Chapter one hundred fifty-four of the Public Laws of eighteen hundred ninety-five, relating to returns of Vital Statistics	141
181	An Act relating to actions for Libel or Slander	143
182	An Act to amend Sections two and sixteen of Chapter forty-eight of the Revised Statutes, relating to Corporations	144
183	An Act to cede the jurisdiction of the State of Maine to the United States of America over so much land as has been or may be hereafter acquired for the public purposes of the United States	146
184	An Act to define the powers and duties of Superintendents of Schools	147
185	An Act to amend Section twenty-nine of Chapter one hundred and sixteen of the Revised Statutes, relating to Fees and Costs of Magistrates	147
186	An Act to repeal Sections twenty-three and twenty-four of Chapter thirty-nine of the Revised Statutes, relating to Paper	148
187	An Act to amend Sections thirty-eight, forty and fifty-one of Chapter sixty-four of the Revised Statutes, relating to Executors and Administrators	148
188	An Act to amend Chapter eleven of the Public Laws of eighteen hundred and eighty-seven, as amended by Chapter forty-four of the Public Laws of eighteen hundred and ninety-nine, authorizing cities and towns to accept legacies, devises and bequests, and to raise money	149
189	An Act to repeal so much of Chapter thirty of the Revised Statutes, as amended by Chapter forty-two, Section five, of the Public Laws of eighteen hundred ninety-nine, as amended by Chapter three hundred seventy-nine of the Private and Special Laws of nineteen hundred one, as prohibits fishing through the ice in Palmer pond, so called, in Mayfield Plantation, in the County of Somerset	151
190	An Act to amend Section one hundred of Chapter forty-seven of the Revised Statutes, as amended by Chapter one hundred sixty-one of the Public Laws of eighteen hundred ninety-five, relating to the investment of funds of Savings Banks,	152
191	An Act to amend Section forty-eight of Chapter two hundred eighty-four of the Public Laws of eighteen hundred and ninety-one, entitled "An Act to consolidate and simplify the laws pertaining to sea and shore fisheries as contained in	

CHAP.		PAGE
	Chapter forty of the Revised Statutes" and in amendments and additions thereto....................................	156
192	An Act to make valid the Elections of Treasurers and Collectors of Taxes, held during the month of March in the year one thousand nine hundred and three................	157
193	An Act relating to the powers and duties of Administrators, de bonis non..	157
194	An Act to abolish issuing separate Executions for Costs, by Disclosure Commissioners	158
195	An Act to amend Chapter thirty-three of the Public Laws of eighteen hundred and eighty-seven, relating to the burial of Widows of Soldiers in Certain Cases...................	159
196	An Act in relation to Lime and Lime Casks................	160
197	An Act to amend Section twelve and following sections of Chapter forty-three of the Revised Statutes in relation to Meridian Lines and a Standard of Length................	162
198	An Act to amend Chapter eighty-seven of the Revised Statutes as amended by Chapter two hundred and eighteen of the Public Laws of eighteen hundred and ninety-three, Chapter one hundred and thirty-three of the Public Laws of eighteen hundred and ninety-five, and Chapter one hundred and twenty of the Public Laws of eighteen hundred and ninety-nine, and Section ninety-two of Chapter eighty-one of the Revised Statutes, relating to the limitations of actions against Executors and Administrators.............	165
199	An Act to increase the salary of the County Attorney of Sagadahoc County	166
200	An Act establishing the salary of the County Attorney for the County of Washington....................................	167
201	An Act in relation to Railroad Surveys.....................	167
202	An Act to establish the salary of the Judge of Probate in the County of Washington...............................	167
203	An Act to provide for the preservation of Town Records of births, marriages and deaths, previous to the year eighteen hundred and ninety-two...........................	168
204	An Act to amend Section four of Chapter ninety-one of the Revised Statutes, relating to Notice of Foreclosure on a mortgage of personal property............................	169
205	An Act to increase and fix the salary of the Assistant Librarian	169
206	An Act relating to the salary of the County Attorney of Somerset County	170
207	An Act to increase the salary of the County Attorney of Piscataquis County	170
208	An Act relating to the salary of the Register of Probate of Sagadahoc County	170
209	An Act to amend Section ten of Chapter sixty of the Revised Statutes, relating to Divorce.............................	171
210	An Act in relation to the salary of the County Attorney of the County of Hancock...................................	171
211	An Act to amend Section one hundred seven of Chapter eleven of the Revised Statutes, relating to Normal Schools,	172
212	An Act to amend Section sixteen of Chapter two hundred and sixty-six of the Public Laws of eighteen hundred and ninety-three, relating to the Militia......................	173

CONTENTS.

CHAP.		PAGE
213	An Act for the protection of the wild Hare or Rabbit......	173
214	An Act relating to Political Caucuses......................	174
215	An Act in relation to Agricultural Societies................	177
216	An Act for the protection of Lobsters with eggs attached....	179
217	An Act to amend Section four of Chapter two hundred and fifty-six of the Public Laws of eighteen hundred and ninety-three as amended by Chapter one hundred and ninety-seven of the Public Laws of eighteen hundred and ninety-seven, relating to the sale and analysis of Commercial Fertilizers,	180
218	An Act to increase the salary of the Justice of the Superior Court for the County of Cumberland......................	181
219	An Act to amend Section one hundred twelve of Chapter eleven of the Revised Statutes, as amended by Chapter thirty-seven of the Public Laws of eighteen hundred and ninety-one, and by Chapter one hundred twenty-one of the Public Laws of eighteen hundred and ninety-five, and by Chapter three hundred eight of the Public Laws of eighteen hundred and ninety-seven, relating to Normal Schools and the Madawaska Training School.........................	181
220	An Act amendatory of Chapter seventy-three, Section eight of the Revised Statutes, relating to the recording of Deeds of Release	182
221	An Act to amend Chapter ninety-six of the Public Laws of eighteen hundred ninety-nine, entitled "An Act to prevent Incompetent Persons from conducting the business of a pharmacist	183
222	An Act to license foreign Executors, Administrators, Guardians and Trustees to receive and dispose of Personal Property	184
223	An Act relating to the Public Health.....................	185
224	An Act relating to Treasurer and Collector of Taxes.......	186
225	An Act to correct Clerical Errors and make plain the meaning of and amend Chapter thirty of the Revised Statutes, as amended by Chapter forty-two of the Public Laws of eighteen hundred ninety-nine, and as amended by Chapters two hundred twenty-two and two hundred seventy-eight of the Public Laws of nineteen hundred one and Chapter three hundred twenty-six of the Private and Special Laws of nineteen hundred one, and acts reported from the Committee on Inland Fisheries and Game, relating to inland fisheries and game	186
226	An Act in relation to the salary of the Register of Probate of the County of Hancock................................	189
227	An Act to create the Maine Mining Bureau................	189
228	An Act appropriating one half of the taxes received from Trust and Banking Companies to the School Fund........	190
229	An Act to amend Section eleven of Chapter thirty of the Revised Statutes as amended by Chapter forty-two of the Public Laws of eighteen hundred ninety-nine and as amended by Chapter two hundred fifty-eight of the Public Laws of nineteen hundred one, relating to Close Time for Game Birds	190
230	An Act to regulate the Sale and Analysis of Concentrated Commercial Feeding Stuffs............................	191
231	An Act to amend Chapter three hundred and seventy-eight of the Public Laws of eighteen hundred and eighty-five, reg-	

CHAP.		PAGE
	ulating the erection of posts and lines for purposes of electricity	194
232	An Act to make certain the meaning of the language "Timber and Grass," relating to the Public Lots, so called, in unincorporated townships in State of Maine.	197
233	An Act providing for a bounty on bears in Oxford County..	197
234	An Act establishing the salary of the County Attorney for the County of Knox.	198
235	An Act relating to Corporations.	199
236	An Act for the protection of Shore Birds.	200
237	An Act to regulate the use of Automobiles and motor Vehicles upon Public Ways.	200
238	An Act to amend Section eight of Chapter one hundred and fifteen of the Revised Statutes, relating to compensation of Members of the Government.	202
239	An Act to establish a bounty on Porcupines, so called, for the better protection of Timber Land.	204
240	An Act fixing a time when other Acts and Resolves shall take effect	205

CONTENTS OF PRIVATE AND SPECIAL LAWS.

SESSION OF 1903.

CHAP.		PAGE
1	An Act to authorize the Franklin Company to reduce its capital stock	3
2	An Act additional to and amendatory of Chapter three hundred and eighteen of the Private and Special Laws of nineteen hundred and one, entitled "An Act to incorporate the Bridgton Water Company".............................	4
3	An Act to authorize the Auburn Savings Bank, of Auburn, Maine, to construct and maintain Safety Deposit Boxes....	6
4	An Act to authorize the Old Orchard Electric Light Company to issue bonds and for other purposes..............	6
5	An Act to amend Sections one and four of Chapter three hundred and thirty-nine of the Private and Special Laws of nineteen hundred and one, being "An Act to incorporate the Winthrop Cold Spring Water Company"............	7
6	An Act authorizing the State Treasurer to purchase unmatured State of Maine bonds.............................	8
7	An Act to amend Chapter sixty-one of the Private and Special Laws of eighteen hundred and ninety-nine, entitled "An Act to establish the Bar Harbor Municipal Court"........	8
8	An Act recognizing Sebasticook Power Company as a corporation legally organized, and to grant to it additional powers	9
9	An Act to provide in part for the Expenditures of Government for the year nineteen hundred and three............	10
10	An Act in relation to the powers of the Union River Light, Gas and Power Company................................	16
11	An Act to amend Chapter two hundred sixty-two of Private and Special Laws of eighteen hundred sixty-three as amended by Chapter two hundred sixty of Private and Special Laws of eighteen hundred eighty-seven, and Chapter fifty-four of Private and Special Laws of eighteen hundred ninety-nine, entitled "An Act to incorporate the Dover and Foxcroft Village Fire Company"......................	17
12	An Act to grant additional powers to the Portsmouth, Kittery and York Street Railway................................	21
13	An Act to authorize the Kennebec Light and Heat Company to issue bonds	23
14	An Act to ratify the mortgage of the Fish River Railroad..	23
15	An Act to ratify the lease of the Fish River Railroad and to authorize the sale of said railroad to the Bangor and Aroostook Railroad Company...................................	24
16	An Act to ratify and confirm the consolidated mortgage made by the Bangor and Aroostook Railroad Company..........	24

CONTENTS.

CHAP.		PAGE
17	An Act to enlarge the powers of the Berwick, Eliot and York Street Railway	25
18	An Act relating to the Bar Harbor Electric Light Company	32
19	An Act to authorize the town of Boothbay Harbor to construct a bridge across the harbor in said town	33
20	An Act to incorporate the Auburn and Turner Railroad Company	33
21	An Act to amend the charter of the Maine General Hospital	36
22	An Act to establish a Street and Sewer Commission for the city of Bath	37
23	An Act to confer additional powers upon the Lincoln County Street Railway	38
24	An Act to authorize the Biddeford and Saco Water Company to issue bonds, and for other purposes	43
25	An Act to incorporate the city of Camden	44
26	An Act to extend the charter of the Eastport Bridge	63
27	An Act to legalize the acts of Saint Francis plantation in the county of Aroostook	64
28	An Act to legalize the doings of the Portland and Rumford Falls Railway	64
29	An Act to increase the corporate powers of the Newport Light and Power Company	64
30	An Act to extend the charter of the Camden Trust Company	66
31	An Act to extend the charter of the Cumberland Trust Company	66
32	An Act to authorize the town of Monson to remove the bodies of deceased persons	67
33	An Act to legalize the doings of the Rumford Falls and Rangeley Lakes Railroad Company	67
34	An Act to extend the powers of the Katahdin Pulp and Paper Company	68
35	An Act to authorize the State Land Agent to convey to the Fish River Railroad Company, rights of way over public lots owned by the state	68
36	An Act to ratify certain doings of the Eliot Bridge Company	69
37	An Act relating to the width of location of the Fish River Railroad	69
38	An Act to authorize the Bangor and Aroostook Railroad Company to extend yard tracks across a way in Houlton	70
39	An Act to amend and extend the charter of the Waldo Street Railway Company	71
40	An Act to amend the charter of the Home for Aged Men in Portland	73
41	An Act to extend the franchises held by the Wiscasset, Waterville and Farmington Railroad Company	74
42	An Act to authorize the Norway and Paris Street Railway to purchase or lease the property and franchises of the Oxford Light Company	75
43	An Act to grant additional powers to the Portland and Brunswick Street Railway	76
44	An Act to amend Section thirty of Chapter four hundred and fifty of the Private and Special Laws of eighteen hundred and ninety-three, incorporating the City of Eastport	78
45	An Act to amend the charter of the Rockland, Thomaston and Camden Street Railway	78

CONTENTS.

CHAP.		PAGE
46	An Act to extend the charter of the Mattanawcook Manufacturing Company	80
47	An Act amendatory of Chapter two hundred seventy-nine of the Private and Special Laws of nineteen hundred and one, entitled "An Act to incorporate the Matagamon Manufacturing Company"	80
48	An Act to amend Chapter sixty-four of the Private and Special Laws of eighteen hundred and ninety-nine as amended by Chapter four hundred and seventy-two of the Private and Special Laws of nineteen hundred and one, relating to the Wilson Stream Dam Company............	81
49	An Act to grant additional powers to the Waterville and Oakland Street Railway...................................	82
50	An Act to incorporate the Swan's Island Telephone and Telegraph Company	83
51	An Act to incorporate the Pittsfield Trust Company.........	85
52	An Act authorizing and empowering the Springer Lumber Company to erect and maintain piers and booms in the Mattawamkeag River	89
53	An Act to amend Chapter twenty-five of the Private and Special Laws of eighteen hundred ninety-nine, relating to taking Eels in Bagaduce river, bay and tributaries........	91
54	An Act to amend the charter of the Augusta, Winthrop and Gardiner Railway	91
55	An Act to incorporate the Squirrel Island Village Corporation	93
56	An Act to amend Chapter one hundred forty-five of the Private and Special Laws of eighteen hundred and ninety-five, entitled "An Act to incorporate the Winn Water and Power Company"	97
57	An Act to incorporate the Pepperell Trust Company........	98
58	An Act to incorporate the International Trust and Banking Company	101
59	An Act to amend an Act entitled "An Act to ratify the mortgage of the Fish River Railroad," approved February eleven, nineteen hundred and three.....................	105
60	An Act additional to and amendatory of Chapter fifty-four of the Private and Special Laws of eighteen hundred and ninety-five, creating the Rumford Falls Village Corporation	106
61	An Act to incorporate the Rangeley Water Company........	106
62	An Act to amend Section five of Chapter forty-two of the Public Laws of eighteen hundred and ninety-nine, as amended by Chapter three hundred and twenty-six of the Private and Special Laws of nineteen hundred and one, relating to fishing through the ice in Thompson pond......	109
63	An Act to amend Chapter two hundred seventy-one of the Private and Special Laws of nineteen hundred one, relating to the Lincoln Electric Railway Company................	110
64	An Act to legalize the doings of the Crosbyville Chapel, at at Bangor, Maine	110
65	An Act in relation to the election of the Members of the School Committee of the City of Portland................	110
66	An Act to grant additional powers to the Vickery Realty Company	111

CONTENTS.

CHAP.		PAGE
67	An Act to incorporate the Central Trust Company........	111
68	An Act to amend the charter of the City of Portland........	116,
69	An Act to extend the charter of the Sanford Trust Company,	118
70	An Act for the better protection of Shell Fish within the town of Georgetown	118
71	An Act to amend Chapter three hundred and forty-six of the Private and Special Laws of eighteen hundred and ninety-seven, entitled "An Act to amend the charter of the city of Westbrook"..	119
72	An Act to authorize the Augusta, Winthrop and Gardiner Railway to supply electricity in the towns of Winthrop and Manchester	119
73	An Act amendatory to Chapter five hundred and seven of the Private and Special Laws of eighteen hundred and eighty-nine, entitled, "An Act to establish the Dover Municipal Court," as amended by Chapter one hundred and ninety-six of the Private and Special Laws of eighteen hundred and ninety-nine	120
74	An Act to incorporate the Mapleton and Presque Isle Railroad Company	122
75	An Act to incorporate the Camden and Liberty Railway.....	123
76	An Act to incorporate the Forest Telegraph and Telephone Company	128
77	An Act authorizing and empowering Samuel W. Hanscom of Reed Plantation, County of Aroostook, to erect and maintain piers and booms in the Mattawamkeag river....	129
78	An Act to incorporate the town of Castle Hill, in the county of Aroostook	130
79	An Act to authorize the county of Piscataquis to negotiate a loan for temporary purposes.............................	131
80	An Act to extend the charter of the South Portland Trust and Banking Company....................................	131
81	An Act to authorize the Bodwell Water Power Company to generate, use, transmit and sell electricity................	132
82	An Act to incorporate the Gardiner Water District.........	133
83	An Act to incorporate the Union Trust Company of Saco, Maine	138
84	An Act to amend Chapter four hundred and eighty-six of the Private and Special Laws of eighteen hundred and eighty-nine, relating to the city of Westbrook...................	142
85	An Act to incorporate the Kineo Trust Company...........	144
86	An Act to authorize the Orono Pulp and Paper Company to generate, use and sell electricity........................	148
87	An Act relating to the taking of lobsters within three miles of the islands of Matinicus and Criehaven, during the months of August and September, in each year..........	149
88	An Act authorizing and empowering Joseph C. Patchell of Reed Plantation, County of Aroostook, to erect and maintain piers and booms in the Mattawamkeag river.........	149
89	An Act to authorize the Penobscot Chemical Fibre Company to generate, use, transmit and sell electricity.............	150
90	An Act to amend Section ten of Chapter three hundred and sixty-six of the Private and Special Laws of eighteen hundred and ninety-seven, entitled "An Act to incorporate the Livermore Falls Water Company".......................	151

CONTENTS.

CHAP.		PAGE
91	An Act to extend the charter of the Bangor and Brewer Steam Ferry Company	151
92	An Act to extend the charter of the Mutual Fire Insurance Company	152
93	An Act to incorporate the Fort Kent Trust Company	153
94	An Act to prevent pollution of the waters of Sebago Lake	156
95	An Act to amend an act incorporating the Trustees of Coburn Classical Institute	156
96	An Act to extend the charter of the Wilton Electric Light and Power Company	157
97	An Act authorizing the City of Rockland to accept donations of money and property to establish and maintain a Free Public Library in Rockland, and to accept conveyances of land for a site therefor	157
98	An Act to amend the charter of the Northport Wesleyan Grove Campmeeting Association	158
99	An Act to incorporate the Knox County General Hospital	160
100	An Act to amend Chapter six hundred and thirteen of the Private and Special Laws of eighteen hundred and ninety-three, entitled "An Act to establish the Western Hancock Municipal Court"	161
101	An Act to incorporate the Union Gas Company	162
102	An Act to incorporate the Lily Water Company	163
103	An Act to legalize the acts and doings of the town of Williamsburg	166
104	An Act extending the charter and changing the name of the Van Buren Trust and Banking Company	166
105	An Act to extend the charter of the Ellsworth Street Railway Company	167
106	An Act in relation to the Hancock County Railway Company,	167
107	An Act to repeal the provisions of Section three of chapter five hundred forty-four of the Special Laws of eighteen hundred eighty-nine, relating to the Bangor Street Railway	168
108	An Act to amend Chapter two hundred fifteen of the Resolves of the State of Maine of eighteen hundred ninety-seven, relating to tuition of Students in Agriculture at University of Maine	169
109	An Act conferring additional powers upon Proprietors of Union Wharf, incorporated by special Act of the Legislature, approved February nine, in the year of our Lord eighteen hundred fifty-six	169
110	An Act to amend Chapter two hundred twenty-nine of the Private and Special Laws of eighteen hundred eighty-three, as amended by Chapter three hundred eighty-three of the Private and Special Laws of eighteen hundred eighty-five, entitled "An Act to incorporate the Passadumkeag Log Driving Company"	170
111	An Act to authorize the erection of piers and booms in the Mattawamkeag River, at Jenkin's Cove	171
112	An Act to incorporate the South West Harbor Trust Company	173
113	An Act in relation to the Trustees of Westbrook Seminary	177
114	An Act to consolidate and amend Chapter seventy-eight of the Special Laws of eighteen hundred and sixty-one, Chap-	

CHAP.		PAGE
	ter three hundred ninety-five of the Special Laws of eighteen hundred sixty-four, Chapter one hundred forty of the Special Laws of eighteen hundred sixty-six, Chapter five hundred thirty-six of the Special Laws of eighteen hundred seventy-four, Chapter three hundred four of the Special Laws of eighteen hundred ninety-five, and Chapter three hundred ninety-eight of the Special Laws of nineteen hundred and one, relating to a Police Court in the City of Rockland	177
115	An Act authorizing the Great Northern Paper Company to locate, erect and maintain piers and booms in the Kennebec river	183
116	An Act relative to the Clinton Electric Light and Power Company	185
117	An Act to incorporate the Saint John River Toll Bridge Company	185
118	An Act to amend Chapter one hundred and fifty-four of the Private and Special Laws of eighteen hundred and ninety-five, relating to the charter of the Wiscasset Water Company	187
119	An Act to amend Chapter two hundred and four of the Private and Special Laws of eighteen hundred and eighty-three, entitled "An Act to establish a Municipal Court in the town of Westbrook".....................................	188
120	An Act to incorporate the Smith Cemetery Association of Palermo, Waldo County, Maine...........................	192
121	An Act additional and amendatory to Chapter three hundred seventy-six of the Private and Special Laws of eighteen hundred eighty-nine, as amended by Chapter four hundred seventy-nine of the Private and Special Laws of nineteen hundred one, to enable the Maine Lake Ice Company to increase its capital stock..................................	193
122	An Act to incorporate Union Power Company.............	193
123	An Act to incorporate the Merrill Trust Company.........	194
124	An Act to amend Chapter three hundred and one of the Private and Special Laws of eighteen hundred fifty, entitled "An Act to incorporate the Portland Widows' Wood Society," as amended by Chapter one hundred forty-five of the Private and Special Laws of eighteen hundred seventy-nine,	198
125	An Act amendatory to Section six of Chapter four hundred and ninety-five of the Special Laws of eighteen hundred and eighty-five, entitled "An Act to incorporate the People's Ferry Company"	200
126	An Act to amend the charter of the Lewiston, Brunswick and Bath Street Railway......................................	200
127	An Act to increase the capital stock of the Ticonic Foot Bridge Company	201
128	An Act to authorize the town of Bucksport to retire its bonded indebtedness and to issue new bonds..............	202
129	An Act relating to the Camden Trotting Park Association..	202
130	An Act to authorize the County Commissioners of Somerset County to borrow a sum of money with which to build an extension to the court house in Skowhegan, in said county,	203
131	An Act to authorize the town of Kennebunk to own and maintain an electric lighting and power plant.............	204

CONTENTS.

CHAP.		PAGE
132	An Act to amend the charter of the city of Auburn.........	206
133	An Act to extend the charter of the Granite Trust Company,	207
134	An Act to provide in part for the Expenditures of Government for the year nineteen hundred and three............	207
135	An Act to grant testimonials of Honorable Service to Soldiers who served in the War with Spain......................	209
136	An Act to amend Resolve in favor of the town of Sanford..	209
137	An Act to amend the charter of the city of Auburn and to provide for a Board of Public Works....................	210
138	An Act to incorporate the Maine Midland Railroad Company,	211
139	An Act relating to the jurisdiction of the Municipal Court of the City of Biddeford.....................................	215
140	An Act concerning the Auburn Free Public Library........	216
141	An Act to amend Chapter one hundred thirty of the Private Laws of eighteen hundred and sixty-six, entitled "An Act to incorporate the Sebec Dam Company," as amended by Section six of Chapter twenty-six of Private and Special Laws of eighteen hundred and ninety-nine.....................	216
142	An Act to amend Chapter one hundred and forty-five of the Private and Special Laws of eighteen hundred and eighty-seven, entitled "An Act to provide sewerage in the town of Houlton"	217
143	An Act to relieve the town of Boothbay Harbor from the duty of building, repairing or maintaining roads, streets or ways on the Isle of Springs....................................	218
144	An Act authorizing Washington County to sell its stock in the Washington County Railroad Company, and authorizing the sale or lease of said railroad............................	219
145	An Act to extend the charter of the Old Orchard Trust and Banking Company	223
146	An Act to incorporate the Tyngstown Water Company.....	223
147	An Act to provide blanks, books and stationery for the Dover Municipal Court	227
148	An Act to amend Chapter two hundred and twenty-seven of the Private and Special Laws of eighteen hundred and eighty, entitled, "An Act to supply the people of Houlton with pure water," as amended by Chapter four hundred and ninety-seven of the Private and Special Laws of eighteen hundred and eighty-nine.................................	227
149	An Act to incorporate the Executive Committee of Huntoon Hill Grange, Number three hundred ninety-eight, Patrons of Husbandry	228
150	An Act to amend the charter of the President and Trustees of Colby College...	229
151	An Act to amend an Act entitled "An Act to authorize the opening of a second channel of Mousam River"..........	230
152	An Act to amend Chapter one hundred and seventy-five of the Private and Special Laws of eighteen hundred and eighty-seven, entitled "An Act to incorporate the Androscoggin Valley Agricultural Society"......................	231
153	An Act to consolidate and amend Chapter one hundred and seventy-seven of the Special Laws of eighteen hundred and eighty-seven, and all acts additional thereto and amendatory thereof, relating to the Old Town Municipal Court.......	231

CHAP.		PAGE
154	An Act for the better protection of Deer in the County of York	239
155	An Act to incorporate the Liberty Water Company	239
156	An Act to extend the charter of the Bluehill Water Company,	242
157	An Act granting a new charter to the Farmington Village Corporation	242
158	An Act to incorporate the Brunswick and Topsham Water District	245
159	An Act to incorporate the Kennebec Valley Railroad Company	251
160	An Act to incorporate the Houlton and Woodstock Electric Railroad Company	255
161	An Act to incorporate the Millinocket Trust Company	258
162	An Act to incorporate the Meduxnekeag Light and Power Company	263
163	An Act to amend the charter of the Portland and Cape Elizabeth Ferry Company	265
164	An Act to enable the Presque Isle Water Company to issue bonds to pay, retire and cancel its outstanding bonds	266
165	An Act relating to the election and term of office of certain members of the Board of Assessors, Board of Overseers of the Poor and female members of the School Committee of the city of Portland	266
166	An Act to authorize the town of Athens to remove the bodies of deceased persons	267
167	An Act to extend the charter of the Winthrop Cold Spring Water Company	268
168	An Act to authorize the Van Buren Water Company to increase its capital stock and bonds	268
169	An Act relating to the Young Women's Christian Association of Portland, Maine	269
170	An Act relating to Gorham Academy	269
171	An Act to enlarge the powers of the Prouts Neck Water Company	270
172	An Act to incorporate the Security Trust Company	271
173	An Act to amend Chapter four hundred seven of the Private and Special Laws of eighteen hundred and forty-six, entitled "An Act to incorporate the Penobscot Log Driving Company"	275
174	An Act to incorporate the West Branch Driving and Reservoir Dam Company	277
175	An Act to consolidate Atlantic Shore Line Railway, Sanford and Cape Porpoise Railway Company, Mousam River Railroad and Sanford Power Company	284
176	An Act to incorporate the Hancock Water, Light and Power Company	288
177	An Act relating to the Fryeburg Electric Light Company	291
178	An Act to extend the charter of the Strong Water Company,	292
179	An Act to incorporate the Libby Meadow Brook Dam Company	292
180	An Act to incorporate the Round Pond Improvement Company	294
181	An Act to amend the charter of the Sanford Light and Water Company and to consolidate with the Springvale Aqueduct Company and Butler Spring Water Company	295

CHAP.		PAGE
182	An Act to incorporate the Van Buren Sewerage Company...	297
183	An Act to incorporate the Saint John River Dam Company..	301
184	An Act to incorporate the Wells Electric Light and Power Company	311
185	An Act to extend the rights, powers and privileges of the Greenville Water Company.	313
186	An Act to incorporate the Sanford Light and Power Company	314
187	An Act to incorporate the Pike Family Association	316
188	An Act to extend the charter of the Hallowell Trust Company	317
189	An Act to incorporate the Wells Telephone Company	317
190	An Act to incorporate the City Trust Company, of Bangor, Maine	319
191	An Act to regulate the taking of codfish, pollock, hake and haddock in the waters of Frenchman's Bay	323
192	An Act to incorporate the Tamarack Club of Patten	324
193	An Act to incorporate the East Branch Improvement Company	325
194	An Act to remove a doubt in the act incorporating the Gardiner Water District	327
195	An Act to amend the charter of the city of Gardiner	327
196	An Act to authorize the Kennebunk Electric Light Company to issue bonds	329
197	An Act to amend an act entitled "An Act to incorporate the City of Old Town"	330
198	An Act to extend the charter of the Union River Water Storage Company	333
199	An Act to incorporate the Brownville and Williamsburg Water Company	333
200	An Act to incorporate the Boothbay Harbor Electric Light and Power Company	336
201	An Act to authorize the Saint John Lumber Company to build piers and booms in the Saint John River in the town of Van Buren	337
202	An Act to authorize the Caratunk Power Company to erect and maintain dams across the Carrabasset River in the towns of Anson and Embden	338
203	An Act to amend Section two of Chapter fifty-six of the Private and Special Laws of one thousand eight hundred and ninety-five, relative to the water supply of Boothbay Harbor	341
204	An Act to incorporate the Hillside Water Company	341
205	An Act additional to the acts which constitute the charter of the trustees of Hebron Academy	343
206	An Act to amend the charter of the Maine Historical Society, permitting said society to hold real and personal estate to the value of five hundred thousand dollars	344
207	An Act to amend the charter of the City of Calais, relating to Ward and District lines	345
208	An Act to prevent the throwing of sawdust and other mill waste into Saint Georges River in the towns of Montville, Searsmont and Appleton	345
209	An Act to change the name of Burnt Island in the town of North Haven to Scallop Island	346

CHAP.		PAGE
210	An Act to make valid certain doings of the Assessors of Norway for the year one thousand nine hundred and two..	346
211	An Act to extend the charter of the Dexter Water Company,	346
212	An Act to incorporate the Searsport Water Company........	347
213	An Act authorizing the County Commissioners of Cumberland County to erect a county building in Portland.......	350
214	An Act to prohibit the use of purse and drag seines in the waters of Sargentville Harbor, known as Billings Cove....	351
215	An Act to construe and continue in force Chapter one hundred and six of the Private and Special Laws of the year one thousand eight hundred and ninety-one, relating to the election of a school committee, and superintendent of schools, for the town of Skowhegan......................	351
216	An Act to establish a School Board for the City of Brewer..	352
217	An Act relative to elections of Treasurer and Collector of Taxes of the City of Augusta...........................	353
218	An Act to enlarge the powers of the Carrabassett Stock Farms,	353
219	An Act to establish a Municipal Court in the city of Eastport ....:........	356
220	An Act to authorize the town of Brunswick to raise money to defray the expense of locating a Water Supply..........	360
221	An Act to regulate the appointment of Constables by the City Council of Portland............................,......	360
222	An Act to authorize the extensions of the Bangor and Aroostook Railroad, in Aroostook, Piscataquis and Penobscot counties	361
223	An Act to establish an additional Normal School to be located at Presque Isle, in the county of Aroostook..............	363
224	An Act to amend the charter of the Lubec Water Company..	364
225	An Act relating to the powers of the Portland and Rumford Falls Railway	365
226	An Act to authorize Frederick J. Merrill of Damariscotta to construct a tide wheel in tide waters of the Damariscotta River	365
227	An Act to incorporate the Rangeley Trust Company of Rangeley, Maine	366
228	An Act to provide in part for the Expenditures of Government for the year nineteen hundred and four..............	370
229	An Act relating to the jurisdiction of the Municipal Court of the City of Auburn....................................	375
230	An Act to incorporate the Castine Gas Company, Castine, Hancock County	375
231	An Act to protect the waters of Lake Auburn..............	377
232	An Act authorizing the town of Anson to purchase with the town of Madison in the county of Somerset, the Norridgewock Falls Bridge.......................................	378
233	An Act to amend the charter of Dead River Log Driving Company	378
234	An Act to authorize the Augusta Trust Company to increase its capital stock	379
235	An Act to incorporate the Mount Abram Cemetery Company.	379
236	An Act to extend the time for the acceptance of the charter of the City of Dexter......................................	380
237	An Act to permit ice fishing in Pease pond on Saturdays of each week during certain months........................	381

CHAP.		PAGE
238	An Act to incorporate the Wilton Trust Company..........	381
239	An Act to incorporate the Somerset Trust Company........	385
240	An Act to incorporate the Lubec Trust and Banking Company	389
241	An Act to supply the town of Lisbon with pure water.......	393
242	An Act authorizing the sale of Norridgewock Falls Bridge..	399
243	An Act authorizing the town of Madison to purchase with the town of Anson in the County of Somerset the Norridgewock Falls Bridge..	399
244	An Act to prevent the throwing of sawdust and other refuse matter into Half Moon Stream, or Sandy Stream or any of the tributaries to Unity Pond, in the County of Waldo.....	400
245	An Act to amend Chapter one hundred forty-three of the Private and Special Laws of eighteen hundred eighty-seven, entitled "An Act to incorporate the Cumberland Illuminating Company"	400
246	An Act to authorize Edward J. Mayo and his assigns to maintain a wharf in Sebec Lake.............................	400
247	An Act to authorize the navigation by steam, of Eagle Lake and the connecting lakes, in the county of Aroostook......	401
248	An Act to incorporate the Maine and New Hampshire Railroad	402
249	An Act to fix the beginning of the open season on fishing in Sebago Lake in Cumberland County.....................	403
250	An Act to authorize the Kennebec Log Driving Company to maintain piers and booms in the Kennebec River above the Augusta Dam	403
251	An Act to prevent the destruction of Smelts in the waters of towns of Lubec and Trescott in the County of Washington,	404
252	An Act to amend Section one of Chapter three hundred and twenty-nine of the Private and Special Laws of nineteen hundred and one, relating to ice fishing in certain lakes and ponds in Kennebec County...............................	404
253	An Act to incorporate the Jonesport Railway Company.....	405
254	An Act to establish the Lubec and Machias Railway Company	408
255	An Act to authorize the Norcross Transportation Company to erect buoys in certain waters of the West Branch of the Penobscot River	411
256	An Act to authorize John M. Jewell to erect and maintain a dam across the Sebasticook River in the town of Clinton..	411
257	An Act to provide for the protection of Deer on the island of Mount Desert	412
258	An Act to prohibit bait fishing, so called, in certain portions of Magalloway river and its tributaries and in various ponds in Oxford County..	412
259	An Act to amend Section one of Chapter one hundred seventy-two of the Private and Special Laws of eighteen hundred ninety-nine, relating to Lobster Traps in Pigeon Hill bay..	413
260	An Act regulating fishing in Quimby pond in the County of Franklin	413
261	An Act to regulate fishing in Kennebago Lake and other lakes and ponds and their tributaries, in Franklin County........	414
262	An Act to authorize the Boston Excelsior Company to locate piers and booms in the Sebec River.......................	414

CONTENTS.

CHAP.		PAGE
263	An Act to amend the charter of the city of Lewiston and to provide for a street, sewer and permanent improvement department	415
264	An Act to extend the charter of the Eastport Street Railway Company	417
265	An Act to incorporate the Waterville and Winslow Bridge Company	418
266	An Act to incorporate the Ellis River Improvement Company,	419
267	An Act to incorporate the Buckfield Water, Power and Electric Light Company	422
268	An Act to incorporate the South Branch Moose River Dam Company	425
269	An Act to incorporate the Ferguson Stream Improvement Company	427
270	An Act to amend the charter of the Union Boom Company	428
271	An Act to extend the charter of Sebasticook Manufacturing and Power Company	429
272	An Act to amend the charter of the Baskahegan Dam Company	430
273	An Act authorizing the town of Fort Fairfield to make a loan,	431
274	An Act to amend and extend the charter of the Waldo Trust Company	431
275	An Act to extend and amend the charter of the Bangor Loan and Trust Company	432
276	An Act amendatory to Chapter three hundred and sixty-nine of the Private and Special Laws of eighteen hundred and eighty-nine, entitled, "An Act regulating the appointment of the members of the police force of the city of Bangor"	433
277	An Act to amend "An Act to establish a Municipal Court for the town of Brunswick."	434
278	An Act to amend the charter of the Moose River Log Driving Company	437
279	An Act to amend the charter of the Bar Harbor Banking and Trust Company	438
280	An Act to incorporate the Fish River Improvement Company,	438
281	An Act to incorporate the Winterport, Frankfort and Prospect Electric Railway	440
282	An Act to incorporate the Lee Telephone Company	442
283	An Act to incorporate the Androscoggin Log Driving Company	444
284	An Act to incorporate the Sullivan Harbor Water Company	449
285	An Act in relation to the Ellsworth Municipal Court	453
286	An Act relating to the Franchise Rights and Privileges of the Milbridge and Cherryfield Electric Railroad Company	456
287	An Act to incorporate the Washington Telephone Company	457
288	An Act to amend An Act entitled "An Act to incorporate the Machias Log Driving Company," approved April eighth, one thousand eight hundred and fifty-four	458
289	An Act to incorporate the Hillside Water Company	459
290	An Act to renew and extend the charter of the Boothbay Harbor Banking Company	462
291	An Act to incorporate the Patten Trust Company	462
292	An Act to incorporate the Cherryfield and Milbridge Street Railway	466
293	An Act relative to the Aroostook Valley Railroad Company	469

CHAP.		PAGE
294	An Act to extnd the charter of the Maine Water and Electric Power Company	470
295	An Act to authorize the Aroostook Valley Railroad Company to purchase or lease the property and franchises of the Presque Isle Electric Light Company	471
296	An Act to incorporate the Village Cemetery Association of Searsport, Waldo County, Maine	472
297	An Act to extend the charter of the Bluehill and Bucksport Electric Railroad Company	473
298	An Act authorizing Samuel D. Warren and others to erect and maintain piers and booms in the Kennebec River	473
299	AnAct to prohibit ice fishing in Number Nine Lake, situated in Township nine, Range three, in the County of Aroostook,	474
300	An Act to prohibit all ice fishing in First or Billings pond, in Bluehill, county of Hancock	475
301	An Act for the Protection of Deer in the counties of Kennebec, Knox, Waldo and Lincoln	475
302	An Act creating a close time on the tributaries to Indian, South and Twitchell ponds, and on Indian pond, in Greenwood, and the tributaries to Bryant pond in Woodstock, in the county of Oxford	476
303	An Act to Legalize the Doings of the Selectmen of the Town of Waltham	476
304	An Act to authorize Bath, West Bath and Brunswick, to build a bridge over the New Meadows River between Brunswick and West Bath	477
305	An Act to amend an act incorporating the Trustees of Bridgton Academy	478
306	An Act in relation to the Bath Military and Naval Orphan Asylum	479
307	An Act opening certain tributaries to Sebec lake to fishing under the general law	479
308	An Act to change the corporate name of "Maine Wesleyan Seminary and Female College"	480
309	An Act to incorporate Washington County General Hospital	481
310	An Act to amend Chapter three hundred eighty-one of the private laws of nineteen hundred and one, relating to open time on Deer in Cumberland county	481
311	An Act to amend Chapter sixty-five of the Private and Special Laws of eighteen hundred seventy-five relative to Petit Menan Point	482
312	An Act to amend the charter of the Penobscot Lumbering Association	483
313	An Act to limit the number of fish that may be taken from Spring lake, in Somerset County, in one day	484
314	An Act to repeal so much of Chapter thirty of the Revised Statutes, as amended by Chapter forty-two, Section five, of the Public Laws of eighteen hundred and ninety-nine, as prohibits fishing in Parlin stream, in Somerset County, from the mouth of Bean brook to Long pond	484
315	An Act to incorporate the Medunkeunk Dam and Improvement Company	485
316	An Act to incorporate the Duck Lake Dam Company	487
317	An Act to prohibit the taking of Clams in the shores or flats within the town of Scarboro	489

CHAP.		PAGE
318	An Act to prohibit the sale of any kind of fish, except eels, taken from certain ponds in Kennebec and Somerset counties	489
319	An Act to prohibit fishing in Morrill Pond in the County of Somerset	490
320	An Act to prevent the destruction of Smelts or Tomcods so called in Steuben Bay	490
321	An Act to regulate the taking of black bass in Upper Kezar Pond in Oxford county, also to prohibit the taking of smelts in any tributary of said pond	491
322	An Act fixing the beginning of the open season for fishing in Little Sebago pond, in the towns of Gray and Windham, in Cumberland county	491
323	An Act to incorporate the Phillips Trust Company	491
324	An Act to incorporate the Merchants Trust Company	495
325	An Act authorizing the Lewiston Trust and Safe Deposit Company to establish a branch at Freeport	499
326	An Act to incorporate the Patten Telegraph and Telephone Company	499
327	An Act to ratify the lease of the Sangerville Improvement Company to the Dover and Foxcroft Light and Heat Company	501
328	An Act to prohibit the throwing of sawdust or other mill refuse into Ellis Stream, so called, in Waldo, Brooks and Belfast, in Waldo County	502
329	An Act additional to the act creating the Rumford Falls Municipal Court	503
330	An Act to amend Section one of Chapter five hundred and sixteen of the Private and Special Laws of eighteen hundred and ninety-seven, entitled "An Act additional relating to the appointment of a Recorder for the Bath Municipal Court"	505
331	An Act to extend the time during which the tolls granted to the Bangor Bridge Company shall continue	506
322	An Act to amend the charter of Maine Investment and Guarantee Company	507
333	An Act to incorporate the Fraternity Temple Company	507
334	An Act to incorporate the Augusta Water District	509
335	An Act to authorize the Phillips and Rangeley Railroad Company to purchase or lease the property and franchises of the Madrid Railroad Company	515
336	An Act to extend and amend the charter of the Bluehill Trust and Banking Company	516
337	An Act to incorporate the Naples Water Company	517
338	An Act to incorporate the Dirigo Electric Light Company of Dexter	519
339	An Act closing Cupsuptic River and its tributaries to all fishing, above the foot of the first falls near its mouth, from July first to May first	523
340	An Act to incorporate the Ashland Trust Company	523
341	An Act to amend the charter of the Augusta Trust Company,	527
342	An Act to permit the Longwood Real Estate Company to construct a wharf in Long Lake, in the town of Naples	527
343	An Act to extend time of construction of Boothbay Railroad	528
344	An Act to incorporate the Brooks Village Corporation	529

CONTENTS.

CHAP.		PAGE
345	An Act for the protection of deer and moose in the County of Sagadahoc	532
346	An Act to incorporate the Maine Coast Telephone Company,	532
347	An Act to prohibit the dumping of herring and all fish offal in the waters of Jonesport and Addison	533
348	An Act to prohibit the throwing of sawdust and other refuse into Norton, Brown or Heath Brooks or their tributaries in the towns of Shapleigh and Limerick	534
349	An Act prohibiting the use of boats or launches of any kind propelled by steam, naphtha, gasolene, or electricity, while hunting sea birds in the waters of Frenchman's Bay, so called, on the coast of Maine	534
350	An Act to regulate fishing in the tributaries of Wilson lake in Wilton, in the County of Franklin	535
351	An Act to prohibit all ice fishing in Lake Webb or Weld pond, so called, in the town of Weld, County of Franklin	535
352	An Act to legalize the acts and doings of Nashville Plantation, Aroostook County	536
353	An Act relating to the new iron bridge over the Presumpscot River in the Town of Falmouth	536
354	An Act to fix qualification for participation in party caucuses in the City of Augusta	537
355	An Act to protect Smelts during their Spawning Season in the Tributaries of the Damariscotta River	538
356	An Act to amend Chapter four hundred and twenty-nine of the Private and Special Laws of nineteen hundred and one, entitled "An Act to establish a municipal court in the town of Winthrop"	538
357	An Act to incorporate the Kibbie Dam Company	544
358	An Act to amend Sections seventeen and nineteen of Chapter one hundred and five of the Private and Special Laws of eighteen hundred and sixty-one, relating to the Election of Mayor, Aldermen, Common Councilmen, Wardens and Ward Clerks, in the city of Lewiston	546
359	An Act to authorize the town of York to construct and maintain Sewers in said Town	548
360	An Act regulating fishing in the streams in Salem and Strong in Franklin County	549
361	An Act regulating the taking of black bass in waters lying wholly or partly in the County of Hancock	549
362	An Act to permit the use of Purse Seines in Damariscotta River	549
363	An Act relating to the Open Season for Fishing in Wilson Lake in the Town of Wilton	550
364	An Act to set off a part of Reed Plantation, and annex the same to Drew Plantation	550
365	An Act authorizing the town of Caribou to hold stock to the extent of four thousand dollars in a company forming for the purpose of erecting a Public Building, or Town Hall	551
366	An Act relating to Fire Wardens in the Town of Bucksport,	552
367	An Act to amend Chapter four hundred and ninety-five of the Private and Special Laws of eighteen hundred ninety-three, relating to the destruction of fish in the Eastern Penobscot River in the town of Orland	552

CHAP.		PAGE
308	An Act to grant additional powers to the Auburn, Mechanic Falls and Norway Street Railway..........................	555
369	An Act to grant certain powers to the Hancock County Trustees of public reservations............................	556
370	An Act to amend an act relating to the Municipal Court for the city of Lewiston......................................	557
371	An Act to extend the powers of the Union River Light, Gas and Power Company..	558
372	An Act to authorize the navigation, by Steam or Electricity, of Range Ponds in the town of Poland.....................	560
373	An Act to supply the people of Bangor with Pure Drinking Water	561
374	An Act to authorize Jacob C. Pike to extend and maintain a Wharf in Lubec Narrows.................................	564
375	An Act to authorize Clarence H. Clark to extend and maintain a wharf in Lubec Narrows............................	564
376	An Act to authorize the Portage Lake Mill Company to build and maintain Piers and Booms, and to operate a Steamboat in Portage Lake	564
377	An Act to incorporate the Peaks Island Water and Light Company	565
378	An Act to authorize Bion M. Pike to maintain and extend a Wharf into the tide waters of Johnson's Bay, in the Town of Lubec, County of Washington...........................	567
379	An Act to authorize Bion M. Pike to maintain and extend a wharf to the harbor line into the tide waters of Lubec Narrows in the town of Lubec, County of Washington.........	567
380	An Act to amend Chapter four hundred and twenty-two of the Private and Special Laws of nineteen hundred and one, relating to the East Pittston Village Corporation..........	567
381	An Act to amend Chapter one hundred and forty-nine of the Private and Special Laws of eighteen hundred and ninety-five, entitled "An Act to divide the town of Sullivan and incorporate the town of Sorrento.........................	569
382	An Act relative to elections of Treasurer and Collector of Taxes of the city of Hallowell............................	570
383	An Act authorizing the acceptance of the conveyance of Widow's Island, Maine, by the State of Maine............	570
384	An Act relative to the treasurer and collector of Taxes of the City of Waterville.......................................	571
385	An Act relative to the Treasurer and Collector of the City of Bangor	571
386	An Act relative to the Treasurer and Collector of Taxes for the town of Brownfield....................................	571
387	An Act in relation to the Treasurer and Collector of Taxes, in the town of Oakfield, in Aroostook County..............	572
388	An Act to incorporate the Houlton and Danforth Electric Railroad Company	572
389	An Act to authorize the Skowhegan and Norridgewock Railway and Power Company to extend its line to and into the town of Smithfield	575
390	An Act to incorporate the Lumberman's Electric Railway Company	575
391	An Act to incorporate the Farmers' Telephone Company.....	579

CHAP.		PAGE
392	An Act to amend Section two of Chapter five hundred eight of the Private and Special Laws of eighteen hundred eighty-five, as amended by Chapter one hundred thirty-four of the Private and Special Laws of eighteen hundred eighty-seven, Chapter five hundred twenty-seven of the Private and Special Laws of eighteen hundred ninety-three, and Chapter four hundred twenty-five of the Private and Special Laws of nineteen hundred one, relating to Norway Municipal Court,	580
393	An Act conferring certain power upon the Trustees of the University of Maine...	581
394	An Act to regulate the Police Force of the City of Portland,	581
395	An Act to make the bridge of the Proprietors of the Wiscasset Bridge, a Public Bridge......................................	585
396	An Act amending the charter of the City of Rockland........	587
397	An Act for the protection of Squirrels and Chipmunks in the County of Knox.......................................	588
398	An Act to amend An Act entitled "An Act authorizing Washington County to sell its stock in the Washington County Railroad Company, and authorizing the sale or lease of said railroad" approved March ten, nineteen hundred three......	588
399	An Act providing temporarily for the payment of Wardens for their services..	590
400	An Act to change the name of the Plantation of Winterville,	591
401	An Act to authorize William C. Farrell and Henry A. Gagnon, to construct a dam or dams across Hammond brook, in Aroostook county, and build and maintain piers in said brook, and improve said brook for driving purposes.......	591
402	An Act to amend Section three of Chapter thirty of the Private and Special Laws of eighteen hundred and seventy-two, relating to the Godfrey Falls Dam Company.........	592
403	An Enabling Act for the annexation of the city of South Portland to Portland	593
404	An Act to incorporate the Piscataquis River Storage Company	597
405	An Act relating to prize logs on the Penobscot river and its tributaries	601
406	An Act to prevent the throwing of sawdust and other mill waste into all tributaries of Seven Tree pond and Crawford pond in Union and Warren...............................	603
407	An Act to consolidate and revise certain laws relating to closing certain lakes and ponds to ice fishing, and to close the tributaries to certain lakes and ponds, and restricting the number of fish that may be taken in one day in certain waters, and defining the manner of fishing in certain waters, and prohibiting the throwing of sawdust and other mill refuse into certain streams, and regulating the method of hunting ducks in certain waters, and regulating the taking of deer in certain counties................................	604
408	An Act to incorporate the Munsungun Telephone Company..	617
409	An Act to authorize A. M. Goddard and others to build and maintain a Movable Sidewalk.............................	618
410	An Act to incorporate the Kittery and York Telephone Company	618

iii

CHAP.		PAGE
411	An Act relating to the Election of a Road Commissioner in the town of Boothbay Harbor....................................	620
412	An Act to incorporate the Tyler-Fogg Trust Company.......	620
413	An Act to amend Section three of Chapter fifty of the Private and Special Laws of eighteen hundred and twenty-one as amended by Chapter one hundred and sixty-one of the Private and Special Laws of eighteen hundred and forty-eight, as amended by Chapter one hundred and seventy-one of the Private and Special Laws of eighteen hundred and sixty-two, relating to extending the time of controlling the water at the alewive fishery at Damariscotta Mills.........	624
414	An Act to enable the County of Sagadahoc to rebuild Merry-meeting Bay Bridge, accept Arrowsic Bridge, and to maintain both bridges free, to accept the Peoples' Ferry, and to acquire in conjunction with the County of Lincoln or town of Dresden the ferry between Richmond and Dresden, to operate the same and to reduce the tolls by at least one-half..	625
415	An Act to annex certain Islands in Casco Bay to the County of Sagadahoc and the town of Phippsburg.................	628
416	An Act for the assessment of a State Tax for the year one thousand nine hundred and three, amounting to the sum of nine hundred seventy thousand four hundred seventy-five dollars and seventy-seven cents.............................	629
417	An Act for the assessment of a State Tax for the year one thousand nine hundred and four, amounting to the sum of nine hundred seventy thousand four hundred seventy-five dollars and seventy-seven cents.............................	676
418	An Act to provide in part for the Expenditures of Government for the year nineteen hundred and three.............	723
419	An Act to provide in part for the Expenditures of Government for the year nineteen hundred and four...............	730
420	An Act in regard to the use of the Roads in Town of Eden..	734
421	An Act to maintain and operate a Draw Bridge at the outlet of Long Lake in the Town of Naples.......................	734
422	An Act in relation to the salary of the Recorder of the Municipal Court of the City of Biddeford.................	735

TITLES OF RESOLVES.

SESSION OF 1903.

CHAP.		PAGE
1	Resolve protesting against the Hay-Bond Treaty...........	3
2	Resolve in aid of the Temporary Home for Women and Children at Portland.....................................	4
3	Resolve providing for a special epidemic or emergency fund,	5
4	Resolve in favor of the Children's Aid Society of Maine......	5
5	Resolve in favor of Nellie E. Flanders of Liberty............	5
6	Resolve in favor of Benjamin Smith of Appleton in Knox County	6
7	Resolve providing for the compensation of Steamboat Inspectors for the years nineteen hundred, nineteen hundred and one, and nineteen hundred and two.......................	6
8	Resolve in favor of King's Daughters Union of Bangor......	6
9	Resolve providing for the preservation of Regimental Rolls in the Adjutant-General's office.........................	7
10	Resolve for State Pensions.................................	7
11	Resolve in favor of Mary C. Rankin, widow of Orlenzo K. Rankin late of Company K, First New England Regiment, Mexican War	7
12	Resolve in favor of the Bath Military and Naval Orphan Asylum	8
13	Resolve in favor of the dairying interests of the State of Maine	8
14	Resolve for the purpose of operating the fish hatcheries and feeding stations for fish and for the protection of Fish......	8
15	Resolve in favor of Allagash Road........................	9
16	Resolves in relation to extra pay of Maine Volunteers in the War with Spain..	9
17	Resolve in favor of the State Reform School..............	10
18	Resolve in favor of Bernhard Pol of Bangor, to re-imburse him for taxes paid through error............................	10
19	Resolve in favor of the purchase of tne Maine State Year Book and Legislative Manual for the years nineteen hundred and three and nineteen hundred and four.............	11
20	Resolve in favor of the town of Sanford.....................	11
21	Resolve providing for paying to the city of Rockland the amount deducted from its school fund for the year one thousand nine hundred and two, on account of imperfect school returns	11
22	Resolves in relation to the completion of the fifth revision of the general and public laws, and appointing a Commissioner therefor	12
23	Resolve to provide means for examinations of claims for State Pensions	13
24	Resolve in favor of establishing a Fish Hatchery and Feeding Station at the Rangeley Lakes...........................	13

CONTENTS.

CHAP.		PAGE
25	Resolve in favor of roads in the Indian Township, Washington County	13
26	Resolve to provide for the expenses of the Maine Industrial School for Girls	14
27	Resolve in favor of establishing a modern Fish hatchery and feeding station at Sebago Lake	14
28	Resolve making appropriations for the Passamaquoddy tribe of Indians	14
29	Resolves authorizing a Temporary Loan for the year nineteen hundred and three	15
30	Resolves authorizing a Temporary Loan for the year nineteen hundred and four	16
31	Resolve making appropriation for Penobscot Tribe of Indians,	16
32	Resolve waiving a forfeiture of the public lot in the southeast quarter of Township Number Four, Hancock County, North Division	17
33	Resolve authorizing the Land Agent to sell certain public lots in E plantation and Portage Lake plantation, in Aroostook County	17
34	Resolve in favor of the Women's Christian Temperance Union	17
35	Resolve in favor of the Society of the Sisters of Charity for the use of the Healy Asylum of Lewiston, Maine	18
36	Resolve in favor of the Young Women's Home of Lewiston,	18
37	Resolve in favor of Albert R. Buck, Chairman of the committee on Maine State Prison	18
38	Resolve in favor of the committee on Revision of the Statutes,	19
39	Resolve in favor of the Town of Trescott	19
40	Resolve in favor of the Maine School for the Deaf	19
41	Resolve in favor of repairing elevator in State House	19
42	Resolve in favor of the Augusta City hospital	20
43	Resolve in favor of the Eastern Maine General Hospital	20
44	Resolve in favor of the Maine Eye and Ear Infirmary	20
45	Resolve in favor of the Hospital of the Society of the Sisters of Charity of Lewiston, Maine	21
46	Resolve in favor of the Central Maine General Hospital	21
47	Resolve in favor of a Maine Soldier's Monument at the Andersonville, Georgia, National Cemetery	21
48	Resolve in favor of the Bar Harbor Medical and Surgical Hospital	22
49	Resolve in favor of the Maine Industrial School for Girls	22
50	Resolve in favor of the Maine Home for Friendless Boys	23
51	Resolve in favor of George B. Haskell, Jacob R. Little and Stephen J. Kelley, in payment of Witnesses', Magistrates' and Officers' fees and disbursements made by them in the city of Lewiston contested election case	23
52	Resolve in favor of Edmund C. Bryant, chairman of the committee on Reform School	23
53	Resolve for an appropriation for the preservation of the remains of Fort William Henry, now the property of the State of Maine	24
54	Resolve to aid in repairing roads in Jerusalem Plantation	24
55	Resolve in favor of the Town of Crystal	24
56	Resolve in favor of the Maine General Hospital	25

CONTENTS.

CHAP.		PAGE
57	Resolve in favor of the Saint Elizabeth's Roman Catholic Orphan Asylum of Portland................................	25
58	Resolve in favor of the Town of Moscow...................	25
59	Resolve in favor of the Committee on Maine State Prison....	26
60	Resolve in favor of C. C. Libby, chairman of the Committee on Education	26
61	Resolve in favor of the town of Island Falls................	26
62	Resolve in favor of the Bangor Children's Home.............	27
63	Resolve in favor of Passamaquoddy Tribe of Indians for the completion of a new church at Pleasant Point, in the Town of Perry	27
64	Resolve in favor of rebuilding the house of the Sisters of Mercy at Peter Dana's Point, within the Jurisdiction of the Passamaquoddy Tribe of Indians.........................	27
65	Resolve for an appropriation for the use of the Commissioner of Sea and Shore Fisheries..............................	28
66	Resolve in favor of Knox County General Hospital..........	28
67	Resolve in favor of the Madawaska Training School........	28
68	Resolve in aid of Caratunk for repairing road from Caratunk village to Pleasant pond in said plantation...........	29
69	Resolve in favor of the Farmington State Normal School....	29
70	Resolve in favor of the Town of Houlton...................	29
71	Resolve authorizing the Land Agent to sell certain public lots in Dallas Plantation, in Franklin County...................	30
72	Resolve in favor of the Committee on Maine State Prison....	30
73	Resolve providing for completing the fireproofing and necessary repairs in the south wing of the State Capitol........	30
74	Resolve providing for repairs to be made on the tomb of Governor Enoch Lincoln	31
75	Resolve providing for the Topographic and Geological Survey for the years nineteen hundred and three and nineteen hundred and four and for extending its work to include Hydrography	31
76	Resolve fixing the valuation of Reed Plantation in Aroostook County and Drew Plantation in Penobscot County........	32
77	Resolve laying a Tax on Counties of the State for the years nineteen hundred and three and nineteen hundred and four,	32
78	Resolve for repairs of highway in Upton, Magalloway Plantation and township C, in the County of Oxford............	33
79	Resolve in favor of Lyman E. Smith of Brunswick, for attendance before Agricultural Committee, nineteen hundred and one	33
80	Resolve in favor of the town of Cutler......................	33
81	Resolve in aid of navigation on Moosehead Lake...........	34
82	Resolve in favor of the Norcross Transportation Company..	34
83	Resolve in relation to the early York deeds.................	35
84	Resolve in favor of the town of Mariaville.................	35
85	Resolve in favor of the re-establishment, where necessary of the boundaries of the lots reserved for public uses in the several plantations and unincorporated places..............	35
86	Resolve to pay for the printing and binding of the report of John A. Morrill, Commissioner for the Revision and consolidation of the Public Laws................................	36
87	Resolve providing for an Epidemic or Emergency Fund......	36

CONTENTS.

CHAP.		PAGE
88	Resolve in favor of the stenographers to the presiding and recording officers of the Senate and House................	36
89	Resolve in favor of the Clerk and Stenographer, and the Messenger to the Judiciary Committee......................	37
90	Resolve in favor of the Trustees of the University of Maine..	37
91	Resolve in favor of Colby College..........................	37
92	Resolve in favor of Castine State Normal School............	38
93	Resolve in favor of the Town of Anson.....................	38
94	Resolve in favor of the Clerk to the Committee on Revision of Statutes	38
95	Resolve in favor of John W. Manson, Secretary of the Committee on Legal Affairs....................................	39
96	Resolve in favor of the Town of Edmunds..................	39
97	Resolve in favor of rebuilding the bridge across the West Branch of the Saint Croix river connecting the town of Princeton with Indian Township..........................	39
98	Resolve in favor of repairing Mattawamkeag Bridge.........	40
99	Resolve providing for a fund for completing the records of the Clerk of Courts of Lincoln County......................	40
100	Resolve in favor of the city of Eastport....................	40
101	Resolve in favor of the City of Rockland, on account of the money paid the Hallowell Industrial School for the care of Mary Newell, a minor and member of the Passamaquoddy Tribe of Indians	41
102	Resolve favoring the establishment of a National Forest Reserve in the White Mountain Region...................	41
103	Resolve in favor of A. A. Burleigh, Chairman of the Committee on Interior Waters	42
104	Resolve in favor of Lee Normal Academy...................	42
105	Resolve in favor of the Eastern Maine Insane Hospital.......	43
106	Resolve in favor of the town of East Livermore..............	43
107	Resolve in favor of the Maine State Library................	44
108	Resolve in favor of G. E. Morrison, Chairman of the Committee on Salaries and of the Committee on Military Affairs...	44
109	Resolve in favor of the Board of Cattle Commissioners of the State of Maine, for the prevention of the Foot and Mouth Disease among Cattle............................	45
110	Resolve providing for the collection of information in regard to the large Bridges within the State.....................	45
111	Resolve in aid of Navigation on Lewey, Long and Big Lakes,	46
112	Resolve in favor of the Maine Insane Hospital..............	47
113	Resolve in favor of Drew Plantation.......................	47
114	Resolve providing for Clerk hire in State Library during legislative session of nineteen hundred and three..........	47
115	Resolve in favor of the Eastern Maine General Hospital....	47
116	Resolve in favor of the Bangor Children's Home...........	48
117	Resolve in favor of State House employees.................	48
118	Resolve in aid of repairing the bridge across the Narraguagus River in the town of Milbridge..........................	48
119	Resolve to aid the town of Frenchville in building a Bridge across Gagnon Stream...................................	49
120	Resolve in favor of Wallagrass Plantation...................	49
121	Resolve abating a part of the State Tax of the town of Bowdoinham for the years nineteen hundred and three and nineteen hundred and four...............................	49

CHAP.		PAGE
122	Resolve in favor of the town of New Sharon..................	50
123	Resolve in favor of C. C. Libby, Chairman of the Committee on Education	50
124	Resolve in favor of George D. Gaddis of East Machias.......	50
125	Resolve to provide for the services of a Stenographer and Typewriter, when needed, and for extra clerk hire in the office of the State Superintendent of Public Schools........	51
126	Resolve in favor of the Western State Normal School at Gorham	51
127	Resolve in favor of J. Calvin Knapp, Secretary for the Committee on State Lands and State Roads.....................	51
128	Resolve in favor of R. E. Randall, Secretary of the Committee on Education	51
129	Resolve in favor of the State Committee of the Young Men's Christian Associations of Maine...........................	52
130	Resolve in favor of Joseph Mitchell, Jr., representative of the Penobscot Tribe of Indians.................................	52
131	Resolve in favor of Lewey Mitchell, representative of the Passamaquoddy Tribe of Indians...........................	52
132	Resolve in favor of the Town of Jackson...................	52
133	Resolve in favor of Albion Oakes, secretary of Committee on Ways and Bridges..	53
134	Resolve in favor of Maine Children's Home Society, Augusta,	53
135	Resolve in favor of Connor Plantation......................	53
136	Resolve in favor of the town of Mariaville, to assist in rebuilding Goodwin's bridge, in said town, which was carried away by an ice jam about two weeks ago.......................	54
137	Resolve waiving a forfeiture of the public lots in the north half of Township Number Four, Hancock County, north division	54
138	Resolve to aid the town of Washburn, in the county of Aroostook, in part payment of the cost and expense incurred by it in building a steel bridge across the Aroostook river......	54
139	Resolve in favor of building a bridge across the Mattawamkeag River in the Town of Bancroft......................	55
140	Resolve in favor of repairing the Bridge across the St. Croix River, near Squirrel Point in Baileyville..................	55
141	Resolve in favor of the Town of Parkman...................	55
142	Resolve in favor of paying the unexpired Licenses of Hawkers and Peddlers	56
143	Resolve on the Pay Roll of the Senate......................	60
144	Resolve to provide for the expense of examination of candidates for the Cecil John Rhodes scholarships..............	60
145	Resolve in favor of Maine State Prison.....................	60
146	Resolve on the Pay Roll of the House......................	69
147	Resolve in favor of an Electric Lighting Plant for the Maine State Prison	69
148	Resolve in relation to the publication and distribution of the Revised Statutes	69

PUBLIC LAWS

OF THE

STATE OF MAINE.

1903.

PUBLIC LAWS

OF THE

STATE OF MAINE.

1903

Chapter 1.

An Act to amend Chapter one hundred and forty-three of the Revised Statutes, relating to Insane Persons.

Be it enacted by the Senate and House of Representatives in Legislature assembled, as follows:

Section 1. Section thirteen of chapter one hundred and forty-three of the revised statutes, as amended by chapter two hundred and forty-four of the public laws of eighteen hundred and ninety-seven, is hereby amended as follows: In line four strike out the word "relative," and instead thereof insert the words 'blood-relative, husband or wife of said alleged insane person;' also in the same line strike out the words "in their town;" also in line six after the word "insane," insert 'shall appoint a time and place for a hearing by them of the allegations of said complaint, and shall cause to be given in hand to the person so alleged to be insane, at least twenty-four hours prior to the time of said hearing, a true copy of said complaint, together with a notice of the time and place of said hearing and that he has the right and will be given

Section 13, chapter 143, R. S., as amended by chapter 244, laws 1897, further amended.

—shall appoint time and place for hearing.

—twenty-four hours notice shall be given.

INSANE PERSONS.

Municipal officers shall constitute board of examiners.

—shall appoint time and place for hearing.

—twenty-four hours notice to be given.

—shall call testimony.

—record shall be kept and copy furnished.

Section 34, chapter 143, R. S., amended.

Preliminary proceedings.

—evidence of two reputable witnesses shall be had.

—certified copy of physicians' certificate shall accompany papers of commitment.

opportunity, then and there to be heard in the matter;" also in line nine, strike out the words "to the hospital" and instead thereof insert the words 'either to the Maine Insane Hospital or to the Eastern Maine Hospital,' so that said section, as amended, shall read as follows:

'Section 13. Insane persons, not thus sent to any hospital, shall be subject to examination as hereinafter provided. The municipal officers of towns shall constitute a board of examiners, and on complaint in writing of any blood-relative, husband or wife of said alleged insane person, or of any justice of the peace, they shall immediately inquire into the condition of any person in said town alleged to be insane; shall appoint a time and place for a hearing by them of the allegations of said complaint, and shall cause to be given in hand to the person so alleged to be insane, at least twenty-four hours prior to the time of said hearing, a true copy of said complaint, together with a notice of the time and place of said hearing and that he has the right and will be given opportunity then and there to be heard in the matter; shall call before them all testimony necessary for a full understanding of the case; and if they think such person insane, and that his comfort and safety, or that of others interested, will thereby be promoted, they shall forthwith send him either to the Maine Insane Hospital or to the Eastern Maine Insane Hospital, with a certificate stating the fact of his insanity, and the town in which he resided or was found at the time of examination, and directing the superintendent to receive and detain him until he is restored or discharged by law, or by the superintendent or trustees. They shall keep a record of their doings, and furnish a copy to any interested person requesting and paying for it.'

Section 2. Section thirty-four of chapter one hundred and forty-three of the revised statutes is hereby amended as follows: Strike out all of said section, and instead thereof insert:

'Section 34. In all cases of preliminary proceedings for the commitment of any person to the hospital, to establish the fact of the insanity of the person to whom insanity is imputed there shall be required the evidence of at least two reputable physicians given by them under oath before the board of examiners, together with a certificate signed by such physicians and filed with said board, that in their opinion such person is insane, such evidence and certificate to be based upon due inquiry and personal examination of the person to whom insanity is imputed; and a certified copy of the physicians' certificate shall accompany the papers of commitment of the insane person to the hospital.'

Section 3. This act shall take effect when approved.

Approved January 22, 1903.

Chapter 2.

An Act to amend Section twenty-eight of Chapter seventy-three of the Revised Statutes, relating to Conveyances.

Be it enacted by the Senate and House of Representatives in Legislature assembled, as follows:

Section 1. Section twenty-eight of chapter seventy-three of the revised statutes is hereby amended by inserting after the word "residence" in the fifth line of said section, the words 'the nature of the instrument, the amount of the consideration named therein and the name of the town or unincorporated place as shown by the instrument, in which the property conveyed is located,' so that said section as hereby amended, shall read as follows:

'Section 28. The register shall certify, on each deed by him recorded, the time when it was received, and it shall be considered as recorded at that time. Within one hour after its delivery to him, he shall enter such time, the names of the grantor and grantee, and their places of residence, the nature of the instrument, the amount of the consideration named therein and the name of the town or unincorporated place as shown by the instrument, in which the property conveyed is located, in a book kept for that purpose, and open to inspection in business hours.'

Section 2. This act shall take effect on the first day of July, nineteen hundred and three.

Approved February 4, 1903.

Chapter 3.

An Act to amend Chapter three hundred and seventy-two of the Public Laws of eighteen hundred and eighty-five, relating to the compensation of the County Commissioners for Oxford County.

Be it enacted by the Senate and House of Representatives in Legislature assembled, as follows:

Chapter three hundred and seventy-two of the public laws of eighteen hundred and eighty-five is amended by striking out the words "two dollars and fifty cents" in the second line of said chapter, and inserting instead thereof, the words 'three dollars,' so that said chapter, as amended, shall read as follows:

'Each county commissioner for Oxford County shall receive three dollars per day while actually employed in the service of

MIGRATORY FISH.

the county, including the time spent in traveling, for which he shall have eight cents a mile for the distance actually traveled; but he shall not have more than one travel in the same hearing or session, nor for more than two adjournments of any regular term, nor for service or travel on more than one petition or case at the same time, nor anything for travel or attendance at the legislature connected with the annual county estimates, nor for any additional trouble or expense of any kind.'

Approved February 4, 1903.

Chapter 4.

An Act to amend Section seventeen of Chapter forty of the Revised Statutes, as amended by Chapter two hundred and sixty-one of the Public Laws of eighteen hundred and eighty-five, and by Chapter sixty-one of the Public Laws of eighteen hundred and ninety-one, relating to Migratory Fish.

Be it enacted by the Senate and House of Representatives in Legislature assembled, as follows:

Section seventeen of chapter forty of the revised statutes, as amended by chapter two hundred and sixty-one of the public laws of the year eighteen hundred and eighty-five, and by chapter sixty-one of the public laws of the year eighteen hundred and ninety-one, is hereby further amended by striking out the word "fifteenth" in the twenty-second line of said section, and substituting in lieu thereof the word 'twenty-fifth,' and by striking out the word "fifty" in the twenty-third line of said section, and substituting in lieu thereof the word 'seventy-five,' so that said section, as amended, shall read as follows:

'Section 17. The taking of mackerel, herring, shad, porgies or menhaden, and the fishing therefor by the use of purse and drag seines, is prohibited in all small bays, inlets, harbors or weirs, where any entrance to the same, or any part thereof from land to land, is not more than three nautical miles in width, under a penalty upon the master or person in charge of such seines, or upon the owners of any vessel or seines employed in such unlawful fishing, of not less than three hundred nor more than five hundred dollars, to be recovered by indictment, or action of debt; one-fourth of the penalty to the complainant or prosecutor, and three-fourths to the county in which the proceedings are commenced; and there shall be a lien upon the vessels, steamers, boats and apparatus used in such unlawful pursuit, until said penalty, with costs of prosecution is paid: but a net for meshing mackerel or porgies, of not more than one hundred meshes in depth, and a net for meshing herring, of not more than one hundred and seventy meshes in depth, and a net for meshing shad, of not more than seventy-five meshes in depth, shall not be deemed a seine; and it shall be lawful to take shad and alewives in the Androscoggin river, and in Merrymeeting bay, from April first to June twenty-fifth in each year, by the use of drag seines, not more than seventy-five fathoms in length, and of not more than fifty meshes in depth.'

—seine defined.

—shad and alewives may be taken in Androscoggin river and in Merrymeeting bay, from April 1 to June 25.

Approved February 11, 1908.

Chapter 5.

An Act to amend Section fifteen of Chapter fifteen of the Revised Statutes, relating to Burying-Grounds.

Be it enacted by the Senate and House of Representatives in Legislature assembled, as follows:

Section fifteen of revised statutes of Maine, eighteen hundred and eighty-three is hereby amended by inserting in the second line thereof, after the word "securities," the words, 'or deposited in savings banks.' So that said section as amended, shall read as follows:

Section 15 of chapter 15, R. S., amended.

'Section 15. Every trust fund authorized by the preceding section shall be safely invested in United States, state, county, city or town securities, or deposited in savings banks: and the annual income only, shall be expended in performance of the requirements of the trust.'

Investment of trust funds.

—expenditure of income.

Approved February 11, 1908.

Chapter 6.

An Act to amend Section twenty-four of Chapter one hundred and two, Public Laws of eighteen hundred and ninety-one, as amended by Chapter two hundred and sixty-seven, Public Laws of eighteen hundred and ninety-three, relating to providing for the printing and distributing ballots at the public expense and regulating voting for State and City Elections.

Be it enacted by the Senate and House of Representatives in Legislature assembled, as follows:

Section 24, chapter 102, public laws of 1891, as amended by chapter 267, laws of 1893, further amended.

Section twenty-four of chapter one hundred and two, public laws of eighteen hundred and ninety-one, as amended by chapter two hundred and sixty-seven, public laws of eighteen hundred and ninety-three is hereby amended by inserting in the twelfth line thereof, after the word "choice" the words: 'Or if the voter places and sticks on and over the name or names of any candidate or candidates for any office or offices, a small strip or strips of paper, commonly known as a sticker or stickers, bearing thereon a name or names other than the name or names of the candidate or candidates so erased or covered up, the name or names of such candidate or candidates so covered shall be considered to be erased from the ballot, and the person or persons whose name or names shall so appear on such strip or strips of paper so placed and stuck on the ballot, shall be deemed to be voted for by the voter as candidate or candidates for such office or offices.' So that said section as amended, shall read as follows:

—voter may place stickers on and over name of any candidates.

How voter shall prepare his ballot.

'Section 24. On receipt of his ballot the voter shall forthwith, and without leaving the enclosed space, retire alone to one of the voting shelves or compartments so provided, and shall prepare his ballot by marking in the appropriate margin or place, a cross (**X**) as follows: He may place such mark within the square above the name of the party group or ticket, in which case he shall be deemed to have voted for all the persons named in the group under such party or designation. And if the voter shall desire to vote for any person or persons, whose name or names are not printed as candidates on the party group or ticket, he may erase any name or names which are printed on the group or party ticket, and under the name or names so erased he may fill in the name or names of the candidates of his choice. Or if the voter places and sticks on and over the name or names of any candidate or candidates for any office or offices, a small strip or strips of paper, commonly known as a sticker or stickers, bearing thereon a name or names other than the name or names of the candidate or candidates so erased or covered up, the name or names of such candidate or candidates so covered shall be considered to be erased from the ballot, and the person or persons

—may erase any name and fill in, etc.

—may place stickers over names.

whose name or names shall so appear on such strip or strips of paper so placed and stuck on the ballot, shall be deemed to be voted for by the voter as candidate or candidates for such office or offices. Or if the voter does not desire to vote for a person or persons whose name or names are printed upon the party group or ticket, he may erase such name or names with the effect that the ballot shall not be counted for the candidate or candidates whose names are so erased. In case of a question submitted to the vote of the people he shall place such mark in the appropriate margin above the answer which he desires to give. Before leaving the voting shelf or compartment, the voter shall fold his ballot without displaying the marks thereon, in the same way it was folded when received by him, and he shall keep the same so folded until he has voted. He shall vote in the manner now provided by law before leaving the enclosed space, and shall deposit his ballot in the box with the official endorsement uppermost. He shall mark and deposit his ballot without undue delay and shall quit said enclosed space as soon as he has voted. No such voter shall be allowed to occupy a voting shelf or compartment already occupied by another, or to remain within said enclosed space more than ten minutes, or to occupy a voting shelf or compartment for more than five minutes in case all of such shelves or compartments are in use, and other voters are waiting to occupy the same. No voter not an election officer or an election clerk, whose name has been checked on the list of the ballot clerks, shall be allowed to re-enter said enclosed space during said election. The presiding election officer or officers, for the time being, shall secure the observance of the provisions of this section.'

Approved February 11, 1903.

Chapter 7.

An Act to fix the salary of the Judge of Probate for Hancock County.

Be it enacted by the Senate and House of Representatives in Legislature assembled, as follows:

Section 1. On and after the first day of January in the year of our Lord one thousand nine hundred and three, the salary of the judge of probate for Hancock county shall be thirteen hundred dollars a year instead of the sum now established by law.

Section 2. This act shall take effect when approved.

Approved February 11, 1903.

Chapter 8.

An Act to amend Section forty-seven of Chapter seventy-seven of the Revised Statutes, relating to the times of holding terms of the Supreme Judicial Court in Knox County.

Be it enacted by the Senate and House of Representatives in Legislature assembled, as follows:

Section 47, chapter 77 of R. S., as amended by section 2, chapter 253, laws of 1901, further amended.

Section 1. Section forty-seven of chapter seventy-seven of the revised statutes, as amended by section two of chapter two hundred and fifty-three of the public laws of the year nineteen hundred and one, is hereby amended so that that paragraph of said section relating to the times of holding the terms of the supreme judicial court in the county of Knox shall read as follows:

—when terms of supreme judicial court shall be held in Knox county.

'Knox, at Rockland, on the first Tuesday of January, first Tuesday of April, and the third Tuesday of September.'

Matters commenced before or after this act takes effect shall be entered at the term substituted by this act.

Section 2. All matters commenced before or after this act takes effect and returnable to and all matters pending in said court, and which would, but for the provisions of this act, be entered and have day at the term of said court to be held on the second Tuesday of March, in the year of our Lord, nineteen hundred and three, as provided by law, shall be entered and have day at the term of the supreme judicial court in said county to be held on the first Tuesday of April, in the year of our Lord, nineteen hundred and three which is substituted by this act for the said March term, and shall have day therein as if originally made returnable to said April term; and any provisions of law applicable to any term of court, the time of holding whereof is changed by this act, are hereby made applicable to the substituted term.

Section 3. This act shall take effect when approved.

Approved February 12, 1903.

TAXATION OF SAVINGS BANKS.   11

CHAP. 9

Chapter 9.   *Chap 184 Act of 1907*

An Act to amend Chapter two hundred fifty-eight of the Public Laws of eighteen hundred and ninety-three as amended by Chapter one hundred thirty of the Public Laws of eighteen hundred and ninety-five, relating to the taxation of Savings Banks.

Be it enacted by the Senate and House of Representatives in Legislature assembled, as follows:

Section 1. Section one of chapter two hundred fifty-eight of the public laws of eighteen hundred and ninety-three as amended by section one of chapter one hundred thirty of the public laws of eighteen hundred and ninety-five is hereby amended by striking out the following words in lines nine to sixteen inclusive; "with aggregates so arranged as to clearly show whether the purchase or acquisition of each item in such detailed statement was prior or subsequent to January first, eighteen hundred and ninety-three. All assets, loans or investments made, purchased or acquired from the proceeds of assets, loans or investments held on said January first and thereafter renewed, sold or paid shall be entered in said statement as acquired subsequent to said January first." So that said section as amended, shall read as follows:

'Section 1. Every savings bank, institution for savings and trust and loan association incorporated under the laws of the state, shall, semi-annually, on the last Saturdays of April and October, make a return, signed and sworn to by its treasurer, of the average amount of its deposits, reserve fund and undivided profits for the six months preceding each of said days, together with a statement in detail of its assets, loans and investments and its deposits within and without the state, in separate columns. Said return shall be made to the bank examiner on or before the first Saturdays of May and November and within thirty days thereafter, he shall fix and determine the market values of the investments aforesaid and transmit the same with such values so determined to the state assessors for the assessment required by section two.'

Section 2. Section two of said chapter two hundred fifty-eight as amended by said chapter one hundred thirty is hereby amended by striking out in lines ten to thirteen the following words; "and also an amount equal to one-seventh of such other assets, loans and investments as by said detailed statement appear to have been acquired prior to January first, eighteen hundred and ninety-three"; also by striking out the word "seventh" in the fourteenth line and inserting instead thereof the word 'fifths;' also by striking out the words "and New Hampshire" in the eighteenth line; also by striking out in lines twenty and twenty-

[margin notes: Section 1, chapter 258, public laws 1893, as amended by section 1, chapter 130, laws of 1895, further amended. Savings banks and trust and loan associations, shall make semi-annual statement of deposits, reserve fund and undivided profits. —shall make a statement of assets, loans, investments and deposits within and without the state. Return shall be made to bank examiner, who shall fix market values, and return to state assessors. Section 2, chapter 258, as amended by chapter 130, further amended.]

CHAP. 9

one the words "severally made, purchased or acquired since said January first"; also by striking out the word "sevenths" in the twenty-second line and inserting in place thereof the word 'fifths'; also by striking out the word "seven" in the twenty-fourth line and inserting in place thereof the word 'five'; and by adding at the end of said section the following words: 'Provided, however, that for the year beginning April first, nineteen hundred and three, and ending April first, nineteen hundred and four, the fractional deduction shall be two-sixths and the rate of assessment shall be six-eighths in order to make for said year a reduction of one-eighth of one per cent from the present rate of taxation.' So that said section as amended, shall read as follows:

State assessors shall determine values of the several franchises.

—rule for determining values.

'Section 2. The state assessors shall thereupon determine the values of the several franchises of the said banks, institutions and associations according to the following rule: From the average amount of deposits, reserve fund and undivided profits so returned by each bank, institution or association there shall in each case be deducted an amount equal to the amount of United States bonds, the shares of corporation stocks such as are by law of this state free from taxation to the stockholders, and the assessed value of real estate owned by the bank, institution or association, and also an amount equal to two-fifths of such other assets, loans and investments as by such statement appear to be loans to persons resident or corporations located and doing business in this state, investments in mortgages on real estate in Maine, securities of this state, public or private, bonds issued by corporations located and doing business in this state or guaranteed by such corporations, provided the corporations issuing such bonds be operated by and physically connected with such guaranteeing corporations, and also an amount equal to two-fifths of the cash on hand and cash deposited within the state. Upon the value of each of said franchises so ascertained the state assessors shall assess an annual tax of five-eighths of one per cent, one-half of said tax to be assessed on or before the fifteenth day of June, and one-half on or before the fifteenth day of December. The state assessors shall thereupon certify said assessments to the treasurer of state, who shall forthwith notify the several banks, institutions and associations interested.

—rate of taxation.

—rate for year ending April first, 1904.

Provided, however, that for the year beginning April first, nineteen hundred and three, and ending April first, nineteen hundred and four, the fractional deduction shall be two-sixths and the rate of assessment shall be six-eighths in order to make for said year a reduction of one-eighth of one per cent from the present rate of taxation.'

Section 3. This act shall take effect when approved.

Approved February 12, 1903.

Chapter 10.

An Act to amend Section thirty-five of Chapter one hundred twenty-four of the Revised Statutes as amended by Chapter twenty-five of the Public Laws of eighteen hundred ninety-one, relating to the Transportation of Animals.

Be it enacted by the Senate and House of Representatives in Legislature assembled, as follows:

Section thirty-five of chapter one hundred twenty-four of the revised statutes as amended by chapter twenty-five of the public laws of eighteen hundred ninety-one is hereby amended by substituting for the words "shall in all cases" in line twelve thereof the word 'may' and by inserting before "separate" in line thirteen thereof, the words 'shall be,' and by adding to the sentence ending with the word "muzzled" in line fifteen thereof, the clause 'except that calves, for a period not to exceed twenty-four hours may be transported in a separate apartment,' so that said section shall read as follows: *[Section 35 of chapter 124, R. S., as amended by chapter 25, laws of 1891, further amended.]*

'Section 35. Railroad companies within the state shall give cars containing cattle, sheep, swine, or other animals, a continuous passage in preference to other freight; and cars loaded with such animals at any station shall take precedence over all other freight. A greater number of animals shall not be loaded into any car than can stand comfortably therein. Animals of one kind only shall be loaded in the same apartment. Young animals shall not be loaded in the same apartment with those larger and mature, except in case of dams with their own and other sucklings which may be transported in the same apartment and shall be separate from other animals. Calves shall have free access to their dams and shall not be muzzled, except that calves for a period not to exceed twenty-four hours may be transported in a separate apartment. During December, January, February and March cars used for the transportation of animals shall be sufficiently boarded on the sides and ends to afford proper protection to such animals in case of storms and severely cold weather.' *[Continuous passage of animals in preference to other freight. —animals of one kind only shall be loaded in same apartment. —calves, how transported.]*

Approved February 18, 1903.

Chapter 11.

An Act to amend Section fifty-seven of Chapter thirty-eight of the Revised Statutes of Maine, relating to the weight of a bushel of Beans.

Be it enacted by the Senate and House of Representatives in Legislature assembled, as follows:

Section fifty-seven of chapter thirty-eight of the revised statutes of Maine is hereby amended by striking out after the word "beans" in the eighth line thereof, the words "sixty-two" and inserting in place thereof the word 'sixty,' so that said section as amended, shall read as follows:

'Section 57. The standard weight of a bushel of potatoes, in good order and fit for shipping, is sixty pounds; of apples, in good order and fit for the market, forty-four pounds; of wheat, sixty pounds; of corn, fifty-six pounds; of barley and buckwheat, forty-eight pounds; of carrots, fifty pounds; of onions in good order and fit for shipping, fifty-two pounds; or ruta baga, sugar beets, mangel wurzel and turnip beets, in like condition, sixty pounds; of English turnips, in like condition, fifty pounds; of beans, sixty pounds; of peas, sixty pounds; of rye and Indian meal, fifty pounds; of oats, thirty pounds, or strike measure; of Turk's Island, or other coarse grades of salt, seventy pounds, and of Liverpool, or other fine grades, sixty pounds; and of hair used in masonry, well dried and cleansed, eleven pounds; and the measure of each of these articles shall be determined as aforesaid at the request of the vendor or vendee; and if either party refuses so to do, he forfeits twenty cents for each bushel, to the person prosecuting thereof within thirty days.'

Approved February 18, 1903.

Chapter 12.

An Act to amend Section eighty-four of Chapter six of the Revised Statutes, relating to county Roads and Bridges in unincorporated townships.

Be it enacted by the Senate and House of Representatives in Legislature assembled, as follows:

Section eighty-four of chapter six of the revised statutes is hereby amended by inserting after the word "counties" in the third line the words 'or where said roads and bridges are rendered impassable by snow,' and inserting after the word "repaired" in said line, the words 'or made passable,' so that said section as amended, shall read as follows:

'Section 84. County commissioners, in case of sudden injury to county roads and bridges in unincorporated townships and tracts of land in their counties, or where said roads and bridges are rendered impassable by snow, may cause them to be repaired or made passable forthwith, or as soon as they deem necessary, and may appoint an agent or agents not members of their own board, to superintend the expenditure therefor, who shall give bond as required in section seventy-eight, if required, the whole expense whereof shall be added to their next assessment on said lands for repairs, authorized by section eighty, which assessment shall create a lien upon said lands for the whole amount thereof as effectually as is now provided in relation to repairs on such county roads. That portion of said assessment which is for repairs of sudden injuries as aforesaid, shall be set down in the assessment in distinct items, in a separate column, and shall not be discharged, under section eighty-one, but shall be enforced as is provided in section eighty-two.'

Approved February 18, 1903.

Chapter 13.

An Act establishing the Salary of the County Treasurer of the County of York.

Be it enacted by the Senate and House of Representatives in Legislature assembled, as follows:

Section 1. From and after the first day of January, in the year of our Lord, one thousand nine hundred and three, the salary of the county treasurer of the county of York shall be seven hundred and fifty dollars annually, payable quarterly on the last days of March, June, September and December, which shall be in full for all services, expenses and travel.

Section 2. All acts and parts of acts inconsistent with this act, are hereby repealed.

Section 3. This act shall take effect when approved.

Approved February 18, 1903.

Chapter 14.

An Act in relation to the salaries of the Justices of the Supreme Judicial Court.

Be it enacted by the Senate and House of Representatives in Legislature assembled, as follows:

Justices of the supreme judicial court, salaries of.

Section 1. From and after the first day of January in the year of our Lord one thousand nine hundred and three, the annual salary of each of the justices of the supreme judicial court, shall be five thousand dollars, payable from the treasury of the state in quarterly payments, on the first days of January, April, July and October.

Section 2. This act shall take effect when approved.

Approved February 18, 1908.

Chapter 15.

An Act to enlarge the powers of the Railroad Commissioners over Street Railroads.

Be it enacted by the Senate and House of Representatives in Legislature assembled, as follows:

Section 11 of chapter 268 of public laws of 1893, amended.

Section 1. Section eleven of chapter two hundred and sixty-eight of the public laws of one thousand eight hundred and ninety-three is hereby amended by striking therefrom the following words: "If the tracks of a street railway cross any steam railroad and a dispute arises in any way in regard to the manner of crossing, the board of railroad commissioners shall upon hearing decide and determine in writing in what manner the crossing shall be made and it shall be made accordingly," and by adding thereto the following words: 'The said corporation may at any time appeal from the decision of such municipal officers determining the form and manner of the construction and maintenance of its railroad and the kind of rail to be used to the board of railroad commissioners who shall upon notice hear the parties and finally determine the questions raised by said appeal;' so that said section as hereby amended, shall read as follows:

Municipal officers may direct manner and form of construction of railways.

'Section 11. Said railways shall be constructed and maintained in such form and manner and with such rails and upon such grade as the municipal officers of the cities and towns where the same are located may direct, and whenever in the judgment of such corporation it shall be necessary to alter the grade of any city, town, or county road said alterations shall be made at the sole expense of said corporation with the assent and in accordance with the directions of said municipal officers. The said corporation may at any time appeal from the decision of said municipal officers determining the form and manner of the construction and maintenance of its railroad and the kind of rail to be used to the board of railroad commissioners who shall upon notice hear the parties and finally determine the questions raised by said appeal.'

Section 2. Section fifteen of chapter two hundred and sixty-eight of the public laws of one thousand eight hundred and ninety-three is hereby amended by adding thereto the following words: 'Any street railway company may appeal from the decision of such municipal officers making any regulation under this section to the board of railroad commissioners who shall upon notice hear the parties and finally determine the questions raised by said appeal,' so that said section as amended, shall read as follows:

'Section 15. The municipal officers of any town shall have power at all times to make all such regulations as to the mode or use of tracks of any street railway, the rate of speed and the removal and disposal of snow and ice from the streets, roads and ways by any street railway company as the public safety and convenience may require. Any street railway company may appeal from the decision of such municipal officers making any regulation under this section to the board of railroad commissioners who shall upon notice hear the parties and finally determine the questions raised by said appeal.'

Approved February 24, 1903.

Chapter 16.

An Act concerning Attorneys at Law.

Be it enacted by the Senate and House of Representatives in Legislature assembled, as follows:

Section 1. Sections twenty-seven, twenty-eight, twenty-nine and thirty of chapter seventy-nine of the revised statutes of eighteen hundred and eighty-three are hereby amended so as to give any justice of the supreme judicial court, in term time or in vacation, the powers therein conferred upon the court, and said sections, as amended, shall read as follows:

CHAP. 17

Collections or settlements shall be paid within ten days after demand.

—claimant may file a motion in writing.

—any justice of the supreme judicial court may require the attorney to appear.

—notice.

—justice may examine.

—shall render decree.

—exceptions may be taken.

—penalty.!

'Section 27. If an attorney at law receives money or any valuable thing on a claim left with him for collection or settlement, and fails to account for and pay over the same to the claimant for ten days after demand, he is guilty of a breach of duty as an attorney; and such claimant may file in the office of the clerk of the supreme judicial court in the county where such attorney resides, a motion in writing, under oath, setting forth the facts; and thereupon any justice of the supreme judicial court in term time or in vacation shall issue a rule, requiring the attorney to appear on a day fixed and show cause why he should not so account and pay, and to abide the order of such justice in the premises; which shall be served by copy in hand at least five days before the return day.'

'Section 28. If he then appears, he shall file an answer to such motion, under oath, and such justice may examine the parties and other evidence pertinent thereto. If he does not appear and answer, the facts set forth in the motion shall be taken as confessed; and in either case such justice shall render such decree as equity requires.'

'Section 29. Either party may allege exceptions to any ruling or decree of such justice; and they shall be allowed unless deemed frivolous.'

'Section 30. If the attorney does not perform the decree of such justice, he shall be committed for contempt until he does, or is otherwise lawfully discharged; and his name shall be struck from the roll of attorneys.'

Section 2. This act shall take effect when approved.

Approved February 24, 1903.

Chapter 17.

An Act for the protection of Railroad Signals.

Be it enacted by the Senate and House of Representatives in Legislature assembled, as follows:

Railroad signals, penalty for injuring or tampering with.

Whoever intentionally and without right injures, destroys, or molests any signal of a railroad corporation, or any line, wire, post, lamp or other structure or mechanism used in connection with any signal on a railroad, or destroys or in any manner interferes with the proper working of any signal on a railroad, shall be punished by fine not exceeding five hundred dollars, or by imprisonment not exceeding two years, or both.

Approved February 25, 1903.

Chapter 18.

An Act to amend Section forty-one of Chapter seventy-seven, of the Revised Statutes, relating to the Supreme Judicial Court.

Be it enacted by the Senate and House of Representatives in Legislature assembled, as follows:

Section forty-one of chapter seventy-seven, of the revised statutes as enacted in section five of chapter two hundred forty-six of the public laws of nineteen hundred and one, is amended by adding after the words 'and a reasonable compensation for making dockets' in the eleventh and twelfth lines thereof, the words 'and for certifying decisions,' so that said section as amended, shall read as follows: *Section 41 of chapter 77 of the R. S. amended.*

'Section 41. The clerks of court in the counties of Kennebec, Penobscot and Cumberland shall be the clerks of the terms of the law court held in their respective counties, and each shall, upon the adjournment of a term thereof holden in his county, transmit to the clerk of the next term all dockets, together with all exhibits and documents in his custody relating to pending causes. The dockets of the law court shall be made from time to time and kept as the court may direct. *—clerks of court in certain counties, shall be clerks of law court. —shall transmit dockets, etc.*

The chief justice, or in his absence, the senior justice present, may allow the several clerks for attendance, not exceeding two and one-half dollars per day, and a reasonable compensation for making dockets and for certifying decisions, which shall be paid by the state; but no entry fee shall be charged.' *—compensation.*

Approved February 25, 1903.

Chapter 19.

An Act extending sundry existing statutes to Street Railroads.

Be it enacted by the Senate and House of Representatives in Legislature assembled, as follows:

Section 1. Section ten of chapter two hundred and sixty-eight of the public laws of one thousand eight hundred and ninety-three, as amended by section three of chapter two hundred and forty-nine of the public laws of one thousand eight hundred and ninety-seven, is further amended by inserting the words 'eighteen as amended by chapter one hundred and twenty-nine of the public laws of one thousand eight hundred and ninety-one' *Section 10 of chapter 268, public laws of 1893, as amended by section 3 of chapter 248, public laws of 1897, further amended.*

CHAP. 19

between the words "seventeen" and "nineteen," by inserting the word 'twenty-one' between the words "twenty and twenty-two," by striking therefrom the word "sixty-eight," by inserting the words 'seventy-eight, seventy-nine, eighty, one hundred and nine' between the words "sixty-eight and one hundred and fourteen" and by inserting between the words "statutes" and "shall" the words 'chapter two hundred and thirty-six of the public laws of one thousand eight hundred and ninety-three,' so that the said section as hereby amended, shall read as follows:

Certain sections of the R. S. made applicable to street railways.

'Section 10. So far as applicable the provisions of sections seventeen, eighteen as amended by chapter one hundred and twenty-nine of the public laws of one thousand eight hundred and ninety-one, nineteen, twenty, twenty-one, twenty-two, twenty-three, twenty-four, twenty-five, twenty-six, twenty-seven, thirty-six, thirty-seven, thirty-eight, thirty-nine, fifty-four, fifty-five, fifty-six, fifty-seven, sixty-six, sixty-seven, seventy-eight, seventy-nine, eighty, one hundred and nine, one hundred and fourteen, one hundred and fifteen, one hundred and sixteen, one hundred and seventeen, one hundred and eighteen, one hundred and twenty-six, one hundred and thirty-five, one hundred and thirty-six as amended, one hundred and thirty-seven, one hundred and thirty-eight, one hundred and thirty-nine, one hundred and forty of chapter fifty-one of the revised statutes, and chapter two hundred and thirty-six of the public laws of one thousand eight hundred and ninety-three shall apply to street railways.'

Proceedings for damages for taking land.

Section 2. In all proceedings now pending or hereafter brought before the county commissioners for the estimation of damages for the taking of land by any street railroad company described in the location of such company now on file, as required by law, section twenty-one of chapter fifty-one of the revised statutes and chapter two hundred and thirty-six of the public laws of one thousand eight hundred and ninety-three shall be applicable thereto.

Section 3. This act shall take effect when approved.

Approved February 25, 1903.

Chapter 20.

An Act to amend Section three, Chapter two hundred two, Public Laws of eighteen hundred eighty-nine entitled, "An Act to fix the salaries of the Judge and Register of Probate and County Commissioners of Waldo county."

Be it enacted by the Senate and House of Representatives in Legislature assembled, as follows:

Section 1. Section three, chapter two hundred two, public laws of eighteen hundred eighty-nine, is hereby amended by striking out section three and insert in the place thereof the following:

'Section 3. On and after the first day of February nineteen hundred and three, the pay of the county commissioners of Waldo county shall be two dollars and fifty cents per day for each day actually employed in the service of said county, including time spent in traveling, for which each commissioner shall have ten cents per mile for the distance actually traveled, but each commissioner shall have no more than one travel during the same hearing or session, or for more than two adjournments of any regular term or for services or travel on more than one petition or case at the same time, or anything for travel or attendance at the legislature, connected with the annual county estimates, or for any additional trouble or expense.'

Section 2. All acts and parts of acts inconsistent with this act, are hereby repealed.

Section 3. This act shall take effect when approved.

Approved February 25, 1903.

Chapter 21.

An Act to abolish Chapter five hundred and eighty-two, Public Laws of eighteen hundred and sixty-eight, relating to taking fish in Frenchman's Bay except by the ordinary process of fishing with hook and line.

Be it enacted by the Senate and House of Representatives in Legislature assembled, as follows:

Sections one, two, three, four, five and six, chapter five hundred and eighty-two of the public laws of eighteen hundred and sixty-eight are hereby repealed.

Approved February 25, 1903.

Chapter 22.

An Act amendatory of and additional to Chapter one hundred and forty-two of the Revised Statutes, relating to the State Reform School.

Be it enacted by the Senate and House of Representatives in Legislature assembled, as follows:

Section 1 of chapter 142 of the R. S. amended.

Section 1. Section one of chapter one hundred and forty-two of the revised statutes is hereby amended so that said section as amended, shall read as follows:

Board of five trustees.

'Section 1. The government of the state reform school, established for the instruction, employment, and reform of juvenile offenders, in the town of South Portland, in the county of Cumberland, is vested in a board of five trustees appointed by the

—appointed by the governor.

governor, with the advice and consent of council, and commissioned to hold their offices during the pleasure of the governor

—tenure.

and council, but not longer than four years under one appointment.

—compensation.

They shall be allowed two dollars a day for their services when employed, and the same sum for every twenty miles

—travel.

traveled. They shall have charge of the general interests of the

—duties.

institution, and see that its affairs are conducted as required by the legislature, and such by-laws as the board may adopt; see that proper discipline is maintained therein; provide employment for the inmates, and bind them out, discharge or remand them,

—superintendent, how appointed.

as hereinafter provided; appoint a superintendent, subject to the approval, and during the pleasure of the governor and council, and appoint such other officers as in their judgment the wants of the institution require; prescribe the duties of all its officers; exercise a vigilant supervision over its concerns, remove its subordinate officers at pleasure, and appoint others in their stead; determine the compensation of the subordinate officers, subject to the approval of the governor and council, and prepare and submit by-laws to the governor and council, which shall be valid when sanctioned by them. They may contract with the attorney

—may contract with attorney general of U. S. for confinement of juvenile offenders.

general of the United States for the confinement and support in the reform school of juvenile offenders against the laws of the United States in accordance with sections five thousand five hundred and forty-nine, and five thousand five hundred and fifty of the revised statutes of the United States.'

Section 2 of chapter 142 of R.S. amended.

Section 2. Section two of said chapter one hundred and forty-two of the revised statutes is hereby amended so that said section, as amended, shall read as follows:

Boys between 8 and 16 may be sentenced to the school.

'Section 2. When a boy between the ages of eight and sixteen years is convicted before any court or trial justice having jurisdiction of the offense, of an offense punishable by imprisonment in the state prison, not for life, or in the county jail, or in any house of correction, such court or justice may order his commitment to the state reform school or sentence him to the punishment provided by law for the same offense. If to the reform school, the commitment shall be conditioned that if such boy is not received or kept there for the full term of his minority, unless sooner discharged by the trustees as provided in section seven, or released on probation as provided in section ten, he shall then suffer the punishment provided by law, as aforesaid, as ordered by the court of justice; but no boy shall be committed to the reform school who is deaf and dumb, non compos, or insane.' —deaf and dumb, non compos or insane shall not be sent.

Section 3. Section three of said chapter one hundred and forty-two is hereby amended so that said section, as amended, shall read as follows: Section 3 of chapter 142, amended.

'Section 3. When a boy is committed to the state reform school, under the provisions of the preceding section, for larceny of property not exceeding one dollar in value; or for assault and battery, malicious mischief, malicious trespass, desecration of the Lord's day, riotous conduct, disturbance of the peace, embezzlement, cheating by false pretenses, vagrancy, or truancy; or for being a common runaway, drunkard, or pilferer; or for any offense punishable in any house of correction, the expenses of conveying such boy to the reform school, and his subsistence and clothing during the time he remains there, not exceeding one dollar a week, shall be defrayed by the town where such boy resides at the time of his commitment, if within the state; otherwise such expense shall be paid by the state.' Expenses, how defrayed.

Section 4. Section four of said chapter one hundred and forty-two is hereby amended so that said section, as amended, shall read as follows: Section 4 of chapter 142, amended.

'Section 4. When any boy is ordered to be committed to the state reform school the court or trial justice by whom such commitment is ordered shall certify in the mittimus the city or town in which such boy resides at the time of his commitment, the age of the boy, and the day on which his term of minority will expire. The finding of the court or justice regarding the age and residence of the boy shall be deemed a decision of a question of fact, and his certificate thereof shall be conclusive evidence of the age and residence of the boy and of the day on which his term of minority will expire. If the said boy is convicted of an offense specified in the preceding section the certificate of the court or trial justice shall be sufficient evidence in the first instance, to charge such city or town in which such boy resides with his expense at the reform school, not exceeding one dollar a week. The superintendent, upon the commitment of such boy shall —age, residence and day when minority expires shall be certified in mittimus.

CHAP. 22

—notification to cities and towns liable, how made.

notify in writing by mail or otherwise, the aldermen of any city, or the selectmen of any town so liable, of the name of the boy committed, the offense with which he is charged, and the duration of his term of commitment. Such written notice shall be sufficient when made, superscribed and directed to said aldermen or selectmen, and deposited, postage prepaid, in the post office.'

Section 6 of chapter 142, amended.

Section 5. Section six of said chapter one hundred and forty-two is hereby amended by striking out after the word "boy" in the first line the words "so convicted and sent to" and inserting in place thereof the words 'committed to,' and by striking out the word "sentence" in the third line of said section and inserting in place thereof the word 'commitment,' so that said section, as amended, shall read as follows:

Board of trustees shall direct the discipline, etc.

'Section 6. Every boy committed to said school, shall there be kept, disciplined, instructed, employed, and governed, under the direction of the board of trustees, until the term of his commitment expires, or he is discharged as reformed, bound out by said trustees according to their by-laws, or remanded to prison under the sentence of the court as incorrigible, upon information of the trustees, as hereinafter provided.'

Section 7 of chapter 142 amended.

Section 6. Section seven of said chapter one hundred and forty-two is hereby amended by striking out after the word "is" in the first line of said section the word "sentenced" and inserting in place thereof the words 'ordered to be committed,' and by striking out the word "convict" in the fifth line of said section and inserting in place thereof the word 'boy,' and by striking out the word "alternative" in the seventh line of said section, and by striking out the word "sentenced" in the ninth line of said section and inserting in place thereof the words 'ordered to be committed,' so that said section, as amended, shall read as follows:

—incorrigible boys, how disposed of.

'Section 7. When a boy is ordered to be committed to said school and the trustees deem it inexpedient to receive him, or he is found incorrigible, or his continuance in the school is deemed injurious to its management and discipline, they shall certify the same upon the mittimus by which he is held, and the mittimus and boy shall be delivered to any proper officer, who shall forthwith commit said boy to the jail, house of correction, or state prison, according to his sentence. The trustees may discharge any boy as reformed; and may authorize the superintendent, under such rules as they prescribe, to refuse to receive boys ordered to be committed to said school, and his certificate thereof shall be as effectual as their own.'

Section 7. Section nine of said chapter one hundred and forty-two is hereby amended, so that said section, as amended, shall read as follows:

Section 9 of chapter 142 amended.

'Section 9. All commitments of boys shall be during their minority unless sooner discharged by order of the trustees, as before provided; and when a boy is discharged from the school at the expiration of his term, whether he be then in the institution or lawfully out on probation, or when discharged as reformed, an appropriate record of such discharge shall be made by the superintendent upon the register of the school required to be kept by provisions of section thirteen of this chapter. Such discharge shall be a full and complete release from all penalties and disabilities created by his sentence and commitment, and the record of the proceedings under which such boy was so committed shall not be deemed to be, nor shall it be subsequently used as, a criminal record against him. Each boy discharged from the institution shall receive an appropriate written discharge, signed by the superintendent. Such discharge, or a copy, duly certified by the superintendent, of the record of discharge upon the register of the school, shall be receivable in evidence and conclusive of the facts therein stated.'

—Commitments shall be made during minority.

—record of discharge shall be made.

—discharge shall be a full and complete release.

Section 8. Section ten of said chapter one hundred and forty-two is hereby amended so that said section, as amended, shall read as follows:

Section 10 of chapter 142, amended.

'Section 10. The trustees may commit, on probation and on such terms as they deem expedient, to any suitable inhabitant of the state, any boy in their charge, for a term within the period of his commitment, such probation to be conditioned on his good behavior and obedience to the laws of the state. Such boy shall, during the term for which he was originally committed to the reform school, be also subject to the care and control of the trustees, and on their being satisfied at any time, that the welfare of the boy will be promoted by his return to the school, they may order his return. On his return to the school, such boy shall there be held and detained under the original mittimus. The trustees may delegate to the superintendent under such rules as they prescribe the powers herein granted to the trustees to commit any boy on probation to any suitable inhabitant of the state, and to return to the reform school any boy so committed when he is satisfied that the welfare of the boy will be promoted by his return. Any boy ordered returned to the reform school may, on the order of the superintendent or other officer of the institution, be arrested and returned to the reform school, or to any officer or agent thereof, by any sheriff, constable or police officer

—trustees may commit boys on probation.

—probation conditioned.

—return to school may be ordered.

or other person; and may also be arrested and returned by any officer or agent of the school.'

Section 11 of chapter 142, repealed.

Section 9. Section eleven of said chapter one hundred and forty-two is hereby repealed.

Section 15 of chapter 142, amended.

Section 10. Section fifteen of said chapter one hundred and forty-two is hereby amended by striking out in the eleventh line of said section the word "sentenced" and inserting in place thereof the word 'committed,' so that said section, as amended, shall read as follows:

Trustees shall visit school, etc.

'Section 15. One or more of the trustees shall visit the school at least once in every four weeks, examine the register and the inmates in the school room and workshop, and regularly keep a record of these visits in the books of the superintendent. Once in every three months, the school, in all its departments, shall be thoroughly examined by a majority of the board of trustees, and a report shall be made, showing the results thereof. Annually, on the first day of December, an abstract of such quarterly reports shall be prepared and laid before the governor and council for the information of the legislature, with a full report of the superintendent, stating particularly among other things, the offense for which each pupil was committed and his place of residence. A financial statement furnishing an accurate detailed account of the receipts and expenditures for the year terminating on the last day of November preceding, shall also be furnished.'

—shall examine once in three months.

—abstract of quarterly reports shall be laid before the governor.

Homeless reformed boys may be returned to overseers of poor.

Section 11. Any boy deemed by the trustees to be reformed who has no suitable home to which he can be sent and for whom, in consequence of physical infirmity or other reason, no suitable home can be found by the trustees, may be discharged by said trustees and returned to the selectmen of the town or the overseers of the poor of the city where such boy resided at the time of his commitment.

Fugitive boys, penalty for aiding or abetting.

Section 12. Any person who shall aid or abet any boy committed to the state reform school in escaping therefrom, or who shall knowingly harbor or conceal any boy who has escaped from said school, shall be fined not less than fifty or more than one hundred dollars, or punished by imprisonment in the county jail not more than sixty days. Any fugitive from the state reform school may, on the order of the superintendent or other officer of the institution, be arrested and returned to the school, or to any officer or agent thereof, by any sheriff, constable, or police officer, or other person; and may also be arrested and returned by any officer or agent of the school.

—fugitives, how arrested and returned.

Section 13. All acts and parts of acts, inconsistent with this act, are hereby repealed.

Section 14. This act shall take effect May one, nineteen hundred three.

Approved February 25, 1903.

Chapter 23.

An Act to amend Section fourteen of Chapter fifty-one of the Revised Statutes, relating to the width of the location of Railroads.

Be it enacted by the Senate and House of Representatives in Legislature assembled, as follows:

Section 1. Section fourteen, chapter fifty-one of the revised statutes is hereby amended so as to read as follows:

'Section 14. A railroad corporation for the location, construction, repair and convenient use of its road may purchase or take and hold as for public uses land and all materials in and upon it; through woodland and forest the land so taken shall not exceed six rods in width unless necessary for excavation, embankment or materials, and through all land other than woodland and forest, the land so taken shall not exceed four rods in width unless necessary for excavation, embankment or materials.'

Section 2. This act shall take effect when approved.

Approved February 25, 1903.

Chapter 24.

An Act to amend Chapter ninety-seven, Section three of the Revised Statutes, relating to Bastard Children and their maintenance.

Be it enacted by the Senate and House of Representatives in Legislature assembled, as follows:

Section three of chapter ninety-seven of the revised statutes of Maine is hereby amended by adding after the last word in said section the following words: 'The cost of commitment and board of the accused while so in jail shall be paid by the county in which said jail is situated. If he gives the required bond after commitment he shall be liberated upon payment of said cost of commitment and board,' so that said section as amended, shall read as follows:

POWERS OF STREET RAILROADS.

CHAP. 25

Accused may be required to give bond.

—may be committed.

—cost of commitment and board shall be paid by county.

'Section 3. When the accused is brought before such or any other justice he may be required to give bond to the complainant, with sufficient sureties, in such reasonable sum as the justice orders, conditioned for his appearance at the next term of the supreme judicial or superior court for the county in which she resides, and for his abiding the order of the court thereon; and if he does not give it he shall be committed to jail until he does. The cost of commitment and board of the accused while so in jail shall be paid by the county in which said jail is situated. If he gives the required bond after said commitment he shall be liberated upon the payment of cost of commitment and board.'

Approved February 26, 1903.

Chapter 25.

An Act to enlarge the powers of Street Railroads in taking Lands.

Be it enacted by the Senate and House of Representatives in Legislature assembled, as follows:

May purchase or take and hold land for gravel pits, etc.

Section 1. Any street railroad corporation may purchase or take and hold, as for public uses, land for borrow and gravel pits, spur tracks thereto, side tracks, turnouts, stations, car barns, pole lines, wires, installing and maintaining power plants, double tracking its road, improving the alignment thereof, changing or avoiding grades, or for avoiding grade crossings of any railroad;

—if owner of land does not consent, may apply to railroad commissioners.

but if the owner of said land does not consent thereto, or if the parties do not agree as to the necessity therefor or the area necessary to be taken, the corporation may make written application to the railroad commissioners, describing the estate and naming the persons supposed to be interested; the commissioners shall thereupon appoint a time for the meeting near the premises, and require notices to be given to the persons so interested as they may direct fourteen days at least before said time; and shall then view the premises, hear the parties, and determine how much, if any, of such real estate is necessary for the reasonable accommodation of the traffic and appropriate business of the corporation. If they find that any of it is so necessary, they shall furnish the corporation with a certificate containing a definite description thereof; and when it is filed with the clerk of courts in the county where the land lies, it shall be deemed and treated as taken; provided, however, that when land is held by a ten-

—meeting shall be appointed.

—proviso.

ant for life and the reversion is contingent as to the persons in whom it may vest on the termination of the life estate, such fact shall be stated in an application and the commissioners shall, in addition to the notice to the tenant for life, give notice by publication to all others interested in such matter as they deem proper.

Section 2. The land taken under section one shall not be entered upon except to make surveys before the certificate aforesaid has been filed with the clerk of courts. All damages shall be determined and paid as provided by chapter fifty-one of the revised statutes for lands taken by railroads, and chapter two hundred and thirty-six of the public laws for one thousand eight hundred and ninety-three shall be applicable thereto. No meeting house, dwelling house, public or private burying grounds shall be so taken without consent of the owners. Nothing herein contained shall authorize the taking of lands already devoted to railroad uses except in cases where the railroad commissioners determine that such lands may be crossed in such manner as to avoid grade crossings with railroads.

Approved February 26, 1908.

Chapter 26

An Act to repeal Sections thirty-four, thirty-five, thirty-six, thirty-seven and thirty-eight of Chapter twenty-six of the Revised Statutes, relating to inquests in cases of suspected Incendiarism.

Be it enacted by the Senate and House of Representatives in Legislature assembled, as follows:

Sections thirty-four, thirty-five, thirty-six, thirty-seven and thirty-eight of chapter twenty-six of the revised statutes are hereby repealed.

Approved February 26, 1908.

Chapter 27.

An Act to amend Chapter fifty-two of the Public Laws of eighteen hundred and ninety-five, relating to the salary of the Register of Probate for the county of Penobscot.

Be it enacted by the Senate and House of Representatives in Legislature assembled, as follows:

Salary of judge of probate, county of Penobscot, established.
—clerk hire.

—fees shall be paid into county treasury.

Section 1. From and after January one, nineteen hundred and three, the register of probate for the county of Penobscot shall receive an annual salary of fifteen hundred dollars, and an additional allowance of eight hundred dollars for clerk hire; said salary and allowance to be paid from the county treasury and to be instead of the salary and fees now provided by law, and all fees now received by said register as register of probate or register of insolvency shall be paid by said register into the county treasury for the use of the county.

Section 2. This act shall take effect when approved.

Approved March 4, 1903.

Chapter 28.

An Act to amend Chapter two hundred and thirty-six of the Public Laws of one thousand eight hundred and ninety-three, relating to the taking of lands or other property by Railroads.

Be it enacted by the Senate and House of Representatives in Legislature assembled, as follows:

Chapter 236 of public laws of 1893, amended.

Chapter two hundred and thirty-six of the public laws of one thousand eight hundred and ninety-three is hereby amended by striking out the words "railroad company" wherever the same occur and substituting in place thereof the words 'railroad or street railroad company,' so that said chapter as amended, shall read as follows:

County commissioners shall have power to prescribe terms and conditions for use of property taken by railroads.

'The county commissioners in awarding damages for land or other property taken by any railroad or street railroad company shall have the power on the application of such railroad or street railroad company to prescribe such terms and conditions in all respects for the use of the land or property taken by the owners thereof and the railroad or street railroad company respectively as will secure the best accommodation of the owners and the proper and convenient use of the same by such railroad or street railroad company. They shall in their award set forth all such terms and conditions so imposed by them. In case of appeal by either party the only question in issue shall be the amount or measure of damages on the terms and conditions imposed by the commissioners.'

Approved March 4, 1903.

Chapter 29

An Act to correct an error in Chapter seventy-nine of the Public Acts of eighteen hundred and ninety-nine, and to amend Section two of Chapter sixty of the Revised Statutes, allowing divorces in state, provided libelee resides therein.

Be it enacted by the Senate and House of Representatives in Legislature assembled, as follows:

Section 1. Section two of chapter sixty of the revised statutes, as amended by chapter one hundred and seventy-nine of the public laws of eighteen hundred and ninety-three, and by chapter seventy-nine of the public laws of eighteen hundred and ninety-nine, is hereby further amended by inserting after the word "proceedings" in the twelfth line of said section of the revised statutes, the following words, 'or if the libellee is a resident of this state,' so that said section as amended, shall read as follows: {Section 2 of chapter 60, R. S. as amended by chapter 179 of public laws of 1893, and by chapter 79 of public laws of 1899, further amended.}

'Section 2. A divorce from the bonds of matrimony may be decreed by the supreme judicial court in the county where either party resides, at the commencement of proceedings, for causes of adultery, impotence, extreme cruelty, utter desertion continued for three consecutive years next prior to the filing of the libel, gross and confirmed habits of intoxication from the use of intoxicating liquors, opium or other drugs, cruel and abusive treatment, or on the libel of the wife, where the husband being of sufficient ability or being able to labor and provide for her, grossly or wantonly and cruelly refuses or neglects to provide suitable maintenance for her; provided that the parties were married in this state or cohabited here after marriage; or if the libelant resides here when the cause of divorce accrued, or had resided here in good faith for one year prior to the commencement of proceedings, or if the libellee is a resident of this state. But when both parties have been guilty of adultery, or there is a collusion between them to procure a divorce, it shall not be granted. Either party may be a witness.' {Divorce may be decreed by supreme court in the county where either party resides, for certain causes.} {—divorce shall not be granted when both parties have been guilty of adultery, or in case of collusion.}

Section 2. This act shall take effect when approved.

Approved March 4, 1903.

Chapter 30.

An Act to repeal Section two hundred of Chapter six of the Revised Statutes as amended by Section ten, Chapter seventy, Public Laws of eighteen hundred ninety-five, relating to Tax Sales.

Be it enacted by the Senate and House of Representatives in Legislature assembled, as follows:

<small>Section 200 of chapter 6 of R. S. as amended by section 10, chapter 70 of laws of 1895, repealed.</small>

Section 1. Section two hundred of chapter six of the revised statutes as amended by section ten, chapter seventy, public laws of eighteen hundred ninety-five is hereby repealed.

Section 2. This act shall take effect when approved.

Approved March 4, 1903.

Chapter 31.

An Act to repeal Section two hundred one, Chapter six of the Revised Statutes, relating to Tax Sales.

Be it enacted by the Senate and House of Representatives in Legislature assembled, as follows:

<small>Section 201 of chapter 6 of R.S., repealed.</small>

Section 1. Section two hundred one of chapter six of the revised statutes is hereby repealed.

Section 2. This act shall take effect when approved.

Approved March 4, 1903.

Chapter 32.

An Act to amend Chapter one hundred sixty-two of the Public Laws of eighteen hundred ninety-five, relating to Tax Sales.

Be it enacted by the Senate and House of Representatives in Legislature assembled, as follows:

<small>Chapter 162, public laws of 1895, amended.</small>

Section 1. Chapter one hundred sixty-two of the public laws of eighteen hundred ninety-five is hereby amended by striking out section three of said chapter.

Section 2. This act shall take effect when approved.

Approved March 4, 1903.

Chapter 33.

An Act to amend Section eighty-three of Chapter six of the Revised Statutes, relating to Tax Sales.

Be it enacted by the Senate and House of Representatives in Legislature assembled, as follows:

Section 1. Section eighty-three of chapter six of the revised statutes is hereby amended by striking out from said section the following words: "but the purchaser or the county shall have a lien on the land sold or forfeited for taxes, costs and interests, and any subsequent taxes legally assessed thereon and paid by either, or those claiming under them; and such sums shall be paid or tendered, before any person shall commence, maintain or defend any suit at law or in equity, involving the title to such lands under such sale or forfeiture, notwithstanding any irregularities or omissions in such sale or forfeiture." Said amended section shall read as follows:

'Section 83. In any trial at law or in equity involving the validity of any sale or forfeiture of such lands, as provided in the preceding section, it shall be prima facie proof of title for the party claiming under it, to produce in evidence the county treasurer's deed, duly executed and recorded, the assessments signed by the county commissioners and certified by them or their clerk to the county treasurer, and to prove that the county treasurer complied with the requirements of law in advertising and selling.'

Section 2. This act shall take effect when approved.

Approved March 4, 1903.

Chapter 34.

An Act to set apart an annual Old Home Week.

Be it enacted by the Senate and House of Representatives in Legislature assembled, as follows:

The week commencing with the second Sunday in August of each year is hereby designated and set apart as Old Home Week; and cities and towns are authorized to raise and appropriate money for the due observance thereof.

Approved March 4, 1903.

CHAP. 35

Chapter 35.

An Act to amend chapter two hundred and ninety-six of the Public Laws of eighteen hundred and ninety-seven, relating to the employment of Superintendents of Schools.

Be it enacted by the Senate and House of Representatives in Legislature assembled, as follows:

Chapter 296, public laws of 1897, amended.

Section 1. Chapter two hundred and ninety-six of the public laws of eighteen hundred and ninety-seven is hereby amended by inserting after the words "superintendent of schools" in the fourteenth line of section two of said chapter, the words 'for a term not exceeding five years' so that said section, as amended by this act, shall read as follows:

Joint committee of towns forming union, shall be agents of each town.

—chairman and secretary shall be chosen.

—duties of joint committee.

—proviso.

'Section 2. The school committees of the towns comprising a union shall form a joint committee and for the purposes of this act said joint committee shall be held to be the agents of each town comprising the union. Said joint committee shall meet annually at a day and place agreed upon by the chairman of the committees of the several towns comprising the union and shall organize by the choice of a chairman and a secretary. They shall determine the relative amount of service to be performed by the superintendent in each town, fix his salary, apportion the amounts thereof to be paid by the several towns, which amount shall be certified to the treasurers of said towns respectively; provided, that the amounts so certified shall be in proportion to the amount of service performed in the several towns. They shall choose by ballot a superintendent of schools, for a term not exceeding five years, in which choice the committee of each town shall have a vote proportional to the town's share of the expenditure for the superintendent's salary.'

Section 2. All acts and parts of acts inconsistent with this act, are hereby repealed.

Approved March 4, 1903.

LOST GOODS AND STRAY BEASTS. 35

CHAP. 36

Chapter 36.

An Act relating to Lost Goods and Stray Beasts.

Be it enacted by the Senate and House of Representatives in Legislature assembled, as follows:

Section 1. Section ten, of chapter ninety-eight of the revised statutes is hereby amended to read as follows: Section 10 of chapter 98 of R.S. amended.

'Section 10. Whoever finds lost money or goods of the value of three dollars or more, shall, if the owner is unknown, within seven days give notice thereof in writing to the clerk of the town where they are found and post a notification thereof in some public place in said town. If the value is ten dollars or more, the finder in addition to the notice to the town clerk and the notification to be posted as aforesaid, shall within one month after finding, publish a notice thereof in some newspaper published in the town, if any, otherwise in some newspaper published in the county.' Money or goods found, finder shall give notice of to clerk of town, within seven days.

—if value be $10 or more, shall publish notice also.

Section 2. Whoever takes up a stray beast shall within seven days give notice thereof in writing, containing a description of its color, and its natural and artificial marks, to the clerk of the town where such beast is taken, and shall cause a notice thereof, containing a like description of the beast to be posted and, if such beast is of the value of ten dollars or more, published in the manner provided in the preceding section; otherwise he shall not be entitled to compensation for any expenses which he may incur relative thereto. Stray beast taken up, notice shall be given to clerk of town within seven days.

—if value be $10 or more, shall publish notice also.

Section 3. Section eleven of the same chapter is hereby amended to read as follows: Section 11, amended.

'Section 11. Every finder of lost goods or stray beasts of the value of ten dollars or more. shall within two months after finding, and before using them to their disadvantage, procure a warrant from the town clerk or a justice of the peace, directed to two persons, appointed by said clerk or justice, not interested except as inhabitants of the town, returnable at said clerk's office, within seven days from its date, to appraise said goods under oath.' Warrant to appraise lost goods or stray beasts shall be procured.

Section 4. Section twelve of the same chapter is hereby amended to read as follows: Section 12 amended.

'Section 12. If the owner of such lost money or goods appears within six months, and if the owner of such stray beasts appears within two months after said notice to the town clerk, and gives reasonable evidence of his ownership to the finder, he shall have restitution of them or the value of the money or goods, paying all necessary charges and reasonable compensation to the finder Owner may have restitution within certain time.

36   LOST GOODS AND STRAY BEASTS.

CHAP. 36

Section 12, amended.

Final disposition of goods if no owner appears.

May sell goods at auction after two months.
—notice.
—proceeds shall be deposited in town treasury.

Restitution, how made.

Section 14, amended.

Penalty if legal notice of finding money or goods is not given.

Lawful charges incurred must be paid.

Damages in land by stray beasts, how recovered.

for keeping, to be adjudged by a justice of the peace of the county, if the owner and the finder cannot agree.'

Section 5. Section thirteen of the same chapter is hereby amended to read as follows:

'Section 13. If no owner appears within six months such money or lost goods shall belong to the finder, by paying one-half their value to the treasurer of said town, after deducting all necessary charges; but if he neglects to pay it on demand, it may be recovered in an action brought by said treasurer in the name of the town.'

Section 6. If the owner does not appear and prove his title within said two months, the finder may sell them at public auction, first giving notice of such sale at least four days before the time of sale, in two public places in the town in which the beasts were taken up; and the proceeds of the sale, after deducting all lawful charges, shall be deposited in the town treasury.

Section 7. If such owner appears within six months after such notice is filed with the town clerk, and proves his title to the beasts, he shall, if they have not been sold have restitution of the same, after paying the charges arising thereon as provided in section four; and if the beasts have been sold, he shall be entitled to receive the money so deposited in the treasury from the proceeds of the sale. If no owner appears within six months, the beasts or the value or price thereof, after deducting said charges, shall as prescribed in section five be equally divided between the finder and the town.

Section 8. Section fourteen of the same chapter is hereby amended to read as follows:

'Section 14. If the finder of lost money or goods, of the value of three dollars or more or if the person taking up such stray beast, neglects to give notice to the town clerk and to cause them to be advertised as herein provided, he forfeits to the owner the full value thereof, unless he delivers or accounts therefor to the owner, in which case he shall forfeit not more than twenty dollars, half to the town and half to the prosecutor.'

Section 9. Whoever takes away a beast taken up as a stray, without paying all lawful charges incurred in relation to the same, shall forfeit to the finder the value thereof.

Section 10. Any person injured in his land by sheep, swine, horses, asses, mules, goats, or neat cattle, in a common or general field, or in a close by itself, may recover his damages by taking up any of the beasts doing it, and giving the notice provided in section two, or in an action of trespass against the person owning or having possession of the beasts at the time of the damage, and there shall be a lien on said beasts, and they may be attached in such action and held to respond to the judgment as in other cases, whether owned by the defendant or only in his possession. But if the beasts were lawfully on the adjoining lands, and escaped therefrom in consequence of the neglect of the person suffering the damage to maintain his part of the partition fence, their owner shall not be liable therefor.

—proviso.

Approved March 4, 1903.

Chapter 37

An Act relating to Houses of Correction.

Be it enacted by the Senate and House of Representatives in Legislature assembled, as follows:

Section 1. Chapter one hundred forty-one of the revised statutes, except sections twenty-three and twenty-four, is hereby repealed.

Chapter 141, R. S., except sections 23 and 24, repealed.

Section 2. A municipal or police court, or trial justice in his county, on complaint under oath may commit to jail or to the house of correction in the town where the person belongs or is found, for a term not exceeding ninety days, all rogues, vagabonds and idle persons going about in any town in the county, begging; persons using any subtle craft, jugglery, or unlawful games, or plays, or for the sake of gain pretending to have knowledge in physiognomy, palmistry, to tell destinies or fortunes or to discover lost or stolen goods; common pipers, fiddlers, runaways, drunkards, night walkers, railers, brawlers and pilferers; persons wanton or lascivious in speech or behavior, or neglecting their callings or employments, misspending what they earn and not providing for the support of themselves and their families; all idle and disorderly persons having no visible means of support, neglecting all lawful calling or employment; and all idle and disorderly persons who neglect all lawful calling or employment and misspend their time by frequenting disorderly houses, houses of ill fame, gaming houses or tippling shops.

Rogues, vagabonds, idle persons, etc., may be committed to jail on complaint to municipal judge or trial justice.

Section 3. A town, at its own expense, may build and maintain a house of correction. Until such house of correction is so built, the almshouse, or any part thereof may be used for that purpose.

Town may maintain a house of correction.

Chap. 37

Overseers of poor shall have charge of house of correction.

Section 4. Such house of correction shall be in charge of the overseers of the poor of the town maintaining the same, who shall have the inspection and government of the same, and may establish from time to time, such rules and orders not repugnant to law, as they deem necessary for governing and punishing persons lawfully committed thereto. When an almshouse is used for a house of correction, the master thereof shall be master of the house of correction; but in other cases the overseers thereof shall appoint a suitable master, removable at their pleasure, and may fix his compensation. The overseers from time to time, shall examine into the prudential concerns and management of such house, and see that the master faithfully discharges his duty.

Overseers shall order supplies of suitable food and clothing to persons committed.

Section 5. Every person committed to such house of correction shall be supplied with suitable food and clothing, and if sick, with such medical attendance and care as the overseers order; and all expenses incurred for commitment and maintenance, exceeding the earnings of the person confined, shall be paid by the town where such prisoner has his legal settlement, or by his kindred as hereinafter provided.

Persons committed to custody may be set to work.

Section 6. The master of such house may set to work all persons committed to his custody, so far as they are able, during the time of their confinement; and if their deportment renders it expedient, he may impose shackles or fetters to prevent resistance or escape, without unnecessarily inflicting pain or interrupting labor.

Insubordination, supply of food may be abridged in cases of.

Section 7. If a prisoner is stubborn, disorderly, idle, refractory, or refuses to perform his appointed task in a proper manner, the master may abridge his supply of food until he complies with the reasonable requirements of the master and overseers.

Actual paupers may be subject to extension of confinement.

Section 8. Notwithstanding the payment of costs and expenses, if the prisoner has actually received relief as a pauper, the overseers of the poor where the house is, or of the town to which he belongs, on complaint to the justice or court by whom he was committed, may procure an extension of the confinement, for not more than thirty days at a time, by the judge or justice; and such application may be renewed, if occasion requires it, on like complaint; and in all cases the prisoners shall be brought before the justice or court to answer to the complaint.

Pauper notice shall be given to towns where prisoner has legal settlement.

Section 9. Such masters shall, within ten days after commitment of any person to such house of correction, give notice thereof to the overseers of the poor of the town where it is situated, and if the prisoner has actually received relief as a pauper, said overseers shall give the same notice thereof to the overseers of the poor of the town of his legal settlement, as is required in other cases in which paupers become chargeable in places where they have no legal settlement.

Section 10. The master shall keep an exact account of the earnings of each prisoner, and of the expenses incurred for commitment and maintenance, specifying the time of his commitment and liberation, and present it, on oath, to the overseers of the poor of the town where such house is established annually and oftener if directed; and the town may recover the amount of such expenses after deducting the earnings of the prisoner, from the town where such prisoner has his legal settlement. *Earnings and expenditures shall be accounted for.*

Section 11. If there are kindred, obliged by law to maintain the prisoner as provided in chapter twenty-four, such master, or the town obliged to pay his account, has the same remedy against such kindred, as is provided in that chapter for towns incurring expense for relief and support of paupers. *Remedy against kindred.*

Section 12. Persons shall be committed to work houses, or houses of correction, only upon conviction of the offenses, acts, or conditions for which such commitments are by law authorized, before some municipal or police court, or trial justice. *Persons shall be committed only on conviction.*

Approved March 4, 1903.

Chapter 38.

An Act relating to Work Houses.

Be it enacted by the Senate and House of Representatives in Legislature assembled, as follows:

Section 1. Chapter twenty-one of the revised statutes is hereby repealed. *Chapter 21, repealed.*

Section 2. Any town may erect or provide a work-house for the employment and support of persons of the following description; all poor and indigent persons, maintained by or receiving alms from the town; all able bodied persons not having estate or means otherwise to maintain themselves, who refuse or neglect to work; all who live a dissolute and vagrant life and exercise no ordinary calling or lawful business sufficient to gain an honest livelihood; and all such persons, as spend their time and property in public houses, to the neglect of their proper business, or by otherwise misspending what they earn, to the impoverishment of themselves and their families, are likely to become paupers. Any work-house may, by vote of the town, *Work house may be provided by any town.* *—persons who may be committed.*

CHAP. 39

—how workhouse may be discontinued.

Overseers of poor shall have charge of.

—may appoint a master of.

Overseers shall hold meetings, and make regulations.

Persons not having legal settlement may be committed.

Persons committed, if able, shall be kept employed.

be discontinued, or applied to other uses. Until such workhouse is thus provided the almshouse or any part thereof may be used for that purpose.

Section 3. Such work-house shall be in charge of the overseers of the poor of the town maintaining the same, who shall have the inspection and government thereof, with power to appoint a master and needful assistants for the more immediate care and superintendence of the persons received or employed therein.

Section 4. The overseers, as occasion requires shall hold meetings on the business of their office; and make needful orders and regulations for such house, to be binding until the next town meeting, when they shall be submitted to the consideration of the inhabitants; and such as are approved at said meeting shall remain in force until revoked by the town.

Section 5. When any person, not having a legal settlement in any town in the state, becomes idle or indigent, he may be committed to the work-house provided for the town in which he resides, to be employed, if able to labor, in the same manner, and to be subject to the lawful regulations of the house.

Section 6. Every person committed to such work-house, if able to work, shall be kept diligently employed during the term of his commitment. For idleness, obstinacy, or disorderly conduct, he may be punished as provided by the lawful regulations of the house.

Approved March 4, 1903.

Chapter 39.

An Act relating to the dedication of Streets.

Be it enacted by the Senate and House of Representatives in Legislature assembled, as follows:

Municipal officers may vacate location of streets in certain cases.

—proceedings.

—damages, by whom paid, and how determined.

Section 1. Where land has been plotted and a plan thereof made, whether recorded or not, showing the proposed location of streets thereon, and lots have been sold by reference to said plan, the municipal officers of the town or city where such land is situated, may on petition of owners of the fee in such of said proposed streets as are named in the petition, vacate in whole or in part the proposed location of any or all such streets as have not been accepted and located as public ways. The proceedings shall be the same as in case of the location of town ways. All damages thereby occasioned shall be paid by the petitioners, and parties aggrieved by the estimate of damages may have them determined in the manner provided respecting damages caused by the location of town ways and with the same right of appeal.

Section 2. This act shall take effect when approved.

Approved March 4, 1903.

Chapter 40.

An Act to repeal Chapter twenty-three of the Revised Statutes, relating to Pounds and Impounding Beasts.

Be it enacted by the Senate and House of Representatives in Legislature assembled, as follows:

Section 1. Chapter twenty-three of the revised statutes is hereby repealed, except section four.

Chapter 23 of R. S., except section 4, repealed.

Section 2. This act shall take effect when approved.

Approved March 4, 1903.

Chapter 41.

An Act to repeal Sections one to thirty-five inclusive, of Chapter thirty-eight of the Revised Statutes, relating to the inspection of Pork and Beef.

Be it enacted by the Senate and House of Representatives in Legislature assembled, as follows:

Section 1. Sections one to thirty-five, inclusive, of chapter thirty-eight is hereby repealed.

Sections 1 to 35 inclusive, of chapter 38, R.S., repealed.

Section 2. This act shall take effect when approved.

Approved March 4, 1903.

Chapter 42.

An Act to repeal Sections seven to twenty-two inclusive of Chapter thirty-nine of the Revised Statutes, relating to the Inspection of Pot and Pearl Ashes and the Inspection of Nails.

Be it enacted by the Senate and House of Representatives in Legislature assembled, as follows:

Section 1. Sections seven to twenty-two inclusive, of chapter thirty-nine of the revised statutes, are hereby repealed.

Sections 7 to 22 inclusive, of chapter 39 of R. S., repealed.

Section 2. This act shall take effect when approved.

Approved March 4, 1903.

Chapter 43.

An Act to repeal Sections fourteen and seventeen, Chapter eight of the Revised Statutes, relating to duties of County Treasurers.

Be it enacted by the Senate and House of Representatives in Legislature assembled, as follows:

Section 14 and section 17 of chapter 8 of R. S., repealed.

Section 1. Section fourteen and section seventeen of chapter eight of the revised statutes are hereby repealed.

Section 2. This act shall take effect when approved.

Approved March 4, 1908.

Chapter 44.

An Act to repeal Section nine of Chapter thirteen of the Revised Statutes, relating to the practice of Medicine and Surgery.

Be it enacted by the Senate and House of Representatives in Legislature assembled, as follows:

Section 9 of chapter 13 of R. S., repealed.

Section 1. Section nine, chapter thirteen of the revised statutes, is hereby repealed.

Section 2. This act shall take effect when approved.

Approved March 4, 1908.

Chapter 45.

An Act to amend Section twelve of Chapter three of the Revised Statutes as amended by Chapter three hundred and thirty-five of the Public Laws of eighteen hundred and eighty-five and to repeal conflicting statutes, relating to the election of Collectors of Taxes.

Be it enacted by the Senate and House of Representatives in Legislature assembled, as follows:

Section 12 of chapter 3, public laws of 1885, further amended.

Section 1. Section twelve of chapter three of the revised statutes as amended by chapter three hundred and thirty-five of the public laws of eighteen hundred and eighty-five is hereby amended by adding thereto the following words: 'nor shall a collector be eligible to or hold the office of treasurer until he has completed his duties under his warrant and had a final settlement with the town.'

—collector of taxes not eligible as treasurer.

Inconsistent acts repealed.

Section 2. Section one hundred and seventy-six of chapter six of the revised statutes and all other acts and parts of acts inconsistent with the preceding section, are hereby repealed.

Section 3. This act shall take effect when approved.

Approved March 4, 1908.

Chapter 46.

An Act to amend Paragraph one, Section six, of Chapter six of the Revised Statutes, relating to Property exempt from Taxation.

Be it enacted by the Senate and House of Representatives in Legislature assembled, as follows:

Section 1. Paragraph one of section six of chapter six of the revised statutes is hereby amended by adding to said paragraph the following words 'and the property of any public municipal corporation of this state, appropriated to public uses,' so said paragraph one of section six will read as follows:

'Section 6. Paragraph I. The property of the United States, and of this state, and the property of any public municipal corporation of this state, appropriated to public uses.'

Section 2. This act shall take effect when approved.

Approved March 4, 1903.

Chapter 47.

An Act to repeal sections forty, forty-two and one hundred twenty-eight of Chapter fifty-one of the Revised Statutes, relating to Railroads.

Be it enacted by the Senate and House of Representatives in Legislature assembled, as follows:

Section 1. Sections forty, forty-two and one hundred twenty-eight of chapter fifty-one of the revised statutes, are hereby repealed.

Section 2. This act shall take effect when approved.

Approved March 4, 1903.

Chapter 48.

An Act to amend Chapter ninety-seven of the Public Laws of eighteen hundred and eighty-seven, relating to assessment of damages resulting from the raising and lowering of Ways.

Be it enacted by the Senate and House of Representatives in Legislature assembled, as follows:

Section 1. Section one of chapter ninety-seven of the public laws of eighteen hundred and eighty-seven, is hereby amended, by adding at the end of said section the following words: 'said complaint to be filed at the term of the supreme judicial court, next to be held within the county where the land is situated,

CHAP. 49

Damages, how assessed, and by whom paid.

after sixty days from the date of assessment' so that said section as amended, shall read as follows:

'Section 1. When a way or street is raised or lowered by a surveyor or person authorized, to the injury of an owner of adjoining land, he may, within a year, apply in writing to the municipal officers and they shall view such way or street and assess the damages, if any have been occasioned thereby, to be paid by the town, and any person aggrieved by said assessment, may, in addition to any other remedy now provided by law, have them determined, on complaint to the supreme judicial court, in the manner prescribed in section eighteen of this chapter, as amended by section five of chapter three hundred and fifty-nine of the laws of eighteen hundred and eighty-five. Said complaint to be filed at the term of the supreme judicial court, next to be held within the county where the land is situated, after sixty days from the date of assessment.'

—complaints to be filed.

Section 2. This act shall take effect when approved.

Approved March 4, 1902.

Chapter 49.

An Act to repeal Chapter twenty-five of the Revised Statutes, except sections eleven and twelve, relating to Watch and Ward in towns.

Be it enacted by the Senate and House of Representatives in Legislature assembled, as follows:

Chapter 25 of R. S., except sections 11 and 12 repealed.

Chapter twenty-five of the revised statutes is hereby repealed, except sections eleven and twelve.

Approved March 4, 1902.

Chapter 50.

An Act to repeal Sections fifty-eight and fifty-nine of Chapter thirty-eight of the Revised Statutes, relating to bounties on Silk, and on Beet Sugar.

Be it enacted by the Senate and House of Representatives in Legislature assembled, as follows:

Sections 58 and 59 of chapter 38, R. S. repealed.

Section 1. Section fifty-eight and section fifty-nine of chapter thirty-eight of the revised statutes are hereby repealed.

Section 2. This act shall take effect when approved.

Approved March 4, 1902.

Chapter 51.

An Act to repeal Section thirty and Section thirty-one of Chapter thirty-nine of the Revised Statutes, relating to Fire Arms.

Be it enacted by the Senate and House of Representatives in Legislature assembled, as follows:

Section 1. Section thirty and section thirty-one of chapter thirty-nine of the revised statutes are hereby repealed. {Sections 30 and 31 of chapter 39, R. S. repealed.}

Section 2. This act shall take effect when approved.

Approved March 4, 1903.

Chapter 52.

An Act to amend Section one hundred twenty-nine of Chapter forty-seven of the Revised Statutes, relating to officers and corporators of Savings Banks.

Be it enacted by the Senate and House of Representatives in Legislature assembled, as follows:

Section one hundred twenty-nine of chapter forty-seven of the revised statutes is hereby amended by striking out all of said section and substituting the following: {Section 129 of chapter 47, R.S. amended.}

'Section 129. Within thirty days after the annual election in the several savings banks, the clerks thereof shall cause to be published in some local newspaper, if any, otherwise in the nearest newspaper, a list of the officers and corporators thereof. {Shall publish list of officers and corporators within 30 days.} They shall also return a copy of such list of officers and corporators to the bank examiner within said thirty days, which shall be kept on file in his office for public inspection. {—shall return copy of list to bank examiner within 30 days.} Any clerk who neglects to give such notice or make such return shall be liable to a penalty of fifty dollars.' {—penalty.}

Approved March 4, 1903.

Chapter 53.

An Act to repeal Sections twenty-one, twenty-two, forty-six, sixty-six and seventy of Chapter two of the Revised Statutes, relating to the duties of Treasurer of State and Secretary of State.

Be it enacted by the Senate and House of Representatives in Legislature assembled, as follows:

Section 1. Sections twenty-one, twenty-two, forty-six, sixty-six and seventy of chapter two of the revised statutes are hereby repealed. {Sections 21, 22, 46, 66 and 70 of chapter 2, R. S. repealed.}

Section 2. This act shall take effect when approved.

Approved March 4, 1903.

Chapter 54.

An Act to repeal section sixty-seven of Chapter two of the Revised Statutes and to amend Section eighty-seven of Chapter six of the Revised Statutes, relating to the duties of the Treasurer of State.

Be it enacted by the Senate and House of Representatives in Legislature assembled, as follows:

Section 67 of chapter 2, R. S., repealed.
Section 1. Section sixty-seven of chapter two of the revised statutes is hereby repealed.

Section 87 of chapter 6, R. S., amended.
Section 2. Section eighty-seven of chapter six of the revised statutes is hereby amended so as to read as follows:

Treasurer of state shall send warrants to assessors, who shall assess sums apportioned to their town.
'Section 87. When a state tax is imposed and required to be assessed by the proper officers of towns, the treasurer of state shall send such warrants, as he is, from time to time, ordered to issue for the assessment thereof, to the assessors requiring them forthwith to assess the sum apportioned to their town or place, and to commit their assessment to the constable or collector for collection.'

Section 3. This act shall take effect when approved.

Approved March 4, 1903.

Chapter 55.

An Act to repeal Sections thirty-nine, forty, forty-one of Chapter three of the Revised Statutes, relating to the returns made by Assessors.

Be it enacted by the Senate and House of Representatives in Legislature assembled, as follows:

Sections 39, 40 and 41 of chapter 3 of R. S., repealed.
Section 1. Sections thirty-nine, forty and forty-one of chapter three of the revised statutes are hereby repealed.

Section 2. This act shall take effect when approved.

Approved March 4, 1903.

Chapter 56.

An Act relating to the duties of Secretary of State.

Be it enacted by the Senate and House of Representatives in Legislature assembled, as follows:

Tables referring to changes in statutes shall be prepared by secretary of state.
Section 1. The secretary of state shall, after final adjournment of each regular session of the legislature, cause tables to be prepared showing what general statutes have been affected by subsequent legislation, in such manner as to furnish ready reference to all changes in such statutes. The tables so pre-

pared shall be printed in the official editions of the laws hereafter published by the state. The compensation for the services herein provided for shall be fixed by the governor and council.

Section 2. This act shall take effect January one, nineteen hundred four.

Compensation, how fixed.

Shall take effect January 1, 1904.

Approved March 5, 1903.

Chapter 57.

An Act to amend Chapter one hundred and fifty-two of the Public Laws of eighteen hundred ninety-five, relating to State Examination and certification of Teachers.

Be it enacted by the Senate and House of Representatives in Legislature assembled, as follows:

Section 1. Chapter one hundred and fifty-two of the public laws of eighteen hundred ninety-five is hereby amended by inserting after the word "examination" in the third line of section four of said chapter the words, 'and certification,' so that said section, as amended, shall read as follows:

Chapter 152, public laws of 1895, amended.

'Section 4. The certificates issued under the provisions of this act shall be accepted by school committees, supervisors and superintendents in lieu of the personal examination and certification required by section eighty-seven, chapter eleven, of the revised statutes and all amendments thereto.'

Certificates shall be accepted by school committees.

Section 2. All acts and parts of acts inconsistent with this act, are hereby repealed.

Approved March 6, 1903.

Chapter 58.

An Act to amend Chapter two hundred and seventy-three of the Public Laws of eighteen hundred eighty-five, relating to the holding of County Teachers' Conventions.

Be it enacted by the Senate and House of Representatives in Legislature assembled, as follows:

Section 1. Chapter two hundred and seventy-three of the public laws of eighteen hundred eighty-five is hereby amended by inserting after the word "counties" in the fourth line of section two of said chapter the following words, namely: 'and also for not more than two days in any year during the sessions of any state teachers' convention approved by the state superintendent of public schools,' so that said section, as amended by this act, shall read as follows:

Chapter 273, public laws of 1885, amended.

CHAP. 59

County conventions, teachers may suspend schools to attend for not more than two days.

—without forfeiture of pay.

—proviso.

'Section 2. Teachers of public schools are hereby authorized to suspend their schools for not more than two days in any year during the sessions of such conventions within their counties and also for not more than two days in any year during the sessions of any state teachers' convention approved by the state superintendent of public schools, unless otherwise directed in writing by the school officers and attend said conventions without forfeiture of pay for the time of such attendance, provided they shall present to the officers employing them certificates signed by the secretaries of such conventions and countersigned by the state superintendent of public schools showing such attendance.'

Section 2. All acts and parts of acts inconsistent with this act, are hereby repealed.

Approved March 6, 1903.

Chapter 59.

An Act establishing the salary of the County Attorney for the County of York.

Be it enacted by the Senate and House of Representatives in Legislature assembled, as follows:

Salary, county attorney, York county, established.

Section 1. The county attorney for the county of York shall receive an annual salary from the treasurer of state of one thousand dollars, payable quarterly on the first day of January, April, July and October of each year, beginning on the first day of April, nineteen hundred and three, instead of the salary now provided by law.

Section 2. All acts and parts of acts inconsistent with this act, are hereby repealed.

Approved March 10, 1903.

Chapter 60.

An Act establishing the salary of the County Attorney for the County of Kennebec.

Be it enacted by the Senate and House of Representatives in Legislature assembled, as follows:

Salary, county attorney, Kennebec county, established.

Section 1. The county attorney for the county of Kennebec shall receive an annual salary from the treasurer of state, of twelve hundred dollars payable quarterly on the first days of January, April, July and October in each year, beginning on the first day of April, one thousand nine hundred and three, instead of the salary now provided by law.

Approved March 10, 1903.

Chapter 61.

An Act to authorize municipalities to make contracts for Water, Gas and Light.

Be it enacted by the Senate and House of Representatives in Legislature assembled, as follows:

Municipal corporations are authorized to contract for a supply of water, gas and electric light for municipal uses for a term of years upon such terms as may be mutually agreed, from time to time to renew the same, and to raise money therefor. All such contracts heretofore made are confirmed and made valid.

Municipal corporations authorized to contract for water, gas and electric light.

Approved March 10, 1903.

Chapter 62.

An Act to prevent injury to Books and works of Art.

Be it enacted by the Senate and House of Representatives in Legislature assembled, as follows:

Section 1. Whoever wantonly mars, defaces or injures a book, picture, statue or painting, belonging to any public library, or library of any association open to the public, or to any literary or educational institution, or any statue erected in any public park or square, or upon any ground open to the public, shall be punished by imprisonment not more than three months, or by a fine not exceeding fifty dollars.

Defacing books, pictures, etc.

—*penalty.*

Section 2. Section eighteen of chapter one hundred and twenty-seven of the revised statutes is hereby repealed.

Section 18, chapter 127, R. S., repealed.

Section 3. This act shall take effect when approved.

Approved March 10, 1903.

Chapter 63.

An Act to amend Chapter two hundred and eighty-five of the Public Laws of nineteen hundred and one, entitled "An Act providing for State Roads and for the improvement thereof."

Be it enacted by the Senate and House of Representatives in Legislature assembled, as follows:

Section 1. Section two of chapter two hundred and eighty-five of the public laws of nineteen hundred and one is hereby amended by striking out the word "one" in the fourth line of said section and inserting in place thereof the word 'two'; also by striking out the word "August" in the eleventh line of said

Section 2 of chapter 285, public laws of 1901, amended.

50 TRUANT OFFICERS.

CHAP. 64

Permanent improvement of roads.

—proviso.

—proviso.

section and inserting in place thereof the word 'September,' so that said section, as amended, shall read as follows:

'Section 2. Towns establishing state roads as aforesaid may, on complying with the conditions hereinafter set forth, receive from the state one-half of the amount actually expended in permanent improvement of said roads, not exceeding two hundred dollars per year; provided that no town shall receive such state aid unless its appropriation and expenditure for such road shall amount to at least one hundred dollars and shall have been exclusive of and in addition to the amount regularly raised in such town for highways and bridges; and provided also, that the amount so expended shall be used before the first day of September in permanent improvement of a continuous portion of said road, and in a manner satisfactory to the county commissioners of the county wherein said road is located. Such aid shall be paid from the state treasury on and after the first day of January, upon certificate by the governor and council as provided by section three.'

Section 6, amended.

Section 2. Section six of said chapter is hereby amended by striking out all of said section after the word "of" in the second line thereof and inserting in place thereof the words 'forty thousand dollars shall be appropriated annually,' so that said section as amended, shall read as follows:

Appropriation.

'Section 6. For the purpose of carrying out the provisions of this act the sum of forty thousand dollars shall be appropriated annually.'

Section 3. This act shall take effect when approved.

Approved March 10, 1903.

Chapter 64.

An Act to amend Section three, Chapter eighty of the Public Laws of eighteen hundred ninety-nine, relating to the election of truant officers and the filling of vacancies occurring in the office of Truant Officer.

Be it enacted by the Senate and House of Representatives in Legislature assembled, as follows:

Section 3 of chapter 80, public laws of 1899, amended.

Section 1. Section three, chapter eighty of the public laws of eighteen hundred ninety-nine, is hereby amended by adding after the word "year" in the last line of said section the following words, namely; 'and shall elect truant officers at their first meeting after the annual meeting of the town, in case the town neglects to do so or the truant officers elect, or any of them, fail to qualify.' So that the last sentence in said section, as amended, shall read as follows, namely:

'Section 3. Superintending school committees shall have power to fill vacancies occurring during the year and shall elect truant officers at their first meeting after the annual meeting of the town, in case the town neglects to do so, or the truant officers elect, or any of them, fail to qualify.'

Section 2. All acts and parts of acts inconsistent with this act, are hereby repealed.

Approved March 10, 1903.

Chapter 65.

An Act to provide for the recording of Plans.

Be it enacted by the Senate and House of Representatives in Legislature assembled, as follows:

Section 1. The county commissioners at the expense of the several counties shall provide suitable books of the best quality of tracing cloth, interleaved with white paper and substantially bound, for the recording of such plans as may be presented for record; and shall provide other books of substantial binding with stubs for the insertion and preservation of such plans as it may not be expedient to copy into the books first mentioned.

In all cases where a plan is to be copied in the first named books the register of deeds may employ a competent draftsman at a fair compensation to make such copy, and shall receive for examining and certifying the same, the sum of fifty cents in addition to the amount paid for making record, and a like sum for furnishing copies from the record.

Said commissioners shall also cause to be made a suitable index to all plans on record, whether filed and recorded before or after the passage of this act.

Section 2. This act shall take effect when approved.

Approved March 10, 1903.

Chapter 66.

An Act to amend Section three of Chapter two hundred and sixteen of the Public Laws of eighteen hundred and ninety-three, relating to the Conveyance of Scholars and to the maintenance of public schools.

Be it enacted by the Senate and House of Representatives in Legislature assembled, as follows:

Section 1. Section three of chapter two hundred and sixteen of the public laws of eighteen hundred and ninety-three, as amended by chapter two hundred and ninety-five of the public laws of eighteen hundred and ninety-seven, and by chapters

CHAP. 66

public laws of 1897, and by chapters 48 and 74, public laws of 1899, and by chapter 208, public laws of 1901, further amended.

Schools may be established or discontinued by towns at annual meeting.

—proceedings and conditions.

—proviso.

—operation of school may be suspended in certain cases.

—how reopened.

—conveyance of pupils.

—proviso.

CONVEYANCE OF SCHOLARS.

forty-eight and seventy-four of the public laws of eighteen hundred and ninety-nine, and by chapter two hundred and three of the public laws of nineteen hundred and one, is further amended by inserting between the words "vote" and "instruct" in the seventeenth line of said section, as last amended, the words 'at the annual meeting, after the said committee shall have made a written recommendation to that effect,' so that said section, as amended by this act, shall read as follows:

'Section 3. This act shall not abolish or change the location of any school legally established at the time of its passage; but any town at its annual meeting, or at a meeting called for the purpose, may determine the number and location of its schools, and may discontinue them or change their location; but such discontinuance or change of location shall be made only on the written recommendation of the superintending school committee, and on conditions proper to preserve the just rights and privileges of the inhabitants for whose benefit such schools were established; provided, however, that in case of any school having, as now established, or which shall hereafter have, too few scholars for its profitable maintenance, the superintending school committee may suspend the operation of such school for not more than one year unless otherwise instructed by the town, but any public school failing to maintain an average attendance for any school year, of at least eight pupils, shall be and hereby is suspended, unless the town in which said school is located shall by vote, at the annual meeting after the said committee shall have made a written recommendation to that effect, instruct its superintending school committee to maintain said school. The superintendent of schools in each town shall procure the conveyance of all public school pupils residing in his town, a part or the whole of the distance, to and from the nearest suitable school, for the number of weeks for which schools are maintained in each year, when such pupils reside at such a distance from the said school as in the judgment of the superintending school committee shall render such conveyance necessary. Provided, however, that the superintending school committee may authorize the superintendent of schools to pay the board of any pupil or pupils at a suitable place near any established school instead of providing conveyance for said pupil or pupils, when in their judgment it may be done at an equal or less expense than by conveyance.'

Section 2. All acts and parts of acts inconsistent with this act, are hereby repealed.

Approved March 11, 1903.

SALARY—EDUCATION OF YOUTH. 53

CHAP. 67

Chapter 67.

An Act relating to the salary of the Sheriff of the county of Aroostook, and fixing the same at five hundred dollars a year.

Be it enacted by the Senate and House of Representatives in Legislature assembled, as follows:

Section 1. The salary of the sheriff of the county of Aroostook shall be five hundred dollars a year, instead of the sum now fixed by law, said salary to be paid in equal quarterly payments. Salary sheriff, Aroostook county, fixed.

Section 2. All acts and parts of acts inconsistent with this act, are hereby repealed.

Section 3. This act shall take effect on the first day of April, nineteen hundred and three.

Approved March 11, 1903.

Chapter 68.

An Act for the better education of Youth.

Be it enacted by the Senate and House of Representatives in Legislature assembled, as follows:

Section 1. Any youth who resides with parent or guardian in any town which does not support and maintain a free high school giving at least one four years' course properly equipped and teaching such subjects as are taught in secondary schools of standard grade in this state may, when he shall be prepared to pursue such four years' course, attend any school in this state which does have such a four years' course and to which he may gain entrance by permission of those having charge thereof, provided said youth shall attend a school or schools of standard grade which are approved by the state superintendent of public schools. In such case the tuition of such youth, not to exceed thirty dollars annually for any one youth, shall be paid by the town in which he resides as aforesaid and towns are hereby authorized and required to raise annually as other school moneys are raised, a sum sufficient to pay such tuition charges. Persons residing in towns not supporting free high schools, may attend in other towns.
—proviso.
—tuition, by whom paid.

Section 2. When any town shall have been required to pay and has paid tuition as aforesaid the superintending school committee of such town shall make a return under oath to the state superintendent of public schools stating the name of each youth for whom tuition has been paid, the amount paid for each, and the name and location of the school which each has attended and thereupon shall be paid, annually in the month of December, from the state treasury out of the appropriation for the Returns to be made.
—partial re-imbursement.

CHAP. 69

support of free high schools, to each town paying tuition and making return as aforesaid, a sum equal to one-half of the amount thus paid by such town not exceeding two hundred fifty dollars.

Section 3. This act shall take effect when approved.

Approved March 11, 1908.

Chapter 69.

An Act to amend Chapter one hundred and ninety-four of the Public Laws of nineteen hundred and one entitled, "An Act additional to Chapter twenty-nine of the Revised Statutes, relating to Bowling Alleys."

Be it enacted by the Senate and House of Representatives in Legislature assembled, as follows:

Chapter 194, public laws of 1901, amended.

Section 1. Chapter one hundred and ninety-four of the public laws of nineteen hundred and one is hereby amended by inserting after the word "alleys" in the second and fifth line the words 'pool, bagatelle and billiard rooms' so that said section as amended, shall read as follows:

Permission may be given to keep open till midnight.

'Section 1. Any person licensed to own, keep and operate a bowling alley, or bowling alleys, pool, bagatelle or billiard rooms in this state under the provisions of chapter twenty-nine of the revised statutes, may be granted permission by the municipal officers of the town or city where said bowling alley or alleys, pool, bagatelle or billiard rooms are situated to keep the same open until midnight, when in the opinion of such municipal officers no person or persons residing in the immediate neighborhood will be disturbed thereby.'

Section 2. This act shall take effect when approved.

Approved March 11, 1908.

Chapter 70.

An Act to amend Chapter two hundred and eighty-four of the Public Laws of nineteen hundred one, relating to Sea and Shore Fisheries.

Be it enacted by the Senate and House of Representatives in Legislature assembled, as follows:

Section 1. Section twenty-one of chapter two hundred and eighty-four of the public laws of nineteen hundred one is hereby amended by striking out the last sentence thereof and inserting the following sentences: Section 21 of chapter 284, public laws of 1901, amended.

'The possession of mutilated lobsters, cooked or uncooked, shall be prima facie evidence that they are not of the required length. Mutilated lobsters.

All lobsters or parts of lobsters sold for use in this state or for export therefrom must be sold and delivered in the shell under a penalty of twenty dollars for each offense, and whoever ships, buys, gives away, sells or exposes for sale, lobster meat after the same shall have been taken from the shell shall be liable to a penalty of one dollar for each pound of meat so bought, sold, given away, exposed for sale or shipped. Any person or corporation in the business of a common carrier of merchandise, who shall knowingly carry or transport from place to place lobster meat after the same shall have been taken from the shell shall be liable to a penalty of fifty dollars upon each conviction thereof. All lobster meat so illegally bought, shipped, sold, given away, exposed for sale or transported shall be liable to seizure and may be confiscated. —must be sold in the shell.
—penalty.
—common carriers, liabilities of.
—meat liable to seizure.

Nothing contained herein, shall be held to prohibit the sale of lobsters that have been legally canned,' so that said section as amended, shall read as follows: —exception.

'Section 21. It is unlawful to catch, buy or sell, give away or expose for sale, or possess for any purpose any lobster less than ten and one-half inches in length, alive or dead, cooked or uncooked, measured in manner as follows; taking the length of the back of the lobster, measured from the bone of the nose to the end of bone of the middle flipper of the tail, the length to be taken in a gauge with a cleat upon each end of the same, measuring ten and one-half inches between said cleats, with the lobster laid and extended upon its back its natural length upon the gauge, without stretching or pulling, and any lobster shorter than the prescribed length when caught shall be liberated alive at the risk and cost of the parties taking them, under a penalty of one dollar for each lobster so caught, bought, sold, exposed for sale or in possession. The possession of mutilated lobsters, cooked or uncooked, shall be prima facie evidence that they are not of the required length. Length of lobsters.
—how measured.
—short lobsters shall be liberated.
—prima facie evidence.

CHAP. 71

—must be sold in the shell.
—penalty.

—Common carrier, liability of.

—exception.

Section 23, amended.

Lobsters for canning, length of, fixed.

—penalty.

All lobsters or parts of lobsters sold for use in this state or for export therefrom must be sold and delivered in the shell under a penalty of twenty dollars for each offense, and whoever ships, buys, sells, gives away or exposes for sale, lobster meat after the same shall have been taken from the shell shall be liable to a penalty of one dollar for each pound of meat so bought, sold, exposed for sale, given away or shipped. Any person or corporation in the business of a common carrier of merchandise, who shall knowingly carry or transport from place to place lobster meat after the same shall have been taken from the shell shall be liable to a penalty of fifty dollars upon each conviction thereof. All lobster meat so illegally bought, shipped, sold, given away, exposed for sale or transported shall be liable to seizure and may be confiscated. Nothing contained herein shall be held to prohibit the sale of lobsters that have been legally canned.'

Section 2. Section twenty-three is hereby amended so that said section, as amended, shall read as follows:

'It shall be unlawful to can lobsters less than ten and one-half inches in length, alive or dead, measured as aforesaid; and for every lobster canned, contrary to the provisions of this section, every person, firm, association or corporation so canning, shall be liable to a penalty of one dollar for every lobster so canned, contrary to the provisions of this section, and a further penalty of three hundred dollars for every day on which such unlawful canning is carried on.'

Approved March 11, 1903.

Chapter 71.

An Act to repeal Section sixteen of Chapter seventy-eight of the Revised Statutes, relating to duties of County Commissioners.

Be it enacted by the Senate and House of Representatives in Legislature assembled, as follows:

Section 16 of chapter 78, R. S., repealed.

Section 1. Section sixteen of chapter seventy-eight of the revised statutes is hereby repealed.

Section 2. This act shall take effect when approved.

Approved March 11, 1903.

Chapter 72.

An Act to repeal Sections seven, eight, nine and ten of Chapter sixty-one of the Revised Statutes, relating to the Rights of Married Women.

Be it enacted by the Senate and House of Representatives in Legislature assembled, as follows:

Section 1. Sections seven, eight, nine and ten of chapter sixty-one of the revised statutes are hereby repealed. *Sections 7, 8, 9 and 10 of chapter 61, R. S., repealed.*

Section 2. This act shall take effect when approved.

Approved March 11, 1903.

Chapter 73.

An Act to amend Chapter two hundred and sixty-six of the Public Laws of eighteen hundred and ninety-three, as amended by Chapter one hundred and twenty-eight of the Public Laws of eighteen hundred and ninety-nine and one hundred and sixty-seven of the Public Laws of nineteen hundred and one, relating to the Militia.

Be it enacted by the Senate and House of Representatives in Legislature assembled, as follows:

Section 1. Section thirty of said act is hereby amended by striking out the word "of" following the word "day" in the thirteenth and twentieth lines, and substituting therefor the word 'following,' so that said section, as amended, shall read as follows: *Section 30, amended.*

'Section 30. All enlistments in the national guard shall be for three years, and shall be made by signing such enlistment book as may be prescribed by the commander-in-chief. An attested copy of the enlistment book, shall at the organization of each company, be made by the clerk and forwarded, together with duplicates of all enlistment papers, forthwith to the adjutant-general. When a soldier re-enlists and is mustered into the service within thirty days from the expiration of his previous term, his service shall be considered as unbroken and continuous, and re-enlistments and musters shall be dated as of the day following such expiration. When the term of service of any enlisted man terminates during a period of furlough and while he is serving in the United States army, should he re-enlist in the national guard within thirty days of his muster out of the United States army, his service shall be considered as continuous, and shall in like manner commence on the day following such expiration, and re-enlistments and musters shall be so dated. When new enlistments or re-enlistments are made in any organization, the commanding officer shall forward duplicate enlistment papers to the adjutant-general.' *Enlistments shall be for three years.* *—re-enlistments.* *—new enlistments.*

Section 41, amended.

Musicians may be enlisted.

—proviso.

Section 46, amended.

Discharge of enlisted men.

Section 2. Section forty-one of said act is hereby amended by striking out the word "discharge" in the seventh line, and substituting therefor the words 'recommended for discharge,' so that said section, as amended, shall read as follows:

'Section 41. Each colonel of a regiment may enlist and muster a band of musicians, not exceeding twenty-five, including one master, one deputy master and one drum major, to be attached to his regiment; provided that the members of such band shall furnish their own uniforms and instruments. They may be recommended for discharge by the colonel at his pleasure.'

Section 3. Section forty-six of said act is hereby amended by striking out all the section following the word "time" in the second line, and inserting the following: 'Enlisted men may also be discharged by the commander-in-chief, upon personal application in writing, approved by intermediate commanding officers, or upon the recommendation of the commanding officer of any company, battery, troop or corps, approved by intermediate commanding officers,' so that said section, as amended, shall read as follows:

'Section 46. The commander-in-chief may, in his discretion, discharge enlisted men at any time. Enlisted men may also be discharged by the commander-in-chief, upon personal application in writing, approved by intermediate commanding officers, or upon the recommendation of the commanding officer of any company, battery, troop or corps, approved by intermediate commanding officers.'

Approved March 11, 1903.

Chapter 74.

An Act to repeal Sections eight, nine, ten, eleven and twelve of Chapter one hundred thirty-three of the Public Laws of eighteen hundred and ninety-seven, relating to Pardons.

Be it enacted by the Senate and House of Representatives in Legislature assembled, as follows:

Sections 8, 9, 10, 11 and 12, public laws of 1897, repealed.

Section 1. Sections eight, nine, ten, eleven and twelve of chapter one hundred thirty-three of the public laws of eighteen hundred and ninety-seven are hereby repealed.

Section 2. This act shall take effect when approved.

Approved March 11, 1903.

Chapter 75.

An Act relating to waiving of the Provisions of Wills by Widows.

Be it enacted by the Senate and House of Representatives in Legislature assembled, as follows:

Section 1. If the election provided by section five of chapter one hundred fifty-seven of the public laws of eighteen hundred and ninety-five is not made within six months after probate of a will, and the estate is thereafter rendered insolvent, and the commissioners are appointed by the judge of probate, such election may be made at any time within six months after the appointment of such commissioners. Such election shall not affect any title to real estate theretofore acquired from the executor or administrator with the will annexed, but the widow or widower may recover from such executor or administrator, if not paid within thirty days after demand therefor in writing, one-third of any sums received from real estate sold before such waiver was filed.

Section 2. This act shall take effect when approved.

Approved March 11, 1903.

Chapter 76.

An Act to amend Chapter one hundred and fifty-nine of the Public Laws of nineteen hundred and one, providing for the retirement of commissioned officers of the militia or the National Guard of the State of Maine.

Be it enacted by the Senate and House of Representatives in Legislature assembled, as follows:

Section one of said act is hereby amended by striking out the word "nine" in the third line, and substituting therefor the word 'six,' and by inserting after the word "years" in the fourth line, the words 'or for the period of nine years not necessarily continuous.' By striking out the words "rank held by him at the time of his discharge from said service or at the time such application is made" in the fifth, sixth and seventh lines, and substituting therefor the words 'highest rank held by him during said service.' By striking out the words "at the time of such discharge or of making such application, has" in the eighth and ninth lines, and substituting therefor the words 'shall have,' so that said section as amended shall read as follows:

'Section 1. Any person who shall have served as a commissioned officer in the militia or the National Guard of this state, for the continuous period of six years, or for the period of nine

CHAP. 77

after specified service.
—proviso.

—retired officers.

—shall be eligible to perform military duty, etc.

—compensation.

—amenable to court martial.

—shall report change of residence.

years not necessarily continuous, may, upon his own application, be placed upon the retired list, with the highest rank held by him during said service, provided, however, that an officer so retired, who shall have remained in the same grade for the continuous period of nine years, shall be retired with increased rank. Retired officers on occasions of ceremony may, and when acting under orders as hereinafter provided, shall wear the uniform of their retired rank. Retired officers shall be eligible to perform military duty, and the commander-in-chief may, in his discretion, by order require them to serve upon military boards, courts of inquiry and courts martial, or to perform any other special or temporary military duty, and for such service they shall receive the same pay and allowances as are provided in law for like service by the officers of the National Guard. All retired officers shall be amenable to courts martial for military offenses as if upon the active list of the National Guard. The names of all officers of retired rank shall be borne upon a separate roster, kept under the supervision of the adjutant-general. Retired officers shall report to the adjutant-general any change in their residence whenever such change occurs.'

Approved March 11, 1903.

Chapter 77.

An Act to amend Chapter ninety-four of the Public Laws of eighteen hundred eighty-seven, relating to Agricultural Societies.

Be it enacted by the Senate and House of Representatives in Legislature assembled, as follows:

Chapter 94, public laws of 1887, amended.

Section 1. Chapter ninety-four of the public laws of eighteen hundred eighty-seven is hereby amended by inserting after the word "county" in the second line the words 'and local,' so said chapter as amended will read as follows:

Receipts exempt from attachment, etc., until expenses and premiums are paid.

'Section 1. The receipts of the Maine State Agricultural Society, the Eastern Maine State Fair and all county and local agricultural societies, are hereby exempted from attachment, trustees process and seizure on execution until current expenses of the fair, purses and premiums awarded by the society are paid, provided that the same are paid within three months from the close of the fair.'

—proviso.

Section 2. This act shall take effect when approved.

Approved March 11, 1903.

RAILROADS—LOAN AND BUILDING ASSOCIATIONS. 61

CHAP. 78

Chapter 78

An Act to amend Section twenty-nine of Chapter eighteen of the Revised Statutes, relating to ways across station grounds of Railroads.

Be it enacted by the Senate and House of Representatives in Legislature assembled, as follows:

Section twenty-nine of chapter eighteen of the revised statutes is hereby amended so that the same shall read as follows: *Section 29 of chapter 18, R. S. amended.*

'Section 29. No way shall be laid out through or across any land or right of way of any railroad corporation, used for station purposes, unless after notice and hearing the railroad commissioners adjudge that public convenience and necessity require it. When the tribunal having jurisdiction over the laying out of such way is satisfied, after hearing, that public convenience and necessity requires such laying out, such proceedings shall be suspended and petition filed by such tribunal with the railroad commissioners for their adjudication hereunder.' *Way shall not be laid out across land of railroad corporations unless after hearing.*

—petition shall be filed with railroad commissioners.

Approved March 11, 1903.

Chapter 79.

An Act to amend Chapter sixty-one, Public Laws of eighteen hundred eighty-seven, relating to Loan and Building Associations.

Be it enacted by the Senate and House of Representatives in Legislature assembled, as follows:

Section 1. Section one hundred thirty-eight of chapter sixty-one, public laws of eighteen hundred eighty-seven, is hereby amended by striking out in the fifth line of said section, the word "six" and inserting in place thereof the word 'five,' so that said section as amended, shall read as follows: *Section 138 of chapter 61, public laws of 1887, amended.*

'Section 138. When each unpledged share of a given series reaches the value of two hundred dollars, all payments of dues thereon shall cease, and the holder thereof shall be paid out of the funds of the association, two hundred dollars therefor, with interest at the rate of five per cent a year, from the time of such maturity to the time of payment; provided, that at no time shall more than one-half of the funds in the treasury be applicable to the payment of such matured shares, without the consent of the directors, and that before paying matured shares, all arrears and fines shall be deducted. Every share shall be subject to a lien for the payment of any unpaid dues, fines, interest, premiums and other charges received thereon, which may be enforced in the manner hereinafter provided.'

Payment of dues shall cease, when value reaches $200.

—how holder of shares shall be paid.

—proviso.

—shares shall be subject to liens for dues.

Section 2. Section one hundred forty-eight of chapter sixty-one, public laws of eighteen hundred eighty-seven as amended by *Section 148 of chapter 61, public laws*

CHAP. 79

of 1897, as amended by chapter 319, laws of 1897, further amended.

section three of chapter three hundred nineteen, public laws of eighteen hundred ninety-seven, is hereby amended by inserting after the word "occurrence" in the ninth line thereof the following words: 'No dividend shall be made at a rate per cent which will make the aggregate amount of said dividend greater than the actual earnings of the association actually collected,' so that said section as amended, shall read as follows:

Profits and losses, when distributed.

—proportion of distribution.

—guaranty fund.

'Section 148. The profits and losses may be distributed annually, semi-annually or quarterly, to the shares then existing, but shall be distributed at least once in each year, and whenever a new series of shares is to be issued. Profits and losses shall be distributed to the various shares existing at the time of such distribution, in proportion to their value at that time, and shall be computed upon the basis of a single share, fully paid to the date of distribution. Losses shall be apportioned immediately after their occurrence. No dividend shall be made at a rate per cent which will make the aggregate amount of said dividend greater than the actual earnings of the association, actually collected. At each periodical distribution of profits, the directors shall reserve as a guaranty fund a sum not less than three nor more than ten per cent of the net profits accruing since the next preceding adjustment, until such fund amounts to five per cent of the dues capital, which fund shall thereafter be maintained and held, and said fund shall be at all times available to meet losses in the business of the association from depreciation in its securities or otherwise.'

Section 149 of chapter 61, public laws of 1897, amended.

Section 3. Section one hundred and forty-nine of chapter sixty-one, public laws of one thousand eight hundred and eighty-seven, is hereby amended by striking out in the sixth line after the word "estate," the word "so" and inserting in place thereof the words 'in whatever manner' and adding after the word "thereto" in the last line the words 'but the bank examiner, upon application of any association may extend said time in which said real estate may be sold,' so that said section as amended, shall read as follows:

May purchase real estate upon which it may have mortgage, etc.
—may sell.

—shall be sold within five years.

'Section 149. Any association may purchase, at any sale, public or private, any real estate upon which it may have a mortgage, judgment, lien or other incumbrance, or in which it may have an interest, and may sell, convey, lease or mortgage at pleasure, the real estate so purchased, to any person or persons whatsoever. All real estate in whatever manner acquired shall be sold within five years from the acquisition of title thereto; but the bank examiner, upon application of any association may extend said time in which said real estate may be sold.'

Approved March 11, 1903.

Chapter 80.

An Act relating to the commitment of the Insane, and to abolish the right of appeal to Justices of the Peace and Quorum.

Be it enacted by the Senate and House of Representatives in Legislature assembled, as follows:

Section 1. Section fifteen of chapter one hundred and forty-three of the revised statutes is hereby repealed.

Section 2. Section sixteen of chapter one hundred and forty-three of the revised statutes is hereby amended so as to read as follows:

'Section 16. If the municipal officers neglect or refuse, for three days after complaint is made to them to examine and decide any case of insanity in their town, complaint may be made by any blood relative, husband or wife of said alleged insane person, or by any justice of the peace, to two justices of the peace and quorum; and the two justices to whom such application is made shall immediately inquire into the condition of such alleged insane person and shall proceed in the manner provided in section thirteen.'

Section 3. Section seventeen of chapter one hundred and forty-three of the revised statutes, is hereby amended so as to read as follows:

'Section 17. Such justices shall keep a record of their doings and furnish a copy thereof to any person interested requesting and paying for it; they shall be entitled to the same fees as for a criminal examination, to be paid by the person or corporation liable in the first instance for the support of the insane person in the hospital.'

Section 4. This act shall take effect when approved.

Approved March 11, 1903.

Chapter 81.

An Act to amend Section four of Chapter eighty-six of the Revised Statutes as amended by Chapter one hundred fifty-seven, Public Laws of eighteen hundred and ninety-three, relating to Trustee Suits.

Be it enacted by the Senate and House of Representatives in Legislature assembled, as follows:

Section 1. Section four of chapter eighty-six of the revised statutes as amended by chapter one hundred fifty-seven of the public laws of eighteen hundred and ninety-three is hereby amended by inserting after the word "firm" in the fifth line of said section the words 'at the place of business of the firm,' and by

CHAP. 82

striking out from the last clause of said section the words "provided legal service shall be afterwards made upon the other members of the firm" so that said section as amended shall read as follows:

<small>Like service on trustee binds all goods.</small>

'Section 4. A like service on the trustee binds all goods, effects, or credits of the principal defendant entrusted to and deposited in his possession, to respond to the final judgment in the action, as when attached by ordinary process. When a partnership is made a trustee in a trustee suit, service upon one member of the firm at the place of business of the firm, shall be a sufficient attachment of the property of the principal defendant in the possession of the firm.'

<small>—partnership</small>
<small>—service on one member of firm.</small>

Section 2. This act shall take effect when approved.

Approved March 11, 1903.

Chapter 82.

An Act to amend Paragraph five of Section sixty-two of Chapter eighty-one of the Revised Statutes, relating to property exempt from Attachment and Execution.

Be it enacted by the Senate and House of Representatives in Legislature assembled, as follows:

<small>Paragraph 5 of section 62 of chapter 81, R. S. amended.</small>

Section 1. Paragraph five of section sixty-two of chapter eighty-one of the revised statutes is hereby amended by inserting after the word "potatoes" in the third line of said paragraph the words 'and other provisions,' and by inserting after the word "bought" in the same line of said paragraph the words 'and necessary.' So that said paragraph will read as follows:

<small>Exemptions.</small>

'Section 62. Paragraph V. All produce of farms until harvested; one barrel of flour; corn and grain necessary for himself and family, not exceeding thirty bushels; all potatoes and other provisions raised or bought, and necessary for himself and family; and all flax raised on one-half acre of land, and all articles manufactured therefrom for the use of himself and family.'

Section 2. This act shall take effect when approved.

Approved March 11, 1903.

Chapter 83.

An Act relating to the attachment of Partnership Property.

Be it enacted by the Senate and House of Representatives in Legislature assembled, as follows:

Section 1. The personal property of any co-partnership, or the interest of any co-partner therein shall be exempt from attachment on mesne process or seizure on execution for any individual debt or liability of such co-partner, but such co-partner's interest in the partnership property may be reached and applied in payment of any judgment against him in the manner provided in section two of chapter thirty-eight of the public laws of eighteen hundred and ninety-one.

Section 2. This act shall take effect when approved.

Approved March 11, 1903.

Personal property of co-partnership exempt from attachment for debt of co-partner.

—co-partners interest, how reached.

Chapter 84.

An Act to authorize Executors and Administrators to provide for the perpetual care of Burial Lots.

Be it enacted by the Senate and House of Representatives in Legislature assembled, as follows:

Section 1. Executors and administrators may pay to cemetery corporations or to cities or towns having burial places therein, a reasonable sum of money for the perpetual care of the lot in which the body of their testate or intestate is buried, and the monuments thereon. The probate court shall determine, after notice to all parties in interest, to whom the same shall be paid and the amount thereof, and such sum shall be allowed in final accounts of such executors and administrators.

Section 2. This act shall take effect when approved.

Approved March 11, 1903.

Care of lots may be provided for by executors and administrators.

—sum to be allowed shall be determined by probate court.

Chapter 85.

An Act relating to commitments by Trial Justices and Judges of Police and Municipal courts.

Be it enacted by the Senate and House of Representatives in Legislature assembled, as follows:

Shall be committed in county where convicted.

Any person sentenced by any trial justice or judge of any municipal or police court to a term of imprisonment in a jail, workhouse or house of correction, not exceeding four months, shall be committed to the jail, workhouse or house of correction in the county in which such person is convicted, provided such

—proviso.

county has a suitable jail, workhouse or house of correction, otherwise such commitment may be to any jail, workhouse or house of correction in the state.

Approved March 12, 1903.

Chapter 86.

An Act relating to Street Railroad Locations.

Be it enacted by the Senate and House of Representatives in Legislature assembled, as follows:

Location may be canceled by municipal officers upon petition of directors.

Section 1. Whenever a location for a street railroad upon any street, road or way has been approved under the general law or any special act with no actual occupation thereof by the rails of such company, such location in whole or in part may be canceled at any time by the municipal officers of the town where so located upon the petition of the directors of the corporation entitled to the same.

Location may be changed under direction of railroad commissioners.

Section 2. Any street railroad corporation, under the direction of the railroad commissioners, may make any changes in the location of its road which it deems necessary or expedient and such changes shall be recorded where the original location was required by law to be recorded.

Approved March 12, 1903.

Chapter 87.

An Act to amend Section one of Chapter one hundred fourteen of the Revised Statutes, relating to Duties payable by Public Officers.

Be it enacted by the Senate and House of Representatives in Legislature assembled, as follows:

Section 1. Section one of chapter one hundred fourteen of the revised statutes is hereby amended so as to read as follows: *Section 1 of chapter 114, R. S., amended.*

'Section 1. No person appointed to the office of the justice of the peace, justice of the peace and of the quorum, commissioner to take depositions and disclosures, trial justice, notary public, coroner, or inspector of fish, women appointed to administer oaths and take acknowledgment of deeds, disclosure commissioners, commissioners appointed under chapter one hundred ten of the revised statutes, assayers of ores and metals shall enter upon the discharge of his official duties until he has paid five dollars to the treasurer of state.' *Duties payable before entering on duties.*

Section 2. This act shall take effect when approved.

Approved March 12, 1903.

Chapter 88.

An Act relating to the Dissolution of Attachments by filing bond.

Be it enacted by the Senate and House of Representatives in Legislature assembled, as follows:

Section 1. Chapter three hundred eleven of the public laws of eighteen hundred and eighty-nine is hereby amended so as to read as follows: "When real estate or personal property is attached on mesne process, and in all cases of attachment on trustee process, the attachment shall be vacated, upon the defendant, or some one in his behalf, delivering to the officer who made such attachment, or to the plaintiff or his attorney, a bond to the plaintiff in such sum not less than the ad damnum of the writ and with such sureties as may be approved by the plaintiff or his attorney, or by any justice or clerk of the supreme judicial or superior courts; conditioned that within thirty days after the rendition of the judgment, or after the adjournment of the court in which it is rendered, or after the certificate of decision of the law court shall be received in the county where the cause is pending, he will pay to the plaintiff or his attorney of record, the amount of said judgment including costs; the bond shall be returned by the officer with the process, for the benefit of the plaintiff, and thereupon all liability of the officer to the plaintiff *Chapter 311, public laws of 1889, amended. —attachment, how vacated by bond. —condition of bond. —return of bond.*

68 ACKNOWLEDGMENT OF DEEDS.

CHAP. 89

—certificate of discharge.

—fee for record.

—in trustee process.

by reason of such attachment shall cease. Upon request the plaintiff or his attorney, shall give to the defendant a certificate acknowledging the discharge of such attachment, which may be recorded in the registry of deeds or town clerk's office, as the case may be, in which the return of the attachment is filed; the register of deeds or town clerk shall be entitled to twenty-five cents for recording the same. If stock in any corporation is attached, such certificate shall be filed with the officer of the corporation, with whom the return of such attachment is filed, and he shall record the same. In trustee process the alleged trustee shall not be liable to the principal defendant for the goods, effects and credits in his hands or possession until such certificate shall be delivered to him, and upon receiving such certificate, he shall be discharged from further liability in said trustee action, and need not disclose, and shall not recover costs."

Sections 85, 86 and 87 of chapter 86, R. S., repealed.

Section 2. Sections eighty-five, eighty-six and eighty-seven of chapter eighty-six of the revised statutes are hereby repealed.

Section 3. This act shall take effect when approved.

Approved March 12, 1903.

Chapter 89.

An Act relating to the Acknowledgment of Deeds.

Be it enacted by the Senate and House of Representatives in Legislature assembled, as follows:

Section 17 of chapter 73, R. S., amended.

Section 1. Section seventeen of chapter seventy-three in revised statutes is hereby amended by striking out in the fifth line the words "justice of the peace, magistrate" and by inserting in place thereof 'clerk of the court of record having the seal'; by adding to said section the seal of such court, or the official seal of such notary shall be affixed to the certificate of acknowledgment. So that said section shall read as follows:

Acknowledgment of deeds, by grantor, before whom.

'Section 17. Deeds shall be acknowledged by the grantors, or one of them, or by their attorney executing the same, before a justice of the peace, or notary public, or women otherwise eligible under the constitution and appointed for the purpose by the governor with the advice and consent of the council in the state or any clerk of a court of record having a seal or notary public within the United States, or before a minister or consul of the United States or notary public in any foreign country. The seal of such court, or the official seal of such notary shall be affixed to the certificate of acknowledgment.'

—seal of court or notary.

Section 2. This act shall take effect when approved.

Approved March 12, 1903.

GUARDIANS—INSANE PERSONS.

Chapter 90.

An Act relating to the authority of courts over Guardians ad litem or next friend.

Be it enacted by the Senate and House of Representatives in Legislature assembled, as follows:

Section 1. No settlement of any suit brought in behalf of an infant by next friend shall be valid unless approved by the court in which the action is pending, or to which the writ is returnable, or affirmed by an entry or judgment. The court may make all necessary orders for protecting the interests of the infant, and may require the guardian ad litem, or next friend, to give bond to truly account for all money received in behalf of the infant.

Section 2. This act shall take effect when approved.

Approved March 12, 1903.

Settlement of suit not valid unless approved by court.
—court may make orders.

Chapter 91.

An Act to amend Chapter sixty-seven of the Revised Statutes and Chapter one hundred forty-three of the Revised Statutes, relating to the appointment of Guardians for persons insane.

Be it enacted by the Senate and House of Representatives in Legislature assembled, as follows:

Section 1. Section five of chapter sixty-seven of the revised statutes is hereby amended so as to read as follows:

'Section 5. Guardians may be appointed, on application as aforesaid, for persons certified by the municipal officers of any town to have been committed by them or their predecessors, to either insane hospital, and there remaining, upon proof of the facts, without personal notice to the parties. In all cases where the municipal officers or overseers of the poor are applicants, if they have given at least fourteen days' notice to such person by serving him with a copy of their application, the judge may adjudicate thereon without further notice, or may order such notice, if any, as he thinks reasonable.'

Section 2. Section six of said chapter sixty-seven is hereby amended so as to read as follows:

'Section 6. In all other cases, the judge shall appoint a time and place for hearing and shall order that notice of the proceedings be given by serving the person for whom a guardian is requested with a copy of the application and order of the court, at least fourteen days before the day of hearing. If upon such

Section 5 of chapter 67, R. S., amended.
Guardians for persons insane, appointment of.
—when notice shall be given.
Section 6 of chapter 67, amended.
Hearing, time and place of.

hearing, he adjudges that such person is insane, a spendthrift, or incapable as aforesaid, he shall appoint a guardian.'

Section 3. Section twenty-seven of chapter one hundred forty-three of the revised statutes is hereby repealed.

Section 4. This act shall take effect when approved.

Approved March 12, 1903.

Chapter 92.

An Act to amend Chapter forty-two of the Public Laws of eighteen hundred ninety-nine, relating to the taking of Black Bass in certain lakes in Kennebec and Somerset Counties, also Sabattus Pond in Androscoggin County, as amended by Chapter two hundred eighty-seven, Public Laws of nineteen hundred one.

Be it enacted by the Senate and House of Representatives in Legislature assembled, as follows:

Section 1. Section one of chapter forty-two of the public laws of eighteen hundred ninety-nine as amended by chapter two hundred eighty-seven of the public laws of nineteen hundred one, is hereby amended by adding thereto after the words "also Keoka lake in Oxford county," the words, 'also Highland lake in the northern part of Cumberland county.'

Section 2. This act shall take effect when approved.

Approved March 12, 1903.

Chapter 93.

An Act to amend Section fifteen of Chapter fifty-one of the Revised Statutes, relating to recording locations of Railroads.

Be it enacted by the Senate and House of Representatives in Legislature assembled, as follows:

Section 1. Section fifteen of chapter fifty-one of the revised statutes is hereby amended by striking out the words "approved by them and recorded" in the fourth line of said section and inserting in the place thereof the words 'who shall endorse the time of the filing thereon and order said location recorded' so that said section, as amended, shall read as follows:

'Section 15. The railroad shall be located within the time and substantially according to the description in its charter; and the location shall be filed with the county commissioners, who shall endorse the time of the filing thereon and order said location recorded. When a corporation, by its first location, fails to acquire the land actually embraced in its roadway, or the location as recorded is defective or uncertain, it may, at any time, correct and perfect its location, and file a new description thereof; and in such case it is liable in damages, by reason of such new or amended location, only for land embraced therein for which the owner had not previously been paid. Any subscriber to the stock, alleging that it has not been located according to its charter, may, before payment of his subscription, make written application to the county commissioners in the county where the deviation is alleged, stating it, who after fourteen days' notice to the corporation, and upon a view and hearing, shall determine whether it has been located as required; if they determine that it has been, no such defense shall be made to any process to enforce payment; if they determine that it has not, the subscription of such applicant is void. The prevailing party recovers costs. Provisions in railroad charters whenever granted, limiting the time within which such railroad shall be completed, shall not affect the portion thereof completed within such time, and all charters under which railroads have been constructed for a portion of the line authorized thereby are confirmed and made valid as to such portion.'

Section 2. This act shall take effect when approved.

Approved March 13, 1903.

Chapter 94.

An Act to amend Section eleven of Chapter sixty-eight of the Revised Statutes, relating to Trust Estates.

Be it enacted by the Senate and House of Representatives in Legislature assembled, as follows:

Section 1. Section eleven of chapter sixty-eight of the revised statutes is hereby amended by striking out the words "according to the will" in the last line of said section and inserting in the place thereof the words 'as will best effect the objects of the trust,' so that said section as amended, shall read as follows:

'Section 11. Any judge of probate, having jurisdiction of the trust, and the supreme judicial court in any county, on application of the trustee, or of any person interested in the trust estate, after notice to all interested, may authorize or require him to sell any real or personal estate held by him in trust, and to invest the proceeds thereof, with any other trust moneys in his hands, in real estate, or in any other manner most for the interest of all concerned therein; and may give such further directions as the case requires, for managing, investing, and dis-

DENTISTRY—JUDGES OF PROBATE—NAVAL RESERVE.

CHAP. 95

posing of the trust fund, as will best effect the objects of the trust.'

Section 2. This act shall take effect when approved.

Approved March 13, 1903.

Chapter 95.

An Act to amend Chapter forty-three of the Public Laws of eighteen hundred ninety-one, relating to the practice of Dentistry.

Be it enacted by the Senate and House of Representatives in Legislature assembled, as follows:

Section 6 of, chapter 43, public laws of 1891, repealed.

Section six of chapter forty-three of the public laws of eighteen hundred ninety-one is hereby repealed.

Approved March 13, 1903.

Chapter 96.

An Act to repeal Section thirty-six of Chapter sixty-three of the Revised Statutes, relating to Examination before Judges of Probate.

Be it enacted by the Senate and House of Representatives in Legislature assembled, as follows:

Section 36 of chapter 63, R. S., repealed.

Section 1. Section thirty-six of chapter sixty-three of the revised statutes is hereby repealed.

Section 2. This act shall take effect when approved.

Approved March 12, 1903.

Chapter 97.

An Act to amend Chapter forty-six of the Public Laws of eighteen hundred and ninety-nine, establishing a Naval Reserve as a part of the National Guard of the State of Maine.

Be it enacted by the Senate and House of Representatives in Legislature assembled, as follows:

Section 1, public laws of 1899, amended.

Section 1. Section one of said act is hereby amended by striking out the word "battalion" in the fifth line thereof and the words which follow, and inserting in place thereof the words 'ship's company'; so that said section, as amended, shall read as follows:

Naval reserve authorized.

'Section 1. There may be allowed, in addition to the national guard of the state of Maine as provided in section twenty-six, chapter two hundred and sixty-six of the laws of eighteen hundred and ninety-three, a naval reserve, to consist in time of peace of not more than one ship's company.'

NAVAL RESERVES. 73

CHAP. 97

Section 2. Section three of said act is hereby amended by striking out the words "battalion may" in the first line thereof, and inserting in place thereof the words 'ship's company shall,' by striking out the words "four" and "an engineer division" in the second line thereof, and inserting in place of the former the word 'eight,' and by adding to said section the words 'in time of war, insurrection, invasion, or imminent danger thereof of not more than sixteen divisions;' so that said section as amended, shall read as follows:

Section 3, public laws of 1889, amended.

'Section 3. In time of peace the authorized ship's company shall consist of not more than eight divisions and in time of war, insurrection, invasion, or imminent danger thereof, of not more than sixteen divisions.'

Ship's company, of what it shall consist.

Section 3. Section four of said act is hereby stricken out and in place thereof the following section is substituted:

Section 4, public laws of 1889, amended.

'Section 4. The ship's company shall be commanded by a lieutenant. There shall be allowed on the staff of the commanding officer of the ship's company, one lieutenant, junior grade, who shall act as executive officer and adjutant, and one assistant surgeon of the rank of lieutenant, junior grade. In addition there shall be on the staff of the commanding officer two chief petty officers of such class as he may designate. Each division shall be commanded by an ensign, excepting that the senior division officer may be commissioned with the rank of lieutenant, junior grade. To each division there shall be allowed, in time of peace, one chief petty officer of such class as the commanding officer of the ship's company may designate and not more than six petty officers and twenty-four enlisted men.'

Officers of ship's company.

Section 4. Section five is hereby stricken out and the following section substituted in place thereof:

Section 5, public laws of 1889, stricken out.

'Section 5. Two divisions shall be considered the equivalent of one company of infantry excepting as is herein provided. To the commanding officer of the ship's company there shall be allowed the sum of twenty-five dollars per annum for the care and custody of such government property as he may be responsible for; to each division commander there shall be allowed the sum of twenty-five dollars per annum for the care of state property and equipment for which he is accountable; to the executive officer or adjutant of the ship's company there shall be allowed the sum of ten dollars per annum. To each division there shall be allowed one clerk who shall receive the sum of ten dollars per annum for his services.'

Two divisions shall be the equivalent of one company of infantry.

—allowances.

Section 5. Section six of said act is hereby amended by striking out the word "the" in the seventh line, and inserting in place thereof the word 'two,' and by striking out the words "of companies" in the eighth line, and inserting in place thereof the

Section 6, public laws of 1889, amended.

words 'a company'; so that said section as amended, shall read as follows:

Administration and instruction.

'Section 6. The system of administration and instruction of the naval reserves shall conform, as nearly as possible, to that of the navy of the United States. Duty shall be performed afloat when possible. When not otherwise provided for, the government of the naval reserve shall be according to the laws and regulations now or hereafter governing the national guard of the state. Two divisions of the naval reserve shall be considered the equivalent of a company of infantry.'

Chapter 46, public laws of 1899, further amended. Election of officers.

Section 6. Said act is hereby further amended by adding the following section thereto:

'Section 9. When the commissions now issued are vacated the lieutenant commanding the ship's company shall be elected by the division commanders. The election of the division commanders shall be as prescribed for the election of company officers.'

Approved March 17, 1903.

Chapter 98.

An Act to regulate the practice of Embalming and the transportation of the bodies of persons who have died of infectious diseases.

Be it enacted by the Senate and House of Representatives in Legislature assembled, as follows:

Rules and regulations to be made uniform.

Section 1. For the preservation of the public health the state board of health is empowered to make such rules and regulations as it may deem necessary, relating to the transportation of the remains of persons who have died of infectious diseases, said rules and regulations so far as may be deemed practicable and safe, to be uniform with those which are now in effect, or which may be in effect in the other North American states and provinces.

Alteration and amendment of rules.

Section 2. The state board of health is also authorized to make, alter or amend rules and regulations governing the preparation and transportation by rail or otherwise of all bodies dead of an infectious, contagious, or other disease.

Registration of undertakers and embalmers.

Section 3. Every person who shall on the approval of this act, be engaged in the business of undertaking and practice of embalming human bodies in this state and shall desire to continue in that business, must, before the first day of September, nineteen hundred three, register his name, age, length of time in the business, and place of residence, with the state board of examiners, and shall receive a certificate certifying that he is a registered undertaker and embalmer, under which he shall have all the privileges of a licensed embalmer.

Section 4. Any person wishing to become an undertaker, an embalmer of dead human bodies, or engage in the business of caring for and preparing dead human bodies for burial, transportation or cremation, as a regular and permanent business or profession, shall have an intelligent comprehension of the art of embalming, and of such rudiments of anatomy, and of the characteristics of, and the dangers from the contagious and infectious diseases, and of the actions and uses of disinfectant agencies, as the state board of health may prescribe as necessary for the protection of the living, before he is permitted to practice said business or profession within this state, and shall also be required to pass an examination before a board of examiners created and empowered by this act.

Section 5. After the examination has been completed the state board of examiners shall judge of the qualification of the applicant, and, if satisfactory, the certificate of a licensed embalmer shall be issued to him, under which he shall have legal authority to prepare bodies dead of infectious or contagious disease for transportation, and to do any work coming within the province of his vocation.

Section 6. The state board of examiners has authority under the law to revoke, for cause, any license it may issue, and the failure to comply with the law and the regulations of the state board of health shall be deemed sufficient provocation for the revocation of a license.

Section 7. Examinations for licenses shall be given by the state board of examiners at least twice annually, at such time and place as they may determine. The examination papers shall contain such questions relating to the subject of embalming as the state board of examiners may deem necessary to determine the qualifications of the applicant for the business, and if found qualified, a certificate, as provided for in section five of this act, shall be granted him.

Section 8. The board of examiners shall consist of four members made up as follows: Two members of the state board of health, one of whom shall be the secretary of the state board of health, and who shall be the clerk of the board, and two practical undertakers and embalmers. The board of examiners shall be appointed by the governor by and with the advice and consent of the executive council, and the three appointive members shall hold office for one, two and three years respectively, and until others are appointed to fill their places. At the expiration of the first term of office of each member, future appointments shall be made for three years. In case of a vacancy due to death, resignation or other cause, the vacancy shall be filled by an

CHAP. 98

Records of examinations shall be kept.

appointment for the unexpired term, as is provided for original appointments.

Section 9. The state board of health may adopt such blanks and forms of procedure as it may deem necessary and best to carry out the provisions of this act, and it shall keep on file a list of all registered and licensed embalmers and a record of examinations, together with the examination papers, all of which shall be open to public inspection.

Restrictions.

Section 10. No person shall inject into any cavity or artery of the body of any person who has died from an accidental or sudden death or under suspicious circumstances, any fluid or substance until a legal certificate of the cause of death from the attending physician has been obtained, nor until a legal investigation has determined the cause of death. If a criminal cause of death is alleged or suspected, no fluid or other substance shall be injected into a body until the cause of death is legally established.

Board shall keep records of licenses issued and of moneys.

Section 11. The board shall keep a record, containing the names and residences of all persons registered hereunder, and a record of all moneys received and disbursed by said board, and said records, or duplicates thereof, shall always be open to inspection in the office of the secretary of the state board of health during regular office hours. Said board shall annually report to the state board of health, on or before the first day of January in each year; the report to contain a full and complete account of all its official acts during the year, together with a statement of the receipts and disbursements of the board and such comments as may be deemed proper.

—shall report to board of health.

Fees.

Section 12. The fee for registration under this act shall be one dollar, and for examination five dollars. The money thus received by the board of examiners shall constitute a permanent fund for carrying out the work provided in this act. From the money thus received the expenses for printing, for stationery, for postage, for other expenses necessarily incurred under the provisions of this act, and for full compensation of the members of the board of examiners, shall be paid. The board of examiners shall be entitled to five dollars each per day and expenses during session. The clerk of the examining board shall be paid one hundred dollars for the first year of his services, and thereafter he shall receive the same compensation as the other members of the board; any balance shall be turned into the treasury of the board of examiners. The clerk of the examining board shall act as treasurer of the board, and shall deposit or otherwise care for any money which may be in the treasury as he may be instructed by vote of the board of examiners.

—disposition of fees.

—compensation of board of examiners.

—of clerk.

—clerk shall act as treasurer.

Section 13. Any person who shall violate any of the provisions of this act, shall be guilty of a misdemeanor, and upon conviction thereof shall be subject to a fine of not less than five dollars nor more than one hundred dollars.

Section 14. All acts and parts of acts inconsistent with this act, are hereby repealed, and this act shall take effect when approved.

Approved March 17, 1903.

Chapter 99.

An Act providing for a license for non-residents to hunt Moose and Deer.

Be it enacted by the Senate and House of Representatives in Legislature assembled, as follows:

Section 1. It shall be unlawful for any person not a bona fide resident of the state, and actually domiciled therein, to hunt, pursue, take, or kill any bull moose or deer at any time without having first procured a license therefor as hereinafter provided. Such licenses shall be issued by the commissioners of inland fisheries and game, upon application in writing and the payment of fifteen dollars, and under such rules and regulations to be established by them, and approved by the governor and council, as may be required to carry out the true intent of this act and not inconsistent herewith.

All money received for such licenses shall be forthwith paid to the state treasurer, and then expended by the commissioners in the protection of moose and deer, under the direction of the governor and council.

Provided, however, that the commissioners of inland fisheries and game shall have authority to adjust and pay, out of the funds received for such licenses, for actual damage done growing crops by deer.

Provided, further, that the governor and council shall have authority to allow the commissioners of inland fisheries and game, out of the funds received for licenses and fines, such compensation as they may deem just and fair for the additional work required of them in carrying out the provisions of this act.

Provided, also, that the governor's council shall, as often as they see fit, examine the books, accounts and vouchers of the commissioners of all moneys received by them for all licenses or other fees and make a report thereon to the governor.

Section 2. Each license shall be provided with three coupons, one of which shall permit the transportation of the carcass of

CHAP. 99

—moose coupon.

—deer coupons.

—transportation of game by licensed hunters.

—moose shipment.

—deer shipment.

one bull moose, or part thereof, and shall be divided into two sections, lettered "A" and "B" respectively, and shall be called the 'moose' coupon; the two other coupons shall permit the transportation of the carcass of one deer, or part thereof, each, and shall be divided into two sections each, lettered "C" and "D" and "E" and "F" respectively, and shall be called the 'deer' coupons.

The holder of a non-resident hunting license shall be entitled to offer for transportation and have transported, within or without this state, by any railroad company, express company, boat, or other transportation company, the carcass of one bull moose, or part of the carcass of one bull moose that he himself has lawfully killed, on the 'moose' coupon attached to said license; also the carcass of one deer, or part of the carcass of one deer, that he himself has lawfully killed, on each of the 'deer' coupons attached to his said license, by presenting to the agent of any transportation company, his license, with the coupons attached to the license at the time when he shall offer the moose or deer for shipment. The agent receiving the carcass or part of a carcass, for shipment shall, if it is a moose, detach section "A" from the 'moose' coupon of the license, cancel the same by writing or stamping thereon the date and place of shipment and his initials, and shall forward the same forthwith to the commissioners of inland fisheries and game, at Augusta, Maine; section "B" of said coupon shall be likewise canceled and shall be attached to the carcass, or part of the carcass, of the bull moose offered for shipment and shall remain attached to the same while it is being transported in this state.

In case of deer received for shipment, the license must be presented to the agent with the coupons attached as aforesaid, and, if but one deer is offered for shipment, the agent shall detach section "C" from the first 'deer' coupon and shall cancel it and forward the same to the commissioners of inland fisheries and game as aforesaid, and section "D" of said coupon shall be likewise canceled and attached to the carcass of the deer, or part thereof, offered for shipment and shall remain attached to the same while it is being transported in this state.

In case two deer are offered for shipment the agent receiving the same for shipment shall detach sections "C" and "E" from the deer coupons and after canceling the same shall forward them to the commissioners as aforesaid, and sections "D" and "F" shall be likewise canceled and attached to the carcasses of the deer, or parts thereof, offered for transportation and shall remain attached to the same while it is being transported in this state.

It shall be unlawful to transport any bull moose or deer, or parts thereof, within this state for any non-resident, otherwise than as provided herein.

Any agent, servant or employee of any transportation company, railroad company, express company, boat or common carrier who shall receive for shipment or transport, or have in his possession with intent to ship or transport, any carcass of a bull moose, or part of the same, or any carcass of a deer or part of the same, for a non-resident, except as herein provided, or who shall refuse or neglect to detach the sections of the coupons as herein provided, or who shall fail to forward to the commissioners of inland fisheries and game, at Augusta, Maine, as herein provided, the sections of coupons by him detached, shall be punished by a fine of not less than twenty-five dollars nor more than one hundred dollars and costs for each offense. —penalties for illegal shipment.

Section 3. Whoever is found guilty of violating any of the provisions of this chapter, or who shall furnish to another person, or permit another person to have or use any license or coupon issued to him, or shall change or alter the same in any manner, or shall have or use any license or coupon issued to another person, or any registered guide who shall knowingly guide any non-resident in hunting who has not a license to hunt as herein provided, shall be punished by a fine of not less than twenty-five dollars nor more than one hundred dollars and costs for each offense. Penalties for violation of this act. —for fraud. —for guiding hunter without license.

Section 4. All acts and parts of acts inconsistent with this act, are hereby repealed. Inconsistent acts, repealed

Section 5. This act shall take effect July first, nineteen hundred three.

Approved March 18, 1903.

Chapter 100.

An Act to amend Chapter three hundred thirty-two of the Public Laws of eighteen hundred ninety-seven, relating to the powers and duties of School Committees and the manner of electing Town Superintendents.

Be it enacted by the Senate and House of Representatives in Legislature assembled, as follows:

Section 1. Section one of chapter three hundred thirty-two of the public laws of eighteen hundred ninety-seven is hereby amended by inserting between the words "annually" and "elect" in the seventh line of said section the words 'and as often as a vacancy shall occur'; and furthermore by striking out after the word "committee" in the ninth line of said section the following Section 1 of chapter 332, public laws of 1897, amended.

CHAP. 101

words, namely; 'but any town may elect a superintendent of schools by ballot at the regular town meeting,' so that said section, as amended, shall read as follows, namely:

Chapter 11, R. S., as amended, further amended.

'Section 1. Chapter eleven of the revised statutes, as now amended, is further amended by adding thereto the following section:

Superintending school committees shall have management of schools, care of buildings, etc.

'Section 129. The management of the schools and the custody and care including repairs and insurance on school buildings and of all school property in every town, shall devolve upon a superintending school committee which shall annually, and as often as a vacancy shall occur, elect a superintendent of schools who shall not be a member of the committee, who shall be, ex officio, secretary of the committee.'

Section 2. All acts and parts of acts inconsistent with this act, are hereby repealed.

Section 3. This act shall take effect when approved.

Approved March 18, 1903.

Chapter 101.

An Act to amend Section one of Chapter two hundred forty-nine of the Public Laws of nineteen hundred and one, in relation to compensation for clerk hire in Adjutant General's office.

Be it enacted by the Senate and House of Representatives in Legislature assembled, as follows:

Section 1 of chapter 249, public laws of 1901, amended.

Section one of chapter two hundred forty-nine of the public laws of nineteen hundred and one is hereby amended by striking out the word "one" in the second line of said section and inserting in its place the word 'three,' and by striking out the word "eighteen" in the third line of said section and inserting in its place the word 'nineteen,' so that said section as amended, shall read as follows:

Clerk hire, amount allowed for.

'Section 1. From and after January first, nineteen hundred and three, the amount allowed for clerk hire in the office of the adjutant general shall be nineteen hundred dollars per annum, payable quarterly, instead of the sum now provided by law.'

Approved March 18, 1903.

Chapter 102.

An Act to amend Section one of Chapter two hundred and forty-two of the Public Laws of eighteen hundred and eighty-nine, in relation to the salary of the Adjutant General.

Be it enacted by the Senate and House of Representatives in Legislature assembled, as follows:

Section one of chapter two hundred and forty-two of the public laws of eighteen hundred and eighty-nine is hereby amended by striking out the words "eighteen hundred and eighty-nine" in the first and second lines of said section and inserting instead thereof the words 'nineteen hundred and three,' and by striking out the word "fifteen" in the third line of said section and inserting in its place the word 'eighteen' so that said section as amended, shall read as follows:

'Section 1. From and after January first, nineteen hundred and three, the salary of the adjutant general shall be eighteen hundred dollars per annum, payable quarterly, instead of the sum now provided by law.'

Approved March 18, 1908.

Chapter 103.

An Act amendatory of Section two of Chapter two hundred and eighty-seven of the Public Laws of eighteen hundred and ninety-three as amended by Chapter thirty-three of the Public Laws of eighteen hundred and ninety-nine, and Chapter one hundred and sixty-three of the Public Laws of nineteen hundred and one, relating to the better protection of Sheep.

Be it enacted by the Senate and House of Representatives in Legislature assembled, as follows:

Section 1. Section two of chapter two hundred and eighty-seven of the public laws of eighteen hundred ninety-three as amended by chapter thirty-three of the public laws of eighteen hundred and ninety-nine, and chapter one hundred and sixty-three of the public laws of nineteen hundred and one, is hereby amended by inserting after the word "keeper" in the first line the words 'upon the first day of April,' and by striking out the word "first" in the second line and adding in place thereof the word 'tenth,' and by striking out the word "from" in said second line and inserting in place thereof the words 'commencing with,' and by inserting after the word "of" in second line the word 'said,' and by inserting after the word "of" as it first appears in the fourth line the word 'said,' and by inserting after the word "licensed" in the twelfth line the words 'as required herein' and by inserting after the word "shall" in the twelfth line the words

CHAP. 104

Dogs shall be registered, numbered, described and licensed.

—shall have collar.

—license fee.

—kennel license.

fee for kennel license.

—exception.

'within ten days after he becomes the owner or keeper of said dog' so that said section shall read as follows:

'Section 2. Every owner or keeper, upon the first day of April of a dog more than four months old, shall annually before the tenth day of said April, cause it to be registered, numbered, described and licensed for one year commencing with the first day of said April, in the office of the clerk of the city, town or plantation where said dog is kept, and shall keep around its neck a collar distinctly marked with the owner's name and its registered number, and shall pay to said clerk for a license the sum of one dollar and fifteen cents for each male dog and each female dog incapable of producing young, and three dollars and fifteen cents for each other female dog, and a person becoming the owner or keeper of a dog after the first day of April, not duly licensed as required herein, shall within ten days after he becomes the owner or keeper of said dog, cause it to be registered, numbered, described and licensed as provided above. Every owner or keeper of dogs, kept for breeding purposes, may receive annually a special kennel license authorizing him to keep such dogs for said purpose, provided he keeps such dogs within a proper enclosure. When the number of dogs so kept does not exceed ten, the fee for such license shall be ten dollars, when the number of dogs so kept exceeds ten, the fee for such license shall be twenty dollars and no fees shall be required for the dogs of such owner or keeper under the age of six months. Dogs covered by kennel license shall be excepted from the provisions of this section requiring registration, numbering and collaring.'

Section 2. This act shall take effect April one in the year of our Lord nineteen hundred and three.

Approved March 18, 1903.

Chapter 104.

An Act establishing the jurisdiction and term of office of Women appointed to solemnize marriages, administer oaths and take acknowledgments of deeds.

Be it enacted by the Senate and House of Representatives in Legislature assembled, as follows:

Authority and tenure.

Section 1. The appointment of any woman under the laws of the state to solemnize marriage, administer oaths and take acknowledgments of deeds shall authorize her to act within and for every county of the state, and said appointment shall continue for the term of seven years.

Section 2. This act shall take effect when approved.

Approved March 18, 1903.

Chapter 105.

An Act to amend Section two of Chapter twenty of the Revised Statutes, relating to Ferries.

Be it enacted by the Senate and House of Representatives in Legislature assembled, as follows:

Section 1. Section two of chapter twenty of the revised statutes is hereby amended by inserting after the word "tolls" in the second line of said section the words 'and shall discontinue such ferries when, in their judgment, it may be expedient,' so that said section, as amended, shall read as follows:

'Section 2. They may establish ferries at such times and places as are necessary, and fix their tolls, and shall discontinue such ferries when, in their judgment, it may be expedient. When no person is found to keep them therefor, the towns in which they are established shall provide a person to be licensed to keep them, and shall pay the expenses, beyond the amount of tolls received, for maintaining them. When established between towns, they shall be maintained by them in such proportions as the commissioners order. For each month's neglect to maintain such ferry or its proportion thereof, a town forfeits forty dollars.'

Section 2. This act shall take effect when approved.

Approved March 18, 1903.

Chapter 106.

An Act to amend Section one hundred and six of Chapter forty-seven of the Revised Statutes, relating to the reserve fund of Savings Banks.

Be it enacted by the Senate and House of Representatives in Legislature assembled, as follows:

Section 1. Section one hundred and six of chapter forty-seven of the revised statutes is hereby amended by striking out the word "five" in the ninth and eleventh lines and inserting in place thereof the word 'ten,' so that said section as amended, shall read as follows:

'Section 106. The trustees, after passing to the reserve fund one-quarter of one per cent of the average amount of deposits for the six months previous to declaring a dividend, not subject to be divided, shall declare dividends, not exceeding two and a half per cent semi-annually except as hereinafter provided, at such times as are required by their by-laws, among depositors of three months standing at least before dividend day. The corporation may by its by-laws include deposits of less standing. The

84 UNCLAIMED DEPOSITS IN SAVINGS BANKS.

CHAP. 107

reserve fund shall be kept constantly on hand, to secure against losses and contingencies, until it amounts to ten per cent of the deposits. All losses shall be passed to the debit of said account. And when said reserve fund amounts to ten per cent of the average amount of deposits for the six months previous to declaring a dividend, all net profits not otherwise divided, thereafter made by said banks, shall be divided every three years ratably among the depositors of one, two and three full years' standing, as extra dividends. No dividends or interest shall be declared, credited or paid, except by a vote of the board of trustees, entered upon their records, whereon shall be recorded the yeas and nays upon such vote. Trustees of savings banks and savings institutions are forbidden to make any semi-annual dividend of a rate per cent which will make the aggregate amount of said dividend greater than the actual earnings of the bank or institution, actually collected.'

—unearned dividends prohibited.

Section 2. This act shall take effect when approved.

Approved March 18, 1903.

Chapter 107.

An Act to amend Chapter one hundred and thirty-six, Public Laws of eighteen hundred and eighty-seven, relating to Unclaimed Deposits in Savings Banks.

Be it enacted by the Senate and House of Representatives in Legislature assembled, as follows:

Chapter 136, public laws of 1887, amended.

Section 1. Chapter one hundred and thirty-six, public laws of eighteen hundred and eighty-seven is hereby amended by striking out all of said chapter and substituting the following:

Treasurer shall publish statement.

'Section 1. The treasurer of every savings bank and institution for savings shall on or before the first day of November annually cause to be published in a newspaper in the place where the bank or institution is located, if any, otherwise in a newspaper published in the nearest place thereto, a statement containing the name, the amount standing to his credit, the last known place of residence or post office address and the fact of death, if known, of every depositor in said bank who shall not have made a deposit therein or withdrawn therefrom any part of his deposit or any part of the dividends thereon, for a period of more than twenty years next preceding; provided, however, that this act shall not apply to the deposits of persons known to the treasurer to be living. Said treasurer shall also transmit a copy of such statement to the bank examiner to be placed on file in his office for

—of name, amount of deposit, last known place of residence of depositors not depositing or withdrawing funds within 20 years.

—proviso.

public inspection. Any treasurer neglecting to comply with the provisions of this statute shall be liable to a penalty of fifty dollars.'

Section 2. This act shall take effect when approved.

Approved March 18, 1903.

Chapter 108.

An Act to amend Section eighty of Chapter eighteen of the Revised Statutes, relating to Injuries on Highways.

Be it enacted by the Senate and House of Representatives in Legislature assembled, as follows:

Section 1. Section eighty of chapter eighteen of the revised statutes, is hereby amended by inserting after the word "town" in the eighth line, the following words: 'Or any person authorized by any commissioner of such county, or any municipal officer, or road commissioner of such town, to act as a substitute for either of them.' So that said section as amended, shall read as follows:

'Section 80. Whoever receives any bodily injury, or suffers damage in his property, through any defect or want of repair or sufficient railing in any highway, town way, causeway or bridge, may recover for the same in a special action on the case, to be commenced within one year from the date of receiving such injury, or suffering damage, of the county or town obliged by law to repair the same, if the commissioners of such county, or the municipal officers, or road commissioners of such town, or any person authorized by any commissioner of such county or any municipal officer, or road commissioner of such town, to act as a substitute for either of them, had twenty-four hours actual notice of the defect or want of repair; but not exceeding two thousand dollars in case of a town; and if the sufferer had notice of the condition of such way previous to the time of the injury he cannot recover of a town unless he has previously notified one of the municipal officers of the defective condition of such way; and any person who sustains injury or damage, as aforesaid, shall within fourteen days thereafter, notify one of the county commissioners of such county, or of the municipal officers of such town, by letter or otherwise, in writing, setting forth his claim for damages and specifying the nature of his injuries and the nature and location of the defect which caused such injury.

86 DOGS.

CHAP. 109
—loss of life, damages for, how recovered.

If the life of any person is lost through such deficiency, his executors or administrators may recover of such county or town liable to keep the same in repair, in an action on the case, brought for the benefit of the estate of the deceased, such sum as the jury may deem reasonable as damages, if the parties liable had said notice of the deficiency which caused the loss of life; at the trial of any such action the court may, on motion of either party, order a view of the premises where the defect or want of repair is alleged, when it would materially aid in a clear understanding of the case.'

Section 2. This act shall take effect when approved.

Approved March 18, 1903.

Chapter 109.

An Act to amend Section one of Chapter thirty of the Revised Statutes, as amended by Chapter one hundred fifteen of the Public Laws of eighteen hundred ninety-five, and Sections three and four of Chapter thirty of the Revised Statutes, in relation to Dogs.

Be it enacted by the Senate and House of Representatives in Legislature assembled, as follows:

Section 1 of chapter 30 of R. S. as amended by chapter 115, public laws of 1895, further amended.

Section one of chapter thirty of the revised statutes as amended by chapter one hundred fifteen of the public laws of eighteen hundred ninety-five is hereby amended by inserting after the word "done" in the fifth line of said section the words 'provided said damage was not occasioned through the fault of the person injured,' so that said section as amended, shall read as follows:

Going at large of dogs, towns may regulate.

—forfeiture for damages done by dogs.

—proviso.

'Section 1. Towns may pass by-laws, to regulate the going at large of dogs therein. When a dog does damage to a person or his property, his owner or keeper and also the parent, guardian, master, or mistress of any minor who owns or keeps such dog, forfeits to the person injured the amount of the damage done, provided said damage was not occasioned through the fault of the person injured; to be recovered by action of trespass.'

Section 3 of chapter 30 of R. S., amended.

Written complaint may be made of dogs at large.

Section 2. Section three of chapter thirty of the revised statutes is hereby amended, so it shall read as follows:

'Section 3. Whoever is so assaulted or finds a dog strolling outside of the premises or immediate care of its owner or keeper, may, within forty-eight hours thereafter, make written complaint before the municipal or police court having jurisdiction in the city or town where the owner or keeper resides, or in case there is no such court, before a trial justice in said town, that he really believes and has reason to believe said dog to be dangerous or vicious; whereupon said court or trial justice shall order said owner or keeper to appear and answer to said complaint by serving said owner or keeper of said dog with a copy of said complaint and order a reasonable time before the day set for a hearing thereon: and if upon hearing, the court or trial justice is satisfied that said complaint is true, he shall order said owner or keeper within twenty-four hours thereafter either to kill or confine said dog or remove and keep same beyond the limits of said town or city; and if said owner or keeper neglects to comply with said order, he shall forfeit to the use of the city or town aforesaid not less than one nor more than ten dollars, to be recovered in an action on the case.' —dog may be confined or killed.

—forfeiture.

Section 3. Section four of chapter thirty of the revised statutes is hereby amended by striking out in the first line of said section the words "after notice so given" and inserting in place thereof the words 'whose owner or keeper neglects to comply with said order,' so that said section as amended, shall read as follows: Section 4 of chapter 30 of R. S., amended.

'Section 4. If a dog, whose owner or keeper neglects to comply with said order, wounds any person by a sudden assault as aforesaid, or wounds or kills any domestic animal, the owner or keeper shall pay the person injured treble damages and costs.' Treble damages and costs when order is neglected.

Approved March 18, 1903.

Chapter 110

An Act in regard to compensation of Town Officers.

Be it enacted by the Senate and House of Representatives in Legislature assembled, as follows:

Towns having four thousand or more inhabitants shall have the right to vote their selectmen a per diem compensation, not exceeding five dollars per day, for time actually spent in the service of the town. Compensation of selectmen in towns of 4,000 inhabitants.

Approved March 18, 1903.

CHAP. 111

EVIDENCE—TREES AND SHRUBS.

Chapter 111.

An Act to amend Section ninety-eight of Chapter eighty-two of the Revised Statutes, relating to Evidence.

Be it enacted by the Senate and House of Representatives in Legislature assembled, as follows:

Section 98 of chapter 82, R. S., amended.

Section 1. Section ninety-eight of chapter eighty-two of the revised statutes, is hereby amended by adding a sixth exception, as follows:

Executors and administrators may testify to facts happening before death of person whom they represent.

'Sixth. In all actions brought by an executor, administrator or other legal representative of a deceased person, such representative party shall not be excused from testifying to any facts admissible upon general rules of evidence, happening before the death of such person, if so requested by the opposite party. But nothing herein shall be so construed as to enable the adverse party to testify against the objection of the plaintiff when the plaintiff does not voluntarily testify.'

Section 2. This act shall take effect when approved.

Approved March 18, 1908.

Chapter 112.

An Act to provide for the protection of Trees and Shrubs from injurious insects and diseases.

Be it enacted by the Senate and House of Representatives in Legislature assembled, as follows:

Inspection of nursery stock.

Section 1. All nursery stock shipped into this state from any other state, country or province shall bear on each box or package a certificate that the contents of said box or package have been inspected by a duly authorized inspecting officer, and that said contents appear to be free from all dangerous insects or diseases. In case nursery stock is brought into the state without such a certificate the consignee shall return it to the consignor at the expense of the latter; provided, however, that any box or package bearing a certificate of fumigation, which shall be an affidavit made before a justice of the peace that all stock sold by the consignor has been fumigated in a manner approved by the state nursery inspector of the state from which said nursery stock is shipped, the same may be accepted as though bearing a proper certificate of inspection.

—nursery stock brought into the state without certificate of inspection, shall be returned.
—proviso.

Penalty for transporting or selling uninspected nursery stock.

Section 2. Any transportation company that shall bring into this state any nursery stock such as trees, shrubs, vines, cuttings or buds, and any transportation company, owner or owners of nursery stock, or persons selling nursery stock as thus defined, who shall transport such stock or cause it to be transported within the state, the same not having attached to each box or package an unexpired official certificate of inspection or an affidavit of fumigation, which shall meet the requirements specified in section one of this act, shall be guilty of a misdemeanor, and on conviction thereof be subject to a fine not exceeding one hundred dollars for each offense.

Section 3. Should any person in the state suspect the presence of San Jose scale or other injurious insects or diseases preying upon trees, shrubs or vines in his possession or within his knowledge he shall forthwith notify the commissioner of agriculture to that effect; and it shall be the duty of said commissioner of agriculture to cause the said trees, shrubs or vines to be inspected by a competent entomologist, who shall forthwith make a report of the results of his enspection and file the same with the commissioner of agriculture at Augusta. If dangerous insects or injurious diseases are found by the entomologist the commissioner of agriculture shall publish the report of the same, and see that the best known treatment is applied to such trees, shrubs or vines for the destruction of the insects or diseases with which the same may be infested. And for the above purposes the commissioner of agriculture or his employes shall have authority to enter private or public grounds and treat any trees, shrubs or vines that may be infested with dangerous insects or injurious diseases.

Section 4. In case of violations of this act it shall be the duty of the commissioner of agriculture to enforce the penalties set down in section two of this act.

Section 5. This act shall take effect when approved.

Approved March 18, 1903.

Chapter 113.

An Act to regulate Costs in the taking of lands or other property for public uses.

Be it enacted by the Senate and House of Representatives in Legislature assembled, as follows:

Section 1. In all proceedings for the estimation of damages for the taking of lands or other property, under any general or special law, if the owner of the land, after an award made by the county commissioners enters an appeal therefrom and fails to obtain a final judgment for an amount greater than the

Chapter 114.

An Act to amend Section six of Chapter three of the Public Laws of eighteen hundred ninety-nine entitled "An Act to amend Section six of Chapter one hundred fifty-six of the Public Laws of eighteen hundred ninety-five entitled 'An Act to amend Section six of Chapter thirty-five of the Revised Statutes," relating to Intelligence Offices.

Be it enacted by the Senate and House of Representatives in Legislature assembled, as follows:

Section 6 of chapter 3, public laws of 1899, amended.

Section 1. Section six of chapter three of the public laws of eighteen hundred ninety-nine is hereby amended by striking out in the second line thereof the words "one dollar each" and inserting in place thereof the words 'the sum of five dollars each into the town treasury;' and by striking out in the tenth line thereof the words, "in excess of one dollar;" and by inserting in the thirteenth line thereof after the word "furnished," the words 'No license shall be granted to a person who is directly or indirectly engaged or interested in the sale of intoxicating liquors,' so that said section as amended, shall read as follows:

Intelligence offices may be licensed by municipal officers.

'Section 6. The municipal officers of any town may on payment of the sum of five dollars each into the town treasury grant licenses to suitable persons for one year, unless sooner revoked after notice and for cause, to keep offices for the purposes of obtaining employment for domestics, servants, or other laborers, except seamen, or of giving information relating thereto, or of doing the usual business of intelligence offices; whoever keeps such an office, without a license, forfeits not exceeding fifty dollars for every day that it is so kept. The keeper of an intelligence office shall not retain any sum of money received from any person seeking employment through the agency of such intelligence office, unless employment of the kind sought for is actually furnished.

—*penalty for keeping intelligence office without license.*

—*license shall not be granted to persons engaged in sale of intoxicants.*

No license shall be granted to a person who is directly or indirectly engaged in or interested in the sale of intoxicating liquors. The keeper of a licensed intelligence office shall cause two copies of this act, printed in type of sufficient size to be legible and easily read, to be conspicuously posted in each room used or occupied for the purposes of such intelligence office. Whoever violates the provisions of this act shall have the license revoked, and shall be punished by fine not exceeding twenty dollars for each offense.'

Section 2. This act shall take effect when approved.

Approved March 19, 1908.

Chapter 115.

An Act in relation to Judges of Municipal Courts.

Be it enacted by the Senate and House of Representatives in Legislature assembled, as follows:

No judge of any municipal court shall give counsel or accept any retainer in relation to any cause, the subject matter of which shall be within the jurisdiction of the court over which he presides, nor in any manner become voluntarily interested, directly or indirectly, in any such cause.

Approved March 19, 1908.

Chapter 116.

An Act to regulate the placing of Permanent Moorings in harbors.

Be it enacted by the Senate and House of Representatives in Legislature assembled, as follows:

Section 1. Selectmen of towns, on request by any person desiring mooring privileges or regulation of mooring privileges for boats or vessels, shall annually appoint a harbor master who shall be subject to all the duties and liabilities of said office as prescribed by law, and in case of the failure or refusal of said harbor master to perform said duties, he shall be subject to a fine of twenty-five dollars, for the benefit of the town, for each wilful neglect or refusal to attend the same. The selectmen may establish his compensation and may for cause by them declared in writing, after due notice to such officer and hearing thereon, if requested, remove him and appoint another in his stead.

Section 2. In all harbors wherein channel lines have been established by the municipal authorities, as provided in chapter two hundred and fifty-nine of the public laws of nineteen hundred and one, and in all other harbors where mooring rights of individuals are claimed to be invaded and protection is sought of

CHAP. 117

—may change location of mooring.

the harbor master, it shall be the duty of the harbor master to assign and to indicate to the master or owner of boats and vessels the location which they may occupy with or for mooring purposes, the kind of mooring to be used, and also to change the location of said moorings from time to time when the crowded condition of such harbor or other conditions render such change desirable; and he shall assign mooring privileges in such waters in all cases where individuals who own the shore rights or have an interest in the same, are complainants, and shall locate suitable mooring privileges therefor for boats and vessels, temporarily or permanently as the case may be, fronting their land, if so requested, but not thereby to encroach upon the natural channel, or channels established by municipal authorities. The municipal officers shall fix the compensation of the harbor master for such services rendered.

—compensation.

Penalty for neglecting to remove or replace moorings.

Section 3. In case of the neglect or refusal of the master or owner of any boat or vessel, to remove his mooring or to replace it by one of different character, when so directed by the harbor master, said harbor master shall cause said mooring to be removed, or shall make such change in the character thereof as required, and shall collect from the master or owner of such boat or vessel the sum of two dollars for either of such services rendered, and also the necessary expenses.

Section 64, chapter 3, R. S., repealed.

Section 4. Section sixty-four of the revised statutes, chapter three, is hereby repealed.

Section 5. This act shall take effect when approved.

Approved March 19, 1903.

Chapter 117.

An Act to amend Chapter seventy-seven of the Public Laws of eighteen hundred and ninety-nine, relating to giving mortgagees a lien for costs of foreclosure under Section five of Chapter ninety of the Revised Statutes.

Be it enacted by the Senate and House of Representatives in Legislature assembled, as follows:

Chapter 77, public laws of 1899, amended.

Chapter seventy-seven of the public laws of eighteen hundred and ninety-nine is hereby amended by inserting after the word "thereof" in the eighth line the following words: 'providing said sum has actually been paid in full or partial discharge of an attorney's fee,' so that said chapter as amended, shall read as follows:

Fee to mortgagee or attorney.

'For the foreclosure of a mortgage by either method prescribed by section five of chapter ninety of the revised statutes as amended by chapter one hundred and sixty-eight of the public laws of eighteen hundred and ninety-three, the mortgagee or the person claiming under him is hereby authorized to charge an attorney's fee of five dollars in addition to the sums actually paid for the publication or service of the notice of foreclosure and for the record thereof, providing said sum has actually been paid in full or partial discharge of an attorney's fee, and said attorney's fee shall be a lien on the mortgaged estate, and shall be included with the amount of mortgage debts and amounts paid for publication or service of said notice and for recording the same, in making up the sum to be tendered by the mortgagor or the person claiming under him in order to be entitled to redeem.'

—fee shall be a lien.

Approved March 19, 1903.

Chapter 118.

An Act relating to proof of Attested Instruments.

Be it enacted by the Senate and House of Representatives in Legislature assembled, as follows:

The signature to an attested instrument or writing, except a will, may be proved in the same manner as if it were not attested.

Signature, how proved.

Approved March 19, 1903.

Chapter 119

An Act to correct an error, and repeal "An Act approved February eleven, nineteen hundred three," relating to Migratory Fish.

Be it enacted by the Senate and House of Representatives in Legislature assembled, as follows:

Section 1. An Act entitled 'An Act to amend section seventeen of chapter forty of the revised statutes, as amended by chapter two hundred and sixty-one of the public laws of eighteen hundred eighty-five, and by chapter sixty-one of the public laws of eighteen hundred ninety-one, relating to Migratory Fish, approved February eleven, nineteen hundred three,' is hereby repealed.

Section 17 of chapter 40, R. S., as amended by chapter 261, public laws of 1885, and by chapter 61, public laws of 1891, repealed.

Section 2. All acts and parts of acts which were expressly or impliedly repealed by the said act of February eleven, nineteen hundred three, are hereby revived and re-enacted.

Acts and parts of acts, re-enacted.

Section 3. This act shall take effect when approved.

Approved March 19, 1903.

SALARY—COUNTY COMMISSIONERS.

Chapter 120.

An Act to amend Section two of Chapter ninety-three of the Public Laws of eighteen hundred and ninety-nine, fixing the salary of the County Commissioners of Kennebec County.

Be it enacted by the Senate and House of Representatives in Legislature assembled, as follows:

Section 2 of chapter 93, public laws of 1899, amended.

Section 1. Section two of chapter ninety-three of the public laws of eighteen hundred and ninety-nine, is hereby amended, by striking out the words, "eighteen hundred and ninety-nine" in the second line thereof, and inserting in place thereof the words, 'nineteen hundred and three;' also by striking out in the fourth line the words, "two dollars and fifty cents" and inserting in place thereof the words, 'three dollars,' so that said section, as amended, shall read as follows:

Salary of county commissioners of Kennebec county, fixed.

'Section 2. From and after the first day of January, in the year of our Lord one thousand nine hundred and three, the salary of each of the county commissioners for the county of Kennebec, shall be three dollars per day, instead of the sum now fixed by law, while actually employed in the service of the county, including the time spent in traveling, for which he shall have ten cents a mile for the distance actually traveled.'

—travel.

Section 2. This act shall take effect when approved.

Approved March 19, 1903.

Chapter 121.

An Act relating to the office of County Commissioner.

Be it enacted by the Senate and House of Representatives in Legislature assembled, as follows:

County commissioner not eligible to be mayor, assessor or selectman.

Section 1. No person holding the office of county commissioner shall at the same time hold either the office of mayor or assessor of a city, or of selectman or assessor of a town.

Section 2. This act shall take effect April first, nineteen hundred and four.

Approved March 19, 1903.

Chapter 122.

An Act to enable cities and towns to establish permanent Fuel Yards.

Be it enacted by the Senate and House of Representatives in Legislature assembled, as follows:

Section 1. Any city or town is hereby authorized and empowered to establish and maintain, within its limits, a permanent wood, coal and fuel yard, for the purpose of selling, at cost, wood, coal and fuel to its inhabitants. The term 'at cost,' as used herein, shall be construed as meaning without financial profit.

Section 2. This act shall take effect when approved.

Approved March 19, 1903.

Chapter 123.

An Act to amend Section twenty-one of Chapter one hundred and sixteen of the Revised Statutes, and Chapter two hundred and twenty-five of the Public Laws of eighteen hundred and ninety-three, relating to fees of Registers of Deeds.

Be it enacted by the Senate and House of Representatives in Legislature assembled, as follows:

Section 1. Section twenty-one of chapter one hundred and sixteen of the revised statutes, is hereby amended by adding thereto the following:

'Recording certificates of limited partnership, fifty cents. Receiving and filing certificate of election of clerk of a corporation, or resignation of such clerk, twenty-five cents. Recording certificates of foreclosure of mortgages, or notices of foreclosure, fifty cents.'

Section 2. Chapter two hundred and twenty-five of the public laws of eighteen hundred and ninety-three, is hereby amended by striking out the words "under seal" in the third line. So that said chapter as amended, shall read as follows:

'Chapter 225. In all cases where books with printed forms are not furnished therefor, registers of deeds shall for receiving, filing and recording any instrument by law entitled to record, in addition to the fees now fixed by law, the sum of fifteen cents for each hundred words or fraction thereof, in excess of five hundred words.'

Section 3. This act shall take effect when approved.

Approved March 20, 1903.

Chapter 124.

An Act to amend Section thirty-five of Chapter ninety-nine of the Revised Statutes, relating to Powers and Duties of Bail Commissioners.

Be it enacted by the Senate and House of Representatives in Legislature assembled, as follows:

Section 35 of chapter 99, R. S., amended.

Section thirty-five of chapter ninety-nine of the revised statutes is hereby amended by adding thereto the following words: 'And such bail commissioners shall receive not exceeding the sum of five dollars in each case in which bail is so taken, the same to be paid by the person so admitted to bail; but the person admitted to bail shall not be required to pay any other fees or charges to any officer for services connected with the giving of such bail,' so that said section thirty-five, as amended, shall read as follows:

Bail commissioner may admit to bail.

—exception.

'Section 35. When a person is confined in a jail for a bailable offense, or for not finding sureties on a recognizance, except when a verdict of guilty has been rendered against him for an offense punishable in the state prison, any such commissioner, on application, may inquire into the case and admit him to bail, and exercise the same power as any justice of the supreme judicial or superior court can; and may issue a writ of habeas corpus, and cause such person to be brought before him for this purpose, and may take such recognizance. And such bail commissioners shall receive not exceeding the sum of five dollars in each case in which bail is so taken, the same to be paid by the person so admitted to bail; but the person admitted to bail shall not be required to pay any other fees or charges to any officer for services connected with the giving of such bail.'

—may issue writ of habeas corpus.

—fees of bail commissioner.

Approved March 23, 1903.

Chapter 125.

An Act to regulate the taking of Bail in Criminal Prosecution.

Be it enacted by the Senate and House of Representatives in Legislature assembled, as follows:

Persons offering to recognize for respondent in criminal prosecution, shall make written sworn statement, describing real estate holden by them.

Section 1. Any person offering to recognize before any trial justice, judge of a police or municipal court, or bail commissioner, as surety for the appearance before any superior or supreme judicial court of any respondent in a criminal prosecution, whether such respondent be an appellant from the finding of a trial justice or judge of a police or municipal court, or be ordered to recognize to await the action of the grand jury, or be arrested in vacation on capias issued on indictment pending in such superior or supreme judicial court, may be required to file with said trial justice, judge of a police or municipal court, or bail commissioner, a written statement signed and sworn to by said surety, describing all real estate owned by said surety within this state with sufficient accuracy to identify it, and giving in detail all incumbrances thereon and the value thereof, such valuation to be based on the judgment of said surety. Said certificate shall remain on file with the original papers in said case and a certified copy thereof be transmitted by the magistrate taking such bail to the clerk of the court before which said respondent so recognizes for his appearance.

Section 2. All bail shall be responsible for the appearance of their principal at all times during the term of court at which they agree to have him, until verdict or certification of the case to the law court on demurrer or exceptions, unless said bail shall have sooner surrendered him into the custody of the sheriff or jailer of the county in which the case is pending. *Shall be responsible for appearance of principal.*

Section 3. All acts and parts of acts inconsistent herewith, are hereby repealed. *Inconsistent acts, repealed.*

Section 4. This act shall take effect when approved.

Approved March 23, 1903.

Chapter 126.

An Act in aid of the soldiers of the Aroostook War

Be it enacted by the Senate and House of Representatives in Legislature assembled, as follows:

Section 1. Any citizen of Maine who has served in the drafted quota of the militia in the Aroostook war, has been honorably discharged and has been unable from his own resources to obtain a livelihood for himself and those dependent upon him, shall be entitled to a pension from the state of Maine of four dollars a month. The same shall be paid in accordance with the regulations provided in sections four, five, six and seven of chapter one hundred and forty-four of the revised statutes and acts additional thereto and amendatory thereof. *Pensions to soldiers of Aroostook war.* *—how paid.*

Section 2. This act shall take effect when approved.

Approved March 24, 1903.

Chapter 127.

An Act fixing the salary of the Judge of Probate of Sagadahoc County.

Be it enacted by the Senate and House of Representatives in Legislature assembled, as follows:

Salary of judge of probate for Sagadahoc county.

Section 1. From and after the first day of January, in the year of our Lord one thousand nine hundred and three, the salary of the judge of probate for the county of Sagadahoc shall be eight hundred dollars per year, instead of the sum now fixed by law.

Section 2. This act shall take effect when approved.

Approved March 24, 1903.

Chapter 128.

An Act to amend Chapter eighty-nine of the Public Laws of eighteen hundred ninety-nine amendatory of Chapter one hundred and sixteen of the Public Laws of eighteen hundred ninety-five as amended by Chapter two hundred and eighty-six of the Public Laws of eighteen hundred ninety-seven and Chapter two hundred and six of the Public Laws of nineteen hundred one, entitled "An Act to provide for the Schooling of Children in unorganized Townships."

Be it enacted by the Senate and House of Representatives in Legislature assembled, as follows:

Chapter 89 of public laws 1899, as amended by chapter 206, public laws of 1901, further amended.

Section 1. Chapter eighty nine of the public laws of eighteen hundred and ninety-nine as amended by chapter two hundred and six of the public laws of nineteen hundred and one, is hereby further amended in section one by substituting for the words "twenty-five cents" in the last provision thereof, the words 'forty cents,' so that said section as amended, shall read as follows:

State superintendent shall cause enumeration to be made when there are two or more children.

—shall provide schooling.

—rights of children when sent to adjoining towns or plantations.

—proviso.

'Section 1. Whenever in any unorganized township in this state there shall be two or more children between the ages of four and twenty-one years, the state superintendent of schools shall cause an enumeration of said children to be made, and returned to him, and shall provide for the schooling of said children, either by establishing a school in the township or by sending the children to schools in adjoining towns or plantations, or both, as shall by him be deemed expedient. In case any of said children are, by the state superintendent, sent to schools in adjoining towns or plantations, said children so sent shall have the same rights in such school as children resident in said town or plantation. Provided, however, that in case the interest on the reserve fund in any unorganized township together with the amount arising from the per capita tax called for in this act, is not sufficient to provide schooling for the children of said town-

SCHOOLING OF CHILDREN. 99

CHAP. 128

ship for at least twenty weeks in a year, the remainder of the expense shall be paid from the fund appropriated by section four of this act, provided, further, that no money shall be expended under this section for the benefit of any township until the inhabitants of said township shall pay to the state treasurer a sum equal to forty cents for each inhabitant thereof.'

Section 2. Section three of said act as amended is hereby further amended by inserting before the last provision thereof beginning with the words 'the state superintendent shall have power to supply school books,' the following: 'Said agents, in the collecting of the per capita tax aforesaid, shall have the same powers and may use the same methods as collectors of taxes in towns are authorized to exercise and use for the collecting of personal and poll taxes committed to them; said agents are further authorized to act as truant officers in their several townships, and may, in their discretion, compel the regular daily attendance at school of every child in their township between the ages of seven and fifteen years by arresting and taking to school any such child when absent therefrom; and any parent or guardian of any such child or children, wilfully refusing to allow said children under his control to attend school, or opposing said agent in arresting and taking said children to school, may be prosecuted by said agent in the name of the state before the nearest trial justice, and, if found guilty, shall forfeit a sum not exceeding twenty dollars for the use of the schools in the township wherein said children are resident, or shall be imprisoned for not exceeding thirty days;' so that said section as amended, shall read:

Section 3, amended.

'Section 3. The state superintendent of schools shall have power to appoint agents for the several townships in which schools shall be established under this act, whose duty it shall be under the direction of the state superintendent to enumerate the pupils, assess and collect the per capita tax, employ the teacher and attend to all necessary details in connection with said schools; for which work he shall be paid a sum not exceeding two dollars per day when actually employed in this duty and actual necessary traveling expenses. Said agents in the collection of the per capita tax aforesaid, shall have the same powers and may use the same methods as collectors of taxes in towns are authorized to exercise and use for the collecting of personal and poll taxes committed to them; said agents are further authorized to act as truant officers in their several townships, and may in their discretion compel the regular daily attendance at school of every child in their townships between the ages of seven and fifteen years by arresting and taking to school any such child

Agents for unincorporated townships.

—duty of.

—compensation.

—may compel regular attendance.

CHAP. 129

when absent therefrom; and any parent or guardian of any such child or children, wilfully refusing to allow said children under his control to attend school, or opposing said agent in arresting and taking said children to school, may be prosecuted by said agent in the name of the state before the nearest trial justice, and if found guilty, shall forfeit a sum not exceeding twenty dollars for the use of the schools in the township wherein said children are resident, or shall be imprisoned for not exceeding thirty days. The state superintendent shall have power to supply school books for the schools established under this act under such conditions as to the purchase and care thereof as he may deem proper.'

—school books, how supplied.

Section 4, amended.

Section 3. Section four of said act as amended is hereby further amended to read as follows:

Appropriation for provisions of this act.

'Section 4. For the purpose of carrying out the provisions of this act, there is hereby appropriated the sum of five thousand dollars annually which sum shall be deducted and set aside therefor by the treasurer of state from the annual school funds of the state.'

Section 4. This act shall take effect when approved.

Approved March 24, 1903.

Chapter 129.

An Act to repeal so much of Section five of Chapter forty-two of the Public Laws of eighteen hundred and ninety-nine, as prohibits fishing in the inlet stream of Squaw Pan lake from Thibadeau's landing to the source of said stream.

Be it enacted by the Senate and House of Representatives in Legislature assembled, as follows:

Squaw Pan lake, inlets of, opened for fishing.

Section 1. So much of section five, so called, of chapter forty-two of the public laws of eighteen hundred and ninety-nine, as prohibits the taking, catching or killing of any fish in the inlet stream or streams of Squaw Pan lake, in the county of Aroostook, from Thibadeau's landing to the source of said stream or streams, said stream or streams being in township eleven, range four, is hereby repealed.

Section 2. This act shall take effect when approved.

Approved March 24, 1903.

Chapter 130.

An Act regulating the sale or exchange of Mortgaged Personal Property.

Be it enacted by the Senate and House of Representatives in Legislature assembled, as follows:

Section 1. No consent by the mortgagee of personal property to the mortgagor for the sale or exchange of the mortgaged personal property shall be valid or be used in evidence in civil process unless in writing and signed by the mortgagee or his assigns. *(Consent for sale or exchange of mortgaged property shall be in writing.)*

Section 2. This act shall take effect on January one, nineteen hundred five.

Approved March 24, 1903.

Chapter 131.

An Act amending Section one of Chapter two hundred eighty-four of the Public Laws of eighteen hundred ninety-three, in relation to Ways.

Be it enacted by the Senate and House of Representatives in Legislature assembled, as follows:

The words "not within" in the third line of said section one are hereby stricken out and the words 'outside of the thickly settled portion of' are substituted in their place; so that said section as amended, will read as follows:

'Section 1. When it is necessary for any person or persons, by themselves, men or teams, to cross or enter upon any tract of land outside of the thickly settled portion of any town, for the purpose of hauling supplies, wood, bark, logs or lumber, or to yard or land the same, such person or persons shall not be liable in an action of trespass therefor, provided, the bond is furnished as provided in section two, but the person or persons carrying on said lumbering operation, shall be liable for all the actual damage done to said land by said men and teams so crossing said land.' *(Not liable for trespass when bond is furnished. —liable for actual damage.)*

Approved March 24, 1903.

102 — DECEASED PERSONS—ELECTRIC POSTS AND WIRES.
CHAP. 132.

Chapter 132.

An Act relating to claims against the estates of Deceased Persons.

Be it enacted by the Senate and House of Representatives in Legislature assembled, as follows:

Section 55 of chapter 64, R. S., amended.

Section fifty-three of chapter sixty-four of the revised statutes is hereby amended by striking out from lines ten, eleven and twelve, the following words: "The claimant may make similar application, and the same proceedings shall, after notice to the other party, be had thereon, if payment is refused, or is not made within thirty days after demand," so that said section as amended, shall read as follows:

Commissioners may be appointed when claims are deemed exorbitant, unjust or illegal.

'Section 53. When one or more claims against the estate of a person deceased, though not insolvent, are deemed by the executor or administrator to be exorbitant, unjust or illegal, on application in writing to the judge of probate, and after notice to the claimants, the judge, if upon hearing, is satisfied that the allegations in said application are true, may appoint two or more commissioners, who shall after being duly sworn, and after notifying the parties as directed in their commission, meet at a convenient time and place, and determine whether any and what amount shall be allowed on each claim, and report to him at such time as he may limit. Sections five, six, seven, eight, twelve, thirteen, fourteen, sixteen and seventeen of chapter sixty-six, apply to such claims, and the proceedings thereon. No action shall be maintained on any claim so committed, unless proved before said commissioners; and their report on all such claims shall be final, saving the right of appeal.'

Approved March 24, 1903.

Chapter 133.

An Act to amend Chapter three hundred and seventy-eight of the Public Laws of eighteen hundred and eighty-five, relating to Electric Posts and Wires.

Be it enacted by the Senate and House of Representatives in Legislature assembled, as follows:

Section 2 of chapter 378 of public laws of 1885, amended.

Section 1. Section two of chapter three hundred and seventy-eight of the public laws of eighteen hundred and eighty-five is hereby amended by adding thereto the following: 'Posts and wires erected and maintained in accordance with the provisions of this chapter shall be deemed legal structures and the party maintaining the same shall be liable on account thereof only for carelessness or negligence in the erection or maintenance of the same,' so that said section as amended, shall read as follows:

'Section 2. No such company, person or association shall construct lines upon and along the highways and public roads of any city or town, without first obtaining a written permit, signed by the mayor and aldermen, or selectmen, specifying where the posts may be located, the kind of posts, and the height at which and the places where the wires may be run. Before granting such permit, fourteen days' public notice thereof shall be given, and residents and owners of property upon the highways to be affected thereby, shall have full opportunity to show cause why such permit should not be granted. Such public notice shall be given by publication in some newspaper printed in such city or town, if any, the last publication to be fourteen days before said hearing; if no newspaper is printed therein, then by posting the same in some public and conspicuous place therein fourteen days before said hearing; when the application for such permit is filed, the mayor or chairman of the selectmen shall indorse thereon what personal notice, if any, shall be given by such company, persons or associations, to the residents and owners of property to be affected thereby. At the hearing, such company, persons or associations, before proceeding, shall first prove that such order of notice has been complied with and public notice given as hereinbefore required, and the adjudication of the mayor and aldermen, or selectmen, that such personal and public notice has been given shall be final and conclusive. If from any cause the notice given appears to have been defective, the municipal officers may order new notice, not exceeding seven days, and adjourn said hearing to time named in said new order of notice. After the erection of the lines, having first given such company, persons, associations or their agents opportunity to be heard, the municipal officers may direct any alteration in the location or erection of such posts, and in the height of the wires. Such permits, specifications and decisions shall be recorded in the records of the city or town. Posts and wires erected and maintained in accordance with the provisions of this chapter shall be deemed legal structures and the party maintaining the same shall be liable on account thereof only for carelessness or negligence in the erection or maintenance of the same.'

Section 2. Section eight of chapter three hundred and seventy-eight of the public laws of eighteen hundred and eighty-five is hereby repealed.

Approved March 24, 1903.

Chapter 134.

An Act in relation to the discharge of debtors in cases now pending in Insolvent Courts.

Be it enacted by the Senate and House of Representatives in Legislature assembled, as follows:

Written application for discharge in pending cases, must be made before January 1, 1904.

Section 1. A discharge shall not be granted to a debtor in any case now pending in the several insolvent courts of this state unless written application is made therefor to the judge before the first day of January, nineteen hundred and four, and in case no such application is made, all proceedings in such case may be dismissed upon motion of any party interested, after such notice, if any, as the judge shall order.

Section 2. This act shall take effect when approved.

Approved March 24, 1903.

Chapter 135.

An Act to amend Chapter eighty-six of the Revised Statutes, relating to Trustee Process.

Be it enacted by the Senate and House of Representatives in Legislature assembled, as follows:

Section 6 of chapter 86, R. S., amended.

Section 1. Section six of chapter eighty-six of the revised statutes is hereby amended, so as to read as follows:

Proceedings in trustee process.

'Section 6. The plaintiff may insert the names of as many persons as trustees as he deems necessary, at any time before the process is served on the principal, but not after; and he may

—may have further service.

have further service made on any trustee, if found expedient, if the service is afterwards made or renewed on the principal;

—costs for services.

but no costs for services shall be taxed for the plaintiff in such case, except for that last made.

—costs in suits discontinued or settled.

When a trustee suit is discontinued or settled by the principal parties thereto, the trustee shall be entitled to no costs, provided the plaintiff or his attorney shall notify the trustee in writing seven days before the return day of the writ that the suit has been discontinued.'

Section 2. This act shall take effect when approved.

Approved March 24, 1903.

Chapter 136.

An Act to repeal so much of Chapter thirty of the Revised Statutes, as amended by Section five of Chapter forty-two of the Public Laws of eighteen hundred ninety-nine, as prohibits fishing through the ice in Dexter pond, in Dexter, Penobscot county.

Be it enacted by the Senate and House of Representatives in Legislature assembled, as follows:

Section 1. So much of chapter thirty, of the revised statutes, as amended by section five of chapter forty-two of the public laws of eighteen hundred ninety-nine, as prohibits fishing through the ice in Dexter pond, in Dexter, Penobscot county, is hereby repealed. *Fishing through the ice in Dexter pond, prohibition removed.*

Section 2. This act shall take effect when approved.

Approved March 24, 1903.

Chapter 137.

An Act to amend Chapter three, Section fifty-nine, Paragraph twelve of the Revised Statutes, relating to dealers in Old Junk.

Be it enacted by the Senate and House of Representatives in Legislature assembled, as follows:

Chapter three, section fifty-nine, paragraph twelve of the revised statutes relating to dealers in old junk is hereby amended by inserting in the second line of said section the words 'and dealers in second hand articles and the pawning of articles with pawnbrokers,' and in the third line of said section the words, 'pawners and pawnbrokers' so that said section as amended, shall read as follows: *Chapter 3, section 59, paragraph 12, R. S., amended.*

'Section 59. Cities may establish ordinances regulating the purchase and sale of articles usually bought by old junk dealers and dealers in second hand articles, and the pawning of articles with pawnbrokers, and may therein prescribe conditions to be observed by buyers and sellers, pawners and pawnbrokers, to prevent or detect the sale or purchase of stolen goods; and suitable penalties may be prescribed in such ordinances.' *Cities may prescribe conditions to be observed by pawnbrokers, old junk dealers, etc.*

Approved March 24, 1903.

Chapter 138.

An Act additional to Chapter sixteen of the Revised Statutes, relating to Public Drains and Sewers.

Be it enacted by the Senate and House of Representatives in Legislature assembled, as follows:

<small>Proceedings public sewer or drain crosses right of way of any railroad.</small>

Section 1. Whenever a public drain or sewer is located and about to be constructed under the general provisions of law, which crosses the right of way of any railroad, unless the municipal officers or committee of the city or town which located the drain or sewer shall agree with the corporation operating such railroad as to the place, manner and conditions of the crossing, the railroad commissioners, upon petition of either party, after notice and hearing, shall determine the place, manner, and conditions of such crossing; all the work within the limits of such railroad location shall be done under the supervision of the officers of the corporation operating said railroad and to the satisfaction of the railroad commissioners, and the expense thereof shall be borne by the city or town in which said drain or sewer is located; provided, however, that any additional expense in the construction of that part of the sewer or drain within the limits of the right of way of said railroad occasioned by the determination of said commissioners shall be borne by said railroad company or by the city or town in which said drain or sewer is located, or shall be apportioned between such company and the city or town as may be determined by said railroad commissioners.

<small>—report of commissioners.</small>

Said commissioners shall make report of their decision in the same manner as in the case of highways located across railroads and subject to the same right of appeal.

Section 2. This act shall take effect when approved.

Approved March 24, 1903.

Chapter 139.

An Act to prohibit Spitting upon the floors of street cars.

Be it enacted by the Senate and House of Representatives in Legislature assembled, as follows:

<small>Spitting on floor of street cars forbidden.</small>

Section 1. Whoever spits upon the floor of any street car shall be fined not less than two nor more than ten dollars to be recovered on complaint.

<small>Copy of law shall be posted in cars.</small>

Section 2. The officers of all street railroad companies shall cause a copy of the preceding section to be posted in their several street cars.

Approved March 24, 1903.

Chapter 140.

An Act to amend Section one of Chapter one hundred eighty-five of the Public Laws of nineteen hundred one, relating to Truants.

Be it enacted by the Senate and House of Representatives in Legislature assembled, as follows:

Section one of chapter one hundred eighty-five of the public laws of nineteen hundred and one is hereby amended by striking out the words in the first and second lines "ages of seven and fourteen inclusive" and inserting in their place 'seventh and fifteenth anniversaries of his birth,' so that said section as amended, shall read as follows:

'Section 1. Every child between the seventh and fifteenth anniversaries of his birth shall attend some public day school during the time such school is in session; provided that necessary absence may be excused by the superintending school committee or superintendent of schools or teachers acting by direction of either; provided also, that such attendance shall not be required if the child obtained equivalent instruction, for a like period of time, in an approved private school or in any other manner approved by the superintending school committee; provided, further, that children shall not be credited with attendance at a private school until a certificate showing their names, residence and attendance at such school signed by the person or persons having such school in charge, shall be filed with the school officials of the town in which said children reside; and provided further, that the superintending school committee may exclude from the public schools any child whose physical or mental condition makes it inexpedient for him to attend.

All persons having children under their control shall cause them to attend school as provided in this section, and for every neglect of such duty shall forfeit a sum not exceeding twenty-five dollars, to the treasurer of the city or town or shall be imprisoned not exceeding thirty days.'

Approved March 24, 1903.

Chapter 141.

An Act to amend Section three of Chapter one hundred and three of the Public Laws of eighteen hundred and ninety-five, relating to Telegraph and Telephone Companies.

Be it enacted by the Senate and House of Representatives in Legislature assembled, as follows:

Section 3 of chapter 103, public laws of 1895, amended.

Section three of chapter one hundred and three of the public laws of eighteen hundred and ninety-five is hereby amended by striking out the following words after the word "incorporation" in the fifth line thereof, namely: "But no corporation organized hereunder shall have authority without special act of the legislature, to construct its lines along the route or routes, used or authorized to be used, by any other telegraph or telephone company, person or firm, or between points connected, or authorized to be connected, by the lines of any such company, person or firm, unless it shall first obtain the consent of such other company, person or firm" so that said section as amended, shall read as follows:

Route or routes along which lines may be constructed.

'Section 3. Corporations organized under the provisions of this act shall have authority, except as herein limited, to construct, maintain and operate lines upon and along the route or routes and between the points stated in its certificate of incorporation.'

Approved March 24, 1903.

Chapter 142.

An Act to amend Section fifty-seven of Chapter eleven of Revised Statutes, as amended by Chapter two hundred eleven of the Public Laws of nineteen hundred one, relating to school house Lots and Grounds.

Be it enacted by the Senate and House of Representatives in Legislature assembled, as follows:

Section 57 of chapter 11, R. S., as amended by chapter 211, public laws of 1901, further amended.

Section fifty-seven of chapter eleven of the revised statutes, as amended by chapter two hundred and eleven of the public laws of nineteen hundred and one is hereby amended by adding after the last word of said section the following:

'And all schoolhouse lots and play grounds that require fencing shall be fenced by the town or city,' so that said section as amended, shall read as follows:

Taking lands for school house locations,

proceedings in.

'Section 57. When a location for the erection or removal of a school house and requisite buildings have been legally designated, and the owner thereof refuses to sell, or, in the opinion of the municipal officers, ask an unreasonable price for it, or resides without the state and has no authorized agent or attorney therein,

FISHING—STATE SCHOOL FOR BOYS. 109

CHAP. 143

they may lay out a school house lot, not exceeding three acres, and appraise the damages therefor; and on payment or tender of such damages, or if such owner does not reside in the state, upon depositing such damages in the treasury of such town or district for his use, the town or district designating it may take such lot to be held and used for the purposes aforesaid; and when such school house has ceased to be thereon for two years, said lot reverts to the owner, his heirs or assigns. And any town or city may take real estate for the enlargement or extension of any location designated for the erection or removal of a school house and requisite buildings and play grounds, as herein provided; but no real estate shall be so taken within fifty feet of a dwelling house, and all school house lots and play grounds that require fencing shall be fenced by the town or city.'

—damages.

—no real estate shall be taken within 50 feet of a dwelling and lots shall be fenced by town or city.

Approved March 24, 1903.

Chapter 143.

An Act to repeal so much of Chapter thirty of the Revised Statutes as amended by Section five of Chapter forty-two of the Public Laws of eighteen hundred ninety-nine, as prohibits fishing through the ice in Indian pond, situated partly in Franklin and partly in Somerset County.

Be it enacted by the Senate and House of Representatives in Legislature assembled, as follows:

Section 1. So much of chapter thirty of the revised statutes, as amended by section five of chapter forty-two of the public laws of eighteen hundred ninety-nine, as prohibits fishing through the ice in Indian pond, situated partly in Franklin and partly in Somerset county, is hereby repealed.

Indian pond, fishing through ice in, prohibition removed.

Section 2. This act shall take effect when approved.

Approved March 24, 1903.

Chapter 144.

An Act to change the name of the State Reform School.

Be it enacted by the Senate and House of Representatives in Legislature assembled, as follows:

Section 1. The name of the State Reform School is hereby changed to the State School for Boys. All public laws and resolves relating to or in favor of said state reform school are hereby amended by striking out said words "state reform school" and "reform school" wherever said words occur in said public

Name changed to State School for Boys.

CHAP. 145

laws and resolves and substituting therefor in each instance the words 'state school for boys.'

Section 2. This act shall take effect when approved.

Approved March 24, 1903.

Chapter 145.

An Act to repeal so much of Chapter thirty of the Revised Statutes, as amended by Chapter forty-two of the Public Laws of one thousand eight hundred and ninety-nine, as prohibits fishing in Goodwin brook, and Higgins stream above the first dam, tributaries to Moose pond, in Somerset county.

Be it enacted by the Senate and House of Representatives in Legislature assembled, as follows:

Goodwin brook and Higgins stream, opened for fishing.

Section 1. So much of chapter thirty of the revised statutes, as amended by section five of chapter forty-two of the public laws of one thousand eight hundred and ninety-nine, as closes Goodwin brook to all fishing, and Higgins stream above the first dam, tributaries to Moose pond, in Somerset county, is hereby repealed.

Section 2. This act shall take effect when approved.

Approved March 25, 1903.

Chapter 146.

An Act to amend an act entitled "An Act to regulate the admission to practice of attorneys, solicitors and counselors, to provide for a board of examiners, and to repeal conflicting acts," approved March seventeen, eighteen hundred ninety-nine.

Be it enacted by the Senate and House of Representatives in Legislature assembled, as follows:

Section 3 of chapter 133, public laws of 1899, amended.

Section 1. Section three of chapter one hundred and thirty-three of the public laws of eighteen hundred and ninety-nine is hereby amended by omitting the words "meet annually at Portland in January, at Bangor in April, at Augusta in October, during the sessions of the supreme judicial court, and also at such other" in the tenth, eleventh, twelfth and thirteenth lines thereof, and by inserting after the words "such board shall" in the tenth line, the words, 'hold at least two sessions annually at such,' so that said section, as amended, shall read as follows:

Board of examiners, appointment of, provided for.

'Section 3. The governor shall on the recommendation of the chief justice of the supreme judicial court, and on and before the first day of July, eighteen hundred and ninety-nine appoint a board of examiners, composed of five competent lawyers of this state, for the examination of applicants for the admission to the bar, whose term of office shall be as follows: One for one year, one for two years, one for three years, one for four years and one for five years, and thereafter each year the governor, on like recommendation, shall appoint one member of the board for the term of five years. Such board shall hold at least two sessions annually at such times and places in the state as the supreme judicial court shall direct, for the purpose of examining all applicants for admission to the bar, as to their legal learning and general qualifications to practice in the several courts of this state as attorneys and counselors at law and solicitors and counselors in chancery and, upon such examinations being had, the board shall issue to such applicants as shall pass the required examination a certificate of qualification stating the standing of the applicants and recommending their admission to the bar. Such board shall elect from their number a secretary and a treasurer and shall make such rules and regulations relative to said examination as to them may seem proper. The president of said board shall be the member whose term of office soonest expires. Three members of said board shall constitute a quorum for the transaction of business.'

Section 2. Section four of said act is hereby amended by inserting after the word "examination" in the tenth line the words 'if deemed necessary,' so that said section as amended, shall read as follows:

'Section 4. The residences and the names of said applicants shall be made to appear to said board and satisfactory evidence shall also be produced by said applicants of their good moral character and of their having pursued the study of the law in the office of some attorney or in some recognized law school or university for at least three years prior to such examination; and a fee to be fixed by said board of not more than twenty dollars shall accompany the application. The applicant shall be required to submit to a written examination which shall be prepared by said board, also to an oral examination by the board, if deemed necessary, and shall be required to answer correctly a minimum of seventy per cent of the questions given him to entitle him to the certificate of the board. The board shall, however, have power to establish such higher grades of standing as to them may seem proper.'

Section 3. Section five of said act is hereby amended so as to read as follows:

'Section 5. The examination papers shall be kept on file in the office of the secretary of the board, and a record kept of

CHAP. 147

file with qualifications of applicant

each application, the name of the applicant, and his qualifications and general standing as ascertained by such examination, and the secretary of the board shall furnish each applicant with a card, showing the proficiency he has attained in each branch or subject upon which he has been examined, whether a certificate is issued or not. Any applicant failing to pass the examination may again apply after six months, by showing to the board that he has diligently pursued the study of the law six months prior to the examination; if such second application is within one year after his first examination, he shall not be required to pay an extra fee for the second examination.'

—applicant failing to pass examination may again apply after six months.

—no extra fee.

Section 6, amended.

Section 4. Section six of said act is hereby amended by omitting the words "as examiners in going to, holding and returning from, such examination" so that said section, as amended, shall read as follows:

Compensation of examiners.

'Section 6. The board of examiners shall receive as compensation for their services five dollars per day for the time actually spent, and the necessary expenses incurred in the discharge of their duties, to be certified by the clerk or one of the justices of the supreme judicial court; provided, however, that all compensation for services and expenses shall not exceed the amounts received as fees from applicants.'

—proviso.

Act shall take effect September 1, 1903.

Section 5. This act shall take effect September first, nineteen hundred and three.

Approved March 26, 1903.

Chapter 147.

An Act to amend Section five of Chapter one hundred thirty-seven of the Revised Statutes as amended by Section one of Chapter two hundred ninety-five of the Public Laws of eighteen hundred ninety-three, relating to Insane Criminals.

Be it enacted by the Senate and House of Representatives in Legislature assembled, as follows:

Section 1. Section five of chapter one hundred thirty-seven of the revised statutes as amended by section one of chapter two hundred ninety-five of the public laws of eighteen hundred ninety-three is hereby further amended, so as to read as follows:

Examiner of insane convicts shall be appointed in each county.

'Section 5. The governor shall appoint in each county in the state a competent physician, who shall be a resident of the county, to act as an examiner of insane convicts in the county jail of the county. When a convict in the state prison or a county jail becomes insane, the warden shall forthwith notify the prison physician, or the jailer shall forthwith notify such examiner in the county, of the fact, and the prison physician

—proceedings when an inmate of prison or jail becomes insane.

INSANE CRIMINALS.

or such examiner, as the case may be, shall forthwith investigate the case and make a personal examination of the convict and if the prison physician or such examiner, as the case may be, finds such convict insane he shall forthwith certify such fact in writing to the governor and council, and the governor and council shall cause the removal of such insane convict to the insane department of the state prison or to either insane hospital until he becomes of sound mind. The fee of such examiner for each examination shall be   dollars. If such convict becomes of sound mind before the expiration of the term of his sentence he shall be returned to the prison or jail from which he was removed. If the term of his sentence has expired he shall be discharged free. Inmates of county jails and persons under indictment, becoming insane before final conviction, may be committed to an insane hospital by the judge of the supreme judicial, or superior court in the county where such person is to be tried or the case is pending, under such limitations as such judge may direct. The superintendent of the insane hospital at Augusta shall visit the insane department of the state prison not less than once each month to advise with the prison physician and warden as to the proper care, treatment and disposition of the convicts in said department. And whenever, in the judgment of said superintendent, any convict of the state prison who may be insane, can be better treated at the insane hospital at Augusta, he may recommend the transfer of said convict to said hospital, and report his conclusions to the governor and council, and thereupon they may order such transfer, and said convict shall be returned to the state prison whenever said superintendent shall consider it advisable to do so; if such person recovers after the expiration of his sentence he shall be discharged free. Whenever any convict in said department at the expiration of his term of sentence shall, in the opinion of said superintendent, prison physician and warden, be so far insane that his discharge will endanger the peace and safety of the community, they shall make a certificate setting forth briefly the facts of his sentence and its expiration and their opinion of his insanity, which certificate shall be by the warden recorded, and thereupon, upon said certificate, which shall be his warrant therefor, said warden shall transfer and commit said insane person to the insane hospital at Augusta. All expenses of said superintendent in connection with said department, as well as those of the commitment, removal and support of said convicts during the term of their sentences shall be paid by the state by order of the governor and council from state prison appropriations.'

Section 2. Section seven of said chapter as amended is hereby further amended, so as to read as follows:

CHAP. 148

Persons insane when convicted may be sentenced to insane department of state prison.

'Section 7. If a person convicted of any crime, in the supreme judicial court or either superior court, is found by the judge of such court to be insane when motion for sentence is made, the court may cause such person to be committed to the insane department of the state prison under such limitations as the court may direct; provided that the crime of which such person is convicted is punishable by imprisonment in the state prison; otherwise such commitment shall be to one of the insane hospitals;

—at expiration of term commitment if still insane, convict may be removed to insane hospital.

if at the expiration of the period of commitment to the insane department of the state prison such person has not become of sound mind in the opinion of the superintendent of the insane hospital at Augusta, prison physician and warden, he shall be removed by them to one of the insane hospitals. Persons committed by a judge of the supreme judicial or a superior court before final conviction, or after conviction and before sentence whether originally committed or subsequently removed thereto, and insane convicts after the expiration of their sentences, shall be supported while in the insane hospital in the manner provided by law in the case of persons committed by municipal officers, and the provisions of sections nineteen to twenty-two inclusive, of chapter one hundred forty-three of the revised statutes shall apply to such cases.'

Section 3. This act shall take effect when approved.

Approved March 26, 1903.

Chapter 148.

An Act to amend Chapter one hundred and one, Public Laws of eighteen hundred and eighty-seven, relating to Paupers.

Be it enacted by the Senate and House of Representatives in Legislature assembled, as follows:

Chapter 101, public laws of 1887, amended.

Section 1. Chapter one hundred and one of the public laws of eighteen hundred and eighty-seven is hereby amended by inserting after the word "found" in the second line the words 'in any town or,' so that said chapter when amended may read as follows:

—state shall reimburse for relief furnished persons having no legal settlement within the state.

'Chapter 101. Whenever persons who have no legal settlement within the state, and needing immediate relief, are found in any town, or in unincorporated places and are brought into an adjoining town obliged by law to care for and furnish relief to such persons, and relief is so furnished, the state shall reimburse said town for such relief so furnished, in the same manner

—when relief is furnished by town, town obliged by law to furnish same.

and under the same restrictions as provided in section twenty-nine, chapter twenty-four of the revised statutes as amended, although the overseers of the poor of said town have no permit in writing from the governor and council to remove the same into their town.'

Section 2. This act shall take effect when approved.

Approved March 26, 1903.

Chapter 149.

An Act relating to suits in equity to quiet Title.

Be it enacted by the Senate and House of Representatives in Legislature assembled, as follows:

Section 1. If, in a suit in equity to quiet or establish the title to land situated in this state or to remove a cloud from the title thereto, the plaintiff, or those under whom he claims, has been in uninterrupted possession of the land described in the bill for ten years or more, claiming an estate of freehold therein, and seeks to determine the claims or rights of any persons who are unascertained, not in being, unknown or out of the state, or who cannot be actually served with process and made personally amenable to the decree of the court, such persons may be made defendants and, if they are unascertained, not in being or unknown, they may be described generally as the heirs, or legal representatives of A B, or such persons as shall become heirs, devisees or appointees of C D, a living person, or persons claiming under A B. It shall not be necessary for the maintenance of such suit that the defendants shall have a claim or the possibility of a claim resting upon an instrument, the cancellation or surrender of which would afford the relief desired; but it shall be sufficient that they claim or may claim by purchase, descent or otherwise, some right, title, interest or estate in the land which is the subject of the suit and that their claim depends upon the construction of a written instrument or cannot be met by the plaintiffs without the production of evidence. Two or more persons who claim to own separate and distinct parcels of land in the same county by titles derived from a common source, or two or more persons who have separate and distinct interests in the same parcel, may join as plaintiffs in any suit brought under the provisions of this section.

Section 2. If in such suit the court finds that actual service cannot be made upon a defendant, it may order notice of the suit to be posted in a conspicuous place on the land or to be published in a newspaper within or without the state, or both, or to be given in such other manner as it considers most effectual,

CHAP. 149

SUITS IN EQUITY.

—court may appoint an agent, guardian ad litem or next friend in certain cases.

and may also require personal notice to be given. Notice given under the provisions of this section shall be constructive service on all the defendants. If, after notice has been given or served as ordered by the court and the time limited in such notice for the appearance of the defendants has expired, the court finds that there are or may be defendants who have not been actually served with process within the state and who have not appeared in the suit, it may of its own motion, or on the representation of any party, appoint an agent, guardian ad litem or next friend or any such defendant, and if any such defendants have or may have conflicting interests, it may appoint different agents, guardians ad litem or next friends to represent them. The cost of appearance of any such agent, guardian ad litem or next friend, including the compensation of his counsel, shall be determined by the court and paid by the plaintiff, against whom execution may issue therefor in the name of the agent, guardian ad litem or next friend.

Court may proceed after process or notification as provided in preceding section.

—suit shall be a proceeding in rem.

Section 3. After all the defendants have been served with process or notified as provided in the preceding section and after the appointment of an agent, the court may proceed as though all the defendants had been actually served with a process. Such suit shall be a proceeding in rem against the land, and a decree establishing or declaring the validity, nature or extent of the plaintiff's title may be entered, and shall operate directly on the land and shall have the force of a release made by or on behalf of all defendants of all claims inconsistent with the title established or declared thereby. The provisions of this and the two preceding sections shall not prevent the court from also exercising jurisdiction in personam against the defendants who have been actually served with process and who are personally amenable to its decrees.

—court may exercise jurisdiction in personam.

May maintain suit in equity to quiet title after ten years open, exclusive.

Section 4. Any person or persons claiming an estate of freehold in wild land or in an interest in common and undivided therein, if the plaintiff and those under whom he claims, has for ten years next prior to the filing of the bill held such open, exclusive, peaceable, continuous and adverse lands in Maine, may maintain a suit in equity to quiet or establish the title thereto or to remove a cloud from the title thereto, as provided in the three preceding sections.

Approved March 26, 1903.

Chapter 150.

An Act additional to Chapter seventy-three of the Revised Statutes, relating to Titles to property.

Be it enacted by the Senate and House of Representatives in Legislature assembled, as follows:

Section 1. Chapter seventy-three of the revised statutes is hereby amended by adding thereto the following section, to wit: *Chapter 73, R. S., amended.*

'Section 30. No agreement that a building erected with the consent of the land owner, by one not the owner of the land upon which it is erected, shall be and remain personal property, shall be effectual against any person, except the owner of such land, his heirs, devisees and persons having actual notice thereof, unless such agreement is in writing and signed by such land owner, or by some one duly authorized for that purpose, and acknowledged and recorded as deeds are required to be acknowledged and recorded under this chapter.' *Agreement that building shall be personal property when erected by one not owner of land, not effectual.*

—exceptions.

Section 2. This act shall not apply to said agreements heretofore entered into and now outstanding.

Approved March 26, 1903.

Chapter 151.

An Act relating to Assaults upon Officers and hindering or obstructing them while in the discharge of their duties.

Be it enacted by the Senate and House of Representatives in Legislature assembled, as follows:

Section 1. Whoever assaults, intimidates, or in any manner wilfully obstructs, intimidates or hinders any sheriff, deputy sheriff, coroner, constable or police officer while in the lawful discharge of his official duties, whether with or without process, shall be punished by a fine of not more than five hundred dollars or by imprisonment for a term of not more than one year. *Assaults upon or interference with officers, how punished.*

Section 2. In offenses under this act, not of an aggravated nature, trial justices may try and punish by a fine of not more than twenty dollars or by imprisonment in the county jail for sixty days and municipal or police courts may punish by a fine of not more than thirty dollars, or sixty days imprisonment. *Jurisdiction of trial justices.*

—of municipal or police courts.

Approved March 26, 1903.

CHAP. 152

Chapter 152.

An Act to amend Section forty-three of Chapter two hundred eighty-four, Public Acts of nineteen hundred one, relating to migratory fish in Mill River.

Be it enacted by the Senate and House of Representatives in Legislature assembled, as follows:

Section 43 of chapter 284, public laws of 1901, amended.

Section forty-three of chapter two hundred and eighty-four of the public laws of nineteen hundred one, is hereby amended by inserting after the words "Augusta dam," in the sixth line, the words, 'nor in Mill river, a tributary of Georges river, in Thomaston, Maine, between said Georges river and the old dam at head of tide waters, in said Mill river,' so that said section, as amended, shall read as follows:

Migratory fish, taking of, in certain waters prohibited.

'Section 43. No salmon, shad, or other migratory fish shall be taken or fished for within five hundred yards of any fishway, dam, or mill race; nor in the Penobscot river between the mouth of the Kenduskeag stream and the water works dam at Treat's falls on said river, nor between the Augusta highway bridge over the Kennebec river and the Augusta dam, nor in Mill river, a tributary of Georges river, in Thomaston, Maine, between said Georges river and the old dam at head of tide waters in said Mill river, nor any salmon five hundred feet above Ferry Point bridge on the Saint Croix river in Calais, between the first days of April and November, except by the ordinary mode of angling with single hook and line or artificial flies; nor shall hook and line or artificial flies be used at any time within one hundred yards of any fishway, dam or mill race; but this section shall not

—exceptions.

apply to the taking of alewives by the town of Warren in the Georges river, and by the town of Waldoboro in Medomak river, under the authority granted said towns by a private and special law of Massachusetts, passed March six, eighteen hundred two, and amendments thereof passed by the legislature of this state; nor shall it apply to the taking of alewives by the town of Woolwich in Nequasset stream; fly fishing shall be allowed up to the bridge across the Denny's river at Lincoln's mill, but not between said bridge and Lincoln's mill dam. But this section shall not apply to the Laconia falls and the Lower falls, so called, of the Saco river, located at Biddeford and Saco; and upon the first three days of each week, from the first of June to the first of September of each year, all persons may dip for salmon, shad, and alewives at the falls last named above. But it shall be lawful for any person to take any salmon, shad or alewives in the waters of Orange river, in the town of Whiting, in the county

—restrictions.

of Washington, up to one hundred and thirty yards of the fishway at the lower dam in said river, subject, however, to all the laws of the state, and laws regulating the taking of such fish in said river. The penalty for any violation of this section is a fine of not more than fifty nor less than ten dollars for each offense, and a further fine of ten dollars for each salmon and one dollar for each shad so taken.'

—penalty.

Approved March 26, 1903.

Chapter 153.

An Act to amend Section five of Chapter seventeen of the Revised Statutes as amended by Chapter one hundred eighty-eight of the Public Laws of eighteen hundred and ninety-three, relating to Nuisances.

Be it enacted by the Senate and House of Representatives in Legislature assembled, as follows:

Section 1. Section five of chapter seventeen of the revised statutes as amended by the public laws of eighteen hundred and ninety-three is hereby amended by striking out all of said section after the words "exceptions hereafter mentioned" in the fifteenth and sixteenth lines thereof and substituting the following: 'Any fence or other structure in the nature of a fence, unnecessarily exceeding six feet in height, maliciously kept and maintained for the purpose of annoying the owners or occupants of adjoining property, shall be deemed a private nuisance.'

Section 2. This act shall take effect when approved.

Section 5 of chapter 17, R. S. as amended by public laws of 1893, further amended.

—fences maliciously maintained, unnecessarily over six feet high, a private nuisance.

Approved March 26, 1903.

Chapter 154.

An Act to repeal so much of Chapter thirty of the Revised Statutes, as amended by Section five of Chapter forty-two of the Public Laws of eighteen hundred ninety-nine, and as amended by Chapter two hundred thirty of the Private and Special Laws of nineteen hundred one, as prohibits fishing through the ice in Large Greenwood pond in Elliottsville and Willimantic, in Piscataquis County.

Be it enacted by the Senate and House of Representatives in Legislature assembled, as follows:

Section 1. So much of chapter thirty of the revised statutes, as amended by section five of chapter forty-two of the public laws of eighteen hundred ninety-nine, and as amended by chapter two hundred thirty of the private and special laws of nineteen hundred one, as prohibits fishing through the ice in Large Greenwood pond, in Elliottsville and Willimantic, in Piscataquis county, is hereby repealed.

Section 2. This act shall take effect when approved.

Fishing through the ice in Large Greenwood pond, prohibition repealed.

Approved March 26, 1903.

Chapter 155.

An Act relating to compensation of County Commissioners of Hancock County.

Be it enacted by the Senate and House of Representatives in Legislature assembled, as follows:

Section 1. On and after January first, in the year of our Lord one thousand nine hundred and three, the pay of each county commissioner of the county of Hancock shall be three dollars and fifty cents for each day actually employed in the service of the county, including the time spent in traveling and each commissioner shall have ten cents a mile for the distance actually traveled.

Section 2. All acts and parts of acts inconsistent with this act, are hereby repealed.

Section 3. This act shall take effect when approved.

Approved March 26, 1903.

Chapter 156.

An Act to exempt Religious Institutions from the Collateral Inheritance Tax.

Be it enacted by the Senate and House of Representatives in Legislature assembled, as follows:

Section 1. Section one of chapter one hundred and forty-six of the public laws of one thousand eight hundred and ninety-three as amended by section one of chapter ninety-six of the laws of one thousand eight hundred and ninety-five, and as further amended by chapter two hundred and twenty-five of the laws of one thousand nine hundred and one, is hereby further amended by inserting the word 'religious' after the word "charitable" so that said section as amended, shall read as follows:

'Section 1. All property within the jurisdiction of this state, and any interest therein, whether belonging to inhabitants of this state, or not, and whether tangible or intangible, which shall pass by will or by the interstate laws of this state, or by deed, grant, sale or gift made or intended to take effect in possession or enjoyment after the death of the grantor, to any person in trust or otherwise, other than to or for the use of the father, mother, husband, wife, lineal descendant, adopted child, the lineal descendant of any adopted child, the wife or widow of a son or the husband of the daughter of a descendant, or any educational, charitable, religious or benevolent institution in this state, shall be liable to a tax of four per cent of its value, above the sum of five hundred dollars, for the use of the state, and all administrators, executors and trustees, and any such grantee under a conveyance made during the grantor's life shall be liable for all such taxes, with lawful interest as hereinafter provided, until the same shall have been paid as hereinafter directed.

Section 2. All such taxes heretofore assessed or to be assessed upon legacies or bequests to religious institutions are hereby abated.'

Approved March 26, 1903.

Chapter 157.

An Act relating to Trespassers.

Be it enacted by the Senate and House of Representatives in Legislature assembled, as follows:

Section 1. In all cases where any person without right now or hereafter dwells upon or in any manner occupies any lands which on the first day of April, eighteen hundred and eighty-three was wild land, any owner of such wild lands or of any legal or equitable interest therein may cause a notice to quit such lands to be served upon such person. Such service shall be made by any sheriff or deputy sheriff by giving the same to such person in hand. Such officer shall make his return upon a copy of such notice certified by him to be a true copy, and within sixty days thereafter such owner may cause such copy and return to be recorded in the registry of deeds in the county or district where said land is located. Proceedings had and taken as above specified shall bar such person who has so entered or dwells upon such wild land from obtaining any rights by adverse possession to the land upon which he has so entered. Provided, however, such person shall be entitled to the benefits of all the provisions of law relating to betterments.

Section 2. This act shall take effect when approved.

Approved March 26, 1903.

COUNTY COMMISSIONERS COURT—DESCENT OF REAL ESTATE.

CHAP. 158

Chapter 158.

An Act to change time of holding sessions of County Commissioners in Aroostook County.

Be it enacted by the Senate and House of Representatives in Legislature assembled, as follows:

Annual sessions of county commissioners of Aroostook county.

Section 1. Section six, chapter seventy-eight of the revised statutes is hereby amended, so far as it relates to holding annual sessions of the county commissioners in the county of Aroostook, so that that part of said section shall read as follows: 'Aroostook, on the first Tuesdays of January, March, May, July, September and November.'

Section 2. This act shall take effect when approved.

Approved March 26, 1903.

Chapter 159.

An Act to amend Section one of Chapter seventy-five of the Revised Statutes, as amended by Chapter one hundred and fifty-seven of the Public Laws of eighteen hundred and ninety-five, and by Chapters one hundred and ninety-three and one hundred and ninety-six of the Public Laws of eighteen hundred and ninety-seven, relating to Descent of Real Estate.

Be it enacted by the Senate and House of Representatives in Legislature assembled, as follows:

Section 1 of chapter 75, R. S., as amended by chapter 157, public laws of 1895, and by chapters 193 and 196, public laws of 1897, further amended.

Section 1. Section one of chapter seventy-five of the revised statutes, as amended by chapter one hundred and fifty-seven of the public laws of eighteen hundred and ninety-five, and also as amended by chapters one hundred and ninety-three and one hundred and ninety-six, of the public laws of eighteen hundred and ninety-seven, is hereby further amended so that said section one, as hereby amended, shall read as follows:

Rules for descent.

'Section 1. The real estate of a person deceased intestate, being subject to the payment of debts, including a wood lot or other land used with the farm or dwelling house although not cleared, and also including wild lands of which he dies seized, but excepting wild lands conveyed by him, though afterwards cleared, descends according to the following rules:

Descent to the widow.

'Rule 1. If he leaves a widow and issue, one-third to the widow. If no issue, one-half to the widow. And if no kindred, the whole to the widow. And to the widower shall descend the

—to the widower.

same shares in his wife's real estate. There shall likewise descend to the widow or widower the same share in all such real estate of which the deceased was seized during coverture, and which has not been barred or released as herein provided. In

DESCENT OF REAL ESTATE. 123

CHAP. 159

any event, one-third shall descend to the widow or widower free from payment of debts. —to widow or widower.

'Rule 2. The remainder of which he dies seized, and if no widow or widower, the whole, shall descend in equal shares to his children, and to the lawful issue of a deceased child by right of representation. If no child is living at the time of his death, to all his lineal descendants; equally, if all are of the same degree of kindred: if not, according to the right of representation. Descent to children.

—to lineal descendants.

'Rule 3. If no such issue, it descends to his father and mother in equal shares. To father and mother.

'Rule 4. If no such issue or father, it descends one-half to his mother. If no such issue or mother, it descends one-half to his father. In either case, the remainder, or if no such issue, father or mother the whole, descends in equal shares to his brothers and sisters, and when a brother or sister has died, to his or her children or grandchildren by right of representation. Alternate rules to father or mother.

—brothers and sisters.

'Rule 5. If no such issue, father, brother or sister, it descends to his mother. If no such issue, mother, brother or sister, it descends to his father. In either case, to the exclusion of the issue of deceased brothers and sisters.

'Rule 6. If no such issue, father, mother, brother or sister, it descends to his next of kin in equal degree; when they claim through different ancestors, to those claiming through a nearer ancestor, in preference to those claiming through an ancestor more remote. Next of kin.

'Rule 7. When a minor dies unmarried, leaving property inherited from either of his parents, it descends to the other children of the same parent, and the issue of those deceased; in equal shares if all are of the same degree of kindred; otherwise, according to the right of representation. Descent of property of unmarried minor.

'Rule 8. If the intestate leaves no widower, widow or kindred, it escheats to the state.' Escheats to the state.

Section 2. This act shall take effect on the first day of May, nineteen hundred and three.

Approved March 26, 1902.

CHAP. 160

Chapter 160

An Act amendatory of Section one of Chapter two hundred and twenty-one of the Public Laws of eighteen hundred and ninety-seven, relating to waiving the provisions of a will by the widow or widower, and to wills in which no provision is made for the widow or widower, and the interest which the widow or widower shall have in the personal estate of the testator or testatrix in such cases.

Be it enacted by the Senate and House of Representatives in Legislature assembled, as follows:

Section 1 of chapter 221, public laws of 1897, amended.

Section 1. Section one of chapter two hundred and twenty-one of the public laws of eighteen hundred and ninety-seven, is hereby amended so that said section one of said chapter, as hereby amended, shall read as follows:

Widow or widower may waive provisions of will within six months after probate.

—written notice to be filed.

'Section 1. When provision is made in the will of a testator or testatrix for his widow or her widower, such widow or widower may, at any time within six months after the probate of such will, waive such provision made for her or for him by filing written notice of such waiver in the probate court having jurisdiction of such will. and when such provision is waived as aforesaid, such widow or widower shall have and receive the same distributive share of the personal estate of such testator or testatrix as is provided by law in intestate estates. When no provision is made in the will of a testator or testatrix for his widow or her widower, such widow or widower shall likewise have and receive the same distributive share of the personal estate of such testator or testatrix as is provided by law in intestate estates, provided such widow or widower shall, within six months after the probate of such will, make, sign and file in the probate court having jurisdiction of such will, written notice that she or he claims such share of the personal estate of such testator or testatrix. Any notice filed under the provisions of this section, shall be recorded in the record books of the probate court where such notice is filed, by the register of probate, but a failure to record such notice shall not in any way affect the rights of any widow or widower.'

—when no provision is made in will, widow or widower shall have such share of personal estate as provided by law in intestate cases.

—written notice shall be filed.

—notice shall be recorded by register of probate.

Act shall not apply where testator or testatrix is deceased June, 1, 1903.

Section 2. This act shall not apply to wills where the testator or testatrix is deceased on the date this act takes effect.

Section 3. This act shall take effect on the first day of June, nineteen hundred and three.

Approved March 26, 1903.

Chapter 161.

An Act relating to bonds to be given by Treasurers of towns and plantations.

Be it enacted by the Senate and House of Representatives in Legislature assembled, as follows:

Section 1. The treasurer of each and every town and plantation, shall, before entering upon the discharge of his official duties, give bond to the inhabitants of his town or plantation, with good and sufficient sureties and for such sum as shall be designated by the municipal officers of his town or plantation, not exceeding, however, twice the amount of the taxes to be collected during the year for which he is treasurer, conditioned for the faithful discharge of all the duties and obligations of his office. If such bond is not furnished and delivered to the municipal officers, within ten days after written demand by the municipal officers on the treasurer therefor, the office of treasurer shall be deemed vacant, and the town or plantation, at any meeting of its inhabitants legally called, may elect a treasurer to fill the vacancy, or the municipal officers may fill the vacancy by written appointment which shall be recorded by the town or plantation clerk in the town or plantation records. The municipal officers shall be the sole judges of the sufficiency of such bond and sureties. Such bond, after its approval and acceptance by the municipal officers, shall be recorded by the town or plantation clerk, and such record shall be prima facie evidence of the contents of such bond, but a failure to so record shall be no defence in any action upon such bond. The municipal officers, however, in their discretion, may accept any surety company authorized to do business in the state, as surety on such bond, and dispense with any further surety or sureties thereon. Any town or plantation may lawfully vote, at its annual meeting, to raise money to be expended by its treasurer, under the direction of the municipal officers, for the purpose of purchasing from any surety company authorized to do business as aforesaid, the bond required by this section.

Treasurer shall give bond before entering on official duties.

—amount of bond.

—office of treasurer vacant if bond is not filed within ten days after written demand.

—vacancy, how filled.

—approval of bond.

—bond shall be recorded.

—municipal officers may accept bond of a surety company.

Town may raise money to pay surety company for treasurer's bond.

Section 2. All acts and parts of acts inconsistent with this act, are hereby repealed.

Act shall take effect June 1, 1903.

Section 3. This act shall take effect on the first day of June, nineteen hundred and three.

Approved March 26, 1903.

FISHING.

Chapter 162.

An Act to repeal so much of Chapter thirty of the Revised Statutes, as amended by Section five of Chapter forty-two of the Public Laws of eighteen hundred and ninety-nine, and as amended by Chapter three hundred seventy-nine of the Private and Special Laws of nineteen hundred and one, as prohibits fishing through the ice in Big Carry pond, or West Carry pond, so called, in Somerset County.

Be it enacted by the Senate and House of Representatives in Legislature assembled, as follows:

Fishing through ice in Big Carry pond, or West Carry pond, prohibition repealed.

Section 1. So much of chapter thirty of the revised statutes, as amended by section five of chapter forty-two of the public laws of eighteen hundred and ninety-nine, and as amended by chapter three hundred seventy-nine of the private and special laws of nineteen hundred and one, as prohibits fishing through the ice in Big Carry pond, or West Carry pond, so called, in Somerset county, is hereby repealed.

Section 2. This act shall take effect when approved.

Approved March 26, 1903.

Chapter 163.

An Act to repeal so much of Chapter thirty of the Revised Statutes, as amended by Section five of Chapter forty-two of the Public Laws of eighteen hundred and ninety-nine, and as amended by Chapter three hundred twenty-nine of the Private and Special Laws of nineteen hundred and one, as prohibits ice fishing in Black, Whittier and Perry ponds, in the towns of Vienna and Chesterville, in Kennebec and Franklin Counties.

Be it enacted by the Senate and House of Representatives in Legislature assembled, as follows:

Fishing through ice in Black, Whittier and Perry ponds, prohibition repealed.

Section 1. So much of chapter thirty of the revised statutes, as amended by section five of chapter forty-two of the public laws of eighteen hundred and ninety-nine, and as amended by chapter three hundred twenty-nine of the private and special laws of nineteen hundred and one, as prohibits fishing through the ice in Black, Whittier and Perry ponds, in the towns of Vienna and Chesterville, in Kennebec and Franklin counties, is hereby repealed.

Section 2. This act shall take effect when approved.

Approved March 26, 1903.

Chapter 164.

An Act to amend Section sixteen, Chapter fifty-one of the Revised Statutes, relating to Railroads.

Be it enacted by the Senate and House of Representatives in Legislature assembled, as follows:

Section 1. Section sixteen of chapter fifty-one of the revised statutes is hereby amended by inserting after the word "stations" in the third line thereof the words 'coal sheds,' so that said section, as amended, shall read as follows:

'Section 16. Any railroad corporation may also purchase or take and hold, as for public uses, land for borrow and gravel pits, necessary tracks, side tracks, stations, coal-sheds, woodsheds, repair shops, and car, engine and freight houses; but if the owner of said land does not consent thereto, or if the parties do not agree as to the necessity therefor or the area necessary to be taken, the corporation may make written application to the railroad commissioners, describing the estate, and naming the persons interested; the commissioners shall thereupon appoint a time for the hearing near the premises, and require notice to be given to the persons interested, as they may direct, fourteen days at least, before said time: and shall then view the premises, hear the parties and determine how much, if any, of such real estate is necessary for the reasonable accommodation of the traffic and appropriate business of the corporation. If they find that any of it is so necessary they shall furnish the corporation with a certificate containing a definite description thereof; and when it is filed with the clerk of courts in the county where the land lies, it shall be deemed and treated as taken; provided, however, that when land is held by a tenant for life, and the reversion is contingent as to the persons in whom it may vest on the termination of the life estate, such fact shall be stated in the application, and the commissioners shall, in addition to the notice to the tenant for life, give notice by publication to all others interested, in such manner as they may deem proper.'

Approved March 26, 1903.

Chapter 165.

An Act to amend Section six of Chapter eleven of the Revised Statutes of Maine, relating to the raising and expending of Common School Funds.

Be it enacted by the Senate and House of Representatives in Legislature assembled, as follows:

Section 1. Section six of chapter eleven of the revised statutes is hereby amended by inserting before the word "schools" in the second line of said section the word 'common' and by adding after the word "deficiency" in the eighth and last line in said section the words 'and all moneys provided by towns, or apportioned by the state for the support of common schools shall be expended for the maintenance of common schools established and controlled by the town by which said moneys are provided or to which said moneys are apportioned,' so that said section as amended, by this act, shall read as follows:

'Section 6. Every town shall raise and expend, annually, for the support of common schools therein, exclusive of the income of any corporate school fund, or of any grant from the revenue or fund from the state, or of any voluntary donation, devise or bequest, or of any forfeiture accruing to the use of schools, not less than eighty cents for each inhabitant, according to the census by which representatives to the legislature were last apportioned, under penalty of forfeiting not less than twice nor more than four times the amount of its deficiency, and all moneys provided by towns, or apportioned by the state for the support of common schools, shall be expended for the maintenance of common schools established and controlled by the town by which said moneys are provided, or to which said moneys are apportioned.'

Section 2. All acts, or parts of acts inconsistent with this act, are hereby repealed.

Section 3. This act shall take effect when approved.

Approved March 26, 1903.

Chapter 166.

An Act to repeal Sections one to forty-seven, inclusive, and Sections forty-nine to eighty-two, inclusive, of Chapter forty-seven of the Revised Statutes, relating to Banks of Discount.

Be it enacted by the Senate and House of Representatives in Legislature assembled, as follows:

Section 1. Sections one to forty-seven, both inclusive, and sections forty-nine to eighty-two, both inclusive, of chapter forty-seven of the revised statutes are hereby repealed. *—Sections 1 to 47, both inclusive, and sections 49 to 82, both inclusive, of chapter 47, R.S., repealed.*

Section 2. The sections declared to be repealed in the foregoing section remain in force for the trial and punishment of all past violations of them; and for the recovery of penalties or forfeitures already incurred; and for the preservation of all rights and their remedies existing by virtue of them; and so far as they apply to any office, trust, judicial proceeding, right, contract, limitation or event already affected by them. *—Sections repealed shall remain in force for past violations, etc.*

Section 3. This act shall take effect when approved.

Approved March 26, 1903.

Chapter 167.

An Act to amend Sections thirty-two, thirty-three, thirty-four, thirty-five of Chapter eighteen of the Revised Statutes, relating to the assessment of damages upon Abutters on City Streets.

Be it enacted by the Senate and House of Representatives in Legislature assembled, as follows:

Section 1. Section thirty-two of said chapter eighteen is hereby amended by striking out the word "thirty" in the third and eighth lines of said section and substituting in place thereof the word 'ten,' so that said section as amended shall read as follows: 'After said assessment has been made upon such lots or parcels and the amount fixed on each, the same shall be recorded by the city clerk, and notice shall be given within ten days after the assessment by delivering to each owner of said assessed lots resident in said city a certified copy of such recorded assessment, or by leaving it at his last and usual place of abode, and by publishing the same three weeks successively in some newspaper published in said city, the first publication to be within said ten days, and the said clerk within ten days shall deposit in the post office of said city, postage paid, a certified copy of such assessment directed to each owner or proprietor residing out of said city, whose place of residence is known to said clerk, and the certificate of said clerk shall be sufficient

—Section 32 of chapter 18, amended.

—assessment shall be recorded by city clerk.

—notice of assessment, how and when to be made.

CHAP. 167

evidence of these facts, and in the registry of deeds shall be the evidence of title in allowing or assessing damages and improvements, so far as notice is concerned.'

Section 33 of chapter 18, amended.

Arbitration when amount of assessment is not satisfactory.

Section 2. Section thirty-three of said chapter eighteen is hereby amended by striking out the entire section and inserting in place thereof the following: 'Any person not satisfied with the amount for which he is assessed, may, within ten days after service of the notice provided for by the preceding section in either manner therein provided, by request in writing given to the city clerk, have the assessment upon his lot or parcel of land determined by arbitration. The municipal officers shall nominate six persons who are residents of said city, two of whom selected by the applicant, with a third resident person selected by said two persons, shall fix the sum to be paid by him, and the report of such referees made to the clerk of said city, and recorded by him, shall be final and binding upon all parties. Said reference shall be had and their report made to said city clerk within thirty days from the time of hearing before the municipal officers as provided in section thirty-one.'

—board of arbitration, how nominated.

Section 34 of chapter 18, amended.

—assessments shall create a lien on land assessed, also on buildings thereon.

Section 3. Section thirty-four of said chapter eighteen is hereby amended by striking out the entire section and inserting in place thereof the following: 'All assessments made under the provisions of section thirty-one, shall create a lien upon each and every lot or parcel of land so assessed, and the buildings upon the same, which lien shall continue one year after said assessments are made, and within ten days after they are made, the clerk of said city shall make out a list of all such assessments, the amount of each, and the name of the person against whom the same is assessed, and he shall certify the list and deliver it to the treasurer of said city; if said assessments are not paid within three months from the date thereof, the treasurer shall sell, at public auction, such of said lots or parcels of land upon which such assessments remain unpaid, or so much thereof, as is necessary to pay such assessments and all costs and incidental charges, he shall advertise and sell the same within one year from the time said assessments are made, as real estate is advertised and sold for taxes under chapter six, and upon such sale, shall make, execute and deliver his deed to the purchaser, which shall be good and effectual to pass the title of such real estate; the sum for which such sale shall be made, shall be the amount of the assessment and all costs and incidental expenses. Any person to whom the right by law belongs, may at any time within one year from the date of said sale redeem such real estate by paying to the purchaser or his assigns the sum for which the same was sold, with interest thereon at the rate of twenty per cent a year, and the costs of re-conveyance.'

—may sell at public auction if assessment is not paid within three months.

—shall advertise and sell within one year.

—deed shall pass title.

—redemption may be within one year.

Section 4. Section thirty-five of said chapter eighteen is hereby amended by striking out the entire section and inserting in place thereof the following: 'If said assessments are not paid, and said city does not proceed to collect said assessments, by a sale of the lots or parcels of land upon which such assessments are made, or do not collect, or is in any manner delayed or defeated in collecting such assessments by a sale of the real estate so assessed, then the said city, in the name of said city, may maintain an action against the party so assessed for the amount of said assessment, as for money paid, laid out and expended, in any court competent to try the same, and in such suit may recover the amount of such assessment, with twelve per cent interest on the same from the date of said assessment and costs.'

Approved March 26, 1903.

Chapter 168.

An Act to amend Chapter one hundred of the Public Laws of eighteen hundred and ninety-one, entitled "An Act to create a Forest Commission and for the protection of forests."

Be it enacted by the Senate and House of Representatives in Legislature assembled, as follows:

Section 1. Section one of chapter one hundred of the public laws of eighteen hundred and ninety-one is hereby amended by striking out the word "two" in the fourth line of said section and inserting in place thereof the word 'four' so that said section, as amended, shall read as follows:

'Section 1. The state land agent is hereby made forest commissioner of the state of Maine, and in addition to the salary now received by him as land agent, he shall receive as compensation for his services as forest commissioner four hundred dollars per annum, and his actual traveling expenses incurred in the performance of his duties, an account of which shall be audited by the governor and council.'

Section 2. Section four of said chapter is hereby amended so that said section, as amended, shall read as follows:

'Section 4. It shall be the duty of the forest commissioner to take measures for the prevention, control and extinguishment of forest fires in all plantations and unorganized townships, and to this end, he shall appoint such number of forest fire wardens to patrol the forests as may be necessary to carry out the provisions of this act, assigning to each warden the territory over and within which he shall have jurisdiction. Fire wardens, so

AUSTRALIAN BALLOT LAW.

CHAP. 169
—terms of wardens.

appointed, shall hold office during the pleasure of said commissioner, be sworn to the faithful discharge of their duties by any officer authorized to administer oaths, and a certificate thereof shall be returned to the office of said commissioner. Said wardens shall perform such duties, at such times, and under such rules and regulations, as the commissioner may prescribe, and they shall receive as compensation two dollars for each day of actual service. Whenever a fire occurs on, or is likely to do damage to, forest lands within the jurisdiction of any such fire warden he shall take immediate action to control and extinguish the same, and for this purpose forest fire wardens are hereby authorized to summon to their assistance citizens of any county in which said fire may be, and every person so summoned and assisting shall be paid fifteen cents for each hour of service rendered by him. Immediately after the extinguishment of a fire the warden in charge shall make return, under oath, to the commissioner, of the expense thereof, including the names of the persons so summoned and assisting, with their post office addresses, and the hours of labor actually performed by each. All expense incurred under the provisions of this section shall be paid from the funds appropriated to and for the use of the forest commission.'

—duties of wardens.

—compensation.

—may summon citizens to their assistance.

—returns of wardens after extinguishment of fire.

Section 3. This act shall take effect when approved.

Approved March 26, 1903.

Chapter 169.

An Act to amend Section six of Chapter two hundred sixty-seven of the Public Laws of eighteen hundred and ninety-three, entitled "An Act to provide for the printing and distributing ballots at the public expense and to regulate voting for State and City Elections."

Be it enacted by the Senate and House of Representatives in Legislature assembled, as follows:

Section 6 of chapter 267, public laws of 1893, amended.

Section six of chapter two hundred and sixty-seven of the public laws of eighteen hundred ninety-three is hereby further amended by inserting after the word "held" in said section the following words: 'and for candidates for electors of president and vice president, on or before the tenth day of October in each year when such election is held,' so that said section as amended shall read as follows:

Nomination certificates for state and county officers shall be filed on or before August

'Section 6. Certificates of nominations and nomination papers for the nomination of candidates for state and county officers and representatives to the legislature, shall be filed with the secretary of state on or before the tenth day of August of each year in which such election is held, and for candidates for electors of president and vice president on or before the tenth of October in each year when such election is held. Such certificates and papers for the nomination of candidates for the offices of mayor and all other offices in cities shall be filed with the city clerks of the respective cities at least seven days, exclusive of Sundays, previous to the day of such election. With nomination papers and certificates shall also be filed the consent in writing of the person nominated.'

Approved March 26, 1903.

Chapter 170.

An Act to amend Section thirty-eight of Chapter twenty-seven of the Revised Statutes and Section forty of Chapter twenty-seven of the Revised Statutes as amended by Chapter one hundred forty of the Public Laws of eighteen hundred and eighty-seven and Chapter one hundred thirty-two of the Public Laws of eighteen hundred and ninety-one, relating to Intoxicating Liquors.

Be it enacted by the Senate and House of Representatives in Legislature assembled, as follows:

Section 1. Section thirty-eight of chapter twenty-seven of the revised statutes is hereby amended by adding thereto the following words, 'whoever violates this section shall be fined one hundred dollars and costs or be imprisoned sixty days,' so that said section as amended shall read as follows:

'Section 38. Whoever shall deposit or have in his possession intoxicating liquors with intent to sell the same in the state in violation of law, or with intent that same shall be sold by any person, or to aid or assist any person in such sale. Whoever violates this section shall be fined one hundred dollars and costs or be imprisoned sixty days.'

Section 2. Section forty of chapter twenty-seven of the revised statutes as amended by chapter one hundred and forty of the public laws of eighteen hundred and eighty-seven, and chapter one hundred and thirty-two of the public laws of eighteen hundred and ninety-one, is hereby amended by striking out the words "or has reason to believe that said person has concealed them about his person, to search said person, and if such liquors are found upon the person or premises, to arrest him" in the sixteenth, seventeenth, eighteenth and nineteenth lines of said section, and insert in the place thereof the words 'to arrest said person' and by striking out the words "found upon the person in the premises described in this section" in the twenty-sixth and twenty-seventh lines of said section and inserting in place thereof the words 'kept and deposited by him in any place,' so that said section as amended shall read as follows:

Chap. 170

Search and seizure process, for intoxicating liquors, proceedings in.

'Section 40. If any person competent to be a witness in civil suits, make sworn complaint before any judge of a municipal or police court or trial justice, that he believes that intoxicating liquors are unlawfully kept or deposited in any place in the state by any person, and that the same are intended for sale within the state in violation of law, such magistrate shall issue his warrant, directed to any officer having power to serve criminal process, commanding him to search the premises described and specially designated in such complaint and warrant, and if said liquors are there found to seize the same, with the vessels in which they are contained, and them safely keep until final action thereon, and make immediate return on said warrant. The name of the person so keeping said liquors as aforesaid, if known to the complainant, shall be stated in such complaint, and the officer shall be commanded by said warrant, if he finds said liquors to arrest said person and hold him to answer as keeping said liquors intended for unlawful sale. Any person who may be suspected of selling from, or keeping for illegal sale in his pockets, intoxicating liquors, may be searched in the same manner and by the same process as is provided for the search of places and if liquors are found upon his person, may be held to answer as though such liquors were kept and deposited by him in any place. If fluids are poured out or otherwise destroyed by the tenant, assistant or other person, when premises are about to be searched, manifestly for the purpose of preventing their seizure by officers authorized to make such search and seizure, such fluids may be held to have been intoxicating and intended for unlawful sale, and the penalties shall be the same as if said liquors had been seized. If the name of the person keeping such liquors is unknown to the complainant, he shall so allege in his complaint, and the magistrate shall thereupon issue his warrant as provided in the first sentence of this section. If upon trial, the court is of the opinion that the liquor was so aforesaid kept and intended for unlawful sale, by the person named in said complaint, or by any other person with his knowledge or consent, he shall be found guilty thereof, and sentenced to a fine of one hundred dollars and costs and in addition thereto be imprisoned sixty days. In default of payment of fine and costs the party shall be imprisoned sixty days additional. The payment of the United States special tax as a liquor seller, or notice of any kind in any place of resort, indicating that intoxicating liquors are there sold, kept or given away unlawfully, shall be held to be prima facie evidence that the person or persons paying said tax, and the party or parties displaying said notices, are common sellers of intoxicating liquors, and the premises so kept by them common nuisances.'

Approved March 26, 1903.

Chapter 171.

An Act to amend Section fifteen of Chapter one hundred and thirty-two of the Revised Statutes, relating to Appeals from Magistrates in criminal cases.

Be it enacted by the Senate and House of Representatives in Legislature assembled, as follows:

Section fifteen of chapter one hundred and thirty-two of the revised statutes is hereby amended so as to read as follows: *Section 15 of chapter 132, R. S., amended.*

'Section 15. Any person aggrieved at the decision or sentence of such magistrate, may within twenty-four hours after such sentence is imposed, Sunday not included, appeal therefrom to the next supreme judicial or superior court in the same county, and the magistrate shall thereupon order such appellant to recognize in a reasonable sum, not less than twenty dollars with sufficient sureties, to appear and prosecute his appeal and to be committed until the order is complied with. When such appeal is not taken before the adjournment of the session of court at which said sentence is imposed, mittimus shall issue and the respondent shall be committed thereon, under such sentence, but if after adjournment and commitment as aforesaid and within said twenty-four hours, application in writing is made to such magistrate to enter such appeal, he shall supersede such commitment by his written order to the jailer or other officer, and the respondent shall be brought before him and such appeal allowed and entered as if claimed before adjournment.' *Persons aggrieved may within 24 hours after sentence, appeal to supreme judicial or superior court.*

Approved March 26, 1903.

Chapter 172

An Act to amend Section forty-four of Chapter two of the Revised Statutes, relating to the publication of the Public Laws.

Be it enacted by the Senate and House of Representatives in Legislature assembled, as follows:

Section 1. Section forty-four of chapter two of the revised statutes, as amended, is hereby further amended by striking out the words "one dollar" in the fifth line and inserting in place thereof the words 'two dollars' so that said section as amended, shall read as follows: *Section 44 of chapter 2, R. S. as amended, further amended.*

'Section 44. He shall cause the public laws passed at each session to be printed within thirty days after the close thereof on extra sheets, on good paper, in good clear nonpareil type, by the publishers of each newspaper; and each printer who so pub- *Compensation to newspapers for publishing and distributing the laws to subscribers.*

ADMINISTRATORS AND EXECUTORS—COLLECTORS' BONDS.

CHAP. 173

lishes and distributes the laws to his subscribers within the state, shall receive ten dollars, besides two dollars for every hundred copies so distributed within the state.'

Section 2. This act shall take effect when approved.

Approved March 26, 1903.

Chapter 173.

An Act relating to defense of actions brought against Administrators and Executors.

Be it enacted by the Senate and House of Representatives in Legislature assembled, as follows:

Heirs, devisees or legatees may petition to defend suit brought against executor or administrator.

Section 1. When suit has been brought against an executor or administrator, any of the heirs, devisees or legatees of the deceased may personally or by attorney, petition the court for leave to defend the suit, setting forth the facts as he believes them to be and his reasons for so desiring to defend, and the court may grant or refuse such leave.

Shall give bond if leave is given to defend.

Section 2. If leave is granted, the petitioner shall give to the administrator or executor bond in such sum as the court orders, to hold the administrator or executor harmless, for any damages or costs occasioned by the suit or by said defense; and an entry of record shall be made that he is admitted to defend such suit.

Section 3. This act shall take effect when approved.

Approved March 27, 1903.

Chapter 174.

An Act relating to Bonds given by Collectors of Taxes.

Be it enacted by the Senate and House of Representatives in Legislature assembled, as follows:

Bond of collector of taxes shall be recorded.

Section 1. The bond given by any collector of taxes to the inhabitants of the town or plantation of which he is collector, shall, after its approval and acceptance by the municipal officers of such town or plantation, be recorded by the town or plantation clerk, in the town or plantation records, and such record shall be prima facie evidence of the contents of such bond, but a failure to so record shall be no defense in any action upon such bond.

Section 2. This act shall take effect on the first day of June, nineteen hundred and three.

Approved March 27, 1903.

Chapter 175.

An Act to amend Chapter two hundred and eighty-six, Public Laws of nineteen hundred and one, relating to taxation of interest bearing deposits in Trust and Banking companies.

Be it enacted by the Senate and House of Representatives in Legislature assembled, as follows:

Chapter two hundred and eighty-six of the public laws of nineteen hundred and one is hereby amended by striking out all of said chapter and substituting the following in place thereof:

'Section 1. Every trust and banking company incorporated under the laws of this state, shall, semi-annually on the last Saturdays of April and October, make a return signed and sworn to by its treasurer, of the average amount of its time deposits and its deposits bearing interest at the rate of three per cent or more per annum for the six months preceding each of said days, together with a statement in detail of the amount of United States bonds, the shares of corporation stocks such as are by law of this state free from taxation to the stockholders. For wilfully making a false return, the corporation treasurer forfeits not less than five hundred, nor more than five thousand dollars. Said return shall be made to the bank examiner, on or before the first Saturdays of May and November, and within thirty days thereafter, he shall fix and determine the market values of the United States bonds, and the shares of corporation stocks returned as aforesaid, and transmit said returns with such values so determined to the board of state assessors for the assessment required by the following section.

'Section 2. The board of state assessors shall thereupon deduct from the average amount of the time and interest bearing deposits so returned, an amount equal to the value so determined of United States bonds, the shares of corporation stocks such as are by law of this state free from taxation to stockholders, and upon the balance so found, assess an annual tax of one-half of one per cent; one-half of said tax shall be assessed on or before the fifteenth day of June on the balance of said deposits so ascertained for the six months ending on and including the last Saturday of April, and one-half on or before the fifteenth day of December on the balance of said deposits so ascertained for the six months ending on and including the last Saturday of October. The board of state assessors shall thereupon certify said assessment to the treasurer of state, who shall forthwith notify the several trust and banking companies interested, and all taxes so assessed shall be paid semi-annually within ten days after the fifteenth days of June and December.

CHAP. 176

If any trust company fail to make return, state assessors shall assess.

—state treasurer shall commence action for debt if tax is not paid.

'Section 3. If any trust company fails to make the returns required by section one of this act the board of state assessors shall make an assessment of state tax upon such company as they think just, with such evidence as they may obtain, and such assessment shall be final. If any company fails to pay the tax required or imposed in this act, the treasurer of state shall forthwith commence an action of debt in the name of the state for the recovery of the same with interest.

'Section 4. All deposits designated in section one of this act are exempt from municipal taxation to the company or the depositor.

'Section 5. This act shall take effect when approved.'

Approved March 27, 1903.

Chapter 176.

An Act to amend Chapter fifty-one of the Revised Statutes, relating to the duties of Railroad Commissioners.

Be it enacted by the Senate and House of Representatives in Legislature assembled, as follows:

Section 114 of chapter 51, R. S., amended.

Section 1. Section one hundred fourteen of chapter fifty-one of the revised statutes is hereby amended by striking out the words "shall give a certificate thereof to the clerk of the corporation, therein stating the condition of the road and rolling stock" from the fifth, sixth and seventh lines and inserting after the word "doings" in the eighth line the words 'therein stating the condition of the road and rolling stock' so that said section, as amended, shall read as follows:

A majority of board of railroad commissioners shall annually examine tracks, etc., of all railroads.

—shall annually make report to the governor of their official doings.

'Section 114. A majority of the board, annually, between the first of April and October, and at any other time on application or whenever they think necessary, shall carefully examine the tracks, rolling stock, bridges, viaducts and culverts of all railroads; and shall annually in December make a report to the governor of their official doings, therein stating the condition of the road and rolling stock, with such facts as they deem of public interest or which he may require; and all persons managing railroads shall give the board such information as they at any time request.'

Section 115 of chapter 51, repealed.

Section 2. Section one hundred fifteen of chapter fifty-one of the revised statutes is hereby repealed.

Approved March 27, 1903.

Chapter 177.

An Act to provide for the assessment and expenditure of the income arising from the Permanent School Fund in certain towns.

Be it enacted by the Senate and House of Representatives in Legislature assembled, as follows:

Section 1. All towns incorporated since seventeen hundred and eighty-eight, not formerly parts of other towns, which fail to account for the permanent school fund arising from sale or lease of school lands in said towns, shall annually raise and expend for the maintenance of common schools not less than forty-five dollars in addition to the amount required by law to be raised and expended for the support of said schools. *Towns failing to account for permanent school funds, shall raise and expend at least $45 in addition to amount required by law.*

Section 2. This act shall take effect January first, nineteen hundred and four.

Approved March 27, 1903.

Chapter 178.

An Act to amend Chapter two hundred and seventy-nine of the Public Laws of eighteen hundred and ninety-seven, as amended by Chapter two hundred and forty of the Public Laws of nineteen hundred and one, relating to the packing of Sardines.

Be it enacted by the Senate and House of Representatives in Legislature assembled. as follows:

Section 1. Section one of chapter two hundred and seventy-nine of the public laws of eighteen hundred and ninety-seven, as amended by chapter two hundred and forty of the public laws of nineteen hundred and one, is hereby further amended so as to read as follows: *Section 1 of chapter 279, public laws of 1897 as amended by chapter 240, public laws of 1901, further amended.*

'Section 1. The commissioner of sea and shore fisheries shall require a strict observation of the following rules. Whoever catches, takes, preserves, sells or offers for sale prior to the tenth day of May, nineteen hundred and three, any herring for canning purposes less than eight inches long, measured from one extreme to the other, or packs or cans sardines of any description, prior to the tenth day of May, nineteen hundred and three, forfeits twenty dollars for every hundred cans so packed or canned, and for every hundred herring so taken; and whoever, beginning with December first, nineteen hundred and three, catches, takes, preserves, sells or offers for sale between the first day of December and the fifteenth day of the following April, any herring for canning purposes less than eight inches long, measured from one extreme to the other, or packs or cans sar- *Packing of sardines and herring, rules to be observed in relation to.* *—prior to May 10, 1903.* *—penalty.* *—between Dec. 1 and April 15, following.*

Chap. 178

—penalty.

—preparation for packing.

—amount and quantity of oil to be used in quarter oils.

—amount of mustard in three-quarter mustards.

—vinegar for one-quarter spiced and three-quarter spiced.

—sealed measures shall be used.

Section 3 of chapter 279, amended.

Sardines, how packed.

—baking in ovens regulated.

dines of any description, between the first day of December and the fifteenth day of the following April, forfeits twenty dollars for every hundred cans so packed or canned, and for every hundred herring so taken; and whoever, after the approval of this act, either bakes, fries, steams, or cooks in any manner, packs or cans any herring or other fish for sardines without first heading and eviscerating the same, and whoever sells, offers for sale or has in his possession for sale any sardines packed without being so headed and eviscerated shall forfeit twenty dollars for every hundred cans so packed, sold, offered for sale or in possession for sale, to be recovered by indictment or action of debt, one-half to the complainant prosecutor, and one-half to the town in which the offense is committed. In packing herring, mackerel or other fish in hermetically sealed cans, either in oil, mustard or vinegar, there shall be used not less than three quarts of oil, of the first quality, pure summer or winter cotton oil, or any food oil of equal quality, for every hundred cans so packed of the size known as quarter oils; three quarts of mustard sauce of good quality for every fifty cans of the size known as three-quarter mustards; and for every one hundred cans of the size known as one-quarter mustards; one gallon of vinegar for every one hundred cans of the size known as one-quarter spiced; and for every fifty cans of the size known as three-quarter spiced or tomato. Proprietors of fish packing factories shall provide sealed measures holding one one-hundredth part of three quarts each, which shall be used in measuring all oil into quarter oil sardine cans, and measures holding one-fiftieth part of a gallon which shall be used in measuring all mustard sauce and vinegar into three-quarter size cans used in packing sardines, and all fish packed as aforesaid shall be when so packed good and sound, except that they shall be cleaned, headed and eviscerated. Whoever packs or cans, or causes to be packed or canned any fish in violation of this section shall forfeit twenty dollars for every one hundred cans or fifty cans as aforesaid, as the case may be, so packed by him or by his employes, to be recovered by complaint.'

Section 2. Section three of said chapter two hundred and seventy-nine is hereby amended by striking out the word "six" in the second line of said section and substituting in place thereof the 'five,' so that said section, as amended, shall read as follows:

'Section 3. No can of sardines shall be packed with less than five fish and no fish shall be packed as sardines unless they have been headed and eviscerated within twenty-four hours from the time they arrive at the factory. No fish shall be baked for sardines in ovens unless they shall first be properly flaked in rows and laid on without overlapping. Whoever flakes, bakes or packs any sardines in violation of this section forfeits five dollars for every hundred fish so flaked, baked or packed, to be recovered by indictment or action for debt, one-half to the complainant or prosecutor, and one-half to the town in which the offense is committed.'

Section 3. This act shall take effect when approved.

Approved March 27, 1903.

Chapter 179.

An Act to repeal so much of Chapter thirty of the Revised Statutes, as amended by Section five of Chapter forty-two of the Public Laws of eighteen hundred and ninety-nine, and as amended by Chapter three hundred and seventy-nine of the Private and Special Laws of nineteen hundred and one, as closes Oaks pond, in Cornville, to ice fishing.

Be it enacted by the Senate and House of Representatives in Legislature assembled, as follows:

Section 1. So much of chapter thirty of the revised statutes, as amended by section five of chapter forty-two of the public laws of eighteen hundred and ninety-nine, and as amended by chapter three hundred and seventy-nine of the private and special laws of nineteen hundred and one, as closes Oaks pond, in Cornville, to ice fishing, is hereby repealed.

Section 2. This act shall take effect when approved.

Approved March 27, 1903.

Chapter 180.

An Act to amend Section four, Section eleven, Section nineteen of Chapter eighteen of the Public Laws of eighteen hundred ninety-one as amended by Chapter one hundred fifty-four of the Public Laws of eighteen hundred ninety-five, relating to returns of Vital Statistics.

Be it enacted by the Senate and House of Representatives in Legislature assembled, as follows:

Section 1. Section four of chapter one hundred eighteen of the public laws of eighteen hundred ninety-one as amended by chapter one hundred fifty-four of the public laws of eighteen hundred ninety-five is hereby amended so as to read as follows:

'Section 4. Whenever any person shall die, or any still-born child be brought forth in this state, the undertaker, town clerk, or other person superintending the burial of said deceased person, shall obtain from the physician attending such bringing forth or

CHAP. 180

VITAL STATISTICS.

last sickness, a certificate, duly signed, setting forth as far as may be, the facts required by section nineteen of chapter one hundred eighteen of the public laws of eighteen hundred ninety-one as amended by section seven of chapter one hundred fifty-four of the public laws of eighteen hundred ninety-five and as further amended hereby; and it shall be the duty of the undertaker, or other person having charge of the burial of said deceased person, to add to said certificate the other facts required by section one of chapter one hundred eighteen of the public laws of eighteen hundred ninety-one; and having duly signed the same, to forward it to the clerk of the town or city where said person died and obtain a permit for burial; and in case of any contagious or infectious disease, said certificate shall be made and forwarded immediately.'

—duty of undertaker.

Section 11 of chapter 118, public laws of 1891, amended.

Section 2. Section eleven of chapter one hundred eighteen of the public laws of eighteen hundred ninety-one is hereby amended so as to read as follows:

Town clerk required to make returns annually to state registrar.

'Section 11. The clerk of every town shall keep a chronological record of all births, marriages, and deaths reported to him and shall in the month of June, nineteen hundred three, transmit a copy of the record of all births, marriages, and deaths occurring during the year of nineteen hundred two to the state registrar, and shall thereafter annually between the fifteenth and the twentieth of January send a copy of the record of all births, marriages, and deaths occurring during the year ending December thirty-one next preceding such said report, to the state registrar, together with the names, residences, and official stations, of all persons who have neglected to make returns to him in relation to the subject matters of such records, which the law required them to make, all to be made upon blanks to be prepared and furnished by the state registrar, and if no births, marriages, or deaths have occurred in the calendar year preceding the aforementioned time for making his annual returns, the town clerk shall send to the state registrar a statement to that effect. Whenever a birth, marriage or death, required by law to be returned to or by such clerk is reported to, or made by him in any year after its occurrence, and subsequent to his return made hereunder, he shall make due return thereof to the state registrar forthwith.'

Section 19, additional, to chapter 118, public laws of 1891, amended.

Section 3. Section nineteen, additional, to chapter one hundred eighteen of the public laws of eighteen hundred ninety-one, which was added thereto by section seven of chapter one hundred fifty-four of the public laws of eighteen hundred ninety-five, is hereby amended so as to read as follows:

LIBEL OR SLANDER. 143

CHAP. 181

'Section 19. A physician who has attended a person during his last illness shall within twenty-four hours after the death of said person make a certificate stating, to the best of his knowledge and belief, the name of the deceased, his age, the disease of which he died, and the date of his death, and shall either deliver it to the person superintending the burial or leave it with the family of the deceased or at the said physician's office where it may be obtained when called for; and a physician or midwife who has attended at the birth of a child dying immediately thereafter, or at the birth of a still-born child, shall, when requested, forthwith furnish for registration a certificate, stating to the best of his knowledge and belief the fact that such child died after birth or was born dead. It shall be a misdemeanor for any person to make a false return in regard to any birth or death.'

Attending physician shall within 24 hours after the death, make a certificate of name, age, disease, and date of birth of deceased.

—certificate, how disposed of.

Approved March 27, 1903.

Chapter 181.

An Act relating to actions for Libel or Slander.

Be it enacted by the Senate and House of Representatives in Legislature assembled, as follows:

Section 1. The defendant in an action for libel, may prove under the general issue, in mitigation of damages, that the charge was made by mistake or through error or by inadvertence, and that he has in writing, within a reasonable time after the publication of the charge, retracted the charge and denied its truth, as publicly and as fully as he made the charge.

Mitigation of damages in action for libel.

Section 2. In actions for libel or slander, and unproved allegation in the pleadings that the matter charged is true, shall not be deemed proof of malice unless the jury on the whole case find that such allegation or the defense thereunder, is made with malicious intent.

Proof of malice, relating to.

Section 3. This act shall not apply to pending actions or to causes of action existing on the date of the approval of this act.

Section 4. This act shall take effect when approved.

Pending actions, and existing causes of actions, not affected by this act.

Approved March 27, 1903.

Chapter 182.

An Act to amend Sections two and sixteen of Chapter forty-eight of the Revised Statutes, relating to Corporations.

Be it enacted by the Senate and House of Representatives in Legislature assembled, as follows:

<small>Section 2 of chapter 48, R. S., amended.</small>

Section 1. Section two of chapter forty-eight of the revised statutes is hereby amended by adding thereto the following words: 'but nothing herein shall prohibit corporations organized under the general law from providing by their by-laws for the division of their directors into classes and their election for a longer term than one year. After the certificate of organization required by law is filed in the office of the secretary of state, directors of all corporations not charged with the performance of any public duty within this state may hold meetings without this state and there transact business and perform all corporate acts not expressly required by statute to be performed within this state. Directors of such corporations may act through committees whose powers shall be defined in the by-laws,' so that said section as amended shall read as follows:

<small>Officers shall be chosen annually.

—tenure.

—shall be not less than three directors.

—director must be a stockholder.

—treasurers shall give bond.

—clerk shall be sworn.

—directors may be divided into classes and may be elected for more than one year.

—may hold meetings without this state for certain purposes.

Section 16 of chapter 48, R. S., amended.</small>

'Section 2. Such officers shall be chosen annually, and shall continue in office until others are chosen and qualified in their stead. There shall not be less than three directors, one of whom shall be by them elected president. No director can hold such office after he ceases to be a stockholder. The treasurer shall give bond for the faithful discharge of his duties, in such sum, and with such sureties, as are required. The clerk shall be sworn and shall record all votes of the corporation in a book kept for that purpose, but nothing herein shall prohibit corporations organized under the general law from providing by their by-laws for the division of their directors into classes and their election for a longer term than one year. After the certificate of organization required by law is filed in the office of the secretary of state, directors of all corporations not charged with the performance of any public duty within this state may hold meetings without this state and there transact business and perform all corporate acts not expressly required by statute to be performed within this state. Directors of such corporations may act through committees whose powers shall be defined in the by-laws.'

Section 2. Section sixteen of chapter forty-eight of the revised statutes is hereby amended by adding the word "anywhere" after the word "business" in line four and by adding thereto the following words: 'but corporations may also be formed hereunder to exercise the following corporate purposes in other states and jurisdiction, namely: the construction and operation of railroads or aiding in the construction thereof, telegraph or telephone companies, and gas or electrical companies, and in all such cases the articles of agreement and certificate of organization shall state that such business is to be carried on only in states and jurisdictions when and where permissible under the laws thereof, and such corporations heretofore organized for the transaction of such business in other states or jurisdictions, if otherwise legally organized and now existing, are hereby declared to be corporations under the laws of this state,' so that said section as amended shall read as follows:

'Section 16. Three or more persons may associate themselves together by written articles of agreement, for the purpose of forming a corporation to carry on any lawful business anywhere, including corporations for manufacturing, mechanical, mining or quarrying business and also corporations whose purpose is the carriage of passengers or freight, or both, upon the high seas, or from port or ports in this state to a foreign port or ports, or to a port or ports in other states, or the carriage of freight or passengers or both, upon any waters where such corporations may navigate; and excepting corporations for banking, insurance, the construction and operation of railroads or aiding in the construction thereof, and the business of savings banks, trust companies or corporations intended to derive profit from the loan or use of money, and safe deposit companies; including the renting of safes in burglar-proof and fire-proof vaults; also excepting telegraph and telephone companies, but corporations may also be formed hereunder to exercise the following corporate purposes in other states and jurisdictions, namely: the construction and operation of railroads or aiding in the construction thereof, telegraph or telephone companies, and gas or electrical companies, and in all such cases the articles of agreement and certificate of organization shall state that such business is to be carried on only in states and jurisdictions when and where permissible under the laws thereof, and such corporations heretofore organized for the transaction of such business in other states or jurisdictions, if otherwise legally organized and now existing, are hereby declared to be corporations under the laws of this state.'

Section 3. This act shall take effect when approved.

Approved March 27, 1903.

Chapter 183.

An Act to cede the jurisdiction of the State of Maine to the United States of America over so much land as has been or may be hereafter acquired for the public purposes of the United States.

Be it enacted by the Senate and House of Representatives in Legislature assembled, as follows:

Jurisdiction of state of Maine ceded to the United States, acquired for public purposes.
—proviso.

Section 1. That the jurisdiction of the state of Maine is hereby ceded to the United States of America over so much land as has been or may be hereafter acquired for the public purposes of the United States: Provided, that the jurisdiction hereby ceded shall not vest until the United States of America shall have acquired the title to the lands, by grant or deed, from the owner or owners thereof, and the evidences thereof shall have been recorded in the office where, by law, the title to such land is required to be recorded; and the United States of America are to retain such jurisdiction so long as such lands shall be used for the purposes in this section mentioned, and no longer; and such jurisdiction is granted upon the express condition that the state of Maine shall retain a concurrent jurisdiction with the United States in and over the said lands, so far as that civil process, in all cases not affecting the real or personal property of the United States, and such criminal or other process as shall issue, under the authority of the state of Maine, against any person or persons charged with crimes or misdemeanors committed within or without the limits of the said lands, may be executed therein, in the same way and manner as if no jurisdiction had been hereby ceded.

—jurisdiction retained while lands are used for public purposes.

—concurrent jurisdiction with U. S.

Ceded lands exempt from taxes, assessments, etc.

Section 2. That all the lands and the tenements which may be granted, as aforesaid, to the United States, shall be and continue, so long as the same shall be used for the purposes in the last section mentioned, exonerated and discharged from all taxes, assessments, and other charges which may be imposed under the authority of the state of Maine.

Section 3. This act shall take effect when approved.

Approved March 28, 1903.

Chapter 184.

An Act to define the powers and duties of Superintendents of Schools.

Be it enacted by the Senate and House of Representatives in Legislature assembled, as follows:

Section 1. Superintendents of schools shall have the power and it shall be their duty to examine and certificate teachers and employ teachers subject to the approval of the superintending school committee.

Section 2. All acts and parts of acts inconsistent with this act, are hereby repealed.

Section 3. This act shall take effect when approved.

Approved March 28, 1903.

Chapter 185.

An Act to amend Section twenty-nine of Chapter one hundred and sixteen of the Revised Statutes, relating to Fees and Costs of Magistrates.

Be it enacted by the Senate and House of Representatives in Legislature assembled, as follows:

Section twenty-nine of chapter one hundred and sixteen of the revised statutes is hereby amended by inserting at the end of the first sentence the words 'other than for copies and the entry fee in the appellant court.' Said section, as amended, will read as follows:

'Section 29. No trial justice, or judge or other officer of any municipal or police court, shall demand or receive any fees for entertaining an appeal or taking a recognizance to prosecute it, in a criminal case, other than for copies and entry fee in the appellant court. The legal fees therefor may be taxed in the bill of costs, and certified and paid like other fees.'

Approved March 22, 1903.

Chapter 186.

An Act to repeal Sections twenty-three and twenty-four of Chapter thirty-nine of the Revised Statutes, relating to Paper.

Be it enacted by the Senate and House of Representatives in Legislature assembled, as follows:

Section 1. Sections twenty-three and twenty-four of chapter thirty-nine of the revised statutes are hereby repealed.

Section 2. This act shall take effect when approved.

Approved March 28, 1903.

Chapter 187.

An Act to amend Sections thirty-eight, forty and fifty-one of Chapter sixty-four of the Revised Statutes, relating to Executors and Administrators.

Be it enacted by the Senate and House of Representatives in Legislature assembled, as follows:

Section 1. Section thirty-eight of chapter sixty-four of the revised statutes is hereby amended by striking out the first fifteen words and inserting in place thereof the following: 'Every executor or administrator within three months after his appointment or within such further time, not exceeding three months, as the judge allows,' so that said section as amended shall read as follows:

'Section 38. Every executor or administrator within three months after his appointment or within such further time, not exceeding three months, as the judge allows, shall cause notice of his appointment to be posted in two or more public places to be specified by the judge in the town where the deceased last dwelt, if in the state, and shall give such further notice as the judge in writing directs.'

Section 2. Section forty of chapter sixty-four is amended so that the same shall read as follows:

'Section 40. An affidavit of the executor or administrator or of the person employed by him to give such notice shall be filed with a copy of the notice in the probate court within one year after his appointment, and the register shall note thereon the time of filing, enter the same on his docket, and record said affidavit, and such record is evidence of the time, place and manner in which the notice was given.

In case an appeal is taken from the appointment of an executor or administrator, then said affidavit shall be filed, noted, entered and recorded as above provided within four months after final decree.

If appeal is taken.

In case of a vacancy in the office of executor or administrator before affidavit has been filed as aforesaid then said affidavit shall be filed as above provided within four months after the appointment of the administrator de bonis non or the administrator with the will annexed. Whenever an executor or administrator fails to give said notice or to file such affidavit as above provided he may be removed from his trust by the judge of probate, in his discretion, upon petition of any interested party.'

—administrator de bonis non, or with will annexed shall file within four months.

Section 3. Section fifty-one of chapter sixty-four of the revised statutes, is amended by striking out the following words in the third and fourth lines "in case of credits and rights to property not in possession" so that said section as amended shall read as follows:

Section 51 of chapter 54, R. S., amended.

'Section 51. Every executor or administrator shall account for the personal property and effects named in the inventory at the appraised value, unless sold under license as provided in the preceding section; but if loss accrues without his fault or negligence, he may be allowed the amount of such loss in his account of administration; and if any goods or effects not sold under license, allowed to the widow, nor distributed to the heirs or devisees, are shown to be of greater value then they are appraised at, he shall account for the difference.'

For what executors and administrators shall account.

Section 4. This act shall take effect when approved.

Approved March 28, 1908.

Chapter 188.

An Act to amend Chapter eleven of the Public Laws of eighteen hundred and eighty-seven, as amended by Chapter forty-four of the Public Laws of eighteen hundred and ninety-nine, authorizing cities and towns to accept legacies, devises and bequests, and to raise money.

Be it enacted by the Senate and House of Representatives in Legislature assembled, as follows:

Section 1. Section one of chapter eleven of the public laws of eighteen hundred and eighty-seven, as amended by chapter forty-four of the public laws of eighteen hundred and ninety-nine is hereby amended by inserting after the word "affairs" in the ninth line thereof the words, 'provided, however, that in cities the acceptance of such devise, bequest or conditional gift may be by vote of the city council instead of by the inhabitants at a special election, if the municipal officers shall so direct.' By inserting

Section 1 of chapter 11, public laws of 1887, as amended by chapter 44, public laws of 1899, further amended.

CHAP. 188

Municipal officers authorized to call meetings to accept legacies.

—notice of object of meeting shall be given.

Section 2 of chapter 11, public laws of 1887, as amended by chapter 44, public laws of 1899, further amended.

Cities and towns may raise money to carry into effect terms of will.

after the word "meeting" in the eleventh line thereof, the words 'of the inhabitants;' by inserting after the word "inhabitants" in the thirteenth line thereof, the words 'or the city council at a regular meeting or at a special meeting called for that purpose;' by inserting after the word "voters" in the fourteenth line thereof, the words, 'or of the members of the city council;' so that said section, as amended, shall read as follows:

'Section 1. Whenever the municipal officers of any city or town are notified in writing by the executors of any will, or by the trustees created by virtue of the terms thereof, that a devise or bequest has been made upon conditions by the testator of said will; or by an individual, that he intends to make a conditional gift, in behalf of said city or town; the municipal officers of said city or town, shall, within sixty days after said notice to them, call a legal meeting of the inhabitants of said city or town qualified to vote upon city or town affairs: provided, however, that in cities the acceptance of such devise, bequest or conditional gift may be by vote of the city council, instead of by the inhabitants at a special election, if the municipal officers shall so direct. Said municipal officers shall give public notice in their warrants, of the objects of said meeting of the inhabitants, and such other notice as said municipal officers shall deem proper. At such meeting, the said inhabitants, or the city council at a regular meeting, or at a special meeting called for that purpose, shall vote upon the acceptance of said devise or bequest or conditional gift, and if a majority of the legal voters, or of the members of the city council, present, then and there vote to accept said devise or bequest or conditional gift, in accordance with the terms contained in said will, and upon the conditions made by the testator or by said individual, said municipal officers of said city or town, shall forthwith notify said executors or trustees, or individual, in writing, of said acceptance by said city or town aforesaid, or the non acceptance thereof.

Section 2. Section two of chapter eleven of the public laws of eighteen hundred and eighty-seven, as amended by chapter forty-four of the public laws of eighteen hundred and ninety-nine is hereby amended by adding to said section the words, 'or of cemetery lots owned by individuals,' so that said section as amended, shall read as follows:

'Section 2. Whenever the executors or trustees of said individual, under any will have fully discharged their duties respecting the payment, delivery or otherwise of any devise or bequest, or conditional gift, to said city or town; and said city or town have accepted said devise or bequest or conditional gift in accordance with the conditions of said will or the terms of said conditional gift as set forth in section one of this chapter, then said city or town shall perpetually comply, and strictly maintain and keep all the conditions and terms contained in said will or said conditional gift by virtue of which said devise or bequest or conditional gift was so made, and any city or town so accepting said devise or bequest, or conditional gift and receiving the same, or enjoying the benefits therefrom, is hereby authorized to raise money to carry into effect the requirements and terms of said will or said conditional gift by virtue of which said devise or bequest or conditional gift was so accepted and received. The provisions of this chapter shall apply only to devises and bequests and gifts, devised and bequeathed or given to cities and towns for educational, benevolent and charitable purposes and objects, or for the care, protection repair and improvement of cemeteries owned by said cities or towns, or of cemetery lots owned by individuals.'

Section 3. This act shall take effect when approved.

Approved March 23, 1903.

Chapter 189.

An Act to repeal so much of Chapter thirty of the Revised Statutes, as amended by Chapter forty-two, Section five, of the Public Laws of eighteen hundred ninety-nine, as amended by Chapter three hundred seventy-nine of the Private and Special Laws of nineteen hundred one, as prohibits fishing through the ice in Palmer Pond, so called, in Mayfield Plantation, in the County of Somerset.

Be it enacted by the Senate and House of Representatives in Legislature assembled, as follows:

Section 1. So much of chapter thirty of the revised statutes, as amended by chapter forty-two, section five, of the public laws of eighteen hundred ninety-nine, and as amended by chapter three hundred seventy-nine of the private and special laws of nineteen hundred one, as prohibits fishing through the ice, in accordance with the general law, in Palmer pond, so called, in Mayfield plantation, in the county of Somerset, is hereby repealed.

Ice fishing in Palmer pond, prohibition repealed.

Section 2. This act shall take effect when approved.

Approved March 28, 1903.

INVESTMENT OF FUNDS IN SAVINGS BANKS.

Chapter 190.

An Act to amend Section one hundred of Chapter forty-seven of the Revised Statutes, as amended by Chapter one hundred sixty-one of the Public Laws of eighteen hundred and ninety-five, relating to the investment of funds of Savings Banks.

Be it enacted by the Senate and House of Representatives in Legislature assembled, as follows:

Section 100 of chapter 47, R. S., as amended by chapter 161, public laws of 1895, further amended. Investment of deposits.

Section 1. Section one hundred of chapter forty-seven of the revised statutes as amended by chapter one hundred sixty-one of the public laws of eighteen hundred and ninety-five, is hereby amended so as to read as follows:

'Section 100. Savings banks and institutions for savings are restricted to and hereafter may invest their deposits as follows:

First, *a:* In the public funds of the United States and District of Columbia.

b: In the public funds of any of the New England states and of the states of New York, Pennsylvania, Maryland, Ohio, Indiana, Kentucky, Michigan, Wisconsin, Minnesota, Iowa, Illinois, Missouri, Kansas and Nebraska.

Second, *a:* In the bonds of the counties, cities and towns of any of the New England states.

b: In the bonds of cities and districts in the states of New York, Pennsylvania, Maryland, Ohio, Indiana, Kentucky, Michigan, Wisconsin, Minnesota, Iowa, Illinois, Missouri, Kansas and Nebraska, having a population of seventy-five thousand or more, when issued for municipal purposes and which are a direct obligation on all the taxable property therein.

c: In the bonds of counties of twenty thousand inhabitants or more in the states of New York, Pennsylvania, Maryland, Ohio, Indiana, Kentucky, Michigan, Wisconsin, Minnesota, Iowa, Illinois, Missouri, Kansas and Nebraska, when issued for municipal purposes, and which are a direct obligation on all the taxable property therein, except when issued in aid of railroads, provided that the net municipal indebtedness of such county does not exceed five per cent of the last preceding valuation of the property therein for the assessment of taxes.

d: In the bonds of any city of ten thousand inhabitants or more in the states of New York, Pennsylvania, Maryland, Ohio, Indiana, Kentucky, Michigan, Wisconsin, Minnesota, Iowa, Illinois, Missouri, Kansas and Nebraska, when issued for municipal purposes and which are a direct obligation on all the taxable property therein, except when issued in aid of railroads, provided the net municipal indebtedness of such city does not exceed five per cent of the last preceding valuation of the property therein for the assessment of taxes.

INVESTMENT OF FUNDS IN SAVINGS BANKS.   153

CHAP. 190

e: In the refunding bonds of counties and cities above enumerated issued to take up at maturity bonds which were legal and constitutional when issued, provided the interest has been fully paid on such original bonds for at least five years last prior to such refunding; provided further that such counties and cities can otherwise meet the foregoing conditions.

f: In the bonds and obligations of school district boards, boards of education and other corporate bodies within such cities, authorized to issue bonds payable primarily from taxes levied on all the taxable property in said district; provided that the population of the district is ten thousand or more, and the population and assessed valuation of the district are equal to at least ninety per cent of the population and the assessed valuation of the city within which such district is located; provided further that the net municipal indebtedness of such district does not exceed five per cent of the last preceding valuation of the property therein for the assessment of taxes.

g: In the bonds or obligations of any municipal or quasi municipal corporation of this state, when such securities are a direct obligation on all the taxable property of said corporation.

Third, *a:* In the railroad bonds of this state.

b: In the first mortgage bonds of any completed railroads of the states of New Hampshire, Vermont, Massachusetts, Rhode Island, Connecticut, New York, New Jersey, Pennsylvania, Maryland, Ohio, Indiana, Kentucky, Michigan, Wisconsin, Minnesota, Iowa, Illinois, Missouri, Kansas and Nebraska.

c: In the first mortgage bonds of the Central Pacific, Union Pacific and Northern Pacific railroads.

d: In the mortgage bonds of any railroad leased to any dividend paying railroad in New England upon terms guaranteeing the payment of a regular stated dividend upon the stock of such leased road and the interest on its bonds.

e: Street railroad companies are not railroad companies within the meaning of the foregoing clauses of this section.

f: In the bonds of street railroads constructed in this state prior to April twenty-seven, eighteen hundred ninety-five, and in the bonds of street railroads in this state constructed after said date and in the first mortgage bonds of any completed street railroad in the states of New Hampshire, Vermont, Massachusetts, Rhode Island, Connecticut, New York, New Jersey, Pennsylvania, Maryland, Ohio, Indiana, Kentucky, Michigan, Wisconsin, Minnesota, Iowa, Illinois, Missouri, Kansas and Nebraska; provided that in the case of street railroads constructed in this state after April twenty-seven, eighteen hundred and ninety-five, and in the case of street railroads in the states above named, an amount of capital stock equal to thirty-three and one-third per cent of the mortgage debt shall have been paid in, in cash, and expended upon the road evidenced by a certificate of the railroad commissioners of the state where the road is located, filed in the office of the secretary of state of this state, that said percentage has been so paid in and expended in addition to the amount of the bonded debt; provided, that in such of the above states as have no railroad commissioners having supervision of street railroads the bank examiner of this state may ascertain the facts and if they meet the foregoing requirement may file certificate thereof with the secretary of state, and all the expenses and compensation of the bank examiner for such service shall be paid by the railroad company seeking to make its bonds a legal investment under this section, whether the same are admitted or not.

Fourth: In the mortgage bonds of any water company in the New England states actually engaged in supplying any city or cities, town or towns, village or villages, or other municipal corporations with water for domestic use and for the extinguishment of fires, whenever such company is earning more than its fixed charges and interest on its debts and its running expenses.

Fifth: In bonds of any corporation other than railroad and water companies, incorporated under the authority of this state, which are earning and are paying a regular dividend of not less than five per cent a year.

Sixth, *a:* In the stock of any bank or banking association incorporated under the authority of this state.

b: In the stock of any bank or banking association incorporated under the authority of the United States, if located within the New England states.

c: In the stock of any railroad company of this state unencumbered by mortgage.

d: In the stock of any dividend paying railroad in New England.

e: In the stock of any railroad leased to any dividend paying railroad in New England upon terms guaranteeing the payment of a regular stated dividend upon the stock of such leased road and the interest on its bonds.

f: In the stock of any corporation, other than railroad and water companies, incorporated under authority of this state which earns and is paying a regular dividend of not less than five per cent a year.

Sixth, *a:* In loans secured by first mortgages of real estate in this state and New Hampshire to an amount not exceeding sixty per cent of the value of such real estate.

b: In notes with a pledge as collateral of any public funds or bonds of any kind, or of any stocks, which the bank or institution would, by this section, be authorized to purchase.

c: In notes with a pledge as collateral of any savings bank deposit book issued by any savings bank in this state.

d: In notes with a pledge as collateral of the stock of any railroad or railroads mentioned in this section, to an amount not exceeding seventy-five per cent of the market value of such stock.

e: In loans to any municipal corporation in this state.

f: In loans secured by a mortgage of such personal property as in the judgment of the trustees it is safe and for the interest of the bank to accept.

g: In loans to any corporation owning real estate in this state and actually conducting in this state the business for which such corporation was created.

Seventh, *a:* The term 'net municipal indebtedness of counties' as used in this section shall be construed to include all bonds which are a direct obligation of the county, less the amount of any sinking fund available in reduction of such debt.

b: The term 'net municipal indebtedness of cities and districts' as used in this section shall be construed to include in the case of either, not only all bonds which are a direct obligation of the cities but also all bonds of the districts or boards within the same as above enumerated, exclusive of any such debt created for a water supply and of the amount of any sinking fund available in reduction of such debt.

c: The number of inhabitants of cities and counties shall be determined by the last previous official census thereof as established by the last United States or state census, or city or county census taken in the same manner as United States or state census, and duly certified to by the clerk or treasurer of such city or the auditor or treasurer of such county.

Eighth: All investments shall be charged and entered on the books of the bank at their cost to the bank, or at par when a premium is paid.'

Approved March 28, 1903.

Chapter 191.

An Act to amend Section forty-eight of Chapter two hundred eighty-four of the Public Laws of eighteen hundred and ninety-one, entitled "An Act to consolidate and simplify the laws pertaining to Sea and Shore Fisheries as contained in Chapter forty of the Revised Statutes" and in amendments and additions thereto.

Be it enacted by the Senate and House of Representatives in Legislature assembled, as follows:

Section 48 of chapter 284, public laws of 1901, amended.

Section 1. That section forty-eight of chapter two hundred eighty-four of the public laws of nineteen hundred and one, are hereby amended by striking out the word "fifteenth" in the twenty-sixth line and inserting therefor the word 'thirtieth,' so that said section as amended will read as follows:

—close time for smelts betwen April and October 1.

—penalty for violation.

—weirs shall be open and nets removed by April 1.

—penalty.

'No smelts shall be taken or fished for in tidal waters except by hook and line between the first days of April and October under a penalty of not less than ten nor more than thirty dollars for each offense, and a further penalty of twenty cents for each smelt so taken, and all weirs for the capture of smelts shall be open and so remain, and all nets used in the smelt and tom cod fishery shall be taken from the water on or before the first day of April under a penalty of not less than twenty nor more than fifty dollars and a further fine of five dollars for each day that any such weir or net remains in violation of law. But weirs with catch pounds covered with nets, the meshes of which are one inch square in the clear, or greater, are not subject to this section. But no smelts caught in such weirs after the first day of April shall be sold or offered for sale in this state nor shall smelts caught in any manner between the first day of April and the first day of October following be offered for sale, sold, or shipped from the state under a penalty of twenty-five dollars for each offense, provided, however, that dip nets may be used between the first day of April and the first day of May and all smelts caught by dip nets between said days may be lawfully offered for sale and sold in this state. provided further that this section does not apply to smelts taken in the Androscoggin river above the Merrymeeting bay bridge between the first days of October and November. Nor to smelts taken in the Penobscot river and its tributaries between the first and thirtieth days of April. Nor to smelts taken in Casco bay between the fifteenth day of September and the first day of October, nor to smelts taken in Taunton bay between the first day of April and the first day of May nor smelts taken in Little Kennebec bay, so called, in the county of Washington between the first day of April and the first day of May.'

—dip nets may be used between April 1 and May 1.

—partial exception on Androscoggin river.

—on Penobscot river.

—on Casco bay.

—on Taunton bay.

—on Little Kennebec bay.

Section 2. This act shall take effect when approved.

Approved March 28, 1903.

Chapter 192.

An Act to make valid the Elections of Treasurers and Collectors of Taxes, held during the month of March in the year one thousand nine hundred and three.

Be it enacted by the Senate and House of Representatives in Legislature assembled, as follows:

Section 1. All elections of treasurers and collectors of taxes in the several cities, towns and plantations held during the month of March in the year one thousand nine hundred and three are hereby confirmed and made valid, and the persons so elected may hold and exercise the duties of their respective offices during the terms for which they were chosen, notwithstanding the provisions of the act approved March four, nineteen hundred and three, entitled "An Act to amend section twelve of chapter three of the revised statutes as amended by chapter three hundred thirty-five of the public laws of eighteen hundred and eighty-five and to repeal conflicting statutes, relating to the election of collectors of taxes."

Section 2. This act shall take effect when approved.

Approved March 28, 1903.

Elections of treasurers and collectors of taxes, held during March 1903, made valid.

Chapter 193.

An Act relating to the powers and duties of Administrators, de bonis non.

Be it enacted by the Senate and House of Representatives in Legislature assembled, as follows:

An administrator de bonis non shall have the power, and it shall be his duty, to collect and receive from his predecessor or his heirs, executors or administrators, and from all other sources, all the property and assets of the estate of the deceased, including the proceeds from the sale of real estate, not already distributed, and shall account for and distribute the same as though he were the original administrator or executor; and all sums recovered on any probate bond shall be a part of the estate, but so much thereof as is recovered on any real estate bond shall be distributed as is provided for the distribution of the proceeds of the sale of real estate.

Approved March 28, 1903.

Administrator de bonis non shall collect property of the deceased, from predecessor.

Chapter 194.

An Act to abolish Issuing separate Executions for Costs, by Disclosure Commissioners.

Be it enacted by the Senate and House of Representatives in Legislature assembled, as follows:

Separate execution for costs shall not be issued.

—exception.

Section 1. No separate execution for costs or for costs and fees, in disclosure proceedings, shall be issued against any judgment debtor by any disclosure commissioner or by any commissioner or magistrate authorized to hear disclosures, except as hereafter provided; but when the petitioner recovers costs or costs and fees against the judgment debtor, either on hearing, default, or otherwise, the commissioner or magistrate shall tax such costs or costs and fees in detail, and make a record thereof, and under his hand and official seal shall indorse upon or annex to the execution in force at the time of disclosure, hearing or default, a certificate certifying that the petitioner has recovered costs or costs and fees and stating therein, in detail, the costs or costs and fees recovered, and also the date of such recovery. A copy of said certificate shall be indorsed upon or annexed to every subsequent execution issued upon the same judgment, or upon any judgment founded thereon. Costs or costs and fees recovered, taxed and certified, as aforesaid, shall be deemed a part of the original judgment for costs recovered against the judgment debtor.

Executions issued prior to this enactment may be renewed.

Section 2. Any and all separate executions for costs or for costs and fees, legally issued by any disclosure commissioner or magistrate, before this act takes effect, may be renewed as now provided by law.

Section 3. All acts and parts of acts inconsistent with this act, are hereby repealed.

Section 4. This act shall take effect on the first day of January, nineteen hundred and four.

Approved March 28, 1903.

BURIAL OF WIDOWS. 159

CHAP. 195

Chapter 195.

An Act to amend Chapter thirty-three of the Public Laws of eighteen hundred and eighty-seven, relating to the Burial of Widows of Soldiers in Certain Cases.

Be it enacted by the Senate and House of Representatives in Legislature assembled, as follows:

Section 1. Section one of chapter thirty-three of the public laws of the year eighteen hundred and eighty-seven is hereby amended by inserting before the word "such" in the sixth line of said section the following: {Section 1 of chapter 33, public laws of 1887, amended.}

'Or whenever the widow of any person who served in the army, navy or marine corps of the United States during the rebellion, and was honorably discharged therefrom, shall die, being at the time of her death a resident of this state and being in destitute circumstances, and having no kindred living within this state and of sufficient ability legally liable for her support, the state shall pay the necessary expenses of her burial;' so that said section as amended shall read as follows:

'Section 1. Whenever any person who served in the army, navy or marine corps of the United States during the rebellion, and was honorably discharged therefrom shall die, being at the time of his death a resident of this state and being in destitute circumstances the state shall pay the necessary expenses of his burial; or whenever the widow of any person who served in the army, navy or marine corps of the United States during the rebellion, and was honorably discharged therefrom shall die, being at the time of her death a resident of this state and being in destitute circumstances and having no kindred living within this state and of sufficient ability legally liable for her support, the state shall pay the necessary expenses of her burial; such expenses shall not exceed the sum of thirty-five dollars in any case, and the burial shall be in some cemetery not used exclusively for the burial of the pauper dead.' {State shall pay burial expenses of destitute soldiers and sailors.} {—burial of widow.}

Section 2. Section two of chapter thirty-three of the public laws of the year eighteen hundred and eighty-seven is hereby amended by adding at the end of said section the following: {Section 2 of chapter 33, public laws of 1887, amended.}

'Or the widow of an honorably discharged soldier or sailor and in destitute circumstances, and having no kindred of sufficient ability, resident in this state legally liable for her burial expenses.' So that said section as amended shall read as follows:

'Section 2. The municipal officers of cities and towns in which such deceased had his residence at the time of his death, shall pay the expenses of his burial, and if he die in an unincorporated place, the town charged with the support of paupers in such {Cities and towns shall be reimbursed such expenses.}

unincorporated place, shall pay the expenses of his burial, and in either case upon satisfactory proof by such town or city to the governor and council of the fact of such death and payment, the governor shall authorize the state treasurer to refund said town or city the amount so paid, said proof shall contain a certificate from the post commander of the post of the Grand Army of the Republic, located nearest the town or city which paid said burial expenses, stating that such person was an honorably discharged soldier or sailor and in destitute circumstances; or the widow of an honorably discharged soldier or sailor and in destitute circumstances, and having no kindred of sufficient ability, resident in this state legally liable for her burial expenses.'

—burial of widow.

Section 3. This act shall take effect when approved.

Approved March 28, 1908.

Chapter 196.

An Act in relation to Lime and Lime Casks.

Be it enacted by the Senate and House of Representatives in Legislature assembled, as follows:

Inspector of lime casks shall be appointed by the governor.
—tenure.
—shall be sworn and give bond.

Section 1. The governor, with the advice and consent of the council shall appoint in each town where lime is manufactured, one resident citizen thereof to be inspector of lime casks therein for four years and until his successor is appointed and qualified, unless sooner removed. He shall be sworn and give bond with sufficient sureties for the faithful performance of his duties before entering thereon to the treasurer of his county, in the following sums: The inspector of Rockland, five thousand dollars; of Thomaston and Rockport, three thousand dollars each; and of every other town, two thousand dollars each, to be approved by the county commissioners; and each lime manufacturer shall designate to the inspector one or more persons to act as deputy inspector for lime casks used by him, from which number the inspector shall appoint as many deputies as are necessary, who shall be sworn and give bond to the treasurer of the county in like manner as his principal in the sum of one thousand dollars. Such deputy shall have sole inspection of lime casks on the premises of the manufacturer by whom he is designated.

—deputy inspector.

Requirements in making of lime casks.

Section 2. Lime casks shall be made of sound and seasoned sawed timber in a workmanlike manner and kiln dried or well fired on the inside, with staves not less than twenty-nine inches in length and three-eighths of an inch thick on the thinnest edge; heads not less than five-eighths of an inch thick and fifteen and one-half inches in diameter when dry and well crozed in; good and strong hoops of oak, ash, beech, birch, maple, cherry or elm wood, not less than one inch wide in the narrowest part and not less than eight in number except when two or more hoops of uniform shape throughout not less than one and one-fourth inches wide are used, the whole number may be reduced to six; each cask shall be not less than twenty-five inches in length between the heads, fifteen and one-fourth inches in width between the chimes and seventeen inches in the clear on the inside at the bilge. No lime casks or barrels to contain lime shall be manufactured and no lime shall be put up for sale in casks or barrels less in size than herein provided and unless made in accordance with this section.

Section 3. All packages containing lime shall have conspicuously on the outside thereof in distinct and plain letters the full name, or initials of the christian name and full surname of the manufacturer followed by the letters "Man'r" with the name of the place or particular locality where manufactured. Nowhere, on any such package shall appear the name, an abbreviation of the name, or any imitation of any name or abbreviation of the name of any city or town, other than that in which the lime contained in such package is manufactured. *Name of manufacturer of lime shall be placed on package.*

Section 4. Every lime manufacturer shall on the first day of January of each year make to the inspector of lime casks in the town where the lime is manufactured, a return, showing the whole amount of lime manufactured by him, the amount put up in packages, and the kind, number and size of such packages and the amount sold or shipped in bulk. *Manufacturers shall annually make returns to inspector of casks.*

Section 5. It shall be the duty of the lime inspectors and their deputies to inspect all lime casks and see that in all respects the provisions of this act are complied with, and for the purpose of performing such duties they shall have the right to stop and inspect casks in transit or offered for sale. They shall be responsible to any person injured by their misconduct, or their failure to perform their official duty, and when judgment is recovered against the inspector or deputy on account of any misdoings in his office and the execution is returned unsatisfied the creditor may avail himself of the benefit of the inspector's or deputy's bond, a copy of which shall be given him on request, in like proceedings as a party injured by the misdoing of a sheriff may avail himself of the bond of such sheriff. *Duties of lime inspectors.* *—may stop casks in transit.*

Section 6. That part of section twenty-four, chapter one hundred sixteen of the revised statutes, under heading "Lime" shall be amended so as to read as follows: For every ordinary cask of lime, and every two hundred pounds of lime put up in *Section 24 of chapter 116, R. S., amended.* *—fees to be paid to inspectors.*

CHAP. 197

barrels and packages other than ordinary casks the manufacturer shall pay to the inspector of lime casks in his town at the time the return thereof is required to be made, one-half of one mill, and in addition shall pay deputy inspectors who inspect the casks used by such manufacturer; and the inspectors and deputies may recover their fees in an appropriate action.

Penalty for violation.

Section 7. Any person convicted of any violation of the provisions of this act shall be punished by fine not exceeding fifty dollars for each offense.

Sections 1, 2, 3, 4, 5, and 6 of chapter 39, R. S., repealed.

Section 8. Sections one, two, three, four, five and six of chapter thirty-nine of the revised statutes are hereby repealed.

Inspectors already appointed shall continue till end of term for which appointed.

Section 9. Inspectors and deputy inspectors appointed and qualified under section one, chapter thirty-nine of the revised statutes shall continue as inspectors and deputies under this act for the times for which they were severally appointed.

Approved March 28, 1903.

Chapter 197.

An Act to amend Section twelve and following Sections of Chapter forty-three of the Revised Statutes, in relation to Meridian Lines and a Standard of Length.

Be it enacted by the Senate and House of Representatives in Legislature assembled, as follows:

Section 1. Section twelve of chapter forty-three of the revised statutes and the subsequent sections of said chapter are hereby amended so as to read as follows:

County commissioners shall erect and maintain meridian line.

'Section 12. The county commissioners, at the expense of their several counties, shall erect and forever maintain therein, at such place or places remote from electrical disturbances as the public convenience requires, a true meridian line to be perpetuated by stone pillars with brass or copper points firmly fixed on the tops thereof, indicating the true range of such meridian;

—record to be kept by clerk of courts.

and shall protect the same and provide a book of records to be kept by the clerk of courts, or by a person appointed by them nearer to such structure, and accessible to all persons wishing to refer thereto.

Clerk of courts shall have care and custody of.

Section 13. Such structures shall be under the care and custody of such clerks; and any surveyor residing in said county or engaged in surveying therein, shall have free access thereto for the purpose of testing the variation of the magnetic needle.

Surveyors shall annually verify compass.

Section 14. When such meridian lines have been established and completed every land surveyor shall, at least annually before making any survey, test and verify his compass, or other instrument using the magnetic needle, by the meridian line so established in the county where his surveys are to be made, and shall enter the declination of such needle from the true meridian in the book mentioned in section twelve, together with the style and make of such instrument and its number, if any, and the date and hour of observation, and subscribe his name thereto for future reference; and shall insert corresponding entries as to date and declination, in his field note books, which field note books shall also show dates at which his surveys are made. Neglect or refusal to comply with the terms of this section shall render such surveyor liable to a penalty of twenty-five dollars for each neglect, to be recovered on complaint in the county where any survey is made, half to the complainant and half to the county.

—shall record declination of needle, etc.

—shall enter same in field note book.

—penalty for neglect.

The provisions of this section shall not apply to such surveys as are made by angles from some fixed, permanent line, or by a solar instrument and independent of the magnetic needle.

—exception.

Section 15. The county commissioners at the expense of the several counties shall also erect and forever maintain therein, at such place or places as the public convenience may require, a standard of length of not less than one hundred feet, with suitable subdivisions marked thereon.

County commissioners shall erect and maintain standard of length.

Such standard may consist of stone monuments permanently fixed with metal plates on the tops thereof, properly marked and protected; or of a steel bar of the necessary length properly marked and suitably placed and protected. All such standards shall be made to correspond with the standard of the United States Bureau of Weights and Measures, and shall be provided with proper means for determining the tension of tapes or chains during comparison.

—monuments to be stone or steel.

Such standards shall be under the care and custody of the clerk of courts, who shall keep a suitable book for the record of comparisons.

—clerk of courts shall have care and custody of standards.

Such standard shall be accessible to any person for comparing any tape, chain, or other linear measure.

—standards shall be accessible.

Every surveyor shall before making surveys in this state, and at least annually, compare his tape or chain used in such surveys with the standard in the county in which he resides or in which surveys are to be made; and shall record the result in the book provided for that purpose, giving description of such tape or chain, with the difference, if any, between the same and such standard, together with the date and temperature and the tension on such tape or chain at the time of comparison. When such standard shall have been completed in any county, any surveyor

—surveyor shall annually compare tape or chain with standard.

—shall record result.

—penalty for neglect.

CHAP. 197

Penalty for injuring meridian lines.

residing or making surveys in such county who shall neglect or refuse to comply with the terms of this section, shall be liable to the penalties and disability set forth in section fourteen of this chapter.

Section 16. Whoever wilfully displaces, alters, defaces, breaks, or otherwise injures any of the pillars or points, plates, enclosures, bars, locks, bolts, or any part of the structure of any meridian line or standard of length shall forfeit not exceeding one hundred dollars, to be recovered by indictment, half to the prosecutor and half to the county, and shall also be liable in an action of debt for the amount necessarily expended in repairing damages caused by his act.

Governor and council to appoint commission to verify meridians.

Section 17. When such meridian line or standard of length is established, repaired or rebuilt in any county, the governor and council shall appoint a competent commissioner, not necessarily a resident of this state, to inspect and verify the same. Such commissioner shall in case of a meridian line verify the same by astronomical observation, and in his report shall give an accurate description of such structures, its latitude and longitude, and the declination of the needle at the time; and in case of a standard of length shall give a description of the structure, its location and exact length as determined by comparison with some authentic standard from the United States Bureau of Weights and Measures. All such reports shall be full and accurate and be deposited in the office of the secretary of state, and a certified copy shall be filed and recorded in the office of the clerk of the courts in the county where such structure is situated.

—**compensation of commissioner.**

Such commissioner shall receive from the state such just compensation as the governor and council shall allow.

Approved March 28, 1903.

Chapter 198.

An Act to amend Chapter eighty-seven of the Revised Statutes as amended by Chapter two hundred and eighteen of the Public Laws of eighteen hundred and ninety-three, Chapter one hundred and thirty-three of the Public Laws of eighteen hundred and ninety-five, and Chapter one hundred and twenty of the Public Laws of eighteen hundred and ninety-nine, and Section ninety-two of Chapter eighty-one of the Revised Statutes, relating to the limitations of actions against Executors and Administrators.

Be it enacted by the Senate and House of Representatives in Legislature assembled, as follows:

Section 1. Section twelve of chapter eighty-seven of the revised statutes as amended by chapter one hundred and twenty of the public laws of eighteen hundred and ninety-nine is hereby amended so as to read as follows: *[Section 12 of chapter 87, R. S., as amended by chapter 190, public laws of 1899, further amended.]*

'Section 12. All claims against estates of deceased persons, except for legacies and distributive shares, shall be presented to the executor or administrator in writing, or filed in the probate court, supported by an affidavit of the claimant, or of some other person cognizant thereof either before or within eighteen months after affidavit has been filed in the probate court that notice has been given by said executor or administrator of his appointment, and no action shall be commenced against such executor or administrator on any such claim until thirty days after the presentation or filing of such claim as above provided. Any claim not so presented or filed shall be forever barred against the estate, except as provided in sections thirteen, fourteen, sixteen and nineteen of chapter eighty-seven. *[Claims against estates shall be filed in writing, with affidavit.] [—claims barred, when.]*

Actions against executors or administrators, on such claims, if brought within one year after notice is given by them of their appointment, shall be continued, without costs to either party, until said year expires and be barred by a tender of the debt within the year, except, actions on claims not affected by the insolvency of the estate, and actions on appeals from commissioners of insolvency or other commissioners appointed by the judge of probate. No action shall be maintained against an executor or administrator on a claim or demand against the estate, except for legacies and distributive shares, and except as provided in sections thirteen and fifteen, unless commenced within eighteen months after affidavit has been filed in the probate court as provided in section forty of chapter sixty-four of the revised statutes. *[—continuance of actions, if brought within one year after notice, to be continued without costs.]*

Executors or administrators residing out of the state at the time of giving notice of their appointment, shall appoint an agent or attorney in the state, and insert therein his name and address. Executors or administrators, removing from the state, *[—executors residing out of state shall appoint agent in the state.]*

SALARY.

CHAP. 199

after giving notice of their appointment, shall appoint an agent or attorney in the state and give public notice thereof; service made on such agent or attorney has the same effect as if made on such executor or administrator. When an executor or administrator, residing out of the state, has no agent or attorney in the state, service may be made on one of his sureties with the same effect as if made on him.'

Section 92 of chapter 81, R. S., amended.

Section 2. Section ninety-two of chapter eighty-one of the revised statutes is hereby amended so as to read as follows:

Provisions in case of death of either party before suit is commenced.

'Section 92. If a person entitled to bring, or liable to any action before mentioned, dies before or within thirty days after the expiration of the time herein limited therefor, and the cause of action survives, the action may be commenced by the executor or administrator at any time within eighteen months after his appointment, and not afterwards, if barred by the other provisions hereof; actions on such claims may be commenced against the executor or administrator, after one year or within one year subject to continuance without costs and within eighteen months after affidavit has been filed in the probate office that notice of his appointment has been given by him, and not afterwards, if barred by the other provisions hereof, except as provided in sections thirteen and fifteen of chapter eighty-seven.'

Pending actions excepted from provisions of this act.

Section 3. This act shall not apply to any pending action nor to any cause of action against estates in which administration has already been granted.

Section 4. This act shall take effect when approved.

Approved March 28, 1903.

Chapter 199.

An Act to increase the Salary of the County Attorney of Sagadahoc County.

Be it enacted by the Senate and House of Representatives in Legislature assembled, as follows:

Salary of county attorney of Sagadahoc county, fixed.

Section 1. On and after January one, nineteen hundred and four, the salary of the county attorney of Sagadahoc county shall be six hundred dollars per annum, payable in quarterly payments, instead of the sum now established by law.

Section 2. This act shall take effect when approved.

Approved March 28, 1903.

Chapter 200.

An Act establishing the Salary of the County Attorney for the County of Washington.

Be it enacted by the Senate and House of Representatives in Legislature assembled, as follows:

Section 1. The county attorney for the county of Washington shall receive an annual salary from the treasury of state, of seven hundred and fifty dollars, payable quarterly on the first days of January, April, July and October in each year, beginning on the first day of April, one thousand nine hundred and three, instead of the salary now provided by law.

Section 2. All acts and parts of acts, inconsistent with this act, are hereby repealed.

Approved March 28, 1903.

Chapter 201.

An Act in relation to Railroad Surveys.

Be it enacted by the Senate and House of Representatives in Legislature assembled, as follows:

Section 1. Any person who shall wilfully or maliciously disturb, remove or destroy any transit point, or benchmarks of any railroad location or survey, shall be punished by a fine not exceeding twenty-five dollars, or imprisonment not exceeding thirty days; and shall in addition be liable in an action of debt for the amount of damage done.

Section 2. This act shall take effect when approved.

Approved March 28, 1903.

Chapter 202.

An Act to establish the Salary of the Judge of Probate in the County of Washington.

Be it enacted by the Senate and House of Representatives in Legislature assembled, as follows:

Section 1. The judge of probate for the county of Washington shall receive an annual salary of eight hundred dollars, instead of the sum now fixed by law, which shall be paid to him out of the county treasury in equal quarterly payments.

Section 2. This act shall take effect when approved.

Approved March 28, 1903.

Chapter 203.

An Act to provide for the Preservation of Town Records of births, marriages and deaths, previous to the year eighteen hundred and ninety-two.

Be it enacted by the Senate and House of Representatives in Legislature assembled, as follows:

Secretary of state shall purchase 500 copies of records of births, marriages and deaths, when conditions have been complied with.

Section 1. Whenever the record of the births, marriages, and deaths, previous to the year eighteen hundred and ninety-two, beginning at the very earliest date, of any town in this state, shall be collected from church records, church registers, records, of clergymen, family bibles, public records and other available sources, and shall be printed and verified in the manner required by the standing committee of the Maine Historical Society, under the editorship of some person selected by said committee, whose services shall be rendered free and without any compensation, and the work shall appear to them to have been prepared with accuracy, the secretary of state shall purchase five hundred copies of such record at a price not exceeding one cent per page; provided, that the written copies of the town records shall become the property of the state, and shall be deposited in the office of the state registrar of vital statistics; and provided, further, that not more than five hundred dollars shall be expended by authority of this act in any one year.

—price.

—proviso.

Distribution of volumes.

Section 2. The volumes purchased, as aforesaid shall be distributed by the state registrar aforesaid as follows: one copy to the office of secretary of state; one copy to the state librarian; one copy to the free public library of each town and city of the state; one copy to each state and territorial library in the United States; one copy to the library of congress; one copy to each incorporated historical society in the state; one copy to the library of each college in the state; and one copy to each registry of deeds. The remainder shall be placed in the state library for the purpose of exchange.

Approved March 28, 1903.

Chapter 204.

An Act to amend Section four of Chapter ninety-one of the Revised Statutes, relating to Notice of Foreclosure on a mortgage of Personal Property.

Be it enacted by the Senate and House of Representatives in Legislature assembled, as follows:

Section four of chapter ninety-one of the revised statutes is hereby amended by inserting in the fifth line thereof after the word "mortgagor" the following words 'cannot be found by reasonable diligence or,' so that said section as amended, shall read as follows: *Section 4 of chapter 91, R. S., amended.*

'Section 4. The mortgagee or his assignee, after condition broken, may give to the mortgagor or his assignee, when his assignment is recorded where the mortgage is recorded, written notice of his intention to foreclose the same, by leaving a copy thereof with the mortgagor or such assignee, or if the mortgagor cannot be found by reasonable diligence or is out of the state, although resident therein, by leaving such copy at his last and usual place of abode, or by publishing it once a week, for three successive weeks in one of the principal newspapers published in the town where the mortgage is recorded. When the mortgagor or his assignee of record is not a resident of the state and no newspaper is published in such town, such notice may be published in any newspaper printed in the county where the mortgage is recorded.' *Notice of foreclosure, how to be given and served.*

Approved March 28, 1903.

Chapter 205.

An Act to increase and fix the salary of the Assistant Librarian.

Be it enacted by the Senate and House of Representatives in Legislature assembled, as follows:

Section 1. The state librarian shall appoint one assistant who shall perform the duties prescribed by him, and shall give bond to the librarian for the faithful performance of the same. The assistant librarian shall receive a salary of twelve hundred dollars, per year, beginning January one, nineteen hundred and three, in full for all of his services of every name and nature. *Salary of assistant librarian.*

Section 2. All acts or parts of acts inconsistent with this act, are hereby repealed. This act shall take effect when approved.

Approved March 28, 1903.

SALARIES.

Chapter 206.

An Act relating to the salary of the County Attorney of Somerset County.

Be it enacted by the Senate and House of Representatives in Legislature assembled, as follows:

Salary of county attorney of Somerset county, fixed.

From and after the first day of January in the year of our Lord one thousand nine hundred and three, the salary of the county attorney for the county of Somerset shall be seven hundred dollars a year.

Approved March 28, 1903.

Chapter 207.

An Act to increase the salary of the County Attorney of Piscataquis County.

Be it enacted by the Senate and House of Representatives in Legislature assembled, as follows:

Salary of county attorney of Piscataquis county, fixed.

Section 1. From and after the first day of January in the year of our Lord one thousand nine hundred and three, the salary of the county attorney for the county of Piscataquis shall be six hundred dollars a year.

Section 2. This act shall take effect when approved.

Approved March 28, 1903.

Chapter 208.

An Act relating to the Salary of the Register of Probate of Sagadahoc County.

Be it enacted by the Senate and House of Representatives in Legislature assembled, as follows:

Salary of register of probate, Sagadahoc county, fixed.

Section 1. On and after the first day of January, in the year of our Lord, nineteen hundred and three, the salary of the register of probate of the county of Sagadahoc shall be seven hundred dollars a year instead of the sum now fixed by law.

Section 2. This act shall take effect when approved.

Approved March 28, 1903.

Chapter 209.

An Act to amend Section ten of Chapter sixty of the Revised Statutes, relating to Divorce.

Be it enacted by the Senate and House of Representatives in Legislature assembled, as follows:

Section 1. Section ten of chapter sixty of the revised statutes is hereby amended by striking out all the words in said section and substituting therefor the following:

'Section 10. When a divorce is decreed to the husband for the fault of the wife, he shall be entitled to one-third, in common and undivided of all her real estate, except wild lands, which shall descend to him as if she were dead; and the court may allow him so much of her personal estate as seems reasonable. In all cases the right, title and interest of the libellee in the real estate of the libellant shall be barred by the decree.'

Section 2. This act shall take effect when approved.

Approved March 23, 1903.

Chapter 210.

An Act in relation to the Salary of the County Attorney of the County of Hancock.

Be it enacted by the Senate and House of Representatives in Legislature assembled, as follows:

Section 1. On and after the first day of January in the year of our Lord one thousand nine hundred and three, the salary of the county attorney of Hancock county shall be seven hundred and fifty dollars per annum, instead of the sum now established by law.

Section 2. This act shall take effect when approved.

Approved March 23, 1903.

Chapter 211.

An Act to amend Section one hundred seven of Chapter eleven of the Revised Statutes, relating to Normal Schools.

Be it enacted by the Senate and House of Representatives in Legislature assembled, as follows:

Section one hundred seven of chapter eleven of the revised statutes is hereby amended by striking out the word "and" in the second line of said section after the word "Castine" and before the word "the," and by adding after the word "Gorham" and before the word "shall" in the second line of said section, 'and Aroostook county normal school at Presque Isle,' so that said section as amended, shall read as follows:

'Section 107. The northern normal school at Farmington, the eastern normal school at Castine, the western normal school at Gorham, and Aroostook county normal school at Presque Isle shall be conducted for the purpose and upon the principles herein set forth.

I. They shall be thoroughly devoted to the training of teachers for their professional labors.

II. The course of study shall include the common English branches in thorough reviews, and such of the higher branches as are especially adapted to prepare teachers to conduct the mental, moral and physical education of their pupils.

III. The art of school management, including the best methods of government and instruction, shall have a prominent place in the daily exercises of said schools.

IV. Said schools, while teaching the fundamental truths of christianity, and the great principles of morality, recognized by law, shall be free from all denominational teachings, and open to persons of different religious connections on terms of equality.

V. The principals of the normal schools and of all other schools in which normal departments are supported, wholly or in part, by the state, shall keep a register containing the names of all students entering such schools or departments, the date of entering and leaving, their ages, number of days' attendance, the length of the term, a list of text-books used, and all other information required in the blanks furnished by the state superintendent. Such register and blanks shall be returned to said superintendent by the first day of each December, and the information so furnished shall appear in his annual report, for the use of the legislature.'

Section 2. This act shall take effect when approved.

Approved March 28, 1903.

Chapter 212.

An Act to amend Section sixteen of Chapter two hundred and sixty-six of the Public Laws of eighteen hundred and ninety-three, relating to the Militia.

Be it enacted by the Senate and House of Representatives in Legislature assembled, as follows:

Section sixteen of said act is hereby amended by striking out the words "in case of war, insurrection or invasion," so that said section as amended, shall read as follows:

'Section 16. The staff of the commander-in-chief shall consist of the adjutant-general, who shall be, ex-officio, chief of staff, quartermaster general and paymaster general with the rank of major general; an inspector general, with the rank of brigadier general; a commissary general, a surgeon general, a judge advocate general, and an inspector general of rifle practice, each with the rank of colonel; two aides-de-camp with the rank of lieutenant colonel, and a military secretary with the rank of major. Provided, however, that the commander-in-chief may appoint such additional staff officers as the public service shall require, and with such rank as he may designate. The staff of the commander-in-chief shall be appointed and commissioned by him and shall hold office during his pleasure and until their successors are appointed and qualified.' {Staff of commander-in-chief.} {—appointment and tenure.}

Approved March 28, 1903.

Chapter 213.

An Act for the protection of the wild Hare or Rabbit.

Be it enacted by the Senate and House of Representatives in Legislature assembled, as follows:

Section 1. There shall be a close time on wild hare or rabbits in which it shall be unlawful to hunt, catch or pursue them, or have them in possession, during the months of April, May, June, July and August of each year, under a penalty of ten dollars and costs for each offense. {Rabbits, close time on.}

Section 2. It shall be unlawful to use any snares, traps or other device in the hunting, pursuing or killing of the common wild hare or rabbits, or to hunt or kill the same except in the ordinary method of shooting with guns in the usual manner. {Manner of hunting rabbits prescribed.}

Section 3. Section two of this bill shall not apply to Hancock county.

Approved March 28, 1903.

Chapter 214.

An Act relating to Political Caucuses.

Be it enacted by the Senate and House of Representatives in Legislature assembled, as follows:

Enrollment a necessary qualification for voting at caucus.

Section 1. No person shall take part or vote in any caucus of any political party unless qualified therefor by enrollment as hereinafter provided.

Enrollment, how made.

Section 2. Any person who is a legal voter may enroll himself as a member of any political party by filing with the clerk of the town of which he is a legal voter a declaration in writing, signed by him, substantially as follows: "I,   , being a legal voter of   , hereby elect to be enrolled as a member of the   party. The following statement of name, residence, place of last enrollment if any, and party of last enrollment if any, is true."

—new enrollment.

A new enrollment may be made at any time, but the person making such new enrollment shall not vote in any political caucus within six months thereafter if he designates a different political party from that named by him in the preceding enrollment.

Clerk shall record enrollment.

Section 3. The clerk of the town where the enrollment is made, as above provided, shall receive and file the same, indorsing thereon the date of filing, and shall record the name, residence, place of last enrollment and date of filing, in a separate book for the enrollment of members of each political party, entering the names alphabetically.

—town clerks shall provide stationery.

Suitable blanks for such enrollment shall be provided by the town clerks and in addition thereto they shall provide books with proper headings, embodying the enrollment statements above provided, which the person desiring to enroll may fill out and sign, thereby enrolling himself with the same effect as by filing such enrollment paper. Such books shall be public records and shall at all times be open to public inspection.

—records shall be open to public.

—enrollment, how made during caucus.

Any voter not previously enrolled may enroll as aforesaid up to the day of holding any caucus and may enroll himself during said caucus by subscribing and making oath to the following statement before the chairman of the caucus. "I,   , do solemnly swear that I am a qualified voter in this town, or ward, and have the legal right to vote in the caucus of the   party. I am a member of that political party and intend to vote for its candidates at the election next ensuing. I have not taken part or voted at the caucus of any other political party in the six months last past."

The secretary of the caucus shall indorse thereon whether the person subscribing and swearing to the same voted in said caucus, and within one week thereafter the secretary shall return said statement with the indorsement thereon to the clerk of the town wherein such caucus is held, and said clerk shall thereupon enroll said voter in the enrollment list of the party designated by him. Said statement shall be preserved as public records and shall be prima facie evidence in any court that said person took said oath and voted in said caucus. *—duty of secretary of caucus, when enrollment is made in caucus.*

Section 5. To facilitate the first enrollment under this act the town committees of each political party shall, on or before January first, nineteen hundred and four, file with the town clerk a list of the legal voters in their respective towns, who are believed by them to be members of their party, giving the exact residence of said voter as near as may be, and such description of said voters, if necessary, as will serve to identify them, and the same shall constitute a legal enrollment under the provisions of this act, of all voters appearing upon the list of only one of such committees, and not otherwise enrolled, and the clerk shall record the same as required in section three with the same effect as if made pursuant to the provisions of section two. But the same may be annulled by the personal enrollment of the voter under the provisions of sections two or four. *Preliminary enrollment by town committees of each political party.*

Section 6. Caucuses and meetings of political parties held for the purpose of nominating candidates or choosing delegates to assemble in convention to nominate any person to any public office whose name shall be placed on the final ballot, unless held under the provisions of this act are hereby declared to be unlawful, and no political party shall have its political ticket placed on the final ballot unless the nominations of its candidates are made in accordance with the provisions of this act, provided that this shall not be construed as preventing citizens' caucuses. *Caucuses must be held under provisions of this act.* *—exceptions.*

Section 7. All votes for the election of delegates to any political convention for the nomination of a candidate for any public office shall be by ballot, written or printed, on plain paper. *Votes for election of delegates shall be by written or printed ballot.*

Section 8. No person shall vote or offer to vote more than once for any candidate or delegate or set of delegates in any one caucus, nor shall he vote or offer to vote in any one caucus held in any caucus district in which he shall not at the same time be a legal voter. No person shall vote or offer to vote in any caucus where candidates or delegates are to be chosen, if he has already voted at the caucus of any other political party in the past six months. *Restrictions on voting.*

Section 9. No person whose right to vote is challenged shall be allowed to vote until he shall have taken the following oath, which shall be administered by the chairman of the caucus: *Oath to be taken by challenged voters.*

"You do solemnly swear that you are a registered voter in this town or ward, and have the legal right to vote in this caucus; that you are a member of the political party holding the same and intend to vote for its candidates at the election next ensuing, and that you have not taken part or voted at the caucus of any other political party in the six months last past." The secretary of the caucus shall make a record of the administration of such oath, as provided in section four of this act, and with the same effect.

Notices of caucuses shall be issued seven days prior to caucuses.

Section 10. Notices of caucuses, signed by the chairman and secretary, shall be issued by each town committee not less than seven days prior to the day on which the caucuses are to be held. They shall be conspicuously posted in at least five places on the highways of each voting precinct, and shall state the place, day and hour of holding such caucuses. In case voting is by check list a sufficient time shall be allowed for all to vote, and the call for the caucus shall state the hours fixed by the committee for the opening and closing of the polls.

Bribery forbidden.

Section 11. No person shall pay or offer to pay to any voter any pecuniary compensation for said voters vote, or to influence his action at any caucus held under the provisions of this act.

Check lists, provisions as to use of.

Section 12. Voting lists as used in the election next preceding any caucus, shall be used as check lists, at such caucuses, if the town committee shall so determine and provide in the call, and such committee shall be required to provide for the use of such list upon written request, filed with the chairman or clerk of the committee, at any time before the call is posted, of voters of the party, to the number of not less than ten in towns of less than two thousand inhabitants; of not less than twenty in towns of two thousand and not exceeding five thousand; and of not less than fifty in towns of five thousand or more inhabitants, according to the last official census of the United States.

It shall be the duty of the officials having charge of such voting lists to furnish certified copies thereof for use in caucuses, upon application of such party committee, the expense thereof to be paid as other expenses of registration are now paid.

No person shall be deprived of his right to vote in such caucus by reason of the fact that his name does not appear on such lists if he shall have become a legally qualified voter of such precinct subsequent to the last election, and shall be otherwise qualified to vote as herein provided.

Penalty for violation of provisions of this act.

Section 13. Any person who violates any of the provisions hereof, or refuses to perform any duty required hereunder, or makes a wilfully false statement of fact in his declaration of enrollment, shall be punished by a fine not exceeding five hundred dollars, or by imprisonment not exceeding six months.

Section 14. This act shall take effect July first, nineteen hundred and three; but shall not apply to caucuses held prior to January first, nineteen hundred and four, nor shall it apply to cities of more than thirty-five thousand inhabitants, nor to cities wherein the calling and holding of caucuses are now regulated by special law until such special law is repealed.

Section 15. This act shall not apply to towns of less than two thousand inhabitants.

Approved March 28, 1903.

Chapter 215.

An Act in relation to Agricultural Societies.

Be it enacted by the Senate and House of Representatives in Legislature assembled, as follows:

Section 1. Section eleven of chapter fifty-eight of the revised statutes, as amended, is hereby amended by striking out that part of said section which relates to the Penobscot and Aroostook Union Agricultural Society, the Waldo and Penobscot Agricultural Society, and the Ossipee Valley Union Agricultural Society, and the appropriations named for each, and by other changes therein, so that said section as amended shall read as follows:

'Section 11. There shall be appropriated annually from the state treasury, beginning in nineteen hundred and four, a sum of money not exceeding one cent and one-quarter to each inhabitant of the state, which shall be divided among the legally incorporated agricultural societies of the state not provided for by special enactment, according to the amount of premiums and gratuities actually paid in full by said societies, provided, that the stipend shall herewith be based entirely upon the premiums and gratuities actually paid in full on exhibition stocks and products, and provided that no society shall receive from the state a sum greater than that actually raised and paid by the society for said purposes. Provided, also, that each of the said societies shall cause the prohibitory liquor law to be enforced on all grounds over which they have control, and not allow gambling in any form or games of chance on said grounds.'

Section 2. Section twelve of chapter fifty-eight of the revised statutes is hereby amended by striking out the words "and also a certificate from the secretary of the board of agriculture that

AGRICULTURAL SOCIETIES.

CHAP. 215

said society has complied with the requirements of section fifteen," and inserting in place thereof the following: 'and also a certificate from the commissioner of agriculture that he has examined into the claim of said society; that in his opinion it has complied with the provisions of section fifteen of this chapter; with section fourteen of this chapter as amended by section two of chapter two hundred eighty-eight of the public laws of one thousand eight hundred ninety-seven and also with section three of this act; that there has been awarded and paid by said society as premiums and gratuities a sum at least equal to the amount apportioned to said society and that the provisions in regard to gambling and the sale of intoxicating liquors have been strictly complied with,' so that said section as amended shall read as follows:

Treasurer shall file certificates with treasurer of state.

'Section 12. None of such payments shall be made to any society until the treasurer thereof files with the treasurer of the state a certificate on oath stating the amount raised by it and containing the specifications required in section fourteen; and also a certificate from the commissioner of agriculture that he has examined into the claim of said society; that in his opinion it has complied with the provisions of section fifteen of this chapter; with section fourteen of this chapter as amended by section two of chapter two hundred eighty-eight of the public laws of one thousand eight hundred ninety-seven and also with section three of this act; that there has been awarded and paid by said society as premiums and gratuities a sum at least equal to the amount apportioned to said society and that the provisions in regard to gambling and the sale of intoxicating liquors have been strictly complied with.'

Society offering premiums on grade males not entitled to stipend.

Section 3. No state stipend shall be paid to any agricultural society offering or paying premiums on grade males and the commissioner of agriculture is hereby authorized to make this a part of the sworn return to be made by the proper officers of all agricultural societies, provided that evidence as to eligibility to registration be accepted as satisfactory proof of purity of blood.

Stipend to Eastern Maine and Maine state agricultural societies, conditional.

Section 4. The payment of the state stipend to the Eastern Maine and Maine State Agricultural societies shall be conditional upon the use of the score card system in the judging of all horses, breeds of cattle, sheep and swine, and of dairy products; the cards to be used for pure bloods to be those adopted by the several breeders' associations. A copy of each score card as filled by the judge shall be delivered to the exhibitor of each individual animal judged. All county societies receiving a three hundred dollar stipend or more, shall be required to faithfully observe the same system and conditions.

Section 5. Section one of chapter one hundred and eight of the public laws of one thousand eight hundred and seventy, and all other acts and parts of acts inconsistent herewith are hereby repealed.

Section 6. This act shall take effect when approved.

Approved March 28, 1903.

Chapter 216.

An Act for the protection of Lobsters with eggs attached.

Be it enacted by the Senate and House of Representatives in Legislature assembled, as follows:

Section 1. The commissioner of sea and shore fisheries is hereby authorized and empowered to purchase at a rate not exceeding twenty-five per cent above the market price, lobsters with eggs attached, caught along the coast of Maine. Whoever catches any such lobsters with eggs attached, may safely store the same in lobster cars or sections of cars used for that purpose only, and may keep them separate from other lobsters until such time as the said commissioner or some person or persons designated by him can gather and pay for them. Said commissioner and his agent shall liberate them in the vicinity of the location where they were caught; or he may at his discretion sell any portion or all of them to the officer in charge of the United States fish hatchery for artificial propagation, the proceeds to be applied to the appropriation made for the enforcement of this act.

Section 2. The sum of seven thousand five hundred dollars, or so much thereof as may be necessary, is hereby appropriated for carrying out the provisions of this act in the year nineteen hundred and three, and five thousand dollars for the year nineteen hundred and four, to be used at the discretion of the commissioner of sea and shore fisheries.

Approved March 28, 1903.

COMMERCIAL FERTILIZERS.

CHAP. 217

Chapter 217.

An Act to amend Section four of Chapter two hundred and fifty-six of the Public Laws of eighteen hundred and ninety-three as amended by Chapter one hundred and ninety-seven of the Public Laws of eighteen hundred and ninety-seven, relating to the sale and analysis of Commercial Fertilizers.

Be it enacted by the Senate and House of Representatives in Legislature assembled, as follows:

Section 4 of chapter 256, public laws of 1893, as amended by chapter 197, public laws of 1897, further amended.

Section 1. Strike out the words "said director" in the fourth line and insert the words 'the state treasurer.' Insert after the words "receipt of" in the ninth line the words 'the treasurer's receipt for.' Strike out the words "The analysis fees received by said director shall be paid immediately by him into the treasury of said experiment station" at the end of said section and insert the following: 'Said director shall present to the governor and council itemized bills showing the cost of analyzing each sample and on approval by them a warrant shall be drawn on the treasurer for payment thereof. Such payments not to exceed in any calendar year the amount of fees received the same year.' So that said section as amended shall read as follows:

Samples of commercial fertilizer shall be deposited with director of Maine experiment station.

—fees for analysis.

'Section 4. Any manufacturer, importer, agent or seller of any commercial fertilizer, who shall deposit with the director of the Maine Experiment Station a sample or samples of fertilizer under the provisions of section two of this act, shall pay annually to the state treasurer an analysis fee as follows: ten dollars for the phosphoric acid, and five dollars each for the nitrogen and potash, contained or said to be contained in the fertilizer, this fee to be assessed on any brand sold in the state, and upon the receipt of the treasurer's receipt for such fee and of the certified statement named in section two of this act, said director shall issue a certificate of compliance with this act. Whenever the manufacturer or importer of a fertilizer shall have filed the statement made in section two of this act and paid the analysis fee, no agent or seller of said manufacturer, importer or shipper shall be required to file such statement or pay such fee. Said director shall present to the governor and council itemized bills showing the cost of analyzing each sample and on approval by them a warrant shall be drawn on the treasurer for the payment thereof. Such payments not to exceed in any calendar year the amount of fees received the same year.'

Approved March 28, 1903.

Chapter 218.

An Act to increase the Salary of the Justice of the Superior Court for the County of Cumberland.

Be it enacted by the Senate and House of Representatives in Legislature assembled, as follows:

Section 1. The salary of the justice of the superior court for the county of Cumberland is hereby fixed at the sum of three thousand dollars per year, from the first day of January, in the year of our Lord nineteen hundred and three, payable quarterly, instead of the sum now provided by law.

Section 2. This act shall take effect when approved.

Approved March 28, 1908.

Chapter 219.

An Act to amend Section one hundred twelve of Chapter eleven of the Revised Statutes, as amended by Chapter thirty-seven of the Public Laws of eighteen hundred and ninety-one, and by Chapter one hundred twenty-one of the Public Laws of eighteen hundred and ninety-five, and by Chapter three hundred eight of the Public Laws of eighteen hundred and ninety-seven, relating to Normal Schools and the Madawaska Training School.

Be it enacted by the Senate and House of Representatives in Legislature assembled, as follows:

Section 1. Section one hundred twelve of chapter eleven of the revised statutes, as amended by chapter thirty-seven of the public laws of eighteen hundred and ninety-one, and by chapter one hundred and twenty-one of the public laws of eighteen hundred and ninety-five, and by chapter three hundred and eight of the public laws of eighteen hundred and ninety-seven, is hereby further amended by inserting in place of the word "three" in the first line thereof the word 'four,' and in place of the words "thirty-one thousand dollars is annually appropriated," in the second and third lines of said section, the words 'the sum of thirty-three thousand dollars is appropriated for the year nineteen hundred three, the sum of forty thousand dollars for the year nineteen hundred four, and the sum of forty-three thousand dollars annually thereafter' so that said section as amended by this act, shall read as follows:

'Section 112. For the support of the four normal schools and the Madawaska Training School, the sum of thirty-three thousand dollars is appropriated for the year nineteen hundred three, the sum of forty thousand dollars for the year nineteen hundred four, and the sum of forty-three thousand dollars annually thereafter, to be expended under the direction of said trustees, which sum the treasurer of state shall deduct for said purpose from any school money raised for the support of common schools. The governor and council may from time to time, as they think proper, draw warrants therefor on said treasurer in favor of said trustees.'

Section 2. This act shall take effect when approved.

Approved March 28, 1903.

Chapter 220.

An Act amendatory of Chapter seventy-three, Section eight, of the Revised Statutes, relating to the recording of Deeds of Release.

Be it enacted by the Senate and House of Representatives in Legislature assembled, as follows:

Section 8, chapter 73, R. S., amended.

Section 1. Section eight of chapter seventy-three of the revised statutes is hereby amended by adding thereto the following words:

'Conveyances of the right, title or interest of the grantor, if duly recorded, shall be as effectual against prior unrecorded conveyances as if they purported to convey an actual title,' so that said section, as amended, shall read:

Not effectual unless recorded.

'Section 8. No conveyance of an estate in fee simple, or fee tail, or for life, or lease for more than seven years, is effectual against any person, except the grantor, his heirs and devisees, and persons having actual notice thereof, unless the deed is recorded as herein provided. Conveyances of the right, title or interest of the grantor, if duly recorded, shall be as effectual against prior unrecorded conveyances, as if they purported to convey an actual title.'

—effectual, if recorded, against prior unrecorded conveyances.

Section 2. This act shall take effect January first, in the year of our Lord nineteen hundred and four.

Approved March 28, 1903.

Chapter 221.

An Act to amend Chapter ninety-six of the Public Laws of eighteen hundred ninety-nine, entitled "An Act to prevent Incompetent Persons from conducting the business of a pharmacist."

Be it enacted by the Senate and House of Representatives in Legislature assembled, as follows:

Section 1. Section two of chapter ninety-six of the public laws of eighteen hundred ninety-nine is hereby amended by striking out the whole of said section and inserting in place thereof the following: <small>Section 2, of chapter 96, public laws of 1899, amended.</small>

'Section 2. A board of commissioners of pharmacy, consisting of three suitable persons, shall be appointed and may be removed for cause by the governor, with the advice and consent of the council. The terms of office of said commissioners shall be so arranged that one member of said board shall be appointed annually for a term of three years from the first day of December in each year. Vacancies caused by death, resignation, removal or inability to perform the duties of the office, shall be filled by appointment for the unexpired term. The Maine Pharmaceutical Association may, at its annual meeting each year, nominate six members of said association, whose names shall be forthwith certified by the president and secretary of said association to the governor, and members of said commission, appointed during any year, shall be selected from the persons whose names are so certified for said year, unless in the opinion of the governor said persons are manifestly unsuitable or incompetent. The compensation of said commissioners of pharmacy shall be five dollars per day, for time actually employed in performance of their official duties, and they shall be paid all necessary expenses incurred therein.' <small>Commissioners of pharmacy, appointment of. —tenure. —vacancies, how filled. —compensation.</small>

Section 2. Section four of said chapter ninety-six of the public laws of eighteen hundred ninety-nine is hereby amended by striking out said section four and inserting in place thereof the following: <small>Section 4, of chapter 96, public laws of 1899, amended.</small>

'Section 4. The board shall keep a record of the names of all persons examined and registered thereunder, and a record of all moneys received and disbursed by said board, a duplicate of which records shall always be open to inspection in the office of the secretary of state. Said board shall annually in December make to the governor and council a report stating the condition of pharmacy in the state, with a full and complete record of all its official acts during the year and of the receipts and disbursements of the board to the last day of the preceding month. Said accounts shall be audited by the governor and council, and when <small>Shall keep record of persons examined and money received. —report annually. —accounts shall be audited by</small>

184 PERSONAL PROPERTY.

CHAP. 222
governor and council.

so audited and allowed by them, said board shall pay any and all balance shown by said accounts to be in its hands and possession, to the treasurer of state on or before the first day of January annually.'

Section 3. This act shall take effect when approved.

Approved March 28, 1903.

Chapter 223.

An Act to license Foreign Executors, Administrators, Guardians and Trustees to receive and dispose of Personal Property.

Be it enacted by the Senate and House of Representatives in Legislature assembled, as follows:

Foreign executors, administrators, guardians or trustees may be licensed.

Section 1. Any executor, administrator, guardian or trustee duly appointed in another state or in a foreign country and duly qualified and acting, who may be entitled to any personal estate in this state, may file an authenticated copy of his appointment in the probate court for any county in which there is real property of his trust or, if there is no such real property, in any county in which there is personal estate of his trust or to which he may be entitled, and may upon petition to said court, after notice to all persons interested, be licensed to collect and receive such personal estate or to sell by public or private sale, or otherwise to dispose of, and to transfer and convey, shares in a corporation or other personal property, if the court finds that there is no executor, administrator, guardian or trustee appointed in this state who is authorized so to collect and receive such personal estate or to dispose of such shares or other personal property, and that such foreign executor, administrator, guardian or trustee will be liable to account for such personal estate or for the proceeds thereof in the state or country in which he was appointed; and that no person resident in this state and interested as a creditor or otherwise objects to the granting of such license or appears to be prejudiced thereby; but no such license shall be granted to a foreign executor or administrator until the expiration of six months after the death of his testator or intestate.

—to collect and receive personal property.

—if no executor, etc., is appointed in this state.

Section 2. This act shall take effect when approved.

Approved March 28, 1903.

Chapter 223.

An Act relating to the Public Health.

Be it enacted by the Senate and House of Representatives in Legislature assembled, as follows:

Section 1. The state board of health is authorized to establish and equip with the proper and necessary apparatus, instruments, and supplies, a state laboratory of hygiene, for the chemical and bacteriological examination of water supplies, milk and food products, and the examination of cases and suspected cases of diphtheria, typhoid fever, tuberculosis, glanders, and other infectious and contagious diseases. *State laboratory of hygiene, authorized.*

Section 2. The state board of health shall appoint a director of such laboratory, who shall hold that position at the pleasure of said board of health. He shall keep a record of all specimens sent to him for examination, and examine these specimens without unnecessary delay, and do such other work, and make such other investigations relating to the public health as said state board of health may from time to time instruct him to do. He shall annually in the month of January make a full report to the state board of health of all matters pertaining to the laboratory, and shall make such other and special reports as the state board of health may ask for. The kind and amount of the work he shall do and the compensation therefor shall be fixed by the state board of health. *Appointment of director of laboratory. —duties of director. —shall report annually.*

Section 3. The services of the laboratory and all investigations therein made shall be free to the people of this state. *Services shall be free.*

Section 4. The sum of two thousand dollars is hereby appropriated for the purpose of procuring the proper and necessary apparatus, instruments, and other supplies for the equipment of such laboratory; and the sum of three thousand dollars per year is hereby appropriated to pay for the services of the director, and of such assistants as may be necessary, to procure the necessary supplies, and to meet the other necessary expenses of said laboratory, which sum shall be expended under the supervision of the state board of health. *Appropriation for equipment.*

Section 5. This act shall take effect when approved.

Approved March 28, 1908.

Chapter 224.

An Act relating to Treasurer and Collector of Taxes.

Be it enacted by the Senate and House of Representatives in Legislature assembled, as follows:

Treasurer and collector may be the same person.

Section 1. That the treasurer and collector of taxes of cities and towns, may be one and the same person.

Section 2. This act shall take effect when approved.

Approved March 28, 1903.

Chapter 225.

An Act to correct Clerical Errors and make plain the meaning of and amend Chapter thirty of the Revised Statutes, as amended by Chapter forty-two of the Public Laws of eighteen hundred ninety-nine, and as amended by Chapters two hundred twenty-two and two hundred seventy-eight of the Public Laws of nineteen hundred one and Chapter three hundred twenty-six of the Private and Special Laws of nineteen hundred one, and acts reported from the Committee on Inland Fisheries and Game, relating to inland fisheries and game.

Be it enacted by the Senate and House of Representatives in Legislature assembled, as follows:

Section 5 of chapter 30, R. S. as amended by chapter 42, public laws of 1899, further amended.

Section 1. Section five of chapter thirty of the revised statutes, as amended by chapter forty-two of the public laws of eighteen hundred ninety-nine. is hereby amended in the first fourteen lines of the same as follows: By inserting the word 'land' before the word "locked" in the third line of said section, and by inserting after the word "first" in the tenth line of said section the words, 'and except Sebago lake, in Cumberland county, on which the close time shall be from October first to April first, and except Wilson pond in Wilton, in Franklin county, on which the close time shall be from October first until the ice is out of said lake the following spring;' and by inserting the words 'or have the same in possession' after the word "state" in the fourteenth line of said section, so that the first fourteen lines of said section, as amended, shall read as follows:

Close time for landlocked salmon, trout, togue and white perch.

—St. Croix river.

—waters of Kennebec county.

—Franklin county.

'Section 5. There shall be an annual close time for landlocked salmon, trout, togue and white perch, as follows: for landlocked salmon, trout and togue, from the first day of October until the ice is out of the pond, lake or river fished in the following spring of each year, except on the Saint Croix river and its tributaries, and on all the waters of Kennebec county, in which the close time shall be from the fifteenth day of September until the ice is out of the ponds and lakes the following spring, and in Franklin county in which the close time shall be from

CLERICAL ERRORS CORRECTED. 187

CHAP. 225

October first till May first, and except Sebago lake, in Cumberland county, on which the close time shall be from October first to May first, and except Wilson pond in Wilton, in Franklin county, on which the close time shall be from October first until the ice is out of said lake the following spring; but for white perch, the close time shall be from the first day of April to the first day of July; no person shall take, catch, kill or fish for, in any manner, any landlocked salmon, trout, togue, or white perch in any of the waters of this state or have the same in possession, in close time.'

—Sebago lake.
—Wilson pond.

Section 2. So much of chapter thirty of the revised statutes, as amended by chapter forty-two, section five, of the public laws of eighteen hundred and ninety-nine, as closes Greely brook and tributaries, situated partly in the towns of Oxford and Norway in the county of Oxford and in the town of Otisfield in the county of Cumberland, is hereby repealed.

Portions of chapter 30, R. S., as amended by chapter 42, section 5, public laws of 1899, repealed.

Section 3. Section twenty-two of chapter thirty of the revised statutes, as amended by chapter forty-two of the public laws of eighteen hundred and ninety-nine, and as amended by chapter two hundred and twenty-two of the public laws of nineteen hundred and one, is hereby amended so as to read as follows:

Section 22 of chapter 30, R. S., as amended, further amended.

'Section 22. The words "close season" and "close time" where used in this act, shall mean the time or period during which by this act it is made unlawful to hunt, shoot, wound, trap, or destroy any bird or animal, or fish for, or catch any fish mentioned or referred to in this act, and the words "open season" where used in this act, shall mean the time or period during which it shall be lawful to take these animals, fish and birds as specified and limited.

Close season and close time defined.

Any person may, at any time, lawfully kill any dog which hunts or chases a moose, caribou or deer, or any dog kept or used for that purpose. Any person owning or having in his possession any dog for the purpose of hunting or chasing moose, caribou or deer, or who permits any dog owned by him or in his possession to hunt or chase moose, caribou or deer, after notice that such dog has chased moose, caribou or deer, shall be punished by a fine of one hundred dollars and costs of prosecution for each offense.

—deer dogs may be killed.
—penalty for having dog for purpose of hunting deer, moose, etc.

Sunday is a close time, on which it is not lawful to hunt, kill or destroy game or birds of any kind, under the penalties imposed therefor during other close time; but the penalties already imposed for the violation of the Sunday laws by the statutes of this state are not hereby repealed or diminished.'

—Sunday is close time for hunting.

Section 4. Section twenty-one of chapter thirty of the revised statutes, as amended by chapter forty-two of the public laws of

Section 21 of chapter 30, R. S., as amended,

CHAP. 225
further amended.

eighteen hundred and ninety-nine, and as amended by chapter two hundred and seventy-eight of the public laws of nineteen hundred and one is hereby amended as follows: By striking out all of said section between the word "November" in the sixth line of said section and the word "any" in the thirteenth line of said section, and inserting instead thereof the words, 'and no registered guide shall guide at the same time or be employed by, at the same time, more than five non-residents in hunting,' and by inserting after the word "deer" in the thirteenth line of said section the words, 'or moose,' and by inserting after the word "contained" in the eighteenth line of said section the words, 'or any guide who shall guide at the same time, or be employed by, at the same time, more than five non-residents in hunting,' so that said section as amended, shall read as follows:

Non-residents entering on wild lands for hunting shall be in charge of registered guide.

'Section 21. It shall be unlawful for non-residents of the state to enter upon the wild lands of the state with intent to camp and kindle fires thereon, while engaged in hunting or fishing, without being in charge of a registered guide, during the months of May, June, July, August, September, October and November, and no registered guide shall guide at the same time, or be employed by, at the same time, more than five non-residents in hunting. Any such non-resident who shall take, catch, or kill any deer or moose, or enter upon the wild lands in this state, with intent to camp and kindle fires thereon, while engaged in hunting or fishing without being in charge of a registered guide, during the months of May, June, July, August, September, October and November, in violation of the provisions herein contained, or any guide who shall guide at the same time, or be employed by, at the same time, more than five non-residents in hunting, shall be fined forty dollars and costs of prosecution for each offense and be subject to imprisonment thirty days.'

—penalty for violation of this section.

Approved March 28, 1903.

Chapter 226.

An Act in relation to the salary of the Register of Probate of the County of Hancock.

Be it enacted by the Senate and House of Representatives in Legislature assembled, as follows:

Section 1. From and after the first day of May, one thousand nine hundred and three, all fees received by the register of probate of Hancock county shall be paid over by him to the county treasurer. *Fees shall be paid to county treasurer, by register of probate.*

Section 2. The salary of the register of probate of Hancock county is hereby fixed at nine hundred dollars per year, payable quarterly. *Salary of register of probate, Hancock county, fixed.*

Section 3. This act shall take effect May first, one thousand nine hundred and three.

Approved March 28, 1903.

Chapter 227.

An Act to create the Maine Mining Bureau.

Be it enacted by the Senate and House of Representatives in Legislature assembled, as follows:

Section 1. The state land agent, the commissioner of agriculture, and the commissioner of labor, are hereby created a mining board to be known as the Maine Mining Bureau. *Maine mining bureau created.*

Section 2. The members of such bureau shall organize by electing from their number a president and a secretary. *President and secretary.*

Section 3. It shall be the duty of such bureau to collect reliable information concerning the deposits of all precious and useful minerals and other valuable subterranean productions in the state that is supposed to exist in quantities sufficient to justify the development of such properties. *Duty of bureau.*

Section 4. Such bureau shall establish a metallurgical cabinet of exhibit of the state in such room in the state house, as the superintendent of public buildings may direct, and in such cabinet they shall properly arrange samples, and specimens of ores, valuable rocks, and metals of the state that they have been able to collect, for safe keeping and preservation of same. *Metallurgical cabinet shall be established.*

Section 5. Said bureau shall once in two years cause to be printed a pamphlet containing such reliable information concerning the mineral resources of the state as it has collected, and distribute at least one thousand copies of such pamphlet each year among the business men and capitalists of other states. *Shall print report once in two years.*

Section 6. This act shall take effect when approved.

Approved March 28, 1903.

CHAP. 228

Chapter 228.

An Act appropriating one half of the taxes received from Trust and Banking Companies to the School Fund.

Be it enacted by the Senate and House of Representatives in Legislature assembled, as follows:

Appropriation to common schools from assessments on trust and banking companies.

Section 1. One-half of the sum assessed upon the deposits of trust and banking companies shall be appropriated to common schools in the manner provided by section three of chapter two hundred fifty-eight of the public laws of eighteen hundred ninety-three, as amended by section three of chapter one hundred thirty-three of the public laws of eighteen hundred ninety-five, relating to the taxation of savings banks, and one-half to the state.

Section 2. This act shall take effect when approved.

Approved March 28, 1903.

Chapter 229.

An Act to amend Section eleven of Chapter thirty of the Revised Statutes as amended by Chapter forty-two of the Public Laws of eighteen hundred ninety-nine and as amended by Chapter two hundred fifty-eight of the Public Laws of nineteen hundred one, relating to Close Time for Game Birds.

Be it enacted by the Senate and House of Representatives in Legislature assembled, as follows:

Section 11, of chapter 30, R. S., as amended by chapter 42, public laws of 1899, as amended by chapter 258, public laws of 1901, further amended.

Section 1. Section eleven of chapter thirty of the revised statutes, as amended by chapter forty-two of the public laws of eighteen hundred ninety-nine, and as amended by chapter two hundred fifty-eight of the public laws of nineteen hundred one, is hereby amended so as to read as follows:

Close time for game birds.

'Section 11. There shall be for game birds an annual close time in which it shall be unlawful to hunt, chase, catch, kill or have them in possession whenever or however killed, as follows:

—duck.

For wood duck, dusky duck, commonly called black duck, teal and gray duck the close time shall be from December first to the first day of the following September of each year; for ruffed

—partridge and woodcock.

grouse, commonly called partridge and woodcock, from the first day of December to September fifteenth next following of each year; for plover, snipe and sandpipers, from the first day of May to the first day of August of each year; and it shall be unlawful

—quail.

to hunt, chase, catch, kill or have in possession at any time any quail. Whoever violates any of the above named provisions of

—penalty.

this section shall be subject to a penalty of not less than five dollars nor more than ten dollars and costs for each bird so killed, caught, chased or had in possession in close time.

—not more than 15 birds

No person shall, in any one day, kill or have in possession more than fifteen of each variety of the above named birds, except sandpipers, the number of which shall not exceed seventy in any one day, during the respective open season for each; nor shall any person at any time kill or have in possession any ruffed grouse, commonly called partridge, woodcock, wood duck, dusky duck, commonly called black duck, teal or gray duck, except for his own consumption within this state, except as hereinafter provided, under a penalty of five dollars and costs for each bird so unlawfully killed or had in possession; nor shall any person at any time sell or offer for sale, any ruffed grouse, commonly called partridge, woodcock, wood duck, dusky duck, commonly called black duck, teal or gray duck within this state under the same penalty; nor shall any person or corporation carry or transport from place to place any of the birds mentioned in this section, in close time, nor in open season unless open to view, tagged and plainly labeled with the owner's name and residence and accompanied by him, unless tagged in accordance with section twenty-six of this chapter, under the same penalty.

Any person, not the actual owner of such bird or birds, who, to aid another in transportation, falsely represents himself to be the owner thereof, shall be liable to the same penalty; nor shall any person or corporation carry or transport at any one time more than fifteen of any one variety of the birds above mentioned as the property of one person, under the same penalty; and it shall be unlawful for a term of ten years, to hunt for, take, catch, kill or destroy the capercailzie, or cock of the woods, so called, black game, so called, or any species of the pheasant, except ruffed grouse, or partridge, under a penalty of fifty dollars for each offense.'

Approved March 28, 1903.

Chapter 230.

An Act to regulate the Sale and Analysis of Concentrated Commercial Feeding Stuffs.

Be it enacted by the Senate and House of Representatives in Legislature assembled, as follows:

Section 1. Every package of any concentrated commercial feeding stuff, as defined in section three of this act, used for feeding farm live stock, sold, offered or exposed for sale in this state, shall have affixed thereunto, in a conspicuous place on the outside thereof, a plainly printed statement clearly and truly certifying the number of net pounds in the package, the name, brand or trade mark under which the article is sold, the name and address of the manufacturer or importer, and a chemical analysis stating the percentage of crude protein, allowing one per cent of nitrogen to equal six and one-fourth per cent of protein, and of crude fat it contains, both constituents to be determined by the methods adopted at the time by the association of official agricultural chemists.

If the feeding stuff is sold in bulk or put up in packages belonging to the purchaser, the agent or dealer shall, upon request of the purchaser, furnish him with the certified statement named in this section.

What the term concentrated commercial feeding stuff shall not include.

Section 2. The term concentrated commercial feeding stuff, as here used, shall not include hays and straws, the whole seeds nor the unmixed meals made directly from the entire grains of wheat, rye, barley, oats, Indian corn, buckwheat and broom corn. Neither shall it include wheat, rye and buckwheat brans or middlings, not mixed with other substances, but sold separately, as distinct articles of commerce, nor wheat bran and middlings mixed together, nor pure grains ground together.

What the term concentrated commercial feeding stuff shall include.

Section 3. The term concentrated commercial feeding stuff, as here used, shall include linseed meals, cottonseed meals, cottonseed feeds, pea meals, cocoanut meals, gluten meals, gluten feeds, maize feeds, starch feeds, sugar feeds, dried brewers' grains, dried distillers' grains, malt sprouts, hominy feeds, cerealine feeds, rice meals, oat feeds, corn and oat chops, corn and oat feeds, corn bran, ground beef or fish scraps, condimental foods, poultry foods, stock foods, patented proprietary or trade marked stock and poultry foods, mixed feeds other than those composed solely of wheat bran and middlings mixed together, or pure grains ground together, and all other materials of similar nature not included in section two of this act.

Appropriation for expenses of analysis.

Section 4. There shall be annually appropriated from the state treasury the sum of one thousand dollars in favor of the treasurer of the Maine Agricultural Experiment Station, the same, or such portion thereof as is found necessary, to be expended by said experiment station in the analysis of concentrated commercial feeding stuffs.

How, by whom and to whom, appropriation may be paid.

Section 5. So much of the appropriation granted under this act shall be paid by the state treasurer to the treasurer of said experiment station as the director of said station may show by his bills has been expended in performing the duties required by this act, such payment to be made quarterly upon the order of the governor and council, who are hereby directed to draw the order for such purpose. The director shall annually publish a statement of the receipts and expenditures under this act.

Penalty for violation of his act.

Section 6. Whoever shall sell, offer or expose for sale or for distribution in this state any concentrated commercial feeding

CONCENTRATED COMMERCIAL FEEDING STUFFS. 193

CHAP. 230

stuff as defined in section three of this act, without complying with the requirements of section one of this act, or any feeding stuff which contains substantially a smaller percentage of constituents than are certified to be contained, shall, on conviction in a court of competent jurisdiction, be fined not more than one hundred dollars for the first offense, and not more than two hundred dollars for each subsequent offense.

Section 7. The director of the Maine Agricultural Experiment Station shall annually analyze, or cause to be analyzed, at least one sample of every concentrated commercial feeding stuff sold or offered for sale under the provisions of this act. Said director is hereby authorized and directed in person or by deputy to take a sample, not exceeding two pounds in weight, for said analysis, from any lot or package of concentrated commercial feeding stuff which may be in the possession of any manufacturer, importer, agent or dealer in this state; said sample should be placed in a suitable jar or bottle, tightly closed and a label placed thereon, stating the name or brand of the feeding stuff or material sampled, the name of the party from whose stock the sample was drawn and the time and place of drawing, and said label shall also be signed by the director or his deputy; provided, however, that when so requested said sample shall be taken in duplicate in the presence of the party or parties in interest or their representatives, in which case one of said duplicate samples shall be retained by the director and the other by the party whose stock was sampled. The sample or samples retained by the director shall be for comparison with the certified statement named in section one of this act. The result of the analysis of the sample or samples so procured, together with such additional information as circumstances advise, shall be published in reports or bulletins from time to time.

Director of Maine agricultural experiment station shall analyze.

—shall take samples.

—shall take sample in duplicate when requested.

Section 8. Any person who shall adulterate any whole or ground grain with milling or manufactured offals, or with any foreign substance whatever, or any bran or middlings made from the several grains with any foreign substance whatever, for the purpose of sale, unless the true composition, mixture or adulteration thereof is plainly marked or indicated upon the packages containing the same, or in which it is offered for sale; or any person who sells or offers for sale any whole or ground grain, bran or middlings which have been so adulterated, unless the true composition, mixture or adulteration is plainly marked or indicated upon the package containing the same, or in which it is offered for sale, shall on conviction in a court of competent jurisdiction be fined not more than one hundred dollars for the first

Adulterations, penalty for.

194 ELECTRICITY.

CHAP. 231

Proceedings for violation of this act.

offense, and not more than two hundred dollars for each subsequent offense.

Section 9. Whenever the directors of the Maine Agricultural Experiment Station becomes cognizant of the violation of any of the provisions of this act, he shall forthwith report such violation to the commissioner of agriculture, and said commissioner shall prosecute the party or parties thus reported. But there shall be no prosecution in relation to the quality of any concentrated commercial feeding stuff if the same shall be found in its constituent parts substantially equivalent to the certified statement named in section one of this act.

Chapter 334, public laws of 1897, and other acts, repealed.

Section 10. Chapter three hundred thirty-four of the public laws of eighteen hundred ninety-seven, and all other acts and parts of acts inconsistent with this act are hereby repealed.

Section 11. This act shall take effect June one, nineteen hundred and three.

Approved March 28, 1903.

Chapter 231.

An Act to amend Chapter three hundred and seventy-eight of the Public Laws of eighteen hundred and eighty-five, regulating the erection of posts and lines for purposes of Electricity.

Be it enacted by the Senate and House of Representatives in Legislature assembled, as follows:

Section 2 of chapter 378, public laws of 1885, amended.

Section 1. Section two of chapter three hundred seventy-eight of the public laws of eighteen hundred and eighty-five is hereby amended by striking out the first six lines thereof and inserting in place thereof the following: 'No such company, person or association shall construct lines upon and along highways and public roads, without first obtaining a written permit, signed by the mayor and aldermen in case of cities, the selectmen in case of towns, and the county commissioners in case of plantations and unorganized townships, specifying the kind of posts, where and how they shall be located and set, and the height of the wire above the ground; and if the line specified in the permit is a telephone line and is not constructed and public telephone service established in connection therewith within eighteen months from the time the decision is filed, the permit shall be void.'

—permit to erect posts must be had from municipal officers.

Also by adding at the end of said section the following words: 'In case of plantations and unorganized townships any person or corporation interested may appeal from the decision of the county commissioners to the supreme judicial court in the manner pro-

—appeal in case of plantations, etc.

vided in sections forty-eight, forty-nine, fifty and fifty-one of chapter eighteen of the revised statutes, relating to highways, and in case of cities and towns as follows: The decision of the mayor and aldermen or the selectmen shall be filed with the clerk of the city or town within one week from their final hearing: and within two weeks from such filing any person or corporation interested may appeal from their decision by filing notice of appeal with a copy of the original petition and adjudication with the clerk of the city or town and with the clerk of the board of county commissioners; the commissioners shall immediately entertain such appeal and give two weeks public notice in a county newspaper of the time and place of hearing, which time shall be within thirty days from the time such appeal is filed; such hearing may be adjourned from time to time, not exceeding thirty days in all, and the commissioners shall file their decision within thirty days from the time the hearing is closed, and transmit a copy of the same to the clerk of the city or town, who shall forthwith record it.' —decision of mayor and aldermen or selectmen shall be filed.

Section 2. Said section is further amended to conform to section one of this act, so that said section as amended shall read as follows: Section 2 of chapter 378, further amended.

'Section 2. No such company, person or association shall construct lines upon and along highways and public roads, without first obtaining a written permit, signed by the mayor and aldermen in case of cities, the selectmen in case of towns, and the county commissioners in case of plantations and unorganized townships, specifying the kind of posts, where and how they shall be located and set, and the height of the wire above the ground; and if the line specified in the permit is a telephone line and is not constructed and public telephone service established in connection therewith within eighteen months from the time the decision is filed, the permit shall be void. Before granting such permit, fourteen days' public notice thereof shall be given, and residents and owners of property upon the highways to be affected thereby, should have full opportunity to show cause why such permit should not be granted. Such public notice shall be given by publication in a county newspaper when the county commissioners are to act, and in some newspaper printed in such city or town, if any, the last publication to be fourteen days before said hearing; if in a town and no newspaper is printed therein, then by posting the same in some public and conspicuous place therein fourteen days before said hearing. When the application for such permit is filed, personal notice, if deemed necessary, may be ordered by such officers and shall be given by such company, persons or associations to the residents and owners of

CHAP. 231

—defective notice.

—appeal may be filed.

property to be affected thereby. At the hearing such company, persons or associations, before proceeding, shall first prove that such order of notice has been complied with and public notice given as hereinbefore required, and the adjudication of the mayor and aldermen, selectmen or county commissioners that such personal and public notice has been given shall be final and conclusive. If from any cause the notice given appears to have been defective, said officers may order new notice, not exceeding seven days, and adjourn said hearing to a time named in said new order of notice. After the erection of the lines, having first given all persons interested an opportunity to be heard, such officers may direct any alteration in the original permit. Such permits, specifications and decisions shall be recorded in the records of the city, town or county commissioners. In case of plantations and unorganized townships any person or corporation interested may appeal from the decision of the county commissioners to the supreme judicial court in the manner provided in sections forty-eight, forty-nine, fifty and fifty-one of chapter eighteen of the revised statutes, relating to highways, and in case of cities and towns as follows: The decision of the mayor and aldermen or the selectmen shall be filed with the clerk of the city or town within one week from their final hearing; and within two weeks from such filing any person or corporation interested may appeal from their decision by filing notice of appeal with a copy of the original petition and adjudication with the clerk of the city or town and with the clerk of the board of county commissioners; the commissioners shall immediately entertain such appeal and give two weeks public notice in a county newspaper of the time and place of hearing, which time shall be within thirty days from the time such appeal is filed; such hearing may be adjourned from time to time, not exceeding thirty days in all, and the commissioners shall file their decision within thirty days from the time the hearing is closed, and transmit a copy of the same to the clerk of the city or town, who shall forthwith record it.'

Section 3. This act shall take effect May one, nineteen hundred three.

Approved March 28, 1903.

Chapter 232.

An Act to make certain the meaning of the language "Timber and Grass," relating to the Public Lots, so called, in unincorporated townships in State of Maine.

Be it enacted by the Senate and House of Representatives in Legislature assembled, as follows:

Section 1. The language 'Timber and Grass,' as relates to the public lots, so called, in unincorporated townships in state of Maine, is hereby construed to mean all growth of every description on said lots. {Timber and grass, meaning of construed.}

Section 2. This act shall take effect when approved.

Approved March 28, 1908.

Chapter 233.

An Act providing for a bounty on bears in Oxford County.

Be it enacted by the Senate and House of Representatives in Legislature assembled, as follows:

A bounty of five dollars for every bear killed in Oxford county by any bona fide resident of this state, and actually domiciled in said state, may be paid by the state treasurer upon the production by the applicant therefor of an inland fish and game warden's certificate in the form set forth in Schedule A hereto. Every warden before issuing any such certificate shall require the applicant therefor to sign and swear to a statement in writing in the form set forth in said Schedule A, which oath said warden is hereby authorized to administer, and shall also require the production by such applicant of the entire skin of the animal for the killing of which such bounty is claimed, with the nose thereof in as perfect a state as when killed, excepting natural decay; and the said warden shall thereupon cut off the whole of the nose from such skin and entirely destroy it by burning. Every such statement in writing, sworn to under the provisions of this section, shall forthwith upon the taking thereof be forwarded by the warden taking the same to the state treasurer.

{Bounty on bears in Oxford county.}
{—certificate of killing shall be sworn to.}
{—entire skin shall be produced.}

[Repealed ch. 36/1913]

Schedule A.

To the Treasurer of the State of Maine:

Claimant's Statement.

I hereby state, that on the   day of   A. D. 190 , at   in the county of Oxford, and State of Maine, I killed the bear, the skin of which I now exhibit to   , game warden, and I claim the bounty allowed by law for killing same.

Dated at this day of A. D. 190 .

Claimant.

Subscribed and sworn to before me the day and year aforesaid.

Game Warden.

Game Warden's Certificate.

I hereby certify, that, as required by law, I have cut off the whole of the nose from the skin of the bear described in the certificate of claimant, made before me the day of A. D. 190 , and have destroyed the same by burning.

Dated at this day of A. D. 190 .

Game Warden.

Approved March 28, 1903.

Chapter 234.

An Act establishing the Salary of the County Attorney for the County of Knox.

Be it enacted by the Senate and House of Representatives in Legislature assembled, as follows:

Salary of county attorney, Knox county, fixed.

Section 1. The county attorney for the county of Knox shall receive an annual salary from the treasurer of state, of seven hundred dollars, payable quarterly on the first days of January, April, July and October in each year, beginning on the first day of April, one thousand nine hundred and three, instead of the salary now provided by law.

Section 2. All acts and parts of acts inconsistent with this act, are hereby repealed.

Approved March 28, 1903.

Chapter 235.

An Act relating to Corporations.

Be it enacted by the Senate and House of Representatives in Legislature assembled, as follows:

Section 1. The secretary of state shall prepare a list of all corporations, giving the corporate name, the name of the treasurer last filed in the office of the secretary of state, and the amount of the annual franchise tax due for the year nineteen hundred and one, except those which have been duly excused as provided by statute or dissolved by decree of court, which have not paid their franchise tax for the year nineteen hundred and one, which list shall be published three times for three consecutive weeks in the month of May, nineteen hundred and three, in three places within the state of Maine:

Namely, Bangor, Augusta and Portland, in such newspaper in each place as the secretary of state may select. Any such corporation so advertised, which shall fail to pay said franchise tax and the expenses of advertising the same, on or before the first day of December, nineteen hundred and three, is hereby declared to have forfeited its charter and the same shall thereafterwards be void.

The data covering the avoiding of said charter; to wit, the fact of the publication of the same and the dates thereof, and the avoidance of said charter by reason of such publication and the failure to pay said over due franchise tax as herein provided, shall be so entered upon the corporation records of the state and be certified by the secretary of state as evidence of the forfeiture thereof. That the sum of three hundred dollars be and hereby is appropriated to pay the expense hereof.

Section 2. Any person or persons who shall undertake to do business, or do business of any kind in behalf of any such corporation, or shall hold out such corporation as doing business, or shall sell, transfer, or put upon the market any stocks or other evidence of indebtedness whatsoever of any such corporation, after the charter thereof has been forfeited as herein provided, shall be subject to a fine of three hundred dollars, for the benefit of the state.

Section 3. This act shall take effect when approved.

Approved March 28, 1903.

Chapter 236.

An Act for the Protection of Shore Birds.

Be it enacted by the Senate and House of Representatives in Legislature assembled, as follows:

License required for hunting shore birds within certain towns and counties.
It shall be unlawful for any person not a bona fide resident of this state, and actually domiciled therein, to hunt, pursue, chase, or kill within the limits of Knox, Lincoln, Waldo and Sagadahoc counties, and the towns of Brunswick, Harpswell and Freeport in the county of Cumberland, any teal, ducks, sea or shore birds without first having procured a license therefor as hereinafter provided.

—*licenses, how issued and obtained.*
Such licenses shall be issued by the commissioners of inland fisheries and game, upon application in writing and the payment of five dollars, and under such rules and regulations to be established by them, and approved by the governor and council, as may be required to carry out the true intent of this act and not inconsistent herewith.

—*license fees be paid to state treasurer.*
All money received for such licenses shall be forthwith paid to the state treasurer, and then expended by the commissioners in the protection of the birds in the counties and towns above named under the direction of the governor and council.

—*penalty for violation.*
Whoever is found guilty of violating any of the provisions of this act shall be punished by a fine of not less than twenty-five dollars nor more than one hundred dollars and costs for each offense.

Approved March 28, 1903.

Chapter 237.

An Act to regulate the use of Automobiles and Motor Vehicles upon Public Ways.

Be it enacted by the Senate and House of Representatives in Legislature assembled, as follows:

Rate of speed of automobiles regulated.
Section 1. No automobile or motor vehicles shall be driven, operated, or caused to be driven or operated, upon any highway, town way, public street, avenue, driveway, park or parkway, at a greater rate of speed than fifteen miles an hour, or upon any highway, town way, public street, avenue, driveway, park or parkway, within the compact or built up portions of any city, town or village, the limits of which shall be fixed by the municipal officers thereof, at a greater rate of speed than eight miles an hour, except where such city or town may by ordinance or by-law permit a greater rate of speed.

AUTOMOBILES.

CHAP. 237

Section 2. No person driving or in charge of an automobile or motor vehicle on any highway, townway, public street, avenue, driveway, park or parkway, shall drive the same at any speed greater than is reasonable and proper, having regard to the traffic and use of the way by others, or so as to endanger the life or limb of any person; and racing any such vehicle on any such ways or parks is hereby forbidden.

Rate of speed of automobiles shall be reasonable and proper.

Section 3. Every person driving or operating an automobile or motor vehicle shall at request and signal by putting up the hand, or by other visible signal, from a person riding or driving a horse or horses or other domestic animals, cause such vehicle to come to a stop as soon as possible and to remain stationary so long as may be necessary to allow such animal or animals to pass.

Shall stop on request of person driving horses or other domestic animals.

Section 4. Every such automobile or motor vehicle shall have attached thereto a suitable bell or other appliance for giving notice of its approach, which, when rung or otherwise operated, may be heard at a distance of three hundred feet; and shall also carry a lighted lamp between one hour after sunset and one hour before sunrise.

Autombile shall have bell.

Section 5. Municipal officers of any city or town may designate places on any streets or ways therein, where, in their judgment, by reason of cliffs, embankments or other exceptional natural conditions, the meeting of automobiles or motor vehicles and horses would be attended with unusual danger. Such designation shall be made by causing the words "automobiles—go slow" to be conspicuously displayed on signboards at the right hand side of each approach to the place to be designated, and not more than one hundred and fifty feet distant therefrom; and an automobile or motor vehicle, before meeting any horse between such limits, shall be brought to a standstill, and shall not proceed, unless by request of the rider or driver of the horse, until such horse shall have passed; and no such vehicle shall pass any place so designated at a greater speed than four miles an hour.

Municipal officers may designate places where meeting with horses would be attended with unusual danger.

—sign boards to be displayed.

Section 6. The violation of any of the provisions of this act shall be punished by fine not exceeding fifty dollars, or by imprisonment not exceeding ten days.

Penalty for violation of this act.

Approved March 28, 1903.

CHAP. 238

COMPENSATION OF MEMBERS OF GOVERNMENT.

Chapter 238.

An Act to amend Section eight of Chapter one hundred and fifteen of the Revised Statutes, relating to compensation of members of the government.

Be it enacted by the Senate and House of Representatives in Legislature assembled, as follows:

Section 8, of chapter 115, R. S., amended.

Section 1. Section eight is hereby amended by striking out, after the word "receive" in the tenth line, the words "one hundred and fifty" and inserting in lieu thereof the words 'three hundred,' and by striking out in the nineteenth line, after the word "receive" the words "three hundred," and insert in place thereof the words 'five hundred' so that said section as amended, shall read as follows:

Executive council, compensation of.

'Each member of the executive council shall receive the same compensation and travel as a representative to the legislature, for serving as a councillor during the session of the council commencing in January and closing immediately after the adjournment of the legislature. For services at other sessions of the council, each councillor shall be paid two dollars for every day's actual attendance, and two dollars for every ten miles travel, one way, from his place of abode to the capitol; and for authorized service on committees, when the council is not in session, three dollars and a half a day and necessary expenses.

—members of house and senate.

Each member of the senate and house of representatives shall receive three hundred dollars for the regular session of the legislature, and two dollars for every ten miles travel from his place of abode, once in each session. He is entitled to mileage on the first day of the session, and fifty dollars of his salary on the first day of each month thereafter, during the session, and the balance at the end thereof; but two dollars shall be deducted from the pay of every member for each day that he is absent from his duties, without being excused by the house to which he belongs.

—president of senate and speaker of house.

The president of the senate and speaker of the house of representatives, shall receive five hundred dollars for each session, with the same mileage as other members, and subject to the same deduction in case of absence. Any member acting as president pro tempore of the senate, or speaker pro tempore of the house, shall receive two dollars a day extra therefor; provided that no member of the legislature shall receive free passes from transportation companies.

—extra session.

When an extra session is called by the governor, the members of the senate and house of representatives shall each be paid two dollars for every day's attendance, and mileage as aforesaid.

The president of the senate and speaker of the house of representatives at such extra session, shall receive, in addition, two dollars for every day's attendance.

The secretary of the senate and the clerk of the house of representatives, eight hundred dollars each in full for all services. Assistant secretary and assistant clerk, six hundred dollars each, in full for all services. Messenger and assistant messengers to senate and to house, two hundred and fifty dollars for each, in full.

Pages to the senate and to the house of representativs, one hundred and fifty dollars for each, in full.

Messenger to governor and council, five hundred dollars, in full for all services and travel.

The salaries of all public officers and the pay of all clerks in public offices not otherwise provided for, shall be from the state treasury in quarterly payments.

The treasurer of state shall make pay rolls and payments according to these provisions.'

Section 2. This act shall be referred at the next state election to the voters of the state and if approved by them shall take effect on the first Wednesday of January nineteen hundred and five.

Section 3. At the said next state election the following question shall be printed upon the official ballot after the list of candidates, in accordance with section ten of chapter one hundred and two of the public laws of eighteen hundred and ninety-one as amended by section one of chapter two hundred and sixty-seven of the public laws of eighteen hundred and ninety-three. "Shall the salary of the executive council and members of the senate and house of representatives be increased to three hundred dollars in place of one hundred and fifty dollars as now provided by law, and the salary of the president of the senate and speaker of the house to five hundred dollars in place of three hundred dollars as now provided by law?" The words "yes" and "no" shall be printed upon such ballot above the aforesaid question so as to leave a blank space, above such question so as to give to each voter a clear opportunity to designate by a cross mark (X) therein opposite to the word "yes" or "no", his answer to the question submitted.

Approved March 28, 1903.

Chapter 239.

An Act to establish a bounty on Porcupines, so called, for the better Protection of Timber Land.

Be it enacted by the Senate and House of Representatives in Legislature assembled, as follows:

Bounty on porcupines. A bounty of twenty-five cents for each and every porcupine, so called, killed in any town or township in this state shall be paid by the treasurer thereof to the person killing it. If the place of killing is in an unorganized township the bounty shall be paid by the treasurer of an adjoining town, if any, otherwise by the treasurer of the town nearest said township. No bounty shall be paid unless the claimant within ten days after he has killed such animal or has returned from the hunting, in which he killed it, exhibits to the town treasurer the entire nose and feet thereof, in as perfect a state as when killed, except natural decay and signs and makes oath to a certificate, in which he shall state that he killed such animal and the time and place showing it to be within the state; and the treasurer shall thereupon entirely destroy said nose and feet by burning; then he shall pay the bounty and take the claimant's receipt therefor upon the same paper with such certificate. The town treasurer shall immediately make upon the same paper a certificate, under oath, addressed to the treasurer of state, that he first destroyed said nose and feet by burning, and then paid said bounty to the claimant. Said certificates and receipts shall annually, in December, be transmitted to the treasurer of state, and by him laid before the governor and council as early as convenient; and when allowed by them shall be paid by the treasurer of state to such towns. The certificates shall be in the following form:

—proofs of killing required.

—duty of town treasurer.

bounties, when and how audited and paid.

Claimant's Certificate.

To the treasurer of   I hereby certify that on the   day of   A. D. 19   , at   , in the State of Maine, I killed the porcupine the nose and feet of which I now exhibit to you; and I claim the bounty allowed by law for killing the same.

Dated at   , this   day of   A. D. 19   .

Subscribed and sworn to before me the day and year aforesaid.

Treasurer of

Claimant's Receipt.

On this   day of   A. D. 19   , I received of treasurer of   ,   dollars, being the bounty allowed by law for killing the porcupine described in the above certificate.

Claimant.

WHEN ACTS AND RESOLVES SHALL TAKE EFFECT.   205

CHAP. 240

Treasurer's Certificate.

I hereby certify that as required by law, I first destroyed by burning the nose and feet of the porcupine described in the foregoing certificate, and then paid to said   the bounty for which I have taken his receipt as above.

Dated at   this   day of   A. D. 19

Treasurer of

Subscribed and sworn to before me the day and year aforesaid.

Justice of the Peace.

Approved March 28, 1903.

Chapter 240.

An Act fixing a time when other Acts and Resolves shall take effect.

Be it enacted by the Senate and House of Representatives in Legislature assembled, as follows:

Section 1. Except as provided in the following section, all acts and resolves passed by the seventy-first legislature, and approved prior to the approval of this act, shall take effect on the twenty-eighth day of April, in the year of our Lord one thousand nine hundred and three. *Acts passed by 71st legislature shall take effect April 28, 1903.*

Section 2. This act shall not apply to acts of incorporation, nor to acts and resolves which by their own terms take effect at times other than the day last named. *Exceptions.*

Section 3. This act shall take effect when approved.

Approved March 28, 1903.

PRIVATE AND SPECIAL LAWS

OF THE

STATE OF MAINE.

1903.

PRIVATE AND SPECIAL LAWS

OF THE

STATE OF MAINE.

1903

Chapter 1.

An Act to authorize the Franklin Company to reduce its capital stock.

Be it enacted by the Senate and House of Representatives in Legislature assembled, as follows:

Section 1. The Franklin Company is hereby authorized from time to time to reduce its present capital stock of one million dollars to an amount not less than two hundred and fifty thousand dollars as hereinafter provided. The stockholders of said corporation may from time to time by a majority vote at any meeting or meetings duly called and held for that purpose reduce said capital stock in such sums or amounts as they may determine, and thereupon the treasurer of the corporation shall send by mail to each stockholder a notice directed to the last known address of such stockholder as shown upon the books of the company, stating the substance of such vote to reduce the capital stock, and each stockholder within three months after such vote shall surrender such portion of his stock as the amount of

_{Authorized to reduce capital stock.}

_{—by majority vote.}

_{—treasurer shall give notice of reduction.}

_{—stockholders shall surrender pro rata.}

BRIDGTON WATER COMPANY.

CHAP. 2

—new certificates shall be issued.

the reduction shall bear to the amount of the capital st standing at the time of the vote so to reduce said stock, each stockholder shall have the same proportion of the r capital stock of the company as before the reduction. stockholder upon the surrender of his certificate of sto accordance with any such vote shall receive a new certificat his proportional share of the remaining capital stock. No dends shall be declared upon any portion of the capital required to be surrendered in accordance with any such vot no dividend shall be paid to any stockholder until he shal surrendered his stock and the new certificate been issued fo proportional share of the remaining capital stock. No certificate shall be issued, however, for fractional parts of a share, but the treasurer shall issue non-interest bearing scrip for such fractional parts of shares which shall be convertible into full shares at par, when presented in amounts of one hundred dollars or multiple thereof. No dividends shall be declared or paid upon fractional parts of shares until the same shall have been converted into full shares by the issue of certificates therefor as herein provided.

—no certificate shall be issued for fractional parts of a share.

Notice of changes shall be given to secretary of state.

Section 2. The corporation shall give notice to the secretary of state of any and all changes in the amount of its capital stock made under the provisions of this act within thirty days thereafter.

Section 3. This act shall take effect when approved.

Approved January 22, 1903.

Chapter 2.

An Act additional to and amendatory of Chapter three hundred and eighteen of the Private and Special Laws of nineteen hundred and one, entitled "An Act to incorporate the Bridgton Water Company."

Be it enacted by the Senate and House of Representatives in Legislature assembled, as follows:

Bridgton Water Company authorized to purchase Bridgton and Harrison Electric Company.

Section 1. Bridgton Water Company is hereby authorized to acquire and hold by purchase all the property, rights, privileges, immunities and franchise of the Bridgton and Harrison Electric Company, a corporation located at Bridgton in the county of Cumberland and state of Maine, upon such terms as may be agreed upon by said corporations, and upon such purchase and transfer said corporation purchasing shall have, hold, possess, exercise and enjoy all the locations, powers, privileges, rights, immunities, franchise, property and estate which at the

—rights of purchaser.

time of such purchase and transfer shall then be had, held, possessed, exercised and enjoyed by said corporation so selling; and said corporation so purchasing from the time of said purchase and transfer may engage in the business of making, generating, selling, distributing and supplying electricity for lighting, heating, manufacturing or mechanical purposes as fully and to the same extent and effect as said corporation so selling has had power and authority prior to such sale and transfer, but under the same restrictions, limitations and conditions applicable to said corporation so selling.

Section 2. Said Bridgton and Harrison Electric Company is hereby authorized to make the sale and transfer authorized by section one of this act at any meeting of its stockholders called for that purpose. *When sale and transfer may be made.*

Section 3. Said corporation so purchasing shall faithfully perform all the obligations of any and all contracts existing at the time of the purchase and transfer aforesaid between said corporation so selling and any town, corporation, village corporation, firm or individual and be subject to all the liabilities of said contracts, and thereupon shall succeed to and enjoy all the rights and benefits of said contracts as fully and to the same extent as if said contracts had been made originally with said corporation so purchasing. *Obligations assumed. —liable for contracts.*

Section 4. All proceedings and suits at law or in equity which may be pending at the time of such transfer to which said corporation so selling shall be a party may be prosecuted or defended by said corporation so purchasing in like manner and with the same effect as if said transfer had not been made. All claims, contracts, rights and causes of action, at law or in equity, in favor of or against said corporation so selling may be enforced by action or suit by or against said corporation so purchasing. *Pending suits —shall be defended by corporation purchasing. —claims may be enforced in favor or against purchaser.*

Section 5. Said corporation so purchasing may issue its bonds to raise funds for the purposes of its business, upon such rates and time as may be deemed expedient, to an amount not exceeding forty thousand dollars in addition to the amount of fifty thousand dollars authorized by section thirteen of said act, and secure all of said bonds by a deed of trust and mortgage of all its property and franchises. *May issue bonds.*

Section 6. The name of said Bridgton Water Company is hereby changed from Bridgton Water Company to Bridgton Water and Electric Company. *Name changed.*

Section 7. Said corporation so purchasing is hereby authorized to increase its capital stock from fifty thousand dollars to ninety thousand dollars. *May increase capital stock.*

AUBURN SAVINGS BANK—OLD ORCHARD ELECTRIC LIGHT CO.

CHAP. 3

May hold real and personal estate.

Section 8. Said corporation so purchasing for all purposes may hold real and personal estate necessary and convenient therefor not exceeding in value two hundred thousand dollars.

Section 9. This act shall take effect when approved.

Approved January 30, 1903.

Chapter 3.

An Act to authorize the Auburn Savings Bank, of Auburn, Maine, to construct and maintain Safety Deposit Boxes.

Be it enacted by the Senate and House of Representatives in Legislature assembled, as follows:

Auburn Savings Bank authorized to construct and rent safety deposit boxes.

Section 1. The Auburn Savings Bank, of Auburn, Maine, is hereby authorized and empowered to construct, own, maintain, operate and rent for hire safety deposit boxes for the safe keeping of personal property; provided, however, that said savings bank shall not be liable for any loss of property deposited in said boxes for safe keeping beyond the sum paid for the hire of the box containing said property so lost; and provided, further, that the construction of said deposit boxes, and their location within the vaults of said bank shall be subject to the approval of the state bank examiner, who shall make careful examination, and certify his approval to said bank.

—liability defined.

—location of boxes subject to approval by bank examiner.

Section 2. This act shall take effect when approved.

Approved February 4, 1903.

Chapter 4.

An Act to authorize the Old Orchard Electric Light Company to issue bonds and for other purposes.

Be it enacted by the Senate and House of Representatives in Legislature assembled, as follows:

Old Orchard Electric Light Company authorized to issue bonds.

Section 1. The Old Orchard Electric Light Company is hereby authorized and empowered to issue its bonds for refunding its outstanding indebtedness and for corporation purposes, in a sum not exceeding one hundred thousand dollars for a time not exceeding twenty years, and upon such rates of interest as said company may deem expedient, and may secure the same by mortgage of the franchises and property of said corporation. And the York Light and Heat Company is hereby authorized to guarantee, assume, and pay said bonds, and all outstanding

—purpose.

—limitations.

—may secure by mortgage.

WINTHROP COLD SPRING WATER COMPANY.

contracts, obligations and liabilities of said Old Orchard Electric Light Company upon such terms as said companies may mutually determine.

Section 2. The York Light and Heat Company is hereby authorized to purchase, hold, own and enjoy the franchises, property, shares of stock, rights, easements, privileges and immunities of the said Old Orchard Electric Light Company. And the said Old Orchard Electric Light Company is hereby authorized to sell, transfer and convey its franchises, property, shares of stock, rights, easements, privileges and immunities to the said York Light and Heat Company, upon such terms as said companies may determine.

And any past sale of said franchises, property, shares of stock, rights, easements, privileges and immunities is hereby confirmed and declared legal and valid.

Section 3. This act shall take effect when approved.

Approved February 4, 1902.

Chapter 5.

An Act to amend Sections one and four of Chapter three hundred and thirty-nine of the Private and Special Laws of nineteen hundred and one, being "An Act to incorporate the Winthrop Cold Spring Water Company."

Be it enacted by the Senate and House of Representatives in Legislature assembled, as follows:

Section 1. Section one of said chapter three hundred and thirty-nine of the private and special laws of nineteen hundred and one is hereby amended by striking out the words "N. M. Carleton" in the first line of said section and inserting instead thereof the following names: 'Joseph Fortier, Lizzie Kelley, L. C. Lee, W. A. Whiting, and W. E. Berry,' so that said section as amended, shall read as follows:

'Section 1. L. T. Carleton, C. H. Gale, Joseph Fortier, Lizzie Kelley, L. C. Lee, W. A. Whiting, W. E. Berry, Charles P. Hannaford, and Adam Fortier of Winthrop in the county of Kennebec, with their associates, successors and assigns, are hereby made a corporation under the name of the Winthrop Cold Spring Water Company, for the purpose of supplying the inhabitants of the town of Winthrop with pure water for domestic purposes, with all the rights and privileges and subject to all the liabilities and obligations of similar corporations under the laws of this state.'

Section 2. Section four of said chapter is hereby amended by striking out the words "shall be one hundred and twenty-five"

STATE OF MAINE BONDS—BAR HARBOR MUNICIPAL COURT.

CHAP. 6

—capit stock.

in the first and second lines of said section and inserting instead thereof the words 'shall not exceed fifty,' so that said section as amended, shall read as follows:

'Section 4. The capital stock of the said corporation shall not exceed fifty thousand dollars, and the stock shall be divided into shares of fifty dollars each.'

Approved February 4, 1903.

Chapter 6.

An Act authorizing the State Treasurer to purchase unmatured State of Maine bonds.

Be it enacted by the Senate and House of Representatives in Legislature assembled, as follows:

State treasurer may purchase and cancel outstanding and unmatured bonds of the state.

Section 1. Whenever, from time to time, in the judgment of the treasurer of state, it may be done to the financial advantage of the state, said treasurer of state, with the advice and consent of the governor and council, shall have the right and authority to purchase, with any funds in the state treasury not otherwise appropriated, and when so purchased to cancel, any of the outstanding, unmatured bonds of the state.

Section 2. This act shall take effect when approved.

Approved February 4, 1903.

Chapter 7.

An Act to amend Chapter sixty-one of the Private and Special Laws of eighteen hundred and ninety-nine, entitled "An Act to establish the Bar Harbor Municipal Court."

Be it enacted by the Senate and House of Representatives in Legislature assembled, as follows:

Section 1, chapter 61, laws 1899, amended.

Bar Harbor municipal court established.

—record and seal.

Section 1. Section one of chapter sixty-one of the private and special laws of eighteen hundred and ninety-nine is hereby amended so that it shall read as follows:

'Section 1. A municipal court is hereby established in the town of Eden, which shall be called the Bar Harbor Municipal Court, and shall be a court of record with a seal. All original processes, issuing from said court, shall be under the teste of the judge, and signed by the judge, or recorder, and shall have the seal of said court affixed.'

Section 3, chapter 61, laws 1899, amended.

Section 2. Section three of said act is hereby amended so that it shall read as follows:

'Section 3. The governor, by and with the consent of the council, may appoint a recorder of said court, who shall hold his said office for the term of four years. Said recorder shall be sworn to the faithful discharge of his duties, and shall give bonds in such sum as the county commissioners shall approve. He may administer oaths and shall have such powers and perform such duties in civil matters as are possessed and performed by clerks of the supreme judicial courts; and in case of the absence of the judge from the court room, or when the office of judge shall be vacant, the said recorder shall have and exercise all the powers of judge by this act, and shall be empowered to sign and issue all papers and processes, in criminal cases, and do all acts relating to criminal proceedings as fully and with the same effect as the judge could do if he were acting in the premises; and the signature of the recorder, as such, shall be sufficient evidence of his right to act instead of the judge. But nothing in this act shall give the recorder authority to act, except as before defined, other than in criminal cases. Said recorder shall receive as compensation for his services the same fees allowed by law to trial justices and clerks of the supreme judicial courts for similar services, except that he shall receive for receiving a complaint and issuing a warrant one dollar.'

Section 3. Section nine of said act is hereby amended so that it shall read as follows:

'Section 9. A term of said court shall be held for the transaction of civil business on the first Wednesday of each month, beginning at ten o'clock in the forenoon; except that for the entry, trial and disposition of actions of forcible entry and detainer, and for the cognizance and trial of criminal actions said court shall be considered in constant session.'

Section 4. Section twenty of said act is hereby amended so that it shall read as follows:

'Section 20. The judge of said court shall receive as compensation a salary of seven hundred and fifty dollars a year to be paid quarterly from the treasury of the county of Hancock, which shall be in full for his services. The fees in civil cases shall be for every blank writ signed by the judge, or recorder, four cents, for entry of each civil action, sixty cents, for trial of issue, two dollars; all other fees not herein specified shall be the same as allowed by law to trial justices and the clerks of the supreme judicial courts, for similar services. All costs in criminal cases shall be taxed the same and paid into court in the same manner as in trial justice courts, except that each warrant issued shall be taxed at one dollar, and each trial of issue shall be taxed at two dollars.'

SEBASTICOOK POWER COMPANY.

CHAP. 8

Section 5. All acts or parts of acts, inconsistent with this act, are hereby repealed.

Section 6. This act shall take effect when approved.

Approved February 4, 1903.

Chapter 8.

An Act recognizing Sebasticook Power Company as a corporation legally organized, and to grant to it additional powers.

Be it enacted by the Senate and House of Representatives in Legislature assembled, as follows:

Sebasticook Power Company authorized to erect dam.

Section 1. Sebasticook Power Company, a corporation organized under the general laws of Maine, located at Pittsfield in said state, is hereby authorized to erect, construct, maintain and repair and extend a dam across the Sebasticook river, with necessary side dams and canals appurtenant thereto across the Sebasticook river upon land which said corporation now owns or may acquire, near the house of Albion Maine, one end of which dam shall rest on land in Pittsfield, in Somerset county, and the other end of which shall rest on land in Burnham, in the county of Waldo, and by means of such dam to flow any and all lands on said river or any of its tributaries above the proposed dam and below any dam now existing, and to erect, maintain and operate mills on or near said dam for the purposes of grinding different kinds of grain, the sawing and finishing of all kinds of lumber, and the manufacturing of woolen and cotton cloths, said mills to be furnished with power from said dam; also for the purposes, notwithstanding the rights of any other corporation, of making, generating, selling, distributing and supplying gas or electricity, or both, for heating, lighting, manufacturing or mechanical purposes in and to the towns of Burnham in said county of Waldo, and Palmyra, Detroit and Pittsfield, in said county of Somerset, or any of them, or to any village corporation in any of the above towns, or to any inhabitant of any of said towns, or to any one doing business in any of said towns, with the right for any and all the above purposes to purchase or otherwise acquire any lands or real estate or any rights of flowage and other rights as may be necessary to accomplish the purposes above set out, to purchase and otherwise acquire, distribute, sell and deal in electrical fixtures and apparatus and all other kinds of merchandise and personal property.

—may flow lands.

—may operate mills.

—may supply gas or electricity.

—may acquire real estate.

—may deal in personal property.

May take and hold lands for purposes of corporation.

Section 2. Said incorporation is hereby empowered to take and hold as for public uses such lands and property as may be necessary for the purpose of said corporation as herein provided,

SEBASTICOOK POWER COMPANY.   11

CHAP. 8

and such material as may be needed for erecting and maintaining its dams and structures, and in case said corporation cannot agree with the owner or owners as to the price to be paid therefor, the same shall be determined by the county commissioners of the county wherein the land or the personal property taken is situated, upon application of any party interested to such county commissioners, in the same manner as damages are assessed for the location, alteration and discontinuance of highways, as provided in chapter eighteen of the revised statutes of eighteen hundred and eighty-three, and acts amendatory thereto and additional thereto, and the same rights of appeal from the decision of said county commissioners shall exist and may be prosecuted in the same manner as provided in chapter eighteen, and acts amendatory thereto and additional thereto. Said corporation is hereby empowered also to flow such lands as may be necessary to carry out the purposes of this act, and said corporation shall be liable to all damages by said flowing, to be ascertained and determined in the manner described in chapter ninety-two of the revised statutes, and acts amendatory thereto and additional thereto.

—price, how determined.

—appeal, how taken.

—may flow lands.

—shall be liable for damages.

Section 3. For the purpose of raising funds to be used in the construction and maintenance of its works, and to carry out the purposes for which it is created, said corporation is also authorized to issue its bonds to an amount not exceeding one hundred thousand dollars, and of such date and denomination and payable at such times as said company may determine, and to secure said bonds, both principal and interest, by mortgage upon all its property, both real and personal, and also upon the franchise of the corporation.

Funds, how to be used.

—may issue bonds.

—may secure bonds by mortgage.

Section 4. Said Sebasticook Power Company is hereby authorized to purchase any or all of the franchise, rights, privileges and property of the Pittsfield Electric Light and Power Company, a corporation organized under the laws of Maine and located at said Pittsfield.

May purchase property of Pittsfield Electric Light and Power Company.

Section 5. The said Pittsfield Electric Light and Power Company is hereby authorized to sell, transfer and convey any or all of its franchise, rights and property to the said Sebasticook Power Company, and its successors.

Pittsfield Electric Light and Power Company may sell its property.

Section 6. The terms, time and manner of said purchase, sale and transfer shall be determined by the mutual agreement of said parties, subject to law, and any contracts already made for such property are hereby ratified.

Section 7. Said Sebasticook Power Company shall immediately upon the transfer be invested with any or all the rights, privileges, immunities and franchises that either or both of said companies may possess.

How method of sale and transfer may be determined.

Section 8. This act shall take effect when approved.

Approved February 4, 1903.

Chapter 9.

An Act to provide in part for the Expenditures of Government for the year nineteen hundred and three.

Be it enacted by the Senate and House of Representatives in Legislature assembled, as follows:

Section 1. In order to provide for the several acts and resolves of the legislature, requiring the payment of money from the treasury, and also to provide for the necessary expenditures of government for the current fiscal year of nineteen hundred and three, the following sums are hereby appropriated out of any moneys in the treasury, and the governor, with the advice and consent of the council, is authorized at any time prior to the first day of January next, to draw his warrant on the treasury for the same.

School fund and mill tax, five hundred ninety thousand two hundred eighty dollars and seventy-seven cents	$590,280 77
Free high schools, forty-six thousand dollars	46,000 00
Normal schools and training school, thirty-one thousand dollars	31,000 00
Aid to academies, twenty-three thousand dollars	23,000 00
Trustees of normal schools, one thousand dollars	1,000 00
Teachers' meetings, one thousand dollars	1,000 00
State examination of teachers, five hundred dollars	500 00
Summer training schools and distribution of educational documents, two thousand five hundred dollars	2,500 00
Schooling of children in unorganized townships, two thousand five hundred dollars	2,500 00
Superintendence of towns comprising school unions, three thousand dollars	3,000 00
Interest on Madawaska territory school fund, three hundred dollars	300 00
Foxcroft Academy, sixty dollars	60 00
Hebron Academy, sixty dollars	60 00
Houlton Academy, one hundred and twenty dollars	120 00
School district number two, Madison, fifty dollars,	50 00
Public debt, seventy thousand dollars	70,000 00

Interest, sixty-five thousand dollars............	65,000 00
Sheriffs and coroners, one thousand dollars......	1,000 00
Costs in criminal prosecutions, one thousand five hundred dollars	1,500 00
Arrest and apprehension of criminals, one thousand five hundred dollars	1,500 00
University of Maine, twenty thousand dollars....	20,000 00
Militia fund, thirty-five thousand two hundred twenty-two dollars and eighty-eight cents	35,222 88
Care of trust deposits, two hundred dollars....	200 00
Advertising land sale and tax act, nine hundred dollars	900 00
Superior court in Waterville, two hundred dollars,	200 00
Maine state library, one thousand dollars.......	1,000 00
Free public libraries, three thousand dollars....	3,000 00
Donation for founding free public libraries, seven hundred dollars	700 00
Traveling libraries, two thousand dollars........	2,000 00
Williams' legacy to Maine insane hospital, forty dollars	40 00
Investigation of the causes of fire, two thousand dollars	2,000 00
Idiotic and feeble minded persons, three thousand dollars	3,000 00
Damage by dogs to domestic animals, ten thousand dollars	10,000 00
Dog licenses refunded, twenty-five thousand three hundred dollars	25,300 00
Pay roll of council, four thousand five hundred dollars	4,500 00
Contingent fund of governor and council, six thousand dollars	6,000 00
Interest on lands reserved for public uses, eight thousand five hundred dollars	8,500 00
Agricultural societies, eight thousand five hundred dollars	8,500 00
Farmers' institutes and dairymen's conference, three thousand dollars.....................	3,000 00
Enforcement of laws relating to sale of impure food, five hundred dollars	500 00
Maine state agricultural society, one thousand dollars	1,000 00
Maine state agricultural society, for industrial exhibits, one thousand dollars	1,000 00
Eastern Maine state fair, one thousand dollars..	1,000 00

Eastern Maine state fair, to encourage pomology, seven hundred fifty dollars	750 00
Bounty on seals, three thousand dollars........	3,000 00
Bureau of industrial and labor statistics, three thousand five hundred dollars	3,500 00
State board of health, five thousand dollars.....	5,000 00
Registration of vital statistics, two thousand five hundred dollars	2,500 00
Trustees of reform school, one thousand two hundred dollars	1,200 00
Visiting committee to reform school, four hundred fifty dollars.........................	450 00
Sanford legacy to reform school, forty-two dollars	42 00
Trustees of insane hospitals, two thousand five hundred dollars	2,500 00
Visiting committee to insane hospitals, eight hundred dollars	800 00
Trustees Maine industrial school for girls, five hundred dollars	500 00
Criminal insane, three thousand five hundred dollars	3,500 00
County taxes, collected in nineteen hundred and two, thirty-eight thousand four hundred fifty dollars and fifty-six cents	38,450 56
Railroad and telegraph tax due towns, one hundred six thousand three hundred ninety-two dollars and nine cents	106,392 09
Lands reserved for public uses, two thousand dollars	2,000 00
Forfeited lands, two thousand dollars.........	2,000 00
Burial expenses of soldiers and sailors, six thousand dollars	6,000 00
Property exempt from taxation, two thousand two hundred dollars	2,200 00
School in state prison, fifty dollars............	50 00
Books for use of convicts in state prison, fifty dollars	50 00
Medicines for state prison, one hundred fifty dollars	150 00
Physician in state prison, two hundred fifty dollars	250 00
Railroad commissioners, twelve thousand four hundred dollars	12,400 00
Investigation of railroad accidents, one thousand dollars	1,000 00

Penobscot Indians, shore rents, three thousand four hundred thirty-four dollars	3,434 00
Engrossing clerk and proof reader, six hundred dollars	600 00
Journal of senate, three hundred dollars	300 00
Journal of house of representatives, three hundred dollars	300 00
Journal of council, one hundred fifty dollars....	150 00
Indexing and filing senate and house papers, one hundred dollars	100 00
Consolidating and indexing laws, one hundred fifty dollars	150 00
Indices, one hundred fifty dollars	150 00
Expenses of state assessors, one thousand five hundred dollars	1,500 00
Expenses of attorney general, four hundred fifty dollars	450 00
Expenses of superintendent of public schools, five hundred dollars	500 00
Expenses of insurance commissioner, one thousand two hundred dollars	1,200 00
Expenses of bank examiner, one thousand two hundred fifty dollars	1,250 00
Expenses and compensation of state liquor assayer, one thousand dollars...............	1,000 00
Expenses of forest commissioner, four hundred dollars	400 00
Expenses of commissioner of agriculture, five hundred dollars	500 00
Expenses of inspector of factories, workshops, mines and quarries, five hundred dollars......	500 00
Expenses of commissioners for the promotion of uniformity of legislation in the United States, two hundred fifty dollars	250 00
Insane state beneficiaries, seventy-six thousand dollars	76,000 00
Water for state house, one thousand eight hundred dollars	1,800 00
Water for state prison, two thousand five hundred dollars	2,500 00
Lights for state prison, three thousand five hundred dollars	3,500 00
Reports of judicial decisions, six thousand four hundred dollars	6,400 00
Trustees of University of Maine, one thousand dollars	1,000 00

UNION RIVER LIGHT, GAS AND POWER COMPANY.

16
CHAP. 10

Printing, thirty-five thousand dollars	35,000 00
Binding and stitching, eighteen thousand dollars,	18,000 00
Support of paupers in unincorporated places, twenty-five thousand dollars	25,000 00
Maine state cattle commission, contagious diseases, ten thousand dollars	10,000 00
Maine state cattle commission, contagious diseases, deficiency, seven thousand five hundred dollars	7,500 00
Clerks of law courts, two thousand dollars	2,000 00
Clerks of law courts for nineteen hundred one and nineteen hundred two, one thousand eight hundred fifty-four dollars and twenty-five cents..	1,854 25
Amounting to the sum of one million three hundred seventy-five thousand nine hundred six dollars and fifty-five cents	$1,375,906 55

Section 2. This act shall take effect when approved.

Approved February 6, 1903.

Chapter 10.

An Act in relation to the powers of the Union River Light, Gas and Power Company.

Be it enacted by the Senate and House of Representatives in Legislature assembled, as follows:

Organization of Union River Light, Gas and Power Company ratified, approved and confirmed.

Section 1. The organization of the Union River Light, Gas and Power Company, a corporation organized at Ellsworth, Hancock county, Maine, under the general laws of said state of Maine, for the purposes set forth in its certificate of organization approved by the attorney general of said state of Maine, October six, in the year of our Lord nineteen hundred and two, and the right of said company to carry out such purposes, except in the towns of Mount Desert and Tremont, are hereby ratified, approved and confirmed.

—except in certain towns.

May issue bonds.

Section 2. Said company is hereby authorized and empowered to issue its bonds for the carrying out of any of its purposes as named in said certificate of organization and in this act prescribed, except in the towns of Mount Desert and Tremont, to an amount not exceeding the sum of one million dollars, on such rates and time as it may deem expedient, and to secure the payment of the principal and interest on such bonds by appropriate mortgages or deeds of trust of all or any part of its property, franchises, rights and privileges now owned, or to be hereafter acquired by it.

—amount of bonds limited.

—bonds may be secured by mortgage.

DOVER AND FOXCROFT WATER DISTRICT. 17

CHAP. 11

Section 3. Upon the consent of the Bar Harbor Electric Light Company being obtained, said Union River Light, Gas and Power Company may carry out the purposes set forth in its said certificate of organization in said towns of Mount Desert and Tremont.

Section 4. This act shall take effect when approved.

Approved February 6, 1903.

How purposes may be carried out in Mount Desert and Tremont.

Chapter 11.

An Act to amend chapter two hundred sixty-two of Private and Special Laws of eighteen hundred sixty-three as amended by chapter two hundred sixty of Private and Special Laws of eighteen hundred eighty-seven, and chapter fifty-four of Private and Special Laws of eighteen hundred ninety-nine, entitled "An Act to incorporate the Dover and Foxcroft Village Fire Company."

Be it enacted by the Senate and House of Representatives in Legislature assembled, as follows:

Section 1. The name of the Dover and Foxcroft Village Fire Company is hereby changed to the Dover and Foxcroft Water District. And all the rights, privileges, franchise and property belonging to said Dover and Foxcroft Village Fire Company shall belong to said Dover and Foxcroft Water District, the same as though originally granted or conveyed to said Dover and Foxcroft Water District, and all liabilities and obligations of the said Dover and Foxcroft Village Fire Company shall be the liabilities and obligations of said Dover and Foxcroft Water District, the same as if incurred by the Dover and Foxcroft Water District. And all suits hereafter brought by or against said corporation shall be in the name of the Dover and Foxcroft Water District whether the cause of action accrues before or after the said change of name.

Name of Dover and Foxcroft Village Fire Company changed.

—Dover and Foxcroft Water District shall own property of.

—shall assume liabilities of.

—suits shall be in name of Dover and Foxcroft Water District.

Section 2. Said Dover and Foxcroft Water District is hereby authorized to raise money by taxation, for the purpose of operating, repairing and extending its water works system, and for the payment of the debts incurred by its purchase, in addition to the purposes now authorized, to be levied and collected in the manner provided by its charter.

May issue money by taxation.

—how levied and collected.

Section 3. Section five of chapter two hundred sixty-two of private and special laws of the year eighteen hundred sixty-three, is hereby amended by inserting after the word "wardens" in the third line thereof, the words, 'And a water board of three members,' so that said section as amended, shall read as follows:

Section 5, chapter 262, laws 1863, amended.

15

CHAP. 11

Officers of corporation.

'Section 5. The officers of said corporation shall consist of a supervisor, clerk, treasurer, collector, three assessors, four or more fire wardens, and a water board of three members, and such other officers as may be provided for in the by-laws of said corporation. Said fire wardens shall have exclusively all the power and authority within the limits of said corporation that fire wardens chosen by the towns in town meetings now have.'

Section 9, chapter 262, laws 1863, amended.

Section 4. Section nine of chapter two hundred sixty-two of private and special laws of eighteen hundred sixty-three is hereby amended so as to read as follows:

May hire money.

'Section 9. Said corporation is hereby authorized to hire money, in addition to the bonded indebtedness authorized by section six of this act, not exceeding the sum of five thousand dollars, for any purpose for which it is authorized to raise money

—purposes for which tax may be levied.

by taxation, and may at any legal meeting called for the purpose, authorize its treasurer to hire any sum not exceeding five thousand dollars, on such terms as the corporation may direct, provided, however, that for any purpose except for the repairing

—purposes for which money may be hired.

or replacing of some part or parts of its water works system it may not hire money as aforesaid, exceeding two thousand dollars.'

—to pay current expenses.

1. To pay the current running expenses for maintaining the water system, and provide for such extensions and renewals as may become necessary.

—to pay interest on bonds.

2. To provide for payment of interest on the bonded indebtedness of said district.

—to provide sinking fund.

3. To provide each year a sum which together with the money provided for in section eight of this act shall be equal to not less than one nor more than three per cent of the purchase price of said water system, which sums shall be turned into a sinking fund to provide for the final extinguishment of the

—disposition of sinking fund.

bonded debt. The amount set aside for the sinking fund shall be devoted to the retirement of the district's bonded obligations, or invested in such securities as savings banks are allowed to hold, said fund shall be invested by the treasurer under the direction of said water board.

Annual sinking fund fixed.

Section 8. Said Dover and Foxcroft Water District shall annually set aside for a period of thirty years, a sum not less than one thousand seven hundred dollars, to be turned into the sinking fund described in paragraph three of section seven of this act, and may raise the whole or any part thereof by taxation.

May sell power.

Section 9. Said Dover and Foxcroft Water District is hereby authorized to sell or lease for manufacturing purposes any power on its dam at Pratt's Rips, so called, at its pumping station, not used by it for supplying water for its water works system,

DOVER AND FOXCROFT WATER DISTRICT.

provided, however, that such sale or lease shall be subject to a reservation of sufficient power for said Dover and Foxcroft Water District for its present or future needs, in supplying water to its said water system, and the extensions thereof.

Section 10. Said water district is hereby authorized to take and hold by purchase or otherwise any land or real estate necessary for reservoirs, or for preserving purity of the water and watersheds, and for laying and maintaining aqueducts for conducting, discharging, distributing and disposing of water. *May take and hold real estate.*

Section 11. Said district shall be liable for all damages that shall be sustained by any person or corporation in their property by taking of any land whatsoever or by excavating through any land for the purpose of laying any pipes or constructing reservoirs. If any person sustaining damage as aforesaid, and said corporation shall not mutually agree upon the sum to be paid therefor, such person may cause his damage to be ascertained in the same manner and under the same conditions, restrictions and limitations as are or may be prescribed in case of damages by laying out of highways. *Shall be liable for damages.* *—how damage may be ascertained.*

Section 12. The corporate property of the said district shall be exempt from taxation. *Property exempt from taxation.*

Section 5. The water board of three members provided for by section three of this act, shall be chosen by ballot at the special meeting of said corporation provided for by this act, one for one year, one for two years and one for three years, and whenever the term of office of a member of said board expires, his successor shall be chosen by ballot to serve the full term of three years, and in case of a vacancy on said board by death or resignation, such vacancy shall be filled in like manner for the unexpired term. Said water board shall have the full management and control of the water works system now owned by said corporation, and establish such rules and regulations as may be necessary for the convenient and proper management of said water works system, employ a superintendent and such other labor as may be necessary for the proper operation of said water works system, fix the amount of the water rentals which shall be uniform throughout said district, and do all things necessary for the proper operation of said system. They shall approve all bills due from the district before payment by the treasurer. They shall meet twice each year on the first Tuesdays of April and October at the office of the district, at which meetings they shall examine and audit the accounts of the superintendent and treasurer. They shall receive for their services five dollars each for each semi-annual meeting actually attended. They may meet at such other times as they may deem necessary for the welfare *Water board, how chosen.* *—tenure of office.* *—powers.* *—shall employ superintendent.* *—shall fix rentals.* *—shall audit accounts.* *—compensation.*

DOVER AND FOXCROFT WATER DISTRICT.

CHAP. 11

of said system, for which additional meetings they may receive two dollars each for each such meeting actually attended.

May issue bonds.

Section 6. Said Dover and Foxcroft Water District is authorized to issue its bonds in amount not exceeding one hundred and forty thousand dollars, for such purposes and on such terms and conditions as it may deem expedient. Said bonds shall have interest coupons attached. Said bonds shall be signed in behalf of said corporation by its treasurer and countersigned by its assessors, and the coupons attached thereto shall be impressed by the facsimile of the signature of its treasurer. Said bonds shall be a legal obligation of said water district, which is hereby declared

—*is quasi municipal corporation.*

to be a quasi municipal corporation within the meaning of section fifty-five, chapter forty-six of the revised statutes, and all of the provisions of said section shall be made applicable thereto. Said bonds, it is hereby declared, shall be public funds of the

—*shall be public funds of the state of Maine.*

state of Maine, within the meaning of section one of chapter one hundred and sixty-one of the public laws of eighteen hundred and ninety-five.

Section 7. All individuals, firms and corporations, whether

Individual firms and corporations shall pay rates established by water board.

private, public or municipal, shall pay to said district the rates established by said water board, for all water used by them. Said rates shall be so established as to provide revenue for the following purposes.

Section 13. The proceedings of the Dover and Foxcroft

Proceedings of Dover and Foxcroft Village Fire Company made valid.

Village Fire Company in calling, holding and acting in a meeting of said corporation held at the engine house of said company in Foxcroft village on the fifteenth of November, in the year of our Lord, nineteen hundred and two, and by adjournment to the town hall in the town of Foxcroft on said date, and all votes, acts and doings of said corporation at said meetings are hereby ratified, confirmed and made valid.

Section 14. The existing debt due from the Dover and Fox-

Debt to Water Syndicate made valid.

croft Village Fire Company to an association of men in Dover and Foxcroft called the Water Syndicate is hereby ratified, confirmed and made valid, and the contract between the Dover and Foxcroft Village Fire Company and the Water Syndicate dated the twenty-second day of November, nineteen hundred and two,

—*contract made valid.*

is hereby ratified, confirmed and made valid.

Section 15. Said district may at a special meeting called and

District may issue bonds after approval of this act.

held in accordance with its previous votes and by-laws, as soon as may be after the approval of this act by the governor, vote to issue the bonds authorized by section six of this act, and choose the water board provided for in section three of this act. The expiration of the terms of office of said water board shall be in one, two and three years, respectively from the next annual meeting of said district.

Section 16. This act shall take effect when approved.

Approved February 6, 1903.

Chapter 12.

An Act to grant additional powers to the Portsmouth, Kittery and York Street Railway.

Be it enacted by the Senate and House of Representatives in Legislature assembled, as follows:

Section 1. The Portsmouth, Kittery and York Street Railway for the purpose of improving the alignment of its road, for changing the grades thereof, for switches, turnouts, side tracks, spur tracks, stations, car barns, gravel pits or power houses, may purchase and take, hold as for public uses any land and all materials in and upon it, except meeting houses, dwelling houses, public or private burying grounds, or land already devoted to any railroad use and may excavate or construct in, through or over such land to carry out its purposes, but the land so taken for switches, spur tracks and side tracks shall not exceed four rods in width unless necessary for excavation, embankment or material. All lands so taken except for switches, turnouts and side tracks shall be subject to the provisions of section sixteen of chapter fifty-one of the revised statutes. It may enter upon such lands to make surveys and locations, and plans of all locations so taken shall be filed with the clerk of courts in the county of York, and when so filed such land shall be deemed and treated as taken. All damages therefor shall be estimated and paid as in the case of taking lands for railroads.

Section 2. The Portsmouth, Kittery and York Street Railway is hereby authorized to sell or lease its property and franchises to any street railroad whose lines as constructed or chartered would form connecting or continuous lines with the lines of said Portsmouth, Kittery and York Street Railway as constructed or chartered, and in such case the corporation so purchasing or leasing such property and franchises shall be entitled to all the privileges and be subject to all appropriate conditions and limitations contained in the charter and franchise of said Portsmouth, Kittery and York Street Railway. Any street railroad company whose lines as constructed or chartered would form connecting or continuous lines with the lines of the said Portsmouth, Kittery and York Street Railway as constructed or chartered is hereby authorized so to purchase or lease the property and franchises of the said Portsmouth, Kittery and York Street Railway.

May consolidate with, or acquire connecting lines.

Section 3. The said Portsmouth, Kittery and York Street Railway is further authorized to consolidate with or to acquire by lease, purchase or otherwise lines, property and franchises of any street railroad or street railroads whose lines as constructed or chartered would form connecting or continuous lines with the lines of the said Portsmouth, Kittery and York Street Railway as constructed or chartered, and in such case the Portsmouth, Kittery and York Street Railway shall be entitled to all the privileges and be subject to all appropriate conditions and limitations contained in the charters and franchises thus united with or acquired. Any street railroad company whose lines as constructed or chartered would form connecting or continuous lines with the lines of the Portsmouth, Kittery and York Street Railway as constructed or chartered is hereby authorized to consolidate with or to lease or to sell its lines, property and franchises as in this section authorized.

Proceedings pending at time of authorized transfer, may be defended by corporation so acquiring the property.

Section 4. All proceedings, suits at law or in equity which may be pending at the time of any transfer authorized by this act to which any corporation so transferring its property and franchises may be a party may be prosecuted or defended by the corporation so acquiring the same in like manner and with like effect as if such transfer had not been made. All claims, contracts, rights and causes of action of or against any corporation so selling or leasing, at law or in equity, may be enforced by suit or action to be begun or prosecuted by or against the corporation so acquiring property and franchises as aforesaid.

Liability of transferee.

Section 5. When any transfer authorized by this act is carried out and fully completed the corporation acquiring any franchise hereunder shall be liable for the then legally existing debts and obligations of the corporation so making such transfer.

Stock and bonds may be issued, secured by mortgage for purposes of this act.

Section 6. Any corporation acquiring property and franchises by virtue of this act may issue its stock to an amount sufficient therefor, and also its bonds secured by appropriate mortgages upon its property and franchise in such amounts as may be required for the purposes of this act, and thereafterwards may issue its stock and bonds in payment and exchange for the stock, bonds, franchises and property of the corporation making any transfer authorized by this act, in such manner and in such amounts as may be agreed upon.

May issue bonds for funding floating debt, etc.

Section 7. The said Portsmouth, Kittery and York Street Railway for the purpose of funding its floating debt, for extensions, additions and improvements, and for the purposes of this act may issue its bonds from time to time as may be deemed expedient, and in such amounts as may be required therefor and secure the same by appropriate mortgages upon its franchise and property.

Section 8. The locations of all rails, posts, wires and fixtures within the limits of any street, road or way as now established by said Portsmouth, Kittery and York Street Railway are hereby confirmed and made valid.

Section 9. This act shall take effect when approved.

Approved February 11, 1903.

Chapter 13.

An Act to authorize the Kennebec Light and Heat Company to issue bonds.

Be it enacted by the Senate and House of Representatives in Legislature assembled, as follows:

Section 1. The Kennebec Light and Heat Company is hereby authorized and empowered to issue bonds for the payment of its indebtedness and for the further construction and improvement of its plant, for such an amount and upon such rate and time as it may deem expedient and necessary, not to exceed the sum of one hundred thousand dollars, and may secure the same by a mortgage or deed of trust of its franchise or franchises, property and estate owned by it or to be hereafter acquired by said corporation, but said mortgage shall not diminish the security of its bonds heretofore issued by said corporation remaining unpaid.

Section 2. This act shall take effect when approved.

Approved February 11, 1903.

Chapter 14.

An Act to ratify the mortgage of the Fish River Railroad.

Be it enacted by the Senate and House of Representatives in Legislature assembled, as follows:

Section 1. The mortgage of the Fish River Railroad, made by the Fish River Railroad Company to the Central Trust Company, dated January one, in the year of our Lord nineteen hundred and two, is hereby made valid, ratified and confirmed.

Section 2. This act shall take effect when approved.

Approved February 11, 1903.

FISH RIVER RAILROAD—BANGOR AND AROOSTOOK RAILROAD.

CHAP. 15

Chapter 15.

An Act to ratify the lease of the Fish River Railroad and to authorize the sale of said railroad to the Bangor and Aroostook Railroad Company.

Be it enacted by the Senate and House of Representatives in Legislature assembled, as follows:

Lease of Fish River Railroad, made valid.

Section 1. The lease of the Fish River Railroad to the Bangor and Aroostook Railroad Company by the Fish River Railroad Company is hereby made valid, ratified and confirmed.

Fish River Railroad Company authorized to sell its property.

Section 2. The Fish River Railroad Company is hereby authorized to sell and convey its railroad and the franchise thereof and all its other property to the Bangor and Aroostook Railroad Company, and the Bangor and Aroostook Railroad Company is hereby authorized to purchase the same.

Section 3. This act shall take effect when approved.

Approved February 11, 1903.

Chapter 16.

An Act to ratify and confirm the consolidated mortgage made by the Bangor and Aroostook Railroad Company.

Be it enacted by the Senate and House of Representatives in Legislature assembled, as follows:

Consolidated refunding mortgage of Bangor and Aroostook R. R. Co. made valid.

Section 1. The consolidated refunding mortgage made by the Bangor and Aroostook Railroad Company to the Old Colony Trust Company as trustee dated July one, nineteen hundred and one, and recorded in Penobscot registry of deeds, volume seven hundred and eleven, page three hundred and ninety-three, in Piscataquis registry of deeds, volume one hundred and thirty-six, page three hundred and forty-seven, in Aroostook registry of deeds, volume one hundred and eighty-three, page three hundred and ninety, and in Aroostook registry of deeds northern district, volume forty, page two hundred and sixty-one, is hereby made valid, ratified and confirmed.

Extensions may be included in mortgage.

Section 2. If the railroad of the Bangor and Aroostook Railroad Company or any of the branches thereof or any of the railroads included in said mortgage, provided the franchises thereof shall have been acquired by the Bangor and Aroostook Railroad Company, be hereafter legally extended, authority is hereby given to said railroad company to include such extensions in said mortgage and to employ any portion of the proceeds of any of the bonds secured by said mortgage to aid in the construction and equipment of such extensions. If the Bangor and

BERWICK, ELIOT AND YORK STREET RAILWAY. 25

CHAP. 17

Aroostook Railroad Company shall hereafter legally acquire the franchises and property of any other railroad company or a controlling interest therein, authority is hereby given to include such acquired railroad or railroads in said mortgage, and to employ any portion of the proceeds of any of the bonds secured by said mortgage for the purpose of acquiring such franchises and property or a controlling interest therein or for retiring any obligations existing upon such acquiring property.

—future acquisition may be included.

Section 3. This act shall take effect when approved.

Approved February 11, 1903.

Chapter 17.

An Act to enlarge the powers of the Berwick, Eliot and York Street Railway.

Be it enacted by the Senate and House of Representatives in Legislature assembled, as follows:

Section 1. The Berwick, Eliot and York Street Railway, is hereby authorized to buy, lease and use the properties and franchises hereinafter named and referred to and to exercise the powers conferred by this act.

Berwick, Eliot and York Street Railway authorized to buy, lease and use certain properties.

Section 2. The said corporation is authorized to hold for its purposes aforesaid so much real and personal estate in this state and in the state of New Hampshire as may be necessary and convenient therefor.

May hold real and personal estate in Maine and in New Hampshire.

Section 3. The said corporation is hereby authorized to purchase or lease the property, capital, stock, rights, privileges, immunities, and franchises of the Berwick and South Berwick Street Railway, the Portsmouth, Kittery and York Street Railway, the Kittery and Eliot Street Railway Company, and the Eliot Bridge Company, or either of them upon such terms as may be agreed upon. And upon such purchase or lease the said Berwick, Eliot and York Street Railway shall have, hold, possess, exercise and enjoy all the locations, powers, privileges, rights, immunities, franchises, property and assets which at the time of such transfer shall then be had, held and possessed or enjoyed by the corporation so selling or leasing, or either of them, and shall be subject to all the duties, restrictions and liabilities to which they or either of them shall then be subject by reason of any charter, contract or general or special law or otherwise.

May purchase Berwick and South Berwick Street Railway, Portsmouth, Kittery and York Street Railway, Kittery and Eliot Street Railway and Eliot Bridge.
—rights so acquired.

—duties, restrictions and liabilities to which they shall then be subject.

Section 4. The Berwick and South Berwick Street Railway, the Portsmouth, Kittery and York Street Railway, the Kittery

Sale of Berwick and South Ber-

and Eliot Street Railway Company, and the Eliot Bridge Company are authorized to make the sales, transfers and leases authorized by section three of this act.

Section 5. The Berwick, Eliot and York Street Railway is further authorized, with the consent of the legislature of New Hampshire, to purchase or lease the property, capital stock, rights, privileges, immunities and franchises of the Dover and Eliot Street Railway, and of the Eliot Bridge Company, a corporation incorporated under the laws of New Hampshire, or either of them upon such terms as may be agreed upon, and upon such purchase or lease the said Berwick, Eliot and York Street Railway shall in such manner as may be permitted by the legislature of New Hampshire, have, hold, possess, exercise and enjoy all the locations, powers, privileges, rights, immunities, franchises, property and assets which at the time of such transfer shall then be had, held and possessed or enjoyed by the corporation so selling or leasing or either of them, and shall be subject to all the duties, restrictions or liabilities to which they or either of them shall then be subject by reason of any charter, contract or general or special law or otherwise, severally in such manner and under such appropriate conditions and limitations as may be imposed by the legislature of the state of New Hampshire.

Section 6. All proceedings, suits at law or in equity which may be pending at the time of such transfers to which either of the corporations named in section three may be a party, may be prosecuted or defended by the said Berwick, Eliot and York Street Railway in like manner and with like effect as if such transfer had not been made. All claims, contracts, rights and causes of action of or against either of the said corporations so selling or leasing, at law or in equity, may be enforced by suit or action to be begun or prosecuted by or against the said Berwick, Eliot and York Street Railway.

Section 7. When the transfers authorized by this act are carried out and fully completed, the Berwick, Eliot and York Street Railway shall be liable for the then legally existing debts and obligations of each and all of the companies so making such transfers.

Section 8. The said Berwick, Eliot and York Street Railway may issue its stocks and bonds in payment and exchange of the stock, bonds, franchises and property of the corporations making the transfers authorized by this act, in such manner and in such amounts as may be agreed upon.

Section 9. The said Berwick, Eliot and York Street Railway is hereby authorized to sell or lease its property and franchises to any street railroad company whose lines as constructed

BERWICK, ELIOT AND YORK STREET RAILWAY.   27

or chartered would form connecting or continuous lines with the CHAP. 17
lines of said Berwick, Eliot and York Stseet Railway as con- authorized to sell or lease its
structed or chartered, and in such case the corporation so property.
purchasing or leasing such property or franchises shall be entitled
to all the privileges and be subject to all appropriate conditions
and limitations contained in the charter and franchises of said
Berwick, Eliot and York Street Railway. Any street railway
company, whose lines as constructed or chartered would form
connecting or continuous lines with the lines of the said Berwick,
Eliot and York Street Railway, as constructed or chartered is
hereby authorized to so purchase or lease the property and franchises of the said Berwick, Eliot and York Street Railway.
Nothing in this section contained shall apply to any property or —exceptions.
franchises within the state of New Hampshire except as may be
authorized by the legislature of said state by appropriate general
or special law.

Section 10. The said Berwick, Eliot and York Street Rail- Authorized to acquire connecting lines.
way is further authorized to acquire by lease, purchase or other-
wise the lines, property and franchises of any street railroad or
street railroads whose lines as constructed or chartered would
form connecting or continuous lines with the lines of the said
Berwick, Eliot and York Street Railway, as constructed or
chartered, and in such case the Berwick, Eliot and York Street
Railway shall be entitled to all the privileges and be subject to
all appropriate conditions and limitations contained in the
charters and franchises then acquired. Any street railway company whose lines as constructed or chartered would form
connecting or continuous lines with the lines of the Berwick,
Eliot and York Street Railway, as constructed or chartered, is
hereby authorized to lease or sell its lines, property and franchises as in this section authorized. Nothing in this section —exceptions.
shall apply to any street railroad company or to any property
and franchises within the state of New Hampshire except as
may be lawful under the general or special laws of that state.

Section 11. The said Berwick, Eliot and York Street Rail- May issue additional stock and bonds.
way may, for the purposes of sections nine and ten, or either of
them, issue such additional stock as may be necessary therefor,
likewise such additional bonds as may be required for the
purposes of said sections or of either of them and secure the
said bonds by appropriate mortgages upon its franchises and —may secure bonds by mortgage.
property, and thereafterwards issue its stock and bonds, or either
of them, in payment and exchange for the stock, bonds, franchises and property of any corporation making transfers under
sections nine and ten, in such manner and in such amounts as
may be agreed upon.

CHAP. 17

Authorized to cross tide waters upon existing bridges.

Section 12. The Berwick, Eliot and York Street Railway is further authorized to cross tide waters and navigable waters within the limits of any or all the towns within which the aforesaid railroads are built or authorized, upon existing bridges or upon bridges or structures of said company erected therefor, provided, however, that said company shall not unnecessarily

—may erect bridges.

obstruct navigation, and that the manner and conditions of its so crossing said waters upon any bridges, and of its erecting and maintaining any such bridges or structures of its own shall first be determined by the municipal officers of the town or towns

—municipal officers shall determine use and location of bridges.

within the limits of which said bridge or structure shall be so erected, maintained or used, and if said company and such municipal officers shall disagree as to the terms prescribing the manner and conditions of such crossing or of erecting and

—appeal to railroad commissioners may be had.

maintaining any such bridge or structure, the same shall after notice and hearing be determined by the railroad commissioners and their decree thereon shall be final.

May strengthen or widen Eliot bridge.

Section 13. In the event of the purchase or lease of the plant, property and franchises of the Eliot Bridge Company, the said Berwick, Eliot and York Street Railway shall thereupon be authorized to construct, operate and maintain a street railroad upon the said bridge so acquired, first strengthening the same to the satisfaction of the railroad commissioners, or, if it so

—may erect independent structure.

elects it may widen the same or erect an independent structure alongside thereof in a manner not inconsistent with the requirements and conditions of the charter of the said Eliot Bridge Company, and all work so done shall be subject to the approval

—may erect piers.

of said railroad commissioners. It may in so doing erect such piers or other structures as may be by it deemed necessary and convenient to the use of said bridge, but nothing in this section shall be construed as permitting said company to obstruct navigation through or at said bridge to an extent greater than is authorized by law at the time of such sale or lease.

May extend its line from terminus.

Section 14. The Berwick, Eliot and York Street Railway, is hereby authorized to construct, operate and maintain from the terminus of the Kittery and Eliot Street Railway Company, as now built, to some convenient point on the line of the said Berwick, Eliot and York Street Railway as now located or built, a street railroad for street traffic for the conveyance of persons and property along and upon said streets, roads and ways, and over and across such lands as said company may deem best for public convenience, with such single or double tracks, sidetracks, switches, turnouts, stations and appurtenances, and with such poles, wires and appliances as shall be reasonably convenient in the premises, with all the powers and privileges incident to or usually granted to similar corporations.

Section 15. The municipal officers of the town or towns in which the extension authorized in section fourteen shall be built, shall determine the distance from the sidewalks or from the side lines of the streets at which the rails of said company shall be laid. The railroad company or any person interested may at any time appeal from such determination to the board of railroad commissioners who shall upon notice hear the parties and finally determine the questions raised by said appeal. In case said Berwick, Eliot and York Street Railway makes any extensions, additions or variations from the lines of the Portsmouth, Kittery and York Street Railway, or under any other franchise by it hereafter acquired created by special act of the legislature, it shall be competent for the railway company or any person interested to at any time appeal from any determination or order of the municipal officers of any town determining the distance from the sidewalks or the side lines of the streets, of the proposed location of the rails of said company to the board of railroad commissioners, who shall upon notice hear the parties and finally determine the questions raised by said appeal.

Section 16. All the said railroad lines to be operated, constructed or maintained under this act shall be constructed and maintained in such form and manner and with such rails and upon such grade as the municipal officers of the towns where the same are located may direct. Such municipal officers shall have power at all times to make such regulations as to the mode of use of any such tracks, the rate of speed and the removal and disposal of snow and ice from the streets, roads and ways as the public safety and convenience may require. The said railroad company may at any time appeal from any such determination, decrees, rules and regulations made and established under this section, to the board of railroad commissioners who shall, upon notice hear the parties and finally determine the questions raised by said appeal.

Section 17. Whenever the said Berwick, Eliot and York Street Railway requires additional land for the purpose of improving the alignment of any part of the road by it to be built or acquired under this act, or if it requires additional land for double tracking its road to be built or acquired hereunder, and is unable to obtain the same by agreement with the owner, it may apply in writing to the railroad commissioners, describing the land required for either or both of said purposes, and naming the persons interested; the commissioners shall thereupon appoint a time for hearing near the premises and requiring notice to be given all persons interested, as they may direct, fourteen days at least before said time; and shall then view the premises,

CHAP. 17

—fourteen days notice which shall be given.

hear the parties and determine how much if any of said real estate is required for either or both of said purposes. If they find that any of it is so required they shall furnish the corporation with a certificate containing a definite description thereof, and when it is filed with the clerk of courts in the county where the land lies it shall be deemed and treated as taken for public uses; provided, however, that where land is held by a tenant for life and the reversion is contingent as to the persons in whom it may vest on the termination of the life estate, such fact shall be stated in the application and the commissioners shall, in addition to the notice to the tenant for life, give notice by publication to all others interested, in such manner as they deem proper. In tak-

—damages, how estimated and paid.

ing such land the corporation shall be subject to the provisions of section seventeen of chapter fifty-one, of the revised statutes, but the damages therefor shall be estimated and paid in the manner hereinafter provided by section twenty of this act. Lands to be taken hereunder shall be subject to the exceptions mentioned in section nineteen.

Copy of location shall be filed with county commissioners of York county.

Section 18. Before beginning construction of the extension authorized by section fourteen, the said company shall first file with the clerk of the county commissioners for York county a copy of its location, defining its courses, distances and boundaries,

—and with railroad commissioners.

accompanied with a map of the proposed route on an appropriate scale, and a like copy and map shall be filed with the board of railroad commissioners.

May take land for location, construction and use of road.

Section 19. The said Berwick, Eliot and York Street Railway, for the location, construction and convenient use of the road authorized by section fourteen hereof, and for the location, construction and convenient use of any extensions, additions to or variations from the railroad lines by it to be acquired hereunder, or in the location, construction and convenient use of any of the lines of railroad to be built under the franchises to be by it acquired hereunder may, for improving the alignment of its road, for changing the grades thereof, for any main track line, switches, turnouts, side tracks, stations, car barns, gravel pits or power houses, purchase or take and hold as for public uses any land and all materials in and upon it, except meeting houses, dwelling houses, private or public burying grounds or lands already devoted to any railroad use, and may excavate or construct in, through or over such land to carry out its purposes, but the land so taken for its main track line, turnouts, switches and side tracks shall not exceed four rods in width unless necessary for excavation and embankment or materials. All lands so taken, except for its main track line, turnouts, switches and side tracks, shall be subject to the provisions of section sixteen, chapter fifty-one, of the revised statutes. It may enter upon any such lands to make surveys and locations, and plans of all locations and lands so taken shall be filed with the clerk of courts in the county of York, and when so filed such land shall be deemed and treated as taken.

Section 20. For the purpose of determining the damages to be paid for lands taken under this act the land owner or said company may, within three years after the filing of such plans and locations with the clerk of courts as hereinbefore provided, apply to the commissioners of said county of York and have such damages assessed as is provided by law wherein land is taken for railroads, so far as the same is consistent with the provisions of this charter, and where inconsistent or at variance with this charter, the charter shall control. The said commissioners shall have the same power to make suitable orders relative to cattle guards, cattle passes and farm crossings, as in the case of railroads. If the company shall fail to pay such land owner or to deposit for his use with the clerk of the county commissioners such sum as may be finally awarded for damages, with costs, within ninety days after final judgment, said location shall be invalid and the company forfeit all right under the same. If such land owner secures more damages than were tendered by said company he shall recover costs, otherwise the company shall recover costs. In case the company shall begin to occupy said lands before rendition of final judgment the land owner may require said company to file its bond with said commissioners in such sum and with such securities as they may approve, conditioned for such payment or deposit; failure to apply for damages within the said three years by said land owner shall be held to be a waiver of the same. No action shall be brought against such company for such taking and occupation of land until after such failure to pay or deposit.

Section 21. The said Berwick, Eliot and York Street Railway may issue its bonds from time to time as may be deemed expedient, and in such amounts as may be required for the purposes of this act, and secure the same by appropriate mortgages upon its franchise and property.

Section 22. The locations of rails, posts, wires and fixtures within the limits of any street, road or way, as now established by any or all of the street railroad companies authorized to sell their properties and franchises under this act, are hereby confirmed and made valid.

Section 23. The said Berwick, Eliot and York Street Railway shall, except as modified by this act, have all the rights and privileges conferred by general law upon street railroad

CHAP. 18

Duties and privileges in New Hampshire defined.

corporations, and be subject to the conditions, restrictions and limitations thereby imposed.

Section 24. The said Berwick, Eliot and York Street Railway is hereby authorized to accept such franchises, powers and privileges as may be conferred upon it by the legislature of the state of New Hampshire, and to perform such acts within said state as may be required or permitted by the said legislature, and this act shall be read and construed as if the several rights and franchises granted by this state and by the legislature of New Hampshire has been included in and granted as a whole by this act.

May change its name.

Section 25. The said Berwick, Eliot and York Street Railway is hereby authorized to change its name to the Portsmouth, Dover and York Street Railway and upon so doing it shall file a certificate thereof in the offices of the secretary of state in this state, and in New Hampshire and a like certificate with the railroad commissioners of said states.

Section 26. This act shall take effect when approved.

Approved February 11, 1903.

Chapter 18.

An Act relating to the Bar Harbor Electric Light Company.

Be it enacted by the Senate and House of Representatives in Legislature assembled, as follows:

Bar Harbor Electric Light Company authorized to extend its lines.

Section 1. The Bar Harbor Electric Light Company is hereby authorized and empowered to build, extend and maintain its poles and wires along and upon the public highways and streets from Bar Harbor, in the town of Eden, to and through Seal Harbor and North East Harbor, in the town of Mount Desert, and South West Harbor in the town of Tremont, for the purpose of supplying light, heat and power by the manufacture and distribution of gas and electricity, as contemplated by its organization and charter, with all the rights, powers and privileges and subject to all the duties and liabilities by law incident to corporations of a similar nature.

—may supply light heat and power.

Section 2. This act shall take effect when approved.

Approved February 11, 1903.

Chapter 19.

An Act to authorize the town of Boothbay Harbor to construct a bridge across the harbor in said town.

Be it enacted by the Senate and House of Representatives in Legislature assembled, as follows:

Section 1. The town of Boothbay Harbor is hereby authorized to lay out, construct and maintain, across the harbor in said town, a suitable highway bridge along side the present foot bridge, running parallel with said foot bridge and adjoining the same. Said highway bridge shall not exceed twenty feet in width and shall be provided with a draw of the same opening as the draw of the present foot bridge. Authority is hereby granted for the erection of all such piers as may be necessary therefor.

Section 2. This act shall take effect when approved.

Approved February 11, 1903.

Chapter 20.

An Act to incorporate the Auburn and Turner Railroad Company.

Be it enacted by the Senate and House of Representatives in Legislature assembled, as follows:

Section 1. W. P. Sawyer of Lewiston, Maine, F. C. Farr of said Lewiston and H. M. Heath of Augusta, Maine, their associates, successors and assigns, are hereby made a corporation under the name of the Auburn and Turner Railroad Company with power to construct, operate and maintain a street railroad for street traffic for the conveyance of persons and property in the city of Auburn and the town of Turner, from the terminus of the Lewiston, Brunswick and Bath Street Railway, at Lake Grove, so called, in Auburn, to some convenient point in the town of Turner, along and over such streets, roads and ways in said city and town and over and across such lands as may seem advisable and necessary to said company, with such single or double tracks, side tracks, switches, turnouts, stations and appurtenances and with such poles, wires and appliances as shall be reasonable in the premises, with all the rights and powers, and subject to all the duties and liabilities incident by law to similar corporations.

Section 2. The capital stock of said corporation shall be one hundred thousand dollars and may be divided into common and

CHAP. 20

Location of rails shall be determined by municipal officers.

—appeal may be had to railroad commissioners.

Municipal officers shall have power to regulate use of track, rate of speed, and removal of snow and ice.

—appeal may be had to railroad commissioners.

Location, etc., shall be filed with clerk of county commissioners.

May take land outside of street limits when needed.

preferred stock as said corporation may determine. It may make and ordain such reasonable by-laws, not inconsistent in law, as its business may require.

Section 3. The municipal officers of said city and town shall determine the distance from the sidewalks, or side lines of any way at which the rails of said company shall be laid. The said company or any person interested therein may appeal from any such determination to the board of railroad commissioners, who shall upon notice hear the parties and finally determine the questions raised by said appeal.

Section 4. The municipal officers of said city and town shall have power at all times to make all such regulations as to the mode and use of said track of the company, the rate of speed and the removal and disposal of snow and ice from the streets, roads and ways as the public safety and convenience may require. Said railroad shall be constructed and maintained in such form and manner and with such rails as said municipal officers may direct. The said company may appeal from any decree of such municipal officers, made under this section to the board of railroad commissioners, who shall upon notice hear the parties and finally determine the questions raised by said appeal.

Section 5. Before beginning construction of its said road, the said company shall first file with the clerk of the county commissioners of Androscoggin county, a copy of its location, defining its courses, distances and boundaries, accompanied with a map of the proposed road on an appropriate scale and another copy shall be filed with the board of railroad commissioners.

Section 6. Such company outside of the limits of streets, roads and ways may for its location, construction and convenient use of its road for its main track line, switches, turnouts, spur tracks, side tracks, stations, car barns, gravel pits and power houses, improving the alignment of its road or changing the grades thereof, purchase or take and hold as for public uses, any lands and all materials in and upon it, excepting meeting houses, dwelling houses and public or private burying grounds and may excavate in, through or over such lands to carry out its purposes but the lands so taken for its main track line, turnouts, switches, spur tracks and side tracks shall not exceed four rods in width, unless necessary for excavations and embankments, or materials. All land so taken except for its main track line, turnouts, switches, spur tracks and side tracks shall be subject to the provisions of section sixteen, chapter fifty-one of the revised statutes. It may enter upon any such lands to make surveys for its location, and plans of all location of lands so taken shall be filed with the clerk of courts in the county of Androscoggin and when so filed such land shall be deemed and treated as taken. All damages for lands taken hereunder, shall be estimated and paid as in the case of taking lands for railroads.

Section 7. The said Auburn and Turner Railroad Company is hereby authorized to sell or lease its property and franchises to any street railroad company whose lines as constructed or chartered would form connecting or continuous lines with the lines of the said Auburn and Turner Railroad Company as constructed or chartered, and in such case the corporation so purchasing or leasing the said property and franchises shall be entitled to all the privileges and be subject to all appropriate conditions and limitations contained in the charter and franchise of the said Auburn and Turner Railroad Company. Any street railroad whose lines as constructed or chartered would form connecting or continuous lines with the lines of the said Auburn and Turner Railroad Company as constructed or chartered, is hereby authorized to so purchase or lease the property and franchises of the said Auburn and Turner Railroad Company.

Section 8. The said corporation is also authorized to consolidate with or to acquire by lease, purchase or otherwise the lines, property and franchises of any street railroad or street railroads whose lines as constructed or chartered would form connecting or continuous lines with the lines of the said Auburn and Turner Railroad Company as constructed or chartered, and in such case the Auburn and Turner Railroad Company shall be entitled to all the privileges and be subject to all appropriate conditions and limitations contained in the charters and franchises thus united with or acquired. Any street railroad company whose lines as constructed or chartered would form connecting or continuous lines with the lines of the Auburn and Turner Railroad Company as constructed or chartered is hereby authorized to consolidate with or to lease or to sell its lines, property and franchise as in this section authorized.

Section 9. The said corporation is authorized to make such connection with the Lewiston, Brunswick and Bath Street Railway as may be mutually agreed upon and to contract with the said Lewiston, Brunswick and Bath Street Railway for the interchange of cars and such mutual running rights as may be deemed proper.

Section 10. Said company for all its purposes may hold real and personal estate necessary and convenient therefor.

Section 11. Upon the filing of the location of the said Auburn and Turner Railroad, as above provided, any location upon the said streets heretofore granted and approved by the municipal officers of the city of Auburn for the Lewiston and Auburn Horse Railroad Company and not then occupied by the rails of the said company, shall be null and void.

36 MAINE GENERAL HOSPITAL.

CHAP. 21
Subject to general laws of this state except as herein modified.

Section 12. All of the general laws of the state applicable to said railroad corporations, except as modified by this charter, are hereby made applicable to the said corporation.

Section 13. This act shall take effect when approved.

Approved February 11, 1903.

Chapter 21.

An Act to amend the charter of the Maine General Hospital.

Be it enacted by the Senate and House of Representatives in Legislature assembled, as follows:

Charter of Maine General Hospital amended.

Section 1. The Maine General Hospital at an annual meeting of the corporation is hereby authorized, if it shall so determine, to increase the number of its directors from nine to twelve.

—how number of directors may be increased.

If the corporation shall decide to increase the number of its directors as aforesaid, it shall at the same annual meeting elect four directors, two of them to hold office for the term of three years, and two of them to hold office for the term of four years. Thereafterwards, annually, two directors shall be chosen by the corporation for the term of four years.

—tenure of office established.

—when the visitors shall appoint one director.

Otherwise the provisions of existing law relating to the hospital remain unchanged, except that when such increase in the number of its directors has been made by the hospital, the visitors shall appoint one additional director to hold office for the term of four years, and at the expiration of the term of any director appointed by the visitors they shall appoint annually one person to be a director for four years; so that the number of directors appointed by the visitors shall be four with terms corresponding to the terms of the directors chosen by the corporation.

Section 2. This act shall take effect when approved.

Approved February 11, 1903.

Chapter 22.

An Act to establish a Street and Sewer Commission for the city of Bath.

Be it enacted by the Senate and House of Representatives in Legislature assembled, as follows:

Section 1. All work done and money expended by the city of Bath in the building and maintenance of streets, sidewalks, bridges, public landings and drains and sewers shall be under the direction of a board to be designated the Street and Sewer Commission, who shall have charge and control of all property and apparatus held by the city of Bath for use in this department and shall have the powers of surveyors of highways. *Bath Street and Sewer Commission, powers and duties of, defined*

Section 2. This board shall consist of five members, including the mayor, who shall be a member, ex-officio. *Board, how constituted.*

Section 3. The other four members to be citizens of Bath, who shall be elected by the voters at the annual municipal election in March, one to be elected each year to serve four years. *How elected.*

Section 4. At the first election of this board four members shall be elected, one to serve one year, one to serve two years, one to serve three years and one to serve four years, the term of each to be determined by lot among the members at their first meeting. *Term of each, how determined.*

Section 5. Any vacancy occurring in the board may be filled for the remainder of the current municipal year by ballot of the city council in joint convention, and at the next municipal election a member shall be elected to fill the vacancy for the unexpired term. *Vacancies, how filled.*

Section 6. No member of the city council shall be eligible for service upon this board, and no two members of the board shall be residents of the same ward. *No member of city council and no two residents of same ward eligible.*

Section 7. This board shall on the third Monday in March organize by the choice of one of its members, other than the mayor, as chairman, and shall elect a secretary whose duty it shall be to keep a record of the proceedings of the board, to notify members of meetings and perform such other duties as the board may elect. *Organization of board.*

Section 8. The board shall also elect a superintendent of streets and sewers who shall have executive charge of work under the direction and control of the board. He may contract for necessary labor and materials subject at all times to the approval of the board, to whom he shall render an account monthly, or oftener if required, of all receipts, expenditures and outstanding bills. *Shall elect a superintendent. —his powers and duties.*

Section 9. The weekly pay roll and all bills not passed upon by the board shall be approved by the chairman of the board, *Pay roll and bills, how approved.*

LINCOLN COUNTY STREET RAILWAY.

CHAP. 23

Compensation of officers.

or in his absence by some member designated by him before being paid from the city treasury.

Section 10. The compensation of the secretary of the board and of the superintendent of streets and sewers shall be fixed by the board and shall be paid from the appropriation made for the work of the board.

Board shall, at beginning of each year, submit estimates, etc., to city council.

Section 11. The board shall, at the beginning of each year, submit to the city council for its guidance in making appropriations, a statement of work proposed to be done in its department, with approximate estimates of cost, and such other information regarding its work as the city council may require, and

—at close of year shall make report.

shall at the close of the year make a full, detailed report to the city council of receipts and expenditures and of work done, and shall have no authority to make expenditures in excess of the amount appropriated for its use by the city council, and no part of said appropriation shall be paid to any member of the board for services as a member of the commission.

When first election under this act shall be held.

Section 12. The first election under this act shall be held at the municipal election next after the act shall have been accepted by the city of Bath, and the other provisions of the act shall take effect at the beginning of the municipal year immediately following, and any and all acts or parts of acts now in force which conflict with the same are hereby repealed.

—inconsistent acts, repealed

Section 13. This act shall take effect when approved.

Approved February 12, 1903.

Chapter 23.

An Act to confer additional powers upon the Lincoln County Street Railway.

Be it enacted by the Senate and House of Representatives in Legislature assembled, as follows:

Lincoln County Street Railway authorized to maintain a street railroad in Wiscasset, Edgecomb, Boothbay, Boothbay Harbor and Newcastle.

Section 1. The Lincoln County Street Railway, a corporation duly created under the general laws of this state, is hereby authorized to construct, operate and maintain a street railroad, for street traffic for the conveyance of persons and property, in the towns of Wiscasset, Edgecomb, Boothbay, Boothbay Harbor, and Newcastle, along and over such streets, roads and ways as shall, from time to time, be determined by the municipal officers of said towns, upon petition of said company, and over and across such lands as may seem advisable and necessary to said company, with such single or double tracks, sidetracks, switches, turnouts, stations and appurtenances, and with such poles, wires and appliances as shall be reasonably convenient in the premises, with all the powers and privileges incident to or usually granted to similar corporations.

LINCOLN COUNTY STREET RAILWAY.

Section 2. The said corporation is further authorized to cross tide waters, and navigable waters, within the limits of any or all of said towns, upon existing bridges, or upon bridges or structures of said company, erected therefor, provided, however, that said company shall not unnecessarily obstruct navigation, and that the manner and conditions of its so crossing said waters upon any bridges, and of its erecting and maintaining any such bridges or structures of its own, shall first be determined by the municipal officers of the town or towns within the limits of which said bridge or structure shall be so erected, maintained or used; and if said company and such municipal officers shall disagree as to the terms prescribing the manner and conditions of such crossing, or of erecting and maintaining any such bridge or structure, the same shall, after notice and hearing, be determined by the railroad commissioners, and their decree thereon shall be final.

Section 3. The said company is authorized to erect, maintain and use such wharves, within the limits of any of said towns, as may be licensed under the general laws of the state, applicable thereto.

Section 4. The said company, in the town of Boothbay Harbor, in addition to the rights conferred under section two, is authorized to cross the tide waters of the harbor in said town, from the north shore thereof, to some point on the existing foot bridge, so called, or to any highway bridge to be hereafterwards erected alongside said foot bridge, and thence, across said foot bridge, or new bridge, and to build, own and use, upon the southerly side of said foot bridge, in the tide waters of said harbor, a wharf, with the following limits: Beginning at a point about two hundred feet westerly from the east end of said foot bridge, thence southerly into said harbor, three hundred and twenty-five feet, thence westerly, at a right angle, one hundred feet, thence at a right angle three hundred and twenty-five feet to said foot bridge, thence easterly, by said foot bridge to the point begun at; but the manner and conditions of crossing said foot bridge or new bridge shall be determined as provided in section two.

Section 5. Said company is hereby authorized to purchase or lease the plant, property and franchises of the Wiscasset Bridge Company, upon such terms as may be mutually agreed upon, and the said Wiscasset Bridge Company is hereby authorized to so make said sale or lease. In the event of any such sale or lease the said Lincoln County Street Railway shall succeed to and enjoy all the rights, privileges, immunities and franchises of the said Wiscasset Bridge Company, and be subject to all the duties and obligations of its charter. The said Lincoln County

CHAP. 23

—may operate its road on bridge when acquired.

—may widen bridge.

Street Railway shall thereupon be authorized to construct, operate and maintain its railroad upon the said bridge so acquired, first strengthening the same to the satisfaction of the railroad commissioners, or if it so elects it may widen the same or erect an independent structure alongside the same, and all work so done shall be subject to the approval of said commissioners. It may widen the draw therein and erect such piers or other structures as may be by it deemed necessary in the convenient use of said bridge, but nothing in this section shall be construed as permitting said company to obstruct navigation through said bridge to an extent greater than is authorized by law at the time of such sale and lease.

Municipal officers shall determine location of railroad on streets, etc.

—appeal may be had to railroad commissioners.

Section 6. The municipal officers of said towns shall, in their written approvals in the location of said railroad upon the streets, roads and ways of the respective towns, therein determine the distance from the sidewalks, or the side lines thereof, at which the rails of said company shall be laid. The said company or any person interested therein may appeal from any such determination to the board of railroad commissioners, who shall upon notice hear the parties and finally determine the questions raised by said appeal.

May make connections and contracts with certain steam railroads.

Section 7. The said corporation is authorized to make such connection with the Maine Central Railroad Company, and the Wiscasset, Waterville and Farmington Railroad Company, as may be mutually agreed upon, and to contract with either or both of said corporations for the interchange of cars as may be deemed proper. Before beginning construction of its said road the said company shall first file with the clerk of the county commissioners for Lincoln county a copy of its location, defining its courses, distances and boundaries, accompanied with a map of the proposed route on an appropriate scale, and another copy shall be filed with the board of railroad commissioners.

—shall file location with clerk of county commissioners for Lincoln county.

May hold land, etc.

Section 8. Such company, outside of the limits of streets, roads and ways, may for its location, construction and convenient use of its road for its main track line, switches, turnouts, side tracks, stations, car barns, gravel pits and power houses, purchase or take and hold as for public uses any land and all materials in and upon it, except meeting houses, dwelling houses, public or private burying grounds, or lands already devoted to any railroad use, and may excavate or construct in, through or over such lands to carry out its purposes, but the land so taken for its main track line, turnouts, switches and side tracks, shall not exceed four rods in width unless necessary for excavation and embankment or materials. All land so taken, except for its main track line, turnouts, switches and side tracks, shall be subject to the provisions of section sixteen of chapter fifty-one of the revised statutes. It may enter upon any such lands to make surveys and locations, and plans of all locations and lands so taken shall be filed with the clerk of courts in the county of Lincoln, and when so filed such land shall be deemed and treated as taken.

Section 9. For the purpose of determining the damages to be paid for such location, occupation and construction, the land owner or said company may, within three years after the filing of such plans of location with the clerk of courts, as hereinbefore provided, apply to the commissioners of said county of Lincoln and have such damages assessed as is provided by law wherein land is taken for railroads, so far as the same is consistent with the provisions of this charter, and where inconsistent or at variance with this charter the charter shall control. Said commissioners shall have the same power to make orders relative to cattle passes, cattle guards and farm crossings as in the case of railroads. If the company shall fail to pay such land owner, or to deposit for his use with the clerk of the county commissioners, such sum as may be finally awarded for damages, with costs, within ninety days after final judgment, the said location shall be invalid and the company forfeit all right under the same. If such land owner secures more damages than were tendered by said company, he shall recover costs, otherwise the company shall recover costs. In case the company shall begin to occupy such lands before rendition of final judgment the land owner may require said company to file its bond with the county commissioners in such sum and with such sureties as they may approve, conditioned for such payment or deposit. Failure to apply for damages within the said three years by said land owner shall be held to be a waiver of the same. No action shall be brought against such company for such taking and occupation of land until after such failure to pay or deposit.

Section 10. The said Lincoln County Street Railway is hereby authorized to sell or lease its property and franchises to any street railroad company whose lines as constructed or chartered would form connecting or continuous lines with the lines of the said Lincoln County Street Railway as constructed or chartered, and in such case the corporation so purchasing or leasing the said property and franchises shall be entitled to all the privileges and be subject to all appropriate conditions and limitations contained in the charter and franchise of the said Lincoln County Street Railway. Any street railroad whose lines as constructed or chartered would form connecting or continuous lines with the lines of the said Lincoln County Railway as constructed or chartered, is hereby authorized to so purchase or lease the property and franchises of the said Lincoln County Street Railway.

CHAP. 23

Authorized to consolidate with or to acquire franchises of connecting or continuous lines.

Section 11. The said corporation is also authorized to consolidate with or to acquire by lease, purchase or otherwise the lines, property and franchises of any street railroad or street railroads whose lines as constructed or chartered would form connecting or continuous lines with the lines of the said Lincoln County Street Railway as constructed or chartered, and in such case the Lincoln County Street Railway shall be entitled to all the privileges and be subject to all appropriate conditions and limitations contained in the charters and franchises thus united with or acquired. Any street railroad company whose lines as constructed or chartered would form connecting or continuous lines with the lines of the Lincoln County Street Railway as constructed or chartered is hereby authorized to consolidate with or to lease or to sell its lines, property and franchise as in this section authorized.

May hold real and personal estate.

Section 12. Said company for all its purposes may hold real and personal estate necessary and convenient therefor.

Municipal officers shall have power to regulate form of rail, grade, rate of speed, and removal of snow and ice.

Section 13. The road of said company shall be constructed and maintained in such form and manner and with such rails and upon such grades as the municipal officers of said towns may direct. Such municipal officers shall have power at all times to make all such regulations as to the mode of use of such tracks, the rate of speed and the removal and disposal of ice and snow from the streets, roads and ways as the public safety and convenience may require. The said company may appeal from any determination in relation to the foregoing to the railroad commissioners whose decision thereon shall after notice and hearing be final.

General laws of the state made applicable.

Section 14. All of the general laws of the state, except as modified by this charter, are hereby made applicable to the said corporation.

Section 15. This act shall take effect when approved.

Approved February 13, 1903.

Chapter 24.

An Act to authorize the Biddeford and Saco Water Company to issue bonds, and for other purposes.

Be it enacted by the Senate and House of Representatives in Legislature assembled, as follows:

Section 1. The Biddeford and Saco Water Company is hereby authorized and empowered to issue its bonds for refunding its outstanding bonds, and for corporation purposes, in a sum not exceeding three hundred and fifty thousand dollars for a time not exceeding twenty years, and upon such rates of interest as said company may deem expedient, and may secure the same by mortgage of the franchises and property of the said corporation.

Section 2. The Biddeford and Saco Water Company is hereby authorized to supply the Old Orchard Water Company with a supply of water for fire and domestic purposes for the town of Old Orchard and the inhabitants thereof, and to guarantee, assume and pay all outstanding bonds, contracts, obligations and liabilities of the said Old Orchard Water Company, upon such terms as said companies have mutually agreed upon, and any guarantee heretofore made is hereby declared legal and valid.

Section 3. The Biddeford and Saco Water Company is hereby authorized to purchase, hold, own and enjoy the franchises, property, shares of stock, rights, easements, privileges and immunities of the said Old Orchard Water Company, and the said Old Orchard Water Company, is hereby authorized to sell, transfer and convey its franchises, property, shares of stock, rights, easements, privileges and immunities to the said Biddeford and Saco Water Company, and upon such terms as said water companies have mutually agreed upon. And upon such purchase, sale and transfer, the said Biddeford and Saco Water Company shall succeed to, and have, hold and enjoy all the rights, easements, privileges and immunities heretofore or hereafter granted to said Old Orchard Water Company, in the town of Old Orchard, in the county of York, and shall thereupon and thereafter have the right and power to supply said town of Old Orchard and the inhabitants thereof, with water for fire and domestic purposes, and have all the powers and privileges, and subject to all the duties, restrictions and liabilities by law incident to such corporations, and any purchases heretofore made are hereby confirmed and declared legal and valid. The provisions of this act shall in no way affect or impair any existing contract or contracts between the town of Old Orchard and the Old Orchard Water Company.

Section 4. This act shall take effect when approved.

Approved February 13, 1903.

Chapter 25.

An Act to incorporate the city of Camden.

Be it enacted by the Senate and House of Representatives in Legislature assembled, as follows:

Corporate name.

Section 1. The inhabitants of the town of Camden, in the county of Knox, shall continue to be a body politic and corporate under the name of the city of Camden, and as such shall have, exercise and enjoy all the rights, immunities, powers, privileges, and franchises, and shall be subject to all the duties and obligations now incumbent upon and pertaining to the said town as a municipal corporation, and may enact reasonable by-laws and regulations for municipal purposes and impose penalties for the breach thereof, not exceeding twenty dollars for any one offense, to be recovered for such uses as the city council may designate.

Rights, powers and privileges.

—may enact laws and regulations.

Municipal affairs vested in mayor and board of aldermen.

Section 2. The administration of all fiscal, prudential and municipal affairs of said city, with the government thereof, shall be vested in an officer to be called the mayor, and one council of ten, being two from each ward, to be denominated a board of aldermen, all of whom shall be inhabitants of said city and legal voters therein. Said mayor and aldermen shall constitute the city council, and shall be sworn or affirmed in the form prescribed by the constitution of the state for state officers.

Duties and powers of mayor.

Section 3. The mayor of said city shall be the chief executive magistrate thereof. It shall be his duty to be vigilant and active in causing the laws and regulations of the city to be executed and enforced, to exercise a general supervision over the conduct of all subordinate officers, and to cause their violation or neglect of duty to be punished. He may call special meetings of the city council, when in his opinion the interest of the city require it, by causing a summons or notification to be given in hand or left at the usual dwelling place of each member thereof. He shall, from time to time, communicate to the city council such measures as the business and interests of the city, may in his opinion, require. He shall preside at the meetings of the city council, but shall have only a casting vote. The salary and compensation of the mayor shall be one hundred dollars per annum for the first three years under this charter. It may then be diminished or increased by the board of aldermen, but not oftener than once in three years. He shall not receive from the city any other compensation for any services by him rendered in any other capacity or agency. The mayor shall, in the month of February annually, prepare and lay before the city council an estimate of the amount of money necessary to be raised for

—may call meetings of the city council.

—salary of mayor.

—shall prepare estimates of money necessary for fiscal year.

CITY OF CAMDEN. 45

CHAP. 25

the current financial year, under the various heads of appropriation, and the ways and means of raising the same; and shall also in the month of December, annually, prepare and lay before the city council a statement of all the receipts and expenditures for each department; and said statement shall be accompanied with a schedule of the property, real and personal, belonging to the city, and the value thereof, and the city debt.

—shall annually prepare statement of receipts and expenditures.

Section 4. The city council shall secure a prompt and just accountability, by requiring bonds with sufficient penalty and surety or sureties, from all persons trusted with the receipt, custody or disbursement of money; the city council shall also have the care and superintendence of the city buildings, and the custody and management of all city property, and trust funds for the benefit of schools, public library, parks, cemeteries, and for any other beneficial purpose whether acquired by purchase, gift or legacy; with power to let or sell what may be legally let or sold, and to purchase and take in the name of the city, real and personal property for municipal purposes, to an amount not exceeding one hundred thousand dollars, in addition to that now held by the town, and Camden Village Corporation, and shall as often as once a year cause to be published for the information of the inhabitants, a particular account of the receipts and expenditures, and a schedule of the city property and the city debt. The city council shall have the power to establish by ordinance, such officers as may be necessary for municipal government, and for the management and care of the city property, not provided for by this act, and to elect such subordinate officers as may be elected by towns under general law of the state, for whose election or appointment other provision is not herein made; to define their duties and fix their compensation; to act upon all matters in which authority is now given to said town of Camden or the selectmen thereof; and to determine what streets, if any, shall be lighted and upon what terms, and how said city shall be supplied with water for municipal purposes and upon what terms. The city council shall appropriate annually, the amount necessary to meet the expenditures of the city for the current municipal year. The city council shall have exclusive authority to lay out, widen, or otherwise alter or discontinue any and all streets and highways in said city, and to estimate and allow all damages sustained by owners of land taken for such purpose. A committee of the council shall be appointed, whose duty shall be to lay out, alter, widen or discontinue any street or way, first giving notice of the time and place of their proceedings to all parties interested, by an advertisement in a newspaper published in said city, for three weeks at least, next previous to

Bonds shall be required from persons trusted with receipt, custody or disbursement of money.

—city council shall have custody and management of all city property, etc.

—in name of city may take real and personal property for municipal purposes.

—shall annually publish account of receipts and expenditures.

—may establish such offices as may be necessary.

—may elect subordinate officers.

—may determine what streets shall be lighted.

—shall appropriate amount necessary for expenditures.

—shall have authority over streets and highways.

—how notice shall be given.

CITY OF CAMDEN.

CHAP. 25

the time appointed; or by giving written notice of their intention, to be posted for seven days, in two public places in the city, and in the vicinity of the way, describing it in said notice. The committee shall first hear all parties interested, and then determine and adjudge whether the public convenience requires such street or way to be laid out, altered or discontinued, and shall make a written return of their proceedings, signed by a majority of them, containing the bounds and descriptions of the street or way, if laid out or altered, and the names of the owners of the land taken, when known, and the damages allowed therefor; the return shall be filed in the city clerk's office at least seven days previous to its acceptance by the city council. The street or way shall not be altered or established until the report is accepted by the city council; and the report so filed shall not be altered or amended before it comes up before the city council for action. A street or way shall not be discontinued by the city council except upon the report of said committee. The committee shall estimate and report the damages sustained by the owners of the lands adjoining that portion of the street or way which is so discontinued; their report shall be filed with the city clerk, seven days, at least, before its acceptance. Any party aggrieved at the action of the city council or the committee thereof, in laying out, and accepting, or in unreasonably refusing to lay out or accept such streets or ways, or the assessment of damages, shall have the same remedy as provided by law in the case of town ways. The city shall not be compelled to construct or open any street or way thus hereafter established until, in the opinion of the city council, the public good requires it to be done; nor shall the city interfere with possession of the land so taken by removing therefrom materials or otherwise, until it is decided to open said street. The city council may regulate the height and width of the sidewalks in any public square, place, street, lane or alley in said city; and may authorize hydrants, drinking fountains, posts and trees to be placed along the edge of the sidewalks, or within the limit of any street or way in said city, and may locate and construct culverts and reservoirs within the limits of any street or way in said city, whenever they deem it needful for protection against fire, and the city shall not be liable for any damages caused by such hydrants, drinking fountains, trees, posts and reservoirs, nor by any poles and wires erected in its streets by any parties authorized by law so to do. Every law, act, ordinance, resolve or order of the city council, excepting rules and orders of a parliamentary character shall be presented to the mayor. If not approved by him, he shall return it with his objections, in writing, at the next stated session of the city council which shall enter the objections at large on its journal, and pro-

—how damages for land taken shall be estimated.

—city council may regulate height and width of sidewalks.

—may authorize hydrants, drinking fountains, posts and trees to be placed.

—city shall not be liable for damages caused by said hydrants, etc.

—acts of city council shall be presented to mayor.

CITY OF CAMDEN. 47

ceed to consider the same. If upon such reconsideration it shall be passed by a vote of two-thirds of all the members of the board of aldermen, it shall have the same force as if approved by the mayor. In case of vacancy in the mayor's office, the above provision shall not apply to any act of the council. In case the mayor fails to either sign or return the bill at the next session, then it becomes a law as though he had signed it.

Section 5. The city clerk shall, before entering upon the duties of his office, be sworn or affirmed by the mayor or a justice of the peace, to the faithful discharge thereof. He shall have care of all journals, records, papers and documents of the city; and shall deliver the same, and all other things entrusted him as city clerk, to his successor in office. He shall be clerk for the city council, and do such acts in his said capacity as the city council may lawfully and reasonably require of him. He shall perform all duties and exercise all the powers by law incumbent upon, or vested in the town clerk of the town of Camden. He shall attend all meetings of the city council, and keep a journal of its acts, voted and proceedings. He shall engross all of the ordinances passed by the city council in a book provided for the purpose, and shall add proper indexes, which book shall be deemed a public record of such ordinances. He shall issue to every person who is appointed to any office by the mayor, or elected to any office by the city council, a certificate of such appointment or election. He shall give notice of the time and place of regular ward meetings. In case of the temporary absence of the city clerk, the city council may elect a clerk, pro tempore, with all powers, duties and obligations of the city clerk, who shall be duly qualified.

Section 6. The assessors, overseers of the poor and health officers shall be elected by the city council on the third Monday of January, or as soon thereafter as may be. At the first election thereof under this act, three persons shall be elected assessors, one of whom shall be elected for one year, one for two years and one for three years, and at each subsequent election one assessor shall be elected for three years, each of whom shall continue in office until some other person shall have been elected and qualified in his place. Three overseers of the poor shall be elected in the same manner as are the assessors, and shall hold office for the same time, and all subsequent elections of these officers shall be in the same manner as all subsequent elections of assessors. The city council may elect an assistant assessor in each ward, whose duty it shall be to furnish the assessors with all necessary information relative to persons and property taxable in his ward. He shall be sworn or affirmed

CHAP. 25
—acts may become valid without approval of mayor, if passed by two-thirds vote of all the aldermen.

City clerk shall be sworn.

—duties of.

—shall attend meetings of city council.

—shall issue certificate of appointment by mayor.

Assessors, overseers of the poor and health officers, their election and tenure.

—assistant assessors may be elected.

CHAP. 25

—taxes shall be assessed, apportioned and collected in manner prescribed by law.

City clerk, treasurer and collector of taxes shall be elected by city council.

—tenure.

—proviso.

—vacancies, how filled.

A street commissioner shall be elected.

—compensation.

—duties of street commissioner.

to the faithful performance of his duty. All taxes shall be assessed, apportioned and collected in the manner prescribed by the laws of this state relative to town taxes, except as herein modified, and the city council may establish further or additional provisions for the collection thereof and of interest thereon.

Section 7. The city council shall elect annually as soon after its organization as may be convenient, by ballot a city clerk, a city treasurer and a collector of taxes, and may elect a city solicitor, who shall hold their offices for the current municipal year following their election and until their respective successors shall be elected and qualified; provided, however, that any of the officers named in this section may be removed at any time by the city council for sufficient cause. Vacancies in the above named offices may be filled by ballot of the city council at any time. All warrants directed to the collector of taxes by the assessors and municipal officers shall run to him and his successors in office, and shall be in the form prescribed by law, changing such parts only as by this act are required to be changed. The method of keeping, vouching and settling his accounts shall be subject to such rules and regulations as the city council may establish. Said collector shall collect all such uncollected taxes and assessments, in whatever year assessed, as may be collected during his term of office; and at the expiration of said term his powers as collector shall wholly cease; all sales, distresses, and all other acts and proceedings, lawfully commenced by him as collector, may be as effectually continued and completed by his successor in office as though done by himself; and all unreturned warrants, which would otherwise be returnable to him, shall be returned to his successor in office.

Section 8. There shall be annually elected by the city council a street commissioner, who shall give bonds to the city in the sum of one thousand dollars, with such sureties as the city council shall approve, for the faithful performance of his duty and shall receive such compensation as the city council shall establish and he shall be removed at their pleasure; and if said office shall become vacant by death, resignation or otherwise, they shall forthwith elect another person to said office to fill such vacancy.

I. It shall be the duty of the street commissioner to superintend the general state of the streets, roads, bridges. sidewalks and lanes of the city; to attend to the repairs of the same, and to remove sidewalks when they are dangerous to travelers; and it shall be the duty of the commissioner to cause permanent bounds, monuments or landmarks to be erected at the termini and angles of all highways and streets now located; or that may hereafter be located by the council, or altered or widened as provided by statute, and shall cause plans thereof to be made and filed with the city clerk when required, after the passage of an order by the city council. He shall make all contracts for labor and material, subject to the approval of the city council, and give notice to the mayor or to any police officer, or constable, of any obstruction or encroachment on the streets. He shall superintend the building and repairs of all sewers, drains or reservoirs, and make contracts for labor and material for the same, subject to the approval of the city council.

—shall make contracts.

—shall superintend building of sewers, etc.

II. He shall perform such duties in his said office as the city council may require, and shall at all times obey the directions of the city council, or its committee, in the performance of his official duties.

—shall obey directions of city council.

III. He shall certify all accounts and bills contracted in the discharge of his official duties, to the council for their examination and allowance at each regular meeting of the council.

—shall certify accounts.

IV. No person or corporation authorized by the city council to dig up any public street or sidewalk in said city, shall begin such digging before furnishing to the street commissioner security satisfactory to him, to restore such street or sidewalk to its original condition.

—no person shall dig up any public street without giving security to street commissioner.

Section 9. The city council first elected under this act, shall, as soon after its organization as may be convenient, elect by ballot three persons, legal voters of said city, to constitute a board of managers of ancient burying grounds, and the public cemeteries of said city, to serve one for three years, one for two years, and one for one year from the third Monday of January then next ensuing. and until their respective successors shall be elected, and thereafter the city council shall annually, on the third Monday in January in the same manner elect one person, a legal voter of said city, to serve on said board of managers for three years then next ensuing, and until his successor is chosen. The said board shall have charge and control of the public cemeteries and burial places belonging to the city and shall serve without pay. The board shall keep deposited at the office of the city clerk, a correct record of its proceedings, which shall be open to public inspection.

City council shall elect board of managers of burying grounds and cemeteries.

—tenure.

—duties.

—shall serve without pay.

Section 10. The city council may, by the affirmative vote of two-thirds of all its members, establish by ordinance, a police department to consist of a city marshal and such other police officers and men as it may prescribe, and may make regulations for the government of the department. Until a department of police shall be established in accordance with the provisions of this act, the mayor shall have the appointment, control and direction of the police force of the city.

Police department, how established.

CITY OF CAMDEN.

Chap. 25

Fire department, how established.

Section 11. The city council may establish a fire department for said city, to consist of a chief engineer and such assistant engineers and other officers and men as it may prescribe, and it may make regulations for the government of the department.

Salaries of city officers, how established.

Section 12. The city council shall establish by ordinance, the regular salaries or remuneration of the officers established by this act, in case the same are not fixed herein, and of such other officers as may be hereafter established, and after the first municipal year no ordinance of the council changing any such salary or remuneration shall take effect until the municipal year succeeding that in which the ordinance is passed. Said council may pass such other ordinances not repugnant to law, as they may see fit.

An appropriation for an amount exceeding one hundred and fifty dollars, shall have affirmative vote of a majority of all the members of city council.

Section 13. In case any ordinance, order, resolution or vote involves the appropriation or expenditure of money to an amount which may exceed one hundred and fifty dollars, the laying of an assessment, or the granting to a person or corporation of any right in, over or under any street or other public ground of said city, the affirmative votes of a majority of all the members of the city council shall be necessary for its passage. Every such ordinance, order, resolution or vote shall be read twice with an interval of at least three days between the two readings before being finally passed, and the vote upon its final passage shall be taken by roll call. No sum appropriated for a specific purpose shall be expended for any other purpose, except by a majority vote of all the members of the council, and no expenditure shall be made, or liability incurred by or in behalf of the city, until an appropriation has been duly voted by the city council, sufficient to meet such expenditures or liability, together with all unpaid liabilities that are payable out of such appropriation; provided, however, that after the expiration of the financial year, and until the passage of the regular annual appropriations, liabilities payable out of a regular appropriation to be contained therein may be incurred to an amount not exceeding one-quarter of the total of such appropriations for the ensuing year. No money shall be paid out of the city treasury except on orders signed by the mayor, designating the fund or appropriation from which said orders are to be paid.

—proceedings.

—no expenditure shall be made until provided for by appropriation.

—money shall be paid from treasury only on order signed by mayor.

Selectmen shall divide town into five wards.

Section 14. It shall be the duty of the selectmen of the town of Camden as soon as may be after this act shall have been accepted by said town as hereinafter provided, to cause a division of said town to be made into five wards, in such manner as includes as nearly as may be, consistently with well defined limits, an equal number of legal voters in each ward, and publish the same in one issue at least of a newspaper published in

CITY OF CAMDEN.

Knox county, before the first election of mayor. For the purpose of organizing the system of government hereby established, and putting the same in operation in the first instance, the selectmen of the town of Camden, for the time being, shall at least seven days before the last Monday of March, next after the acceptance of this charter, issue their warrants for calling meetings of the said voters in each ward at such place and hour of the day as they shall deem expedient, for the purpose of choosing a warden and clerk for each ward, and also to give their vote for a mayor to be taken from the city at large, and two aldermen for each ward; and the transcript of the records of each ward, specifying the votes given for mayor and two aldermen, certified by the warden and clerk of said ward, shall, on the evening of the day of said first election be returned to the said selectmen of the said town of Camden, whose duty it shall be to examine and compare the same; and in case such election shall not be completed at the first election, to forthwith issue new warrants until such elections shall be completed according to the provisions of this act; and to give notice thereof to the several persons elected. At said first meeting any legal voter of said ward may call the citizens to order and preside until a warden shall have been chosen; and at said first meeting, a list of voters in each ward, prepared and corrected by the selectmen of the town of Camden for the time being, shall be delivered to the clerk of each ward when elected, to be used as provided by law in town meetings. And on the second Monday of January annually, thereafter, the qualified voters of each ward shall vote on one ballot for city and ward officers as provided by law for elections in cities, all of which officers, except the mayor, shall be residents of the wards or districts where elected. Said officers shall be elected by a plurality of the votes given, and shall hold their offices from the third Monday of January, and until others shall be elected and qualified in their places; all city and ward officers shall be held to discharge the duties of the offices to which they have been respectively elected, notwithstanding the removal, after their election, out of their respective wards into any other ward in the city, but they shall not so be held after they have taken up their permanent residence out of the city; the ward clerk within twenty-four hours after such election, shall deliver to the ward officers elected, certificates of their election, and shall forthwith deliver to the city clerk a certified copy of the record of such election, a plain and intelligible abstract of which shall be entered by the city clerk upon the city records. If the person elected at the first election shall refuse to accept the office, the said board shall issue their warrants for another election; and thereafter in case of a vacancy

CHAP. 25
—shall call ward meetings.

—purpose for which ward meeting shall be called.

—how returns shall be made

—when annual elections shall be held.

—officers shall be elected by plurality of votes given.

—certificates of election shall be delivered within twenty-four hours.

—vacancies, how filled.

CHAP. 25

in the office of mayor, or any alderman, warden or ward clerk, by death, resignation or otherwise, it shall be filled for the remainder of the term by a new election to be called as provided for other city elections, and held within twenty days after the vacancy occurs. The oath or affirmation prescribed by this act shall be administered to the mayor by the city clerk or any justice of the peace in said city. The aldermen elect shall meet on third Monday of January at seven o'clock in the evening, except those first elected who shall meet one week after the first election when the oath or affirmation required by the second section of this act shall be administered to the members present, by the mayor or any justice of the peace in said city. The city council shall by ordinance determine the times of holding stated or regular meetings of the council, and shall also in like manner determine the manner of calling special meetings, and the persons by whom the same shall be called, but, until otherwise provided by ordinance, special meetings shall be called by the mayor, by causing a notification to be given in hand, or left at the usual residence of each member.

—aldermen elect shall meet on third Monday of January.

—stated or regular meetings, time of holding, how determined.

—special meetings shall be called by the mayor.

Section 15. After the organization of a city government, and the qualification of a mayor, and when a quorum of the city council shall be present, said council, the mayor presiding, shall proceed to choose a permanent chairman, who in the absence of the mayor, shall preside at all meetings of the council, and in case of any vacancy in the office of mayor, he shall exercise all the powers and perform all the duties of that office so long as such vacancy shall remain; he shall continue to have a vote in the board but shall not have the veto power. The board of aldermen in the absence of the mayor and permanent chairman shall choose a chairman, pro tempore, who shall exercise the powers of permanent chairman.

City government shall choose a chairman.

—duties and powers.

Section 16. Every officer of the city, except the mayor, shall at the request of the city council, appear before said council and give such information as may be required, and answer any questions that may be asked by the council in relation to any matter, act or thing connected with his office, or the discharge of the duties thereof.

City officers shall, upon request, give information to the council.

Section 17. The aldermen shall not be entitled to receive any salary or other compensation during the year for which they are elected, for their services, nor be eligible to any office of profit or emolument, the salary of which is payable by the city during said term, and all departments, boards, officers and committees acting under the authority of the city and entrusted with the expenditure of public money, shall expend the same for no other purpose than that for which it is appropriated and shall be

Aldermen shall receive no salary.

CITY OF CAMDEN. 53

CHAP. 25

accountable therefor to the city in such manner as the city council shall direct.

Section 18. All officers of the police and health departments shall be appointed by nomination by the mayor, and confirmed by the aldermen, and may be removed by the city council for cause. Except as otherwise provided in this act, all subordinate officers shall be elected annually, in such manner as the city council shall provide, on the third Monday of January, or as soon thereafter as may be, and their term of office shall be one year, and until others are qualified in their place. *Officers of police and health departments, how appointed and removed.*

Section 19. The superintending school committee of the town of Camden consisting of three members, whose terms of office expire, one in March, nineteen hundred and three, one in March, nineteen hundred and four, and one in March, nineteen hundred and five, shall be continued as the superintending school committee of the city of Camden. Upon the expiration of the terms of the members of said committee and thereafter at its annual meeting to elect subordinate city officers, the city council shall elect a person to fill the place of each member whose term expires, who shall hold office for three years. The city council shall have power to increase the number of members of said committee, so electing such additional members that the term of an equal number thereof, as nearly as possible, shall expire in one, two and three years from the date of such increase in number. No member of the committee shall receive any compensation for his services as such. The members of said committee duly elected shall meet and organize as soon after the election of any new member or members as may be. A majority of the board shall constitute a quorum for the transaction of business. They shall have all the powers and perform all the duties in regard to the care and management of the public schools of said city which are now conferred upon the superintending school committees by the laws of this state, except as otherwise provided in this act. They shall annually, and whenever there is a vacancy, elect a superintendent of schools for the current municipal year, who shall not be a member of the board of superintending school committee, and who shall have the care and supervision of said public schools under their direction, and act as secretary of that board. They shall fix his salary at the time of his election, which shall not be increased or diminished during the year for which he is elected, and may at any time dismiss him, if they deem it necessary, proper or expedient. A suitable and convenient room shall be furnished by the city for the meeting of said committee, wherein shall be kept their records open to the inspection of the citizens. The said committee shall annually in *Superintending school committee of town continued as committee for the city.*

—how members of superintending school committee shall be elected.

—tenure.

—powers and duties.

—superintendent of schools shall be elected.

—city council shall fix his salary.

—records shall be public.

CHAP. 25

the month of December furnish to the city council, an estimate in detail of the several sums required during the ensuing municipal year for the support of said public schools, and they shall not increase the expenditures beyond the amount appropriated therefor.

Drains and sewers, city council may lay out, etc.

Section 20. Part I. The city council may make, lay and maintain all such drains or common sewers, as they adjudge to be necessary for the public convenience, or the public health, through the public streets, or through lands of any person or corporation, and may repair the same whenever it is necessary as hereinafter provided. All such drains and sewers shall be the property of the city, and shall be constructed in such manner and of such dimensions as the city council deem best.

—may take land for sewers.

Part II. When such drains or sewers are laid through the land of any person or corporation, and the land taken therefor, the proceedings shall be the same as provided by revised statute and this act in the case of laying out streets.

—may make sewer assessments.

Part III. The city council shall adjudge what lots or parcels of land are to be benefited by such drains or sewers, and establish outlines of same and estimate what sums shall be assessed upon such lots and parcels of land, or the owners thereof, towards defraying the expense of constructing such drains or sewers, the whole of said assessment not to exceed one-half of the cost of such drains or sewers.

—five resident tax payers may apply for construction of local sewers.

Part IV. Upon the application of five resident tax payers for the construction of drains or sewers in a locality, the city council, if it deems them necessary, may proceed to construct such drains or sewers in manner as herein provided.

City council shall adjudge what lands are benefited and assess same equitably.

Part V. When such drains or sewers are completed, the city council shall adjudge what lots or parcels of land are benefited by such drains or sewers, and estimate and assess upon such lots and parcels of land and against the owners thereof, if known, such sum not exceeding such benefit, as they may deem just and equitable towards defraying the expenses of constructing and completing such drains or sewers which shall forever thereafter be maintained and kept in order by said city; the city council shall file with the clerk of said city the amount assessed upon each lot or parcel of land so assessed and the name of the owner of each lot or parcel of land, if known, and the clerk of said city shall record the same in a book for that purpose, and within ten days after filing such notice each person so assessed shall be notified of such assessment by having an authentic copy of said assessment with an order of notice signed by the clerk, stating the time and place for a hearing on the subject matter of said assessment given to the person so assessed, or left at his usual place of abode

—notification of assessment, how made.

CITY OF CAMDEN. 55

CHAP. 25

in said city; if he has no place of abode in said city, then such notice shall be given to or left at the place of abode of his tenant or lessee, if he has one in said city; if he has no tenant or lessee in said city, then by posting the same in some conspicuous place in the vicinity of the lot or parcel of land so assessed, at least thirty days before said hearing; or such notice may be given by publishing the same in a newspaper published in said city, three weeks successively, the first publication to be not less than thirty nor more than sixty days before said hearing; if there be no newspaper published in said city, said publication may be made in the same way in any newspaper published in the county of Knox; a return made by copy of such notice by any constable of said city, or the production of the paper containing such notice shall be conclusive evidence that such notice has been given, and upon such hearing, the city council shall have power to revise, increase or diminish any such assessment, and all such revision, increase or diminution shall be stated in writing and recorded by the city clerk.

Part VI. Any person who is aggrieved by the doings of said city council in laying out and constructing said drains or sewers, or in making said assessments, may appeal therefrom to the next term of the supreme judicial court which shall be holden in the county of Knox, more than thirty days from and after the day when the hearing last mentioned is concluded, excluding the day of the commencement of the session of said term of court; the appellants shall serve written notice of such appeal upon said city council fourteen days, at least before the session of the court, and shall at the first term, file a complaint setting forth the facts of the case; either party shall be entitled to a trial by jury, or the matter in dispute may, if parties so agree, be decided by a committee of reference, and the court shall render such judgment and decree in the premises as the nature of the case may require; at the trial exceptions may be taken to the ruling of the judge as in other cases. —appeal from sewer assessment, how made.

Part VII. All assessments made under the provisions of this act shall create a lien upon each and every lot or parcel of land so assessed, and within ten days after they are made the clerk of said city shall make out a list of all assessments, the amount of each assessment, the name of the persons, if known, against whom the same are assessed, to be by him certified; and he shall deliver the same to the treasurer of said city, and if said assessments are not paid within three months from the date of said assessments, then the treasurer shall proceed and sell such of said lots or parcels of land, upon which such assessments remain unpaid, or so much thereof, at public auction, as is necessary to —sewer assessment, a lien.

CITY OF CAMDEN.

CHAP. 25

pay such assessments and all costs and incidental charges, in the same way and manner that real estate is advertised and sold for taxes under the laws of this state, said treasurer being hereby invested with all the powers in advertising and selling said lots or parcels of land, that any treasurer or collector of taxes of a town may now or hereafter have for said purposes under said laws of this state; and upon such sale the treasurer shall make, execute and deliver his deed to the purchaser thereof, which shall be good and effectual to pass the title to such real estate.

—land sold for sewer assessment may be redeemed.

Part VIII. Any person to whom the right by law belongs, may, at any time within one year from the date of said sale, redeem such real estate by paying to the purchaser or his assigns, the sum for which the same was sold with interest thereon at the rate of twelve per centum per annum, with cost of reconveyance.

Assessments may be collected by suit.

Part IX. If said assessments are not paid and said city does not proceed to collect them by a sale of the lots or parcels of land upon which they are made, or does not collect, or is in any way delayed or defeated in collecting such assessments, by sale of the real estate so assessed, then the said city may, in the name of such city, sue for and maintain an action against the parties so assessed for the amount of said assessment, as for money paid, laid out and expended, in any court competent to try the same, and in such suit may recover the amount of such assessment with twelve per cent interest on the same from the date of said assessment, and costs; provided, however, that if any lot, when sold in the manner before provided, shall not sell for enough to pay the amount of said assessment with interest and costs the owner thereof shall be under no personal liability for the same.

City shall have a seal.

Section 21. Said city shall have a seal, which shall be in the custody of the clerk, and such seal shall bear as its principal device a mountain which shall be as nearly as may be, a representation of "Mount Battie," and for its inscription the name of said city and the date on which said city's existence shall begin under this act.

A municipal court established.

—name.

Section 22. A municipal court shall be, and is hereby established in and for said city, to be denominated the municipal court of Camden, which shall be a court of record having a seal to be established by the judge of said court, which court shall consist of one judge who shall be an inhabitant of the county of Knox, of sobriety of manners and learned in the law, who shall be appointed as provided in the constitution and who shall have and exercise concurrent authority and jurisdiction with trial justices, justices of the peace and of the quorum, over all matters and

CITY OF CAMDEN. 57

CHAP. 25

things within their jurisdiction, and such authority and jurisdiction additional thereto as is conferred upon him by this act.

Section 23. Said municipal court shall have jurisdiction as follows: Exclusive jurisdiction in all matters and things where both parties interested, or the plaintiff and the person or persons summoned as trustees, shall be inhabitants of or residents in said city, or, in case said parties are corporations, have an established place of business in said city; and said court shall also have exclusive jurisdiction over all such criminal offenses committed within the limits of said city, as are cognizable by justices of the peace or trial justices, and under similar restrictions and limitations except as hereinafter otherwise provided. And said court shall have concurrent jurisdiction with the supreme judicial court and the police court of the city of Rockland in all personal actions where the debt or damage demanded, exclusive of costs, is over twenty dollars and not over one hundred dollars, and in all actions of replevin, when it appears that the sum demanded for the penalty, forfeiture or damages does not exceed one hundred dollars, or that the property in the beasts or other chattels is in question and the value thereof does not exceed one hundred dollars, and either defendant or person summoned as trustees, is a resident, or, if a corporation, has an established place of business in Knox county; but this jurisdiction shall not include proceedings under the divorce laws or complaints under the mill act, so called, nor jurisdiction over actions in which the title to real estate according to the pleadings filed in the case by either party is in question except as is provided in chapter ninety-four, sections six and seven of the revised statutes. If any defendant in any action in said court where the amount claimed in the writ exceeds twenty dollars, or his agent or attorney, shall, on the return day of the writ, file in said court, a motion asking that said cause be removed to the supreme judicial court, and deposit with the judge the sum of two dollars for copies and entry fee in said supreme court, to be taxed in his costs if he prevails, the said action shall be removed into the said supreme judicial court for said county and the judge shall forthwith cause certified copies of the writ, officers' return and defendant's motion to be filed in the clerk's office of the supreme judicial court, and shall pay the entry fee thereof; and said action shall be entered on the docket of the term next preceding said filing, unless said court shall be in session, when it shall be entered forthwith, and shall be in order for trial at the next succeeding term. If no such motion is filed, the said municipal court shall proceed and determine said action, subject to the right of appeal in either party as herein provided in other cases. The pleadings in such cases shall be the same as

—Jurisdiction of municipal court.

—concurrent jurisdiction.

—pleadings.

58 CITY OF CAMDEN.

CHAP. 25

—costs, how taxed.

in the supreme judicial court. In any action in which the plaintiff recovers not over twenty dollars debt or damages, the costs shall be taxed the same as before trial justices, except that the plaintiff shall have two dollars for his writ. When the defendant prevails in any action in which the sum claimed in the writ is not over twenty dollars, he shall recover two dollars for his pleadings and other costs as before trial justices. In actions where the amount recovered by the plaintiff, exclusive of costs, exceeds twenty dollars, or the amount claimed exceeds twenty dollars, where the defendant prevails, the costs of parties, trustees and witnesses shall be the same as in the supreme judicial court, except the costs to be taxed for attendance shall be two dollars and fifty cents for each term and for trial of issue, eighty cents. All the provisions of the statutes of this state, relative to the attachment of real and personal property and the levy of executions, shall be applicable to actions in this court, and executions on judgments rendered therein. Actions may be referred, and judgment on the referee's report may be rendered in the same manner and with the same effect as in the supreme judicial court. Said court shall also have exclusive jurisdiction in all cases of forcible entry and detainer arising in said city.

—shall have jurisdiction in cases of simple larceny.

Said court shall have jurisdiction of all cases of simple larceny, and where the property alleged to be stolen shall not exceed the value of thirty dollars, and of all cases of cheating by false pretenses, where the property, money or other thing alleged to have been fraudulently obtained, shall not exceed in value the sum of thirty dollars, and shall have power to try the same, and in either of said cases, to award sentence upon conviction by fine not exceeding fifty dollars, or imprisonment in the county jail with or without labor, for a term not exceeding ninety days. He shall have exclusive jurisdiction of all offenses arising in said city, which are by any law or statute within the jurisdiction of a trial justice, and concurrent jurisdiction with trial justices of the county of Knox, and with the police court of the city of Rockland, of all such offenses arising in said county, out of said city of Camden, except in the said city of Rockland; and shall have exclusive jurisdiction of all offenses against the ordinances and by-laws of said city of Camden.

Terms shall be held on the third Monday in each month.

Section 24. Said court shall be held on the third Monday of each month at ten o'clock in the forenoon, for the transaction of civil business, at such place within said city as the judge shall determine, but the city may at any time provide a court room, in which case the court shall be held therein, and all civil processes shall be made returnable accordingly. Said court may be adjourned from time to time by the judge, but it shall be considered in constant session for the cognizance of criminal actions.

CHAP. 25

Section 25. It shall be the duty of the judge of said court to make and keep the records thereof, or cause the same to be made and kept, and to perform all duties required of similar tribunals in this state; and copies of said records, duly certified by said judge, shall be legal evidence in all courts. The judge may appoint in writing, a recorder, who shall be a trial justice for the county of Knox, duly qualified, who shall be sworn by said judge, who shall keep the records of said court when requested so to do by the judge; in case of the absence from the court room, or sickness of the judge, or when the office of the judge shall be vacant, the recorder shall have and exercise all the powers of the judge, and perform all duties required of said judge by this act, and shall be empowered to sign and issue all processes and papers, and do all acts as fully and with the same effect as the judge could do were he acting in the premises; and the signature of the recorder, as such shall be sufficient evidence of his right to act instead of the judge. When the office of judge is vacant, the recorder shall be entitled to the fees; in all other cases he shall be paid by the judge and shall hold his said office at the discretion of said judge.

Duties of the judge.

—judge may appoint a recorder.

—duties of recorder.

Section 26. Any person aggrieved at any judgment or sentence of said court may appeal to the supreme judicial court in the same manner as from a judgment or sentence of a trial justice, and all such appeals shall be in order for trial at the first term of said appellate court after such appeal is taken. Final judgment in said municipal court may be re-examined in the supreme judicial court on a writ of error or on a petition for review, and when the judgment is reversed, the supreme judicial court shall render such judgment as said municipal court should have rendered, and when a review is granted it shall be tried in said supreme judicial court.

Appeals, how taken.

Section 27. Writs and processes issued by said court shall be in the usual form, signed by the judge and under the seal of said court. They shall be served as like precepts are required to be served when issued by trial justices, except original writs in civil actions, which shall be served not less than seven nor more than sixty days before the sitting of the court at which the same are made returnable.

Writs and processes.

Section 28. Said court is hereby authorized to administer oaths, render judgment, issue executions, punish for contempt, and compel attendance, as in the supreme judicial court, and make all such rules and regulations, not repugnant to law, as may be necessary and proper for the administration of justice.

Court authorized to administer oaths, etc.

CHAP. 25

Actions shall be entered on the first day of the term, in the forenoon.

Section 29. Actions in said court shall be entered on the first day of the term in the forenoon, and not afterwards, except by special permission. When a defendant legally served, fails to enter his appearance by himself or attorney, on the first day of the return term, he shall be defaulted; but if he afterwards appears during the term, the court may, for sufficient cause, permit the default to be taken off. Pleas in abatement must be filed on or before the day of the entry of the action. The defendant may file his pleadings, which shall be the general issue, with a brief statement of special matter of defense on the return day of the writ, and must file them on or before the first day of the next term, or he shall be defaulted, unless the court for good cause, enlarge the time, for which it may impose reasonable terms. Actions in which the defendant files his pleadings on the return day and all actions of forcible entry and detainer seasonably answered to shall be in order for trial at the return term and shall remain so until tried or otherwise disposed of, unless continued by consent or on motion of either party for good cause, in which latter case the court may impose such terms as it deems reasonable; but all other actions unless defaulted or otherwise disposed of, shall be continued as of course and be in order for trial at the next term.

—pleas in abatement, when filed.

Purposes for which trial justices or justice of peace may preside in absence of judge and recorder.

Section 30. If at any regular or adjourned term of said court to be held for civil business, the judge or recorder is not present at the place for holding said court within two hours after the time for opening said court, then any trial justice or justice of the peace and quorum in the county of Knox, may preside for the purpose of entering and continuing actions and filing papers in said court, and may adjourn said court from time to time, not exceeding one week at any one time without detriment to any action returnable or pending, and may in his discretion adjourn said court without day, in which event all actions returned or pending shall be considered as continued to the next term.

Fees of judge.

Section 31. The judge of said court shall furnish his own blanks and may demand and receive therefor the sums allowed by law to trial justices for like blanks, and may also demand and receive the same fees allowed to trial justices and clerks of the supreme judicial court for like services, except that he may demand and receive for a complaint and warrant in criminal cases, one dollar; for the entry of a civil action, fifty cents; for the trial of an issue, civil or criminal, two dollars for the first day and one dollar for each day after the first, occupied in such trial, to be paid to him by the plaintiff in civil cases before trial, who shall recover the same as costs if he prevails in the suit, and the fees so received by said judge shall be payment in full for his services. Provided, that the city council may, at any time, by vote, determine to pay him a salary, which shall be accepted by him instead of said fees, in which case he shall pay all fees of office by him received into the city treasury.

Section 32. Trial justices are hereby restricted from exercising any jurisdiction in the city of Camden over any matter or thing, civil or criminal, except such as are in the jurisdiction of justices of the peace and of the quorum; provided, that the said restrictions shall be suspended until the judge of said court shall enter upon the duties of his office. Any civil action in which the judge is interested but which otherwise would be within the exclusive jurisdiction of said court, may be brought and disposed of by the police court of the city of Rockland in the same manner and with the same effect as other matters therein. Nothing in this act shall be construed to interfere with actions which have been brought and are pending before trial justices in the town of Camden, but all such actions shall be disposed of by such trial justices the same as if this act had not passed.

Section 33. General meetings of the citizens qualified to vote in the city affairs may, from time to time, be held to consult upon the public good, to instruct their representatives, and to take any lawful measures to obtain redress of any grievances, according to the rights secured to the people by the constitution of the state; and such meetings shall be duly warned by the mayor and aldermen upon requisition of twenty qualified voters. The city clerk shall act as clerk of such meetings, and record the proceedings upon the city records.

Section 34. Chapter two hundred and sixty-six of the private and special laws of eighteen hundred and sixty seven, incorporating the Camden Village Corporation, and all laws amendatory thereof and additional thereto, are hereby repealed and said village corporation is hereby abolished, and on the acceptance of this act by the voters of the town of Camden as hereinafter provided, all the property of said village corporation, both real and personal, together with all moneys of said corporation in the hands of the treasurer thereof, or under his control, becomes the property of the city of Camden, and the city of Camden shall assume all obligations of said Camden Village Corporation then existing, and all indebtedness, both temporary and bonded, and shall provide for the payment thereof according to the terms under which said indebtedness was contracted. All persons upon whom taxes have been legally assessed by said Camden Village Corporation, and who have not paid the same, shall be required to make payment thereof to the several collectors to whom warrants for the collection of said taxes have been issued,

CHAP. 25

treasurer of city of Camden.

and said collectors shall pay over the same to the treasurer of the city of Camden. All rights, contracts, claims, immunities, privileges and franchises which might be exercised by said Camden Village Corporation may be exercised and enforced by the city of Camden as its successor; and all privileges, exemptions and immunities granted by the said Camden Village Corporation, if any, shall remain binding upon the city of Camden. The treasurer of said Camden Village Corporation is hereby authorized and empowered to execute and deliver to said city of Camden a deed of the real estate of said Camden Village Corporation.

—proviso.

Provided, however, that this section shall not take effect, until after this act is accepted by the voters of said town of Camden as hereinafter provided and this section has been accepted by the voters of said Camden Village Corporation at a corporation meeting duly called for that purpose.

Rights in any suit, etc. not affected by passage of this act.

Section 35. The passage of this act shall not affect any right accruing or accrued, or any suit, prosecution or other legal proceeding pending at the time when it shall take effect by acceptance as herein provided for, and no penalty or forfeiture previously incurred shall be affected thereby. All persons holding office in said town of Camden at the time this act shall be accepted as aforesaid, shall continue to hold such offices until the organization of the city government hereby authorized shall be effected and until their respective successors shall be chosen and qualified.

Acceptance of this act to be submitted to voters.

Section 36. A town meeting may be held at the usual place of meeting in said town, for the purpose of submitting the question of the acceptance of this act to the legal voters of said town at any time within five years after the approval thereof, except in the months of September and November. At such meeting

—when polls shall be open.

the polls shall be opened from nine o'clock in the forenoon until five o'clock in the afternoon, and the vote shall be by written or printed ballots under an article in the warrant calling said meeting to read as follows, namely: "To see if the town will vote to accept the act passed by the legislature in the year of our Lord, one thousand nine hundred and three, entitled 'An Act to incorporate the city of Camden.'" The town may elect a committee

—how ballots may be received, sorted and counted.

to assist in receiving, sorting and counting the ballots, and a check list shall be used. The affirmative vote of a majority of the voters present and voting thereon shall be required for its acceptance. If at any meeting so held this act shall fail to be thus accepted, it may, at the expiration of six months or more from any such meeting, be again thus submitted for acceptance, but not after the period of five years from the approval thereof. Such meetings shall be called as provided for by the general laws of the state for calling and holding meetings for the transaction of town business.

Section 37. So much of this act as authorizes the submission of the acceptance thereof to the legal voters of said town, and so much as authorized the submission of the provisions of section thirty-six of this act to the legal voters of said Camden Village Corporation for acceptance, shall take effect upon its approval, but it shall not take further effect unless accepted by the legal voters of said town, as herein prescribed. If this act is accepted by said town as aforesaid, then all acts and parts of acts, inconsistent with this act and not specially repealed thereby, are hereby repealed.

Act takes partial effect when approved.

—further effect when accepted by legal voters.

Approved February 12, 1903.

Chapter 26.

An Act to extend the charter of the Eastport Bridge.

Be it enacted by the Senate and House of Representatives in Legislature assembled, as follows:

Section 1. The charter incorporating certain persons for the purpose of building a bridge uniting the towns of Eastport and Perry, passed June twenty-seventh, eighteen hundred and twenty, being chapter fourteen of the private and special laws of eighteen hundred and twenty, and the right to take toll thereunder, which charter was extended for two years, by an act approved March twenty-sixth, eighteen hundred and ninety-five, being chapter two hundred and eighty-three of the private and special laws of eighteen hundred and ninety-five, and was again extended for six years, by an act approved March tenth, eighteen hundred and ninety-seven, being chapter four hundred and fifteen of the private and special laws of eighteen hundred and ninety-seven, are hereby extended for the term of six years, from September twentieth, nineteen hundred and three; provided, that the rate of tolls to be charged and collected shall not exceed those now charged and collected.

Charter extended.

—proviso.

Section 2. This act shall take effect when approved.

Approved February 13, 1903.

64 ST. FRANCIS PL.—PORTLAND AND RUMFORD FALLS RAILWAY.

CHAP. 27

Chapter 27.

An Act to legalize the acts of Saint Francis plantation in the county of Aroostook.

Be it enacted by the Senate and House of Representatives in Legislature assembled, as follows:

Saint Francis plantation, made a legal corporation.

Section 1. That the acts and doings of the plantation of Saint Francis in Aroostook county be made legal and the said Saint Francis plantation be and become a legal corporation.

Section 2. This act shall take effect when approved.

Approved February 18, 1903.

Chapter 28.

An Act to legalize the doings of the Portland and Rumford Falls Railway.

Be it enacted by the Senate and House of Representatives in Legislature assembled, as follows:

Portland and Rumford Falls Railway, capital stock increased and doings made valid.

Section 1. The acts and doings of the Portland and Rumford Falls Railway in increasing its capital stock and in issuing the same are hereby ratified, confirmed and made valid.

Section 2. This act shall take effect when approved.

Approved February 18, 1903.

Chapter 29.

An Act to increase the corporate powers of the Newport Light and Power Company.

Be it enacted by the Senate and House of Representatives in Legislature assembled, as follows:

Organization of Newport Light and Power Company ratified.

Section 1. The organization of the Newport Light and Power Company, a corporation organized under the general laws of the state of Maine, and having an established place of business at Newport, Maine, is hereby ratified, approved and confirmed, and said Newport Light and Power Company is hereby authorized and empowered to carry on the business of making, generating, selling, distributing and supplying gas and electricity

—powers conferred.

for lighting, heating, manufacturing or mechanical purposes in said town of Newport, and in the adjoining towns of Plymouth in the county of Penobscot, and Detroit and Palmyra in the county of Somerset in said state with all the rights, privileges and powers and subject to all the restrictions and liabilities by

NEWPORT LIGHT AND POWER COMPANY.

law incident to corporations of a similar nature. Said Newport Light and Power Company is further authorized and empowered to purchase, erect, manage and control saw, grist and lumber mills and factories for the manufacture of woolen and cotton goods and such other articles as may be incidental to the same or beneficial to the corporation.

—rights, powers, restrictions, liabilities, etc.

Section 2. Said corporation may hold real and personal estate necessary and convenient for its purposes aforesaid, and is also authorized and empowered to purchase, hold, own and dispose of the capital stock and bonds in other corporations.

Section 3. Said corporation is hereby empowered to set poles and erect wires in and through the streets and ways of the said towns of Newport, Plymouth, Detroit and Palmyra for the purpose of furnishing electric lights for public and private use in said towns, under such reasonable restrictions as may be imposed by the municipal officers thereof, subject to the general laws of the state regulating the erection of posts and lines for the purposes of electricity; it is also empowered to transmit electricity for lease or sale to such points in said towns as may be feasible, in such manner as may be expedient, and, subject to the general laws aforesaid, it may erect and maintain all posts, wires and fixtures necessary therefor. Said corporation shall have the right to lay gas pipes in any of the public streets or highways in said towns of Newport, Plymouth, Detroit and Palmyra; the permit of the municipal officers of said towns having first been obtained in writing, and to re-lay and repair the same, subject to such regulations as the health and safety of the citizens and the security of public travel may require, and as may be prescribed by the authorities thereof.

May set poles and erect wires in streets of certain towns.

—may lay gas pipes in streets of certain towns

Section 4. The said company shall be liable in all cases to repay to said towns all sums of money that said towns may be obliged to pay or any indictment or judgment recovered against said towns occasioned by any obstruction or taking up, or displacement of any way, highway, railroad or street by said company in said towns, provided, however, that said company shall have notice whenever such damages are claimed by said towns, from the municipal officers and shall be allowed to defend the same at its own expense.

Shall be liable for damages occasioned by obstructions, etc.

Section 5. Said company shall not be allowed to obstruct or impair the use of any public or private drain or sewer, but may cross the same, being responsible to the owners or other person for any injury occasioned thereby in an action on the case.

Shall not obstruct sewers.

Section 6. Said corporation is hereby authorized to issue its bonds in such amounts and on such time as it may, from time to time determine, not exceeding the amount of capital stock sub-

May issue bonds.

CHAP. 30
—may mortgage its franchises and property.
Certain towns may hold stock in the corporation.

scribed for, in aid of the purposes specified in this act, and to secure the same by a mortgage of its franchises and property.

Section 7. The towns of Newport, Plymouth, Detroit or Palmyra or any manufacturing or machine company having a place of business in said towns, may take and hold stock in said corporation, and contract with said corporation for gas or electricity for light or power.

Section 8. This act shall take effect when approved.

Approved February 18, 1903.

Chapter 30.

An Act to extend the charter of the Camden Trust Company.

Be it enacted by the Senate and House of Representatives in Legislature assembled, as follows:

Camden Trust Company, rights, powers and privileges extended.

Section 1. The rights, powers and privileges of the Camden Trust Company, which were granted by chapter four hundred and three of the private and special laws of nineteen hundred and one are hereby extended for two years from the approval of this act; and the persons named in said act, their associates and successors, shall have all the rights, powers and privileges that were granted them by said act, to be exercised in the same manner and for the same purposes as specified in said act.

Section 2. This act shall take effect when approved.

Approved February 18, 1903.

Chapter 31.

An Act to extend the charter of the Cumberland Trust Company.

Be it enacted by the Senate and House of Representatives in Legislature assembled, as follows:

Cumberland Trust Company, rights, powers and privileges extended.

Section 1. The rights, powers and privileges of the Cumberland Trust Company which were granted by chapter three hundred and sixty-seven of the private and special laws of nineteen hundred and one, are hereby extended for two years from the approval of this act; and the persons named in said act, their associates and successors, shall have all the rights, powers and privileges that were granted them by said act, to be exercised in the same manner and for the same purposes as specified in said act.

Section 2. This act shall take effect when approved.

Approved February 18, 1903.

Chapter 32

An Act to authorize the town of Monson to remove the bodies of deceased persons.

Be it enacted by the Senate and House of Representatives in Legislature assembled, as follows:

Section 1. The town of Monson is hereby authorized to take up from the old burying-ground in the village in said town the bodies and remains of all deceased persons buried therein, and all head stones and markers at the graves therein, and remove the said bodies and remains to the new burying-ground in said town and there decently bury the same, and properly reset such head stones and markers over such dead bodies and remains, at the expense of said town; and to sell and convey all the rights and interest said town has in the old burying-ground; provided, that said town of Monson at any legal meeting or meetings, duly called and notified, shall agree thereto by a majority vote of its legal voters present and voting.

Section 2. This act shall take effect when approved.

Approved February 18, 1903.

Chapter 33.

An Act to legalize the doings of the Rumford Falls and Rangeley Lakes Railroad Company.

Be it enacted by the Senate and House of Representatives in Legislature assembled, as follows:

Section 1. The acts and doings of the Rumford Falls and Rangeley Lakes Railroad Company, in increasing its capital stock and in issuing the same are hereby ratified, confirmed and made valid.

Section 2. This act shall take effect when approved.

Approved February 18, 1903.

Chapter 34.

An Act to extend the powers of the Katahdin Pulp and Paper Company.

Be it enacted by the Senate and House of Representatives in Legislature assembled, as follows:

Katahdin Pulp and Paper Company, powers increased.

—may manufacture and deal in lumber.

—may generate electricity and other power.

Section 1. The Katahdin Pulp and Paper Company, a corporation organized under the general laws of the state, in addition to the powers which it already possesses, is hereby authorized and empowered to manufacture lumber of all kinds; to buy, sell and otherwise deal in the manufactured products of lumber; to carry on lumber operations in the woods, and to supply others carrying on such operations; and to buy and sell logs and other lumber. Said company is also authorized and empowered to generate and create electricity and other power for manufacturing and other purposes within the town of Lincoln, in the county of Penobscot, and to lease or sell the same, also to supply the inhabitants of said town, or any village corporation within said town, with water, lights and heat for domestic, sanitary and municipal purposes, including the extinguishment of fires, and generally to do all things necessary and convenient for carrying on the business of the company, including the carrying on of a general mercantile business in connection with any of the purposes of the company.

Doings made valid.

Section 2. The acts and doings of the stockholders and directors of said company in building and equipping its saw mill at said Lincoln, are hereby ratified, confirmed and made valid.

Section 3. This act shall take effect when approved.

Approved February 18, 1903.

Chapter 35.

An Act to authorize the State Land Agent to convey to the Fish River Railroad Company, rights of way over public lots owned by the state.

Be it enacted by the Senate and House of Representatives in Legislature assembled, as follows:

Right of way over public lots may be deeded to Fish River Railroad Company.

Section 1. The state land agent is hereby authorized, empowered and directed, when thereto requested by the Fish River Railroad Company to execute to said railroad company, for a nominal consideration on behalf of the state, a deed of right of way, six rods wide, over such public lots owned by the state as are crossed by the railroad of said company; the center line of said six rods to be the center line of the location of said railroad.

Section 2. This act shall take effect when approved.

Approved February 18, 1903.

Chapter 36.

An Act to ratify certain doings of the Eliot Bridge Company.

Be it enacted by the Senate and House of Representatives in Legislature assembled, as follows:

Section 1. All of the corporate acts of the Eliot Bridge Company at its meetings held in the state of New Hampshire are hereby ratified, confirmed and made valid. *Corporate acts made valid.*

Section 2. The votes, acts and doings of the said company in empowering the Eliot Bridge Company of New Hampshire to erect, maintain, own and operate the entire bridge authorized by the legislatures of Maine and New Hampshire to be so erected and owned by both of said corporations are hereby ratified. confirmed and made valid and in uniting with the said Eliot Bridge Company of New Hampshire by admitting the stockholders thereof as stockholders thereof as associate members of the Eliot Bridge Company of this state are hereby ratified, confirmed and made valid. *Votes, acts and doings of Eliot Bridge Company made valid.*

Section 3. The Eliot Bridge Company, so incorporated under the laws of New Hampshire, is hereby declared to be a corporation of this state so far as may be necessary to exercise within this state the franchises appertaining to said bridge. *Eliot Bridge Company declared to be a corporation.*

Section 4. The Eliot Bridge Company, incorporated under the laws of this state, is hereby authorized to hold meetings within the state of New Hampshire. *May hold meetings in New Hampshire.*

Section 5. This act shall take effect when approved.

Approved February 18, 1903.

Chapter 37.

An Act relating to the width of the location of the Fish River Railroad.

Be it enacted by the Senate and House of Representatives in Legislature assembled, as follows:

Section 1. The Fish River Railroad Company is hereby authorized and empowered to purchase or to take and hold as for public uses, so much of the land and the real estate through woodland and forest, of private persons and corporations adjoining and in addition to its present location of four rods in width as may be necessary for the location, construction and convenient operation of the railway of said company, and they shall also have the right to take, remove and use for the construction or repair of said railroad and branches and appurtenances, any earth, gravel, stone, timber or other materials on or from the *Fish River Railroad Company may take land to widen its location.*

BANGOR AND AROOSTOOK RAILROAD COMPANY.

CHAP. 38
—proviso.

—proviso.

—damages, how paid or determined.

land so taken, provided, however, that said land so taken together with its present location of four rods, shall not exceed six rods in width, except where greater width is necessary for the purposes of excavation or embankment; and provided, also, that in all cases said corporation shall pay for such lands, estate or materials so taken and used, such price as they and the respective owner or owners thereof may agree upon, and in case said parties shall not otherwise agree, the damages to be paid by said corporation for the lands, estates and materials authorized to be taken by this act, shall be ascertained and determined in the same manner and under the same conditions and limitations as are by law provided in the case of damages for taking their original location of four rods.

Section 2. This act shall take effect when approved.

Approved February 18, 1903.

Chapter 38.

An Act to authorize the Bangor and Aroostook Railroad Company to extend yard tracks across a way in Houlton.

Be it enacted by the Senate and House of Representatives in Legislature assembled, as follows:

Bangor and Aroostook Railroad Company empowered to extend yard tracks.

Section 1. The Bangor and Aroostook Railroad Company is hereby authorized and empowered to extend one or more of its Houlton yard tracks across the town way in Houlton leading from the Military Road to the Farmers Starch Factory to and upon land of Albert A. Burleigh, his consent in writing having been first filed with said company. The railroad commissioners, upon petition therefor, being filed with them by said company shall, after notice and hearing, prescribe the manner and conditions of the crossing of said way by any such track, and said company shall make and maintain such crossings, as said commissioners shall determine.

—railroad commissioners shall prescribe manner and conditions of crossing.

Section 2. This act shall take effect when approved.

Approved February 18, 1903.

Chapter 39.

An Act to amend and extend the charter of the Waldo Street Railway Company.

Be it enacted by the Senate and House of Representatives in Legislature assembled, as follows:

Section 1. The rights, powers and privileges of the Waldo Street Railway Company which were granted by chapter two hundred and fifty-three of the private and special laws of eighteen hundred and ninety-one, as amended by chapter six hundred and thirty-seven of the private and special laws of eighteen hundred and ninety-three, as further amended by chapter three hundred and nine of the private and special laws of eighteen hundred and ninety-five, as amended by chapter five hundred and eleven of the private and special laws of eighteen hundred and ninety-seven, as amended by chapter one hundred and thirty-two of the private and special laws of eighteen hundred and ninety-nine, as amended by chapter two hundred and twenty of the private and special laws of nineteen hundred and one, are hereby extended for two years from the passage of this act, and the persons named in said act, their associates, successors and assigns shall have all the rights, powers and privileges that were granted them by said act, to be exercised in the same manner and for the same purposes as specified in said act.

Section 2. The said corporation in addition to the powers conferred upon it by its charter is hereby authorized to construct, maintain and use its street railroad from the boundary line between the towns of Camden and Lincolnville to and into the town of Camden to a connection with the Rockland, Thomaston and Camden Street Railway, in the manner and under the rights and subject to the limitations of its charter.

Section 3. The said Waldo Street Railway Company for the location, construction and convenient use of its road for any main track line, switches, turnouts, side tracks, stations, car barns, gravel pits or power houses or for improving the alignment of its road or changing the grades thereof may purchase or take and hold as for public uses any land and all materials in and upon it, except meeting houses, dwelling houses, private or public burying grounds or lands already devoted to railroad use, and may excavate or construct in, through or over such lands to carry out its purposes, but the land so taken for its main track line, turnouts, switches and side tracks shall not exceed four rods in width unless necessary for excavation, embankments or materials. All lands so taken except for its main track line, turnouts, switches and side tracks shall be subject to the provisions of

Chap. 39

—may enter upon lands to make surveys.

—damages, how estimated and paid.

May sell or lease its property and franchises.

—connecting lines may purchase.

May consolidate, lease or purchase.

Suits at law, how prosecuted, defended, etc.

section sixteen of chapter fifty-one of the revised statutes. It may enter upon any such lands to make surveys and locations, and plans of all locations and lands so taken shall be filed with the clerk of courts for the county where the land lies, and when so filed such lands shall be deemed and treated as taken. All damages therefor shall be estimated and paid as in the case of taking of lands by railroads.

Section 4. The Waldo Street Railway Company is hereby authorized to sell or lease its property and franchises to any street railroad whose lines as constructed or chartered would form connecting or continuous lines with the lines of the said Waldo Street Railway Company as constructed or chartered, and in such case the corporation so purchasing or leasing such property and franchises shall be entitled to all the privileges and be subject to all appropriate conditions and limitations contained in the charter and franchise of the said Waldo Street Railway Company. Any street railroad company whose lines as constructed or chartered would form connecting or continuous lines with the lines of the said Waldo Street Railway Company as constructed or chartered is hereby authorized to so purchase or lease the property and franchises of the said Waldo Street Railway Company.

Section 5. The said Waldo Street Railway Company is further authorized to consolidate with or to acquire by lease, purchase or otherwise lines, property and franchises of any street railroad or street railroads whose lines as constructed or chartered would form connecting or continuous lines with the lines of the said Waldo Street Railway Company as constructed or chartered, and in such case the Waldo Street Railway Company shall be entitled to all the privileges and be subject to all appropriate conditions and limitations contained in the charters and franchises thus united with or acquired. Any street railroad company whose lines as constructed or chartered would form connecting or continuous lines with the lines of the Waldo Street Railway Company as constructed or chartered is hereby authorized to consolidate with or to lease or to sell its lines, property and franchises as in this section authorized.

Section 6. All proceedings, suits at law or in equity which may be pending at the time of any transfer authorized by this act to which any corporation so transferring its property and franchises may be a party, may be prosecuted or defended by the corporation so acquiring the same in like manner and with like effect as if such transfer had not been made. All claims, contracts, rights and causes of action of or against any corporation so selling or leasing, at law or in equity, may be enforced by suit or action to be begun or prosecuted by or against the corporation so acquiring property and franchises as aforesaid.

Section 7. When any transfer authorized by this act is carried out and fully completed the corporation acquiring any franchise hereunder shall be liable for the then legally existing debts and obligations of the corporation so making such transfer. *Liability for debts fixed, in case of transfer.*

Section 8. Any corporation acquiring property and franchises by virtue of this act may issue its stock to an amount sufficient therefor, and also its bonds secured by appropriate mortgages upon its franchise and property in such amounts as may be required for the purposes of this act, and thereafterwards may issue its stock and bonds in payment and exchange for the stock, bonds, franchises and property of the corporation making any transfer authorized by this act, in such manner and in such amounts as may be agreed upon. *May issue stock and bonds.*

Section 9. This act shall take effect when approved.

Approved February 18, 1903.

Chapter 40.

An Act to amend the charter of the Home for Aged Men in Portland.

Be it enacted by the Senate and House of Representatives in Legislature assembled, as follows:

Section 1. The Home for Aged Men in Portland, a corporation organized under the provisions of chapter one hundred and thirty-three of the private and special laws of eighteen hundred and eighty-one, amended by chapter two hundred and sixty-seven of the private and special laws of eighteen hundred an eighty-three, is authorized and empowered for the purposes of its organization, to receive, take and hold, by deed, devise, bequest, or otherwise, and sell, exchange, convey, or otherwise dispose of property, real and personal, to the amount of five hundred thousand dollars, including all gifts, conveyances, devises and bequests heretofore made to said corporation. *Home for Aged Men in Portland, charter amended. —may hold and dispose of property. —amount.*

Section 2. This act shall take effect when approved.

Approved February 18, 1903.

Chapter 41.

An Act to extend the franchises held by the Wiscasset, Waterville and Farmington Railroad Company.

Be it enacted by the Senate and House of Representatives in Legislature assembled, as follows:

Franklin, Somerset and Kennebec Railway Company, rights extended.

Section 1. All of the rights, powers and privileges of the Franklin, Somerset and Kennebec Railway Company, now held by the Wiscasset, Waterville and Farmington Railroad Company which were granted by chapter four hundred and sixty-seven of the private and special laws of one thousand eight hundred and ninety-seven, are hereby extended to January first, one thousand nine hundred and five.

Waterville and Wiscasset Railroad Company, rights extended.

Section 2. All of the rights, powers and privileges of the Waterville and Wiscasset Railroad Company, now held by the Wiscasset, Waterville and Farmington Railroad Company which were granted by chapter three hundred and seventeen of the laws of one thousand eight hundred and ninety-five are hereby extended to January first, one thousand nine hundred and five.

Wiscasset and Quebec Railroad Company, rights conferred upon successor.

Section 3. All the rights, powers, privileges and immunities conferred upon the Wiscasset and Quebec Railroad Company by section two of chapter one hundred and twenty-six of the private and special laws for one thousand eight hundred and ninety-nine are hereby conferred upon the Wiscasset, Waterville and Farmington Railroad Company as successor to the Wiscasset and Quebec Railroad Company and the said Wiscasset, Waterville and Farmington Railroad Company is hereby given two years from the approval of this act for the location and construction of its road as therein and thereby authorized.

Section 4. This act shall take effect when approved.

Approved February 18, 1903.

Chapter 42.

An Act to authorize the Norway and Paris Street Railway to purchase or lease the property and franchises of the Oxford Light Company.

Be it enacted by the Senate and House of Representatives in Legislature assembled, as follows:

Section 1. The Norway and Paris Street Railway, a corporation existing under the general laws of the state, is hereby authorized to purchase or lease the property, capital stock, rights, privileges, immunities and franchises of the Oxford Light Company upon such terms as may be agreed upon, and upon such purchase or lease the said Norway and Paris Street Railway shall have, hold, possess, exercise and enjoy all the locations, powers, privileges, rights, immunities, franchises, property and assets, which at the time of said transfer shall then be had, held, possessed or enjoyed by the said Oxford Light Company, and shall be subject to all the duties, restrictions and liabilities to which the said Oxford Light Company shall then be subject by reason of any charter, contract or general or special law, or otherwise. *— Norway and Paris Street Railway authorized to purchase the Oxford Light Company. —liabilities, etc.*

Section 2. All proceedings, suits at law or in equity, which may be pending at the time of such transfer, to which the said Oxford Light Company may be a party, may be prosecuted or defended by the said Norway and Paris Street Railway in like manner and with like effect as if such transfer had not been made. All claims, contracts, rights and causes of action of or against the said Oxford Light Company, at law or in equity, may be enforced by suit or action to be begun or prosecuted by or against the said Norway and Paris Street Railway. *Pending proceedings, and suits, how prosecuted and defended.*

Section 3. The Oxford Light Company is hereby authorized to make the sale or lease authorized by section one of this act. *Oxford Light Company authorized to sell or lease.*

Section 4. The said Norway and Paris Street Railway may increase its capital stock to such amount as may be necessary for the purposes of this act, and further may issue its stock and bonds in payment and exchange for the stock, bonds, franchises and property of the said Oxford Light Company, in such manner and in such amounts as may be agreed upon. *Norway and Paris Street Railway may increase capital stock.*

Section 5. When the transfer authorized in this act is carried out and fully completed the Norway and Paris Street Railway shall be liable for the then lawfully existing debts, obligations and contracts of the said Oxford Light Company. *Shall be liable for debts of Oxford Light Company.*

Section 6. The said Norway and Paris Street Railway may issue its bonds from time to time upon such rates and terms as may be deemed expedient, for the purpose of funding its floating *May issue bonds.*

CHAP. 43

—may mortgage its property.

—may change name.

Location of posts, wires and fixtures made valid.

debt and also in such amounts as may be required for the purposes of this act, and secure the same by appropriate mortgages upon its franchises and property by it then held or thereafterwards to be acquired.

Section 7. The said Norway and Paris Street Railway is hereby authorized to change its corporate name and to file proper certificate thereof in the office of the secretary of state in the manner required by the general law.

Section 8. The locations of all posts, wires and fixtures of the said Norway and Paris Street Railway and of the Oxford Light Company as now established and maintained, are hereby confirmed and made valid.

Section 9. This act shall take effect when approved.

Approved February 18, 1903.

Chapter 43.

An Act to grant additional powers to the Portland and Brunswick Street Railway.

Be it enacted by the Senate and House of Representatives in Legislature assembled, as follows:

Portland and Brunswick Street Railway authorized to sell or lease its property.

Section 1. The Portland and Brunswick Street Railway is hereby authorized to sell or lease its property and franchises to any street railroad company whose lines as constructed or chartered would form connecting or continuous lines with the lines of the Portland and Brunswick Street Railway as constructed or chartered, and in such case the corporation so purchasing or leasing said property and franchises shall be entitled to all the privileges and be subject to all appropriate conditions and limitations contained in the charter and franchises of the said Portland and Brunswick Street Railway. Any street railroad company whose lines as constructed or chartered would form connecting or continuous lines with the lines of the Portland and Brunswick Street Railway as constructed or chartered is hereby authorized to so purchase or lease the property and franchises of the said Portland and Brunswick Street Railway.

—any connecting lines may purchase property of.

Portland and Brunswick Street Railway authorized to consolidate with connecting lines.

Section 2. The said Portland and Brunswick Street Railway is further authorized to consolidate with or to acquire by lease, purchase or otherwise the lines, property and franchises of any street railroad or street railroads whose lines as constructed or chartered would form connecting or continuous lines with the lines of the said Portland and Brunswick Street Railway as constructed or chartered, and in such case the said Portland

and Brunswick Street Railway shall be entitled to all the privileges and be subject to all appropriate conditions and limitations contained in the charter and franchises thus united with or acquired. Any street railroad whose lines as constructed or chartered would form connecting or continuous lines with the lines of the said Portland and Brunswick Street Railway as constructed or chartered is hereby authorized to consolidate with or to lease or to sell its lines, property and franchise as in this act authorized.

Section 3. All proceedings, suits at law or in equity which may be pending at the time of any transfer hereby authorized to which any corporation making such transfer may be a party may be prosecuted or defended by the said corporation so acquiring the same in like manner and with like effect as if such transfer had not been made. All claims, contracts, rights and causes of action of or against any corporation making such transfer, at law or in equity, may be enforced by suit or action to be begun or prosecuted by or against the corporation so acquiring property or franchises thereunder. *Pending proceedings, how prosecuted and defended.*

Section 4. When any transfer authorized by this act is carried out and fully completed the corporation acquiring property and franchises thereunder shall be liable for the then legally existing debts and obligations of the corporation so making such transfer. *Liabilities for debts, etc.*

Section 5. Any corporation so acquiring property and franchises hereunder may issue its stock for the purposes thereof, and also its bonds in such amounts as may be required for the purposes of this act and secure the same by appropriate mortgages upon its franchise and property and thereupon may likewise issue such stock and bonds in payment and exchange for the stock, bonds, franchises and property of the corporation making any transfer authorized by this act in such manner and in such amounts as may be agreed upon. *Stock and bonds may be issued by purchaser, for certain purposes.*

Section 6. The location of the rails, posts, wires and fixtures of the said Portland and Brunswick Street Railway as now established in Brunswick, Freeport and Yarmouth are hereby confirmed and made valid. *Location of posts, wires and fixtures made valid.*

Section 7. This act shall take effect when approved.

Approved February 18, 1903.

Chapter 44.

An Act to amend Section thirty of Chapter four hundred and fifty of the Private and Special Laws of eighteen hundred and ninety-three, incorporating the city of Eastport.

Be it enacted by the Senate and House of Representatives in Legislature assembled, as follows:

Section 30, of chapter 450, laws of 1893, amended.

Section 1. Section thirty of chapter four hundred and fifty of the private and special laws of eighteen hundred and ninety-three is hereby amended by striking out in paragraph four all after the word "marshal," and inserting in lieu thereof the words 'who shall exercise all the powers and be subject to the duties prescribed for constables by the laws of the state'; so that said paragraph four, as amended, shall read as follows:

—city marshal, powers and duties of.

'IV. A city marshal who shall exercise all the powers and be subject to the duties prescribed for constables by the laws of the state.'

Section 2. This act shall take effect when approved.

Approved February 18, 1903.

Chapter 45.

An Act to amend the charter of the Rockland, Thomaston and Camden Street Railway.

Be it enacted by the Senate and House of Representatives in Legislature assembled, as follows:

Rockland, Thomaston Camden Street Railway authorized to sell its property.

Section 1. The Rockland, Thomaston and Camden Street Railway is hereby authorized to sell or lease its property and franchises to any street railroad company whose lines as constructed or chartered would form connecting or continuous lines with the lines of the said Rockland, Thomaston and Camden Street Railway as constructed or chartered, and in such case the corporation so purchasing or leasing said property and franchises shall be entitled to all the privileges and be subject to all appropriate conditions and limitations contained in the charter and franchises of the said Rockland, Thomaston and Camden Street Railway. Any street railroad company whose lines as constructed or chartered would form connecting or continuous lines with the lines of the Rockland, Thomaston and Camden Street Railway as constructed or chartered is hereby authorized to so purchase or lease the property and franchises of the said Rockland, Thomaston and Camden Street Railway.

—any connecting lines may purchase property of.

Section 2. The said Rockland, Thomaston and Camden Street Railway is further authorized to consolidate with or to acquire by lease, purchase or otherwise the lines, property and franchises of any street railroad or street railroads whose lines as constructed or chartered would form connecting or continuous lines with the lines of the said Rockland, Thomaston and Camden Street Railway as constructed or chartered, and in such case the said Rockland, Thomaston and Camden Street Railway shall be entitled to all the privileges and be subject to all appropriate conditions and limitations contained in the charter and franchises thus united with or acquired. Any street railroad whose lines as constructed or chartered would form connecting or continuous lines with the lines of the said Rockland, Thomaston and Camden Street Railway as constructed or chartered is hereby authorized to consolidate with or to lease or to sell its lines, property and franchise as in this act authorized. *Rockland, Thomaston and Camden street Railway authorized to consolidate with connecting lines.*

Section 3. All proceedings, suits at law or in equity which may be pending at the time of any transfer hereby authorized to which any corporation making such transfer may be a party may be prosecuted or defended by the said corporation so acquiring the same in like manner and with like effect as if such transfer had not been made. All claims, contracts, rights and causes of action of or against any corporation making such transfer, at law or in equity, may be enforced by suit or action to be begun or prosecuted by or against the corporation so acquiring property or franchises thereunder. *Pending proceedings, how prosecuted and defended.*

Section 4. When any transfer authorized by this act is carried out and fully completed the corporation acquiring property and franchises thereunder shall be liable for the then legally existing debts and obligations of the corporation so making such transfer. *Liability for debts, etc.*

Section 5. Any corporation so acquiring property and franchises hereunder may issue its stock for the purposes thereof, and also its bonds in such amounts as may be required for the purposes of this act and secure the same by appropriate mortgages upon its franchise and property and thereupon may likewise issue such stock and bonds in payment and exchange for the stock, bonds, franchises and property of the corporation making any transfer authorized by this act in such manner and in such amounts as may be agreed upon. *Stock may be issued by purchase for certain purposes.*

Section 6. The location of the rails, posts, wires and fixtures of the said Rockland, Thomaston and Camden Street Railway as now established and maintained in Camden, Rockland, Thomaston and Warren are hereby confirmed and made valid. *Locating rails, posts, etc., made valid.*

Section 7. This act shall take effect when approved.

Approved February 18, 1903.

Chapter 46.

An Act to extend the charter of the Mattanawcook Manufacturing Company.

Be it enacted by the Senate and House of Representatives in Legislature assembled, as follows:

Right, powers and privileges extended.
Sesction 1. The right, powers and privileges of the Mattanawcook Manufacturing Company, which were granted by chapter two hundred eighty of the private and special laws of nineteen hundred one, are hereby extended, and the persons named in said act, their associates, successors and assigns, shall have all the rights, powers and privileges that were granted them by said act, to be exercised in the same manner and for the same purposes as specified in said act.

Section 2. This act shall take effect when approved.

Approved February 18, 1903.

Chapter 47.

An Act amendatory of Chapter two hundred seventy-nine of the Private and Special Laws of nineteen hundred and one, entitled "An Act to incorporate the Matagamon Manufacturing Company."

Be it enacted by the Senate and House of Representatives in Legislature assembled, as follows:

Section 9, of chapter 279, of special laws of 1901, amended.
Section 1. Section nine of chapter two hundred seventy-nine of the private and special laws of nineteen hundred and one is hereby amended by striking out the words "five hundred thousand" in the second line thereof, and inserting in place thereof the words 'one million,' so that said section as amended, shall read as follows:

Capital stock shall not exceed one million dollars.
'Section 9. The capital stock of said company shall not exceed one million dollars, divided into shares of one hundred dollars each. And for the purpose of carrying out any of the provisions for which said company is incorporated, it is hereby authorized

—may issue bonds.
and empowered to issue its bonds in such form and amount and on such time and rates as it may deem expedient, not exceeding

—may mortgage its property.
the amount of its capital stock actually subscribed for, and secure the same by mortgage of its property and franchises.'

Section 2. This act shall take effect when approved.

Approved February 18, 1903.

Chapter 48.

An Act to amend Chapter sixty-four of the Private and Special Laws of eighteen hundred and ninety-nine as amended by Chapter four hundred and seventy-two of the Private and Special Laws of nineteen hundred and one, relating to the Wilson Stream Dam Company.

Be it enacted by the Senate and House of Representatives in Legislature assembled, as follows:

Section 1. The organization of the Wilson Stream Dam Company, a corporation chartered by a special act of the legislature, chapter sixty-four of the private and special laws of eighteen hundred and ninety-nine, as amended by chapter four hundred and seventy-two of the private and special laws of nineteen hundred and one, the certificate of which organization was filed in the office of the secretary of state, December seventeen, nineteen hundred and two, is hereby ratified and confirmed, and all acts of said corporation done in pursuance of said charter and amendment, are hereby made valid and legal. *—Organization of Wilson Stream Dam Company ratified and confirmed.*   *—acts made valid.*

Section 2. And said charter is hereby further amended by striking out all of section four of said chapter sixty-four of the private and special laws of eighteen hundred and ninety-nine, and inserting the following: 'Said corporation in addition to the powers already conferred upon it, is hereby further authorized and empowered at all times to store and hold, by means of the dams mentioned in said original charter and said amendment, water for all domestic, sanitary, manufacturing, industrial, municipal and commercial purposes, and said corporation can use said water for any and all said purposes, and to create power for any and all such purposes, and said corporation can in any manner sell, lease, or otherwise dispose of, the use of said water for any and all such purposes, or to create power for any and all such purposes, to any person, party or corporation, municipal or otherwise. Provided, however, the water stored in said dams shall be used at all times so far as necessary for log driving purposes on said Wilson stream.' *Charter further amended.* *—may store and hold water for certain purposes.* *—proviso.*

Approved February 18, 1903.

Chapter 49.

An Act to grant additional powers to the Waterville and Oakland Street Railway.

Be it enacted by the Senate and House of Representatives in Legislature assembled, as follows:

Section 1. The Waterville and Oakland Street Railway is hereby authorized to sell or lease its property and franchises to any street railroad whose lines as constructed or chartered would form connecting or continuous lines with the lines of the said Waterville and Oakland Street Railway as constructed or chartered, and in such case the corporation so purchasing or leasing such property and franchises shall be entitled to all the privileges and be subject to all appropriate conditions and limitations contained in the charter and franchises of said Waterville and Oakland Street Railway. Any street railroad company whose lines as constructed or chartered would form connecting or continuous lines with the lines of the said Waterville and Oakland Street Railway as constructed or chartered is hereby authorized to so purchase or lease the property and franchises of the said Waterville and Oakland Street Railway.

Section 2. The said Waterville and Oakland Street Railway is further authorized to consolidate with or acquire by lease, purchase or otherwise lines, property and franchises of any street railroad or street railroads whose lines as constructed or chartered would form connecting or continuous lines with the lines of the said Waterville and Oakland Street Railway as constructed or chartered, and in such case the Waterville and Oakland Street Railway shall be entitled to all the privileges and be subject to all appropriate conditions and limitations contained in the charters and franchises thus united with or acquired. Any street railroad company whose lines as constructed or chartered would form connecting or continuous lines with the lines of the Waterville and Oakland Railway Company as constructed or chartered is hereby authorized to consolidate with or to lease or to sell its lines, property and franchises as in this section authorized.

Section 3. All proceedings, suits at law or in equity which may be pending at the time of any transfer authorized by this act to which any corporation so transferring its property and franchises may be a party may be prosecuted or defended by the corporation so acquiring the same in like manner and with like effect as if such transfer had not been made. All claims, contracts, rights and causes of action of or against any corporation so selling or leasing, at law or in equity, may be enforced by suit or action to be begun or prosecuted by or against the corporation so acquiring property and franchises as aforesaid.

Section 4. When any transfer authorized by this act is carried out and fully completed the corporation acquiring any franchise hereunder shall be liable for the then legally existing debts and obligations of the corporation so making such transfer.

Liabilities for debts, etc.

Section 5. Any corporation acquiring property and franchises by virtue of this act may issue its stock to an amount sufficient therefor, and also its bonds secured by appropriate mortgages upon its franchise and property in such amounts as may be required for the purposes of this act, and thereafterwards may issue its stock and bonds in payment and exchange for the stock, bonds, franchises and property of the corporation making any transfer authorized by this act, in such manner and in such amounts as may be agreed upon.

May issue stock and bonds for certain purposes.
—may mortgage its property.

Section 6. This act shall take effect when approved.

Approved February 18, 1903.

Chapter 50.

An Act to incorporate the Swan's Island Telephone and Telegraph Company.

Be it enacted by the Senate and House of Representatives in Legislature assembled, as follows:

Section 1. H. W. Joyce, H. W. Small and H. P. Jones, their associates, successors and assigns, are hereby created a body corporate by the name of the Swan's Island Telephone and Telegraph Company, with all the powers, rights and privileges, and subject to all the duties and obligations granted and prescribed by the general laws of this state relating to corporations; with power by that name to sue and be sued; to have a common seal and to establish any and all by-laws and regulations for the management of their affairs not repugnant to the laws of this state.

Corporators.

—powers, etc

Section 2. Said corporation shall have the right to locate, construct, maintain, operate, and own, lines of telephone and telegraph from any point in the village of Bass Harbor, town of Tremont, Hancock county, Maine, to Lopaus Point so called in said Tremont, thence across Bluehill bay, so called, to Burnt Point in Swan's Island in said county, thence to any point in said Swan's Island.

Location of lines.

Section 3. Said company shall have the right, within the limits aforesaid, to locate, construct and maintain its line upon and along any public way, bridge or private lands, but in such manner as not to incommode or endanger the customary use of

May construct along public ways, etc.

such way or bridge. With the right to cut down trees, remove obstacles when necessary, within the limits aforesaid, except ornamental, fruit or shade trees, and with the power to establish and collect tolls on said line, provided, that the right to construct and maintain said lines shall be subject to the provisions of chapter three hundred and seventy-eight, public laws of eighteen hundred and eighty-five, and all rights and powers granted by this act shall be exercised in accordance with said chapter three hundred and seventy-eight.

Damages, how estimated. Section 4. If the land of any individual or corporation is taken under this act and the parties cannot agree on the damages occasioned thereby, they shall be estimated, secured and paid as for land taken for highways.

May connect with, or sell or lease to other lines. Section 5. Said corporation is hereby authorized to connect its line or lines with those of any other company, or to sell or lease its line either before or after completion to any other telephone or telegraph company, upon such terms as may be mutually agreed upon, which sale or lease shall be binding upon the parties; or to purchase or lease any other line or lines of telephone or telegraph, upon such terms and conditions as may be mutually agreed upon.

Amount of capital stock, how fixed. Section 6. The amount of capital stock shall be fixed by vote of the corporation, but not to exceed eight thousand dollars, and said corporation may purchase, hold, sell and convey real estate and personal property necessary for the purposes contemplated in this charter.

First meeting, how called. Section 7. Any one of the corporators named in this act, may call the first meeting of this company by mailing a written notice to each of the other corporators, seven days at least, before the day of meeting, naming the time, place and purposes of such meeting; and at such meeting, a president, secretary, treasurer and directors may be chosen, by-laws adopted and any corporate business transacted.

Operations shall commence within two years. Section 8. This charter shall be null and void unless operations shall actually commence hereunder within two years from date of the passage of this act.

Section 9. This act shall take effect when approved.

Approved February 18, 1908.

Chapter 51.

An Act to incorporate the Pittsfield Trust Company.

Be it enacted by the Senate and House of Representatives in Legislature assembled, as follows:

Section 1. James M. Chalmers, Charles E. Vickery, Llewellyn Parks, E. J. Ney, Fred R. Smith, George H. Morse, C. S. Philbrick, Leroy W. Coons, Thomas E. Getchell, Wilson L. Frost, Benjamin S. Mathews, Walter M. Priley, Benjamin D. Priley, Guy W. Lord, Frank L. Smith, Frank Weeks, Ira A. Sutherland, Benjamin E. Cornell, George E. Stevens, Elmer D. Smith, E. E. Bagley and Franz Bagley or such of them as may by vote, accept the charter, with their associates, successors or assigns, are hereby made a body corporate and politic to be known as the Pittsfield Trust Company, and as such shall be possessed of all the powers, privileges and immunities and subject to all the duties and obligations conferred on corporations by law. *Corporators. —corporate name. —powers.*

Section 2. The corporation hereby created shall be located at Pittsfield, in the county of Somerset and state of Maine, and may establish agencies in any part of the state. *Location.*

Section 3. The purposes of said corporation and the business which it may perform, are; first, to receive on deposit, money, coin, bank notes, evidences of debt, accounts of individuals, companies, corporations, municipalities and states, allowing interest thereon, if agreed, or as the by-laws of said corporation may provide; second, to borrow money, to loan money on credits, or real estate, or personal security, and to negotiate loans and sales for others; third, to own and maintain safe deposit vaults, with boxes, safes and other facilities therein, to be rented to other parties for the safe keeping of moneys, securities, stocks, jewelry, plate, valuable papers and documents, and other property susceptible of being deposited therein, and may receive on deposit for safe keeping, property of any kind entrusted to it for that purpose; fourth, to hold and enjoy all such estate, real, personal and mixed, as may be obtained by the investment of its capital stock or any other moneys and funds that may come into its possession in the course of its business and dealings, and the same sell, grant, and dispose of; fifth, to act as agent for issuing, registering and countersigning certificates, bonds, stocks, and all evidences of debt or ownership in property; sixth, to hold by grant, assignment, transfer, devise or bequest any real or personal property or trusts duly created, and to execute trusts of every description; seventh, to act as assignee, receiver, executor, administrator and guardian, and no surety shall be necessary upon the bond of the corporation, unless the court or officer *Purposes. —may own and maintain safe deposit vaults. —may hold estate, real personal and mixed. —may act as trustee, etc. —administrators, etc., may deposit with.*

PITTSFIELD TRUST COMPANY.

Chap. 51

approving such bond shall require it; eighth, to do in general all the business that may lawfully be done by trust and banking companies.

Capital stock.

—shall not commence business until $50,000 has been paid in.

SECTION 4. The capital stock of said corporation shall not be less than fifty thousand dollars, divided into shares of one hundred dollars each, with the right to increase the said capital stock at any time, by vote of the shareholders, to any amount not exceeding five hundred thousand dollars. Said corporation shall not commence business as a trust or banking company until stock to the amount of at least fifty thousand dollars shall have been subscribed and paid in, in cash.

Shall not loan money on the security of its own capital stock.

—exception.

SECTION 5. Said corporation shall not make any loan or discount on the security of the shares of its own capital stock, nor be the purchaser or holder of any such shares unless necessary to prevent loss upon a debt previously contracted in good faith; and all stock so acquired shall, within six months from the time of its acquisition, be disposed of at public or private sale.

Board of trustees.

—tenure.

—executive board.

—vacancies, how filled.

SECTION 6. All the corporate powers of this corporation shall be exercised by a board of trustees, who shall be residents of this state, whose number and term of office shall be determined by a vote of the shareholders at the first meeting held by the incorporators and at each annual meeting thereafter. The affairs and powers of the corporation may, at the option of the shareholders, be entrusted to an executive board of five members, to be, by vote of the shareholders, elected from the full board of trustees. The trustees of said corporation shall be sworn to the proper discharge of their duties, and they shall hold office until others are elected and qualified in their stead. If a trustee or director dies, resigns, or becomes disqualified for any cause, the remaining trustees or directors may appoint a person to fill the vacancy until the next annual meeting of the corporation. The oath of office of such trustee or director shall be taken within thirty days of his election, or his office shall become vacant. The clerk of such corporation shall, within ten days, notify such trustees or directors of their election, and within thirty days shall publish the list of all persons who have taken the oath of office as trustees or directors.

Board of investment, how constituted.

—shall keep record of all loans.

SECTION 7. The board of directors or trustees of said corporation shall constitute the board of investment of said corporation. Said directors or trustees shall keep in a separate book, specially provided for the purpose, a record of all loans, and investments of every description, made by said institution substantially in the order of time when such loans or investments are made, which shall show that such loans or investments have been made with the approval of the investment committee of said corporation, which shall indicate such particulars respecting such loans or investments as the bank examiner shall direct. This book shall be submitted to the directors and to the bank examiner whenever requested. Such loans or investments shall be classified in the book as the bank examiner shall direct. No loan shall be made to any officer or director of said banking or trust company except by the approval of a majority of the executive board in writing, and said corporation shall have no authority to hire money or to give notes unless by vote of the said board duly recorded.

Section 8. No person shall be eligible to the position of a director or trustee of said corporation who is not the actual owner of five shares of the stock.

Section 9. Said corporation, after beginning to receive deposits, shall, at all times, have on hand in lawful money, as a reserve, not less than fifteen per cent of the aggregate amount of its deposits which are subject to withdrawal on demand, provided, that in lieu of lawful money, two-thirds of said fifteen per cent may consist of balances payable on demand, due from any national or state bank.

Section 10. All the property or money held in trust by this corporation shall constitute a special deposit and the accounts thereof of said trust department shall be kept separate and such funds and the investments or loans of them shall be specially appropriated to the security and payment of such deposits, and not be subject to any other liabilities of the corporation; and for the purpose of securing the observance of this proviso, said corporation shall have a trust department in which all business pertaining to said trust property shall be kept separate and distinct from its general business.

Section 11. An administrator, executor, assignee, guardian or trustee, any court of law or equity, including courts of probate and insolvency, officers and treasurers of towns, cities, counties, and savings banks of the state of Maine may deposit any moneys, bonds, stocks, evidences of debt or of ownership in property, or any personal property, with said corporation, and any of said courts may direct any person deriving authority from them to so deposit the same.

Section 12. Each shareholder of this corporation shall be individually responsible, equally and ratably, and not one for the other, for all contracts, debts and engagements of such corporation, to a sum equal to the amount of the par value of the shares owned by each, in addition to the amount invested in said shares.

CHAP. 51 PITTSFIELD TRUST COMPANY.

Reserve fund.

Section 13. Such corporation shall set apart as a surplus fund not less than ten per cent of its earnings in each and every year until such fund with the accumulated interest thereon, shall amount to one-fourth of the capital stock of said corporation.

Taxation of shares.

Section 14. The shares of said corporation shall be subject to taxation in the same manner and rate as are the shares of national banks.

Shall be subject to examination by bank examiner.

Section 15. Said corporation shall be subject to examination by the bank examiner, who shall visit it at least once in every year, and as much oftener as he may deem expedient. At such visits he shall have free access to its vaults, books and papers, and shall thoroughly inspect and examine all the affairs of said corporation, and make such inquiries as may be necessary to ascertain its condition and ability to fulfill all its engagements. If upon examination of said corporation the examiner is of the opinion that its investments are not in accordance with law, or said corporation is insolvent, or its condition is such as to render its further proceedings hazardous to the public or to those having funds in its custody, or is of the opinion that it has exceeded its powers or failed to comply with any of the rules or restrictions provided by law, he shall have such authority and take such action as is provided for in the case of savings banks by chapter forty-seven of the revised statutes. He shall preserve in a permanent form a full record of his proceedings, including a statement of the condition of said corporation. A copy of such statement shall be published by said corporation immediately after the annual examination of the same in some newspaper published where said corporation is established. If no paper is published in the town where said corporation is established, then it shall be published in a newspaper printed in the nearest city or town. The necessary expenses of the bank examiner while making such examination shall be paid by the corporation.

—keep record and publish statement annually.

First meeting, how called.

Section 16. Any three of the corporators named in this act may call the first meeting of the corporation by mailing a written notice, signed by all, postage paid, to each of the other corporators, seven days at least before the day of the meeting, naming the time, place and purpose of such meeting, and at such meeting the necessary officers may be chosen, by-laws adopted, and any other corporate business transacted.

Section 17. This act shall take effect when approved.

Approved February 18, 1903.

Chapter 52.

An Act authorizing and empowering the Springer Lumber Company to erect and maintain piers and booms in the Mattawamkeag river.

Be it enacted by the Senate and House of Representatives in Legislature assembled, as follows:

Section 1. The Springer Lumber Company, a corporation organized under the general laws of the state, its successors and assigns, are hereby authorized and empowered to locate, erect and maintain in the Mattawamkeag river between a line drawn across said river at the mouth of Wytopitlock stream and a line drawn across said river five hundred yards above the bridge connecting Drew plantation, in the county of Penobscot, and Reed plantation, in the county of Aroostook, piers and booms for the purpose of collecting, holding, separating and sorting out logs and other lumber coming down said Mattawamkeag river. Provided, however, that at least two sorting gaps are constructed, maintained and used for the passage of logs and other lumber through said booms. Said piers and booms shall be so located, constructed, maintained and used that logs and lumber running down said river belonging to other parties and not destined for use and manufacture at the mills of said company, its successors or assigns, shall not be unreasonably impeded or delayed, and in no case shall logs and other lumber be delayed longer than twenty-four hours, and the logs or lumber of other parties, when stopped for sorting, shall be turned by as soon as they practically can be sorted and separated from logs and lumber destined for use and manufacture at said mills, and any stray logs or other lumber not destined for use and manufacture at the mills of said company, if found in the booms of said company, shall be turned out by said company upon written demand of the owner or owners thereof, at its own charge and expense.

Section 2. Said Springer Lumber Company, its successors and assigns, by aid of such piers and booms are hereby authorized and empowered to separate and sort out from the logs and other lumber coming down said river all logs and other lumber destined and intended for use and manufacture at the mills of said company, provided, however, if upon the approach of the rear of any drive of logs to the booms of said company herein authorized to be constructed and maintained, it shall appear to the person in charge of such drive that said company has not sufficient men to sort and turn by the logs or other lumber arriving at said booms, so that such drive may be unreasonably impeded or delayed, such person, upon notice in writing to said company left at its office, shall have the right to put men of his own selection upon said booms, to expedite the sorting and

CHAP. 52

turning by of the logs and other lumber in such drive, who shall be paid by said Springer Lumber Company, and the additional cost, if any, of making such drive through said booms in consequence of such erections and piers of said company shall be paid by said Springer Lumber Company, but nothing herein contained shall make said company liable for any delay caused by said piers and booms. And said company is also authorized and empowered to hold within the piers and booms mentioned in this act and located, erected and maintained as aforesaid, all logs and other lumber coming down said Mattawamkeag river which are destined and intended for use and manufacture at the mills of said company.

May appoint agent.

—duties of agent.

—list of marks shall be furnished.

—compensation.

Section 3. The Mattawamkeag Log Driving Company, a corporation existing under the laws of the state, shall have the right at any time to appoint an agent who is hereby authorized and empowered, and whose duty it shall be, to take charge of and superintend the sorting of the logs and other lumber running through the booms herein authorized, and said company at the beginning of every driving season, or at the time of the appointment of such agent, shall furnish such agent a list of marks upon all logs and other lumber intended to be manufactured at the mills of the company, and such agent shall see to it that the logs and other lumber not intended to be manufactured at the mills of the company are not unreasonably detained in or by said booms. The compensation of such agent shall not exceed two dollars fifty cents per day, and shall be paid by said Springer Lumber Company.

May hold lands.

—may pass and repass over lands of other persons.
—purposes.

—damages, how assessed.
—appeal.

Section 4. Said Springer Lumber Company, its successors and assigns, may enter upon, take and hold such lands as may be necessary for the location, erection and maintenance of the piers and booms mentioned in this act and connecting the same with the shores, and may with their agents and teams, pass and repass over said shores and to and from the same, over the lands of other persons, for the purposes aforesaid, and for the operation and management of said piers and booms, and the damages for such taking shall be assessed and recovered as follows. If any person sustaining damages as aforesaid cannot agree with said company upon the sum to be paid therefor, either party on petition to the county commissioners of the county in which the land so taken is situated, may have the damages assessed by them and subsequent proceedings and right of appeal thereon shall be had in the same manner and under the same conditions, restrictions and limitations as are by law prescribed in the case of damages occasioned by the laying out of highways.

Section 5. This act shall take effect when approved.

Approved February 18, 1903.

Chapter 53.

An Act to amend Chapter twenty-five of the Private and Special Laws of eighteen hundred ninety-nine, relating to taking Eels in Bagaduce river, bay and tributaries.

Be it enacted by the Senate and House of Representatives in Legislature assembled, as follows:

Chapter twenty-five of the private and special laws of eighteen hundred ninety-nine, is hereby amended by striking out in the fourth and fifth lines the words "first day of April and first day of November" and inserting therein the words, 'fifteenth day of April and the first day of February,' so that said section as amended, shall read as follows:

'Section 1. It shall be unlawful to take or fish for any eels in any manner whatever in the Bagaduce river, Bagaduce bay or any of the tributaries of said river or bay between the fifteenth day of April and the first day of February of each year.'

Approved February 18, 1903.

Chapter 54.

An Act to amend the charter of the Augusta, Winthrop and Gardiner Railway.

Be it enacted by the Senate and House of Representatives in Legislature assembled, as follows:

Section 1. The Augusta, Winthrop and Gardiner Railway, originally incorporated by the name of the Lewiston, Winthrop and Augusta Street Railway, is hereby authorized to sell or lease its property and franchises or any part thereof to any street railroad company whose lines as constructed or chartered would form connecting or continuous lines with the lines of the said Augusta, Winthrop and Gardiner Railway as constructed or chartered, and in such case the corporation so purchasing or leasing said property and franchises shall be entitled to all the privileges and be subject to all appropriate conditions and limitations contained in the charter and franchises of such Augusta, Winthrop and Gardiner Railway. Any street railroad company whose lines as constructed or chartered would form connecting or continuous lines with the lines of the said Augusta, Winthrop and Gardiner Railway as constructed or chartered is hereby authorized to so purchase or lease the property and franchises of the said Augusta, Winthrop and Gardiner Railway.

Section 2. The said Augusta, Winthrop and Gardiner Railway is further authorized to consolidate with or to acquire by

CHAP. 54

Railway authorized to consolidate with connecting lines.

lease, purchase or otherwise the lines, property and franchises of any street railroad or street railroads whose lines as constructed or chartered would form connecting or continuous lines with the lines of the said Augusta, Winthrop and Gardiner Railway as constructed or chartered, and in such case the Augusta, Winthrop and Gardiner Railway shall be entitled to all the privileges and be subject to all appropriate conditions and limitations contained in the charters and franchises thus united with or acquired. Any street railroad company whose lines as constructed or chartered would form connecting or continuous lines with the lines of the said Augusta, Winthrop and Gardiner Railway as constructed or chartered is hereby authorized to consolidate with or to lease or to sell its lines, property and franchises as in this section authorized.

Pending proceedings, how prosecuted and defended.

Section 3. All proceedings, suits at law or in equity which may be pending at the time of any such transfer to which the corporation making such transfer may be a party may be prosecuted or defended by the corporation so acquiring the same in like manner and with like effect as if such transfer had not been made. All claims, contracts, rights and causes of action of or against any corporation making any such transfer, at law or in equity, may be enforced by suit or action to be begun or prosecuted by or against the corporation so acquiring property and franchises hereunder.

Liabilities for debts, etc.

Section 4. Any transfer authorized by this act when carried out and fully completed the corporation so acquiring any property thereunder shall be liable for the then legally existing debts and obligations of any corporation so making such transfer.

May issue stock and bonds for certain purposes.

—may mortgage its property.

Section 5. Any corporation acquiring property and franchises hereunder may issue its stock therefor and also its bonds, secured by appropriate mortgages upon its franchises and property in such amounts as may be required for the purposes of this act, and thereupon may issue such stock and bonds in payment and exchange for the stock, bonds, franchises and property of the corporation making any transfer authorized by this act in such manner and in such amounts as may be agreed upon.

Section 6. This act shall take effect when approved.

Approved February 18, 1903.

Chapter 55.

An Act to Incorporate the Squirrel Island Village Corporation.

Be it enacted by the Senate and House of Representatives in Legislature assembled, as follows:

Section 1. The territory embraced within the limits of Squirrel Island in the town of Southport, in the county of Lincoln, together with the inhabitants thereon and certain owners of real estate thereon as hereinafter specified is hereby created a body politic and corporate by the name of the Squirrel Island Village Corporation.

Section 2. Said corporation is hereby authorized and vested with the power at any legal meeting called for the purpose to raise money for the following purposes: To create and maintain a fire department with all the necessary equipment, appliances and apparatus for the prevention and extinguishment of fires; to build, repair and maintain roads, streets and ways, sidewalks, sewers and other sanitary works, including the collection and removal of offal and garbage; to care for and beautify that portion of the island which has been or may hereafter be reserved for and dedicated to public uses to be enjoyed in common by all the owners of lots on the island and to that end to build roads and walks upon and through said public lands and to plant and care for trees in the roads and streets and upon said public lands; to build, repair and maintain public wharves and landings; to establish and maintain police and night watch; to procure water for fire, domestic and other purposes and to produce or procure light for public use and for the use of the inhabitants of the island, and for such purposes to contract with any individual, firm or corporation to furnish such water or light for either or both of the purposes named and to establish reasonable rates to be paid by the inhabitants of the island using such water or light for domestic purposes; to construct, maintain and operate telephone or telegraph lines or to aid in such construction, maintenance and operation and to that end and for that purpose to contract with any corporation, firm or individual therefor; and to defray any and all other necessary or proper corporate charges.

Section 3. The town of Southport is hereby relieved from any and all duty to build, repair or maintain roads, streets or ways upon Squirrel Island or to build school houses or maintain schools thereon or to perform any of the duties for which said corporation is authorized by section two of this act to raise money, and said town shall not be liable for defects in streets, ways or roads on said island nor for failure to perform any duty

SQUIRREL ISLAND VILLAGE CORPORATION.

—village corporation shall be liable.

from which it is relieved by this act, but said corporation shall assume all of said duties and be liable for said defects in streets, ways and roads and for failure to perform the duties assumed as the town of Southport would have been liable except for this act, which liability may be enforced under the same conditions, in the same manner and with the same remedies as are provided by law in relation to towns.

Laying out, discontinuing and altering town ways.

Section 4. Said corporation and the overseers thereof shall have the same power and duties in laying out, discontinuing and altering town ways on Squirrel Island which the town of Southport and the selectmen now have to be exercised and performed under the same conditions and limitations and in the same manner that they are now exercised and performed by said town and its selectmen.

Taxes.

Section 5. The town of Southport shall annually pay over to the treasurer of said corporation out of the taxes collected from the inhabitants and estates on Squirrel Island a sum equal to sixty per centum of all the town taxes, exclusive of the state and county tax, collected from said inhabitants and estates.

Assessments, how made.

Section 6. All moneys which shall be raised for the purposes named in section two of this act or for any other purpose, for which the corporation may lawfully raise money, shall be assessed upon the taxable polls and estates embraced within the limits of the corporation by the assessors of the town of Southport in the same manner as is provided by law for the assessment of town and county taxes. For the purposes of taxation under this act the person or persons entitled to the use or occupation of any lot of land on said island shall be deemed the owner thereof and be taxed for said lot and the improvements, if any, thereon.

Officers of corporation.

Section 7. The officers of said corporation shall be a clerk, who shall be a resident of this state, a treasurer and five overseers, who shall be chosen by ballot and such other officers as the by-laws of said corporation may require. Said corporation is empowered to adopt at any legal meeting called for that purpose a code of by-laws for the government of the same and for the proper management of its prudential affairs and other purposes connected therewith, provided said by-laws are not repugnant to the laws of the state. Such code of by-laws may be altered or amended at any legal meeting of the corporation in the call for which notice of the proposed change has been given.

—by-laws may be adopted.

—officers shall be sworn.

The officers aforesaid shall be sworn before the clerk or a justice of the peace and the treasurer shall give bond to said corporation in such sum as the overseers may direct, which bond shall be approved by the overseers and clerk.

SQUIRREL ISLAND VILLAGE CORPORATION. 95

CHAP. 55

Section 8. Any person who is a legal voter in said corporation may be elected or appointed to any office therein, but shall cease to hold said office whenever he ceases to be such legal voter.

Who may hold office.

Section 9. Said overseers shall be the general municipal officers of said corporation and shall have general charge of its affairs and of the expenditure of all money therein except so far as the same may be committed to other officers or persons.

General municipal officers.

Section 10. Upon a certificate being filed with the assessors of the town of Southport by the clerk of this corporation of the amount of money voted to be raised at any meeting for any of the purposes aforesaid, it shall be the duty of said assessors or their successors in office, at the time of the next annual assessment of town and county taxes in said town of Southport to assess the total amounts certified by the clerk of this corporation upon the polls and estates of persons residing within the limits of said corporation and upon the estates of non-resident proprietors thereof and to certify and deliver the lists of the assessments so made to the collector of the town of Southport, whose duty it shall be to collect the same in like manner as county and town taxes are by law collected and said collector shall pay over all moneys collected by him to the treasurer of said corporation whenever the overseers shall so direct. It shall be the duty of the treasurer of said corporation to receive all moneys belonging to the corporation and to pay it out only upon the written order or direction of the overseers and to keep a regular account of all moneys received and paid out and to exhibit the same to the overseers whenever requested, and said town of Southport shall have the same power to direct the mode of collecting said taxes that it has in the collection of the town taxes and said collector shall have the same rights and powers to recover any taxes committed to him under the provisions of this act by suit that he has for the collection of town taxes committed to him and the town of Southport shall have the same right to recover taxes assessed under this act by suit that it has to recover town taxes assessed therein. The collector of Southport shall be entitled to receive the same percentage for the collection of taxes assessed under this act and the same fees in connection with the collection thereof which he receives for the collection of the town taxes.

Assessors of Southport shall assess taxes for village corporation.

—tax collector of Southport shall collect.

—duties of treasurer.

—shall make exhibit to board of overseers.

—compensation of collector of taxes.

Section 11. All persons residing within the limits of said corporation, who would be legal voters in the town of Southport and every person of lawful age who owns one or more shares of stock of the Squirrel Island Association and is in possession of one or more lots of land on said island by virtue of the ownership of said stock shall be legal voters at any meeting of said corporation at which they are present. The overseers

Legal voters in meetings of corporation.

CHAP. 55

—overseers shall determine, and prepare list of.

—votes, how taken.

—proviso.

First election of officers.

—tenure.

When charter may be accepted.

—first meeting, how called.

—subsequent meetings, how called.

of said corporation shall determine who are the legal voters at any meeting and shall prepare a list of said voters at least twenty-four hours before every meeting, which said list they may amend or correct at any time before said meeting or during its progress. The vote upon any proposition at any meeting shall be taken and checked by this list upon the demand of five legal voters; provided, however, that every person who by virtue of a joint ownership of himself and some other person or persons of a share of said stock and by agreement with the other joint owners, is in possession of a certain aliquot part of a lot of land on said island upon which he has a dwelling house owned and controlled by himself exclusively, shall be deemed a legal voter at any meeting of the corporation at which he is present and provided further that the majority in interest of the joint owners of any share of stock may designate in writing one of such owners to represent such share who shall be a legal voter at any meeting of the corporation at which he is present, but no person shall be entitled to more than one vote in any meeting either for himself or as representing the joint owners of any share of stock.

Section 12. The first election of officers shall be at the meeting at which this charter is accepted. Said officers shall hold their respective offices until the next annual meeting of the corporation, at which said meeting officers shall be elected and thereafterwards at each annual meeting, but in any event all officers duly elected shall hold office until their successors are elected and duly qualified. The annual meeting of said corporation shall be held on the last Saturday of July in each year.

Section 13. This charter may be accepted at any time within five years from its approval by the governor, but only one meeting to vote thereon shall be called in any one calendar year. Albert H. Davenport, Martin V. B. Chase, Josiah S. Maxcy and Edward W. Hall, or either of them, may call all meetings of the corporation previous to the acceptance of the charter and the election of officers, and notify the persons entitled to vote therein to meet at some suitable time and place, on said Squirrel Island, by posting of notices in two public places on said island seven days at least before the time of holding said meeting; all subsequent meetings shall be called and notified by the overseers as town meetings are called and notified by the selectmen; either of the above named persons are authorized to preside at any meeting previous to the acceptance of the charter until the meeting is organized and until a moderator shall have been chosen by ballot and sworn; at all meetings of the corporation a moderator shall be chosen in the manner, and with the same power as in town meetings.

WINN WATER AND POWER COMPANY. 97

CHAP. 56

Section 14. The Squirrel Island Association is hereby authorized to sell, convey, lease or otherwise dispose of any and all real estate or interests therein which it now has to the Squirrel Island Village Corporation and said latter corporation is hereby authorized to purchase, take title to, lease or otherwise acquire said real estate or interests therein and to hold, manage and control the same for the benefit of said corporation and the members thereof and for the purpose of enabling the corporation to accomplish the objects for which it was created.

Squirrel Island Association may sell its property to village corporation.

Section 15. This act shall take effect when approved by the governor so far as to authorize the calling of a meeting or meetings of said corporation for the purpose of, voting upon the acceptance of this charter, and whenever this charter shall be accepted by a majority of the voters of said corporation at a legal meeting called for that purpose, then the same shall take and have complete effect in all its parts.

When this act shall take effect.

—pre-requisites.

Approved February 18, 1903.

Chapter 56.

An Act to amend Chapter one hundred forty-five of Private and Special Laws of eighteen hundred and ninety-five, entitled "An Act to incorporate the Winn Water and Power Company."

Be it enacted by the Senate and House of Representatives in Legislature assembled, as follows:

Section 1. Section ten of chapter one hundred forty-five of the private and special laws of eighteen hundred and ninety-five is hereby amended by striking out in the second line of said section the word "one," and inserting in place thereof the word 'two,' so that said section as amended, shall read as follows:

Section 10 of chapter 145 of private and special laws of 1895, amended.

'Section 10. The capital stock of said company shall not exceed two hundred thousand dollars, divided into shares of fifty dollars each. Said company may hold real and personal estate necessary and convenient for its purposes aforesaid.'

Capital stock.

Section 2. The rights, powers and privileges of said company are hereby extended, and the organization of said company as now existing is hereby confirmed.

Rights extended.
—organization confirmed.

Section 3. This act shall take effect when approved.

Approved February 18, 1903.

Chapter 57.

An Act to incorporate the Pepperell Trust Company.

Be it enacted by the Senate and House of Representatives in Legislature assembled, as follows:

Corporators.

Section 1. George F. West, Gilman N. Deering, J. B. E. Tartre, George E. Morrison, Jere G. Shaw, Carlos H. McKenney and Kenneth W. Sutherland or such of them as may by vote accept this charter, with their associates, successors and assigns, are hereby made a body corporate and politic to be known as the Pepperell Trust Company, and as such shall be possessed of all the powers, privileges and immunities and subject to all the duties and obligations conferred on corporations by law.

—corporate name.
—powers.

Location.

Section 2. The corporation hereby created shall be located at Biddeford, York county, Maine.

—purposes.

Section 3. The purposes of said corporation and the business which it may perform, are; first, to receive on deposit, money, coin, bank notes, evidences of debt, accounts of individuals, companies, corporations, municipalities and states, allowing interest thereon, if agreed, or as the by-laws of said corporation may provide; second, to borrow money, to loan money on credits, or real estate, or personal security, and to negotiate loans and sales for others; third, to own and maintain safe deposit vaults, with boxes, safes and other facilities therein, to be rented to other parties for the safe keeping of moneys, securities, stocks, jewelry, plate, valuable papers and documents, and other property susceptible of being deposited therein, and may receive on deposit for safe keeping, property of any kind entrusted to it for that purpose; fourth, to act as agent for issuing, registering and countersigning certificates, bonds, stocks, and all evidences of debt or ownership in property; fifth, to hold by grant, assignment, transfer, devise or bequest any real or personal property or trusts duly created, and to execute trusts of every description; sixth, to act as assignee, trustee, administrator, receiver, executor, and no surety shall be necessary upon the bond of the corporation, unless the court or officer approving such bond shall require it; seventh, to do in general all the business that may lawfully be done by trust and banking companies, but said corporation shall not have the power or authority to establish branches.

—may own and maintain safe deposit vaults.

—may act as trustee, etc.

—shall not have power to establish branches.

Capital stock.

Section 4. The capital stock of said corporation shall not be less than fifty thousand dollars, divided into shares of one hundred dollars each, with the right to increase the said capital stock at any time, by a vote of the shareholders, to any amount not exceeding five hundred thousand dollars. Said corporation shall not commence business as a trust or banking company, until

—shall not commence business until $50,000 has been paid in.

stock to the amount of at least fifty thousand dollars shall have been subscribed and paid in, in cash.

Section 5. Said corporation shall not make any loan or discount on the security of the shares of its own capital stock, nor be the purchaser or holder of any such shares unless necessary to prevent loss upon a debt previously contracted in good faith; and all stock so acquired shall, within six months of the time of its acquisition, be disposed of at public or private sale.

Shall not loan money on security of its own capital stock.

—proviso.

Section 6. All the corporate powers of this corporation shall be exercised by a board of trustees, who shall be residents of this state, whose number and term of office shall be determined by a vote of the shareholders at the first meeting held by the incorporators and at each annual meeting thereafter. The affairs and powers of the corporation may, at the option of the shareholders, be entrusted to an executive board of five members to be, by vote of the shareholders, elected from the full board of trustees.

Board of trustees.

—tenure.

—executive board.

The trustees of said corporation shall be sworn to the proper discharge of their duties, and they shall hold office until others are elected and qualified in their stead. If a trustee or director dies, resigns, or becomes disqualified for any cause, the remaining trustees or directors may appoint a person to fill the vacancy until the next annual meeting of the corporation. The oath of office of such trustee or director shall be taken within thirty days of his election, or his office shall become vacant. The clerk of such corporation shall, within ten days, notify such trustees or directors of their election, and within thirty days shall publish the list of all persons who have taken the oath of office as trustees or directors.

—vacancies, how filled.

Section 7. The board of trustees or directors of said corporation shall constitute the board of investment of said corporation. Said trustees or directors shall keep in a separate book, specially provided for the purpose, a record of all loans, and investments of every description, made by said institution substantially in the order of time when such loans or investments are made, which shall show that such loans or investments have been made with the approval of the investment committee of said corporation, which shall indicate such particulars respecting such loans or investments as the bank examiner shall direct. No loan shall be made to any officer or director of said banking or trust company except by the unanimous approval of the executive board in writing, and said corporation shall have no authority to hire money or to give notes unless by vote of the said board duly recorded.

Board of investment, how constituted.

—shall keep record of all loans.

—loan to directors, how approved.

Section 8. No person shall be eligible to the position of a director or a trustee of said corporation who is not the actual owner of ten shares of the stock.

Owner of less than ten shares not eligible to be a director.

CHAP. 57

Reserve fund shall be in lawful money.

Section 9. Said corporation, after beginning to receive deposits, shall, at all times, have on hand in lawful money, as a reserve, not less than fifteen per cent of the aggregate amount of its deposits which are subject to withdrawal on demand, provided, that in lieu of lawful money, two-thirds of said fifteen per cent may consist of balances payable on demand, due from any national or state bank.

Trust funds shall constitute a special deposit.

Section 10. All the property or money held in trust by this corporation shall constitute a special deposit and the accounts thereof and of said trust department shall be kept separate and such funds and the investment or loans of them shall be specially appropriated to the security and payment of such deposits, and not be subject to any other liabilities of the corporation; and for the purpose of securing the observance of this proviso, said corporation shall have a trust department in which all business pertaining to such trust property shall be kept separate and distinct from its general business.

Administrators, etc., may deposit with.

Section 11. An administrator, executor, assignee, guardian or trustee, any court of law or equity, including courts of probate and insolvency, officers and treasurers of towns, cities, counties, and savings banks of the state of Maine may deposit any money, bonds, stocks, evidences of debt or ownership in property, with said corporation, and any of said courts may direct any person deriving authority from them to so deposit the same.

Responsibility of shareholders.

Section 12. Each shareholder of this corporation shall be individually responsible, equally and ratably, and not one for the other, for all contracts, debts and engagements of such corporation, to a sum equal to the amount of the par value of the shares owned by each, in addition to the amount invested in said shares.

Guaranty fund.

Section 13. Such corporation shall set apart as a guaranty fund not less than ten per cent of its earnings in each and every year until such fund with the accumulated interest thereon, shall amount to one-fourth of the capital stock of said corporation.

Taxation of shares.

Section 14. The shares of said corporation shall be subject to taxation in the same manner and rate as are the shares of national banks.

Shall be subject to examination by bank examiner.

Section 15. Said corporation shall be subject to examination by the bank examiner, who shall visit it at least once in every year, and as much oftener as he may deem expedient. At such visits he shall have free access to its vaults, books and papers, and shall thoroughly inspect and examine all the affairs of said corporation, and make such inquiries as may be necessary to ascertain its condition and ability to fulfill its engagements. If upon examination of said corporation the examiner is of the opinion that its investments are not in accordance with law, or said corporation is insolvent, or its condition is such as to render its further proceedings hazardous to the public or to those having funds in its custody, or is of the opinion that it has exceeded its powers or failed to comply with any of the rules or restrictions provided by law, he shall have such authority and take such action as is provided for in the case of savings banks by chapter forty-seven of the revised statutes. He shall preserve in a permanent form a full record of his proceedings, including a statement of the condition of said corporation. A copy of such statement shall be published by said corporation immediately after the annual examination of the same in some newspaper published where said corporation is established. If no paper is published in the town where said corporation is established, then it shall be published in a newspaper printed in the nearest city or town. The necessary expenses of the bank examiner while making such examination shall be paid by the corporation. —shall keep a record and publish statement annually.

Section 16. Any five of the corporators named in this act may call the first meeting of the corporation by mailing a written notice, signed by all, postage paid, to each of the other corporators, seven days at least before the day of the meeting. naming the time, place and purpose of such meeting, and at such meeting the necessary officers may be chosen, by-laws adopted, and any other corporate business transacted. First meeting, how called.

Section 17. This act shall take effect when approved.

Approved February 18, 1903.

Chapter 58.

An Act to incorporate the International Trust and Banking Company.

Be it enacted by the Senate and House of Representatives in Legislature assembled, as follows:

Section 1. Prescott M. Pirington, Frank N. Beckett, George W. Lord, William J. Fowler, George R. Gardner, George A. Curran, of Calais, in the county of Washington and state of Maine, and Charles W. Young, Gilbert W. Gagnon, Irving R. Todd, of Saint Stephen in the county of Charlotte and the Province of New Brunswick, or such of them as may by vote accept the charter, with their associates, successors and assigns, are hereby made a body corporate and politic to be known as the International Trust and Banking Company, and as such shall be possessed of all the powers, privileges and immunities and Corporators. —corporate name. —powers.

102 INTERNATIONAL TRUST AND BANKING COMPANY.

CHAP. 58

subject to all the duties and obligations conferred on corporations by law.

Location.

Section 2. The corporation hereby created shall be located at Calais, Washington county, Maine, and shall have office for the transaction of business in said city.

Purposes.

Section 3. The purposes of said corporation and the business which it may perform, are; first, to receive on deposit, money, coin, bank notes, evidences of debt, accounts of individuals, companies, corporations, municipalities and states, allowing interest thereon, if agreed, or as the by-laws of said corporation may provide; second, to borrow money, to loan money on credits, or real estate, or personal security, and to negotiate loans and sales for others; third, to own and maintain safe deposit vaults, with boxes, safes and other facilities therein, to be rented to other parties for the safe keeping of moneys, securities, stocks, jewelry, plate, valuable papers and documents, and other property susceptible of being deposited therein, and may receive on deposit for safe keeping, property of any kind entrusted to it for that purpose; fourth, to hold and enjoy all such estate, real, personal and mixed, as may be obtained by the investment of its capital stock or any other moneys and funds that may come into its possession in the course of its business and dealings, and the same sell, grant, and dispose of; fifth, to act as agent for issuing, registering and countersigning certificates, bonds, stocks, and all evidences of debt or ownership in property; sixth, to hold by grant, assignment, transfer, devise or bequest any real or personal property or trusts duly created, and to execute trusts of every description; seventh, to act as assignee, receiver, executor, and no surety shall be necessary upon the bond of the corporation, unless the court or officer approving such bond shall require it; eighth, to do in general all the business that may lawfully be done by trust and banking companies.

—may own and maintain safe deposit boxes.

—may act as trustee, etc.

Capital stock.

Section 4. The capital stock of said corporation shall not be less than fifty thousand dollars, divided into shares of one hundred dollars each, with the right to increase the said capital stock at any time, by vote of the shareholders, to any amount not exceeding two hundred thousand dollars. Said corporation shall not commence business as a trust or banking company until stock to the amount of at least twenty-five thousand dollars shall have been subscribed and paid in, in cash.

—shall not commence business until at least $25,000 has been paid in.

Shall not loan money on security of its own capital stock.

Section 5. Said corporation shall not make any loan or discount on the security of the shares of its own capital stock, nor be the purchaser or holder of any such shares unless necessary to prevent loss upon a debt previously contracted in good faith;

INTERNATIONAL TRUST AND BANKING COMPANY. 103

and all stock so acquired shall, within six months of the time of its acquisition, be disposed of at public or private sale.

Section 6. All the corporate powers of this corporation except as herein otherwise provided, shall be exercised by a board of directors, a majority of whom shall be residents of this state, whose number and term of office shall be determined by a vote of the shareholders at the first meeting held by the incorporators and at each annual meeting thereafter. The affairs and powers of the corporation may, at the option of the shareholders, expressed in their by-laws, be entrusted to an executive board of five members to be, by vote of the shareholders, elected from the full board of directors, and three of said board shall be a quorum to transact business. The directors of said corporation shall be sworn to the proper discharge of their duties, and they shall hold office until others are elected and qualified in their stead. If a director dies, resigns, or is removed by the election and qualification of another in his place, or becomes disqualified for any cause, the remaining directors may appoint a person to fill the vacancy until the next annual meeting of the corporation. The oath of office of such director shall be taken within thirty days of his election, or his office shall be declared vacant. The clerk of such corporation shall, within ten days, notify such directors of their election, and within thirty days shall publish the list of all persons who have taken the oath of office as directors.

Section 7. The executive board of directors of said corporation shall constitute the board of investment of said corporation. Said corporation shall keep in a separate book, specially provided for the purpose, a record of all loans, and investments of every description, made by said institution substantially in the order of time when such loans or investments are made, which shall show that such loans or investments have been made with the approval of the executive board of said corporation, which shall indicate such particulars respecting such loans or investments as the bank examiner shall direct. This book shall be submitted to the directors and to the bank examiner whenever requested. Such loans or investments shall be classified in the book as the bank examiner shall direct.

No loan shall be made to any officer or director of said banking or trust company except by the approval of a majority of the executive board in writing, and said corporation shall have no authority to hire money or to give notes unless by vote of the said board duly recorded.

Section 8. No person shall be eligible to the position of a director of said corporation who is not the actual owner of ten shares of the stock.

INTERNATIONAL TRUST AND BANKING COMPANY.

CHAP. 58

Reserve fund.

Section 9. Said corporation, after beginning to receive deposits, shall, at all times, have on hand in lawful money, as a reserve, not less than fifteen per cent of the aggregate amount of its deposits which are subject to withdrawal on demand, provided, that in lieu of lawful money, two-thirds of said fifteen per cent may consist of balances payable on demand, due from any national or state bank.

Trust funds shall constitute a special deposit.

Section 10. All the property or money held in trust by this corporation shall constitute a special deposit and the accounts thereof and of said trust department shall be kept separate and such funds and the investment or loans of them shall be specially appropriated to the security and payment of such deposits, and not be subject to any other liabilities of the corporation; and for the purpose of securing the observance of this proviso, said corporation shall have a trust department in which all business pertaining to such trust property shall be kept separate and distinct from its general business.

Administrators, etc., may deposit with.

Section 11. An administrator, executor, assignee, guardian or trustee, any court of law or equity, including courts of probate and insolvency, officers and treasurers of towns, cities, counties, and savings banks of the state of Maine may deposit any moneys, bonds, stocks, evidences of debt or of ownership in property, or any personal property, with said corporation, and any of said courts may direct any person deriving authority from them to so deposit the same.

Responsibility of shareholders.

Section 12. Each shareholder of this corporation shall be individually responsible, equally and ratably, and not one for the other, for all contracts, debts and engagements of such corporation, to a sum equal to the amount of the par value of the shares owned by each, in addition to the amount invested in said shares.

Surplus fund.

Section 13. Such corporation shall set apart as a surplus fund not less than ten per cent of its earnings in each and every year until such fund with the accumulated interest thereon, shall amount to one-fourth of the capital stock of said corporation.

Taxation of shares.

Section 14. The shares of said corporation shall be subject to taxation under the laws of this state in the same manner and rate as are or may be the shares of national banks.

Shall be subject to examination by bank examiner.

Section 15. Said corporation shall be subject to examination by the bank examiner, who shall visit it at least once in every year, and as much oftener as he may deem expedient. At such visits he shall have free access to its vaults, books and papers, and shall thoroughly inspect and examine all the affairs of said corporation, and make such inquiries as may be necessary to ascertain its condition and ability to fulfill all its engagements. If upon examination of said corporation the examiner is of the opinion that its investments are not in accordance with law, or said corporation is insolvent, or its condition is such as to render its further proceedings hazardous to the public or to those having funds in its custody, or is of the opinion that it has exceeded its powers or failed to comply with any of the rules or restrictions provided by law, he shall have such authority and take such action as is provided for in the case of savings banks by chapter forty-seven of the revised statutes and amendments or additions thereto. He shall preserve in a permanent form a full record of his proceedings, including a statement of the condition of said corporation. A copy of such statement shall be published by said corporation immediately after the annual examination of the same in some newspaper published where such corporation is established. If no paper is published in the town where said corporation is established, then it shall be published in a newspaper printed in the nearest city or town. The necessary expenses of the bank examiner while making such examination shall be paid by the corporation.

Section 16. Any three of the corporators named in this act may call the first meeting of the corporation by mailing a written notice, signed by all, postage paid, to each of the other corporators, seven days at least before the day of the meeting, naming the time, place and purpose of such meeting, and at such meeting the necessary officers may be chosen, by-laws adopted, and any other corporate business transacted.

Section 17. This act shall take effect when approved.

Approved February 18, 1903.

Chapter 59.

An Act to amend an act entitled "An Act to ratify the mortgage of the Fish River Railroad," approved February eleven, nineteen hundred and three.

Be it enacted by the Senate and House of Representatives in Legislature assembled, as follows:

Section 1. Section one of an act entitled "An Act to ratify the mortgage of the Fish River Railroad," approved February eleven, nineteen hundred and three, is hereby amended by substituting for the word "Central" therein the word 'City' so that said section as amended, shall read as follows:

'Section 1. The mortgage of the Fish River Railroad made by the Fish River Railroad Company to the City Trust Company dated January one in the year of our Lord nineteen hundred and two, is hereby made valid, ratified and confirmed.'

Section 2. This act shall take effect when approved.

Approved February 18, 1903.

Chapter 60.

An Act additional to and amendatory of Chapter fifty-four of the Private and Special Laws of eighteen hundred and ninety-five, creating the Rumford Falls Village Corporation.

Be it enacted by the Senate and House of Representatives in Legislature assembled, as follows:

Rumford Falls Village Corporation, limits extended.

Section 1. The limits of the Rumford Falls Village Corporation as described in section one of chapter fifty-four of the private and special laws of eighteen hundred and ninety-five are hereby extended and enlarged by adding thereto the following described land in the town of Rumford together with all the inhabitants and property thereon, namely: All the land that is located on the northerly side of the Androscoggin river in the town of Rumford, above Rumford Falls, which was known as the Charles F. Wheeler farm, said farm being situated between the southerly and westerly line of the Rufus Virgin farm, so called, and the farm owned by William M. Blanchard and now occupied by his son George E. Blanchard.

Provisions shall apply to land, inhabitants and property.

Section 2. All the provisions of chapter fifty-four referred to in section one of this act shall apply to all the land, inhabitants and property on the same, described in section one of this act the same as if said land, inhabitants and property had been described and included in section one of said chapter fifty-four. And the same shall become a part of the Rumford Falls Village Corporation from and after the date of the approval of this act.

Approved February 19, 1903.

Chapter 61.

An Act to incorporate the Rangeley Water Company.

Be it enacted by the Senate and House of Representatives in Legislature assembled, as follows:

Corporators.

Section 1. Phineas Richardson, Whiting L. Butler, Walter F. Oakes, John A. Russell, Harry A. Furbish, G. Lafayette Kempton, John R. Toothaker and G. A. Proctor, with their associates and successors, are hereby made a corporation, under

—corporate name.
—purposes.

the name of the Rangeley Water Company, for the purpose of supplying the inhabitants of the town of Rangeley and adjoining plantations with suitable water for industrial, manufacturing, domestic, sanitary and municipal purposes, including the extinguishment of fire; with all the rights and privileges, and subject to all the liabilities and obligations of similar corporations under the laws of this state.

Section 2. For any of the purposes aforesaid, the said corporation is hereby authorized to take and use water from the lakes, ponds, rivers, streams, springs, or other waters in the towns of Rangeley and Madrid, and in the plantations of Greenvale, Sandy River, Rangeley and Dallas; to conduct and distribute the same into and through any of the said towns and plantations; and to survey for, locate, construct and maintain suitable and convenient dams, reservoirs, buildings, machinery, lines of pipes, aqueducts, structures and appurtenances.

Authorized to take water from lakes, etc. in certain towns.

—may construct dams, lines of pipe, etc.

Section 3. The said corporation is hereby authorized to lay, construct and maintain its lines of pipe under, in and over any river or other stream of water in any of the said towns or plantations, and to build and maintain all necessary structures therefor, at such places as may be necessary for the said purposes of the said corporation; and to cross any water course, private or public sewer, or to change the direction thereof, where necessary for the said purposes of the said corporation, but in such manner as not to obstruct or impair the use thereof, and the said corporation shall be liable for any injury or damage caused thereby.

May lay pipes across rivers.

Section 4. The said corporation is hereby authorized to lay, construct and maintain in, under, through, along, over and across the highways, ways, streets, railroads and bridges in the said towns and plantations named in section two of this act, and to take up, replace and repair, all such aqueducts, pipes, hydrants and other structures and fixtures as may be necessary and convenient for the said purposes of said corporation; and said corporation shall be responsible for all damages to the said towns and plantations and to all corporations, persons and property, occasioned by such use of said highways, ways and streets. Whenever the said corporation shall lay down or construct any fixtures in any highway, way or street, it shall cause the same to be done with as little obstruction to public travel as may be practicable, and shall at its own expense, without unnecessary delay, cause the earth and pavement then removed by it, to be replaced in proper condition.

May lay pipes in streets, etc.

—damages.

Section 5. The said corporation is hereby authorized to take and hold, by purchase or otherwise, any lands necessary for flowage, and also for its dams, reservoirs, gates, hydrants, buildings and other necessary structures, and may locate, erect, lay and maintain aqueducts, lines of pipe, hydrants and other necessary structures or fixtures in, over and through any land for the said purposes, and excavate in and through such land for such location, construction and erection. And in general to do any acts necessary, convenient or proper, for carrying out any of the said purposes of said corporation. It may enter upon such

May take lands for flowage, etc.

CHAP. 61

—may enter lands for surveys.
—plans of location shall be published.

lands to make surveys and locations, and shall file in the registry of deeds for the county of Franklin, plans of such locations and lands, showing the property taken, and within thirty days thereafter publish notice of such filing in some newspaper in said county, such publication to be continued three weeks successively. Not more than two rods in width of land shall be occupied by any one line of pipe or aqueduct.

Damages may be assessed by county commissioners.

Section 6. Should the said corporation and the owner of any land required for the said purposes of said corporation, be unable to agree upon the damages to be paid for such location, taking, holding and construction, the land owner may within twelve months after the said filing of plans of location, apply to the commissioners of said county of Franklin, and cause such damages to be assessed in the same manner and under the same conditions, as are prescribed by law in the case of damages by the laying out of railroads. If the said corporation shall fail to pay such land owner, or deposit for his use with the clerk of the county commissioners aforesaid, such sums as may be finally awarded as damages, with costs when recovered by him, within ninety days after notice of final judgment shall have been received by the clerk of courts of the said county, the said location shall be thereby invalid and the said corporation shall forfeit all rights under the same, as against the owner of the land. The said cor-

—may make tender to land owner.

poration may make a tender to any land owner damaged under the provisions of this act, and if such land owner recovers more damages than was tendered him by the said corporation, he shall recover costs, otherwise the said corporation shall recover costs. In case the said corporation shall begin to occupy such land before the rendition of final judgment, the land owner may require the said corporation to file its bond to him with the said county commissioners in such sum and with such sureties as they may approve, conditioned for the payment of the damages that may be awarded. No action shall be brought against the said corporation for such taking, holding and occupation, until after such failure to pay or deposit as aforesaid. Failure to apply for damages within the said twelve months shall be held to be a waiver of the same.

May make contracts with United States, the state of Maine, towns, etc.

Section 7. The said corporation is hereby authorized to make contracts with the United States, the state of Maine, the county of Franklin, the towns and plantations named in section two of this act, and Rangeley Village Corporation in the said town of Rangeley, and with the inhabitants of said towns, plantations and village corporation, or any corporations doing business therein, for the supply of water and power for the purposes contemplated in this act; and the said towns, plantations and village corporation, by their proper officers, are hereby authorized to enter into contract with the said water company for a supply of water for any and all purposes mentioned in this act, and for such exemptions from public burdens as the said towns and the said water company may agree upon, which when made, shall be legal and binding upon all parties thereto.

Section 8. The capital stock of the said water company shall be twenty thousand dollars, which may be increased to any sum not exceeding fifty thousand dollars, by a majority vote of the stockholders of the said water company; and the stock shall be divided into shares of one hundred dollars each. *Capital stock*

Section 9. The said water company for all its purposes, may hold real and personal estate necessary and convenient therefor, to the amount of fifty thousand dollars. *May hold real and personal estate to the value of $50,000.*

Section 10. The said water company may issue its bonds for the construction of its works, of any and all kinds, upon such rates and time as it may deem expedient not to exceed the amount of the capital stock subscribed for, and secure the same by mortgage of its franchise and property. *May issue bonds. —may mortgage its property.*

Section 11. The first meeting of said water company shall be called by a written notice thereof, signed by any two of the named incorporators, served upon each named incorporator by giving him the same in hand, or by leaving the same at his last and usual place of abode at least seven days before the time of meeting, or by publishing said notice in some newspaper published in said county of Franklin. *First meeting how called.*

Section 12. This act shall take effect when approved.

Approved February 20, 1903.

Chapter 62.

An Act to amend Section five of Chapter forty-two of the Public Laws of eighteen hundred and ninety-nine, as amended by Chapter three hundred and twenty-six of the Private and Special Laws of nineteen hundred and one, relating to fishing through the ice in Thompson pond.

Be it enacted by the Senate and House of Representatives in Legislature assembled, as follows:

Section 1. So much of section five of chapter forty-two of the public laws of eighteen hundred and ninety-nine, as amended by chapter three hundred and twenty-six of the private and special laws of nineteen hundred and one, as prohibits fishing through the ice in Thompson pond, situated partly in Oxford and partly in Cumberland county, in accordance with the general law of the state, permitting fishing through the ice during February, March and April, is hereby repealed. *Ice fishing in Thompson pond, prohibition repealed.*

Section 2. This act shall take effect when approved.

Approved February 20, 1903.

Chapter 63.

An Act to amend Chapter two hundred seventy-one of the Private and Special Laws of nineteen hundred one, relating to the Lincoln Electric Railway Company.

Be it enacted by the Senate and House of Representatives in Legislature assembled, as follows:

Charter amended.

Section 1. Section eleven of chapter two hundred seventy-one of the private and special laws of nineteen hundred one is hereby amended by striking out the word "two," in the third line, and inserting in place thereof, the word 'four,' so that said section as amended shall read as follows:

Shall be void unless operations are commenced within four years.

'Section 11. This charter shall be null and void unless operations for building this railroad shall have been actually commenced without four years from date of the passage of this act.'

Section 2. This act shall take effect when approved.

Approved February 20, 1903.

Chapter 64.

An Act to legalize the doings of the Crosbyville Chapel, at Bangor, Maine.

Be it enacted by the Senate and House of Representatives in Legislature assembled, as follows:

Acts and doings legalized.

Section 1. All acts and doings of the Crosbyville Chapel, Bangor, Maine, from the date of incorporation to the present date are hereby legalized.

Section 2. This act shall take effect when approved.

Approved February 24, 1903.

Chapter 65.

An Act in relation to the election of the Members of the School Committee of the City of Portland.

Be it enacted by the Senate and House of Representatives in Legislature assembled, as follows:

School committee, shall be elected.

—time fixed.

—plurality shall determine the choice of members.

Section 1. The members of the school committee of the city of Portland, including the female members of said committee, shall hereafter continue to be elected on the first Monday in December at the annual municipal election and in the same manner now provided for by law, except that a plurality of the votes given at such election shall determine the choice of members of said committee.

Section 2. This act shall take effect when approved.

Approved February 24, 1903.

Chapter 66.

An Act to grant additional powers to the Vickery Realty Company.

Be it enacted by the Senate and House of Representatives in Legislature assembled, as follows:

Section 1. The Vickery Realty Company is hereby authorized to maintain in the streets by it now occupied in the city of Augusta a system of aqueducts for a domestic supply of water from the springs by it now owned and to supply therefrom water for such domestic use to and upon the real estate by it now supplied, the number of takers thereon not to be increased, with all the rights and subject to all the duties, restrictions and liabilities imposed by law or by the ordinances of said city upon corporations using the streets of said city for similar purposes.

Section 2. For the purpose of confirming the title of said company to its easements in the lands now occupied by its aqueduct it is hereby authorized to take an easement in such lands, not exceeding two rods in width, by filing in the registry of deeds for the county of Kennebec plans for such location and lands showing the property and the easement therein taken, and within thirty days thereafter it shall publish notices of such filing in some newspaper in said county for three weeks successively. The damages therefor shall be assessed and paid in the same manner and under the same conditions as are or may be prescribed by law in the case of damages by the laying out of highways.

Section 3. The said corporation for the said purposes may hold real and personal estate necessary and convenient therefor.

Section 4. This act shall take effect when approved.

Approved February 24, 1903.

Chapter 67.

An Act to incorporate the Central Trust Company.

Be it enacted by the Senate and House of Representatives in Legislature assembled, as follows:

Section 1. George Burnham, Jr., Franklin R. Barrett, Charles S. Fobes, Herbert J. Brown, Franklin C. Payson, Arthur K. Hunt and George H. Richardson, all of Portland, county of Cumberland, state of Maine, or such of them as may by vote accept this charter, with their associates, successors and assigns, are hereby made a body corporate and politic to be known as the Central Trust Company, and as such shall be possessed of

112   CENTRAL TRUST COMPANY.

Chap. 67

Location.

all the powers, privileges and immunities and subject to all the duties and obligations conferred on corporations by law.

Section 2. The corporation hereby created shall be located at Portland, Cumberland county, Maine, and may have two offices for the transaction of business in said city.

Purposes.

Section 3. The purposes of said corporation and the business which it may perform, are; first, to receive on deposit, money, coin, bank notes, evidences of debt, accounts of individuals, companies, corporations, municipalities and states, allowing interest thereon, if agreed, or as the by-laws of said corporation may provide; second, to borrow money, to loan money on credits, or real estate, or personal or collateral security, and to negotiate purchases, loans and sales for others; third, to erect, construct, own, maintain and operate safe deposit vaults, with boxes, safes and other facilities therein, to be rented to other parties for the safe keeping of moneys, securities, stocks, jewelry, plate, valuable papers and documents, and other property susceptible of being deposited therein, and to receive on deposit for safe keeping, property of any kind entrusted to it for that purpose; fourth, to hold and enjoy all such estate, real, personal and mixed as may be obtained by the investment of its capital stock or any other moneys and funds that may come into its possession in the course of its business and dealings, and the same sell, grant and dispose of; fifth, to act as agent for issuing, registering and countersigning certificates, bonds, stocks, and all evidences of debt or ownership in property; sixth, to hold by grant, assignment, transfer, devise or bequest, any real or personal property or trusts duly created, and to execute trusts of every description; seventh, to act as executor, receiver or assignee, with the same powers and duties as are conferred and imposed by law upon natural persons acting in the same capacities and subject to the same control of the court having jurisdiction of the same in all proceedings relating to the exercise of these powers; all papers may be signed and sworn to by any officer designated by the corporation for that purpose, and the officers shall be subject to citation and examination in the same manner and to the same extent as natural persons acting in the same capacities. No sureties shall be required upon the bond of the corporation when acting in said capacities, unless the court or officer approving said bond shall require it; eighth, to guarantee the payment of the principal and interest of all obligations secured by mortgages of real estate running to said Central Trust Company; to issue its own bonds or obligations based upon real or personal property conveyed to it in trust to secure the payment of such bonds or obligations and the interest thereon; ninth, to hold for

—may rent deposit boxes.

—may act as agent.

—may act as trustee.

—may guarantee payment.

—may issue bonds.

CENTRAL TRUST COMPANY. 113

CHAP. 67

safe keeping all kinds of personal or mixed property and to act as agents for the owners thereof, and of real estate for the collection of income on the same and for the sale of the same; tenth, to do in general all the business that may lawfully be done by trust and banking companies.

—may act as agents of owners of property.

Section 4. The capital stock of said corporation shall not be less than fifty thousand dollars, divided into shares of one hundred dollars each, with the right to increase the said capital stock at any time, by a vote of the shareholders, to any amount not exceeding five hundred thousand dollars. Said corporation shall not commence business as a trust or banking company, until stock to the amount of at least fifty thousand dollars shall have been subscribed and paid in, in cash.

Capital stock.

—shall not commence business until $50,000 has been paid in.

Section 5. Said corporation shall not make any loan or discount on the security of the shares of its own capital stock, nor be the purchaser or holder of any such shares unless necessary to prevent loss upon a debt previously contracted in good faith; and all stock so acquired shall, within six months from the time of its acquisition, be disposed of at public or private sale.

Shall not make loan on security of its own capital stock.

—proviso.

Section 6. All the corporate powers of this corporation shall be exercised by a board of directors or trustees, who shall be residents of this state, whose number and term of office shall be determined by a vote of the shareholders at the first meeting held by the incorporators and at each annual meeting thereafter. The affairs and powers of the corporation may, at the option of the shareholders, be entrusted to an executive board of five members to be, by vote of the shareholders, elected from the full board of directors or trustees. The directors or trustees of said corporation shall be sworn to the proper discharge of their duties, and they shall hold office until others are elected and qualified in their stead. If a director or trustee dies, resigns, or becomes disqualified for any cause, the remaining directors or trustees may appoint a person to fill the vacancy until the next annual meeting of the corporation. The oath of office of such director or trustee shall be taken within thirty days of his election, or his office shall become vacant. The clerk of such corporation shall, within ten days, notify such directors or trustees of their election, and within thirty days shall publish the list of all persons who have taken the oath of office as directors or trustees.

Board of trustees.

—number and tenure.

—executive board.

—vacancies, how filled.

Section 7. The board of directors or trustees of said corporation shall constitute the board of investment of said corporation. Said directors or trustees shall keep in a separate book, specially provided for the purpose, a record of all loans, and investments of every description, made by said institution sub-

Board of investment.

—shall keep a record.

21

stantially in the order of time when such loans or investments are made, which shall show that such loans or investments have been made with the approval of the executive committee of said corporation, which shall indicate such particulars respecting such loans or investments as the bank examiner shall direct. This book shall be submitted to the directors or trustees and to the bank examiner whenever requested. Such loans or investments shall be classified in the book as the bank examiner shall direct.

—loans to directors or agent, how made.

No loan shall be made to any officers, director or agent of said company or to other persons in its employ, until the proposition to make such loan shall have been submitted by the person desiring the same to the board of directors of such bank, or to the executive committee of such board, if any, and accepted and approved by a majority of such board or committee. Such approval, if the loan is made, shall be spread upon the records of the corporation; and this record shall, in every instance, give the names of the directors authorizing the loan. Said corporation shall have no authority to hire money or to give notes unless by vote of the said board or of said committee duly recorded.

Holders of less than ten shares not eligible to be directors or trustees.

Section 8. No person shall be eligible to the position of a director or trustee of said corporation who is not the actual owner of ten shares of stock.

Reserve fund.

Section 9. Said corporation, after beginning to receive money on deposit shall at all times have on hand, as a reserve, in lawful money of the United States, an amount equal to at least fifteen per cent of the aggregate amount of all its deposits which are subject to withdrawal upon demand or within ten days; and whenever said reserve of such corporation shall be below said percentage of such deposits, it shall not increase its liabilities by making any new loans until the required proportion between the aggregate amount of such deposits and its reserve fund shall be restored; provided, that in lieu of lawful money two-thirds of said fifteen per cent may consist of balances payable on demand, due from any national bank, and one-third of said fifteen per cent may consist of lawful money and bonds of the United States or of this state, the absolute property of such corporation.

—proviso.

Trust funds shall constitute a special deposit.

Section 10. All the property or money held in trust by this corporation shall constitute a special deposit and the accounts thereof and of said trust department shall be kept separate, and such funds and the investment or loans of them shall be specially appropriated to the security and payment of such deposits, and not be subject to any other liabilities of the corporation; and for the purpose of securing the observance of this proviso, said corporation shall have a trust department in which all business pertaining to such trust property shall be kept separate and distinct from its general business.

Section 11. An administrator, executor, assignee, guardian or trustee, any court of law or equity, including courts of probate and insolvency, officers and treasurers of towns, cities, counties, and savings banks of the state of Maine may deposit any moneys, bonds, stocks, evidences of debt or of ownership in property, or any personal property, with said corporation, and any of said courts may direct any person deriving authority from them to so deposit the same. *Administrators, executors, etc. may deposit in.*

Section 12. Each shareholder of this corporation shall be individually responsible, equally and ratably, and not one for the other, for all contracts, debts and engagements of such corporation, to a sum equal to the amount of the par value of the shares owned by each, in addition to the amount invested in said shares. *Responsibility of shareholders.*

Section 13. Said corporation shall set apart as a guaranty fund not less than ten per cent of its net earnings in each and every year until such fund with the accumulated interest thereon, shall amount to one-fourth of the capital stock of the company. The said surplus shall be kept to secure against losses and contingencies, and whenever the same becomes impaired it shall be reimbursed in the manner provided for its accumulation. *Guaranty fund.*

Section 14. The shares of said corporation shall be subject to taxation in the same manner and at the same rate as are the shares of national banks. *Taxation.*

Section 15. Said corporation shall be subject to examination by the bank examiner, who shall visit it at least once in every year, and as much oftener as he may deem expedient. At such visits he shall have free access to its vaults, books and papers, and shall thoroughly inspect and examine all the affairs of said corporation, and make such inquiries as may be necessary to ascertain its condition and ability to fulfill all its engagements. If upon examination of said corporation the examiner is of the opinion that its investments are not in accordance with law, or said corporation is insolvent, or its condition is such as to render its further proceedings hazardous to the public or to those having funds in its custody, or is of the opinion that it has exceeded its powers or failed to comply with any of the rules or restrictions provided by law, he shall have such authority and take such action as is provided for in the case of the savings banks by chapter forty-seven of the revised statutes. He shall preserve in a permanent form a full record of his proceedings, including a statement of the condition of said corporation. A copy of such statement shall be published by said corporation immedi- *Shall be subject to examination by bank examiner.*

—statement shall be published.

116 CITY OF PORTLAND.

CHAP. 68

ately after the annual examination of the same in some newspaper published where said corporation is established. If no paper is published in the town where said corporation is established, then it shall be published in a newspaper printed in the nearest city or town. The necessary expenses of the bank examiner while making such examination shall be paid by the corporation.

First meeting, how called.

Section 16. Any three of the corporators named in this act may call the first meeting of the corporation by mailing a written notice, signed by all, postage paid, to each of the other corporators, seven days at least before the day of the meeting, naming the time, place and purpose of such meeting, and at such meeting the necessary officers may be chosen, by-laws adopted, and any other corporate business transacted.

Section 17. This act shall take effect when approved.

Approved February 25, 1903.

Chapter 68.

An Act to amend the charter of the City of Portland.

Be it enacted by the Senate and House of Representatives in Legislature assembled, as follows:

Section 12, of chapter 275, of special laws of 1863, as amended by chapter 384, of special laws of 1901, further amended.

Section 1. Section twelve of chapter two hundred seventy-five of the private and special laws of the state of Maine, approved March twenty-four, eighteen hundred sixty-three, as amended by chapter three hundred eighty-four of the private and special laws of the state of Maine, approved March nineteen, nineteen hundred one, is hereby further amended by striking out the word "majority" in the fifth line of said section and substituting therefor the word 'plurality,' so that said section twelve as amended, shall read as follows:

Election of mayor, ward officers and constables.

'Section 12. The mayor shall be elected by the inhabitants of the city, voting in their respective wards. One alderman, three common councilmen, a warden and clerk, and two constables, shall be elected by each ward, being residents in the ward where elected. All said officers shall be elected by ballot by a plurality of the votes given; and shall hold their office one year from the second Monday in December, and until others shall be elected and qualified in their places. All city and ward officers shall be held to discharge the duties of the offices to which they have been respectively elected, notwithstanding their removal after their election out of their respective wards into any other

—plurality shall elect.

CITY OF PORTLAND.   117

CHAP. 68

wards in the city; but they shall not so be held after they have taken up their permanent residence out of the city.'

Section 2. Section thirteen of said chapter two hundred and seventy-five as amended by said chapter three hundred and eighty-four is hereby further amended by striking out the word "majority" at the end of the fifteenth line of said section and substituting therefor the word 'plurality,' so that said section thirteen as amended, shall read as follows: *Section 13 of chapter 275 of special laws of 1880, as amended by chapter 284 of special laws of 1901, furthe1 amended.*

'Section 13. On the first Monday in December annually the qualified electors of each ward shall ballot for mayor, one alderman, three common councilmen, a warden and clerk, and two constables, on one ballot. The ward clerk, within twenty-four hours after such election, shall deliver to the persons elected, certificates of their election, and shall forthwith deliver to the city clerk a certified copy of the record of such election, a plain and intelligible abstract of which shall be entered by the city clerk on the city records. If the choice of any such officers is not effected on that day, the meeting shall be adjourned to another day, not more than two days thereafter, to complete such election, and may so adjourn from time to time, until the election is complete. The board of aldermen shall, as soon as conveniently may be, examine the copies of the records of the several wards, certified as aforesaid, and shall cause the person who shall have been elected mayor by a plurality of the votes given in all the wards, to be notified in writing of his election. But if it shall appear that no person shall have been so elected, or if the person elected shall refuse to accept the office, the said board shall issue their warrants for another election; and in case the citizens shall fail on a second ballot to elect a mayor, the city council in convention shall, from the four highest candidates voted for at the second election and returned, elect a mayor for the ensuing year; and in case of a vacancy in the office of mayor by death, resignation or otherwise, it shall be filled for the remainder of the term by a new election in the manner hereinbefore provided for the choice of said officer. The oath or affirmation prescribed by this act, shall be administered to the mayor by the city clerk or any justice of the peace in said city. The aldermen and common councilmen elect, shall on the second Monday in December, at ten o'clock in the forenoon, meet in convention, when the oath or affirmation required by the second section of this act shall be administered to the members of the two boards present, by the mayor or any justice of the peace, after which the board of common council shall be organized by the election of a president and clerk. The city council shall, by ordinance, determine the time of holding stated or regular meetings of the

—When election shall be held.

—certificates of election shall be delivered within 24 hours.

—when no choice is made, subsequent proceedings.

—vacancy in office of mayor, how filled.

—oath of office, by whom administered.

—when stated or regular meetings shall be held.

SANFORD TRUST COMPANY—SHELL FISH.

board, and shall also, in like manner, determine the manner of calling special meetings and the persons by whom the same shall be called; but until otherwise provided by ordinance special meetings shall be called by the mayor by causing a notification to be left at the usual residence or place of business of each member of the board or boards to be convened.'

Section 3. This act shall take effect when approved.

Approved February 25, 1903.

Chapter 69.

An Act to extend the charter of the Sanford Trust Company.

Be it enacted by the Senate and House of Representatives in Legislature assembled, as follows:

Charter extended for two years.

Section 1. The rights, powers and privileges of the Sanford Trust Company which were granted by chapter four hundred and sixty-nine, of the private and special laws of one thousand nine hundred and one, are hereby extended for two years from the approval of this act and the persons named in said act, their associates and successors shall have all the rights, powers and privileges that were granted them by said act to be exercised in the same manner and for the same purposes as specified in said act.

Section 2. This act shall take effect when approved.

Approved February 25, 1903.

Chapter 70.

An Act for the better protection of Shell Fish within the town of Georgetown.

Be it enacted by the Senate and House of Representatives in Legislature assembled, as follows:

Shell fish shall not be taken in the town of Georgetown without written permit.

Section 1. No shell fish shall be taken from any flats within the limits of the town of Georgetown, in Sagadahoc county, except by written permit of the municipal officers of the town and payment to the town for the privilege at such price as said town may establish at any town meeting, any existing law to the contrary notwithstanding; provided, that without such permit, any inhabitant within said town, or any person temporarily resident therein, or the riparian owner of such flats, may take there-

—proviso.

from for the immediate use of himself or his family, not exceeding one bushel at any one tide.

Section 2. Any person taking shell fish contrary to the provisions of this act, shall be punished for each offense by a fine not exceeding ten dollars, or by imprisonment not exceeding thirty days, or by both, and it shall be the duty of the municipal officers of Georgetown to make complaint for any violation of this act.

Penalty.

Approved February 25, 1903.

Chapter 71.

An Act to amend Chapter three hundred and forty-six of the Private and Special Laws of eighteen hundred and ninety-seven, entitled "An Act to amend the charter of the City of Westbrook."

Be it enacted by the Senate and House of Representatives in Legislature assembled, as follows:

Section two of chapter three hundred and forty-six of the private and special laws of eighteen hundred and ninety-seven, entitled "An Act to amend the charter of the City of Westbrook," is hereby amended by striking out the words "second Monday in March" in the third sentence of said section, and inserting in place thereof the words 'first Monday in January.'

Section 2 of chapter 346 of special laws of 1897, amended.

Approved February 25, 1903.

Chapter 72.

An Act to authorize the Augusta, Winthrop and Gardiner Railway to supply electricity in the towns of Winthrop and Manchester.

Be it enacted by the Senate and House of Representatives in Legislature assembled, as follows:

Section 1. The Augusta, Winthrop and Gardiner Railway is hereby authorized to make, generate, sell, distribute and supply electricity for lighting, heating, manufacturing and mechanical purposes in the towns of Winthrop and Manchester, and in so doing shall have all the rights and be subject to all the duties and liabilities of corporations exercising similar powers under the general laws of the state.

Augusta, Winthrop and Gardiner Railway authorized to supply electricity to towns of Winthrop and Manchester.

Section 2. The said company is authorized to make contracts with the towns of Winthrop and Manchester, and any village corporation therein, and with corporations and inhabitants of said towns for the purpose of supplying light, heat and power

May make contracts with Winthrop and Manchester to supply electricity.

CHAP. 73

as contemplated by this act. The said towns, through their selectmen, or any village corporation therein through the assessors thereof, are severally authorized to contract with the said company from time to time for a supply of electricity for public purposes from year to year or for a term of years, as they may deem expedient and to raise money therefor.

May increase its capital stock.

Section 3. The said company for the purposes of this act may increase its capital stock and issue the same therefor to an amount not exceeding thirty thousand dollars.

May issue bonds.

Section 4. The said company may issue its bonds for the purposes of this act from time to time and in such amount and on such rates and time as it may deem expedient, and secure the same by appropriate mortgages upon its property and franchises.

Locations of posts, wires, etc.

Section 5. The locations of all posts, wires and fixtures of the said corporation as now established and maintained are hereby confirmed and made valid.

Section 6. This act shall take effect when approved.

Approved February 25, 1903.

Chapter 73.

An Act amendatory to Chapter five hundred and seven of the Private and Special Laws of eighteen hundred and eighty-nine, entitled, "An Act to establish the Dover Municipal Court," as amended by Chapter one hundred and ninety-six of the Private and Special Laws of eighteen hundred and ninety-nine.

Be it enacted by the Senate and House of Representatives in Legislature assembled, as follows:

Section 6 of chapter 507 of special laws of 1889, as amended by chapter 196 of special laws of 1899, further amended.

Section six of said chapter is amended by inserting in the fourth line thereof between the word "exceed" and the word "hundred," the word 'two,' instead of the word "one" so that said section, as amended, shall read as follows:

Original jurisdiction of Dover municipal court.

'Section 6. Said court shall have original jurisdiction concurrent with the supreme judicial court as follows; first, of all civil actions wherein the debt or damage demanded, exclusive of costs, does not exceed two hundred dollars, in which any person, summoned as trustee resides within the county of Piscataquis, or, if a corporation has an established place of business in said county, or in which, no trustee being named in the writ, any defendant resides in said county, or if no defendant resides within the limits of this state, any defendant is served with process in said county, or the goods, estate or effects of any defendant are found within said county and attached on the original writ; second, of the assaults and batteries described in section twenty-eight of chapter one hundred and eighteen of the revised statutes; of all larcenies described in sections one, six, seven, nine and eleven of chapter one hundred and twenty of the revised statutes, when the value of the property is not alleged to exceed thirty dollars, of the offense described in section twenty-one of chapter one hundred and twenty-two of the revised statutes; of all offenses and crimes described in sections one and four of chapter one hundred and twenty-three of the revised statutes; of all offenses described in section six and in sections twenty-nine to forty-five inclusive, of chapter one hundred and twenty-four of the revised statutes; of the offense described in section five of chapter one hundred and twenty-five of the revised statutes; of all offenses described in section one of chapter one hundred and twenty-six of the revised statutes, when the value of the property or thing alleged to have been fraudulently obtained, sold, mortgaged or pledged, is not alleged to exceed thirty dollars; and of all offenses described in sections two, nine, sixteen, seventeen and twenty-one of chapter one hundred and twenty-seven of the revised statutes, when the value of the property destroyed or the injury done, is not alleged to exceed thirty dollars; and may punish for either of said crimes or offenses, by fine not exceeding fifty dollars, and by imprisonment not exceeding three months, provided, that when the offenses described in section twenty-eight of chapter one hundred and eighteen, section twenty-one of chapter one hundred and twenty-two, and sections one and four of chapter one hundred and twenty-three, are of a high and aggravated nature, the judge of said court may cause persons charged with such offenses to recognize with sufficient sureties to appear before the supreme judicial court, and in default thereof commit them; third, of all other crimes, offenses and misdemeanors committed in said county, which are by law punishable by fine not exceeding fifty dollars, and by imprisonment not exceeding three months, and are not within the exclusive jurisdiction of some other municipal or police court.'

Approved February 25, 1908.

Chapter 74.

An Act to incorporate the Mapleton and Presque Isle Railroad Company

Be it enacted by the Senate and House of Representatives in Legislature assembled, as follows:

Corporators
Section 1. John W. Dudley, Allen M. Dudley, Micajah H. Dudley, Francis C. Dudley, Sanford S. Dudley, Lionel E. Dudley, Melvin A. Dudley and J. Perley Dudley, all of Castle Hill,

—corporate name.
their associates, successors and assigns, are hereby created and constituted a body corporate by the name of the Mapleton and Presque Isle Railroad Company, with all the powers, franchises, rights and privileges, and subject to all the duties, obligations and restrictions, conferred and imposed upon railroad corporations by the laws of this state.

Officers.
Section 2. The officers of said corporation shall be a president, vice-president, secretary, treasurer, board of directors, and such others as may be provided by the by-laws, rules and regulations of the corporation, not repugnant to the laws of the state.

Capital stock.
Section 3. The capital stock of said corporation shall consist of six hundred shares of the par value of one hundred dollars each.

Powers.
Section 4. Said corporation is authorized to locate, construct, equip, maintain and operate a railroad of standard gauge, with one or more tracks or sets of rails. with all suitable bridges, tunnels, viaducts, culverts, drains, turnouts, and all other necessary appendages. from the village of Mapleton to Presque Isle, with the right to connect with the Bangor and Aroostook Railroad.

—location.
Said line to be located as near as practicable according to the survey of September, nineteen hundred and two, made by Charles I. Haynes, civil engineer, under the direction of the aforesaid corporators.

Limitations.
Section 5. If said corporation shall not have been organized, and the location of its line from Mapleton to Presque Isle, as provided in section four of this act according to actual surveys, shall not have been filed with the county commissioners of the county of Aroostook, on or before the first day of January, in the year of our Lord one thousand nine hundred and five, or if said corporation shall fail to complete said line of railroad on or before the first day of January, in the year of our Lord one thousand nine hundred and seven, in either of the above mentioned cases, this act shall be null and void so far as said line is concerned.

May sell or lease its lines.
Section 6. Said corporation may sell or lease its line or lines to any other railroad corporation, which latter company is hereby

authorized to enter with such contract for sale or lease, and the directors of the two corporations may enter into contract for the running of the road, and for the purchase, sale or lease thereof, as the directors of the two contracting companies, in the exercise of their best judgment and discretion may deem for the advantage of their respective corporations, subject to the approval of a majority of the stock in each corporation.

Section 7. Provided, however, that said corporation shall not locate its road until the capital stock required by section three has been subscribed in good faith by responsible parties, and five per cent paid thereon in cash to the directors of said corporation, and an affidavit made by a majority of said directors, and recorded in the office of the secretary of state, that the amount of the stock required by section three has been in good faith subscribed and five per cent paid thereon as aforesaid, and that it is intended in good faith to construct, maintain and operate said road. The secretary of state shall record said affidavit upon payment of five dollars. *Capital stock shall be subscribed before location of road.*

Section 8. Said corporation or its successors or assigns shall have authority to use either steam or electricity in the operation of said road. *May use steam or electricity.*

Section 9. This charter is granted because the objects sought to be accomplished cannot be fully attained and accomplished under the general laws for the formation of railroad companies.

Section 10. This act shall take effect when approved.

Approved February 25, 1903.

Chapter 75.

An Act to Incorporate the Camden and Liberty Railway.

Be it enacted by the Senate and House of Representatives in Legislature assembled, as follows:

Section 1. Thomas W. Lawson, Holly M. Bean, Charles W. Emery, Charles E. Littlefield, Reuel Robinson, Charles C. Griffin, Herbert L. Shepherd, E. Frank Knowlton, John G. Crowley, William E. Schwartz, Lucius C. Morse and Robert L. Bean, their associates, successors and assigns, are hereby constituted a corporation by the name of the Camden and Liberty Railway, with authority to construct, maintain and operate by electricity or other motive power, a street railway with all necessary and convenient power stations, car houses and lines of poles, wires, appliances, appurtenances and conduits, with convenient single *Corporators.*

—corporate name.

CAMDEN AND LIBERTY RAILWAY.

CHAP. 75
—location.

—proviso.

—alteration, location of poles, etc., may be directed by municipal officers.

—may purchase or take land.

—land taken shall not exceed four rods in width.

—may fix rates for transportation of persons and property.

or double tracks, side tracks, switches or turnouts, to connect with the Rockland, Thomaston and Camden Street Railway, from such points in the town of Camden, and thence through said Camden and the towns of Lincolnville, Hope, Searsmont, Appleton, Montville, and Liberty, or any of said towns, to any points in said Liberty, upon and over such public highways, and upon and over such other streets and ways in said towns, or any of them, as shall, from time to time, be fixed and determined by the municipal officers of said towns, and assented to in writing by said corporation; provided, however, that all tracks of said railway shall be laid at such distances from the sidewalks in any of said towns as the municipal officers thereof shall, in their order fixing the routes and locations of said railway, determine to be for public safety and convenience. The written assent of said corporation to any vote of the municipal officers of either of said towns, prescribing from time to time, the routes of said railway therein, shall be filed with the clerk of said town, and shall be taken and deemed the location thereof, and such location prescribed by said municipal officers shall include the location of all tracks, side tracks, switches or turnouts and conduits of said railway, together with the location and kind of poles and the height at which and the places where the wires may run, for operating said railway or for other purposes. After the erection of the lines, having first given said corporation or its agents opportunity to be heard, the said municipal officers of either of said towns may direct any alteration in the location or erection of such poles and in the height of the wires, the same to be filed with the clerk of said town as aforesaid, and said corporation shall not be required to have any other license or permit for the location or maintenance of said poles or wires. Outside of the limits of highways, roads, streets or ways, for the location, construction or convenient use of its road, said corporation may purchase or take and hold by its location as for public uses, land and all materials in and upon it, whenever for any reason it appears to be impracticable to locate such railway within the limits of said highways, roads, streets or ways, and it shall be so found by the board of railroad commissioners, but the land so taken shall not exceed four rods in width unless necessary for excavation, embankments or materials; and the location of said railway upon land taken by virtue of this section shall be filed and the estimation and payment of damages for land so taken shall be made in accordance with the provisions of chapter fifty-one of the revised statutes. Said corporation shall have power from time to time, to fix such rates of compensation for transporting persons and property as it may think expedient, and shall have all the powers and be subject to all the liabilities of corporations as set forth in the forty-sixth chapter of the revised statutes and acts amendatory thereof and additional thereto. Said corporation is also authorized to carry on the business of an express company.

Section 2. Said corporation may operate electric generators by steam or water power or both, and for that reason may purchase, lease, hold and operate such water powers and privileges in the counties of Knox and Waldo as it may deem necessary or convenient. It may purchase, lease, erect, or otherwise acquire, and maintain hotels, casinoes, cottages and pleasure grounds on the line of its road. Said corporation is also authorized and empowered to carry on the business of lighting by electricity such public streets in the towns of Lincolnville, Hope, Searsmont, Appleton, Montville, and Liberty, or any of said towns, and such buildings and places therein, public and private, as may be agreed upon by said corporation and the owners having control of such buildings or places to be lighted, and may contract with any of said towns for the lighting of said public streets, buildings and places, and may furnish motive power by electricity within any of said towns, and may build and operate manufactories and works for providing and supplying electricity, light and power, and may purchase, lease and hold real and personal property, and do all other acts and things necessary and convenient for carrying on said business. It may construct, lay, maintain and operate lines of poles, wires, appliances and conduits for the transmission of electricity for light or power, upon, under, along and over any and all streets and ways in said towns with the consent and under the direction of the municipal officers thereof. It may take and hold as for public uses, land necessary for the construction and operation of its lines, and land so taken and damages therefor may be estimated, secured and determined and paid as in case of railroads; provided, however, that the right of taking lands or other property as for public uses shall not extend to property to be used for any of the other purposes enumerated in this section.

Section 3. The municipal officers of said town through or into which the road of said corporation may run, shall have power, at all times, to make all regulations as to the rate of speed, the removal of snow and ice from the streets, roads and ways by said corporation at its expense, and the manner of use of tracks of said railway within each of said towns as public convenience and safety may require.

Section 4. Said corporation shall keep and maintain in repair such portions of the streets and ways as shall be occupied by the

CHAP. 75

streets in repair.

—liable for damages.

tracks of said railway, and shall make all other repairs of said streets, roads and ways within either of said towns which may be rendered necessary by the occupation of the same by said railway, and if not repaired upon reasonable notice, such repairs may be made by said towns at the expense of said corporation. Said corporation shall repay to any town, any sum of money which such town may have been compelled to pay on any judgment, for damages caused by a defect or want of repair in the streets thereof, due to the negligence of said corporation, or any judgment for damages caused by the neglect of said corporation in the erection or maintenance of poles, wires or appurtenances connected with its business; provided, said corporation may have notice in writing of any suit wherein such damages are claimed, within seven days after process is served upon the town, and shall be allowed to defend the same at its own expense. Said corporation shall not be allowed to obstruct or impair the use of any public or private drain or sewer, telegraph or telephone wire, but may cross, or when necessary, change the direction of any private wire or pipe, drain or sewer, in such manner as not to obstruct or impair the use thereof, being responsible to the owner or other person for any injury occasioned thereby, in an action on the case.

Penalty for obstructing tracks.

Section 5. If any person shall wilfully or maliciously obstruct said corporation in the use of its roads or tracks or the passing of cars, carriages or other vehicles of said corporation thereon, such person and all who shall aid or abet therein, shall be punished by a fine not exceeding two hundred dollars or with imprisonment in the county jail for a period not exceeding sixty days.

Capital stock.

Section 6. The capital stock of said corporation shall not exceed five hundred thousand dollars, to be divided into shares of one hundred dollars each.

May acquire necessary real and personal property.

Section 7. Said corporation shall have the power to lease, purchase or hold such real estate or personal property as may be necessary and convenient for the accomplishment of its purposes.

Manner of construction shall be under direction of municipal officers.

Section 8. Said railway shall be constructed and maintained, in the streets and ways in each of said towns wherein it may be located, in such form and manner and upon such grades and with such rails as the municipal officers of said town shall direct, and whenever in the judgment of said corporation it shall be necessary to alter the grade of any street or way, said alteration may be made at the sole expense of said corporation, provided the same shall be assented to by the municipal officers of the town wherein said grade so sought to be changed is located. If the tracks of said corporation's railway cross any other railroad and a dispute arises in any way in regard to the manner of crossing, the board of railroad commissioners of this state shall, upon hearing, decide and determine in writing in what manner the crossing shall be made, and it shall be constructed accordingly. *—railroad commissioners shall determine the manner of crossing other railroads.*

Section 9. Said corporation may change the location of said railway in any of said streets and ways at any time by first obtaining the written consent of the municipal officers of the town in which the change is so sought to be made, and to make additional locations subject to the foregoing provisions and conditions. *Location of, how changed.*

Section 10. Nothing in this act shall be construed to prevent the proper authorities of either of said towns from entering upon and taking up any of the streets or ways in either of said towns, occupied by said railway, for any purpose for which they may lawfully take up the same. *Proper town authorities may enter upon or take up streets or ways.*

Section 11. No other person or corporation shall be permitted to construct or maintain any railroad for similar purposes over the same streets or ways, or between the same points, that may be lawfully occupied or connected by the railway of this corporation, but any person or corporation lawfully operating any street railroad to any point which this corporation's tracks extend, may enter upon, connect with and use the same on such terms and in such manner as may be agreed upon between the parties, or if they shall not agree, to be determined by the railroad commissioners for the state of Maine; and this corporation may enter upon, connect with and use the street railroad of any other corporation or person, under the same conditions and provisions. *Exclusive franchise given.*

Section 12. Said corporation is hereby authorized to issue bonds in such amount and on such time as may from time to time be determined, in aid of the purposes specified in this act, and to secure the same by a mortgage of its franchises and property. It is also hereby authorized to lease or sell all of its property and franchises upon such terms as it may determine. *May issue bonds. —may mortgage its property.*

Section 13. The first meeting of said corporation may be called by any two of said corporators giving actual notice in writing to their several associates, and said corporation may make such by-laws as are proper and not contrary to the laws of the state. *First meeting, how called.*

Section 14. This charter shall be null and void unless operations for building said railway shall have been actually commenced within two years from the time when this act shall take effect.

Approved February 25, 1903.

Chapter 76.

An Act to incorporate the Forest Telegraph and Telephone Company.

Be it enacted by the Senate and House of Representatives in Legislature assembled, as follows:

Corporators. Section 1. Lemuel Brehaut, M. J. Brehaut, Wilfred L. Eaton, Frederick W. Hinckley, Albert A. Williams, Charles A. Rolfe, their associates, successors and assigns, are hereby created a body politic by the name of the Forest Telegraph and Telephone Company, with all the rights, privileges and powers, and subject to all the duties and obligations granted and prescribed by the general laws of this state relating to corporations.

—corporate name.

May operate telegraph and telephone lines in Washington, Hancock, Penobscot and Aroostook counties. Section 2. Said corporation is hereby authorized to construct, own, maintain and operate lines of telegraph and telephone throughout the counties of Washington, Hancock, Penobscot and Aroostook, and within and between any or all of the cities, towns and islands of said counties, and in any part or parts of said counties, commencing and terminating at such points as they may determine, and to do all things that may be necessary or convenient therefor; to erect poles and lay pipes, or other conduits for the supporting and containing such wires and cables as it may determine upon, along, across, within or under any street, highway, public way, bridge, line of railroad or private land; to stretch wires and cables over or lay them under tide water all in such manner as not to unnecessarily incommode or endanger the customary public use thereof; first having obtained therefor, the consent required by law of the municipal officers in case of streets, highways, or public ways, and the consent of the directors of any railroad along the right of way of which the same shall pass; and to collect tolls and rentals for the use thereof and the right to cut down trees, except ornamental trees and shade trees and to remove obstructions when necessary.

—powers.

Damage for land taken, how estimated. Section 3. If the land of any individual or corporation is taken under this act and the parties cannot agree on the damage occasioned thereby, it shall be taken and damages estimated, secured and paid in the manner provided in the case of land taken for railroads.

May connect with other lines. Section 4. Said corporation is hereby authorized and empowered to connect its line or lines with those of any other telegraph or telephone company, corporation or individual, or to sell or lease its line or lines of telegraph, or telephone together with property rights and franchises, either before or after completion, to any other telegraph or telephone company, corporation or individual, upon such terms as may be mutually agreed upon, which sale or lease shall be binding upon the parties; or may purchase or lease any other lines or line of telegraph or telephone upon such terms and conditions as may be mutually agreed upon.

Section 5. The capital stock of the company shall be fifty thousand dollars but the corporation may hereafter from time to time increase or decrease the same by a majority vote of the stockholders whenever it shall be deemed necessary or for the best interests of the company. The maximum amount of capital stock shall not exceed five hundred thousand dollars. The said corporation may purchase, hold, sell, lease and convey all real and personal property necessary for the purposes contemplated in this act.

Section 6. Said corporation is hereby authorized and empowered to issue its bonds in such amounts at such times and on such rates as it may from time to time determine, and secure the same by a mortgage of its property and franchises.

Section 7. Any two of the corporators named in this act may call a first meeting of the corporation at any time within one year from the date of the approval of this act, by mailing a written notice signed by both, postage paid, to each of the other corporators, seven days at least before the day of the meeting, naming the time, place and purposes of such meeting and at such meeting a president, clerk, treasurer and directors may be chosen, by-laws adopted and any corporate business transacted.

Section 8. This act is not to interfere with or infringe upon the rights in Penobscot county of the Chamberlain Lake Telephone and Telegraph Company organized under the general law prior to this act.

Section 9. This act shall take effect when approved.

Approved February 25, 1903.

Chapter 77.

An Act authorizing and empowering Samuel W. Hanscom of Reed Plantation, County of Aroostook, to erect and maintain piers and booms in the Mattawamkeag river.

Be it enacted by the Senate and House of Representatives in Legislature assembled, as follows:

Section 1. Samuel W. Hanscom, his heirs and assigns, are hereby authorized and empowered to locate, erect and maintain, piers and booms in the Mattawamkeag river, commencing at a point on the westerly side of said river six hundred yards above the bridge across said river connecting Drew plantation, county of Penobscot and Reed plantation, county of Aroostook, and extending up westerly side of said river to Prouty rips, so called.

Logs and other lumber shall not be impeded by said piers and booms.

Section 2. Said piers and booms shall be so constructed that logs, pulp wood, and other lumber shall not be impeded or delayed in its passage down said river, and expense of such delay, if any, shall be paid by said Hanscom.

How piers and booms shall be constructed.

Section 3. Said booms and piers shall also be so constructed that logs or other lumber belonging to other parties shall not run under and be retained in the booms of said Hanscom; and if any logs, lumber, or other floatable material not owned by said Hanscom be found within said booms, they shall upon notice in writing be turned out of said booms at said Hanscom's expense.

—lumber detained in said booms shall be turned out.

Agent may be appointed.

Section 4. The Mattawamkeag Log Driving Company, or any individual log owners, driving logs by the boom down said river, shall have the right to appoint an agent who is hereby authorized and empowered to see that none of the logs are held and retained in said booms, and the said Hanscom shall pay the said agent the sum of two dollars and fifty cents per day.

—compensation, how paid.

Section 5. This act shall take effect when approved.

Approved February 25, 1903.

Chapter 78.

An Act to incorporate the town of Castle Hill, in the county of Aroostook.

Be it enacted by the Senate and House of Representatives in Legislature assembled, as follows:

Town of Castle Hill, incorporated.

Section 1. Township number twelve, range four, west from the east line of the state, in the county of Aroostook, and known as Castle Hill plantation, is hereby incorporated into a town by the name of Castle Hill, and the inhabitants of said town are hereby vested with all the powers, privileges, immunities and liabilities of other towns.

First town meeting, how called.

Section 2. The present board of assessors of Castle Hill plantation are hereby authorized and required to call the first meeting of the town under this act, for the choice of town officers, by issuing their warrant for the same seven days prior to the time of said meeting, which shall be holden in the month of March of the present year.

Shall own property and assume liabilities of Castle Hill plantation.

Section 3. The town hereby created shall be possessed of all the property and effects belonging to said plantation, and shall assume all the liabilities thereof.

Section 4. This act shall take effect when approved.

Approved February 25, 1903.

Chapter 79.

An Act to authorize the county of Piscataquis to negotiate a loan for temporary purposes.

Be it enacted by the Senate and House of Representatives in Legislature assembled, as follows:

Section 1. The county commissioners of Piscataquis county may raise by temporary loan a sum not exceeding twenty-five thousand dollars, and cause notes or obligations of said county with coupons for lawful interest to be issued for payment thereof. <small>Piscataquis county authorized to make temporary loan.</small>

Section 2. All notes and obligations of the county of Piscataquis issued for the purpose of securing temporary loans, amounting January first, nineteen hundred three, to nineteen thousand dollars, are hereby ratified, confirmed and made valid. <small>Validity of notes and obligations made valid.</small>

Section 3. This act shall take effect when approved.

Approved February 25, 1903.

Chapter 80.

An Act to extend the charter of the South Portland Trust and Banking Company.

Be it enacted by the Senate and House of Representatives in Legislature assembled, as follows:

Section 1. The rights, powers and privileges of the South Portland Trust and Banking Company, which were granted by chapter four hundred and eighty-seven of the private and special laws of nineteen hundred and one, are hereby extended for two years from the approval of this act; and the persons named in said act, their associates and successors, shall have all the rights, powers and privileges that were granted them by said act, to be exercised in the same manner and for the same purposes as specified in said act. <small>Charter extended for two years.</small>

Section 2. This act shall take effect when approved.

Approved February 25, 1903.

Chapter 81.

An Act to authorize the Bodwell Water Power Company to generate, use, transmit and sell electricity.

Be it enacted by the Senate and House of Representatives in Legislature assembled, as follows:

May make and generate electricity at certain points on Penobscot river.

Section 1. The Bodwell Water Power Company is hereby specially authorized and empowered to make and generate electricity upon its property situated on the Penobscot river between the towns of Old Town and Milford, and also on the dam or dams which it proposes to erect on the Stillwater branch of the Penobscot river at Gilman falls, so called, in connection with its dams erected and to be erected on the Penobscot river, and to use said electricity as a motive power in the use and development of its property, and also to sell the same for manufacturing and heating purposes, and also to carry and conduct electricity made and generated upon its property between the towns of Old Town and Milford to and into any towns or cities in the county of Penobscot, state of Maine, and to use the same in all ways for its own purposes, and to sell the same for manufacturing purposes in units of not less than twenty-five horse power and also for heating purposes, but not for electric lighting or street railway purposes.

—may use electricity as a motive power.

Authorized to operate lines, etc.

Section 2. Said company is hereby authorized and empowered to construct, lay, maintain and operate lines of wire or other material for the transmission of such electricity under and across any stream or river, and under, along, upon and over streets, ways and bridges in said cities and towns.

Restrictions and rights.

Section 3. In erecting poles and laying said lines of wire, upon, along and over streets, ways and bridges, and under any stream or river, said corporation shall be subject to the laws of the state applicable to corporations which are authorized to make, generate, sell, distribute and supply electricity for manufacturing purposes, and shall have all the rights and powers of such corporations in the erection of poles and conduits and the constructions, laying and maintaining lines of wire.

Section 4. This act shall take effect when approved.

Approved February 25, 1902.

Chapter 82.

An Act to incorporate the Gardiner Water District.

Be it enacted by the Senate and House of Representatives in Legislature assembled, as follows:

Section 1. The following territory and the people within the same, namely: Wards one, two, three, four and five in the city of Gardiner and that part of ward six in said city, which is bounded on the north by ward three, on the east by Kennebec river, on the south by Richmond and on the west by the Marston road, so called, in said Gardiner, shall constitute a body politic and corporate under the name of the Gardiner Water District, for the purpose of supplying the inhabitants of said district and of the towns of Randolph, Pittston and Farmingdale, and such municipalities, together with the city of Gardiner, with pure water for domestic and municipal purposes. *Limits of district defined. —corporate name. —purpose.*

Section 2. Said district is hereby authorized for the purposes aforesaid to take and hold sufficient water of the Cobbosseecontee river, and may take and hold by purchase or otherwise any land or real estate necessary for erecting dams, power, reservoirs, or for preserving the purity of the water and water shed, and for laying and maintaining aqueducts for taking, discharging and disposing of water. *May take and hold water of Cobbosseecontee river. —may take land, etc.*

Section 3. Said district shall be liable for all damages that shall be sustained by any person or corporation in their property by the taking of any land whatsoever, or water, or by flowage, or by excavating through any land for the purpose of laying pipes, building dams or constructing reservoirs. If any person sustaining damage as aforesaid and said corporation shall not mutually agree upon the sum to be paid therefor, such person may cause his damages to be ascertained in the same manner and under the same conditions, restrictions and limitations as are or may be prescribed in the case of damages by the laying out of highways. *Damages, how estimated.*

Section 4. Said district is hereby authorized to lay in and through the streets and highways thereof and of said towns of Pittston, Randolph and Farmingdale, and to take up, repair and replace all such pipes, aqueducts and fixtures as may be necessary for the objects above set forth, and whenever said district shall lay any pipes or aqueducts in any street or highway it shall cause the same to be done with as little obstruction as possible to the public travel, and shall at its own expense without unnecessary delay cause the earth and pavement removed by it to be replaced in proper condition. *May lay pipes, etc.*

CHAP. 82

Board of trustees.

—president and clerk shall be elected by trustees.

—tenure.

—may establish by-laws.

—compensation.

May purchase property of Maine Water Company in certain towns, etc.

May take plant and property after May 1, 1903.

—may file petition addressed to any justice of supreme judicial court.

Section 5. All the affairs of said water district shall be managed by a board of trustees composed of three members to be chosen by the municipal officers of the city of Gardiner, but no member of the city council shall during the term for which he is elected be chosen one of said board of trustees. As soon as convenient after the members of said board have been chosen, said trustees shall hold a meeting at the city rooms in the city of Gardiner, and organize by the election of a president and clerk, adopt a corporate seal and when necessary may choose a treasurer and all other needful officers and agents for the proper conduct and management of the affairs of said district. At said first meeting they shall determine by lot the term of office of each trustee so that one shall serve for one year, one for two years and one for three years; and whenever the term of office of a trustee expires the said municipal officers of the city of Gardiner shall appoint a successor to serve the full term of three years; and in case any other vacancy arises it shall be filled in like manner for the unexpired term. They may also ordain and establish such by-laws as are necessary for their own convenience and the proper management of the affairs of the district. The term of office of trustees shall begin on the first Monday of April. Said trustees may procure an office and incur such expenses as may be necessary. Each member shall receive in full compensation for his services an allowance of one hundred dollars per annum.

Section 6. Said water district is hereby authorized and empowered to acquire by purchase or by the exercise of the right of eminent domain, which right is hereby expressly delegated to said district for said purpose, the entire plant, property and franchises, rights and privileges now held by the Maine Water Company within said district and said towns of Pittston, Randolph and Farmingdale, including all lands, waters, water rights, dams, reservoirs, pipes, machinery, fixtures, hydrants, tools and all apparatus and appliances owned by said company and used or useable in supplying water in said district and towns and any other real estate in said district.

Section 7. In case said trustees fail to agree with said Maine Water Company upon the terms of purchase of the above mentioned property on or before May first, nineteen hundred and three, said water district through its trustees is hereby authorized to take said plant, property and franchises as for public uses by petition therefor in the manner hereinafter provided. And said water district through its trustees is hereby authorized on or before May fifth, nineteen hundred and three, to file a petition in the clerk's office of the supreme judicial court for the county of Kennebec in term time or in vacation, addressed to any justice of said court, who after notice to said Maine Water Company and its mortgagees, shall after hearing and within thirty days after the filing of said petition appoint three disinterested appraisers none of whom shall be residents of the county of Kennebec, one of whom shall be learned in the law, for the purpose of fixing the valuation of said plant, property and franchises. The said appraisers shall have the power of compelling attendance of witnesses and the production of books and papers pertinent to the issue, and may administer oaths; and any witness, or person in charge of such books or papers, refusing to attend, or to produce the same, shall be subject to the same penalties and proceedings, so far as applicable as witnesses summoned to attend the supreme judicial court. The appraisers so appointed shall after due notice and hearing fix the valuation of said plant, property and franchises at what they are fairly and equitably worth, so that the said Maine Water Company shall receive just compensation for all the same. The first day of July, nineteen hundred and three, shall be the date as of which the valuation aforesaid shall be fixed, from which day interest on said award shall run and all net rents and profits accruing thereafter shall belong to said water district. The report of said appraisers, or of a majority of them, shall be filed in said clerk's office in term time or vacation within five months after their appointment, and such single justice, or in case of his inability to act then any justice designated for the purpose by the chief justice, may, after notice and hearing, confirm or reject the same, or recommit it if justice so requires. The award of the appraisers shall be conclusive as to valuations. Upon the confirmation of said report the court so sitting shall thereupon, after hearing, make final decree upon the entire matter, including the application of the purchase money, discharge of incumbrances and transfer of the property, jurisdiction over which is hereby conferred, with the same power to enforce said decree as in equity cases. Upon request of either party the justice so making such final decree shall make separate findings of law and fact. All such findings of fact shall be final, but either party aggrieved may take exceptions to any rulings of law so made, the same to be accompanied only by such parts of the case as are necessary to a clear understanding of the questions raised thereby. Such exceptions shall be claimed on the docket within ten days after such final decree is signed, entered and filed, and notice thereof has been given by the clerk to the parties or their counsel, and said exceptions so claimed shall be made up, allowed and filed within said time unless further time is granted by the court or by agreement of parties. They shall be entered at the next term

CHAP. 82
—when exceptions shall be entered.

of the law court to be held after the filing of said decree and there heard, unless otherwise agreed, or the law court shall for good cause order a further time for hearing thereon. Upon such hearing the law court may confirm, reverse or modify the decree of the court below, or remand the cause for further proceedings as it deems proper. During the pendency of such exceptions the cause shall remain on the docket of the court below marked "law" and decree shall be entered thereon by a single justice in term time or in vacation, in accordance with the certificate and opinion of the law court. Before said plant, property and franchises are transferred in accordance with such final decree, and before payment therefor, the court sitting in said county of Kennebec, by a single justice thereof as hereinbefore provided, shall, upon motion of either party, after notice and hearing, take account of all receipts and expenditures properly had or incurred by the Maine Water Company belonging to the period from and after July first, nineteen hundred and three, and all the net rents and profits accruing thereafter, and shall order the net balance due to either party to be added to or deducted from the amount to be paid under said final decree, as the case may be. All findings of law or fact by such single justice at such hearing shall be final. On payment or tender by said district of the amount so fixed and the performance of all other terms and conditions so imposed by the court, said entire plant, property and franchises shall become vested in said water district and be free from all liens, mortgages and incumbrances theretofore created by the Gardiner Water Company or the Maine Water Company. After the filing of said petition it shall not be discontinued or withdrawn by said water district, and the said Maine Water Company may thereafterwards on its part cause said valuation to be made as herein provided, and shall be entitled to appropriate process to compel said water district to perform the terms of the final decree, and to pay for said plant, property and franchises in accordance therewith.

Contracts now existing shall be assumed.

Section 8. All valid contracts now existing between the Gardiner Water Company or the Maine Water Company and any persons or corporations for supplying water within said district and in the said towns of Pittston, Randolph and Farmingdale, shall be assumed and carried out by said Gardiner Water District.

May issue bonds.

Section 9. For accomplishing the purposes of this act said water district, through its trustees, is authorized to issue its bonds to an amount sufficient to procure funds to pay the expenses incurred in the acquisition of the property of said Maine Water Company, and the purchase thereof, and for further extensions, additions and improvements of said plant. Said bonds shall be a legal obligation of said water district which is hereby declared to be a quasi municipal corporation within the meaning of section fifty-five, chapter forty-six of the revised statutes, and all the provisions of said section shall be applicable thereto. The said bonds shall be a legal investment for savings banks.

Section 10. All individuals, firms and corporations, whether private, public or municipal, shall pay to the treasurer of said district the rates established by said board of trustees for the water used by them, and said rates shall be uniform within the territory supplied by the district. Said rates shall be so established as to provide revenue for the following purposes:

I. To pay the current running expenses for maintaining the water system and provide for such extensions and renewals as may become necessary.

II. To provide for payment of the interest on the indebtedness of the district.

III. To provide each year a sum equal to not less than one nor more than four per cent of the entire indebtedness of the district, which sum shall be turned into a sinking fund to provide for the final extinguishment of the funded debt. The money set aside for the sinking fund shall be devoted to the retirement of the obligations of the district or invested in such securities as savings banks are allowed to hold.

IV. If any surplus remains at the end of the year it may be paid to the city of Gardiner and the towns of Farmingdale and Randolph in the same proportions as each of said municipalities and its inhabitants contribute to the gross earnings of said water system.

Section 11. All incidental powers, rights and privileges necessary to the accomplishment of the main object herein set forth are granted to the corporation hereby created.

Section 12. This act shall take effect when approved by a majority vote of the legal voters within said district at the annual municipal election in March in the year one thousand nine hundred and three, or at an election to be specially called and held for the purpose within thirty days after the approval of this act as the municipal officers of the city of Gardiner may determine. The board of registration shall make and provide a separate check list for such of the voters within said district as are then legal voters within ward six of said city and all warrants issued to said ward shall be varied accordingly to show that only such voters therein are entitled to vote hereon. Such election, if a special one, shall be called, advertised and conducted accord-

138 UNION TRUST COMPANY.

CHAP. 83

ing to the law relating to municipal elections, provided, however, that the board of registration shall not be required to prepare or the city clerk to post a new list of voters and for this purpose said board shall be in session the two secular days next preceding such election, the first day thereof to be devoted to regulation of voters and the last day to enable the board to verify the corrections of said lists and to complete and close up its records of said sessions. The city clerk shall reduce the subject matter of this act to the following question: "Shall the act to incorporate the Gardiner Water District be accepted?" and the voters shall indicate by a cross placed against the words "yes" or "no" their opinion of the same. The result shall be declared by the mayor and aldermen and due certificate thereof filed by the city clerk with the secretary of state. This act shall take effect when approved by the governor so as necessary to empower the calling and holding of such election.

—tenor of vote.

Sections 2, 3 and 4 of this act void unless under certain conditions.

Section 13. Sections two, three and four of this act shall be inoperative, null and void, unless the said water district shall first acquire by purchase, or by the exercise of the right of eminent domain as in this act provided, the plant, property and franchises, rights and privileges now held by the Maine Water Company within said district and said towns of Pittston, Randolph and Farmingdale.

Costs and expenses, how paid.

Section 14. All costs and expenses arising under the provisions of this act shall be paid and borne as directed by the court in the final decree provided by section seven.

Section 15. This act shall take effect when approved.

Approved February 26, 1903.

Chapter 83.

An Act to incorporate the Union Trust Company of Saco, Maine.

Be it enacted by the Senate and House of Representatives in Legislature assembled, as follows:

Corporators.

Section 1. James O. Bradbury, William J. Maybury, Fred C. Bradbury of Saco, Frank H. Libby, William J. Mewer of Old Orchard, James W. Meserve of Buxton, J. F. Googins, C. E. Atwood of Biddeford, Lendall W. Nash of Kennebunk, or such of them as may by vote accept this charter, with their associates, successors and assigns, are hereby made a body corporate and politic to be known as the Union Trust Company, and as such shall be possessed of all the powers, privileges and immunities and subject to all the duties and obligations conferred on corporations by law.

—corporate name.

—powers, etc.

Section 2. The corporation hereby created shall be located at Saco, in the county of York and state of Maine.

Section 3. The purposes of said corporation and the business which it may perform, are; first, to receive on deposit, money, coin, bank notes, evidences of debt, accounts of individuals, companies, corporations, municipalities and states, allowing interest thereon, if agreed, or as the by-laws of said corporation may provide; second, to borrow money, to loan money on credits, or real estate, or personal security, and to negotiate loans and sales for others; third, to own and maintain safe deposit vaults, with boxes, safes and other facilities therein, to be rented to other parties for the safe keeping of moneys, securities, stocks, jewelry, plate, valuable papers and documents, and other property susceptible of being deposited therein, and may receive on deposit for safe keeping, property of any kind entrusted to it for that purpose; fourth, to act as agent for issuing, registering and countersigning certificates, bonds, stocks, and all evidences of debt or ownership in property; fifth, to hold by grant, assignment, transfer, devise or bequest, any real or personal property or trusts duly created and to execute trusts of every description; sixth, to act as assignee, receiver or executor, and no surety shall be necessary upon the bond of the corporation, unless the court or officer approving such bond shall require it; seventh, to do in general all the business that may be lawfully done by trust and banking companies, but said corporation shall not have the power or authority to establish branches.

Section 4. The capital stock of said corporation shall not be less than fifty thousand dollars, divided into shares of one hundred dollars each, with the right to increase the said capital stock at any time, by vote of the shareholders, to any amount not exceeding five hundred thousand dollars. Said corporation shall not commence business as a trust or banking company, until stock to the amount of at least fifty thousand dollars shall have been subscribed and paid in, in cash.

Section 5. Said corporation shall not make any loan or discount on the security of the shares of its own capital stock, nor be the purchaser or holder of any such shares unless necessary to prevent loss upon a debt previously contracted in good faith; and all stock so acquired shall, within six months from the time of its acquisition, be disposed of at public or private sale.

Section 6. All the corporate powers of this corporation shall be exercised by a board of trustees, who shall be residents of this state, whose number and term of office shall be determined by a vote of the shareholders at the first meeting held by the incorporators and at each annual meeting thereafter. The affairs and powers of the corporation may, at the option of the shareholders, be entrusted to an executive board of five members to be, by vote of the shareholders, elected from the full board of trustees. The trustees of said corporation shall be sworn to the proper discharge of their duties, and they shall hold office until others are elected and qualified in their stead. If a trustee or director dies, resigns, or becomes disqualified for any cause, the remaining trustees or directors may appoint a person to fill the vacancy until the next annual meeting of the corporation. The oath of office of such trustee or director shall be taken within thirty days of his election, or his office shall become vacant. The clerk of such corporation shall, within ten days, notify such trustees or directors of their election, and within thirty days shall publish the list of all persons who have taken the oath of office as trustees or directors.

Section 7. The board of trustees or directors of said corporation shall constitute the board of investment of said corporation. Said trustees or directors shall keep in a separate book, specially provided for the purpose, a record of all loans, and investments of every description, made by said institution substantially in the order of time when such loans or investments are made, which shall show that such loans or investments have been made with the approval of the investment committee of said corporation, which shall indicate such particulars respecting such loans or investments as the bank examiner shall direct. This book shall be submitted to the trustees or directors and to the bank examiner whenever requested. Such loans or investments shall be classified in the book as the bank examiner shall direct. No loan shall be made to any officer or director of said banking or trust company except by the unanimous approval of the executive board in writing, and said corporation shall have no authority to hire money or to give notes unless by vote of the said board duly recorded.

Section 8. No person shall be eligible to the position of a director or a trustee of said corporation who is not the actual owner of ten shares of the stock.

Section 9. Said corporation, after beginning to receive deposits, shall, at all times, have on hand in lawful money, as a reserve, not less than fifteen per cent of the aggregate amount of its deposits which are subject to withdrawal on demand, provided, that in lieu of lawful money, two-thirds of said fifteen per cent may consist of balances, payable on demand, due from any national or state bank.

Section 10. All the property or money held in trust by this corporation shall constitute a special deposit and the accounts thereof and of said trust department shall be kept separate, and such funds and investments or loans of them shall be specially appropriated to the security and payment of such deposits, and not be subject to any other liabilities of the corporation; and for the purpose of securing the observance of this provision, said corporation shall have a trust department in which all business pertaining to such trust property shall be kept separate and distinct from its general business.

Special deposit.

Section 11. An administrator, executor, assignee, guardian or trustee, any court of law or equity, including courts of probate and insolvency, officers and treasurers of towns, cities, counties, and savings banks of the state of Maine may deposit any moneys, bonds, stocks, evidences of debt or of ownership in property, or any personal property, with said corporation, and any of said courts may direct any person deriving authority from them to so deposit the same.

Administrators, etc., may deposit with.

Section 12. Each shareholder of this corporation shall be individually responsible for all contracts, debts and engagements of said corporation to a sum equal to the amount of the par value of the shares owned by him, in addition to the amount invested in said shares.

Responsibility of shareholders.

Section 13. Such corporation shall set apart as a guaranty fund not less than ten per cent of its net earnings in each and every year until such fund with the accumulated interest thereon, shall amount to one-fourth of the capital stock of said corporation.

Guaranty fund.

Section 14. The shares of said corporation shall be subject to taxation in the same manner and rate as are the shares of national banks.

Taxation of shares.

Section 15. Said corporation shall be subject to examination by the bank examiner, who shall visit it at least once in every year, and as much oftener as he may deem expedient. At such visits he shall have free access to its vaults, books and papers, and shall thoroughly inspect and examine all the affairs of said corporation, and make such inquiries as may be necessary to ascertain its condition and ability to fulfill all its engagements. If upon examination of said corporation the examiner is of the opinion that its investments are not in accordance with law or said corporation is insolvent, or its condition is such as to render its further proceedings hazardous to the public or to those having funds in its custody, or is of the opinion that it has exceeded its powers or failed to comply with any of the rules or restrictions provided by law, he shall have such authority and take such action as is provided for in the case of savings banks by chapter forty-seven of the revised statutes. He shall preserve in a per-

Shall be subject to examination by bank examiner.

142 CITY OF WESTBROOK.

CHAP. 84

—statement shall be published.

manent form a full record of his proceedings, including a statement of the condition of said corporation. A copy of such statement shall be published by said corporation immediately after the annual examination of the same in some newspaper published where said corporation is established. If no paper is published in the town where said corporation is established, then it shall be published in a newspaper printed in the nearest city or town. The necessary expenses of the bank examiner while engaged in making such examination shall be paid by said corporation.

First meeting, how called.

Section 16. Any five of the corporators named in this act may call the first meeting of this corporation by mailing a written notice, signed by all, postage paid, to each of the other corporators, seven days at least before the day of the meeting, naming the time, place and purpose of such meeting, and at such meeting the necessary officers may be chosen, by-laws adopted, and any other corporate business transacted.

Section 17. This act shall take effect when approved.

Approved February 26, 1908.

Chapter 84.

An Act to amend Chapter four hundred and eighty-six of the Private and Special Laws of eighteen hundred and eighty-nine, relating to the city of Westbrook.

Be it enacted by the Senate and House of Representatives in Legislature assembled, as follows:

Section 4 of chapter 486, special laws of 1889, amended.

Section 1. Section four of said chapter four hundred eighty-six is hereby amended by striking out the words "second Monday in March" in the third sentence of said section, and inserting in place thereof the words 'first Monday in January.' Section five of said chapter is hereby amended by striking out the words "first Monday in March" in the first sentence of said section, and inserting in place thereof the words 'second Monday in December.' Section nine of said chapter is hereby amended by striking out the words "second Monday in March" in the first sentence of said section, and inserting in place thereof the words 'first Monday in January'; and by striking out the words "second Monday in March" in the fourth sentence of said section, and inserting in place thereof the words 'first Monday in January.'

Section 17 of chapter 486, amended.

Section 2. Section seventeen of said chapter is hereby amended by inserting after the fourth sentence thereof the following: 'Whenever any ordinance, order, resolution or vote of the city council involves an appropriation or expenditure of

CITY OF WESTBROOK. 143

money, the mayor may approve it as a whole or he may approve or disapprove specific items thereof, and the portions approved shall then be in force in like manner as if no part thereof had been disapproved, and the items disapproved shall thereupon take the course herein provided for orders and ordinances disapproved as a whole.'

CHAP. 84
—mayor may approve appropriations in whole or in part.

Section 3. Section twenty-three of said chapter is hereby amended by striking out the words "second Monday in March" in the third sentence of said section, and inserting in place thereof the words 'first Monday in January.' Section twenty-nine of said chapter is hereby amended by striking out the words "third Monday in March" in the first sentence of said section, and inserting in place thereof the words 'second Monday in January'; and by striking out the words "third Monday in March" in the third sentence of said section, and inserting in place thereof the words 'second Monday in January.'

Section 23, chapter 486, amended.

Section 4. Section thirty of said chapter is hereby amended by striking out the following sentence thereof: "The above named officers and boards shall be appointed on or before the third Monday in March, annually, and shall hold their respective offices for the term of one year, unless sooner removed, or, in the case of boards, until a majority of the members thereof are appointed and qualified," and inserting in place thereof the following sentences: 'The above named officers shall be appointed on the first Monday of January, or as soon thereafter as may be, and, with the exception of the overseers of the poor, shall hold their respective offices for the term of one year, unless sooner removed. The overseers of the poor shall serve three years, unless sooner removed. In January of the year of our Lord one thousand nine hundred and four, the mayor shall appoint one overseer to serve one year, one to serve two years, and one to serve three years, and thereafter one overseer shall be appointed annually to serve three years, as above.'

Section 30 of chapter 486, amended.

Overseers of poor.

Section 5. The terms of office of all city officers that would otherwise expire on the second or third Mondays of March in the year of our Lord one thousand nine hundred and four shall expire on the first and second Mondays, respectively, of January of that year, or as soon thereafter as other officers have qualified for the places.

Terms of city officers, expiration of.

Section 6. All acts and parts of acts inconsistent herewith, are hereby repealed.

Approved February 26, 1903.

Chapter 85.

An Act to incorporate the Kineo Trust Company.

Be it enacted by the Senate and House of Representatives in Legislature assembled, as follows:

Corporators.
Section 1. Elbridge A. Thompson, Henry Hudson, John F. Hughes, Crowell C. Hall, Edward J. Mayo, Liston P. Evans, John F. Arnold, Frank E. Guernsey, or such of them as may by vote accept this charter, with their associates, successors and assigns, are hereby made a body corporate and politic to be

—corporate name.
known as the Kineo Trust Company, and as such shall be possessed of all the powers, privileges and immunities and subject to all the duties and obligations conferred on corporations by law, except as otherwise provided herein.

Location.
Section 2. The corporation hereby created shall be located at Dover, Piscataquis county, state of Maine.

Purposes.
Section 3. The purposes of said corporation and the business which it may perform, are; first, to receive on deposit, money, coin, bank notes, evidences of debt, accounts of individuals, companies, corporations, municipalities and states, allowing interest thereon, if agreed, or as the by-laws of said corporation may provide; second, to borrow money, to loan money on credits,

—may maintain safe deposit vaults.
or real estate, or personal security, and to negotiate loans and sales for others; third, to own and maintain safe deposit vaults, with boxes, safes and other facilities therein, to be rented to other parties for the safe keeping of moneys, securities, stocks, jewelry, plate, valuable papers and documents, and other property susceptible of being deposited therein, and may receive on deposit for safe keeping, property of any kind entrusted to it for that

—ay act as agent.
purpose; fourth, to act as agent for issuing, registering and countersigning certificates, bonds, stocks, and all evidences of debt or ownership in property; fifth, to hold by grant, assignment, transfer, devise or bequest, any real or personal property

—may execute trusts.
or trusts duly created and to execute trusts of every description; sixth, to act as assignee, receiver, executor, and no surety shall be necessary upon the bond of the corporation, unless the court or officer approving such bond shall require it; seventh, to do in general all the business that may be lawfully done by trust and banking companies.

Capital stock.
Section 4. The capital stock of said corporation shall not be less than fifty thousand dollars, divided into shares of one hundred dollars each, with the right to increase the said capital stock

—shall not commence business until $50,000 has been paid in.
at any time, by vote of the shareholders, to any amount not exceeding one hundred thousand dollars. Said corporation shall not commence business as a trust or banking company, until stock

KINEO TRUST COMPANY. 145

CHAP. 85

to the amount of at least fifty thousand dollars shall have been subscribed and paid in, in cash.

Section 5. Said corporation shall not make any loan or discount on the security of the shares of its own capital stock, nor be the purchaser or holder of any such shares unless necessary to prevent loss upon a debt previously contracted in good faith; and all stock so acquired shall, within six months from the time of its acquisition, be disposed of at public or private sale. *Shall not make common security of shares of its own capital stock.*

Section 6. All the corporate powers of this corporation shall be exercised by a board of trustees, who shall be residents of this state, whose number and term of office shall be determined by a vote of the shareholders at the first meeting held by the incorporators and at each annual meeting thereafter. The affairs and powers of the corporation may, at the option of the shareholders, be entrusted to an executive board of five members to be, by vote of the shareholders, elected from the full board of trustees. The trustees of said corporation shall be sworn to the proper discharge of their duties, and they shall hold office until others are elected and qualified in their stead. If a trustee or director dies, resigns, or becomes disqualified for any cause, the remaining trustees or directors may appoint a person to fill the vacancy until the next annual meeting of the corporation. The oath of office of such trustee or director shall be taken within thirty days of his election, or his office shall become vacant. The clerk of such corporation shall, within ten days, notify such trustees or directors of their election, and within thirty days shall publish the list of all persons who have taken the oath of office as trustees or directors. *Board of trustees. —number and tenure, how determined. —executive board. —vacancies, how filled.*

Section 7. The board of trustees or directors of said corporation shall constitute the board of investment of said corporation. Said trustees or directors shall keep in a separate book, specially provided for the purpose, a record of all loans, and investments of every description, made by said institution substantially in the order of time when such loans or investments are made, which shall show that such loans or investments have been made with the approval of the investment committee of said corporation, which shall indicate such particulars respecting such loans or investments as the bank examiner shall direct. This book shall be submitted to the trustees or directors and to the bank examiner whenever requested. Such loans or investments shall be classified in the book as the bank examiner shall direct. No loan shall be made to any officer or director of said banking or trust company except by the unanimous approval of the executive board in writing, and said corporation shall have no authority *Board of investment. —shall keep record of loans. —loan to officer or director, how made.*

23

to hire money or to give notes unless by vote of the said board duly recorded.

Director or trustee shall own ten shares of stock.

Section 8. No person shall be eligible to the position of a director or a trustee of said corporation who is not the actual owner of ten shares of the stock.

Section 9. Said corporation, after beginning to receive deposits, shall, at all times, have on hand in lawful money, as a reserve, not less than fifteen per cent of the aggregate amount of its deposits which are subject to withdrawal on demand, provided, that in lieu of lawful money, two-thirds of said fifteen per cent may consist of balances, payable on demand, due from any national or state bank.

Trust funds shall constitute a special deposit.

Section 10. All the property or money held in trust by this corporation shall constitute a special deposit and the accounts thereof and of said trust department shall be kept separate, and such funds and investments or loans of them shall be specially appropriated to the security and payment of such deposits, and not be subject to any other liabilities of the corporation; and for the purpose of securing the observance of this provision, said corporation shall have a trust department in which all business pertaining to such trust property shall be kept separate and distinct from its general business.

Administrators, etc., may deposit funds in.

Section 11. An administrator, executor, assignee, guardian or trustee, any court of law or equity, including courts of probate and insolvency, officers and treasurers of towns, cities, counties, and savings banks of the state of Maine may deposit any moneys, bonds, stocks, evidences of debt or of ownership in property, or any personal property, with said corporation, and any of said courts may direct any person deriving authority from them to so deposit the same.

Responsibility of shareholders.

Section 12. Each shareholder of this corporation shall be individually responsible, equally and ratably, and not one for the other, for all contracts, debts and engagements of such corporation to a sum equal to the amount of the par value of the shares owned by each, in addition to the amount invested in said shares.

Guaranty fund.

Section 13. Such corporation shall set apart as a guaranty fund not less than ten per cent of its net earnings in each and every year until such fund with the accumulated interest thereon, shall amount to one-fourth of the capital stock of said corporation.

Taxation of shares.

Section 14. The shares of said corporation shall be subject to taxation in the same manner and rate as are the shares of national banks.

Shall be subject to examination

Section 15. Said corporation shall be subject to examination by the bank examiner, who shall visit it at least once in every year, and as much oftener as he may deem expedient. At such visits he shall have free access to its vaults, books and papers, and shall thoroughly inspect and examine all the affairs of said corporation, and make such inquiries as may be necessary to ascertain its condition and ability to fulfill all its engagements. If upon examination of said corporation the examiner is of the opinion that its investments are not in accordance with law or said corporation is insolvent, or its condition is such as to render its further proceedings hazardous to the public or to those having funds in its custody, or is of the opinion that it has exceeded its powers or failed to comply with any of the rules or restrictions provided by law, he shall have such authority and take such action as is provided for in the case of savings banks by chapter forty-seven of the revised statutes. He shall preserve in a permanent form a full record of his proceedings, including a statement of the condition of said corporation. A copy of such statement shall be published by said corporation immediately after the annual examination of the same in some newspaper published where said corporation is established. If no paper is published in the town where said corporation is established, then it shall be published in a newspaper printed in the nearest city or town. The necessary expenses of the bank examiner while engaged in making such examination shall be paid by the corporation.

Section 16. Any five of the corporators named in this act may call the first meeting of this corporation by mailing a written notice, signed by all, postage paid, to each of the other corporators, seven days at least before the day of the meeting, naming the time, place and purpose of such meeting, and at such meeting the necessary officers may be chosen, by-laws adopted, and any other corporate business transacted.

Section 17. This act shall take effect when approved.

Approved February 26, 1903.

Chapter 86.

An Act to authorise the Orono Pulp and Paper Company to generate, use and sell electricity.

Be it enacted by the Senate and House of Representatives in Legislature assembled, as follows:

May make and generate electricity upon Stillwater branch of Penobscot river in Old Town.

—may conduct electricity into Old Town.

—shall not sell power outside of Old Town.

Section 1. The Orono Pulp and Paper Company is hereby specially authorized and empowered to make and generate electricity upon its property situated upon the Stillwater branch of the Penobscot river in Old Town, in Penobscot county, and to transmit and conduct such electricity to and into the cities of Old Town, Bangor, Brewer, and the towns of Orono and Veazie, and to use the same in all ways for its own purposes, and to sell the same for power and manufacturing purposes in units of not less than twenty-five horse power, and also for heating purposes, but not for electric lighting or street railway purposes; provided, however, that prior to March one, nineteen hundred and five, said company shall not sell or otherwise dispose of power to any other person or corporation to be used outside of said Old Town.

May build works, etc.

Section 2. Said company is hereby authorized and empowered to build and operate manufactories and works for generating and making electricity upon its said property, and to erect, lay, construct, maintain and operate lines of wire or other material for the transmission of such electricity under and across any stream or river, and under, along, upon and over streets, ways and bridges in said cities and towns.

Shall be subject to general laws in erecting poles, etc.

Section 3. In erecting poles and lines of wire along, upon and over streets, ways and bridges, and in constructing and laying lines of wire under any stream, river, street or highway, said corporation shall be subject to the general laws of the state applicable to corporations which are authorized to make, generate, sell, distribute and supply electricity for power and manufacturing purposes, and shall have all the rights and powers of such corporations in the erection and construction of poles and conduits, and the construction, laying and maintaining cables and lines of wire.

Section 4. This act shall take effect when approved.

Approved February 26, 1903.

Chapter 87.

An Act relating to the taking of lobsters within three miles of the islands of Matinicus and Criehaven, during the months of August and September, in each year.

Be it enacted by the Senate and House of Representatives in Legislature assembled, as follows:

Section 1. No person shall take, catch, kill or destroy any lobster or lobsters within three miles of the islands of Matinicus and Criehaven, between the first day of August and the first day of October in each and every year. <small>Close time on lobsters within three miles of Matinicus and Criehaven, from August 1 to October 1.</small>

Section 2. Any person violating the provisions of the foregoing section shall be punished by a fine of one dollar for each and every lobster taken, caught, killed or destroyed contrary to the provisions of the foregoing section. Trial justices and judges of police and municipal courts shall have jurisdiction of all offenses under this act. <small>Penalty, one dollar for each lobster.</small>

Section 3. This act shall take effect on the first day of August, nineteen hundred and three.

Approved February 26, 1903.

Chapter 88.

An Act authorizing and empowering Joseph C. Patchell of Reed Plantation, County of Aroostook, to erect and maintain piers and booms in the Mattawamkeag river.

Be it enacted by the Senate and House of Representatives in Legislature assembled, as follows:

Section 1. Joseph C. Patchell, his heirs and assigns, is hereby authorized and empowered to locate, erect and maintain piers and booms in the Mattawamkeag river, commencing at a point on the westerly side of said river twenty-five yards above Prouty rips, so called, and extending up the westerly side of said river to a point opposite the mouth of Hawkins brook. <small>Joseph C. Patchell authorized to locate piers and booms in Mattawamkeag river.</small>

Section 2. Said piers and booms shall be so constructed that logs, pulp wood, and other lumber shall not be impeded or delayed in this passage down said river, and expense of such delay, if any, shall be paid by said Patchell. <small>Logs and other lumber shall not be impeded by said piers and booms.</small>

Section 3. Said booms and piers shall also be so constructed that logs or other lumber belonging to other parties shall not run under and be retained in the booms of said Patchell; and if any logs, lumber, or other floatable material not owned by said Patchell be found within said booms, they shall upon notice in writing be turned out of said booms at said Patchell's expense. <small>How constructed. —lumber detained in said booms, how turned out.</small>

PENOBSCOT CHEMICAL FIBRE COMPANY.

CHAP. 89

Agent may be appointed.

Section 4. The Mattawamkeag Log Driving Company, or any individual log owners, driving logs by the boom down said river, shall have the right to appoint an agent who is hereby authorized and empowered to see that none of the logs are held and retained in said booms, and the said Patchell shall pay the said agent the sum of two dollars and fifty cents per day.

—compensation, how paid.

Passage for logs and lumber shall be provided.

Section 5. Said Patchell shall also provide a suitable passage through his booms for logs and other lumber being driven out of Finn brook, so called.

Section 6. This act shall take effect when approved.

Approved February 26, 1903.

Chapter 89.

An Act to authorize the Penobscot Chemical Fibre Company to generate, use, transmit and sell electricity.

Be it enacted by the Senate and House of Representatives in Legislature assembled, as follows:

May make and generate electricity upon Penobscot river between Old Town and Bradley.

Section 1. The Penobscot Chemical Fibre Company is hereby specially authorized and empowered to make and generate electricity upon its property situated upon the Penobscot river between the towns of Old Town and Bradley, and also on any dam or dams which it may erect on its property situated on said Penobscot river as aforesaid, and to use said electricity as a motive power in the use and development of its property, and also to sell the same for manufacturing and heating purposes and also to carry and conduct electricity made and generated upon its property between the towns of Old Town and Bradley to and into any towns or cities in county of Penobscot, state of Maine, and to use the same in all ways for its own purposes, and to sell the same for manufacturing purposes in units of not less than twenty-five horse power and also for heating purposes, but not for electric lighting or street railway purposes.

—may conduct electricity into any towns or cities in county of Penobscot.

May lay lines under and across rivers, etc.

Section 2. Said company is hereby authorized and empowered to construct, lay, maintain and operate lines of wire or other material for the transmission of such electricity under and across any stream or river, and under, along, upon and over streets, ways and bridges in said cities and towns.

Subject to laws of the state in laying lines.

Section 3. In erecting poles and laying said lines of wire, upon, along and over streets, ways and bridges, and under any stream or river, said corporation shall be subject to the laws of the state applicable to corporations which are authorized to make, generate, sell, distribute and supply electricity for manufacturing purposes, and shall have all the rights and powers of such corporations in the erecting of poles and conduits and the construction, laying and maintaining lines of wire.

Section 4. This act shall take effect when approved.

Approved February 26, 1903.

Chapter 90.

An Act to amend Section ten of Chapter three hundred and sixty-six of the Private and Special Laws of eighteen hundred and ninety-seven, entitled "An Act to incorporate the Livermore Falls Water Company."

Be it enacted by the Senate and House of Representatives in Legislature assembled, as follows:

Section 1. Section ten of chapter three hundred and sixty-six of the private and special laws of eighteen hundred and ninety-seven, entitled "An Act to incorporate the Livermore Falls Water Company," is hereby amended by striking out the words "the amount of its capital stock subscribed for" in the third and fourth lines, and inserting in the place thereof the words 'one hundred thousand dollars,' so that said section as amended, shall read as follows:

'Section 10. Said corporation may issue its bonds for the construction of its works upon such rates and time as it may deem expedient, to the amount not exceeding one hundred thousand dollars, and secure the same by mortgage of the franchises and property of the said company.'

Section 2. This act shall take effect when approved.

Approved February 26, 1903.

Chapter 91.

An Act to extend the charter of the Bangor and Brewer Steam Ferry Company.

Be it enacted by the Senate and House of Representatives in Legislature assembled, as follows:

Section 1. The charter of the Bangor and Brewer Steam Ferry Company, with all the rights and privileges and all the responsibilities attaching to said company by virtue of the several acts creating, extending and relating thereto, shall continue and remain in force for twenty years from the eighth day of February, in the year of our Lord, nineteen hundred three.

MUTUAL FIRE INSURANCE COMPANY.

CHAP. 92
—proviso.

Provided, however, that the said company shall run its boats each day during the season from five-thirty o'clock, in the morning, until eleven o'clock at night; and shall properly light its ferry slips, so long as its boats shall run; and also light the approaches to the ice, in the winter.

May collect toll of 5 cents from each passenger, after 9 o'clock, P. M.

Section 2. Said corporation shall have the right to collect a toll of five cents for each passenger carried upon its boats, after nine o'clock in the evening; instead of the toll established by its original charter.

Section 3. This act shall take effect when approved.

Approved February 26, 1903.

Chapter 93.

An Act to extend the charter of the Mutual Fire Insurance Company.

Be it enacted by the Senate and House of Representatives in Legislature assembled, as follows:

Charter extended.

Section 1. The rights, powers and privileges of the Mutual Fire Insurance Company which were granted by chapter five hundred and thirty-four of the private and special laws for the year eighteen hundred and ninety-seven and extended by chapter seventy-one of the private and special laws of eighteen hundred and ninety-nine and again extended by chapter two hundred and ninety of the private and special laws of nineteen hundred and one, are hereby further extended for two years from the approval of this act.

Section 2. This act shall take effect when approved.

Approved February 26, 1903.

Chapter 93.

An Act to Incorporate the Fort Kent Trust Company.

Be it enacted by the Senate and House of Representatives in Legislature assembled, as follows:

Section 1. John A. Nadeau, George V. Cunliffe, William H. Cunliffe, Joseph Archambault, Michel Michaud, Jesse J. Wheelock, Dosithe Daigle, Thomas H. Phair, John P. Donworth, Eloi R. Michaud, Thomas J. Cochran or such of them as may by vote accept this charter, with their associates, successors and assigns, are hereby made a body corporate and politic to be known as the Fort Kent Trust Company, and as such shall be possessed of all the powers, privileges and immunities and subject to all the duties and obligations conferred on corporations by law.

Section 2. The corporation hereby created shall be located at Fort Kent, in the county of Aroostook, and state of Maine.

Section 3. The purposes of said corporation and the business which it may perform, are; first, to receive on deposit, money, coin, bank notes, evidences of debt, accounts of individuals, companies, corporations and municipalities, allowing interest thereon, if agreed, or as the by-laws of said corporation may provide; second, to borrow money, to loan money on credits, or real estate, or personal security, and to negotiate loans and sales for others; to guarantee the payment of the principal and interest of all obligations secured by mortgages of real estate running to the said Fort Kent Trust Company; third, to hold for safe keeping all kinds of personal or mixed property, and to let deposit boxes for hire, and to act as agent for the owners thereof, and of real estate, for collection of income on the same and for sale of the same, and to act as agent for issuing, registering and countersigning certificates, bonds, stocks, and all evidences of debt or ownership in property; fourth, to hold by grant, assignment, or transfer, any real or personal property or trusts duly created and to execute trusts of every description; fifth, to act as assignee or receiver, and no surety shall be necessary upon the bond of the corporation, unless the court or officer approving such bond shall require it; sixth, to hold and enjoy all such estates, real, personal, and mixed, as may be obtained by the investment of its capital stock or any other moneys and funds that may come into its possession in the course of its business and dealings, and the same sell, grant, mortgage and dispose of, except as provided in section ten; seventh, to do in general all the business that may lawfully be done by trust or banking companies.

CHAP. 93

Administrators, assignees, etc., may deposit in.

Section 4. An administrator, assignee, guardian or trustee, any court of law or equity, including courts of probate and insolvency, officers and treasurers of towns, cities, counties and savings banks of the state of Maine, may deposit any moneys, bonds, stocks, evidences of debt or of ownership in property, or any personal property with said corporation, and any of said courts may direct any person deriving authority from them to so deposit the same.

Capital stock.

—shall not commence business until $50,000 has been paid in.

Section 5. The capital stock of said corporation shall be fifty thousand dollars divided into shares of one hundred dollars each, with the right to increase said capital at any time, by vote of the shareholders, to any amount not exceeding one million of dollars. Said corporation shall not commence business until stock to the amount of fifty thousand dollars shall have been subscribed for and paid in. Said corporation may hold real estate such as may be necessary for its immediate accommodation in the transaction of its business, not exceeding thirty thousand dollars in value.

Reserve fund.

Section 6. Said corporation after beginning to receive deposits, shall at all times have on hand, in lawful money, as a reserve, not less than twenty-five per cent of the aggregate amount of its deposits, which are subject to withdrawal on demand, provided, that in lieu of lawful money, two-thirds of said twenty-five per cent may consist of balances payable on demand, due from any national or state bank.

Taxation of shares.

Section 7. The shares of said corporation shall be subject to taxation in the same manner and amount as are the shares of national banks.

Shall be subject to examination by bank examiner.

Section 8. Said corporation shall be subject to examination by the bank examiner, who shall visit it at least once in every year, and as much oftener as he may deem expedient. At such visits he shall have free access to its vaults, books and papers, and shall thoroughly inspect and examine all the affairs of said corporation, and make such inquiries as may be necessary to ascertain its condition and ability to fulfill all its engagements. He shall preserve, in a permanent form a full record of his proceedings, including a statement of the condition of said corporation. A copy of such statement shall be published by said corporation immediately after the annual examination of the same, in some newspaper published in said county of Aroostook.

—statement shall be published.

Responsibility of shareholders.

Section 9. The shareholders of this corporation shall individually be responsible, equally and ratably, and not one for the other, for all contracts, debts and engagements of said corporation to a sum equal to the amount of the par value of the shares owned by each, in addition to the amount invested in said shares.

Section 10. All property or money held in trust by this corporation shall constitute a special deposit, and the accounts thereof and of said trust department, shall be kept separate, and such funds and the investment or loan of them shall be especially appropriated to the security and payment of such deposits and not be subject to any other liabilities of the corporation and for the purpose of securing the observance of this proviso, said corporation shall have a trust department in which all business pertaining to such trust department shall be kept separate and distinct from its general business.

Section 11. All the corporate powers of this corporation shall be exercised by a board of trustees, whose number, not less than five, shall be determined by the stockholders at their first meeting. Their term of office shall be for one year and until their successors shall have been chosen and qualified, except that the trustees first chosen shall hold office until the next annual meeting of the stockholders. The affairs and powers of the corporation may, at the option of the stockholders, be entrusted to an executive board of three members to be elected by the stockholders from the full board of trustees. The board of trustees or the executive board, if one be chosen, shall constitute the board of investment of said corporation. No loan shall be made to an officer or trustee of said corporation, except by the unanimous approval of the trustees or the executive board in writing, and said corporation shall have no authority to hire money or to give notes, unless by vote of said trustees or of said executive board duly recorded.

Section 12. Any one of the corporators named in this act may call the first meeting of this company, which shall be held at said Fort Kent, by mailing a written notice, postage paid, to each of the other corporators, seven days at least before the day of meeting, naming the time and place in said Fort Kent, and purposes of such meeting.

Section 13. This act shall take effect when approved.

Approved February 26, 1903.

Chapter 94.

An Act to prevent the pollution of the waters of Sebago Lake.

Be it enacted by the Senate and House of Representatives in Legislature assembled, as follows:

Restrictions on building on shores or islands of Sebago lake.

Section 1. No person or corporation shall use or occupy any structure hereafter built upon or near the shores of Sebago lake in the county of Cumberland, or upon any of the islands of said lake, for such purposes or in such manner that the sewage or drainage therefrom shall enter the waters of said lake or pollute the same.

Sewage, etc., shall not be discharged into said lake.

Section 2. No sewage, drainage, refuse or polluting matter of such kind and amount as either by itself or in connection with other matter will corrupt or impair the quality of the water of said Sebago lake, or render it injurious to health, shall be discharged into said lake, but nothing herein shall prohibit the cultivation and use of the soil in the ordinary methods of agriculture if no human excrement is used thereon within three hundred feet of the shores of said lake.

Supreme judicial court shall have power to enjoin.

Section 3. The supreme judicial court shall have jurisdiction in equity to enjoin, prevent or restrain any violation of the provisions of this act.

Section 4. This act shall take effect when approved.

Approved February 26, 1903.

Chapter 95.

An Act to amend an act incorporating the Trustees of Coburn Classical Institute.

Be it enacted by the Senate and House of Representatives in Legislature assembled, as follows:

Section 2 of chapter 333 of private and special laws of 1901, amended.

Section 1. Section two of chapter three hundred thirty-three of the private and special laws of nineteen hundred and one, is hereby amended by striking out of the second line thereof the word "seventeen" and inserting in its place the word 'twenty', so that said section two, as amended, shall read:

Board of trustees not exceeding twenty shall be elected.

'Section 2. Said corporation shall be governed and its powers exercised by a board of not exceeding twenty trustees, of which the president of Colby College and the principal of Coburn Classical Institute for the time being shall, ex-officio, be members.

—number, how fixed.

At the organization of the corporation, the number of other trustees shall be fixed by the by-laws and shall be divided as

WILTON ELECTRIC LIGHT AND POWER CO.—CITY OF ROCKLAND. 157

CHAP. 96
—tenure.

nearly as may be into three classes; one class shall be elected for one year, one for two years and one for three years; and at each annual meeting thereafter, members shall be elected by the board in place of those whose terms shall expire, and any vacancies in the other classes shall be filled.'

Section 2. This act shall take effect when approved.

Approved February 27, 1908.

Chapter 96.

An Act to extend the charter of the Wilton Electric Light and Power Company.

Be it enacted by the Senate and House of Representatives in Legislature assembled, as follows:

Section 1. That the rights, powers and privileges of the Wilton Electric Light and Power Company which were granted by chapter three hundred and twenty-four of the private and special laws of nineteen hundred and one, are hereby renewed and extended for and during a term of two years from the date of the approval of this act and the persons named in said act, their associates and successors shall have all the rights, powers and privileges that were granted them by said act to be exercised in the same manner and for the same purposes as provided therein.

Charter extended for two years.

Section 2. This act shall take effect when approved.

Approved February 27, 1908.

Chapter 97.

An Act authorizing the City of Rockland to accept donations of money and property to establish and maintain a Free Public Library in Rockland, and to accept conveyances of land for a site therefor.

Be it enacted by the Senate and House of Representatives in Legislature assembled, as follows:

Section 1. The city of Rockland is hereby authorized to receive and accept donations and bequests of money and property to an amount not exceeding one hundred thousand dollars for the purpose of establishing and maintaining a free public library in said Rockland, and of erecting a suitable building therefor, and also to accept conveyances of land for a site for said building, which shall be forever held by said city for the

Donations and bequests may be received for free library.

—may erect building and accept conveyances of land for site.

158 NORTHPORT WESLEYAN GROVE CAMPMEETING ASSOCIATION.

CHAP. 98

purpose aforesaid. And all acts and votes of said city, or of the city council, for the establishment and maintenance of a free public library in said city are hereby ratified and confirmed, and made valid.

Trustees.

Section 2. The management and control of said library, and of the buildings and grounds connected therewith, shall be vested in a board of trustees, to be designated "Trustees of the Rockland Public Library," consisting of the mayor, who shall be, ex officio, a member thereof, and of such a number of other trustees, inhabitants of the city of Rockland, as the city council may determine upon, to be elected by ballot in joint convention, all of whom shall serve as trustees without compensation.

—mayor shall be, ex-officio, member.

—members, how elected.

Section 3. All acts or parts of acts inconsistent with this act, are hereby repealed.

Section 4. This act shall take effect when approved.

Approved March 4, 1902.

Chapter 98.

An Act to amend the charter of the Northport Wesleyan Grove Campmeeting Association.

Be it enacted by the Senate and House of Representatives in Legislature assembled, as follows:

Chapter 319 of special laws of 1873, as amended by chapter 458 of special laws of 1901, further amended.

Section 1. Chapter three hundred and nineteen of the private and special laws of the state of Maine, for the year eighteen hundred and seventy-three, being "An Act to incorporate the Northport Wesleyan Grove Campmeeting Association," as amended by chapter four hundred and fifty-eight of the private and special laws of the state of Maine, for the year nineteen hundred and one, is hereby further amended by adding after the word "same" in the twentieth line of section one, the following words, 'and to erect and maintain fences on all lines bounding the lands of the association, with gates at public entrances, with full power to control the same'; and to add to said section after the word "state" in the twenty-seventh line, the following words, 'and the association is authorized to appoint a health officer whose jurisdiction shall be within the bounds of the lands of the said association in the town of Northport, who shall have authority to act, and be subject to the same restrictions, as is provided by statute with reference to local health officers'; so that said section as amended, shall read as follows:

—may erect fences on lines bounding lands of association.

—may appoint health officer.

Corporators.

'Section 1. Isaac H. W. Wharff, Henry B. Dunbar, Frank H. Nickerson, Norris E. Bragg, Gardner L. Ferrand, Nathan

A. Nickerson and Thomas F. Jones, trustees, their associates and successors; the preachers of the East Maine Conference of the Methodist Episcopal church, their associates and successors; with one representative from each Methodist Episcopal church or society having a cottage or lot on the campground, said representative to be elected or selected as set forth in section two of this act, are hereby constituted a body politic and corporate by the name of the Northport Wesleyan Grove Campmeeting Association, with full power by that name to sue and be sued, to plead and be impleaded, to take and hold by gift or purchase, property, real and personal, to the amount not exceeding fifty thousand dollars, to build and maintain streets, paths, walks, by-ways, parks, and sewers for the drainage of cottages and lands situated within the bounds of the lands of said association and full power to control the same; and to erect and maintain fences on all lines bounding the lands of the association, with gates at public entrances, with full power to control the same; with full control over the laying of all pipes for furnishing water or gas, and setting poles for supplying electricity for any purposes whatsoever, and also full control of establishing of all electric railroads within the bounds of the property of said association, to sell and convey the same and to establish such by-laws and regulations as are necessary for the further and proper management of their affairs, consistent with the laws of the state. And said association is authorized to appoint a health officer whose jurisdiction shall be within the bounds of the lands of said association in the town of Northport, who shall have the same authority to act, and be subject to the same restrictions, as are provided by statute with reference to local health officers.'

—corporate name.

—powers.

—health officer.

—powers of health officer.

Section 2. This act shall take effect when approved.

Approved March 4, 1903.

CHAP. 99

Chapter 99.

An Act to incorporate the Knox County General Hospital.

Be it enacted by the Senate and House of Representatives in Legislature assembled, as follows:

Corporators. Section 1. A. F. Crockett, W. T. White, L. B. Keen, Elmer S. Bird, John Lovejoy, E. S. Farwell, S. T. Kimball, M. S. Bird, F. R. Spear, John F. Gregory, W. M. Spear, F. B. Adams, C. A. Crockett, John T. Berry, Thomas Hawken, N. F. Cobb, J. H. McNamara, A. R. Smith, S. M. Bird, W. H. Bird, W. W. Case, F. A. Thorndike, H. I. Hix, N. T. Farwell, E. A. Burpee, W. W. Spear, E. A. Butler, S. W. McLoon, John Bird, W. S. White, A. J. Bird, E. K. Glover, E. F. Glover and F. W. Fuller of Rockland in the county of Knox; J. M. Wakefield, George Walker and N. B. Eastman of Warren; W. G. Alden, W. F. Hart, S. G. Ritterbush, E. W. Boynton, C. W. Follansbee, Williston Grinnell and W. E. Schwartz of Camden; H. L. Shepherd, J. H. Carleton, R. W. Carleton, Frank Carleton and S. Y. Weidman of Rockport; John E. Walker, P. M. Studley, J. E. Moore and Edwin Smith of Thomaston; G. C. Horn and F. M. Smith of South Thomaston; Willis Adams of Saint George, their associates and successors, are hereby incorporated and made a body politic by the name of the Knox County General Hospital, and by that name may sue and be sued, may have a common seal, and shall have all the immunities and privileges and be subject to all the liabilities of like corporations.

—corporate name.

May hold lands, tenements, etc. Section 2. Said corporation may take, receive, purchase, hold and possess lands and tenements in fee simple or otherwise, and dispose of and sell the same, and may receive of and from all persons disposed to aid its benevolent purposes, and grants and devises of real estate, and any donations, subscriptions, and bequests of money, or other property, to be used for the erection, support and maintenance of a general hospital for the sick, to be located within the city of Rockland.

May establish by-laws and regulations. Section 3. The said corporation shall have the power to make and establish such by-laws and regulations as may be necessary for the choice of proper officers, to prescribe their duties and powers, and to provide generally for the internal government and economy of the hospital, such by-laws and regulations not being repugnant to the constitution and by-laws of this state.

May establish training school for nurses. Section 4. The said corporation is authorized to establish a training school for nurses, and to issue diplomas as shall be fit and proper.

Section 5. This act shall take effect when approved.

Approved March 4, 1903.

Chapter 100.

An Act to amend Chapter six hundred and thirteen of the Private and Special Laws of eighteen hundred and ninety-three, entitled "An Act to establish the Western Hancock Municipal Court."

Be it enacted by the Senate and House of Representatives in Legislature assembled, as follows:

Section 1. Section nine of chapter six hundred and thirteen of the private and special laws of eighteen hundred and ninety-three is hereby amended by striking out the words "on the fourth Tuesday of each of the months of May, July, September and November in the town of Deer Isle" and inserting in place thereof the words 'on the fourth Tuesday of each of the months of January, February, March, April, May, July, September, October, November and December in the town of Deer Isle,' so that said section as amended, shall read as follows: *Section 9 of chapter 613 of special laws of 1893, amended.*

'Section 9. A term of said court shall be held for the transaction of civil business as follows: On the second Tuesday of each of the months of January, March, July and September in the town of Bluehill. On the second Tuesday of each of the months of February, May, June, August, November and December in the town of Bucksport. On the fourth Tuesday of each of the months of January, February, March, April, May, July, September, October, November and December in the town of Deer Isle. On the fourth Tuesday of the months of June and August in the town of Castine. Beginning at ten o'clock in the forenoon at such place in either of the towns named in this section, as the judge shall determine. For the cognizance and trial of criminal actions said court shall be considered in constant session. In all cases it may be adjourned from time to time by the judge.' *When terms of court shall be held.*

Section 2. This act shall take effect when approved.

Approved March 4, 1903.

Chapter 101.

An Act to incorporate the Union Gas Company.

Be it enacted by the Senate and House of Representatives in Legislature assembled, as follows:

Corporators.
—corporate name.

Section 1. Fred A. Alden, H. L. Robbins, F. E. Burkett, and their associates and assigns, are hereby constituted a body politic and corporate, by the name of the Union Gas Company, for the purpose of supplying light, heat and power by the manufacture of gas acetylene in the town of Union with all the privileges and subject to all the duties, restrictions and liabilities by law incident to corporations of a similar nature.

Location.
—may light by acetylene.
—may furnish power.

Section 2. Said company shall be located in the town of Union, in Knox county and is authorized and empowered to carry on the business of lighting by acetylene such public streets in said town and such buildings and places therein, public and private, as may be agreed upon by said corporation and the owners or those having control of said buildings and places to be lighted, and may furnish motive power by acetylene within said town, and may build and operate manufactories and works for providing and supplying acetylene, light and power and may lease, purchase and hold real and personal estate for the purposes of the corporation to the amount of its capital stock, and to construct, lay, maintain and operate lines of pipe for the transmission of acetylene, underground, under and along any and all streets and ways, under the direction of the municipal officers of said town.

Shall be liable for damages caused by obstructing streets, etc.
—proviso.

Section 3. The said company shall be liable in all cases to repay to the town all sums of money that said town may be obliged to pay on any indictment or judgment recovered against said town occasioned by any obstruction or taking up, or displacement of any way, highway, railroad or street by said company in said town; provided, however, that said company shall have notice whenever such damages are claimed by said town from the municipal officers and shall be allowed to defend the same at its own expense.

May cross sewers.

Section 4. Said company shall not be allowed to obstruct or impair the use of any public or private drain or sewer, but may cross the same, being responsible to the owners or other person for any injury occasioned thereby in an action on the case.

Town of Union may contract with, for light, etc.

Section 5. The town of Union, by its municipal officers, is hereby authorized to contract with said company from time to time as is deemed expedient for the supply of light, heat and power for said town.

LILY WATER COMPANY.

CHAP. 102

Section 6. The capital stock of said company shall not exceed ten thousand dollars, and shall be divided into shares of fifty dollars each. *Capital stock.*

Section 7. Said corporation is hereby authorized to issue its bonds in such amount and on such time as it may from time to time determine, not exceeding the amount of capital stock subscribed for, in aid of the purpose specified in this act and to secure the same by a mortgage of its franchises and property. It is also hereby authorized to lease all of its property and franchises upon such terms as it may determine. *May issue bonds.* *—may mortgage its property.*

Section 8. The first meeting of said corporation may be called by the first incorporator, but failing to do so, either of the other incorporators may by a written notice signed by him, stating the time and place thereof, and sent by mail to his associates five days before said meeting. *First meeting, how called.*

Section 9. This charter shall be null and void unless operations shall actually commence hereunder within two years from the date of the passage of this act. *Shall commence within two years.*

Approved March 4, 1903.

Chapter 102.

An Act to incorporate the Lily Water Company.

Be it enacted by the Senate and House of Representatives in Legislature assembled, as follows:

Section 1. Augustus O. Gross, Henry W. Sargent and Elmer P. Spofford, their associates, successors and assigns, are hereby created into a body corporate, by the name of the Lily Water Company, for the purpose of supplying the town of Deer Isle in the county of Hancock, and the inhabitants of said town with water for industrial, manufacturing, domestic, sanitary and municipal purposes, including the extinguishing of fires and sprinkling of streets. *Corporators.* *—corporate name.* *—purposes.*

Section 2. Said corporation for said purposes, may flow, detain, take, collect, store, use and distribute water from any pond or stream flowing from any pond, in said Deer Isle, and may locate, construct and maintain dams, cribs, reservoirs, locks, gates, sluices, aqueducts, pipes, hydrants, and all other necessary structures therefor. *May take water.* *—may construct dams, etc.*

Section 3. Said company is hereby authorized to lay, construct and maintain under, through, along and across the highways, ways, streets, railroads, bridges in said town, and to take *May cross highways.*

—shall be responsible for damages.

up, replace and repair all such sluices, aqueducts, pipes, hydrants and structures as may be necessary for the purposes of their incorporation, under such reasonable restrictions and conditions as the selectmen of said town may impose. And said company shall be responsible for all damages to all corporations, persons and property occasioned by the use of such highways, ways and streets, and shall further be liable to pay said town all sums recovered against said town for damages from obstruction caused by said company, and for all expenses, including reasonable counsel fees, incurred in defending such suits, with interest on the same.

May cross sewers.

Section 4. Said company shall have power to cross any water course, private or public sewer, or to change the direction thereof when necessary for the purposes of their incorporation, but in such manner as not to obstruct or impair the use thereof, and said company shall be liable for any injury caused thereby. Whenever said company shall lay down any fixtures in any highway, way or street, or make any alterations or repairs upon its works in any highway, way or street, it shall cause the same to be done with as little obstruction to public travel as may be practicable, and shall, at its own expense without unnecessary delay, cause any earth or pavements removed by it to be placed in proper condition.

May take lands.

Section 5. Said company can take and hold any lands necessary for flowage, and also for its dams, reservoirs, locks, gates, hydrants, and other necessary structures, and may locate, lay and maintain sluices, aqueducts, pipes, hydrants, and other necessary structures and fixtures in, over and through any land for its said purposes, and excavate in and through such lands for such locations, and dig, excavate and remove for its own use the rock, substance and earth at the bed of Torrey's pond, so called, in said Deer Isle. It may enter upon such lands to make surveys and locations, and shall file in the registry of deeds in said county

—may enter upon lands to make surveys.

of Hancock, plans of such location and lands, and within thirty days thereafter publish notice thereof in some newspaper in said county, such publication to be continued three weeks successively.

Damages, how assessed.

Section 6. Should the company and owner of such land be unable to agree upon the damages to be paid for such location, holding and construction, the land owner may within twelve months after such taking apply to the commissioners of said county of Hancock, and cause such damages to be assessed in the same manner and under the same conditions, restrictions and limitations as are by law prescribed in the case of damages resulting from the laying out of highways, so far as such laws are consistent with this act. Said company may make a tender to any land owner damaged under the provisions of this act, and if such owner recovers more damages than were tendered to him by said company, he shall recover costs, otherwise said company shall recover costs.

—may make tender for.

Section 7. Said company is hereby authorized to make contracts with the United States and with corporations and the said town of Deer Isle, for the purpose of supplying water as contemplated by this act. And said town of Deer Isle is hereby authorized by its selectmen to enter into contract with said company for a supply of water for any and all purposes mentioned in this act, including the remission of taxes upon real estate, fixtures, franchise and plant of said corporation.

May make contracts to supply water.

Section 8. If said company find it necessary to lay its pipes over tide waters, it may build and maintain all necessary piers and other structures causing as little obstruction to navigation as possible.

May build piers.

Section 9. The capital stock of said company shall not exceed one hundred thousand dollars, and said stock shall be divided into shares of fifty dollars each.

Capital stock.

Section 10. Said company for all of its said purposes may hold real and personal estate necessary and convenient therefor, not exceeding in amount one hundred thousand dollars.

May hold real and personal estate.

Section 11. Said company may issue its bonds for the construction of its works of any and all kinds, upon such rates and times as it may deem expedient, not exceeding the sum of one hundred thousand dollars and secure the same by mortgage of the franchise, income and property of said company.

May issue bonds.

—may mortgage its property.

Section 12. The first meeting of said company may be called by a written notice thereof, signed by any one incorporator herein named, served upon each incorporator by giving in hand or leaving the same at his place of last and usual abode seven days before the time of meeting.

First meeting how called.

Section 13. This act shall take effect when approved.

Approved March 4, 1902.

CHAP. 103

Chapter 103.

An Act to legalize the acts and doings of the town of Williamsburg.

Be it enacted by the Senate and House of Representatives in Legislature assembled, as follows:

Acts and doings legalized.
All acts and doings of the town of Williamsburg, Maine, prior to this date are hereby legalized and made valid.

Approved March 4, 1903.

Chapter 104.

An Act extending the charter and changing the name of the Van Buren Trust and Banking Company.

Be it enacted by the Senate and House of Representatives in Legislature assembled, as follows:

Charter extended.
Section 1. Chapter two hundred and seventy-six of the private and special laws of eighteen hundred and ninety-five entitled "An Act to Incorporate the Van Buren Trust and Banking Company," as amended by chapter one hundred and thirty-one of the private and special laws of eighteen hundred and ninety-nine, as extended by chapter three hundred and thirty-seven of the private and special laws of nineteen hundred and one is hereby continued in force and the persons named in said act, as amended, are hereby given a period of two years from the date of the approval of this act in which to organize and commence business.

Name changed.
Section 2. The name of the Van Buren Trust and Banking Company is hereby changed to Van Buren Trust Company.

Section 3. This act shall take effect when approved.

Approved March 4, 1903.

Chapter 105.

An Act to extend the charter of the Ellsworth Street Railway Company.

Be it enacted by the Senate and House of Representatives in Legislature assembled, as follows:

Section 1. The rights, powers and privileges of the Ellsworth Street Railway Company which were granted by chapter three hundred ninety-one of the private and special laws for the year eighteen hundred eighty-nine, as extended and enlarged by chapter five hundred fifteen of the private and special laws for the year eighteen hundred ninety-three, chapter eighty-one of the private and special laws for the year eighteen hundred ninety-five, chapter four hundred fifty-six of the private and special laws for the year eighteen hundred ninety-seven, chapter one hundred thirty-three of the private and special laws for the year eighteen hundred ninety-nine and chapter two hundred sixty-seven of the private and special laws for the year nineteen hundred one, are hereby extended for two years additional, and the persons named in said acts, their associates and successors, shall have the rights, powers and privileges that were granted to them by said acts to be exercised by them for the same purposes as specified in said acts. *Charter extended.*

Section 2. This act shall take effect when approved.

Approved March 4, 1902.

Chapter 106.

An Act in relation to the Hancock County Railway Company.

Be it enacted by the Senate and House of Representatives in Legislature assembled, as follows:

Section 1. The organization of the Hancock County Railway Company, a corporation established by chapter three hundred one of the private and special laws of the state of Maine, for the year nineteen hundred one, as now existing, is hereby ratified and confirmed, and all the rights, powers and privileges conferred by said chapter three hundred one are hereby vested in said corporation, and the further period of two years from the date when this act takes effect is hereby granted said corporation in which to commence actual business under its charter. *Charter extended.*

Section 2. Said corporation, the Hancock County Railway Company, is hereby authorized and permitted by a vote of its stockholders representing a majority of the stock issued, to *May increase capital stock.*

CHAP. 107

May issue bonds.

increase its capital stock to any amount not exceeding one million dollars.

Section 3. Said corporation, the Hancock County Railway Company, is hereby authorized and permitted to issue its bonds for the construction of its works, maintenance or operation of the same, of any or all kinds, upon such rates and time as it may deem expedient, not however exceeding in total amount the amount of one million dollars, and to secure the payment of the principal and interest on such bonds by appropriate mortgages or deeds of trust of all or any part of its property, franchises, rights and privileges now owned or to be hereafter acquired by it.

May operate branches.

Section 4. Said corporation, the Hancock County Railway Company is hereby granted the further right to build, equip, maintain and operate a branch or branches of its line in all or any of the towns of Ellsworth, Surry, Bluehill, Brooklin, Sedgwick, Brooksville, Castine or Penobscot, in said county of Hancock, with like privileges respectively in each of said towns, and subject to like restrictions respectively in each of said towns as provided by said chapter three hundred one of the laws of nineteen hundred one for the construction of its main line.

Section 5. This act shall take effect when approved.

Approved March 4, 1903.

Chapter 107.

An Act to repeal the provisions of Section three of Chapter five hundred forty-four of the Special Laws of eighteen hundred eighty-nine, relating to the Bangor Street Railway.

Be it enacted by the Senate and House of Representatives in Legislature assembled, as follows:

Section 3 of chapter 544 of special laws of 1889, repealed.

Section 1. The provisions of section three of chapter five hundred and forty-four of the special laws of eighteen hundred eighty-nine are hereby repealed.

Section 2. This act shall take effect when approved.

Approved March 4, 1903.

Chapter 108.

An Act to amend Chapter two hundred fifteen of the Resolves of the State of Maine of eighteen hundred ninety-seven, relating to tuition of Students in Agriculture at University of Maine.

Be it enacted by the Senate and House of Representatives in Legislature assembled, as follows:

That chapter two hundred fifteen of the resolves of the state of Maine of eighteen hundred ninety-seven, is hereby amended by adding to the same the words 'and to students pursuing the courses in agriculture', so that said section as amended, shall read as follows:

'That said trustees are hereby directed to charge all students a reasonable tuition but they may abate said tuition to such worthy pupils resident in the state as may be financially unable to pay the same, and to students pursuing the courses in agriculture.'

Approved March 4, 1908.

Chapter 109.

An Act conferring additional powers upon Proprietors of Union Wharf, incorporated by special Act of the Legislature, approved February nine, in the year of our Lord eighteen hundred fifty-six.

Be it enacted by the Senate and House of Representatives in Legislature assembled, as follows:

Section 1. In addition to the powers conferred upon the proprietors of Union Wharf by its charter, said corporation is hereby authorized to acquire, hold, mortgage and dispose of real estate and personal property in the city of Portland, to an amount not exceeding in value one hundred thousand dollars in addition to the value of the property now held by it.

Section 2. This act shall take effect when approved.

Approved March 4, 1908.

Chapter 110.

An Act to amend Chapter two hundred twenty-nine of the Private and Special Laws of eighteen hundred eighty-three, as amended by Chapter three hundred eighty-three of the Private and Special Laws of eighteen hundred eighty-five, entitled "An Act to incorporate the Passadumkeag Log Driving Company."

Be it enacted by the Senate and House of Representatives in Legislature assembled, as follows:

Chapter 229, as amended by chapter 383, further amended.

Section 1. Said chapter two hundred twenty-nine as amended by said chapter three hundred eighty-three is hereby amended by striking out sections two, three and four and inserting in place thereof the following sections:

Company may drive logs.

—in Nickatous stream.

—in the Passadumkeag river.

'Section 2. Said company may drive at the cost and expense of the owners thereof the logs and other timber that may be seasonably in the Nickatous stream between the dam at the foot of Nickatous lake and the mouth of said stream, and the logs and other timber that may be seasonably in the Passadumkeag river between the mouth of said stream and Suponic pond, to the Passadumkeag boom or the Penobscot boom where logs are usually sorted, as designated by the owners of such logs and other timber.'

Owner of logs shall file statement on or before March 15.

—directors shall assess cost.

—clerk shall keep record of assessments.

'Section 3. Every owner of logs and other timber to be driven by said company shall file with the clerk of said company on or before the fifteenth day of March in that year a written statement signed by such owner or his authorized agent, stating the amount of logs or other timber to be driven as aforesaid, and the mark or marks thereon, together with the place from which such logs and other timber are to be driven and their place of destination. After the directors shall have ascertained the amount necessary to defray the cost of driving such logs and other timber and the other expenses for the season, they shall assess to the owners thereof the amount necessary to drive such logs and other timber together with other necessary expenses, such assessment to be based upon the boom scale. If logs or other timber are driven by said company which have not been returned as aforesaid, the directors may assess the owner of such logs and other timber, as his proportion of such expenses, such sum or sums as may be considered by the directors just and equitable; and the clerk of the company shall keep a record of all assessments and of all expenses upon which such assessments are based, which shall be open to the inspection of persons interested.'

Payment shall be made or secured within 30 days of assessment.

'Section 4. The directors shall give to the treasurer of the company a list of the assessments made by them, and owners of logs and other timber shall pay or satisfactorily secure the amounts of their several assessments within twenty days from the date of such assessment, and said company shall have a lien upon all logs and other timber by it driven for the expenses of driving the same and for the other expenses of the company, which lien shall have precedence of all other claims, except laborers' liens, and shall continue for ninety days after the logs and other timber shall arrive at their place of destination for sale or manufacture, and may be enforced by attachment, but such lien may be discharged by giving a bond with sufficient sureties to said company approved by its board of directors, conditioned that such expenses shall be seasonably paid.'

—lien established.

—lien, how discharged.

Section 2. This act shall take effect when approved.

Approved March 4, 1903.

Chapter 111.

An Act to authorize the erection of piers and booms in the Mattawamkeag River, at Jenkin's Cove.

Be it enacted by the Senate and House of Representatives in Legislature assembled, as follows:

Section 1. Marion E. Sprague of Drew, in the county of Penobscot, his successors and assigns, are hereby authorized and empowered to erect and maintain in the Mattawamkeag river, at or near Jenkin's cove, so called, piers and booms for the purpose of collecting, separating, sorting and holding logs and other lumber coming down said river. Said piers and booms shall be located as follows; a sorting boom at said Jenkin's cove, and holding booms upon the northerly side of said river extending from said sorting boom to a point one hundred rods above the head of Ox Bow island and from a point one-fourth of a mile above the mouth of Mud brook, so called, to the mills of said Sprague, situated below said Jenkin's cove in Reed plantation. At least two sorting gaps shall be constructed, maintained and used for the passage of logs and other lumber through said booms. Said piers and booms shall be so located, constructed, maintained and used that logs and other lumber running down said river, belonging to other parties, and not destined for use and manufacture at the mills of said Sprague, his successors and assigns, shall not be unreasonably impeded or delayed, and in no case shall logs or other lumber be delayed longer than twenty-four hours, and the logs or lumber of other parties, when stopped for sorting shall be turned by as soon as they practically can be sorted and separated from logs and other lumber destined for

Marion E. Sprague, authorized to erect piers and booms in Mattawamkeag river.

—location.

—sorting gaps.

—logs shall not be delayed longer than 24 hours.

use and manufacture at the mills of said Sprague, and any stray logs or other lumber not destined for use and manufacture, at the mills of said Sprague, if found in said booms, shall be turned out by him upon written demand of the owner or owners thereof, at his own charge and expense.

Said Sprague may sort out logs for his mill.

Section 2. Said Sprague, his successors and assigns, by aid of such piers and booms are hereby authorized and empowered to separate and sort out from the logs and other lumber coming down said river, all logs and other lumber destined and intended for use and manufacture at the mills of said Sprague; provided,

—proviso.

however, if upon the approach of the rear of any drive of logs to the booms herein authorized to be constructed and maintained, it shall appear to the person in charge of such drive that said Sprague has not sufficient men to sort and turn by the logs or other lumber arriving at said booms, so that such drive may be unreasonably impeded or delayed, such person, upon notice in writing to said Sprague, shall have the right to put men of his own selection upon said booms, to expedite the sorting and turning by of the logs and other lumber in such drive, who shall be paid by said Sprague; and the additional cost, if any, of making such drive through said booms in consequence of such erections and piers of said Sprague shall be paid by said Sprague; but nothing herein contained shall make said Sprague liable for any delay caused by said piers and booms. And said Sprague is also authorized and empowered to hold within the piers and booms mentioned in this act and located, erected and maintained as aforesaid, all logs and other lumber coming down said Mattawamkeag river which are destined and intended for use and manufacture at the mills of said Sprague.

Mattawamkeag Log Driving Company may appoint agent.

Section 3. The Mattawamkeag Log Driving Company, a corporation existing under the laws of the state, shall have the right at any time to appoint an agent who is hereby authorized and empowered, and whose duty it shall be, to take charge of

—duties of agent.

and superintend the sorting of the logs and other lumber running through the booms herein authorized, and said Sprague at the beginning of every driving season, or at the time of the appointment of such agent, shall furnish such agent a list of marks upon all logs and other lumber intended to be manufactured at the mills of said Sprague, and such agent shall see to it that the logs and other lumber not intended to be manufactured at the mills of said Sprague are not unreasonably detained in or by said booms.

—compensation of agent.

The compensation of such agent shall not exceed two dollars fifty cents per day, and shall be paid by said Sprague.

May enter upon and take lands.

Section 4. Said Sprague, his successors and assigns, may enter upon, take and hold such lands as may be necessary for the location, erection and maintenance of the piers and booms mentioned in this act and connecting the same with the shores, and may with their agents and teams, pass and repass over said shores and to and from the same, over the lands of other persons, for the purpose aforesaid, and for the operation and management of said piers and booms, and the damages for such taking shall be assessed and recovered as follows; if any person sustaining damages as aforesaid cannot agree with said Sprague upon the sum to be paid therefor, either party on petition to the county commissioners of the county in which the land so taken is situated, may have the damages assessed by them, and subsequent proceedings and right of appeal thereon shall be had in the same manner and under the same conditions, restrictions and limitations as are by law prescribed in the case of damages occasioned by the laying out of highways. —damages, how assessed.

Section 5. This act shall take effect when approved.

Approved March 4, 1903.

Chapter 112

An Act to incorporate the South West Harbor Trust Company.

Be it enacted by the Senate and House of Representatives in Legislature assembled, as follows:

Section 1. J. D. Phillips, B. H. Mayo, E. A. Lawler, A. L. Somes, George R. Fuller and A. E. Farnsworth, or such of them as may by vote accept this charter, with their associates, successors and assigns, are hereby made a body corporate and politic to be known as the South West Harbor Trust Company, and as such shall be possessed of all the powers, privileges and immunities and subject to all the duties and obligations conferred on corporations by law. Corporators. —corporate name.

Section 2. The corporation hereby created shall be located at South West Harbor, Maine. Location.

Section 3. The purposes of said corporation and the business which it may perform, are; first, to receive on deposit, money, coin, bank notes, evidences of debt, accounts of individuals, companies, corporations, municipalities and states, allowing interest thereon, if agreed, or as the by-laws of said corporation may provide; second, to borrow money, to loan money on credits, or real estate, or personal security, and to negotiate loans and sales for others; third, to own and maintain safe deposit vaults, with boxes, safes and other facilities therein, to Purposes. —may own safe deposit vaults.

CHAP. 112

—may act as agent.

—may execute trusts.

—shall not establish branches.

Capital stock.

—shall not commence business until $25,000 has been paid in.

Shall not loan money on security of its own capital stock.

Board of trustees.
—number and tenure.

—executive board.

—vacancies, how filled.

be rented to other parties for the safe keeping of moneys, securities, stocks, jewelry, plate, valuable papers and documents, and other property susceptible of being deposited therein, and may receive on deposit for safe keeping, property of any kind entrusted to it for that purpose; fourth, to act as agent for issuing, registering and countersigning certificates, bonds, stocks, and all evidences of debt or ownership in property; fifth, to hold by grant, assignment, transfer, devise or bequest, any real or personal property or trusts duly created, and to execute trusts of every description; sixth, to act as assignee, receiver, executor, and no surety shall be necessary upon the bond of the corporation, unless the court or officer approving such bond shall require it; seventh, to do in general all the business that may lawfully be done by trust and banking companies, but said corporation shall not have the power or authority to establish branches.

Section 4. The capital stock of said corporation shall not be less than twenty-five thousand dollars, divided into shares of one hundred dollars each, with the right to increase the said capital stock at any time, by vote of the shareholders, to any amount not exceeding five hundred thousand dollars. Said corporation shall not commence business as a trust or banking company, until stock to the amount of at least twenty-five thousand dollars shall have been subscribed and paid in, in cash.

Section 5. Said corporation shall not make any loan or discount on the security of the shares of its own capital stock, nor be the purchaser or holder of any such shares unless necessary to prevent loss upon a debt previously contracted in good faith; and all stock so acquired shall, within six months from the time of its acquisition, be disposed of at public or private sale.

Section 6. All the corporate powers of this corporation shall be exercised by a board of trustees, who shall be residents of this state, whose number and term of office shall be determined by a vote of the shareholders at the first meeting held by the incorporators and at each annual meeting thereafter. The affairs and powers of the corporation may, at the option of the shareholders, be entrusted to an executive board of five members to be, by vote of the shareholders, elected from the full board of trustees. The trustees of said corporation shall be sworn to the proper discharge of their duties, and they shall hold office until others are elected and qualified in their stead. If a trustee or director dies, resigns, or becomes disqualified for any cause, the remaining trustees or directors may appoint a person to fill the vacancy until the next annual meeting of the corporation. The oath of office of such trustee or director shall be taken within thirty days of his election, or his office shall become vacant. The clerk of such corporation shall, within ten days, notify such trustees or directors of their election, and within thirty days shall publish the list of all persons who have taken the oath of office as trustees or directors.

Section 7. The board of trustees or directors of said corporation shall constitute the board of investment of said corporation. Said trustees or directors shall keep in a separate book, specially provided for the purpose, a record of all loans, and investments of every description, made by said institution substantially in the order of time when such loans or investments are made, which shall show that such loans or investments have been made with the approval of the investment committee of said corporation, which shall indicate such particulars respecting such loans or investments as the bank examiner shall direct. This book shall be submitted to the trustees or directors and to the bank examiner whenever requested. Such loans or investments shall be classified in the book as the bank examiner shall direct. No loan shall be made to any officer or director of said banking or trust company except by the unanimous approval of the executive board in writing, and said corporation shall have no authority to hire money or to give notes unless by vote of the said board duly recorded.

Board of investment.
—shall keep record of loans.
—loans to officers or directors, how made.

Section 8. No person shall be eligible to the position of a director or a trustee of said corporation who is not the actual owner of ten shares of the stock.

Director or trustee must own ten shares of stock.

Section 9. Said corporation, after beginning to receive deposits, shall, at all times, have on hand in lawful money, as a reserve, not less than fifteen per cent of the aggregate amount of its deposits which are subject to withdrawal on demand, provided, that in lieu of lawful money, two-thirds of said fifteen per cent may consist of balances, payable on demand, due from any national or state bank.

Reserve fund.

Section 10. All the property or money held in trust by this corporation shall constitute a special deposit and the accounts thereof and of said trust department shall be kept separate, and such funds and the investment or loans of them shall be specially appropriated to the security and payment of such deposits, and not be subject to any other liabilities of the corporation; and for the purpose of securing the observance of this proviso, said corporation shall have a trust department in which all business pertaining to such trust property shall be kept separate and distinct from its general business.

Trust funds shall constitute a special deposit.

Section 11. An administrator, executor, assignee, guardian or trustee, any court of law or equity, including courts of probate and insolvency, officers and treasurers of towns, cities, counties,

Administrators, etc., may deposit in.

176 CHAP. 112

SOUTH WEST HARBOR TRUST COMPANY.

and savings banks of the state of Maine may deposit any moneys, bonds, stocks, evidences of debt or of ownership in property, or any personal property, with said corporation, and any of said courts may direct any person deriving authority from them to so deposit the same.

Responsibility of shareholders.

Section 12. Each shareholder of this corporation shall be individually responsible, equally and ratably, and not one for the other, for all contracts, debts and engagements of such corporation, to a sum equal to the amount of the par value of the shares owned by each in addition to the amount invested in said shares.

Guaranty fund.

Section 13. Such corporation shall set apart as a guaranty fund not less than ten per cent of its earnings in each and every year until such fund with the accumulated interest thereon, shall amount to one-fourth of the capital stock of said corporation.

Taxation of shares.

Section 14. The shares of said corporation shall be subject to taxation in the same manner and rate as are the shares of national banks.

Shall be subject to examination by bank examiner

Section 15. Said corporation shall be subject to examination by the bank examiner, who shall visit it at least once in every year, and as much oftener as he may deem expedient. At such visits he shall have free access to its vaults, books and papers, and shall thoroughly inspect and examine all the affairs of said corporation, and make such inquiries as may be necessary to ascertain its condition and ability to fulfill all its engagements. If upon examination of said corporation the examiner is of the opinion that its investments are not in accordance with law, or said corporation is insolvent, or its condition is such as to render its further proceedings hazardous to the public or to those having funds in its custody, or is of the opinion that it has exceeded its powers or failed to comply with any of the rules or restrictions provided by law, he shall have such authority and take such action as is provided for in the case of savings banks by chapter forty-seven of the revised statutes. He shall preserve in a permanent form a full record of his proceedings, including a statement of the condition of said corporation. A copy of such statement shall be published by said corporation immediately after the annual examination of the same in some newspaper published where said corporation is established. If no paper is published in the town where said corporation is established, then it shall be published in a newspaper printed in the nearest city or town. The necessary expenses of the bank examiner while making such examination shall be paid by the corporation.

—statement shall be published.

First meeting, how called.

Section 16. Any five of the corporators named in this act may call the first meeting of the corporation by mailing a written notice, signed by all, postage paid, to each of the other corporators, seven days at least before the day of the meeting, naming the time, place and purpose of such meeting, and at such meeting the necessary officers may be chosen, by-laws adopted, and any other corporate business transacted.

Section 17. This act shall take effect when approved.

Approved March 4, 1908.

Chapter 113.

An Act in relation to the Trustees of Westbrook Seminary.

Be it enacted by the Senate and House of Representatives in Legislature assembled, as follows:

Section 1. Women shall be eligible to membership on the board of Trustees of Westbrook Seminary, which board shall consist of not less than three nor more than twenty-seven members to be elected by the board as heretofore and hold office for the term of six years, vacancies by death, resignation or otherwise to be filled by election of members for the unexpired term. Not more than one-third of the number shall be clergymen, and eight members shall constitute a quorum if there are more than fifteen members, but if less a majority shall be a quorum. *Women shall be eligible as trustees. —tenure of office of trustees. —quorum.*

Section 2. The election and qualifications of the present and all past acting members of the board of trustees and all their acts and doings in their official capacity are hereby confirmed, legalized and made valid. *Former elections of trustees made valid.*

Approved March 4, 1908.

Chapter 114.

An Act to consolidate and amend Chapter seventy-eight of the Special Laws of eighteen hundred and sixty-one, Chapter three hundred ninety-five of the Special Laws of eighteen hundred sixty-four, Chapter one hundred forty of the Special Laws of eighteen hundred sixty-six, Chapter five hundred thirty-six of the Special Laws of eighteen hundred seventy-four, Chapter three hundred four of the Special Laws of eighteen hundred ninety-five, and Chapter three hundred ninety-eight of the Special Laws of nineteen hundred and one, relating to a Police Court in the City of Rockland.

Be it enacted by the Senate and House of Representatives in Legislature assembled, as follows:

Section 1. There is hereby established in the city of Rockland, a court to be denominated the police court for the city of Rockland, to consist of one judge, who shall be appointed, com- *Rockland police court established.*

CHAP. 114.

—seal, and
court of
record.

Jurisdiction.

Concurrent
jurisdiction
with supreme
judicial court
when debt is
above $20 and
does not
exceed $100.

—exceptions.

—shall not
include
actions when
titles to real
estate is
in question.

—how actions
may be
removed to
supreme
judicial court
in certain
cases.

missioned and qualified in the manner provided by the constitution of this state, and be a citizen of said city, and so continue while he remains in office. Said police court shall be a court of record with a seal to be affixed to all original processes issued therefrom. The present judge shall continue in office until the end of the term for which he was appointed.

Section 2. Said judge shall, except where interested, exercise jurisdiction over all such matters and things, civil and criminal, within the county of Knox, as justices of the peace or trial justices may exercise, and under similar restrictions and limitations, and concurrent jurisdiction with justices of the peace and quorum and trial justices in cases of forcible entry and detainer in said county; and exclusive jurisdiction in all such matters and things where both parties interested, or the plaintiff and the person or persons summoned as trustees, shall be inhabitants of or residents in said city; and said court shall also have exclusive jurisdiction over all such criminal offenses committed within the limits of said city, as are cognizable by justices of the peace or trial justices, and under similar restrictions and limitations. And said court shall have concurrent jurisdiction with the supreme judicial court in all personal actions where the debt or damage demanded, exclusive of costs, is over twenty dollars and not over one hundred dollars, and in all actions of replevin, when it appears that the sum demanded for the penalty, forfeiture or damages does not exceed one hundred dollars, or that the property in the beasts or other chattels is in question and the value thereof does not exceed one hundred dollars and either defendant, or a person summoned as trustee is resident in Knox county; but this jurisdiction shall not include proceedings under the divorce laws or complaints under the mill act, so called, nor jurisdiction over actions in which the title to real estate according to the pleadings filed in the case by either party is in question except as provided in chapter ninety-four, sections six and seven of the revised statutes. If any defendant, in any action in said court where the amount claimed in the writ exceeds twenty dollars, or his agent or attorney shall, on the return day of the writ, file in said court a motion asking that said cause be removed to the supreme judicial court and deposit with the judge the sum of two dollars for copies and entry fee in said supreme court, to be taxed in his costs if he prevails, the said action shall be removed into the supreme judicial court for said county, and the judge shall forthwith cause certified copies of the writ, officer's return and defendant's motion to be filed in the clerk's office of the supreme judicial court, and shall pay the entry fee thereof; and said action shall be entered on the docket of the term next preceding said filing, unless said court shall then be in session, when it shall be entered forthwith, and shall be in order for trial at the next succeeding term. If no such motion is filed, the said police court shall proceed and determine said action, subject to the right of appeal in either party as hereinafter provided. The pleadings in such cases shall be the same as in the supreme judicial court. In any action in which the plaintiff recovers not over twenty dollars debt or damage, the costs to be taxed shall be the same as before trial justices, except that the plaintiff shall have two dollars for his writ. Where the defendant prevails in any action in which the sum claimed in the writ is not over twenty dollars, he shall recover two dollars for his pleadings and other costs as before trial justices. In actions where the amount recovered by the plaintiff, exclusive of costs, exceeds twenty dollars, or the amount claimed exceeds twenty dollars, where the defendant prevails, the cost of parties, trustees and witnesses shall be the same as in the supreme judicial court, except the costs to be taxed for attendance shall be two dollars and fifty cents for each term, not exceeding three terms, and for trial of issue, eighty cents. All the provisions of the statutes of this state relative to the attachment of real and personal property and the levy of executions, shall be applicable to actions in this court, and executions on judgments rendered therein. Actions may be referred and judgments on the referees report may be rendered in the same manner and with the same effect as in the supreme judicial court.

—costs, how taxed.

—costs.

Section 3. Said judge shall have jurisdiction in all cases of simple larceny when the property alleged to have been stolen shall not exceed in value the sum of fifty dollars, and on conviction award sentence of imprisonment in the county jail or house of correction not exceeding one year, or fine not exceeding one hundred dollars; of offenses described in section four of chapter one hundred and thirty-two of the revised statutes, where they are not of a high and aggravated nature, and on conviction, may punish by fine not exceeding fifty dollars, or by imprisonment in the county jail for a term not exceeding six months, and all violations of the tramp law, and of offenses described in section four of chapter one hundred and forty-one of the revised statutes, and on conviction, may be punished by imprisonment in the county jail or house of correction not exceeding six months. And shall have exclusive jurisdiction of all offenses against the ordinances and by-laws of said city, though the penalty therefor may accrue to said city; and in the prosecutions on any such ordinances or by-laws, or any special law of the state relating to said city, such by-law, ordinance or special law need not be

Judge shall have jurisdiction in cases of simple larceny when value of property does not exceed $50, etc.

CHAP. 114

Judge shall have jurisdiction in cases of cheating by false pretences when amount obtained does not exceed $20.

recited in the complaint or process, nor the allegations therein be more particular than in prosecutions on a public statute.

Section 4. Said judge shall have jurisdiction of all cases of cheating by false pretences, where the property, money, or other thing alleged to have been fraudulently obtained shall not exceed in value the sum of twenty dollars, and shall have power to try the same and award sentence upon a conviction, by fine not exceeding twenty dollars, or imprisonment in the county jail, or in the house of correction to hard labor for a term not exceeding ninety days. The same proceedings may be had before said court, and in the same manner against persons keeping houses of ill fame, resorted to for purposes of prostitution or lewdness, on complaint as before a justice of the peace or trial justice.

Warrants shall be issued by the judge.

Section 5. All warrants issued upon complaints for offenses committed within the limits of the city shall be issued by the judge of said court, and shall be made returnable before said court, and no justice of the peace or trial justice, in said county of Knox, shall in any manner take cognizance of, or exercise jurisdiction over any crime or offense committed within the limits of said city except as hereinafter provided.

Jurisdiction of justices of the peace and trial justices restricted.

Section 6. The several justices of the peace in said city shall continue to have and exercise all the power and authority vested in them by the laws of the United States; but no such justice of the peace, nor any trial justice for said Knox county, shall exercise any civil or criminal jurisdiction otherwise, except as hereinafter provided, unless in civil cases where the said judge is interested, under a penalty of twenty dollars for each offense, to be recovered by indictment in any court proper to try the same;

—exceptions.

but nothing in this act shall be construed to prevent said justices of the peace or trial justices, administering oaths, taking acknowledgments of deeds and other writings, acting as arbitrators or referees, or doing any business other than that especially devolving upon said court.

Appeals may be taken to supreme judicial court.

Section 7. Any persons aggrieved at any judgment or sentence of said court may appeal to the supreme judicial court in the same manner as from a judgment or sentence of a trial justice, and all such appeals shall be in order for trial at the first term of said appellate court after such appeal is taken. Final

—final judgment may be reexamined on writ of error.

judgment in said police court may be re-examined in the supreme judicial court on a writ of error, on a petition for review, and when the judgment is reversed the supreme judicial court shall render such judgment as said police court should have rendered, and when a review is granted it shall be tried in said supreme judicial court.

POLICE COURT IN ROCKLAND.   181

CHAP. 114

Section 8. The judge of the police court in the city of Rockland shall render an account of, and pay over all fines and forfeitures by him received upon convictions and sentences before him, to the treasurer of the county of Knox within six months after he receives the same, and for any neglect, he shall forfeit and pay in each instance double the amount, to be recovered in an action of debt in the name of the county treasurer.

Fines and forfeitures shall be paid to county treasurer.

Section 9. Said police court shall be holden on the first Tuesday of each month, at nine o'clock in the forenoon, for the transaction of civil business, except for actions of forcible entry and detainer which shall be held on each Tuesday at the hour aforesaid, and all civil processes shall be made returnable accordingly; said court shall be considered in constant session for the trial of criminal offenses; and said court may be adjourned from time to time at the discretion of the judge. Said court to be held at such place as such city shall provide for that purpose. It shall be the duty of the judge of said court to make and keep the records of said court or cause the same to be done, and to perform all other duties required of similar tribunals; the copies of the records of said court duly certified by the judge, shall be legal evidence in any court of this state. The fees in all cases, civil and criminal before said court, except as provided in section two of this act, shall be the same as are now taxable by justices of the peace or trial justices, provided that the price of blank writs, which shall be signed by the judge of said court and bear the seal of said court, shall be three cents; and said judge shall keep an account of said fees, and pay the same quarterly into the treasury of the said city.

Terms of court, when held.

—judge shall cause records to be kept.

Section 10. When the office of judge of said court shall be vacant in consequence of resignation, death, or removal of the judge's residence from said city, the trial justices of said city, if it have any, or if not, the trial justices of the adjoining towns, may perform all acts and duties appertaining to the office of trial justice during the continuance of such vacancy; and all proceedings instituted during such a vacancy shall be finally determined by the trial justice instituting the same; and when such a vacancy occurs, all the proceedings and business pending in said court shall stand continued to the first Tuesday of the month next after such vacancy shall be filled.

Trial justices may act in cases of resignation, death or removal of judge's residence.

Section 11. In case of sickness, absence from the city or other disability of the judge to attend at the regular times of holding said court for the transaction of civil business as provided in section nine, the said court shall stand adjourned until the next term, and so from term to term, without cost to either party, until the judge is able to attend; and during such sickness,

In case of absence or disability of judge, court shall stand adjourned.

CHAP. 114

—may appoint person to enter actions.

—criminal jurisdiction shall devolve on trial justices if judge cannot perform the duties.

Writs and processes, form of.

—powers of court.

—City marshal, deputy marshal and police officers shall attend court when requested.

City of Rockland shall provide rooms for court, stationery, etc.

—salary of judge.

—judge shall not act as attorney in cases within jurisdiction of court.

Judge may appoint a recorder.

absence, or other disability, any person that the judge may appoint may enter actions at the regular term and make such entries under them as necessary. If the judge is unable to perform the other duties of his office, the criminal jurisdiction of said court shall devolve exclusively upon the trial justices mentioned in section ten, and all proceedings instituted during that time shall be finally determined by the trial justices before whom the same are instituted.

Section 12. The writs and processes in civil actions, issued from said court, shall be the same as now provided by law, and shall be served in time and manner as now provided by law in case of writs issued by trial justices, and be obeyed and executed throughout the state, and the costs and fees allowed to parties and attorneys in actions in this court shall be the same as allowed by law in actions before trial justices except as otherwise provided in this act. Said court is hereby authorized to administer oaths, render judgment, issue executions, certify copies of its records, punish for contempt and compel attendance, and to make all such rules and regulations not repugnant to law as may be necessary and proper for the administration of justice and to facilitate its business; and the provisions of law relating to practice and proceedings in the aforesaid matters in the supreme judicial court in civil cases, are hereby extended to said court as far as applicable; and all acts relating to courts and judicial proceedings are hereby modified so as to give full effect to this act. The city marshal, the deputy marshal and the police officers of the said city shall be in attendance on said court when requested to do so by the judge for the purpose of preserving order, and shall execute all legal orders to them directed by the court.

Section 13. Said city of Rockland shall have power and it shall be its duty to raise money to provide suitable room or rooms in which to hold said court, and to furnish the same in an appropriate manner, including stationery, record books, fuel, lights, and other things necessary to accommodate said court. The judge of said court shall receive from said city in quarter-yearly payments, at the close of each quarter, an annual salary of eight hundred dollars, which shall be in full for all fees pertaining to said office, except copies; and the judge of said court shall not act as counsel or attorney in any case within the exclusive jurisdiction of said court, nor in such matter or thing which may depend on or have relation to any case, matter or thing which has been or is depending in said court.

Section 14. The judge of said court may if he chooses at his own expense, appoint a recorder for said court during his pleasure, who shall be a justice of the peace for said county, and a citizen of said Rockland, who may make the records of said court.

Section 15. Any trial justice of said city, if it has any, and if not, of either of the adjoining towns, may take cognizance of any action, matter or thing within the jurisdiction of a trial justice, wherein the judge of said court or recorder is a party interested. *When judge or recorder is interested, action may be brought before trial justice.*

Section 16. All civil actions which shall at the time this act takes effect be pending in said police court, or be returnable thereto, and all other actions, suits, matters, and things which may then be pending in said police court, and all writs, warrants, recognizances and processes returnable to, and which would have had day therein, had not this act been passed, shall thereupon be returnable to, have day in and be fully acted upon by the police court established by this act; and the said police court shall have full power and authority to grant any execution to carry into effect any judgment rendered in said police court heretofore existing, in the same manner as the said police court might have done had not this act passed. *Pending actions, how disposed of.*

Section 17. The records and papers of any police or municipal court now or heretofore existing in said Rockland shall be treated and be the records and papers of this court and certified as such. *Existing records and papers, how treated.*

Section 18. All acts and parts of acts inconsistent with this act and all acts heretofore passed in relation to any police or municipal court in said Rockland, are hereby repealed. *Inconsistent acts repealed.*

Section 19. This act shall so far take effect when approved as to make valid writs and processes made returnable to terms of court held hereunder, if they are otherwise properly brought. *When this act shall take effect.*

Approved March 4, 1908.

Chapter 115.

An Act authorizing the Great Northern Paper Company to locate, erect and maintain piers and booms in the Kennebec river.

Be it enacted by the Senate and House of Representatives in Legislature assembled, as follows:

Section 1. The Great Northern Paper Company, its successors and assigns, are hereby authorized and empowered to locate, erect and maintain in the Kennebec river, between land of the Great Northern Paper Company and land of B. P. J. Weston in the town of Madison and the land of the heirs of George W. Walker and land of B. F. Walker in the town of Anson, piers and booms for the purpose of collecting, holding *Great Northern Paper Company authorized to erect piers and booms in Kennebec river. —purpose.*

CHAP. 115

—works, how constructed.

and sorting logs, pulp wood and other lumber coming down said Kennebec river. Said works shall be so constructed as to provide for the prompt and convenient passage of all logs, pulp wood and other lumber that may come within the same, without unreasonable or unnecessary delay; and it shall be the duty of said Great Northern Paper Company to sort and turn out at least twenty-two thousand five hundred logs per day on the average, each week, through said booms, when there is that number therein; but in case said Great Northern Paper Company does not sort and turn out the required number, the Kennebec Log Driving Company, upon notice to said Great Northern Paper Company in writing, left at its office, shall have the right to put men of its own selection upon said booms at the charge and expense of said Great Northern Paper Company, in order that the required number of logs may be put through the same; but nothing herein contained shall make said Great Northern Paper Company liable for any delay caused by said piers and booms except as herein otherwise specified. Any stray logs, pulp wood or other lumber not destined for use and manufacture at the mills of said Great Northern Paper Company, if found in the storage booms of said Great Northern Paper Company shall be turned out thereof by said Great Northern Paper Company at its own charge and expense upon demand in writing of the owners thereof or of said Kennebec Log Driving Company. All damages for flowage caused by the construction of said piers and booms shall be determined by the county commissioners of Somerset county.

—stray logs, etc., shall be turned out.

—damage for flowage.

Liabilities.

Section 2. Said Great Northern Paper Company shall be liable to indemnify the Kennebec Log Driving Company and the log owners for any logs or damage by reason of logs or other lumber lodged on lands adjoining the waters affected by any works constructed under this act whenever said lodgment is caused by any jam produced by said works.

May take lands.

Section 3. Said Great Northern Paper Company, its successors and assigns, may take such lands as may be necessary for the erection and maintenance of said piers and booms mentioned in section one and connect the same with the shores, and may with their agents and teams pass and repass over said shores to and from the same over the lands of other persons, for the purposes aforesaid and for the operation and management of said booms. Said company shall be held liable to pay all damages that shall be sustained by any person or persons by the taking of any lands or rights of way and for any other injuries resulting from said acts; and if any person sustaining damage as aforesaid shall not agree with said company upon the sum

—liabilities.

to be paid therefor, either party on petition to the county commissioners of Somerset county may have said damage assessed by them; and subsequent proceedings and rights of appeal thereon shall be had in the same manner and under the same conditions, restrictions and limitations as are by law prescribed in the case of damages by the laying out of highways.

—damages, and subsequent proceedings.

Section 4. This act shall take effect when approved.

Approved March 4, 1903.

Chapter 116.

An Act relative to the Clinton Electric Light and Power Company.

Be it enacted by the Senate and House of Representatives in Legislature assembled, as follows:

Section 1. The Clinton Electric Light and Power Company, a corporation organized under the general laws of the state of Maine, is hereby authorized to make, generate, sell, distribute and supply gas and electricity for lighting, heating, manufacturing and mechanical purposes in the town of Clinton.

Clinton Electric Light and Power Company authorized to supply gas and electricity in town of Clinton.

Section 2. The inhabitants of the town of Clinton are hereby authorized to contract with said company for lighting said town for such time and upon such terms as they may by vote determine.

Inhabitants may contract for lighting town.

Section 3. This act shall take effect when approved.

Approved March 4, 1903.

Chapter 117.

An Act to incorporate the Saint John River Toll Bridge Company.

Be it enacted by the Senate and House of Representatives in Legislature assembled, as follows:

Section 1. Allen E. Hammond, Peter C. Keegan, Charles A. Milliken, Arthur W. Brown, Thomas Malcolm, Thomas J. Cochran, John M. Stevens, Henry A. Gagnon and Earle H. Gowing, their associates, successors and assigns, are hereby constituted a body corporate and politic, by the name of the Saint John River Toll Bridge Company, for the purpose of erecting and keeping in repair a bridge across the Saint John river between the town of Van Buren, in the county of Aroostook, in the state

Corporators.

—corporate name.

CHAP. 117

—may unite with a similar corporation.

—may purchase and hold real estate.

Location of bridge.

—manner of construction.

Toll established.

—rate of toll.

of Maine, and the parish of Saint Leonards, in the county of Madawaska, in the province of New Brunswick, and for said purpose and all others herein mentioned or incidental thereto, may consolidate or unite with any corporation organized for a similar purpose, acting in behalf of, or under, or by virtue of an act or authority granted by the legislature of the province of New Brunswick, or the parliament of the dominion of Canada, and all of the authority which may be conferred by such act of the legislature or parliament aforesaid, is likewise authorized and granted by this act, to the corporation formed by such consolidation, even though not specifically mentioned herein; and said corporation, or the corporation formed by such consolidation, shall have power to purchase and hold such personal and real estate as may be necessary for the use and purposes of said corporation, and the more advantageous carrying on of its business and accomplishment of its objects; may prosecute and defend suits at law, may have and use a common seal, may make by-laws for the management of their concerns, not repugnant to the laws of the state, and shall enjoy all the other powers and privileges incident to or usually granted to similar corporations.

Section 2. Said bridge shall be erected across the Saint John river opposite Van Buren village, in the town of Van Buren, in the most practicable place, shall be constructed of good materials, of a suitable height from the water, and not less than twenty-four feet wide, with suitable and sufficient coverings and railings for the safety of passengers, and sufficient passage ways shall be left for the passage of boats, rafts, logs and timber.

Section 3. A toll is hereby granted and established for the benefit of this corporation or the corporation formed by such consolidation, according to the rates following, namely: For every foot passenger five cents, for each horse and rider eight cents, for each sleigh, sled, cart, wagon, chaise, chair or sulky drawn by one beast ten cents, for each sleigh, sled, cart or wagon drawn by two beasts fifteen cents, for each additional horse or beast beyond two in sleighs, sleds, carts or wagons five cents, for droves of neat cattle, horses, mules and asses, three cents, for sheep and swine two cents each, and no additional toll shall be charged for persons actually traveling in any of the vehicles above named, but this exception shall not extend to persons taken in for the purpose of avoiding toll, and only one person as a driver to each team shall be allowed to pass free of toll, and said tolls may be commuted by this corporation or such corporation formed by the union or consolidation as aforesaid, by taking of him or them a smaller sum for the season, or for tickets sold in quantities.

WISCASSET WATER COMPANY. 187

CHAP. 118

Section 4. At the place of collecting tolls, this corporation, or the corporation formed by such union or consolidation, shall keep constantly exposed to the public view a board or sign upon which shall be plainly printed the rates of toll aforesaid; and whenever the toll gatherer shall be absent from the toll house, the gates shall be left open and the bridge toll free, and said toll shall commence on the day when the bridge is first opened for passengers.

Rates of toll shall be kept exposed to public view.

Section 5. If this corporation or a corporation formed by the union or consolidation of this corporation as provided for in this act, shall fail to begin the erection of such bridge within four years from the approval of this act, and to have the same ready for use by the first of May, in the year of our Lord one thousand nine hundred and eight, then this act shall be void and of no effect.

Time of commencement of erection, and of completion of bridge, fixed.

Section 6. The capital stock of said corporation shall be forty thousand dollars, which may be increased to fifty thousand dollars by a vote of said corporation, and be divided into shares of one hundred dollars each, and said company may issue bonds to an amount not exceeding the amount of its capital stock, for the construction of its bridge, to be secured by mortgage on its real and personal estate and franchise.

Capital stock.

—may issue bonds secured by mortgage.

Section 7. Any three of the persons named in the first section of this act, may call the first meeting of the corporation intended to be formed under the provisions of this act, by giving in hand to each of the corporators, or by mailing to him a notice of the time and place of meeting for the purpose of organizing, seven days before the day of meeting.

First meeting, how called.

Section 8. This act shall take effect when approved.

Approved March 4, 1903.

Chapter 118.

An Act to amend Chapter one hundred and fifty-four of the Private and Special Laws of eighteen hundred and ninety-five, relating to the charter of the Wiscasset Water Company.

Be it enacted by the Senate and House of Representatives in Legislature assembled, as follows:

Section nine of chapter one hundred and fifty-four of the private and special laws of eighteen hundred and ninety-five, is hereby amended as follows: the word "eight" in the first line of said section is stricken out and the word 'ten' inserted so that said section shall read as follows:

Section 9 of chapter 154 of the special laws of 1895, amended.

WESTBROOK MUNICIPAL COURT.

CHAP. 119

Shall commence construction within ten years.

'Section 9. This act shall become null and void in ten years from the approval thereof, unless the corporation shall have organized and commenced the actual construction of its works under this charter.'

Approved March 4, 1903.

Chapter 119.

An Act to amend Chapter two hundred and four of the Private and Special Laws of eighteen hundred and eighty-three, entitled "An Act to establish a Municipal Court in the town of Westbrook."

Be it enacted by the Senate and House of Representatives in Legislature assembled, as follows:

Section 1. Chapter two hundred and four of the private and special laws of eighteen hundred and eighty-three is hereby amended by striking out all after the enacting clause and substituting the following sections:

Westbrook municipal court established.

—judge, qualifications of.

—how appointed.

'Section 1. A municipal court is hereby established in and for the city of Westbrook, to be denominated the municipal court for the city of Westbrook, and to consist of one justice who shall be an inhabitant of said city and a person learned in the law and of sobriety of manners. Said judge shall be appointed as provided in the constitution for the appointment of judges of municipal and police courts; and shall be, ex-officio, a justice of the peace and of the quorum for the state, and have and exercise concurrent jurisdiction with trial justices of the county of Cumberland over all matters and things within their jurisdiction, and such authority and jurisdiction, additional thereto as are conferred upon him by this act.'

Exclusive original jurisdiction of court.

—original jurisdiction concurrent with superior court of county of Cumberland, wherein debt or damages do not exceed $50.

'Section 2. Said court shall have exclusive original jurisdiction of all offenses against the ordinances and by-laws of said city, and of the local board of health therein, and of such criminal offenses and misdemeanors committed therein, as are cognizable by trial justices; and of all civil actions wherein the debt or damages demanded do not exceed twenty dollars, and both parties reside in said city, except when the judge of said court is interested in any such action as party or attorney; and original jurisdiction concurrent with the superior court of the county of Cumberland in all civil actions wherein the debt or damages demanded do not exceed fifty dollars, exclusive of costs, in which any party to the action or person summoned as trustee shall reside, or, if not an inhabitant of the state, shall be commorant or have a place of business, in said city.'

'Section 3. Said court shall also have original jurisdiction concurrent with the superior court of the county of Cumberland, of the assaults and batteries described in section twenty-eight of chapter one hundred and eighteen of the revised statutes of eighteen hundred and eighty-three, and of all larcenies described in sections one, six, seven and nine of chapter one hundred and twenty of the revised statutes of eighteen hundred and eighty-three, when the value of the property is not alleged to exceed fifty dollars, and may punish for either of said crimes or offenses by a fine not exceeding fifty dollars, or by imprisonment not exceeding four months; provided, that when the offenses described in section twenty-eight of chapter one hundred and eighteen, and in sections one, six, seven and nine, of chapter one hundred and twenty aforesaid, are of a high and aggravated nature, the judge of said court may cause persons charged with such offenses to recognize with sufficient sureties to appear before the superior court of Cumberland county; and in default thereof commit them. Said court shall also have original jurisdiction, concurrent with said superior court, of the offense described in section six of chapter one hundred and twenty-four of the revised statutes of eighteen hundred and eighty-three.'

'Section 4. Nothing in this act shall be construed to give said court jurisdiction in any civil action in which the title to real estate, according to the pleadings and brief statements filed therein by either party, is in question; and all such actions brought therein shall be removed to the supreme judicial court, or otherwise disposed of as in like cases before a trial justice.'

'Section 5. Said court shall be held Saturday of each week, at ten o'clock in the forenoon for the transaction of civil business, at such place in the village of Saccarappa or Cumberland Mills in said city, as the city council shall provide, and all civil processes shall be made returnable accordingly; and it may be adjourned from time to time, by the judge at his discretion; but it shall be considered in constant session for the cognizance of criminal actions. The judge of said court may punish contempts against his authority by fine or imprisonment, or either, compel the attendance of witnesses, and administer oaths in civil and criminal cases.'

'Section 6. If said judge is prevented by any cause from attending at the time said court is to be held for civil business, it may be adjourned from day to day by a constable of said city, or any deputy sheriff residing therein, without detriment to any action then returnable or pending, until he can attend, when said action shall be entered or disposed of with the same effect as if it were the first day of the term; and it may be so adjourned

CHAP. 119

without day when necessary, in which event, pending actions shall be considered as continued, and actions then returnable may be returned and entered at the next term with the same effect as if originally made returnable at said term.'

Seal.

—records, how kept.

'Section 7. The seal of said court shall remain as already established; and in addition to the judicial duties imposed upon the judge of said court by this act, he shall cause the records of said court to be kept in a legible hand or typewritten, or printed in whole or in part by some person of either sex to be appointed by himself for the purpose; and perform all other duties required of similar tribunals in this state; and copies of such records duly certified by said judge shall be legal evidence in all courts. All writs and processes issuing from said court shall be in the usual forms, bear the teste of the judge, and be signed by him; and shall be served as like precepts are required to be served when issued by trial justices. But warrants in criminal cases issuing from said court shall be made returnable before the same; and no writ in a civil action shall be made returnable at a term of said court to begin more than two calendar months after the commencement of the action.'

—writs and processes, form of.

Actions, when entered.

—pleas or motions in abatement, when filed.

'Section 8. Actions in said court shall be entered on the first day of the term, and not afterwards, except by special permission. When a defendant legally served, fails to enter his appearance by himself or his attorney on the first day of the return term, he shall be defaulted; but if he afterwards appears during the term, the court may, for sufficient cause, permit the default to be taken off. Pleas or motions in abatement must be filed on or before the day of the entry of the action. The defendant may file his pleadings, which shall be the general issue with a brief statement of special matter of defense, on or before the return day of the writ, and must file them on or before the first day of the next term, or he shall be defaulted, unless the court, for good cause, enlarge the time, for which it may impose reasonable terms. All actions of forcible entry and detainer, seasonably answered to, shall be in order for trial at the return term, and shall remain so until tried or otherwise finally disposed of, unless continued by consent or on motion of either party for good cause, in which latter case, the court may impose such terms as it deems reasonable; but all other actions, unless defaulted or finally disposed of, shall be continued as of course, and be in order for trial at the next term.'

—forcible entry and detainer.

Costs and fees allowed to parties, attorneys and witnesses.

'Section 9. The costs and fees allowed to parties, attorneys and witnesses in all actions in said court shall be the same as allowed by trial justices in actions before them, when the debt or damages recovered do not exceed twenty dollars exclusive of costs, except that the plaintiff if he prevails shall be allowed one dollar for his writ, and the defendant if he prevails one dollar for his pleadings. But in all actions in which the amount recovered exceeds twenty dollars exclusive of costs, the costs and fees allowed to parties, attorneys and witnesses shall be the same as in the superior court for the county of Cumberland, except that the defendant if he prevails shall be allowed two dollars for his pleadings.'

'Section 10. The judge of said court shall demand and receive the same fees as are allowed to trial justices in similar cases, except that he shall receive one dollar for a complaint and warrant in criminal actions, twenty-five cents for the entry and five cents for a blank writ in a civil action. An accurate account of the fees so received by said judge shall be by him laid before the county commissioners of Cumberland county, and he shall pay the same into the county treasury quarterly on or before the first days of January, April, July and October of each year.' *Fees allowed to judge.*

—shall pay fees into county treasury.

'Section 11. The judge of said court shall receive a salary of eight hundred dollars per year to be paid him in quarterly payments from the county treasury of Cumberland county, which shall be in full for his services as such judge; and he shall receive an additional sum not to exceed two hundred dollars per year, at the discretion of said county commissioners, to defray the cost of keeping the records of said court. All blanks, civil and criminal, dockets and record books, required by said court, shall be furnished by the county of Cumberland.' *Salary of judge.*

'Section 12. All the provisions of the statutes of this state in relation to attachments of real and personal property, and the levy of execution on the same shall be applicable to actions brought in said court, which shall have authority to issue execution to be satisfied in the same manner as though issuing from the supreme judicial court, except that no such execution shall be levied on real estate unless the debt or damages therein exceed the sum of twenty dollars.' *Attachments of real and personal property, and levy of execution.*

'Section 13. Any party may appeal from a sentence or judgment of said court to the then next term for civil or criminal business, as the case may require, of the court having jurisdiction within the county of Cumberland, by appeal from trial justices and such appeal shall be taken and prosecuted in the same manner from a sentence or judgment of a trial justice.' *Appeal, how taken.*

'Section 14. Trial justices are hereby restricted from exercising any jurisdiction in said Westbrook over any matter or thing, civil or criminal, except such as are within the jurisdiction of justices of the peace and of the quorum, and except that they may issue warrants in complaints for criminal offenses *Jurisdiction of trial justices restricted.*

CHAP. 120

SMITH CEMETERY ASSOCIATION.

returnable before said court; or in case of the death, disability, or long continued absence from the state, of the judge, before themselves or some other trial justice within and for said county.'

Chapter 408 of special laws of 1885, and chapter 635 of special laws of 1898, repealed.

'Section 15. Chapter four hundred and eight of the private and special laws of eighteen hundred and eighty-five and chapter six hundred and thirty-five of the private and special laws of eighteen hundred and ninety-three are hereby repealed.'

Section 2. This act shall take effect when approved.

Approved March 4, 1903.

Chapter 120.

An Act to incorporate the Smith Cemetery Association of Palermo, Waldo County, Maine.

Be it enacted by the Senate and House of Representatives in Legislature assembled, as follows:

Corporators.

Section 1. Mitchell Delany, Leander A. Bowler, George M. Rowe, Samuel Marden and Henry S. Couillard, their associates, successors and assigns, are hereby made a corporation by the name of the Smith Cemetery Association, for the purpose of enlarging, improving and caring for the Smith cemetery, so called, in the town of Palermo.

—corporate name.

Powers.

Section 2. Said association shall have power to purchase land, to enlarge and improve said cemetery, to lay out lots and to sell the same, to receive and hold trust funds for the care or improvement of said cemetery or any part thereof.

Officers.

Section 3. The officers of said association shall be a president, vice president, secretary, treasurer and superintendent. The president, vice president, secretary, treasurer and superintendent, together with three or more members of the association who shall be elected by the association, shall constitute the executive committee. Said executive committee shall have full control of all work and improvements, the laying out of all moneys and the investment of all trust funds of the association.

Regular meetings.

—tenure of officers.

Section 4. Regular meetings of said association for the choice of officers and the transaction of any business that may legally come before said meetings shall be held annually on the first Saturday in May. Officers so chosen shall hold office for the term of one year or until their successors are elected.

First meeting how called.

Section 5. The first meeting of said corporation shall be called by written notice thereof, signed by any two corporators herein named, served upon each corporator, by giving him the same in hand, or by leaving same at his last usual place of abode, seven days before the time of said meeting.

Approved March 4, 1903.

Chapter 121.

An Act additional and amendatory to Chapter three hundred seventy-six of the Private and Special Laws of eighteen hundred eighty-nine, as amended by Chapter four hundred seventy-nine of the Private and Special Laws of nineteen hundred one, to enable the Maine Lake Ice Company to increase its capital stock.

Be it enacted by the Senate and House of Representatives in Legislature assembled, as follows:

Section 1. The Maine Lake Ice Company is hereby authorized and empowered to increase its capital stock to an amount not exceeding one million dollars, and is further authorized and empowered to issue its bonds, to pay, retire and cancel its outstanding bonds and the mortgage securing the same, and for the further construction and improvement of its works and plant, and for other purposes of its incorporation, and for such amount and upon such rate and time as it may deem expedient, not to exceed the sum of one million dollars; and to secure such bonds by mortgage or deed of trust of all, or any part of its franchise, property, rights and privileges now owned or to be hereafter acquired.

Capital stock increased.

—may issue bonds.

—may mortgage property.

Section 2. Said corporation may hold real and personal property to an amount not exceeding one million dollars.

May hold real and personal property not to exceed $1,000,000.

Section 3. This act shall take effect when approved.

Approved March 4, 1908.

Chapter 122.

An Act to incorporate Union Power Company.

Be it enacted by the Senate and House of Representatives in Legislature assembled, as follows:

Section 1. Deola C. Getchell, George C. Cary, Edward E. Talbot, with their associates, successors and assigns, are hereby made a corporation under the name of Union Power Company, for the purpose of manufacturing, generating, selling, leasing, transmitting, distributing and supplying electricity for heating, manufacturing and mechanical purposes not including lighting, in the towns of Machias and Machiasport.

Corporators.

—corporate name.

—purposes.

Section 2. Said corporation for the purposes aforesaid is hereby authorized to set poles and to construct, lay, maintain and operate lines of wires or other material in, through, under, over and along any and all streets and ways of said towns, and under or over tide waters in said towns, subject, however, to the per-

May set poles, etc.

Chap. 123 —restrictions.	mission of the municipal officers thereof and under such reasonable restrictions as they may impose and subject to the general laws of the state regulating the erection of poles and wires for electrical purposes.
Capital stock.	Section 3. The capital stock of said company shall not exceed fifty thousand dollars, divided into shares of the par value of one hundred dollars each.
May issue bonds. —may mortgage property. —proviso.	Section 4. Said company is hereby authorized to issue its bonds for the construction of its works upon such rates and terms as it may deem expedient, and secure the same by mortgage of the franchise and property of said company. But the amount of said bonds so issued shall not exceed fifty thousand dollars in all, and shall not exceed the amount of capital stock subscribed for.
First meeting, how called.	Section 5. The first meeting of said company may be called by written notice thereof, signed by any incorporator herein named, serving upon each incorporator by a copy of the same in hand or mailed, postage paid, at least seven days prior to the day named therein for such meeting.
Shall organize and commence construction within two years.	Section 6. This act shall become null and void in two years from the time when the same takes effect, unless the corporation shall have organized and commenced the construction of its works under this charter.
	Section 7. This act shall take effect when approved.

Approved March 4, 1908.

Chapter 123.

An Act to incorporate the Merrill Trust Company.

Be it enacted by the Senate and House of Representatives in Legislature assembled, as follows:

Corporators.	Section 1. Edgerton R. Burpee, Horace C. Chapman, Milton S. Clifford, Henry F. Dowst, William Engel, Edwin G. Merrill, Henry Prentiss, Wilson D. Wing and Frederick H. Appleton, or such of them as may by vote accept this charter, with their associates, successors and assigns, are hereby made a body corporate and politic, to be known as the Merrill Trust Company,
—corporate name.	and as such shall be possessed of all the powers, privileges and immunities, and subject to all the duties and obligations conferred on corporations by law.
Location.	Section 2. The corporation hereby created shall be located at Bangor, Penobscot county, Maine.
Purposes.	Section 3. The purposes of said corporation and the business which it may perform, are; first, to receive on deposit money,

coin, bank notes, evidences of debt, accounts of individuals, companies, corporations, municipalities and states, allowing interest thereon, if agreed, or as the by-laws of said corporation may provide; second, to borrow money, to loan money on credits or real estate, or personal or collateral security, and to negotiate loans and sales for others; third, to purchase, erect, own, maintain and operate safe deposit vaults with boxes, safes and other facilities therein to be rented to other parties for the safe keeping of moneys, securities, stocks, jewelry, plate, valuable papers and documents, and other property susceptible of being deposited therein, and to receive on deposit for safe keeping property of any kind entrusted to it for that purpose; fourth, to hold and enjoy all such estate real, personal and mixed as may be obtained by the investment of its capital stock or any other moneys and funds that may come into its possession in the course of its business and dealings, and the same sell, grant and dispose of; fifth, to act as agent for issuing, registering and countersigning certificates, bonds, stocks and all evidences of debt or ownership in property; sixth, to hold by grant, assignment, transfer, devise or bequest any real or personal property or trusts duly created, and to execute trusts of every description; seventh, to act as executor, administrator, guardian, receiver or assignee with the same powers and duties as are imposed by law upon natural persons acting in the same capacities, and subject to the same control of the court having jurisdiction of the same in all proceedings relating to the exercise of these powers; all papers may be signed and sworn to by any officer designated by the corporation for that purpose, and the officers shall be subject to citation and examination in the same manner and to the same extent as natural persons acting in the same capacities. No sureties shall be required upon the bond of the corporation when acting in said capacities unless the court or officer approving said bond shall require it; eighth, to hold for safe keeping all kinds of personal or mixed property, and to act as agents for the owners thereof, and of real estate for the collection of income on the same and for the management and sale of the same; ninth, to do in general all the business that may lawfully be done by trust and banking companies.

Section 4. The capital stock of said corporation shall not be less than one hundred thousand dollars, divided into shares of one hundred dollars each, with the right to increase the said capital stock at any time, by vote of the shareholders, to any amount not exceeding five hundred thousand dollars. Said corporation shall not commence business as a trust or banking company, until stock to the amount of at least one hundred thousand dollars shall have been subscribed and paid in, in cash.

CHAP. 123

Shall not make loan on security of its own capital stock.

Section 5. Said corporation shall not make any loan or discount on the security of the shares of its own capital stock, nor be the purchaser or holder of any such shares unless necessary to prevent loss upon a debt previously contracted in good faith; and all stock so acquired shall, within six months from the time of its acquisition, be disposed of at public or private sale.

Board of directors.

Section 6. All the corporate powers of this corporation shall be exercised by a board of directors, who shall be residents of this state, whose number and term of office shall be determined by a vote of the shareholders at the first meeting held by the incorporators and at each annual meeting thereafter.

—executive board.

The affairs and powers of the corporation may, at the option of the shareholders, be entrusted to an executive board of five members to be, by vote of the shareholders, elected from the full board of directors. The directors of said corporation shall be sworn to the proper discharge of their duties, and they shall hold office until others are elected and qualified in their stead.

—vacancies, how filled.

If a director dies, resigns, or becomes disqualified for any cause, the remaining directors may appoint a person to fill the vacancy until the next annual meeting of the corporation. The oath of office of such director shall be taken within thirty days of his election, or his office shall become vacant. The clerk of such corporation shall, within ten days, notify such directors of their election, and within thirty days shall publish the list of all persons who have taken the oath of office as directors.

Board of investment.

Section 7. The board of directors of said corporation shall constitute the board of investment of said corporation.

—shall keep record of loans.

Said directors shall keep in a separate book, specially provided for the purpose, a record of all loans, and investments of every description, made by said institution substantially in the order of time when such loans or investments are made, which shall show that such loans or investments have been made with the approval of the investment committee of said corporation, which shall indicate such particulars respecting such loans or investments as the bank examiner shall direct. This book shall be submitted to the trustees or directors and to the bank examiner whenever requested. Such loans or investments shall be classified in the book as the bank examiner shall direct.

—loans to officers or directors, how made.

No loan shall be made to any officer or director of said banking or trust company except by the unanimous approval of the executive board in writing, and said corporation shall have no authority to hire money or to give notes unless by vote of the said board duly recorded.

Directors must own at least ten shares of stock.

Section 8. No person shall be eligible to the position of a director of said corporation who is not the actual owner of ten shares of the stock.

MERRILL TRUST COMPANY.   197

CHAP. 123

Section 9. Said corporation, after beginning to receive deposits, shall, at all times, have on hand in lawful money, as a reserve, not less than fifteen per cent of the aggregate amount of its deposits which are subject to withdrawal on demand, provided, that in lieu of lawful money, two-thirds of said fifteen per cent may consist of balances, payable on demand, due from any national or state bank. *Reserve fund.*

Section 10. All the property or money held in trust by this corporation shall constitute a special deposit and the accounts thereof and of said trust department shall be kept separate, and such funds and the investment or loans of them shall be specially appropriated to the security and payment of such deposits, and not be subject to any other liabilities of the corporation; and for the purpose of securing the observance of this proviso, said corporation shall have a trust department in which all business pertaining to such trust property shall be kept separate and distinct from its general business. *Trust funds shall constitute a special deposit.*

Section 11. An administrator, executor, assignee, guardian or trustee, any court of law or equity, including courts of probate and insolvency, officers and treasurers of towns, cities, counties, and savings banks of the state of Maine may deposit any moneys, bonds, stocks, evidences of debt or of ownership in property, or any personal property, with said corporation, and any of said courts may direct any person deriving authority from them to so deposit the same. *Administrators, etc., may deposit in.*

Section 12. The shareholders of this corporation shall be individually responsible, equally and ratably, and not one for the other, for all contracts, debts and engagements of said corporation, to a sum equal to the amount of the par value of the shares owned by each in addition to the amount invested in said shares. *Responsibility of shareholders*

Section 13. Such corporation shall set apart as a guaranty fund not less than ten per cent of its net earnings in each and every year until such fund with the accumulated interest thereon, shall amount to one-fourth of the capital stock of said corporation. *Guaranty fund.*

Section 14. The shares of said corporation shall be subject to taxation in the same manner and rate as are the shares of national banks. *Taxation.*

Section 15. Said corporation shall be subject to examination by the bank examiner, who shall visit it at least once in every year, and as much oftener as he may deem expedient. At such visits he shall have free access to its vaults, books and papers, and shall thoroughly inspect and examine all the affairs of said corporation, and make such inquiries as may be necessary to *Shall be subject to examination by bank examiner.*

198 PORTLAND WIDOWS' WOOD SOCIETY.

CHAP. 124

—statement shall be published.

ascertain its condition and ability to fulfill all its engagements. If upon examination of said corporation the examiner is of the opinion that its investments are not in accordance with law, or said corporation is insolvent, or its condition is such as to render its further proceedings hazardous to the public or to those having funds in its custody, or is of the opinion that it has exceeded its powers or failed to comply with any of the rules or restrictions provided by law, he shall have such authority and take such action as is provided for in the case of savings banks by chapter forty-seven of the revised statutes. He shall preserve in a permanent form a full record of his proceedings, including a statement of the condition of said corporation. A copy of such statement shall be published by said corporation immediately after the annual examination of the same in some newspaper published where said corporation is established. If no paper is published in the town where said corporation is established, then it shall be published in a newspaper printed in the nearest city or town. The necessary expenses of the bank examiner while making such examination shall be paid by the corporation.

First meeting, how called.

Section 16. Any five of the corporators named in this act may call the first meeting of the corporation by mailing a written notice, signed by all, postage paid, to each of the other corporators, seven days at least before the day of the meeting, naming the time, place and purpose of such meeting, and at such meeting the necessary officers may be chosen, by-laws adopted, and any other corporate business transacted.

Section 17. This act shall take effect when approved.

Approved March 5, 1902.

Chapter 124.

An Act to amend Chapter three hundred and one of the Private and Special Laws of eighteen hundred fifty, entitled "An Act to incorporate the Portland Widows' Wood Society," as amended by Chapter one hundred forty-five of the Private and Special Laws of eighteen hundred seventy-nine.

Be it enacted by the Senate and House of Representatives in Legislature assembled, as follows:

Section 2 of chapter 301 of special laws of 1850, amended.

Section 1. Section two of chapter three hundred and one of the private and special laws of eighteen hundred and fifty is hereby amended so that, as amended, said section shall read as follows:

Shall have a seal, may sue and be sued.

'Section 2. Said corporation shall have a seal, may sue or be sued in its corporate capacity, and appoint an agent or attorney to prosecute and defend suits with the power of substitution.'

PORTLAND WIDOWS' WOOD SOCIETY.

CHAP. 124

Section 2. Section three of said chapter three hundred and one, as amended by chapter one hundred and forty-five of the private and special laws of eighteen hundred and seventy-nine, is hereby further amended so that, as amended, said section shall read as follows:

Section 8 of chapter 301, as amended by chapter 145 of special laws of 1879, further amended.

'Section 3. Said corporation may take and hold by gift, bequest, devise, purchase, or otherwise, real and personal property to an amount not exceeding two hundred thousand dollars in value; and may manage and dispose of the same in any manner consistent with the purposes of said corporation, and with the terms under which said property is acquired by it.'

May take and hold property by gift, etc.

Section 3. Section four of said chapter three hundred and one, as amended by said chapter one hundred and forty-five, is hereby further amended so that, as amended, said section shall read as follows:

Section 4 of chapter 301, as amended by said chapter 145, further amended.

'Section 4. Said corporation may annually elect a president, vice president, treasurer, secretary, and such other officers and such number of directors as it may deem expedient; and may adopt by-laws and regulations, not repugnant to the laws of the state, for the management of its affairs, including the manner of calling and conducting its meetings, conditions of membership, constitution of a quorum, and the bestowal and distribution of its charities.'

Officers.

Section 4. Section six of said chapter three hundred and one, as amended by said chapter one hundred and forty-five, is hereby further amended so that, as amended, said section shall read as follows:

Section 6 of chapter 301, as amended by said chapter 145, further amended.

'Section 6. No officer or member of said corporation, except the treasurer, the secretary, and the distributors of fuel, shall receive any salary or other pecuniary compensation for his services.'

Who shall receive salary.

Section 5. Section seven of said chapter three hundred and one, as amended by said chapter one hundred and forty-five, is hereby further amended so that, as amended, said section shall read as follows:

Section 7 of chapter 301, as amended by said chapter 145, further amended.

'Section 7. The treasurer shall give a bond for the faithful performance of his duties in such sum and with such surety or sureties as the board of directors may require.'

Treasurer shall give bond.

Section 6. Section five of said chapter three hundred and one of the private and special laws of eighteen hundred and fifty, is hereby repealed.

Section 5 of chapter 301 of special laws of 1850, repealed.

Section 7. This act shall take effect when approved.

Approved March 6, 1903.

Chapter 125.

An Act amendatory to Section six of Chapter four hundred and ninety-five of the Special Laws of eighteen hundred and eighty-five, entitled "An Act to incorporate the People's Ferry Company."

Be it enacted by the Senate and House of Representatives in Legislature assembled, as follows:

Section six of chapter four hundred and ninety-five of special laws of eighteen hundred and eighty-five is hereby amended so that said section, as amended, shall read as follows:

'Section 6. The time for running said boat or boats, unless prevented by accident or unavoidable casualty shall on week days be not later than six o'clock in the forenoon and not less than two round trips per hour shall be run up to and until six and one-half o'clock in the afternoon, and on Sundays the time for running shall be not later than eight o'clock in the forenoon and not less than two round trips per hour shall be run up to and until six o'clock in the afternoon.

And the said People's Ferry Company is hereby given the further power and authority to run as many other trips before, after and during the above mentioned hours as it may deem for its best interests in addition to those required, using for these trip or trips a boat or boats for teams, freight and passengers or a boat or boats for passengers and freight only as the said company may deem expedient.'

This act shall take effect when approved.

Approved March 6, 1903.

Chapter 126.

An Act to amend the charter of the Lewiston, Brunswick and Bath Street Railway.

Be it enacted by the Senate and House of Representatives in Legislature assembled, as follows:

Section 1. The locations of the rails, posts, wires and fixtures of the Lewiston and Auburn Horse Railroad Company, the Bath Street Railway and of the Lewiston, Brunswick and Bath Street Railway in the streets, roads and ways of Auburn, Lewiston, Webster, Lisbon, Topsham, Brunswick, West Bath and Bath are hereby confirmed and made valid. This section shall apply only to locations heretofore legally and finally approved.

Section 2. The said Lewiston, Brunswick and Bath Street Railway is hereby authorized to sell or lease its property and franchises to any street railroad company whose lines as constructed or chartered would form connecting or continuous lines with the lines of the said Lewiston, Brunswick and Bath Street Railway as constructed or chartered, and in such case the corporation so purchasing or leasing said property and franchises shall be entitled to all the privileges and be subject to all appropriate conditions and limitations contained in the charter and franchises of the said Lewiston, Brunswick and Bath Street Railway. Any street railroad whose lines as constructed or chartered would form connecting or continuous lines with the lines of the said Lewiston, Brunswick and Bath Street Railway as constructed or chartered is hereby authorized to so purchase or lease the property and franchises of the said Lewiston, Brunswick and Bath Street Railway.

—connecting lines authorized to purchase or lease.

Section 3. This act shall take effect when approved.

Approved March 6, 1903.

Chapter 127.

An Act to increase the capital stock of the Ticonic Foot Bridge Company.

Be it enacted by the Senate and House of Representatives in Legislature assembled, as follows:

Section 1. Section five of chapter thirty-seven of the private and special laws of eighteen hundred and ninety-nine is hereby amended by striking out the word "twenty-five" in the second line and inserting instead thereof the word 'forty' so that said section as amended, shall read as follows:

Section 5 of chapter 37 of special laws of 1899, amended.

'Section 5. Said corporation may issue stock to an amount not exceeding forty thousand dollars and may issue bonds not exceeding the amount of stock issued.'

Amount of capital stock. —bonds.

Section 2. This act shall take effect when approved.

Approved March 6, 1903.

Chapter 128.

An Act to authorize the town of Bucksport to retire its bonded indebtedness and to issue new bonds.

Be it enacted by the Senate and House of Representatives in Legislature assembled, as follows:

Town of Bucksport authorized to retire its bonded indebtedness.

Section 1. The town of Bucksport is hereby authorized to retire its bonded indebtedness, by purchase or exchange, at the maturity thereof in such form and amount, and with such rates of interest, and payable at such times and in such manner as shall be determined by vote of said town, under a proper article in the warrant at a legal town meeting; provided, however, that nothing herein contained shall authorize any increase in the indebtedness of said town.

—proviso.

May pass votes to carry out provisions of this act.

Section 2. To carry into effect the provisions of this act, said town is hereby authorized to pass such votes as may be deemed necessary and proper to enter into and make any contract or agreement not inconsistent with the laws of this state.

Section 3. This act shall take effect when approved.

Approved March 6, 1903.

Chapter 129.

An Act relating to the Camden Trotting Park Association.

Be it enacted by the Senate and House of Representatives in Legislature assembled, as follows:

Powers and privileges.

Section 1. The Camden Trotting Park Association, a corporation organized under the general laws of the state of Maine, and located at Camden, in the county of Knox, shall have and exercise all the powers, rights and privileges granted to and exercised by agricultural societies and similar corporations.

Shall have police power.

Section 2. Said corporation shall have all the police powers, together with all other powers and privileges, at all of its exhibitions of whatever name and nature, which are conferred upon agricultural societies by sections sixteen, seventeen and eighteen of chapter fifty-eight of the revised statutes.

Prohibitions, restrictions, forfeitures and penalties.

Section 3. The prohibitions, restrictions, forfeitures, and penalties provided by section nineteen of chapter fifty-eight of the revised statutes, shall be applicable to all exhibitions of said corporation.

Passing within enclosure of,

Section 4. Whoever, contrary to the regulations of said corporation, shall enter or pass within the enclosure of its exhibition or fair grounds, shall forfeit to such corporation a sum not exceeding five dollars, to be recovered on complaint.

Section 5. This act shall take effect when approved.

Approved March 6, 1903.

Chapter 130.

An Act to authorize the County Commissioners of Somerset County to borrow a sum of money with which to build an extension to the Court house in Skowhegan, in said county.

Be it enacted by the Senate and House of Representatives in Legislature assembled, as follows:

Section 1. The treasurer of the county of Somerset is hereby authorized to procure a loan, on the faith and responsibility of said county, of such sum or sums of money as the county commissioners of said county shall by order direct, not exceeding in all twenty-five thousand dollars, exclusive of and in addition to loans provided for by section seventeen of chapter seventy-eight of the revised statutes, as amended by chapter two hundred and seventy-six of the public laws of the state of Maine for the year eighteen hundred and eighty-nine, to be expended by and under the direction of the county commissioners of said county for the purpose of enlarging, improving and repairing the county court house and appurtenances thereof, in said county, the interest on said sum or sums to be paid annually, and the principal to be reimbursed by said county at such time or times as said commissioners may agree upon, but the whole amount to be paid within twenty years; and the said treasurer is hereby authorized to issue his scrip as county treasurer therefor, with coupons for interest attached, or to issue interest bearing, negotiable promissory notes of said county therefor, payable in manner as aforesaid, such scrip, and coupons and notes to be signed by the treasurer and countersigned by the county commissioners of said county.

Section 2. But said county commissioners shall not authorize the loan hereinbefore provided until after notice and public hearing thereon by said county commissioners, which hearing shall be given at the court house in Skowhegan the second Tuesday of June, nineteen hundred three, and notice thereof, setting forth the time, place and purposes of said hearing shall be given by publication in each and every newspaper published in said county, the first publication in each newspaper to be at least thirty days before said hearing.

204 KENNEBUNK.

CHAP. 131

May take land contiguous to court house lot.

Section 3. For the purpose of carrying out the provisions of this act, the county commissioners of Somerset county are authorized to take by eminent domain, any land that may be necessary, contiguous to the court house lot, in said Skowhegan. They shall file in the registry of deeds' office in the county of Somerset, plans of the location of any land taken under the provisions of this act, and no entry shall be made on any land, except to make surveys, until the expiration of ten days from said filing; and with such plans the said commissioners may file in the office of the registry of deeds aforesaid, a statement of the damages they are ready to pay any person for any property so taken, and if the amount finally awarded does not exceed such sum, the county shall recover costs against such person, otherwise such person shall recover costs against the county. If any person is aggrieved by the award of damages made by the said county commissioners, they may appeal to the next term of the supreme judicial court for the county of Somerset, to be held at said Skowhegan, after thirty days from the date of the filing of said plans and statement in the office of the registry of deeds, and all subsequent proceedings shall be had in the same manner and under the same conditions, restrictions and limitations as are by law provided in the case of damages by the laying out of highways.

—damages, how awarded.

—appeal, how taken.

Section 4. This act shall take effect when approved.

Approved March 6, 1903.

Chapter 131.

An Act to authorize the town of Kennebunk to own and maintain an electric lighting and power plant.

Be it enacted by the Senate and House of Representatives in Legislature assembled, as follows:

Kennebec, town of, authorized to own electric lighting and power plant.

Section 1. The town of Kennebunk is hereby authorized to acquire, own, and maintain an electric lighting and power plant, and for such purpose said town is vested with power to raise money at its annual meeting, or at any legal meeting called for the purpose, for the purchase or lease of lands, water power, dams, manufactories and works for providing and supplying electricity, and for the purchase of dynamos and other apparatus necessary for equipping and properly maintaining an electric lighting and power plant.

—purposes.

May support lines of wire, etc., over streets and roads.

Section 2. Said town is also authorized to construct, lay, maintain and support lines of wire or other material for the transmission of electricity upon, under, along and over any and all streets and roads within the limits of said town, and for such purpose to erect, establish and maintain in and along said streets and roads all necessary poles, pipes and apparatus, provided that said poles, pipes and apparatus are so erected, established and maintained as not to unreasonably interfere with the public use of said streets and roads.

Section 3. Said town is also authorized to use the electricity by it manufactured and generated to light its streets, roads and public squares, and all buildings or parts of buildings owned, used or occupied by it; and said town is further authorized to sell, distribute and furnish electricity for lighting, heating and power to individuals and corporations within that part of said town which lies northerly of a straight line extending southwesterly from the center of Durrell's bridge, so called, on the Kennebunk river to the Wells town line and passing through a point on Fernald's Hill where the town way to Crescent Surf intersects with the road to Stony bridge, but said town shall not have like authority to sell, distribute and furnish electricty to individuals or corporations within that part of said town lying south of said line, and the rights of the Kennebunk Electric Light Company to sell and distribute electricity within said town shall not be limited by this act.

Section 4. Said town is further authorized to purchase or lease the rights, privileges, properties and franchises of any corporation organized for furnishing electricity for lighting or power within the territory of said town, and such corporation is hereby empowered to sell, transfer, convey or lease its rights, privileges, properties and franchises to said town.

Section 5. This act shall take effect when approved.

Approved March 7, 1903.

CHAP. 132

CITY OF AUBURN.

Chapter 132.

An Act to amend the charter of the City of Auburn.

Be it enacted by the Senate and House of Representatives in Legislature assembled, as follows:

Section 3 of chapter 471 of laws of 1868, amended.

Section 1. Section three of chapter four hundred and seventy-one of the laws of eighteen hundred sixty-eight is hereby amended by striking out in the sixth line of said section the word "majority," and inserting in place thereof the word 'plurality,' so that said section as amended shall read as follows:

Election of officers.

'Section 3. The mayor shall be an inhabitant of said city, and shall be elected from the citizens at large by the inhabitants thereof voting in their respective wards. One alderman and three common councilmen shall be elected by each ward, and shall be residents of the wards for which they are elected. All of said officers shall be elected by ballot by a plurality of the votes given, and shall hold their offices for one year from the third Monday in March and until others shall be elected in their places, and shall be sworn to the faithful performance of the duties of their respective offices.'

—by plurality.

Section 2 of chapter 173 of special laws of 1883, amended.

Section 2. Section two of chapter one hundred and seventy-three of the special laws of eighteen hundred eighty-three is hereby amended by striking out in the third line of said section the word "majority," and inserting in the place thereof the word 'plurality,' so that said section as amended shall read as follows:

Superintending school committee, elected by plurality.

'Section 2. The qualified voters in each ward shall at the annual municipal election next after the passage of this act, by a plurality of the votes cast, elect two of the residents of said ward as members of the superintending school committee, one of whom shall hold his office for the term of two years, and one for the term of one year, and the members of said committee in each ward so elected shall determine their respective terms of office by lot.'

Plurality of votes cast shall determine election of officers.

Section 3. All officers of the city of Auburn required by law to be elected by a majority of the votes cast shall hereafter be elected by a plurality of the votes cast, at any election.

Section 4. This act shall take effect when approved.

Approved March 7, 1903.

Chapter 133.

An Act to extend the charter of the Granite Trust Company.

Be it enacted by the Senate and House of Representatives in Legislature assembled, as follows:

Section 1. The rights, powers and privileges of the Granite Trust Company, which were granted by chapter three hundred and fifty-one of the private and special laws of nineteen hundred and one, are hereby extended for two years from the approval of this act; and the persons named in said act, their associates and successors, shall have all the rights, powers and privileges that were granted them by said act, to be exercised in the same manner and for the same purposes as specified in said act.

Section 2. This act shall take effect when approved.

Approved March 10, 1903.

Rights extended.

Chapter 134.

An Act to provide in part for the Expenditures of Government for the year nineteen hundred and three.

Be it enacted by the Senate and House of Representatives in Legislature assembled, as follows:

Section 1. In order to provide for the several acts and resolves of the legislature, requiring the payment of money from the treasury, and also to provide for the necessary expenditures of government for the current fiscal year of nineteen hundred and three, the following sums are hereby appropriated out of any moneys in the treasury, and the governor, with the advice and consent of the council, is authorized at any time prior to the first day of January next, to draw his warrant on the treasury for the same.

Act of appropriation for 1903.

Salaries of public officers, ninety-five thousand one hundred dollars	$95,100 00
Subordinate officers of state prison, ten thousand six hundred dollars	10,600 00
Private secretary to the governor, one thousand two hundred dollars	1,200 00
Clerks in secretary of state's office, three thousand two hundred dollars	3,200 00
Clerks in state treasurer's office, four thousand dollars	4,000 00
Clerks in adjutant general's office, one thousand eight Hundred dollars	1,800 00

Clerk in superintendent of schools' office, one thousand dollars	1,000 00
Clerk in commissioner of agriculture's office, one thousand dollars	1,000 00
Pension clerk, one thousand two hundred dollars..	1,200 00
Clerks in bank examiner's office, one thousand five hundred dollars	1,500 00
Clerk in state assessors' office, one thousand dollars,	1,000 00
Stenographers to justices supreme judicial court, twelve thousand dollars	12,000 00
Messenger to governor and council, five hundred dollars	500 00
Stenographer and typewriter, six hundred dollars,	600 00
Contingent fund of secretary of state, three hundred dollars	300 00
Contingent fund of state treasurer, eight hundred dollars	800 00
Indexing papers and records in land office, one thousand dollars	1,000 00
Transportation of documents, two thousand five hundred dollars	2,500 00
Transportation of mail, fifty dollars..............	50 00
Stationery, seven thousand dollars...............	7,000 00
Postage, six thousand dollars....................	6,000 00
Foreman, engineer and mail carrier, two thousand seven hundred dollars	2,700 00
Night watch, two thousand four hundred dollars...	2,400 00
Porters and laborers, six thousand dollars........	6,000 00
Furniture and repairs, eight thousand dollars....	8,000 00
Fuel and lights, seven thousand dollars..........	7,000 00
Freight and trucking, six hundred dollars........	600 00
Military pensions, three thousand five hundred dollars	3,500 00
Education of the blind, seven thousand dollars....	7,000 00
Inspectors of state prison and jails, one thousand five hundred dollars	1,500 00
Inspectors of steamboats, three thousand five hundred dollars	3,500 00
Inspector of dams and reservoirs, one hundred dollars	100 00

Amounting to the sum of one hundred ninety-four thousand six hundred fifty dollars............ $194,650 00

Section 2. This act shall take effect when approved.

Approved March 10, 1903.

Chapter 135.

An Act to grant testimonials of Honorable Service to Soldiers who served in the War with Spain.

Be it enacted by the Senate and House of Representatives in Legislature assembled, as follows:

Section 1. The governor is hereby authorized to issue testimonials of appropriate design to all soldiers who served in the war with Spain, and have been honorably discharged, and to widows or next of kin in such as have deceased. _{Testimonials to soldiers of Spanish war.}

Section 2. The sum of one thousand five hundred dollars, or as much thereof as may be necessary, is hereby appropriated for the purpose of carrying out the provisions of this act. _{Appropriation for.}

Section 3. This act to take effect when approved.

Approved March 10, 1903.

Chapter 136.

An Act to amend Resolve in favor of the town of Sanford.

Be it enacted by the Senate and House of Representatives in Legislature assembled, as follows:

Section 1. The resolve in favor of the town of Sanford approved March fourth, nineteen hundred three is hereby amended by striking out the word "two" in the second line and inserting in its place the word 'three' so that said resolve as amended, shall read as follows:

Resolved, That there be paid out of the school fund for the year one thousand nine hundred and three, to the town of Sanford, the sum of eight hundred fifty-nine dollars and twenty-three cents, being the amount due said town, on account of its failure to make its annual return by reason of sickness of superintendent.

Approved March 10, 1903.

Chapter 137.

An Act to amend the charter of the city of Auburn and to provide for a Board of Public Works.

Be it enacted by the Senate and House of Representatives in Legislature assembled, as follows:

Board of public works established.
—powers and duties of.
Section 1. A board, to be known as the Board of Public Works, is hereby established in and for the city of Auburn, which shall have and exercise all the powers and be charged with all the duties relative to the construction, maintenance, care and control of the streets, highways, bridges, sidewalks, drains and sewers in said city which are now conferred or imposed upon the city council, municipal officers and commissioner of streets, by the charter and ordinances of said city, and the general laws of the state; but this act shall not be construed to deprive the city council or municipal officers of said city of the jurisdiction conferred by law over proceedings for the location, alteration or discontinuance of streets in said city or of proceedings for the location of tracks in and upon the surface of said streets.

Election of board.
Section 2. This board shall consist of five members, one from each ward, who shall be elected by the city council in the month of March.

Tenure.
Section 3. At the first election one member shall be elected for one year, one for two years, one for three years, one for four years, and one for five years, and after the first election one member to be chosen each year for a term of five years unless it becomes necessary to fill a vacancy caused by death or resignation, in which event the election shall be for the unexpired term of the incumbent whose place has been made vacant, and such vacancy may be filled for the remainder of such unexpired term by ballot of the city council in joint convention.

Persons not eligible.
Section 4. No member of the city council shall be eligible for service upon this board.

Organization of board.
Section 5. This board shall on the third Monday in March or soon thereafter as practicable organize by the choice of one of its members as chairman, and shall elect a secretary whose duty it shall be to keep a record of the proceedings of the board, to notify members of meetings and perform such other duties as the board may direct.

Superintendent of streets and sewers.
—powers.
Section 6. The board shall also elect a superintendent of streets and sewers who shall have executive charge of work under the direction and control of the board and shall at all times conform to all rules and directions of said board. Said superintendent may contract for necessary labor and materials subject at all times to the approval of the board, to whom he

shall render an account monthly, or oftener if required, of all receipts, expenditures and outstanding bills.

Section 7. The weekly pay roll and all bills not passed upon by the board shall be approved by the chairman of the board, or in his absence by some member designated by him before being paid from the city treasury. *Approval of pay roll and bills.*

Section 8. The compensation of the superintendent of streets and sewers shall be fixed by the board and shall be paid from the appropriation made for the work of the board. *Compensation of superintendent of streets and sewers.*

Section 9. The board shall, at the beginning of each financial year, submit to the city council for its guidance in making appropriations, a statement of work proposed to be done in its department, with approximate estimates of cost, and such other information regarding its work as may seem to them proper or the city council may require, and shall at the close of the year make a full, detailed report to the city council of receipts and expenditures and of work done; said board shall have no authority to make expenditures in excess of the amount appropriated for its use by the city council, and no part of said appropriation shall be paid to any member of the board for services as a member of the board. *Board shall submit to city council a statement of proposed work. —with estimates of cost. —at close of year shall make full report. —shall not exceed appropriation.*

Section 10. This act shall take effect when accepted by the city council of the city of Auburn, and the first election of commissioners hereunder shall be held on the third Monday of March, nineteen hundred three, or as soon thereafter as practicable, if this act shall then have been accepted; otherwise, immediately upon such acceptance. All other acts or parts of acts now in force which conflict with this act, are hereby repealed. *Provisions for acceptance of this act.*

Section 11. This act shall take effect when approved so far as necessary to authorize the city council of the city of Auburn to take action relative to its acceptance.

Approved March 10, 1903.

Chapter 138.

An Act to Incorporate the Maine Midland Railroad Company.

Be it enacted by the Senate and House of Representatives in Legislature assembled, as follows:

Section 1. Edward P. Borden, of Philadelphia, in the state of Pennsylvania, Thomas B. Wanamaker, of Philadelphia, state of Pennsylvania, William P. Oglesby, of Philadelphia, state of Pennsylvania, Charles Eisenlohr, of Philadelphia, state of Pennsylvania, Arthur C. Denniston, of Philadelphia, state of Pennsyl- *Corporators.*

CHAP. 138

—corporate name.

vania, William D. Hewitt, of Burlington, state of New Jersey, Leonard Atwood, of Farmington, in the state of Maine, Edmond Eaton, of Livermore Falls, in the state of Maine, Philip H. Stubbs, of Strong, in the state of Maine, their associates, successors and assigns, are hereby made a corporation by the name of the Maine Midland Railroad Company, for the purpose of buying or leasing the property, capital stock, rights, privileges, immunities and franchises of the Wiscasset, Waterville and Farmington Railroad Company, and of thereafterwards exercising the powers of this act.

Capital stock.

—board of directors.

Section 2. The capital stock of such corporation shall consist of not more than twenty thousand shares, of the par value of one hundred dollars each, the amount to be fixed from time to time by the corporation. The immediate government of its affairs shall be vested in a board of directors to consist for one year from the time of the incorporation of said company of the corporators herein named and subsequently thereto said directors shall be chosen in accordance with the by-laws made and provided by said company, which by-laws, not inconsistent with law, said corporation shall have the power to make, ordain and publish.

May hold real and personal estate.

Section 3. The said corporation is authorized to hold for its purposes aforesaid so much real and personal estate as may be necessary and convenient therefor.

May purchase Wiscasset, Waterville and Farmington R. R. Co.

Section 4. The said corporation is further authorized to purchase or lease the property, capital stock, rights, privileges, immunities and franchises of the Wiscasset, Waterville and Farmington Railroad Company upon such terms as may be agreed upon; and upon such purchase or lease, the said Maine Midland Railroad Company shall have, hold, possess, exercise and enjoy all the locations, powers, privileges, rights, immunities, franchises, property and assets which at the time of such transfer shall then be had, held, possessed or enjoyed by the corporation so selling or leasing, and shall be subject to all the duties, restrictions and liabilities which the said Wiscasset, Waterville and Farmington Railroad Company shall then be subject to by reason of any contract, charter, or general or special law, or otherwise.

Wiscasset, Waterville and Farmington R. R. Co. may sell.

Section 5. The Wiscasset, Waterville and Farmington Railroad Company is hereby authorized to sell or lease its property, capital stock, rights, privileges, immunities and franchises to the said Maine Midland Railroad Company, upon such terms as may be mutually agreed upon, but any such sale or lease shall be made subject to all the outstanding liabilities of the said Wiscasset, Waterville and Farmington Railroad Company. In case of such sale or lease the said Maine Midland Railroad Company may mortgage the franchises and property so acquired for the security of any bonds or other indebtedness authorized by this act, but all such mortgages shall be subject to the outstanding bonds or other indebtedness of the said Wiscasset, Waterville and Farmington Railroad Company existing at the time of said sale or lease.

Section 6. All proceedings, suits at law or in equity, which may be pending at the time of such transfer, to which the said Wiscasset, Waterville and Farmington Railroad Company may be a party, may be prosecuted or defended by the said Maine Midland Railroad Company in like manner and with like effect as if such transfer had not been made. All claims, contracts, rights and causes of action of or against said corporation so selling or leasing, at law or in equity, may be enforced by suit or action to be begun or prosecuted by or against said Maine Midland Railroad Company. *Pending proceedings, how prosecuted and defended.*

Section 7. The said Maine Midland Railroad Company may issue its stocks and bonds in payment and exchange for the stocks, bonds, franchises and property of the Wiscasset, Waterville and Farmington Railroad Company as authorized by this act, in such manner and in such amounts as may be agreed upon. *May issue its stocks and bonds.*

Section 8. When the transfer authorized by this act is carried out and fully completed, the Maine Midland Railroad Company shall be liable for the then existing legal debts and obligations of the Wiscasset, Waterville and Farmington Railroad Company. *Liability for debts after transfer.*

Section 9. Upon and after completion of the aforesaid sale or lease the said Maine Midland Railroad Company shall be and hereby is authorized to locate, construct, equip, maintain and operate a railroad commencing at some point near the village of Farmington Falls, at or near the present track or road bed of the Wiscasset, Waterville and Farmington Railroad Company near said village of Farmington Falls, thence through the towns of Farmington, Chesterville, Fayette and East Livermore, a distance of seventeen and a half miles, to some point in the village of Livermore Falls to connect with the Portland and Rumford Falls Railway, with all the powers and subject to all the liabilities incident to a railroad corporation under the general laws of the state. Said location in Livermore Falls village after crossing the Maine Central Railroad and the manner and conditions of its connection with the Portland and Rumford Falls Railway shall be under the direction of and subject to the approval of the railroad commissioners. *May extend line. —through certain towns. —to connect with Portland and Rumford Falls Ry.*

Section 10. The said corporation is further authorized to carry on the business of an express company upon its own lines, and also to maintain and operate telephone and telegraph lines *Express, telegraph and telephone business, to do, authorized.*

Chap. 138
—hotels, etc.

for public use along its location and to its principal offices, as the same may be located. It may also erect and maintain hotels, cottages and pleasure grounds and own and operate steamboats upon any lakes and ponds near its location, but the right to take land or other property shall not extend to property to be used for purposes authorized by this section, and all such land or property so to be used shall be acquired by purchase and in no other way.

Toll granted.

Section 11. A toll is hereby granted for the benefit of said corporation upon all passengers and property which may be carried over its railroads or in any of its steamboats, and upon all telegraph and telephone messages which may be transmitted over its lines, at such rates as may be established by its directors, subject to such general laws as are or may be from time to time established.

Connecting lines, may purchase.

Section 12. The said corporation is authorized to purchase or lease the property and franchises of any connecting railroad corporation in the state, or to purchase and hold the stock and bonds of any such corporation and all such connecting corporations, or any corporation, association or person claiming rights under the stock, bonds, mortgages or franchises of any such corporation are hereby authorized to make such sales or leases, and all such property, franchises, stocks and bonds so acquired may be pledged or mortgaged to secure the bonds herein authorized. Said corporation is hereby authorized to make connection with any other railroad or railroads on such terms as may be mutually agreed upon and as may be provided by the general laws of the state, and to lease its property and road either before or after it shall have been completed upon such terms as it may determine, subject in all cases to the approval of a majority of the outstanding stock in each corporation.

Location shall be filed.

Section 13. Said corporation shall organize and the location of its railroad according to actual survey shall be filed with the county commissioners of Franklin county and of Androscoggin county on or before the first day of December, in the year of our Lord nineteen hundred and three, and the said corporation shall be and hereby is given until the thirty-first day of December, in the year of our Lord nineteen hundred and five, within which to build and operate its said railroad.

May receive aid from towns, etc.

Section 14. The said company may receive from any town or from any person or body corporate. municipal or politic, aid towards the construction, equipment and maintenance of the railway line or the objects contemplated by this act, by the way of gifts, subsidies or bonuses in land, money or securities, or by loans or by the way of guaranty, or by providing rights of way for such lines or any part thereof or objects free of expense to the company, upon such terms or conditions as may be agreed upon.

Section 15. The directors may make and issue as paid up stock shares in the company, and may allot and hand over such shares, and also mortgage bonds of the company, in payment of right of way, plant, rolling stock or materials of any kind, and also for services of, or work done, by contractors, engineers, solicitors or other persons who may have been, are, or may be engaged in promoting the undertaking and interests of the company, and in whole or partial payment for the purchase, lease or other acquisition of railways, lands and other property; and such allotments of stock or bonds shall be binding on the company, and the paid up stock shall not be assessable thereafter for calls or other purposes. *Paid up stock and mortgage bonds.*

Section 16. The said corporation may issue its bonds from time to time upon such rates and times as may be deemed expedient, and in such amounts as may be required for the purposes of this act, and secure the same by appropriate mortgages upon its franchises and property. *May issue bonds.*

Section 17. The first meeting of said corporation may be called by any two corporators within named by notice thereof in writing signed by said two corporators, and given in hand or mailed to each of the other corporators at least ten days before said meeting, and any corporator may act at such meeting by written proxy. *First meeting.*

Section 18. Nothing in this act shall be construed as affecting the rights as now provided by law of minority stockholders in any company or corporation to be affected hereby. *Minority stockholders.*

Section 19. This act shall take effect when approved.

Approved March 10, 1903.

Chapter 139.

An Act relating to the jurisdiction of the Municipal Court of the City of Biddeford.

Be it enacted by the Senate and House of Representatives in Legislature assembled, as follows:

Section 1. The jurisdiction of the municipal court of the city of Biddeford in civil causes is hereby enlarged from one hundred dollars, as now established by law, to two hundred dollars. *Jurisdiction enlarged.*

Section 2. In taxing costs in all civil suits in said court, where issue has been joined, one dollar shall be allowed for trial instead of the sums now fixed by law. *Costs in civil suits.*

216   AUBURN PUBLIC LIBRARY—SEBEC DAM COMPANY.

CHAP. 140
Cognizance of simple larcenies, etc.

Section 3. Said court may take cognizance of simple larcenies when the property alleged to be stolen shall not exceed in value fifty dollars, and of the offenses described in sections six, seven and nine of chapter one hundred and twenty of the revised statutes, and in sections one and four of chapter one hundred and twenty-six of the revised statutes, where the value of the property does not exceed fifty dollars; of offenses described in section four of chapter one hundred and thirty-two of the revised statutes, where they are not of a high and aggravated nature, and on conviction, may punish by fine not exceeding fifty dollars, or by imprisonment in the county jail for a term not exceeding six months.

Section 4. This act shall take effect when approved.

Approved March 10, 1903.

Chapter 140.

An Act concerning the Auburn Free Public Library.

Be it enacted by the Senate and House of Representatives in Legislature assembled, as follows:

Acts and doings of, ratified.

Section 1. All the acts and doings of the city of Auburn concerning the establishment of a free public library are hereby ratified, confirmed and made valid.

Section 2. This act shall take effect when approved.

Approved March 10, 1903.

Chapter 141.

An Act to amend Chapter one hundred thirty of the Private Laws of eighteen hundred and sixty-six, entitled "An Act to incorporate the Sebec Dam Company," as amended by Section six of Chapter twenty-six of Private and Special Laws of eighteen hundred and ninety-nine.

Be it enacted by the Senate and House of Representatives in Legislature assembled, as follows:

Chapter 130 of private laws of 1866, as amended by chapter 26 of private laws of 1899, further amended.

Chapter one hundred thirty of the private laws of eighteen hundred sixty-six, as amended by chapter twenty-six of private laws of eighteen hundred ninety-nine, is hereby amended by adding to said chapter sections five and six, which shall read as follows:

Use of water restricted from July 1, to October 15.

'Section 5. Said company shall not be allowed, from July first to October fifteenth of each year, to draw the water from said dam below one foot above the bottom of the flood gates in the present dam, as now constructed, except the use of said waters for manufacturing and other purposes for which power may be used on said dam and for creating power for the same and manufacturing on Sebec river, and the proper repair of said dam. Before said repairs are to be made notice shall be given to each cottage owner, mill owner and steamboat owner on Sebec lake and to the proprietors of the hotels on Sebec lake and at Sebec village by written notice through the mail, postage paid, to the last known address of each cottage, mill and steamboat owner and hotel keeper, two weeks before drawing the water down to make said repairs and by publication of said notice in some newspaper published in the county of Piscataquis, three consecutive weeks, the last publication to be fourteen days before commencing to draw the water. If any question arises as to the necessity for repairs such question shall be determined by the county commissioners of the county of Piscataquis on written application of any person or persons interested as hereinbefore set out whose decision shall be final. If no petition is filed with the county commissioners within fourteen days from the date of the last publication of the notice aforesaid and notice thereof served upon Sebec Dam Company, said Sebec Dam Company shall proceed to make said repairs. All expenses of the county commissioners shall be paid by the petitioner or petitioners.

Any person injured by any violation of the provisions of this charter shall have a remedy by injunction and by an action for damages.'

'Section 6. This act shall take effect when approved.'

Approved March 10, 1903.

Chapter 142.

An Act to amend Chapter one hundred and forty-five of the Private and Special Laws of eighteen hundred and eighty-seven, entitled "An Act to provide sewerage in the town of Houlton."

Be it enacted by the Senate and House of Representatives in Legislature assembled, as follows:

Section two of said act is hereby amended to read as follows:

'Section 2. Said corporation may acquire and hold real and personal estate necessary and convenient for the purposes aforesaid, not exceeding in amount one hundred thousand dollars; may sell and convey the same; may issue certificates of stock to an amount not exceeding the amount of its capital stock act-

TOWN OF BOOTHBAY HARBOR.

CHAP. 143

—may issue certificates of stock.
—bonds to amount of $50,000 may be held by savings banks of Maine.

ually paid in; and may issue and sell bonds to an amount not exceeding fifty thousand dollars, to aid in the construction, repairs and improvements of its works, and said bonds to the amount of fifty thousand dollars may be purchased and held by the savings banks of Maine.'

Approved March 10, 1903.

Chapter 143.

An Act to relieve the town of Boothbay Harbor from the duty of building, repairing or maintaining roads, streets or ways on the Isle of Springs.

Be it enacted by the Senate and House of Representatives in Legislature assembled, as follows:

Isle of Springs Association created.

—purposes.

Section 1. The Isle of Springs Association is hereby created a municipal corporation for the following purposes, namely: for the laying out, construction and maintenance of wharves, ways, sewers and sidewalks, and for furnishing and supplying water and lights for the use of the residents of said Isle of Springs.

Boothbay Harbor relieved from certain duties.

Section 2. The town of Boothbay Harbor is hereby relieved from any and all duty to build, repair or maintain roads, streets or ways upon the Isle of Springs, or to build school houses or maintain schools thereon. The said town shall not be required to build sewers or other sanitary works upon said island, nor to afford protection against fires, nor to maintain police and night watch.

Taxes collected from inhabitants, how disposed of.

Section 3. The town of Boothbay Harbor shall annually pay over to the treasurer of the Isle of Springs Association out of the taxes collected from the inhabitants and estates on Isle of Springs a sum equal to sixty per centum thereof, exclusive of the state and county tax.

Expenditures of amount so paid by town, regulated.

Section 4. The amount so paid by the town shall be expended by said association for the erection, maintenance and repairs of a wharf or wharves, roads, ways and walks upon said island, and for the maintenance of a water supply, light and drainage for the benefit of residents of said island.

Section 5. This act shall take effect when accepted by the Isle of Springs Association.

Approved March 10, 1903.

Chapter 144.

An Act authorizing Washington County to sell its stock in the Washington County Railroad Company, and authorizing the sale or lease of said railroad.

Be it enacted by the Senate and House of Representatives in Legislature assembled, as follows:

Section 1. Whenever a proposition for the purchase of the holdings of Washington county in the preferred stock of the Washington County Railroad Company shall be made in writing by the holders of the other shares of the stock of said corporation to the county commissioners of said county, or by any other person or corporations said proposition stating in substance that upon a legal transfer of such preferred stock to them, the said holders of the other shares of the stock of said corporation or such other person or corporations as may submit a proposition will pay to said county commissioners for the use of said county a certain definite sum of money, or when such holders of the other shares of the stock of said corporation or any other person or corporations, shall make any other proposition for the purchase of said preferred stock or the exchange thereof for other securities, if said commissioners shall approve said proposition, they shall submit it to the determination of the legal voters of said county at such time as they may designate, subject to the provisions of this act, and thereupon there shall be submitted to the voters of the several cities, towns and organized plantations in the county of Washington the following proposition: "Shall the county commissioners be empowered to dispose of the holdings of the county in the preferred stock of the Washington County Railroad Company in accordance with the written proposition made therefor?" and the warrants issued for calling such meetings shall contain a copy of such written proposition, and it is hereby made the duty of the county commissioners of said county to appoint a day for meetings to vote thereon, and to notify the municipal officers of the cities, towns and plantations thereof, leaving a sufficient time for calling said meetings in the usual form for city or town meetings.

Said commissioners shall cause to be prepared printed forms for the warrants and returns of said meetings and transmit them with their notifications to city, town and plantation officers as above prescribed.

Section 2. The municipal officers of the cities, towns and plantations in said county shall call meetings on the day appointed by issuing and posting warrants therefor as for municipal elections. No such meetings shall be opened before ten o'clock in the forenoon nor later than one o'clock in the after-

CHAP. 144

Vote, how taken.

—returns.

Canvass of returns.

Sale may be made if majority of ballots favor acceptance of proposition.

Transfers of stock shall be sufficient to transfer title.

Proceeds of sale shall constitute a special fund.

noon and the polls shall be kept open until five o'clock in the afternoon and then be closed.

Section 3. At said meetings the vote shall be taken by printed or written ballots and those in favor of accepting said proposition shall vote "yes" and those opposed to it "no" and the ballots cast shall be sorted and counted and the vote declared in open meeting and recorded. The meetings shall be presided over and conducted as at municipal elections and the municipal officers shall make returns thereof to the county commissioners by depositing in some post office in said county within twenty-four hours after the close of said polls their return of the votes cast, postpaid, directed to the clerk of courts at Machias in said county, to be transmitted by mail, or personally deliver the same to said clerk of courts within that time.

Section 4. The county commissioners shall meet at the court house in said Machias within twenty days after said meeting, canvass the returns and declare the result, and the result shall then be recorded by the clerk of courts and be certified on the record by said commissioners and said clerk, which record shall be the only record required of the vote cast under this act.

Section 5. If said commissioners, upon canvass of said returns shall declare that a majority of the ballots returned at said meetings were in favor of the acceptance of said proposition, then said commissioners are hereby authorized and empowered and directed for and in behalf of said county to sell upon such terms as shall be contained in said proposition the holdings of said county in the preferred stock of the Washington County Railroad Company, and to that end said commissioners are hereby authorized and empowered to execute for and in behalf of said county all transfers of said stock necessary to complete such sale and all written agreements setting forth the terms of such contract for sale.

Section 6. Any and all transfers of stock made under the provisions of this act shall be sufficient to transfer the title to such stock to the purchaser or purchasers and any written contract relating to the sale of said stock so executed shall be binding upon the county, and the county commissioners shall for and in behalf of said county do and perform all things to be done and performed by said county as in said contract provided.

Section 7. All the proceeds of such sale shall be held as a separate fund by the county treasurer of said county and shall not be expended or paid out except as herein provided. Such proceeds shall be kept invested in such funds as are legal investments for savings banks under the laws of this state, and all such investments shall be made under the direction of the county treasurer, the county attorney and the county commissioners of said county. The principal of said fund shall be applied to the payment and redemption of bonds issued by said county for the purchase of said stock. The interest of said fund shall be applied toward paying the interest of said bonds each year if needed for that purpose. When all of said bonds have been retired any of said fund which then remains shall be turned into the county treasury for the general purposes of said county. Whenever under the provisions of this section the county officers aforesaid deem it for the best interest of the county, they shall out of said fund, purchase the bonds of Washington county and immediately cancel the same.

—principal shall be applied to payment of bonds.

—interest, how applied.

Section 8. The words 'county commissioners' in this act shall be construed to mean the board of county commissioners for the time being of Washington county and any action taken hereunder may be by a majority thereof, the intention being that at any time the county commissioners of said county then in office are in accordance with this act fully empowered to represent, act for and bind the county in relation to said stock as herein provided, and nothing in this act shall be construed as taking away or in any manner impairing the option and rights which the holders of the other shares of stock in said Washington County Railroad Company now possess to purchase the holdings of said county in said preferred stock.

Words 'county commissioners' defined.

Section 9. The Washington County Railroad Company is hereby authorized to sell or lease its railroad, franchises and all other assets of the company to any railroad company operating a railroad wholly or partly in this state, and any railroad company so operating a railroad in this state is authorized to acquire by lease or purchase the railroad, franchises and all other assets of said Washington County Railroad Company and to operate said railroad when acquired with all the rights, franchises and privileges attached thereto.

May sell or lease its railroad.

Section 10. Any railroad company operating a railroad wholly or partly in this state is authorized to purchase and hold the whole or any number of the shares of the preferred or common stock of the Washington County Railroad Company, and upon acquiring a majority of the shares of the common stock of said corporation to guarantee the payment of the whole or any part of the principal and interest of the outstanding mortgage bonds of the Washington County Railroad Company or of any bonds hereafter issued by it.

Authority to purchase given.

Section 11. The directors of any railroad company holding stock in the Washington County Railroad Company purchased under the provisions of this act may designate the person or per-

Proxy of directors of other railroads, holding stock

CHAP. 144
In Washington R. R. Co., may vote at meetings.

sons who shall vote upon said stock so held by it at any meeting of the stockholders of said Washington County Railroad Company, and any stockholder or director of the railroad company so holding stock in the Washington County Railroad Company may be a director thereof.

May issue bonds.

Section 12. The Washington County Railroad Company for the purposes hereafter named is hereby authorized to issue its bonds in such amount and with such rate of interest that the annual interest charge thereon shall not exceed the annual interest charge upon the present outstanding mortgage bonds, and to secure the same by a mortgage of its railroad, franchises, property and privileges; provided said mortgage shall be authorized

—proviso.

by a majority vote of the holders of the common stock in said company at a legal meeting called therefor, in the call for which the purposes of said meeting shall be stated, and shall also be consented to in writing by the owner or owners of all of the preferred stock in said company. The proceeds of such last named mortgage bonds shall be applied to the payment, redemp-

—proceeds of mortgage, how applied.

tion or purchase of said first mortgage bonds, or to the purchase of the preferred stock, which when purchased may be retired and canceled. When all of said bonds shall have been so paid, redeemed or purchased and the first mortgage discharged, and the preferred stock purchased and paid for so the county of Washington is not a holder of said stock, any balance remaining may be applied to the improvement or betterment of said road.

Bonds exempt from taxation for unexpired part of 20 years.

Section 13. Any bonds issued under this act shall be exempt from taxation for the unexpired portion of the term of twenty years mentioned in section three of chapter ninety of the private laws of the year eighteen hundred ninety-five and in the contract made thereunder in accordance with the terms of said section and contract.

Section 14. This act shall take effect when approved.

Approved March 10, 1903.

Chapter 145.

An Act to extend the charter of the Old Orchard Trust and Banking Company.

Be it enacted by the Senate and House of Representatives in Legislature assembled, as follows:

Section 1. The rights, powers and privileges of the Old Orchard Trust and Banking Company, which were granted by chapter three hundred and forty-nine of the private and special laws of nineteen hundred and one, are hereby extended for two years from the approval of this act; and the persons named in said act, their associates and successors, shall have all the rights, powers and privileges that were granted them by said act, to be exercised in the same manner and for the same purposes as specified in said act. *Charter extended.*

Section 2. This act shall take effect when approved.

Approved March 11, 1903.

Chapter 146.

An Act to incorporate the Tyngstown Water Company.

Be it enacted by the Senate and House of Representatives in Legislature assembled, as follows:

Section 1. F. J. Goodspeed, Herman Sanborn and C. N. Blanchard of Wilton with their associates and successors, be and are hereby made a corporation under the name of the Tyngstown Water Company, for the purpose of supplying the inhabitants of the town of Wilton with pure water for domestic, sanitary and municipal purposes, including the extinguishment of fires; and such corporation shall possess all the powers and privileges and be subject to all the liabilities and obligations imposed upon corporations by law, except as herein otherwise provided. *Corporators. —corporate name. —purposes. —liabilities.*

Section 2. The place of business of said corporation shall be at Wilton, in the county of Franklin and state of Maine. *Location.*

Section 3. For any of the purposes aforesaid the said corporation is hereby authorized to take and use water from Wilson lake, Varnum pond, or from any spring in actual use for domestic purposes or any pond, brook or other waters in the town of Wilton, or from Hills pond in Perkins plantation, to conduct and distribute the same into and through the said town of Wilton; and to survey for, locate, construct and maintain all suitable and convenient dams, reservoirs, sluices, hydrants, buildings, machinery, lines of pipe, aqueducts, structures and appurtenances. *May take water in town of Wilton and in Perkins plantation.*

CHAP. 146

May lay pipes.

Section 4. The said corporation is hereby authorized to lay, construct and maintain its lines of pipe in Perkins plantation, Washington plantation and in the town of Wilton, and to build and maintain all necessary structures therefor, at such places as shall be necessary for the said purposes of said corporation; and to cross any water course, private or public sewer, or to change the direction thereof, when necessary for their said purpose of incorporation, but in such a manner as not to obstruct or impair the use thereof, and the said corporation shall be liable for any injury caused hereby.

May construct under highways, etc.

Section 5. The said corporation is hereby authorized to lay, construct and maintain in, under, through, along, over and across the highways, ways, streets, railroads and bridges in the said town, and to take up, replace and repair, all such aqueducts, sluices, pipes, hydrants and other structures and fixtures, as may be necessary and convenient for any of the said purposes of the

—liabilities.

said corporation, under such reasonable restrictions and conditions as the selectmen of the said town may impose; and the said corporation shall be responsible for all damage to the said town, and to all corporations, persons and property, occasioned by such use of the highway, ways and streets.

Whenever the said corporation shall lay down or construct any pipes or fixtures in any highway, way or street, or make any alteration or repairs upon its works, in any highway, way or street, it shall cause the same to be done with as little obstruction to public travel as may be practicable, and shall at its own expense, without unnecessary delay, cause the earth and pavement then removed by it, to be placed in proper condition.

May take land for flowage, etc.

Section 6. The said corporation is hereby authorized to take and hold by purchase or otherwise any land necessary for flowage, and also for its dams, reservoirs, gates, hydrants, buildings and other necessary structures, and may locate, erect, lay and maintain aqueducts, hydrants, lines of pipes, and other necessary structures or fixtures in, over and through any land for the said purposes, and excavate in and through such land for such location, construction and erection.

—may make surveys.

And in general to do any act necessary, convenient or proper for carrying out any of the said purposes of incorporation. It may enter upon such land to make surveys and locations, and shall file in the registry of deeds in the county of Franklin, plans of such locations and lands, showing the property taken, and within thirty days thereafter publish notices of such filing in

—width of location limited.

some newspaper in said county, such publication to be continued three weeks successively. Not more than two rods in width of land shall be occupied by more than one line of pipe or aqueduct.

Section 7. Should the said corporation and the owner of such land be unable to agree upon the damages to be paid for such location, taking, holding, flowing and construction, the land owner or said corporation may, within twelve months after said filing of plans of location, apply to the commissioners of said county of Franklin, and cause such damages to be assessed in the same manner and under the same conditions as are prescribed by law in the case of damages by the laying out of highways, so far as such law is consistent with the provisions of this act. If said corporation shall fail to pay such land owner, or deposit for his use with the clerk of the county commissioners aforesaid such sum as may be finally awarded as damages, with costs when recovered by him, within ninety days after notice of final judgment shall have been received by the clerk of courts of said county, the said location shall be thereby invalid, and the said corporation shall forfeit all rights under the same as against such land owner. In case the said corporation shall begin to occupy such land before the rendition of final judgment the land owner may require the said corporation to file its bond to him with the said county commissioners, in such sum and with such sureties as they may approve, conditioned for said judgment or deposits. No action shall be brought against the said corporation for such taking, holding and occupation until after such failure to pay or deposit as aforesaid.

Section 8. Any person suffering damage by the taking of water by said company as provided by this act, may have his damages assessed in the manner provided in the preceding section, and payment therefor shall be made in the same manner and with the same effect. No action shall be brought for the same until after expiration of the time of payment and a tender by said company may be made with the same effect as in the preceding section.

Section 9. The said corporation is hereby authorized to make contracts with the United States, the state of Maine, the county of Franklin, the town of Wilton and with any village corporation in the said town, and with the inhabitants thereof, or any corporation doing business therein, for the supply of water for any and all the purposes contemplated in this act; and the said town and any village corporation in the said town by their proper officers, are hereby authorized to enter into any contract with the said corporation for a supply of water for any and all purposes mentioned in this act, and in consideration thereof to relieve said corporation from such public burdens by abatement or otherwise as said town, village corporation, and the said corporation may

226 TYNGSTOWN WATER COMPANY.

CHAP. 146

Corruption of water supply.

—penalty.

Capital stock.

May hold real and personal property.

May issue bonds.

—may mortgage its property.

First meeting, how called.

Purchase of system after 20 years, authorized.

—price, how fixed.

agree upon, which when made, shall be legal and binding upon all parties thereto.

Section 10. Whoever shall knowingly or maliciously corrupt the water supply of the said corporation, whether frozen or not, or in any way render such water impure, or whoever shall wilfully or maliciously injure any of the works of the said corporation, shall be punished by a fine not exceeding one thousand dollars, or by imprisonment not exceeding two years, and shall be liable to the said corporation for three times the actual damage, to be recovered in any proper action.

Section 11. The capital stock of the said corporation shall be twenty-five thousand dollars, which may be increased to any sum not exceeding fifty thousand dollars, by a majority vote of the stockholders of the said corporation; and the stock shall be divided into shares of fifty dollars each.

Section 12. The said corporation, for all its said purposes, may hold real and personal estate necessary and convenient therefor, not exceeding fifty thousand dollars.

Section 13. The said corporation may issue its bonds for the construction of its works, of any and all kinds upon such rates and time as it may deem expedient, to an amount not exceeding its capital stock subscribed for, and secure the same by mortgage of its franchise and property.

Section 14. The first meeting of the corporation shall be called by a written notice therefor, signed by any two of the named incorporators, served upon each named incorporator by giving him the same in hand, or by leaving the same at his last and usual place of abode, at least seven days before the time of meeting, or by publishing said notice in some newspaper published in the county of Franklin.

Section 15. At any time after twenty years from the date of the approval of this act the town of Wilton, or any village corporation within the limits of said town of Wilton, if its inhabitants shall so vote, by a two-thirds vote, at a legal meeting called therefor, shall have the right to purchase the system of water works constructed by this company in said town for supplying said town and the inhabitants thereof, together with the franchises of this company relating thereto, at a price to be agreed upon between said company and said town or village corporation; and if such price cannot be agreed upon, then at a price, which shall be determined by a commission of three competent and disinterested men, one of whom shall be selected by said company, one by said town of Wilton, or by said village corporation, and the third by the two so selected if they can agree, if not, then by the chief justice of the supreme judicial court of Maine. The award of said commissioners, not less than cost, shall be binding upon said company and said town, or village corporation, and said town or village corporation shall pay the amount of said award for said system of water works and franchises within ninety days from the date when such award shall be rendered. The costs of said commission shall be borne equally by the said company and said town or village corporation.

—costs, how borne.

Section 16. This act shall take effect when approved.

Approved March 11, 1908.

Chapter 147.

An Act to provide blanks, books and stationery for the Dover Municipal Court.

Be it enacted by the Senate and House of Representatives in Legislature assembled, as follows:

Section 1. It shall be the duty of the county commissioners of the county of Piscataquis to furnish and provide at the expense of the county, all books, blanks, and all necessary stationery and supplies required for the use of the Dover Municipal Court in the town of Dover, in the transaction of the civil and criminal business of said court, including proper books for the record of all cases arising in said court, at a cost not exceeding one hundred dollars per year.

Books, blanks, etc., to be supplied for use of court.

Section 2. All acts or parts of acts, conflicting with this act, are hereby repealed.

Repeal of conflicting acts.

Section 3. This act shall go into effect on the first day of April in the year of our Lord one thousand nine hundred and three.

When act shall take effect.

Approved March 11, 1908.

Chapter 148.

An Act to amend Chapter two hundred and twenty-seven of the Private and Special Laws of eighteen hundred and eighty, entitled, "An Act to supply the people of Houlton with pure water," as amended by Chapter four hundred and ninety-seven of the Private and Special Laws of eighteen hundred and eighty-nine.

Be it enacted by the Senate and House of Representatives in Legislature assembled, as follows:

Section 1. Section one of said chapter two hundred and twenty-seven is hereby amended by adding thereto at the end of said section the following:

Section 1 of chapter 227, amended.

CHAP. 149
—public sewers provided for.

'And for the purpose of providing the town and village of Houlton a system of public sewers and drainage, for the comfort, convenience and health of the people of said Houlton.'

Section 2 of chapter 227, as amended by chapter 497, special laws of 1889, further amended.

Section 2. Section two of said chapter two hundred and twenty-seven as amended by chapter four hundred and ninety-seven of the private and special laws of eighteen hundred eighty-nine is hereby amended to read as follows:

May acquire real and personal estate.

'Section 2. Said corporation may acquire and hold real and personal estate, necessary and convenient for the purposes aforesaid, and the stock in whole or in part of the Houlton Sewerage Company, not exceeding in all two hundred thousand dollars;

—may issue stock.

may sell and convey the same, may issue certificates of stock to an amount not exceeding fifty thousand dollars; and may issue

—may issue bonds.

and sell bonds to an amount not exceeding one hundred thousand dollars; to aid in the construction, extension, improvement and repairs of its works, and to pay any existing debts whether represented by bonds, notes or accounts, and for the purchase of the

—bonds may be held by savings banks of Maine.

whole or any part of the stock of the Houlton Sewerage Company; and said bonds to the amount of one hundred thousand dollars may be purchased and held by the savings banks of Maine.'

Approved March 11, 1903.

Chapter 149.

An Act to incorporate the Executive Committee of Huntoon Hill Grange, Number three hundred ninety-eight, Patrons of Husbandry.

Be it enacted by the Senate and House of Representatives in Legislature assembled, as follows:

Corporators.

Section 1. Silas Y. Jackson, William S. Damon, Ezra S. Perkins, and their successors, are hereby created a body politic

—corporate name.

and corporate, by the name of the executive committee of the Huntoon Hill Grange, Number three hundred ninety-eight,

—purpose.

Patrons of Husbandry, for the purpose of holding real and personal estate, and managing and disposing of the same for the use and benefit of said grange.

May hold real or personal property.

Section 2. Said corporation may take by purchase, devise or otherwise any real or personal property and hold the same, for the purposes aforesaid, to an amount not exceeding four

—exemption from taxation.

thousand dollars, exempt from taxation, and may manage and dispose of the same at the discretion of said grange.

Officers.

Section 3. Said corporation shall choose annually such officers as may be necessary for their own government, and have the right to prosecute actions at law and in equity, and adopt a seal and code of by-laws not inconsistent with the laws of the state.

Section 4. Vacancies by death, resignation or otherwise shall be filled by said Huntoon Hill Grange from the membership thereof.

Vacancies, how filled.

Section 5. Any two persons named in this act, may call the first meeting of this corporation, by written notice, delivered or mailed each corporator, at least five days before the time of said meeting.

First meeting how called.

Section 6. This act shall take effect when approved.

Approved March 11, 1908.

Chapter 150.

An Act to amend the charter of the President and Trustees of Colby College.

Be it enacted by the Senate and House of Representatives in Legislature assembled, as follows:

Section 1. That section three of the act entitled "An Act to establish a Literary Institution in the District of Maine, within this commonwealth," passed by the general court of Massachusetts and approved February twenty-seven, eighteen hundred thirteen, and from time to time amended, be further amended by inserting after the word "trustees" in the eleventh line thereof the following words; 'except as hereinafter provided,' and by adding to the end of said section the following words: 'And provided also that nine of the trustees shall be elected by the Alumni association of Colby college, to be known as Alumni Trustees and to be elected, three each year, for terms of three years, in such manner as said association may provide.' So that said section three as amended, shall read as follows:

Colby College, charter amended.

'Section 3. Be it further enacted, that for the more orderly conducting the business of the said corporation, the president and trustees shall have full power and authority, from time to time as they shall determine, to elect a vice president, treasurer and secretary of said corporation, and to declare the tenure and duties of their respective offices, and also to remove any trustee from the said corporation, when in their judgment he shall be rendered incapable by age or other ways, of discharging the duties of his office, and to fill up all vacancies in the said corporation, by electing such persons for trustees, except as hereinafter provided, as they shall judge best: Provided nevertheless,

Vice president, treasurer and secretary may be elected by president and trustees.

—may declare tenure of and remove trustees.

—proviso.

CHAP. 151

—proviso.

—alumni trustees.

that the number of the said corporation, including the president of the said institution, and the treasurer for the time being, shall never be greater than thirty-one, nor less than twenty-one: And provided also, that nine of the trustees shall be elected by the Alumni association of Colby college to be known as Alumni Trustees and to be elected, three each year, for terms of three years, in such manner as said association may provide.'

When trustees shall be elected.

Section 2. The first three of the trustees herein provided for shall, for their first term, be elected during the year nineteen hundred four, the second three during the year nineteen hundred five and the third three during the year nineteen hundred six.

Section 3. This act shall take effect when approved.

Approved March 11, 1903.

Chapter 151.

An Act to amend An Act entitled "An Act to authorize the opening of a second channel of Mousam River."

Be it enacted by the Senate and House of Representatives in Legislature assembled, as follows:

Section 1 of chapter 92 of special laws of 1887, amended.

Section one of chapter ninety-two of the private and special laws of eighteen hundred eighty-seven is hereby amended by striking out all words after the word "river" in the ninth line of said section, and inserting in place thereof the following: 'and should it prove necessary for the economical execution of above purpose, they are authorized to build dams or other artificial obstructions required,' so that said section as amended, shall read as follows:

Corporators.

—may cut channel.

—may build dams.

'Section 1. Hartley Lord, Robert W. Lord, Owen Wentworth, Emery Andrews and Sidney T. Fuller, together with such persons as they shall associate with themselves, their heirs and assigns, are hereby authorized and empowered to cut a channel from any point below Clay Hill bridge, so called, in Mousam river, so called, in Kennebunk, through the lands of Owen Wentworth and others, to the Cove, so called, which lies easterly of Gillespie's point, so that sail and row boats may pass to and from said cove into said river, and should it prove necessary for the economical execution of above purpose, they are authorized to build dams or other artificial obstructions of any kind required.'

Approved March 11, 1903.

Chapter 152.

An Act to amend Chapter one hundred and seventy-five of the Private and Special Laws of eighteen hundred and eighty-seven, entitled "An Act to incorporate the Androscoggin Valley Agricultural Society."

Be it enacted by the Senate and House of Representatives in Legislature assembled, as follows:

Section 1. Chapter one hundred and seventy-five of the private and special laws of eighteen hundred and eighty-seven is hereby amended by adding after section two of said act the following section: Chapter 175 of special laws of 1887, amended.

'Section 3. Said society is hereby authorized to construct and maintain on its fair grounds a grand stand, and to issue stock therefor to an amount not exceeding twenty-five hundred dollars, and bonds to an equal amount of the stock so issued, secured by mortgage on said grand stand; and the net proceeds derived from said grand stand after its construction shall be applied exclusively to the payment of the interest on said bonds and the retirement thereof.'

Section 2. This act shall take effect when approved.

Approved March 11, 1903.

Chapter 153.

An Act to consolidate and amend Chapter one hundred and seventy-seven of the Special Laws of eighteen hundred and eighty-seven, and all acts additional thereto and amendatory thereof, relating to the Old Town Municipal Court.

Be it enacted by the Senate and House of Representatives in Legislature assembled, as follows:

Section 1. The Old Town Municipal Court shall continue to be a court of record with a seal and all original processes issuing from said court shall be in the name of the state, under the teste of the judge, or, if the office of judge is vacant, or the recorder thereof, signed either by the judge or recorder, and shall have the seal of said court affixed.

Section 2. Said court shall consist of one judge, who shall be a member of the bar of this state, residing in the county of Penobscot, be appointed in manner and for the term provided by the constitution of Maine, and he shall be, ex-officio, a justice of the peace and of the quorum within and for each and every of the several counties through the state. The said judge shall enter, or cause to be entered on the docket of said court all civil and criminal actions, with full minutes of the proceedings in and

CHAP. 153

—tenure of present judge.

disposition of the same, which docket shall be at all times open to inspection, and he shall perform all other duties required of similar tribunals in this state. Copies of the records of said court, duly certified by the judge or recorder thereof, shall be legal evidence in all courts. The present judge of said court shall continue in office until the end of the term for which he was appointed and no judge of said court shall act as attorney or counsel in any action, cause, matter or thing within the exclusive jurisdiction thereof.

Recorder, appointment and tenure.

—shall give bond.

—powers and duties of recorder.

Section 3. The governor, by and with the advice and consent of the council, may appoint a recorder of said court, who shall be qualified as provided in the constitution and hold his office for the term of four years. Said recorder, while in office, shall be a resident of the city of Old Town, give bond to the county of Penobscot in the sum of five hundred dollars to be approved by the commissioners of said county. The said recorder may administer oaths; when requested so to do by the judge, he shall keep the records of said court; he shall be empowered to sign and issue all papers and processes, receive and file pleas and motions, hear complaints and issue warrants in criminal matters, make and sign processes of commitment, but the same shall be heard and determined as now provided by law, and all papers, processes, complaints, warrants or processes of commitment, drawn and signed by the judge of said court shall be equally valid. In the absence of the judge, or when he is engaged in the transaction of civil business, or when the office of judge shall be vacant, the said recorder shall have and exercise all the powers of the judge by this act, and do all acts as fully and with the same effect as the judge could do if he were acting in the premises, and the signature of the recorder, as such shall be sufficient evidence of his right to act instead of the judge, but, except when the office of judge is vacant, the said recorder shall not have authority to hear and determine civil causes.

Jurisdiction of court.

Section 4. Said court shall have original and exclusive jurisdiction as follows: First, of all cases of forcible entry and detainer respecting estates within the city of Old Town or either of the towns of Milford, Bradley, Alton, Argyle, Greenbush and Greenfield, in said county of Penobscot. Second, of all such criminal offenses and misdemeanors committed in said city or either of said towns as are within the jurisdiction of trial justices. Third, of all offenses against the ordinances and by-laws of said city or either of said towns. Fourth, said court shall have original jurisdiction concurrent with trial justices in all such matters, civil or criminal, within the county of Penobscot, as are by law within the jurisdiction of trial justices within said county and are not placed within the exclusive jurisdiction of said court by this section, and in all such civil matters, excepting, however, actions of forcible entry and detainer respecting estates within the city of Bangor, the said court shall have jurisdiction though either party interested, or a person summoned as trustee, resides in said city of Bangor.

Section 5. Said court shall have original jurisdiction concurrent with the supreme judicial court as follows: First, of all civil actions wherein the debt or damages demanded, exclusive of costs, does not exceed two hundred dollars, in which any person summoned as trustee resides within the county of Penobscot, or, if a corporation, has its office or an established or usual place of business in said county; or in which, if such actions are not commenced by trustee process, any defendant resides in said county, or, if no defendant resides within the limits of this state, any defendant is served with process in said county, or the goods, estate, or effects of any defendant are found within said county and attached on the original writ, but no proceedings under the laws relating to divorce shall be included within the jurisdiction of said court. Second, of petitions relating to the support of wives and children under the provisions of chapter one hundred and thirty-six of the public laws enacted in the year one thousand eight hundred and ninety-five, and amendments thereof and additions thereto, if the defendant resides in the county of Penobscot. Third, of the assaults and batteries described in section twenty-eight of chapter one hundred and eighteen of the revised statutes; of all offenses described in sections one, six, seven, nine and eleven of chapter one hundred and twenty of the revised statutes, when the value of the property is not alleged to exceed thirty dollars; of the offense described in section twenty-one of chapter one hundred and twenty-two of the revised statutes; of all offenses described in sections one and four of chapter one hundred and twenty-three of the revised statutes; of the offenses described in sections one and four of chapter one hundred and twenty-six of the revised statutes, when the value of the money, goods, other property, or thing, alleged to have been fraudulently obtained, sold, conveyed, mortgaged or pledged, or fraudulently removed or concealed, is not alleged to exceed thirty dollars, and on conviction may punish for either of said crimes or offenses by fine not exceeding one hundred dollars and by imprisonment in the county jail for not more than six months; and also of the offenses described in section six of chapter one hundred and twenty-four of the revised statutes, and on conviction may punish therefor by imprisonment in the county jail for not more than sixty days and by fine not exceeding one hundred dollars.

CHAP. 153

—warrants, by whom issued and to whom returnable.

Fourth, of all other crimes and offenses committed in said county which are by law punishable by fine not exceeding one hundred dollars and by imprisonment not exceeding six months, and of all such other crimes and offenses committed in said county jurisdiction whereof is expressly conferred upon municipal courts by any general statute, and, upon conviction, may punish therefor as provided by law. Warrants may be issued by any municipal court or trial justice in said county, upon complaint for offenses committed in said city of Old Town or either of the towns mentioned in section four of this act, but all such warrants shall be made returnable before said Old Town Municipal Court, and no other municipal court, and no trial justice, shall have or take cognizance of any crime or offense committed in said city or in either of said towns.

When title to real estate is in question, shall not have jurisdiction.

Section 6. Said court shall not have jurisdiction of any civil action wherein the title to real estate, according to the pleading or brief statement filed therein by either party, is in question; and all such actions brought in said court shall be removed to the supreme judicial court or otherwise disposed of as in like actions before a trial justice, provided, that nothing herein contained shall prevent said court from proceeding in accordance with the provisions of sections six and seven of chapter ninety-four of the revised statutes.

When judge is interested or related, how actions may be brought.

Section 7. Any action, civil or criminal, in which the judge of said court is interested or related to either of the parties by consanguinity or affinity, within the sixth degree according to the rules of the civil law, or within the degree of second cousin inclusive, but which would otherwise be within the exclusive jurisdiction of said court, may be brought before and disposed of by any trial justice or any other municipal court in said county, in the same manner as other actions before said trial justice or municipal courts. If any action wherein said judge is so interested or related to either party is made returnable before this court, the parties thereto, by themselves or their attorneys, may in writing consent that said judge shall hear and dispose of the same, or such actions shall be disposed of as follows; civil actions, wherein the debt or damages demanded, exclusive of costs, exceed twenty dollars, shall, upon motion, be removed to the supreme judicial court for said county; all other civil actions, and all criminal actions, shall be removed and entered before any such trial justice within said county as may be agreed upon in writing by the parties entering an appearance in such action, or, if no trial justice is agreed upon, before any other municipal court in said county, and such trial justice or other municipal court shall have and take cognizance of such action and dispose of the same as if originally returnable before such justice or court, provided, that nothing in this section contained shall prevent any civil action wherein the title to real estate is in question, from being disposed of in accordance with the provisions of the preceding section. In any action in which said city of Old Town or either of the towns hereinbefore named is a party, or is summoned as trustee, this court shall not lose its jurisdiction by reason of the said judge or recorder being an inhabitant of or owning property in such city or either of said towns, but in any such case the action may, upon written motion of either party, filed before trial, be removed to the supreme judicial court for said county.

—In actions in which city of Old Town is interested, court shall not lose jurisdiction.

Section 8. A term of said court shall be held for the transaction of civil business on the third Tuesday of each month, beginning at ten of the clock in the forenoon. Said court shall also be held on every Tuesday at the usual hour, for the purpose of filing pleas in abatement, the motion mentioned in section eighteen of this act and for the entry and trial of actions of forcible entry and detainer and such actions shall be returnable accordingly and be heard and judgment entered therein on the return day of the writ unless continued for good cause. For the cognizance and trial of criminal cases, and for the entry, hearing and determination of petitions under the provisions of chapter one hundred and thirty-six of the public laws enacted in the year eighteen hundred and ninety-five, said court shall be considered as in constant session. In all cases said court may be adjourned from time to time.

Terms, when held.

—constant session in certain cases.

Section 9. Said court shall be held at such place as the city of Old Town shall provide and said city shall have power and it shall be its duty to raise money to provide a proper place for said court and its officers and suitably furnish, warm and light the same. The salary of the judge of said court is hereby continued at one thousand dollars, annually; that of the recorder is hereby fixed at two hundred dollars, annually, and both of said salaries are to be paid quarterly, with all other expenses of said court, from the treasury of the county of Penobscot.

Location of court.

--salary of judge.

—salary of recorder.

Section 10. The city marshal or one of his deputies shall be in attendance on said court when requested so to do by the judge or recorder, for the purpose of preserving order, and shall execute all legal orders and processes to him directed by the court.

Officers in attendance on court.

Section 11. All fines and forfeitures and fees of the judge and recorder of said court imposed and collected by said court in all criminal cases and all fees of said judge and recorder in civil and criminal cases received by said judge or recorder, shall be accounted for and paid over quarterly into the treasury of said

Fines and forfeitures, how accounted for, and to whom paid.

CHAP. 153

Trial justices, when and for what purposes they may preside.

county for the use of the county; and all fees of said court paid after commitment to any jailer shall be paid by him monthly into said treasury.

Section 12. If at any regular or adjourned term of said court to be held for civil business the judge or recorder is not present at the place for holding said court within two hours after the time for opening said court, then any trial justice or justice of the peace in the county of Penobscot may preside for the purpose of entering and continuing actions and filing papers in said court, and may adjourn said court from time to time, not exceeding one week at any one time, without detriment to any action returnable or pending, and may in his discretion, adjourn said court without day, in which event all actions returned or pending, shall be considered as continued to the next term. No trial justice or justice of the peace shall be disqualified from presiding for the purpose mentioned in this section, by reason of his being interested in any action returnable before or pending in said court.

Appeals, how taken.

Section 13. Any party may appeal from any judgment or sentence of said court to the supreme judicial court in the same manner as from a judgment or sentence of a trial justice.

Writs and processes, forms and service of.

Section 14. Writs and processes issued by said court shall be in the usual forms, and shall be served as like precepts are required to be served when issued by trial justices.

Attachments and levy.

Section 15. All the provisions of the statutes relating to attachment of real and personal property and the levy of executions, shall be applicable to actions brought in this court and executions on judgments rendered therein, provided, that property may be attached in addition to the ad damnum, sufficient to satisfy the costs of suit, and the writs may be framed accordingly.

Civil actions, when entered.

—when in order for trial.

—proviso.

—default.

—pleas in abatement.

—pleadings.

Section 16. All civil actions in said court shall be entered on the first day of the term and not afterwards, except by special permission; and they shall be in order for trial, except actions of forcible entry and detainer, at the next regular monthly term after the entry if not otherwise disposed of, provided, that any action shall be considered in order for trial at the return term when the party so desiring shall have given written notice thereof to the adverse party seven days at least before the sitting of said court. When a defendant, legally summoned, fails to enter his appearance by himself or his attorney on the first day of the return term, he shall be defaulted; but if he afterward appear during said term, the court may for sufficient cause, permit the default to be taken off. Pleas in abatement must be filed on or before the first day of the first regular weekly term held after the entry of the action. The pleadings shall be the same as in the

OLD TOWN MUNICIPAL COURT.   237

CHAP. 153

supreme judicial court, and all provisions of law relative to practice and proceedings in civil actions in the supreme judicial court are hereby made applicable and extended to this court except so far as they are modified by the provisions of this act.

Section 17. Actions pending in this court may be referred in the same manner as in the supreme judicial court, and on the report of the referee to said municipal court, judgment may be rendered in the same manner and with the same effect as in the supreme judicial court, except that the referees' fees shall not be paid by the county but be taxed as costs. *Pending actions.*

Section 18. If any defendant, his agent or attorney, in any civil action in this court in which the debt or damage demanded or claimed in the writ exceeds twenty dollars, shall, on or before the first day of the second regular weekly term of said court after the entry of said action file in said court a motion asking that said cause be removed to the supreme judicial court, and deposit with the judge or recorder the sum of two dollars for copies and entry fee in said supreme court, to be taxed in his costs if he prevails, the said action shall be removed into the supreme judicial court for said county, and shall be entered at the next ensuing term of the supreme judicial court after such removal; and the judge or recorder of said municipal court shall forthwith cause certified copies of the writ, return of the officer and defendant's motion to be filed in the clerk's office of said supreme judicial court and shall pay the entry fee thereof. If no such motion is filed, the said municipal court shall proceed and determine said action, subject to the right of appeal in either party as now provided by law. *Actions may be removed to supreme judicial court, in certain cases.* *—proceedings.*

Section 19. Exceptions may be alleged and cases certified on an agreed statement of facts, or upon evidence reported by the judge in all civil actions as in the supreme judicial court, and the same shall be entered, heard and determined at the law term thereof as if the same had originated in the supreme judicial court for said county of Penobscot; and decisions of the law court in all such cases, shall be certified to said municipal court for final disposition with the same effect as in cases originating in said supreme judicial court. *Exceptions, etc.*

Section 20. Said municipal court may render judgment and issue execution, punish for contempt and compel attendance, as in the supreme judicial court, make all such rules and regulations, not repugnant to law, as may be necessary and proper for the administration of justice, and is clothed with all such power as is necessary for the performance of its duties under this act. *Powers of court.*

Section 21. In any action in which the plaintiff recovers for the penalty, forfeiture, debt or damage not over twenty dollars, *Costs, how taxed.*

238 OLD TOWN MUNICIPAL COURT.

CHAP. 153

or property, the value of which does not exceed that sum, the costs shall be taxed as before trial justices, except that the plaintiff shall have two dollars for his writ. Where the defendant prevails in any action in which the sum claimed in the writ is not over twenty dollars, or property, the value of which does not exceed that sum, he shall recover two dollars for his pleadings, and other costs as before trial justices. In actions where the amount recovered by the plaintiff, exclusive of costs, exceeds twenty dollars, or property, the value of which exceeds that sum, or the amount claimed, or the value of the property recovered exceeds twenty dollars where the defendant prevails, the costs of the parties, trustees and witnesses shall be the same as in the supreme judicial court, except the costs to be taxed for attendance shall be two dollars and fifty cents for each term, for as many terms as may be allowed by the court.

Fees.

Section 22. The price of blank writs and summonses with the seal of the court, signed by the judge or recorder, shall be four cents, and all other fees in civil cases shall be the same as are taxable by a trial justice, except as otherwise provided in sections eighteen and twenty-one. For every warrant issued in criminal cases there shall be allowed one dollar, and for the trial of an issue in such cases one dollar may be charged for the first day and two dollars for each subsequent day actually employed. All other fees in criminal cases shall be the same as are taxable by trial justices.

Trial justices, jurisdiction restricted.

Section 23. Trial justices are hereby restricted from exercising any jurisdiction in said city of Old Town or either of the towns named in section four of this act over any matter or thing, civil or criminal, except such as are within the jurisdiction of justices of the peace and quorum and except as provided in sections five, seven and twelve of this act, provided, that whenever the offices of judge and recorder are together vacant any trial justice shall have and exercise the same jurisdiction 'as though this municipal court had never been established.

Inconsistent acts, repealed.

Section 24. All acts and parts of acts inconsistent herewith are hereby repealed, but nothing in this act shall be construed to authorize said court to infringe upon the executive jurisdictions heretofore conferred upon other municipal courts in said county of Penobscot except so far as such exclusive jurisdictions may be affected by the provisions of section four of this act.

Revised statutes, meaning of, defined.

Section 25. The expression, revised statutes, as used in this act relates to the revision of the statutes of the year eighteen hundred and eighty-three and shall be held to include all additions thereto and amendments thereof.

Section 26. This act shall take effect when approved.

Approved March 11, 1903.

Chapter 154.

An Act for the better protection of Deer in the County of York.

Be it enacted by the Senate and House of Representatives in Legislature assembled, as follows:

Section 1. No person shall take, catch, kill, chase or hunt any deer in the county of York, except during the month of October of each year, and no person shall during the open season in this county, take, catch, kill or have in possession more than two deer or parts thereof. Whoever shall violate any of the provisions of this section shall be subject to a penalty of one hundred dollars and costs for each offense. *Close time on deer, in York county.*

Section 2. This act shall take effect on the first day of October, in the year of our Lord one thousand nine hundred and three.

Approved March 11, 1903.

Chapter 155.

An Act to incorporate the Liberty Water Company.

Be it enacted by the Senate and House of Representatives in Legislature assembled, as follows:

Section 1. Lucius C. Morse, J. J. Walker, W. J. Knowlton, Arthur Ritchie and A. C. Crockett, and such persons as they may associate with themselves in the enterprise, and their successors, are hereby incorporated into a corporation by the name of the Liberty Water Company, for the purpose of supplying the town of Liberty, in the county of Waldo, and the inhabitants of said town, with pure water for industrial, manufacturing, domestic, sanitary and municipal purposes, including extinguishment of fires. *Corporators. —corporate name. —purposes.*

Section 2. Said company, for said purposes, may detain, collect, take, store, use and distribute water from Saint George's lake or stream, or any other water source or sources, in said town of Liberty. *May take water in town of Liberty.*

Section 3. Said company is hereby authorized to lay, construct, and maintain in, under, through, along and across the highways, ways, streets and bridges in said town, and to take up, replace and repair all such sluices, aqueducts, pipes, hydrants, and structures as may be necessary for the purposes of their incorporation, under such reasonable restrictions and conditions as the selectmen may impose. And said company shall be *May lay pipes, in and across highways, etc.*

LIBERTY WATER COMPANY.

CHAP. 155

responsible for all damage to all corporations, persons and property occasioned by the use of such highways, ways and streets, and shall pay to said town all sums recovered against said town for damages from obstruction caused by said corporation, and for all expenses, including reasonable counsel fees incurred in defending such suits, with interest on the same.

May cross water courses, etc.

—damages.

Section 4. Said company shall have power to cross any water course, public or private sewer, or to change the direction thereof when necessary for the purpose of their corporation, but in such manner as not to obstruct or impair the use thereof, and said company shall be liable for any injury caused thereby. Whenever said company shall lay down any fixture in any highway, way or street, or make any alterations or repairs upon its works in any highway, way or street, it shall cause the same to be done with as little obstruction to public travel as may be practicable, and shall, at its own expense, without unnecessary delay, cause the earth and pavements thus removed by it, to be replaced in proper condition.

May lay pipes in highways.

—may build dams.

Section 5. Said company is hereby authorized to lay, construct and maintain its pipes under the highways, ways and streets in said Liberty and to build and maintain all necessary structures thereof, to build dams and reservoirs for storage of water across any brook or stream in said Liberty.

May take lands.

Section 6. Said company may take and hold any lands necessary for reservoirs, hydrants and other necessary structures, and may locate, lay and maintain pipes, hydrants and other necessary structures or fixtures in, over and through any land for its purposes, and excavate in and through such lands for such locations, construction and maintenance. It may enter upon such lands to make surveys and locations and shall file in the registry of deeds in said county of Waldo, plans for such locations and lands showing the property taken.

—may make surveys.

Damages, how assessed.

Section 7. Should the said company and the owner of such land, be unable to agree upon the damages to be paid for such location, taking, holding and construction, the land owner may within twelve months after said filing of plans of location, apply to the county commissioners of said county of Waldo and cause such damages to be assessed in the same manner and under the same conditions, restrictions and limitations, as are by law prescribed in the case of damages by the laying out of highways, so far as such law is consistent with the provisions of this act.

May contract to supply water.

Section 8. Said corporation is hereby authorized to make contracts with the United States, and with corporations and inhabitants of said town of Liberty, or any village corporation or association in said town, for the purpose of supplying water as contemplated by this act, and said town of Liberty, or part thereof, is hereby authorized by its selectmen to enter into contract with said company for a supply of water for any and all purposes mentioned in this act, and for such exemption from public burden as said town and said company may agree, which, when made, shall be legal and binding upon all parties thereto. Any village corporation in said town through its assessors, is also authorized to contract with said company for water for all public purposes.

Section 9. Whoever shall wilfully or maliciously corrupt the water of said company, whether frozen or not, or in any way render such water impure, or whoever shall wilfully or maliciously injure any of the works of said company, shall be punished by fine not exceeding one thousand dollars, or by imprisonment not exceeding two years, and shall be liable to said company for three times the actual damage, to be recovered in any proper action.

Corruption of water, how punished.

Section 10. The capital stock of said company shall be ten thousand dollars, which may be increased to fifty thousand dollars by a vote of said company, and said stock shall be divided into shares of twenty-five dollars each.

Capital stock.

Section 11. Said company for all of its said purposes, may hold real and personal estate necessary and convenient therefor, not exceeding in amount one hundred thousand dollars.

May hold real and personal property.

Section 12. Said company may issue its bonds for the construction of its works of any and all kinds, upon such rates and time as it may deem expedient, not exceeding the sum of fifty thousand dollars, and secure the same by mortgage of the franchise and property of said company.

May issue bonds.

—may mortgage property.

Section 13. The first meeting of said company may be called by a written notice thereof, signed by any three corporators herein named, served upon each corporator by giving him the same in hand or by leaving the same at his last usual place of abode, seven days before the time of meeting.

First meeting, how called.

Section 14. This act shall take effect when approved.

Approved March 11, 1908.

Chapter 156.

An Act to extend the charter of the Bluehill Water Company.

Be it enacted by the Senate and House of Representatives in Legislature assembled, as follows:

Charter extended.
Section 1. The rights, powers and privileges of the Bluehill Water Company, which were granted by chapter three hundred and fifty-three of the private and special laws of eighteen hundred and eighty-nine, and amended and extended by chapter four hundred and ninety-nine of the private and special laws of eighteen hundred and ninety-seven and extended by chapter one hundred and nine of the private and special laws of eighteen hundred and ninety-nine, and further extended by chapter three hundred and thirteen of the private and special laws of nineteen hundred and one, are hereby extended for two years additional; and the persons named in said act and amendment, their associates and successors, shall have all the rights, powers and privileges that were granted them by said act, to be exercised in the same manner and for the same purpose as specified in said act.

Section 2. This act shall take effect when approved.

Approved March 11, 1903.

Chapter 157.

An Act granting a new charter to the Farmington Village Corporation.

Be it enacted by the Senate and House of Representatives in Legislature assembled, as follows:

Corporate limits.
Section 1. The territory in the town of Farmington, comprising front lots number twenty-four, twenty-five, twenty-six and twenty-seven, on the east side of Sandy river, together with the inhabitants thereon, shall continue to be a body politic and **—corporate name.** corporate by the name of the Farmington Village Corporation, with all the rights and privileges provided by the general laws of the state relating to corporations.

May raise money by taxation on loan.
Section 2. Said corporation is hereby authorized and vested with power at all legal meetings called for the purpose, to raise money by taxation or loan, including the power to issue bonds or notes therefor, for the following purposes:

—may own and operate water works.
To own, operate and maintain the entire water works and rights acquired by purchase of the Farmington Water Company in accordance with chapter four hundred and thirty-four of the private and special laws of Maine enacted by the legislature of eighteen hundred and ninety-seven, and to make extensions,

FARMINGTON VILLAGE CORPORATION.

CHAP. 157

additions or improvements of the same and to repair and rebuild the same anywhere within the limits of the town of Farmington, and to adopt all rules and regulations for operating said water works, including fixing and establishing the water rates and shall hereafter own and operate said Farmington Water Company's entire works and rights, and exercise and enjoy and have all the rights and franchise that was granted to said Farmington Water Company as fully as if granted to said Farmington Village Corporation direct. —may adopt rules and regulations.

To organize and maintain an efficient fire department, and to adopt all rules and regulations for governing the same. —may organize and maintain fire department.

To appoint by its assessors two or more persons annually whose duties and power shall be the same as those of fire wardens of towns. —fire wardens.

To organize and maintain such a police department as may be necessary for the security of property, the protection of life, and the promotion of good order and quiet within its corporation limits, and to adopt all rules and regulations necessary for governing and controlling said department. —police department.

To purchase lands for village parks or commons, and to expend money in the improvement of land used for this purpose, and also to plant and care for shade trees. —parks and commons.

To receive, hold and manage devises, bequests, or gifts for any of the above purposes. —hold devises, etc.

Also shall have exclusive authority to grant licenses for exhibitions or shows within the limits of said corporation as the municipal officers of the town now have by law, with the right to collect the same fees for said licenses as are now provided by law for like licenses by the municipal officers of towns, and the same penalties and forfeitures may be enforced by said corporation for exhibitions or shows within its limits without license as are provided by law for exhibitions or shows without license from the municipal officers of towns. —may grant licenses.

Section 3. Any money raised by said corporation for the purposes aforesaid, shall be assessed upon the property and polls within the territory aforesaid by the assessors of said corporation in the same manner as is by law provided for the assessment of town taxes. Assessments.

Section 4. After a vote of the said corporation to raise money for any of the purposes enumerated in this charter, it shall be the duty of the assessors as soon as may be, to assess said amount upon the polls and estates of the persons residing in the territory aforesaid, and upon the estates of non-resident proprietors thereof, and to certify and deliver lists of assessments so made, to the collector whose duty it shall be to collect the same in like Assessors, duties of.

—collector, duties of.

CHAP. 157

—treasurer, duties of

manner as county and town taxes are by law collected by towns, and to pay over the same to the treasurer of said corporation, who shall receive the same and pay it out to order or direction of the corporation, and keep a regular account of all moneys received and paid out, and exhibit the same to the assessors whenever requested; and said corporation shall have the same power to direct the mode of collecting said taxes as towns have in the collection of town taxes.

Officers.

Section 5. The officers of said corporation shall consist of a clerk, treasurer, collector, three assessors, and such other officers as the by-laws of the corporation may require the assessors to appoint.

By-laws, adoption of.

Section 6. Said corporation at the next annual meeting after the adoption of this charter, or at any legal meeting called for that purpose, shall adopt a code of by-laws not repugnant to this charter or the laws of this state, for the efficient management of the municipal affairs of said corporation. The by-laws aforesaid may be amended at any legal meeting of the corporation called for that purpose.

Assessors, clerk and treasurer, election of.

Section 7. The assessors, clerk and treasurer of said corporation shall be elected by ballot at the annual meeting to be held in the month of January.

—tenure of clerk and treasurer.

The clerk and treasurer shall hold office each for one year, or until successors are chosen and qualified. The assessors shall appoint a collector. At the first annual meeting of the corporation after the adoption of this charter, one assessor shall be elected by ballot for one year, one for two years, and one for three years, and thereafter one assessor shall be elected at each annual meeting for the term of three years.

—collector, appointment of.

—assessors, election of.

Clerk, shall keep record of meetings.

Section 8. The clerk shall keep a record of all the doings and proceedings at the meetings of the said corporation.

Bonds of collector and of treasurer.

Section 9. The collector and treasurer shall give bonds in double the amount of the taxes so raised, to the inhabitants of said corporation, which bond shall be approved by the assessors and clerk.

Meetings, how called.

Section 10. The meetings of said corporation shall be called by publishing the warrant of the assessors in any newspaper printed within the limits of the corporation; the publication of which shall be at least seven days before the time of holding said meeting; or by posting copies of said warrant in three public places within the limits of said corporation, at least seven days before said meeting.

If the assessors unreasonably refuse to call a meeting of the corporation, any ten or more legal voters may apply to a justice of the peace within the corporation, who may issue his warrant for calling such a meeting, as prescribed in the statutes for calling town meetings.

Section 11. All persons liable to be taxed for polls, residing in the limits of said corporation, shall be legal voters at any meeting of said corporation. *Legal voters.*

Section 12. All acts and parts of acts, inconsistent with this act, are hereby repealed. Provided, however, the repeal of the said acts shall not affect any act done, or any act accruing, or accrued, or any suit or proceeding had or commenced in any civil case before the time when such repeal shall take effect, under the acts hereby repealed, and before the time when repeal shall take effect, shall be affected by the repeal. And provided, also, that all persons who, at the time said repeal shall take effect, shall hold any office under the said acts or by-laws of the Farmington Village Corporation, shall continue to hold the same until others are elected and qualified in their stead, as provided in this act. *Inconsistent acts repealed. —proviso. —proviso.*

And provided, also, that all acts of legislature, relating to the Farmington Village Corporation and the by-laws, rules and regulations of the Farmington Village Corporation in force at time of the passage of this act if not inconsistent therewith shall remain in force and are not repealed by this act. *—proviso.*

Section 13. This act shall be void unless at a legal meeting of the corporation called for the purpose, the legal voters of the corporation shall vote, by ballot on the question of accepting this charter, and if a majority shall vote in favor of its acceptance, then it shall take effect at the next annual, nineteen hundred four, meeting of the corporation, and its officers shall be elected according to its provisions. *Charter, ratification of.*

Approved March 11, 1903.

Chapter 158.

An Act to Incorporate the Brunswick and Topsham Water District.

Be it enacted by the Senate and House of Representatives in Legislature assembled, as follows:

Section 1. The territory and people constituting the towns of Brunswick and Topsham shall constitute a body politic and corporate under the name of the Brunswick and Topsham Water District, for the purpose of supplying the inhabitants of said district and said municipalities with pure water for domestic and municipal purposes. *Corporate limits.*

246 BRUNSWICK AND TOPSHAM WATER DISTRICT.

CHAP. 158

May take water in said district.

—exception.

Damages, liability for.

May lay pipes in streets and highways.

Board of trustees.

—how chosen.

—shall have seal.

—tenure of trustees.

—vacancies, how filled.

Section 2. Said district is hereby authorized for the purposes aforesaid to take and hold sufficient water of any surface or underground brooks, streams and springs in said district, excepting Thompson's brook and the tributaries thereof, and may take and hold by purchase or otherwise any land or real estate necessary for erecting dams, power, reservoirs, or for preserving the purity of the water and water shed, and for laying and maintaining aqueducts for taking, discharging and disposing of water.

Section 3. Said district shall be liable for all damages that shall be sustained by any persons or corporations in their property by the taking of any land whatsoever, or water, or by flowage, or by excavating through any land for the purpose of laying pipes, building dams or constructing reservoirs. If any person sustaining damage as aforesaid and said corporation shall not mutually agree upon the sum to be paid therefor, such person may cause his damages to be ascertained in the same manner and under the same conditions, restrictions and limitations as are or may be prescribed in the case of damages by the laying out of highways.

Section 4. Said district is hereby authorized to lay in and through the streets and highways thereof, and to take up, repair and replace all such pipes, aqueducts and fixtures as may be necessary for the objects above set forth, and whenever said district shall lay any pipes or aqueducts in any street or highway it shall cause the same to be done with as little obstruction as possible to the public travel, and shall at its own expense without unnecessary delay cause the earth and pavement removed by it to be replaced in proper condition.

Section 5. All the affairs of said water district shall be managed by a board of trustees composed of three members, two to be chosen by the municipal officers of Brunswick, and one by the municipal officers of Topsham. As soon as convenient after the members of said board have been chosen, said trustees shall hold a meeting at the town building at Brunswick, and organize by the election of a president and clerk, adopt a corporate seal and when necessary may choose a treasurer and all other needful officers and agents for the proper conduct and management of the affairs of said district. At said first meeting they shall determine by lot the term of office of each trustee so that one shall serve for one year, one for two years and one for three years; and whenever the term of office of a trustee expires, the body which appointed said trustee shall appoint a successor to serve the full term of three years, and in case any other vacancy arises it shall be filled in like manner for the unexpired term. They may also ordain and establish such by-laws as are necessary for their own convenience and the proper management of the affairs of the district. The term of office of trustees shall begin on the first Monday of April, in the year of our Lord nineteen hundred three. Said trustees may procure an office and incur such expenses as may be necessary. Each member shall receive in full compensation for his services an allowance of one hundred dollars per annum.

—compensation of trustees.

Section 6. Said water district is hereby authorized and empowered to acquire by purchase or by the exercise of the right of eminent domain, which right is hereby expressly delegated to said district for said purpose, the entire plant, property and franchises, rights and privileges now held by the Maine Water Company within said district, excepting the Thompson's brook and its tributaries, but including all other lands, waters, water rights, dams, reservoirs, pipes, machinery, fixtures, hydrants, tools, apparatus and appliances in said district, owned by said company and used or usable in supplying water therein, and any other real estate in said district.

Maine Water Company, property of, in district may be acquired.

Section 7. In case said trustees fail to agree with said Maine Water Company upon the terms of purchase of the above mentioned property on or before January first, nineteen hundred and four, said water district through its trustees is hereby authorized to take said plant, property and franchises as for public uses by petition therefor in the manner hereinafter provided. And said water district through its trustees is hereby authorized on or after January first, nineteen hundred and four, to file a petition in the clerk's office of the supreme judicial court for the county of Cumberland or Sagadahoc in term time or in vacation, addressed to any justice of said court, who after notice to said Maine Water Company and its mortgagees, shall after hearing and within thirty days after the filing of said petition appoint three disinterested appraisers, none of whom shall be residents of the town of Brunswick or the county of Sagadahoc, one of whom shall be learned in the law, for the purpose of fixing the valuation of said plant, property and franchises, and of assessing the additional damages, if any, suffered by the said Maine Water Company, by reason of the taking of said plant, property and franchises, and of the severance thereof from the entire water system and franchises as now operated, composed of Brunswick, Bath, West Bath and Woolwich ; it being the intent of this act that the amount of said valuation and of said additional damages, if any, taken together, shall be so fixed as to equal the difference between the valuation, before severance, of the entire plant, property and franchises of said company in Brunswick, West Bath, Bath and

Eminent domain, how applied to property of Maine Water Co.

—petition.

—appraisers.

—assessing additional damages.

CHAP. 158

Woolwich, and the valuation, after severance, of the plant, property and franchises of said company in the easterly part of Brunswick, and in West Bath, Bath and Woolwich, as aforesaid, both said last named valuations to be determined under the principles of eminent domain. The said appraisers shall have the power of compelling the attendance of witnesses and the production of books and papers pertinent to the issue, and may administer oaths; and any witness, or person in charge of such books and papers refusing to attend, or to procure the same, shall be subject to the same penalties and proceedings, so far as applicable, as witnesses summoned to attend the supreme judicial court. The appraisers so appointed shall, after due notice and hearing, fix all valuations of plants, properties and franchises and assess all damages, if any, in the manner heretofore detailed by this act, so that said Maine Water Company shall receive just compensation for the taking of said Brunswick plant, property and franchises and for the severance thereof from the entire water system and franchises above described. The first day of January, nineteen hundred and four, shall be the date as of which the valuation aforesaid shall be fixed, from which day interest on said award shall run and all net rents and profits accruing thereafter shall belong to said water district. The report of said appraisers, or of a majority of them, shall be filed in said clerk's office in term time or vacation as soon as may be after their appointment, and such single justice, or in case of his inability to act, then any justice designated for the purpose by the chief justice, may, after notice and hearing, confirm or reject the same, or recommit it if justice so requires. Before a commission is issued to the appraisers, either party may ask for instructions to the appraisers, and all questions of law arising upon said requests for instructions or upon any other matters in issue may be reported to the law court for determination before the appraisers proceed to fix the valuation of the property and assess the additional damages, if any. The award of the appraisers shall be conclusive as to valuations and damages. Upon the confirmation of said report the court so sitting shall thereupon, after hearing, make final decree upon the entire matter, including the application of the purchase money, discharge of incumbrances and transfer of the property, jurisdiction over which is hereby conferred, with the same power to enforce said decree as in equity cases. Upon request of either party the justice so making such final decree shall make separate findings of law and fact. All such findings of fact shall be final, but either party aggrieved may take exceptions to any rulings of law so made, the same to be accompanied only by such parts of the case as are necessary to a clear under-

BRUNSWICK AND TOPSHAM WATER DISTRICT. 249

CHAP. 158

standing of the questions raised thereby. Such exceptions shall
be claimed on the docket within ten days after such final decree
is signed, entered and filed, and notice thereof has been given
by the clerk to the parties or their counsel, and said exceptions so
claimed shall be made up, allowed and filed within said time
unless further time is granted by the court or by agreement of
parties. They shall be entered at the next term of the law court
to be held after the filing of said decree and there heard, unless
otherwise agreed, or the law court shall for good cause order a
further time for hearing thereon. Upon such hearing the law
court may confirm, reverse or modify the decree of the court
below, or remand the cause for further proceedings as it deems
proper. During the pendency of such exceptions the cause shall
remain on the docket of the court below marked 'law' and decree
shall be entered thereon by a single justice in term time or in
vacation, in accordance with the certificate and opinion of the law
court. Before said plant, property and franchises are transferred
in accordance with such final decree, and before payment therefor,
the court sitting in said county of Cumberland or Sagadahoc,
by single justice thereof as hereinbefore provided, shall, upon
motion of either party, after notice and hearing, take account of
all receipts and expenditures properly had or incurred by the
Maine Water Company belonging to this period, from and after
January first, nineteen hundred four, and all net rents and
profits accruing thereafter, and shall order the net balance to be
added to, or deducted from, the amount to be paid under such
final decree, as the case may be. All findings of law or fact by
such single justice at such hearing shall be final. On payment
or tender by said district of the amount so fixed, including such
additional damages, if any, and the performance of all other terms
and conditions so imposed by the court, said entire plant, property
and franchises in said district westerly of the Thompson's brook
plant shall become vested in said water district and be free from
all liens, mortgages and incumbrances theretofore created by the
Pejepscot Water Company, the Bath Water Supply Company,
or the Maine Water Company. After the filing of said petition
it shall not be discontinued or withdrawn by said water district,
and the said Maine Water Company may thereafterwards on its
part cause said valuation and assessment to be made as herein
provided and shall be entitled to appropriate process to compel
said water district to perform the terms of the final decree, and
to pay for said plant, property and franchises in accordance
therewith.

Exceptions shall be filed within 10 days.

Section 8. All valid contracts now existing between the
Pejepscot Water Company or the Maine Water Company and

Existing contracts shall be assumed.

CHAP. 158

any persons or corporations for supplying water within said district shall be assumed and carried out by said Brunswick and Topsham Water District.

May issue bonds.

Section 9. For accomplishing the purposes of this act said water district, through its trustees, is authorized to issue its bonds to an amount sufficient to procure funds to pay the expenses incurred in the acquisition of the property of said Maine Water Company, and the purchase thereof, and for further extensions, additions and improvements of said plant, and to secure a new source of supply. Said bonds shall be a legal obligation of said water district, which is hereby declared to be a quasi municipal corporation within the meaning of section fifty-five, chapter forty-six of the revised statutes, and all the provisions of said section shall be applicable thereto. The said bonds shall be a legal investment for savings banks.

—declared to be a quasi municipal corporation.

—bonds shall be a legal investment for savings banks.

Rates.

Section 10. All individuals, firms and corporations, whether private, public or municipal, shall pay to the treasurer of said district the rates established by said board of trustees for the water used by them, and said rates shall be uniform within the district. Said rates shall be so established as to provide revenue for the following purposes:

—running expenses.

I. To pay the current running expenses for maintaining the water system and provide for such extensions and renewals as may become necessary.

—payment of interest.

II. To provide for payment of the interest on the indebtedness of the district.

—sinking fund.

III. To provide each year a sum equal to not less than one nor more than four per cent of the entire indebtedness of the district, which sum shall be turned into a sinking fund to provide for the final extinguishment of the funded debt. The money set aside for the sinking fund shall be devoted to the retirement of the obligations of the district or invested in such securities as savings banks are allowed to hold.

Taxation.

Section 11. The property of said district shall be exempt from taxation.

Powers granted.

Section 12. All incidental powers, rights and privileges necessary to the accomplishment of the main object herein set forth are granted to the corporation hereby created.

This act to take effect when approved by ballot.

Section 13. This act shall take effect when approved by a majority vote by ballot of the inhabitants of each of said towns, at their annual meeting in March in the year one thousand nine hundred and three or at a special meeting to be called and held for the purpose within sixty days after the approval of this act. This act shall take effect when approved by the governor so far as necessary to empower the calling and holding of such meeting.

The approval of this act in the manner provided by this section shall constitute an acceptance by said water district of the methods of appraisal prescribed by section seven hereof, and shall bind said water district and said water company thereto.

Section 14. Sections two, three and four of this act shall be inoperative, null and void, unless the said water district shall first acquire by purchase, or by the exercise of the right of eminent domain, as in this act provided, the plant, property and franchises, rights and privileges now held by the Maine Water Company within said district. *Sections 2, 3 and 4 inoperative until purchase, etc., is made.*

Section 15. All costs and expenses arising under the provisions of this act shall be paid and borne as directed by the court in the final decree provided by section seven. *Costs and expenses, how borne and paid.*

Approved March 11, 1903.

Chapter 159.

An Act to incorporate the Kennebec Valley Railroad Company.

Be it enacted by the Senate and House of Representatives in Legislature assembled, as follows:

Section 1. William M. Ayer and A. R. Small both of Oakland, Maine, and R. W. Dunn and William T. Haines, both of Waterville, Maine, their associates, successors and assigns are hereby made a corporation by the name of the Kennebec Valley Railroad Company, for the purpose of buying or leasing the property, capital stock, rights, privileges, immunities and franchises of the Somerset Railway, and of thereafterwards exercising the powers of this act. *Corporators. —corporate name. —purposes*

Section 2. The capital stock of said corporation shall consist of not more than ten thousand shares of the par value of one hundred dollars each, the amount to be fixed from time to time by the corporation. The immediate government of its affairs shall be vested in a board of directors to be chosen as the by-laws of said corporation may provide, not in conflict with the general laws of the state, who shall hold their offices until others are chosen and qualified in their places. It shall have power to make, ordain and establish all necessary by-laws not inconsistent with said general laws. *Capital stock. —board of directors. —tenure. —powers.*

Section 3. The said corporation is authorized to hold for the purposes of this act so much real and personal estate as may be necessary and convenient therefor. *May hold real and personal estate.*

Section 4. The said corporation is further authorized to purchase or lease the property, capital stock, rights, privileges, *Somerset Ry. may purchase property of.*

CHAP. 159

immunities and franchises of the Somerset Railway upon such terms as may be mutually agreed upon. And upon such purchase or lease the said Kennebec Valley Railroad Company shall have, hold, possess, exercise and enjoy all the locations, powers, privileges, rights, immunities, franchises, property and assets which at the time of such transfers shall then be had, held, and possessed or enjoyed by said Somerset Railway, and shall be subject to all the duties, restrictions and liabilities to which the said Somerset Railway shall then be subject by reason of any charter, contract or general or special law or otherwise.

Somerset Ry. may sell its property.

Section 5. The Somerset Railway is hereby authorized to sell or lease its property, capital stock, rights, privileges, immunities and franchises to the said Kennebec Valley Railroad Company or to any other connecting railroad company upon such terms as may be mutually agreed upon, but any such sale or lease shall be made subject to all the outstanding liabilities of the said Somerset Railway. In case of such sale or lease to the said Kennebec Valley Railroad Company it may mortgage the franchises and property so acquired for the security of any bonds, or other indebtedness authorized by this act, but all such mortgages shall be subject to the outstanding bonds or other indebtedness of the said Somerset Railway existing at the time of said sale or lease.

Pending proceedings, how prosecuted or defended.

Section 6. All proceedings, suits at law or in equity, which may be pending at the time of any such sale or lease, to which the said Somerset Railway may be a party, may be prosecuted or defended by the said Kennebec Valley Railroad Company in like manner and with like effect as if such transfer had not been made. All claims, contracts, rights and causes of action of or against said Somerset Railway, at law or in equity, may be enforced by an action to be begun or prosecuted by or against said Kennebec Valley Railroad Company.

May issue stock and bonds.

Section 7. Said Kennebec Valley Railroad Company may issue its stock and bonds in payment and exchange for the stock, franchises and property of the Somerset Railway in such manner and in such amounts as may be agreed upon.

Existing debts, who liable for.

Section 8. When the transfer authorized by this act is carried out and fully completed the Kennebec Valley Railroad Company shall be liable for the then legal existing debts and obligations of said Somerset Railway.

Location of road.

Section 9. Upon and after the completion of the aforesaid sale or lease the said Kennebec Valley Railroad Company shall be and hereby is authorized to locate, construct, equip, maintain and operate a railroad from some point in the town of Bingham, in the county of Somerset, by the most feasible route within the valley of the Kennebec river, by such course within said territory to some point or place on the west shore of Moosehead lake, as the directors of said corporation in the exercise of their best judgment shall deem most favorable and best calculated to promote public convenience, with all the powers and subject to all the liabilities incident to railroad corporations under the general laws of the state.

Section 10. Said corporation is further authorized to carry on the business of an express company upon its own lines, and also to maintain and operate telegraph and telephone lines for public use along its location and to its principal offices as the same may be located. It may also erect and maintain hotels, cottages and pleasure grounds, own and operate steamboats upon any lakes and ponds near its location, acquire and own interests in timber lands and water powers, operate and manage the same either alone or in connection with others, build dams, improve streams and do all things necessary, proper and convenient in connection with the ownership and management of timber lands or water powers, but the right to take land or other property shall not extend to property to be used for the purposes authorized by this section, except for telegraph and telephone lines, and all such land or property so to be used shall be acquired by purchase and in no other way. *May carry on express business.* *—may own steamboats.*

Section 11. A toll is hereby granted for the benefit of said corporation upon all passengers and property which may be carried over its railroads or in any of its steamboats, and upon all telephone and telegraph messages which may be transmitted over its lines, at such rates as may be established by its directors, subject to such general laws as are or may from time to time be established. *Tolls granted*

Section 12. Said corporation may make connections with any other railroad or railroads on such terms as may be mutually agreed upon. It may also sell or lease its railroad, franchises, and property, either before or after its road shall have been completed, upon such terms as it may determine, subject in all cases to the approval of a majority of the outstanding stock in each corporation. *Connections with other railroads.*

Section 13. Said corporation may purchase or lease the property and franchises of any connecting railroad in this state, or purchase or hold the stock and bonds of any such corporation, and all such connecting corporations or any corporation, association or persons claiming rights in stock, bonds, mortgages or franchises of any such corporation are hereby authorized to make such sale or lease. All such property, franchises, stock, bonds or leasehold interests so acquired may be pledged or *May acquire connecting railroads.*

mortgaged to secure the bonds herein authorized, or any other lawful indebtedness.

Section 14. Said corporation shall organize, and the location of its railroad, according to actual survey, shall be filed with the county commissioners of Somerset county on or before the first day of December, in the year of our Lord nineteen hundred and six, and if it shall, before the thirty-first day of December of the same year complete, equip and operate ten miles of said railroad within its said location, then the said corporation shall be and hereby is given until the thirty-first day of December, in the year of our Lord nineteen hundred and sixteen, within which to build and operate the remaining portion of its said railroad within its said location.

Section 15. If the said railroad company shall build as aforesaid at least ten miles of its railroad within its location aforesaid under the rights given to it by this act, within and during the period expiring on said thirty-first day of December, in the year of our Lord nineteen hundred and six, no railroads shall be built parallel to said railroad which shall at any time within five miles from the line of said railroad so located. It is the intention of this section to encourage the building of said railroad within the location as herein provided, and to prevent its paralleling by any other railroad within the time within which it is authorized to build its said railroad within the location hereinbefore provided, but not to prohibit the building of any railroad which may in good faith be built to connect with or cross said railroad without running in the same general direction as the location aforesaid.

Section 16. The said corporation is hereby authorized to enter into a contract with the state of Maine for the transportation over its said railroad of troops and munitions of war free of charge, other than as herein provided, for a period of twenty years after the construction and operation of the aforesaid first ten miles of railroad by this corporation, and to receive thereafter from the state annually for such term of twenty years an amount which shall equal ninety-five per cent of the tax collected in the corresponding year by said state from said corporation upon its railroad and other real and personal property used in connection with the maintenance and operation of said railroad, including its stock and franchise but not including timber lands, water powers, hotels, cottages or steamboat property. Whenever such contract shall be prepared and signed by the president and directors of said railroad company and approved by a majority of its stockholders at a meeting duly called for that purpose, it shall be presented to the state treasurer and it is hereby made the duty of said treasurer to execute said contract in behalf of said state, and thereafterwards the state treasurer shall pay over to the said corporation each year during the term of said contract the amount provided in this section.

Section 17. Said corporation may issue its bonds from time to time upon such rates and times as may be deemed expedient, and in such amounts as may be required for the purposes of this act, and secure the same by appropriate mortgages upon its franchises and property. *May issue bonds.*

Section 18. The first meeting of said corporation may be called by any corporator within named by notice thereof in writing signed by said corporator and given in hand or mailed to each of the other corporators, at least seven days before said meeting, and any corporator may act at said meeting, by written proxy. *First meeting, how called.*

Section 19. Nothing in this act shall be construed as affecting the rights as now provided by law for minority stockholders in any company or corporation to be affected hereby. *Rights of minority stockholders.*

Section 20. This act shall take effect when approved.

Approved March 11, 1903.

Chapter 160.

An Act to incorporate the Houlton and Woodstock Electric Railroad Company.

Be it enacted by the Senate and House of Representatives in Legislature assembled, as follows:

Section 1. George Ingraham, Joseph A. Browne, Clarence H. Pearce, John Watson, Don A. H. Powers, Ransford W. Shaw, Charles D. Merritt, John B. Madigan, Leland O. Ludwig, Frank M. Hume, Hudson T. Frisbie, Willard S. Lewin, James Archibald and Harry M. Briggs, their associates, successors and assigns, are hereby constituted a corporation by the name of the Houlton and Woodstock Electric Railroad Company, with authority to construct, maintain and use a street railroad, to be operated by horse power or electricity with convenient single and double tracks, side tracks, switches or turnouts, with any necessary or convenient line of poles, wires, appliances, appurtenances or conduits, from the east line of the town of Houlton westward across the town of Houlton to and into the towns of Hodgdon, Linneus, New Limerick, Littleton and Ludlow, in the county of Aroostook, and from and to such other points and upon and over such other streets and ways, in the towns of Houlton, Hodgdon, Linneus, New Limerick, Littleton and Ludlow, as shall from *Corporators. —corporate name. Location of route.*

256 HOULTON AND WOODSTOCK ELECTRIC RAILROAD COMPANY.

CHAP. 160

—proviso.

time to time be fixed and determined by the municipal officers of said towns, and assented to in writing by said corporation, and shall also have authority to construct, maintain and use said railroad over and upon any lands where the land damages have been mutually settled by said corporation and the owners thereof; provided, however, that all tracks of said railroad shall be laid at such distances from the sidewalk in any of said towns as the municipal officers thereof shall, in their order fixing the routes and locations of said railroad, determine to be for public safety and convenience. The written assent of said corporation to any vote of the municipal officers of either of said towns, prescribing from time to time, the routes of said railroad therein, shall be filed with the clerk of said town, and shall be taken and deemed to be the location thereof. Said corporation shall have power, from time to time, to fix such rates of compensation for transporting persons and property as it may think expedient, and shall have all the powers and be subject to all the liabilities of corporations as set forth in the forty-sixth chapter of the revised statutes.

Municipal officers may regulate rate of speed, removal of snow, etc.

Section 2. The municipal officers of said towns shall have power, at all times, to make all regulations as to the rate of speed, the removal of snow and ice from the streets, roads and ways by said company at its expense, and the manner of use of tracks of said railroad within each of said towns as public convenience and safety may require.

Repairs on portions of streets occupied.

Section 3. Said corporation shall keep and maintain in repair such portions of the streets and ways as shall be occupied by the tracks of said railroad, and shall make all other repairs of said streets, roads and ways within either of said towns which in the opinion of the municipal officers of said towns may be rendered necessary by the occupation of the same by said railroad and if not repaired upon reasonable notice, such repairs may be made by said towns at the expense of said corporation.

Obstruction of tracks, how punished.

Section 4. If any person shall wilfully or maliciously obstruct said corporation in the use of its roads or tracks or the passing of the cars or carriages of said corporation thereon, such person and all who shall aid or abet therein, shall be punished by a fine not exceeding two hundred dollars or with imprisonment in the county jail for a period not exceeding sixty days.

Capital stock.

Section 5. The capital stock of said corporation shall not exceed two hundred and fifty thousand dollars, to be divided into shares of one hundred dollars each.

May hold real and personal estate.

Section 6. Said corporation shall have the power to lease, purchase or hold such real or personal estate as may be necessary and convenient for the purpose of management of said road.

Section 7. Said railroad shall be constructed and maintained in each of said towns, in such form and manner and upon such grade and with such rails as the municipal officers of said town shall direct, and whenever in the judgment of the said corporation it shall be necessary to alter the grade of any street or way, said alteration may be made at the sole expense of said corporation, provided, the same shall be assented to by the municipal officers of the town wherein said grade so sought to be changed is located. If the tracks of said corporation's railroad cross any other railroad, and a dispute arises in any way in regard to the manner of crossing, the board of railroad commissioners of this state shall, upon hearing, decide and determine in writing in what manner the crossing shall be made, and it shall be constructed accordingly.

Section 8. Said corporation may change the location of said railroad at any time by first obtaining the written consent of the municipal officers of the town in which the change is so sought to be made, and to make additional locations subject to the foregoing provisions and conditions.

Section 9. Nothing in this act shall be construed to prevent the proper authorities of either of said towns from entering upon and taking up any of the streets or ways in either of said towns, occupied by said railroad for any purpose for which they may lawfully take up the same.

Section 10. No other person or corporation shall be permitted to construct or maintain any railroad for similar purposes over the same streets or ways that may be lawfully occupied by this corporation, but any person or corporation lawfully operating any horse or electric railroad to any point to which this corporation's tracks extend, may enter upon, connect with and use the same on such terms and in such manner as may be agreed upon between the parties, or if they shall not agree, to be determined by the railroad commissioners for the state of Maine.

Section 11. Said corporation is hereby authorized to issue bonds in such amount, and on such time as may from time to time be determined, in aid of the purposes specified in this act, and to secure the same by a mortgage of its franchises and property. It is also hereby authorized to lease all of its property and franchise upon such terms as it may determine.

Section 12. The first meeting of said corporation may be called by any two of said corporators giving actual notice in writing to their several associates, and said corporation may make such by-laws as are proper and not contrary to the laws of the state.

MILLINOCKET TRUST COMPANY.

Chap. 161

When charter shall be void.

Section 13. This charter shall be null and void unless operations for building said railway shall have been actually commenced within two years from the passage of this act.

Section 14. This act shall take effect when approved.

Approved March 12, 1903.

Chapter 161.

An Act to incorporate the Millinocket Trust Company.

Be it enacted by the Senate and House of Representatives in Legislature assembled, as follows:

Corporators.

Section 1. Garret Schenck, A. Ledyard Smith, George H. Parks, George W. Stearns, James F. Kimball and S. J. Gonya or such of them as may by vote accept this charter with their associates, successors and assigns, are hereby made a body corporate and politic to be known as the Millinocket Trust Company, and as such shall be possessed of all powers, privileges and immunities and subject to all the duties and obligations conferred and imposed by law on similar corporations.

—corporate name.

Location.

Section 2. The corporation hereby created shall be located at Millinocket, Penobscot county, Maine.

Purposes.

Section 3. The purposes of said corporation and the business which it may perform, are; first, to receive on deposit, money, coin, bank notes, evidences of debt, accounts of individuals, companies, corporations, municipalities and states, allowing interest thereon, if agreed, or as the by-laws of said corporation may provide; second, to borrow money, to loan money on credit, or real estate, or personal or collateral security, and to negotiate loans and sales for others; third, to erect, construct, own, maintain and operate safe deposit vaults, with boxes, safes and other facilities therein, to be rented to other parties for the safe keeping of moneys, securities, stocks, jewelry, plate, valuable papers and documents, and other property susceptible of being deposited therein, and to receive on deposit for safe keeping, property of any kind entrusted to it for that purpose; fourth, to hold and enjoy all such estate, real, personal and mixed, as may be obtained by the investment of its capital stock or any other moneys and funds that may come into its possession in the course of its business and dealings, and the same sell, grant and dispose of; fifth, to act as agent for issuing, registering and countersigning certificates, bonds, stocks, and all evidences of debt or ownership in property; sixth, to hold by grant, assignment,

—may own safe deposit vaults.

—may act as agent.

transfer, devise or bequest, any real or personal property or trusts duly created, and to execute trusts of every description; seventh, to act as executor, administrator, guardian, receiver or assignee, with the same powers and duties as are conferred and imposed by law upon natural persons acting in the same capacities and subject to the same control of the court having jurisdiction of the same in all proceedings relating to the exercise of these powers; all papers may be signed and sworn to by any officer designated by the corporation for that purpose, and the officers shall be subject to citation and examination in the same manner and to the same extent as natural persons acting in the same capacities. No sureties shall be required upon the bond of the corporation when acting in said capacities, unless the court or officer approving said bond shall require it; eighth, to guarantee the payment of the principal and interest of all obligations secured by mortgages of real estate running to said Millinocket Trust Company; ninth, to hold for safe keeping all kinds of personal or mixed property and to act as agents for the owners thereof, and of real estate for the collection of income on the same and for the sale of the same; tenth, to do in general all the business that may lawfully be done by trust and banking companies.

Section 4. The capital stock of said corporation shall not be less than fifty thousand dollars, divided into shares of one hundred dollars each, with the right to increase the said capital stock at any time, by vote of the shareholders, to any amount not exceeding five hundred thousand dollars. Said corporation shall not commence business as a trust or banking company, until stock to the amount of at least fifty thousand dollars shall have been subscribed and paid in, in cash.

Section 5. Said corporation shall not make any loan or discount on the security of the shares of its own capital stock, nor be the purchaser or holder of any such shares unless necessary to prevent loss upon a debt previously contracted in good faith; and all such stock so acquired shall, within six months from the time of its acquisition, be disposed of at public or private sale.

Section 6. All the corporate powers of this corporation shall be exercised by a board of directors or trustees, three-fifths of whom at least, shall be residents of this state, whose number and term of office shall be determined by a vote of the shareholders at the first meeting held by the incorporators and at each annual meeting thereafter. The affairs and powers of the corporation may, at the option of the shareholders, be entrusted to an executive board of three members to be, by vote of the shareholders, elected from the full board of directors or trustees. The

Chap. 161

MILLINOCKET TRUST COMPANY.

directors or trustees of said corporation shall be sworn to the proper discharge of their duties, and they shall hold office until others are elected and qualified in their stead. If a director or trustee dies, resigns, or becomes disqualified for any cause, the remaining directors or trustees may appoint a person to fill the vacancy until the next annual meeting of the corporation. The oath of office of such director or trustee, shall be taken within thirty days of his election, or his office shall become vacant. The clerk of such corporation shall, within ten days, notify such directors or trustees of their election, and within thirty days shall publish the list of all persons who have taken the oath of office as directors or trustees.

—vacancies, how filled.

Board of investment.

Section 7. The board of directors or trustees of said corporation shall constitute the board of investment of said corporation. Said directors or trustees shall keep in a separate book, specially provided for the purpose, record of all loans, and investments of every description, made by said institution substantially in the order of time when such loans or investments are made, which shall show that such loans or investments have been made with the approval of the executive committee of said corporation, which shall indicate such particulars respecting such loans or investments as the bank examiner shall direct. This book shall be submitted to the directors or trustees and to the bank examiner whenever requested. Such loans or investments shall be classified in the book as the bank examiner shall direct. No loan shall be made to any officers, director or agent of said company or to other persons in its employ, until the proposition to make such loan shall have been submitted by the person desiring the same to the board of directors of such bank, or to the executive committee of such board, if any, and are accepted and approved by a majority of such board or committee. Such approval, if the loan is made, shall be spread upon the records of the corporation; and this record shall, in every instance, give the names of the directors authorizing the loan. Said corporation shall have no authority to hire money or to give notes unless by vote of the said board or of said committee duly recorded.

—loans to directors, how made.

Directors must own at least ten shares of stock.

Section 8. No person shall be eligible to the position of a director or trustee of said corporation who is not the actual owner of ten shares of its stock.

Reserve fund.

Section 9. Said corporation after beginning to receive money on deposit shall at all times have on hand, as a reserve, in lawful money of the United States, an amount equal to at least fifteen per cent of the aggregate amount of all its deposits which are subject to withdrawal upon demand or within ten days; and whenever said reserve of such corporation shall be below said percentage of such deposits, it shall not increase its liabilities by making any new loans until the required proportion between the aggregate amount of such deposits and its reserve fund shall be restored; provided, that in lieu of lawful money two-thirds of said fifteen per cent may consist of balances payable on demand, due from any national bank, and one-third of said fifteen per cent may consist of lawful money and bonds of the United States or of this state, the absolute property of such corporation.

—proviso.

Section 10. All the property or money held in trust by this corporation shall constitute a special deposit and the accounts thereof and of said trust department shall be kept separate, and such funds and the investment or loans of them shall be specially appropriated to the security and payment of such deposits, and not be subject to any other liabilities of the corporation; and for the purpose of securing the observance of this proviso, said corporation shall have a trust department in which all business pertaining to such trust property shall be kept separate and distinct from its general business.

Trust funds shall constitute a special deposit.

Section 11. An administrator, executor, assignee, guardian or trustee, any court of law or equity, including courts of probate and insolvency, officers and treasurers of towns, cities, counties and savings banks of the state of Maine may deposit any moneys, bonds, stocks, evidences of debt or of ownership in property, or any personal property, with said corporation, and any of said courts may direct any person deriving authority from them to so deposit the same.

Administrators, executors, etc. may deposit in.

Section 12. Each shareholder of this corporation shall be individually responsible, equally and ratably, and not one for the other, for all contracts, debts and engagements of such corporation, to a sum equal to the amount of the par value of the shares owned by each in addition to the amount invested in said shares.

Responsibility of shareholders.

Section 13. Said corporation shall set apart as a guaranty fund not less than ten per cent of its net earnings in each and every year until such fund, with the accumulated interest thereon, shall amount to one-fourth of the capital stock of the company. The said surplus shall be kept to secure against losses and contingencies, and whenever the same becomes impaired it shall be reimbursed in the manner provided for its accumulation.

Guaranty fund.

Section 14. The shares of said corporation shall be subject to taxation in the same manner and at the same rate as are the shares of national banks.

Taxation.

Section 15. Said corporation shall be subject to examination by the bank examiner, who shall visit it at least once in every year, and as much oftener as he may deem expedient. At such visits he shall have free access to its vaults, books and papers,

Shall be subject to examination by bank examiner.

and shall thoroughly inspect and examine all the affairs of said corporation, and make such inquiries as may be necessary to ascertain its condition and ability to fulfill all its engagements.

—proceedings when business becomes hazardous.

If upon examination of said corporation the examiner is of the opinion that its investments are not in accordance with law, or said corporation is insolvent, or its condition is such as to render its further proceedings hazardous to the public or to those having funds in its custody, or is of the opinion that it has exceeded its powers or failed to comply with any of the rules or restrictions provided by law, he shall have such authority and take such action as is provided for in the case of savings banks by chapter forty-seven of the revised statutes. He shall preserve in a permanent form a full record of his proceedings, including a statement of the condition of said corporation. A copy of such statement shall be published by said corporation immediately after the annual examination of the same in some newspaper published where said corporation is established. If no paper is published in the town where said corporation is established, then it shall be published in a newspaper printed in the nearest city or town. The necessary expenses of the bank examiner while making such examination shall be paid by the corporation.

First meeting, how called.

Section 16. Any three of the corporators named in this act may call the first meeting of the corporation by mailing a written notice signed by all three, postage paid, to each of the other corporators, seven days at least before the day of the meeting, naming the time, place and purpose of such meeting, and at such meeting the necessary officers may be chosen, by-laws adopted, and any other corporate business transacted.

Section 17. This act shall take effect when approved.

Approved March 12, 1903.

Chapter 162.

An Act to incorporate the Meduxnekeag Light and Power Company.

Be it enacted by the Senate and House of Representatives in Legislature assembled, as follows:

Section 1. George Ingraham, Joseph A. Browne, Clarence H. Pearce, John Watson, Don A. H. Powers, Ransford W. Shaw, Charles D. Merritt, John B. Madigan, Hudson T. Frisbie, Willard S. Lewin, Leland O. Ludwig, Frank M. Hume, James Archibald and Martin Lawlis, their associates, successors and assigns, are hereby made and constituted a body corporate by the name of the Meduxnekeag Electric Light and Power Company, with all the rights, powers and privileges and subject to all the duties and obligations conferred and imposed on corporations by law, except as otherwise provided herein. *Corporators.* *—corporate name.*

Section 2. Said company is hereby authorized and empowered to furnish power for manufacturing and mechanical purposes; and to generate, make, sell, distribute and supply electricity and electrical power for lighting, heating, manufacturing, mechanical and transportation purposes, in the towns of Monticello, Littleton, Houlton, Hodgdon, Linneus, New Limerick, Oakfield and Ludlow, in the county of Aroostook; and may transport and sell the same in Carleton county, New Brunswick, and may build and operate manufactories and works for the providing and supplying of electricity and light and power and may lease, purchase and hold real and personal estate for the proper object of the corporation to the amount of one hundred and fifty thousand dollars, and to construct, lay, maintain and operate lines of wire and other material for the transmission of electricity, under ground, upon, under and along and over any and all streets and ways in said towns under the direction of the municipal officers of said towns; and in public places in such a manner as not to endanger the appropriate public use thereof, and to establish and maintain, under directions of said municipal officers all necessary posts, pipes, supports and appurtenances as may be necessary, and terminating at such places in said towns as may be expedient. *Powers.*

Section 3. For the erecting of said wires above ground and for laying same or pipes thereof under ground, or for taking up, replacing and repairing the same, said company shall first obtain the consent of the municipal officers of said towns and perform all said acts as directed by said municipal officers. *Consent of municipal officers shall direct laying of pipes, etc.*

Section 4. Damages for any land or easement taken for the purposes of erecting or laying said lines, if the parties cannot agree, shall be estimated, secured and paid as in the case of lands taken for railroads. *Damages, how estimated, secured and paid.*

Section 5. Nothing contained in this act will be construed to affect or diminish the liability of said corporation for any injury to private property, by depreciating the value thereof or otherwise, but any legal remedies existing shall continue.

Section 6. The municipal officers of the various towns through which said company's lines may pass, or property be found shall at all times have the power to regulate and control the acts and doings of said corporation, which may in any manner affect the health and safety of the public or become a nuisance to the said towns.

Section 7. The capital stock of said company shall not exceed one hundred and fifty thousand dollars, and shall be divided into shares of ten dollars each.

Section 8. Said company is hereby authorized to take and hold by purchase any electric light plant or power station now within the limits of said towns, and hold and use said property, for the purpose herein mentioned.

Section 9. Said company is hereby authorized to issue bonds for the construction of its works upon such rates and such amounts as may be deemed necessary, not to exceed one hundred and fifty thousand dollars in all, and not to exceed the amount of the capital stock subscribed for, and to secure the same by mortgage or deed of trust upon its franchises and property.

Section 10. Any two of the corporators named in this act may call the first meeting of the corporation by mailing a written notice signed by both, postage paid, to each of the corporators, seven days at least before the day of the meeting, naming the time and place and purpose of said meeting; a president, secretary, and directors and other necessary officers may be chosen, by-laws adopted and any corporate business transacted.

Section 11. This act may be accepted at any regular meeting of the corporation by a majority of the members present.

Section 12. This act shall take effect when approved.

Approved March 12, 1903.

Chapter 163.

An Act to amend the charter of the Portland and Cape Elizabeth Ferry Company.

Be it enacted by the Senate and House of Representatives in Legislature assembled, as follows:

Section 1. Section four of the charter of the Portland and Cape Elizabeth Ferry Company, approved February seventeen, eighteen hundred and seventy-two, and amended by chapter four hundred and seventeen of the private and special laws of eighteen hundred and ninety-three, approved February twenty-third, eighteen hundred and ninety-three, is hereby further amended by striking out the following:

"The time for running said boat or boats shall be from six o'clock in the forenoon to eight o'clock in the afternoon, from the first day of April to the first day of October; and from six and a half o'clock in the forenoon, to seven o'clock in the afternoon, from the first day of October to the first day of April, in each year"; and by substituting in place thereof the following: 'The time for running said boat or boats, unless prevented by accident or unavoidable casualty, shall on week days be from six o'clock in the forenoon to six and a half o'clock in the afternoon; and on Sundays from eight o'clock in the forenoon to six o'clock in the afternoon'; so that said section, as amended, shall read as follows:

'Section 4. The time for running said boat or boats, unless prevented by accident or unavoidable casualty, shall on week days be from six o'clock in the forenoon to six and a half o'clock in the afternoon; and on Sundays from eight o'clock in the forenoon to six o'clock in the afternoon. And if said corporation shall neglect to furnish suitable and proper attendance, and suitable, safe and proper boat or boats at any time within the hours prescribed for running the same for the transportation of passengers or freight, as authorized by this act, said corporation shall forfeit and pay for each case of such neglect the sum of ten dollars, to be recovered in an action of the case by the person aggrieved thereby, in any court of competent jurisdiction; said corporation shall also be liable in a like action to the party injured, for loss and damage occasioned by the neglect or want of proper care on the part of said corporation, its agents or servants. But the requirement for running said boat or boats during the hours above prescribed shall not be construed as preventing said company from running its boat or boats at other times; and said company may run its boat or boats during such other hours as it may, from time to time, deem that the public accommodation requires.'

Section 2. This act shall take effect when approved.

Approved March 12, 1903.

Chapter 164.

An Act to enable the Presque Isle Water Company to issue bonds to pay, retire and cancel its outstanding bonds.

Be it enacted by the Senate and House of Representatives in Legislature assembled, as follows:

<small>Authorized to issue bonds to pay and cancel outstanding bonds.</small>

Section 1. The Presque Isle Water Company is hereby authorized and empowered to issue its bonds to pay, retire and cancel its outstanding bonds, and the mortgage securing the same, and for the further construction and improvement of its works and for other purposes of said company, for an amount not exceeding fifty thousand dollars, and upon such rate and time as it may be deemed expedient, and to secure the same by mortgage or deed of trust of all or any part of its franchise, property, rights and privileges now owned or to be hereafter acquired.

<small>—and for improvements.</small>

<small>—limit as to amount.</small>

Section 2. This act shall take effect when approved.

Approved March 12, 1903.

Chapter 165.

An Act relating to the election and term of office of certain members of the Board of Assessors, Board of Overseers of the Poor and female members of the School Committee of the city of Portland.

Be it enacted by the Senate and House of Representatives in Legislature assembled, as follows:

<small>Election of assessor, and overseers of poor declared legal.</small>

Section 1. The term of office of the member of the board of assessors and of the members of the board of overseers of the poor of the city of Portland which have been elected by the city council of said city for a term of three years from the second Monday in March, in the year of our Lord nineteen hundred and one, shall expire on the second Monday in December, nineteen hundred and three, and the elections of a member of said board of assessors and four members of said board of overseers of the poor on the second Monday in December, in the year of our Lord nineteen hundred and two, by said city council, are hereby declared to be legal, and all acts performed by either of said

<small>—acts of, made valid.</small>

officers since their election and qualification for said offices are hereby confirmed and made valid, and their term of office shall be for three years, or until their successors are elected and qualified.

Section 2. The election of a female member of the school committee of the city of Portland for a term of two years at the annual municipal election in December, in the year of our Lord nineteen hundred and two, is hereby declared to be legal, and all her acts as a member of said committee since her election and qualification are hereby confirmed and made valid, and all future elections of the female members of said committee shall be at the annual municipal elections in December and for a term of two years.

Section 3. This act shall take effect when approved.

Approved March 12, 1903.

Chapter 166.

An Act to authorize the town of Athens to remove the bodies of deceased persons.

Be it enacted by the Senate and House of Representatives in Legislature assembled, as follows:

Section 1. The town of Athens is hereby authorized to take up from the old burying ground in the village in said town the bodies and remains of all deceased persons buried therein, and all headstones and markers at the graves therein, and remove the said bodies and remains to the new burying ground in said town and there decently bury the same, and properly reset such head stones and markers over such dead bodies and remains, at the expense of said town; and to sell and convey all the right and interest said town has in the old burying ground; provided that said town of Athens at any legal meeting or meetings, duly called and notified, shall agree thereto, by a majority vote of its legal voters present and voting.

Section 2. This act shall take effect when approved.

Approved March 12, 1903.

Chapter 167.

An Act to extend the charter of the Winthrop Cold Spring Water Company.

Be it enacted by the Senate and House of Representatives in Legislature assembled, as follows:

Charter extended for two years.
Section 1. The rights, powers and privileges of the Winthrop Cold Spring Water Company which were granted by chapter three hundred and thirty-nine of the private and special laws of nineteen hundred and one are hereby extended for a period of two years from the approval of this act, and the persons named in said act, their associates and successors, shall have all the rights and powers and privileges that were granted them by said act, to be exercised in the same manner and for the same purposes as provided therein.

Section 2. This act shall take effect when approved.

Approved March 12, 1903.

Chapter 168.

An Act to authorize the Van Buren Water Company to increase its capital stock and bonds.

Be it enacted by the Senate and House of Representatives in Legislature assembled, as follows:

Capital stock, increase of, authorized.
Section 1. The Van Buren Water Company is hereby authorized to increase its capital stock to any amount not exceeding fifty thousand dollars by a majority vote of its stockholders and to issue bonds to an amount not exceeding its authorized capital stock; said bonds to be secured by a mortgage of its works and franchises and to bear interest at a rate not exceeding five per cent per annum.

Section 2. This act shall take effect when approved.

Approved March 12, 1903.

Chapter 169.

An Act relating to the Young Women's Christian Association of Portland, Maine.

Be it enacted by the Senate and House of Representatives in Legislature assembled, as follows:

Section 1. The Young Women's Christian Association of the city of Portland, Maine, a corporation organized under the laws of this state and located at said Portland in said county of Cumberland is hereby authorized and empowered to hold by deed, devise, bequest or otherwise, property, personal and real to the amount of fifty thousand dollars. *Authorized to hold by deed, bequest or otherwise property to the amount of $50,000.*

Section 2. The acts and doings of the meeting of said corporation held on the twelfth day of May, in the year of our Lord nineteen hundred and two, are hereby ratified, confirmed and declared to be legal and valid. *Certain acts and doings made valid.*

Section 3. This act shall take effect when approved.

Approved March 12, 1903.

Chapter 170.

An Act relating to Gorham Academy.

Be it enacted by the Senate and House of Representatives in Legislature assembled, as follows:

Section 1. The trustees of the Gorham Academy in the county of Cumberland, a corporation created in eighteen hundred and three is hereby continued with all the powers and privileges thereto belonging, the same as though chapter three hundred and seventy-four of the special laws of eighteen hundred and fifty, entitled "An Act to change Gorham Academy to a Female Seminary" and chapter forty-three of the special laws of eighteen hundred and sixty-one, entitled "An Act to amend An Act to change Gorham Academy to a Female Seminary approved August twentieth, eighteen hundred and fifty" had not been passed. *Trustees continued, with all powers and privileges.*

Section 2. Said academy shall be devoted exclusively to the education of boys. *Education of boys exclusively.*

Section 3. The present trustees of the Gorham Seminary, with such associates and successors as they may from time to time elect, are hereby constituted the trustees of the Gorham Academy. They may determine the number of trustees, the tenure of office and what number shall constitute a quorum of the board of said trustees, and how many thereof shall be residents of Gorham. *Present trustees with successors, constituted the trustees of Gorham Academy.*

CHAP. 171

Property shall vest in trustees.

Section 4. All the property of the Gorham Seminary shall vest in and revert to the trustees of the Gorham Academy in the county of Cumberland, whenever the trustees of said seminary shall vote to accept this act.

May hold property to amount of $500,000.

Section 5. Said academy corporation shall be allowed to hold real and personal property to the amount of five hundred thousand dollars.

Section 6. All acts and parts of acts inconsistent with this act, are hereby repealed.

Approved March 12, 1908.

Chapter 171.

An Act to enlarge the powers of the Prouts Neck Water Company.

Be it enacted by the Senate and House of Representatives in Legislature assembled, as follows:

Authorized to make, sell and distribute gas and electricity.

Section 1. The Prouts Neck Water Company, incorporated under chapter four hundred and ninety of the private and special laws of Maine approved March twenty-second, nineteen hundred and one, is hereby authorized to make, generate, sell, distribute and supply gas or electricity, or both, for lighting, heating, manufacturing and mechanical purposes, and to supply that part of

—may supply Scarborough.

the town of Scarborough in the county of Cumberland which is situate and lies south of the eastern division of the Boston and Maine Railroad, and the inhabitants thereof, with electric light and electric power, and to carry on the business of lighting by electricity or otherwise such public streets in the territory aforesaid and such buildings and places therein, public and private, as may be agreed upon by said corporation and the owners or those having control of such places to be lighted, and of furnishing power by electricity or otherwise within said territory; and

—may provide works, etc.

may build and operate factories and works for providing and supplying electric light and power, and may take, lease, purchase and hold real estate and personal estate therefor, and construct, lay, maintain and operate lines of wire or other material for the transmission of electricity or power upon, along, and over any and all streets and ways, under the direction of the municipal officers of said town.

Section 2. This act shall take effect when approved.

Approved March 12, 1908.

SECURITY TRUST COMPANY.

Chapter 172.

An Act to incorporate the Security Trust Company.

Be it enacted by the Senate and House of Representatives in Legislature assembled, as follows:

Section 1. F. S. Walls of Vinalhaven, and H. I. Hix, Maynard S. Bird, S. T. Kimball, all of Rockland, or such of them as may by vote accept this charter, with their associates, successors and assigns, are hereby made a body corporate and politic to be known as the Security Trust Company, and as such shall be possessed of all the powers, privileges and immunities and subject to all the duties and obligations conferred on corporations by law. —Corporators. —corporate name.

Section 2. The corporation hereby created shall be located at Rockland, Knox county, Maine, and may have two offices for the transaction of business in said city. —Location.

Section 3. The purpose of said corporation and the business which it may perform, are; first, to receive on deposit, money, coin, bank notes, evidences of debt, accounts of individuals, companies, corporations, municipalities and states, allowing interest thereon, if agreed, or as the by-laws of said corporation may provide; second, to borrow money, to loan money on credits, or real estate, or personal security, and to negotiate loans and sales for others; third, to own and maintain safe deposit vaults, with boxes, safes and other facilities therein, to be rented to other parties for the safe keeping of moneys, securities, stocks, jewelry, plate, valuable papers and documents, and other property susceptible of being deposited therein, and may receive on deposit for safe keeping, property of any kind entrusted to it for that purpose; fourth, to hold and enjoy all such estate, real, personal and mixed, as may be obtained by the investment of its capital stock or any other moneys and funds that may come into its possession in the course of its business and dealings, and the same sell, grant and dispose of; fifth, to act as agent for issuing, registering and countersigning certificates, bonds, stocks, and all evidences of debt or ownership in property; sixth, to hold by grant, assignment, transfer, devise, or bequeath, any real or personal property or trusts, duly created, and to execute trusts of every description; seventh, to act as assignee, receiver, executor, and no surety shall be necessary upon the bond of the corporation, unless the court or officer approving such bond shall require it; eighth, to do in general all the business that may lawfully be done by trust and banking companies. —Purpose and business. —may own and rent safe deposit vaults. —may act as agent. —may execute trusts.

Section 4. The capital stock of said corporation shall not be less than twenty-five thousand dollars, divided into shares of one —Capital stock.

SECURITY TRUST COMPANY.

Chap. 172

—shall not commence business until $50,000 has been paid in.

hundred dollars each, with the right to increase the said capital stock at any time, by vote of the shareholders, to any amount not exceeding two hundred thousand dollars. Said corporation shall not commence business as a trust or banking company, until stock to the amount of at least fifty thousand dollars shall have been subscribed and paid in, in cash.

Shall not make a loan on security of its own capital stock.

Section 5. Said corporation shall not make any loan or discount on the security of the shares of its own capital stock, nor be the purchaser or holder of any such shares unless necessary to prevent loss upon a debt previously contracted in good faith; and all stock so acquired shall, within six months from the time of its acquisition, be disposed of at public or private sale.

Board of directors.

—number and tenure.

—executive board.

—vacancies, how filled.

Section 6. All the corporate powers of this corporation shall be exercised by a board of directors, who shall be residents of this state, whose number and term of office shall be determined by a vote of the shareholders at the first meeting held by the incorporators and at each annual meeting thereafter. The affairs and powers of the corporation may, at the option of the shareholders, be entrusted to an executive board of seven members to be, by vote of the shareholders, elected from the full board of directors. The directors of said corporation shall be sworn to the proper discharge of their duties, and they shall hold office until others are elected and qualified in their stead. If a director dies, resigns, or becomes disqualified for any cause, the remaining directors may appoint a person to fill the vacancy until the next annual meeting of the corporation. The oath of office of such director shall be taken within thirty days of his election, or his office shall become vacant. The clerk of such corporation shall, within ten days, notify such directors of their election, and within thirty days shall publish the list of all persons who have taken the oath of office as directors.

Board of investment.

—loans to directors, how made.

Section 7. The board of directors of said corporation shall constitute the board of investment of said corporation. Said directors shall keep a separate book, specially provided for the purpose, a record of all loans, and investments of every description, made by said institution, substantially in the order of time when such loans or investments are made, which shall show that such loans or investments have been made with the approval of the investment committee of said corporation, which shall indicate such particulars respecting such loans or investments as the bank examiner shall direct. This book shall be submitted to the directors and to the bank examiner whenever requested. Such loans or investments shall be classified in the book as the bank examiner shall direct. No loan shall be made to any officer or director of said banking or trust company except by the approval of a majority of the executive board in writing, and said corporation shall have no authority to hire money or to give notes unless by vote of said board duly recorded.

Section 8. No person shall be eligible as a member of the executive committee of said corporation who is not the actual owner of ten shares of the stock. *Director shall shall own ten shares of stock.*

Section 9. Said corporation, after beginning to receive deposits, shall, at all times, have on hand in lawful money, as a reserve, not less than fifteen per cent of the aggregate amount of its deposits which are subject to withdrawal on demand, provided, that in lieu of lawful money, two-thirds of said fifteen per cent may consist of balances, payable on demand, due from any national or state bank. *Reserve fund*

Section 10. All the property or money held in trust by this corporation, shall constitute a special deposit and the accounts thereof and of said trust department shall be kept separate, and such funds and the investment or loans of them shall be specially appropriated to the security and payment of such deposits, and not be subject to any other liabilities of the corporation; and for the purpose of securing the observance of this proviso, said corporation shall have a trust department in which all business pertaining to such trust property shall be kept separate and distinct from its general business. *Trust funds shall constitute a special deposit.*

Section 11. An administrator, executor, assignee, guardian, or trustee, any court of law or equity, including courts of probate and insolvency, officers and treasurers of towns, cities, counties and savings banks of the state of Maine may deposit any moneys, bonds, stocks, evidences of debt or of ownership in property, or any personal property, with said corporation, and any of said courts may direct any person deriving authority from them to so deposit the same. *Administrators, executors, etc., may deposit with.*

Section 12. Each shareholder of this corporation shall be individually responsible, equably and ratably, and not one for the other, for all contracts, debts and engagements of such corporation to a sum equal to the amount of the par value of the shares owned by each in addition to the amount invested in said shares. *Responsibility of shareholders.*

Section 13. Such corporation shall set apart as a surplus fund not less than ten per cent of its earnings in each and every year until such fund with the accumulated interest thereon, shall amount to one-fourth of the capital stock of said corporation. *Surplus fund.*

Section 14. The shares of said corporation shall be subject to taxation in the same manner and rate as are the shares of national banks. *Taxation.*

Chap. 172

Shall be subject to examination by bank examiner.

Section 15. Said corporation shall be subject to examination by the bank examiner, who shall visit it at least once in every year, and as much oftener as he may deem expedient. At such visits he shall have free access to its vaults, books and papers, and shall thoroughly inspect and examine all the affairs of said corporation, and make such inquiries as may be necessary to ascertain its condition and ability to fulfill all its engagements.

—proceedings when supposed to be insolvent.

If upon examination of said corporation the examiner is of the opinion that its investments are not in accordance with law, or said corporation is insolvent, or its condition is such as to render its further proceedings hazardous to the public or to those having funds in its custody, or is of the opinion that it has exceeded its powers or failed to comply with any of the rules or restrictions provided by law, he shall have such authority and take such action as is provided for in the case of savings banks by chapter forty-seven of the revised statutes. He shall preserve in a permanent form a full record of his proceedings, including a statement of the condition of said corporation. A copy of such statement shall be published by said corporation immediately after the annual examination of the same in some newspaper published where said corporation is established. If no paper is published in the town where said corporation is established, then it shall be published in a newspaper printed in the nearest city or town. The necessary expenses of the bank examiner while making examination shall be paid by the corporation.

—statement shall be published.

First meeting, how called.

Section 16. Any three of the corporators named in this act may call the first meeting of the corporation by mailing a written notice signed by all three, postage paid, to each of the other corporators, seven days at least before the day of the meeting, naming the time, place and purpose of such meeting, and at such meeting the necessary officers may be chosen, by-laws adopted, and any other corporate business transacted.

Section 17. This act shall take effect when approved.

Approved March 12, 1908.

Chapter 173.

An Act to amend Chapter four hundred seven of the Private and Special Laws of eighteen hundred and forty-six, entitled "An Act to incorporate the Penobscot Log Driving Company."

Be it enacted by the Senate and House of Representatives in Legislature assembled, as follows:

Section 1. Section one of chapter four hundred seven of the private and special laws of eighteen hundred and forty-six, entitled "An Act to incorporate the Penobscot Log Driving Company," as amended by chapter two hundred forty-three of the private and special laws of eighteen hundred forty-nine is hereby further amended by striking out of said section everything between the period in the thirteenth line and the period in the eighteenth line, and inserting in place thereof the following: 'Said company shall drive all logs and other timber that may be in the West branch of the Penobscot river for that purpose between the head of Shad pond and the East branch of said river to such place of destination on said river as may be designated by the owners of such logs and other timber or by the directors of said company, such place not to be below the Penobscot boom where logs are usually sorted and rafted,' so that said section as amended, shall read as follows:

'Section 1. That Ira Wadleigh, Samuel P. Strickland, Hastings Strickland, Isaac Farrar, William Emerson, Amos M. Roberts, Leonard Jones, Franklin Adams, James Jenkins, Aaron Babb and Cyrus S. Clark, their associates, and successors, be, and they are hereby made and constituted a body politic and corporate, by the name and style of the Penobscot Log Driving Company, and by that name may sue and be sued, prosecute and defend, to final judgment and execution, both in law and in equity, and may make and adopt all necessary regulations and by-laws not repugnant to the constitution and laws of this state, and may adopt a common seal, and the same may alter, break and renew at pleasure, and may hold real and personal estate not exceeding the sum of fifty thousand dollars at any one time and may grant and vote money. Said company shall drive all logs and other timber that may be in the West branch of the Penobscot river for that purpose between the head of Shad pond and the East branch of said river to such place of destination on said river as may be designated by the owners of such logs and other timber or by the directors of said company, such place not to be below the Penobscot boom where logs are usually sorted and rafted. And said company may for the purposes aforesaid clear out and improve the navigation of the river between the points aforesaid, remove obstructions, break jams and erect

CHAP. 173

booms, where the same may be lawfully done, and shall have all the powers and privileges, and be subject to all the liabilities incident to corporations of a similar nature.'

Section 3 of chapter 407, amended.

Section 2. Section three of said chapter four hundred seven is hereby amended by striking out in the second and third lines of said section the words "between said Chesuncook dam and said East branch," and by inserting after the word "Branch" in the fourth line the words 'below Shad pond,' so that said section as amended, shall read as follows:

Statement of logs to be driven shall be filed by owner.

'Section 3. Every owner of logs or other timber which may be in said West branch or which may come therein during the season of driving and intended to be driven down said West branch below Shad pond, shall on or before the fifteenth day of May, in that year, file with the clerk a statement in writing, signed by such owner or owners, his or their authorized agent, of all such logs or timber, of the number of feet, board measure, of all such logs and other timber, and the marks thereon, and the directors, or one of them, shall require such owner or owners or agents

—shall make oath to statement.

presenting such statement, to make oath that the same is, in his or their judgment and belief, true, which oath the directors, or either of them, are hereby empowered to administer. And if any owner shall neglect or refuse to file a statement in the man-

—assessment of delinquents.

ner herein prescribed, the directors may assess such delinquent or delinquents for his or their proportion of such expenses, such sum or sums as may be by the directors considered just and equitable. And the directors shall give public notice of the time and place of making such assessments, by publishing the same

—public notice of assessments.

in some newspaper printed in Bangor, two weeks in succession, the last publication to be before making such assessments. And any assessment or assessments when the owner or owners of any mark of logs or other timber is unknown to the directors, may be set to the mark upon such logs or other timber. And the clerk shall keep a record of all assessments, and of all expenses upon which such assessments are based, which shall at all times be open to all persons interested.'

Chapter 407, further amended.

Section 3. Said chapter four hundred and seven is further amended by striking out all of section five and inserting in place thereof the following section:

Assessments shall be secured or paid within 30 days.

'Section 5. The directors annually shall give the treasurer a list of the assessments made by them, and owners of logs and other timber shall be required to pay or satisfactorily secure the amount of their several assessments within thirty days from the

—lien on logs and lumber.

date of such assessment, and said company shall have a lien on all logs and other timber by it driven for the expense of driving the same and for the other expenses of the company, which lien shall have precedence of all other claims, except laborers' liens, and shall continue for ninety days after the logs or other timber shall arrive at their place of destination for sale or manufacture and may be enforced by attachment, but such lien may be discharged by a bond with sufficient sureties given to the company conditional that all such expenses shall be seasonably paid.'

—lien shall have precedence.

Section 4. Said chapter four hundred and seven is hereby further amended by adding thereto the following section:

Chapter 407, further amended.

'Section 6. Every person or corporation owning timber lands on the west branch of the Penobscot river, or its tributaries, and every owner of logs or other timber cut upon said West branch, or its tributaries, and intended to be driven down said river below Shad pond, shall be members of this company. Every such timberland owner shall be entitled to one vote, and every such owner of logs or other timber shall be entitled to one vote for every one hundred thousand feet of logs or other timber intended to be driven to any point on said river between Shad pond and the Penobscot boom.'

Owners of timber lands shall be members of this company

—voting powers.

Section 5. All acts or parts of acts, inconsistent herewith are hereby repealed.

Section 6. This act shall take effect when approved.

Approved March 13, 1903.

Chapter 174.

An Act to incorporate the West Branch Driving and Reservoir Dam Company.

Be it enacted by the Senate and House of Representatives in Legislature assembled, as follows:

Section 1. Frederick H. Appleton, J. Fred Webster, Fred A. Gilbert, J. Sanford Barnes, Jr., Payne Whitney, R. Somers Hayes and Garret Schenck, their associates, successors and assigns, are hereby created a body politic and corporate by the name of the West Branch Driving and Reservoir Dam Company.

Corporators.

—corporate name.

Section 2. The capital stock of said company shall be fixed by said company and shall not be less than two hundred thousand dollars, and may be increased from time to time by a vote representing a majority of the capital stock issued.

Capital stock.

Section 3. When this charter shall have been accepted by the corporators and said company shall have been organized and subscriptions to the capital stock thereof to an amount at least of two hundred thousand dollars shall have been made in good faith, and fifty thousand dollars at least on such subscriptions

Eminent domain, when and to what extent it may be exercised.

shall have been actually paid in cash into the treasury of said company, said West Branch Driving and Reservoir Dam Company may then exercise the power of eminent domain to the extent that thereunder it may take and hold all the dams, real estate, piers, booms, wing dams, side dams and steamboats now owned by the Penobscot Log Driving Company except the dam at the outlet of Millinocket lake which is to be and remain the property of the Penobscot Log Driving Company. Said West Branch Driving and Reservoir Dam Company may file in the registries of deeds in Penobscot and Piscataquis counties a written statement of its determination to exercise said power of eminent domain and thereupon said dams, real estate, piers, booms, wing dams, side dams and steamboats shall be and become the property of said West Branch Driving and Reservoir Dam Company and all the powers, rights and privileges of the Penobscot Log Driving Company pertaining to the driving of logs and the improving of the West branch of the Penobscot river above the head of Shad pond on said West branch but not below the head of said Shad pond shall be and become the powers, rights and privileges of the West Branch Driving and Reservoir Dam Company, and all the duties of said Penobscot Log Driving Company pertaining to the driving of logs between the head of Chesuncook lake and the head of Shad pond shall be and become the duties of said West Branch Driving and Reservoir Dam Company which shall thereafter be holden to perform said duties except as modified by the provisions of this act.

The value of said dams, real estate, piers, booms, wing dams, side dams and steamboats so taken shall be determined by agreement between said companies or if said companies shall fail to agree then by a commission of three disinterested persons to be appointed as follows: Either of said corporations, or any person interested, may file in the clerk's office of the supreme judicial court in and for the county of Penobscot, either in term time or vacation, a petition to said court for the appointment of such commission, to consist of three disinterested persons, and upon such petition said court, after such notice as said court may deem proper, shall appoint such commission. Such commission shall as soon as may be, but after reasonable notice, hear the parties, their proofs and arguments and determine the value of said dams, real estate, piers, booms, wing dams, side dams and steamboats. The commission shall have power to compel the attendance of witnesses and the production of books and papers pertinent to the issue, and may administer oaths, and any witness or person in charge of such books or papers refusing to attend or to produce the same shall be subject to the same penalties and proceedings, so far as applicable, as witnesses summoned to attend the supreme judicial court. The commission, or a majority thereof, after such hearing, shall report to the court in said county in term time what in its judgment is a fair and just value of the dams, real estate, piers, booms, wing dams, side dams and steamboats, which it is directed to appraise and all other findings which it may have been directed by the court to make, and return such papers and proofs taken by it as the court has directed or may from time to time direct it to return. —commission shall report to court.

The court may confirm such report or reject it, or recommit the same, or submit the subject matter thereof to a new commission. —court may confirm, reject or recommit report.

The expenses of said commission shall be paid one-half by each of said companies. —expenses of commission, by whom paid.

All proceedings of the court with reference to any matter herein raising a question of law shall be subject to exceptions. When all such exceptions, if any shall be taken, shall be disposed of, and any such report shall have been accepted and confirmed by said court, said court shall render judgment against said West Branch Driving and Reservoir Dam Company for the amount finally determined in such report as accepted and confirmed by said court. —exceptions, if taken, how disposed of.

Section 4. If the amount of said judgment with the amount of all other assets of said Penobscot Log Driving Company, not including said Millinocket dam and not including the franchise of said Penobscot Log Driving Company, shall not be sufficient to pay in full all outstanding notes and other legal liabilities of said Penobscot Log Driving Company said West Branch Driving and Reservoir Dam Company shall make good the deficiency and be holden to guarantee the payment in full of all such notes and other legal liabilities after all said assets of the Penobscot Log Driving Company shall have been reduced to money and applied towards the payment of the said notes and other legal liabilities, and by accepting the charter hereby granted said West Branch Driving and Reservoir Dam Company shall be holden to have guaranteed to make good any such deficiency and to so guarantee the payment of the said notes and other legal liabilities of the Penobscot Log Driving Company. Liabilities of Penobscot Log Driving Company, how paid or guaranteed.

Said West Branch Driving and Reservoir Dam Company may assume the defense of any claims which may be made against the said Penobscot Log Driving Company, and prosecute, in the name of said Penobscot Log Driving Company, any claim which it may have against other parties, and no settlement of any claim belonging to said Penobscot Log Driving Company —pending claims, by whom defended on prosecution.

280 WEST BRANCH DRIVING AND RESERVOIR DAM COMPANY.

CHAP. 174

Logs and lumber, driving of, regulated.

or against it shall be made without the consent of said West Branch Driving and Reservoir Dam Company.

Section 5. From and after the time when said West Branch Driving and Reservoir Dam Company shall have filed in the registries of deeds for Penobscot and Piscataquis counties a written statement of its determination to exercise the power of eminent domain, as provided in section three of this act, said West Branch Driving and Reservoir Dam Company shall drive all logs and other lumber that may be in the West branch of the Penobscot river between the head of Chesuncook lake and the head of said Shad pond into said Shad pond, but if said Shad pond shall become filled with logs then against the rear of said logs in said pond, and the booms and piers at the head of Chesuncook lake acquired by the Penobscot Log Driving Company from the West Branch Chesuncook Boom Company shall be within the chartered limits of this company.

At least one drive each year shall be made.

—shall start drive not later than June 25.

—shall complete drive Aug. 20, 1903, and thereafter Aug. 5, of each year.

Section 6. Said West Branch Driving and Reservoir Dam Company shall make at least one drive each year, with due diligence, from the head of Chesuncook lake into said Shad pond in the manner aforesaid and shall start said drive from the head of Chesuncook lake as soon as all logs for said drive shall arrive there but not later than June twenty-fifth, in each year in any event and shall complete the same in nineteen hundred three by the twentieth day of August and thereafter by the fifth day of August in each year. Said company shall be under no obligation to drive from the head of Chesuncook lake any logs which shall not be there when the rear of said drive shall be started as aforesaid, nor under any obligation to drive the same season any logs which shall not be delivered to it before the rear of said drive shall pass the point of attempted delivery.

Prices for driving logs.

Section 7. Said West Branch Driving and Reservoir Dam Company shall receive for driving the logs as aforesaid into Shad pond the following prices per thousand feet board measure: From the head of Chesuncook lake, seventy cents; from the foot of Chesuncook lake, fifty-three cents; from Sourdnahunc, fifty cents; from the head of Ambijejus lake, thirty cents; from the foot of Pemadumcook lake, sixteen and one-fourth cents; from North Twin dam, eleven cents, and for logs driven to the sorting booms of the Great Northern Paper Company, or the Twin Lakes Lumber Company; from the head of Chesuncook lake, fifty cents; from the foot of Chesuncook lake, thirty-three cents; from Sourdnahunc, thirty-three cents. And from any place to any place within the limits aforesaid not specified above, the price shall be as near as may be in proportion to the above prices.

These prices shall continue in force for ten years and thereafter until changed by the legislature.

Section 8. All owners of logs and other lumber which shall be driven by said company shall pay three-quarters of the amount due for driving their respective logs and lumber at the prices above set forth as soon as such logs or other lumber shall arrive at their respective places of destination, and shall pay the balance of said amount as soon as such logs or other lumber shall be scaled after arriving at their respective places of destination, but at all events within three months from the time when such logs or other lumber shall pass from the control of said company. And the number of feet driven shall be found by using as a basis the boom scale of the Penobscot boom, or what shall be equivalent to such scale.

Section 9. The West Branch Driving and Reservoir Dam Company is hereby given a lien on all logs and lumber which it shall drive for the driving of the same as provided in this act, which lien shall have precedence of all other claims except liens reserved to the state and laborers' liens. Such lien shall continue for six months after the logs or lumber shall arrive at the place of destination for sale or manufacture and may be enforced by attachment.

Section 10. Said company in any and all dams which may be owned or controlled by it may store water for the use of any mills or machinery which may use West branch water, subject to the provision that day and night throughout the year the flow of water down the West branch, so long as there shall be any stored water shall not be less than two thousand cubic feet per second, measured in the canal and at the stone dam of the Great Northern Paper Company, at Millinocket, and subject to the further provision that in the spring of each year in advance of the freshet season the water shall be drawn down in all the dams which may be owned or controlled by the company, in accordance with any direction which the commission to be appointed under the provision of this section may give. The supreme judicial court, or any justice thereof, sitting in equity, in term time or vacation, may summarily enforce the specific performance of any of the provisions of this section. There shall be a commission of three persons appointed by the chief justice of the supreme judicial court upon petition of said company or any person interested, after such notice as he shall order and hearing. The chief justice of the supreme judicial court may at any time remove any member of such commission upon petition of said company or any person interested after such notice as he shall order and hearing, if he shall determine that a change in such commission ought to be made. Should any vacancy occur in such commission by death, resignation or otherwise, it shall be filled by the chief justice after such notice as he shall order and hearing. The expenses of said commission shall be paid by said West Branch Driving and Reservoir Dam Company.

May clear out and improve navigation of West branch.

Section 11. Said company in order to facilitate the driving of logs and lumber, and to facilitate the storage of water for use as aforesaid, may clear out and improve the navigation of said West branch, remove obstructions, break jams and erect booms where the same may lawfully be done all within the limits aforesaid.

May rebuild dams.

—may raise height of Chesuncook dam.

—of North Twin dam.

—of dam between North Twin and Millinocket.

—damages for flowage, how recovered.

Section 12. Said company is hereby given the power to rebuild in such manner as it may see fit, any dams which it may acquire as aforesaid of the Penobscot Log Driving Company, and may raise the height of the same so that the Chesuncook dam may hold back six feet more water than the present dam, and the North Twin dam may hold back five feet more water than the present dam and may raise the dam between North Twin and Millinocket lakes to retain the stored water in North Twin lake, and the damages for any flowage caused by such increased height of any of said dams may be recovered in accordance with the provisions of chapter ninety-two of the revised statutes.

May build dam near Sourdnahunc falls.

—near Ambijejus falls.

—damages for flowage, how recovered.

Section 13. Said company is hereby authorized to erect and maintain a dam across the West branch of Penobscot river in the vicinity of Sourdnahunc falls, and another dam across said West branch in the vicinity of Ambijejus falls for the purpose of facilitating the driving of logs and lumber and damages for any flowage caused by such dams may be recovered in accordance with the provisions of chapter ninety-two of the revised statutes.

May take lands for certain purposes.

—proceedings.

—damages, how assessed and paid.

Section 14. Said company for the purpose of rebuilding, constructing or maintaining dams as authorized in this act is hereby given the right to purchase or take and hold any lands necessary for erecting and abutting such dam or dams. Said company shall file in the registry of deeds' office in the county where any land so taken may be situated, plans of the location of all land so taken in such county, and no entry for the purpose of taking lands shall be made on any lands owned by other persons except to make surveys, until the expiration of ten days from the time of said filing. Said company shall also publish in some newspaper published in the city of Bangor, Maine, within ten days after such plans shall be filed, a statement that it has filed in the registry of deeds' office plans of the location of all lands so taken in such county. Said company shall be held liable to pay all damages for the land so taken, and if any person sustaining damages as aforesaid shall not agree with the company upon the sum to be paid therefor, either party on petition to the county commissioners of the county where such land is situated may have the damages assessed for the taking of said land and subsequent proceedings and right of appeal thereupon shall be had in the same manner and under the same conditions, restrictions and limitations as are by law prescribed in the case of damages by the laying out of highways.

Section 15. After said West Branch Driving and Reservoir Dam Company shall have delivered the rear of any annual drive of logs into Shad pond in manner aforesaid it shall allow to flow out of North Twin dam at such times and at such rates of discharge as the Penobscot Log Driving Company may request for the purpose of driving said logs to the Penobscot boom or their several places of destination above said boom, water equivalent to the amount of water held back by said dam as now constructed when there is a thirteen foot head at said dam measured from the bottom of the dam, or so much thereof as shall be called for by said Penobscot Log Driving Company for said purpose, and in determining the quantity of water which the Penobscot Log Driving Company shall be entitled to request for driving purposes, the two thousand cubic feet per second specified in section ten shall be considered a part thereof at such times and at such times only as water is being allowed to flow from said dam at the instance and request of the Penobscot Log Driving Company. *Water for driving logs from Shad pond to destination, how supplied.*

If before the rear of the drive shall be delivered in Shad pond in manner aforesaid in any year, a jam shall occur in the West branch below Shad pond and the Penobscot Log Driving Company or its agent shall notify the West Branch Driving and Reservoir Dam Company to stop turning logs out of Quakish lake, said company shall stop turning logs out of said lake until otherwise notified and the time of getting the rear into Shad pond in manner aforesaid that year may be postponed by the West Branch Driving and Reservoir Dam Company by as much time as the said company was prevented from turning logs out of Quakish lake as aforesaid. *—provisions when jam occurs in West branch below Shad pond.*

Section 16. The first meeting of said corporation shall be called at Bangor, in the county of Penobscot, by a notice signed by any two of the corporators named in section one, setting forth the time, place and purpose of the meeting, and such notice shall be mailed to each of the corporators, postage paid, seven days at least before the day of such meeting. Any corporator may be represented at said first meeting by proxy. *First meeting, how called.*

Section 17. This act shall take effect when approved.

Approved March 12, 1903.

284

CHAP. 175

Chapter 175.

An Act to consolidate Atlantic Shore Line Railway, Sanford and Cape Porpoise Railway Company, Mousam River Railroad and Sanford Power Company.

Be it enacted by the Senate and House of Representatives in Legislature assembled, as follows:

Name changed to Atlantic Shore Line Railway.

Section 1. The name of the Atlantic Shore Line Railway Company, a corporation organized under the general laws of the state of Maine, is hereby changed to Atlantic Shore Line Railway.

Atlantic Shore Line Railway, authorized to acquire certain other lines.

Section 2. The Atlantic Shore Line Railway is hereby authorized to acquire by lease, purchase of stock or otherwise the street railroads franchises and all other assets of the Mousam River Railroad and of the Sanford and Cape Porpoise Railway Company, and of the Sanford Power Company, respectively, and of any other connecting street railroads, and to operate said street railroads, when acquired, with all the rights, franchises and privileges attached respectively thereto as a part of its street railway system; and to raise funds for the above purpose, or for any extension of its said system, said Atlantic Shore Line Railway is further authorized to issue shares of its capital stock or bonds secured by mortgage, or either, to such amount as may be found expedient; and the Mousam River Railroad and the Sanford and Cape Porpoise Railway Company and the Sanford Power Company, and any other connecting street railroads are hereby respectively authorized to lease or sell their railroads, property and franchises to the Atlantic Shore Line Railway.

Authorized to furnish light, heat and power in town of Sanford.

Section 3. The Atlantic Shore Line Railway is hereby authorized to engage in the business of furnishing electric light, heat and power in the town of Sanford, subject, however, to the general laws of the state regulating the erection of posts, wires and lines for the purposes of electricity, with all the powers and privileges and subject to all the duties, restrictions and liabilities by law incident to corporations having similar corporate purposes.

Pending proceedings, how prosecuted and defended.

Section 4. All proceedings, suits at law or in equity which may be pending at the time of such transfers to which either of the corporations named in section two may be a party, may be prosecuted or defended by the said Atlantic Shore Line Railway in like manner and with like effect as if such transfer had not been made. All claims, contracts, rights and causes of action of or against either of the said corporations so selling or leasing, at law or in equity, may be enforced by suit or action to be begun or prosecuted by or against the said Atlantic Shore Line Railway.

—claims, contracts, rights and causes of action, how enforced.

Section 5. When the transfers authorized by this act are carried out and fully completed, the Atlantic Shore Line Railway shall be liable for the then legally existing debts and obligations of each and all of the companies so making such transfers.

Shall be liable for debts of acquired properties.

Section 6. The said Atlantic Shore Line Railway is farther authorized to acquire by lease, purchase or otherwise the lines, property and franchises of any street railroad or street railroads whose lines as constructed or chartered would form connection or continuous lines with the lines of said Atlantic Shore Line Railway, as constructed or chartered, and in such case the Atlantic Shore Line Railway shall be entitled to all the privileges and be subject to all appropriate conditions and limitations contained in the charters and franchises then acquired. Any street railway company whose lines as constructed or chartered would form connecting or continuous lines with the lines of the Atlantic Shore Line Railway, as constructed or chartered, is hereby authorized to lease or sell its lines, property and franchises as in this section authorized.

May acquire connecting or continuous lines.

Section 7. The said Atlantic Shore Line Railway may, for the purposes of sections two, three and five, or either of them, issue such additional stock as may be necessary therefor, likewise such additional bonds as may be required for the purposes of said sections or of either of them and secure the said bonds by appropriate mortgages upon its franchises and property, and thereafterwards issue its stock and bonds, or either of them, in payment and exchange for the stock, bonds, franchises and property of any corporation making transfers under sections two, three and five, in such manner and in such amounts as may be agreed upon.

May issue additional stock for purposes of sections 2, 3 and 5.

—and issue additional bonds.

Section 8. The Atlantic Shore Line Railway is further authorized to cross tide waters and navigable waters within the limits of any or all the towns within which the aforesaid railroads are built or authorized, upon existing bridges or upon bridges or structures of said company erected therefor, provided, however, that said company shall not unnecessarily obstruct navigation, and that the manner and conditions of its so crossing said waters upon any bridges, and of its erecting and maintaining any such bridges or structures of its own shall first be determined by the municipal officers of the town or towns within the limits of which said bridge or structure shall be so erected, maintained or used, and if said company and such municipal officers shall disagree as to the terms prescribing the manner and conditions of such crossing or of erecting and maintaining any such bridge or structure, the same shall after notice and hearing be determined by the railroad commissioners and their decree thereon shall be final.

May cross tide waters.

—proviso.

CHAP. 175

May construct a street railroad.

Section 9. The Atlantic Shore Line Railway is hereby authorized to construct, operate and maintain a street railroad for street traffic for the conveyance of persons and property along and upon said streets, roads and ways, and over and across such lands as said company may deem best for public convenience, with such single or double tracks, side tracks, switches, turnouts, stations, and appurtenances, and with such poles, wires and appliances as shall be reasonably convenient in the premises, with all the powers and privileges incident to or usually granted to similar corporations.

Distance of rails from sidewalk, etc., shall be determined by municipal officers.

—appeal, how taken.

Section 10. The municipal officers of the town or towns in which said Atlantic Shore Line Railway is located shall determine the distance from the sidewalks or from the side lines of the streets at which the rails of said company shall be laid. The railway company or any person interested may at any time appeal from such determination to the board of railroad commissioners, who shall upon notice hear the parties and finally determine the questions raised by said appeal. In case said Atlantic Shore Line Railway makes any extensions, additions or variations from the lines of the Sanford and Cape Porpoise Railway Company or under any other franchise by it hereafter acquired created by special act of the legislature, it shall be competent for the railway company or any person interested to at any time appeal from any determination or order of the municipal officers of any town determining the distance from the sidewalks or the side lines of the streets, of the proposed location of the rails of said company to the board of railroad commissioners, who shall upon notice hear the parties and finally determine the questions raised by said appeal.

Grade, rate of speed, removal of snow from tracks, etc., regulated by municipal officers.

Section 11. All the said railroad lines to be operated, constructed or maintained under this act shall be constructed and maintained in such form and manner and with such rails and upon such grade as the municipal officers of the towns where the same are located may direct. Such municipal officers shall have power at all times to make such regulations as to the mode of use of any such tracks, the rate of speed and the removal and disposal of snow and ice from the streets, roads and ways as the public safety and convenience may require. The said railroad company may at any time appeal from any such determination, decrees, rules and regulations made and established under this section, to the board of railroad commissioners, who shall, upon notice, hear the parties and finally determine the questions raised by said appeal.

Additional land, how same may be acquired.

Section 12. Whenever the said Atlantic Shore Line Railway requires additional land for the purpose of improving the alignment of any part of the road by it to be built or acquired under this act, or if it requires additional land for double tracking its road to be built or acquired hereunder, and is unable to obtain the same by agreement with the owner, it may apply in writing to the railroad commissioners, describing the land required for either or both of said purposes, and naming the persons interested; the commissioners shall thereupon appoint a time for hearing near the premises and requiring notice to be given to all persons interested, as they may direct, fourteen days at least before said time; and shall then view the premises, hear the parties and determine how much if any of said real estate is required for either or both of said purposes. If they find that any of it is so required they shall furnish the corporation with a certificate containing a definite description thereof, and when it is filed with the clerk of courts in the county where the land lies it shall be deemed and treated as taken for public uses; provided, however, that where land is held by a tenant for life and the reversion is contingent as to the persons in whom it may vest on the termination of the life estate, such fact shall be stated in the application and the commissioners shall, in addition to the notice to the tenant for life, give notice by publication to all others interested, in such manner as they deem proper. In taking such land the corporation shall be subject to the provisions of section seventeen of chapter fifty-one of the revised statutes, but the damages therefor shall be estimated and paid in the manner hereinafter provided by section thirteen of this act.

Section 13. For the purpose of determining the damages to be paid for lands taken under this act the land owner or said company may, within three years after the filing of such plans and locations with the clerk of courts as hereinbefore provided, apply to the commissioners of said county of York and have such damages assessed as is provided by law wherein land is taken for railroads, so far as the same is consistent with the provisions of this charter, and where inconsistent or at variance with this charter, the charter shall control. The said commissioners shall have the same power to make suitable orders relative to cattle guards, cattle passes, and farm crossings, as in the case of railroads. If the company shall fail to pay such land owner or to deposit for his use with the clerk of the county commissioners such sum as may be finally awarded for damages, with costs, within ninety days after final judgment, said location shall be invalid and the company forfeit all rights under the same. If such land owner secures more damages than were tendered by said company he shall recover costs, otherwise the company shall recover costs. In case the company shall begin to occupy said

CHAP. 176

—failure to apply for damages for three years, held a waiver.

lands before rendition of final judgment the land owner may require said company to file its bond with said commissioners in such sum and with such securities as they may approve, conditioned for such payment or deposit; failure to apply for damages within the said three years by said land owner shall be held to be a waiver of the same. No action shall be brought against such company for such taking and occupation of land until after such failure to pay or deposit.

Established locations confirmed.

Section 14. The locations of rails, posts, wires and fixtures within the limits of any street, road or way, as now established by any or all of the street railroad companies, authorized to sell their properties and franchises under this act, are hereby confirmed and made valid.

Rights and privileges.
—restrictions.

Section 15. The said Atlantic Shore Line Railway shall, except as modified by this act, have all the rights and privileges conferred by general law upon street railroad corporations, and be subject to the conditions, restrictions and limitations thereby imposed.

Section 16. This act shall take effect when approved.

Approved March 12, 1903.

Chapter 176.

An Act to Incorporate the Hancock Water, Light and Power Company.

Be it enacted by the Senate and House of Representatives in Legislature assembled, as follows:

Corporators.
—corporate name.

Section 1. George H. Grant, Isadore L. Halman and John S. Sanger, their associates, successors and assigns, are hereby made a corporation under the name of the Hancock Water, Light and Power Company.

Capital stock.

—may hold real and personal estate.

Section 2. The capital stock of said corporation shall not be less than twenty-five thousand dollars divided into shares of twenty-five dollars each. The capital stock may by vote of the corporation be increased to two hundred and fifty thousand dollars. Said corporation is authorized to hold such real and personal estate as may be necessary and proper for the purposes of its incorporation.

Purposes.

Section 3. The purposes of said corporation shall be to supply water for public and private use, and for any and all purposes in the town of Hancock in Hancock county; to generate and supply light by electricity, gas or otherwise for public and private use, and for any and all purposes in the towns of Hancock and Sullivan, in said county; and to generate, sell, distribute

tribute and supply electric or other power for any and all purposes in the aforesaid towns of Hancock and Sullivan.

Section 4. Said corporation is hereby authorized for the purposes aforesaid, to erect and maintain dams, reservoirs, filters and standpipes; and to lay and maintain pipes and aqueducts necessary or proper for accumulating, storing, conducting, discharging, distributing, disbursing, supplying and selling water; said corporation may take and hold by purchase or otherwise any real estate necessary therefor, and may take, store and use the water of any river, stream, lake, pond, spring or well in the town of Hancock, and may excavate through any lands when necessary for the purposes of the corporation.

May erect dams, reservoirs, etc.
—may lay pipes.

Section 5. Said corporation is hereby authorized for the purposes aforesaid, to carry on the business of lighting by electricity, gas or otherwise, the public streets and such buildings and places in the towns of Hancock and Sullivan aforesaid, both public and private, as may be agreed upon by said corporation, and the owners, or those having control of such places, to be lighted; and may furnish motive power by electricity or otherwise within said towns, and may build, maintain and operate works, plants and manufactories for the purposes of generating, providing, supplying and selling electricity, gas or other light and power of any kind, and may take and hold by purchase or otherwise any real estate necessary therefor, and may construct, lay, erect, maintain and operate pipe lines, or lines of wire, or other material, and poles and wires for the transmission of gas, electricity and power, any or all of them, upon, under, along and over any and all streets and ways in the towns of Hancock and Sullivan.

May furnish light in towns of Hancock and Sullivan.
—may furnish power by electricity.

Section 6. Said corporation is hereby authorized to lay down in and through the streets and ways of the said town of Hancock, and to take up, replace and repair all such pipes, aqueducts and fixtures as may be necessary for the purposes of its incorporation under such reasonable restrictions as may be imposed by the selectmen of said town, and said corporation shall be responsible for all damage to persons and property occasioned by its use of such streets and ways, and shall further be liable to pay to said town all sums recovered against it for damages from obstructions caused by said corporation.

May lay pipes in town of Hancock.
—damages by use of streets.

Section 7. Said corporation shall be held liable to pay all damages that shall be sustained by any person by the taking of water, land or other property, or by flowage, or by excavating through any land for the purposes of laying down pipes and aqueducts, building dams, reservoirs and also damages for any other injuries resulting from said acts; and if any person sustain-

Damages for land taken.

CHAP. 176

—appeal.

ing damage as aforesaid, and said corporation cannot mutually agree upon the compensation to be made therefor, either party on petition to the county commissioners of Hancock county may have the damages assessed by them; and subsequent proceedings and rights of appeal shall be had in the same manner, and under the same conditions, restrictions and limitations as are by law provided in case of damages by the laying out of highways.

May make contracts for light, heat and power.

—towns of Hancock and Sullivan may contract for light, etc.

Section 8. The said corporation is hereby authorized to make contracts with the United States, the state of Maine and the town of Hancock and with corporations and inhabitants of said town for the purpose of supplying water, light and power as contemplated by this act; and with the town of Sullivan and with corporations and inhabitants of said town for the purpose of supplying light and power as contemplated by this act. And the said towns of Hancock and Sullivan, through its selectmen, are hereby authorized to enter into contracts with said corporation for the purpose of supplying light and power, and, in the case of the town of Hancock, water, as contemplated by this act; and also for such exemption from public burden as the said towns, or either of them, and said corporation may agree upon, which when made shall be legal and binding upon all parties thereto.

May cross sewers.

Section 9. Said corporation shall have power to cross any public or private sewer, or to change the direction thereof when necessary for the purposes of said corporation, but in such a manner as not to obstruct or impair the use thereof, and said corporation shall be liable for any injury caused thereby. Whenever said corporation shall lay down any pipes in any street, or make any alteration or repairs upon its works in any street it shall cause the same to be done with as little obstruction to public travel as may be practicable, and shall at its own expense without unnecessary delay cause the earth removed to be replaced in proper condition.

Proceedings when land, water or other property is taken.

Section 10. When said corporation shall take any water, land or other property under the powers herein granted it shall cause a statement of such waters, and a description of such land, or other property, with a plan thereof to be filed in the registry of deeds for Hancock county, and within ten days of such filing a copy of such statement or description shall be published three weeks successively in some public newspaper printed in Ellsworth in said Hancock county. Such water, land or other property shall be deemed to have been taken at the date of such filing. The corporation shall take no water, land, or other property, until such filing of statement or description, but may make all needful explorations and surveys on any land or water in said towns prior to such filing.

FRYEBURG ELECTRIC LIGHT COMPANY. 291

CHAP. 177

Section 11. Said corporation may issue its bonds for the construction of its works upon such rates and terms as it may deem expedient not exceeding one hundred thousand dollars, and secure the same by mortgage of the franchise and property of said company. {May issue bonds.}

Section 12. The lease for nine hundred ninety-nine years from the Hancock Point Water Company, a corporation created by act of the legislature of Maine approved February one, eighteen hundred eighty-seven, to George H. Grant of all its franchises, plant, real and personal property, said lease being dated May eleven, nineteen hundred one, is hereby ratified and made valid; and the said George H. Grant is hereby authorized to assign and convey to the corporation hereby created all and the same property and property rights acquired by him under and by virtue of said lease from the Hancock Point Water Company, and the said corporation hereby created may thereafterwards have, hold and exercise all the rights, titles, privileges and advantages heretofore held or enjoyed by the Hancock Point Water Company and leased to said Grant as fully and effectually as if originally granted to and held by said corporation hereby created; but expressly subject to all the terms, restrictions, limitations and conditions as set forth in the aforesaid lease from the Hancock Point Water Company to George H. Grant. {Lease from Hancock Point Water Company, confirmed.} {—terms, restrictions, etc.}

Section 13. The first meeting of said corporation may be called by a public notice published in the Ellsworth American five days before the day of meeting, said call to be signed by any one of the corporators herein named. {First meeting, how called.}

Section 14. This act shall take effect when approved.

Approved March 17, 1903.

Chapter 177.

An Act relating to the Fryeburg Electric Light Company.

Be it enacted by the Senate and House of Representatives in Legislature assembled, as follows:

Section 1. The organization of the Fryeburg Electric Light Company under the general law of the state is hereby ratified and confirmed. {Organization ratified and confirmed.}

Section 2. Permission is hereby given to said company to exercise its corporate powers of making, generating, selling, distributing and supplying gas or electricity or both for lighting, heating, manufacturing and mechanical purposes within the town of Fryeburg, county of Oxford, provided said corporation {May exercise corporate powers in Fryeburg.} {—proviso.}

STRONG WATER CO.—LIBBY MEADOW BROOK DAM COMPANY.

CHAP. 178

shall first acquire by purchase or otherwise the existing electrical plant now in operation in said town.

Section 3. This act shall take effect when approved.

Approved March 17, 1903.

Chapter 178.

An Act to extend the charter of the Strong Water Company.

Be it enacted by the Senate and House of Representatives in Legislature assembled, as follows:

Charter extended.

Section 1. The rights, powers and privileges of the Strong Water Company which were granted by chapter one hundred and forty-seven of the private and special laws of the year eighteen hundred and ninety-nine as amended by chapter two hundred and thirty-three of the private and special laws of the year nineteen hundred and one, are hereby extended for two years additional; and the persons named in said acts, their associates and successors, shall have all the rights, powers and privileges that were granted to them by said acts, to be exercised in the same manner and for the same purposes as specified in said acts.

Section 2. This act shall take effect when approved.

Approved March 17, 1903.

Chapter 179.

An Act to incorporate the Libby Meadow Brook Dam Company.

Be it enacted by the Senate and House of Representatives in Legislature assembled, as follows:

Corporators.

—corporate name.

Section 1. Marion E. Sprague, O. L. Sprague and Alonzo R. Page, their associates, successors and assigns, are hereby incorporated under the name of Libby Meadow Brook Dam Company.

May erect dams on Libby Meadow brook.

—may remove obstructions.

Section 2. Said company may erect and maintain dams with suitable gates and sluice ways upon Libby Meadow brook, a tributary of the Mattawamkeag river, and may clear and remove obstructions therefrom, build necessary side dams, piers and booms therein and otherwise improve said stream for the purpose of facilitating the driving of logs and other lumber down the same, and for the above purposes said company may take necessary land and materials for building such dams and making such improvements and may flow contiguous land so far as necessary, and if interested parties cannot agree upon the amount of damages to be paid by said company for the land and materials so taken, such damages shall be ascertained and determined by the county commissioners of the county where the land so taken is situated or the materials so used are found, in the same manner and under the same conditions and limitations as is provided by law in the case of damages occasioned by laying out of highways, and the amount of damages so determined shall be paid by said company and the damages arising from the flowing of lands may be recovered in accordance with provisions of chapter ninety-two of the revised statutes.

Section 3. Said company may demand and receive a toll upon all logs and other lumber which may pass over or through said dams and improvements, to be fixed by the directors of said company, but said tolls shall not exceed ten cents per thousand feet, board measure. Said company shall have a lien upon the logs or other lumber which may pass over or through any of its dams or improvements, until the full amount of such tolls is paid, to be enforced by attachment, but the logs of each mark shall only be holden for the unpaid tolls of such mark.

Section 4. The capital stock of the company shall not exceed three thousand dollars.

Section 5. When said company shall have received from tolls its outlay on all dams and improvements and for the repairs made upon the same up to that time, including the amount paid on account of flowage or other damages and six per cent interest thereon then the tolls herein provided shall be fixed at a sufficient amount to keep said dams and other improvements in repair.

Section 6. The first meeting of the company shall be called by a notice signed by one of the corporators named in section one, mailed to each of the other corporators, at least seven days before the day of such meeting.

Section 7. This act shall take effect when approved.

Approved March 17, 1903.

Chapter 180.

An Act to incorporate the Round Pond Improvement Company.

Be it enacted by the Senate and House of Representatives in Legislature assembled, as follows:

Corporators.
Section 1. John R. Toothaker, Abram Ross, John W. Ross, Lyman J. Kempton, Eugene I. Herrick, Gilbert L. Kempton, Harry A. Furbish, Whiting L. Butler and Fred W. Soule, their associates, successors and assigns, are hereby created a body corporate by the name of the Round Pond Improvement Company, with all the rights and privileges of similar corporations.

—corporate name.

May improve inlets and outlets of Round pond, and Dodge pond.
Section 2. Said corporation may deepen, widen and otherwise improve, the streams which constitute the main inlets of Round pond and the outlet of said pond, the main inlet of Dodge pond and the outlet of said Dodge pond, connecting the same with Rangeley lake, and may erect and maintain dams, side booms and sluices on said streams, all in the town of Rangeley in the county of Franklin, for the purpose of making said streams floatable and raising and holding a head of water for driving logs and other lumber; may flow lands contiguous to said streams so far as may be necessary for holding or driving logs or other lumber; may erect and maintain dams, side booms and sluices, at the outlet of said Round pond and at the outlet of said Dodge pond, and may hold at high water mark the water in said ponds for such periods as may be necessary for holding or driving logs or other lumber; and may take land and materials for erecting and maintaining said dams, side booms and sluices, and making said improvements.

—may erect dams, etc.

—may flow contiguous lands.

Damages for taking land, liable for.
Section 3. Said corporation shall be liable for all damages sustained by any person for the taking of any land or other property, and for damages caused by flowage, and if the party or parties sustaining such damages and said corporation cannot mutually agree upon the amount of the same, either party may petition the county commissioners of said county of Franklin, and may have such damages assessed by the said commissioners, and subsequent proceedings and rights of appeal thereon shall be had in the same manner as by law provided in case of damages in laying out highways.

Tolls.
Section 4. Said corporation may demand and receive as a toll the sum of twenty cents for every thousand feet of logs, or other lumber, board measure, woods scale, which may pass over the improvements and dams made by said corporation, and said corporation shall have a lien on all logs and other lumber that shall pass over said improvements and dams, until the full amount of such toll is paid, but the logs of each particular mark

—lien for toll.

only shall be holden to pay the toll on such mark, and if said toll is not paid within thirty days after such logs, or a major part of them, shall arrive in Rangeley lake, in said county, or at the place of manufacture, said corporation may seize said logs and sell at public sale so many thereof as may be necessary to pay such toll, costs and charges, ten days' notice of the time and place of such sale being given in some newspaper published in said county of Franklin.

Section 5. This act shall take effect when approved.

Approved March 17, 1903.

Chapter 181.

An Act to amend the charter of the Sanford Light and Water Company and to consolidate with the Springvale Aqueduct Company and Butler Spring Water Company.

Be it enacted by the Senate and House of Representatives in Legislature assembled, as follows:

Section 1. The organization of the Sanford Light and Water Company under the general laws of the state, as recorded in the book of corporations in the office of the secretary of state in volume ten, page five hundred and twenty-one is hereby confirmed and made valid, and said company is hereby declared to be a corporation for the purposes therein specified, and all the acts and doings of said company since the filing of the certificate thereof in the secretary of state's office, are made valid as acts of such corporation, the same as if incorporated by a special act, with all the rights and privileges and subject to all the duties, obligations and liabilities of such corporations.

Organization of Sanford Light and Water Company, confirmed.
—declared to be a corporation.
—acts and doings made valid.

Section 2. Said corporation is hereby authorized to acquire by lease, purchase of stock or otherwise, the franchises and all other assets of the Springvale Aqueduct Company and of the Butler Spring Water Company respectively, and to operate said companies, when acquired, with all the rights, franchises and privileges attached respectively thereto as a part of its water system; and to raise funds for the above purpose, or for any extension of its system, said Sanford Light and Water Company is further authorized to issue shares of its capital stock or bonds secured by a mortgage, or either, to such amount as may be found expedient; and the Springvale Aqueduct Company and the Butler Spring Water Company are hereby respectively authorized to lease or sell their property and franchises to the Sanford Light and Water Company.

Purchase of Springvale Aqueduct Company and Butler Spring Water Company, authorized.
—may issue capital stock or bonds.

Chapter 175.

An Act to consolidate Atlantic Shore Line Railway, Sanford and Cape Porpoise Railway Company, Mousam River Railroad and Sanford Power Company.

Be it enacted by the Senate and House of Representatives in Legislature assembled, as follows:

Name changed to Atlantic Shore Line Railway.

Section 1. The name of the Atlantic Shore Line Railway Company, a corporation organized under the general laws of the state of Maine, is hereby changed to Atlantic Shore Line Railway.

Atlantic Shore Line Railway, authorized to acquire certain other lines.

Section 2. The Atlantic Shore Line Railway is hereby authorized to acquire by lease, purchase of stock or otherwise the street railroads franchises and all other assets of the Mousam River Railroad and of the Sanford and Cape Porpoise Railway Company, and of the Sanford Power Company, respectively, and of any other connecting street railroads, and to operate said street railroads, when acquired, with all the rights, franchises and privileges attached respectively thereto as a part of its street railway system; and to raise funds for the above purpose, or for any extension of its said system, said Atlantic Shore Line Railway is further authorized to issue shares of its capital stock or bonds secured by mortgage, or either, to such amount as may be found expedient; and the Mousam River Railroad and the Sanford and Cape Porpoise Railway Company and the Sanford Power Company, and any other connecting street railroads are hereby respectively authorized to lease or sell their railroads, property and franchises to the Atlantic Shore Line Railway.

Authorized to furnish light, heat and power in town of Sanford.

Section 3. The Atlantic Shore Line Railway is hereby authorized to engage in the business of furnishing electric light, heat and power in the town of Sanford, subject, however, to the general laws of the state regulating the erection of posts, wires and lines for the purposes of electricity, with all the powers and privileges and subject to all the duties, restrictions and liabilities by law incident to corporations having similar corporate purposes.

Pending proceedings, how prosecuted and defended.

Section 4. All proceedings, suits at law or in equity which may be pending at the time of such transfers to which either of the corporations named in section two may be a party, may be prosecuted or defended by the said Atlantic Shore Line Railway in like manner and with like effect as if such transfer had not been made. All claims, contracts, rights and causes of action of or against either of the said corporations so selling or leasing, at law or in equity, may be enforced by suit or action to be begun or prosecuted by or against the said Atlantic Shore Line Railway.

—claims, contracts, rights and causes of action, how enforced.

Section 5. When the transfers authorized by this act are carried out and fully completed, the Atlantic Shore Line Railway shall be liable for the then legally existing debts and obligations of each and all of the companies so making such transfers.

<small>Shall be liable for debts of acquired properties.</small>

Section 6. The said Atlantic Shore Line Railway is farther authorized to acquire by lease, purchase or otherwise the lines, property and franchises of any street railroad or street railroads whose lines as constructed or chartered would form connection or continuous lines with the lines of said Atlantic Shore Line Railway, as constructed or chartered, and in such case the Atlantic Shore Line Railway shall be entitled to all the privileges and be subject to all appropriate conditions and limitations contained in the charters and franchises then acquired. Any street railway company whose lines as constructed or chartered would form connecting or continuous lines with the lines of the Atlantic Shore Line Railway, as constructed or chartered, is hereby authorized to lease or sell its lines, property and franchises as in this section authorized.

<small>May acquire connecting or continuous lines.</small>

Section 7. The said Atlantic Shore Line Railway may, for the purposes of sections two, three and five, or either of them, issue such additional stock as may be necessary therefor, likewise such additional bonds as may be required for the purposes of said sections or of either of them and secure the said bonds by appropriate mortgages upon its franchises and property, and thereafterwards issue its stock and bonds, or either of them, in payment and exchange for the stock, bonds, franchises and property of any corporation making transfers under sections two, three and five, in such manner and in such amounts as may be agreed upon.

<small>May issue additional stock for purposes of sections 2, 3 and 5.</small>

<small>—and issue additional bonds.</small>

Section 8. The Atlantic Shore Line Railway is further authorized to cross tide waters and navigable waters within the limits of any or all the towns within which the aforesaid railroads are built or authorized, upon existing bridges or upon bridges or structures of said company erected therefor, provided, however, that said company shall not unnecessarily obstruct navigation, and that the manner and conditions of its so crossing said waters upon any bridges, and of its erecting and maintaining any such bridges or structures of its own shall first be determined by the municipal officers of the town or towns within the limits of which said bridge or structure shall be so erected, maintained or used, and if said company and such municipal officers shall disagree as to the terms prescribing the manner and conditions of such crossing or of erecting and maintaining any such bridge or structure, the same shall after notice and hearing be determined by the railroad commissioners and their decree thereon shall be final.

<small>May cross tide waters.</small>

<small>—proviso.</small>

CHAP. 175

May construct a street railroad.

Section 9. The Atlantic Shore Line Railway is hereby authorized to construct, operate and maintain a street railroad for street traffic for the conveyance of persons and property along and upon said streets, roads and ways, and over and across such lands as said company may deem best for public convenience, with such single or double tracks, side tracks, switches, turnouts, stations, and appurtenances, and with such poles, wires and appliances as shall be reasonably convenient in the premises, with all the powers and privileges incident to or usually granted to similar corporations.

Distance of rails from sidewalk, etc., shall be determined by municipal officers.

—appeal, how taken.

Section 10. The municipal officers of the town or towns in which said Atlantic Shore Line Railway is located shall determine the distance from the sidewalks or from the side lines of the streets at which the rails of said company shall be laid. The railway company or any person interested may at any time appeal from such determination to the board of railroad commissioners, who shall upon notice hear the parties and finally determine the questions raised by said appeal. In case said Atlantic Shore Line Railway makes any extensions, additions or variations from the lines of the Sanford and Cape Porpoise Railway Company or under any other franchise by it hereafter acquired created by special act of the legislature, it shall be competent for the railway company or any person interested to at any time appeal from any determination or order of the municipal officers of any town determining the distance from the sidewalks or the side lines of the streets, of the proposed location of the rails of said company to the board of railroad commissioners, who shall upon notice hear the parties and finally determine the questions raised by said appeal.

Grade, rate of speed, removal of snow from tracks, etc., regulated by municipal officers.

Section 11. All the said railroad lines to be operated, constructed or maintained under this act shall be constructed and maintained in such form and manner and with such rails and upon such grade as the municipal officers of the towns where the same are located may direct. Such municipal officers shall have power at all times to make such regulations as to the mode of use of any such tracks, the rate of speed and the removal and disposal of snow and ice from the streets, roads and ways as the public safety and convenience may require. The said railroad company may at any time appeal from any such determination, decrees, rules and regulations made and established under this section, to the board of railroad commissioners, who shall, upon notice, hear the parties and finally determine the questions raised by said appeal.

Additional land, how same may be acquired.

Section 12. Whenever the said Atlantic Shore Line Railway requires additional land for the purpose of improving the alignment of any part of the road by it to be built or acquired under this act, or if it requires additional land for double tracking its road to be built or acquired hereunder, and is unable to obtain the same by agreement with the owner, it may apply in writing to the railroad commissioners, describing the land required for either or both of said purposes, and naming the persons interested; the commissioners shall thereupon appoint a time for hearing near the premises and requiring notice to be given to all persons interested, as they may direct, fourteen days at least before said time; and shall then view the premises, hear the parties and determine how much if any of said real estate is required for either or both of said purposes. If they find that any of it is so required they shall furnish the corporation with a certificate containing a definite description thereof, and when it is filed with the clerk of courts in the county where the land lies it shall be deemed and treated as taken for public uses; provided, however, that where land is held by a tenant for life and the reversion is contingent as to the persons in whom it may vest on the termination of the life estate, such fact shall be stated in the application and the commissioners shall, in addition to the notice to the tenant for life, give notice by publication to all others interested, in such manner as they deem proper. In taking such land the corporation shall be subject to the provisions of section seventeen of chapter fifty-one of the revised statutes, but the damages therefor shall be estimated and paid in the manner hereinafter provided by section thirteen of this act.

Section 13. For the purpose of determining the damages to be paid for lands taken under this act the land owner or said company may, within three years after the filing of such plans and locations with the clerk of courts as hereinbefore provided, apply to the commissioners of said county of York and have such damages assessed as is provided by law wherein land is taken for railroads, so far as the same is consistent with the provisions of this charter, and where inconsistent or at variance with this charter, the charter shall control. The said commissioners shall have the same power to make suitable orders relative to cattle guards, cattle passes, and farm crossings, as in the case of railroads. If the company shall fail to pay such land owner or to deposit for his use with the clerk of the county commissioners such sum as may be finally awarded for damages, with costs, within ninety days after final judgment, said location shall be invalid and the company forfeit all rights under the same. If such land owner secures more damages than were tendered by said company he shall recover costs, otherwise the company shall recover costs. In case the company shall begin to occupy said

HANCOCK WATER, LIGHT AND POWER COMPANY.

CHAP. 176

—failure to apply for damages for three years, held a waiver.

lands before rendition of final judgment the land owner may require said company to file its bond with said commissioners in such sum and with such securities as they may approve, conditioned for such payment or deposit; failure to apply for damages within the said three years by said land owner shall be held to be a waiver of the same. No action shall be brought against such company for such taking and occupation of land until after such failure to pay or deposit.

Established locations confirmed.

Section 14. The locations of rails, posts, wires and fixtures within the limits of any street, road or way, as now established by any or all of the street railroad companies, authorized to sell their properties and franchises under this act, are hereby confirmed and made valid.

Rights and privileges.

—restrictions.

Section 15. The said Atlantic Shore Line Railway shall, except as modified by this act, have all the rights and privileges conferred by general law upon street railroad corporations, and be subject to the conditions, restrictions and limitations thereby imposed.

Section 16. This act shall take effect when approved.

Approved March 13, 1903.

Chapter 176.

An Act to incorporate the Hancock Water, Light and Power Company.

Be it enacted by the Senate and House of Representatives in Legislature assembled, as follows:

Corporators.

—corporate name.

Section 1. George H. Grant, Isadore L. Halman and John S. Sanger, their associates, successors and assigns, are hereby made a corporation under the name of the Hancock Water, Light and Power Company.

Capital stock.

—may hold real and personal estate.

Section 2. The capital stock of said corporation shall not be less than twenty-five thousand dollars divided into shares of twenty-five dollars each. The capital stock may by vote of the corporation be increased to two hundred and fifty thousand dollars. Said corporation is authorized to hold such real and personal estate as may be necessary and proper for the purposes of its incorporation.

Purposes.

Section 3. The purposes of said corporation shall be to supply water for public and private use, and for any and all purposes in the town of Hancock in Hancock county; to generate and supply light by electricity, gas or otherwise for public and private use, and for any and all purposes in the towns of Hancock and Sullivan, in said county; and to generate, sell, distribute

HANCOCK WATER, LIGHT AND POWER COMPANY.   289

CHAP. 176

tribute and supply electric or other power for any and all purposes in the aforesaid towns of Hancock and Sullivan.

Section 4. Said corporation is hereby authorized for the purposes aforesaid, to erect and maintain dams, reservoirs, filters and standpipes; and to lay and maintain pipes and aqueducts necessary or proper for accumulating, storing, conducting, discharging, distributing, disbursing, supplying and selling water; said corporation may take and hold by purchase or otherwise any real estate necessary therefor, and may take, store and use the water of any river, stream, lake, pond, spring or well in the town of Hancock, and may excavate through any lands when necessary for the purposes of the corporation.

May erect dams, reservoirs, etc.
—may lay pipes.

Section 5. Said corporation is hereby authorized for the purposes aforesaid, to carry on the business of lighting by electricity, gas or otherwise, the public streets and such buildings and places in the towns of Hancock and Sullivan aforesaid, both public and private, as may be agreed upon by said corporation, and the owners, or those having control of such places, to be lighted; and may furnish motive power by electricity or otherwise within said towns, and may build, maintain and operate works, plants and manufactories for the purposes of generating, providing, supplying and selling electricity, gas or other light and power of any kind, and may take and hold by purchase or otherwise any real estate necessary therefor, and may construct, lay, erect, maintain and operate pipe lines, or lines of wire, or other material, and poles and wires for the transmission of gas, electricity and power, any or all of them, upon, under, along and over any and all streets and ways in the towns of Hancock and Sullivan.

May furnish light in towns of Hancock and Sullivan.

—may furnish power by electricity.

Section 6. Said corporation is hereby authorized to lay down in and through the streets and ways of the said town of Hancock, and to take up, replace and repair all such pipes, aqueducts and fixtures as may be necessary for the purposes of its incorporation under such reasonable restrictions as may be imposed by the selectmen of said town, and said corporation shall be responsible for all damage to persons and property occasioned by its use of such streets and ways, and shall further be liable to pay to said town all sums recovered against it for damages from obstructions caused by said corporation.

May lay pipes in town of Hancock.

—damages by use of streets.

Section 7. Said corporation shall be held liable to pay all damages that shall be sustained by any person by the taking of water, land or other property, or by flowage, or by excavating through any land for the purposes of laying down pipes and aqueducts, building dams, reservoirs and also damages for any other injuries resulting from said acts; and if any person sustain-

Damages for land taken.

32

ing damage as aforesaid, and said corporation cannot mutually agree upon the compensation to be made therefor, either party on petition to the county commissioners of Hancock county may have the damages assessed by them; and subsequent proceedings and rights of appeal shall be had in the same manner, and under the same conditions, restrictions and limitations as are by law provided in case of damages by the laying out of highways.

Section 8. The said corporation is hereby authorized to make contracts with the United States, the state of Maine and the town of Hancock and with corporations and inhabitants of said town for the purpose of supplying water, light and power as contemplated by this act; and with the town of Sullivan and with corporations and inhabitants of said town for the purpose of supplying light and power as contemplated by this act. And the said towns of Hancock and Sullivan, through its selectmen, are hereby authorized to enter into contracts with said corporation for the purpose of supplying light and power, and, in the case of the town of Hancock, water, as contemplated by this act; and also for such exemption from public burden as the said towns, or either of them, and said corporation may agree upon, which when made shall be legal and binding upon all parties thereto.

Section 9. Said corporation shall have power to cross any public or private sewer, or to change the direction thereof when necessary for the purposes of said corporation, but in such a manner as not to obstruct or impair the use thereof, and said corporation shall be liable for any injury caused thereby. Whenever said corporation shall lay down any pipes in any street, or make any alteration or repairs upon its works in any street it shall cause the same to be done with as little obstruction to public travel as may be practicable, and shall at its own expense without unnecessary delay cause the earth removed to be replaced in proper condition.

Section 10. When said corporation shall take any water, land or other property under the powers herein granted it shall cause a statement of such waters, and a description of such land, or other property, with a plan thereof to be filed in the registry of deeds for Hancock county, and within ten days of such filing a copy of such statement or description shall be published three weeks successively in some public newspaper printed in Ellsworth in said Hancock county. Such water, land or other property shall be deemed to have been taken at the date of such filing. The corporation shall take no water, land, or other property, until such filing of statement or description, but may make all needful explorations and surveys on any land or water in said towns prior to such filing.

Section 11. Said corporation may issue its bonds for the construction of its works upon such rates and terms as it may deem expedient not exceeding one hundred thousand dollars, and secure the same by mortgage of the franchise and property of said company.

May issue bonds.

Section 12. The lease for nine hundred ninety-nine years from the Hancock Point Water Company, a corporation created by act of the legislature of Maine approved February one, eighteen hundred eighty-seven, to George H. Grant of all its franchises, plant, real and personal property, said lease being dated May eleven, nineteen hundred one, is hereby ratified and made valid; and the said George H. Grant is hereby authorized to assign and convey to the corporation hereby created all and the same property and property rights acquired by him under and by virtue of said lease from the Hancock Point Water Company, and the said corporation hereby created may thereafterwards have, hold and exercise all the rights, titles, privileges and advantages heretofore held or enjoyed by the Hancock Point Water Company and leased to said Grant as fully and effectually as if originally granted to and held by said corporation hereby created; but expressly subject to all the terms, restrictions, limitations and conditions as set forth in the aforesaid lease from the Hancock Point Water Company to George H. Grant.

Lease from Hancock Point Water Company, confirmed.

—terms, restrictions, etc.

Section 13. The first meeting of said corporation may be called by a public notice published in the Ellsworth American five days before the day of meeting, said call to be signed by any one of the corporators herein named.

First meeting, how called.

Section 14. This act shall take effect when approved.

Approved March 17, 1903.

Chapter 177.

An Act relating to the Fryeburg Electric Light Company.

Be it enacted by the Senate and House of Representatives in Legislature assembled, as follows:

Section 1. The organization of the Fryeburg Electric Light Company under the general law of the state is hereby ratified and confirmed.

Organization ratified and confirmed.

Section 2. Permission is hereby given to said company to exercise its corporate powers of making, generating, selling, distributing and supplying gas or electricity or both for lighting, heating, manufacturing and mechanical purposes within the town of Fryeburg, county of Oxford, provided said corporation

May exercise corporate powers in Fryeburg.

—proviso.

shall first acquire by purchase or otherwise the existing electrical plant now in operation in said town.

Section 3. This act shall take effect when approved.

Approved March 17, 1903.

Chapter 178.

An Act to extend the charter of the Strong Water Company.

Be it enacted by the Senate and House of Representatives in Legislature assembled, as follows:

Charter extended.
Section 1. The rights, powers and privileges of the Strong Water Company which were granted by chapter one hundred and forty-seven of the private and special laws of the year eighteen hundred and ninety-nine as amended by chapter two hundred and thirty-three of the private and special laws of the year nineteen hundred and one, are hereby extended for two years additional; and the persons named in said acts, their associates and successors, shall have all the rights, powers and privileges that were granted to them by said acts, to be exercised in the same manner and for the same purposes as specified in said acts.

Section 2. This act shall take effect when approved.

Approved March 17, 1903.

Chapter 179.

An Act to incorporate the Libby Meadow Brook Dam Company.

Be it enacted by the Senate and House of Representatives in Legislature assembled, as follows:

Corporators.
—corporate name.
Section 1. Marion E. Sprague, O. L. Sprague and Alonzo R. Page, their associates, successors and assigns, are hereby incorporated under the name of Libby Meadow Brook Dam Company.

May erect dams on Libby Meadow brook.
—may remove obstructions.
Section 2. Said company may erect and maintain dams with suitable gates and sluice ways upon Libby Meadow brook, a tributary of the Mattawamkeag river, and may clear and remove obstructions therefrom, build necessary side dams, piers and booms therein and otherwise improve said stream for the purpose of facilitating the driving of logs and other lumber down the same, and for the above purposes said company may take necessary land and materials for building such dams and making

such improvements and may flow contiguous land so far as necessary, and if interested parties cannot agree upon the amount of damages to be paid by said company for the land and materials so taken, such damages shall be ascertained and determined by the county commissioners of the county where the land so taken is situated or the materials so used are found, in the same manner and under the same conditions and limitations as is provided by law in the case of damages occasioned by laying out of highways, and the amount of damages so determined shall be paid by said company and the damages arising from the flowing of lands may be recovered in accordance with provisions of chapter ninety-two of the revised statutes.

—may flow contiguous lands.

—damages, how ascertained and determined.

Section 3. Said company may demand and receive a toll upon all logs and other lumber which may pass over or through said dams and improvements, to be fixed by the directors of said company, but said tolls shall not exceed ten cents per thousand feet, board measure. Said company shall have a lien upon the logs or other lumber which may pass over or through any of its dams or improvements, until the full amount of such tolls is paid, to be enforced by attachment, but the logs of each mark shall only be holden for the unpaid tolls of such mark.

Tolls.

—lien.

Section 4. The capital stock of the company shall not exceed three thousand dollars.

Capital stock.

Section 5. When said company shall have received from tolls its outlay on all dams and improvements and for the repairs made upon the same up to that time, including the amount paid on account of flowage or other damages and six per cent interest thereon then the tolls herein provided shall be fixed at a sufficient amount to keep said dams and other improvements in repair.

Revision of tolls, when to be had.

Section 6. The first meeting of the company shall be called by a notice signed by one of the corporators named in section one, mailed to each of the other corporators, at least seven days before the day of such meeting.

First meeting, how called.

Section 7. This act shall take effect when approved.

Approved March 17, 1903.

Chapter 180.

An Act to incorporate the Round Pond Improvement Company.

Be it enacted by the Senate and House of Representatives in Legislature assembled, as follows:

Corporators.

Section 1. John R. Toothaker, Abram Ross, John W. Ross, Lyman J. Kempton, Eugene I. Herrick, Gilbert L. Kempton, Harry A. Furbish, Whiting L. Butler and Fred W. Soule, their associates, successors and assigns, are hereby created a body corporate by the name of the Round Pond Improvement Company, with all the rights and privileges of similar corporations.

—corporate name.

May improve inlets and outlets of Round pond, and Dodge pond.

—may erect dams, etc.

—may flow contiguous lands.

Section 2. Said corporation may deepen, widen and otherwise improve, the streams which constitute the main inlets of Round pond and the outlet of said pond, the main inlet of Dodge pond and the outlet of said Dodge pond, connecting the same with Rangeley lake, and may erect and maintain dams, side booms and sluices on said streams, all in the town of Rangeley in the county of Franklin, for the purpose of making said streams floatable and raising and holding a head of water for driving logs and other lumber; may flow lands contiguous to said streams so far as may be necessary for holding or driving logs or other lumber; may erect and maintain dams, side booms and sluices, at the outlet of said Round pond and at the outlet of said Dodge pond, and may hold at high water mark the water in said ponds for such periods as may be necessary for holding or driving logs or other lumber; and may take land and materials for erecting and maintaining said dams, side booms and sluices, and making said improvements.

Damages for taking land, liable for.

Section 3. Said corporation shall be liable for all damages sustained by any person for the taking of any land or other property, and for damages caused by flowage, and if the party or parties sustaining such damages and said corporation cannot mutually agree upon the amount of the same, either party may petition the county commissioners of said county of Franklin, and may have such damages assessed by the said commissioners, and subsequent proceedings and rights of appeal thereon shall be had in the same manner as by law provided in case of damages in laying out highways.

Tolls.

—lien for toll.

Section 4. Said corporation may demand and receive as a toll the sum of twenty cents for every thousand feet of logs, or other lumber, board measure, woods scale, which may pass over the improvements and dams made by said corporation, and said corporation shall have a lien on all logs and other lumber that shall pass over said improvements and dams, until the full amount of such toll is paid, but the logs of each particular mark only shall be holden to pay the toll on such mark, and if said toll is not paid within thirty days after such logs, or a major part of them, shall arrive in Rangeley lake, in said county, or at the place of manufacture, said corporation may seize said logs and sell at public sale so many thereof as may be necessary to pay such toll, costs and charges, ten days' notice of the time and place of such sale being given in some newspaper published in said county of Franklin.

Section 5. This act shall take effect when approved.

Approved March 17, 1903.

Chapter 181.

An Act to amend the charter of the Sanford Light and Water Company and to consolidate with the Springvale Aqueduct Company and Butler Spring Water Company.

Be it enacted by the Senate and House of Representatives in Legislature assembled, as follows:

Section 1. The organization of the Sanford Light and Water Company under the general laws of the state, as recorded in the book of corporations in the office of the secretary of state in volume ten, page five hundred and twenty-one is hereby confirmed and made valid, and said company is hereby declared to be a corporation for the purposes therein specified, and all the acts and doings of said company since the filing of the certificate thereof in the secretary of state's office, are made valid as acts of such corporation, the same as if incorporated by a special act, with all the rights and privileges and subject to all the duties, obligations and liabilities of such corporations.

Section 2. Said corporation is hereby authorized to acquire by lease, purchase of stock or otherwise, the franchises and all other assets of the Springvale Aqueduct Company and of the Butler Spring Water Company respectively, and to operate said companies, when acquired, with all the rights, franchises and privileges attached respectively thereto as a part of its water system; and to raise funds for the above purpose, or for any extension of its system, said Sanford Light and Water Company is further authorized to issue shares of its capital stock or bonds secured by a mortgage, or either, to such amount as may be found expedient; and the Springvale Aqueduct Company and the Butler Spring Water Company are hereby respectively authorized to lease or sell their property and franchises to the Sanford Light and Water Company.

CHAP. 181

May hold real and personal property.

Section 3. Said corporation may take and hold by purchase or otherwise, real and personal estate necessary and convenient for the purposes aforesaid, not exceeding one hundred thousand dollars in amount.

May take water from Square pond and from Mousam or Long pond.

Section 4. For the purposes aforesaid, or for the preservation and purity of said water, said corporation is hereby authorized to take and use water from Square pond and from Mousam or Long pond in the towns of Acton and Shapleigh, and conduct and distribute the same in and through the towns of Acton, Shapleigh and Sanford; to survey for, locate, lay, erect and

—may maintain dams, etc.

maintain suitable dams, reservoirs and machinery, pipes, aqueducts and fixtures, but shall not lay, erect and maintain dams on any water power privileges, known to be such, or occupy any adjoining lands that do not belong to such corporation; to carry its pipes or aqueducts under or over any water course, bridge, street, railroad, highway or other way; to enter upon and excavate any highway or other way, in such manner as least to

—other powers.

obstruct the same: to enter, pass over and excavate any lands; and to take and hold by purchase or otherwise, any real estate, rights of way or of water, and in general do any acts necessary, convenient or proper for carrying out any of the purposes of its incorporation. And said corporation is further authorized, for the purpose of making all needed repairs or service connections, to lay its pipes through any public or private lands or ways, with the right to enter upon the same and dig therein; but no entry shall be made on any private lands or ways, except to make surveys, until said corporation shall file in the registry of deeds in the county of York, plans of the location of all lands and water rights which it may wish to take under the provisions

—plans of location shall be filed.

of this act, nor until the expiration of ten days from such filing; and with such plan, the corporation may file a statement of the damages it is willing to pay to any person for any property so taken, and if the amount awarded finally, does not exceed that sum, the company shall recover costs against such person, otherwise such person shall recover costs against the company.

Damages, liable for.

Section 5. Said corporation shall be held liable to pay all damages that shall be sustained by any persons by the taking of any land, water, right of way or other property, or by excavating through any land for the purpose of surveying, locating, laying or building dams, reservoirs, pipes, aqueducts and other necessary fixtures, and for any other injuries resulting from said acts; and if any person sustaining damages as aforesaid, shall not agree with said corporation upon the sum to be paid therefor,

—damages, how assessed.

either party, upon petition to the county commissioners of York county, within twelve months after said plans are filed, may have said damages assessed by them, and subsequent proceedings and right of appeal thereon, shall be had in the same manner, and under the same conditions, restrictions, and limitations as are by law prescribed in the case of damages by the laying out of highways. Failure to apply for damages within said twelve months shall be held to be a waiver of the same.

Section 6. Said corporation is hereby authorized to lay down and maintain in and through the streets and ways of said town of Sanford and adjoining towns, all such pipes, aqueducts and fixtures as may be necessary for the purposes hereinbefore mentioned. Said company shall have power to cross any water course, private or public sewer, or to change the direction thereof where necessary for the purposes of its incorporation, but in such manner as not to obstruct or impair the use thereof. *May lay pipes.* *—may cross sewers, etc.*

Section 7. Said company may establish and fix, from time to time, rates for the use of water and collect the same. Said town of Sanford is hereby authorized to enter into a contract with said company for a supply of water for all municipal purposes, which, when made shall be legal and binding upon all parties thereto. *Water rates.*

Section 8. This act shall take effect when approved.

Approved March 17, 1903.

Chapter 182.

An Act to Incorporate the Van Buren Sewerage Company.

Be it enacted by the Senate and House of Representatives in Legislature assembled, as follows:

Section 1. Peter C. Keegan, Allen E. Hammond, James Crawford, Arthur Brown, Earl H. Gowing, Henry A. Gagnon, Joseph F. Theriault, Simeon Cyr and Remi Cyr, with their associates, successors and assigns are hereby made a corporation under the name of the Van Buren Sewerage Company for the purpose of providing a system of sewers and drainage for the town and village of Van Buren for the comfort, convenience and health of the people of Van Buren, with all the rights, powers and privileges and immunities incident or properly belonging to such corporations. *Corporators.* *—corporate name.*

Section 2. Said corporation may acquire and hold real and personal estate necessary and convenient for the purposes aforesaid not exceeding in amount fifty thousand dollars, may sell and convey the same, may issue certificates of stock to an amount not *May hold real and personal estate to amount of $50,000.*

CHAP. 182

—may issue stock and bonds.

exceeding twenty-five thousand dollars and may issue and sell bonds to the amount of twenty-five thousand dollars secured by mortgage of its works and franchise, to aid in the construction of its works.

May take lands.

Section 3. Said corporation is hereby authorized to take and hold by purchase or otherwise any land or real estate or easement therein necessary for forming basins, reservoirs and outlets, for erecting buildings for pumping works and for laying and maintaining conduits for carrying and collecting, discharging and disposing of sewerage matter and waters and for any other objects necessary, convenient and proper for the purposes of this act.

May construct conduits into Saint John river.

Section 4. Said corporation may construct conduits, in manner aforesaid in and through said village of Van Buren to and into the Saint John river and its tributaries, the discharge therefrom to be at such point in said river and tributaries as is most convenient, and convey through the same sewerage, surface water and the natural flowage of existing water courses and secure and maintain basins, reservoirs and outlets;

—may construct flush tanks, etc.

may construct and maintain flush tanks, manholes, lampholes and all usual appliances, public and private; may build and maintain pumping stations and buildings, constructions and appliances for collecting, holding, distributing and disposing of sewerage matter,

—fees for entering sewers.

may establish regulations for the use of sewers and fix and collect the prices to be paid for entering the same and also the annual rentals for using thereof, and said corporation is hereby authorized for the purposes aforesaid, having first obtained the permission of the municipal officers of said town and under such restrictions and regulations as said officers may prescribe, to lay down through the streets, highways and lands of said town, and take up, replace and repair all such conduits, pipes and fixtures as may be necessary for the objects of its incorporation; to carry and lay conduits under any watercourse way, public or private, or railroad in the manner prescribed by law, and to cross any drain or sewer or if necessary to change its direction in such manner as not to obstruct the use thereof, and to enter and dig up any such street, road or way, for the purpose of laying pipes beneath the surface thereof, for placing manholes or other fixtures and for maintaining and repairing the same and in general to do any other act or things necessary, convenient and proper to be done for the purpose of this act.

—may occupy streets.

Easement, filing and record of.

Section 5. Said corporation shall file in the registry of deeds for the northern district of Aroostook county, a certificate containing a description of the land taken, or on which an easement may be taken under the provisions of this act and a statement of the purposes for which it is taken, to be recorded by the register and such land or easement shall be deemed to be taken upon the filing of such certificate.

Section 6. Such corporation shall be liable to pay all damages that shall be sustained by any person in his property by the taking of any land or easement therein, under the provisions of this act; and if any person sustaining damages as aforesaid and said corporation shall not mutually agree upon the sum to be paid therefor, such person may cause his damages to be ascertained in the same manner and under the same conditions and limitations as are by law prescribed in the case of damages by the location of railroads.

Section 7. Said corporation, at all times, after it shall commence receiving pay for the facilities supplied by it, shall be bound to permit the owners of all premises abutting upon its lines of pipes and conduits, to enter the same with all proper sewerage upon conformity to the rules and regulations of said company, and payment of the prices and rentals established therefor.

Section 8. Any person who shall place or leave any offensive or injurious matter or materials on the conduits, catch basins or receptacles of said corporation, contrary to its regulations, or shall wilfully injure any conduit, pipe, reservoir, flush tank, catch basin, manhole, lamp hole, outlet, engine, pump or other property held, owned or used by said corporation for the purposes of this act, shall pay twice the amount of damages to said corporation to be recovered in any proper action; and every such person, on conviction of either of said acts of wilful injury aforesaid, shall be punished by fine not exceeding two hundred dollars and by imprisonment not exceeding one year.

Section 9. Said corporation shall be liable to any person injured by any fault of said corporation or its agents, or any defect in the highways occasioned by the construction of the works of said company, during said construction or after the same have been completed, or while the same shall be undergoing repairs or extensions are being made; and said corporation shall also be liable to the town of Van Buren for any and all cost, damage and expense which said town may suffer or be put to by reason of the default, neglect, negligence or carelessness of said corporation or of any of its officers, servants or agents.

Section 10. The affairs of said corporation shall be controlled by a board of directors consisting of not less than five members, who shall be citizens of the town of Van Buren, and elected annually by a vote of the stockholders of the corporation, and such board of directors shall choose such other officers as may, from time to time, be required by the by-laws of the corporation.

CHAP. 182

Town may take over works of.

Section 11. Should the town of Van Buren, at a meeting duly called for the purpose, vote to take over the works of said company, and at any time subsequent to the first day of January, in the year of our Lord nineteen hundred eight, inform the said company of its intention to take over the said works, then and

—proceedings.

in that case, the said company will, within sixty days after receipt of notice of such intention of the said town and upon the tender of the fair market value, at the time of the said works including all the rights and franchises of the company, convey and make over to the said town the said sewer works and system in their entirety as they then exist and make, execute, acknowledge and deliver such deeds, conveyances, transfers or other instruments as may be necessary to secure to the town all and every right, title and interest whether in law or in equity which the said company may have in said sewer works and system.

Consideration when taken over shall be fair market value.

Section 12. Should said sewer works and system be taken over by the town as aforesaid, the consideration to be paid by the town therefor shall be the fair market value of the said works at the time of taking, including the rights and franchises of the said company, as may be agreed upon by the said parties thereto.

—referees, in case mutual agreement is not had.

And should said parties be unable to agree upon the amount to be so paid, the same shall be left to the determination of three persons to be chosen as follows, namely: one who shall not be a lawyer, to be selected by the company; one who shall not be a lawyer, to be chosen by the municipal officers of the town, and another who shall be learned in the law, to be chosen by the chief justice of the supreme court, whose finding in the matter shall be final and conclusive between the parties.

Board of directors.

Section 13. The affairs of said corporation shall be controlled by a board of directors consisting of not less than five members, who shall be citizens of the town of Van Buren, and elected annually by a vote of the stockholders of the corporation; and the board of directors shall choose such other officers as may from time to time be required by the by-laws of the corporation.

First meeting, how called.

Section 14. Any two of the persons mentioned in the first section of this act, may call the first meeting of said corporation, by publishing notice therefor two weeks in a newspaper printed in the county of Aroostook.

Approved March 17, 1903.

SAINT JOHN RIVER DAM COMPANY.

Chapter 183.

An Act to incorporate the Saint John River Dam Company.

Be it enacted by the Senate and House of Representatives in Legislature assembled, as follows:

Section 1. Albert A. Burleigh of Houlton, Charles A. Milliken of Augusta, James W. Parker of Portland, George A. Murchie of Calais, Maine, Redfield Proctor of Proctor, Vermont, Abner W. Hayford of Boston, Massachusetts, Allan E. Hammond and Peter C. Keegan of Van Buren, Maine, John Costigan of Ottawa, Ontario, James Robinson of Millerton, New Brunswick, Thomas J. Cochran and John M. Stevens of Edmundston, New Brunswick, Thomas Crockett of River-Du-Loup, Province of Quebec, and Thomas Clair of Saint Francis, New Brunswick, their associates, successors and assigns, are hereby constituted a body corporate and politic under the name of the Saint John River Dam Company, hereinafter called the 'company' which term shall hereinafter, as to all rights, powers, duties and obligations herein conferred on which may be conferred by the legislature of New Brunswick or the parliament of Canada, include the consolidated or amalgamated corporation contemplated by this act. *Corporators. —corporate name.*

Section 2. The persons named in section one of this act shall be the first or provisional directors of the company, a majority of whom shall constitute a quorum, and they shall have all the powers which are ordinarily possessed and exercised by directors in other similar corporations, and shall hold office until such time as said corporation shall be fully organized and shall have the power to choose a president, treasurer and a clerk to hold office until others are chosen in their stead and may make all by-laws required for the transaction of the business and management of the affairs of the corporation, not inconsistent with the laws of the state, including the mode of calling the first meeting for permanent organization of this or of any corporation formed by the consolidation or amalgamation of this corporation with any other corporation or corporations authorized under this act. *Provisional directors. —quorum. —tenure. —powers.*

Section 3. The capital stock of the company shall be two hundred thousand dollars, which by vote of the stockholders may be increased to an amount not exceeding one million dollars, divided into shares of one hundred dollars each, and may be assessed by the directors from time to time as they deem necessary, but no assessment subsequent to the allotment of shares shall exceed ten per cent, nor be made at less intervals than two months. Said company is also hereby authorized to issue bonds to an amount not exceeding three hundred thousand dollars, in *Capital stock. —shares may be assessed. —may issue bonds.*

CHAP. 183

Head office, where located.

—may accept franchises from legislature of New Brunswick or parliament of Canada.

—franchises may be carried on jointly.

—proviso.

'Logs,' and 'local logs,' meaning of expressions defined.

May construct dam in Saint John river,

denominations of one hundred, five hundred and one thousand dollars, secured by mortgage upon the property of said company, and its franchises, for the building of the dam and other works provided for in this act, and the payment of damages for land taken and land flowed by virtue of the authority conferred by this act.

Section 4. The head office of the company shall be in Van Buren, in the county of Aroostook, at which all meetings of the stockholders shall be held; but the directors may meet elsewhere, as provided by the by-laws of the company, and such meetings may be held in the province of New Brunswick. The company is hereby authorized to accept such franchises, powers and privileges as may be conferred upon it by the legislature of New Brunswick or the parliament of Canada, and to perform such acts within New Brunswick or Canada as may be required or permitted by said legislature or parliament, and this company may consolidate or amalgamate and build, maintain and carry on its works and the franchises hereby granted jointly with the works built under and the franchises granted by said legislature or parliament or all or either of them as one single enterprise, and any organization of such corporation in the ordinary manner whether in accordance with the laws of the state, province or dominion shall be deemed valid and legal in the courts of the state; and any mortgage of its property, real or personal, and franchises given to any individual or individuals, corporation or corporations or to any trustee to secure an issue of notes or bonds which shall be executed in accordance with the laws of the state, province or dominion, shall be deemed valid, effectual and binding to all intents and purposes within the state, provided the same has been duly recorded in the northern registry of deeds for Aroostook county, and this act shall be read and construed as if the several rights and franchises granted by this state and the provincial legislature and the dominion parliament, or either or any of them had been included in and granted as a whole by this act.

Section 5. In this act, unless the context otherwise requires, the expression 'logs' shall mean logs, timber and wood of any kind, the expression 'local logs' shall mean logs, timber and wood of any kind in respect to the holding, collecting, securing, separating. sorting out, rafting or driving of which above the boundary line between Maine and New Brunswick near Grand Falls, the owner or owners thereof have requested the company to take charge.

Section 6. The company may construct, equip, maintain and operate a dam, with the right of flowage, in the Saint John river, at or near the Winding Ledges in the town of Fort Kent, in the county of Aroostook and state of Maine, from any point along the bank or shore of said river to the boundary line in said river between the United States and Canada, to, and may connect said dam with a dam to be built from the opposite shore of said river in the parish of Saint Francis, in the province of New Brunswick, provided and whenever authority to build such dam from the said shore in the province of New Brunswick, and to make such connection has been or may be obtained by this or some other company in the dominion of Canada, and may build, maintain and operate all such other dams, wing dams, sluices, conduits, booms, side booms, sheer booms, piers, wharfs, slips, buildings and other works above said dam to a point opposite the mouth of the Saint Francis river, and below said dam to the boundary line between Maine and New Brunswick near Grand Falls, in the county of Victoria and province aforesaid, in the river Saint John or any of its tributaries within the state, necessary for the purposes of the company.

Said dam shall be constructed in such a manner as will permit of the safe passage and transmission of all logs, and shall be maintained free of charge, for the use of all persons, except to the owner or owners of local logs who may desire to pass or transmit their logs, and the company shall be liable to pay damages to any owners of property injured by any overflowing of the waters of said river Saint John, caused by said dam.

The company shall be liable to pay to any persons injured, except to the owners of local logs, compensation for any loss, damage, expense, detention, obstruction or any unnecessary delay, caused by the said dams, wing dams, conduits, booms, sheer booms, side booms, piers, wharfs, slips, buildings or other works of the company, or by the erection and maintenance of said dams and other works, in the driving and floating down the river Saint John of any logs, except local logs.

The company shall, without delay, build and maintain in the said dams such fish ways and of such design as may be prescribed by law.

Section 7. The company, by means of and through the works aforesaid, may hold, collect, secure, separate, sort out, raft and drive over the said dam all logs including local logs, that may come into or be driven within the company's booms above the said dam; and may, in addition to its own logs, contract to hold, collect, secure, separate, sort out, raft and drive to their destination, all local logs coming over said dam or into the Saint John river out of any river or stream or in any other manner whatsoever, below said dam and above the boundary line near Grand

CHAP. 183

—proviso.

Falls, that may be intended for any and all sawmills or pulp mills or other manufactories that are now or may be hereafter built and operated along the river Saint John below said dam and above the boundary line near Grand Falls, provided, however, all logs, except local logs which shall come into or be driven within the company's booms, shall, without any unnecessary delay, be separated by the company from the company's logs and from local logs and be driven out of the said booms into the river at the expense of the company.

—Madawaska Log Driving Company may place men at booms.

—purposes for which men may be so placed.

The Madawaska Log Driving Company may place one or more men, if necessary, at the said booms and at the expense of the company hereby incorporated, to see that all logs in the manner herein provided, except the company's logs and local logs are all and properly passed by and if not passed by to the satisfaction of the said log driving company, may itself take charge of and pass by all logs except local logs and the logs of the company, hereby incorporated.

Prize or unmarked logs, regulations relating to.

Section 8. Subject to any provisions of any act of the legislature of the province of New Brunswick, the company shall not take or hold within its booms any prize or unmarked logs, and any person interested may go upon the property of the company at any reasonable time and in a reasonable manner and search for such prize or unmarked logs, but the company shall have its proper proportion of the proceeds of the sale thereof, provided, however, the company may, by and with the consent in writing of all the owners of logs operating on the Saint John river or any tributary thereof above said dam, which consent must be served upon the company at least two months before the driving season opens, hold said prize or unmarked logs in their booms to be disposed of as hereinafter provided; and provided, also, the holding of said prize or unmarked logs in the company's booms shall be optional with the company, unless a bond satisfactory to the company shall have been given to the company to indemnify it against any damages that may arise by reason of the holding in its booms of said prize or unmarked logs.

—proviso.

—proviso.

Piers, booms and other works shall not unnecessarily obstruct river.

Section 9. Such piers, booms and other works authorized to be placed in the river Saint John by the company shall be so constructed and maintained by the company as to not unnecessarily obstruct, hinder or delay the free and uninterrupted passage down the said river to and below the said dam all logs, except local logs and logs of the company.

Local logs, company's duty relative thereto.

Section 10. It shall be the duty of the company and it is hereby required to hold, collect, secure, separate and sort out within its booms above its dam, and whenever requested so to do, drive over the dam, all local logs which shall come into or be driven within the company's booms at any time between the opening of the spring and the river being entirely free from ice and the first day of November in each and every year during the continuance of this act, providing the owner or owners of said local logs shall have furnished the company with the mark or marks of said local logs a reasonable time before the opening of the spring and at least fifteen days before said local logs come within the company's booms and after so furnishing said marks all logs bearing any of said marks shall be considered local logs so soon as they come within the said booms and shall be under the full control, and be liable to boomage and other charges of the company.

—proviso.

Section 11. The company shall be entitled to and may charge a reasonable compensation for holding, collecting, securing, separating, sorting out, booming and for other work done in connection with said local logs, within its booms above said dams, and may by by-laws from time to time fix uniform tolls and charges therefor on the different kinds of logs, which said by-laws shall be subject to the approval of the governor and council, and the company may also fix by contract with the owner or owners of said local logs, the charges to be made by the company for all local logs contracted for by and with the company to be driven or rafted and driven to their destination above the Grand Falls and below said dam; and the company shall have a lien on said local logs whether manufactured or not, in respect to which boomage and other charges, including those for driving or rafting and driving of the company have not been paid for a period of two months after said logs have reached their destination; and if said logs have not gone out of the possession of the company, the company may retain said local logs or a sufficient part thereof to pay the same and all other expenses afterwards incurred in connection therewith, until the same are paid; and if the owner or owners of said local logs shall not, within ten days after said local logs have been surveyed by the company, pay the same, the company shall be entitled to a reasonable compensation for keeping said local logs which shall be deemed to be at the risk of the owner or owners thereof, and the company is hereby authorized, if default in the payment of all said charges against said local logs continue another ten days, to sell them or so much thereof as shall be sufficient to pay all of said charges and expenses at public auction on giving ten days' notice of the time and place of sale to be published in the newspaper published in Aroostook county at the place nearest to Fort Kent or by sending a notice of the time and place of sale by registered letter to the person or persons who furnished the mark or marks on the

Tolls and charges.

—lien on local logs.

—proceedings for collection of tolls and charges.

said local logs, at least ten days before such sale, and after deducting from the proceeds of such sale, all charges and also the expenses of keeping said local logs and the expenses of such sale as well as all other incidental expenses, shall render the surplus, if any, to the owner or owners of said local logs.

Measurement of local logs.

Section 12. All local logs shall be measured by a competent surveyor duly sworn, who shall be employed and paid by the company, whose survey shall be conclusive upon the parties, unless the owner or owners of such local logs shall give notice to the company within three days after the said local logs have been surveyed, of his or their dissent to such survey, then and in such case the differences shall be settled and determined in the manner prescribed by section fifteen of this act.

Prize or unmarked logs, regulations for.

Section 13. Under and by virtue of the authority that may be conferred upon the company by section eight of this act and subject to the provisions contained in said section, the company may from time to time as the directors may deem expedient, between the hours of ten o'clock in the forenoon and two o'clock in the afternoon, sell by public auction at a public place in Fort Kent aforesaid, first giving fifteen days' notice by advertisement in the newspaper published in Aroostook county nearest to Fort Kent, all such prize or unmarked logs, except such as may be in joints or shackle booms, as may be found within the booms of the company during the season, and shall, at the time of such

—shall post survey bill.

sale, exhibit and post up for the information of purchasers a survey bill of all such prize or unmarked logs in the said booms and so offered for sale as aforesaid, and after deducting the costs and charges of selling same, together with the boom fees, which are hereby authorized to be charged according to the scale fixed for local logs, shall, at the winding up of the year's operation,

—net proceeds of sale, how distributed.

distribute the net proceeds of such sales among the several persons having marked logs in the said booms, or who may have had marked logs therein previous to the time of such sale during the season and on which boomage charges have been paid to the company, in fair and just proportion according to the quantity of marked logs such person or persons may have coming through said booms; provided nothing herein contained shall give to the

—proviso.

company the right to sell any logs which at the time of such sale shall be in the custody of the law, or shall be adjudged the property of any person claiming same.

Loss of local logs, liability of company for.

Section 14. The company shall not be liable for the loss of any local logs which may pass out of or by the said booms, or escape therefrom, unless such loss is occasioned by the neglect or default of the company, or the neglect or default of its agents or servants; provided, always, that the company shall be bound to use and follow due diligence to collect together and pick up and secure and raft all such local logs which may pass out of or escape from or run below the said booms, before the same go over the Grand Falls, the expense of such following, picking up, securing, rafting and delivering to be a charge on the said local logs and be paid by the owner or owners thereof, when such escape is not the result of the negligence or default of the company or its officers.

Section 15. All questions of difference or dispute of any kind relating to the quantity of local logs, or to the mode of rafting or other work done in connection with the said local logs, shall be submitted to the award or arbitrament and determination of three persons indifferently chosen between the parties; the award or determination of them or of any two of them, shall be final and conclusive between the parties, which referees or any two of them shall also determine and award by whom and how the expenses of such reference shall be paid; provided, always that such reference may be made to one person, if the parties can agree upon such one, who shall be vested with the like powers herein assigned to the three referees. *Arbitrament of differences or disputes.*

Section 16. The company may, by means of and through the works aforesaid, carry on the business of lumberers and manufacturers of lumber and lumber products in all its branches, including the manufacture of pulp and paper and other business incident thereto and connected therewith, and may erect and operate lumber mills and pulp and paper mills on or near the river Saint John or any of its tributaries above the boundary line near Grand Falls, and may, for all and any of said purposes, purchase, hold, lease or otherwise acquire lands, limits and rights to cut logs, and other property, real or personal, movable or immovable, and may get and manufacture logs and may improve, extend, manage, develop, lease, exchange, sell or deal in any other way in lumber and lumber products of all kinds, including pulp and paper. *Additional powers of the company.*

Section 17. The company may purchase or otherwise acquire any business within the objects of the company, and any lands, property, privileges, water powers, rights, contracts and liabilities appertaining thereto and may let or sublet any property of the company and may sell or otherwise dispose of the business, property or undertaking of the company, or any part thereof, for such consideration as the company thinks fit, and in particular for shares, debentures or securities of any other company. *May acquire any business, lands, property, privileges, etc., within the objects of the company.*

Section 18. The company may construct, maintain and operate for its own use or otherwise tramways to be worked by electricity or otherwise, from the said dams to the boundary line *May construct tramways.*

near Grand Falls and for such purposes may erect poles and do all other things necessary therefor.

May supply power for any purpose.

Section 19. The company, by means of and through the works aforesaid, may supply persons with water, hydraulic, electric or other power for use or for any purpose by means of wires, cables, machinery or other appliances, including said dams and appliances connected therewith, at such rates and upon such conditions as are agreed upon between the company and such person; and may construct, maintain and operate works for the production, sale and distribution of electric and pneumatic power, light, heat and driving logs and lumber.

The company may also erect poles and do all other things necessary for the transmission of power as fully and effectually as the circumstances of the case may require, subject, however, to the following provisions, that is to say.

—shall not interfere with travel.

(a) The company shall not interfere with the public right of travel or in any way obstruct the entrance to any door or gateway or free access to any building.

—wires, height of, fixed.

(b) The company shall not permit any wires to be less than twenty-two feet above such highway or other public place.

—poles, character of and how set.

(c) All poles shall be so nearly as possible straight and perpendicular and shall in cities and towns be painted, if so required by any by-laws of the municipality or other authority having jurisdiction over the same.

—wires cut by officer at fire, entitled to no damage for.

(d) The company shall not be entitled to damages on account of its poles or wires being cut by the direction of the officer in charge of a fire brigade at any fire, if, in the opinion of such officer, it is advisable that such poles or wires be cut.

—shade trees, etc., not to be cut down without authority for.

(e) The company shall not cut down or mutilate any shade, fruit or ornamental tree without the approval of the municipal officers of the municipality in which it is situate, and then only so far as it may be necessary.

—opening up of streets for poles or wires subject to approval by municipal officers.

(f) The opening up of streets for the erection of poles or for carrying wires under ground, shall be subject to the direction and approval of the municipal officers and shall be done in such manner as the said municipal officers direct, and they may also designate the places where such poles shall be erected and such street, square or other public place shall, without any unnecessary delay, be restored, so far as possible, to its former condition, by and at the expense of the company.

—consent of owner required before entering private property.

(g) Nothing herein contained shall be deemed to authorize the company to enter upon any private property for the purpose of erecting, maintaining or repairing any of its works, without the previous assent of the owner or occupant of the property for the time being.

ST. JOHN RIVER DAM COMPANY. 309

CHAP. 183

(h) If, for the purpose of removing buildings, or in the exercise of the public right of travel, it is necessary that the said wires or poles be temporarily removed by cutting or otherwise, the company shall at its own expense, upon reasonable notice in writing from any person requiring it, remove such poles and in default of the company so doing, such person may remove such wires and poles at the expense of the company. The said notice may be given either at any office of the company or to any agent or officer of the company in the municipality wherein are the wires or poles required to be moved, or in case of a municipality wherein there is no such agent or officer, then, either at the head office or to any agent or officer of the company in the nearest or adjoining municipality to that in which such wires or poles are.

—temporary removal of poles and wires, shall be at expense of company.

—notice in writing shall be given.

—service of notice, how made.

(i) The company shall be responsible for all damage which it causes to ornamental, shade or fruit trees and otherwise for all unnecessary damages which it may cause in carrying out or maintaining any of its works.

—ornamental shade or fruit trees, damage to, company responsible for.

(j) Subject to the foregoing provisions, the company, for the purposes of constructing and maintaining its works, with the consent of the municipal officers or other authority having jurisdiction over the same, enter on any highway, square or other public place and so often as the company thinks proper, may, with like consent, break up and open any highway or other public place.

—may enter on any highway, square or other public place.

Section 20. Lands actually required for the construction, maintenance and operation of the company's mills, dams, wing dams, sluices, conduits, booms, side booms, sheer booms, piers, wharves, slips, buildings, roads, tramways, and other works of the company, and all lands which may be flowed by a dam not exceeding twelve feet in height, may be purchased by the company or taken and held as for public uses, and said company shall file in the registry of deeds for the northern district of Aroostook county, plans of all lands so taken in said county, and no entry for the purposes of taking lands shall be made on any lands owned by other persons except to make surveys, until the expiration of ten days from the time of said filing and with such plan the company may file a statement of the damages it is willing to pay to any person for the property so taken, and if the amount finally awarded does not exceed that sum, the company shall recover costs against such person, otherwise such person shall recover costs against the company. Said company shall be liable to pay all damages for the land so taken, and if any person sustaining damages as aforesaid shall not agree with the company upon the sum to be paid therefor, either party on petition to the county commissioners of the county of Aroostook, within twelve months after such plans are filed, may have the damages for the

Lands required for purposes of company may be purchased or taken and held as for public uses.

—proceedings.

—shall be liable for all land taken.

CHAP. 183

taking of said lands assessed, and the subsequent proceedings and right of appeal thereupon shall be had in the same manner and under the same conditions, restrictions and limitations as are by law prescribed in the case of damages by the laying out of highways, failure to apply for such damages within the twelve months shall be held to be a waiver of the same.

Payment for lands or other property acquired, how made.

Section 21. The company may purchase, lease and acquire timber and other lands including the property of the incorporators or any of them, and the whole or any part of the good will, stock in trade, assets and property, real and personal, movable or immovable, of the incorporators or other persons in connection with said business, subject to the obligations, if any, affecting the same, and may pay therefor wholly in cash or wholly or partly in fully paid up or partly paid up shares of the company or wholly or partly in debentures of the company or otherwise and may mortgage, sell or otherwise dispose thereof.

May make, endorse or accept negotiable instruments.
—proviso.

Section 22. The company may make, endorse, accept or otherwise execute cheques, promissory notes, bills of exchange, warehouse receipts, bills of lading and other negotiable instruments; provided, however, that nothing in this section contained shall be construed to authorize the company to issue any note or bill payable to bearer or intended to be circulated as money or bill of a bank.

Loans, authority for, how given.

Section 23. The directors, under the authority of a resolution of the shareholders passed at any special meeting called for the purpose, or at any annual meeting at which shareholders representing at least two-thirds in value of the issued capital stock of the company are present or represented by proxy, may from time to time, at their discretion, borrow moneys for the purposes of the company, and secure the repayment thereof in such manner and upon such terms and conditions as they see fit, and for this purpose may mortgage, pledge, hypothecate or charge the assets and property of the company; provided the aggregate amount so borrowed shall not, at any time be greater than seventy-five per cent of the actual paid up stock of the company; but this limitation shall not apply to commercial paper discounted by the company.

—may mortgage property.

Marks on logs and lumber, registry of.

Section 24. Said corporation shall keep at its office or at said dam, a book in which shall be registered the marks of each and every operator cutting logs and lumber on the waters of the Saint John river above the dam of said corporation, which book shall be open to inspection at all seasonable hours to any and all persons interested in lumbering operations, either as operators or employees of operators, or of any log driving association. It shall also be the duty of the clerk of said corporation to obtain from the clerk of the Fredericton Boom Company, a copy of the record of all marks registered in the books of said corporation, and of parties operating on the Saint John waters above said dam.

Section 25. Said corporation shall provide a suitable passage for or means of transporting boats and water craft of all kinds by the dam in question, for all persons having occasion to use the same, or in lieu thereof shall convey said boats or water craft by said dam free of expense to the owner or person or persons using or in possession of same. *Passage of boats by the dam provided for.*

Section 26. The construction of said works shall be commenced within three years and completed within six years from the passage of this act, otherwise the powers hereby granted shall cease and be null and void as respects so much of the said works as then remain uncompleted. *Limit of charter.*

Approved March 18, 1903.

Chapter 184.

An Act to incorporate the Wells Electric Light and Power Company.

Be it enacted by the Senate and House of Representatives in Legislature assembled, as follows:

Section 1. George G. Hatch, Joseph D. Eaton, John Rankin, Freeman E. Rankin, George H. Littlefield and Joseph H. Littlefield, their associates, successors and assigns, are hereby made a body corporate by the name of the Wells Electric Light and Power Company, with all the powers, rights and privileges, and subject to all the duties and obligations conferred and imposed on corporations by law, except as otherwise provided herein. *Corporators. —corporate name.*

Section 2. Said company is authorized and empowered to carry on the business of lighting by electricity such public streets of the town of Wells, and such buildings and places therein, public and private, as may be agreed upon by said corporation and the owners or those having control of such places to be lighted; and may furnish motive power by electricity within the limits of said town of Wells; and may build and operate manufactories and works for the providing and supplying of electricity and light and power, and may lease, purchase and hold real and personal estate for the proper objects of the corporation, and to construct, lay, maintain and operate lines of wire or other material for the transmission of electricity, submarine, under ground, upon, under and along and over any and all streets and *May light streets, buildings and places in town of Wells. —may furnish power. —may hold real and personal estate.*

WELLS ELECTRIC LIGHT AND POWER COMPANY.

CHAP. 184

ways under the direction of the municipal officers of said Wells; and in public places in such a manner as not to endanger the appropriate public use thereof, and to establish and maintain, under direction of said municipal officers, all necessary posts, pipes, supports and appurtenances, and terminating at such points as may be expedient.

Consent of municipal officers shall be obtained before erecting wires, etc.

Section 3. For the erecting said wires above ground and for laying the same, or pipes thereof, submarine or under ground, and for taking up, replacing and repairing the same, said company shall first obtain the consent of the municipal officers of said town, and perform all said acts as directed by said municipal officers; and said company shall repay to said Wells any sum which said town may have been compelled to pay on any judgment for any damages caused by a defect or want of repair in the streets or ways thereof, due to the neglect of said company, or on any judgment for damages caused by the negligence of said company in the erecting and maintaining of any posts, wires or appurtenances connected with said business.

Shall not unnecessarily obstruct streets.

Section 4. Said company, at its own expense, without unnecessary delay, shall remove any and all obstructions in any street or way, made in erecting or laying the lines for such purposes, and cause earth disturbed to be properly replaced. It shall not be allowed to obstruct or impair the use of any public or private drain, or gas pipe, or sewer, telegraph or telephone wire, but may cross, or when necessary, change the direction of any private wire or pipe, drain or sewer, in such manner as not to obstruct or impair the use thereof, being responsible to the owner or other person for any injury occasioned thereby, in an action on the case.

Damages for land taken.

Section 5. Damages for any land taken for the purposes of erecting or laying said lines, if the parties cannot agree, shall be estimated, secured and paid as in the case of lands taken for railroads.

Liability for injury to private property.

Section 6. Nothing contained in this act shall be construed to affect or diminish the liability of said corporation for any injury to private property, by depreciating the value thereof or otherwise, but any legal remedies existing shall continue. The selectmen of said Wells, for the time being, shall at all times, have the power to regulate and control the acts and doings of said corporation, which may in any manner affect the health and safety, or become a nuisance to the inhabitants of said town.

Capital stock.

Section 7. The capital stock of said company shall not exceed thirty thousand dollars, divided into shares of fifty dollars each.

May issue bonds.

Section 8. Said company is hereby authorized to issue bonds for the construction of its works upon such rates and time, and to such amount as it may deem necessary, not to exceed thirty thousand dollars in all, and not to exceed the amount of capital stock subscribed for, and to secure the same by mortgage or deed of trust upon its franchise and property.

Section 9. Manufactories and other business corporations doing business in said Wells are hereby authorized to subscribe for and hold stock in said company.

Section 10. Any two of the corporators named in this act may call the first meeting of the corporation by mailing a written notice, signed by both, postage paid, to each of the corporators, seven days at least before the day of the meeting, naming the time, place and purpose of said meeting; a president, secretary and directors may be chosen, by-laws adopted, and any corporate business transacted.

First meeting, how called.

Section 11. This act may be accepted at any regular meeting of said association by a majority of the members present.

Section 12. This act shall take effect when approved.

Approved March 18, 1903.

Chapter 185.

An Act to extend the rights, powers and privileges of the Greenville Water Company.

Be it enacted by the Senate and House of Representatives in Legislature assembled, as follows:

Section 1. The rights, powers and privileges of the Greenville Water Company, which were granted by chapter four hundred and ninety-six of the private and special laws of the year one thousand nine hundred and one, are hereby extended for and during the period of two years from the twenty-second day of March in the year one thousand nine hundred and three and all the rights, powers and privileges that were granted by said act may and shall be exercised in the same manner and for the same purposes as provided in said act.

Charter extended.

Section 2. This act shall take effect when approved.

Approved March 18, 1903.

Chapter 186.

An Act to incorporate the Sanford Light and Power Company.

Be it enacted by the Senate and House of Representatives in Legislature assembled, as follows:

Corporators. Section 1. Charles A. Bodwell, Will J. Bodwell and Stillman A. Bodwell, their associates, successors and assigns, are hereby made a body corporate by the name of Sanford Light and Power Company, with all the powers, rights and privileges and subject to all the duties and obligations conferred and imposed on corporations by law, except as otherwise provided herein.

—corporate name.

Purposes. Section 2. The purposes of said corporation are the making, generating, selling, distributing and supplying electricity or gas, or both, for lighting, heating, manufacturing or mechanical purposes in the town of Sanford, with all the rights, privileges and powers, and subject to all the restrictions and liabilities by law incident to corporations of a similar nature.

Capital stock. Section 3. The capital stock of said corporation shall be fifty thousand dollars, divided into shares of one hundred dollars each.

May set poles, extend wires, lay pipe, etc. Section 4. Said corporation is hereby empowered to set poles and extend wires and lay its pipe and construct and maintain its lines in, upon, along, over, across and under the roads and streets in said town of Sanford for the purpose of furnishing electric or gas lights and for heating, manufacturing or mechanical purposes, for public and private use in said town under such reasonable restrictions as may be imposed by the municipal officers thereof, subject to the general laws of the state regulating the erection of posts and lines and laying pipes for the purposes of electricity or gas.

—under reasonable restrictions imposed by municipal officers.

May make contracts for light, heat and power. Section 5. Said corporation is hereby authorized to make contracts with said town of Sanford and with other corporations and individuals for the purpose of supplying electricity or gas for light, heat and power as contemplated by this act, and said town by its selectmen and other corporations are hereby authorized to enter into contracts with said company for the supplying of electricity or gas for light, heat and power, and for such exemptions from public burden as such town and such corporations and said company agree upon which when made, shall be legal and binding upon all parties thereto.

Shall repair streets when disturbed or obstructed by its operations. Section 6. Said company, at its own expense, without unnecessary delay, shall remove any and all obstructions in any street or way made in erecting or laying the lines for such purposes, and cause earth disturbed to be properly replaced. It shall not be allowed to obstruct or impair the use of any public or private drain, or gas pipe, sewer, telegraph, telephone or rail-

—may cross, but shall not obstruct sewers, etc.

SANFORD LIGHT AND POWER COMPANY.

road wire, but may cross, or when necessary, change the direction of any private wire or pipe, drain or sewer, in such manner as not to obstruct or impair the use thereof, being responsible to the owner or other person for any injury occasioned thereby in an action on the case.

Section 7. Said corporation may issue its bonds upon such rates and time as it may deem expedient and in such an amount as may be required for the objects of its incorporation and for the purposes authorized by this act, and secure the same by mortgage upon the franchise and property of said company.

May issue bonds.

Section 8. The said corporation is hereby authorized to acquire by lease or purchase the power plant and pole line of the Mousam River Railroad used for lighting purposes, and the poles and wire line of the Sanford Light and Water Company, and the Mousam River Railroad and the Sanford Light and Water Company are hereby respectively authorized to lease or sell their power plant and pole line used for lighting purposes to said Sanford Light and Power Company.

May purchase plant and pole line of Mousam River R. R.

—poles and wire line of Sanford Light and Water Co.

Section 9. The charter hereby granted shall be null and void if said Sanford Light and Power Company shall fail to lease or purchase and take over within one year from the approval of this act, all the electric light property and plant now in operation in Sanford by the Mousam River Railroad and the Sanford Light and Water Company.

Limitations of this charter.

Section 10. The first meeting of said corporation may be called by written notice thereof signed by any two corporators herein named served upon each corporator by a copy of the same in hand or mailed, postage paid, at least seven days prior to the day named therein for such meeting.

First meeting how called.

Section 11. This act shall take effect when approved.

Approved March 18, 1903.

Chapter 187.

An Act to incorporate the Pike Family Association.

Be it enacted by the Senate and House of Representatives in Legislature assembled, as follows:

Corporators.

Section 1. Edwin B. Pike, Joseph T. Pike, Glifford L. Pike, Walter N. Pike, Ezra B. Pike, John Q. Evans, Gordon B. Pike, their associates and successors, are hereby constituted a corporation under the name of the Pike Family Association, and by that name shall have power to prosecute and defend suits at law, have and use a common seal and change the same at pleasure, take and hold for the objects of their association, by gift, grant, bequest, purchase or otherwise, any estate real or personal, the annual income of which shall not exceed fifty thousand dollars, and to sell and convey any estate, real or personal, which the interests of said association may require to be sold and conveyed.

—corporate name.

—powers.

Purposes to which property and funds shall be applied.

Section 2. All property and estate, real or personal, which at any time may come into the possession of the said corporation shall be applied, to the promotion of historical and genealogical research, in home or foreign lands, to the publication of any historical or genealogical research, in home or foreign lands, to the publication of any historical or genealogical matter pertaining to the family of which it may become possessed, to the maintenance, by purchase or otherwise, of a suitable building for its corporate meetings and the preservation of its property, and to the perpetuation, by tablet, monument or otherwise, of the names of those who have made the family name illustrious.

May issue stock.

Section 3. The said corporation is hereby given authority to issue stock to the amount of one hundred thousand dollars to be divided into shares of one dollar each which shall be forever unassessable.

May adopt rules.

Section 4. The said corporation may adopt such rules and by-laws, the same not being repugnant to the laws of this state, as they may deem expedient for the management of their affairs. They may choose all necessary officers, and they shall be and they are hereby invested with all the powers, privileges, rights and immunities incident to similar corporations.

—may choose officers.

Corporation meetings, when and where to be held.

Section 5. The said corporation may hold its meetings, biannual, annual or special, in any of the states or territories of the United States, and may choose its officers therefrom.

First meeting at U. S. hotel, Boston, Mass., Sept. 27, 1904.

Section 6. The first meeting of the said corporation may be held in the United States Hotel in Boston, Massachusetts, on Tuesday, the twenty-seventh day of September, nineteen hundred and four, at ten o'clock in the forenoon, or at such other place and time as Edwin B. Pike, Joseph T. Pike and Glifford

L. Pike, or any two of them may determine by giving seasonable notice of said meeting to all the persons named as corporators.

Section 7. The treasurer, before entering upon his duties, shall give a bond, approved by the directors, for the faithful discharge of the same.

<small>Treasurer shall give bond.</small>

Section 8. This act shall take effect when approved.

Approved March 18, 1903.

Chapter 188.

An Act to extend the charter of the Hallowell Trust Company.

Be it enacted by the Senate and House of Representatives in Legislature assembled, as follows:

Section 1. The rights, powers and privileges of the Hallowell Trust Company, which were granted by chapter four hundred and seventy-five of the private and special laws of nineteen hundred and one, are hereby extended for two years from the approval of this act; and the persons named in said act, their associates and successors, shall have all the rights, powers and privileges that were granted them by said act, to be exercised in the same manner and for the same purposes as specified in said act.

<small>Charter extended.</small>

Section 2. This act shall take effect when approved.

Approved March 18, 1903.

Chapter 189.

An Act to incorporate the Wells Telephone Company.

Be it enacted by the Senate and House of Representatives in Legislature assembled, as follows:

Section 1. George G. Hatch, Joseph D. Eaton, Freeman E. Rankin, John Rankin, George H. Littlefield and Joseph H. Littlefield, their associates and successors are hereby created a corporation by the name of the Wells Telephone Company, with all the powers, rights and privileges, and subject to all the duties and obligations of similar corporations under the general laws of this state.

<small>Corporators.

—corporate name.</small>

Section 2. Said corporation is hereby authorized to construct, own, maintain and operate telephone line or lines anywhere in

<small>Powers and authority.</small>

318 WELLS TELEPHONE COMPANY.

CHAP. 189 the towns of Wells, York and North Berwick, in the county of York and state of Maine, having obtained consent of the several municipalities, and said company shall have a right to locate and construct its lines upon and along any public highway or bridge in said towns, but in such a manner as not to incommode or endanger the customary public use thereof.

May connect with other lines.
Section 3. Said corporation is hereby authorized and empowered to connect its line or lines with those of any other telephone company or corporation on such terms as may be agreed upon, or to sell or lease its line or lines of telephone and property in whole or part, either before or after completion to any other telephone company or corporation, as provided by law or upon such terms as may be agreed by the contracting parties, which sale or lease shall be binding upon the parties; or may purchase or lease any other line or lines of telephone upon such terms and conditions as may be agreed by the parties thereto.

Damages, how estimated, secured and paid.
Section 4. If the land of any individual or corporation is taken under this act, and the parties cannot agree on the damages occasioned thereby, they shall be estimated, secured and paid in the manner provided in case of land taken for railroads.

Capital stock.
Section 5. The capital stock of said corporation shall be of such amount as said corporation may, from time to time determine to be necessary, but not exceeding the sum of one hundred thousand dollars, for the sole purpose of owning, leasing, constructing, maintaining and operating the line or lines of telephone hereby authorized and contemplated. And the said corporation may purchase, hold, lease, sell and convey all real estate and personal property necessary for the purposes contemplated in this charter.

First meeting, how called.
Section 6. Any one of the incorporators named in this act may call the first meeting of the corporation by mailing a written notice signed by himself, postage paid, to each of the other corporators, seven days at least before the day of the meeting, naming the time, place and purposes of such meeting, and at such meeting a president, secretary, treasurer and directors may be chosen, by-laws adopted, present amount of capital stock fixed, and any corporate business transacted.

Section 7. This act shall take effect when approved.

Approved March 18, 1903.

Chapter 190.

An Act to incorporate the City Trust Company, of Bangor, Maine.

Be it enacted by the Senate and House of Representatives in Legislature assembled, as follows:

Section 1. George W. E. Barrows, William E. Brown, Arthur Chapin, George H. Nutter, J. Albert Dole, Joseph G. Blake, Augustus B. Farnham, William P. Dickey, J. Norman Towle, Eugene Danforth, Charles E. Woodward, and E. C. Ryder, all of Bangor, county of Penobscot, state of Maine, or such of them as may by vote accept this charter, with their associates, successors and assigns, are hereby made a body corporate and politic to be known as the City Trust Company, and as such shall be possessed of all the powers, privileges and immunities and subject to all the duties and obligations conferred on corporations by law, except as otherwise provided herein. *Corporators. —corporate name.*

Section 2. The corporation hereby created shall be located at Bangor, Penobscot county, Maine. *Location.*

Section 3. The purposes of said corporation and the business which it may perform, are: *Purposes.*

First, to receive on deposit, money, coin, bank notes, evidences of debt, accounts of individuals, companies, corporations, municipalities and states, allowing interest thereon, if agreed, or as the by-laws of said corporation may provide;

Second, to borrow money, to loan money on credits, or real estate, or personal or collateral security, and to negotiate loans and sales for others;

Third, to erect, construct, own, maintain and operate safe deposit vaults, with boxes, safes and other facilities therein, to be rented to other parties, for the safe keeping of moneys, securities, stocks, jewelry, plate, valuable papers and documents, and other property susceptible of being deposited therein, and to receive on deposit for safe keeping, property of any kind entrusted to it for that purpose;

Fourth, to hold and enjoy all such estate, real, personal and mixed, as may be obtained by the investment of its capital stock or any other moneys and funds that may come into its possession in the course of its business and dealings, and the same sell, grant, and otherwise dispose of;

Fifth, to act as agent for issuing, registering and countersigning certificates, bonds, stocks, and all evidences of debt or ownership in property;

Sixth, to hold by grant, assignment, transfer, devise or bequest, any real or personal property or trusts duly created, and to execute trusts of every description;

Seventh, to act as agent for a person or corporation, and also to act as executor, receiver or assignee, with the same powers and duties as are conferred and imposed by law upon natural persons acting in the same capacities and subject to the same control of the court having jurisdiction of the same in all proceedings relating to the exercise of these powers; all papers may be signed and sworn to by any officer designated by the corporation for that purpose, and the officers shall be subject to citation and examination in the same manner and to the same extent as natural persons acting in the same capacities. No sureties shall be required upon the bond of the corporation when acting in said capacities, unless the court or officer approving said bond shall require it;

Eighth, to guarantee the payment of the principal and interest of all obligations secured by mortgages of real estate running to said City Trust Company;

Ninth, to hold for safe keeping all kinds of personal or mixed property and to act as agents for the owners thereof, and of real estate for the collection of income on the same and for the sale of the same;

Tenth, to do in general all the business that may lawfully be done by trust and banking companies.

Capital stock.

—shall not commence business until $50,000 has been paid in.

Section 4. The capital stock of said corporation shall not be less than fifty thousand dollars, divided into shares of one hundred dollars each, with the right to increase the said capital stock at any time, by vote of the shareholders, to any amount not exceeding five hundred thousand dollars. Said corporation shall not commence business as a trust or banking company, until stock to the amount of at least fifty thousand dollars shall have been subscribed and paid in, in cash.

Shall not make loan on security of its own capital stock.

Section 5. Said corporation shall not make any loan or discount on the security of the shares of its own capital stock, nor be the purchaser or holder of any such shares unless necessary to prevent loss upon debt previously contracted in good faith: and all stock so acquired shall, within six months from the time of its acquisition, be disposed of at public or private sale.

Board of directors.

—executive board.

Section 6. All the corporate powers of this corporation shall be exercised by a board of directors or trustees, who shall be residents of this state, whose number and term of office shall be determined by a vote of the shareholders at the first meeting held by the incorporators and at each annual meeting thereafter. The affairs and powers of the corporation may, at the option of the shareholders, be entrusted to an executive board of five members to be, by vote of the shareholders, elected from the full board of directors or trustees. The directors or trustees of said corporation shall be sworn to the proper discharge of their duties, and they shall hold office until others are elected and qualified in their stead. If a director or trustee dies, resigns, or becomes disqualified for any cause, the remaining directors or trustees may appoint a person to fill the vacancy until the next annual meeting of the corporation. The oath of office of such director or trustee, shall be taken within thirty days of his election, or his office shall become vacant. The clerk of such corporation shall, within ten days, notify such directors or trustees of their election, and within thirty days shall publish the list of all persons who have taken the oath of office as directors or trustees. *—vacancies, how filled.*

Section 7. The board of directors or trustees of said corporation shall constitute the board of investment of said corporation. Said directors or trustees shall keep in a separate book, specially provided for the purpose, record of all loans, and investments of every description, made by said institution substantially in the order of time when such loans or investments are made, which shall show that such loans or investments have been made with the approval of the executive committee of said corporation, which shall indicate such particulars respecting such loans or investments as the bank examiner shall direct. This book shall be submitted to the directors or trustees and to the bank examiner whenever requested. Such loans or investments shall be classified in the book as the bank examiner shall direct. No loan shall be made to any officers, director or agent of said company or to other persons in its employ, until the proposition to make such loan shall have been submitted by the person desiring the same to the board of directors of such bank, or to the executive committee of such board, if any, and accepted and approved by a majority of such board or committee. Such approval, if the loan is made, shall be spread upon the records of the corporation; and this record shall, in every instance, give the names of the directors authorizing the loan. Said corporation shall have no authority to hire money or to give notes unless by vote of the said board or of said committee duly recorded. *Board of investment.* *—shall keep record of loans.* *—loan to officers, how made.*

Section 8. No person shall be eligible to the position of a director or trustee of said corporation who is not the actual owner of ten shares of stock. *Director must own ten shares of stock.*

Section 9. Said corporation after beginning to receive money on deposit shall at all times have on hand, as a reserve, in lawful money of the United States, an amount equal to at least fifteen per cent of the aggregate amount of all its deposits which are subject to withdrawal upon demand or within ten days; and whenever said reserve of such corporation shall be below said percentage of such deposits, it shall not increase its liabilities by *Reserve fund.*

CHAP. 190

making any new loans until the required proportion between the aggregate amount of such deposits and its reserve fund shall be restored; provided, that in lieu of lawful money two-thirds of said fifteen per cent may consist of balances payable on demand, due from any national bank, and one-third of said fifteen per cent may consist of lawful money and bonds of the United States or of this state, the absolute property of such corporation.

Trust funds shall constitute special deposit.

Section 10. All the property or money held in trust by this corporation shall constitute a special deposit and the accounts thereof and of said trust department shall be kept separate, and such funds and the investment or loans of them shall be specially appropriated to the security and payment of such deposits, and not be subject to any other liabilities of the corporation; and for the purpose of securing the observance of this proviso, said corporation shall have a trust department in which all business pertaining to such trust property shall be kept separate and distinct from its general business.

Administrators, etc., may deposit in.

Section 11. An administrator, executor, assignee, guardian or trustee, any court of law or equity, including courts of probate and insolvency, officers and treasurers of towns, cities, counties and savings banks of the state of Maine may deposit any moneys, bonds, stocks, evidences of debt or of ownership in property, or any personal property, with said corporation, and any of said courts may direct any person deriving authority from them to so deposit the same.

Responsibility of shareholders.

Section 12. Each shareholder of this corporation shall be individually responsible, equally and ratably, and not one for the other, for all contracts, debts and engagements of such corporation, to a sum equal to the amount of the par value of the shares owned by each in addition to the amount invested in said shares.

Guaranty fund.

Section 13. Said corporation shall set apart as a guaranty fund not less than ten per cent of its net earnings in each and every year until such fund, with the accumulated interest thereon, shall amount to one-fourth of the capital stock of the company. The said surplus shall be kept to secure against losses and contingencies, and whenever the same becomes impaired it shall be reimbursed in the manner provided for its accumulation.

Taxation.

Section 14. The shares of said corporation shall be subject to taxation in the same manner and at the same rate as are the shares of national banks.

Shall be subject to examination by bank examiner.

Section 15. Said corporation shall be subject to examination by the bank examiner, who shall visit it at least once in every year, and as much oftener as he may deem expedient. At such visits he shall have free access to its vaults, books and papers, and shall thoroughly inspect and examine all the affairs of said corporation, and make such inquiries as may be necessary to ascertain its condition and ability to fulfill all its engagements. If upon examination of said corporation, the examiner is of the opinion that its investments are not in accordance with law, or said corporation is insolvent, or its condition is such as to render its further proceedings hazardous to the public or to those having funds in its custody, or is of the opinion that it has exceeded its powers or failed to comply with any of the rules or restrictions provided by law, he shall have such authority and take such action as is provided for in the case of savings banks by chapter forty-seven of the revised statutes. He shall preserve in a permanent form a full record of his proceedings, including a statement of the condition of said corporation. A copy of such statement shall be published by said corporation immediately after the annual examination of the same in some newspaper published where said corporation is established. If no paper is published in the town where said corporation is established, then it shall be published in a newspaper printed in the nearest city or town. The necessary expenses of the bank examiner while making such examination shall be paid by the corporation.

Section 16. Any three of the corporators named in this act may call the first meeting of the corporation by mailing a written notice signed by all, postage paid, to each of the other corporators, seven days at least before the day of the meeting, naming the time, place and purpose of such meeting, and at such meeting the necessary officers may be chosen, by-laws adopted, and any other corporate business transacted. *First meeting, how called.*

Section 17. This act shall take effect when approved.

Approved March 18, 1908.

Chapter 191.

An Act to regulate the taking of codfish, pollock, hake and haddock in the waters of Frenchman's Bay.

Be it enacted by the Senate and House of Representatives in Legislature assembled, as follows:

Section 1. No person shall use more than one trawl, not exceeding five hundred hooks for the purpose of taking or destroying any codfish, pollock, hake or haddock, in the waters of Frenchman's bay inside or northerly of a straight line drawn from the south side of Round or Bald Porcupine island to the south end of Jordan's island. *Use of trawl restricted in Frenchman's bay.*

TAMARACK CLUB.

Chap. 192

Penalty for violation of this act.

Section 2. Any person violating the provisions of this act shall be liable to a fine of ten dollars for each offense.

Section 3. This act shall take effect on the first day of April, one thousand nine hundred and three.

Approved March 18, 1903.

Chapter 192.

An Act to incorporate the Tamarack Club of Patten.

Be it enacted by the Senate and House of Representatives in Legislature assembled, as follows:

Corporators.

Section 1. William W. Pond, Sylvester L. Huston, Halbert P. Gardner, G. Frank Woodbury, Halbert G. Robinson and all persons who are or may hereafter become associated with them, are hereby created a corporation by name of Tamarack Club,

—*corporate name.*

for the purpose of establishing and maintaining a club house in the town of Patten, in this state, and of promoting literary and social intercourse among its members; and by that name shall have power to sue and be sued, and possess all the rights and privileges of corporations under the laws of this state.

—*purposes.*

May elect officers and hold property to value of $25,000.

Section 2. Said corporation may elect such officers as it may deem necessary, and may take, hold and convey real and personal property to an amount not exceeding twenty-five thousand dollars, and may adopt such constitution, by-laws, rules and regulations, not repugnant to the laws of this state, as they may deem necessary for the management of their affairs, including the power to fix and limit the right of members in and to the corporate property, and the manner in which the same shall determine.

First meeting, how called.

Section 3. The first meeting of the corporators may be called by any one of the persons named in the first section of this act, by giving to each said corporator seven days' notice of the time and place of said meeting.

Section 4. This act shall take effect when approved.

Approved March 18, 1903.

Chapter 193.

An Act to incorporate the East Branch Improvement Company.

Be it enacted by the Senate and House of Representatives in Legislature assembled, as follows:

Section 1. Nathaniel M. Jones, Fred W. Ayer, Halbert P. Gardner, Herbert W. Marsh, James W. Sewall and George H. Hamlin, their associates, successors and assigns, are hereby incorporated under the name of the East Branch Improvement Company.

<small>Corporators.</small>

<small>—corporate name.</small>

Section 2. The capital stock of said company shall not exceed one hundred thousand dollars, divided into shares of one hundred dollars each, and, in order to carry out the purposes for which said company is incorporated, it is hereby authorized and empowered to issue its bonds in such form and amount and on such rates as it may deem expedient, not exceeding the amount of its capital stock, and may secure the same by mortgage of its property and franchises.

<small>Capital stock.</small>

<small>—may issue bonds.</small>

Section 3. Said company is hereby authorized and empowered to take and hold by virtue of any conveyances made to it, the franchises, real estate, canals, sluiceways, piers, dams, wing dams, side dams, booms, steamboats, improvements and other property of the Telos Canal Company and the Grand Lake Dam Company, both of which were incorporated by special acts of the legislature of Maine, approved August seven, eighteen hundred forty-six, and of the East Branch Dam Company, incorporated by special act of the legislature of Maine, approved April twenty-six, eighteen hundred fifty-two, which said companies are hereby authorized and empowered to sell, assign and convey by deeds duly executed by the presidents of the several companies, to said East Branch Improvement Company such franchises, real estate, canals, sluiceways, piers, dams, wing dams, side dams, booms, steamboats, improvements, and other property owned or possessed by them at the time of such transfer, and upon receiving such conveyances said East Branch Improvement Company is hereby authorized and empowered to exercise all the powers and privileges of said Telos Canal Company, said Grand Lake Dam Company and said East Branch Dam Company, including the assessment and collection of tolls in accordance with all acts of the legislature relating thereto, and the duties of the said several companies shall be and become the duties of said East Branch Improvement Company, which said company shall thereafter be holden to perform such duties.

<small>May take and hold property of certain other corporations.</small>

Section 4. In addition to the rights and powers now possessed by said Telos Canal Company, said Grand Lake Dam Company and said East Branch Dam Company, said East

<small>May build additional dams.</small>

Chap. 193

Branch Improvement Company, for the purpose of facilitating the driving of logs and other lumber, shall have the power to build additional dams upon its own land or land acquired for that purpose, with suitable gates and sluiceways, repair or rebuild any dams it may acquire from said companies as aforesaid, increasing the height of the same, remove obstructions and erect necessary piers, booms, side booms and other works, in the waters of the East branch of the Penobscot river and its natural tributaries above Grand Lake dam, and said company shall also have the power to rebuild the dam at the foot of Grand lake, increasing the height of the same not exceeding five feet and the additional damages for flowage caused by such new dams or by the increased height of existing dams may be recovered in accordance with the provisions of chapter ninety-two of the revised statutes; provided, however, after the drive in any year shall arrive in the Penobscot boom, or the drive which shall have been abandoned, the water stored by such dams shall be allowed to flow so that the volume and flow shall be, as nearly as practicable, equal and continuous for the whole twenty-four hours of each day thereafter until such stored water has run through said dams. Nothing in this act shall be construed as giving said company the right to increase the height of the dam at the outlet of Chamberlain lake or enlarge the Telos canal as constructed by the Telos Canal Company.

—may rebuild and increase height of dam at foot of Grand lake.

Section 5. Said company is hereby authorized and empowered to make contracts with any person or corporation to drive logs and other lumber into the Penobscot boom or to their place of destination for sale or manufacture, charging such compensation therefor as shall be agreed upon between said company and such person or corporation; provided, however, said company shall not drive logs or other lumber below said Grand Lake dam except by virtue of a contract with the Penobscot East Branch Log Driving Company. And said company shall have a lien upon the logs driven by virtue of such contract, which lien shall have precedence of all other claims, except laborers' liens, and shall continue for ninety days after the logs or lumber shall arrive at place of destination for sale or manufacture, and may be enforced by attachment.

May make contracts to drive logs.

—compensation.

Section 6. The first meeting of said corporation shall be called at Bangor, in the county of Penobscot, by a notice signed by one of the corporators named in section one, setting forth the time, place and purposes of the meeting, and such notice shall be mailed to each of the corporators, postage paid, at least seven days before the day of such meeting.

First meeting, how called.

Section 7. This act shall take effect when approved.

Approved March 18, 1903.

Chapter 194.

An Act to remove a doubt in the act incorporating the Gardiner Water District.

Be it enacted by the Senate and House of Representatives in Legislature assembled, as follows:

Section 1. An Act entitled "An Act to incorporate the Gardiner Water District" approved February twenty-six, shall take effect if approved by a majority vote of the legal voters voting at the election held under the provisions of said act. *Act shall take effect if approved by legal voters.*

Section 2. This act shall take effect when approved.

Approved March 18, 1903.

Chapter 195.

An Act to amend the charter of the City of Gardiner.

Be it enacted by the Senate and House of Representatives in Legislature assembled, as follows:

Section 1. Section four of the act entitled "An Act to incorporate the city of Gardiner" is hereby amended by inserting in the twenty-sixth line thereof after the word "treasury" the following: 'And all bills and claims against the city of any and every nature shall be paid by the city treasurer upon presentation of the same, itemized, and approved in writing by the city official by whose authority the expenditures represented by them shall have been incurred; and he shall retain all such bills properly receipted, as his vouchers for moneys by him paid out.' *Section 4 of "An Act to incorporate the city of Gardiner," amended.* *—itemized and approved bills only, are to be paid by treasurer.*

Section 2. Section three of said act as amended by chapter four hundred fifty-five of the laws of eighteen hundred and eighty-five is hereby amended by striking out the last ten lines thereof and substituting therefor the following: 'The aldermen and common councilmen shall receive no compensation for their services as such. Except as above provided, neither the mayor nor any member of the city council shall, during the term for which he may be elected, be chosen to any salaried office.' *Section 3 of said act as amended by chapter 455, laws of 1885, amended.* *—aldermen and councilmen shall serve without pay.*

Section 3. The mayor with the advice and consent of the board of aldermen, shall annually, on the third Monday in March, appoint a city marshal, who shall be the chief of police and who shall have all the powers and exercise all the duties that now appertain to the constables of towns. *City marshal*

The city marshal shall, with the advice and consent of the municipal officers, appoint all police officers. The number of regular and special police officers shall be determined from time *—police officers.*

CITY OF GARDINER.

CHAP. 185

to time by the municipal officers, and their duties shall be regulated by the city marshal.

—tenure of police officers.

All regular police officers shall hold office during good behavior and until removed by the city marshal, with the consent of the municipal officers. All special police officers shall be appointed each year, and may be removed in the same manner as the regular officers.

—powers and duties of police officers.

All police officers shall have all the powers and exercise all the duties in criminal matters that now appertain to the constables of towns.

Section nineteen of "An Act to incorporate the city of Gardiner" is hereby repealed.

Highway and sewer commissioners.

Section 4. The care, construction, repair and maintenance of the streets, roads, ways, sidewalks and bridges, and the care, construction, repair and maintenance of the sewers in said city is hereby invested in a board of commissioners to be known as highway and sewer commissioners. At the annual municipal election next after this section shall have been accepted as provided in section five, the people shall elect three commissioners, whose terms of office shall expire respectively, in one, two and three years from the time of such election, and annually thereafter, at the municipal election they shall elect one such commissioner for a term of three years. In case of a vacancy the mayor, with the advice and consent of the aldermen, shall appoint a suitable person to serve until the municipal election next following, when, if there still remains a portion of the term unexpired, the people shall elect a person to serve during such remainder. The commissioner who has served the longest shall be the chairman of the board, provided, however, that in its first organization, the person elected to serve for one year shall be the chairman of the board, to be succeeded by the person who was elected for two years.

—election and tenure of.

—powers and duties of commissioners.

The board shall have full charge of the maintenance and repair of the streets, roads, ways, sidewalks, bridges, sewers, culverts, drains and catch basins. It shall appoint some competent person who shall not be a member of the board as superintendent of streets, who shall perform all the duties incumbent upon the present street commissioner of the city, which office is hereby abolished, and when necessary, may employ a competent engineer.

—shall be agents in reference to sewers, of municipal officers.

For the construction, repair and maintenance of drains and sewers the board shall be the authorized agents of the municipal officers, and shall only act under their direction; and nothing in this act shall be construed to divest the municipal officers of any duties relating thereto, which are by law imposed upon them.

Section 5. At a special election called for that purpose, the voters of said city shall have the right by majority vote to accept or reject sections three and four of this act; neither of which shall take effect until it shall have been so accepted, and upon being so accepted, section three shall take effect on the third Monday of March next following its acceptance, section four shall take effect as therein provided and sections one and two shall take effect when approved, provided, that nothing in section two shall be held to prohibit any member of the city council from holding any office to which he may be elected prior to July one, nineteen hundred and three.

Section 6. All acts and parts of acts, inconsistent with the provisions of this act, are hereby repealed.

Section 7. For the purpose of calling the special election, provided for in section five, this act shall take effect when approved.

Approved March 18, 1903.

Chapter 196.

An Act to authorize the Kennebunk Electric Light Company to issue bonds.

Be it enacted by the Senate and House of Representatives in Legislature assembled, as follows:

Section 1. The Kennebunk Electric Light Company, a corporation organized under the general laws of the state of Maine, and located at Kennebunk, county of York, is hereby authorized and empowered to issue coupon or registered bonds, to provide means for constructing its lines and plant, funding its floating debt, or for the payment of money borrowed for any lawful purpose, upon vote at a legal meeting of its stockholders, and may mortgage or pledge as security for the payment of the principal and interest of such bonds, a part or all of its property and franchises. Such bonds may be issued in sums of not less than one hundred dollars each, payable at periods not exceeding twenty years from the date thereof, and in such amount as shall not exceed, including that of bonds previously issued, the capital stock of said corporation.

Section 2. This act shall take effect when approved.

Approved March 18, 1903.

Chapter 197.

An Act to amend an act entitled "An Act to incorporate the City of Old Town."

Be it enacted by the Senate and House of Representatives in Legislature assembled, as follows:

Section 20 of chapter 71, private and special laws of 1891, as amended by chapter 210, laws of 1895, further amended.

Section 1. Section twenty of chapter seventy-one of the private and special laws of eighteen hundred ninety-one incorporating the city of Old Town, as amended by chapter two hundred and ten of private laws of eighteen hundred ninety-five is hereby further amended by adding after the words "city engineer" in the fourth line the words, 'city clerk, city attorney and city marshal' and by striking out the words "street superintendent" in the fifth line and in the fourteenth line and inserting the words 'members of a street board' and adding after the words "city engineer" in the thirteenth line the words 'city clerk, city attorney and city marshal;' after the word "board" in the eighteenth line insert 'school board and street board;' after the word "member" in the twentieth line insert 'of each board;' after the word "undertakers" in the last line add the following:

'Said school board shall elect a superintendent of schools who shall hold office for one year beginning the first Monday of April; but said school board may by a majority vote remove said superintendent for sufficient reason.

Said street board shall elect a superintendent of streets who shall hold office for one year beginning the first Monday of April; but said street board may by a majority vote remove said superintendent for sufficient reason. Said board shall have all the powers and perform all the duties of surveyors of highways and road commissioners of towns, and shall have general oversight and care of the streets, sidewalks and public places and make all contracts for labor and materials and have general care of the property of the street department,' so that said section shall read as follows:

Certain subordinate officers to be elected by city council.

'Section 20. The subordinate officers of said city to be elected by the city council shall be three overseers of the poor, three assessors, treasurer, collector of taxes, members of the school board, two street commissioners, city engineer, city clerk, city attorney and city marshal, chief engineer of the fire department, members of a street board, city physician, constables, truant officers, members of a cemetery board, fence viewers, surveyors of lumber, measurers of wood and bark, and such other officers as by law are allowed to be elected by towns, except as otherwise hereby provided, and also such as are provided for by the by-laws or ordinances of the city. The overseers of the poor, assessors, treasurer, members of the school board, street commissioners, city engineer, city clerk, city attorney and city marshal, chief engineer of the fire department, members of the cemetery board, members of a street board, and city physician shall be elected by written ballot; and the other officers elected by the city council, may be elected by any method agreed upon by said council. The cemetery board, school board and street board shall consist of as many members as there are wards of the city; and the city council shall so fix the term of office of said members that the term of one member of each board shall expire each year. Said cemetery board shall elect the undertakers of the city who shall hold office for one year beginning on the first Monday of April; but said cemetery board may by a majority vote for sufficient cause remove any or all of said undertakers.

Said school board shall elect a superintendent of schools who shall hold office for one year beginning the first Monday of April; but said school board may by a majority vote remove said superintendent for sufficient reason.

Said street board shall elect a superintendent of streets who shall hold office for one year beginning the first Monday of April; but said street board may by a majority vote remove said superintendent for sufficient reason. Said board shall have all the powers and perform all the duties of surveyors of highways and road commissioners of towns, and shall have general oversight and care of the streets, sidewalks and public places, and make all contracts for labor and materials and have general care of the property of the street department.'

Section 2. Section twenty-one of said chapter seventy-one as amended by aforesaid chapter two hundred ten, private and special laws of eighteen hundred ninety-five, is hereby amended by striking out in said amended section the words "city clerk, city attorney, city marshal and" in the second and third lines, so that section twenty-one when amended, shall read as follows:

'Section 21. The mayor, with the consent of the board of aldermen, shall appoint such number of police officers as shall, from time to time, be fixed by the city council; and also, except as otherwise hereby provided, all other officers, who, by the laws of the state, may be appointed by the mayor and aldermen of cities or by the municipal officers of towns.'

Section 3. Section twenty-seven of said chapter seventy-one is hereby amended by striking out the words "the superintending school committee" in the first line and inserting the words 'school board' and by striking out the words "but this change of designation shall not be construed as affecting its power and obligation to perform any duty imposed by statute upon the superintending school committee of the city of Old Town, nor as affecting in any way the right of the members of the superintending school committee of said city who shall, at the time when this act takes effect, be holding such office, to continue to hold the same until the expiration of the original term of office for which they were respectively elected by said city," and by striking out all of said section after the words "city council" in the nineteenth line, and by 'inserting instead the following words; 'the salary of the superintendent of schools shall be fixed by the school board and shall be paid from the city treasury as salaries of teachers are paid; the members of said board shall receive no salary or compensation for their services. Said board shall have and perform all the powers and duties conferred by law upon the superintending school committee and school agents.' So that the said section shall read as follows:

Duties of school board.

'Section 27. The school board of said city shall perform all the duties and be vested with all the powers of the superintending school committee of a town under the laws of this state. It shall be officially designated and known as the school board of said city. The said school board shall elect a chairman annually, and may appoint some suitable person, not a member of said board, to be superintendent of schools, and may adopt such rules and regulations for the management of schools and transaction of its business as are not inconsistent with the laws of the state. It shall have the supervision and care of all school property subject to the general supervision and control of the city council. The salary of the superintendent of schools shall be fixed by the school board and shall be paid from the city treasury as salaries of teachers are paid; the members of said board shall receive no salary or compensation for their services. Said board shall have and perform all the powers and duties conferred by law upon the superintending school committee and school agents.'

Section 42 of chapter 71, repealed.

Section 4. Section forty-two of said chapter seventy-one is hereby repealed.

Section 5. All acts or parts of acts inconsistent with the provisions of this act, or with the amendments hereto are hereby repealed.

Section 6. This act shall take effect when approved.

Approved March 18, 1903.

Chapter 198.

An Act to extend the charter of the Union River Water Storage Company.

Be it enacted by the Senate and House of Representatives in Legislature assembled, as follows:

Section 1. The rights, powers and privileges of the Union River Water Storage Company which were granted by chapter three hundred twenty-five of the private and special laws of the state of Maine for the year nineteen hundred and one, are hereby extended for two years additional, and the persons named in said act, their associates and successors, shall have all the rights, powers and privileges that were granted to them by said act, to be exercised in the same manner and for the same purposes specified in said act. *Charter extended.*

Section 2. This act shall take effect when approved.

Approved March 18, 1903.

Chapter 199.

An Act to incorporate the Brownville and Williamsburg Water Company.

Be it enacted by the Senate and House of Representatives in Legislature assembled, as follows:

Section 1. Edwin M. Johnston, Urban H. Sumner, Ezekiel Chase and Frank E. Guernsey, their associates and successors, are hereby made a corporation by the name of the Brownville and Williamsburg Water Company, for the purpose of supplying the inhabitants of the towns of Brownville and Williamsburg with pure water for domestic, sanitary, municipal and commercial purposes, including the extinguishment of fires, and such corporation shall possess all the powers, privileges and be subject to all the liabilities and obligations imposed upon corporations by law except as herein otherwise provided. *Corporators. —corporate name. —purposes.*

Section 2. For any of the purposes aforesaid, the said corporation is hereby authorized to take and use water from springs of water in lands owned by Urban H. Sumner, situated in the town of Williamsburg in said county, or from any spring, pond, brook or other waters in the towns of Brownville and Williamsburg, to conduct and distribute the same into and through the said towns of Brownville and Williamsburg, and to survey for, locate, construct and maintain all suitable and convenient dams, reservoirs, sluices, hydrants, buildings, machinery, lines of pipe, aqueducts, structures and appurtenances. *May take water from waters of Brownville and Williamsburg.*

May lay pipes in Brownville and Williamsburg.

Section 3. The said corporation is hereby authorized to lay, construct and maintain its lines of pipe in the towns of Brownville and Williamsburg, and to build and maintain all necessary structures therefor, at such places as shall be necessary for the purposes of said corporation, and to cross any water course, private or public sewer, or to change the direction thereof, when necessary for their said purposes of incorporation, but in such manner as not to obstruct or impair the use thereof, and the said corporation shall be liable for any injury caused thereby.

May occupy streets.

Section 4. The said corporation is hereby authorized to lay, construct and maintain in, under, through, along, over and across the highways, ways, streets, railroads and bridges in said towns, and to take up, replace and repair all such aqueducts, sluices, pipes, hydrants and other structures and fixtures as may be necessary and convenient for any of the said purposes of the said corporation, under such reasonable restrictions and conditions as the selectmen of the said towns may impose, and the said corporation shall be responsible for all damages to the said towns, and to all corporations, persons and property, occasioned by such use of the highway, ways and streets. Whenever the said corporation shall lay down or construct any pipes or fixtures in any highway, way or street, or make any alterations thereof, or repairs upon its works, in any highway, way or street, it shall cause the same to be done with as little obstruction to public travel as may be practical, and shall at its own expense without unnecessary delay, cause the earth and pavement then removed by it, to be replaced in proper condition.

May take land for flowage.

Section 5. The said corporation is hereby authorized to take and hold by purchase or otherwise, any land necessary for flowage, and also for its dams, reservoirs, gates, hydrants, buildings and other necessary structures, and may locate, erect, lay and maintain aqueducts, hydrants, lines of pipes and other necessary structures or fixtures, in, over and through any land for the said purpose, and excavate in and through such lands for said location, construction and erection, and in general do any act necessary, convenient or proper for carrying out any of the said purposes of incorporation. It may enter such land and make surveys and locations, and shall file in the registry of deeds in the county of Piscataquis, plans of such locations and lands, showing the property taken, within thirty days thereafter publish notices of such filing in some newspaper in said county, said publication to be continued three weeks successively.

—shall file location.

Damages for location, how assessed.

Section 6. Should the said corporation and the owner of such land be unable to agree upon the damages to be paid for such location, taking, holding, flowing and construction, such damages shall be assessed in accordance with the law applicable to the assessment of damages for ways taken by railroads. If said corporation shall fail to pay such land owner, or deposit for his use with the clerk of the county commissioners aforesaid, such sum as may be finally awarded as damages, with costs when recovered by him, within ninety days after notice of final judgment shall have been received by the clerk of courts of said county, the said location shall be thereby invalid, and the said corporation shall forfeit all rights under the same, as against such land owner. In case the said corporation shall begin to occupy such land before the rendition of final judgment the land owner may require the said corporation to file its bond to him with the county commissioners, in such sum and with such sureties as they may approve conditioned for said judgment or deposits. No action shall be brought against the said corporation for such taking, holding and occupation until after such failure to pay or deposit as aforesaid.

Section 7. Any person suffering damage by the taking of water by said company as provided by this act, may have his damages assessed in the manner provided in the preceding section, and payment therefor shall be made in same manner and with the same effect. No action shall be brought for the same until after the expiration of the time of payment. *Damages for taking water, how assessed.*

Section 8. In case of failure to agree with any railroad company as to place, manner and condition of crossing its railroad with such pipe, the place, manner and conditions of such crossings shall be determined by the railroad commissioners, and all works within the limits of the railroad location and lands shall be done under the supervision and to the satisfaction of the officers and agents of the railroad company, but at the expense of said water company. *Disagreements as to crossing of railroads referred to commissioners.*

Section 9. The said corporation is hereby authorized to make contracts with the towns of Brownville and Williamsburg and with any village corporation in said town, and with the inhabitants thereof, of any corporation doing business therein, for the supply of water for any and all the purposes contemplated in this act: and the said town and any village corporations in the said town by their proper officers, are hereby authorized to enter into any contract with the said corporation for a supply of water for any and all purposes mentioned in this act, and in consideration thereof to relieve said corporation from such public burdens by abatement or otherwise as said town, village corporation, and the said corporation may agree upon, which, when made, shall be legal and binding upon all parties thereto. *May make contracts to supply water.*

Section 10. Whoever shall knowingly or maliciously corrupt the water supply of the said corporation, whether frozen or not, *Pollution of water.*

BOOTHBAY HARBOR ELECTRIC LIGHT AND POWER COMPANY.

CHAP. 200

—penalty for.

or in any way render such water impure, or whoever shall wilfully or maliciously injure any of the works of the said corporation, shall be punished by a fine not exceeding one thousand dollars, or by imprisonment not exceeding two years, and shall be liable to the said corporation for three times the actual damage, to be recovered in any proper action.

Capital stock.

Section 11. The capital stock of the said corporation shall be twenty-five thousand dollars and the said stock shall be divided into shares of twenty-five dollars each.

May hold real estate not to exceed $25,000.

Section 12. The said corporation, for all its said purposes, may hold real and personal estate necessary and convenient therefor, not exceeding twenty-five thousand dollars.

May issue bonds.

Section 13. The said corporation may issue its bonds for the construction of its works, of any and all kinds upon such rates and time as it may deem expedient, to an amount not exceeding its capital stock, and secure the same by mortgage of its franchise and property.

First meeting, how called.

Section 14. The first meeting of said corporation may be called by written notice therefor, signed by two of the incorporators herein named, served upon each corporator by giving him the same in hand or by leaving the same at his last and usual place of abode, seven days at least before said meeting.

Section 15. This act shall take effect when approved.

Approved March 18, 1903.

Chapter 200.

An Act to incorporate the Boothbay Harbor Electric Light and Power Company.

Be it enacted by the Senate and House of Representatives in Legislature assembled, as follows:

Corporators.

—corporate name.

Section 1. Luther Maddocks of Boothbay Harbor, E. W. Gross of Auburn and Frank Ridlon of Boston, Massachusetts, are hereby incorporated under the name of the Boothbay Harbor Electric Light and Power Company.

Rights, duties and liabilities.

Section 2. Said corporation is hereby authorized to make, generate, sell, distribute and supply electricity for lighting, heating, manufacturing and mechanical purposes in the towns of Boothbay Harbor, Boothbay, Southport, Edgecomb and Wiscasset, with all the rights and powers and subject to all the duties and liabilities of similar corporations organized under the general laws of the state.

CHAP. 201

Section 3. The capital stock shall not exceed one hundred thousand dollars, to be fixed by the corporation from time to time.

Capital stock.

Section 4. The said corporation is authorized to purchase the property rights and privileges of the E. W. Gross Company used in supplying electricity in said Boothbay Harbor and Boothbay and on such purchase it shall succeed to and enjoy all such rights and privileges of said firm and be subject to all liabilities whether imposed by law or by contract or otherwise.

May purchase E. W. Gross Co.

Section 5. The location of the posts, wires and fixtures of the said E. W. Gross Company in the streets of said Boothbay Harbor and Boothbay, and its municipal contracts are hereby confirmed and made valid.

Location of posts of E. W. Gross Co. made valid.

Section 6. The towns aforesaid, or any municipal corporation therein, are authorized to contract with said corporation for a supply of electricity for municipal purposes for a term of years, and to renew the same, and to raise money therefor.

Boothbay and Boothbay Harbor may contract for electricity.

Section 7. The said corporation, for the purposes of this act, is authorized to issue its bonds from time to time in such amounts and on such rates and time, as it may deem expedient, and secure the same by appropriate mortgages upon its franchises.

May issue bonds.

Section 8. The first meeting may be called by written notice therefor naming the time and place signed by either of said corporators and sent by mail or given in hand to the other corporators three days before such meeting. Any corporator may act at such meeting by written proxy.

First meeting, how called.

Section 9. This act shall take effect when approved.

Approved March 18, 1903.

Chapter 201.

An Act to authorize the Saint John Lumber Company to build piers and booms in the Saint John River in the town of Van Buren.

Be it enacted by the Senate and House of Representatives in Legislature assembled, as follows:

The Saint John Lumber Company, a corporation organized and existing under the laws of the state of Maine, its successors and assigns are hereby authorized to build and maintain piers and booms in connection therewith in the Saint John river at a point near to the mills of the said company in the town of Van Buren, and thence from the mainland to or near to the foot of island number three in said town, and also from the mainland

St. John Lumber Co. authorized to build piers and booms in St. John river in town of Van Buren

338

CARATUNK POWER COMPANY.

CHAP. 202

opposite or nearly opposite the upper end of island number four to said island number four, and also at any other point or points between the lower end of island number three and the upper end of island number four aforesaid, as may appear necessary or convenient in the carrying on of the business of said company in holding and manufacturing lumber.

Approved March 18, 1903.

Chapter 202.

An Act to authorize the Caratunk Power Company to erect and maintain dams across the Carrabasset River in the towns of Anson and Embden.

Be it enacted by the Senate and House of Representatives in Legislature assembled, as follows:

Caratunk Power Co. authorized to maintain dam across Carrabasset river.

Section 1. The Caratunk Power Company, a corporation organized and existing under the laws of the state of Maine, and having its established place of business at Fairfield, in the county of Somerset, is hereby authorized to erect and maintain a dam across the Carrabasset river, upon that part of said river that constitutes the town line between Anson and Embden, also a

—proviso.

dam across the said Carrabasset river, about half a mile below Cleveland rips, so called, provided that suitable sluices, for the passage of logs and lumber, shall be constructed and maintained in said dams, for manufacturing and other purposes, with all of

—liabilities and obligations.

the rights and privileges, and subject to the liabilities and obligations of similar corporations, under the laws of this state. Provided, that nothing herein shall be construed as authorizing said company to take any water power by right of eminent domain.

May cut and maintain canals.

Section 2. Said corporation is hereby authorized to cut and maintain canals from said dams, and to erect and maintain necessary side dams, appurtenant thereto, and for the purpose of constructing and maintaining said dams and canals, may take, occupy and enclose any land adjoining the same, which may be necessary for building or repairing the same, and other necessary purposes and may blow up and remove any rocks in said river, and dig any of the land near said river, when necessary to said

—may enter upon land for surveys.

purposes. And may enter upon any land for the purpose of making necessary preliminary surveys, and setting marks and monuments therefor, and may take and hold by purchase or otherwise, any real estate, rights of way or of water, and may also take and occupy any land necessary for the construction and maintenance of a road from the end of said dam, on each side of the said Carrabasset river, to the highways leading from Anson to New Portland.

Section 3. Said company is authorized to make contracts with any municipalities, corporation or individual, for the supply either of water power or electricity, and may establish written regulations for the supply of the same, and may sell or lease any power not used by it on the dams aforesaid.

Section 4. Said company shall have authority to construct and maintain its lines, poles, wires and fixtures, for the transmission of electricity, along, over, across and under the roads and streets in the towns of Madison, Starks, Anson, Cornville, Solon and Embden; also to generate and supply electricity in said towns, subject, however, to the conditions and restrictions provided in chapter one hundred and two of the public laws of eighteen hundred and ninety-five, so far as applicable to the use of said roads and streets. Provided, that said company shall not supply electricity for any purpose within the territorial limits of the town of Anson without the consent of the Carrabasset Stock Farms Company, except within the limit of one mile of the westerly terminus of the Norridgewock Falls bridge. No pole lines shall be established within one mile of the limits of the village of North Anson. Provided, further, said company shall not construct and maintain lines, poles, wires and fixtures in the town of Madison until the same shall have been approved by a major vote of those present and voting at a legal meeting of voters of said town acting under a proper article in the warrant calling said meeting.

Section 5. Said company shall be liable in all cases to repay to said towns all sums of money that said towns, or either of them, may be obliged to pay on any judgment recovered against them, or either of them, for damages occasioned by any obstruction, taking up or displacement of any street or road by said company, together with counsel fees, and other expenses necessarily incurred in defending the same; provided, however, that said company shall have notice of any suit wherein such damages shall be claimed, and shall be allowed to defend the same at its own expense.

Section 6. Said company shall file in the registry of deeds for the county of Somerset, plans of the location of all lands and rights of way, taken under the provisions of this act, and no entry shall be made on any land, except to make surveys as aforesaid, until the expiration of ten days from such filing; and with such plan, the company may file a statement of the damages it is ready to pay to any person, for any property so taken, and if the amount finally awarded does not exceed that sum, the company shall recover costs against said person, otherwise such person shall recover costs against the company.

CHAP. 202

Liable to pay damages for taking of lands, rights of way or water.

Section 7. Said corporation shall be held liable to pay all damages that shall be sustained by any person or corporation, by the taking of any lands, rights of way or of water, or other property as aforesaid, and if such person or corporation, sustaining damages, as aforesaid, shall not agree with said company upon the sum to be paid therefor, either party, on petition to the county commissioners of Somerset county, within twelve months after such plans are filed, may have said damages assessed by them, and subsequent proceedings and rights of appeal thereon, shall be had in the same manner and under the same restrictions and limitations as are by law prescribed in the case of damages by the laying out of highways. Failure to apply for damages within said twelve months shall be held to be a waiver of the same. For all damages occasioned by flowage, said corporation shall not be liable to an action at common law, but the person injured may have a remedy by complaint for flowage, in which the same proceedings shall be had as in a complaint for flowage under the mill acts of this state.

—damages for flowage.

Capital stock may be increased.

Section 8. Said company is hereby authorized to increase its capital stock from time to time in such manner and under such restrictions as are provided for increasing the capital stock of corporations organized under the general law, and may issue its bonds to an amount not exceeding the amount of capital stock, and secure the same by mortgage upon its franchise and property.

Madison Village Corporation may purchase.

Section 9. At any time the Madison Village Corporation by a majority vote at a legal meeting called therefor, shall have the right to purchase the franchise and property of said company at a price to be agreed upon between said company and said village corporation; and if such price cannot be agreed upon, then at a price which shall be determined by a commission of three competent and disinterested persons, one of whom shall be selected by said company, one by said village corporation, and the third by the two so selected if they can agree, if not, then by the chief justice of the supreme judicial court of Maine. The award of said commissioners shall be binding upon said company and said village corporation, and said village corporation shall pay the amount of said award for said property and franchise within ninety days after said award shall have been rendered. The cost of said commission shall be borne equally by said company and said village corporation.

—proceedings if price cannot be agreed upon.

Section 10. This act shall take effect when approved.

Approved March 18, 1903.

Chapter 203.

An Act to amend Section two of Chapter fifty-six of the Private and Special Laws of one thousand eight hundred and ninety-five, relative to the water supply of Boothbay Harbor.

Be it enacted by the Senate and House of Representatives in Legislature assembled, as follows:

Section 1. Section two of chapter fifty-six of the private and special laws of one thousand eight hundred and ninety-five is hereby amended by adding the words 'Southport, Squirrel Island, Mouse Island, and other adjacent islands. Said town of Boothbay Harbor is also authorized and empowered to sell water to the town of Boothbay and the town of Southport, and to any company, individual, firm or corporation in either of said towns or in either of the adjacent islands,' so that said section as amended, shall read as follows:

'Section 2. Said town is further authorized and empowered, in case it obtains control of said corporation either directly by purchase, or indirectly through ownership of stock, to take water from Adams pond in the town of Boothbay, sufficient for all domestic, sanitary, municipal and commercial purposes, and to take and convey the same, through the towns of Boothbay, Boothbay Harbor and Southport, and to Squirrel Island, Mouse Island, and other adjacent islands. Said town is also authorized and empowered, to sell water to the towns of Boothbay and Southport, and to any company, individual, firm or corporation in either of said towns, or either of the adjacent islands.'

Section 2. This act shall take effect when approved.

Approved March 18, 1903.

Chapter 204.

An Act to incorporate the Hillside Water Company.

Be it enacted by the Senate and House of Representatives in Legislature assembled, as follows:

Section 1. Levi Jones, L. E. Jones, L. B. Jones, E. R. Jones and F. H. Jones, with their associates, successors and assigns, are hereby made a corporation under the name of the Hillside Water Company, for the purpose of supplying the inhabitants of the town of Winthrop with pure water for domestic and manufacturing purposes, with all the rights and privileges and subject to all the liabilities and obligations of similar corporations under the laws of this state.

HILLSIDE WATER COMPANY.

CHAP. 204

May take water from springs or wells.

Section 2. For any of the purposes aforesaid the said corporation is hereby authorized to take and use water from any springs or wells that they may acquire by purchase of the owner thereof; to conduct and distribute the same into and through said town of Winthrop by pipes or aqueducts in the usual manner.

May lay pipes in streets of own of Winthrop.

Section 3. The said corporation is hereby authorized to lay, construct and maintain in, under, through, along, over and across the highways, ways, streets and bridges in the said town of Winthrop under such reasonable restrictions as the selectmen of said town may impose, and to take up, replace and repair all such aqueducts, pipes and hydrants and other structures and fixtures as may be necessary and convenient for the said purposes of said corporation; and the corporation shall be responsible for all damages to the said town and to all corporations, persons and property, occasioned by such use of the said highways, ways and streets. Whenever the said corporation shall lay down or

—duties when laying pipes in streets.

construct any fixtures in any highway, way or street, or make any alterations or repairs upon its works in any highway, way or street, it shall cause the same to be done with as little obstruction to public travel as may be practicable, and shall at its own expense, without unnecessary delay, cause the earth and pavement then removed by it to be replaced in proper condition. The location of all pipes heretofore laid by any of said incorporators for the purposes specified herein are hereby ratified and confirmed.

Capital stock.

Section 4. The capital stock of the said corporation shall be five thousand dollars, and the stock shall be divided into shares of one hundred dollars each.

May hold property to value of $5,000.

Section 5. The said corporation for all its said purposes, may hold real and personal estate necessary and convenient therefor, to the amount of five thousand dollars.

First meeting, how called.

Section 6. The first meeting of said corporation shall be called by a written notice thereof, signed by any one of the named incorporators, served upon each named incorporator by giving the same in hand or by leaving the same at his last and usual place of abode, at least seven days before the time of meeting, or by mailing such notice, postage paid, to each incorporator directed to his place of residence seven days at least before the time of said meeting.

May sell its rights, or buy rights of any other water company in town of Winthrop.

Section 7. Said corporation may sell all its rights, property and franchises to any other water company in said Winthrop and may buy all the rights, property and franchises of any other water company in said Winthrop.

Section 8. This act shall take effect when approved.

Approved March 18, 1908.

Chapter 205.

An Act additional to the acts which constitute the charter of the trustees of Hebron Academy.

Be it enacted by the Senate and House of Representatives in Legislature assembled, as follows:

Section 1. All acts and doings of the trustees of Hebron Academy in the town of Hebron, county of Oxford, in constructing and acquiring a line of poles and wires thereon from Mechanic Falls village in the town of Mechanic Falls, county of Androscoggin, to Hebron Academy in the town of Hebron aforesaid, for the purpose of obtaining electricity for lighting purposes in the buildings and property of Hebron Academy, is hereby approved and declared to be legal and valid, and the contract now in force between the trustees of Hebron Academy and the Mechanic Falls Water and Electric Light and Power Company is hereby approved, and the trustees of Hebron Academy are hereby granted the right to maintain said line of poles and wires, for said purposes, between said points, subject to existing provisions of law, and to make and execute additional contract or contracts with said Mechanic Falls Water and Electric Light and Power Company, or any other person or corporation to furnish electricity to be used within said town of Hebron.

Section 2. The trustees of Hebron Academy are hereby authorized and empowered to construct and maintain a line of poles and wires thereon, at any point within the town of Hebron, subject to all existing provisions of law or laws hereinafter enacted, regulating the use of electricity, and when said pole line is established, shall have the right to make contracts with persons or corporations for the lighting of streets or buildings within said town of Hebron, and collect and receive such compensation therefor as may be mutually agreed between the parties and may sell or lease their pole lines, franchises and fixtures belonging to the same, at any time when they deem it for their interest.

Approved March 19, 1903.

Chapter 206.

An Act to amend the charter of the Maine Historical Society, permitting said society to hold real and personal estate to the value of five hundred thousand dollars.

Be it enacted by the Senate and House of Representatives in Legislature assembled, as follows:

Section 1 of chapter 118, private and special laws of 1822, amended.

Section 1. Section one of chapter one hundred and eighteen of the private and special laws of eighteen hundred twenty-two is hereby amended by striking out after the word "estate," in the twenty-fifth line of said section, the words, "to an amount not exceeding the yearly value of five thousand dollars and personal estate not exceeding at any one time fifty" and inserting in lieu thereof the words 'and personal property, to an amount not exceeding five hundred,' so that said section as amended, shall read as follows:

Corporators.

'Section 1. Be it enacted by the senate and house of representatives in legislature assembled, that William Allen, Albion K. Parris, Prentiss Mellen, William P. Preble, Ichabod Nichols, Edward Payson, Joshua Wingate, Junior, Stephen Longfellow, Junior, George Bradbury, Ashur Ware, Edward Russell, Benjamin Orr, Benjamin Hasey, William King, Daniel Rose. Benjamin Ames, Isaac Lincoln, Benjamin Vaughan, Nathan Weston, Junior, Daniel Coney, Robert H. Gardiner, Sanford Kingsbery, Eliphalet Gillet, Thomas Bond, John Merrick, Peleg Sprague, James Parker, Ariel Mann, Ebenezer T. Warren, Benjamin Tappan. Reuel Williams, James Bridge, Hezekiah Packard, Samuel E. Smith, William Abbott, Leonard Jarvis, John Wilson, William D. Williamson. Jacob McGaw, David Sewall, John Holmes, Jonathan Cogswell, Josiah W. Seaver, William A. Hayes, Joseph Dane, Ether Shepley, Enoch Lincoln, Horatio G. Balch and Judah Dana, with their fellows, or associates, and successors be, and they hereby are, made a body politic and corporate, by the name of the Maine Historical Society; and by that name may sue and be sued, plead and be impleaded; and may have a common seal, which they may alter at pleasure; and may hold real estate and personal property to an amount not exceeding five hundred thousand dollars; and may choose a president, librarian, treasurer, and such other officers as they may think proper; and may make and ordain by-laws for the government of said society; provided the same are not repugnant to the constitution and laws of this state.'

—corporate name.

Section 2. This act shall take effect when approved.

Approved March 19, 1903.

Chapter 207.

An Act to amend the charter of the City of Calais, relating to Ward and District lines.

Be it enacted by the Senate and House of Representatives in Legislature assembled, as follows:

Section nine of chapter three hundred and twenty-five of the private acts of eighteen hundred and eighty-three is hereby amended by inserting in the fourth line after the word "ward" the word 'lines,' and by inserting in the fifth line before the word "district" the words 'may alter or abolish existing' and by inserting in the fifth line after the word "lines" the words 'and may establish voting districts in any ward and fix the lines thereof,' so that said first sentence shall read as follows:

'Section 9. The city shall remain divided into seven wards, and ward seven shall remain as now divided into district number one and district number two, and the council may, once in ten years revise and, if needful, alter the ward lines, and may alter or abolish existing district lines, and may establish voting districts in any ward and fix the lines thereof so as to preserve, as nearly as may be, an equal number of voters in each ward.'

Approved March 19, 1903.

Chapter 208.

An Act to prevent the throwing of sawdust and other mill waste into Saint Georges river in the towns of Montville, Searsmont and Appleton.

Be it enacted by the Senate and House of Representatives in Legislature assembled, as follows:

Section 1. No person or persons shall cast or throw into the Saint Georges river in the towns of Montville and Searsmont, in the county of Waldo, and Appleton in the county of Knox, any sawdust, edgings, heading turnings, shavings, bark or other mill waste, or place or deposit such mill waste, or other refuse, along the banks in such a manner that the same shall fall or be washed into said Saint Georges river.

Section 2. Any person violating the provisions of section one shall be subject to a penalty of not less than five dòllars and not more than fifty dollars, to be recovered in an action of debt by any party injured, or by indictment.

Approved March 19, 1903.

Chapter 209.

An Act to change the name of Burnt Island in the town of North Haven to Scallop Island.

Be it enacted by the Senate and House of Representatives in Legislature assembled, as follows:

Burnt island, name changed to Scallop island.

Section 1. The island known by the name of Burnt island being and lying near the northeast point of the town of North Haven, containing fifteen acres more or less, belonging to Francis W. Chandler of Boston, Massachusetts, is hereby changed to the name of Scallop island.

Section 2. This act shall take effect when approved.

Approved March 19, 1903.

Chapter 210.

An Act to make valid certain doings of the Assessors of Norway for the year one thousand nine hundred and two.

Be it enacted by the Senate and House of Representatives in Legislature assembled. as follows:

Assessors of town of Norway, acts of, made valid

Section 1. The acts and doings of the assessors of the town of Norway in assessing and committing for the year one thousand nine hundred and two a tax of twenty-seven thousand two hundred forty dollars and ninety-seven cents, instead of the amount authorized by law, are hereby ratified, confirmed and made valid.

Section 2. This act shall take effect when approved.

Approved March 19, 1903.

Chapter 211.

An Act to extend the charter of the Dexter Water Company.

Be it enacted by the Senate and House of Representatives in Legislature assembled, as follows:

Charter extended.

The time within which the Dexter Water Company, a corporation created by chapter two hundred and fifty-two of the private and special laws of nineteen hundred and one, entitled "An Act to supply the town of Dexter with pure water," approved February thirteenth, nineteen hundred and one, may organize and have its works in actual operation is hereby extended to February thirteenth, nineteen hundred and five. The said town

SEARSPORT WATER COMPANY. 347

of Dexter shall pay all damages sustained by any person or corporation by taking of any water, water source, water right or easement, or by any other thing done by said town under the authority of this act, which shall be determined and assessed in the same manner as is provided in section three for land taken under the provisions of this act. Damages shall not be allowed for taking water from Dexter pond, otherwise known as Silver lake.

CHAP. 212
—town of Dexter shall pay damages for taking water, etc.

—exception.

Approved March 19, 1903.

Chapter 212.

An Act to incorporate the Searsport Water Company.

Be it enacted by the Senate and House of Representatives in Legislature assembled, as follows:

Section 1. J. W. Black, A. H. Nichols, L. C. Morse, C. E. Adams, their associates, successors and assigns, are hereby made a corporation by the name of the Searsport Water Company, for the purpose of supplying the town of Searsport, in the county of Waldo, and the inhabitants of said town, with pure water for domestic, sanitary and municipal purposes, including extinguishment of fires.

Corporators.

—corporate name.

Section 2. Said company, for said purposes, may retain, collect, take, store, use and distribute water from any springs, except such springs as are in actual use for domestic purposes, ponds, streams, or other water sources, in said Searsport, or from Boyd's pond in Stockton Springs, and may locate, construct and maintain cribs, reservoirs, aqueducts, gates, pipes, hydrants and all other necessary structures therefor.

May take water.

Section 3. Said company is hereby authorized to lay, construct and maintain in, under, through, along and across the highways, ways, streets, railroads and bridges in said towns, and to take up, replace and repair all such sluices, aqueducts, pipes, hydrants and structures as may be necessary for the purposes of its incorporation, so as not to unreasonably obstruct the same, under such reasonable restrictions and conditions as the selectmen of said towns may impose. It shall be responsible for all damages to persons and property occasioned by the use of such highways, ways and streets, and shall further be liable to pay to said town all sums recovered against said towns for damages for obstruction caused by said company, and for all expenses, including reasonable counsel fees incurred in defending such suits, with interest on the same, provided said company shall have notice of such suits and opportunity to defend the same.

May lay pipes.

—responsible for damages.

CHAP. 212

May cross sewers.

—shall not unnecessarily obstruct travel.

Section 4. Said company shall have power to cross any water course, private and public sewer, or to change the direction thereof when necessary for the purposes of its incorporation, but in such manner as not to obstruct or impair the use thereof, and it shall be liable for any injury caused thereby. Whenever said company shall lay down any fixture in any highway, way or street, or make any alterations or repairs upon its works in any highway, way or street, it shall cause the same to be done with as little obstruction to public travel as may be practicable, and shall, at its own expense, without unnecessary delay, cause the earth and pavements there removed by it to be replaced in proper condition.

May take lands.

—may enter on lands and make surveys.

Section 5. Said company may take and hold any waters as limited in section two and also any lands necessary for reservoirs, and other necessary structures, and may locate, lay and maintain aqueducts, pipes, hydrants and other necessary structures or fixtures in, over and through any lands for its said purposes, and excavate in and through such lands for such location, construction and maintenance. It may enter upon such lands to make surveys and location, and shall file in the registry of deeds for said county of Waldo, plans of such location and lands, showing the property taken, and within thirty days thereafter, publish notice of such filing in some newspaper in said county, such publication to be continued three weeks successively. Not more than one rod in width of land shall be occupied by any one line of pipe or aqueduct.

In case of disagreement, how damages shall be assessed.

Section 6. Should the said company and the owner of such land so taken be unable to agree upon the damages to be paid for such location, taking, holding and construction, the damages shall be assessed in accordance with the law applicable to the assessment of damages for ways taken by railroads, so far as such law is consistent with the provisions of this act. If said company shall fail to pay such land owner, or deposit for his use with the clerk of the county commissioners aforesaid, such sum as may be finally awarded as damages, with costs when recovered by him, within ninety days after notice of final judgment shall have been received by the clerk of courts of said county, the said location shall be thereby invalid, and said company forfeit all rights under the same as against such land owner. Said company may make a tender to any land owner damaged under the provisions of this act, and if such land owner recovers more damages than were tendered him by said company, he shall recover costs, otherwise said company shall recover costs. In case said company shall begin to occupy such lands before the rendition of final judgment, the land owner may require said company to file its bond to him with said county commissioners, in such sum and with such sureties as they approve, conditioned for said payment or deposit. No action shall be brought against said company for such taking, holding and occupation, until after such failure to pay or deposit as aforesaid. Failure to apply for damages within three years by the land owner, shall be held to be a waiver of the same.

Section 7. Any person suffering damage by the taking of water by said company as provided by this act, may have his damages assessed in the manner provided in the preceding section, and payment therefor shall be made in the same manner and with the same effect. No action shall be brought for the same until after the expiration of the time of payment. And a tender by said company may be made with the same effect as in the preceding section. *Damages for taking water how assessed*

Section 8. Said corporation is hereby authorized to make contracts with the United States, and with corporations, and inhabitants of said town of Searsport or any village corporation therein for the purpose of supplying water as contemplated by this act; and said town of Searsport by its selectmen, or such village corporation by its assessors, is hereby authorized to enter into contract with said company for a supply of water for public uses, on such terms and for such time as the parties may agree, which when made, shall be legal and binding on all parties thereto, and said town of Searsport for this purpose may raise money in the same manner as for other town charges. *May make contracts.*

Section 9. The capital stock of said company shall be fifty thousand dollars, and said stock shall be divided into shares of twenty-five dollars each. *Capital stock*

Section 10. Said company for all of its said purposes, may hold real and personal estate necessary and convenient therefor, not exceeding in amount two hundred thousand dollars. *May hold property not to exceed $200,000.*

Section 11. Said company may issue its bonds for the construction of its works of any and all kinds upon such rates and time as it may deem expedient, to an amount not exceeding in all the capital stock of said corporation subscribed for, and secure the same by mortgage or mortgages of the franchise and property of said company. *May issue bonds.*

Section 12. The first meeting of said company may be called by a written notice thereof, signed by any corporator herein named, served upon each corporator by giving him the same in hand, or by leaving the same at his last usual place of abode, seven days before the time of meeting. *First meeting, how called.*

Section 13. This act shall become null and void in two years from the day when the same shall take effect, unless said com- *Must organize and commence*

CHAP. 213
business within two years.

pany shall have organized and commenced actual business under this charter.

Section 14. This act shall take effect when approved.

Approved March 19, 1903.

Chapter 213.

An Act authorizing the County Commissioners of Cumberland County to erect a county building in Portland.

Be it enacted by the Senate and House of Representatives in Legislature assembled, as follows:

County commissioners authorized to build a county building.

The county commissioners of the county of Cumberland are authorized to erect and maintain in the city of Portland a county building of modern, fire proof construction, containing suitable court rooms, registries, county offices, library rooms and such other rooms, accommodations and conveniences as to such commissioners may seem necessary or desirable, and for that purpose to acquire suitable land, either by purchase, exchange or by taking as for public uses, and in order to provide for the payment thereof to borrow money and issue interest bearing bonds of said county. Said county commissioners shall cause any land so taken to be surveyed, located and so described that the same can be identified, and shall cause a plan and description thereof to be filed in their office and there recorded. The filing of said plan and description shall vest the title to said land in said county, or its grantees, to be held during the pleasure of said county.

—may acquire land.

—plan of land acquired shall be filed.

—compensation for land, how determined in case of disagreement.

If compensation for land taken as aforesaid is not agreed upon, the owner of said land shall have just compensation therefor, to be determined by a commission of three disinterested persons, not residents of said county of Cumberland, appointed by any justice of the supreme judicial court, upon petition of the owner of said land or of said county commissioners, directed to said court and filed in said court at any time within one year after said plan and description are filed in the office of said county commissioners as aforesaid. Such commission shall, after hearing, make its award and return the same to said court within six months from date of its appointment. The supreme judicial court may confirm such award or reject it or recommit it or submit the subject matter thereof to a new commission. Such commission shall have full power to summon and examine witnesses, call for books and papers for the determination of said compensation and may fix the time and place of hearing and adjourn the same from time to time.

Said county commissioners are authorized to dispose of the interest of said county in and to the land at the corner of Congress and Myrtle streets in said Portland whereon the city building of said city is located, and to adjust with said city all matters, whether of contract or otherwise relating to said land.

Commissioners may sell land at corner of Congress and Myrtle streets in Portland.

Approved March 19, 1903.

Chapter 214.

An Act to prohibit the use of purse and drag seines in the waters of Sargentville Harbor, known as Billings Cove.

Be it enacted by the Senate and House of Representatives in Legislature assembled, as follows:

Section 1. The use of purse and drag seines is hereby prohibited in the waters of Sargentville harbor, known as Billings cove, under a penalty of not less than five, nor more than fifty dollars.

Purse and drag seines, use in Billings cove, prohibited.

Section 2. This act shall take effect when approved.

Approved March 19, 1903.

Chapter 215.

An Act to construe and continue in force Chapter one hundred and six of the Private and Special Laws of the year one thousand eight hundred and ninety-one, relating to the election of a school committee, and superintendent of schools, for the town of Skowhegan.

Be it enacted by the Senate and House of Representatives in Legislature assembled, as follows:

Chapter one hundred six of the private and special laws of the year eighteen hundred ninety-one is hereby re-enacted, and shall be construed to authorize the town of Skowhegan to act either under the provisions thereof or according to the general statutes, and to change from one method to the other, at any annual meeting, provided the warrant contains a proper article for that purpose.

Chapter 106, private and special laws of 1891, re-enacted.

Approved March 19, 1903.

Chapter 216.

An Act to establish a School Board for the City of Brewer.

Be it enacted by the Senate and House of Representatives in Legislature assembled, as follows:

Membership of school board.

Section 1. The school board of the city of Brewer shall consist of three members, who shall be chosen by the city council in the following manner, namely: at the first meeting of the city council after the passage of this act, three citizens of the city, either male or female, shall be chosen to serve as members of the school board, who shall hold office as provided in section two of this act, and each succeeding year the incoming council shall, at its first meeting, choose one member of said school board, who shall serve for three years, to take the place of the retiring member, as provided in said section two of this act, and all vacancies in said school board shall be filled by the city council for the remainder of the term in which the same occur.

Tenure of members elect, how determined.

Section 2. The school board so chosen by the city council in March nineteen hundred and three, shall, at its first meeting decide by lot, which of its members shall serve for three years, which for two years, and the remaining member shall serve for one year, and shall be chairman of the board for that year; and each subsequent year, the member whose term of office expires at the end of that year, shall be the chairman of the board.

Powers and duties of chool board.

Section 3. The school board chosen under this act shall have all the powers, and perform all the duties of superintending school committees, as provided in chapter eleven of the revised statutes of eighteen hundred and eighty-three, and acts additional thereto and amendatory thereof.

Inconsistent acts, repealed.

Section 4. All the provisions of chapter four hundred fifty-three, of the private and special laws of eighteen hundred and eighty-nine, entitled "An Act to amend an act entitled, 'An Act to incorporate the city of Brewer,' that are inconsistent with the provisions of this act," are hereby repealed.

Section 5. This act shall take effect when approved.

Approved March 19, 1903.

Chapter 217.

An Act relative to elections of Treasurer and Collector of Taxes of the City of Augusta.

Be it enacted by the Senate and House of Representatives in Legislature assembled, as follows:

Section 1. The treasurer and collector of taxes of the city of Augusta may be one and the same person.

Section 2. The election on March sixteen, nineteen hundred and three, of James R. Townsend as treasurer and collector of taxes of the city of Augusta is hereby made legal and valid.

Election of James R. Townsend made legal.

Section 3. This act shall take effect when approved.

Approved March 19, 1903.

Chapter 218.

An Act to enlarge the powers of the Carrabassett Stock Farms.

Be it enacted by the Senate and House of Representatives in Legislature assembled, as follows:

Section 1. The Carrabassett Stock Farms, a corporation organized under the general law and having an established place of business at Anson in the county of Somerset, is hereby authorized to supply the inhabitants of Anson with water suitable for industrial, domestic, sanitary and municipal purposes, including the extinguishment of fire; and shall have all the rights and privileges and be subject to all the liabilities and obligations of similar corporations under the general laws of this state.

Carrabassett Stock Farms authorized to supply inhabitants of Anson with water.

Section 2. For any of the purposes aforesaid or for the preservation and purity of said water, said corporation is hereby authorized to take and use water from the Carrabassett river or its tributaries, or from any springs, wells or ponds in said town of Anson; to conduct and distribute the same into and through the said town of Anson; to survey for, locate, lay, erect and maintain suitable dams, reservoirs, stand pipes, machinery, pipes, aqueducts and fixtures; to carry its pipes or aqueducts under, in and over the Carrabassett river, or under, over or along any water course, bridge, street, railroad, highway or other way; and said corporation is further authorized to enter upon and excavate any highway, or other way, in such manner as least to obstruct the same; to enter, pass over and excavate any lands, and to take and hold, by purchase or otherwise, any real estate, rights of way or of water, and in general do any acts necessary, convenient or proper, for carrying out any of the purposes here-

May take water.

—may conduct and distribute water.

—may lay pipes.

CHAP. 218

inbefore specified. And said corporation is further authorized, for the purpose of making all needed repairs or service connections, to lay its pipes through any public or private lands or ways, with the right to enter upon the same or dig therein, and said corporation may make written regulations for the use of said water, and change the same from time to time.

Plans of land and water taken shall be filed in registry of deeds.

Section 3. Said corporation shall file in the registry of deeds in the county of Somerset, plans of all lands and water rights taken under the provisions of this act; and no entry shall be made upon any lands, except to make surveys, until the expiration of ten days from said filing; and with such plan, the corporation may file a statement of the damage it is willing to pay the owner for any property so taken, and if the amount finally awarded does not exceed that sum, the company shall recover costs against such owner, otherwise such owner shall recover costs against the company.

Liable for damages by use of streets.

Section 4. Said corporation shall be held liable to pay all damages that shall be sustained by any persons, to themselves or their property, occasioned by the use of such streets and ways, and shall pay to said town all sums recovered against said town for damage from obstruction caused by said corporation, and for all expense, including reasonable counsel fees incurred in defending such suits, with interest on the same; but said corporation may assume the defense of suits brought to recover damages as aforesaid; and also for all damages sustained by any persons by the taking of any land, water, rights of way or other property,

—damages for taking lands, etc.

or by excavating through any land for the purpose of laying or building any dams, reservoirs, pipes and aqueducts, and for any other injuries resulting from said acts. And if any person sustaining damage as aforesaid, shall not agree with said corporation upon the sum to be paid therefor, either party, on petition

—proceedings in case of disagreement on damages to be paid.

to the county commissioners of Somerset county, within twelve months after said plans are filed, may have said damage assessed by them, and subsequent proceedings, and right of appeal thereon, shall be had in the same manner and under the same conditions, restrictions and limitations, as are by law prescribed in the case of damages by the laying out of highways. Failure to apply for damages within said twelve months, shall be held to be a waiver of the same.

May make contracts to supply water.

Section 5. Said corporation is hereby authorized to make contracts with the United States, the state of Maine, the county of Somerset, the town of Anson or any village corporation in said town and with the inhabitants thereof or any corporation for the purpose of supplying water as contemplated by this act. And said town of Anson by its municipal officers, or any village corporation by its proper officers, are hereby authorized to enter into contract with said company for a supply of water for any and all purposes mentioned in this act and for such exemptions from public burdens as said town or village corporation and said company may agree, which when made, shall be legal and binding upon all parties thereto.

Section 6. Whoever shall wilfully or maliciously injure any of the property of said corporation, or knowingly corrupt the sources of its water supply, or any of its tributaries so as to affect the purity of the water taken by said corporation, or in any manner pollute them as aforesaid whether frozen or not, shall be punished by a fine not exceeding one thousand dollars, or by imprisonment not exceeding two years, and shall be liable to said corporation for three times the actual damage, to be recovered in any proper action.

Section 7. Said corporation for all its purposes may hold real and personal estate necessary and convenient therefor, not exceeding two hundred thousand dollars.

Section 8. Said corporation, for the construction of its works of any and all kinds, is authorized to issue its bonds in such form and amount, and on such time and rates as it may deem expedient, and secure the same by mortgage of its franchise and property.

Section 9. Said corporation is hereby authorized to take by eminent domain, land, water and water power necessary for its purposes; also to store water in Middle Carrying Place pond in Middle Carrying Place and Rowe pond in Pleasant Ridge, and for that purpose may take material and build dams on the outlets of said ponds and raise the water therein, and widen and deepen the said outlets.

Section 10. For damages caused by flowing lands adjacent to said ponds, said corporation shall be liable to the process provided by the mill act.

Section 11. This act shall take effect when approved.

Approved March 20, 1903.

Chapter 219.

An Act to establish a Municipal Court in the city of Eastport.

Be it enacted by the Senate and House of Representatives in Legislature assembled, as follows:

Eastport municipal court established.

Section 1. A municipal court is hereby established in and for the city of Eastport in our county of Washington, which shall be denominated the Eastport Municipal Court, shall be a court of record, with a seal, and shall consist of one judge who shall be an attorney at law and reside in said Eastport. He shall cause to be entered on the docket of said court all civil and criminal actions, with full minutes of the proceedings in and disposition of the same, which docket shall be at all times open to inspection, and he shall perform all other duties required of similar tribunals in this state; and copies of the records of said court, duly certified by said judge, shall be legal evidence in all courts. He shall not act as attorney or counsel in any action, matter or thing within the jurisdiction of said court.

—qualifications and duties of judge.

Recorder, appointment of.

Section 2. The judge shall appoint a recorder of said court, who shall be an attorney at law and reside in said Eastport, and hold his office for four years. He shall be sworn by said judge, and keep the records of said court when requested to do so by said judge. In case of absence from the court room or sickness of the judge, or when the office of judge shall be vacant, the recorder shall have and exercise all the powers of said judge, and perform all the duties of said judge by this act, and the signature of the recorder, as such, shall be sufficient evidence of his right to act instead of the judge. In the absence of both judge and recorder, any justice of the peace of the city of Eastport, may preside for the purpose of entering and continuing actions and filing papers in said court, and may adjourn the same from day to day, or till the next regular term.

—may preside in absence of judge.

—justice of the peace may preside in absence of judge and recorder.

Exclusive original jurisdiction of court.

Section 3. Said court shall have exclusive original jurisdiction of all civil actions in which the debt or damage demanded do not exceed twenty dollars, and both parties, or one of the parties or a person summoned in good faith and on probable grounds as trustee, reside in said city of Eastport; and shall have exclusive original jurisdiction of all offenses committed against the ordinances and by-laws of said city, and all such criminal offenses and misdemeanors committed therein as are cognizable by trial justices; provided, that warrants may be issued on complaints for offenses committed in said city of Eastport, by any trial justice in said county, but all such warrants shall be made returnable before said court, and no trial justice shall take cognizance of any crime or offense committed in said city, or any civil action of which said court has exclusive jurisdiction. Said court shall have original jurisdiction concurrent with trial justices of all such matters and things, civil and criminal, within the city of Eastport, and the towns of Cutler, Whiting, Perry and Pembroke as are by law within the jurisdiction of trial justices in said county.

Section 4. Said court shall have original jurisdiction, concurrent with the supreme judicial court, of all civil actions in which the debt or damage demanded, exclusive of costs, do not exceed one hundred dollars, in which either party, or a person summoned in good faith and on probable grounds as trustee, reside in said city of Eastport, or in the towns of Cutler, Whiting, Perry or Pembroke, or having his residence beyond the limits of this state, is served with process within said county. Said court shall have original jurisdiction, concurrent with the supreme judicial court in said county, of all larcenies described in sections one, six, seven, eight, and nine of chapter one hundred and twenty of the revised statutes, when the value of the property is not alleged to exceed thirty dollars; of all the cases of cheating by false pretenses, described in section one of chapter one hundred and twenty-six of the revised statutes, when the value of the property or other thing alleged to have been fraudulently obtained or sold does not exceed thirty dollars; of the assaults and batteries described in section twenty-eight of chapter one hundred and eighteen of the revised statutes and of the offense described in section six of chapter one hundred and twenty-four of the revised statutes, and may punish for either of said offenses by fine not exceeding fifty dollars, and by imprisonment not exceeding three months; and of all other crimes, offenses and misdemeanors committed in said county which are by law punishable by fine not exceeding fifty dollars, and by imprisonment not exceeding three months; provided, that said court shall not try civil actions in which the title to real estate according to pleadings filed in the case of either party, is in question, except as provided in chapter ninety-four, sections six and seven, of the revised statutes.

Section 5. A term of said court shall be held on the first Tuesday of each month, beginning at ten o'clock in the forenoon at such place in the city of Eastport as said city shall provide for the transaction of civil business, and all civil processes shall be made returnable accordingly; provided, however, that said court shall be held on every Tuesday at the usual hour, for the entry and trial of actions of forcible entry and detainer, and such actions shall be returnable accordingly, and be heard and determined and judgment entered on the return day of the writ, unless

EASTPORT MUNICIPAL COURT.

Forms of writs and processes.

—service of writs and processes.

continued for good cause. Said court may adjourn from time to time, but shall be considered as in constant session for the trial of criminal offenses.

Section 6. Writs and processes issued by said court shall be in the usual forms, signed by the judge or recorder, and under the seal of said court. They shall be served as like precepts are required to be served when issued by trial justices, except original writs in civil actions, which shall be served not less than seven nor more than sixty days before the sitting of the court at which the same are made returnable. All the provisions of the statutes of the state relative to the attachment of real and personal property and the levy of executions, shall be applicable to actions in this court and executions on judgments rendered therein; provided that property may be attached equal in value to ad damnum, and in addition thereto sufficient to satisfy the costs of suit, and the writ may be framed accordingly.

Civil actions, when entered.

Section 7. All civil actions in said court shall be entered the first day of the term and not afterwards, except by special permission, and they shall be in order for trial at the next term after the entry, if not otherwise disposed of. The pleading shall be the same as in the supreme judicial court, and all provisions of law relative to practice and proceedings in the supreme judicial court, in civil actions, as are hereby made applicable and extended to this court, except so far as they are modified by the provisions of this act.

Proceedings when defendant claims jury trial.

Section 8. If any defendant, his agent or attorney, in any action in said court in which the debt or damage claimed in the writ exceeds twenty dollars, shall on or before the first day of the second term claim a jury trial, and shall deposit with the judge of said court one dollar and fifty cents for copies and entry in the supreme judicial court, to be taxed in his costs if he prevails, the said action shall be removed on motion into and entered at the next term of the supreme judicial court, for said county, and the judge of said municipal court shall forthwith cause certified copies of the writ, return of the officer and all other papers in the case to be filed in the clerk's office of said supreme court.

Reference of pending actions.

Section 9. Actions pending in this court may be referred in the same manner as in the supreme judicial court, and on report of the referees to said municipal court. Judgment may be rendered in the same manner and with like effect as in the supreme judicial court.

Appeals.

Section 10. Any party may appeal from any judgment or sentence of said municipal court to the supreme judicial court, in the same manner as from a judgment or sentence of a trial justice.

CHAP. 219

Section 11. Exceptions may be alleged in cases certified on agreed statement of facts, or upon evidence reported by the judge in all civil actions, as in the supreme judicial court, and the same shall be entered, heard and determined at the next law term, or by agreement of parties may be certified at and to the chief justice of the supreme judicial court and when so certified to be argued in writing on both sides within thirty days; and the supreme judicial court, sitting as a court of law, shall have the same jurisdiction over all questions of law arising on said exceptions, statements and reports, as if they originated in the supreme judicial court for the county of Washington; and all the provisions of law and rules of the supreme judicial court relative to the transfer of actions and other matters from the supreme judicial court in said county shall apply to the transfer of actions from the said municipal court to said law court. Decisions of the law court on all cases from said municipal court, shall be certified to the judge of said municipal court, with the same effect as in cases originating in the supreme judicial court in said county.

Section 12. The costs and fees allowed to parties and attorneys in civil actions before said court, in which the debt or damages recovered do not exceed twenty dollars, shall be the same as are allowed in actions before trial justices, except the plaintiff, if he prevails, shall be allowed two dollars for his writ; and the defendant, if he prevails, one dollar for his fees. But in all actions in which the amount recovered exceeds twenty dollars, the costs and fees of parties and attorneys shall be same as in the supreme judicial court, except that the defendant, if he prevails, shall be allowed two dollars for his pleadings.

Section 13. The fees of the judge, or the recorder acting as judge, which they may demand and receive in full payment for their services, shall be the same as are allowed to the trial justices and clerks of the supreme judicial court for similar services, except he shall receive for every blank writ signed by him four cents; for the entry of each civil action fifty cents; for every warrant issued by him one dollar; and for the trial of an issue in civil or criminal cases one dollar and two dollars for each day actually employed after the first. All fines and penalties awarded and received by said judge, or said recorder, shall be accounted for and paid over as if the same had been awarded and received by a trial justice, and for neglect to do so they shall be subject to like penalties with trial justices.

Section 14. The city marshal of the city of Eastport or one of his deputies, shall be in attendance on said court when requested so to be by the judge or recorder, for the purpose of preserving order and he shall execute all legal orders and processes to him directed by said court.

Section 15. The city of Eastport shall provide suitable rooms for said court and furnish the same in an appropriate manner.

Section 16. Any trial justice in the county of Washington may take cognizance of any action, matter or thing within his jurisdiction, wherein the judge or recorder of said court is a party or interested.

Section 17. This act shall take effect when approved.

Approved March 20, 1903.

Chapter 220.

An Act to authorize the town of Brunswick to raise money to defray the expense of locating a water supply.

Be it enacted by the Senate and House of Representatives in Legislature assembled, as follows:

Section 1. The town of Brunswick is hereby authorized to raise or appropriate money to defray any expense that may be incurred by the Brunswick and Topsham Water District in locating a water supply for said district; and said district is hereby authorized to reimburse said town for any money actually expended under this act.

Section 2. This act shall take effect when approved.

Approved March 20, 1903.

Chapter 221.

An Act to regulate the appointment of Constables by the City Council of Portland.

Be it enacted by the Senate and House of Representatives in Legislature assembled, as follows:

Section 1. The city council of the city of Portland may, at the time of the election of subordinate city officers, or as soon thereafter as may be, elect not exceeding nine city constables and their term of office shall be for one year and until others are qualified in their place.

Section 2. The provisions of section one shall not be construed as repealing or amending the provisions of sections twelve and thirteen of chapter two hundred and seventy-five of the special laws of eighteen hundred and sixty-three, entitled, "An Act to confer certain powers on the city of Portland."

Section 3. All acts and parts of acts inconsistent with this act, are hereby repealed.

Section 4. This act shall take effect when approved.

Approved March 20, 1903.

Chapter 222.

An Act to authorize extensions of the Bangor and Aroostook Railroad, in Aroostook, Piscataquis and Penobscot counties.

Be it enacted by the Senate and House of Representatives in Legislature assembled, as follows:

Section 1. For and during a period of ten years from and after this passage of this act, the Bangor and Aroostook Railroad Company is hereby authorized and empowered to build in one or more of the counties of Penobscot, Piscataquis and Aroostook but only in that part of said counties west of that part of the Bangor and Aroostook Railroad which runs from Brownville to Van Buren and north of that part of the Canadian Pacific Railroad which extends from the west line of the state to said part of said Bangor and Aroostook Railroad extensions of its railroad, and extensions of any line of railroad the franchise of which it may, under legislative authority acquire, and extensions of such extensions and branches to connect with its said railroad, and branches to connect with any railroad which it may acquire as aforesaid or with any such extension by complying with the provisions of this act. *Bangor and Aroostook R. R. Co. authorized to build extensions.*

Section 2. Whenever said company shall desire to build any such extensions or any such branch, it may present to the railroad commissioners a petition setting forth its said desire, accompanied with a map of the proposed route as near as may be of such extension, or such branch as the case may be, on an appropriate scale. *Proceedings when extensions are desired.*

The board of railroad commissioners shall, on presentation of such petition, appoint a day for a hearing thereon and the petitioner shall give such notice thereof as said board shall order, in order that all persons interested may have an opportunity to appear and be heard thereon.

If the board of railroad commissioners after such notice and hearing shall find that public convenience or necessity requires the construction of such railroad, said board shall file with the secretary of state a certificate of that fact, together with a copy

BANGOR AND AROOSTOOK RAILROAD.

CHAP. 222

of said petition, and shall furnish said railroad company with a like certificate, and thereupon said railroad company shall be and become possessed of the right to build, equip and operate such branch or extension.

Provisions relating to increase of capital stock.

Section 3. The provisions of chapter one hundred eighty-six of the public laws of the year eighteen hundred ninety-seven, and any acts amendatory thereof shall not apply to the issuance of an increase of the capital stock of said company to an amount in the aggregate of not more than six thousand dollars per mile for each mile of any extension or branch which said company may be authorized to build pursuant to the provisions of this act.

Provisions of Section 6 of chapter 51, R. S., to be complied with.

Before commencing the construction of any such extension or branch the provisions of section six of chapter fifty-one of the revised statutes so far as they may be applicable shall be complied with and thereafter all the provisions of the general railroad law, except as the same are modified by this act, shall be applicable to every such extension and branch.

Provisions of section 1 of chapter 122, as amended, shall apply to Fish River R. R.

Section 4. The provisions of section one of chapter one hundred and twenty-two of the private and special laws of the year eighteen hundred ninety-one, as amended by chapter three hundrd and sixty-two of the private and special laws of the year eighteen hundred ninety-three, shall apply to the Fish River Railroad, provided the Bangor and Aroostook Railroad Company shall with legislative consent acquire said railroad and the franchise thereof, and shall apply to any extensions and any branches which may be built under the authority given in this act.

—*proviso.*

May enter into agreements with state of Maine, amending contract.

Section 5. Said Bangor and Aroostook Railroad Company is hereby authorized to enter into agreements from time to time with the state of Maine amending the contract between said parties heretofore executed pursuant to section four of chapter one hundred twenty-two of the private and special laws of the year eighteen hundred ninety-one so as to include in said contract the present railroad owned by said company, the Fish River Railroad, whenever said company shall, pursuant to legislative authority, acquire said Fish River Railroad and the franchise thereof, and so as to include from time to time all extensions and branches which may be built by the Bangor and Aroostook Railroad Company under the authority given in this act.

Whenever any such agreement shall be executed by said company and be approved by vote of its board of directors and shall be presented to the treasurer of the state it shall be his duty to execute said contract in behalf of the state and thereafter he shall carry out the provisions of said contract as at the time amended during the term of said contract.

Section 6. This act shall take effect when approved.

Approved March 20, 1903.

Chapter 223.

An Act to establish an additional Normal School to be located at Presque Isle, in the county of Aroostook.

Be it enacted by the Senate and House of Representatives in Legislature assembled, as follows:

Section 1. Another normal school, to be known as Aroostook County Normal School, is hereby created and established, upon such plan as the board of trustees of normal schools may direct.

Aroostook County Normal School, established.

Section 2. Said normal school shall be located at Presque Isle, in the county of Aroostook, provided and upon condition that the inhabitants of said town of Presque Isle, shall, within six months after the date of the approval of this act, donate and cause to be conveyed to the state, for the use and purposes of such school, the lot of land and buildings thereon, in the village portion of said Presque Isle, now owned by said inhabitants, and which was conveyed to said inhabitants by Robert Codman as Bishop of the Episcopal Church in Maine, by deed dated April ninth, nineteen hundred and two, and recorded in the Aroostook registry of deeds, southern district, volume one hundred ninety-two, page three hundred twenty-four, containing five acres more or less. Said inhabitants of said town of Presque Isle, at any legal meeting of said inhabitants called and held within said six months, are hereby authorized and empowered, by a majority vote of the legal voters voting at said meeting, to donate said lot of land and buildings thereon to said state for the use and purposes aforesaid, and to instruct and direct the selectmen of said town, to make, execute and deliver, for and in behalf of said inhabitants, a proper deed conveying said lot of land and buildings thereon to the state, for the use and purpose aforesaid. Said deed shall be delivered to the board of trustees of normal schools, who are hereby authorized and empowered to accept and receive the same for and in behalf of said state, and when so delivered, it shall be conclusive evidence of the legality of the meeting of said inhabitants to be held as aforesaid and of all the proceedings at such meeting, and the title to said lot of land and all buildings thereon, shall be forever vested in said state for the

Location.
—proviso.

use and purposes aforesaid. And said trustees, upon such conveyance and delivery of such deed, are authorized, instructed and directed to procure teachers and put in operation such school, and cause the same to be conducted at a cost per year not greater than that of either of the present normal schools, such cost to be deducted and paid from the public school funds.

Appropriation for repairing and erecting buildings.

Section 3. The sum of five thousand dollars is hereby appropriated for the year nineteen hundred and three, and a like sum of five thousand dollars for the year nineteen hundred and four, the same or so much of the same as may be necessary, to be used by said trustees in repairing buildings upon said lot of land, and in erecting any other necessary and needful buildings on said lot of land.

Proviso.

Section 4. But said sums shall not be available unless said lot and buildings are donated to the state as provided in section two of this act.

Section 5. This act shall take effect when approved.

Approved March 20, 1903.

Chapter 224.

An Act to amend the charter of the Lubec Water Company.

Be it enacted by the Senate and House of Representatives in Legislature assembled, as follows:

Section 6 of chapter 489, private and special laws of 1901, amended.

Section 1. Section six of chapter four hundred and eighty-nine of the private and special laws of nineteen hundred and one is hereby amended by inserting after the word "town" in the thirteenth line the following words: 'The above commissioners, with such additional commissioners as the town may, from time to time, elect, shall apply the surplus funds arising from said system solely for the purpose of the liquidation of the water works loan,' so that said section as amended, shall read as follows:

Water commissioners shall be elected by ballot.

'Section 6. For the purpose of carrying into effect the provisions of this act, the town of Lubec, at a meeting duly called therefor, may, as soon as this act takes effect, and shall, as soon as the town comes into ownership, control or management of a system of water works, by building, purchase, or otherwise, elect by ballot three water commissioners, the three first chosen as

—tenure.

aforesaid, shall serve, one for one year, one for two years, and one for three years, and thereafterwards one commissioner shall be elected annually in the month of March to serve for a term of three years. Said commissioners are authorized to fix the water rates and determine the conditions and manner of the water supply, and shall have the general control and management of the water system owned by the town. The above commissioners, with such additional commissioners as the town may, from time to time, elect, shall apply the surplus funds arising from said system solely for the purpose of the liquidation of the water works loan. They shall receive such compensation for their services as may be fixed by the town.'

Section 2. This act shall take effect when approved.

Approved March 23, 1903.

Chapter 225.

An Act relating to the powers of the Portland and Rumford Falls Railway.

Be it enacted by the Senate and House of Representatives in Legislature assembled, as follows:

Section 1. The Portland and Rumford Falls Railway is hereby authorized and empowered to guarantee the payment, both principal and interest, or either, of the bonds of other railroad corporations, upon such terms as said corporations may mutually agree.

Section 2. The Portland and Rumford Falls Railway is hereby authorized and empowered to lease the Rumford Falls and Rangeley Lakes Railway and any other railroad that may connect with the latter railroad on such terms as may be mutually agreed upon.

Section 3. This act shall take effect when approved.

Approved March 23, 1903.

Chapter 226.

An Act to authorize Frederick J. Merrill of Damariscotta to construct a tide wheel in tide waters of the Damariscotta River.

Be it enacted by the Senate and House of Representatives in Legislature assembled, as follows:

Section 1. Frederick J. Merrill is hereby authorized to build and maintain a tide wheel in the tide waters of the Damariscotta river, and within the limits herein described, as follows:

Beginning on the east shore of said Damariscotta river, on the land of said Frederick J. Merrill, at low water mark, thence

CHAP. 227

running northwesterly forty feet, and of width sufficient to successfully run and operate said wheel, provided said wheel shall not obstruct navigation.

Section 2. This act shall take effect when approved.

Approved March 23, 1903.

Chapter 227.

An Act to Incorporate the Rangeley Trust Company of Rangeley, Maine.

Be it enacted by the Senate and House of Representatives in Legislature assembled, as follows:

Corporators.

Section 1. H. A. Furbish, James B. Dill, F. E. Timberlake and N. P. Noble or such of them as may by vote accept this charter, their associates, successors and assigns, are hereby made a body corporate and politic to be known as the Rangeley Trust Company, and as such shall be possessed of all the powers, privileges and immunities and subject to all the duties and obligations conferred on corporations by law.

—corporate name.

Location.

Section 2. The corporation hereby created shall be located at Rangeley, in the county of Franklin and state of Maine.

Purposes.

Section 3. The purposes of said corporation and the business which it may perform are; first, to receive on deposit, money, coin, bank notes, evidences of debt, accounts of individuals, companies, corporations, municipalities and states, allowing interest thereon, if agreed, or as the by-laws of said corporation may provide; second, to borrow money, to loan money on credits, or real estate, or personal security, and to negotiate loans and sales for others; third, to own and maintain safe deposit vaults, with boxes, safes and other facilities therein, to be rented to other parties for the safe keeping of moneys, securities, stocks, jewelry, plate, valuable papers and documents, and other property susceptible of being deposited therein, and may receive on deposit for safe keeping, property of any kind entrusted to it for that purpose; fourth, to act as agent for issuing, registering and countersigning certificates, bonds, stocks, and all evidences of debt or ownership in property; fifth, to hold by grant, assignment, transfer, devise or bequest, any real or personal property or trusts duly created, and to execute trusts of every description; sixth, to act as assignee, receiver or executor, and no surety shall be necessary upon the bond of the corporation, unless the court or officer approving the same shall require it: seventh, to do in general all the business that may be lawfully done by trust and

—may own safe deposit vaults.

—may act as agent.

banking companies, but said corporation shall not have the power or authority to establish branches.

Section 4. The capital stock of said corporation shall not be less than twenty-five thousand dollars, divided into shares of one hundred dollars each, with the right to increase the said capital stock at any time, by vote of the shareholders, to any amount not exceeding one hundred thousand dollars. Said corporation shall not commence business as a trust or banking company until stock to the amount of at least fifty thousand dollars shall have been subscribed and paid in, in cash.

Capital stock.

—shall not commence business till at least $50,000 shall be paid in.

Section 5. Said corporation shall not make any loan or discount on the security of the shares of its own capital stock, nor be the purchaser or holder of any such shares unless necessary to prevent loss upon a debt previously contracted in good faith; and all stock so acquired shall, within six months from the time of its acquisition, be disposed of at public or private sale.

Shall not make loan on security of its own capital stock.

Section 6. All the corporate powers of this corporation shall be exercised by a board of trustees, who shall be residents of this state whose number and term of office shall be determined by a vote of the shareholders at the first meeting held by the incorporators and at each annual meeting thereafter. The affairs and powers of the corporation may, at the option of the shareholders, be entrusted to an executive board of five members to be, by vote of the shareholders, elected from the full board of trustees. The trustees of said corporation shall be sworn to the proper discharge of their duties, and they shall hold office until others are elected and qualified in their stead. If a trustee or director dies, resigns, or becomes disqualified for any cause, the remaining trustees or directors may appoint a person to fill the vacancy until the next annual meeting of the corporation. The oath of office of such trustees or director shall be taken within thirty days of his election, or his office shall become vacant. The clerk of such corporation shall, within ten days, notify such trustees or directors of their election and within thirty days shall publish the list of all persons who have taken the oath of office as trustees or directors.

Board of trustees.

—number and tenure.

—executive board.

—vacancies, how filled.

Section 7. The board of trustees or directors of said corporation shall constitute the board of investment of said corporation. Said trustees or directors shall keep in a separate book, specially provided for the purpose, a record of all loans and investments of every description, made by said institution substantially in the order of time when such loans or investments are made, which shall show that such loans or investments have been made with the approval of the investment committee of said corporation, which shall indicate such particulars respecting such

Board of investment.

—shall keep record of loans.

CHAP. 227

—loan to officer or director, how made.

loans or investments as the bank examiner shall direct. This book shall be submitted to the trustees or directors and to the bank examiner whenever requested. Such loans or investments shall be classified in the book as the bank examiner shall direct. No loan shall be made to any officer or director of said banking or trust company except by the unanimous approval of the executive board in writing, and said corporation shall have no authority to hire money or to give notes unless by vote of the said board duly recorded.

Director must own at least ten shares of stock.

Section 8. No person shall be eligible to the position of a director or a trustee of said corporation who is not the actual owner of ten shares of the stock.

Reserve fund.

Section 9. Said corporation, after beginning to receive deposits, shall, at all times, have on hand in lawful money, as a reserve, not less than fifteen per cent of the aggregate amount of its deposits, which are subject to withdrawal on demand, provided, that in lieu of lawful money, two-thirds of said fifteen per cent may consist of balances, payable on demand, due from any national or state bank.

Trust funds shall constitute a special deposit.

Section 10. All the property or money held in trust by this corporation, shall constitute a special deposit and the accounts thereof and of said trust department shall be kept separate, and such funds and the investment or loans of them shall be specially appropriated to the security and payment of such deposits, and not be subject to any other liabilities of the corporation; and for the purpose of securing the observance of this proviso, said corporation shall have a trust department in which all business pertaining to such trust property shall be kept separate and distinct from its general business.

Administrators, executors, etc. may deposit in.

Section 11. An administrator, executor, assignee, guardian or trustee, any court of law or equity, including courts of probate and insolvency, officers and treasurers of towns, cities, counties and savings banks of the state of Maine may deposit any moneys, bonds, stocks, evidences of debt or of ownership in property, or any personal property, with said corporation, and any of said courts may direct any person deriving authority from them to so deposit the same.

Responsibility of shareholders.

Section 12. Each shareholder of this corporation shall be individually responsible for all contracts, debts and engagements of said corporation, to a sum equal to the amount of the par value of the shares owned by him in addition to the amount invested in said shares.

Guaranty fund.

Section 13. Such corporation shall set apart as a guaranty fund not less than ten per cent of its net earnings in each and every year until such fund, with the accumulated interest thereon, shall amount to one-fourth of the capital stock of said corporation.

Section 14. The shares of said corporation shall be subject to taxation in the same manner and rate as are the shares of national banks. *Taxation.*

Section 15. Said corporation shall be subject to examination by the bank examiner, who shall visit it at least once in every year, and as much oftener as he may deem expedient. At such visits he shall have free access to its vaults, books and papers, and shall thoroughly inspect and examine all the affairs of said corporation, and make such inquiries as may be necessary to ascertain its condition and ability to fulfill all its engagements. If upon examination of said corporation, the examiner is of the opinion that its investments are not in accordance with law, or said corporation is insolvent, or its condition is such as to render its further proceedings hazardous to the public or to those having funds in its custody, or is of the opinion that it has exceeded its powers or failed to comply with any of the rules or restrictions provided by law, he shall have such authority and take such action as is provided for in the case of savings banks by chapter forty-seven of the revised statutes. He shall preserve in a permanent form a full record of his proceedings, including a statement of the condition of said corporation. A copy of such statement shall be published by said corporation immediately after the annual examination of the same in some newspaper published where said corporation is established. If no paper is published in the town where said corporation is established, then it shall be published in a newspaper printed in the nearest city or town. The necessary expenses of the bank examiner while engaged in making such examination shall be paid by said corporation. *Shall be subject to examination by bank examiner.*

Section 16. Any five of the corporators named in this act may call the first meeting of this corporation by mailing a written notice signed by all, postage paid, to each of the other corporators, seven days at least before the day of the meeting, naming the time, place and purpose of such meeting, and at such meeting the necessary officers may be chosen, by-laws adopted, and any other corporate business transacted. *First meeting, how called.*

Section 17. This act shall take effect when approved.

Approved March 23, 1903.

CHAP. 228.

Chapter 228.

An Act to provide in part for the Expenditures of Government for the year nineteen hundred and four.

Be it enacted by the Senate and House of Representatives in Legislature assembled, as follows:

Appropriations.
Section 1. In order to provide for the several acts and resolves of the legislature, requiring the payment of money from the treasury, and also to provide for the necessary expenditures of government for the year nineteen hundred and four, the following sums are hereby appropriated out of any moneys in the treasury, and the governor, with the advice and consent of the council, is authorized, at any time between the first day of January, nineteen hundred and four, and the first day of January nineteen hundred and five, to draw his warrant on the treasury for the same.

School fund and mill tax, six hundred thousand dollars,	$600,000 00
Free high schools, forty-six thousand dollars,	46,000 00
Normal schools and training school, thirty-one thousand dollars,	31,000 00
Aid to academies, twenty-three thousand dollars,	23,000 00
Trustees of normal schools, one thousand dollars,	1,000 00
Teachers' meetings, one thousand dollars,	1,000 00
State examination of teachers, five hundred dollars,	500 00
Summer training schools and distribution of educational documents, two thousand five hundred dollars,	2,500 00
Schooling of children in unorganized townships, two thousand five hundred dollars,	2,500 00
Superintendence of towns comprising school unions, three thousand dollars,	3,000 00
Interest on Madawaska territory school fund, three hundred dollars,	300 00
University of Maine, twenty thousand dollars,	20,000 00
Trustees of University of Maine, one thousand dollars,	1,000 00
Foxcroft academy, sixty dollars,	60 00
Hebron academy, sixty dollars,	60 00
Houlton academy, one hundred twenty dollars,	120 00
School district number two, Madison, fifty dollars,	50 00
Public debt, seventy thousand dollars,	70,000 00
Interest, sixty-five thousand dollars,	65,000 00
Salaries of public officers, ninety-five thousand one hundred dollars,	95,100 00

EXPENDITURES OF GOVERNMENT.

CHAP. 228

Private secretary to the governor, one thousand two hundred dollars,	1,200 00
Stenographers to justices of supreme judicial court, twelve thousand dollars,	12,000 00
Clerks in secretary of state's office, three thousand two hundred dollars,	3,200 00
Clerks in state treasurer's office, four thousand dollars,	4,000 00
Clerks in adjutant general's office, one thousand eight hundred dollars,	1,800 00
Clerk in superintendent of schools' office, one thousand dollars,	1,000 00
Clerk in commissioner of agriculture's office, one thousand dollars,	1,000 00
Pension clerk, one thousand two hundred dollars,	1,200 00
Clerks in bank examiner's office, one thousand five hundred dollars,	1,500 00
Clerk in state assessors' office, one thousand dollars,	1,000 00
Subordinate officers of state prison, ten thousand six hundred dollars,	10,600 00
Messenger to governor and council, five hundred dollars,	500 00
Stenographer and typewriter, six hundred dollars,	600 00
Foreman, engineer and mail carrier, two thousand seven hundred dollars,	2,700 00
Night watch, two thousand four hundred dollars,	2,400 00
Porters and laborers, six thousand dollars,	6,000 00
Contingent fund of governor and council, six thousand dollars,	6,000 00
Pay roll of council, four thousand dollars,	4,000 00
Journal of council, one hundred fifty dollars,	150 00
Indices, one hundred fifty dollars,	150 00
Contingent fund of secretary of state three hundred dollars,	300 00
Contingent fund of state treasurer, eight hundred dollars,	800 00
County taxes collected in nineteen hundred and three, thirty-five thousand dollars,	35,000 00
Trustees of reform school, one thousand two hundred dollars,.	1,200 00
Visiting committee to reform school, four hundred fifty dollars,	450. 00
Sanford legacy to reform school, forty-two dollars,	42 00

Insane state beneficiaries, seventy-six thousand dollars,	76,000 00
Criminal insane, three thousand five hundred dollars,	3,500 00
Trustees of insane hospitals, two thousand five hundred dollars,	2,500 00
Visiting committee to insane hospitals, eight hundred dollars,	800 00
Education of the blind, seven thousand dollars,	7,000 00
Idiotic and feeble minded persons, three thousand dollars,	3,000 00
Support of paupers in unincorporated places, twenty-five thousand dollars,	25,000 00
Expenses of state assessors, one thousand five hundred dollars,	1,500 00
Expenses of attorney general, four hundred fifty dollars,	450 00
Expenses of superintendent of public schools, five hundred dollars,	500 00
Expenses of insurance commissioner, one thousand two hundred dollars,	1,200 00
Expenses of bank examiner, one thousand two hundred fifty dollars,	1,250 00
Expenses of forest commissioner, four hundred dollars,	400 00
Expenses of commissioner of agriculture, five hundred dollars,	500 00
Expenses of inspector of factories, workshops, mines and quarries, five hundred dollars,	500 00
Expenses of commissioners for the promotion of uniformity of legislation in the United States, two hundred fifty dollars,	250 00
Expenses and compensation of state liquor assayers, one thousand dollars,	1,000 00
Printing, thirty-five thousand dollars,	35,000 00
Binding and stitching, eighteen thousand dollars,	18,000 00
Stationery, eight thousand dollars,	8,000 00
Postage, six thousand dollars,	6,000 00
Agricultural societies, eight thousand five hundred dollars,	8,500 00
Maine state agricultural society, one thousand dollars,	1,000 00
Maine state agricultural society for industrial exhibits, one thousand dollars,	1,000 00
Eastern Maine state fair, one thousand dollars,	1,000 00

EXPENDITURES OF GOVERNMENT.

CHAP. 228

Eastern Maine state fair, to encourage pomology, seven hundred fifty dollars,	750 00
Burial expenses of soldiers and sailors, six thousand dollars,	6,000 00
Sheriffs and coroners, one thousand dollars,	1,000 00
Costs in criminal prosecutions, one thousand five hundred dollars,	1,500 00
Superior court in Waterville, two hundred dollars,	200 00
Reports of judicial decisions, three thousand two hundred dollars,	3,200 00
Advertising land sale and tax act, nine hundred dollars,	900 00
Investigation of the causes of fire, two thousand dollars,	2,000 00
Williams' legacy to Maine insane hospital, forty dollars,	40 00
Maine state cattle commission, contagious diseases, ten thousand dollars,	10,000 00
Railroad and telegraph tax due towns, one hundred fifteen thousand dollars,	115,000 00
Damage by dogs to domestic animals, ten thousand dollars,	10,000 00
Dog licenses refunded, thirty thousand dollars,	30,000 00
Bounty on seals, three thousand dollars,	3,000 00
Farmers' institutes and dairymen's conference, three thousand dollars,	3,000 00
Enforcement of laws relating to sale of impure food, five hundred dollars,	500 00
Arrest and apprehension of criminals, one thousand five hundred dollars,	1,500 00
Lands reserved for public uses, two thousand dollars,	2,000 00
Interest on lands reserved for public uses, nine thousand two hundred and fifty dollars,	9,250 00
Forfeited lands, two thousand dollars,	2,000 00
Fuel and lights, seven thousand dollars,	7,000 00
Furniture and repairs, eight thousand dollars,	8,000 00
Freight and trucking, six hundred dollars,	600 00
Military pensions, three thousand five hundred dollars,	3,500 00
Maine state library, one thousand dollars,	1,000 00
Free public libraries, three thousand dollars,	3,000 00
Donations for founding free public libraries, seven hundred dollars,	700 00
Traveling libraries, two thousand dollars,	2,000 00

State board of health, five thousand dollars,	5,000 00
Registration of vital statistics, two thousand five hundred dollars,	2,500 00
Bureau of industrial and labor statistics, three thousand five hundred dollars,	3,500 00
Water for state house, one thousand eight hundred dollars,	1,800 00
Water for state prison, two thousand five hundred dollars,	2,500 00
Light for state prison, three thousand five hundred dollars,	3,500 00
School in state prison, fifty dollars,	50 00
Physician in state prison, two hundred fifty dollars,	250 00
Medicine for state prison, one hundred fifty dollars,	150 00
Books for use of convicts in state prison, fifty dollars,	50 00
Transportation of documents, two thousand dollars,	2,000 00
Transportation of mail, fifty dollars,	50 00
Property exempt from taxation, two thousand two hundred dollars,	2,200 00
Expenses of Australian ballot, eleven thousand dollars,	11,000 00
Care of trust deposits, two hundred dollars,	200 00
Militia fund, thirty-five thousand two hundred twenty-two dollars and eighty-eight cents,	35,222 88
Indexing papers and records in land office, one thousand dollars,	1,000 00
Trustees Maine industrial school for girls, five hundred dollars,	500 00
Railroad commissioners, twelve thousand four hundred dollars,	12,400 00
Investigation of railroad accidents, one thousand dollars,	1,000 00
Inspectors of state prison and jails, one thousand five hundred dollars,	1,500 00
Inspectors of steamboats, three thousand five hundred dollars,	3,500 00
Inspector of dams and reservoirs, one hundred dollars,	100 00
Amounting to the sum of one million five hundred eighty-two thousand four hundred forty-four dollars and eighty-eight cents,	$1,582,444 88

Section 2. This act shall take effect when approved.

Approved March 24, 1903.

Chapter 229.

An Act relating to the jurisdiction of the Municipal Court of the City of Auburn.

Be it enacted by the Senate and House of Representatives in Legislature assembled, as follows:

Section 1. Section two, paragraph three, of chapter one thirty-five of the private and special laws of eighteen hundred and seventy-five, entitled "An Act to establish a municipal court in the city of Auburn," as amended by chapter one hundred and eighty-six of the private and special laws of the same year, chapter fifty-one of the private and special laws of eighteen hundred and eighty-one, chapter one hundred and fifty-two of the private and special laws of eighteen hundred and ninety-one and chapter sixty-two of the private and special laws of eighteen hundred and ninety-five, is hereby amended by striking out the word "twenty" in the fifth line of said paragraph and inserting instead thereof the word 'ten.' *Section 2, paragraph 3, of chapter 135, private and special laws of 1875, as amended by chapter 186, private and special laws of 1875, chapter 51 of laws of 1881, chapter 152, laws of 1891 and chapter 62, laws of 1895, further amended.*

Section 2. This act shall take effect when approved.

Approved March 24, 1903.

Chapter 230.

An Act to incorporate the Castine Gas Company, Castine, Hancock County.

Be it enacted by the Senate and House of Representatives in Legislature assembled, as follows:

Section 1. W. A. Walker, W. G. Sargent, H. W. Sargent, C. W. Waldron and George M. Warren, their associates and assigns, are hereby constituted a body politic and corporate, by the name of the Castine Gas Company, for the purpose of supplying light, heat and power by the manufacture of gas in the town of Castine, with all the privileges and subject to all the duties, restrictions and liabilities by law incident to corporations of a similar nature. *Corporators. —corporate name.*

Section 2. Said company is authorized and empowered to carry on the business of lighting by gas such public streets in the said town and such buildings and places therein, public and private, as may be agreed upon by said corporation and the owners or those having control of said buildings and places to be lighted, and may furnish motive power by gas within said town, and may build and operate manufactories and works for providing and supplying gas, light and power, and may lease, purchase and hold real and personal estate for the purposes of the corpo- *May furnish light and power by gas.* *—may hold real and personal property.*

Chap. 230

ration to the amount of its capital stock, and to construct, lay, maintain and operate lines of pipe for the transmission of gas, underground, over, under and along any and all streets and ways, under the direction of the municipal officers of said town.

Shall repay town for damages occasioned by obstruction of streets.

Section 3. The said company shall be liable in all cases to repay to the town all sums of money that said town may be obliged to pay on any indictment or judgment recovered against said town occasioned by any obstruction or taking up, or displacement of any way, highway, railroad or street by said company in said town; provided, however, that said company shall

—proviso.

have notice whenever such damages are claimed by said town from the municipal officers and shall be allowed to defend the same at its own expense.

May cross sewers, etc.

Section 4. Said company shall not be allowed to obstruct or impair the use of any public or private drain or sewer but may cross the same, being responsible to the owners or other persons for any injury occasioned thereby in an action on the case.

Municipal officers of Castine may contract with town for gas.

Section 5. The town of Castine, by its municipal officers, is hereby authorized to contract with said company from time to time as is deemed expedient for the supply of light, heat and power for said town.

Capital stock.

Section 6. The capital stock of said company shall not exceed ten thousand dollars, and shall be divided into shares of fifty dollars each.

—may issue bonds.

Section 7. Said corporation is hereby authorized to issue its bonds in such amount and on such time as it may from time to time determine, not exceeding the amount of capital stock subscribed for, in aid of the purpose specified in this act and to secure the same by a mortgage of its franchises and property. It is also hereby authorized to lease all of its property and franchises upon such terms as it may determine.

First meeting, how called.

Section 8. The first meeting of said corporation may be called by the first incorporator, but failing to do so, either of the other incorporators may by a written notice signed by him, stating the time and place thereof, and sent by mail to his associates five days before said meeting.

Shall commence hereunder within two years.

Section 9. This charter shall be null and void unless operations shall actually commence hereunder within two years from the date of the passage of this act.

Approved March 24, 1903.

Chapter 231.

An Act to protect the waters of Lake Auburn.

Be it enacted by the Senate and House of Representatives in Legislature assembled, as follows:

Section 1. No person shall hereafter maliciously injure any of the property of the Auburn water commissioners, the city of Auburn, or of the city of Lewiston, used by either of said corporations in connection with its water supply, nor corrupt the waters of Lake Auburn or any of its tributaries so as to render them impure, nor throw the bodies of dead animals or other offensive materials into the waters of said Lake Auburn or any of its tributaries, or leave the same upon the lake when frozen, nor in any manner wilfully destroy or injure any dam, reservoir, aqueduct, pipe, hydrant or other property held under or used by said Auburn water commissioners, the city of Auburn or the city of Lewiston in connection with their water supply, and any person violating the provisions of this act shall pay three times the amount of damages occasioned to said Auburn water commissioners, the city of Auburn or the city of Lewiston, to be recovered in any proper action, and any person convicted of any wilful violation of this act shall be punished by a fine not exceeding one thousand dollars and by imprisonment not exceeding one year, but nothing in this act shall be construed as taking away or limiting the right to harvest ice from said lake.

Section 2. No structure shall hereafter be built upon or near the shores of said Lake Auburn or any island in said lake, in such manner or in such location that the drainage therefrom shall pollute the waters thereof. The supreme judicial court shall have jurisdiction in equity to prevent and restrain any violation of this section.

Section 3. This act shall take effect when approved.

Approved March 24, 1903.

378 ANSON—DEAD RIVER LOG DRIVING COMPANY.

CHAP. 232

Chapter 232.

An Act authorizing the town of Anson to purchase with the town of Madison in the county of Somerset, the Norridgewock Falls Bridge.

Be it enacted by the Senate and House of Representatives in Legislature assembled, as follows:

Anson, town of, authorized to raise money to purchase bridge.

Section 1. The town of Anson in the county of Somerset is hereby authorized and empowered to raise money by taxation or by temporary loan or loans, to be paid out of money raised by taxation during the year in which they are made; to purchase with the town of Madison the bridge across the Kennebec river between the said towns of Anson and Madison, erected by and belonging to the proprietors of Norridgewock Falls Bridge.

Authorized to purchase bridge, with town of Madison.

Section 2. Said town of Anson is hereby authorized and empowered to take and purchase with the said town of Madison said bridge and franchise, with all the rights, powers, privileges and appurtenances thereto belonging, on the payment to said proprietors of said bridge such sum therefor as may be mutually agreed upon by said towns and said proprietors; each town to pay such part of such sum, or purchase price, as they shall mutually agree upon; provided, that after such purchase said bridge shall be declared free for public travel and use.

—proviso.

Section 3. This act shall take effect when approved.

Approved March 24, 1903.

Chapter 233.

An Act to amend the charter of Dead River Log Driving Company.

Be it enacted by the Senate and House of Representatives in Legislature assembled, as follows:

Section 7 of chapter 279, private and special laws of 1880, amended.

Section 1. Section seven of chapter two hundred and seventy-nine of private and special laws of eighteen hundred and eighty is hereby amended as follows, namely; by striking out the word "Wednesday" in the fourth line thereof and inserting in its place the word 'Tuesday,' so that said section as amended, shall read as follows:

Day of holding annual meeting, changed.

'Section 7. The first meeting of said company may be called by any one of the corporators named in this act, by written notice to each member. Annual meetings shall be called by the clerk, on the third Tuesday of February in each year, or at such times as the company may vote, by giving fourteen days' notice in some newspaper published in Kennebec or Somerset counties;

special meetings may be called by order of the directors, with like notice.'

Section 2. Section two of said chapter two hundred and seventy-nine of private and special laws of eighteen hundred and eighty is hereby amended by striking out the word "five" in the second line of said section and inserting in its place the word 'seven,' so that said section shall read as follows:

'Section 2. The officers of said company shall be a clerk, treasurer and board of seven directors, all of whom shall be chosen by ballot and sworn, and a master driver and such other officers and agents as may be deemed necessary, may be appointed by the directors unless chosen at the annual meeting. The directors shall, at the first meeting, elect one of their number, who shall be president of the company. A majority of the board of directors shall constitute a quorum for doing business. The treasurer shall give bonds to the acceptance of the directors.'

Approved March 24, 1903.

Chapter 234.

An Act to authorize the Augusta Trust Company to increase its capital stock.

Be it enacted by the Senate and House of Representatives in Legislature assembled, as follows:

Section 1. The Augusta Trust Company is hereby authorized to increase its capital stock from time to time to an amount not exceeding five hundred thousand dollars.

Section 2. This act shall take effect when approved.

Approved March 24, 1903.

Chapter 235.

An Act to incorporate the Mount Abram Cemetery Company.

Be it enacted by the Senate and House of Representatives in Legislature assembled, as follows:

Section 1. Eben E. Rand, Llewellyn P. Bryant, O. P. Farrington, Walter B. Rand, Charles E. Stowell, Harry M. Swift, their associates, successors and assigns and such other persons as are owners of lots in the cemetery situated at Locke's Mills, in the town of Greenwood, in the county of Oxford, are hereby created a corporation by the name of the Mount Abram Cemetery Company.

CHAP. 236

May purchase land to the value of $5,000.

Section 2. The corporation hereby created may purchase and hold such land as may be necessary for the present or future requirements of said corporation not to exceed five thousand dollars and may hold such personal property as may be needed or appropriate to the purposes of this corporation and may convey lots for burial purposes by their corporate deeds, but nothing in this section shall limit the right to take land by petition to the municipal officers of the town in accordance with chapter fifteen of the revised statutes.

May have corporate seal.

Section 3. Said corporation may have a corporate seal to be used in its conveyances and may make and establish such by-laws for the government of its concerns as may be necessary, not conflicting with the laws of the state.

Board of directors.

Section 4. Said corporation by its board of directors shall have the care, control and general management of the cemetery.

Owners of lots shall be members of corporation.

Section 5. All persons who are or shall be owners of lots in said cemetery shall be members of this corporation and each member shall be entitled to one ballot.

Officers.

—tenure.

Section 6. The officers of this corporation shall be a president, secretary, treasurer and a board of directors of not less than five, who shall hold their offices until others are chosen.

First meeting.

Section 7. Either of the corporators is hereby authorized to call the first meeting of the corporation by posting notices thereof in three public places in the vicinity, seven days before said meeting.

Section 8. This act shall take effect when approved.

Approved March 24, 1903.

Chapter 236.

An Act to extend the time for the acceptance of the charter of the City of Dexter.

Be it enacted by the Senate and House of Representatives in Legislature assembled, as follows:

Time extended for acceptance of charter.

The time within which the charter of the city of Dexter, granted by chapter seventeen of the private and special laws of eighteen hundred and ninety-five, entitled "An Act to incorporate the city of Dexter," approved February seventh, eighteen hundred and ninety-five, may be submitted for acceptance to the legal voters of the town of Dexter as provided in section twenty-four of said act, is hereby extended to February seventh, nineteen hundred and eight.

Approved March 24, 1903.

Chapter 237.

An Act to permit ice fishing in Pease pond on Saturdays of each week during certain months.

Be it enacted by the Senate and House of Representatives in Legislature assembled, as follows:

Section 1. So much of section five of chapter forty-two of the public laws of eighteen hundred ninety-nine as prohibits fishing through the ice in Pease pond, in the town of Wilton, Franklin county, on Saturdays of each week during the months of February, March and April, is hereby repealed.

Saturday ice fishing in Pease pond, prohibition repealed.

Section 2. This act shall take effect when approved.

Approved March 24, 1903.

Chapter 238.

An Act to incorporate the Wilton Trust Company.

Be it enacted by the Senate and House of Representatives in Legislature assembled, as follows:

Section 1. A. B. Adams, C. F. Blanchard, F. J. Goodspeed, Milton Holmes and C. N. Blanchard, or such of them as may by vote accept this charter, with their associates, successors or assigns, are hereby made a body corporate and politic to be known as the Wilton Trust Company, and as such shall be possessed of all the powers, privileges and immunities and subject to all the duties and obligations conferred on corporations by law.

Corporators.

—corporate name.

Section 2. The corporation hereby created shall be located at Wilton, Franklin county, Maine.

Location.

Section 3. The purposes of said corporation and the business which it may perform are; first, to receive on deposit, money, coin, bank notes, evidences of debt, accounts of individuals, companies, corporations, municipalities and states, allowing interest thereon, if agreed, or as the by-laws of said corporation may provide; second, to borrow money, to loan money on credits, or real estate, or personal security, and to negotiate loans and sales for others; third, to own and maintain safe deposit vaults, with boxes, safes and other facilities therein to be rented to other parties for the safe keeping of moneys, securities, stocks, jewelry, plate, valuable papers and documents, and other property susceptible of being deposited therein, and may receive on deposit for safe keeping, property of any kind entrusted to it for that purpose; fourth, to hold and enjoy all such estate, real,

Purposes.

—may rent safe deposit boxes.

WILTON TRUST COMPANY.

CHAP. 238

personal and mixed, as may be obtained by the investment of its capital stock or any other moneys and funds that may come into its possession in the course of its business dealings, and the same sell, grant, and dispose of; fifth, to act as agent for issuing, registering and countersigning certificates, bonds, stocks, and all evidences of debt or ownership, in property; sixth, to hold by grant, assignment, transfer, devise or bequest, any real or personal property or trusts duly created, and to execute trusts of every description; seventh, to act as assignee, receiver, executor, and no surety shall be necessary upon the bond of the corporation unless the court or officer approving such bond shall require it; eighth, to do in general all the business that may lawfully be done by trust and banking companies.

Capital stock.

Section 4. The capital stock of said corporation shall not be less than twenty-five thousand dollars, divided into shares of one hundred dollars each, with the right to increase the said capital stock at any time, by a vote of the shareholders, to any amount not exceeding two hundred thousand dollars. Said corporation shall not commence business as a trust or banking company until stock to the amount of at least twenty-five thousand dollars shall have been subscribed and paid in, in cash.

—shall not commence business till $25,000 shall have been paid in.

Shall not loan money on security of its own capital stock.

Section 5. Said corporation shall not make any loan or discount on the security of the shares of its own capital stock, nor be the purchaser or holder of any such shares unless necessary to prevent loss upon a debt previously contracted in good faith; and all stock so acquired shall, within six months from the time of its acquisition, be disposed of at public or private sale.

Board of trustees.

Section 6. All the corporate powers of this corporation shall be exercised by a board of trustees, who shall be residents of this state, whose number and term of office shall be determined by a vote of the shareholders at the first meeting held by the incorporators and at each annual meeting thereafter. The affairs and powers of the corporation may, at the option of the shareholders, be entrusted to an executive board of five members to be, by vote of the shareholders, elected from the full board of trustees. The trustees of said corporation shall be sworn to the proper discharge of their duties, and they shall hold office until others are elected and qualified in their stead. If a trustee or director dies, resigns, or becomes disqualified for any cause, the remaining trustees or directors may appoint a person to fill the vacancy until the next annual meeting of the corporation. The oath of office of such trustee or director shall be taken within thirty days of his election, or his office shall become vacant. The clerk of such corporation shall, within ten days, notify such trustees or directors of their election and within thirty days shall publish

—executive board.

Vacancies, how filled.

the list of all persons who have taken the oath of office as trustees or directors.

Section 7. The board of directors or trustees of said corporation shall constitute the board of investment of said corporation. Said directors or trustees shall keep in a separate book, specially provided for the purpose, a record of all loans and investments of every description, made by said institution substantially in the order of time when such loans or investments are made, which shall show that such loans or investments have been made with the approval of the investment committee of said corporation, which shall indicate such particulars respecting such loans or investments as the bank examiner shall direct. This book shall be submitted to the directors and to the bank examiner whenever requested. Such loans or investments shall be classified in the book as the bank examiner shall direct. No loan shall be made to any officer or director of said banking or trust company except by the approval of a majority of the executive board in writing, and said corporation shall have no authority to hire money or to give notes unless by vote of the said board duly recorded. *Board of investment.*

—shall keep record of loans.

—loan to directors, how made.

Section 8. No person shall be eligible to the position of a director or trustee of said corporation who is not the actual owner of five shares of the stock. *Director must own five shares of stock.*

Section 9. Said corporation, after beginning to receive deposits, shall, at all times, have on hand in lawful money, as a reserve, not less than fifteen per cent of the aggregate amount of its deposits, which are subject to withdrawal on demand, provided, that in lieu of lawful money, two-thirds of said fifteen per cent may consist of balances, payable on demand, due from any national or state bank. *Reserve fund.*

Section 10. All the property or money held in trust by this corporation, shall constitute a special deposit and the accounts thereof and of said trust department shall be kept separate, and such funds and the investments or loans of them shall be specially appropriated to the security and payment of such deposits, and not be subject to any other liabilities of the corporation; and for the purpose of securing the observance of this proviso, said corporation shall have a trust department in which all business pertaining to such trust property shall be kept separate and distinct from its general business. *Trust funds shall constitute a special deposit.*

Section 11. An administrator, executor, assignee, guardian or trustee, any court of law or equity, including courts of probate and insolvency, officers and treasurers of towns, cities, counties and savings banks of the state of Maine may deposit any moneys, bonds, stocks, evidences of debt or of ownership in property, or any personal property, with said corporation, and *Administrators, etc., may deposit in.*

384 WILTON TRUST COMPANY.

CHAP. 238

any of said courts may direct any person deriving authority from them to so deposit the same.

Responsibility of shareholders.

Section 12. Each shareholder of this corporation shall be individually responsible, equally and ratably, and not one for the other, for all contracts, debts and engagements of such corporation, to a sum equal to the amount of the par value of the shares owned by each in addition to the amount invested in said shares.

Surplus fund.

Section 13. Such corporation shall set apart as a surplus fund not less than ten per cent of its earnings in each and every year until such fund, with the accumulated interest thereon, shall amount to one-fourth of the capital stock of said corporation.

Taxation.

Section 14. The shares of said corporation shall be subject to taxation in the same manner and rate as are shares of national banks.

Shall be subject to examination by bank examiner.

Section 15. Said corporation shall be subject to examination by the bank examiner, who shall visit it at least once in every year, and as much oftener as he may deem expedient. At such visits he shall have free access to its vaults, books and papers, and shall thoroughly inspect and examine all the affairs of said corporation, and make such inquiries as may be necessary to ascertain its condition and ability to fulfill all its engagements. If upon examination of said corporation, the examiner is of the opinion that its investments are not in accordance with law, or said corporation is insolvent, or its condition is such as to render its further proceedings hazardous to the public or to those having funds in its custody, or is of the opinion that it has exceeded its powers or failed to comply with any of the rules or restrictions provided by law, he shall have such authority and take such action as is provided for in the case of savings banks by chapter forty-seven of the revised statutes. He shall preserve in a permanent form a full record of his proceedings, including a statement of the condition of said corporation. A copy of such statement shall be published by said corporation immediately after the annual examination of the same in some newspaper published where said corporation is established. If no paper is published in the town where said corporation is established, then it shall be published in a newspaper printed in the nearest city or town. The necessary expenses of the bank examiner while making such examination shall be paid by the corporation.

First meeting, how called.

Section 16. Any three of the corporators named in this act may call the first meeting of the corporation by mailing a written notice signed by all, postage paid, to each of the other corporators, seven days at least before the day of the meeting, naming the time, place and purpose of such meeting, and at such meeting the necessary officers may be chosen, by-laws adopted, and any other corporate business transacted.

Section 17. This act shall take effect when approved.

Approved March 24, 1903.

Chapter 239.

An Act to Incorporate the Somerset Trust Company.

Be it enacted by the Senate and House of Representatives in Legislature assembled, as follows:

Section 1. C. H. Clark, K. C. Gray, C. A. Wilbur, John F. Hill, George E. Macomber, Byron Boyd, F. G. Kinsman, J. Manchester Haynes and Arthur W. Whitney, or such of them as may by vote accept this charter, with their associates, successors and assigns, are hereby made a body corporate and politic to be known as the Somerset Trust Company, and as such shall be possessed of all the powers, privileges and immunities and subject to all the duties and obligations conferred on corporations by law. {Corporators. —corporate name.}

Section 2. The corporation hereby created shall be located at Madison, Somerset county, Maine. {Location.}

Section 3. The purposes of said corporation and the business which it may perform are; first, to receive on deposit, money, coin, bank notes, evidences of debt, accounts of individuals, companies, municipalities and states, allowing interest thereon, if agreed, or as the by-laws of said corporation may provide; second, to borrow money, to loan money on credits, or real estate, or personal security, and to negotiate loans and sales for others; third, to own and maintain safe deposit vaults, with boxes, safes and other facilities therein, to be rented to other parties for the safe keeping of moneys, securities, stocks, jewelry, plate, valuable papers and documents, and other property susceptible of being deposited therein, and may receive on deposit for safe keeping, property of any kind entrusted to it for that purpose; fourth, to act as agent for issuing, registering and countersigning certificates, bonds, stocks, and all evidences of debt or ownership, in property; fifth, to hold by grant, assignment, transfer, devise or bequest, any real or personal property or trusts duly created, and to execute trusts of every description: sixth, to act as assignee, receiver, executor, and no surety shall be necessary upon the bond of the corporation unless the court or officer approving such bond shall require it; seventh, to do {Purposes. —may own safe deposit vaults.}

in general all the business that may lawfully be done by trust and banking companies, but said corporation shall not have the power or authority to establish branches.

Capital stock.

Section 4. The capital stock of said corporation shall not be less than fifty thousand dollars, divided into shares of one hundred dollars each, with the right to increase the said capital stock at any time, by a vote of the shareholders, to any amount not exceeding five hundred thousand dollars. Said corporation shall not commence business as a trust or banking company until stock to the amount of at least fifty thousand dollars shall have been subscribed and paid in, in cash.

—shall not commence business until at least $50,000 shall have been paid in.

Shall not make loans on security of its own capital stock.

Section 5. Said corporation shall not make any loan or discount on the security of the shares of its own capital stock, nor be the purchaser or holder of any such shares unless necessary to prevent loss upon a debt previously contracted in good faith; and all stock so acquired shall, within six months from the time of its acquisition, be disposed of at public or private sale.

Board of trustees.

Section 6. All the corporate powers of this corporation shall be exercised by a board of trustees, who shall be residents of this state, whose number and term of office shall be determined by a vote of the shareholders at the first meeting held by the incorporators and at each annual meeting thereafter. The affairs and powers of the corporation may, at the option of the shareholders, be entrusted to an executive board of five members to be, by vote of the shareholders, elected from the full board of trustees. The trustees of said corporation shall be sworn to the proper discharge of their duties, and they shall hold office until others are elected and qualified in their stead. If a trustee or director dies, resigns, or becomes disqualified for any cause, the remaining trustees or directors may appoint a person to fill the vacancy until the next annual meeting of the corporation. The oath of office of such trustee or director shall be taken within thirty days of his election, or his office shall become vacant. The clerk of such corporation shall, within ten days, notify such trustees or directors of their election and within thirty days shall publish the list of all persons who have taken the oath of office as trustees or directors.

—number and tenure of.

—executive board.

—vacancies, how filled.

Board of investment.

Section 7. The board of trustees or directors of said corporation shall constitute the board of investment of said corporation. Said trustees or directors shall keep in a separate book, specially provided for the purpose, a record of all loans and investments of every description, made by said institution substantially in the order of time when such loans or investments are made, which shall show that such loans or investments have been made with the approval of the investment committee of said

—shall keep record of loans.

corporation, which shall indicate such particulars respecting such loans or investments as the bank examiner shall direct. This book shall be submitted to the trustees or directors and to the bank examiner whenever requested. Such loans or investments shall be classified in the book as the bank examiner shall direct. No loan shall be made to any officer, or director of said banking or trust company except by the unanimous approval of the executive board in writing, and said corporation shall have no authority to hire money or to give notes unless by vote of the said board duly recorded. —loan shall not be made to directors.

Section 8. No person shall be eligible to the position of a director or a trustee of said corporation who is not the actual owner of ten shares of the stock. Director must own ten shares of stock.

Section 9. Said corporation, after beginning to receive deposits, shall, at all times, have on hand in lawful money, as a reserve, not less than fifteen per cent of the aggregate amount of its deposits, which are subject to withdrawal on demand, provided, that in lieu of lawful money, two-thirds of said fifteen per cent may consist of balances, payable on demand, due from any national or state bank. Reserve fund.

Section 10. All the property or money held in trust by this corporation, shall constitute a special deposit and the accounts thereof and of said trust department shall be kept separate, and such funds and the investment or loans of them shall be specially appropriated to the security and payment of such deposits, and not be subject to any other liabilities of the corporation; and for the purpose of securing the observance of this provision, said corporation shall have a trust department in which all business pertaining to such trust property shall be kept separate and distinct from its general business. Trust funds shall constitute a special deposit.

Section 11. An administrator, executor, assignee, guardian or trustee, any court of law or equity, including courts of probate and insolvency, officers and treasurers of towns, cities, counties and savings banks of the state of Maine may deposit any moneys, bonds, stocks, evidences of debt or of ownership in property, or any personal property, with said corporation, and any of said courts may direct any person deriving authority from them to so deposit the same. Administrators, executors, etc., may deposit in.

Section 12. Each shareholder of this corporation shall be individually responsible, equally and ratably, and not one for the other, for all contracts, debts and engagements of such corporation, to a sum equal to the amount of the par value of the shares owned by each in addition to the amount invested in said shares. Responsibility of shareholders.

Section 13. Such corporation shall set apart as a guaranty fund not less than ten per cent of its earnings in each and every Guaranty fund.

CHAP. 239

year until such fund, with the accumulated interest thereon, shall amount to one-fourth of the capital stock of said corporation.

Taxation.

Section 14. The shares of said corporation shall be subject to taxation in the same manner and rate as are the shares of national banks.

Shall be subject to examination by bank examiner

Section 15. Said corporation shall be subject to examination by the bank examiner, who shall visit it at least once in every year, and as much oftener as he may deem expedient. At such visits he shall have free access to its vaults, books and papers, and shall thoroughly inspect and examine all the affairs of said corporation, and make such inquiries as may be necessary to ascertain its condition and ability to fulfill all its engagements. If upon examination of said corporation, the examiner is of the opinion that its investments are not in accordance with law, or said corporation is insolvent, or its condition is such as to render its further proceedings hazardous to the public or to those having funds in its custody, or is of the opinion that it has exceeded its powers or failed to comply with any of the rules or restrictions provided by law, he shall have such authority and take such action as is provided for in the case of savings banks by chapter forty-seven of the revised statutes. He shall preserve in a permanent form a full record of his proceedings, including a statement of the condition of said corporation. A copy of such statement shall be published by said corporation immediately after the annual examination of the same in some newspaper published where said corporation is established. If no paper is published in the town where said corporation is established, then it shall be published in a newspaper printed in the nearest city or town. The necessary expenses of the bank examiner while making such examination shall be paid by the corporation.

First meeting, how called.

Section 16. Any two of the corporators named in this act may call the first meeting of the corporation by mailing a written notice signed by both, postage paid, to each of the other corporators, seven days at least before the day of the meeting, naming the time, place and purpose of such meeting, and at such meeting the necessary officers may be chosen, by-laws adopted, and any other corporate business transacted.

Section 17. This act shall take effect when approved.

Approved March 24, 1903.

Chapter 240.

An Act to incorporate the Lubec Trust and Banking Company.

Be it enacted by the Senate and House of Representatives in Legislature assembled, as follows:

Section 1. Llewellyn Powers, Edward M. Lawrence, Frank M. Tucker, Clarence H. Clark, Bion M. Pike, Jacob C. Pike, Chester L. Pike, Elias P. Lawrence, Robert J. Peacock of Lubec, Elias P. Grimes of Jonesboro, and Jasper Wyman of Milbridge, or such of them as may by vote accept the charter, with their associates, successors and assigns, are hereby made a body corporate and politic to be known as the Lubec Trust and Banking Company, and as such shall be possessed of all the powers, privileges and immunities and subject to all the duties and obligations conferred on corporations by law. *Corporators.* *—corporate name.*

Section 2. The corporation hereby created shall be located at Lubec, Washington county, Maine, and shall have offices for the transaction of business in said town. *Location.*

Section 3. The purposes of said corporation and the business which it may perform are: first, to receive on deposit, money, coin, bank notes, evidences of debt, accounts of individuals, companies, corporations, municipalities and states, allowing interest thereon, if agreed, or as the by-laws of said corporation may provide; second, to borrow money, to loan money on credits, or real estate, or personal security, and to negotiate loans and sales for others; third, to own and maintain safe deposit vaults, with boxes, safes and other facilities therein, to be rented to other parties for the safe keeping of moneys, securities, stocks, jewelry, plate, valuable papers and documents, and other property susceptible of being deposited therein, and may receive on deposit for safe keeping, property of any kind entrusted to it for that purpose; fourth, to hold and enjoy all such estate, real, personal and mixed, as may be obtained by the investment of its capital stock or any other moneys and funds that may come into its possession in the course of its business and dealings and the same sell, grant, and dispose of; fifth, to act as agent for issuing, registering and countersigning certificates, bonds, stocks, and all evidences of debt or ownership, in property; sixth, to hold by grant, assignment, transfer, devise or bequest, any real or personal property or trusts duly created, and to execute trusts of every description; seventh, to act as assignee, receiver, executor, and no surety shall be necessary upon the bond of the corporation unless the court or officer approving such bond shall require it; eighth, to do in general all the business that may lawfully be done by trust and banking companies. *Purposes.* *—may own and rent safe deposit vaults.* *—may execute trusts.* *—may act as assignee, etc.*

CHAP. 240

Capital stock.

—shall not commence business till $25,000 has been paid in.

Shall not make loans on security of its own capital stock.

Board of directors.

—number and tenure of.

—executive board.

—vacancies, how filled.

Board of investment.

—shall keep record of loans.

Section 4. The capital stock of said corporation shall not be less than fifty thousand dollars, divided into shares of one hundred dollars each, with the right to increase the said capital stock at any time, by vote of the shareholders, to any amount not exceeding two hundred thousand dollars. Said corporation shall not commence business as a trust or banking company until stock to the amount of at least twenty-five thousand dollars shall have been subscribed and paid in, in cash.

Section 5. Said corporation shall not make any loan or discount on the security of the shares of its own capital stock, nor be the purchaser or holder of any such shares unless necessary to prevent loss upon a debt previously contracted in good faith; and all stock so acquired shall, within six months from the time of its acquisition, be disposed of at public or private sale.

Section 6. All the corporate powers of this corporation except as herein otherwise provided, shall be exercised by a board of directors, a majority of whom shall be residents of this state, whose number and term of office shall be determined by a vote of the shareholders at the first meeting held by the incorporators and at each annual meeting thereafter. The affairs and powers of the corporation may, at the option of the shareholders, expressed in their by-laws, be entrusted to an executive board of five members to be, by vote of the shareholders, elected from the full board of directors, and three of said board shall be a quorum to transact business. The directors of said corporation shall be sworn to the proper discharge of their duties, and they shall hold office until others are elected and qualified in their stead. If a director dies, resigns, or is removed by the election and qualification of another in his place or becomes disqualified for any cause, the remaining directors may appoint a person to fill the vacancy until the next annual meeting of the corporation. The oath of office of such director shall be taken within thirty days of his election, or his office shall be declared vacant. The clerk of such corporation shall, within ten days, notify such directors of their election and within thirty days shall publish the list of all persons who have taken the oath of office as directors.

Section 7. The executive board of directors of said corporation shall constitute the board of investment of said corporation. Said corporation shall keep in a separate book, specially provided for the purpose, a record of all loans and investments of every description, made by said institution substantially in the order of time when such loans or investments are made, which shall show that such loans or investments have been made with the approval of the executive board of said corporation, which shall indicate such particulars respecting such loans or investments as the bank examiner shall direct. This book shall be submitted to the directors and to the bank examiner whenever requested. Such loans or investments shall be classified in the book as the bank examiner shall direct. No loan shall be made to any officer or director of said banking or trust company except by the approval of a majority of the executive board in writing, and said corporation shall have no authority to hire money or to give notes unless by vote of the said board duly recorded. —loan to director, how made.

Section 8. No person shall be eligible to the position of a director of said corporation who is not the actual owner of ten shares of the stock. Director must own ten shares of stock.

Section 9. Said corporation, after beginning to receive deposits, shall, at all times, have on hand in lawful money, as a reserve, not less than fifteen per cent of the aggregate amount of its deposits, which are subject to withdrawal on demand, provided, that in lieu of lawful money, two-thirds of said fifteen per cent may consist of balances, payable on demand, due from any national or state bank. Reserve fund.

Section 10. All the property or money held in trust by this corporation, shall constitute a special deposit and the accounts thereof and of said trust department shall be kept separate, and such funds and the investments or loans of them shall be specially appropriated to the security and payment of such deposits, and not be subject to any other liabilities of the corporation; and for the purpose of securing the observance of this proviso, said corporation shall have a trust department in which all business pertaining to such trust property shall be kept separate and distinct from its general business. Trust funds shall constitute a special deposit.

Section 11. An administrator, executor, assignee, guardian or trustee, any court of law or equity, including courts of probate and insolvency, officers and treasurers of towns, cities, counties and savings banks of the state of Maine may deposit any moneys, bonds, stocks, evidences of debt or of ownership in property, or any personal property, with said corporation, and any of said courts may direct any person deriving authority from them to so deposit the same. Administrators, etc., may deposit in.

Section 12. Each shareholder of this corporation shall be individually responsible, equally and ratably, and not one for the other, for all contracts, debts and engagements of such corporation, to a sum equal to the amount of the par value of the shares owned by each in addition to the amount invested in said shares. Responsibility of shareholders.

Section 13. Such corporation shall set apart as a surplus fund not less than ten per cent of its earnings in each and every year Guaranty fund.

LUBEC TRUST AND BANKING COMPANY.

CHAP. 240

Taxation.

until such fund, with the accumulated interest thereon, shall amount to one-fourth of the capital stock of said corporation.

Section 14. The shares of said corporation shall be subject to taxation under the laws of this state, in the same manner and rate as are or may be the shares of national banks.

Shall be subject to examination by bank examiner.

Section 15. Said corporation shall be subject to examination by the bank examiner, who shall visit it at least once in every year, and as much oftener as he may deem expedient. At such visits he shall have free access to its vaults, books and papers, and shall thoroughly inspect and examine all the affairs of said corporation, and make such inquiries as may be necessary to ascertain its condition and ability to fulfill all its engagements. If upon examination of said corporation, the examiner is of the opinion that its investments are not in accordance with law, or said corporation is insolvent, or its condition is such as to render its further proceedings hazardous to the public or to those having funds in its custody, or is of the opinion that it has exceeded its powers or failed to comply with any of the rules or restrictions provided by law, he shall have such authority and take such action as is provided for in the case of savings banks by chapter forty-seven of the revised statutes, and amendment or additions thereto. He shall preserve in a permanent form a full record of his proceedings, including a statement of the condition of said corporation. A copy of such statement shall be published by said corporation immediately after the annual examination of the same in some newspaper published where said corporation is established. If no paper is published in the town where such corporation is established, then it shall be published in a newspaper printed in the nearest city or town. The necessary expenses of the bank examiner while making such examination shall be paid by the corporation.

First meeting, how called.

Section 16. Any three of the corporators named in this act may call the first meeting of the corporation by mailing a written notice signed by all, postage paid, to each of the other corporators, seven days at least before the day of the meeting, naming the time, place and purpose of such meeting, and at such meeting the necessary officers may be chosen, by-laws adopted, and any other corporate business transacted.

Section 17. This act shall take effect when approved.

Approved March 24, 1908.

Chapter 241.

An Act to supply the town of Lisbon with pure water.

Be it enacted by the Senate and House of Representatives in Legislature assembled, as follows:

Section 1. The town of Lisbon, by its municipal officers or by a commission as hereinafter provided, acting for and in behalf of said town, is authorized and empowered to take water from any river, lake, pond, stream, brook, spring or other water sources, natural or artificial, except the springs owned by the Sylvester Aqueduct Company, within the towns of Lisbon, Bowdoin, or Webster, and from the Little River stream, a part of which is in Topsham, sufficient for domestic purposes in said Lisbon, including a sufficient quantity to extinguish fires, supply hotels, laundries, livery stables, business places and private dwellings, as well as for the sprinkling of lawns and streets, and for manufacturing purposes; and for the purposes aforesaid, to convey any of the waters aforesaid by aqueducts or pipes, sunk to any depth desirable for said purposes, and to lay such aqueducts or pipes under or over any water course, stream, brook, street, railroad, highway or other way, in such manner as not unreasonably to obstruct the same; and to lay down, in and through streets and ways in said town of Lisbon, and take up, replace and repair all such aqueducts, pipes or service pipes, as may be necessary to carry out the purposes of a complete system of water works.

Section 2. The town of Lisbon, by said municipal officers, or by said commission, may make any necessary contract with any person, company or corporation for acquiring the ownership of any aqueduct company or corporation, owning a system of water works, or any part thereof, in said town of Lisbon, whereby the said town of Lisbon, by its municipal officers or said commission, may be entitled to purchase the whole at any one time, or to purchase the same in installments through a period of years.

Section 3. For the purpose of carrying out the provisions of this act, said town of Lisbon, by its municipal officers, or said commission, shall have power and is hereby authorized to take and hold by purchase or otherwise, any lands or real estate, excepting the springs owned by the Sylvester Aqueduct Company, necessary for laying and maintaining pipes, aqueducts, locks, gates, hydrants, dams, standpipes and reservoirs, for taking, conducting, conveying, holding, discharging and distributing, and for roadways to be used as approaches thereto, doing no unnecessary damage.

CHAP. 241

—may enter on lands for surveys and locations.

—shall file and publish notice of location of land taken.

The said town, by its municipal officers, or said commission, may enter upon said lands or real estate so taken and held to make surveys and locations, and shall file in the registry of deeds in the county in which such lands or property lies, plans of such lands and locations, showing the property taken within said county, and within thirty days thereafter shall publish notice of such taking and filing in some newspaper published in said county wherein said land is taken, such publication to be continued three weeks successively, and such filing in the registry of deeds shall be in lieu of any other filing now required by law. Said town of Lisbon, by its municipal officers, or by said commission, may permit the use, for said purposes, of any lands so taken by it, by any person, company or corporation, with which it has made such a contract as is described in section two, whereby the said town of Lisbon may be entitled to acquire the ownership of any aqueduct or system of water works or any part thereof in said town of Lisbon.

County commissioners shall assess damages in case of disagreement.

Section 4. Should the said town of Lisbon, by its municipal officers or said commission, and the owner of such land be unable to agree upon the damages to be paid for such taking, location and holding, the land owner or the town of Lisbon by its municipal officers, or said commission, may within twelve months after the filing of said plans and location, apply to the commissioners of the county wherein said land lies, who shall cause such damages to be assessed in the same manner, and under the same conditions, restrictions, limitations and rights of appeal as are by law prescribed in the case of damages for the laying out of railroads, so far as such law is consistent with the provisions of this act.

May contract for construction.

Section 5. The town of Lisbon, by its municipal officers or said commission, is authorized and empowered to contract with any person or corporation to construct aqueducts, pipes, locks, gates, hydrants, dams, standpipes and reservoirs and any other structures necessary for a system of water works, upon lands taken as hereinbefore prescribed. And in case any such company or corporation is organized to construct any such aqueduct, it is empowered to place all or any part of its capital stock in the name of a trustee, or trustees, and to contract that said trustee, or trustees, shall sell and deliver the same to the said town of Lisbon in installments from year to year, as may be agreed upon.

—may place all or a part of its capital stock in hands of trustee.

Water commissioners.

—election of.

Section 6. For the purpose of carrying into effect the provisions of this act, the town of Lisbon, at a meeting duly called therefor, may as soon as this act takes effect, if it so elects, or at any time thereafter elect by ballot three water commissioners, whose duty it shall be to perform all such acts for the town as are necessary and convenient for the full operation of this act, and such as may be prescribed by town ordinance or lawfully directed by the municipal officers of said town.

The three persons first chosen, as aforesaid shall serve one for one year, one for two years, one for three years from the date of the annual March meeting, following their election. Their terms of service being designated by the municipal officers of the town of Lisbon, and thereafter one commissioner shall be elected by ballot annually at the annual March meeting, to serve for the term of three years. —tenure.

The municipal officers of said town of Lisbon may fill any vacancy occurring by death, resignation or otherwise. Until such water commissioners are elected, the municipal officers of said town of Lisbon shall perform the duties of the water commissioners. —vacancies, how filled.

Section 7. Said municipal officers of said town of Lisbon, or said water commissioners, in case water commissioners are elected as hereinbefore provided, are authorized to fix the rates for water to be paid monthly, quarterly, semi-annually or annually by persons or corporations supplied with the same, or by the state of Maine if so supplied and in the same manner determine the conditions and methods of such supply, and shall have general charge and control of the town's water system. Municipal officers or water commissioners may fix water rates.

Section 8. Said town of Lisbon, through its municipal officers, or said commission, is authorized for the purpose of carrying into effect the provisions of this act, to dig up and excavate any highway in said town, lay pipes therein, and fill the trenches under the directions of the road commissioner of said town or such person as may be acting in that capacity for the time being. May dig up streets, lay pipes, etc., under direction of road commissioner.

Section 9. Whenever said town of Lisbon, or said trustee, company or corporation of which either may obtain control, as provided in section two, either directly or through ownership of stock, shall, under section one, take water from any of the sources therein named, it shall file in the registry of deeds, in the county in which such source of supply is located, a notice of such taking, describing the size, location and depth of the pipe, or pipes, through which said water is to be taken from said source or sources. Shall file location of water supply.

The said town of Lisbon, or said trustee, company or corporation shall pay all damages sustained by any person or corporation in property, by the taking of any water, water sources, water right, or easement, or by anything done by said town, or by said trustee, company or corporation first named in this section, under the authority of this act, which shall be determined and assessed in the same manner as provided in section four, for land taken under the provisions of this act. —town, liable for damages. —damages, how assessed.

LISBON WITH PURE WATER.

CHAP. 241

May issue bonds.

Section 10. For the purpose of raising money to carry out the provisions of this act, the town of Lisbon may issue its bonds, with interest coupons, in behalf of said town, signed by the municipal officers of said town, and the treasurer of said town, when authorized by a vote of said town, to an amount which, taken in connection with the other indebtedness of the town, will not exceed the amount limited by the state of Maine. And such bonds shall be signed by the municipal officers of the town and the treasurer of said town, but the coupons need be signed by the treasurer only, and shall be designated 'The Lisbon Water Loan.'

May put water in one village at a time.

Section 11. Under the provisions of this act the said town of Lisbon, by a majority vote at a meeting called for the purpose or at the regular March meeting, may proceed and put in water works for one village at a time.

Aggregate amount of water rates.

Section 12. The rates for the supply of water under this act shall be fixed so that all expenses for repairs and management shall be paid annually, together with interest, and such amounts as the town may determine to be paid annually on the principal expenditures.

May transfer rights herein granted, if town so votes.

Section 13. In case said town of Lisbon, in a legal town meeting, shall refuse to vote to proceed as a municipality under the rights, powers and authority herein granted, with the work of supplying the town of Lisbon with pure water, or shall fail to take any action in regard to the matter, within a period of one year from the date of the approval of this act, then said town at a legal town meeting called and held for the purpose, or at the annual March meeting, is hereby granted the authority, provided a majority of its legal voters present so vote, to transfer the rights, powers, authority and privileges herein granted to the town of Lisbon, to a corporation which shall be organized for the purpose of supplying said town with pure water.

—terms of transfer, if made.

Said transfer to be made upon such terms, and under such conditions, restrictions and limitations as shall be determined by said town in a legal town meeting and W. E. Plummer, H. E. Coolidge, G. W. Curtis, William Parkin, E. T. Smith, A. E. Jordan, C. A. Julia, H. E. Plummer, J. H. Brewster and their associates are hereby constituted a corporation for such purpose of supplying the town of Lisbon with pure water.

May hold real estate.

Section 14. Said corporation for said purpose may hold real estate not exceeding in value two hundred thousand dollars.

May take water.

Section 15. Said corporation shall have the right to take water from any river, lake, pond, stream, brook, spring or other water sources, natural or artificial, except the springs owned by the Sylvester Aqueduct Company, within said towns of Lisbon, Bowdoin, or Webster, and from the Little River stream, a part

—exception.

of which is in Topsham, and to convey the same upon such conditions and under such restrictions as are prescribed in section one of this act.

Section 16. Said corporation shall have the right to take lands or real estate, necessary for laying and maintaining pipes, aqueducts, locks, gates, hydrants, dams, stand pipes, reservoirs, and water works structures, upon such conditions and under such restrictions as are prescribed in section three of this act. *May take lands.*

Section 17. Said corporation shall have the right to lay its pipes or aqueducts under or over any water course, street, railroad, highway or other way, and in and through the streets and ways in said town of Lisbon, in such manner, and under such restrictions as are prescribed in section one of this act. *May lay pipes.*

Section 18. Said corporation shall have the right to settle damages for the taking and holding of land or real estate, for the location of its pipes, aqueducts, locks, gates, hydrants, dams, stand pipes, reservoirs and waterworks structures, and their maintenance upon such terms and conditions, and in such manner, as is prescribed in section four of this act. *Damages, how settled.*

Section 19. If it shall be necessary for said corporation to lay pipes or aqueducts across or under the tracks or location of any railroad company, and said corporation shall fail to agree with such railroad company, as to place, manner and condition of crossing its railroad, with such pipes or aqueducts, the place, manner and condition of said crossing shall be determined by the railroad commissioners, and all work within the limits of the railroad location shall be done under the supervision and to the satisfaction of the officers and agents of the railroad company, but at the expense of said corporation. *Railroad commissioners shall determine manner of laying pipes across railroad locations.*

Section 20. Said corporation shall be responsible for all damages to persons or property, occasioned by the use and occupancy of said streets and ways, for the laying of its pipes and aqueducts and the construction of its locks, gates, hydrants, dams, stand pipes, reservoirs and water works structures, and shall pay to said town all sums recovered against said town for damages from obstruction caused by said corporation, and for all expenses, including reasonable counsel fees incurred in defending suits for such damages. *Liability for damage caused by occupancy of streets.*

Section 21. Said town of Lisbon at any time after the expiration of three years from the opening for use and service of a system of water works constructed by said corporation, and after a vote in a legal town meeting to that effect has been passed, shall have the right to purchase, and by this act said corporation is required to sell, to said town, said system of water works, including everything appertaining thereto, and if said town and *Town of Lisbon may purchase plant after three years of opening of water service*

CHAP. 241

corporation cannot agree upon the terms, upon such terms and at such price as shall be determined and fixed by the chief justice of the supreme court of the state of Maine after due hearing of the parties interested, and from the decision of said chief justice there shall be no appeal.

May make contracts for supplying water.

Section 22. Said corporation may make contracts with the state of Maine, the town through which the pipes of the system may be laid, or with the corporations and individuals of said town, for supplying water as contemplated in this act, and said corporation may establish and fix from time to time rates for the use of said water, and collect the same and the town of Lisbon in legal town meeting may authorize its municipal officers to contract for a supply of water for the extinguishment of fires, flushing of sewers or other purposes, for a term of years with said corporation.

Capital stock.

Section 23. The capital stock of said corporation shall not exceed two hundred thousand dollars and may be divided into shares of fifty dollars each.

—may issue bonds.

Section 24. Said corporation may issue bonds for the construction of its works, upon such rates and time as it may deem expedient, not exceeding in amount the amount of capital stock subscribed for, and secure the same by mortgage on the franchise and property of said corporation.

Charter null and void after two years.

Section 25. If said corporation shall not be organized and have its works in actual operation within two years from the date of approval of this act, the rights and privileges herein granted shall be null and void.

First meeting, how called.

Section 26. The first meeting of said corporation may be called by a notice, signed by any one of the corporators, served upon each corporator, by giving him the same in hand, or by leaving the same at his last and usual place of abode, seven days before the time of meeting.

Section 27. Except as herein otherwise provided, this act shall take effect when approved.

Approved March 24, 1903.

Chapter 242

An Act authorizing the sale of Norridgewock Falls Bridge.

Be it enacted by the Senate and House of Representatives in Legislature assembled, as follows:

Section 1. The proprietors of the Norridgewock Falls Bridge, owners of a bridge across the Kennebec river between the towns of Anson and Madison, in the county of Somerset, are hereby authorized to sell said bridge with all the privileges, franchises and appurtenances thereunto belonging, to the said towns of Anson and Madison, for such sum as shall be mutually agreed upon by the said proprietors and the said towns; provided that the owners of a majority of the stock present and voting at a meeting of the stockholders legally called for the purpose shall assent thereto; and provided further, that when said sale shall have been made and said bridge with all its rights, powers, franchises and appurtenances transferred and conveyed to the said, all the rights, powers and privileges of the said proprietors of Norridgewock Falls Bridge shall thereafter cease.

Section 2. This act shall take effect when approved.

Sale of Norridgewock Falls bridge, authorized.

Approved March 24, 1903.

Chapter 243.

An Act authorizing the Town of Madison to purchase with the Town of Anson in the County of Somerset the Norridgewock Falls Bridge.

Be it enacted by the Senate and House of Representatives in Legislature assembled, as follows:

Section 1. The town of Madison in the county of Somerset is hereby authorized and empowered to raise money by taxation, or otherwise, to purchase with the said town of Anson the bridge across the Kennebec river between the said towns of Madison and Anson, erected by and belonging to the proprietors of Norridgewock Falls Bridge.

Town of Madison authorized to raise money to purchase bridge.

Section 2. Said town of Madison is hereby authorized and empowered to take and purchase with the said town of Anson said bridge and franchise, with all the rights, powers, privileges and appurtenances thereto belonging, on the payment to said proprietors of said bridge such sum therefor as may be mutually agreed upon by said towns and said proprietors; each town to pay such part of such sum, or purchase price, as they shall mutually agree upon; provided, that after such purchase said bridge shall be declared free for public travel and use.

Authorized to purchase bridge with town of Anson.

Section 3. This act shall take effect when approved.

Approved March 24, 1903.

Chapter 244.

An Act to prevent the throwing of sawdust and other refuse matter into Half Moon Stream or Sandy Stream or any of the tributaries to Unity Pond, in the County of Waldo.

Be it enacted by the Senate and House of Representatives in Legislature assembled, as follows:

Throwing of refuse matter into tributaries of Unity pond, prohibited.
It shall be unlawful for any person to put, or allow the same to be done by any person within his employ, any sawdust, slabs, edgings, or other refuse matter into Half Moon stream or Sandy stream or any of the tributaries to Unity pond, in the county of Waldo, under a penalty of not less than fifty nor more than one hundred dollars and costs for each offense.

Approved March 24, 1903.

Chapter 245.

An Act to amend Chapter one hundred forty-three of the Private and Special Laws of eighteen hundred eighty-seven, entitled "An Act to incorporate the Cumberland Illuminating Company."

Be it enacted by the Senate and House of Representatives in Legislature assembled, as follows:

Authorized to increase capital stock.
Section 1. The Portland Lighting and Power Company, which was incorporated under the name of Cumberland Illuminating Company, is hereby authorized to increase its capital stock from five hundred thousand dollars to one million dollars.

Section 2. This act shall take effect when approved.

Approved March 24, 1903.

Chapter 246.

An Act to authorize Edward J. Mayo and his assigns to maintain a wharf in Sebec Lake.

Be it enacted by the Senate and House of Representatives in Legislature assembled, as follows:

Edward J. Mayo authorized to extend wharf into Sebec lake.
Section 1. Edward J. Mayo and his assigns, are hereby authorized to erect, maintain and control a private wharf from his shore front a few feet westerly from the boat house of said Mayo and W. E. Parsons, extending one hundred and forty feet into the waters of Sebec lake in the town of Foxcroft and county of Piscataquis, substantially as now located.

Section 2. This act shall take effect when approved.

Approved March 24, 1903.

Chapter 247.

An Act to authorize the navigation, by steam, of Eagle Lake and the connecting lakes, in the county of Aroostook.

Be it enacted by the Senate and House of Representatives in Legislature assembled, as follows:

Section 1. Allston Cushing, Parker P. Burleigh, P. N. Burleigh, and P. C. Newbegin, their associates, successors and assigns, are hereby authorized to clear and enlarge, dredge bars, remove stones, and to build dams and locks in the thoroughfares between the Fish river lakes in Aroostook county; and they are hereby authorized to make and construct bridges, and to raise bridges in a proper and suitable manner to convene the public travel across the highways passing between said lakes, or to provide draws in the same, at their own cost and expense, subject to approval of the county commissioners of Aroostook county; and they are hereby vested with the right of employing and navigating every kind of boat or water craft, propelled by steam, for carrying passengers or freight on said lakes and thoroughfares, at such times as they may deem practical, for a term of twenty years. *Navigation of Eagle and connecting lakes and improvement of, authorized.*

Section 2. Any person or corporation who shall use or employ on said lakes or thoroughfares, any boat or other water crafts, for the carriage of freight or passengers, shall pay a toll to said corporators, their associates, successors or assigns, for the use of said improved thoroughfares or locks, said toll to be established by the county commissioners of Aroostook county. All logs or timber not loaded on boats or other water crafts shall have free passage through said thoroughfares. *Toll established.*

Section 3. If the persons named in this act, or their associates or assigns, shall, for the term of two years after the passage of this act, fail to make the improvements in said thoroughfares so that the same can be navigated by steam, then this act shall be void. *Time limited.*

Section 4. This act shall take effect when approved.

Approved March 24, 1903.

Chapter 248.

An Act to incorporate the Maine and New Hampshire Railroad.

Be it enacted by the Senate and House of Representatives in Legislature assembled, as follows:

Corporators.

Section 1. Leslie C. Cornish, Edward E. Hastings, Henry Andrews, A. C. Kennett and George B. James, their associates, successors and assigns, are hereby made and constituted a body corporate and politic by the name of Maine and New Hampshire Railroad, with all the powers, rights and privileges and subject to all the duties, restrictions and obligations, conferred and imposed on railroad corporations by the laws of the state.

—corporate name.

—duties and restrictions.

Powers conferred on corporation.

Section 2. Said corporation is hereby authorized and empowered to survey, locate, construct, operate, maintain, alter and keep in repair a railroad, with one or more sets of rails, commencing at and connecting with the Maine Central Railroad at some convenient point at Steep Falls in the town of Standish in the county of Cumberland, and extending thence across the Saco river through the towns of Limington and Hollis in the county of York, to and connecting with the Boston and Maine Railroad in the town of Hollis at some convenient point on the west side of the Saco river.

May make connections with other railroads.

Section 3. Said corporation is hereby authorized to make connections with any other railroad or railroads on such terms as may be mutually agreed upon, and to lease its road and property either before or after it shall have been completed, on such terms as it may determine, subject in all cases to the approval of the stockholders in each corporation.

May acquire connecting railroads of same gauge.

Section 4. The said corporation is authorized to purchase or lease the property and franchises of any connecting railroad corporation of the same gauge or to purchase and hold the stock and bonds of any such corporation, and all such connecting corporations or association or person claiming rights under the stock, bonds, mortgages or franchises of any such corporations are hereby authorized to make such sales or leases. All such property, franchises, stock and bonds, so acquired, may be pledged or mortgaged to secure the bonds hereinafter authorized.

May issue bonds.

Section 5. Said corporation is authorized to issue its bonds from time to time to such an amount as may be required for the purposes as the directors may deem advisable, and to secure the same by mortgage of its road, franchises and property, or in any other manner.

May maintain bridges across Saco river.

Section 6. Said corporation is empowered to erect and maintain bridges across the Saco river and to build and operate side tracks to any mills on said Saco river in any of the towns named in this act.

Section 7. The capital stock of said corporation shall not exceed fifty thousand shares of one hundred dollars each.

Capital stock.

Section 8. The officers of said corporation may be elected annually, the powers and duties of the officers and the number constituting the board of directors shall be such as may be required or prescribed in the by-laws of the corporation.

Officers.

Section 9. The first meeting of said corporation may be called by any two corporators within named by notice thereof in writing by said two corporators, and given in hand or mailed to each of the other corporators at least ten days before said meeting, and any corporator may act at such meeting by written proxy.

First meeting, how called.

Section 10. This act shall take effect when approved.

Approved March 24, 1903.

Chapter 249.

An Act to fix the beginning of the open season on fishing in Sebago Lake in Cumberland County.

Be it enacted by the Senate and House of Representatives in Legislature assembled, as follows:

Section 1. Open season for fishing in Sebago lake in Cumberland county, shall begin April first of each year instead of when the ice is out, as now provided by law.

Open season in Sebago lake, April 1.

Section 2. This act shall take effect when approved.

Approved March 24, 1903.

Chapter 250.

An Act to authorize the Kennebec Log Driving Company to maintain piers and booms in the Kennebec River above the Augusta Dam.

Be it enacted by the Senate and House of Representatives in Legislature assembled, as follows:

Section 1. The Kennebec Log Driving Company is hereby authorized and empowered to locate and maintain in the Kennebec river between the Augusta dam and Five Mile island boom, so called, piers and booms for the purpose of holding, sorting and rafting logs and other lumber coming down said river.

Kennebec Log Driving Company authorized to erect piers and booms.

Section 2. Said piers and booms shall be so constructed as not to impede the use or navigation of said river.

Shall not obstruct navigation.

Section 3. This act shall take effect when approved.

Approved March 24, 1903.

SMELTS—FISHING IN KENNEBEC COUNTY.

Chapter 251.

An Act to prevent the destruction of Smelts in the waters of towns of Lubec and Trescott in the County of Washington.

Be it enacted by the Senate and House of Representatives in Legislature assembled, as follows:

Purse seines or gill nets, use of, prohibited in waters of Lubec and Trescott.

Section 1. All persons are hereby prohibited from taking smelts in the waters of the towns of Lubec and Trescott in the county of Washington, by the means of purse or drag seines, or gill nets.

Penalty for violation of this act.

Section 2. Whoever shall violate the provisions of this act, shall on conviction of the same before any municipal court or trial justice of said county of Washington, be punished by a fine not less than ten dollars, nor more than twenty dollars, or by imprisonment in the county jail, for a term of not less than ten days, and imprisoned in said jail for same time, for non-payment of fine.

Section 3. This act shall take effect when approved.

Approved March 24, 1903.

Chapter 252.

An Act to amend Section one of Chapter three hundred and twenty-nine of the Private and Special Laws of nineteen hundred and one, relating to ice fishing in certain lakes and ponds in Kennebec County.

Be it enacted by the Senate and House of Representatives in Legislature assembled, as follows:

Section 1, chapter 329, private and special laws of 1901, amended.

Section one of chapter three hundred and twenty-nine of the private and special laws of nineteen hundred and one is hereby amended by inserting after the word "Sidney" in the tenth line of said section the words, 'except Messalonskee lake, or Snow pond, so called,' so that said section as amended, shall read as follows:

Ice fishing permitted and regulated in certain ponds in Kennebec county.

'Section 1. It shall be lawful for citizens of this state to fish through the ice, in the day time, with not more than five set lines to a family, and when under the immediate personal control of the person fishing, and to catch not exceeding twenty pounds or one fish in one day, and convey the same to their own homes for consumption therein, but not otherwise, in the following named lakes and ponds situated wholly or partly in Kennebec county, namely:

All of the ponds and lakes situated wholly or partly in the town of Sidney except Messalonskee lake, or Snow pond, so called, Cochnewagon pond in Monmouth, Dexter, Berry, Ford,

Pickerel and Wayne ponds, situated wholly or partly in the town of Wayne, also all of the lakes or ponds situated in Readfield with the exception of Lake Maranocook, also all of the lakes and ponds situated wholly or partly in the town of Litchfield with the exception of Jimmy pond, so called, also all the lakes and ponds situated on the east side of the Kennebec river in Kennebec county with the exception of Three Mile pond, so called, in China, Windsor and Vassalboro, in which last named pond it shall be lawful to catch pickerel on Saturdays only of each week, also Horseshoe pond in West Gardiner; but nothing in this act shall be construed as permitting ice fishing at any time in Lake Cobbosseecontee, situated partly in Monmouth, Winthrop, Manchester, West Gardiner and Litchfield.'

Approved March 24, 1903.

Chapter 253.

An Act to incorporate the Jonesport Railway Company.

Be it enacted by the Senate and House of Representatives in Legislature assembled, as follows:

Section 1. Edward B. Sawyer, George F. Mansfield, William H. Faulkingham and Fred A. Chandler, their associates, successors and assigns are hereby constituted a corporation under the name of the Jonesport Railway Company, with authority to construct, maintain, equip and operate a line or lines of single or double track railway, to be operated by steam or electricity, with the necessary side tracks, switches and turnouts and other appliances for the passing of cars, carriages or other vehicles upon or along the streets or ways in the towns of Jonesport, Jonesboro, Addison, Columbia Falls, Columbia and Harrington. *Corporators.*

—corporate name.

Section 2. Said company shall have authority to extend its railway over the bridge across the navigable tide waters of Indian river in Jonesport and Addison, also over the bridge across the navigable tide waters of Branch stream, in the town of Addison. *May extend its railway over bridges.*

Section 3. Said company may purchase and hold or lease real estate in said towns for railway purposes, and also for the purpose of car houses, power houses and waiting rooms, to the amount deemed necessary by the directors. And in case the company is unable to agree with the owners of the land required under this section, and necessary for the convenience of the company, the taking of such land shall be done as provided in chapter fifty-one of the revised statutes. *May acquire lands for railway purposes.*

CHAP. 253

May use animal or electric power.

Section 4. Said railroad shall be occupied and used by said company with animal or electric power. The municipal officers of each of said towns shall have power at all times to make all such regulations valid and binding within the limits of their towns only, as to the rate of speed of cars or trains, and the removal of snow and ice from the streets, roads and highways from and alongside of its tracks at the expense of said railway company, as the public convenience and safety may require.

—municipal officers may regulate speed of cars, removal of snow, etc.

Municipal officers shall control laying of tracks.

Section 5. The tracks of said company shall be laid in such parts of the streets, roads or highways as the municipal officers of either of said towns shall direct; and poles may be set at convenient places and distances along the streets, roads or highways over which the tracks of the railroad shall be laid, from which trolley wires may be suspended for the operation of cars by electricity, at such points as the municipal officers may direct.

Manner of construction.

Section 6. Said road shall be constructed in such form and manner and with such rails and appliances that so much of the streets, roads and ways as are occupied thereby shall be safe and convenient for travelers, and said road shall be liable to an action on any case for any loss or damage which any person may sustain by reason of any failure to comply with this provision.

Railroad commissioners shall determine manner of crossing railroad locations.

Section 7. The company may lay its tracks across the tracks of any steam railroad, but the manner and terms of the crossing shall be determined by the railroad commissioners before the crossing is made.

May lease, consolidate with or acquire other lines.

Section 8. Said company is hereby authorized to lease all of its property and franchises on such terms as it may determine; also to consolidate with or to acquire by lease, purchase or otherwise the lines, property or franchises of any other street railway, whose lines as constructed or chartered would form connecting or continuing lines with the lines of this company, and in such case this company shall be entitled to all the privileges and be subject to all the appropriate conditions and limitations contained in the charters thus united with or acquired. Whenever any person or corporation shall be lawfully operating any railroad to any point to which this company's tracks extend, this company may enter upon, connect with and use the same on such terms and in such manner as may be agreed upon between the parties.

Repairs of streets by the company.

Section 9. This company shall keep and maintain in repair, such portion of the streets, town or county roads as shall be occupied by the tracks of this railroad, and shall make all other repairs of said streets or roads which may be rendered necessary by the occupation of the same by said railroad, and if not repaired upon reasonable notice, such repairs may be made by the town in which the necessity exists, at the expense of said company, and said town may recover all expenses in an action of money paid for the use of said railroad company.

Said company shall be liable for any loss or damage which any person may sustain by reason of any carelessness, neglect or misconduct of its agents or servants, or by reason of any defect in so much of said streets or roads as is occupied by said railway, if such defect arises from neglect or misconduct of the company, its servants or agents. *—liable for damages for neglect or misconduct of agents.*

Section 10. If any person shall wilfully and maliciously obstruct said corporation in the use of its roads or tracks, or the passing of the cars of said company thereon, and all who shall aid and abet therein, shall be fined not exceeding two hundred dollars, or imprisoned in the county jail not exceeding sixty days. *Obstruction of tracks. —penalty.*

Section 11. Said company may from time to time, fix such rates of compensation for transporting persons or property, as it may deem expedient, and generally shall have the powers and be subject to all the liabilities of corporations as set forth in the forty-sixth chapter of the revised statutes and amendments thereto. *May fix rates of transportation.*

Section 12. Said corporation may change the location of said railroad by first obtaining the written consent of the municipal officers of said towns, and make additional locations on the aforementioned highways subject to the foregoing provisions and conditions and in no event to cross or go north of said Sturgeon creek. *Change of location, how obtained.*

Section 13. Nothing in this act shall be construed to prevent the proper authorities of said town from entering upon and temporarily taking up the soil in any street, town or county road occupied by said railroad, for any purpose for which they may now lawfully take up the same. *Proper authorities may take up streets.*

Section 14. No other corporation or person shall be permitted to construct or maintain any railroad for similar purposes over the same streets, roads and ways, that may be lawfully occupied by this corporation. *Exclusive franchise.*

Section 15. Said town shall not be liable to pay for any damage to persons or property occasioned by any neglect or fault of said railway during construction. *Damages during construction.*

Section 16. The directors of this company, from time to time, may raise or borrow for the use and purpose, of the company, any sum or sums not exceeding four hundred thousand dollars by the issue of bonds or debentures in sums of not less than one hundred dollars, and not exceeding the amount of capital stock subscribed for on such terms and credit as they may think proper, and may pledge or mortgage all the tools, property, *May borrow money. May issue bonds. —may mortgage property.*

408 LUBEC AND MACHIAS RAILWAY COMPANY.

CHAP. 254

—proviso.

franchises and incomes of the company, or any part thereof for the repayment of money so raised or borrowed and the interest thereon, provided always, that the consent of the majority in value of the stockholders of the company shall be first had and obtained at a regular or special meeting to be called and held for that purpose.

First meeting, how called.

Section 17. The first meeting of the incorporation under this act, may be called by either of the corporators giving notice to the others in writing at least seven days before the time of said meeting, of the time and place of said meeting.

Section 18. This act shall take effect when approved.

Approved March 24, 1903.

Chapter 254.

An Act to establish the Lubec and Machias Railway Company.

Be it enacted by the Senate and House of Representatives in Legislature assembled, as follows:

Corporators.

—corporate name.

—purposes.

—route.

— may cross rivers and tide waters.

Section 1. Bion M. Pike, Jacob C. Pike, Robert J. Peacock, Clarence H. Clark and James H. Gray, their associates and successors, are constituted a corporation under the name of the Lubec and Machias Railway Company, for the purpose of building, constructing, maintaining and operating by electrical, steam, or other power, a railway for passenger and freight transportation, with such single or double tracks, side tracks, switches, turnouts, stations and appurtenances, and with such poles, wires, appliances and appurtenances, as may seem advisable and desirable to said company, from any point in the town of Lubec, through the towns of Trescott, Whiting, Cutler, East Machias and Machiasport, if necessary, to some point in the town of Machias as may seem to said company desirable, together with the right to cross the rivers and tide waters of the East Machias and Machias rivers, within the limits of the said towns of East Machias, Machiasport and Machias upon the bridges of said towns of East Machias, Machiasport and Machias, or upon bridges of said company, erected therefor, and also with the right to lay their said tracks within the limits of said town of Lubec, and within the limits of the towns of Trescott, Whiting, Cutler, East Machias, Machiasport and Machias, as may be assented to in writing by the municipal officers of said towns at any meeting thereof upon petition of said company, and together, also, with the right to cross tide waters and navigable and fresh water streams within the limits of any of said towns mentioned, upon existing bridges or upon bridges of said company, erected therefor, provided, however, that said railway company shall not unnecessarily obstruct navigation, and that the manner and conditions of its so crossing said Machias river, tide waters, navigable waters or fresh water stream or rivers, upon any bridges, and of its erecting and maintaining any bridges of its own, shall first be determined by the municipal officers of the towns within the limits of which said bridges shall be so erected, maintained or used.

—proviso.

Section 2. Said railway shall be of a gauge not to exceed five feet, and the land occupied by said company for its main track line, exclusive of turnouts, switches, side tracks, stations or appurtenances, shall nowhere exceed four rods in width. Said company shall have power, from time to time, to fix such rates of compensation for transportation of passengers or freight as it may think expedient, and in general, shall have and enjoy all the powers and privileges incident to or usually granted to similar corporations.

Gauge of railway shall not exceed five feet.

—may fix rates of transportation.

Section 3. Said company shall further have power to occupy any lands reasonably necessary for its tracks, switches, turnouts, stations, appurtenances or appliances, and to excavate or construct in, through or over such lands to carry out its purposes. It may enter upon such lands to make surveys and locations, and shall file in the registry of deeds in said county of Washington, plans of such locations and land, and within thirty days thereafter, publish notice thereof in some newspaper in said county, such publication to be continued for three weeks successively.

May occupy lands.

—shall file location.

Section 4. For the purpose of determining the damages to be paid for such location, occupation and construction, the land owner or said railway company, may within three years after the filing of plans of location, apply to the commissioners of said county of Washington, and have such damages assessed as is provided by law in cases wherein land is taken for railroads, so far as the same is consistent with the provisions of this charter, and where inconsistent, or at variance with this charter, the charter shall control. If the railway company shall fail to pay such land owner, or to deposit for his use with the clerk of the county commissioners such sum as may be finally awarded as damages, with costs, within ninety days after final judgment, the said location shall be thereby invalid, and the company forfeit all right under the same. If such land owner secures more damages than were tendered by said company, he shall recover costs, otherwise the company shall recover costs. In case the said company shall begin to occupy such land before the rendition of final judgment, the land owner may require said

Damages, how determined.

CHAP. 254

company to file its bond to him with the county commissioners, in such sum and with such sureties as they approve, condition for said payment or deposit. Failure to apply for damages within said three years by the land owner shall be held to be a waiver of the same. No action shall be brought against said railway company for such taking and occupation of land until after such failure to pay or deposit as aforesaid.

Capital stock. Section 5. The capital stock of said company shall be fixed at the first meeting of said company, with the right to increase up to seven hundred thousand dollars, and shall be divided into shares of one hundred dollars each.

May hold real and personal estate. Section 6. Said company for all its said purposes may hold real and personal estate sufficient, necessary and convenient therefor.

—may issue bonds. Section 7. Said company may issue its bonds for the construction of its works, maintenance or operation of the same of any or all kinds, upon such rates and terms as it may deem expedient, not exceeding the sum of twenty-five thousand dollars *—limitation of issue.* per mile, and not exceeding in total amount the amount of capital stock of said company at the time of the issuance of said bonds, and to secure the same by mortgage of any property and franchise of the said company.

Municipal officers may regulate speed, removal of snow, ice, etc. Section 8. The municipal officers of said towns shall have power at all times to make all such regulations as to rates of speed, removal of snow and ice, keeping in repair that portion of street between the rails, and adjacent to them outside, and the mode of use of the tracks of said company, within street limits of any of said towns, as the public safety and convenience may require.

First meeting, how called. Section 9. The first meeting of said company shall be called by a written notice signed by any one corporator above named, stating the time and place of meeting, served upon the other corporators above named, either personally or by leaving the same at the last and usual place of abode of each, at least seven days before the time of such meeting, or said first meeting may be called by a written notice signed by any one corporator, above named, stating the time and place of meeting, published in the Lubec Herald, a newspaper published at Lubec, in said county of Washington, at least fourteen days before the time of such meeting. In either case, the certificate of the signer of the notice shall be sufficient proof as to the service or publication of the notice.

May construct branch lines. Section 10. The said Lubec and Machias Railway is hereby granted the further right to build, equip, maintain and operate a branch of its line, with the same privileges, and subject to the restrictions conferred upon it in the preceding sections, from any point of its line or tracks within the town of Lubec to any point within the limits of said town of Lubec, or to any point within the limits of any of the towns above mentioned in this act.

Approved March 24, 1903.

Chapter 255

An Act to authorize the Norcross Transportation Company to erect buoys in certain waters of the West Branch of the Penobscot River.

Be it enacted by the Senate and House of Representatives in Legislature assembled, as follows:

The Norcross Transportation Company, a corporation organized under the laws of this state, is hereby authorized and empowered to erect and maintain buoys as guides to navigation in the North Twin lake, in North Twin thoroughfare, in Pemadumcook lake and thoroughfare, and Ambigigus lake and thoroughfare. Said buoys shall be erected at the places and in the manner approved by one of the steamboat inspectors. *Norcross Transportation Co., authorized to erect guides to navigation*

Approved March 24, 1903.

Chapter 256.

An Act to authorize John M. Jewell to erect and maintain a dam across the Sebasticook River in the town of Clinton.

Be it enacted by the Senate and House of Representatives in Legislature assembled, as follows:

Section 1. John M. Jewell of Clinton, his heirs and assigns, are hereby authorized to erect and maintain a dam across the Sebasticook river in the town of Clinton upon Hunters rips about one-half mile below the mouth of the Fifteenth Mile stream, and to make, generate and supply electricity for heating, manufacturing, traction and mechanical purposes within the town of Clinton. Said Jewell, his heirs and assigns shall provide suitable sluices or roll ways for the passage of logs or lumber over said dam. *Dam across Sebasticook river, authorized. —location of dam.*

Section 2. Said John M. Jewell, his heirs and assigns, are authorized for the purpose of constructing, maintaining and repairing said dam, to take as for public uses, occupy and inclose any lands adjoining the same which may be necessary therefor, not exceeding in all one acre, and may remove any and all rocks in said river when necessary. *May occupy adjoining lands.*

412 DEER—FISHING IN MAGALLOWAY RIVER.

CHAP. 257
Liable for damages.
—proceedings in case of disagreement.

Section 3. Said Jewell, his heirs and assigns, shall be held liable to pay all damages that shall be sustained by any person or persons by taking and holding any lands for the purpose of constructing and maintaining or repairing said dam, or by flowage; and if any person or persons sustaining damages as aforesaid shall not agree with said Jewell, his heirs and assigns, upon the sum to be paid therefor, either party, upon petition to the county commissioners of Kennebec county within twelve months after said damage is sustained as aforesaid, may have said damage assessed by said commissioners and subsequent proceedings and right of appeal thereon shall be had in the same manner and under the same conditions, restrictions and limitations as are prescribed by law in case of damages by the laying out of highways. Failure to petition for said damage within twelve months after the same is sustained shall be held to be a waiver of the same.

Section 4. This act shall take effect when approved.

Approved March 24, 1903.

Chapter 257.

An Act to provide for the protection of Deer on the island of Mount Desert.

Be it enacted by the Senate and House of Representatives in Legislature assembled, as follows:

Close time for deer, Mt. Desert island.

It shall be unlawful for any person to hunt, chase, pursue, catch or kill any deer at any time in the towns of Eden, Mount Desert and Tremont, in Hancock county, under the penalty provided in the general law for illegal hunting or killing of deer.

Approved March 24, 1903.

Chapter 258.

An Act to prohibit bait fishing, so called, in certain portions of the Magalloway river and its tributaries and in various ponds in Oxford county.

Be it enacted by the Senate and House of Representatives in Legislature assembled, as follows:

Bait fishing prohibited in certain waters in Oxford county.

Section 1. It shall be unlawful to fish for in any way or catch any fish of any kind in the Magalloway river above Aziscohos falls, in Oxford county, or in any of the tributaries of said river north of said Aziscohos falls, or in Sunday pond, Long pond, Parmachenee lake, Wells pond, Otter pond, Rump pond, Billings ponds, Barker's pond, M. T. Abbey pond, Upper and

Lower Black ponds, Cupsuptic pond, or Lincoln pond, all situated in the county of Oxford, except by the ordinary method of casting with artificial flies or fly fishing.

Section 2. Whoever violates any of the provisions of this act shall be subject to the same penalties as provided for illegal fishing in the general law of the state.

Approved March 24, 1903.

Chapter 259.

An Act to amend Section one of Chapter one hundred seventy-two of the Private and Special Laws of eighteen hundred ninety-nine, relating to Lobster Traps in Pigeon Hill bay.

Be it enacted by the Senate and House of Representatives in Legislature assembled, as follows:

Section 1. No person shall between the first day of July and the first day of September in each year, set any lobster trap or device for catching lobsters, in the waters of Pigeon Hill bay, so called, under a penalty of ten dollars for every trap or device so set. *(Use of lobster traps forbidden between July 1 and September 1.)*

All traps or devices so set shall be subject to confiscation by the officer finding same.

Section 2. This act shall take effect when approved.

Approved March 24, 1903.

Chapter 260.

An Act regulating fishing in Quimby pond in the County of Franklin.

Be it enacted by the Senate and House of Representatives in Legislature assembled, as follows:

Section 1. It shall be unlawful for any person to take, catch, kill or have in possession more than six fish in all in Quimby pond, so called, in Rangeley, in the county of Franklin, in any one day, and so much of section five of chapter forty-two of the public laws as is inconsistent with this act is hereby repealed. *(Six fish only, shall be taken in one day from Quimby pond.)*

Section 2. Whoever violates any of the provisions of this act shall be subject to a penalty of not less than ten dollars nor more than thirty dollars and costs for each offense. *(Penalty.)*

Approved March 24, 1903.

Chapter 261.

An Act to regulate fishing in Kennebago Lake and other lakes and ponds and their tributaries, in Franklin County.

Be it enacted by the Senate and House of Representatives in Legislature assembled, as follows:

Fishing in certain waters in Franklin county, regulated.

Section 1. It shall be unlawful to fish for, in any way, or catch any fish of any kind, in Kennebago lake, John's pond, Flat Iron pond, Blanchard pond and in all the streams flowing into the same, situated in the county of Franklin, except in the ordinary method of casting with artificial flies or fly fishing; it shall also be unlawful to fish for, catch or kill in any one day, more than ten fish in any of the following named waters; Kennebago lake, Little Kennebago lake, John's pond, Flat Iron pond, Blanchard pond, the Seven Ponds, so called, and in any of the streams flowing into any of the above named lakes or ponds; also, in the stream flowing out of Little Kennebago lake to the dam at the head of Kennebago Falls, and in the stream flowing out of Kennebago lake, commencing four rods above the Berlin Mills Company's bridge, and continuing down said stream to its junction with the stream flowing from Little Kennebago lake.

So much of section five of chapter forty-two of the public laws of one thousand eight hundred and ninety-nine as is inconsistent with this act, is hereby repealed.

Penalty.

Section 2. Whoever violates any of the provisions of this act shall be subject to a penalty of not less than ten dollars nor more than thirty dollars and costs for each offense.

Approved March 24, 1903.

Chapter 262.

An Act to authorize the Boston Excelsior Company to locate piers and booms in the Sebec River.

Be it enacted by the Senate and House of Representatives in Legislature assembled, as follows:

Erection of piers and booms in Sebec river authorized.

—location of piers and booms.

—shall not impede common use of river.

Section 1. The Boston Excelsior Company, a corporation existing under the laws of the state of Maine, its successors and assigns, are hereby authorized and empowered to locate, erect and maintain in the Sebec river, opposite the land and shore rights of said company in the town of Milo, county of Piscataquis, piers and booms for the purpose of collecting and holding logs and other lumber coming down said Sebec river that belongs to said company. Said piers and booms shall be so located, constructed, maintained and used as not to impede or to unreasonably obstruct the common use of said Sebec river or to unreasonably delay logs and lumber running down said Sebec river, belonging to other parties and not detained for use and manufacture at the mills of said company, its successors or assigns.

Section 2. Said Boston Excelsior Company, its successors and assigns, by aid of such piers and booms, are hereby authorized and empowered to separate and sort out from the logs and other lumber coming down said Sebec river, all logs, and other lumber destined and intended for use and manufacture at the mills of said company, and said company is also hereby authorized and empowered to hold within the piers and booms mentioned in this act and located, erected and maintained as aforesaid, all logs and other lumber coming down said Sebec river which are destined and intended for use and manufacture at the mills of said company, erected upon said Sebec river.

May sort out lumber intended for its own mills.

Section 3. The organization of the Boston Excelsior Company under the general laws of the state of Maine, and the acts, doings and votes of said company at the annual meeting of its stockholders on the last Tuesday of January, in the year nineteen hundred and two, enlarging the purposes of its organization are hereby ratified, confirmed and made valid.

Organization, acts and doings, made valid.

Section 4. Said Boston Excelsior Company is hereby authorized and empowered to issue its bonds for the purposes of its business on such rates and time as it may deem expedient and to secure the payment of the principal and interest on such bonds by appropriate mortgages or deeds of trust on any or part of its property, franchises, rights and privileges now owned or to be hereafter acquired by it.

—may issue bonds.

Section 5. This act shall take effect when approved.

Approved March 24, 1903.

Chapter 263.

An Act to amend the charter of the city of Lewiston and to provide for a street, sewer and permanent improvement department.

Be it enacted by the Senate and House of Representatives in Legislature assembled, as follows:

Section 1. A board, to be known as the Board of Public Works, is hereby established in and for the city of Lewiston, which shall have and exercise all the powers and be charged with all the duties relative to the construction, maintenance, care and control of the streets, highways, bridges, sidewalks, drains and sewers in said city which are now conferred or imposed upon the city council, municipal officers and commissioners of

Board of public works, established.

—powers and duties.

streets, by the charter and ordinances of said city, and the general laws of the state.

Membership of board.

Section 2. The board shall consist of seven members, one of whom shall be the mayor, ex-officio; and one of said board shall be chosen annually, in the month of February, by the municipal officers, and shall be sworn to the faithful discharge of his duties, and shall hold his office for the term of six years unless removed by the city council for cause. In case a member of the board is elected to and accepts the office of mayor, his office as member of this board shall be vacated and such vacancy shall be filled as hereinafter provided.

—tenure.

Election of members.

Section 3. At the first election which shall be held in the month of February, one thousand nine hundred and four, or as soon thereafter as may be, one member shall be elected for one year, one for two years, one for three years, one for four years, one for five years and one for six years, and after the first election one member to be chosen each year for a term of six years, as hereinbefore provided, unless it becomes necessary to fill a vacancy caused by death, resignation, or removal, in which event the election shall be for the unexpired term of the incumbent whose place has been made vacant, and such vacancy may be filled for the remainder of such unexpired term by ballot of the municipal officers.

—proviso.

Members of city council not eligible.

Section 4. No member of the city council shall be eligible for service upon this board, except as hereinbefore provided.

When board shall organize.

Section 5. This board shall, on the third Monday in March, organize by the choice of one of its members as chairman, and shall elect a secretary, whose duty it shall be to keep a record of the proceedings of the board, to notify members of meetings and perform such other duties as the board may elect.

Superintendent of streets and sewers.

Section 6. The board shall also elect a superintendent of streets and sewers who shall have executive charge of work under the direction and control of the board. Said superintendent may contract for necessary labor and materials, subject at all times to the approval of the board, to whom he shall render an account monthly, or oftener if required of all receipts, expenditures and outstanding bills.

Chairman of board shall approve bills.

Section 7. The weekly pay roll and all bills not passed upon by the board shall be approved by the chairman of the board, or in his absence by some member designated by him, before being paid from the city treasury.

Compensation of superintendent of streets and sewers.

Section 8. The compensation of the superintendent of streets and sewers shall be fixed by the board and shall be paid from the appropriation made for the work of the board.

Section 9. The board shall, at the beginning of each financial year, submit to the city council for its guidance in making appropriations, a statement of work proposed to be done in its department, with approximate estimates of cost, and such other information regarding its work as the city council may require, and shall at the close of the year make a full, detailed report to the city council of receipts and expenditures and of work done, and shall have no authority to make expenditures in excess of the amount appropriated for its use by the city council, and no part of said appropriation shall be paid to any member of the board for services as a member of the board.

Board shall submit estimates as basis for appropriations.

Section 10. This act shall take effect on the third Monday of March in the year of our Lord one thousand nine hundred and four, except for the purposes enumerated in section three hereof; and for the purposes enumerated in said section three, this act shall take effect on the first day of February in the year of our Lord one thousand nine hundred and four. All acts and parts of acts inconsistent herewith are hereby repealed.

When this act shall take effect.

Approved March 24, 1903.

Chapter 264.

An Act to extend the charter of the Eastport Street Railway Company.

Be it enacted by the Senate and House of Representatives in Legislature assembled, as follows:

Section 1. The rights, powers and privileges of the Eastport Street Railway Company which were granted by chapter four hundred and sixty-five of the laws of eighteen hundred and ninety-seven, and extended by chapter one hundred and seventeen of the laws of eighteen hundred and ninety-nine, and further extended by chapter two hundred and sixty-eight of the private and special laws of nineteen hundred and one, are hereby further extended for and during the period of two years from the seventeenth day of March nineteen hundred and three, and all the rights, powers and privileges that were granted and acquired by virtue of or under said acts may and shall be exercised in the same manner and for the same purposes as provided in said chapter four hundred and sixty-five.

Charter extended till March 17, 1905.

Section 2. This act shall take effect on the seventeenth day of March, nineteen hundred and three.

Approved March 25, 1903.

Chapter 265.

An Act to Incorporate the Waterville and Winslow Bridge Company.

Be it enacted by the Senate and House of Representatives in Legislature assembled, as follows:

Corporators.

Section 1. Godfrey P. Farley, of Wiscasset, W. D. Patterson, of said Wiscasset, A. M. Card, of Head Tide, F. C. Thayer, W. B. Arnold, C. W. Davis, G. K. Boutelle and G. F. Terry, severally of Waterville, Leonard Atwood, of Farmington, and E. J. Lawrence, of Fairfield, their associates, successors and assigns,

--corporate name.

—location of bridge.

are hereby made a corporation by the name of the Waterville and Winslow Bridge Company, with power to build a bridge across the Kennebec river between Waterville and Winslow below the present highway bridge, with such terminals as will permit the use of said bridge by the Wiscasset, Waterville and Farmington Railroad Company, its successors and assigns, with all the powers and subject to all the liabilities of corporations.

Capital stock.

Section 2. The capital stock of said corporation shall not exceed one hundred thousand dollars to be fixed from time to time by the corporation.

May take and hold lands.

Section 3. Said corporation is hereby authorized to take and hold as for public uses lands necessary for the purposes of its incorporation by filing a plan and description thereof in the office of the clerk of courts for Kennebec county, and all damages therefor shall be estimated and paid in the same manner as when lands are taken for railroads. No meeting houses, dwelling houses, lands used for private or public burying grounds, or land of the Maine Central Railroad Company shall be taken hereunder.

May lease bridge with option of purchase.

Section 4. The said corporation and the Wiscasset, Waterville and Farmington Railroad Company, its successors and assigns, are hereby authorized to contract for the use of said bridge, by lease or otherwise, with an option of purchase, upon such terms as may be mutually agreed and to execute all necessary instruments therefor; provided, however, that such bridge shall not be used until approved as to safety by the railroad commissioners, and it shall at all times be subject to the orders of said commissioners in all matters affecting the public safety in the use thereof in the same manner as bridges owned by railroad corporations.

—proviso.

May issue bonds.

Section 5. Said corporation is hereby authorized for the purposes of this act to issue its bonds in such amounts and on such rates and time as it deems expedient and secure the same by appropriate mortgages upon its property and franchises.

ELLIS RIVER IMPROVEMENT COMPANY. 419

CHAP. 266

Section 6. This first meeting of said corporators shall be called either by notice by him signed given in hand, or mailed, to the others at least seven days before such meeting. Any corporator may act at such meeting by proxy.

First meeting, how called.

Section 7. This act shall take effect only when the directors of the Wiscasset, Waterville and Farmington Railroad Company, its successors and assigns, shall file a written assent hereto in the office of the secretary of state, and to empower the filing of such assent it shall take effect when approved by the governor.

When this act shall take effect.

Approved March 25, 1903.

Chapter 266.

An Act to incorporate the Ellis River Improvement Company.

Be it enacted by the Senate and House of Representatives in Legislature assembled, as follows:

Section 1. Frank P. Thomas, Richmond L. Melcher, Hollis C. Dunton and Y. A. Thurston, their associates and assigns, are hereby incorporated under the name of the Ellis River Improvement Company, with all the powers and privileges of similar corporations.

Corporators.

—corporate name.

Section 2. Said corporation is authorized to build dams, booms, side dams, sheer booms, remove rocks, dredge, make embankments and other improvements on the Ellis river, and any or all of its tributaries, in the county of Oxford, Maine; as may be necessary to facilitate the driving of logs and lumber down the same, and for the purpose of carrying out the intentions herein provided said corporation may purchase and hold real and personal estate sufficient for carrying on the business of the corporation, and may grant and raise by loan or assessment for the same such sums of money and in such manner as the directors may from time to time vote. Said corporation may also make and adopt all necessary regulations and by-laws not repugnant to the constitution and laws of the state and adopt a common seal.

Powers.

May purchase and hold real and personal estate.

—may raise money by loan or assessment.

Section 3. The officers of said company shall be a clerk, treasurer, and a board of three or five directors, to be chosen by ballot, and such other officers as may be deemed necessary, who may be appointed by the directors, unless they shall be chosen at the annual meeting, all of whom shall hold their offices until the next annual meeting, or until others are chosen or appointed in their stead. The clerk, treasurer and directors shall be sworn to the faithful performance of their duties. The treasurer shall give a bond to the acceptance of the directors. The directors

Officers.

—tenure.

—election of president.

ELLIS RIVER IMPROVEMENT COMPANY.

CHAP. 266

shall, at their meeting, elect one of their number who shall be the president of the company. And no person shall be eligible to the office of director except he be a member of the corporation.

Who may become members of the company.

Section 4. Any person, or corporation, or their agents, owning logs or other lumber to be driven on said river or its tributaries, at the date of the annual meeting in each year, may become members of the Ellis River Improvement Company, and shall so continue for two years at least, from that date, and shall have all the privileges and be subject to all the liabilities thereto.

—voting powers of members.

Said members shall be entitled to vote at any meeting of the company as follows; one vote each for any member having or representing fifty thousand feet of logs or lumber in the river to be driven; with an additional vote for each additional fifty thousand feet; the same to be determined by the directors. And it shall be the duty of the directors to keep an itemized account of all expenses incurred for all improvements made under this act;

—directors may assess an equitable tax on owners of logs driven.

and ascertain the number of feet, full scale, and ownership of said logs and other lumber driven annually on said river or any of its tributaries, and assess thereon, to owners if known, or to owners unknown, making such discount for logs or lumber driven less than the whole distance as in their opinion may be right and equitable, a tax sufficient to pay interest on or cost of investment, expenses of maintenance, damages and losses for improvements made and such other expenses as may be voted by the company

—company shall have lien on logs driven.

or the directors. And said company shall have a lien on all logs and other lumber that may be driven for the expense of such improvements as is herein contemplated, which shall not be discharged until all assessments shall be finally paid. The directors shall keep a record of the assessments in the office of the clerk, which shall be open to the inspection of all persons interested.

Collection of assessments, how made.

Section 5. The directors shall give the treasurer a list of all assessments by them made, with a warrant in due form under their hands. And it shall be the duty of the treasurer immediately after he shall receive from the directors a list of assessments in due form, to notify in writing all the owners, where known, of the amount assessed upon their several marks, and all owners of logs and other lumber shall be required to pay or satisfactorily secure the amount of their several assessments on demand, and in default of payment of the whole or any part of any member's assessment, the treasurer shall have power to take possession of a sufficient quantity of the logs or other lumber of any mark owned or assessed to said member, and advertise the same for sale at public auction, by posting up in some conspicuous place in Rumford Falls, in the town of Rumford, also by publication in some newspaper published in Rumford Falls a notice of such sale stating therein the names of the persons taxed, if known, with the mark or marks assessed, with the amount of the assessment unpaid, ten days at least before the day of the sale; and unless such assessments, with all expenses incurred, are previously paid, he may then proceed to sell to the highest bidder a sufficient quantity of such logs or other lumber to pay such assessment, with all proper costs, together with ten per cent interest from the date of said assessment; such sale to be at the office of the company, or where the logs are situated.

Section 6. Any owner or owners of logs and other lumber on said river, or its tributaries, may take and use on his or their logs or other lumber any mark not in use by any other person on said river, or tributaries, and such mark shall be left with the clerk of said company and shall be by him recorded in a book kept for that purpose which shall be at all time open to the inspection of all persons interested; and if any other person or corporation shall use such mark on any logs or other lumber on said river, or its tributaries, after such mark shall be recorded, or any mark so closely resembling such other mark already recorded and in use, as to be calculated to mislead or require more than ordinary care to identify and select such logs or other lumber in the usual course of handling the same, such offender or offenders shall forfeit and pay the sum of two dollars for every log so marked, to be recovered in action of debt in any court of competent jurisdiction, to the use of the person or corporation injured thereby. *Record of marks used shall be made by clerk of company.*

Section 7. For the purpose of carrying out the provisions of this act, when there are no highways conveniently near leading to the river, or its tributaries, the company may have the right to cross on foot and with teams the land of private persons or corporations in some places reasonably convenient, and in such a location calculated to do the least damage to the owner thereof. *May cross private lands for purposes of this act.*

Section 8. Any other person or corporation having logs or lumber to be driven on said river, or its tributaries, and not desirous of becoming a member of this corporation, may use said river, or its tributaries, for driving or floating their said logs or lumber, and reasonable compensation for the use of the same for driving or floating the same shall be determined and secured according to the provisions hereinbefore stated. *Persons not members of corporation, may use river for driving.*

Section 9. In case of any disagreement as to the rights of owners hereunder the same shall forthwith be determined by referees agreed upon by the parties or after notice and hearing appointed by any judge of the supreme judicial court, sitting in term time or vacation, in either of the counties of Oxford or Androscoggin. *Proceedings in case of disagreement as to rights of owners.*

Chap. 267

Annual meeting.

Section 10. The annual meeting of the corporation until otherwise provided, shall be held in the town of Rumford or Andover, in the county of Oxford, and the manner, place and time of calling annual and special meetings of the company and meetings of the directors may be determined by a vote of the company, at any meeting thereof. The first meeting of the company for the purpose of the acceptance of this act and for the organization of the same may be called at Rumford Falls by any associate named herein, on giving at least seven days' notice of the time and place of said meeting.

—first meeting, how called.

Damages for carrying out provisions of this act, how recovered.

Section 11. Any person or corporation sustaining any damage by reason of the carrying out the provisions of this act shall be entitled to recover and receive the same in the manner as is now or may hereafter be provided by law, for recovering damages in the laying out of highways.

Section 12. This act shall take effect when approved.

Approved March 25, 1903.

Chapter 267.

An Act to incorporate the Buckfield Water, Power and Electric Light Company.

Be it enacted by the Senate and House of Representatives in Legislature assembled, as follows:

Corporators.

Section 1. Horace A. Irish, Osborne McConathy, Cyrus M. Irish, Isaac W. Shaw, Ralph H. Morrill and Frederick R. Dyer, or such of them as shall vote to accept this charter, with their associates, successors and assigns are hereby made a body corporate by the name of the Buckfield Water, Power and Electric Light Company, and as such shall possess all the powers and be subject to all the duties and obligations conferred and imposed on corporations by law, except as otherwise provided herein.

—corporate name.

Location.

Section 2. The place of business of said corporation shall be at Buckfield, in the county of Oxford and state of Maine and its business shall be confined to the town of Buckfield.

Business of the company.

Section 3. The business to be carried on by said company shall be to furnish water for the extinguishment of fires and for domestic, sanitary and municipal uses, to said village of Buckfield and vicinity and the inhabitants thereof, to create, sell and lease water power for manufacturing purposes, to furnish electric lights for lighting streets of said village and to dispose of electric light to individuals and corporations.

May take water in Buckfield,

Section 4. Said company is hereby authorized, for the purposes aforesaid, to take, detain and use the water of North pond in Sumner and Buckfield, Swan pond in Hartford, or any other suitable source of water supply in the towns of Buckfield, Hartford and Sumner in said Oxford county and to erect and maintain reservoirs and dams, and lay down and maintain pipes and aqueducts necessary for the proper accumulating, conducting, discharging, distributing and disposing of water and forming proper reservoirs thereof; and said company may take and hold by purchase or otherwise any lands or real estate necessary therefor, and may excavate through any lands, when necessary for the purposes of this incorporation. Provided however that should this company take water from said North pond it shall, in consideration thereof, build and maintain a good and sufficient dam of a height sufficient to hold the reasonable flowage of said pond.

Section 5. Said company is authorized to erect and maintain a dam or dams across North Pond brook, so called, at a point or points between North pond and the west branch of Nezinscot river in said Buckfield.

Section 6. Said company is further authorized to cut and maintain canals from said dam or dams, and for the purpose of constructing a dam or dams and canals, may take, occupy and inclose any lands adjoining the same which may be necessary for building or repairing the same and other necessary purposes on each side thereof, and may blow up and remove any rocks in said stream and dig up any land in said stream when necessary.

Section 7. Said company is hereby authorized to lay down pipes, and to set poles and extend wires in and through the streets and ways in said town of Buckfield, and to take up, replace and repair all such pipes, aqueducts, poles and fixtures as may be necessary for the purposes of this incorporation, under such reasonable restrictions as may be imposed by the selectmen of said town, and all provisions of this act relating to the construction, repairs, maintaining or operating works for furnishing electric light shall be subject to the provisions of chapter three hundred seventy-eight of the public laws of eighteen hundred and eighty-five.

Section 8. Said company shall have power to cross any water course, public or private sewer, or to change the direction thereof for the purposes of this incorporation, but in such manner as not to obstruct or impair the use thereof, and said company shall be liable for all injury thereby. Whenever said company shall lay down any fixture in any highway, way or street or make any alteration or repairs upon its works in any highway, way or street it shall cause the same to be done with as little obstruction to public travel as may be practicable, and shall at its own expense, without unnecessary delay, cause the earth then removed by it, to be replaced in proper condition.

May cross Nezinscot river with pipes.

Section 9. Said company is authorized to lay and maintain its pipes in, under and over the Nezinscot river and to build and maintain all necessary structures therefor.

Liability for damages.

Section 10. Said company shall be held liable to pay all damages that may be sustained by any persons by taking any lands, water, rights of way or other property or by excavating through any land for the purpose of surveying for locating, laying or building dams, canals, reservoirs, pipes, hydrants or other structures, by taking and holding any lands necessary for flowage, by setting posts and extending wires, and for any other injuries resulting from said acts, and if any person sustaining damage as aforesaid, and said corporation cannot mutually agree upon the sum to be paid therefor, such person may cause his damages to be ascertained in the same manner and under the same conditions, restrictions and limitations as are by law prescribed in the case of damage by laying out of railroads.

May contract to supply water and electric light.

Section 11. Said company is authorized to make contracts with the said town of Buckfield, with any village corporation that now, or hereafter may exist in said town, and with other corporations and individuals for the purpose of supplying water or electric light as contemplated by this act; and said town, by their selectmen, and said village corporation, by their assessors, are hereby authorized to enter into contracts with the said company for the supply of water and electric lights, and for such exemption from public burden as said town and said corporation and said company agree upon, which when made, shall be legal and binding upon all parties thereto. Said company is authorized to sell or lease any water not used by it on the dams aforesaid.

Capital stock.

Section 12. The capital stock of said company shall not exceed one hundred thousand dollars, divided into shares of fifty dollars each; said company may hold real and personal estate necessary and convenient for its purposes aforesaid.

May issue bonds.

Section 13. For the purpose of carrying out the foregoing provisions or either of them, said company is authorized to issue its bonds in such form and amount and on such time and rates, not exceeding the amount of its capital stock subscribed, as it may deem expedient, and secure the same by mortgage of its property and franchises.

First meeting, how called.

Section 14. The first meeting of said company shall be called at Buckfield on a notice in writing signed by any two of the corporators named in section one, such notice shall be served in hand, or by mail postage prepaid at least seven days before the day appointed therefor. At such meeting any corporator may be represented and act by proxy.

Section 15. This act shall take effect when approved.

Approved March 25, 1903.

Chapter 268.

An Act to incorporate the South Branch Moose River Dam Company.

Be it enacted by the Senate and House of Representatives in Legislature assembled, as follows:

Section 1. Chauncey S. Skinner, Dean C. French and Carl D. French, their associates and assigns, are hereby incorporated under the name of the South Branch Moose River Dam Company, with all the powers and privileges of similar corporations. Corporators. —corporate name.

Section 2. Said company is hereby authorized to erect, purchase and maintain dams, side dams and piers on the South Branch of Moose river and its tributaries in Township one, Range seven, west of Bingham's Kennebec Purchase and in Lowelltown, so called, in the county of Franklin, and to widen, deepen and otherwise improve the same for the purpose of raising a head of water and of facilitating the driving of logs and lumber upon the same. Powers.

Section 3. Said company for the above purposes may take all necessary land and materials for building said dams and piers and making improvements, and may flow contiguous lands so far as necessary to raise suitable heads of water; and if the parties cannot agree upon the damages, the corporation shall pay the proprietors for the land and materials so taken; such damages shall be ascertained and determined by the county commissioners of the county of Franklin, in the same manner and under the same conditions and limitations as provided by law in the case of damage by laying out of highways; and for the damage occasioned by flowing land said company shall not be liable to an action at common law, but the person injured may have a remedy by complaint for flowage, in which case the same proceedings shall be had as when a complaint is made under the statutes of this state for flowing lands occasioned by raising a head of water for the working of mills. May take land and materials. —may flow lands. —proceedings for damages when parties cannot agree.

Section 4. Said company may demand and receive tolls for the passage of all logs and lumber over their dams and improvements as follows: For all logs and lumber landed in said South Branch above the upper dam, so called, a sum not exceeding Tolls for passage of logs.

CHAP. 268

—scale at which tolls shall be reckoned.

—lien on logs driven.

fifty-five cents per thousand feet; for all logs and lumber landed on said stream between said upper dam and the next lower dam a sum not exceeding fifty cents per thousand feet; for all logs and lumber landed on said stream between said last mentioned dam and the next lower dam a sum not exceeding forty-five cents per thousand feet; and for all logs and lumber landed in said stream between said last mentioned dam and the lowest dam a sum not exceeding forty cents per thousand feet. All the above tolls to be reckoned at the survey or scale adopted by the Kennebec Log Driving Company. Said South Branch Moose River Dam Company shall have a lien upon all logs and lumber which may pass over any of its dams and improvements until the full amount of tolls is paid; but the logs of each particular mark shall only be holden to pay the toll on such mark; and if said toll is not paid within thirty days after said logs or lumber, or the major part thereof, shall have arrived within the limits of the Kennebec Log Driving Company, said South Branch Moose River Dam Company may seize, hold and sell at public auction such part of said logs as shall be necessary to pay such tolls, with all incidental costs and charges thereon, after ten days' notice in writing of the time and place of said sale given to the owner of such logs or lumber.

Account of cost and toll receipts to be open for inspection.

Section 5. An account of the cost of said improvements shall be kept by the treasurer of said South Branch Moose River Dam Company, and also of its receipts for tolls, which shall be open to inspection at all reasonable times to any person interested in the same.

Reduction of tolls, when to take effect.

Section 6. When said corporation shall have received from tolls its outlay on dams, improvements and repairs made up to that time, with six per cent interest thereon, then the tolls shall be reduced to a sum sufficient to keep the works in repair; the treasurer of the Kennebec Log Driving Company, for the time being, is appointed to audit the accounts and determine the cost of said dams, improvements and repairs.

Membership of company.

Section 7. Any or all owners of lands from which logs or lumber are cut which pass through or over said dams or improvements shall have a right to take an interest in said company.

Voting rights of members.

Section 8. The amount invested shall at all meetings be represented by a fixed convenient number of votes which shall be cast by the owners of the lands from which logs or lumber are cut which pass through or over its dams or improvements; and each owner shall have the right to vote in proportion to his interest in said lands by paying his proportion of the cost of building and maintaining said dams and improvements.

Referees to determine voting rights

Section 9. In case of any disagreement as to the rights of owners hereunder, the same shall be forthwith determined by referees agreed upon by the parties, or by the county commissioners of Franklin county, if the parties cannot agree.

When in dispute.

Section 10. This act shall take effect when approved.

Approved March 25, 1903.

Chapter 269.

An Act to Incorporate the Ferguson Stream Improvement Company.

Be it enacted by the Senate and House of Representatives in Legislature assembled, as follows:

Section 1. Micajah Hudson, Samuel M. Gile and Henry Hudson, their associates and successors be and are hereby created a body politic and corporate under the name and corporate style of the Ferguson Stream Improvement Company; and by that name may sue and be sued, prosecute and defend to final judgment and execution both in law and equity and may make and adopt all regulations and laws not repugnant to the constitution and laws of the state of Maine; adopt a common seal and may purchase and hold personal and real estate sufficient for carrying on the business of said Ferguson Stream Improvement Company; and may grant and raise money by loan or assessment for the same. Said company may erect and maintain a dam or dams with side booms on said Ferguson stream in the towns of Wellington and Cambridge at such points or places as may be desirable for the purpose of raising a head of water to facilitate the driving of logs and lumber down said Ferguson stream into Main stream, so called, and to raise a head of water to be held for manufacturing purposes when not required in the driving of logs or lumber. Said company for the purpose aforesaid may remove rocks and other obstructions in said Ferguson stream and may take land and material for building said dams and side dams and making said improvements by making compensation to the owners thereof. Said company shall have all the powers and privileges and be subject to all the liabilities incident to corporations of a similar nature.

Corporators.

—corporate name.

—powers.

—may erect dams on Ferguson stream.

—may remove obstructions.

—powers, privileges and restrictions.

Section 2. The officers of said company shall be a clerk, treasurer and a board of three directors to be chosen by ballot and such other officers as may be deemed necessary who may be appointed by said directors all of whom shall hold their offices until the next annual meeting or until others are chosen or appointed in their stead. The clerk, treasurer and directors shall be sworn to faithfully perform all of their duties. The

Officers.

—tenure.

428   UNION BOOM COMPANY.

CHAP. 270
—president.

treasurer shall give bond to the acceptance of said directors. The directors shall at their first meeting elect one of their number who shall be the president of said company. No person shall be eligible to the office of director unless he is a member of said corporation.

Tolls, rates of.

Section 3. The said corporation may demand and receive a toll upon all logs and lumber which shall pass through and over said dams and improvements of said company of twenty-five cents for each thousand, board measure, woods scale, or twelve and one-half cents per cord and said corporation shall have a lien on all logs and lumber which may pass over and through any of its said dams and improvements for the payment of said tolls, but the logs of each particular mark shall be holden only for the tolls of such mark, and if such toll is not paid within twenty days after such logs or a major part of them shall arrive at the place of sale or manufacture, said corporation may seize such logs or lumber and sell at public auction so many thereof as may be necessary to pay such toll, costs and charges, notice of the time and place of such sale being first given ten days prior to said sale in some newspaper printed in Skowhegan in the county of Somerset and in some newspaper printed in the county of Piscataquis.

Approved March 25, 1903.

Chapter 270.

An Act to amend the charter of the Union Boom Company.

Be it enacted by the Senate and House of Representatives in Legislature assembled, as follows:

Section 4, chapter 286, private and special laws of 1901, amended.

Section 1. Section four of chapter two hundred eighty-six of the private and special laws of nineteen hundred one is hereby amended by striking out in the fourth line of said section the words "Rumford Falls in the town of Rumford, county of Oxford" and substituting in place thereof the words 'Portland in the county of Cumberland,' so that said section as amended, shall read as follows:

Capital stock.
—location of office.
—first meeting, how called.

'Section 4. The capital stock of said corporation shall be ten thousand dollars, and the stock shall be divided into shares of one hundred dollars each. The office of said corporation shall be at Portland in the county of Cumberland and state of Maine. The first meeting of said corporation shall be called by a written notice thereof signed by any one of the incorporators named therein, by giving the same to them either in the hand or by mailing such notice properly addressed, postage prepaid, seven days at least before the time of said meeting.'

Section 2. This act shall take effect when approved.

Approved March 25, 1903.

Chapter 271.

An Act to extend the charter of Sebasticook Manufacturing and Power Company.

Be it enacted by the Senate and House of Representatives in Legislature assembled, as follows:

Section 1. That the rights, powers and privileges of the Sebasticook Manufacturing and Power Company, which were granted by chapter eighty-six of the private and special laws of one thousand eight hundred and ninety-nine and extended for the term of two years by chapter four hundred seventeen of the private and special laws of one thousand nine hundred and one, are hereby further extended for and during a term of two years from the date of the approval of this act, with the exception of the right to manufacture, generate, sell, distribute and supply electricity for lighting purposes in the town of Clinton, and with the further exception that said company shall have no right to flow any mill privilege upon which a dam is now built without the consent of the owners thereof. The persons named in said act, their associates and successors shall have all the rights, powers and privileges that were granted them thereby to be exercised in the same manner and for the same purposes as specified therein, except as modified by this act.

Charter extended.

—exception.

Section 2. Said company is also authorized to engage in manufacturing with all the rights and powers and subject to all the restrictions and liabilities incident to manufacturing corporations under the laws of this state.

Section 3. This act shall take effect when approved.

Approved March 25, 1903.

Chapter 272.

An Act to amend the charter of the Baskahegan Dam Company.

Be it enacted by the Senate and House of Representatives in Legislature assembled, as follows:

Section 1, chapter 313, acts and resolves of 1864, amended.

Section one of chapter three hundred thirteen of the acts and resolves of eighteen hundred sixty-four, entitled "An Act to incorporate the Baskahegan Dam Company," is hereby amended so that it shall read as follows:

Corporators.

'Section 1. John Pomroy of Bancroft, James S. Hamilton of Orono, Joseph D. Smith of Veazie and Davis R. Stockwell, Joab W. Palmer, Benjamin Johnson, Walter Brown, Isaiah Stetson, George Stetson, William H. McCrillis and Thomas W. Baldwin of Bangor, their associates, successors and assigns, are hereby created a body corporate under the name of the Baskahegan Dam Company with all the general powers, rights and duties of other corporations under the laws of this state, for the purpose of erecting and maintaining a dam at Baskahegan falls near the mouth of Baskahegan stream in Bancroft in the county of Aroostook, and another dam at the outlet of Baskahegan lake in township number nine, range three, in the county of Washington, both for the purpose of facilitating the driving of logs and lumber out of said Baskahegan stream, and when necessary all the water stored in said dams shall be used for the purpose of driving logs, and said company shall have the rights to store water in both of said dams for the purpose of manufacturing, generating electricity, or for any other power and may use and make contracts for the sale of said stored water with any corporations or persons for the purposes aforesaid, and receive payment therefor, said company may also make improvements in the navigation of said Baskahegan stream.'

—corporate name.

—purposes.

Section 2. This act shall take effect when approved.

Approved March 25, 1903.

Chapter 273.

An Act authorizing the town of Fort Fairfield to make a loan.

Be it enacted by the Senate and House of Representatives in Legislature assembled, as follows:

Section 1. The inhabitants of the town of Fort Fairfield are hereby authorized to procure by loan on the faith and credit of the town, a sum of money not exceeding thirty thousand dollars, for the purpose of erecting, equipping and furnishing a school building; and they may issue bonds therefor on such terms and conditions as the town shall vote.

Section 2. This act shall take effect when approved.

Approved March 25, 1903.

Chapter 274.

An Act to amend and extend the charter of the Waldo Trust Company.

Be it enacted by the Senate and House of Representatives in Legislature assembled, as follows:

Section 1. Section two of chapter five hundred of the private and special laws of nineteen hundred and one is hereby amended by striking therefrom the words "either at Frankfort or Winterport" and inserting instead thereof the word 'Belfast,' so that said section as amended, shall read as follows:

'Section 2. The corporation hereby created shall be located at Belfast, Waldo county, Maine.'

Section 2. The time within which the Waldo Trust Company must organize and commence business under its charter as hereby amended is hereby extended until two years from the date of the approval of this act.

Section 3. This act shall take effect when approved.

Approved March 25, 1903.

Chapter 275.

An Act to extend and amend the charter of the Bangor Loan and Trust Company.

Be it enacted by the Senate and House of Representatives in Legislature assembled, as follows:

Charter extended.
Section 1. The rights, powers and privileges of the Bangor Loan and Trust Company which were granted in and by chapter four hundred and four of the private and special laws for the year nineteen hundred and one, are hereby extended for two years from the approval of this act.

Name changed.
Section 2. The name of said company is hereby changed from the Bangor Loan and Trust Company to the Bangor Trust Company.

Section 3 of chapter 404, private and special laws 1901, amended.
Section 3. Section three of said chapter four hundred and four of the private and special laws for the year nineteen hundred and one is hereby amended by striking out all of said section after the word "seventh" in the twenty-first line thereof, to and including the word "eighth" in the twenty sixth line thereof, so that said section as amended, shall read as follows:

Purposes.
'Section 3. The purposes of said corporation and the business which it may perform, are: first, to receive on deposit, money, coin, bank notes, evidences of debt, accounts of individuals, companies, corporations, municipalities and states, allowing interest thereon, if agreed, or as the by-laws of said corporation may provide; second, to borrow money, to loan money on credits, or real estate, or personal security, and to negotiate loans and sales for others; third, to own and maintain safe deposit vaults, with boxes, safes and other facilities therein, to be rented to other parties for the safe keeping of moneys, securities, stocks, jewelry, plate, valuable papers and documents, and other property susceptible of being deposited therein and may receive on deposit for safe keeping property of any kind entrusted to it for that purpose; fourth, to act as agent for issuing, registering and countersigning certificates, bonds, stocks, and all evidences of debt or ownership in property; fifth, to hold by grant, assignment, transfer, devise or bequest, any real or personal property or trust duly created, and to execute trusts of every description; sixth, to act as assignee, receiver, executor, and no surety shall be necessary on the bond of the corporation unless the court or officer approving such bond shall require it; seventh, to do in general all the business that may lawfully be done by trust and banking companies.'

Section 4. This act shall take effect when approved.

Approved March 25, 1903.

Chapter 276.

An Act amendatory to Chapter three hundred and sixty-nine of the Private and Special Laws of eighteen hundred and eighty-nine, entitled "An Act regulating the appointment of the members of the police force of the city of Bangor."

Be it enacted by the Senate and House of Representatives in Legislature assembled, as follows:

Chapter three hundred and sixty-nine of the private and special laws of eighteen hundred and eighty-nine is hereby amended by adding thereto the following sections:

'Section 10. Any officer of the police force who shall receive injuries while in the discharge of his duties whereby death results within six months from the time of receiving said injuries, leaving a widow or minor children under the age of sixteen years, such widow shall be placed upon a pension roll of said city, from the date of said officer's death, at the rate of twelve dollars per month during her widowhood, and shall also be paid two dollars per month for each child of such officer under sixteen years of age; and in case of death or remarriage of such widow leaving a child or children of such officer under the age of sixteen years, such pension shall be paid to such child or children until the age of sixteen.'

'Section 11. The city is hereby authorized to place upon said list the widow of Patrick Henry Jordan and her children, who was shot while in the discharge of his duties, in accordance with the above section ten.'

'Section 12. The city treasurer is hereby authorized to pay said pension monthly upon proof of death of such officer.'

Section 13. This act shall take effect when approved.

Approved March 25, 1903.

Chapter 277.

An Act to amend "An Act to establish a Municipal Court for the town of Brunswick."

Be it enacted by the Senate and House of Representatives in Legislature assembled, as follows:

Chapter 195, public laws of 1850, as amended by chapter 565, special laws of 1874, further amended.

Chapter one hundred and ninety-five of the public laws of eighteen hundred and fifty, as amended by chapter five hundred and sixty-five of the private and specal laws of eighteen hundred and seventy-four, is hereby further amended so as to read as follows:

Brunswick municipal court established.

'Section 1. A municipal court is hereby established in and for the town of Brunswick, in the county of Cumberland, which shall be called the municipal court for the town of Brunswick; and said court shall consist of one judge, a citizen of said town, who shall be appointed by the governor, with the consent of the council, and who shall be duly sworn.

Concurrent jurisdiction.

'Section 2. The judge of said court shall, except when interested, exercise concurrent jurisdiction with trial justices over all such matters and things, civil and criminal, within said county of Cumberland, as are by law within the jurisdiction of trial justices; also concurrent jurisdiction with trial justices in cases of forcible entry and detainer in said county, and exclusive jurisdiction in all civil actions, if otherwise cognizable by a trial justice, in which both parties interested, or either of the principal parties and a person summoned as trustee, are inhabitants of or residents in said town; also exclusive jurisdiction in all cases of forcible entry and detainer in said town; also concurrent original jurisdiction with the superior court for the county of Cumberland, in all civil actions at law where the damage does not exceed one hundred dollars, in which both parties interested or either of the principal parties and a person summoned as trustee are inhabitants of or residents in the county of Cumberland. Actions may be referred, and judgment on the referee's report may be rendered, in the same manner and with the same effect as in said superior court.

—exclusive jurisdiction.

Proceedings for removal of action to superior court.

'Section 3. If any defendant in any action in said court, where the amount claimed in the writ exceeds twenty dollars, or his agent or attorney, shall, on the return day of the writ, file in said court his pleadings, and a motion asking that said action be removed to the superior court in the county of Cumberland, and deposit with the judge the sum of two dollars and ten cents for copies and entry fee in said superior court, to be taxed in his costs if he prevails, the said action shall be removed into the said superior court. The judge shall forthwith cause certified copies of the writ, officer's return, and defendant's motion and pleadings, to be filed in the clerk's office of said superior court within ten days, and shall pay the entry fee thereof, and said action shall be entered on the docket of the following term of said superior court, unless said court shall then be in session, when it shall be entered forthwith, and shall be in order for trial at that term. If no such motion and pleadings are filed, the said municipal court shall proceed and determine said action, subject to the right of appeal in either party as now provided by law. The pleadings in such cases shall be the same as in the said superior court.

'Section 4. The said court may take cognizance of all larcenies at common law or by statute, when the property alleged to have been stolen shall not exceed in value thirty dollars, of offenses described in sections one and four of chapter one hundred and twenty-six of the revised statutes, when the value of the property shall not exceed thirty dollars, and of offenses described in section four of chapter one hundred and thirty-two of the revised statutes, when they are not of a high and aggravated nature; and on conviction may punish by fine not exceeding twenty dollars, or by imprisonment in the county jail not exceeding ninety days; and shall have exclusive jurisdiction of all offenses against the by-laws of the town of Brunswick; and in prosecution on said by-laws, they need not be recited in complaint, nor the allegations therein be more particular than in prosecutions on a public statute. *Jurisdiction in larceny, etc*

'Section 5. Any person aggrieved by any sentence or judgment awarded by said judge, may appeal therefrom in the same manner as if sentence or judgment were awarded by a trial justice, and under such recognizance as said court may require. *Appeals, how taken.*

'Section 6. The said judge shall enter, or cause to be entered on the docket of said court, all civil and criminal actions, with full minutes of the proceedings in and disposition of the same, which docket shall be at all times open to inspection; and copies of the records of said court, duly certified by the judge or recorder thereof, shall be legal evidence in all courts. All writs and processes returnable before said court, wherein the debt or damages demanded exceed twenty dollars, shall be served fourteen days at least before the return day thereof. *Docket.* *—service of writs and processes.*

'Section 7. The court shall be held weekly, on Monday, at nine of the clock in the forenoon, at such place as shall be provided by the town of Brunswick, and all civil processes shall be made returnable accordingly; and the judge may adjourn from day to day if necessary. The said court shall be considered in constant session for the trial of criminal actions. *Time and place of holding court.*

CHAP. 277

Recorder, appointment of.

—tenure.

—powers of recorder.

'Section 8. The governor, by and with the consent of the council, shall appoint a recorder of said court, who shall reside in said Brunswick, and hold his office for the term of four years. In case of the absence of the judge from the court room, or when said judge shall be an interested party, or when the office of judge shall be vacant, the recorder shall have and exercise all the powers of the judge, including the authority to sign original writs and processes. When the office of judge shall be vacant, the recorder shall be entitled to the fees; in all other cases he shall be paid by the judge.

Fees.

'Section 9. The judge of said court shall tax, in all criminal proceedings, the same fees and at the same rates, as are allowed by law in the Portland municipal court. In civil actions the fees shall be the same as in actions before trial justices, except that the judge may demand four cents for every blank writ signed by him, and thirty cents for entry of each civil action. In actions wherein the damages demanded exceed twenty dollars, the fee shall be two dollars for the trial of an issue. All fees, civil and criminal, shall inure to the county of Cumberland, and shall be paid over to the treasurer of said county quarterly, on the last days of March, June, September and December.

Costs, how taxed.

'Section 10. In all actions in which the amount recovered shall not exceed twenty dollars, the same costs shall be taxed and allowed as in actions before trial justices, except that the plaintiff, if he prevails, shall have two dollars for his writ. In all actions in which the amount recovered shall exceed twenty dollars, the costs and fees of parties and attorneys shall be the same as in the superior court, except that the defendant, if he prevails, shall be allowed two dollars for his pleadings.

Salary of judge.

'Section 11. The judge of said court shall receive an annual salary of six hundred dollars in full for all services, payable quarterly on the last days of March, June, September and December, from the treasury of Cumberland county.

Court room, how provided.

'Section 12. The town of Brunswick shall provide and furnish a suitable court room, for the purpose of holding said court therein, and shall heat and light the same. All other expenses of said court, including blank books of record, docket and blanks necessary for the use of said court, shall be paid from the treasury of the county of Cumberland.

'Section 13. This act shall take effect April first, nineteen hundred and three.'

Approved March 25, 1903.

Chapter 278.

An Act to amend the charter of the "Moose River Log Driving Company."

Be it enacted by the Senate and House of Representatives in Legislature assembled, as follows:

Section 1. Section one of chapter one hundred seventy-nine of private and special laws of eighteen hundred seventy-nine, is hereby amended as follows: By striking out, in the thirteenth and fourteenth lines, the words "Moose River bridge," and inserting in their place the words 'head of Attian pond and of Wood pond,' so that said section as amended, shall read as follows: *Section 1, chapter 179, private laws of 1879, amended.*

'Section 1. That Elias Milliken, Joseph S. Bradstreet, Franklin Smith, C. B. Foster and Abner Coburn, their associates and successors be and they are hereby made a body politic and corporate by the name and style of Moose River Log Driving Company, and by that name may sue and be sued, prosecute and defend to final judgment and execution, both in law and in equity, and may make and adopt any and all regulations and by-laws not repugnant to the constitution and laws of the state, and may adopt a common seal, may hold real and personal estate, sufficient to carry on successfully the business of the Moose River Log Driving Company, and may grant and vote money for the same. And said company shall drive all logs and other timber coming into Moose river, between the head of Attian pond and of Wood pond and Moosehead lake for the purpose of being driven to market. And said company may for the purposes aforesaid remove obstructions, erect booms and dams, where the same may be lawfully done, and may use steam or other power for the purpose of towing logs and booms, and shall have all the powers and privileges and be subject to all the liabilities, incident to corporations of a similar nature.' *Corporators. —corporate name. —powers. —limits, extended.*

Section 2. Section seven of said act is amended by striking out the word "Wednesday" in the fourth line thereof, and inserting in its place the word 'Tuesday,' so that said section, as amended, shall read as follows: *Section 7, amended.*

'Section 7. The first meeting of said company may be called by any one of the corporators named in this act, by written notice to each member. Annual meetings shall be called by the clerk on the third Tuesday of February in each year, or at such times as the company may vote, by giving fourteen days' notice in some newspaper published in Kennebec or Somerset county; special meetings may be called by order of the directors, with like notice.' *Day of annual meeting changed.*

Approved March 25, 1903.

Chapter 279.

An Act to amend the charter of the Bar Harbor Banking and Trust Company.

Be it enacted by the Senate and House of Representatives in Legislature assembled, as follows:

Chapter one hundred and ninety-six of the private and special laws of eighteen hundred eighty-seven, entitled "An Act to incorporate the Bar Harbor Trust and Banking Company," is hereby amended in the following particulars:

Title of act amended.

Section 1. The title of said act is hereby amended so as to read "An Act to incorporate the Bar Harbor Banking and Trust Company."

Section 10, repealed.

Section 2. Section ten of said chapter one hundred ninety-six is hereby repealed.

Authorized to establish branch.

Section 3. Said Bar Harbor Banking and Trust Company is hereby authorized and empowered to establish a branch in the town of Mount Desert, Hancock county, Maine.

Section 4. This act shall take effect when approved.

Approved March 25, 1903.

Chapter 280.

An Act to incorporate the Fish River Improvement Company.

Be it enacted by the Senate and House of Representatives in Legislature assembled, as follows:

Corporators.

Section 1. George B. Dunn, Frank Stetson, John Mullin, L. F. Bradbury, F. G. Dunn, C. C. Bradbury, William C. Donnell and Walter H. Sawyer, their associates, successors and assigns, are hereby created a body politic and corporate by the name of the Fish River Improvement Company.

—corporate name.

Capital stock.

Section 2. The capital stock of the corporation shall be one hundred thousand dollars, but the stockholders may by a vote representing a majority of the stock issued, increase the amount of the capital stock from time to time, to any amount.

Purposes.

Section 3. The purposes of said company shall be to hold, store, regulate and control the flow of the waters of the Fish river, of Eagle lake, Square lake, Cross lake, Mud lake, Long lake and Nadeau lake, otherwise known as Saint Froid lake in the county of Aroostook, connecting and tributary waters of said Fish river in aid of navigation on said lakes and so that the flow of the waters of said Fish river below the outlet of Eagle lake shall be as nearly as practicable uniform; to dredge, widen, straighten and improve the channels of said Fish river above the outlet of Eagle lake and remove obstructions and bars in the same and in any of said ponds and connecting and tributary waters; to erect and maintain wing dams, and side dams, booms and piers in said waters.

Section 4. Said corporation may erect and maintain dams on land which it may acquire, below the outlet of Eagle lake and below the outlet of Nadeau lake, otherwise known as Saint Froid lake, and may hold, store, regulate and control the waters raised by said dams and draw down the same as may be required for the purposes aforesaid, and said corporation is hereby empowered to flow such land as may be necessary to carry out the provisions of this act, and said corporation shall be liable for all damage caused by said flowage, to be ascertained and determined in the manner prescribed in chapter ninety-two of the revised statutes. Said corporation may use the power if any which may be developed at the said dams below the outlet of Eagle lake and below the outlet of Nadeau lake for manufacturing or mechanical purposes and for generating electricity and may sell or lease such power and distribute and sell such electricity to manufacturing plants on the Fish river or its tributaries and for lighting, heating, manufacturing, mechanical and transportation purposes in Eagle Lake plantation, Wallagrass plantation, Fort Kent, and Winterville plantation, all in Aroostook county.

Section 5. During the construction and after the completion of said dam below the outlet of Eagle lake, said corporation shall throughout each working day allow, at least, six hundred cubic feet of water per second to pass said dam into the main river, provided, that the quantity of water flowing into Eagle lake is sufficient to yield the above quantity.

Section 6. Said corporation may issue its bonds for corporate purposes of any and all kinds upon such rates and time and in such amounts as it may deem expedient and secure the same by mortgage of its franchise and property.

Section 7. The first meeting of said corporation shall be called by a written notice thereof, signed by any four named incorporators served upon each named incorporator by giving him the same in hand, or by leaving the same or mailing the same to him postage paid, at his last and usual place of abode at least seven days before the time of meeting, or by publishing said notice in some newspaper published in the county of Aroostook.

Section 8. This act shall take effect when approved.

Approved March 25, 1903.

Chapter 281.

An Act to incorporate the Winterport, Frankfort and Prospect Electric Railway.

Be it enacted by the Senate and House of Representatives in Legislature assembled, as follows:

Corporators.

—corporate name.

—powers.

—route.

—locations shall be filed with clerk of courts.

—may fix transportation rates.

May maintain line of wires.

Section 1. Charles A. McKenney, Frank C. Young, Charles R. Hill and Ellery Bowden of Winterport and Albert Peirce of Frankfort, their associates, successors and assigns are hereby constituted a corporation by the name of the Winterport, Frankfort and Prospect Electric Railway with authority to construct, maintain and operate by electricity or animal power, a street railway with convenient single or double tracks, side tracks or turnouts, with all necessary or convenient lines of poles, wires, appliances, appurtenances and conduits, from the terminus of the Bangor, Hampden and Winterport Railway in Hampden through the town of Hampden to Winterport, in and through the towns of Winterport, Frankfort and Prospect to Stockton Springs upon streets and highways to be fixed and determined by the municipal officers of said respective towns, after the right of way has been granted by the respective towns, and assented to in writing by said corporation; build and maintain bridges with draws across navigable tide waters in each of said towns upon location and upon terms to be established and made by the county commissioners of the counties in which the bridge is located, and may also maintain and operate said railway upon and over any lands where the land damages have been mutually settled by said corporation and owners thereof; provided, however, that all tracks of said railway shall be laid at such distances from the sidewalks of said towns as the respective municipal officers thereof shall in their order fixing the routes of said railway determine to be for the public safety and convenience. The written assent of said corporation to any vote of said towns or of the municipal officers of said towns, prescribing from time to time the routes of said railway, shall be filed with respective clerks of said towns, and the assent to the location of bridges by county commissioners shall be filed with the clerk of courts, in the county where said bridge is to be built, and shall be taken and deemed to be the location thereof. Said corporation shall have power from time to time to fix such rates of compensation for transporting persons or property as it may think expedient and generally shall have all the powers and be subject to all the liabilities of corporations as set forth in the forty-sixth chapter of the revised statutes.

Section 2. Said corporation is hereby authorized to build and forever maintain, on the line of location of its track and line of

WINTERPORT, FRANKFORT AND PROSPECT ELECTRIC RAILWAY.

wires transmitting power and supplying lights and power, any and all necessary bridges, across tide waters where vessels can navigate, in either of the towns named in this act, and especially across Marsh river in said Frankfort, upon location, terms and conditions, to be determined by the commissioners of the county in which said bridge is to be built, after due notice and a public hearing thereon, and forever maintain draws in such bridges, cross said bridges with wires and maintain the same in accordance with regulations that may be established by said commissioners from time to time; which rules and regulations shall be printed and a copy thereof be posted in each car run by said company. Provided, always, that after the county commissioners have once established their rules and regulations they shall not be changed in any particular, until after thirty days written notice to said corporation to the end that a hearing may be had thereon.

—may cross navigable waters.

—proviso.

Section 3. Said corporation is also authorized to make, generate, sell, distribute and supply electricity for lighting, heating, manufacturing or mechanical purposes in any of the towns hereinbefore mentioned with all the rights, privileges and powers and subject to all the restrictions and liabilities incident by law to corporations organized for said last named purposes.

May supply electricity for light, heat and power.

Section 4. The capital stock of said corporation shall not exceed five hundred thousand dollars, to be divided into shares of one hundred dollars each.

Capital stock.

Section 5. Said corporation may change the location of said railway, by first obtaining the written consent of the municipal officers of said town, and make additional locations, subject to the foregoing provisions and conditions; provided that the location of any bridge across tide waters where vessels can navigate shall not be changed without the consent of the county commissioners.

Change of location.

Section 6. Nothing in this act shall be construed to prevent the proper authorities of said towns, from entering upon and temporarily taking up the soil in any street, town or county road occupied by said railway, for any purpose for which they may now lawfully take up the same.

Municipal officers may occupy streets.

Section 7. Such corporation is hereby authorized to lease all of its property and franchises on such terms as it may determine, also to consolidate with or to acquire by lease, purchase, or otherwise, the lines, property and franchises of any other street railway, whose lines as constructed or chartered would form connecting or continuous lines with the lines of this company, and in such case this corporation shall be entitled to all the privileges, and be subject to all appropriate conditions and limitations contained in the charter thus united with or acquired. Whenever

May sell or lease its property to connecting lines.

any person or corporation shall be lawfully operating any street railway to any point to which this corporation's tracks extend, this corporation may enter upon, connect with and use the same on such terms and in such manner as may be agreed upon between the parties, and may acquire by purchase or lease for a term of years and operate any ferry way on the Penobscot river connecting with its roads.

Shall not be required to run cars during snow blockade.

Section 8. Said corporation shall not be required to run cars upon its road when the line of the road is blocked with snow and ice, or when the convenience or wants of the public do not demand it. And said corporation is permitted to run omnibuses instead of rail cars during such time as the tracks may be blocked.

May use existing poles, trees or structures for its wires.

—price, how determined.

Section 9. Whenever it is practicable to use existing poles or any electric light, telephone or telegraph company, or any tree or structure of any kind, for any of the wires of said corporation and the owners thereof consent to the free use of the same, or at a price satisfactory to said corporation shall have the right to use the same; and the decision as to the practicability of such use shall be left to three persons skilled in the science of electricity, one chosen by said corporation, one by the municipal officers, and the third by the two so chosen; the decision of the majority of said board shall be final and the expense of said tribunal shall be borne by said corporation. In the erection and maintenance of its poles, posts, lamps and wires, said corporation shall be subject to the general laws of the state, regulating the erection of posts and lines for the purposes of electricity.

First meeting, how called.

Section 10 The first meeting of said corporation shall be called in the manner provided in the revised statutes, chapter forty-six, section three.

Section 11. This act shall take effect when approved.

Approved March 25, 1903.

Chapter 282.

An Act to incorporate the Lee Telephone Company.

Be it enacted by the Senate and House of Representatives in Legislature assembled, as follows:

Corporators.

—corporate name.

Section 1. F. L. Riggs, H. L. Haskell, J. W. Burke, C. C. Burke and G. H. Haskell, their associates and successors, are hereby made a body corporate by the name of the Lee Telephone Company, with all the rights, powers and privileges, and subject to all the duties and obligations of similar corporations under the general laws of this state, with power by that name to sue and be sued, to have a common seal, to establish all by-laws and regulations for the management of its affairs not repugnant to the laws of this state and to do and perform any and all legal acts, incident to similar corporations.

Section 2. Said corporation is hereby authorized to construct, own, maintain and operate telephone line or lines anywhere in the towns of Springfield, Lee, Lincoln and Winn, all within the county of Penobscot and state of Maine, having obtained consent of the several municipalities, and said corporation shall have the right to locate and construct its lines upon and along any public highway or bridge in said towns, but in such a way as not to incommode or endanger the customary use thereof; and shall have the power to establish and collect tolls on said lines. *Location of line.* *—may collect tolls.*

Section 3. Said corporation is hereby authorized and empowered to connect its lines with those of any other telephone company or corporation on such terms as may be mutually agreed upon, or to sell or lease its line or lines of telephone and property in whole or in part, either before or after completion to any other telephone company or corporation, as provided by law or upon such terms as may be agreed by the contracting parties, which sale or lease shall be binding upon the parties; or may purchase or lease any other line or lines of telephone upon such terms and conditions as may be agreed by the parties thereto. *May connect with other lines.*

Section 4. If the land of any individual or corporation is taken under this act, and the parties cannot agree upon the damages occasioned thereby, they shall be estimated, secured and paid in the manner provided in the case of land taken for railroads. *Damages, how determined.*

Section 5. The capital stock of said corporation shall be of such an amount as said corporation may, from time to time determine to be necessary, but not exceeding the sum of ten thousand dollars, for the sole purpose of owning, leasing, constructing, maintaining and operating the line or lines of telephone hereby authorized and contemplated. And the said corporation may purchase, hold, lease, sell and convey all real estate and personal property necessary for the purposes contemplated in this charter. *Capital stock.* *—may hold real and personal property.*

Section 6. Any one of the incorporators named in this act may call the first meeting of the corporation by mailing a written notice signed by himself, postage paid, to each of the other incorporators, seven days at least before the day of the meeting, naming the time, place and purposes of such meeting, and at such meeting a president, secretary, treasurer and directors may be chosen, by-laws adopted, present amount of capital stock fixed, and any corporate business transacted. *First meeting how called.*

Section 7. This act shall take effect when approved.

Approved March 25, 1903.

Chapter 283.

An Act to incorporate the Androscoggin Log Driving Company.

Be it enacted by the Senate and House of Representatives in Legislature assembled, as follows:

Corporators.

Section 1. Charles E. Oak, Edwin Riley, Frank P. Thomas, Richmond L. Melcher, Hollis C. Dunton and Waldo Pettingill,

—corporate name.

their associates and assigns are hereby incorporated under the name of the Androscoggin Log Driving Company with all the powers and privileges of similar corporations.

Charter limits from state line to Livermore Falls.

Section 2. Said corporation is authorized to build side dams, shear booms, remove rocks, dredge, make embankments and other improvements on the Androscoggin river in the counties of Oxford, Franklin and Androscoggin from the boundary line between Maine and New Hampshire to the village of Livermore Falls in the town of East Livermore in the county of Andros-

—shall drive logs and lumber.

coggin to facilitate the driving of logs and lumber down the same and said company shall drive to such places of destination on said Androscoggin river between the points aforesaid as may be designated by the owners of the same all logs, or other lumber belonging to said company or any other person or corporation represented by any member of said corporation that may be in said river between said points for the purpose of being driven or floated down the same together with such other logs or lumber as is hereinafter provided, and for the purpose of carrying out

—may hold real and personal estate.

the intentions herein provided said corporation may purchase and hold real and personal estate sufficient for carrying on the business of the corporation, and may grant and raise by loan or assessment for the same such sums of money and in such manner as the directors may from time to time vote. Said corporation may also make and adopt all necessary regulations and by-laws not repugnant to the constitution and laws of the state and adopt a common seal and change or renew the same at pleasure.

Officers.

Section 3. The officers of said company shall be a clerk, treasurer, and a board of three or five directors, to be chosen by ballot, and such other officers as may be deemed necessary,

—tenure.

who may be appointed by the directors, unless they shall be chosen at the annual meeting, all of whom shall hold their offices

—shall be sworn.

until the next annual meeting, or until others are chosen or appointed in their stead. The clerk, treasurer and directors shall be sworn to the faithful performance of their duties. The treasurer shall give a bond to the acceptance of the directors.

—president.

The directors shall, at their first meeting, elect one of their number who shall be the president of the company. And no person shall be eligible to the office of director except he be a member of the corporation.

ANDROSCOGGIN LOG DRIVING COMPANY. 445

CHAP. 283

Membership, how made up.

Section 4. Any person, or corporation, or their agents, owning logs or other lumber to be driven on said river at the date of the annual meeting in each year, may become members of the Androscoggin Log Driving Company, and shall so continue for two years at least, from that date, and shall have all the privileges and be subject to all the liabilities thereto. Said members shall be entitled to vote at any meeting of the company as follows: One vote each for any member having or representing one hundred thousand feet of logs or lumber in the river to be driven, with an additional vote for every additional fifty thousand feet of logs or lumber, the same to be determined by the amount driven the year before on which they have paid taxes or dues provided any were so driven during the previous year.

—voting powers of members.

Section 5. The members of said company owning logs or other lumber to be driven down said rivers, shall, on or before the first day of May in that year, file with the clerk of the company, a correct statement in writing, signed by a sworn surveyor, of all such logs or timber of the number of feet, full scale, with the mark or marks thereon, together with the place from which the logs are to be driven and their destination. And it shall be the duty of the directors to keep a separate and distinct account of all expenses incurred for driving the logs and other lumber between the New Hampshire line and Rumford Falls, and between Rumford Falls, and each of the following mills, dams or booms, viz: The boom next below Canton Point, so called, the dam or mill at Riley, so called, the dam or mill at Jay Bridge, so called, the dam or mill at Otis Falls, so called, the dams or mills at Livermore Falls, so called, together with such other point of destination on said river between the two points first named and any other intermediate points and ascertain the number of feet, full scale, and ownership of said logs and other lumber driven between said points, and assess thereon, to owners if known, or to owners unknown, making such discount for logs driven less than the whole distance as in their opinion may be right and equitable, a distinct and separate tax sufficient to pay said expenses, with such further sums as may be necessary to pay interest or cost of investment in whole or in part, expense of maintenance, damages and losses for piers, booms, buoys. dams and such other expenses as may be voted by the company or the directors. And the directors shall have power whenever they may deem it necessary or expedient, to cause a survey to be made of any or all logs driven or secured by the company, and the expense of such survey shall be assessed on such logs in the same manner as is herein provided for assessing the expenses of driving and securing the same. If any owner or

Statement of logs to be driven shall be filed.

—expense account, how to be kept.

—directors shall assess such tax as shall pay expenses.

—may cause survey to be made.

CHAP. 283

agent shall refuse or neglect to file such a statement in the manner herein prescribed, the directors may assess such delinquent or delinquents for his or their proportion of expenses, such sum or sums as may be by the directors considered just and equitable, and such assessment shall be final; said assessment to be made at any time after the first day of July at the discretion of the directors. And said company shall have a lien on all logs and other lumber by them driven for the expense of driving, booming and securing, which shall not be discharged until all assessments shall be finally paid. The directors shall keep a record of the assessments in the office of the clerk, which shall be open to the inspection of all persons interested.

Assessments shall be given to treasurer.

Section 6. The directors shall give the treasurer a list of all assessments by them made, with a warrant in due form under their hands. And it shall be the duty of the treasurer immediately after he shall receive from the directors a list of assessments in due form, to notify in writing all the owners, where known, of the amount assessed upon their several marks, and all owners of logs and other lumber shall be required to pay or satisfactorily secure the amount of the several assessments on demand, and in default of payment of the whole or any part of any member's assessment, the treasurer shall have power to take possession of a sufficient quantity of the logs or other lumber of any mark owned or assessed to said member and advertise the same for sale at public auction, by posting up in some conspicuous place in Rumford Falls, in the town of Rumford, also by publication in some newspaper published in Rumford Falls a notice of such sale, stating therein the names of the persons taxed, if known, with the mark or marks assessed, with the amount of assessment unpaid, ten days at least before the day of the sale; and unless such assessments, with all expenses incurred, are previously paid, he may then proceed to sell to the highest bidder a sufficient quantity of such logs or other lumber to pay such assessment, with all proper costs, together with twelve per cent, interest from the date of said assessment; such sales to be at the office of the company, or where the logs are situated.

—treasurer shall notify owners of logs.

—proceedings when assessment is not paid.

Unmarked logs may be disposed of.

Section 7. All logs or other lumber, after coming within the limits of the corporation, and not having thereon some mark designating the owner or owners thereof, shall be the property of said company; and said logs or other lumber shall be disposed of by order of the directors, and the proceeds paid into the treasury of said company to defray expenses; provided, however, that nothing in this or the following section shall be construed to impair the right of any person to claim any log or other lumber which he may have put into said river without such mark of

—proviso.

ownership. And any such person, upon furnishing reasonable proof of such ownership, shall be entitled to receive all logs or other lumber which, at any time before the sale thereof he may so prove to be his, or to receive the proceeds of the sale of the same, provided they have been sold by said company; all such claims to be made and proof to be furnished within one year from the date of sale of the same by the company.

Section 8. It shall not be lawful for any person or corporation, other than the Androscoggin Log Driving Company, to mark, or cause to be marked, any log or other lumber put into said rivers or their tributaries, usually called prize logs. And if any person or corporation shall take any, carry away or otherwise convert to his or their use, without the consent of said company, any prize log or prize lumber, he or they shall be subject to all the liabilities provided for similar offenses in the laws of the state, which specially provide for securing to owners their property in logs, masts, spars and other lumber. *Prize logs.*

Section 9. Any owner or owners of logs or other lumber on said rivers or their tributaries may take and use on his or their logs or other lumber any mark not in use by any other person on said river or tributaries, and such mark shall be left with the clerk of said company and shall be by him recorded in a book kept for that purpose, which shall be at all times open to the inspection of all persons interested; and if any other person or corporation shall use such mark on any logs or other lumber on said river or its tributaries after such mark shall be recorded, or any mark so closely resembling such other mark already recorded and in use, as to be calculated to mislead or require more than ordinary care to identify and select such logs or other lumber in the usual course of handling the same, such offender or offenders shall forfeit and pay the sum of two dollars for every log so marked, to be recovered in action of debt in any court of competent jurisdiction, to the use of the person or corporation injured thereby. *Marks shall be recorded by clerk.*

Section 10. Whenever the directors of the Androscoggin Log Driving Company shall judge it for the interest of the owners of logs and other lumber remaining in the booms or in any place exposed to loss to collect and deposit them in suitable and convenient places and properly secure the same they are hereby authorized so to collect and deposit such logs and lumber thus situated and to use all reasonable care safely to keep the same, until removed by the owners thereof or are otherwise disposed of in the manner provided in this act. *Logs exposed to loss may be secured, and held for owners.*

Section 11. Upon all logs and other timber thus collected and deposited, the directors shall assess the expense actually *Expense on logs collected*

CHAP. 283

and secured, how assessed.

incurred thereon, with such additional sums as may be deemed necessary to cover necessary future expenditures upon them while in charge; and said company shall have a lien upon the logs and other lumber and may hold the same and sell as provided in section five for the full payment of all expenses; or the treasurer may recover such assessments, and all other assessments, made by virtue of this act, in an action of debt in the name of the Androscoggin Log Driving Company in any court in the counties of Oxford or Androscoggin competent to try the same, to the use of the person prosecuting therefor.

Proceedings when logs are not called for by owners.

Section 12. If any logs or other lumber shall remain in the depositories upon the first day of September next ensuing, upon which the assessments have not been paid, the directors may immediately thereafter advertise for three weeks successively in newspapers printed in the city of Lewiston and at Rumford Falls notifying all owners of logs and other lumber deposited under this act, to remove the same within thirty days from said first day of September; and all logs not removed before the expiration of thirty days, and upon which the assessments have not been paid, may be sold at public auction, and the proceeds therefor, after deducting all unpaid assessments and necessary expenses of sale, shall be paid upon demand by the treasurer of the company to the owners of logs and other lumber then sold; provided, however, this shall not apply to logs that are in booms the first day of September or that may come in after that date by reason of a late drive of such logs.

May cross private lands.

Section 13. For the purpose of carrying out the provisions of this act, when there are no highways conveniently near leading to the river, the company may have the right to cross on foot and with teams the land of private persons or corporations in some place reasonably convenient, and in such a location calculated to do the least damage to the owner thereof, and for all damages sustained by any person or corporation under the provisions of this act unless otherwise herein provided, they shall be estimated and determined in the same way as damages for the laying out of highways.

Restrictions.

Section 14. This corporation is not authorized to make any change in the river bed or in any dam now existing in said river, or put any obstructions that will change the flow of the water at any point at or near any mill, dam or boom on the same, without the written approval of the owner of said mill, dam or boom.

Persons not members of this company, may have logs driven.

Section 15. Any other person or corporation having logs or lumber to be driven on said river, and not desirous of becoming a member of this corporation, may have the same driven to their place of destination within the limits of this corporation, after having given reasonable notice in writing of this said request, and the service for driving the same shall be determined and secured according to the provisions hereinbefore stated.

Section 16. In case of any disagreement as to the rights of owners hereunder the same shall forthwith be determined by referees agreed upon by the parties or after notice and hearing appointed by any judge of the supreme judicial court sitting in term time or vacation in either of the counties of Oxford, Androscoggin or Cumberland. Referees in cases of disagreement.

Section 17. The annual meeting of this corporation until otherwise provided, shall be held in the town of Rumford, in the county of Oxford, and the manner, place and time of calling annual and special meetings of the company and meeting of the directors may be determined by a vote of the company, at any meeting thereof. The first meeting of the company for the purpose of the acceptance of this act and for the organization of the same may be called at Rumford Falls by any associate named herein, on giving at least seven days notice of the time and place of said meeting. Annual meeting. First meeting how called.

Section 18. This act shall take effect when approved.

Approved March 25, 1903.

Chapter 284.

An Act to incorporate the Sullivan Harbor Water Company.

Be it enacted by the Senate and House of Representatives in Legislature assembled, as follows:

Section 1. Moses Hawkins, Charles P. Simpson, Stanislaus Wilson, Emery B. Dunbar, Harvey W. Dunbar, Fred W. Bridgham, Spiro V. Bennis and William O. Emery, and such persons as they may associate with themselves in the enterprise, their successors and assigns, are hereby made a corporation under the name of the Sullivan Harbor Water Company, for the purpose of supplying the town of Sullivan, in the county of Hancock, Maine, and the inhabitants of said town, with pure water for domestic, sanitary, municipal and public uses, including the extinguishment of fires. Corporators. —corporate name.

Section 2. Said Sullivan Harbor Water Company may take and hold by purchase or otherwise, real and personal estate necessary and convenient for the purposes aforesaid. May hold real and personal estate.

Section 3. Said Sullivan Harbor Water Company is hereby authorized for the purposes aforesaid to take, collect, store, flow, May take water from Long pond.

CHAP. 284

—proviso.

May lay pipes in town of Sullivan.

—shall be liable for damages.

May cross sewers, etc.

—liable for damages thereby.

May cross pipes of Long Pond Water Co.

May take lands for flowage, etc.

use, detain, distribute and convey to the town of Sullivan and any part thereof, water from Long pond, in said Sullivan, and is also authorized to locate, construct and maintain dams, cribs, reservoirs, locks, gates, sluices, aqueducts, pipes, conduits, standpipes, hydrants and other necessary structures therefor, provided, however, that said Sullivan Harbor Water Company shall not at any time enter said Long pond and take water therefrom at a lower level than the Long Pond Water Company may be taking water therefrom at that time.

Section 4. Said Sullivan Harbor Water Company is hereby authorized to lay, construct and maintain in, under, through, along and across the highways, ways, streets, railroads and bridges in said town, and to take up, replace and repair all such sluices, aqueducts, pipes, hydrants and structures as may be necessary for the purposes of their incorporation, under such reasonable restrictions and conditions as the selectmen of said town may impose. And said Sullivan Harbor Water Company shall be responsible for all damages to all corporations, persons and property occasioned by the said use of such highways, ways and streets, and shall further be liable to pay to said town all sums recovered against said town for damages from obstructions caused by said Sullivan Harbor Water Company, and for all expenses, including reasonable counsel fees incurred in defending such suits, with interest on the same.

Section 5. Said Sullivan Harbor Water Company shall have power to cross any water course, public or private sewer, or to change the direction thereof where necessary for the purposes of its incorporation, but in such manner as not to obstruct or impair the use thereof; and said company shall be liable for any injury caused thereby. Whenever said Sullivan Harbor Water Company shall lay down any fixtures in any highway, way or street, or make any alterations or repairs upon its works in any highway, way or street, it shall cause the same to be done with as little obstruction to public travel as may be practicable, and shall at its own expense, without unnecessary delay, cause the earth and pavements then removed by it to be replaced in proper condition.

Section 6. Said Sullivan Harbor Water Company shall have power to cross any pipes, sluices or aqueducts of the Long Pond Water Company, when necessary for the purposes of its incorporation, but in such manner as not to injure the same, or to obstruct or impair the use thereof, and for any injury caused thereby the said Sullivan Harbor Water Company shall be liable.

Section 7. Said Sullivan Harbor Water Company may take and hold any lands necessary for flowage, and also for its dams,

SULLIVAN HARBOR WATER COMPANY. 451

CHAP. 284

cribs, reservoirs, stand pipes, locks, gates, hydrants and other necessary structures, and may locate, lay and maintain sluices, aqueducts, pipes, conduits, hydrants and other necessary structures, or fixtures in, over and through any lands for its said purposes, and excavate in and through such lands for such location, construction and maintenance. It may enter upon such lands to make surveys and locations, and shall file in the registry of deeds, in said county of Hancock, plans of such locations and lands, showing the property taken, and within thirty days thereafter publish notice of such filing in some newspaper in said county, such publication to be continued three weeks successively. Such water, land or other property shall be deemed to have been taken at the date of such filing. Said Sullivan Harbor Water Company, however, may make all needful explorations, surveys and levels on any land prior to such filing.

—may enter on lands for surveys.

Section 8. Said Sullivan Harbor Water Company shall be held liable to pay all legal damages that shall be sustained by any person by the taking of any land or other property, or by flowage, or by excavating through any land for the purposes of laying down pipes, sluices, aqueducts and conduits, building dams, cribs, reservoirs, locks, gates, stand pipes, hydrants and other necessary structures, and also damages for any other injuries resulting from said acts, and when any person sustaining damages as aforesaid and said corporation cannot mutually agree upon the sum to be paid therefor, said corporation or such person may cause such damages to be ascertained in the same manner and under the same conditions, restrictions and limitations as are by law prescribed in the case of damages by laying out of steam railroads, so far as such law is consistent with the provisions of this act. The Long Pond Water Company shall be reimbursed by way of damages by said Sullivan Harbor Water Company for such proportion of the former's expenditures in improving Long pond, and in settling with or purchasing the rights of George C. Lyman (or Lynam) or persons claiming under him, as may be determined to be equitable.

Liability for land taken

—damages, how determined.

Section 9. The cost of maintaining hereafter the improvements now made for the benefit of the storage or water supply in said Long pond, of erecting and maintaining other improvements for the same purposes shall be equitably shared by said Long Pond Water Company and said Sullivan Harbor Water Company.

Costs of maintenance of joint improvements.

In case said two companies cannot agree as to what should be done in the way of construction, improvements or repairs, or how the expense thereof should be shared under this section, these matters may be determined by the chief justice of the

—proceedings in case of disagreement.

supreme judicial court of the state of Maine, for the time being, upon petition of either company and upon hearing thereon after such notice as said chief justice may order.

May make contracts for supplying water.

Section 10. Said Sullivan Harbor Water Company is hereby authorized to make contracts with the United States and with corporations and inhabitants of said town of Sullivan for the purposes of supplying water, as contemplated by this act. And said town of Sullivan is hereby authorized by its selectmen to enter into contract with said Sullivan Harbor Water Company for a supply of water for any and all purposes mentioned in this act, and for such exemption from public burden as said town and said company may agree, which, when made, shall be legal and binding upon all parties thereto.

Pollution of water.

Section 11. Whoever shall wilfully or maliciously corrupt the water of said pond or streams, or any of the tributaries thereto, whether frozen or not, or in any way render such waters impure, whether frozen or not, or whoever shall wilfully or maliciously injure any of the works of said Sullivan Harbor Water Company, shall be punished by fine not exceeding one thousand dollars, or by imprisonment not exceeding two years,

—penalty.

and shall be liable to said company for three times the actual damage, to be recovered in any proper action.

Capital stock.

Section 12. The capital stock of said company shall be fifty thousand dollars and said stock shall be divided into shares of twenty-five dollars each.

May issue bonds.

Section 13. Said Sullivan Harbor Water Company may issue its bonds for the carrying out of any of its purposes, to an amount not exceeding the sum of fifty thousand dollars, on such rates and time as it may deem expedient, and secure the payment of the principal and interest on such bonds by appropriate mortgages or deeds of trust of all or any part of its property, franchises, rights and privileges owned or hereafter acquired by it.

First meeting, how called.

Section 14. The first meeting of said Sullivan Harbor Water Company may be called by written notice thereof signed by any two of the incorporators herein named served upon each of the other incorporators by giving him the same in hand, or by leaving the same at his last usual place of abode, or by mailing the same to him at his last known residence or place of business, or by publishing the same in some newspaper in the county of Hancock, state of Maine, at least five days before the time of such meeting.

Section 15. This act shall take effect when approved.

Approved March 26, 1903.

Chapter 285.

An Act in relation to the Ellsworth Municipal Court.

Be it enacted by the Senate and House of Representatives in Legislature assembled, as follows:

Section 1. The jurisdiction of said court is hereby established as follows: Said court shall have original jurisdiction; first, of all cases of forcible entry and detainer respecting estates in the county of Hancock; second, of all such criminal offenses and misdemeanors committed in the said county as are by law within the jurisdiction of trial justices; third, of all offenses against the ordinances and by-laws of either of the towns in said county, and in the prosecutions on any such ordinances or by-laws, or such by-law or ordinance need not be recited in the complaint or process, nor the allegations therein be more particular than in prosecutions on a public statute. Warrants may be issued by any trial justice in said county upon complaints for offenses committed in the city of Ellsworth, but all such warrants issued by any trial justice in said Ellsworth shall be made returnable before said court, and no trial justice in said Ellsworth shall have or take cognizance of offenses committed within said city of Ellsworth. *Original jurisdiction of court.*

Section 2. Said court shall have original jurisdiction concurrent with trial justices in all such matters civil and criminal, within the county of Hancock, as are by law within the jurisdiction of trial justices within said county, and are not placed within the exclusive jurisdiction of said court by the preceding section. *Original jurisdiction concurrent with trial justices.*

Section 3. Said court shall have original jurisdiction concurrent with the supreme judicial court as follows; first, of all civil actions wherein the debt or damages demanded, exclusive of costs, does not exceed one hundred dollars, in which any person summoned as trustee resides within the county of Hancock, or, if a corporation has an established place of business in said county of Hancock; or in which if such actions are not commenced by a trustee process, any defendant resides in said county, or, if no defendant resides within the limits of this state, any defendant is served with process in said county, or the goods, estate, or effects of any defendant are found within said county and attached on the original writ; but no proceedings under the laws relating to divorce shall be included within the jurisdiction of said court; second, of the assaults and batteries described in section twenty-eight of chapter one hundred and eighteen of the revised statutes; of all larcenies described in sections one, six, seven, nine and eleven of chapter one hundred and twenty of the revised statutes, when the value of the property is not alleged to exceed thirty dollars; of the offense described in section *Original jurisdiction concurrent with supreme judicial court*

CHAP. 285

twenty-one of chapter one hundred and twenty-two of the revised statutes; of all offenses described in sections one and four of chapter one hundred and twenty-three of the revised statutes; of all offenses described in section six and in sections twenty-nine to forty-five, inclusive, of chapter one hundred and twenty-four of the revised statutes; of the offense described in section five of chapter one hundred and twenty-five of the revised statutes; of all offenses described in section one of chapter one hundred and twenty-six of the revised statutes, when the value of the property or thing alleged to have been fraudulently obtained, sold, mortgaged or pledged, is not alleged to exceed thirty dollars; and of all offenses described in sections two, nine, sixteen, seventeen and twenty-one of chapter one hundred and twenty-seven of the revised statutes, when the value of the property destroyed or injury done is not alleged to exceed thirty dollars, and all amendments thereto: and may punish for either of said crimes or offenses by fine not exceeding fifty dollars, and by imprisonment not exceeding three months, provided, that when the offenses described in section twenty-eight of chapter one hundred and eighteen, section twenty-one of chapter one hundred and twenty-two, and sections one and four of chapter one hundred and twenty-three, are of a high and aggravated nature, the judge of said court may cause persons charged of such offenses, to recognize with sufficient sureties to appear before the supreme judicial court, and in default thereof commit them; third, of all other crimes, offenses and misdemeanors committed in said county which are by law punishable by fine not exceeding fifty dollars, and by imprisonment not exceeding three months, and are not within the exclusive jurisdiction of some other municipal or police court.

No jurisdiction in civil actions when title to real estate is in question, etc.

Section 4. Said court shall not have jurisdiction in any civil action wherein the title of real estate, according to the pleading or brief statement filed therein by either party, is in question; and all such actions brought in said court shall be removed to the supreme judicial court, or otherwise disposed of as in like cases before a trial justice; provided, that nothing herein contained, shall prevent said court from proceeding in accordance with the provisions of sections six and seven of chapter ninety-four of the revised statutes; neither shall said court have jurisdiction under the divorce laws, complaints under the mill act, so called, nor proceedings under the bastardy act, and the judge of said court shall not act in the capacity of a disclosure commissioner.

Terms for transaction

Section 5. Said court shall hold a term for the transaction of civil business at Ellsworth on the first Tuesday of each month beginning at ten o'clock in the forenoon, and shall remain in session for four days; but said term may be continued or adjourned for such time, or to such day as may be ordered by the judge; said court shall be considered constantly in session for the transaction of criminal business.

of civil business, when held.

In case of the absence of the judge from the court room or of his inability to attend to the business of the court by reason of relationship, interest or other disability, or in case of his death, all the powers of the judge may be exercised by the recorder whose acts and proceedings shall be as valid and effectual as if performed by the judge, and said recorder shall continue to perform the duties of said judge until his return, or until such disability is removed, or until his successor is appointed and qualified.

—recorder may act in absence of judge.

Section 6. All original processes, both civil and criminal, issuing from said court shall be under teste of the judge, and signed by the recorder or by the judge, and shall have the seal of said court affixed.

Form of original processes.

Section 7. The recorder of said court shall receive as compensation a salary of four hundred dollars per year to be paid quarterly from the treasury of the county of Hancock, and in addition thereto he shall receive fees in all civil cases.

Salary of recorder.

Section 8. Said municipal court may render judgment, issue execution, punish for contempt and compel attendance as in the supreme judicial court; make all such rules and regulations not repugnant to law as may be necessary and proper for the prompt administration of justice, and is clothed with all such lawful power as is necessary for the performance of its duties under this act, or any prior act in relation to said court not hereby repealed.

Powers of municipal court.

Section 9. All fees, fines and costs in criminal actions in said court shall be paid to the recorder, and he shall keep a correct account thereof, and shall annually on the first day of January make a detailed statement thereof, and pay the same to the county treasurer.

Fees, fines and costs in criminal actions.

Said recorder shall keep two dockets in which shall be entered respectively all proceedings in criminal and civil matters, and the entries therein shall include the names of the parties, their counsel and notes of all motions, judgments or other proceedings in the cases, including rendition of judgment and the issuing of execution; and it shall not be necessary to further extend, or otherwise record any of such proceedings, and such docket entries shall be legal evidence as records in the courts of this state.

—recorder shall keep two dockets.

Section 10. All prior acts or parts of acts inconsistent with this act, are hereby repealed.

Section 11. This act shall take effect when approved.

Approved March 25, 1903.

Chapter 286.

An Act relating to the franchise, rights and privileges of the Milbridge and Cherryfield Electric Railroad Company.

Be it enacted by the Senate and House of Representatives in Legislature assembled, as follows:

Rights and privileges declared to be in full force.

Section 1. The franchises, rights and privileges of the Milbridge and Cherryfield Electric Railroad Company are hereby declared to be and are in full force, effect and legal existence, as also are all the official permits and official approvals heretofore obtained by said company relative to its incorporation and to the location of its proposed railroad from a point in the town of Cherryfield so as to connect with the Washington County Railroad at or near the upper corner, so called, to a point at or near the junction of Main street and the Steuben road, so called, near the store of A. Wallace in the town of Milbridge, both in the county of Washington and state of Maine.

Route of, defined.

Section 2. The Milbridge and Cherryfield Electric Railroad Company aforesaid is hereby authorized and empowered to construct, maintain and operate as an extension of its proposed railroad as above set forth, its railroad over, along and upon the highway or public way extending from a point at or near the junction of Main street and the Steuben road, so called, near the store of A. Wallace in said town of Milbridge to the steamboat wharf and landing of the Portland, Mount Desert and Machias Steamboat Company in said Milbridge, provided said electric railroad company shall first obtain the official permit required by the laws of Maine from the selectmen of the town of said Milbridge, and the official approval of location required by law from the board of railroad commissioners of Maine relating to said proposed extension.

May increase capital stock.

Section 3. Said Milbridge and Cherryfield Electric Railroad Company is hereby authorized to increase the capital stock of said company fifty thousand dollars.

Location of route to be approved.

Section 4. Said Milbridge and Cherryfield Electric Railroad Company is hereby authorized to construct, maintain and operate its proposed railroad between the points heretofore set forth over, along and upon the highway or public way leading from Cherryfield village in said Cherryfield to Milbridge village in said Milbridge located on the easterly side of the Narraguagus river or in part over, along and upon the highway or public way on the westerly side of said river, between the two points as above set forth, provided said company shall have obtained or may obtain the official permits from the municipal officers of said towns, and official approvals of the board of railroad commissioners as the law provides; and further provided, that if said railroad is constructed, maintained and operated on said highway or public way across the navigable tide-waters of the Narraguagus river in the town of Milbridge, it shall be located and constructed so as to comply with the authority and permission heretofore granted said Milbridge and Cherryfield Electric Railroad Company by chapter three hundred and four of the private and special laws of nineteen hundred and one of the state of Maine.

Section 5. This act shall be null and void unless said corporation shall on or before the first day of December, in the year of our Lord, nineteen hundred and three, expend an amount equal to ten per cent of its capital stock, as stated in its articles of association, in the construction of its railroad. This fact shall be determined by the railroad commissioners, after notice and hearing, and a certificate of their determination shall be filed in the office of the secretary of state. *Shall expend 10 per cent of capital stock prior to Dec. 1, 1903.*

Section 6. This act shall take effect when approved.

Approved March 25, 1903.

Chapter 287.

An Act to incorporate the Washington Telephone Company.

Be it enacted by the Senate and House of Representatives in Legislature assembled, as follows:

Section 1. A. R. Gilson, P. S. Dorsey and F. L. Shaw, their associates, successors and assigns, are hereby created a body corporate by the name of the Washington Telephone Company, with all the powers, rights and privileges and subject to all the duties and obligations of similar corporations. *Corporators. —corporate name.*

Section 2. Said corporation shall have the right to locate, construct, maintain, operate and own lines of telephone in, upon and along any public way in any of the following towns: Machias, Marshfield, East Machias, Whitneyville, Centerville, Northfield, Wesley, Township Number Thirty-one, Cooper, Township Number Eighteen, Township Number Nineteen, Township Number Fourteen, Marion, Cutler, Machiasport, Roque Bluff, Jonesboro, Jonesport, Addison and Columbia Falls in the county of Washington. *Location of lines.*

Section 3. Said corporation is hereby authorized to connect its line or lines with those of any other company, or to lease its line or lines to any other company upon such terms as may be mutually agreed upon. *May connect with other lines.*

CHAP. 288
Capital stock.

Section 4. The amount of capital stock shall be fixed by vote of the corporation, but not to exceed ten thousand dollars and said corporation may purchase, hold, sell and convey real estate and personal property necessary for the purposes contemplated in this charter.

First meeting, how called.

Section 5. Any of the corporators named in this act may call the first meeting of this company by mailing a written notice to each of the other corporators, seven days at least, before the day of meeting, naming the time, place, and purposes of such meeting; and at such meeting, a president, secretary, treasurer and directors may be chosen, by-laws adopted and any corporate business transacted.

Section 6. This act shall take effect when approved.

Approved March 25, 1903.

Chapter 288.

An Act to amend An Act entitled "An Act to incorporate the Machias Log Driving Company," approved April eighth, one thousand eight hundred and fifty-four.

Be it enacted by the Senate and House of Representatives in Legislature assembled, as follows:

Section 11, repealed.

Section 1. Section eleven of an act entitled "An Act to incorporate the Machias Log Driving Company," approved April eighth, one thousand eight hundred and fifty-four, is hereby repealed.

Section 2. Said act is hereby amended by adding thereto the following:

—duration of membership.

'All persons or corporations or their agents owning logs or other timber to be driven on said waters at the date of the annual meeting in each year shall be members of the Machias Log Driving Company and shall continue so for two years at least from that date and shall have all the privileges and be subject to all the liabilities thereof.'

Section 3. This act shall take effect when approved.

Approved March 25, 1903.

Chapter 289.

An Act to incorporate the Hillside Water Company.

Be it enacted by the Senate and House of Representatives in Legislature assembled, as follows:

Section 1. Albert Peirce, William Heagan, A. S. Newman, Fred Shaw, Hayward Peirce, C. C. Emerson and A. T. Snow, their associates, successors and assigns, are hereby made a corporation by the name of the Hillside Water Company for the purpose of supplying the town of Frankfort in the county of Waldo and the inhabitants of said town with pure water for domestic, sanitary and municipal purposes, including the extinguishment of fires.   *Corporators.* *—corporate name.*

Section 2. Said company for said purposes may retain, collect, take, store, use and distribute water from any springs, ponds, streams and other water sources in said Frankfort and may locate, construct and maintain cribs, reservoirs, aqueducts, gates, pipes, hydrants and all other necessary structures therefor.   *May take water in town of Frankfort.*

Section 3. Said company is hereby authorized to lay, construct and maintain in, under, through, along and across the highways, ways, streets, railroads and bridges in said towns, and to take up, replace and repair all such sluices, aqueducts, pipes, hydrants and structures as may be necessary for the purposes of its incorporation, so as not to unreasonably obstruct the same, under such reasonable restrictions and conditions as the selectmen of said town may impose. It shall be responsible for all damages to persons and property occasioned by the use of such highways, ways and streets and shall further be liable to pay to said towns all sums recovered against said towns for damages for obstructions caused by said company, and for all expenses incurred in defending such suits, with interest on the same, provided said company shall have notice of such suits and opportunity to defend the same.   *May lay pipes, etc.* *—liability for damages.*

Section 4. Said company shall have power to cross any water course, private and public sewer, or to change the direction thereof when necessary for the purposes of its incorporation, but in such manner as not to obstruct or impair the use thereof, and it shall be liable for any injury caused thereby. Whenever said company shall lay down any fixture in any highway, way or street, or make any alterations or repairs upon its works in any highway, way or street, it shall cause the same to be done with as little obstruction to public travel as may be practicable, and shall, at its own expense, without unnecessary delay, cause the earth and pavements there removed by it to be replaced in proper condition.   *May cross sewers, etc.*

460 HILLSIDE WATER COMPANY.

CHAP. 289

May take lands.

—location shall be filed.

—width of location.

Proceedings when parties disagree as to damages for taking land.

Damages for taking of water, how assessed

Section 5. Said company may take and hold any waters as limited in section two and also any lands necessary for reservoirs, and other necessary structures, and may locate, lay and maintain aqueducts, pipes, hydrants and other necessary structures or fixtures in, over and through any lands for its said purposes, and excavate in and through such lands for such location, construction and maintenance. It may enter upon such lands to make surveys and location, and shall file in the registry of deeds for said county of Waldo, plans of such location and lands, showing the property taken, and within thirty days thereafter, publish notice of such filing in some newspaper in said county, such publication to be continued three weeks successively. Not more than one rod in width of land shall be occupied by any one line of pipe or aqueduct.

Section 6. Should the said company and the owner of such land so taken be unable to agree upon the damages to be paid for such location, taking, holding and construction, either party may, within twelve months after said filing of plans of location, apply to the commissioners of said county of Waldo, and cause such damages to be assessed in the same manner and under the same conditions, restrictions and limitations as are by law prescribed in the case of damages by the laying out of railroads, so far as such law is consistent with the provisions of this act. If said company shall fail to pay such land owner, or deposit for his use with the clerk of the county commissioners aforesaid, such sum as may be finally awarded as damages, with costs when recovered by him, within ninety days after notice of final judgment shall have been received by the clerk of courts of said county, the said location shall be thereby invalid, and said company forfeits all rights under the same as against such land owner. Said company may make a tender to any land owner damaged under the provisions of this act, and if such land owner recovers more damages than were tendered him by said company, he shall recover costs, otherwise said company shall recover costs. In case said company shall begin to occupy such lands before the rendition of final judgment, the land owner may require said company to file its bond to him with said county commissioners, in such sum and with such sureties as they approve, conditioned for said payment or deposit. No action shall be brought against said company for such taking, holding and occupation, until after such failure to pay or deposit as aforesaid. Failure to apply for damages within three years by the land owner, shall be held to be a waiver of the same.

Section 7. Any person suffering damage by the taking of water by said company as provided by this act, may have his

HILLSIDE WATER COMPANY.

damages assessed in the manner provided in the preceding section, and payment therefor shall be made in the same manner and with the same effect. No action shall be brought for the same until after the expiration of the time of payment. And a tender by said company may be made with the same effect as in the preceding section.

Section 8. Said corporation is hereby authorized to make contracts with the United States, and with corporations, and inhabitants of said town of Frankfort or any village corporation therein for the purpose of supplying water as contemplated by this act; and said town of Frankfort, or such village corporation, is hereby authorized to enter into contracts with said company for a supply of water for public uses, on such terms and for such time as the parties may agree, which when made, shall be legal and binding on all parties thereto, and said town of Frankfort for this purpose may raise money in the same manner as for other town charges. *May supply water.*

Section 9. The capital stock of said company shall be ten thousand dollars, and said stock shall be divided into one thousand shares of ten dollars each. *Capital stock*

Section 10. Said company for all of its said purposes, may hold real and personal estate necessary and convenient therefor. *May hold real and personal estate.*

Section 11. Said company may issue its bonds for the construction of its works of any and all kinds upon such rates and time as it may deem expedient, to an amount not exceeding in all the capital stock of said corporation subscribed for, and secure the same by mortgage or mortgages of the franchise and property of said company. *May issue bonds.*

Section 12. The first meeting of said company may be called by a written notice thereof, signed by any corporator herein named, served upon each corporator by giving him the same in hand, or by leaving the same at his last usual place of abode, seven days before the time of meeting. *First meeting, how called.*

Section 13. Said town of Frankfort at any time after the expiration of five years from the opening for use and service of a system of water works constructed by said corporation and after a vote in a legal town meeting to that effect has been passed, shall have the right to purchase, and by this act said corporation is required to sell to said town said system of water works including everything appertaining thereto, and if said town and corporation cannot agree upon the terms, upon such terms and that such price as shall be determined and fixed by the chief justice of the supreme court of the state of Maine, after due hearing of the parties interested, and from the decision of said chief justice there shall be no appeal. *Town may purchase works after five years.*

CHAP. 290

Charter void in two years unless business is commenced.

Section 14. This act shall become null and void in two years from the day when the same shall take effect, unless said company shall have organized and commenced actual business under this charter.

Consent of Winterport Water Co. to be obtained.

Section 15. The rights herein provided shall not be exercised by said incorporators without the consent in writing of the Winterport Water Company, a corporation located at Winterport in said county, first obtained.

Section 16. This act shall take effect when approved.

Approved March 25, 1903.

Chapter 290.

An Act to renew and extend the charter of the Boothbay Harbor Banking Company.

Be it enacted by the Senate and House of Representatives in Legislature assembled, as follows:

Charter extended for two years.

The charter incorporating certain persons into a body corporate and politic to be known as the Boothbay Harbor Banking Company, being chapter one hundred and forty-one of the private and special laws of eighteen hundred and ninety-nine, which was renewed and extended by chapter three hundred and fifty-three of the private and special laws of nineteen hundred and one, is hereby renewed and extended for a further term of two years.

Approved March 25, 1903.

Chapter 291.

An Act to incorporate the Patten Trust Company.

Be it enacted by the Senate and House of Representatives in Legislature assembled, as follows:

orporators.

Section 1. N. M. Jones, H. P. Gardner, Don. A. H. Powers, Albert A. Burleigh, I. K. Stetson, James McNutty, R. D. Gardner, S. L. Huston, George W. Cooper and Laroy Miles, or such of them as may by vote accept this charter, with their associates, successors and assigns, are hereby made a body corporate and politic to be known as the Patten Trust Company, and as such shall be possessed of all the powers, privileges and immunities and subject to all the duties and obligations conferred on corporations by law.

—corporate name.

PATTEN TRUST COMPANY. 463

Section 2. The corporation hereby created shall be located at Patten, Penobscot county, Maine.

CHAP. 291
Location.

Section 3. The purposes of said corporation and the business which it may perform are; first, to receive on deposit, money, coin, bank notes, evidences of debt, accounts of individuals, companies, municipalities and states, allowing interest thereon, if agreed, or as the by-laws of said corporation may provide; second, to borrow money, to loan money on credits, on real estate, or personal security, and to negotiate loans and sales for others; third, to own and maintain safe deposit vaults, with boxes, safes and other facilities therein, to be rented to other parties for the safe keeping of moneys, securities, stocks, jewelry, plate, valuable papers and documents, and other property susceptible of being deposited therein, and may receive on deposit for safe keeping, property of any kind entrusted to it for that purpose; fourth, to act as agent for issuing, registering and countersigning certificates, bonds, stocks, and all evidences of debt or ownership, in property; fifth, to hold by grant, assignment, transfer, devise or bequest, any real or personal property or trusts duly created, and to execute trusts of every description; sixth, to act as assignee, receiver, executor, and no surety shall be necessary upon the bond of the corporation unless the court or officer approving such bond shall require it; seventh, to do in general all the business that may lawfully be done by trust and banking companies, but said corporation shall not have the power or authority to establish branches.

Purposes.

—may own safe deposit vaults.

—may execute trusts.

—shall not establish branches.

Section 4. The capital stock of said corporation shall not be less than twenty-five thousand dollars, divided into shares of one hundred dollars each, with the right to increase the said capital stock at any time, by a vote of the shareholders, to any amount not exceeding one hundred thousand dollars. Said corporation shall not commence business as a trust or banking company until stock to the amount of at least twenty-five thousand dollars shall have been subscribed and paid in, in cash.

Capital stock.

—shall not commence business till $25,000 has been paid in.

Section 5. Said corporation shall not make any loan or discount on the security of the shares of its own capital stock, nor be the purchaser or holder of any such shares unless necessary to prevent loss upon a debt previously contracted in good faith; and all stock so acquired shall, within six months from the time of its acquisition, be disposed of at public or private sale.

Shall not make loan on security of its own shares.

Section 6. All the corporate powers of this corporation shall be exercised by a board of trustees, who shall be residents of this state, whose number and term of office shall be determined by a vote of the shareholders at the first meeting held by the incorporators and at each annual meeting thereafter. The affairs and

Board of trustees.

464   PATTEN TRUST COMPANY.

CHAP. 291

—executive board.

powers of the corporation may, at the option of the shareholders, be entrusted to an executive board of five members to be, by vote of the shareholders, elected from the full board of trustees. The trustees of said corporation shall be sworn to the proper discharge of their duties, and they shall hold office until others are elected and qualified in their stead. If a trustee or director dies, resigns, or becomes disqualified for any cause, the remaining trustees or directors may appoint a person to fill the vacancy until the next annual meeting of the corporation. The oath of office of such trustee or director shall be taken within thirty days of his election, or his office shall become vacant. The clerk of such corporation shall, within ten days, notify such trustees or directors of their election and within thirty days shall publish the list of all persons who have taken the oath of office as trustees or directors.

—vacancies, how filled.

Board of investment.

Section 7. The board of trustees or directors of said corporation shall constitute the board of investment of said corporation. Said trustees or directors shall keep in a separate book, specially provided for the purpose, a record of all loans and investments of every description, made by said institution substantially in the order of time when such loans or investments are made, which shall show that such loans or investments have been made with the approval of the investment committee of said corporation, which shall indicate such particulars respecting such loans or investments as the bank examiner shall direct. This book shall be submitted to the trustees or directors and to the bank examiner whenever requested. Such loans or investments shall be classified in the book as the bank examiner shall direct. No loan shall be made to any officer, or director of said banking or trust company except by the unanimous approval of the executive board in writing, and said corporation shall have no authority to hire money or to give notes unless by vote of the said board duly recorded.

—shall keep record of loans.

Director shall own five shares of stock.

Section 8. No person shall be eligible to the position of a director or a trustee of said corporation who is not the actual owner of five shares of the stock.

Reserve fund.

Section 9. Said corporation, after beginning to receive deposits, shall, at all times, have on hand in lawful money, as a reserve, not less than fifteen per cent of the aggregate amount of its deposits, which are subject to withdrawal on demand, provided, that in lieu of lawful money, two-thirds of said fifteen per cent may consist of balances, payable on demand, due from any national or state bank.

Trust funds shall constitute

Section 10. All the property or money held in trust by this corporation, shall constitute a special deposit and the accounts thereof and of said trust department shall be kept separate, and such funds and the investment or loans of them shall be specially appropriated to the security and payment of such deposits, and not be subject to any other liabilities of the corporation; and for the purpose of securing the observance of this provision, said corporation shall have a trust department in which all business pertaining to such trust property shall be kept separate and distinct from its general business.

Special deposit.

Section 11. An administrator, executor, assignee, guardian or trustee, any court of law or equity, including courts of probate and insolvency, officers and treasurers of towns, cities, counties and savings banks of the state of Maine may deposit any moneys, bonds, stocks, evidences of debt or of ownership in property, or any personal property, with said corporation, and any of said courts may direct any person deriving authority from them to so deposit the same.

Administrators, etc., may deposit in.

Section 12. Each shareholder of this corporation shall be individually responsible, equally and ratably, and not one for the other, for all contracts, debts and engagements of such corporation, to a sum equal to the amount of the par value of the shares owned by each in addition to the amount invested in said shares.

Responsibility of shareholders

Section 13. Such corporation shall set apart as a guaranty fund not less than ten per cent of its earnings in each and every year until such fund, with the accumulated interest thereon, shall amount to one-fourth of the capital stock of said corporation.

Guaranty fund.

Section 14. The shares of said corporation shall be subject to taxation in the same manner and rate as are the shares of national banks.

Taxation.

Section 15. Said corporation shall be subject to examination by the bank examiner, who shall visit it at least once in every year, and as much oftener as he may deem expedient. At such visits he shall have free access to its vaults, books and papers, and shall thoroughly inspect and examine all the affairs of said corporation, and make such inquiries as may be necessary to ascertain its condition and ability to fulfill all its engagements. If upon examination of said corporation, the examiner is of the opinion that its investments are not in accordance with law, or said corporation is insolvent, or its condition is such as to render its further proceedings hazardous to the public or to those having funds in its custody, or is of the opinion that it has exceeded its powers or failed to comply with any of the rules or restrictions provided by law, he shall have such authority and take such action as is provided for in the case of savings banks by chapter forty-

Shall be subject to examination by bank examiner.

seven of the revised statutes. He shall preserve in a permanent form a full record of his proceedings, including a statement of the condition of said corporation. A copy of such statement shall be published by said corporation immediately after the annual examination of the same in some newspaper published where said corporation is established. If no paper is published in the town where said corporation is established, then it shall be published in a newspaper printed in the nearest city or town. The necessary expenses of the bank examiner while making such examination shall be paid by the corporation.

First meeting, how called.

Section 16. Any two of the corporators named in this act may call the first meeting of the corporation by mailing a written notice signed by both, postage paid, to each of the other corporators, seven days at least before the day of the meeting, naming the time, place and purpose of such meeting, and at such meeting the necessary officers may be chosen, by-laws adopted, and any other corporate business transacted.

Section 17. This act shall take effect when approved.

Approved March 25, 1903.

Chapter 292.

An Act to Incorporate the Cherryfield and Milbridge Street Railway.

Be it enacted by the Senate and House of Representatives in Legislature assembled, as follows:

Corporators.

Section 1. E. K. Wilson, William M. Nash, Samuel N. Campbell, severally of Cherryfield, and Jasper Wyman and George A. Sawyer, both of Milbridge, are hereby made a corporation under the name of the Cherryfield and Milbridge Street Railway with authority to construct, operate and maintain a street railroad, for street traffic for the conveyance of persons and property, in the towns of Cherryfield and Milbridge, along and over such streets, roads and ways therein as shall, from time to time, be deemed best for the public convenience by the said company, and over and across such lands as to it may seem advisable and necessary, with such single or double tracks, side tracks, switches, turnouts, stations and appurtenances, and with such poles, wires and appliances as shall be reasonably convenient in the premises, with all the powers and privileges incident to or usually granted to similar corporations.

—corporate name.

—location of route.

May cross tide and navigable waters.

Section 2. The said corporation is further authorized to cross tide waters and navigable waters, within the limits of any or both of said towns, upon existing bridges, or upon bridges or structures of said company erected therefor, with such draws and piers as may be reasonably necessary, provided, however, that said company shall not unnecessarily obstruct navigation, and that the manner of its so crossing said waters and of its so erecting and maintaining any such bridges or structures of its own, shall first be determined by the municipal officers of the town or towns within the limits of which said bridge or structure shall be so erected, maintained or used; and if said company and such municipal officers shall disagree as to the terms prescribing the manner of such crossing, or of erecting and maintaining any such bridge or structure, the same shall, after notice and hearing, be determined by the railroad commissioners, and their decree thereon shall be final.

—proviso.

Section 3. The said company is authorized to erect, maintain and use such wharves, within the limits of any of said towns, as may be licensed under the general laws of the state, applicable thereto.

May erect wharves.

Section 4. The municipal officers of said towns shall determine the distance from the sidewalks, or the side lines of the roads, at which the rails of said company shall be laid. The said company or any person interested therein may appeal from any such determination to the board of railroad commissioners, who shall upon notice hear the parties and finally determine the questions raised by said appeal.

Municipal officers shall determine location of rails in streets.

Section 5. Before beginning construction of its said road the said company shall first file with the clerk of the county commissioners for Washington county a copy of its location, defining its courses, distances and boundaries, accompanied with a map of the proposed route on an appropriate scale, and another copy shall be filed with the board of railroad commissioners.

Location shall be filed with county commissioners.

Section 6. Such company, outside the limits of streets, roads and ways, may for its location, construction and convenient use of its road for its main track line, switches, turnouts, sidetracks, stations, car barns, gravel pits, spur tracks thereto, pole lines, wires, and power houses purchase or take and hold as for public uses any land and all materials in and upon it, except meeting houses, dwelling houses, public or private burying grounds or lands already devoted to railroad uses, and may excavate or construct in, through or over such lands to carry out its purposes, but the land so taken for its main track line, turnouts, switches and side tracks, shall not exceed four rods in width unless necessary for excavation and embankment or materials. All land so taken, except for its main track line, turnouts, switches and side tracks, shall be subject to the provisions of section sixteen of chapter fifty-one of the revised statutes. It may enter upon any

May take land as for public uses.

—damages for land taken.

468 CHERRYFIELD AND MILBRIDGE STREET RAILWAY.

CHAP. 292

—may enter on lands for surveys.

such lands to make surveys and locations, and plans of all locations and lands so taken shall be filed with the clerk of courts in the county of Washington, and when so filed such land shall be deemed and treated as taken.

County commissioners may determine damages.

Section 7. For the purpose of determining the damages to be paid for such location, occupation and construction, the land owner or said company may, within three years after the filing of such plans of location with the clerk of courts, as hereinbefore provided, apply to the commissioners of said county of Washington and have such damages assessed as is provided by law wherein land is taken for railroads, so far as the same is consistent with the provisions of their charter, and where inconsistent or at variance with this charter the charter shall control. Said commissioners shall have the same power to make orders relative to cattle passes, cattle guards and farm crossings as in the case of railroads. If the company shall fail to pay such land owner, or to deposit for his use with the clerk of the county commissioners, such sum as may be finally awarded for damages, with costs, within ninety days after final judgment, the said location shall be invalid and the company forfeit all right under the same. If such land owner secures more damages than were tendered by said company, he shall recover costs, otherwise the company shall recover costs. In case the company shall begin to occupy such lands before rendition of final judgment the land owner may require said company to file its bond with the county commissioners in such sum and with such sureties as they may approve, conditioned for such payment or deposit. Failure to apply for damages within said three years by said land owner shall be held to be a waiver of the same. No action shall be brought against such company for such taking and occupation of land until after such failure to pay or deposit.

—cattle passes, cattle guards and farm crossings.

Municipal officers may direct construction, removal of snow, etc.

Section 8. The road of said company shall be constructed and maintained in such form and manner and with such rails and upon such grades as the municipal officers of said towns may direct. Such municipal officers shall have power at all times to make all such regulations as to the mode of use of such tracks, the rate of speed and the removal and disposal of ice and snow from the streets, roads and ways as the public safety and convenience may require. The said company may appeal from any determination in relation to the foregoing to the railroad commissioners, whose decision thereon shall after notice and hearing be final.

May connect with Washington County R. R. Co.

Section 9. The said corporation is authorized to make such connection with the Washington County Railroad Company as may be agreed and to contract with it for interchange of cars.

Section 10. The said corporation is authorized to cross the railroad of the Washington County Railroad Company in such manner and under such conditions as shall be determined by the railroad commissioners. *May cross location of Washington County R. R. Co.*

Section 11. In addition to its main line, the said company is authorized to build and operate such branches in said towns as the public convenience may require. *May build branches.*

Section 12. Said company for all its purposes may hold real and personal estate necessary and convenient therefor. *May hold real and personal estate.*

Section 13. The capital stock of said corporation shall not exceed one hundred thousand dollars. It may issue its bonds in such amounts and on such rates and time as it deems expedient and secure the same by appropriate mortgages upon its franchises and property. *Capital stock.*

Section 14. All of the general laws of the state, except as modified by this charter, are hereby made applicable to the said corporation. *General laws made applicable.*

Section 15. This act shall be null and void unless said corporation shall on or before the first day of December, in the year of our Lord nineteen hundred three, expend an amount equal to ten per cent of its capital stock, as stated in its articles of association, in the construction of its railroad. This fact shall be determined by the railroad commissioners, after notice and hearing, and a certificate of their determination shall be filed in the office of the secretary of state. *Shall expend ten per cent of capital stock prior to Dec. 1, 1903.*

Section 16. This act shall take effect when approved.

Approved March 25, 1903.

Chapter 293.

An Act relative to the Aroostook Valley Railroad Company.

Be it enacted by the Senate and House of Representatives in Legislature assembled, as follows:

Section 1. The Aroostook Valley Railroad Company, a corporation created under the general laws of the state, is hereby authorized to file its petition in the office of the clerk of the supreme judicial court for the county of Penobscot, in term time or in vacation, addressed to any justice of said court, praying for a decree of said court to determine whether the railroad commissioners have lawful authority, under the general laws of the state and the special laws now in force relative to the Bangor and Aroostook Railroad Company, to approve the location of the road of said Aroostook Valley Railroad Company now on file *Authorized to file petition for decree relative to approval of location.*

CHAP. 294

in the office of the railroad commissioners, and like authority to determine whether public convenience requires the construction of such road upon such location.

Court shall hear the cause.

Section 2. The court shall under such notice thereon to the Bangor and Aroostook Railroad Company as it deems proper, and such other notice by publication or otherwise as to the court may seem necessary, hear the cause in term time or in vacation, and a certificate of its determination shall be filed with the clerk of the board of railroad commissioners. Such cause may by consent of parties be reported to the law court, appeal taken, or exceptions filed, severally to be taken, heard and determined in the same manner as in equity causes.

Section 3. This act shall take effect when approved.

Approved March 25, 1903.

Chapter 294.

An Act to extend the charter of the Maine Water and Electric Power Company.

Be it enacted by the Senate and House of Representatives in Legislature assembled, as follows:

Charter extended.

Section 1. The time within which the Maine Water and Electric Power Company shall actually commence business under its charter is hereby extended to two years from the approval hereof; provided, however, this act shall be null and void unless the sum of five thousand dollars is expended before the next session of the legislature in the development and improvement of the water power under the charter of said company; and provided further that three thousand of said five thousand dollars shall be expended on or before March fifteenth, one thousand nine hundred and four.

—proviso.

Section 2. This act shall take effect when approved.

Approved March 25, 1903.

Chapter 295.

An Act to authorize the Aroostook Valley Railroad Company to purchase or lease the property and franchises of the Presque Isle Electric Light Company.

Be it enacted by the Senate and House of Representatives in Legislature assembled, as follows:

Section 1. The Aroostook Valley Railroad Company, a corporation existing under the laws of the state, is hereby authorized to purchase or lease the property, capital stock, rights, privileges, immunities and franchises of the Presque Isle Electric Light Company upon such terms as may be agreed upon, and upon such purchase or lease the said Aroostook Valley Railroad Company shall have, hold, possess, exercise and enjoy all the locations, powers, privileges, rights, immunities, franchises, property and assets, which at the time of said transfer shall then be had, held, possessed or enjoyed by the said Presque Isle Electric Light Company, and shall be subject to all the duties, restrictions and liabilities to which the said Presque Isle Electric Light Company shall then be subject by reason of any charter, contract or general or special law, or otherwise. *Authorized to acquire the Presque Isle Electric Light Co.*

Section 2. All proceedings, suits at law or in equity, which may be pending at the time of such transfer, to which the said Presque Isle Electric Light Company may be a party, may be prosecuted or defended by the said Aroostook Valley Railroad Company in like manner and with like effect as if such transfer had not been made. All claims, contracts, rights and causes of action of or against the said Presque Isle Electric Light Company at law or in equity, may be enforced by suit or action to be begun or prosecuted by or against the said Aroostook Valley Railroad Company. *Pending proceedings, how prosecuted and defended*

Section 3. The Presque Isle Electric Light Company is hereby authorized to make the sale or lease authorized by section one of this act. *Sale authorized.*

Section 4. The said Aroostook Valley Railroad Company may increase its capital stock to such amount as may be necessary for the purposes of this act, and further may issue its stock and bonds in payment and exchange for the stocks, bonds, franchises and property of the said Presque Isle Electric Light Company, in such manner and in such amounts as may be agreed upon. *May increase capital stock.*

Section 5. When the transfer authorized in this act is carried out and fully completed, the Aroostook Valley Railroad Company shall be liable for the then lawfully existing debts, obligations and contracts of the said Presque Isle Electric Light Company. *Liability for debts and contracts.*

Section 6. This act shall take effect when approved.

Approved March 25, 1908.

Chapter 296.

An Act to incorporate the Village Cemetery Association of Searsport, Waldo county, Maine.

Be it enacted by the Senate and House of Representatives in Legislature assembled, as follows:

Corporators.

Section 1. Cyrus True, J. W. Black, E. Hopkins, J. A. Colson and L. M. Sargent, their associates, successors and assigns, are hereby made a corporation by the name of the Village Cemetery Association, for the purpose of enlarging, improving and caring for the Village cemetery, so called, in the town of Searsport.

—corporate name.

May purchase lease and lay out lots.

Section 2. Said association shall have power to purchase land, to enlarge and improve said cemetery, to lay out lots and to sell the same, to receive and hold trust funds for the care or improvement of said cemetery or any part thereof.

Officers.

Section 3. The officers of said association shall be a president, vice president, secretary, treasurer and superintendent. The president, vice president, secretary, treasurer and superintendent, together with three or more members of the association who shall be elected by the association, shall constitute the executive committee. Said executive committee shall have full control of all work and improvements, the laying out of all moneys and the investment of all trust funds of the association.

—executive committee.

Annual meetings.

Section 4. Regular meetings of said association for the choice of officers and the transaction of any business that may legally come before said meetings shall be held annually on the first Saturday in May. Officers so chosen shall hold office for the term of one year or until their successors are elected.

First meeting, how called.

Section 5. The first meeting of said corporation shall be called by written notice thereof, signed by any two corporators herein named, served upon each corporator, by giving him the same in hand, or by leaving same at his last usual place of abode, seven days before the time of said meeting.

Approved March 25, 1903.

Chapter 297.

An Act to extend the charter of the Bluehill and Bucksport Electric Railroad Company.

Be it enacted by the Senate and House of Representatives in Legislature assembled, as follows:

Section 1. The rights, powers and privileges of the Bluehill and Bucksport Electric Railroad Company, which were granted by chapter one hundred and fifty-seven of the private and special laws of eighteen hundred and ninety-nine, are hereby extended for two years additional; and the persons named in said act, their associates and successors, shall have all the rights, powers and privileges that were granted them by said act, to be exercised in the same manner and for the same purposes as specified in said act. *[Charter extended.]*

Section 2. This act shall take effect when approved.

Approved March 25, 1903.

Chapter 298.

An Act authorizing Samuel D. Warren and others to erect and maintain piers and booms in the Kennebec River.

Be it enacted by the Senate and House of Representatives in Legislature assembled, as follows:

Section 1. Samuel D. Warren, Mortimer B. Mason, Fiske Warren and John E. Warren, their successors and assigns are hereby authorized and empowered to locate, erect and maintain in the Kennebec river and in the city of Augusta and towns of Vassalboro and Sidney, piers and booms for the purpose of holding all logs, pulp wood and other lumber coming down said river and destined for use or manufacture by them or either of them substantially as follows: A deposit boom with suitable piers beginning at a point on the easterly side of the Kennebec river at or near land of J. S. Nicholas, and extending northerly to a point southerly of and near Five Mile Island, so called, and distant from the easterly shore of said river about one-third of its width; also a sorting boom substantially as follows: Beginning at a point on the westerly shore of said river near the line between Augusta and Sidney thence extending across said river in a southeasterly direction with suitable piers. Said piers and booms shall be so constructed as not to impede the use or navigation of said river, and not to occasion any unreasonable delay or obstruction in the driving of any logs or lumber owned by other parties. All other logs than those provided for by this sec- *[Piers and booms in Kennebec river authorized. —deposit boom. —sorting boom. —use or navigation of river shall not be impeded.]*

CHAP. 299

tion, if held by, or found in either of said booms, shall be turned out thereby by said Samuel D. Warren and others at their own charge and in no case shall the delay in so turning out exceed forty-eight hours after demand made by the Kennebec Log Driving Company or by the log owner; and they shall, when required by the Kennebec Log Driving Company or by other log owners, turn out of said sorting boom, not less than fifteen thousand logs daily, if the elements will permit the same. Said Samuel D. Warren and others shall at their own expense, break and also put through their boom any jam of logs occasioned by their said piers.

—may take lands.

Section 2. Said Samuel D. Warren, Mortimer B. Mason, Fiske Warren and John E. Warren, their successors and assigns, may enter upon, take and hold such lands as may be necessary for the erection and maintenance of the piers and booms mentioned in this act, and connected by same with the shores, and may, with their agents and teams, pass and repass over said shores and to and from the same over the lands of other persons for the purposes aforesaid and for the operation and management of said booms, making compensation therefor as provided in the case of damages for lands taken in laying out highways.

—compensation for land taken.

Section 3. This act shall take effect when approved.

Approved March 26, 1903.

Chapter 299.

An Act to prohibit ice fishing in Number Nine Lake, situated in Township nine, Range three, in the County of Aroostook.

Be it enacted by the Senate and House of Representatives in Legislature assembled, as follows:

Ice fishing in Number Nine lake, prohibited.

It shall be unlawful to fish for, take, catch or kill, in any way, any fish in Number Nine lake, situated in Township nine, Range three, in the county of Aroostook, from October first to June first of each year, under a penalty of not less than ten dollars nor more than thirty dollars and costs for each offense, and one dollar additional for each fish caught, taken or killed in violation of this act.

—penalty.

Approved March 26, 1903.

Chapter 300.

An Act to prohibit all ice fishing in First or Billings pond, in Blue Hill, county of Hancock.

Be it enacted by the Senate and House of Representatives in Legislature assembled, as follows:

Section 1. It shall be unlawful to fish for, take, catch or kill any fish, from October first to May first of each year, in First or Billings pond, in the town of Bluehill, in the county of Hancock, for a period of five years from October first, nineteen hundred and three.

Ice fishing in First or Billings pond, prohibited.

Section 2. Whoever violates any of the provisions of this act shall be punished by a fine of not less than ten nor more than thirty dollars and costs for each offense, and a further penalty of one dollar for each fish caught, taken or killed in violation of this act.

Penalty for violation.

Approved March 26, 1903.

Chapter 301.

An Act for the protection of Deer in the Counties of Kennebec, Knox, Waldo and Lincoln.

Be it enacted by the Senate and House of Representatives in Legislature assembled, as follows:

Section 1. No person shall in any manner hunt, take, catch or kill any deer in Kennebec, Knox, Waldo and Lincoln counties between December first and October fifteenth next following; and no person shall between October fifteenth and December first inclusive next following take, catch or kill more than two deer, not more than one of which shall be a doe or fawn; nor shall any person have in possession any deer or part thereof killed in violation of this section.

Protection of deer in Kennebec, Knox, Waldo and Lincoln counties.

Section 2. The penalties provided by the general law for like offenses shall be the penalties for a violation of this act. Except where inconsistent with this act the general law shall apply to deer in each of said counties.

Penalty for violation.

Approved March 26, 1903.

Chapter 302.

An Act creating a close time on the tributaries to Indian, South and Twitchell ponds, and on Indian pond, in Greenwood, and the tributaries to Bryant pond in Woodstock, in the county of Oxford.

Be it enacted by the Senate and House of Representatives in Legislature assembled, as follows:

Close time for fishing in certain waters in Oxford county.

Section 1. It shall be unlawful for any person, at any time, to fish for, take, catch or kill any kind of fish in any of the tributaries to Indian pond, South pond and Twitchell pond, situated in the town of Greenwood, or the tributaries to Bryant pond in the town of Woodstock.

Indian pond.

Section 2. It shall be unlawful for any person to fish for, take, catch or kill any kind of fish in Indian pond, above named, for three years from April first, nineteen hundred and three.

Penalty for violation.

Section 3. Whoever violates any of the provisions of this act shall be subject to the same penalty as is provided in the general law for illegal fishing.

Approved March 26, 1903.

Chapter 303.

An Act to legalize the doings of the selectmen of the town of Waltham.

Be it enacted by the Senate and House of Representatives in Legislature assembled, as follows:

Doings of selectmen of Waltham made valid.

Section 1. The doings of the selectmen of the town of Waltham in the county of Hancock for the year nineteen hundred, whereby the board of selectmen acted as fire wardens and assessed taxes to pay expense of same are hereby made legal and valid.

Section 2. This act shall take effect when approved.

Approved March 26, 1903.

Chapter 304.

An Act to authorize Bath, West Bath and Brunswick, to build a bridge over the New Meadows River between Brunswick and West Bath.

Be it enacted by the Senate and House of Representatives in Legislature assembled, as follows:

Section 1. The city of Bath and the towns of West Bath and Brunswick or any one or two of said municipalities, are hereby authorized to erect a free bridge over New Meadows river, from land in Brunswick to land in West Bath, and between the bridge of the Maine Central Railroad Company and the steamboat landing above Bull Rock bridge; said free bridge to be built of good materials, substantially made, well railed, and convenient for the passage of travelers thereon. *Free bridge over New Meadows river authorized.*

Section 2. If one of said municipalities shall erect and complete said bridge, the said municipalities shall thereafter have the same control thereof, and be under the same liability to keep it in repair, as if were wholly within the limits of said municipality, and, on the completion of said bridge, said municipality shall file with the secretary of state its certificate in writing, under the hands of its municipal officers, that it has erected and completed said bridge under this act. If two or all of said municipalities shall erect and complete said bridge, the cost of construction shall be apportioned among them, and the said control and liability shall devolve upon them, or any of them, as they may agree in writing, under the hands of their municipal officers, before the work of construction shall begin, and a copy of such agreement attested by the clerk of each of the contracting parties, together with the certificate of each of said contracting parties, under the hands of its municipal officers, that the bridge has been erected and completed according to such agreement, shall be filed with the secretary of state, on the completion of the work of construction. Each of said municipalities is hereby authorized to raise money by taxation or otherwise, for the purposes aforesaid. *Either municipality building bridge, the same shall control.* *—If two or all build said bridge, cost shall be apportioned.*

Section 3. The county commissioners of Sagadahoc and Cumberland counties may authorize the use of any part of the materials composing Bull Rock bridge, so far as the same may be suitable for the purpose, in the construction of the new bridge, and may, at any time, close said Bull Rock bridge to travel, or discontinue the same. Until said bridge is so closed to travel, or discontinued, either or both of said towns may aid the city of Bath in the alteration or repair of said bridge, and may raise or appropriate money therefor. Said Bull Rock bridge, shall be discontinued on the completion of the new bridge, if not pre- *County commissioners may allow materials of Bull Rock bridge to be used.* *—may close Bull Rock bridge.*

Approved March 26, 1903.

Chapter 305.

An Act to Amend an Act Incorporating the Trustees of Bridgton Academy.

Be it enacted by the Senate and House of Representatives in Legislature assembled, as follows:

Section 1, chapter 105, laws of Massachusetts of 1808, amended.

Section 1. Section one of chapter one hundred and five of laws of Massachusetts of eighteen hundred and eight entitled "An Act to establish an academy at Bridgetown in the county of Cumberland," is hereby amended by striking out the word "fifteen" and by inserting in lieu thereof the word 'twenty,' so that said section as amended shall read as follows:

Academy established at Bridgetown.

'Section 1. Be it enacted by the Senate and House of Representatives, in General Court assembled, and by the authority of the same, that an academy shall be, and hereby is established at Bridgetown, in the county of Cumberland, and that Mr. Samuel Andrews, Mr. Robert Andrews, Mr. Aaron Beman,

—corporators.

Stephen Chase, Esquire, the Reverend Nathan Church, Mr. David Clark, Doctor Ezra Dean, Samuel Farnsworth, Esquire, Mr. Benjamin Kimball, Enoch Perley, Esquire, and Mr. Seba Smith, all of said Bridgetown; the Reverend Daniel Gould, of Bethel, the Reverend Lincoln Ripley, of Waterford, Mr. Jonathan Bernard, of   , and Mr. Nathaniel Burnham of Harrison, be, and they are hereby appointed the trustees of the said academy, and they and their successors in the said trust, are hereby made and declared to be a body politic and corporate,

—corporate name.

by the name of the Trustees of Bridgetown Academy; and the said trustees shall have, hold and continue in perpetual succession, with all the powers and privileges usually given to, and exercised and enjoyed by other academies; but the number of

—number of trustees.

the said trustees, shall not be less than nine, nor more than twenty, and five of whom may be a quorum for doing business. And the said trustees may keep and use a common seal, which they may alter or change when they see cause; and all deeds or other instruments, made by the said corporation, shall be signed and sealed with their seal, and executed, delivered and acknowledged by the secretary and treasurer of the said corporation by order of the trustees, and shall be binding on the said corporation, and shall be good and valid in law.'

Section 2. This act shall take effect when approved.

Approved March 26, 1903.

Chapter 306.

An Act in relation to the Bath Military and Naval Orphan Asylum.

Be it enacted by the Senate and House of Representatives in Legislature assembled, as follows:

Section 1. Chapter one hundred and sixty-three of the private and special laws of eighteen hundred and sixty-six is hereby amended by adding the following section: {Chapter 163, special laws of 1866, amended.}

'Section 7. The trustees are authorized and empowered, at their discretion, to admit to the Home, children or grandchildren of the veterans of the civil war when they have been deserted by either of their parents, also orphans or half orphans of veterans of the Spanish war who were residents of Maine, also orphans of any citizens of Maine, should the capacity of the Home, at any time, be more than sufficient to care for orphans eligible for admittance under the preceding section of this chapter.' {Admissions to the asylum}

Section 2. This act shall take effect when approved.

Approved March 26, 1903.

Chapter 307.

An Act opening certain tributaries to Sebec lake to fishing under the general law.

Be it enacted by the Senate and House of Representatives in Legislature assembled, as follows:

Section 1. It shall be lawful to fish for, take, catch and kill fish, in accordance with the general law of the state, in all of the streams flowing into Sebec lake, in Piscataquis county, except Wilson stream and Ship pond stream. {Open season for certain tributaries of Sebec lake.}

Section 2. This act shall take effect when approved.

Approved March 26, 1903.

Chapter 308.

An Act to change the corporate name of "Maine Wesleyan Seminary and Female College."

Be it enacted by the Senate and House of Representatives in Legislature assembled, as follows:

Name changed.

Section 1. The corporate name of the trustees of "Maine Wesleyan Seminary and Female College" as altered and amended by chapters one hundred ninety-five and three hundred ten of the special laws of eighteen hundred eighty-three is hereby amended by striking out the word "Female" and inserting in lieu thereof the word 'Woman's' so that the same shall hereafter be "Maine Wesleyan Seminary and Woman's College."

Powers, rights and privileges, made valid to Maine Wesleyan Seminary and Woman's College.

Section 2. All donations, gifts, grants, conveyances, devises, and bequests heretofore made to the trustees of the Readfield Religious and Charitable Society; to the trustees of the Maine Wesleyan Seminary; to the trustees of the Maine Wesleyan Seminary and Female Collegiate Institute; to the Maine Wesleyan Seminary and Female College, or that shall hereafter be made to either of said corporations or to the trustees thereof, shall be deemed good and valid and shall be and become the property of said "Maine Wesleyan Seminary and Woman's College" as if made to the said seminary and college, or to the trustees thereof, and shall be held by said trustees as if made to them, and the said trustees shall have the same right to prosecute in their corporate name any action at law or in equity upon any contract or liability heretofore made or existing with the trustees of the Readfield Religious and Charitable Society; the trustees of the Maine Wesleyan Seminary; the trustees of the Maine Wesleyan Seminary and Female Collegiate Institute; or with the Maine Wesleyan Seminary and Female College, as the said body politic, under whatever name, might have done if the name thereof had not been changed; and also to defend any suit which may be brought against them upon any such contract or liability; and all acts of said trustees in their corporate capacity are here ratified.

Section 3. This act shall take effect when approved.

Approved March 26, 1903.

Chapter 309.

An Act to incorporate Washington County General Hospital.

Be it enacted by the Senate and House of Representatives in Legislature assembled, as follows:

Section 1. John A. McDonald of East Machias, Frank L. Shaw, Samuel B. Hunter and A. L. Smith of Machias, R. L. Holland of Calais, James B. Grady of Eastport, Fred A. Chandler of Addison, and George A. Sawyer of Milbridge, and their associates, are hereby created a corporation, and a body politic under the name Washington County General Hospital, with all the powers and privileges of similar corporations. {Corporators. —corporate name.}

Section 2. Said corporation is authorized to establish, maintain and carry on a hospital at Machias in the county of Washington, for the treatment of persons requiring the aid of medical or surgical skill, care and attendance, and for the purpose of conducting a training school for nurses. {Purposes.}

Section 3. Said corporation is authorized and empowered for the purposes of its organization, to receive, take and hold, by deed, devise, bequest, or otherwise, property, personal and real, to the amount of two hundred and fifty thousand dollars. {May hold property to the amount of $250,000.}

Section 4. Any two of the incorporators named in this act may call the first meeting of this company, which shall be held at said Machias, by mailing a written notice, postage paid, to each of the other corporators, seven days at least before the day of meeting, naming the time and place in said Machias, and purposes of such meeting. {First meeting, how called.}

Section 5. This act shall take effect when approved.

Approved March 26, 1903.

Chapter 310.

An Act to amend chapter three hundred eighty-one of the private laws of nineteen hundred and one, relating to open time on Deer in Cumberland county.

Be it enacted by the Senate and House of Representatives in Legislature assembled, as follows:

Section one of chapter three hundred eighty-one of the private and special laws of nineteen hundred and one is hereby amended by inserting after the word "Windham," in the fourth line, the words 'Freeport and Pownal,' so that said section as amended shall read as follows: {Section 1, chapter 381, special laws of 1901, amended.}

CHAP. 311

Open time on deer in certain towns in Cumberland county.

'Section 1. It shall be lawful to hunt, chase and kill deer in the towns of Baldwin, Bridgton, Casco, Gorham, Gray, Harrison, Naples, New Gloucester, Otisfield, Raymond, Sebago, Standish, Windham, Freeport and Pownal, in Cumberland county, from October first to November first.'

Approved March 26, 1903.

Chapter 311.

An Act to amend Chapter sixty-five of the Private and Special Laws of eighteen hundred seventy-five, relative to Petit Menan Point.

Be it enacted by the Senate and House of Representatives in Legislature assembled, as follows:

Chapter 65, special laws of 1875, amended.

Section 1. Chapter sixty-five of the private and special laws of eighteen hundred seventy-five is hereby amended by adding thereto the following:

Open season for hunting on shores of Great and Chair ponds.

'Provided however that residents of the state shall from the first day of October in each year to the first day of June in the following year, if not otherwise prohibited by law, have the right to shoot, hunt and kill birds on the shores of said point lying south of Chair pond on the east and Yellow Birch head on the west and upon the shores of Great and Chair ponds.

Petit Menan point, relative to hunting deer on portion of.

Any person who shall hunt, shoot or kill deer at any time or shall hunt any game with a dog on any part of said Petit Menan point south of the line described in said chapter sixty-five shall be deemed a trespasser and be subject to the provisions and liable to the penalties provided by said act.'

Section 2. This act shall take effect when approved.

Approved March 26, 1903.

Chapter 312

An Act to amend the charter of the Penobscot Lumbering Association.

Be it enacted by the Senate and House of Representatives in Legislature assembled, as follows:

Section 1. Chapter two hundred and ninety-eight of the private and special laws of eighteen hundred and fifty-four, approved April five, eighteen hundred and fifty-four, entitled "An Act to incorporate the Penobscot Lumbering Association and to amend the charter of the Penobscot Boom Corporation," is amended as follows:

'Section eighteen of said chapter two hundred and ninety-eight of the private and special laws of eighteen hundred and fifty-four is amended so that said section eighteen, as amended, shall then read as follows: 'In order to meet all payments and expenses of every character due from the association, they shall have power and it shall be their duty to make and enforce assessments therefor, either after the payments or expenses or in anticipation of the same, which assessments shall be pro rata upon all logs or other lumber of which the same number of sticks make a thousand feet, board measure; but in making the assessment in each year said association shall first ascertain the average number of logs or other lumber out of the total quantity rafted for such year that will make a thousand feet, board measure, by adopting as a basis of calculation the average number required for a thousand feet, board measure, the previous year, and upon such average number of logs or other lumber making a thousand feet, board measure, there shall be one level, average rate of assessment, and in addition to said level, average rate of assessment there shall be an increase of one-half a cent per thousand feet, board measure, for every log or stick required to make a thousand feet, board measure, in excess of said average number, namely: logs or other lumber of which it takes to make a thousand feet, board measure, one more stick than said average number, shall have an additional assessment of one-half a cent per one thousand feet, board measure, two more sticks, one cent per thousand feet, board measure, three more sticks, one and one-half cents per thousand feet, board measure, and so on in a like manner of increase; and there shall be a similar rate of decrease from said level, average rate of assessment of one-half a cent per one thousand feet, board measure, when a less number than said average number of logs or other lumber make a thousand feet, board measure, all of which to be ascertained or estimated as the by-laws may prescribe. For all such assessments a lien upon the lumber shall exist enforcible as pointed out in the

CHAP. 313

—proceedings if owner wishes to take lumber before assessment is made.

seventh section of the charter of the Penobscot Boom Corporation, and in the sixth section of the act additional thereto approved March twenty-first, eighteen hundred and thirty-eight. If any owner shall wish to take his lumber before the assessment thereon has been made, he shall be permitted to do it upon paying to the treasurer in advance such sum as he shall prescribe, the amount to be made equal and just after the amount to have been assessed shall be ascertained. In addition to the lien aforesaid the association shall have a remedy by action of assumpsit against the owner or any person to whom the lumber so assessed may have been transferred by mortgage, pledge or other way of security.'

—remedy by action of assumpsit, in addition to lien.

Section 2. This act shall take effect when approved.

Approved March 26, 1903.

Chapter 313.

An Act to limit the number of fish that may be taken from Spring lake, in Somerset County, in one day.

Be it enacted by the Senate and House of Representatives in Legislature assembled, as follows:

Spring lake, fish to be taken from in one day.

No person shall take, catch, kill or carry away more than two fish of any kind, eels and suckers excepted, or ten pounds of fish, in any one day from Spring lake, so called, in Somerset county, under a penalty of not less than ten dollars nor more than thirty dollars and costs for each offense and a further penalty of one dollar for each fish caught, taken or killed in violation of this act.

—penalty for violation.

Approved March 26, 1903.

Chapter 314.

An Act to repeal so much of chapter thirty of the Revised Statutes, as amended by Chapter forty-two, Section five, of the Public Laws of eighteen hundred and ninety-nine, as prohibits fishing in Parlin stream, in Somerset County, from the mouth of Bean brook to Long pond.

Be it enacted by the Senate and House of Representatives in Legislature assembled, as follows:

Fishing in Parlin stream, prohibition repealed.

Section 1. So much of chapter thirty of the revised statutes, as amended by chapter forty-two, section five, of the public laws of eighteen hundred and ninety-nine, as prohibits fishing in Parlin stream, in Somerset county from the mouth of Bean brook to Long pond, is hereby repealed.

Section 2. This act shall take effect when approved.

Approved March 26, 1903.

Chapter 315.

An Act to incorporate the Madunkeunk Dam and Improvement Company.

Be it enacted by the Senate and House of Representatives in Legislature assembled, as follows:

Section 1. John G. Fleming, James F. Kimball, Nathaniel M. Jones, George W. Smith, Alvarius Hathaway, Samuel C. Fleming and George H. Haynes, their associates, successors and assigns, are hereby incorporated under the name of the Madunkeunk Dam and Improvement Company. *Corporators. —corporate name.*

Section 2. Said company is authorized to erect and maintain dams, sluices and side dams on the Madunkeunk stream, in the county of Penobscot, and its tributaries, to remove rocks therefrom, and to widen, deepen and otherwise improve said stream and its tributaries for the purpose of facilitating the driving of logs and other lumber down the same. Said dams to be located as follows: One at or near the mouth of the Ebhors stream, a tributary of said Madunkeunk; one on the east branch of said stream at or near the old dam; one at the foot of Beaver pond, so called; one on Trout brook, a tributary of said stream, at or near the foot of the meadows; and one on the Ebhors stream at a point to be hereafter determined by said company. Said company is hereby authorized to purchase any dams now constructed and in use at or near the aforesaid points. Said company is also authorized to locate, erect and maintain in the Penobscot river at or near the mouth of said Madunkeunk stream piers and booms for the purpose of affording owners of logs and other lumber coming down said stream facilities for collecting, holding and sorting out the same; provided, said piers and booms shall be so located, constructed, maintained and used that they will not in any way interfere with the free navigation of said Penobscot river or the passage of logs or rafts of lumber down said river. Said company, its successors and assigns, by aid of such piers and booms is hereby authorized to separate and sort out the logs and other lumber coming out of said stream and belonging to different owners whenever requested to do so by such owners, receiving such compensation therefor as may be agreed upon between such owners and said company. Said company is also hereby authorized and empowered to hold within the piers and booms mentioned in this act and located, erected and maintained as aforesaid, all logs, pulp wood and other lumber coming down said Madunkeunk stream when so requested by the owners thereof, or when necessary for the protection of such logs and other lumber. *Powers. —location of dams. —location of piers and booms. —proviso. —may sort logs. —compensation for sorting. —on request of owners may hold logs, etc.*

CHAP. 315

Damages for flowage.

Section 3. Any damages arising from flowing of land by said dams may be recovered in accordance with the provisions of chapter ninety-two of the revised statutes.

Tolls.

Section 4. Said company may demand and receive a toll upon all logs and other lumber which may pass over or through said dams or other improvements, including said booms, to be fixed by said company, but not to exceed fifteen cents per thousand feet stumpage scale, or, when such logs or other lumber have not been scaled for stumpage, by the scale rendered at the place of destination of such logs and other lumber, and said company shall have a lien upon such logs and other lumber until the full amount of toll is paid, to be enforced by attachment, said lien to continue for ninety days after such logs and other lumber shall arrive at their place of destination.

Reduction of tolls.

Section 5. When said company shall have received from tolls its outlay upon all dams, improvements and repairs made up to that time, including any damages paid for flowage or otherwise, together with six per cent interest thereon, then the tolls herein provided for shall be reduced to a sum sufficient to keep said dams and improvments in reasonable repair.

Capital stock.

Section 6. Said company may issue its capital stock to an amount not exceeding ten thousand dollars, to be divided into shares of one hundred dollars each.

First meeting, how called.

Section 7. The first meeting of said company shall be called at Lincoln, in the county of Penobscot, by a notice signed by any one of the corporators named in section one, setting forth the time, place and purposes of the meeting, and such notice shall be mailed to each of the other corporators, postage paid, seven days at least before the day of such meeting.

Section 8. This act shall take effect when approved.

Approved March 26, 1903.

Chapter 316.

An Act to incorporate the Duck Lake Dam Company.

Be it enacted by the Senate and House of Representatives in Legislature assembled, as follows:

Section 1. Charles L. Hathaway, Charles D. Whittier and George W. Banton, their associates, successors and assigns are hereby created a corporation by the name of the Duck Lake Dam Company, with all the powers and privileges of similar corporations. — Corporators. —Corporate name.

Section 2. The said corporation may for the purposes of driving logs, raising a head of water therefor and facilitating the business thereof erect and maintain a dam or dams on Duck lake at or near its outlet in township numbered four, north division, in the county of Hancock, and said corporation may, at its election, erect, construct and maintain piers, sluices, embankments, dam or dams, abutments, side dams and other improvements at or near the foot of said Duck lake, and also on Duck brook running from said Duck lake through a part of said township numbered four and a part of township numbered three, north division, in said county of Hancock, into Nicatous lake; and remove rocks and other obstructions in said Duck lake and Duck brook and otherwise improve the passageway therein for driving logs. Powers.

Section 3. The said corporation is authorized to enter upon and take such land, property or material upon said townships, or either of them, as said corporation may find necessary to construct its works, dams and other improvements and locate the same, and also flow contiguous lands, provided said corporation shall pay to the proprietor or proprietors of the land, property or material so taken such damages, unless the parties agree, as shall be ascertained and determined by the county commissioners of said county of Hancock, in the same manner and under the same conditions and limitations as are by law provided in case of damage by laying out of public highways, with the same right to have a jury to determine the damages; and for the damage occasioned by flowing land the said corporation shall not be liable to an action at common law, but the party injured may have a remedy by a complaint for flowage, in which the same proceedings shall be had as when a complaint is made under a statute of this state for flowing lands occasioned by raising a head of water for the working of mills; and said corporation may hold by purchase or otherwise other property real and personal necessary or convenient for its purposes. May take lands. —may flow contiguous lands. —damages, how determined.

Section 4. Said corporation may demand and receive as toll for each and every thousand feet board measure of all logs and Tolls.

CHAP. 316

lumber which either may be put into waters above its dam at or near the foot of said Duck lake and pass over its said dam or which may pass down said Duck brook, to be ascertained by the woods scale or boom scale at the option of said corporation, the following sums, namely: From below the mouth of Spencer brook ten cents per thousand; between the mouth of Spencer brook and Duck lake, twenty-five cents per thousand; and from above the dam at or near the foot of said Duck lake, forty cents per thousand: and said corporation shall have a lien upon all logs and lumber which either may pass over its said dam at or near the foot of said Duck lake or which may pass down said Duck brook until the full amount of toll of all the logs and lumber which may pass over its said dam or down said Duck brook, is fully paid, but the logs or lumber of each particular mark shall only be holden to pay the toll of such mark, and if said toll is not paid within thirty days after said logs and lumber shall arrive at the place of destination for sale or manufacture said corporation may sell at public auction in Bangor, after ten days notice in some newspaper printed in said Bangor, so much of said logs and lumber as may be sufficient to pay said toll and incidental charges. Said corporation may also proceed to collect its dues for tolls by action at law or, if necessary, by suit in equity.

Reduction of tolls.

Section 5. When said corporation shall, from tolls received by it, be reimbursed for all costs, expenses and incidental charges for erecting and maintaining its dam or dams, sites, works and other improvements, with interest at nine per centum per annum, there shall then be a reduction of tolls to a sum sufficient in the opinion of the directors of said company to keep said dam or dams, sites, works and the other improvements, if any, in repair for protecting and preserving them and paying said interest charge.

Section 6. This act shall take effect when approved.

Approved March 26, 1903.

Chapter 317.

An Act to prohibit the taking of Clams in the shores or flats within the Town of Scarboro.

Be it enacted by the Senate and House of Representatives in Legislature assembled, as follows:

Section 1. No person shall take or dig or destroy in any manner clams in any of the shores or flats within the town of Scarboro from the first day of April until the first day of October in each year under a penalty of not less than ten or more than one hundred dollars for each and every violation of this statute. *Close time on clams in Scarboro.*

Section 2. The aforesaid section shall not apply to inhabitants or residents of said town taking clams for the consumption of himself and family nor to hotel keepers within the town taking clams for the use of their hotels. *Inhabitants may take clams for own use*

Section 3. This act shall take effect when approved.

Approved March 26, 1903.

Chapter 318.

An Act to prohibit the sale of any kind of fish, except eels, taken from certain ponds in Kennebec and Somerset counties.

Be it enacted by the Senate and House of Representatives in Legislature assembled, as follows:

Section 1. It shall be unlawful for any person to sell, or offer for sale, any kind of fish, except eels, at any time, taken from any of the following named lakes and ponds and their tributaries lying wholly or in part in the counties of Kennebec and Somerset, to wit: East, North, Little, Great, Long, McGraw, Ellis and Snow ponds, under a penalty of not less than ten nor more than thirty dollars and costs for each offense, and a further fine of one dollar for each fish sold in violation of this law. *Sale of fish taken from certain ponds in Kennebec and Somerset counties, prohibited.*

Section 2. This act shall take effect May first, nineteen hundred three.

Approved March 26, 1903.

CHAP. 319

Chapter 319.

An Act to prohibit fishing in Morrill Pond in the County of Somerset.

Be it enacted by the Senate and House of Representatives in Legislature assembled, as follows:

Close time on fishing in Morrill pond.

It shall be unlawful to fish for, take, catch, or kill any kind of fish in Morrill pond in the county of Somerset at any time before the first day of April in the year of our Lord nineteen hundred and five. Whoever violates the provision of this section shall be subject to the same penalties as provided for illegal fishing in the general law.

Approved March 26, 1903.

Chapter 320.

An Act to prevent the destruction of Smelts or Tomcods so called in Steuben Bay.

Be it enacted by the Senate and House of Representatives in Legislature assembled, as follows:

Smelts and tomcods protected in Steuben bay.

Section 1. All persons are forbidden to take the fish known as smelts and tomcods in that part of Steuben and Joys bays above the Narrows at Rogers point so called in the town of Steuben, by the use of weirs or set nets, from the first day of April to the first day of January, in each year for the term of three years, from and after the passage of this act.

Penalty.

Section 2. If any person shall violate the provisions of this act, he shall pay for each and every violation the sum of ten dollars, to be recovered in an action of debt, one-half to the person who may prosecute and the other half to the use of the town where the offense is committed.

Section 3. This act shall take effect when approved.

Approved March 26, 1903.

Chapter 321.

An Act to regulate the taking of black bass in Upper Kezar Pond in Oxford County, also to prohibit the taking of smelts in any tributary of said Pond.

Be it enacted by the Senate and House of Representatives in Legislature assembled, as follows:

Section 1. It shall be unlawful for any one person in one day, to take more than ten black bass from Upper Kezar pond in Oxford county. It shall also be unlawful at any time, to take black bass from said Upper Kezar pond less than twelve inches in length.

Taking of black bass in Upper Kezar pond, to regulate.

Section 2. It shall be unlawful at any time to take smelts from any tributary of Upper Kezar pond in Oxford county.

Smelts protected in tributaries of pond.

Section 3. Whoever shall violate any provisions of this act shall be subject to the same penalty provided for illegal fishing under the general law.

Approved March 26, 1903.

Chapter 322.

An Act fixing the beginning of the open season for fishing in Little Sebago pond, in the towns of Gray and Windham, in Cumberland county.

Be it enacted by the Senate and House of Representatives in Legislature assembled, as follows:

Section 1. The open time for fishing in Little Sebago pond, in the towns of Gray and Windham, in Cumberland county, shall begin as soon as the ice is out of said pond instead of on June fifteenth as now provided by law.

Open season for fishing, Little Sebago pond.

Section 2. This act shall take effect when approved.

Approved March 26, 1903.

Chapter 323.

An Act to incorporate the Phillips Trust Company.

Be it enacted by the Senate and House of Representatives in Legislature assembled, as follows:

Section 1. Joel Wilbur, E. H. Shepard, Frank H. Wilbur, F. N. Beal, Weston Lewis, G. A. French, N. P. Noble, Josiah S. Maxcy, F. E. Timberlake, Edward Greenwood, A. M. Greenwood, Fremont Scamman, J. W. Brackett, or such of them as may by vote accept this charter, with their associates, successors

Corporators.

CHAP. 323

—corporate name.

and assigns, are hereby made a body corporate and politic to be known as the Phillips Trust Company, and as such shall be possessed of all the powers, privileges and immunities and subject to all the duties and obligations conferred on corporations by law.

Location.

Section 2. The corporation hereby created shall be located at Phillips, Maine.

Purposes.

Section 3. The purposes of said corporation and the business which it may perform, are; first, to receive on deposit, money, coin, bank notes, evidences of debt, accounts of individuals, companies, corporations, municipalities and states, allowing interest thereon, if agreed, or as the by-laws of said corporation may provide; second, to borrow money, to loan money on credits, or real estate, or personal security, and to negotiate loans and sales for others; third, to own and maintain safe deposit vaults, with boxes, safes and other facilities therein, to be rented to other parties for the safe keeping of moneys, securities, stocks, jewelry, plate, valuable papers and documents, and other property susceptible of being deposited therein, and may receive on deposit for safe keeping, property of any kind entrusted to it for that purpose; fourth, to act as agent for issuing, registering and countersigning certificates, bonds, stocks, and all evidences of debt or ownership, in property; fifth, to hold by grant, assignment, transfer, devise or bequest, any real or personal property or trusts duly created, and to execute trusts of every description; sixth, to act as assignee, receiver, executor, and no surety shall be necessary upon the bond of the corporation unless the court or officer approving such bond shall require it; seventh, to do in general all the business that may lawfully be done by trust and banking companies.

—may own safe deposit vaults.

—may execute trusts.

Capital stock.

Section 4. The capital stock of said corporation shall not be less than twenty-five thousand dollars, divided into shares of one hundred dollars each, with the right to increase the said capital stock at any time, by a vote of the shareholders, to any amount not exceeding five hundred thousand dollars. Said corporation shall not commence business as a trust or banking company, until stock to the amount of at least twenty-five thousand dollars shall have been subscribed and paid in, in cash.

Shall not make loan on security of its own stock.

Section 5. Said corporation shall not make any loan or discount on the security of the shares of its own capital stock, nor be the purchaser or holder of any such shares unless necessary to prevent loss upon a debt previously contracted in good faith; and all stock so acquired shall, within six months from the time of its acquisition, be disposed of at public or private sale.

Board of trustees.

Section 6. All the corporate powers of this corporation shall be exercised by a board of trustees, who shall be residents of this state, whose number and term of office shall be determined by a vote of the shareholders at the first meeting held by the incorporators and at each annual meeting thereafter. The affairs and powers of the corporation may, at the option of the shareholders, be entrusted to an executive board of five members to be, by vote of the shareholders, elected from the full board of trustees. The trustees of said corporation shall be sworn to the proper discharge of their duties, and they shall hold office until others are elected and qualified in their stead. If a trustee or director dies, resigns, or becomes disqualified for any cause, the remaining trustees or directors may appoint a person to fill the vacancy until the next annual meeting of the corporation. The oath of office of such trustee or director shall be taken within thirty days of his election, or his office shall become vacant. The clerk of such corporation shall, within ten days, notify such trustee or directors of their election and within thirty days shall publish the list of all persons who have taken the oath of office as trustees or directors.

—executive board.

—vacancies, how filled.

Section 7. The board of trustees or directors of said corporation shall constitute the board of investment of said corporation. Said trustees or directors shall keep in a separate book, specially provided for the purpose, a record of all loans, and investments of every description, made by said institution substantially in the order of time when such loans or investments are made, which shall show that such loans or investments have been made with the approval of the investment committee of said corporation, which shall indicate such particulars respecting such loans or investments as the bank examiner shall direct. This book shall be submitted to the trustees or directors and to the bank examiner whenever requested. Such loans or investments shall be classified in the book as the bank examiner shall direct. No loan shall be made to any officer, or director of said banking or trust company except by the unanimous approval of the executive board in writing, and said corporation shall have no authority to hire money or to give notes unless by vote of the said board duly recorded.

Board of investment.

—shall keep record of loans.

—loans to directors, how made.

Section 8. No person shall be eligible to the position of a director or a trustee of said corporation who is not the actual owner of ten shares of the stock.

Director must own ten shares of stock.

Section 9. Said corporation, after beginning to receive deposits, shall, at all times, have on hand in lawful money, as a reserve, not less than fifteen per cent of the aggregate amount of its deposits which are subject to withdrawal on demand, provided, that in lieu of lawful money, two-thirds of said fifteen per cent may consist of balances, payable on demand, due from any national or state bank.

Reserve fund.

CHAP. 323

Trust funds shall constitute a special deposit.

Section 10. All the property or money held in trust by this corporation shall constitute a special deposit and the accounts thereof and of said trust department shall be kept separate, and such funds and the investment or loans of them shall be specially appropriated to the security and payment of such deposits, and not be subject to any other liabilities of the corporation; and for the purpose of securing the observance of this proviso, said corporation shall have a trust department in which all business pertaining to such trust property shall be kept separate and distinct from its general business.

Administrators, etc., may deposit in.

Section 11. An administrator, executor, assignee, guardian or trustee, any court of law or equity, including courts of probate and insolvency, officers and treasurers of towns, cities, counties and savings banks of the state of Maine may deposit any moneys, bonds, stocks, evidences of debt or of ownership in property, or any personal property, with said corporation, and any of said courts may direct any person deriving authority from them to so deposit the same.

Responsibility of shareholders.

Section 12. Each shareholder of this corporation shall be individually responsible, equally and ratably, and not one for the other, for all contracts, debts and engagements of such corporation, to a sum equal to the amount of the par value of the shares owned by each in addition to the amount invested in said shares.

Guaranty fund.

Section 13. Such corporation shall set apart as a guaranty fund not less than ten per cent of its earnings in each and every year until such fund with the accumulated interest thereon, shall amount to one-fourth of the capital stock of said corporation.

Taxation.

Section 14. The shares of said corporation shall be subject to taxation in the same manner and rate as are the shares of national banks.

Shall be subject to examination by bank examiner.

Section 15. Said corporation shall be subject to examination by the bank examiner, who shall visit it at least once in every year, and as much oftener as he may deem expedient. At such visits he shall have free access to its vaults, books and papers, and shall thoroughly inspect and examine all the affairs of said corporation, and make such inquiries as may be necessary to ascertain its condition and ability to fulfill all its engagements. If upon examination of said corporation, the examiner is of the opinion that its investments are not in accordance with law, or said corporation is insolvent, or its condition is such as to render its further proceedings hazardous to the public or to those having funds in its custody, or is of the opinion that it has exceeded its powers or failed to comply with any of the rules or restrictions provided by law, he shall have such authority and take such action as is provided for in the case of savings banks by chapter forty-seven of the revised statutes. He shall preserve in a permanent form a full record of his proceedings, including a statement of the condition of said corporation. A copy of such statement shall be published by said corporation immediately after the annual examination of the same in some newspaper published where said corporation is established. If no paper is published in the town where said corporation is established, then it shall be published in a newspaper printed in the nearest city or town. The necessary expenses of the bank examiner while making such examination shall be paid by the corporation.

—shall publish statement.

Section 16. Any one of the corporators named in this act may call the first meeting of the corporation by mailing a written notice, signed by all, postage paid, to each of the other corporators, seven days at least before the day of the meeting, naming the time, place and purpose of such meeting, and at such meeting the necessary officers may be chosen, by-laws adopted, and any other corporate business transacted.

First meeting, how called.

Section 17. This act shall take effect when approved.

Approved March 26, 1903.

Chapter 324.

An Act to incorporate the Merchants Trust Company.

Be it enacted by the Senate and House of Representatives in Legislature assembled, as follows:

Section 1. Henry P. Cox, Charles F. Bolton, Erlon M. Richardson and Horace B. Wentworth of Portland, in the county of Cumberland and George C. Wing of Auburn, in the county of Androscoggin and the state of Maine, or such of them as may by vote accept the charter, with their associates, successors and assigns, are hereby made a body corporate and politic to be known as the Merchants Trust Company, and as such shall be possessed of all the powers, privileges and immunities and subject to all the duties and obligations conferred on corporations by law.

Corporators.

—corporate name.

Section 2. The corporation hereby created shall be located at Auburn, Androscoggin county, Maine.

Location.

Section 3. The purposes of said corporation and the business which it may perform, are; first, to receive on deposit, money, coin, bank notes, evidences of debt, accounts of individuals,

Purposes.

CHAP. 324

—may maintain safe deposit vaults.

—may execute trusts.

Capital stock

—shall not commence business till $50,000 has been paid in.

Shall not make loan on security of its own stock.

Board of directors.

—executive board.

companies, corporations, municipalities and states, allowing interest thereon, if agreed, or as the by-laws of said corporation may provide; second, to borrow money, to loan money on credits, on real estate, or personal security, and to negotiate loans and sales for others; third, to own and maintain safe deposit vaults, with boxes, safes and other facilities therein, to be rented to other parties for the safe keeping of moneys, securities, stocks, jewelry, plate, valuable papers and documents, and other property susceptible of being deposited therein, and may receive on deposit for safe keeping, property of any kind entrusted to it for that purpose; fourth, to hold and enjoy all such estate, real, personal and mixed as may be obtained by the investment of its capital stock or any other moneys and funds that may come into its possession in the course of its business and dealings, and the same sell, grant and dispose of; fifth, to act as agent for issuing, registering and countersigning certificates, bonds, stocks and all evidences of debt or ownership in property; sixth, to hold by grant, assignment, transfer, devise or bequest, any real or personal property or trusts duly created, and to execute trusts of every description; seventh, to act as assignee, receiver, executor, and no surety shall be necessary upon the bond of the corporation, unless the court or officer approving such bond shall require it; eighth, to do in general all the business that may lawfully be done by trust and banking companies.

Section 4. The capital stock of said corporation shall not be less than fifty thousand dollars, divided into shares of one hundred dollars each, with the right to increase the said capital stock at any time, by vote of the shareholders, to any amount not exceeding five hundred thousand dollars. Said corporation shall not commence business as a trust or banking company, until stock to the amount of at least fifty thousand dollars shall have been subscribed and paid in, in cash.

Section 5. Said corporation shall not make any loan or discount on the security of the shares of its own capital stock, nor be the purchaser or holder of any such shares unless necessary to prevent loss upon a debt previously contracted in good faith; and all stock so acquired shall, within six months from the time of its acquisition, be disposed of at public or private sale.

Section 6. All the corporate powers of this corporation shall be exercised by a board of directors, who shall be residents of this state, whose number and term of office shall be determined by a vote of the shareholders at the first meeting held by the incorporators and at each annual meeting thereafter. The affairs and powers of the corporation may, at the option of the shareholders, be entrusted to an executive board of not less than five members

MERCHANTS TRUST COMPANY.   497

to be, by vote of the shareholders, elected from the full board of directors. The directors of said corporation shall be sworn to the proper discharge of their duties, and they shall hold office until others are elected and qualified in their stead. If a director dies, resigns, or becomes disqualified for any cause, the remaining directors may appoint a person to fill the vacancy until the next annual meeting of the corporation. The oath of office of such director shall be taken within thirty days of his election, or his office shall become vacant. The clerk of such corporation shall, within ten days, notify such directors of their election, and within thirty days shall publish the names of all persons who have taken the oath of office as directors.

Section 7. The board of directors of said corporation shall constitute the board of investment of said corporation. The treasurer shall keep in a separate book, specially provided for the purpose, a record of all loans, and investments of every description, made by said institution substantially in the order of time when such loans or investments are made, which shall show that such loans or investments have been made with the approval of the board of investment, and which shall indicate such particulars, respecting such loans or investments as the bank examiner shall direct. This book shall be submitted to the directors and to the bank examiner whenever requested. Such loans or investments shall be classified in the book as the bank examiner shall direct. No loan shall be made to any officer, or director of said banking or trust company except by the approval of the executive board in writing, and said corporation shall have no authority to hire money or to give notes unless by vote of the said board duly recorded.

Section 8. No person shall be eligible to the position of a director of said corporation who is not the actual owner of ten shares of the capital stock.

Section 9. Said corporation, after beginning to receive deposits, shall, at all times, have on hand in lawful money, as a cash reserve, not less than fifteen per cent of the aggregate amount of its deposits which are subject to withdrawal on demand, provided, that in lieu of lawful money, two thirds of said fifteen per cent may consist of balances, payable on demand, due from any national or state bank.

Section 10. All the property or money held in trust by this corporation shall constitute a special deposit and the accounts thereof and of said trust department shall be kept separate, and such funds and the investment of loans of them shall be specially appropriated to the security and payment of such deposits, and not be subject to any other liabilities of the corporation; and for

CHAP. 324

—vacancies, how filled.

Board of investment.

—shall keep record of all loans.

—loans to directors, how made.

Director must own ten shares of stock.

Reserve fund.

Trust funds shall constitute a special deposit.

45

the purpose of securing the observance of this proviso, said corporation shall have a trust department in which all business pertaining to such trust property shall be kept separate and distinct from its general business.

Administrators, etc., may deposit in.

Section 11. An administrator, executor, assignee, guardian or trustee, any court of law or equity, including courts of probate and insolvency, officers and treasurers of towns, cities, counties and savings banks of the state of Maine may deposit any moneys, bonds, stocks, evidences of debt or of ownership in property, or any personal property, with said corporation, and any of said courts may direct any person deriving authority from them to so deposit the same.

Responsibility of shareholders.

Section 12. Each shareholder of this corporation shall be individually responsible, equally and ratably, and not one for the other, for all contracts, debts and engagements of such corporation, to a sum equal to the amount of the par value of the shares owned by each in addition to the amount invested in said shares.

Surplus fund.

Section 13. Such corporation shall set apart as a surplus fund not less than ten per cent of its net earnings in each and every year until such fund with the accumulated interest thereon, shall amount to one-fourth of the capital stock of said corporation.

Taxation.

Section 14. The shares of said corporation shall be subject to taxation in the same manner and rate as are the shares of national banks.

Shall be subject to examination by bank examiner.

Section 15. Said corporation shall be subject to examination by the bank examiner, who shall visit it at least once in every year, and as much oftener as he may deem expedient. At such visits he shall have free access to its vaults, books and papers, and shall thoroughly inspect and examine all the affairs of said corporation, and make such inquiries as may be necessary to ascertain its condition and ability to fulfill all its engagements. If upon examination of said corporation, the examiner is of the opinion that its investments are not in accordance with law, or said corporation is insolvent, or its condition is such as to render its further proceedings hazardous to the public or to those having funds in its custody, or is of the opinion that it has exceeded its powers or failed to comply with any of the rules or restrictions provided by law, he shall have such authority and take such action as is provided for in the case of savings banks by chapter forty-seven of the revised statutes. He shall preserve in a permanent form a full record of his proceedings, including a statement of the condition of said corporation. A copy of such statement shall be published by said corporation immediately after the

—shall publish statement.

annual examination of the same in some newspaper published where said corporation is established. If no paper is published in the town where said corporation is established, then it shall be published in a newspaper printed in the nearest city or town. The necessary expenses of the bank examiner while making such examination shall be paid by the corporation.

First meeting, how called.

Section 16. Any one of the corporators named in this act may call the first meeting of the corporation by mailing a written notice, signed by all, postage paid, to each of the other corporators, seven days at least before the day of the meeting, naming the time, place and purpose of such meeting, and at such meeting the necessary officers may be chosen, by-laws adopted, and any other corporate business transacted.

Section 17. This act shall take effect when approved.

Approved March 26, 1903.

Chapter 325.

An Act authorizing the Lewiston Trust and Safe Deposit Company to establish a branch at Freeport.

Be it enacted by the Senate and House of Representatives in Legislature assembled, as follows:

Freeport branch.

Section 1. The Lewiston Trust and Safe Deposit Company is hereby authorized to establish a branch at Freeport, in the county of Cumberland.

Section 2. This act shall take effect when approved.

Approved March 26, 1903.

Chapter 326.

An Act to incorporate the Patten Telegraph and Telephone Company.

Be it enacted by the Senate and House of Representatives in Legislature assembled, as follows:

Corporators.
—corporate name.
—rights, powers, privileges, duties and liabilities.

Section 1. James McNulty, Fred W. Ayer, Nathaniel M. Jones, Halbert P. Gardner and George G. Weeks, their associates, successors and assigns, are hereby made a body corporate by the name of the Patten Telegraph and Telephone Company, with all the rights, powers and privileges and subject to all the duties and liabilities provided by the general laws of this state relating to similar corporations, with power by that name to sue

CHAP. 326

—route of lines.

and be sued, to have, own, sell, real estate and personal property, to establish all by-laws and regulations for the management of its affairs not repugnant to the laws of this state, and to do and perform any and all other acts legal and incident to similar corporations. The said corporation shall have the right to locate, construct, to own, maintain and operate telegraph and telephone lines from some convenient point in the town of Sherman, through the towns of Stacyville and Patten, and from there by the most feasible and advantageous routes to Eagle lake, Grand lake and Moosehead lake, and from its main line to any lumber or sporting camp in unincorporated places.

Consent of municipal officers shall be obtained as to location on streets.

Section 2. Said company shall have the right within the limits aforesaid to locate, construct, maintain and operate its lines of telegraph and telephone upon and along any public highway, bridge, or upon the line of any railroad, first having obtained consent therefor of the municipal officers of any town where it is proposed to construct said lines, and of the officers of any railroad company over which the same are to be built, but in such a manner as not to incommode or endanger the customary use of said way, bridge or railroad, with the right to cut down trees and remove obstacles where necessary within the limits aforesaid, except ornamental, fruit or shade trees, and with the power to establish and collect tolls on said lines.

May acquire real estate and personal property.

Section 3. The company is hereby authorized to take, purchase, hold and dispose of such real estate and personal property as may be necessary to carry out the provisions of this act, and in the case of real estate taken the damages therefor when the parties cannot agree shall be estimated, secured and paid as in the case of land taken for highway.

May carry on telephone or telegraph business.

Section 4. Said corporation is hereby authorized to carry on the business of practical telegraphic and telephonic connections by the use of any proper telegraph or telephone appliances or inventions, and may attach its wires or any appliances to buildings or trees, provided that the owners of such buildings or trees shall first give their consent.

Capital stock.

Section 5. The capital stock of said corporation shall be such an amount as said corporation may from time to time deem necessary for all the purposes contemplated by their act, the same to be fixed by vote of said corporation.

May issue bonds.

Section 6. Said corporation may issue its bonds for the construction and operation of its lines and conduct of its business for such amount not exceeding the amount of capital stock, and on such time and rates of interest as said corporation may determine, and may secure the same by a mortgage of its franchise and property.

SANGERVILLE IMPROVEMENT COMPANY.

Section 7. Said corporation is hereby authorized and empowered to connect its lines with the lines of any other telephone and telegraph company by contract with said company or to lease or to sell its own lines at any time. *May connect with other lines.*

Section 8. Any one of the corporators named in this act may call the first meeting of this company by mailing or giving in hand written notice to each of the other incorporators seven days at least before the day of said meeting, naming the time, place and purpose of said meeting, and at such meeting if a majority of such corporators shall be present, a president, secretary, treasurer and directors may be chosen, by-laws adopted and other corporate business transacted. *First meeting, how called.*

Section 9. This act shall take effect when approved.

Approved March 26, 1903.

Chapter 327.

An Act to ratify the lease of the Sangerville Improvement Company to the Dover and Foxcroft Light and Heat Company.

Be it enacted by the Senate and House of Representatives in Legislature assembled, as follows:

Section 1. The proceedings of the incorporation and organization of the Sangerville Improvement Company are hereby confirmed and made valid, and all the proceedings of said corporation in calling, holding and acting in a meeting of said corporation held at Dover, in the county of Piscataquis, at the office of Frank E. Guernsey, on the twenty-seventh day of September, in the year of our Lord nineteen hundred and two, and all the proceedings of said corporation in calling, holding and acting in a meeting of said corporation, held at Sangerville in said county on the ninth day of October, in the year of our Lord nineteen hundred and two, and all the votes, acts and doings of said corporation at said meeting are hereby ratified, confirmed and made valid. *Incorporation and organization made valid.*

Section 2. The existing lease of date of October ninth, in the year of our Lord nineteen hundred and two, between said Sangerville Improvement Company and Dover and Foxcroft Light and Heat Company is hereby ratified, confirmed and made valid. *Existing lease made valid.*

Section 3. The Dover and Foxcroft Light and Heat Company is authorized and empowered, as lessee, or in case of purchase of the plant, property and franchise of the Sangerville Improvement Company, to supply the town of Sangerville and the inhabitants thereof with light, heat and power by the manufacture of electricity. *May supply light, heat and power in Sangerville.*

CHAP. 328

Town of Sangerville may contract for street lighting.

Section 4. The town of Sangerville is hereby authorized to enter into a contract with the Dover and Foxcroft Light and Heat Company for street lighting for a term of years.

Sangerville Improvement Co. authorized to sell its property.

Section 5. The Sangerville Improvement Company is hereby authorized to sell and the Dover and Foxcroft Light and Heat Company to buy the plant, property and franchise, and all the rights and privileges of the Sangerville Improvement Company in its corporate capacity in accordance with the terms of the lease mentioned in section two of this act, or at any time that said Sangerville Improvement Company may agree, to sell its plant, property, franchise and corporate rights to said Dover and Foxcroft Light and Heat Company during the term of said lease as well as at the time specified in said lease that said sale or purchase may take place.

Section 6. This act shall take effect when approved.

Approved March 26, 1903.

Chapter 328.

An Act to prohibit the throwing of sawdust or other mill refuse into Ellis Stream, so called, in Waldo, Brooks and Belfast, in Waldo County.

Be it enacted by the Senate and House of Representatives in Legislature assembled, as follows:

Throwing of sawdust into Ellis stream, prohibited.

It shall be unlawful for any person to put, or allow the same to be done by any person within his employ, any sawdust, slabs, edgings, or other refuse matter into Ellis stream, so called, situated in Waldo, Brooks and Belfast, in Waldo county, under a penalty of not less than fifty nor more than one hundred dollars and costs for each offense.

Approved March 26, 1903.

Chapter 329.

An Act additional to the act creating the Rumford Falls Municipal Court.

Be it enacted by the Senate and House of Representatives in Legislature assembled, as follows:

Section 1. Actions pending in the Rumford Falls Municipal court may be referred to one referee in the same manner as in the supreme judicial court, and on report of the referee to said municipal court, judgment may be rendered in the same manner and with like effect as in the supreme judicial court. *Pending actions may be referred, as in supreme court.*

This section shall not apply to actions within the jurisdiction of trial justices, fees of the referee to be approved by the the judge, certified and paid as in the supreme judicial court.

Section 2. Exceptions may be alleged and cases certified on an agreed statement of facts, or upon evidence reported by the judge in all civil actions as in the supreme judicial court, and the same shall be entered, heard and determined at the law term thereof as if the same had originated in the supreme judicial court for the county of Oxford; and decisions of the law court in all such cases, shall be certified to the judge of said municipal court for final disposition with the same effect as in cases originating in said judicial court. *Exceptions may be alleged, etc., as in supreme court.*

Section 3. The governor, by and with the consent of the council, shall appoint a recorder of said court, who shall be an attorney at law and duly sworn, hold his office for a term of four years, and shall reside in the town of Rumford or Mexico. Said recorder shall keep the records of said court, when requested so to do by the judge; and in the absence or inability of the judge the recorder shall have and exercise all the powers of the judge, and perform all the duties required of said judge by law, and shall be empowered to sign and issue all processes and papers, and all acts as fully and with the same effect as the judge could do were he acting in the premises; and the signature of the recorder as such, shall be sufficient evidence of his right to act instead of the judge. When the office of the judge is vacant, or the judge is absent or unable to act, the recorder shall be entitled to the fees; in all other cases he shall be paid by the judge. *Recorder, appointment and qualifications of.* *—duties.*

Section 4. In addition to such jurisdiction as said court now has by law the Rumford Falls Municipal Court shall have original jurisdiction concurrent with the supreme judicial court, in all civil actions wherein the debt or damage demanded does not exceed three hundred dollars, in which any defendant or person summoned as trustee shall reside, or have a place of business in said county of Oxford, or, if not an inhabitant of the state, shall be commorant in the county of Oxford. *Original concurrent with supreme judicial court.*

CHAP. 329

Attachable property, jurisdiction over.

Section 5. When any defendant has any attachable property within the county of Oxford and the same has been attached, said court shall have the same jurisdiction over said defendant and his property that the supreme judicial court has in similar cases and said municipal court shall order such service or notice as said supreme judicial court might order in like cases.

Proceedings when defendant demands jury trial.

Section 6. If any defendant, or his attorney, in any civil action in this court in which the debt or damage demanded or claimed in the writ exceeds twenty dollars, shall, on or before the first day of the first regular monthly term of said court held after the entry of said action, file in said court a motion setting forth therein that he has a good defense to said action, and intends in good faith to make such defense and claims a jury trial, and shall at the same time deposit with the judge or recorder of said court, one dollar and sixty-five cents for copies and entry in the supreme judicial court, to be taxed in his costs if he prevails, the said action shall forthwith be removed into the supreme judicial court, for said county of Oxford and shall be entered at the next ensuing term of the supreme judicial court after such removal; and the judge or recorder of said municipal court shall forthwith cause certified copies of the writ, return of the officer and all other papers in the case to be filed in the clerk's office of said supreme judicial court.

Shall not have jurisdiction in towns partly on west side of G. T. R. R.

Section 7. The Rumford Falls Municipal Court shall not have or exercise jurisdiction in any criminal matter where the offense complained of is alleged to have been committed in any town in Oxford county situated in part or in whole on the westerly side of the Grand Trunk Railroad.

Section 8. All acts and parts of acts inconsistent with this act are hereby repealed.

Approved March 26, 1903.

Chapter 330.

An Act to amend Section one of Chapter five hundred and sixteen of the Private and Special Laws of eighteen hundred and ninety-seven, entitled "An Act additional relating to the appointment of a Recorder for the Bath Municipal Court."

Be it enacted by the Senate and House of Representatives in Legislature assembled, as follows:

Section 1. Section one of chapter five hundred and sixteen of the private and special laws of eighteen hundred and ninety-seven is hereby amended by striking out the words "When the office of judge is vacant, the recorder shall be entitled to the fees; in all other cases he shall be paid by the judge," in the eleventh, twelfth and thirteenth lines of said section; and inserting instead the words 'The said recorder shall receive a salary of seventy-five dollars per annum, which shall be in full for all services performed by him, and which shall be paid him in the same manner as the salary of the judge of said court is now provided to be paid,' so that said section, as hereby amended, shall read as follows: *(Section 1, chapter 516, private and special laws of 1897, amended.)*

'Section 1. There shall be appointed by the governor, for said court, a recorder, who shall keep the records of said court when requested so to do by the judge; and in case of the absence of the judge from the court room, or when the office of judge shall be vacant, the recorder shall have and exercise all the powers of the judge and perform all the duties required of said judge, and shall be empowered to sign and issue all processes and papers, and to do all acts as fully and with the same effect as the judge could do were he acting in the premises, and the signature of the recorder as such, shall be sufficient evidence of his right to act instead of the judge. The said recorder shall receive a salary of seventy-five dollars per annum, which shall be in full for all services performed by him, and which shall be paid him in the same manner as the salary of the judge of said court is now provided to be paid. Said recorder shall reside in Bath, and shall hold his office until another is appointed in his stead.' *(Recorder, appointment and duties of.)*

Section 2. This act shall take effect when approved.

Approved March 26, 1903.

Chapter 331.

An Act to extend the time during which the tolls granted to the Bangor Bridge Company shall continue.

Be it enacted by the Senate and House of Representatives in Legislature assembled, as follows:

Continuance of tolls granted.

Section 1. The tolls granted by chapter five hundred and twenty-nine of the special laws of eighteen hundred and twenty-eight, and chapter three hundred and twenty-five of the special laws of eighteen hundred and forty-six, are hereby extended so that they shall continue from the date of the approval of this act, subject to revision at any time by the legislature, until all tolls so collected, together with all incomes of whatever nature, collectively, equal the amount of sixty thousand dollars, together with the cost of a new steel bridge and the running expenses, with interest on all moneys so invested at five per cent.

Chapter 208, special laws of 1895, and chapter 360, special laws of 1901, repealed.

Section 2. The provisions of chapter two hundred and eight of the special laws of eighteen hundred and ninety-five and of chapter three hundred and sixty of the special laws of nineteen hundred and one, are hereby repealed.

May borrow money for specified purposes.

Section 3. Bangor Bridge Company is hereby authorized to borrow such a sum of money as shall be necessary to pay for making the bridge a steel bridge throughout, similar to the present middle span of said bridge, and to thoroughly repair the piers and abutments of said bridge and to secure the payment of the same by a mortgage upon its bridge property.

When bridge shall become free.

Section 4. The said bridge and all appurtenances of said bridge company shall then become free without further compensation to its owners.

Books shall be open to mayors and treasurers of Bangor and Brewer.

Section 5. The books of said company shall be open to inspection at all times to the mayors and treasurers of Bangor and Brewer.

When this act may take effect.

Section 6. This act shall not take effect until the supreme judicial court shall in appropriate proceedings therefor determine that the cities of Bangor and Brewer and the county of Penobscot are not liable to said bridge company for the amount heretofore awarded for the value of the bridge, property and appurtenances of said bridge company under chapter three hundred and sixty, private and special laws of nineteen hundred and one, now of record in said court, in such proportions as have been or may be legally apportioned under said chapter three hundred and sixty, and in addition for the cost and interest thereon of the new steel span erected by said bridge company under the instructions of the special committee of the city governments of Bangor and Brewer, upon the agreement of said committee that said cities should pay such cost and interest.

Section 7. If the bridge, property and appurtenances of said bridge company shall hereafter be taken under any special or general law as for public uses, in assessing or determining the value thereof nothing shall be allowed for franchise.

Provisions if bridge be taken as for public uses.

Approved March 26, 1903.

Chapter 332.

An Act to amend the charter of Maine Investment and Guarantee Company.

Be it enacted by the Senate and House of Representatives in Legislature assembled, as follows:

Section 1. Section four of chapter two hundred twenty-eight of the private and special laws of one thousand eight hundred and ninety-one are hereby amended by adding to said section after the word "individual" in the last line, the words 'or trust company' so that said section as amended, shall read as follows:

Section 4, chapter 228, private and special laws of 1891, amended.

'Section 4. Said corporation may also make loans and advances; take and hold mortgages and other forms of security on real and personal property and hold and deal in the stocks and securities of other corporations, firms or persons in the same manner as an individual or trust company may lawfully do.'

May make loans, hold mortgages, etc.

Approved March 26, 1903.

Chapter 333.

An Act to incorporate the Fraternity Temple Company.

Be it enacted by the Senate and House of Representatives in Legislature assembled, as follows:

Section 1. Joseph E. Hall, Charles F. Bragg, Henry O. Pierce, Albert F. Smith and Victor Brett, their associates and successors, are hereby made a corporation under the name of the Fraternity Temple Company with all the rights, privileges and immunities of corporations under chapter fifty-five of the revised statutes of Maine and, subject thereto, all the rights, privileges, duties and responsibilities conferred upon corporations under the general laws of this state.

Corporators.

—corporate name.

Section 2. The capital stock of said company shall consist of not more than six thousand shares of the par value of ten dollars, the amount to be fixed from time to time by the corporation. The immediate government of its affairs shall be vested

Capital stock.

CHAP. 333

Board of directors.

in a board of directors to consist, for one year from the time of the corporation of said company, of the corporators herein named, together with an advisory board to be composed of representatives of the various fraternal, benevolent, educational or social organizations owning stock in the company, said organizations, whether incorporated or not, being hereby authorized to purchase, hold or sell stock in the company, and for this purpose shall have all the rights, powers and privileges of corporations. Such representatives to be elected by their respective organizations and to be admitted to said board upon presentation of their proper credentials of election. The powers of said boards and their subsequent election may be governed by by-laws which said corporation shall, within the scope of its legal authority, have power to make, ordain and publish.

Purposes of the corporation.

Section 3. The purposes of said corporation shall be as follows: To provide a permanent home and meeting place for such fraternal, benevolent, educational and social organizations as may desire to obtain quarters therein, said home and meeting place to be erected in the city of Bangor and to be known as the Fraternity Temple; to conduct entertainments and to transact all business incident thereto in said Temple; to rent such rooms in said Temple as may not be required for the uses of such organizations; to collect such rents from all tenants as will meet the necessary expense of maintaining the building and meeting the obligations incurred in its behalf; to provide all necessary equipment and furniture for said Temple and to do all acts and transact any business in said Temple not repugnant to law or inconsistent with the foregoing purposes.

May raise money.

Section 4. The said corporation is further authorized to raise money for the purchase of real estate and the erection of said Temple by issuing stock, bonds, mortgage or other evidences of indebtedness in such manner and upon such terms as may be determined by the directors, but no stockholder shall be liable on any such indebtedness beyond the amount remaining unpaid on his stock subscription. The corporation shall be further authorized to sell or lease the right to build upon its walls, to any other fraternal organization, above the height required for its own uses, and in case of the sale of such right no mortgage which the said corporation may execute shall apply to the portion built by its grantee.

—liability of stockholders.

Beneficiary powers.

Section 5. Any member of a fraternal beneficiary organization organized under or doing business in this state under the laws of Maine may, in case of the loss by death or desertion of all the members of his immediate family, make said corporation his beneficiary, and said corporation shall be included within the class now allowed by law as beneficiaries, provided, no portion of any funds so received by said company shall be disbursed as dividends to individual stockholders, but may be applied towards the discharge of any obligations of the company on account of the building of such temple or making improvements or additions thereto, and when not required for such purpose shall be distributed among such fraternities having quarters in the building and owning stock in the company, as pay sick benefits to its members; such fraternities shall receive from such funds in proportion to its stock in the corporation.

—beneficiary funds, how applied and used.

Section 6. The said company for all its said purposes may hold real estate and personal property sufficient, necessary and convenient therefor.

May hold real estate.

Section 7. The first meeting of the corporation may be held at any time within sixty days after the passage and approval of this act by all the foregoing corporators participating therein and signing written waiver of notice thereof, otherwise any of the corporators may call said first meeting by giving the notice required by law in such case, and a majority of the corporators may hold such meeting. In either case all necessary business, the election of officers and the adoption of by-laws may be transacted at such meeting.

First meeting, how called.

Approved March 26, 1903.

Chapter 334.

An Act to Incorporate the Augusta Water District.

Be it enacted by the Senate and House of Representatives in Legislature assembled, as follows:

Section 1. The following territory and the people within the same, namely: Wards one, two, three, four, six, seven and eight in the city of Augusta, shall constitute a body politic and corporate under the name of the Augusta Water District, for the purpose of supplying the inhabitants of said district and of the towns of Chelsea, Vassalborough, China and Manchester, and such municipalities, together with the city of Augusta, with pure water for domestic and municipal purposes.

Corporate limits.

—purpose.

Section 2. Said district is hereby authorized for the purposes aforesaid to take and hold sufficient water of the Kennebec river and China lake, and may take and hold by purchase or otherwise any land or real estate necessary for erecting dams, power, reservoirs, or for preserving the purity of the water and water shed, and for laying and maintaining aqueducts for taking, discharging and disposing of water. Nothing in this act shall

May take water of Kennebec river and China lake.

—shall not increase flowage on China lake.

authorize said district to increase the present flowage upon China lake.

Section 3. Said district shall be liable for all damages that shall be sustained by any person or corporation in their property by the taking of any land whatsoever, or water, or by flowage, or by excavating through any land for the purpose of laying pipes, building dams or constructing reservoirs. If any person sustaining damage as aforesaid and said corporation shall not mutually agree upon the sum to be paid therefor, such person may cause his damages to be ascertained in the same manner and under the same conditions, restrictions and limitations as are or may be prescribed in the case of damages by the laying out of highways.

Section 4. Said district is hereby authorized to lay in and through the streets and highways thereof and of said towns of Chelsea, Vassalborough, China and Manchester, and to take up, repair and replace all such pipes, aqueducts and fixtures as may be necessary for the objects above set forth, and whenever said district shall lay any pipes or aqueducts in any street or highway it shall cause the same to be done with as little obstruction as possible to the public travel, and shall at its own expense without unnecessary delay cause the earth and pavement removed by it to be replaced in proper condition.

Section 5. All the affairs of said water district shall be managed by a board of trustees composed of three members to be chosen by the municipal officers of the city of Augusta, but no member of the city council shall during the term for which he is elected be chosen one of said board of trustees. As soon as convenient after the members of said board have been chosen, said trustees shall hold a meeting at the city rooms in the city of Augusta, and organize by the election of a president and clerk, adopt a corporate seal and when necessary may choose a treasurer and all other needful officers and agents for the proper conduct and management of the affairs of said district. At said first meeting they shall determine by lot the term of office of each trustee so that one shall serve for one year, one for two years and one for three years; and whenever the term of office of a trustee expires the said municipal officers of the city of Augusta shall appoint a successor to serve the full term of three years; and in case any other vacancy arises it shall be filled in like manner for the unexpired term. They may also ordain and establish such by-laws as are necessary for their own convenience and the proper management of the affairs of the district. The term of office of the trustees shall begin on the first Monday of August. Said trustees may procure an office and incur such expenses as may be necessary. Each member shall receive in full compensation for his services an allowance of three hundred dollars per annum.

Section 6. Said water district is hereby authorized and empowered to acquire by purchase or by the exercise of the right of eminent domain, which right is hereby expressly delegated to said district for said purpose, the entire plant, property and franchises, rights and privileges now held by the Augusta Water Company within said district and said towns of Chelsea, Vassalborough, China and Manchester, including all lands, waters, water rights, dams, reservoirs, pipes, machinery, fixtures, hydrants, tools and all apparatus and appliances owned by said company and used or usable in supplying water in said district and towns and any other real estate in said district. *May acquire Augusta Water Co.*

Section 7. In case said trustees fail to agree with said Augusta Water Company upon the terms of purchase of the above mentioned property on or before November first, nineteen hundred and three, said water district through its trustees is hereby authorized to take said plant, property and franchises as for public uses by petition therefor in the manner hereinafter provided. And said water district through its trustees is hereby authorized on or before November sixth, nineteen hundred and three, to file a petition in the clerk's office of the supreme judicial court for the county of Kennebec in term time or in vacation, addressed to any justice of said court, who after notice to said Augusta Water Company and its mortgagees, shall after hearing and within thirty days after the filing of said petition appoint three disinterested appraisers none of whom shall be residents of the county of Kennebec, one of whom shall be learned in the law, for the purpose of fixing the valuation of said plant, property and franchises. The said appraisers shall have the power of compelling attendance of witnesses and the production of books and papers pertinent to the issue, and may administer oaths; and any witness, or person in charge of such books or papers, refusing to attend, or to produce the same, shall be subject to the same penalties and proceedings, so far as applicable as witnesses summoned to attend the supreme judicial court. The appraisers so appointed shall after due notice and hearing fix the valuation of said plant, property and franchises at what they are fairly and equitably worth, so that the said Augusta Water Company shall receive just compensation for all the same. The first day of March, nineteen hundred and four, shall be the date as of which the valuation aforesaid shall be fixed, from which day, interest on said award shall run and all net rents and profits accruing thereafter shall belong to said water district. *Proceedings in case of disagreement as to terms of purchase.* —appraisers. —powers of appraisers. —duties of appraisers. —date when valuation shall be fixed.

AUGUSTA WATER DISTRICT.

CHAP. 334
--further proceedings.
The report of said appraisers or of a majority of them, shall be filed in said clerk's office in term time or vacation within five months after their appointment, and such single justice, or in case of his inability to act then any justice designated for the purpose by the chief justice, may, after notice and hearing, confirm or reject the same, or recommit it if justice so requires. The award of the appraisers shall be conclusive as to valuations. Upon the confirmation of said report the court so sitting shall thereupon, after hearing, make final decree upon the entire matter, including the application of the purchase money, discharge of incumbrances and transfer of the property, jurisdiction over which is hereby conferred, with the same power to enforce said decree as in equity cases. Upon request of either party the justice so making such final decree shall make separate findings of law and fact. All such findings of fact shall be final, but either party aggrieved may take exceptions to any rulings of law so made, the same to be accompanied only by such parts of the case as are necessary to a clear understanding of the questions raised thereby. Such exceptions shall be claimed on the docket within ten days after such final decree is signed, entered and filed, and notice thereof has been given by the clerk to the parties or their counsel, and said exceptions so claimed shall be made up, allowed and filed within said time unless further time is granted by the court or by agreement of parties. They shall be entered at the next term of the law court to be held after the filing of said decree and there heard, unless otherwise agreed, or the law court shall for good cause order a further time for hearing thereon. Upon such hearing the law court may confirm, reverse or modify the decree of the court below, or remand the cause for further proceedings as it seems proper. During the pendency of such exceptions the cause shall remain on the docket of the court below marked "law" and decree shall be entered thereon by a single justice in term time or in vacation, in accordance with the certificate and opinion of the law court. Before said plant, property and franchises are transferred in accordance with such final decree, and before the payment therefor, the court sitting in said county of Kennebec, by a single justice thereof as hereinbefore provided, shall, upon motion of either party, after notice and hearing, take account of all receipts and expenditures properly had or incurred by the Augusta Water Company belonging to the period from and after March first, nineteen hundred and four, and all the net rents and profits accruing thereafter, and shall order the net balance due to either party to be added to or deducted from the amount to be paid under said final decree, as the case may be. All findings of law or fact by such single

justice at such hearing shall be final. On payment or tender by said district of the amount so fixed and the performance of all other terms and conditions so imposed by the court, said entire plant, property and franchises shall become vested in said water district and be free from all liens, mortgages and incumbrances theretofore created by the Augusta Water Company. After the filing of said petition it shall not be discontinued or withdrawn by said water district, and the said Augusta Water Company may thereafterwards on its part cause said valuation to be made as herein provided, and shall be entitled to appropriate process to compel said water district to perform the terms of the final decree, and to pay for said plant, property and franchises in accordance therewith.

Section 8. All valid contracts now existing between the Augusta Water Company and any persons or corporations for supplying water within said district and in the said towns of Chelsea, Vassalborough, China and Manchester, shall be assumed and carried out by said Augusta Water District. *Existing valid contracts shall be assumed.*

Section 9. For accomplishing the purposes of this act said water district, through its trustees, is authorized to issue its bonds to an amount sufficient to procure funds to pay the expenses incurred in the acquisition of the property of said Augusta Water Company, and the purchase thereof, and to secure a new source of water supply or the improvement of the present supply. Said bonds shall be a legal obligation of said water district which is hereby declared to be a quasi municipal corporation within the meaning of section fifty-five, chapter forty-six of the revised statutes, and all the provisions of said section shall be applicable thereto. The said bonds shall be a legal investment for savings banks. *May issue bonds.*

Section 10. All individuals, firms and corporations, whether private, public or municipal, shall pay to the treasurer of said district the rates established by said board of trustees for the water used by them, and said rates shall be uniform within the territory supplied by the district. Said rates shall be so established as to provide revenue for the following purposes: *Water rates.*

I. To pay the current running expenses for maintaining the water system and provide for such extensions and renewals as may become necessary.

II. To provide for payment of the interest on the indebtedness of the district.

III. To provide each year a sum equal to not less than one nor more than five per cent of the entire indebtedness of the district, which sum shall be turned into a sinking fund to provide for the final extinguishment of the funded debt. The money

CHAP. 334

set aside for the sinking fund shall be devoted to the retirement of the obligations of the district or invested in such securities as savings banks are allowed to hold.

IV. If any surplus remains at the end of the year it may be paid to the city of Augusta.

Section 11. All incidental powers, rights and privileges necessary to the accomplishment of the main object herein set forth are granted to the corporation hereby created.

When this act shall take effect.

Section 12. This act shall take effect when approved by a majority vote of the legal voters within said district voting at an election to be specially called and held for the purpose on the fourth Monday of June, nineteen hundred and three. The board of registration shall make and provide a separate check list for such of the voters within said district as are then legal voters of said city and all warrants issued to said city shall be varied accordingly to show that only such voters therein are entitled to vote hereon. Such special election, shall be called, advertised and conducted according to the law relating to municipal elections, provided, however, that the board of registration shall not be required to prepare or the city clerk to post a new list of voters and for this purpose said board shall be in session the three secular days next preceding such election, the first two days thereof to be devoted to registration of voters and the last day to enable the board to verify the corrections of said lists and to complete and close up its records of said sessions. The city clerk shall reduce the subject matter of this act to the following question: "Shall the act to incorporate the Augusta Water District be accepted?" and the voters shall indicate by a cross placed against the words "yes" or "no" their opinion of the same. The result shall be declared by the mayor and aldermen and due certificate thereof filed by the city clerk with the secretary of state. This act shall take effect when approved by the governor so as necessary to empower the calling and holding of such election.

When certain sections of this act shall be void.

Section 13. Sections two, three and four of this act shall be inoperative, null and void, unless the said water district shall first acquire by purchase, or by the exercise of the right of eminent domain as in this act provided, the plant, property and franchises, rights and privileges now held by the Augusta Water Company within said district and said towns of Chelsea, Vassalborough, China and Manchester.

Costs and expenses, how borne and paid.

Section 14. All costs and expenses arising under the provisions of this act shall be paid and borne as directed by the court in the final decree provided by section seven.

Section 15. This act shall take effect when approved.

Approved March 26, 1903.

Chapter 335

An Act to authorize the Phillips and Rangeley Railroad Company to purchase or lease the property and franchises of the Madrid Railroad Company.

Be it enacted by the Senate and House of Representatives in Legislature assembled, as follows:

Section 1. The Phillips and Rangeley Railroad Company, a corporation existing under the general laws of the state, is hereby authorized to purchase or lease the property, capital stock, rights, privileges, immunities and franchises of the Madrid Railroad Company upon such terms as may be agreed upon, and upon such purchase or lease the said Phillips and Rangeley Railroad Company shall have, hold, possess, exercise and enjoy all the locations, powers, privileges, rights, immunities, franchises, property and assets, which at the time of said transfer shall then be had, held, possessed or enjoyed by the said Madrid Railroad Company, and shall be subject to all the duties, restrictions and liabilities to which the said Madrid Railroad Company shall then be subject by reason of any charter, contract or general or special law, or otherwise. *Authorized to purchase property of Madrid R. R. Co.*

Section 2. All proceedings, suits at law or in equity, which may be pending at the time of such transfer, to which the said Madrid Railroad Company may be a party, may be prosecuted or defended by the said Phillips and Rangeley Railroad Company in like manner and with like effect as if such transfer had not been made. All claims, contracts, rights and causes of action of or against the said Madrid Railroad Company, at law or in equity, may be enforced by suit or action to be begun or prosecuted by or against the said Phillips and Rangeley Railroad Company. *Pending proceedings, etc., how prosecuted or defended.*

Section 3. The Madrid Railroad Company is hereby authorized to make the sale or lease authorized by section one of this act. *Sale of Madrid R. R. authorized.*

Section 4. The said Phillips and Rangeley Railroad Company may increase its capital stock to such amount as may be necessary for the purposes of this act, and further may issue its stock and bonds in payment and exchange for the stock, bonds, franchises and property of the said Madrid Railroad Company, in such manner and in such amounts as may be agreed upon. *May increase capital stock.*

Section 5. When the transfer authorized in this act is carried out and fully completed the Phillips and Rangeley Railroad Company shall be liable for the then lawfully existing debts, obligations and contracts of the said Madrid Railroad Company. *Liability for debts, etc., of Madrid R. R. Co.*

Section 6. The said Phillips and Rangeley Railroad Company may issue its bonds from time to time upon such rates and terms *May issue bonds.*

as may be deemed expedient for the purpose of funding its floating debt and also in such amounts as may be required for the purposes of this act, and secure the same by appropriate mortgages upon its franchises and property by it then held or thereafterwards to be acquired.

Section 7. This act shall take effect when approved.

Approved March 27, 1903.

Chapter 326.

An Act to extend and amend the charter of the Bluehill Trust and Banking Company.

Be it enacted by the Senate and House of Representatives in Legislature assembled, as follows:

Charter extended.

Section 1. The rights, powers and privileges of the Bluehill Trust and Banking Company, which were granted by chapter two hundred and seventy-two of the private and special laws of eighteen hundred and ninety-five, and extended by chapter three hundred and ninety-one of the private and special laws of eighteen hundred and ninety-seven, and further extended by chapter one hundred and thirty of the private and special laws of eighteen hundred and ninety-nine, and further extended by chapter three hundred and fifty-six of the private and special laws of nineteen hundred and one, are hereby extended for two years from the approval of this act; and the persons named in said act, their associates and successors, shall have all the rights, powers and privileges that were granted them by said act, to be exercised in the same manner and for the same purposes as specified in said act.

Section 4, chapter 272, private and special laws of 1895, amended.

Section 2. Section four of chapter two hundred and seventy-two of the private and special laws of eighteen hundred and ninety-five is hereby amended by striking out the word "fifty" in the second and seventh lines of said section and substituting therefor in each instance the word 'twenty-five,' so that said section as amended shall read as follows:

Capital stock.

—shall not commence business till $25,000 has been paid in.

'The capital stock of said corporation shall not be less than twenty-five thousand dollars, divided into shares of one hundred dollars each, with the right to increase the said capital stock at any time by a vote of the shareholders to any amount not exceeding five hundred thousand dollars. Said corporation shall not commence business as a trust or banking company, until stock to the amount of at least twenty-five thousand dollars shall have been subscribed and paid in, in cash.'

Section 3. Section eight of chapter two hundred and seventy-two of the private and special laws of eighteen hundred and ninety-five is hereby amended by striking out the word "ten" in the third line and substituting therefor the word 'three,' so that said section as amended shall read as follows: 'No person shall be eligible to the position of a director or trustee of said corporation who is not the actual owner of three shares of the stock.'

Section 4. This act shall take effect when approved.

Approved March 27, 1903.

Chapter 337.

An Act to Incorporate the Naples Water Company.

Be it enacted by the Senate and House of Representatives in Legislature assembled, as follows:

Section 1. Llewellyn Barton, Charles L. Goodridge, John H. Card of Portland, Clarence L. Barker of Boston and Harry H. Cannell of Naples, their associates, successors and assigns, are hereby made a corporation by the name of the Naples Water Company, for the purpose of supplying the village of Naples, in the county of Cumberland, and the inhabitants of said town, with pure water, for domestic, sanitary and municipal purposes, including the extinguishment of fires, with all the rights and privileges and subject to all the liabilities and obligations of similar corporations under the laws of this state.

Section 2. Said company for said purposes, may retain, collect, take, store, use and distribute water from any springs or wells, that it may acquire by purchase of the owner thereof, ponds, streams, or other water sources in said Naples, and may locate, construct and maintain cribs, reservoirs, dams, standpipes, gates, hydrants, pipes and all other necessary structures to conduct and distribute the same through said town of Naples in the usual manner.

Section 3. The place of business of said corporation shall be at Naples in the county of Cumberland and state of Maine, and its business shall be confined to the town of Naples in said county.

Section 4. Said corporation is hereby authorized for the purposes aforesaid, to lay, construct and maintain in, under, through, along and across the highways, ways, streets, railroads and bridges in said towns, and to take up, replace and repair all such sluices, aqueducts, pipes, hydrants and structures as may be necessary for the purposes of its incorporation, so as not to unreasonably obstruct the same, under such reasonable restric-

518   NAPLES WATER COMPANY.

CHAP. 337

—responsibility for damages in laying pipes.

tions and conditions as the selectmen of said town may impose. It shall be responsible for all damage to persons and property occasioned by the use of such highways, ways and streets, and shall further be liable to pay to said town all sums recovered against said town for damages for obstruction caused by said company, and for all expenses including reasonable counsel fees incurred in defending such suits with interest on the same, provided said company shall have notice of such suits and opportunity to defend the same.

May cross sewers, etc.

Section 5. Said company shall have power to cross any water course, private and public sewer, or to change the direction thereof, when necessary for the purposes of its incorporation, but in such manner as not to obstruct or impair the use thereof, and it shall be liable for any injury caused thereby. Whenever said company shall lay down any fixtures in any highway, way or street, or make any alterations or repairs, upon its works in any highway, way or street, it shall cause the same to be done with as little obstruction to public travel as may be practicable, and shall, at its own expense, without unnecessary delay, cause the earth and pavements there removed by it, to be replaced in proper condition.

Liability for damages for land, flowage, etc.

—proceedings in case of disagreement.

Section 6. Said corporation shall be held liable to pay all damages that shall be sustained by any person by the taking of any land or other property, or by flowage, or by excavating through any land for the purposes of laying down pipes and aqueducts, building dams, reservoirs, and also damages for any other injuries resulting from said acts; and if any person sustaining damage as aforesaid, and said corporation cannot mutually agree upon the sum to be paid therefor, either party on petition to the county commissioners of Cumberland county, may have the damages assessed by them; and subsequent proceedings and rights of appeal thereon, shall be had in the same manner and under the same conditions, restrictions and limitations, as are by law provided in case of land taken for railroads.

May hold real and personal estate.

Section 7. Said corporation may hold real and personal estate necessary and convenient for all its said purposes to the amount of twenty-five thousand dollars.

—may issue bonds.

Section 8. Said corporation may issue its bonds for the construction of its work, upon such rates and terms as it may deem expedient, not exceeding twenty-five thousand dollars, and secure the same by mortgage of the franchise and property of said company.

Capital stock.

Section 9. The capital stock of said corporation shall be twenty-five thousand dollars, said stock to be divided into shares of ten dollars each.

First meeting, how called.

Section 10. The first meeting of this corporation, may be called by written notice, signed by any one of the incorporators and served upon each of the other incorporators, at least seven days before the day of said meeting.

Section 11. This act shall become null and void in four years from the time when the same takes effect, unless the corporation shall have organized and commenced the construction of its works under this charter. *Must commence construction within four years.*

Section 12. Said corporation is hereby authorized to make contracts with said town of Naples, and with other corporations and individuals, for the purpose of supplying water, for municipal and other purposes; and said town by its selectmen, is hereby authorized to enter into contract with said company for the supply of water, with such exemption from public burden as said town and said company may agree upon, which, when made, shall be legal and binding upon all parties thereto. *May contract to supply water.*

Section 13. This act shall take effect when approved.

Approved March 27, 1903.

Chapter 338.

An Act to incorporate the Dirigo Electric Light Company of Dexter.

Be it enacted by the Senate and House of Representatives in Legislature assembled, as follows:

Section 1. Edwin Bunker, Norman H. Fay, Owen W. Bridges, William C. Elder, Atwood J. Cobb, John W. Springall and Elmer Weymouth, their associates, successors and assigns are hereby made a body corporate by the name of the Dirigo Electric Light Company, with all the powers, rights and privileges, subject to all the duties and obligations conferred and imposed upon corporations by law, except as otherwise provided herein. *Corporators. —corporate name.*

Section 2. Said company is authorized and empowered to carry on the business of lighting by electricity such public streets in the towns of Dexter, Garland and Corinna, outside of the limits of Corinna village, and such buildings and places therein, public or private as may be agreed upon by said corporation and the owners or those having control of such places to be lighted; and may furnish motive power by electricity within the limits of said towns of Dexter, Garland and Corinna, outside of the limits of Corinna village; and may build and operate factories and works for the providing and supplying of electricity and light and power and may contract with any other electric light and power company for the same purpose; and may lease, purchase and hold real and personal estate for the proper objects of *Powers.*

the corporation to the amount of fifteen thousand dollars and to construct, lay, maintain and operate lines of wire or other material for the transmission of electricity, submarine, underground, upon, under and along and over any and all streets and ways under the direction of the municipal officers of said Dexter, Garland and Corinna, outside of the limits of said Corinna village; and in public places in such a manner as not to endanger the appropriate public use thereof, and to establish and maintain, under direction of said municipal officers, all necessary posts, pipes, supports and appurtenances, and terminating at such points as may be expedient.

May set poles, etc.

—in towns of Dover, Newport and Detroit.

Section 3. Said corporation is hereby empowered to set and maintain poles, wires and fixtures necessary for the transmission of electricity through the streets and ways of the towns of Dover, in the county of Piscataquis, Newport, in the county of Penobscot, and Detroit, in the county of Somerset, under such reasonable restrictions as may be imposed by the municipal officers thereof, and subject to and in accordance with the general laws of the state regulating the erection of posts and lines for the purposes of electricity, with the right to cut down trees and remove obstacles when necessary within the limits aforesaid, excepting ornamental, fruit or shade trees.

Restriction of powers.

Section 4. None of the powers granted to said corporation by section three shall be used by it for the sale of light, heat or power, in Dover, Newport or Detroit where corporations organized under special charter are now exercising some of their chartered powers without the written consent of said corporations, nor within the limits of Corinna village without first obtaining the consent of Leslie F. Ireland who has an established lighting plant in said Corinna village, or by first obtaining the consent of a majority of the legal voters residing within said village limits, at a meeting of said voters called for such purpose after seven days notice.

Municipal officers may direct erection of wires, etc.

Section 5. For the erecting said wires above ground and for laying the same, or pipes thereof, submarine or under ground, and for taking up, replacing and repairing the same, said company shall first obtain the consent of the municipal officers of said towns, and perform all acts as directed by said municipal officers; and said company shall repay to said Dexter, Dover, Garland, Corinna, Newport and Detroit any sum which said towns may have been compelled to pay on any judgment for any damages caused by a defect or want of repair in the streets or ways thereof, due to the neglect of said company, or on any judgment for damages caused by the negligence of said company in the erecting and maintaining of any posts, wires or appurtenances connected with said business.

Section 6. Said company, at its own expense, without unnecessary delay, shall remove any and all obstructions in any street or way, made in erecting or laying the lines for such purposes; and cause earth disturbed to be properly replaced. It shall not be allowed to obstruct or impair the use of any public or private drain, or gas pipe or sewer, telegraph or telephone wire, but may cross, or when necessary, change direction of any private wire or pipe, drain or sewer, in such manner as not to obstruct or impair the use thereof, being responsible to the owner or other person for any injury occasioned thereby, in an action on the case.

Restrictions and duties in occupancy of streets.

Section 7. Damages for any land taken for the purposes of erecting or laying said lines, if the parties cannot agree, shall be estimated, secured and paid as in the case of lands taken for railroads.

Proceedings in case of disagreement as to damages.

Section 7. Nothing contained in this act shall be construed to affect or diminish the liability of said corporation for any injury to private property, by depreciating the value thereof or otherwise, but any legal remedies existing shall continue. The selectmen of said Dexter, Dover, Garland, Corinna, Newport and Detroit for the time being, shall, at all times, have the power to regulate and control the acts and doings of said corporation, which may in any manner affect the health or safety, or become a nuisance to the inhabitants of said towns.

Liable for injury to private property.

Section 9. The capital stock of said company shall not exceed fifty thousand dollars divided into shares of fifty dollars each.

Capital stock.

Section 10. Said company is hereby authorized to issue bonds for the construction of its works upon such rates and time, and to such amount as it may deem necessary, not to exceed twenty-five thousand dollars in all, and not to exceed the amount of capital stock subscribed for, and to secure the same by mortgage or deed of trust upon its franchise and property.

May issue bonds.

Section 11. Manufactories and other business corporations doing business in said Dexter, Dover, Garland, Corinna, Newport and Detroit are hereby authorized to subscribe and hold stock in said company.

Subscriptions to stock authorized.

Section 12. Any two of the corporators named in this act may call the first meeting of the corporation by mailing a written notice, signed by both, postage paid, to each of the corporators seven days at least before the day of the meeting, naming the time, place and purpose of said meeting; a president, secretary and directors may be chosen, by-laws adopted and any corporate business transacted.

First meeting, how called.

Section 13. This act may be accepted at any regular meeting of said association by a majority of the members present.

Acceptance of this act.

CHAP. 338

Charter may become null and void.

Section 14. The charter hereby granted shall be null and void if the Dexter Electric Light and Power Company shall, on or before the first day of December, in the year of our Lord nineteen hundred and three, increase its supply of electricity by one hundred horse power, available for all night service, together with such electrical appliances as will enable said corporation to utilize said additional power for the purposes of electricity under the obligations of its charter.

Further proceedings under this section.

Upon petition therefor by the said Dexter Electric Light and Power Company, filed in the clerk's office of the supreme judicial court for Penobscot county, during the month of January, in the year of our Lord, nineteen hundred and four, any justice of the supreme judicial court, in term time or vacation, after notice to said Dirigo Electric Light Company, or if not then organized, to any incorporator thereof, and after hearing thereon may extend said time a reasonable period if it appears to such justice that said Dexter Electric Light and Power Company has been prevented from the full performance of the condition herein by inevitable accident or unavoidable cause.

Upon application made by the Dirigo Electric Light Company, filed in the clerk's office of the supreme judicial court for Penobscot county, during the month of February, in the year of our Lord, nineteen hundred and four, or during the thirty days next following the aforesaid extension of time of completion, any justice of the supreme judicial court, after notice and hearing, in term time or vacation, shall determine finally and without appeal whether the aforesaid conditions have been substantially performed, and whether the charter hereby granted is or is not null and void; and such findings, signed by such justice, shall be returned to and entered of record in the office of the clerk of courts of the county of Penobscot.

Approved March 27, 1903.

Chapter 339.

An Act closing Cupsuptic River and its tributaries to all fishing, above the foot of the first falls near its mouth, from July first to May first.

Be it enacted by the Senate and House of Representatives in Legislature assembled, as follows:

Section 1. It shall be unlawful to fish at any time for any kind of fish in the Cupsuptic river or its tributaries, above the foot of the first falls near its mouth, except from May first to July first of each year. <small>Close season, Cupsuptic river and tributaries.</small>

Section 2. Whoever violates any of the provisions of this act shall be subject to a penalty of not less than ten nor more than thirty dollars and costs for each offense, and a further penalty of one dollar for each fish caught, taken or killed in violation of this act. <small>Penalty for violation.</small>

Approved March 27, 1903.

Chapter 340.

An Act to incorporate the Ashland Trust Company.

Be it enacted by the Senate and House of Representatives in Legislature assembled, as follows:

Section 1. E. G. Dunn, G. B. Haywood, E. R. McKay, N. S. Coffin, C. A. Trafton, H. L. Dobson, F. G. Dunn, H. M. Chapman, S. S. Thornton, W. B. Hallett, all of Ashland, or such of them as may by vote accept this charter, with their associates, successors and assigns, are hereby made a body corporate and politic to be known as the Ashland Trust Company, and as such shall be possessed of all the powers, privileges and immunities and subject to all the duties and obligations conferred on corporations by law. <small>Corporators. —corporate name.</small>

Section 2. The corporation hereby created shall be located at Ashland, Aroostook county, Maine, and may have two offices for the transaction of business in said town. <small>Location.</small>

Section 3. The purposes of said corporation and the business which it may perform, are: first, to receive on deposit, money, coin, bank notes, evidences of debt, accounts of individuals, companies, corporations, municipalities and states, allowing interest thereon, if agreed, or as the by-laws of said corporation may provide; second, to borrow money, to loan money on credits, or real estate, or personal security, and to negotiate loans and sales for others; third, to own and maintain safe deposit vaults, with boxes, safes and other facilities therein, to be rented to other <small>Purposes. —may maintain safe deposit vaults.</small>

524 ASHLAND TRUST COMPANY.

CHAP. 340

parties for the safe keeping of moneys, securities, stocks, jewelry, plate, valuable papers and documents, and other property susceptible of being deposited therein, and may receive on deposit for safe keeping, property of any kind entrusted to it for that purpose; fourth, to hold and enjoy all such estate, real, personal and mixed, as may be obtained by the investment of its capital stock, or any other moneys and funds that may come into its possession in the course of its business and dealings, and the same sell, grant and dispose of; fifth, to act as agent for issuing, registering and countersigning certificates, bonds, stocks and all evidences of debt or ownership in property; sixth, to hold by grant, assignment, transfer, devise or bequeath, any real or personal property or trusts duly created, and to execute trusts of every description; seventh, to act as assignee, receiver, executor, and no surety shall be necessary upon the bond of the corporation, unless the court or officer approving such bond shall require it; eighth, to do in general all the business that may lawfully be done by trust and banking companies.

—may execute trusts.

Capital stock.

Section 4. The capital stock of said corporation shall not be less than twenty-five thousand dollars, divided into shares of one hundred dollars each, with the right to increase the said capital stock at any time, by vote of the shareholders, to any amount not exceeding two hundred thousand dollars. Said corporation shall not commence business as a trust or banking company, until stock to the amount of at least twenty-five thousand dollars shall have been subscribed and paid in, in cash.

—shall not commence business till $25,000 has been paid in.

Shall not make loans on security of its own capital stock.

Section 5. Said corporation shall not make any loan or discount on the security of the shares of its own capital stock, nor be the purchaser or holder of any such shares unless necessary to prevent loss upon a debt previously contracted in good faith; and all stock so acquired shall, within six months from the time of its acquisition, be disposed of at public or private sale.

Board of directors.

Section 6. All the corporate powers of this corporation shall be exercised by a board of directors, who shall be residents of this state, whose number and term of office shall be determined by a vote of the shareholders at the first meeting held by the incorporators and at each annual meeting thereafter. The affairs and powers of the corporation may, at the option of the shareholders, be entrusted to an executive board of seven members to be, by vote of the shareholders, elected from the full board of directors. The directors of said corporation shall be sworn to the proper discharge of their duties, and they shall hold office until others are elected and qualified in their stead. If a director dies, resigns, or becomes disqualified for any cause, the remaining directors may appoint a person to fill the vacancy until the next

—executive board.

—vacancies, how filled.

annual meeting of the corporation. The oath of office of such director shall be taken within thirty days of his election, or his office shall become vacant. The clerk of such corporation shall, within ten days, notify such directors of their election, and within thirty days shall publish the list of all persons who have taken the oath of office as directors.

Section 7. The board of directors of said corporation shall constitute the board of investment of said corporation. Said directors shall keep a separate book, specially provided for the purpose, a record of all loans, and investments of every description, made by said institution substantially in the order of time when such loans or investments are made, which shall show that such loans or investments have been made with the approval of the investment committee of said corporation, which shall indicate such particulars, respecting such loans or investments as the bank examiner shall direct. This book shall be submitted to the directors and to the bank examiner whenever requested. Such loans or investments shall be classified in the book as the bank examiner shall direct. No loan shall be made to any officer or director of said banking or trust company except by the approval of a majority of the executive board in writing, and said corporation shall have no authority to hire money or to give notes unless by vote of said board duly recorded.

Section 8. No person shall be eligible as a member of the executive committee of said corporation who is not the actual owner of ten shares of the stock.

Section 9. Said corporation, after beginning to receive deposits, shall, at all times, have on hand in lawful money, as a reserve, not less than fifteen per cent of the aggregate amount of its deposits which are subject to withdrawal on demand, provided, that in lieu of lawful money, two-thirds of said fifteen per cent may consist of balances, payable on demand, due from any national or state bank.

Section 10. All the property or money held in trust by this corporation shall constitute a special deposit and the accounts thereof and of said trust department shall be kept separate, and such funds and the investment or loans of them shall be specially appropriated to the security and payment of such deposits, and not be subject to any other liabilities of the corporation; and for the purpose of securing the observance of this proviso, said corporation shall have a trust department in which all business pertaining to such trust property shall be kept separate and distinct from its general business.

Section 11. An administrator, executor, assignee, guardian or trustee, any court of law or equity, including courts of probate and insolvency, officers and treasurers of towns, cities, counties and savings banks of the state of Maine may deposit any moneys, bonds, stocks, evidences of debt or of ownership in property, or any personal property, with said corporation, and any of said courts may direct any person deriving authority from them to so deposit the same.

Responsibility of shareholders.

Section 12. Each shareholder of this corporation shall be individually responsible, equally and ratably, and not one for the other, for all contracts, debts and engagements of such corporation, to a sum equal to the amount of the par value of the shares owned by each in addition to the amount invested in said shares.

Surplus fund.

Section 13. Such corporation shall set apart as a surplus fund not less than ten per cent of its earnings in each and every year until such fund with the accumulated interest thereon, shall amount to one-fourth of the capital stock of said corporation.

Taxation.

Section 14. The shares of said corporation shall be subject to taxation in the same manner and rate as are the shares of national banks.

Shall be subject to examination by bank examiner

Section 15. Said corporation shall be subject to examination by the bank examiner, who shall visit it at least once in every year, and as much oftener as he may deem expedient. At such visits he shall have free access to its vaults, books and papers, and shall thoroughly inspect and examine all the affairs of said corporation, and make such inquiries as may be necessary to ascertain its condition and ability to fulfill all its engagements. If upon examination of said corporation, the examiner is of the opinion that its investments are not in accordance with law, or said corporation is insolvent, or its condition is such as to render its further proceedings hazardous to the public or to those having funds in its custody, or is of the opinion that it has exceeded its powers or failed to comply with any of the rules or restrictions provided by law, he shall have such authority and take such action as is provided for in the case of savings banks by chapter forty-seven of the revised statutes. He shall preserve in a permanent form a full record of his proceedings, including a statement of the condition of said corporation. A copy of such statement shall be published by said corporation immediately after the annual examination of the same in some newspaper published where said corporation is established. If no paper is published in the town where said corporation is established, then it shall be published in a newspaper printed in the nearest city or town. The necessary expenses of the bank examiner while making such examination shall be paid by the corporation.

—shall publish statement.

CHAP. 341

Section 16. Any three of the corporators named in this act may call the first meeting of the corporation by mailing a written notice, signed by all, postage paid, to each of the other corporators, seven days at least before the day of meeting, naming the time, place and purpose of such meeting, and at such meeting the necessary officers may be chosen, by-laws adopted, and any other corporate business transacted.

First meeting, how called.

Section 17. This act shall take effect when approved.

Approved March 27, 1903.

Chapter 341.

An Act to amend the charter of the Augusta Trust Company.

Be it enacted by the Senate and House of Representatives in Legislature assembled, as follows:

Section 1. The Augusta Trust Company, originally chartered under the name of the Augusta Safe Deposit and Trust Company, but now a lawfully existing corporation under the laws of this state under the name of the Augusta Trust Company, is hereby authorized to establish a branch at Madison, in the county of Somerset.

Authorized to establish branch at Madison.

Section 2. All of the acts and doings of the said corporation in the change of its name from the Augusta Safe Deposit and Trust Company to the Augusta Trust Company are hereby ratified and confirmed.

Change of name ratified.

Section 3. This act shall take effect when approved.

Approved March 27, 1903.

Chapter 342

An Act to permit the Longwood Real Estate Company to construct a wharf in Long Lake, in the Town of Naples.

Be it enacted by the Senate and House of Representatives in Legislature assembled, as follows:

Section 1. The Longwood Real Estate Company, a corporation duly established and existing under the laws of this state, its successors or assigns, are hereby authorized and empowered to construct and maintain a wharf at the foot of Long lake in the town of Naples, county of Cumberland, near the Casino, and

Construction of wharf authorized.

BOOTHBAY RAILROAD.

CHAP. 343

to extend the same, far enough into said lake, to allow the landing of boats and steamers.

Section 2. This act shall take effect when approved.

Approved March 27, 1903.

Chapter 343.

An Act to extend time of construction of Boothbay Railroad.

Be it enacted by the Senate and House of Representatives in Legislature assembled, as follows:

Time of construction, extended.

Section 1. The time within which the Boothbay Railroad Company may commence construction of its line is hereby extended to March first in the year nineteen hundred and five.

Conditional extension of charter.

Section 2. This extension of the charter of the Boothbay Railroad Company is granted upon the condition that said company shall abandon so much of its location now on file or of any location by it to be hereafter filed as may be included in any location hereafter filed by the Lincoln County Street Railway and any such location, or part thereof, so to be abandoned shall be null and void whenever said Lincoln County Street Railway shall file a location so conflicting therewith and shall construct its railroad thereon but nothing herein contained shall apply to any part of the location of the Boothbay Railroad Company built upon by said railroad company or then under contract for construction in good faith and subsequently built upon under such contract.

Section 3. This act shall take effect when approved.

Approved March 27, 1903.

Chapter 344.

An Act to incorporate the Brooks Village Corporation.

Be it enacted by the Senate and House of Representatives in Legislature assembled, as follows:

Section 1. All that part of the town of Brooks embraced within the following bounds, namely: Beginning on the west line of the town of Monroe, near the railroad crossing next east from the dwelling house of P. B. Clifford, thence running south by land of A. E. Carpenter, on said Carpenter's east line, to land of N. A. Cilley, thence running westerly on south lines of lands of N. A. Cilley and C. F. Bessey to land of J. B. McTaggart, thence running westerly on south lines of lands of J. B. McTaggart, Clara E. Ames and Joseph N. Ginn to the old Belfast road, so called, thence westerly on south line of land of Joseph N. Ginn, and north line of land of Robert Nickerson, south lines of lands of F. W. Gibbs and F. B. Thompson, to the road running from Belfast to Unity, thence westerly on south line of land of Frank Quimby, to land of C. T. Scribner, thence southerly on east lines of lands of C. T. Scribner, C. F. Foss, Mary E. Webber and George Johnson to land of C. H. Dickey, thence westerly on north line of land of C. H. Dickey, and south lines of lands of George Johnson and E. L. Prime to the east line of the town of Knox, thence northerly on east line of the town of Knox to the south line of the town of Jackson, thence easterly on the south line of the town of Jackson to the west line of the town of Monroe, thence southerly on the west line of the town of Monroe to the place of beginning, together with the inhabitants thereon, be and the same is hereby created a body corporate by the name of Brooks Village Corporation, with all the rights and privileges granted by the laws of the state to similar corporations. —Territorial limits.
—corporate name.

Section 2. Said corporation is hereby authorized and vested with power, at any legal meeting called for the purpose, or at its annual meeting, to raise money by taxation, or otherwise, including the power to issue bonds or notes therefor, provided the whole amount does not at any one time exceed five per cent of the assessed valuation of such corporation; for the purpose of organizing and maintaining within the limits of said corporation, an efficient fire department; for building, renting, purchasing, repairing, and maintaining engine houses, hook and ladder carriage houses and lockups or police stations; for purchasing, repairing and maintaining fire engines, hose, ladders, buckets, machines and other apparatus for the extinguishment and prevention of fire; for the location, construction, and repair of May raise money.
—proviso.
—fire department.

CHAP. 344

—for schoolhouses.

—sidewalks.

—sewers.

—police.

—lighting of streets.

reservoirs and aqueducts; for the procuring of water and pumps, pipes, hydrants and machinery for handling and distributing the same; for building, repairing and maintaining schoolhouses; for building, repairing and maintaining sidewalks; for building, repairing and maintaining sewers; for setting out, maintaining and caring for shade trees; for maintaining and improving the common lands, for the purchasing and renting of real estate for any of the above purposes; to pay for the services of one or more police officers, night watchmen or any other officers to whom the said corporation may vote a salary or other compensation; to erect and maintain lamp posts and lamps, and provide for lighting the streets within the limits of said corporation; and for school purposes, and may receive, hold and manage devises, bequests or gifts for and any of the above purposes.

May take lands for schoolhouses.

Section 3. For the purpose of building schoolhouses, said corporation shall have all the powers, that towns now have, for taking land for schoolhouses and play grounds, and the proper officers of the town of Brooks, shall have the same power in such taking, as they would have if it was the town taking said land, so far as it relates to the locating and appraising said land, and all such taking shall be governed by the same laws.

Assessments, how and by whom made.

Section 4. Any money raised by taxation by said corporation for the purposes aforesaid, shall be assessed upon the property and polls within the territory by the assessors of said corporation, in the same manner as is provided by law for the assessment of county and town taxes, and said assessors may copy the last valuation of said property by the assessors of the town of Brooks, and assess the taxes thereon, if said corporation shall so direct, and may abate any tax by them so assessed; the tax on polls not to exceed the sum of one dollar to any one person in one year.

Duties of assessors.

—duty of collector.

Section 5. Upon a certificate being filed with the assessors of said corporation by the clerk thereof of the amount of money raised at any meeting for the purposes aforesaid, it shall be the duty of said assessors, as soon as may be, to assess said amount upon the polls and estates of the persons residing on the territory aforesaid and upon the estates of non-resident proprietors thereof, and lists of the assessment so made, to certify and deliver to the collector, whose duty it shall be to collect the same in like manner as county and town taxes are by law collected by towns, and pay over the same to the treasurer of said corporation, who shall receive the same and pay it out to order or direction of the said corporation, and keep a regular account of all moneys received and paid out, and exhibit the same to the assessors whenever requested; and said corporation shall have the same power to direct the mode of collecting said taxes as towns have in the collection of town taxes.

Section 6. The officers of said corporation shall consist of a clerk, treasurer, assessors, collector and such other officers as may be provided for in the by-laws of said corporation. *Officers.*

Section 7. Said corporation at any legal meeting thereof, may adopt a code of by-laws for the government of the same, provided, the said by-laws are not repugnant to the laws of the state. *By-laws.*

Section 8. All officers of said corporation shall be chosen by ballot and sworn to the faithful performance of their duties; the first election to be at the meeting of the legal voters of said corporation, at which this charter is accepted, and the annual election of officers shall be in the month of March. *First election*

Section 9. The collector shall give bonds in double the amount of the tax so raised, and the treasurer in such sum as the assessors direct, which bonds shall be approved by the assessors and clerk. *Bonds of collector and of treasurer.*

Section 10. E. C. Holbrook, E. G. Roberts, E. A. Carpenter, F. R. York, or either of them are hereby authorized to call the first meeting of the said corporation, and to notify the legal voters thereof to meet at some suitable time and place within the limits aforesaid, by posting up notices in two public and conspicuous places within said limits, seven days at least before the time of said meeting; and either of said persons are authorized to preside at said meeting until after its organization, and until after a moderator shall have been chosen by ballot and sworn, and at all meetings of said corporation a moderator shall be chosen in the manner and with the same powers as in town meetings. *First meeting, how called.*

Section 11. All persons liable to be taxed for polls residing in the limits of said corporation, shall be legal voters at any meeting of said corporation. *Poll tax payers shall be voters.*

Section 12. This act shall take effect when approved by the governor, so far as to empower the first meeting of said corporation to be called. *Approval of this act.*

Section 13. In the meeting prescribed in section ten of this act for the first meeting of said corporation, the legal voters shall vote by ballot on the question of accepting this charter; and if the majority shall vote in favor of its acceptance then it shall take effect in all its parts, and the corporation shall proceed to organize and choose its officers as provided in section eight of this act. There shall be but one meeting called each year for the purpose of the acceptance of this charter. *Acceptance of charter.*

Approved March 27, 1903.

532   DEER—MAINE COAST TELEPHONE COMPANY.

CHAP. 345

Chapter 345.

An Act for the protection of deer and moose in the County of Sagadahoc.

Be it enacted by the Senate and House of Representatives in Legislature assembled, as follows:

Close time for deer and moose in Sagadahoc county.

It shall be unlawful to hunt, chase, catch or kill any deer or moose, in the county of Sagadahoc, until October first, nineteen hundred and five, under the penalty provided in the general law of the state for the illegal hunting and killing of deer and moose.

Approved March 27, 1903.

Chapter 346.

An Act to incorporate the Maine Coast Telephone Company.

Be it enacted by the Senate and House of Representatives in Legislature assembled, as follows:

Corporators.

—corporate name.

—powers and privileges.

Section 1. George A. Sawyer and Charles M. Cole, their associates and successors, are hereby made a body corporate by the name of the Maine Coast Telephone Company, with all the rights, powers and privileges, and subject to all the duties and obligations of similar corporations under the general laws of this state, with power by that name to sue and be sued, to have a common seal, to establish all by-laws and regulations for the management of its affairs not repugnant to the laws of this state and to do and perform any and all legal acts, incident to similar corporations.

Location of route.

Section 2. Said corporation is hereby authorized to construct, own, maintain and operate telephone line or lines anywhere in the towns of Milbridge, Steuben and Harrington, all within the county of Washington and state of Maine, having obtained consent of the several municipalities, and said corporation shall have the right to locate and construct its lines upon and along any public highway or bridge in said towns, but in such a way as not to incommode or endanger the customary use thereof; and shall have the power to establish and collect tolls on said lines.

May connect with other lines.

Section 3. Said corporation is hereby authorized and empowered to connect its lines with those of any other telephone company or corporation on such terms as may be mutually agreed upon, or to sell or lease its line or lines of telephone and property in whole or in part, either before or after completion to any other telephone company or corporation, as provided by law or upon such terms as may be agreed by the contracting parties, which sale or lease shall be binding upon the parties; or may purchase or lease any other line or lines of telephone upon such terms and conditions as may be agreed by the parties thereto.

Section 4. If the land of any individual or corporation is taken under this act, and the parties cannot agree upon the damages occasioned thereby, they shall be estimated, secured and paid in the manner provided in the case of land taken for railroads.

Proceedings in case of disagreement as to damages.

Section 5. The capital stock of said corporation shall be of such an amount as said corporation may, from time to time determine to be necessary, but not exceeding the sum of ten thousand dollars, for the sole purpose of owning, leasing, constructing, maintaining and operating the line or lines of telephone hereby authorized and contemplated. And the said corporation may purchase, hold, lease, sell and convey all real estate and personal property necessary for the purposes contemplated in this charter.

Capital stock.

—may hold real and personal estate.

Section 6. Any one of the incorporators named in this act may call the first meeting of the corporation by mailing a written notice signed by himself, postage paid, to each of the other incorporators, seven days at least before the day of the meeting, naming the time, place and purposes of such meeting, and at such meeting a president, secretary, treasurer and directors may be chosen, by-laws adopted, present amount of capital stock fixed, and any corporate business transacted.

First meeting how called.

Section 7. This act shall take effect when approved.

Approved March 27, 1903.

Chapter 347.

An Act to prohibit the dumping of herring and all fish offal in the waters of Jonesport and Addison.

Be it enacted by the Senate and House of Representatives in Legislature assembled, as follows:

Section 1. The dumping of herring and all fish offal is hereby prohibited in the waters adjacent to the towns of Jonesport and Addison, in the county of Washington, under a penalty of not less than ten nor more than fifty dollars for each offense.

Dumping of fish offal in certain waters, prohibited. —penalty.

Section 2. All fines or penalties imposed under this act may be recovered by indictment or action of debt, one-fourth of the penalty to party prosecuting and three-fourths to town school fund in the town where the offense may be committed.

Fines, how recovered.

Section 3. This act shall take effect August first, nineteen hundred and three.

Approved March 27, 1903.

Chapter 348.

An Act to prohibit the throwing of sawdust and other refuse into Norton, Brown or Heath Brooks or their tributaries in the towns of Shapleigh and Limerick.

Be it enacted by the Senate and House of Representatives in Legislature assembled, as follows:

Throwing of sawdust into certain waters, prohibited.

Section 1. No person shall cast or throw into Norton brook, in the town of Shapleigh, or into Brown or Heath brooks in the town of Limerick, in the county of York, or into any of the tributaries of said brooks, any sawdust, shavings, bark or other mill waste, or place or deposit such mill waste or other refuse along the banks in such manner that the same shall fall or be washed into said brooks or their tributaries.

Penalty.

Section 2. Whoever violates any of the provisions of this act shall be subject to a penalty of not less than five dollars nor more than fifty dollars for each offense.

Section 3. This act shall take effect when approved.

Approved March 27, 1903.

Chapter 349.

An Act prohibiting the use of boats or launches of any kind propelled by steam, naphtha, gasoline, or electricity, while hunting sea birds in the waters of Frenchmans' bay, so called, on the coast of Maine.

Be it enacted by the Senate and House of Representatives in Legislature assembled, as follows:

Hunting of sea birds in certain waters, by use of launches, prohibited.

Section 1. It shall be unlawful for any person at any time to use boats or launches of any kind propelled by steam, naphtha, gasoline, or electricity, or any other mode than the ordinary sail boat or row boat in chasing, hunting or gunning any sea birds, duck or water fowl in any of the waters of Frenchman's Bay, so called, on the coast of Maine, under a penalty of not less than twenty-five dollars nor more than one hundred dollars and costs of prosecution for each offense.

—penalty.

Frenchman's Bay, defined.

Section 2. For the purposes of this act Frenchman's Bay is defined and bounded as follows: On the north by the towns of Hancock and Sulivan; on the east by the towns of Gouldsboro and Winter Harbor; on the south by Mount Desert Island and a straight line from Schoodic point, so called, to Great Head, so called; on the west by Thompson's toll bridge.

Approved March 27, 1903.

Chapter 350.

An Act to regulate fishing in the tributaries of Wilson lake in Wilton, in the County of Franklin.

Be it enacted by the Senate and House of Representatives in Legislature assembled, as follows:

Section 1. So much of section five of chapter forty-two of the public laws of eighteen hundred and ninety-nine as prohibits fishing in the tributaries of Wilson lake in Wilton, in the county of Franklin, except in Coos brook from its entrance into said Wilson lake to the upper side of the Wilkins bridge over said Coos brook, and the Holland brook from its junction with Coos brook to the upper side of the Coos bridge over said Holland brook, is hereby repealed.

Section 2. This act shall take effect when approved.

Approved March 27, 1903.

Chapter 351.

An Act to prohibit all ice fishing in Lake Webb or Weld pond, so called, in the town of Weld, County of Franklin.

Be it enacted by the Senate and House of Representatives in Legislature assembled, as follows:

Section 1. It shall be unlawful to fish for, take, catch or kill any kind of fish in Lake Webb or Weld pond, so called, in the town of Weld, Franklin county, between October first and May first of the following year.

Section 2. Whoever violates any of the provisions of this act shall be punished by a fine of not less than ten nor more than thirty dollars and costs for each offense and a further fine of one dollar for each fish caught, taken or killed in violation of this law.

Approved March 27, 1903.

Chapter 352.

An Act to legalize the acts and doings of Nashville Plantation, Aroostook County.

Be it enacted by the Senate and House of Representatives in Legislature assembled, as follows:

Acts of Nashville plantation, legalized.

Section 1. All acts and doings of Nashville plantation, Aroostook county, Maine, prior to this date are hereby legalized and made valid.

May raise money for repair of winter roads.

Section 2. Said plantation may raise money at any annual meeting for the breaking, opening and repairing of snow roads, and to keep its winter roads passable for public travel, to be expended by the assessors of said plantation.

Section 3. This act shall take effect when approved.

Approved March 27, 1903.

Chapter 353.

An Act relating to the new iron bridge over the Presumpscot River in the Town of Falmouth.

Be it enacted by the Senate and House of Representatives in Legislature assembled, as follows:

County of Cumberland may acquire bridge over Presumpscot river.

Section 1. When the town of Falmouth, in the county of Cumberland, shall release to said county by deed all the rights of said town in and to the new iron bridge over the Presumpscot river, on the new Gray road in said Falmouth, and shall cause said deed to be recorded in the Cumberland registry of deeds, the said county shall thereupon be vested with all the rights and powers, and be subject to all the obligations and liabilities of said town, in respect to said bridge; and the county commissioners of said county shall thereafter, at the expense of said county, inspect, repair and maintain, said bridge, and, when necessary, rebuild the same. Said town of Falmouth is hereby authorized to convey its rights in said bridge as aforesaid.

—rights and liabilities of county, in respect to.

Section 2. This act shall take effect when approved.

Approved March 27, 1903.

Chapter 354.

An Act to fix qualification for participation in party caucuses in the City of Augusta.

Be it enacted by the Senate and House of Representatives in Legislature assembled, as follows:

Section 1. No person shall participate in any caucus of any political party unless qualified therefor by enrollment as hereinafter provided. Any person violating this section, or making any wilfully false statement of fact in his declaration of enrollment, shall be punished by fine not exceeding five hundred dollars or by imprisonment not exceeding six months. *Participants in caucus must be enrolled. —penalty for false statement.*

Section 2. Any person who is a legally qualified voter, may enroll himself as a member of any political party by filing with the city clerk of the city of Augusta, a declaration in writing, signed by him, of his election to enroll himself as a member of the party designated by him, which declaration shall be substantially as follows: *Legal voters may enroll.*

I,   being a legally qualified voter of the   of   hereby elect to enroll myself as a member of the   party. The following statement of name, residence, place of last enrollment if any, and party of last enrollment, if any, is true. *—form of declaration.*

Name.   Street.   Number.   Place of last enrollment.   Party of last enrollment.

Date.   Signature.

A new enrollment may be made at any time. No person shall vote in any caucus in said city unless he has been enrolled as herein provided as a member of the party holding such a caucus for a period of at least six months preceding such caucus. *—new enrollments.*

Section 3. The city clerk of the city of Augusta, where the enrollment is made as above provided shall receive and file the same, indorsing thereon the date of filing, and shall record the name, residence, place of last enrollment, party of last enrollment, and date of filing, in a separate book, entering the names alphabetically. *City clerk shall file enrollment.*

Suitable blanks for filing such enrollment shall be provided by the city clerk, and in addition thereto he shall provide books with proper headings embodying the enrollment statements above provided, which the person desiring to enroll may sign and fill out, thereby enrolling himself with the same effect as by filing such enrollment paper. *—blanks and books, how provided.*

Such books shall be public records, and shall at all times be open to public inspection, and kept in the office of the city clerk. *Books shall be public records.*

Section 4. This act shall take effect July first, nineteen hundred and three.

Approved March 27, 1903.

Chapter 355.

An Act to protect Smelts during their spawning season in the tributaries of the Damariscotta River.

Be it enacted by the Senate and House of Representatives in Legislature assembled, as follows:

Close time for smelts in tributaries of Damariscotta river.

Section 1. It shall be unlawful to fish for smelts in the waters of any of the tributaries of the Damariscotta river, in the county of Lincoln, in any manner whatever, from the first day of April to the tenth day of May of each year, on any days excepting Monday and Thursday of each week, on either of which days any person may take or catch a quantity not exceeding fifteen pounds.

Penalty for violating provisions of section 1.

Section 2. The penalty for a violation of the provisions of section one of this act shall be a fine of not less than five nor more than twenty dollars, which shall, upon conviction, be paid one-half to the county of Lincoln and one-half to the person making the complaint; and in case of non-payment, the party convicted shall be confined in the county jail for a period not less than ten days nor more than sixty days.

Trial justices have jurisdiction under this act.

Section 3. Trial justices shall have jurisdiction in all cases coming under this act, and in case of an appeal from the decision of such a justice, the bond required shall in no case be less than three hundred dollars.

Section 4. This act shall take effect when approved.

Approved March 27, 1903.

Chapter 356.

An Act to amend Chapter four hundred and twenty-nine of the Private and Special Laws of nineteen hundred and one, entitled "An Act to establish a municipal court in the town of Winthrop."

Be it enacted by the Senate and House of Representatives in Legislature assembled, as follows:

Section 1, chapter 429, private and special laws of 1901, amended.

Section 1. Section one of chapter four hundred and twenty-nine of the private and special laws of nineteen hundred and one is hereby amended by adding, after the words "municipal court" in the fourth line, the words 'which shall be a court of record and have a seal,' and by adding after the word "quorum" in the eighth line the words 'for the state,' so that said section, as amended, shall read as follows:

Municipal court established.

'Section 1. A municipal court is hereby established in and for the towns of Winthrop, Monmouth, Wayne and Fayette, in the county of Kennebec, to be denominated as the Winthrop

Municipal Court, which shall be a court of record and have a seal; said court shall consist of one judge, who shall reside during his continuance in said office, in said town of Winthrop or Monmouth and who shall be appointed, qualified and hold his office as provided in the constitution, and who shall be, ex-officio, a justice of the peace and of the quorum for the state, and have and exercise a concurrent authority and jurisdiction with trial justices over all matters and things by law within their jurisdiction and such authority and jurisdiction additional thereto as is conferred upon him by this act.'

Section 2. Section two is hereby amended so as to read as follows:

'Section 2. Said court shall have jurisdiction as follows: exclusive jurisdiction of all such criminal offenses and misdemeanors committed within said towns of Winthrop, Monmouth, Wayne and Fayette as are cognizable by trial justices and concurrent jurisdiction with trial justices in the county of Kennebec of all like offenses and misdemeanors, not herein placed within its exclusive jurisdiction, when committed in the towns of Readfield, Mount Vernon, Vienna, Rome, Belgrade and Manchester, in said county; exclusive original jurisdiction of all civil actions wherein the debt or damages demanded do not exceed twenty dollars, and both parties, or any plaintiff, and a person summoned as trustee, resides in either of said towns named in section one of this act, including prosecutions for penalties in which either of said towns are interested, and actions of forcible entry and detainer arising therein; and concurrent jurisdiction with trial justices in said county of all other civil actions and other proceedings cognizant by them, not within the exclusive jurisdiction of said court; provided that any action, civil or criminal, in which the judge may be interested or related to either of the parties by consanguinity or affinity within the sixth degree, according to the rules of the civil law, or within the degree of second cousin inclusive, but which otherwise would be within the exclusive jurisdiction of said court, may be brought in and disposed of by any other municipal or police court in said county in the same manner and with like effect as other actions therein; original jurisdiction concurrent with the superior court of the offenses committed in Winthrop, Monmouth, Wayne and Fayette, described in sections one, six, seven and nine of chapter one hundred and twenty of the revised statutes, when the alleged value of the property exceeds twenty dollars, but does not exceed fifty dollars; of the offenses described in section twenty-eight of chapter one hundred and eighteen of the revised statutes; of the offenses described in sections one and four of chapter one

Chap. 356

—proviso.

hundred and twenty-six of the revised statutes, when the alleged value of the property fraudulently obtained, mortgaged or sold, or fraudulently removed or concealed, does not exceed fifty dollars, and on conviction may punish for either of said offenses by fine not exceeding one hundred dollars and by imprisonment in the county jail for not more than six months; and also of the offense described in section six of chapter one hundred and twenty-four of the revised statutes, and on conviction may punish therefor by fine not exceeding fifty dollars and by imprisonment in the county jail not more than thirty days; and also of the offenses described in section four of chapter one hundred and forty-one of the revised statutes, and on conviction may sentence therefor to imprisonment in the county jail not more than ninety days; and of the offenses described in sections seventeen and twenty-two of chapter one hundred and twenty-eight of the revised statutes, as amended, relating to tramps, and on conviction may punish therefor as therein provided; original jurisdiction concurrent with the superior court in said county of all civil actions in which the debt or damages demanded, exceed twenty dollars, but do not exceed three hundred dollars and the defendant or a person summoned as trustee resides within Kennebec county; provided, however, that any action wherein the debt or damage demanded exceeds twenty dollars, brought in said court, shall be removed by order of the judge, or in his absence, by order of the recorder, into the superior court, on motion of the defendant, filed at the return term, if he files therewith, at the same time, an affidavit that he believes he has a good defense to said action, in whole or in part, and in good faith intends to make such defense, and deposits with the judge or recorder the fee of the clerk of the court above for entering said action therein; and when such removal has been ordered, the judge shall file in the superior court, at its next term in the county, an attested copy of the writ in such action, and of said motion and affidavit, and order of court thereon, and pay to the clerk of said court the fee for entering the same, for which services he shall be entitled to the same fees allowed for the necessary copies in actions carried up by appeal, to be paid to him by the defendant and recovered by him with his costs, if he prevailed in the suit; in any action in which either of the towns named in section one of this chapter is a party, or is summoned as a trustee, this court shall not lose jurisdiction by reason of the residence or the ownership of property in such town by the judge or recorder: but in such case the action may, upon written motion of either party, filed at the return term, be removed to the superior court.'

Section 3. Section five of said chapter is hereby amended by adding, after the word "judge" in the fifth line, the words 'or by the recorder and be of equal force and validity when signed by either,' so that said section, as amended, shall read as follows:

'Section 5. Writs in civil actions commenced in said court shall be in the usual forms, and all such writs and all other precepts and processes, civil or criminal, issued by said court, shall bear teste of the judge under seal of said court, and be signed by the judge, or by the recorder and be of equal force and validity when signed by either. All such writs shall be made returnable at one of the next four terms of said court held after seven days from their date, and service thereof may be made at any time not less than seven days before the return day thereof, except that when any defendant or trustee named in any such writ is a corporation, service upon such corporation must be made at least thirty days before the return day.'

Section 4. Section six of said chapter is hereby amended by striking out in the thirteenth and fourteenth lines the words "if said judge is prevented by any cause from attending at the time said court is to be held for civil business" and inserting in place thereof, the words 'if at any regular or adjourned term of said court to be held for civil business, neither the judge nor the recorder is present at the place used for holding said court within two hours after the time for opening said court, then' and also by striking out in the seventeenth line the word "he" and inserting in place thereof the words 'either the judge or recorder,' so that said section, as amended, shall read as follows:

'Section 6. Said court shall be held on the first and third Mondays of each month, for the entry, trial and determination of civil actions of all kinds that may lawfully be brought before it, and for the transaction of other civil business, and upon each other Monday for the entry, trial and determination of actions of forcible entry and detainer only, at ten of the clock in the forenoon, at such suitable place as the judge may determine, until the town of Winthrop shall provide a court room, when the court shall be held therein, and all civil processes shall be made returnable accordingly; and it may be adjourned from time to time by the judge, at his discretion, but it shall be considered in constant session for the cognizance of criminal actions. Provided that, if at any regular or adjourned term of said court to be held for civil business, neither the judge nor the recorder is present at the place used for holding said court within two hours after the time for opening said court, then it may be adjourned from day to day by a constable of Winthrop or a deputy sheriff of the county of Kennebec, without detriment to any action then return-

CHAP. 356

WINTHROP MUNICIPAL COURT.

able or pending, until the judge or recorder can attend, when said action may be entered or disposed of with the same effect as if it were the first day of the term; and it may be so adjourned without day when necessary, in which event, pending actions shall be considered as continued, and actions then returnable may be returned and entered at the next term with the same effect as if originally made returnable at said term.'

Section 7, amended.

Section 5. Section seven of said chapter is hereby amended by adding, in the fifth line, after the words "said judge" the words 'or recorder,' by striking out in the fifth, sixth, seventh and eighth lines the following: "the judge may appoint, in writing, a recorder, who shall be a trial justice for the county of Kennebec, duly qualified, who shall be sworn by said judge," and inserting in place thereof the following words: 'The governor, by and with the advice and consent of the council, may appoint a recorder of said court, who, at the time of his appointment shall be a resident of said Winthrop, duly qualified,' and also by adding in the seventeenth line after the words "the judge" the words 'without any recital of the act hereinbefore named authorizing him to act,' and also by striking out the twentieth line and inserting in place thereof the words 'for four years,' so that said section, as amended, shall read as follows:

Records of court.

'Section 7. It shall be the duty of said judge of said court to make and keep the records thereof or cause the same to be made and kept, and to perform all other duties, required of similar tribunals in this state; and copies of said records duly certified by said judge or recorder, shall be legal evidence in all courts. The governor, by and with the advice and consent of the council, may appoint a recorder of said court, who, at the time of his appointment, shall be a resident of Winthrop, duly qualified, who shall keep the records of said court when requested so to do by the judge; and in case of absence from the court room, or sickness of the judge, or when the office of judge shall be vacant, the recorder shall have and exercise all the powers of the judge, and perform all the duties required of said judge by this act, and shall be empowered to sign and issue all processes and papers, and to do all acts as fully and with the same effect as the judge could do were he acting in the premises; and the signature of the recorder, as such, shall be sufficient evidence of his right to act instead of the judge without any recital of the act hereinbefore named authorizing him to act. When the office of judge is vacant, the recorder shall be entitled to the fees; in all other cases he shall be paid by the judge, and shall hold his said office for four years.'

—recorder, appointment of.

Section 14, amended.

Section 6. Section fourteen of said chapter is hereby amended by adding after the word "use" in the fourth line, the words 'and it shall be deemed and denominated as the court room, though used also for other purposes, if approved by the judge,' so that said section, as amended, shall read as follows:

'Section 14. It shall be the duty of the town of Winthrop to provide a suitable court room in said Winthrop, conveniently situated and appropriately fitted up and furnished, in which to hold said court, and keep the same in proper condition for use, and it shall be deemed and denominated as the court room, though used also for other purposes, if approved by the judge, and also to provide for said court an appropriate seal, and all blanks, blank books, dockets, stationery and other things necessary in the transaction of its business; and said town is hereby authorized to appropriate money therefor.'

Court room, how provided, furnished and equipped.

Section 7. Section fifteen of said chapter is hereby amended by adding, after the word "quorum" in the fifth line, the words 'and except that they may issue warrants on complaints for criminal offenses committed in said towns to be returned before said municipal court,' so that said section, as amended shall read as follows:

Section 15, amended.

'Section 15. Trial justices are hereby restricted from exercising any jurisdiction in the towns of Winthrop, Monmouth, Wayne and Fayette, over any matter or thing, civil or criminal, except such as are within the jurisdiction of justices of the peace and quorum and except that they may issue warrants on complaints for criminal offenses committed in said towns to be returned before said municipal court; provided, that such restrictions shall be suspended until the judge of said court shall enter upon the duties of his office. Nothing in this act shall be construed to interfere with actions which have been brought and are pending before trial justices in the towns of Winthrop, Monmouth, Wayne and Fayette at the time when the judge of said court shall enter upon the duties of his office, but all such actions shall be disposed of by such trial justices the same as if this act had not passed.'

Jurisdiction of trial justices restricted.

Section 8. All acts and parts of acts, inconsistent with this act, are hereby repealed.

Section 9. This act shall take effect when approved.

Approved March 27, 1903.

Chapter 357.

An Act to incorporate the Kibbie Dam Company.

Be it enacted by the Senate and House of Representatives in Legislature assembled, as follows:

Corporators.
—corporate name.

Section 1. Charles A. Dean, Frank E. Boston, William W. Thomas and William J. Lanigan, their associates and assigns are hereby incorporated under the name of the Kibbie Dam Company, with the powers and privileges of similar corporations.

May erect dams, etc.

—may improve channel.

Section 2. Said company is hereby authorized to erect and maintain dams, side dams and piers on Kibbie stream and its tributaries in the townships of Kibbie and township number one, range seven, west of Bingham's Kennebec Purchase in the county of Franklin and township number four, range five and number five, range six in Bingham's Kennebec Purchase in the county of Somerset, to remove rocks and trees and to excavate ledges therefrom, and to widen, deepen and otherwise improve the same for the purpose of raising a head of water and of making said stream and its tributaries floatable, and of facilitating the driving of logs and lumber upon the same.

May take lands.

—may flow contiguous lands.

—damages, how determined.

Section 3. Said company for the above purposes may take all necessary land and materials for building said dams and piers and making improvements, and may flow contiguous lands so far as necessary to raise suitable heads of water; and if the parties cannot agree upon the damages, the corporation shall pay the proprietors for the land and materials so taken; such damages shall be ascertained and determined by the county commissioners of the county where the land and materials so taken lie, in the same manner and under the same conditions and limitations as provided by law in the case of damage by laying out of highways; and for the damage occasioned by flowing said land said company shall not be liable to an action at common law, but the person injured may have a remedy by complaint for flowage, in which case the same proceedings shall be had as when a complaint is made under the statutes of this state for flowing lands occasioned by raising a head of water for the working of mills.

Tolls.

Section 4. Said company may demand and receive tolls for the passage of all logs and lumber over their dams and improvements as follows: for all logs and lumber landed in said Kibbie stream above the upper West Branch dam, a sum not exceeding forty-five cents per thousand feet; for all logs and lumber landed on said stream between said upper West Branch dam and the north line of the Rockwood strip, so called, in Kibbie township, a sum not exceeding thirty-five cents per thousand feet; for all logs and lumber landed on said stream between said north line of the Rockwood strip and the flowage line of lower Kibbie dam, situated near the west line of township four, range five, a sum not exceeding twenty-five cents per thousand feet; for all logs and lumber landed in said stream between said flowage line and lower Kibbie dam, a sum not exceeding fifteen cents per thousand feet; and for all logs and lumber landed on said stream between said lower Kibbie dam and the mouth of Kibbie stream, a sum not exceeding ten cents per thousand feet. All the above tolls to be reckoned at the survey or scale adopted by the Kennebec Log Driving Company. Said Kibbie Dam Company shall have a lien upon all logs and lumber which may pass over any of its dams and improvements until the full amount of tolls is paid; but the logs of each particular mark shall only be holden to pay the toll on such mark; and if said toll is not paid within thirty days after said logs or lumber, or the major part thereof, shall have arrived within the limits of the Kennebec Log Driving Company, said Kibbie Dam Company may seize, hold and sell at public auction such part of said logs or lumber as shall be necessary to pay such tolls, with all incidental costs and charges thereon, after ten days' notice in writing of the time and place of said sale given to the owner of such logs or lumber. *—shall have lien on logs.*

Section 5. An account of the cost of said improvements shall be kept by the treasurer of said Kibbie Dam Company, and also of its receipts for tolls, which shall be open to inspection at all reasonable times to any person interested in the same. *Accounts shall be open to inspection.*

Section 6. When said corporation shall have received from tolls its outlay on dams, improvements and repairs made up to that time, with six per cent interest thereon, then the tolls shall be reduced to a sum sufficient to keep the works in repair; the treasurer of the Kennebec Log Driving Company, for the time being, is appointed to audit the accounts and determine the cost of said dams, improvements and repairs. *Reduction of tolls.*

Section 7. Any or all owners of lands from which logs or lumber are cut which pass through or over said dams or improvements shall have a right to take an interest in said company. *Owners of timber lands may take interest in company.*

Section 8. The amount invested shall at all meetings be represented by a fixed, convenient number of votes which shall be cast by the owners of the lands from which logs or lumber are cut which pass through or over its dams or improvements; and each owner shall have the right to vote in proportion to his interest in said lands by paying his proportion of the cost of building and maintaining said dams and improvements. *Voting powers of members.*

OFFICERS IN LEWISTON.

CHAP. 358
Referees to be agreed on in case of disagreement.

Section 9. In case of any disagreement as to the rights of owners hereunder, the same shall be forthwith determined by referees agreed upon by the parties, or by the county commissioners of the county where the land lies, if the parties cannot agree.

Section 10. This act shall take effect when approved.

Approved March 27, 1903.

Chapter 358.

An Act to amend Sections seventeen and nineteen of Chapter one hundred and five of the Private and Special Laws of eighteen hundred and sixty-one, relating to the Election of Mayor, Aldermen, Common Councilmen, Wardens and Ward Clerks, in the city of Lewiston.

Be it enacted by the Senate and House of Representatives in Legislature assembled, as follows:

Section 17 of chapter 105, private and special laws of 1861, amended.

Section 1. Section seventeen of chapter one hundred and five of the private and special laws of eighteen hundred and sixty-one is hereby amended by striking out the word "majority" in the fifth line of said section and inserting in place thereof the word 'plurality,' so that said section, as amended, shall read as follows:

Election of officers.

'Section 17. The mayor shall be elected from the citizens at large, by the inhabitants of the city voting in their respective wards. One alderman and three common councilmen shall be elected by each ward, being residents in the wards where elected.

—tenure.

All said officers shall be elected by ballot, by a plurality of the votes given, and shall hold their offices one year from the third Monday in March, and until others shall be elected in their places; provided, however, that if the city shall be divided into

—proviso.

less than seven wards, then one or two, as the case may be, of the aldermen shall be elected at large by the inhabitants of the city, the whole number of aldermen in no case to be more than seven, as provided in section second of this act.'

Section 19 of chapter 105, private laws of 1861, amended.

Section 2. Section nineteen of said chapter is hereby amended by striking out the words "the choice of" in the eleventh line, all of the twelfth, thirteenth, fourteenth, fifteenth, sixteenth, seventeenth and eighteenth lines, together with the word "number" in the nineteenth line, all in said section, and substituting in place thereof the words 'there be no choice of alderman, common councilmen, warden or ward clerk'; also by striking out the word "majority" in the twenty-third line of said section and substituting in place thereof the word 'plurality'; also by striking out the words "and in case the citizens should," in the twenty-seventh line, all of the twenty-eighth, twenty-ninth, thirtieth and thirty-first lines, together with the words "elected, and notified as aforesaid" in the thirty-second line, all in said section; also by striking out the word "number" in the thirty-third line of said section and substituting in place thereof the word 'plurality,' so that said section, as amended, shall read as follows:

'Section 19. On the first Monday of March, annually, the qualified electors of each ward shall ballot for a mayor, one alderman and three common councilmen, warden and ward clerk; all the votes given for the said several officers respectively, shall be sorted, counted, declared and registered in open ward meeting, by causing the names of persons voted for and the number of votes given for each to be written on the ward record at length. The ward clerk, within twenty-four hours after such election, shall deliver to the persons elected alderman and common councilmen, certificates of their election and shall forthwith deliver to the city clerk a certified copy of the records of such election; provided, however, that if there be no choice of alderman, common councilmen, warden or ward clerk, the balloting shall be continued from day to day until a choice is thus effected. The board of aldermen shall as soon as conveniently may be, examine the copies of the records of the several wards, certified as aforesaid, and shall cause the person who shall have been elected mayor, by a plurality of votes given in all the wards, to be notified in writing of his election; but if it shall appear that no person shall have been elected, or if the person elected shall refuse to accept the office, the said board shall issue their warrants for another election; if no one shall then have such plurality, further elections shall in the same manner be ordered till a choice shall be made, by some one having the highest number of votes; and in case of a vacancy in the office of mayor by death, resignation or otherwise, it shall be filled for the remainder of the term by a new election in the manner hereinbefore provided for the choice of said officer; and in the meantime the president pro tempore of the board of aldermen shall perform the duties of mayor. The oath prescribed by this act shall be administered to the mayor by the city clerk, or any justice of the peace in said city. The aldermen and common councilmen elect, shall, on the third Monday of March, at ten of the clock in the forenoon, meet in convention, when the oath required by the second section of this act shall be administered to the members of the two boards present, by the mayor or any justice of the peace, and thereupon the two boards shall separate, and the board of common council shall be organized by the election of a president and clerk.'

Approved March 28, 1903.

Chapter 359.

An Act to authorize the Town of York to construct and maintain Sewers in said town.

Be it enacted by the Senate and House of Representatives in Legislature assembled, as follows:

Town of York authorized to maintain sewers.

Section 1. The town of York is hereby authorized to construct and maintain a system or systems of sewers within said town in such places and such manner as may be determined by the inhabitants of said town at any legal town meeting, and to make appropriations necessary therefor.

Authorized to lay pipes, etc.

Section 2. Said town is authorized, for the purposes aforesaid, to construct, lay down and maintain all such pipes or other structures as may be necessary for properly conducting, discharging and disposing of sewerage; and to excavate in and through any land in said town when necessary for the purpose aforesaid.

May cross tide waters.

Section 3. Said town is authorized to lay, extend and maintain its pipes into, under and across tidal waters, and to build and maintain all structures necessary therefor, but in such manner as not to obstruct navigation.

May cross railroads.

Section 4. Said town is authorized to lay, construct and maintain in, through, under and along any railroads and water courses in said town all pipes and other structures necessary or convenient for the purposes herein set forth, and to take up, replace and repair the same when necessary. Provided, that in case of crossing any railroad at any point outside the limits of any highway, unless said town of York shall agree with the corporation, person or persons owning and operating such railroad, as to place, manner and conditions of such crossings, the railroad commissioners shall determine the place, manner and conditions thereof; and all work within the limits of the location of such railroad shall be done under the supervision and to the satisfaction of the officials of such railroad, but at the expense of said town.

—proviso.

Rights, powers and privileges.

Section 5. To carry out the purposes aforesaid said town of York is hereby granted all the rights, powers and privileges which towns, and their municipal officers, have under the first sixteen sections of chapter sixteen of the revised statutes, as amended, and under chapter two hundred and eighty-five of the public laws of eighteen hundred eighty-nine, relating to drains and sewers.

Section 6. This act shall take effect when approved.

Approved March 28, 1903.

Chapter 360.

An Act regulating fishing in the streams in Salem and Strong in Franklin County.

Be it enacted by the Senate and House of Representatives in Legislature assembled, as follows:

It shall be unlawful for any person to take, catch, kill, or have in possession in any one day more than twenty-five fish in all taken in any of the streams lying wholly or partly in the towns of Freeman, Salem and Strong in the county of Franklin, and it shall be unlawful for any person to fish for, take, catch or kill any fish in any of these streams except on Tuesdays, Thursdays and Saturdays of each week during open season, under a penalty of not less than ten dollars nor more than thirty dollars and costs for each offense, and one dollar for each fish caught, taken or killed in violation of the provisions of this act.

Fishing regulated in Freeman, Salem and Strong.

—penalties.

Approved March 28, 1903.

Chapter 361.

An Act regulating the taking of black bass in waters lying wholly or partly in the County of Hancock.

Be it enacted by the Senate and House of Representatives in Legislature assembled, as follows:

It shall be unlawful for any person to take, catch, kill or have in possession in any one day more than twenty-five pounds of black bass, in any of the waters lying wholly or partly in the towns of Eden, Mount Desert, Tremont, Hancock, Sullivan, Franklin, Eastbrook, Waltham, townships number seven, number ten, and number twenty-one in the county of Hancock.

Fishing for black bass in Hancock county, to regulate.

Approved March 28, 1903.

Chapter 362.

An Act to permit the use of Purse Seines in Damariscotta River.

Be it enacted by the Senate and House of Representatives in Legislature assembled, as follows:

Section 1. The use of purse seines in Damariscotta river, for the purpose of catching all fish except smelts and alewives, from the mouth of said river to a point known as the "Ledges," is hereby permitted and made legal from the first day of July to the first day of November, inclusive, in each year.

Section 2. This act shall take effect when approved.

Use of purse seines restricted.

Approved March 28, 1903.

Chapter 363.

An Act relating to the open season for fishing in Wilson Lake in the town of Wilton.

Be it enacted by the Senate and House of Representatives in Legislature assembled, as follows:

Section 1. The open season for fishing in Wilson lake in the town of Wilton, shall begin as soon as the lake is free from ice, instead of May first in each year, as is now provided by law.

Section 2. All acts and parts of acts inconsistent herewith are hereby repealed.

Section 3. This act shall take effect when approved.

Approved March 28, 1903.

Chapter 364.

An Act to set off part of Reed Plantation, and annex the same to Drew Plantation.

Be it enacted by the Senate and House of Representatives in Legislature assembled, as follows:

Section 1. All that part of Reed Plantation in the county of Aroostook, which was set off from Drew Plantation, in the county of Penobscot, and annexed to said Reed Plantation by and under the provisions of chapter five hundred and fourteen of the private and special laws of eighteen hundred and eighty-nine, is hereby set off from said Reed Plantation and annexed to said Drew Plantation, and said chapter five hundred and fourteen is hereby repealed. And for the purpose of reimbursing the said county of Aroostook for the cost and expense incurred by said county of Aroostook in the construction of the bridge heretofore built by the said counties of Aroostook and Penobscot, across the Mattawamkeag river, which said bridge connects that part of said Reed hereby set off and annexed to said Drew, with said Drew, the said county of Penobscot shall pay and is hereby authorized, directed, instructed and empowered to pay to said county of Aroostook, the sum of one thousand dollars. Said sum shall be paid on or before the first day of July, nineteen hundred and three. If said sum is not paid as aforesaid, the inhabitants of said county of Aroostook may maintain an action at law therefor against the inhabitants of said county of Penobscot, and shall have judgment for said sum or so much of said sum as remains unpaid on the said first day of July. All county taxes assessed for the years nineteen hundred and three and four on said part of said Reed hereby set off annexed to said Drew as aforesaid, shall belong to said county of Penobscot, and if collected by said county of Aroostook, shall be paid to said county of Penobscot, and the inhabitants of said county of Penobscot may maintain an action therefor against the inhabitants of said county of Aroostook, if said county of Aroostook collects said taxes and refuses to pay the same to said county of Penobscot. The state board of assessors is hereby given full power and authority to adjust, settle and determine any and all questions which may arise concerning state taxes assessed for the years nineteen hundred and three and four, on said part of said Reed Plantation hereby set off and annexed to said Drew Plantation.

And said state board of assessors is also hereby given full power and authority to adjust, settle and determine any and all questions which may arise concerning any public lot or public lots on said part of said Reed Plantation hereby set off and annexed to said Drew Plantation or the disposition of the income received from any such lot or lots.

Section 2. This act shall take effect when approved.

Approved March 28, 1903.

Chapter 365.

An Act authorizing the Town of Caribou to hold stock to the extent of four thousand dollars in a company forming for the purpose of erecting a public building, or town hall.

Be it enacted by the Senate and House of Representatives in Legislature assembled, as follows:

Section 1. The citizens of the town of Caribou are hereby authorized to take and pay for and hold stock to the extent of four thousand dollars in a corporation forming for the purpose of erecting and maintaining a public building or town hall.

Section 2. The vote of the citizens of the town of Caribou, whereby they voted to take, pay for and hold stock to the extent of four thousand dollars, in a corporation forming for the purpose of erecting and maintaining a public building or town hall, is hereby ratified and approved.

Section 3. This act shall take effect when approved.

Approved March 28, 1903.

Chapter 366.

An Act relating to Fire Wardens in the Town of Bucksport.

Be it enacted by the Senate and House of Representatives in Legislature assembled, as follows:

Duties of fire wards.

Section 1. That the fire wards in the town of Bucksport be on duty day and night and that they have charge of the property of the town used by the fire department, that they audit all bills and keep a correct account of the expenditures and report to the selectmen annually.

Section 2. This act shall take effect when approved.

Approved March 28, 1903.

Chapter 367.

An Act to amend Chapter four hundred and ninety-five of the Private and Special Laws of eighteen hundred ninety-three, relating to the destruction of fish in the Eastern Penobscot River in the town of Orland.

Be it enacted by the Senate and House of Representatives in Legislature assembled, as follows:

24 hours close time on alewives in Eastern Penobscot river.

Section 1. From and after the passage of this act no person unless authorized by the commissioner of sea and shore fisheries shall be allowed to take any alewives in the Eastern Penobscot river in the town of Orland, in the county of Hancock, with any large net, seine, spear, scoop-net, or in any weirs between sunrise on Sunday of each week and sunrise on Monday of each week, under a penalty of twenty cents for each and every alewive so taken.

Further regulations.

Section 2. No person shall be allowed to take any alewive in said river within said town at any time above a point five hundred yards below the lower dam, under a penalty of fifty cents for each and every alewive so taken.

Taking of alewives on certain days regulated.

Section 3. Any of the alewives in said river above a point five hundred yards below the lower dam may be taken by the town of Orland on Mondays, Tuesdays and Wednesdays of each week from the first day of May to the fifteenth day of July, if the town so votes at its annual meeting, and fish may be taken by the town during the season of nineteen hundred three.

Committee to be chosen by selectmen.

—by town.

Section 4. The selectmen shall appoint a committee of not more than three persons to superintend the taking and disposal of said fish for the year nineteen hundred three. After nineteen hundred three the committee may be chosen or appointed as the town may vote.

Section 5. No person shall be allowed to build or place in or across said river below the extreme low water mark or in or across said river above a point five hundred yards below the lower dam, any boxes or traps, weirs or nets so as to prevent said fish from passing up or down said river, under a penalty of twenty-five dollars. *Placing of seines, traps, weirs, etc., regulated.*

Section 6. All nets, seines, craft, boats, barrels, tubs and salt used in taking or securing fish in violation of the provisions of this act, and all horses, wagons, carts and harnesses, used in moving fish taken from the lock at the lower falls or the fishway at the upper falls, and all fish so taken shall be forfeited, and when so used may be seized by the fish commissioner or his deputies or wardens and proceeded against as in the case of forfeiture of personal property. *Forfeitures for illegal fishing.*

Section 7. The Eastern River and Sluice Company shall be required from the first day of May to the fifteenth day of July in each year to keep open, at their own expense, the large gates at the lower end and the small gates at the upper end of said lock so as to afford sufficient water for the fish to pass in at all times when tide waters are in said lock at the lower falls, except when boats, timber, rafts, spars or other lumber may be passing through said gates, and to cause some suitable person to attend the gates at the lock in order to lock in the fish and enable those which have come into or passed through the lock to go up to the fishway at the upper dam, and in case of neglect or refusal to keep open and attend said gates as aforesaid said company shall forfeit and pay the sum of ten dollars for each and every day they shall so neglect or refuse to keep open and attend said gates. *Gates of lock to be kept open for passage of fish.*

—*exception.*

Section 8. The Eastern River and Sluice Company shall be required from the first day of May to the fifteenth day of July in each year, at their own expense, to keep the fishway at the upper dam on said river in repair and running order so as to enable the fish at all times to pass through into Great pond, so called, and in case of neglect or refusal to keep in repair and running order said fishway, the aforesaid company shall forfeit and pay the sum of ten dollars for each and every day they shall neglect or refuse to keep in repair and running order said fishway. *Fishway shall be kept in repair.*

Section 9. No person shall catch or kill any young alewives on their way down through said fishways, locks or river under a penalty of ten dollars for each and every offense. *Alewives protected in passing down river.*

Section 10. All weirs on said river now built or that shall be built shall be constructed with a suitable gate which shall be at least eighteen inches wide and shall extend from the top of *Construction of weirs, manner of prescribed.*

CHAP. 367

—gate of weir shall be open from sunrise, Sunday, till sunrise, Monday.

the pond to the bottom of the floor, which gate the owner or occupant of said weir shall keep open from sunrise on Sunday of each week until sunrise on Monday of each week, under a penalty of ten dollars to be forfeited by said owner or occupant for each and every day they shall refuse or neglect so to keep open said gate. All material used in building weirs shall be removed from said river on or before the first day of October, and if any owner or occupant of a weir shall refuse or neglect to remove said material he shall forfeit and pay the sum of twenty dollars, to be recovered by the commissioner of sea and shore fisheries or his deputies or wardens.

—weirs shall be renewed Oct. 1.

Weirs forbidden from 1903 to 1906, both inclusive.

Section 11. No weirs shall be built on said Eastern Penobscot river in the town of Orland, during the years nineteen hundred and three, nineteen hundred and four, nineteen hundred and five and nineteen hundred and six.

Throwing of waste material into river, prohibited.

Section 12. No mill waste, slabs, edgings, bark, chips, shavings, sawdust or other waste shall be thrown or put into the Eastern Penobscot river or any of its tributaries in the town of Orland, except under such rules and regulations as the commissioner of sea and shore fisheries may prescribe. Whoever violates any of the provisions of this section shall be punished by a fine of not less than five dollars nor more than one hundred dollars.

Fines and penalties, to whom paid.

Section 13. All fines and penalties recovered under this act shall be paid to the state treasurer to be added to and made a part of the appropriation for sea and shore fisheries.

Section 14. This act shall be enforced by the state commissioner of sea and shore fisheries.

Section 15. All acts and parts of acts inconsistent with the provisions of this act are hereby repealed.

Section 16. No legislation hereafter enacted shall be held to affect this act unless it specifically refers thereto.

Section 17. This act shall take effect when approved.

Approved March 28, 1903.

Chapter 368.

An Act to grant additional powers to the Auburn, Mechanic Falls and Norway Street Railway.

Be it enacted by the Senate and House of Representatives in Legislature assembled, as follows:

Section 1. The Auburn, Mechanic Falls and Norway Street Railway is hereby authorized to sell or lease its property and franchises to any street railroad whose location as approved by the railroad commissioners would form connecting or continuous locations with the approved location of said Auburn, Mechanic Falls and Norway Street Railway, and in such case the corporation so purchasing or leasing such property and franchises shall be entitled to all the privileges belonging to said Auburn, Mechanic Falls and Norway Street Railway and shall be subject to all appropriate conditions and limitations contained in its charter and franchises. *Authorized sell or lease to connecting lines.*

—privileges of purchaser or lessor.

Any street railroad company whose location as approved would form continuous or connecting locations with the location of said Auburn, Mechanic Falls and Norway Street Railway, as said railroad is approved by the railroad commissioners, is hereby authorized to so purchase or lease the property and franchises of the said Auburn, Mechanic Falls and Norway Street Railway. *—connecting line authorized to purchase or lease.*

Section 2. The Auburn, Mechanic Falls and Norway Street Railway is further authorized to consolidate with or acquire by lease, purchase or otherwise, lines, property and franchises of any street railroad or street railroads whose locations as approved by the railroad commissioners, would form connecting or continuous locations with the location of said Auburn, Mechanic Falls and Norway Street Railway, as said location is approved by the railroad commissioners; and in such case the Auburn, Mechanic Falls and Norway Street Railway shall be entitled to all the privileges of said street railroad or street railroads, and be subject to all appropriate conditions and limitations contained in the charters and franchises thus united with or acquired. Any street railroad company, whose location as approved by the railroad commissioners would form connecting or continuous locations with the location of the Auburn, Mechanic Falls and Norway Street Railway, as approved by the railroad commissioners, is hereby authorized to consolidate with or to lease, or to sell its lines, property and franchises, as in this section authorized. *May consolidate with connecting lines.*

Section 3. All proceedings, suits at law or in equity which may be pending at the time of any transfer authorized by this act to which any corporation so transferring its property and franchises may be a party may be prosecuted or defended by *Pending proceedings, how prosecuted or defended.*

CHAP. 369

Liabilities of acquiring corporation.

Acquiring corporation may issue stock and bonds.

the corporation so acquiring the same in like manner and with like effect as if such transfer had not been made. All claims, contracts, rights and causes of action of or against any corporation so selling or leasing, at law or in equity, may be enforced by suit or action to be begun or prosecuted by or against the corporation so acquiring property and franchises as aforesaid.

Section 4. When any transfer authorized by this act is carried out and fully completed the corporation acquiring any franchise hereunder shall be liable for the then legally existing debts and obligation of the corporation so making such transfer.

Section 5. Any corporation acquiring property and franchises by virtue of this act may issue its stock to an amount sufficient therefor, and also its bonds secured by appropriate mortgages upon its franchise and property in such amounts as may be required for the purposes of this act, and thereafterwards may issue its stock and bonds in payment and exchange for the stock, bonds, franchises and property of the corporation making any transfer authorized by this act, in such manner and in such amounts as may be agreed upon.

Section 6. This act shall take effect when approved.

Approved March 28, 1903.

Chapter 369.

An Act to grant certain powers to the Hancock County Trustees of public reservations.

Be it enacted by the Senate and House of Representatives in Legislature assembled, as follows:

Incorporation made valid.

Section 1. The incorporation of the Hancock County Trustees of public reservations, a corporation organized at Bar Harbor, Maine, under the revised statutes of Maine, chapter fifty-five, is hereby ratified and confirmed.

May acquire lands for free public uses.

Section 2. Said corporation shall have power to acquire, by devise, gift or purchase, and to own, arrange, hold, maintain and improve, for free public use, lands in Hancock county, Maine, which by reason of scenic beauty, historical interest, sanitary advantages, or for other reasons, may be available for the purpose.

Lands shall be exempt from taxation.

Section 3. Lands and improvements thereon, held by said corporation, for free public use, shall be exempt from state, county or town taxation.

Section 4. This act shall take effect when approved.

Approved March 28, 1903.

Chapter 370.

An Act to amend an act relating to the Municipal Court for the city of Lewiston.

Be it enacted by the Senate and House of Representatives in Legislature assembled, as follows:

Section 1. Chapter six hundred and twenty-six of the private and special laws of the year eighteen hundred and seventy-four amending chapter six hundred and thirty-six of the private and special laws of the year eighteen hundred and seventy-one, establishing a municipal court for the city of Lewiston, is hereby amended by striking out the word "forty" in the eleventh line of section twelve of said chapter six hundred twenty-six, and substituting therefor the words 'seventy-five;' so that said section twelve of said chapter six hundred and twenty-six as amended shall read as follows:

'Section 12. The governor, by and with the advice of the council, shall appoint a clerk of said court, who shall be a citizen of said Lewiston, and who shall hold his office for the term of four years, who shall be sworn, and who shall give bond to the treasurer of said city in the sum of two thousand dollars, to be approved by said judge; and who shall be entitled to demand and receive for his services the same fees allowed by law to trial justices in matters relating to civil business, except the trial fee; provided, that for the entry of an action and recording the same he shall be allowed sixty cents; for taxing costs, recording judgment in each criminal case, one dollar and ten cents; for each recognizance of persons charged with crime for their appearance at the supreme judicial court, and for certifying and returning the same, with or without sureties, twenty-five cents; for making and recording each libel for liquors seized, fifty cents; for making each process of commitment, twenty-five cents; said fees to be allowed and paid in the same manner as fees in criminal matters on approval of the judge of said court. In case of the absence of said clerk, or vacancy in said office, the judge of said court may appoint a clerk, who shall be sworn by said judge, and act during said absence, or till the vacancy is filled.'

Section 2. This act shall take effect when approved.

Approved March 28, 1903.

Chapter 371.

An Act to extend the powers of the Union River Light, Gas and Power Company.

Be it enacted by the Senate and House of Representatives in Legislature assembled, as follows:

May purchase property of Ellsworth Water Co.

Section 1. The Union River Light, Gas and Power Company is hereby authorized to purchase, hold, own and enjoy the franchises, property, shares of stock, rights, easements, privileges and immunities of the Ellsworth Water Company, and the said Ellsworth Water Company is hereby authorized to sell, transfer and convey its franchises, property, shares of stock, rights, easements, privileges and immunities to the said Union River Light, Gas and Power Company upon such terms as said companies may determine between themselves, and upon such purchase and sale and transfer, the said Union River Light, Gas and Power Company shall succeed to and have, hold and enjoy all the rights, franchises, easements, privileges and immunities heretofore and hereafter acquired by or granted to said Ellsworth Water Company and have all the powers and privileges and be subject to all the duties, restrictions and liabilities by law incident to such corporations.

—shall succeed to rights and restrictions of.

May purchase property of Bar Harbor Electric Light Co.

Section 2. The Union River Light, Gas and Power Company is hereby authorized to purchase, hold, own and enjoy the franchises, property, shares of stock, rights, easements, privileges and immunities of the Bar Harbor Electric Light Company and the said Bar Harbor Electric Light Company is hereby authorized to sell, transfer and convey its franchises, property, shares of stock, rights, easements, privileges and immunities to the said Union River Light, Gas and Power Company upon such terms as these said companies may determine between themselves, and upon such purchase and sale and transfer, the said Union River Light, Gas and Power Company shall succeed to and have, hold and enjoy all the rights, franchises, easements, privileges and immunities heretofore and hereafter acquired by or granted to said Bar Harbor Electric Light Company, and have all the powers and privileges and be subject to all the duties, restrictions and liabilities by law incident to such corporations.

—shall succeed to rights and restrictions of.

May supply gas and electricity in Hancock county.

Section 3. In addition to its other purposes as set forth in its certificate of organization, approved by the attorney general of the state of Maine, October sixth, in the year of our Lord nineteen hundred and two, said Union River Light, Gas and Power Company is hereby authorized and empowered to make, generate, sell, lease, conduct, distribute and supply gas or any by-products thereof, electricity, or electrically transmitted energy or power, for any or all purposes, anywhere within the limits of any or all towns, townships, plantations and cities, in the county of Hancock, said state of Maine, provided, however, that none of the rights or privileges granted said Union River Light, Gas and Power Company under this section shall be exercised within the limits of the city of Ellsworth, Hancock county, Maine, unless and until said Union River Light, Gas and Power Company shall first purchase a majority of the outstanding capital stock of said Ellsworth Water Company and such of the minority stock as is hereinafter provided and provided also that none of the rights and privileges granted said Union River Light, Gas and Power Company under this section shall be exercised within the limits of the towns of Eden, Mount Desert or Tremont, unless and until, said Union River Light, Gas and Power Company shall purchase a majority of the outstanding capital stock of said Bar Harbor Electric Light Company and such of the minority stock as is hereinafter provided and provided also that no electricity or electrically transmitted energy or power shall be so sold, leased, distributed or supplied by said Union River Light, Gas and Power Company within the limits of the town of Castine, in said Hancock county, for electric lighting purposes, unless and until said Union River Light, Gas and Power Company shall purchase a majority of the outstanding capital stock of said Castine Water Company and such of the minority stock as is hereinafter provided. Any stockholder in the Ellsworth Water Company, the Bar Harbor Electric Light Company or the Castine Water Company may within thirty days after the approval of this act file a written notice with the clerk of the corporation of which he is a member expressing his willingness to sell his stock in such corporation to the Union River Light, Gas and Power Company at a price to be agreed upon or if not agreed upon to be fixed by any justice of the supreme judicial court after petition therefor by said Union River Light, Gas and Power Company and notice and hearing and the said Union River Light, Gas and Power Company shall purchase such stock from such stockholder, or the subsequent holder thereof, in each case before the exercise of the rights in this section granted in the town or towns where such corporation is authorized to do business under its franchises as respectively stated in the provisos of this section.

In exercising the rights or privileges granted under this section, the said Union River Light, Gas and Power Company shall have all the powers and privileges, and be subject to all the duties, restrictions and liabilities by law incident to such corporations.

560   NAVIGATION OF RANGE PONDS.

CHAP. 372

May furnish gas and electricity in certain towns in Penobscot county.

Section 4. In addition to its other purposes as set forth in its certificate of organization and the rights herein above granted said Union River Light, Gas and Power Company is hereby authorized to make, generate, sell, lease, conduct, distribute and supply gas or any by-products thereof, electricity or electrically transmitted energy or power anywhere within the limits of the towns of Orrington, Eddington, Holden, Clifton and the city of Brewer, in Penobscot county, state of Maine, so far as reasonably necessary and convenient to enable said Union River Light, Gas and Power Company to supply same to the Eastern Manufacturing Company, its successors and assigns, owners or tenants of the real estate and plant or any part thereof situated in said city of Brewer and now occupied by said Eastern Manufacturing Company.

—duties, restrictions and liabilities.

In exercising the rights or privileges granted under this section, the said Union River Light, Gas and Power Company shall have all the powers and privileges, and be subject to all the duties, restrictions and liabilities by law incident to such corporations.

Section 5. This act shall take effect when approved.

Approved March 28, 1903.

Chapter 373.

An Act to authorize the navigation by steam or electricity, of Range Ponds in the Town of Poland.

Be it enacted by the Senate and House of Representatives in Legislature assembled, as follows:

Corporators.

Section 1. Edward P. Ricker, Alvin B. Ricker and Hiram W. Ricker, their associates and assigns, are hereby authorized to clear, deepen and widen the channels or canals connecting the upper and the middle of the Range ponds in Poland, county of Androscoggin, at their own expense, but shall in no way interfere with the dam at the outlet of the middle of said Range ponds, or do any act to change the water levels of said ponds. And said incorporators, their associates and assigns, for the passage thereunder of boats suitable for the navigation of said ponds, may raise to a reasonable height, the highway bridge over the stream between the upper and middle of said ponds, at their own expense but so as not to hinder public travel over said bridge.

—powers.

Corporation may have exclusive right of navigation.

Section 2. After such improvements shall have been made, at an expense of not less than fifteen hundred dollars, the said incorporators, their associates and assigns, shall have the exclusive right of navigation on said ponds, the channels and streams connecting the same, by boats or other water craft propelled by steam, naphtha or electricity, for the carriage of passengers for hire, for the period of ten years from approval of this act, except that any other person or company owning boats or water craft, propelled by steam, naphtha or electricity, shall have the right to use the same on said ponds, the channels and streams connecting the same, for the carriage of passengers for hire, upon the payment of their proportional part of said improvements so made, to these incorporators, their associates or assigns, taking into account the number of boats used which are propelled by steam, naphtha or electricity. And after said payment, such person or company shall have the same right of navigation in said ponds, their connecting streams and channels, as the foregoing incorporators, their associates and assigns, have under this act.

Section 3. If the sum of one thousand dollars shall not be expended within two years from the date of the approval of this act in making said improvements upon said ponds, then this act shall become void.

Section 4. This act shall take effect when approved.

Approved March 28, 1903.

Chapter 373.

An Act to supply the people of Bangor with pure drinking water.

Be it enacted by the Senate and House of Representatives in Legislature assembled, as follows:

Section 1. F. W. Ayer, I. K. Stetson, J. P. Bass, P. H. Gillin, J. F. Whitcomb, C. H. Haynes and J. O. Whitney, with their associates and successors are hereby made a corporation by the name of the Bangor Water Power Company, for the purpose of conveying to the city of Bangor a supply of pure water for drinking purposes.

Section 2. Said corporation may hold real and personal estate necessary and convenient for the purpose aforesaid, not exceeding in amount six hundred thousand dollars.

Section 3. Said corporation is hereby authorized, for the purpose aforesaid, to take and hold the water of Hat Case pond, so called, in the town of Dedham, and streams tributary thereto in said town, and the water of Fitts pond, so called, in the town of Clifton, and the streams tributary thereto in said town of Clifton, and may also hold by purchase or otherwise any land or real estate necessary for erecting dams and reservoirs and for laying and maintaining aqueducts for conducting, discharging, distributing and disposing of water, and for forming reservoirs thereof.

Damages, liability for.

Section 4. Said corporation shall be liable to pay all damages that shall be sustained by any persons in their property, by the taking of any land or mill privilege, or by flowing or excavating through any land for the purpose of laying down pipes, building dams, or constructing reservoirs; and if any person sustaining damage as aforesaid and said corporation shall not mutually agree upon the sum to be paid therefor, such damage shall be assessed in the same manner and under the same conditions, restrictions and limitations, as are by law prescribed in the case of damages for land taken by railroads.

—damages, how assessed.

Capital stock.

Section 5. The capital stock of said company shall not exceed six hundred thousand dollars, and shall be divided into shares of one hundred dollars each. Said capital stock shall be applied exclusively to the supply and distribution of water for the purposes set forth in this act.

Shall operate works within six years.

Section 6. If said corporation shall not be organized, and its works put into actual operation within six years from the approval of this act, it shall be null and void.

Liability for injury to private property.

Section 7. Nothing contained in this act shall be construed to affect or diminish the liability of said corporation, for any injury to private property, by depreciating the value thereof or otherwise, but said corporation shall be liable therefor in an action on the case.

May lay pipes, etc.

Section 8. The said company are hereby authorized to lay down in and through the streets of said city, and to take up, replace and repair, all such pipes, aqueducts and fixtures as may be necessary for the objects of their incorporation, first having obtained the consent of the city council therefor, and under such restrictions and regulations as said city council and water board may see fit to prescribe; and any obstruction in any street of said city, or taking up or displacement of any portion of any street, without such consent of the city council, or contrary to the rules and regulations that may be prescribed as aforesaid, shall be considered a nuisance, and said company shall be liable to indictment therefor, and to all the provisions of the law applicable thereto, and said company shall in all cases be liable to repay said city all sums of money that said city may be obliged to pay on any judgment recovered against said city for damages occasioned by any obstructions or taking up or displacement of any street by said company whatever, with or without the consent of the city council, together with counsel fees and other expenses incurred by said city in defending any suit to recover damages aforesaid, with interest on the same, to be recovered in an action for money paid to the use of said company.

—restrictions and regulations.

Section 9. Whenever the company shall lay down any pipes or aqueducts in any street, or make any alteration or repairs upon their works in any street, they shall cause the same to be done with as little obstruction to the public travel as may be practicable, and shall at their own expense, without unnecessary delay, cause all earth and pavement removed by them to be replaced in proper condition. They shall not in any case be allowed to obstruct or impair the use of any public or private drain, or common sewer or reservoir, but said company shall have the right to cross, or when necessary, to change the direction of any private drain in such a manner as not to obstruct or impair the use thereof, being liable for any injury occasioned by any such crossing or alteration to the owner thereof or any other person, in an action upon the case.

Shall not unnecessarily obstruct public travel.

—may cross, but shall not obstruct sewers.

Section 10. If in the erection and construction of the works herein provided for, it shall become necessary to erect any dam, or permanent works over tide waters, the said company is hereby authorized to erect, construct and maintain the same, first having the approval of the city council of said city.

May erect permanent works over tide waters

Section 11. The mayor and aldermen, for the time being, shall at all times have the power to regulate, restrict, and control the acts and doings of said corporation which may in any manner affect the health, safety or convenience of the inhabitants of said city.

Mayor and aldermen shall have control of acts and doings of.

Section 12. The first meeting of said corporation may be called by a notice signed by two of the corporators, published five days successively before the day fixed for such meeting in any newspaper published in Bangor.

First meeting how called.

Section 13. The city of Bangor shall have the right at any time within one year from the date of approval of this act, to take, exercise and control all the property, rights, powers and privileges of said corporation, on paying to said corporation the amount of money actually paid in and expended under the provisions of this act; and in case said city and said corporation shall not agree upon the sum to be paid therefor, the supreme judicial court, at any term thereof holden in the county of Penobscot, upon application of said city, shall appoint three commissioners, whose duty it shall be to hear the parties and determine what amount has been expended under the provisions of this act, the report of whom, or the major part of them, when made and accepted by the court, shall be final; and upon payment of that sum, the franchise of said corporation, with all the property, rights, powers and privileges, shall vest in and belong to said city of Bangor.

City of Bangor may take works.

Section 14. This act shall be taken and deemed to be a public act, and shall be in force from and after its approval.

Approved March 28, 1903.

Chapter 374.

An Act to authorize Jacob C. Pike to extend and maintain a wharf in Lubec Narrows.

Be it enacted by the Senate and House of Representatives in Legislature assembled, as follows:

Jacob C. Pike authorized to erect wharf.

Jacob C. Pike, his associates and assigns, are hereby authorized to erect and maintain a wharf from the shore front of his land to the United States harbor line in Cobscook bay, town of Lubec.

Approved March 28, 1903.

Chapter 375.

An Act to authorize Clarence H. Clark to extend and maintain a wharf in Lubec Narrows.

Be it enacted by the Senate and House of Representatives in Legislature assembled, as follows:

Clarence H. Clark authorized to erect wharf.

Clarence H. Clark, his associates and assigns, are hereby authorized to erect and maintain a wharf from the shore front of his land to the United States harbor line in Cobscook bay, town of Lubec.

Approved March 28, 1903.

Chapter 376.

An Act to authorize the Portage Lake Mill Company to build and maintain piers and booms, and to operate a steamboat in Portage Lake.

Be it enacted by the Senate and House of Representatives in Legislature assembled, as follows:

Portage Lake Mill Co. authorized to build piers, etc.

The Portage Lake Mill Company is hereby authorized and empowered to build, maintain and control piers, booms and hitching posts in the southerly end of Portage lake in the county of Aroostook, opposite land owned by said company, and the adjoining lands, to enable said company to hold and retain logs and lumber to be manufactured at the mill of said company, in Portage Lake plantation, in said county of Aroostook, but said piers and booms shall be so constructed as not to interfere with or obstruct the landing or channel leading to said landing on the state road, so called; and said company is hereby also authorized and empowered to own and operate a boat, propelled by steam or other power, to tow logs across said lake and for other purposes, in said Portage lake.

—may operate boat for towage, etc.

Approved March 28, 1903.

Chapter 377.

An Act to Incorporate the Peaks Island Water and Light Company.

Be it enacted by the Senate and House of Representatives in Legislature assembled, as follows:

Section 1. Edgar E. Rounds, Walter S. Crandall, and Emma Rounds, their associates, successors and assigns, are hereby constituted a body corporate and politic by the name of the Peaks Island Water and Light Company for the purpose of supplying Peaks Island in the city of Portland with pure water.

Corporators.
—corporate name.

Section 2. Said corporation for said purpose is hereby authorized to hold real and personal estate, necessary and convenient therefor, to the amount of fifty thousand dollars.

May hold real and personal estate.

Section 3. Said corporation is hereby authorized to erect and maintain reservoirs, and lay down and maintain all pipes and aqueducts necessary for the proper accumulation, conduct, discharge, distribution and disposition of water and forming proper reservoirs thereof; and said corporation may take and hold, by purchase or otherwise, any lands or real estate necessary therefor, and may make excavations through any lands whatever when necessary for the purpose of this corporation.

May erect reservoirs, and lay pipes.

—may excavate through lands.

Section 4. Said corporation shall be held liable to pay all damages that may be occasioned to any person by the taking of any land or other property, or by the flowage, or by excavation through any land for the purpose of laying down pipes and aqueducts, building reservoirs, and also damages for any other injuries resulting from said acts; and if any person sustaining damage as aforesaid and said corporation cannot agree upon the sum to be paid therefor, such person may cause his damages to be ascertained in the same manner and under the same limitations, conditions and restrictions as are by law prescribed in the case of damages by the laying out of railroads.

Liability for damages.

Section 5. The capital stock of said corporation shall be twenty thousand dollars, which may be increased to fifty thousand dollars by a vote of said corporation, and be divided

Capital stock.

PEAKS ISLAND WATER AND LIGHT COMPANY.

CHAP. 377

—may issue bonds.

into shares of one hundred dollars each, and said corporation may issue bonds to raise money for the construction of said works and their extension and repair, to an amount not exceeding twenty-five thousand dollars, to be secured by mortgage upon its real estate, works and franchise.

May lay pipes, aqueducts and other fixtures.

Section 6. Said corporation is hereby authorized to lay down, in and through the streets and ways of said Peaks Island, and take up, replace and repair all pipes, aqueducts and fixtures as may be necessary for the purposes of their incorporation, under such reasonable restrictions as may be imposed by the municipal officers of said city. Said corporation shall be responsible for all damages to persons and property occasioned by the use of such streets and ways and shall also be liable to said city for damages from obstructions caused by said corporation and for all expenses.

—liability for damages by use of streets.

May contract to supply water.

Section 7. Said corporation is hereby authorized to make contracts with the city of Portland, and with any or all corporations or individuals for the purposes of supplying said corporations with water for fire and other municipal purposes, or any other corporation or individuals with water for any other purposes whatsoever.

Shall not unnecessarily obstruct public travel.

Section 8. Said corporation in making any changes, additions or improvements upon its works in any streets of said Peaks Island shall cause the same to be done with as little obstruction to public travel as may be practicable, and shall at its own expense, without unnecessary delay, cause the earth and pavements removed by it to be replaced in proper condition.

Injury to property of corporation, or pollution of water.

Section 9. Any person who shall wilfully injure any of the property of said corporation or who shall knowingly corrupt the wells out of which said water company's water is obtained, in any manner whatever, or render them impure whether the same be frozen or not, or who shall wilfully destroy any reservoir or aqueduct, pipes, hydrant or other property held or owned by said corporation for the purposes of this act, shall be punished by a fine not exceeding one thousand dollars, or by imprisonment less than one year, and shall be liable to said corporation for three times the actual damage, to be recovered in any proper action.

—punishment for.

First meeting, how called.

Section 10. The first meeting of said corporation may be called by a written notice thereof, signed by one corporator herein named, served upon each corporator by giving him the same in hand, or by leaving the same at his last and usual place of abode, seven days before the time of meeting.

Section 11. This act shall take effect when approved.

Approved March 28, 1903.

Chapter 378.

An Act to authorize Bion M. Pike to maintain and extend a wharf into the tide waters of Johnson's Bay, in the town of Lubec, County of Washington.

Be it enacted by the Senate and House of Representatives in Legislature assembled, as follows:

Section 1. Bion M. Pike and his assigns are hereby authorized to maintain a wharf in the town of Lubec, known as the Ferry wharf and to extend same for a distance of fifty feet into the tide waters of Johnson's bay in the town of Lubec, county of Washington.

Section 2. This act shall take effect when approved.

Bion M. Pike authorized to maintain wharf.

Approved March 28, 1903.

Chapter 379.

An Act to authorize Bion M. Pike to maintain and extend a wharf to the harbor line into the tide waters of Lubec Narrows in the town of Lubec, County of Washington.

Be it enacted by the Senate and House of Representatives in Legislature assembled, as follows:

Section 1. Bion M. Pike and his assigns are hereby authorized to maintain and extend a wharf from his shore front into the tide waters of Lubec narrows to the harbor line in the town of Lubec, county of Washington.

Section 2. This act shall take effect when approved.

Bion M. Pike authorized to maintain wharf.

Approved March 28, 1903.

Chapter 380.

An Act to amend Chapter four hundred and twenty-two of the Private and Special Laws of nineteen hundred and one, relating to the East Pittston Village Corporation.

Be it enacted by the Senate and House of Representatives in Legislature assembled, as follows:

Section 1. Section eleven of chapter four hundred and twenty-two of the private and special laws of nineteen hundred and one is hereby amended by striking out all of said section after the word "bridges" in the seventh line thereof and adding thereto the following: "The provisions of chapter two hundred and eighty-five of the public laws of nineteen hundred and one, and of acts

Section 11, chapter 422, private and special laws of 1901, amended.

CHAP. 380

Assessors to control maintenance of highways.

amendatory thereof and additional thereto, shall apply to said corporation; and said corporation and the assessors thereof shall have all the rights and privileges, duties and obligations, which towns and the municipal officers thereof now have or may hereafter have under said act,' so that said section shall read as follows:

'Section 11. The assessors of said corporation are hereby given the exclusive supervision and control of maintaining and repairing the highways and bridges within the limits of said corporation; and for that purpose the same rights and powers are conferred upon said assessors as are now, or may hereafter be, conferred by law upon road commissioners and selectmen of towns in relation to maintaining and repairing ways and bridges. The provisions of chapter two hundred eighty-five of the public laws of nineteen hundred one and of acts amendatory thereof and additional thereto shall apply to said corporation; and said corporation and the assessors thereof shall have all the rights and privileges, duties and obligations, which towns and the municipal officers thereof now have or may hereafter have under said act.'

Section 12, chapter 422, private laws of 1901, amended.

Section 2. Section twelve of said chapter is hereby amended by inserting after the word "corporation" in the eleventh line, the following: 'also the town treasurer of said town shall pay to the treasurer of said corporation on the first day of February of each year, its proportional part, according to the foregoing valuation, of all sums of money expended on highways and bridges in said town by the municipal officers of said town from money not voted at any town meeting of said town but used from other appropriations or drawn from the treasury,' so that said section shall read as follows:

Division of highway assessment.

'Section 12. The town treasurer of the town of Pittston shall pay to the treasurer of said corporation one-half of such proportion of all moneys voted for highways and bridges and for the payment of unpaid highway bills, at any and all town meetings of said town including that of nineteen hundred one, by the first day of September, and the remaining one-half of such proportion by the first day of the following January of each year, as the valuation of the property and estates within said corporation, as fixed by the assessors of said town for the purposes of taxation, bears to the valuation of the property and estates within said town of Pittston, including said corporation; also the town treasurer of said town shall pay to the treasurer of said corporation on the first day of February of each year, its proportional part, according to the foregoing valuation, of all sums of money expended on highways and bridges and for all other highway purposes in said town by the municipal officers of said town from money not voted at any town meeting of said town but used from other appropriations or drawn from the treasury; and said money shall be expended upon the highways and bridges within the limits of said corporation by and under the supervision of said corporation assessors. Said corporation may raise money for the maintaining and repairing ways and bridges within the limits of said corporation, in addition to the foregoing, and direct the same to be assessed as other taxes are assessed in said corporation, and the same shall be expended by and under the supervision of the assessors of said corporation.'

Approved March 28, 1903.

Chapter 381.

An Act to amend Chapter one hundred and forty-nine of the Private and Special Laws of eighteen hundred and ninety-five, entitled "An Act to divide the town of Sullivan and incorporate the town of Sorrento."

Be it enacted by the Senate and House of Representatives in Legislature assembled, as follows:

Section 1. Section one of chapter one hundred and forty-nine of the private and special laws of eighteen hundred and ninety-five is hereby amended by inserting after the words "Simpson's Island" in the twelfth line of said section the words 'Sheldrake or Sullivan's Island, Ash Island, and Junk of Pork together with the shore or flats belonging to said islands,' so that said section as amended, shall read as follows:

'Section 1. All that part of the town of Sullivan in the county of Hancock, and state of Maine, known as Waukeag Neck, which lies south of Long Cove, west of Bass Cove, and southwest of a line running from Long Cove to Bass Cove, described as follows, namely; beginning at the center of the stream which runs in a northwesterly direction into said Long Cove at the point where said stream joins said Long Cove at mean high water mark just west of the bridge crossing said stream, thence south, thirty-seven degrees east about seventeen hundred and sixty feet to said Bass Cove, including Ingal's Island, Bean's Island, Dram Island, Calf Island, Seward Island, Preble or Simpson's Island, Sheldrake or Sullivan's Island, Ash Island, and Junk of Pork, together with the shore or flats belonging to said islands, together with the inhabitants thereof, is hereby incorporated into a separate town by the name of Sorrento; and said town is hereby invested with all the powers and privileges and subject to all the duties and obligations incident to other towns of the state.'

Section 2. This act shall take effect when approved.

Approved March 28, 1903.

Chapter 382.

An Act relative to elections of Treasurer and Collector of Taxes of the City of Hallowell.

Be it enacted by the Senate and House of Representatives in Legislature assembled, as follows:

Treasurer and collector.

Section 1. The treasurer and collector of taxes of the city of Hallowell may be one and the same person.

Election of Charles K. Howe, made legal.

Section 2. The election on March nine, nineteen hundred and three, of Charles K. Howe as treasurer and collector of taxes of the city of Hallowell, is hereby made legal and valid.

Section 3. This act shall take effect when approved.

Approved March 28, 1903.

Chapter 383.

An Act authorizing the acceptance of the conveyance of Widow's Island, Maine, by the State of Maine.

Be it enacted by the Senate and House of Representatives in Legislature assembled, as follows:

Widow's island accepted for public purposes.

That, pursuant to an act of Congress approved March two, nineteen hundred and three, the state of Maine hereby accepts, to be used for public purposes, Widow's island situated in Fox island thoroughfare on the coast of Maine, with all of the buildings and improvements thereon, subject to all of the terms and conditions of said act of Congress; and that the governor of the state of Maine, be and is hereby, authorized and instructed to procure and receive the conveyance thereof to the state of Maine; and to take such action as may be necessary to properly care for and protect the same until it may be used for some public purpose by the state of Maine.

Approved March 28, 1903.

Chapter 384.

An Act relative to Treasurer and Collector of Taxes of the City of Waterville.

Be it enacted by the Senate and House of Representatives in Legislature assembled, as follows:

Section 1. The treasurer and collector of taxes of the city of Waterville, may be one and the same person.

Section 2. This act shall take effect when approved.

Approved March 28, 1903.

Chapter 385.

An Act relative to the Treasurer and Collector of the City of Bangor.

Be it enacted by the Senate and House of Representatives in Legislature assembled, as follows:

Section 1. The treasurer and collector of taxes in and for the city of Bangor, may be one and the same person.

Section 2. This act shall take effect when approved.

Approved March 28, 1903.

Chapter 386.

An Act relative to the Treasurer and Collector of Taxes for the Town of Brownfield.

Be it enacted by the Senate and House of Representatives in Legislature assembled, as follows:

Section 1. The treasurer and collector of taxes in and for the town of Brownfield, may be one and the same person.

Section 2. This act shall take effect when approved.

Approved March 28, 1903.

Chapter 387.

An Act in relation to the Treasurer and Collector of Taxes, in the Town of Oakfield, in Aroostook County.

Be it enacted by the Senate and House of Representatives in Legislature assembled, as follows:

Treasurer and collector may be same person.

Section 1. That the treasurer and collector of taxes in the town of Oakfield, in Aroostook county, may be one and the same person.

Section 2. This act shall take effect when approved.

Approved March 28, 1903.

Chapter 388.

An Act to incorporate the Houlton and Danforth Electric Railroad Company.

Be it enacted by the Senate and House of Representatives in Legislature assembled, as follows:

Corporators.

Section 1. Veazie E. Price, Joseph A. Brown, John Watson, Clarence H. Pierce, Don A. H. Powers, Ransford W. Shaw, Charles D. Merritt, John B. Madigan, Hudson T. Frisbie, Willard S. Lewin, James Archibald and Frank W. Titcomb, their

—corporate name.

associates, successors and assigns, are hereby constituted a corporation by the name of the Houlton and Danforth Electric Railroad Company, with authority to construct, maintain and use a street railroad, for the purpose of carrying passengers, freight and mail, to be operated by electricity or any other motive power, with convenient single or double tracks, side tracks, switches or turnouts, with any necessary or convenient line of

—route.

poles, wires, appliances, appurtenances or conduits, from Houlton in the county of Aroostook, upon and over any public highway leading from said Houlton to and through the towns of Hodgdon, Cary plantation, Amity, Orient and Weston in the county of Aroostook, to and through Danforth, in the county of Washington, as shall from time to time be fixed and determined by the municipal officers of said towns, and assented to in writing by said corporation and the owners thereof, providing, however, that all tracks of said railroad shall be laid at such distance from the sidewalks in any of said towns as the municipal officers thereof shall in their order fixing the routes and locations of said railroad, determined to be for public safety and convenience.

—location to be filed with town clerks

The written assent of said corporation to any vote of the municipal officers of either of said towns, prescribed from time to time, the routes of said railroad therein shall be fixed with the clerk of said town, and shall be taken and deemed to be the location thereof. Said corporation shall have power, from time to time to fix such rates of compensation for transporting persons and property as it may think expedient, and shall have all the powers and shall be subject to all the liabilities of corporations as set forth in the forty-sixth chapter of the revised statutes, not inconsistent with the express provisions of this act. —corporation may fix rates of transportation.

Section 2. Said corporation shall also have authority to construct, maintain and use said railroad over and upon lands outside of the limits of streets and highways where the land damages have been mutually settled by said corporation and the owners thereof. *May construct road outside street limits.*

Section 3. The municipal officers of said towns shall have power at all times to make all regulations as to the rate of speed, the removal of snow and ice from the streets, roads and ways by said company at its expense, and the manner of use of tracks of said railroad within each of said towns as public convenience and safety may require. *Municipal officers may regulate speed, removal of snow and ice, etc.*

Section 4. Said corporation shall keep and maintain in repair such portion of the streets and ways as shall be occupied by the tracks of said railroad, and shall make all other repairs of said street, roads and ways within either of said towns which in the opinion of the municipal officers of said towns may be rendered necessary by the occupation of the same by said railroad and if not repaired upon reasonable notice, such repairs may be made by said towns at the expense of said corporation. *Shall repair portions of streets occupied by tracks.*

Section 5. If any person shall wilfully or maliciously obstruct said corporation in the use of its roads or tracks or the passing of the cars or carriages of said corporation thereon, such persons and all who shall aid or abet therein, shall be punished by a fine not exceeding two hundred dollars or with imprisonment in the county jail for a period of not exceeding sixty days. *Penalty for obstruction of tracks.*

Section 6. The capital stock of said corporation shall not exceed five hundred thousand dollars, to be divided into shares of one hundred dollars each. *Capital stock*

Section 7. Said corporation shall have the power to lease, purchase or hold real or personal estate as may be necessary and convenient for the purpose of constructing, equipping, operating and managing said road. *May hold real and personal estate.*

Section 8. Said railroad shall be constructed and maintained in each of said towns, in such form and manner and upon such grade and with such rails as the municipal officers of said towns shall direct, and whenever, in the judgment of the said corporation it shall be necessary to alter the grade of any street *Municipal officers may control manner of construction.*

CHAP. 388

—manner of crossing location of railroad, by whom determined.

or way, said alteration may be made at the sole expense of said corporation, provided, the same shall be assented to by the municipal officers of the town wherein said grade so sought to be changed is located. If the tracks of said corporation's railroad cross any other railroad, and a dispute arises in any way in regard to the manner of crossing, the board of railroad commissioners of this state shall, upon hearing, decide and determine in writing in what manner the crossing shall be made, and it shall be constructed accordingly.

Location, how changed.

Section 9. Said corporation may change the location of said railroad at any time by first obtaining the written consent of the municipal officers of the town in which the change is so sought to be made, and to make additional locations subject to the foregoing provision and conditions.

Town authorities may occupy streets.

Section 10. Nothing in this act shall be construed to prevent the proper authorities of either of said towns from entering upon and taking up any of the streets or ways in either of said towns, occupied by said railroad for any purpose for which they may lawfully take up the same.

Exclusive franchise.

Section 11. No other person or corporation shall be premitted to construct or maintain any railroad for similar purposes over the same streets or ways that may be lawfully occupied by this corporation, but any person or corporation lawfully operating any horse or electric railroad to any point to which this corporation's tracks extend, may enter upon, connect with and use the same on such terms and in such manner as may be agreed upon between the parties, or if they shall not agree, to be determined by the railroad commissioners for the state of Maine.

May issue bonds.

Section 12. Said corporation is hereby authorized to issue bonds in such amount, and on such time as may from time to time be determined, in aid of the purpose specified in this act and to secure the same by mortgage of its franchises and property. It is also hereby authorized to lease all of its property and franchises upon such terms as it may determine.

First meeting, how called.

Section 13. The first meeting of said corporation may be called by any two of said corporators giving actual notice in writing to their several associates, and said corporation may make such by-laws as are proper and not contrary to the laws of the state.

Shall commence construction within four years.

Section 14. This charter shall be null and void unless operations for building said railway shall have been actually commenced within four years from the passage of this act.

Section 15. Said corporation shall not be required to run cars upon their road during the winter season nor when the convenience or wants of the public do not require it.

Shall not be required to operate road in winter.

Section 16. This act shall take effect when approved.

Approved March 28, 1903.

Chapter 389.

An Act to authorize the Skowhegan and Norridgewock Railway and Power Company to extend its line to and into the town of Smithfield.

Be it enacted by the Senate and House of Representatives in Legislature assembled, as follows:

Section 1. The Skowhegan and Norridgewock Railway and Power Company is hereby authorized to extend its street railroad from or near its present terminus in the town of Norridgewock, to and into the town of Smithfield over streets, roads and ways to be determined by the selectmen of said towns, with all the powers and privileges and subject to all the duties and liabilities incident to street railroad corporations except as modified by this act.

Authorized to extend line of its road.

Section 2. All proceedings for the extension of said railroad shall be had under the general laws of this state regulating similar extensions, except, however, that the petition to the railroad commissioners for approval of location shall omit the prayer for such commissioners to determine whether public convenience requires the construction of such road.

Proceedings.

Section 3. Said company may discontinue the running of its cars during such portion of the winter months as it may find expedient.

May discontinue service in winter.

Section 4. This act shall take effect when approved.

Approved March 28, 1903.

Chapter 390.

An Act to incorporate the Lumbermen's Electric Railway Company.

Be it enacted by the Senate and House of Representatives in Legislature assembled, as follows:

Section 1. E. B. Curtis, O. M. Vose, A. R. Gilson, A. D. McFaul, C. Sullivan, E. P. Grimes, W. E. Tupper, W. F. Pope, S. N. Tobey, C. Hollis White and F. L. Shaw, their associates, successors and assigns are hereby constituted a cor-

Corporators.

576   LUMBERMEN'S ELECTRIC RAILWAY COMPANY.

CHAP. 390

—corporate name.

poration under the name of the Lumbermen's Electric Railway Company, with authority to construct, maintain, equip and operate a line or lines of single or double track railway, to be operated by electricity, with the necessary side tracks, switches and turnouts and other appliances for the passing of cars, carriages or other vehicles upon or along the streets or ways in the towns of Machias, Machiasport, East Machias, Jonesboro and in any or all the towns, townships and lumber regions lying on and along Chandler's river, Machias river and the East Machias river.

—powers.

May cross tide waters.

Section 2. Said company shall have authority to extend its railway over the bridge across the navigable tide waters of Chandler's river, Machias river, Middle river and East Machias river, in Washington county.

May purchase or lease real estate.

Section 3. Said company may purchase and hold or lease real estate in said towns for railway purposes, and also for the purpose of car houses, power houses and waiting rooms, to the amount deemed necessary by the directors. And in case the company is unable to agree with the owners of the land required under this section, and necessary for the convenience of the company, the taking of such land shall be done as provided in chapter fifty-one of the revised statutes.

Animal or electric power may be used.

Section 4. Said railroad shall be occupied and used by said company with animal or electric power. The municipal officers of each of said towns shall have power at all times to make all such regulations valid and binding within the limits of their towns only, as to the rate of speed of cars or trains, and the removal of snow and ice from the streets, roads and highways from and alongside of its tracks at the expense of said railway company, as the public convenience and safety may require.

Municipal officers may designate location in streets.

Section 5. The tracks of said company shall be laid in such parts of the streets, roads or highways as the municipal officers of either of said towns shall direct; and poles may be set at convenient places and distances along the streets, roads or highways over which the tracks of the railroad shall be laid, from which trolley wires may be suspended for the operation of cars by electricity, at such points as the municipal officers may direct.

Manner of construction.

Section 6. Said road shall be constructed in such form and manner and with such rails and appliances that so much of the streets, roads and ways as are occupied thereby shall be safe and convenient for travelers, and said road shall be liable to an action on any case for any loss or damage which any person may sustain by reason of any failure to comply with this provision.

May cross tracks of steam railroad.

Section 7. The company may lay its tracks across the tracks of any steam railroad, but the manner and terms of the crossing

LUMBERMEN'S ELECTRIC RAILWAY COMPANY. 577

CHAP. 390

shall be determined by the railroad commissioners before the crossing is made.

Section 8. Said company is hereby authorized to lease all of its property and franchises on such terms as it may determine; also to consolidate with or to acquire by lease, purchase or otherwise the lines, property or franchises of any other street railway, whose lines as constructed or chartered would form connecting or continuing lines with the lines of this company, and in such case this company shall be entitled to all the privileges and be subject to all the appropriate conditions and limitations contained in the charters thus united with or acquired. Whenever any person or corporation shall be lawfully operating any railroad to any point to which this company's tracks extend, this company may enter upon, connect with and use the same on such terms and in such manner as may be agreed upon between the parties. *May sell or lease to connecting line.*

Section 9. This company shall keep and maintain in repair such portion of the streets, town or county roads as shall be occupied by the tracks of this railroad, and shall make all other repairs of said streets or roads which may be rendered necessary by the occupation of the same by said railroad, and if not repaired upon reasonable notice, such repairs may be made by the town in which the necessity exists, at the expense of said company, and said town may recover all expenses in an action of money paid for the use of said railroad company. *Repairs of streets occupied.*

Said company shall be liable for any loss or damage which any person may sustain by reason of any carelessness, neglect or misconduct of its agents or servants, or by reason of any defect in so much of said streets or roads as is occupied by said railway, if such defect arises from neglect or misconduct of the company, its servants or agents. *—liability for damages.*

Section 10. If any person shall wilfully and maliciously obstruct said corporation in the use of its roads or tracks, or the passing of the cars of said company thereon, and all who shall aid and abet therein, shall be fined not exceeding two hundred dollars, or imprisoned in the county jail not exceeding sixty days. *Obstruction of tracks, penalty for.*

Section 11. Said company may, from time to time, fix such rates of compensation for transporting persons or property, as it may deem expedient, and generally shall have the powers and be subject to all the liabilities of corporations as set forth in the forty-sixth chapter of the revised statutes and amendments thereto. *Rates of transportation.*

Section 12. Said corporation may change the location of said railroad by first obtaining the written consent of the *Change of location, how made.*

50

CHAP. 390

municipal officers of said towns, and make additional locations on the afore mentioned highways subject to the foregoing provisions and conditions and in no event to cross or go north of said Sturgeon Creek.

Town may enter on streets for lawful purposes.

Section 13. Nothing in this act shall be construed to prevent the proper authorities of said town from entering upon and temporarily taking up the soil in any street, town or county road occupied by said railroad, for any purpose for which they may now lawfully take up the same.

Exclusive franchise.

Section 14. No other corporation or person shall be permitted to construct or maintain any railroad for similar purposes over the same streets, roads and ways, that may be lawfully occupied by this corporation.

Liability for damages during construction.

Section 15. Said town shall not be liable to pay for any damage to persons or property occasioned by any neglect or fault of said railway during construction.

May borrow money.

Section 16. The directors of this company, from time to time, may raise or borrow for the use and purpose, of the company, any sum or sums not exceeding four hundred thousand dollars by the issue of bonds or debentures in sums of not less than one hundred dollars, and not exceeding the amount of capital stock subscribed for on such terms and credit as they may think proper, and may pledge or mortgage all the tools, property, franchises and incomes of the company, or any part thereof for the repayment of money so raised or borrowed and the interest thereon provided, always, that the consent of the majority in value of the stock holders of the company shall be first had and obtained at a regular or special meeting to be called and held for that purpose.

—may issue bonds.

First meeting, how called.

Section 17. The first meeting of the incorporation under this act, may be called by either of the corporators giving notice to the others in writing at least seven days before the time of said meeting, of the time and place of said meeting.

Section 18. This act shall take effect when approved.

Approved March 28, 1903.

Chapter 391.

An Act to incorporate the Farmers' Telephone Company.

Be it enacted by the Senate and House of Representatives in Legislature assembled, as follows:

Section 1. Augustus W. Gilman and C. C. Dunham, their associates and successors, are hereby created a corporation by the name of the Farmers' Telephone Company, with all the powers, rights and privileges, and subject to all the duties and obligations of similar corporations under the general laws of this state. {Corporators. —corporate name.}

Section 2. Said corporation is hereby authorized to construct, own, maintain and operate a telephone line or lines anywhere in the towns of Foxcroft and Guilford in Piscataquis county, along and upon any public highway or bridge in said towns, subject to the control of the municipal officers of said towns, but in such a manner as not to incommode or endanger the customary public uses thereof; and said company may cut down any trees standing within the limits of any highway except ornamental or shade trees, where necessary for the erection, use and safety of its lines. {Route.}

Section 3. Said corporation is hereby authorized and empowered to connect its line or lines with those of any other telephone company or corporation upon such terms as may be agreed upon, or to sell or lease its line or lines and property in full or in part, before or after completion, to any other telephone company or corporation, upon such terms as may be agreed upon by the contracting parties. {May connect with other lines.}

Section 4. In case of the taking of any real estate necessary to carry out the provisions of this act the damages therefor, when the parties cannot agree, shall be assessed and paid in accordance with the law applicable to the assessment of damages for ways taken by railroads. {Damages for land taken.}

Section 5. The capital stock of said company shall be of such amount as said company may from time to time determine to be necessary, but not to exceed the sum of ten thousand dollars, which capital stock shall be divided into shares of twenty-five dollars each. {Capital stock.}

Section 6. Said company is hereby authorized to purchase, hold, lease, sell and convey all the real and personal estate necessary for the purposes contemplated in this charter. {May hold real and personal estate.}

Section 7. The first meeting of the incorporators named in this act shall be called for the purpose of organization under this act, by a written notice signed by one of the corporators, directed to each of the corporators, seven days at least before the date {First meeting, how called.}

580 NORWAY MUNICIPAL COURT.

CHAP. 392

of meeting, naming the time and place of meeting and purposes of such meeting, and at such meeting a president, secretary and treasurer, and three directors may be chosen, by-laws adopted, present amount of capital stock fixed, and any corporate business transacted.

Section 8. This act shall take effect when approved.

Approved March 28, 1903.

Chapter 392.

An Act to amend Section two of Chapter five hundred eight of the Private and Special Laws of eighteen hundred eighty-five, as amended by Chapter one hundred thirty-four of the Private and Special Laws of eighteen hundred eighty-seven, Chapter five hundred twenty-seven of the Private and Special Laws of eighteen hundred ninety-three, and Chapter four hundred twenty-five of the Private and Special Laws of nineteen hundred one, relating to Norway Municipal Court.

Be it enacted by the Senate and House of Representatives in Legislature assembled, as follows:

Section 2, chapter 508 of private and special laws of 1885, as amended, further amended.

Section 1. Section two of chapter five hundred and eight of the private and special laws of eighteen hundred and eighty-five, as amended by chapter one hundred and thirty-four of the private and special laws of eighteen hundred and eighty-seven; chapter five hundred and twenty-seven of the private and special laws of eighteen hundred and ninety-three, and chapter four hundred and twenty-five of the private and special laws of nineteen hundred and one, is hereby amended in the third clause of said section and in the fourth line of said clause by striking out the word "and" and inserting in lieu thereof the word 'or,' so that said third clause of said section two, as amended, shall read as follows:

Original jurisdiction concurrent with supreme judicial court.

'Third: Original jurisdiction, concurrent with the supreme judicial court, of all civil actions in which the debt or damage demanded does not exceed two hundred dollars, and both parties or the defendant or a person summoned as a trustee reside in the county of Oxford. Provided, that any action, civil or criminal, in which the judge is interested but which would otherwise be within the exclusive jurisdiction of said court, may be brought before and disposed of by any trial justice within said county, in the same manner and with like effect as other actions before said tribunals.'

—proviso.

Approved March 28, 1903.

Chapter 393.

An Act conferring certain power upon the Trustees of the University of Maine.

Be it enacted by the Senate and House of Representatives in Legislature assembled, as follows:

Section 1. The trustees of the University of Maine are hereby empowered to guarantee loans for the construction, upon the grounds of said university, of society houses, which shall serve as student dormitories, provided that nothing herein contained shall be construed as binding the state of Maine to pay said loans, or any of them, or any part thereof, or any interest thereon; and provided further that no appropriation therefor shall hereafter be asked of the state of Maine. *May guarantee loans for construction of society houses.*

Section 2. This act shall take effect when approved.

Approved March 28, 1903.

Chapter 394.

An Act to regulate the Police Force of the City of Portland.

Be it enacted by the Senate and House of Representatives in Legislature assembled, as follows:

Section 1. The police force of the city of Portland shall hereafter consist of a chief of police, two captains of police, two police inspectors, not more than four sergeants of police, and not exceeding fifty-five policemen, which officers shall rank in the order named, and a police matron. The mayor shall have power and authority to appoint watchmen to serve without pay from said city, and in the event of any extraordinary demand upon the police force of said city, which demand the police force herein provided for, and the reserve police force authorized by this act are insufficient to meet, the mayor may appoint temporarily as many special policemen as the public needs and safety may require, but the term of office of all watchmen and special policemen thus appointed, shall in no event exceed a period of six months, and the term of office of such special policemen shall not be extended beyond the period of the extraordinary demand for which they were appointed, and all members of the police force mentioned in this section, excepting the police matron, shall have within the limits of the city of Portland, all the common law and statutory powers of constables, except the service of civil process, and all the powers given to watchmen or police officers under the statutes of this state. *Police force, its membership.* *—mayor may appoint watchmen.* *—special policemen.*

CHAP. 394

Tenure of present police force.

Section 2. All policemen now holding office in said city of Portland, excepting watchmen not paid by said city, and special policemen, shall continue in office, and all future appointments of policemen shall be made by the mayor from the reserve force hereinafter created, or from such special policemen who have, previous to the acceptance of this act, as hereinafter provided, been in active service on the police force of said city for a period of more than six months, and who, in the judgment of the mayor, have the requisite qualifications for efficient policemen, and the term of office of each policeman holding under the terms of this act, or by appointment by the mayor, shall be during good behavior of such policeman, or until retired under such pension rules as the city council may from time to time establish, but all policemen not otherwise removed, shall be honorably discharged on arriving at the age of sixty-five years.

—future appointments, how made.

Sergeants of police.

Section 3. As soon as may be after the acceptance of this act, as hereinafter provided, the mayor shall appoint from the present regular police force of said city of Portland, as many sergeants of police, not exceeding four, as in his judgment, the needs of the city require, two captains of police, and shall by appropriate rules assign their respective duties, and all future appointments to said offices mentioned in this section, including the filling of vacancies, shall be made by the mayor from the policemen, or from the officers ranking below the office to be filled, and such future appointments shall be made in accordance with such system of promotion as the mayor may establish, and said sergeants and captains shall hold office during good behavior, or until retired under such pension rules as the city council may from time to time establish, but all sergeants and captains not otherwise removed, shall be honorably discharged at the age of sixty-five years. The mayor shall designate two policemen to serve as police inspectors, during his pleasure, who shall resume their duties as policemen when other police inspectors are designated in their places. The mayor shall also appoint a police matron, a resident of Portland, who shall hold office for a term of five years, unless sooner removed by the mayor for cause.

—police inspectors.

Chief of police.

Section 4. As soon as may be after the acceptance of this act, as hereinafter provided, the mayor shall appoint from the present officers of police, or from the citizens at large a chief of police who shall hold office until the first day of January, in the year of our Lord one thousand nine hundred and five, or until his successor is appointed and qualified, and all future appointments to said office, except to fill a vacancy for an unexpired term, shall be for a term of one year from the first day of Jan-

POLICE FORCE IN PORTLAND.

uary, in each year beginning with the year nineteen hundred and five unless sooner terminated as hereinafter provided or until a successor is appointed and qualified.

Section 5. The mayor shall have full power to make all needful rules and regulations for the government of the police of said city, and enforce said rules and regulations, if necessary, by suspending any policeman, sergeant, captain, or chief of police, for cause, from duty, without pay, for a period not exceeding thirty days, and may remove any of them, also any watchman, at any time for sufficient cause, after notice and public hearing, which cause shall be expressed in the order of removal; and the mayor may, for cause, and after notice and public hearing, reduce any captain or sergeant to a lower grade. The mayor shall also have power to fill any vacancies occuring for any reason in any of the offices mentioned in this act.

Powers of mayor.

Section 6. From the men certified by the police examining board of the city of Portland, as possessing the required qualifications and as having successfully passed the competitive examination now required of all candidates for appointment as policemen of said city, the mayor may at any time designate not exceeding ten, in the order of their rank obtained under such competitive examination, beginning with the highest, who shall constitute a reserve police force, and all additions thereafter made to said reserve force shall be made by the mayor as the needs of the police department of said city may require, and in the manner aforesaid, the applicant holding the highest rank under the civil service rules then in effect, being always next in order for promotion to said reserve force, but said reserve force shall at no time consist of more than ten men. The members of said reserve force may be called upon at any time by the chief of police or the mayor to do police duty, and shall have all the power and authority conferred upon policemen by this act, and shall serve on said reserve force at least six months before being eligible to appointment as policemen. Any member may be rejected and his name stricken from said reserve force by the mayor at any time, for unreasonably refusing to go on duty when called on, or after six months of active service, provided the mayor shall have become satisfied that said member does not possess the necessary qualifications of an efficient policeman.

Reserve police force.

Section 7. The compensation of the chief of police, captains of police, police inspectors, sergeants, policemen, special policemen, and members of the reserve force, when on duty, and the matron, shall be fixed by the city council, and said compensation having been once fixed shall not be decreased except by action of the city council. The city council shall appropriate such sums annually as may be necessary to carry on efficiently

Compensation of police force.

the work of the police department, the same to be expended under the direction of the mayor, but at no time shall the mayor have authority to create liabilities for the maintenance of the police department in excess of the amount appropriated for that purpose by the city council, or to create any liability for said city for any purpose unless a specific fund for that purpose be first provided by appropriation, or otherwise, by the city council.

Inconsistent acts, repealed. Section 8. All acts and parts of acts and ordinances and by-laws of the city of Portland, in so far as they are inconsistent with this act, except as hereinafter provided, are hereby repealed, but all the powers of the police of the city of Portland as now organized, and the authority of the mayor and board of aldermen over the same shall continue in full force until the appointment and organization of the police under this act, and all rules and regulations established by the mayor and board of aldermen governing the police of said city of Portland shall continue in force until new rules and regulations are established by the mayor under the provisions of this act.

Legal voters shall vote on acceptance of this act. Section 9. At the annual municipal election following the passage of this act, the legal voters of the city of Portland shall be called upon to give in their votes upon the acceptance of this act at meetings in the several wards in said city, duly warned by the mayor and aldermen. The vote shall be taken upon the same ballot on which the votes are given for the municipal and ward officers and shall be in answer to the following question: Shall the act passed by the legislature of the state of Maine, in the year nineteen hundred and three, entitled "An Act to regulate the police force of the city of Portland," be accepted? Those in favor of the acceptance of said act shall vote "Yes," and those opposed, "No." The same proceedings shall be had for the sorting, counting, declaring and recording of the returns of said votes as is provided for the election of mayor, and the board of aldermen shall at the time it canvasses the returns of the votes of the several wards for mayor, compare the returns of the several ward officers of the votes upon the question of the acceptance of this act; and if it appears that a majority of the votes given upon the acceptance of this act are in favor thereof, the mayor shall be so notified and shall forthwith make proclamation of the fact, and this act shall thereupon take full effect.

Section 10. So much of this act as authorizes the submission of the question of its acceptance to the legal voters of the city of Portland, shall take effect upon its passage, but it shall not take further effect unless accepted by the legal voters of said city as hereinbefore provided.

Approved March 28, 1903.

Chapter 395.

An Act to make the bridge of the Proprietors of the Wiscasset Bridge, a Public Bridge.

Be it enacted by the Senate and House of Representatives in Legislature assembled, as follows:

Section 1. The county commissioners of the county of Lincoln are hereby directed to lay out a a county road across the bridge and approaches thereto of the proprietors of the Wiscasset bridge sometimes called the Wiscasset Bridge Company, upon petition therefor by responsible persons in said county, after notice and hearing, in the manner required by the general laws of the state regulating the laying out of highways. The damages therefor shall be ascertained and determined in the same manner as in taking lands for highways, and shall be paid by the said county. *Wiscasset bridge made part of county road.* —*damages, how determined.*

Section 2. Said bridge and its approaches shall thereafter be a public highway and shall be thereupon made safe and convenient for public travel by the said county commissioners and maintained by the county of Lincoln free of toll. *Bridge and approaches a public highway.*

Section 3. For the foregoing purpose the sum of ten thousand dollars is hereby appropriated, and the governor and council are hereby authorized to draw their warrant therefor, and to pay the same to the treasurer of the county of Lincoln upon the certificate of the commissioners of the county of Lincoln that said highway across said bridge has been legally established and that the bridge and the approaches thereto have been made safe and convenient as required by law. *Appropriation for.*

Section 4. The county commissioners of said county are hereby authorized and empowered for the purpose of defraying the cost of outlay for the purchase and repairs of said bridge so far as the same shall fall upon the county of Lincoln to issue the bonds of said county made payable in not more than forty years from date, with annual interest not to exceed five per centum per annum, payable semi-annually, signed by the county treasurer and countersigned by said county commissioners. Said bonds to be of such denominations as the county commissioners may deem advisable. *Lincoln county may issue bonds.*

Section 5. From and after the acceptance of this act in the manner hereafter provided, the county commissioners of said county shall include in their annual estimates of county taxes the sums necessary therefor, together with a sum equal to one per centum of the bonds issued in virtue of this act, which sum shall be set aside yearly until, with its past and prospective accretions, it shall be sufficient to provide for the payment of *Sinking fund provided.*

CHAP. 395

said bonds at maturity and said sum and accretions shall constitute a sinking fund for the payment of said bonds and shall be invested in such interest bearing securities as said commissioners shall approve or in such bonds.

This act void unless accepted by legal voters of county.

Section 6. No part of this act shall take effect unless and until it is accepted as a whole by the legal voters of Lincoln county by a majority vote of the voters voting at meetings in the several towns and municipalities of said county, duly notified and warned by the county commissioners, to be held on the first Monday of June next, for the purpose of accepting or rejecting this act, at which meeting the vote shall be by ballot as follows:

—form of ballot.

"Shall the act making the Wiscasset Bridge free be accepted?" and each voter shall express his opinion thereon by marking the same opposite the word "yes" or "no," as the case may be. The ballots shall be received, sorted, counted and declared as votes for town officers are, and shall be recorded by the town clerk, and true copies thereof sealed and attested, shall be transmitted to the county commissioners of said county within six days. The commissioners shall open and declare the votes so returned. If errors appear in the returns they shall be corrected by the commissioners by proper evidence, and if a majority of the ballots returned have "yes" upon them, it shall be deemed to be an acceptance of this act, and the same shall then be in force; but if there should be a majority of ballots with "no" thereon, it shall be deemed a rejection of the same.

—if act is rejected another special election may be held.

If said act is so rejected at said election, it shall be the duty of the county commissioners upon the petition of twenty-five per cent of the voters of said county, to order another special election to be held in the manner aforesaid at any time within three months thereafter. The clerk of courts for the county of Lincoln shall make due returns to the secretary of state of the results of the election so to be held, and the certificate of said clerk shall be filed with the secretary of state with this act.

Section 7. This act shall take effect when approved by the governor, so far as is necessary to authorize the calling and holding of the election herein provided for.

Approved March 28, 1903.

CITY OF ROCKLAND.

CHAP. 396

Chapter 396.

An Act amending the charter of the City of Rockland.

Be it enacted by the Senate and House of Representatives in Legislature assembled, as follows:

Section eleven of private and special laws of eighteen hundred and eighty-nine, is hereby amended by inserting after the word "who" in the tenth line of said section, the words 'under the control of and subject to the approval of the city council,' so that said section as amended shall read as follows: Section 11, private and special laws of 1889, amended.

'Section 11. The city council shall annually, on the second Monday in March, or as soon thereafter as may be convenient, by ballot in joint convention, elect for the ensuing year the following officers: A city clerk, a city treasurer, a chief of police, who shall be styled the city marshal, and who shall exercise all the powers and perform all the duties of a constable, one overseer of the poor, one assessor of taxes, a road commissioner, or in lieu of a road commissioner, a board of road commissioners, consisting of three members, who, under the control of and subject to the approval of the city council, shall have charge of all the work and expenditure upon the streets, sidewalks and sewers; and when the city council shall by vote decide to elect a board of commissioners as aforesaid they shall be elected, one for three years, one for two years, and one for one year; after the first election one member thereof shall be elected annually; a collector of taxes, and one or more city constables. All said officers and agents shall hold their offices during the ensuing year and until others are elected and qualified in their stead, unless sooner removed by the city council; and all moneys received and collected for and on account of the city by any officer or agent thereof, shall forthwith be paid into the city treasury. The city council shall take care that moneys shall not be paid from the treasury unless granted or appropriated; shall secure a prompt and just accountability by requiring bonds with sufficient penalties and sureties from all persons trusted with the receipt or custody of public money; shall have the care and superintendence of the city public buildings and the custody and management of all city property, with power to let or sell what may be legally let or sold, and to purchase in the name of the city such real or personal property, not exceeding the sum of two hundred thousand dollars, including the property now owned by the city, as they deem of public utility. And the city council shall, as often as once a year, cause to be published for the information of the inhabitants, an account of receipts and expenditures and a schedule of the city property, and no money shall be paid from the city treasury unless the same be appropriated by the city council and upon a warrant signed by the mayor, which warrant shall state the appropriation under which the same is drawn.

Approved March 28, 1903.

Chapter 397.

An Act for the protection of Squirrels and Chipmunks in the County of Knox.

Be it enacted by the Senate and House of Representatives in Legislature assembled, as follows:

Protection of squirrels in Knox county.

Section 1. Whoever, within the limits of the county of Knox, kills or has in his possession, except alive, any gray squirrel, red squirrel or chipmunk, forfeits five dollars for each of said animals so killed or had in possession, to be recovered on complaint.

Section 2. This act shall take effect when approved.

Approved March 28, 1903.

Chapter 398.

An Act to amend An Act entitled, "An Act authorizing Washington County to sell its stock in the Washington County Railroad Company, and authorizing the sale or lease of said railroad," approved March ten, nineteen hundred three.

Be it enacted by the Senate and House of Representatives in Legislature assembled, as follows:

Section 1, of act approved March 10, 1903, amended.

Section 1. Section one of an act authorizing Washington county to sell its stock in the Washington County Railroad Company, and authorizing the sale or lease of said railroad, approved March tenth, nineteen hundred and three, is hereby amended by striking out in the sixteenth and seventeenth lines of said section the words "if said commissioners shall approve said proposition they shall submit it" and inserting in place thereof the words 'said commissioners shall call together the Washington county delegation for the time being to the Maine legislature and if a majority of said commissioners and delegation acting jointly shall approve said proposition said commissioners shall submit such proposition,' so that said section, as amended, shall read as follows:

CHAP. 398

'Section 1. Whenever a proposition for the purchase of the holdings of Washington county in the preferred stock of the Washington County Railroad Company shall be made in writing by the holders of the other shares of the stock of said corporation to the county commissioners of said county, or by any other person or corporations said proposition stating in substance that upon a legal transfer of such preferred stock to them, the said holders of the other shares of the stock of said corporation or such other person or corporations as may submit a proposition will pay to said county commissioners for the use of said county a certain definite sum of money, or when such holders of the other shares of the stock of said corporation or any other person or corporations, shall make any other proposition for the purchase of said preferred stock or the exchange thereof for other securities, said commissioners shall call together the Washington county delegation for the time being to the Maine legislature and if a majority of said commissioners and delegation acting jointly shall approve said proposition said commissioners shall submit such proposition to the determination of the legal voters of said county at such time as they may designate, subject to the provisions of this act, and thereupon there shall be submitted to the voters of the several cities, towns and organized plantations in the county of Washington the following proposition: "Shall the county commissioners be empowered to dispose of the holdings of the county in the preferred stock of the Washington County Railroad Company in accordance with the written proposition made therefor?" and the warrants issued for calling such meetings shall contain a copy of such written proposition, and it is hereby made the duty of the county commissioners of said county to appoint a day for meetings to vote thereon, and to notify the municipal officers of the cities, towns and plantations thereof, leaving a sufficient time for calling said meetings in the usual form for city or town meetings.

Said commissioners shall cause to be prepared printed forms for the warrants and returns of said meetings and transmit them with their notifications to city, town and plantation officers as above prescribed.'

Section 2. Section twelve of said act is hereby amended by inserting at the beginning thereof the words, 'After Washington county shall have sold its preferred stock in accordance with the provisions of this act;' also by striking out in the eighteenth, nineteenth and twentieth lines the words "and the preferred stock purchased and paid for so the county of Washington is not a holder of said stock," so that said section, as amended shall read as follows:

CHAP. 399

May issue bonds after stock is sold.

'Section 12. After Washington county shall have sold its preferred stock in accordance with the provisions of this act, the Washington County Railroad Company for the purposes hereafter named is hereby authorized to issue its bonds in such amount and with such rate of interest that the annual interest charge thereon shall not exceed the annual interest charge upon the present outstanding mortgage bonds, and to secure the same by a mortgage of its railroad, franchises, property and privileges:

—proviso.

provided said mortgage shall be authorized by a majority vote of the holders of the common stock in said company at a legal meeting called therefor, in the call for which the purposes of said meeting shall be stated, and shall also be consented to in writing by the owner or owners of all of the preferred stock in said company. The proceeds of such last named mortgage bonds shall be applied to the payment, redemption or purchase of said first mortgage bonds, or to the purchase of the preferred stock, which when purchased may be retired and canceled. When all of said bonds shall have been so paid, redeemed or purchased and the first mortgage discharged, any balance remaining may be applied to the improvement or betterment of said road.'

Section 3. This act shall take effect when approved.

Approved March 28, 1903.

Chapter 399.

An Act providing temporarily for the Payment of Wardens for their services.

Be it enacted by the Senate and House of Representatives in Legislature assembled, as follows:

Provision for payment of fish and game wardens.

Section 1. Until there shall be funds available to pay inland fish and game wardens for their services, the governor is authorized to draw his warrant for the payment of the same on the state treasurer from the amount appropriated for the operation of the fish hatcheries and feeding stations for fish and for the protection of fish, and such amount thus drawn shall be returned to said fund as soon as it is received for licenses or fines.

Section 2. This act shall take effect when approved.

Approved March 28, 1903.

Chapter 400.

An Act to change the name of the Plantation of Winterville.

Be it enacted by the Senate and House of Representatives in Legislature assembled, as follows:

In honor of his excellency the governor, the name of Winterville plantation in the county of Aroostook is hereby changed, and the name shall be hereafter known as Hill plantation.

Winterville plantation, name changed.

Approved March 28, 1903.

Chapter 401.

An Act to authorize William C. Farrell and Henry A. Gagnon to construct a dam or dams across Hammond brook, in Aroostook county, and build and maintain piers in said brook, and improve said brook for driving purposes.

Be it enacted by the Senate and House of Representatives in Legislature assembled, as follows:

Section 1. William C. Farrell and Henry A. Gagnon, their heirs and assigns, are hereby authorized to erect and maintain a dam or dams, with piers, booms and sluices, on Hammond brook, in Cyr plantation, in Aroostook county, and improve said stream by removing therefrom, trees, brush, rocks, or other obstructions, to facilitate the driving of logs and lumber down said stream, and the holding of logs and lumber to be manufactured at the mill of said Farrell, situated on said stream.

Dam, piers, booms and sluices authorized on Hammond brook.

Section 2. Said Farrell and Gagnon, their heirs and assigns, may purchase land and materials for building said dams and making said improvements, and flow contiguous lands so far as necessary to raise suitable heads of water, and land necessary for landing logs and lumber on said stream. And if the parties owning lands flowed or used for landings cannot agree upon the damages therefor, the said damages shall be estimated by the county commissioners for the county of Aroostook, as provided by law in case of taking lands for public highways, and for the damage occasioned by flowing land, the said Farrell and Gagnon, their heirs and assigns, shall not be liable to an action at common law, but the person injured may have a remedy, by complaint for flowing, in the manner provided by chapter ninety-two of the revised statutes.

May purchase land.

—and flow contiguous lands.

—damages, how estimated.

Section 3. Said Farrell and Gagnon, their heirs and assigns, may demand and receive toll for the passage of logs and lumber cut and hauled above the mill of said Farrell, and driven over

Tolls.

CHAP. 402

—lien for payment of tolls.

—lien, how enforced.

—when tolls shall cease.

said dam or dams and improvements, including logs to be manufactured at said mill, of ten cents for each thousand feet, board measure, woods scale, and said Farrell and Gagnon, their heirs and assigns, shall have a lien upon all logs and lumber which may pass over any of their dams and improvements for the payment of said tolls, and said Farrell and Gagnon, their heirs and assigns, may hold said logs or lumber, or such quantity thereof as shall be necessary to pay such toll and costs and charges, in the pond at said Farrell's mill, and unless such toll is paid within ten days after the first of such logs or lumber liable to toll as aforesaid, have reached said pond, said Farrell and Gagnon, their heirs and assigns, may seize said logs or lumber and sell at public sale, such quantity thereof as shall be necessary to pay such toll and costs and charges, notice of the time and place of sale ten days before such sale being first given in some newspaper printed in the county of Aroostook, and said Farrell and Gagnon, their heirs and assigns, shall keep an account of all expenditure for improvements, and tolls as aforesaid, and when the amount of said tolls equals the expenditure and interest at six per cent, said tolls shall cease.

Section 4. This act shall take effect when approved.

Approved March 28, 1903.

Chapter 403.

An Act to amend Section three of Chapter thirty of the Private and Special Laws of eighteen hundred and seventy-two, relating to the Godfrey Falls Dam Company.

Be it enacted by the Senate and House of Representatives in Legislature assembled, as follows:

Section 3, chapter 30, private and special laws of 1872, amended.

Section 1. Section three of chapter thirty of the private and special laws of eighteen hundred and seventy-two is hereby amended by adding after the word "boom" in the seventeenth line the following, 'or their place of sale or manufacture,' and by adding after the word "may" in said seventeenth line the words 'then, or at any time thereafter,' so that said section as amended shall read as follows:

Tolls.

'Section 3. Said corporation may demand and receive as a toll the sum of seventy-five cents for each and every thousand feet board measure of all logs and lumber cut and not more than thirty feet in length and two dollars for each and every thousand feet board measure of all logs and lumber more than thirty feet in length put into the lakes, ponds and streams above their dam at or near the head of Godfrey's Falls, and which may pass over their dam at, or near, the head of said Godfrey's Falls, to be ascertained by the woods scale or boom scale at the option of said corporation; and said corporation shall have a lien upon all logs and lumber which may pass over said dam at or near the head of said Godfrey's Falls until the full amount of toll of all the logs and lumber which may pass over said dam at or near the head of said Godfrey's Falls is paid; but logs of a particular mark shall only be holden to pay the toll of such mark; and if said toll is not paid within ten days after such logs and lumber shall arrive at the Penobscot boom or at their place of sale or manufacture said corporation may then, or at any time thereafter, sell at public auction in Bangor after ten days' notice in some newspaper printed in Bangor so much of said logs and lumber as may be sufficient to pay said toll and incidental charges.'

—lien established.

Section 2. This act shall take effect when approved.

Approved March 28, 1903.

Chapter 403.

An Enabling Act for the annexation of the city of South Portland to Portland.

Be it enacted by the Senate and House of Representatives in Legislature assembled, as follows:

Section 1. Upon the acceptance of this act as hereinafter provided, the city of South Portland shall be annexed to and be a part of the city of Portland, and the inhabitants and territory of the city of South Portland shall be subject to the charter and ordinances of the city of Portland, and to the acts amendatory thereof and supplemental thereto, except as herein otherwise provided.

Annexation of South Portland to city of Portland.

Section 2. The city of Portland as herein enlarged shall be divided into eleven wards, and until the city council shall have revised the ward lines in the manner provided by law, ward ten shall consist of that part of the city of South Portland, lying westerly of the following described line, namely: Beginning at the center of the draw in Portland bridge; thence along the center of Ocean street through City and Dyer squares to the Cape Elizabeth line. Ward eleven shall consist of that part of South Portland lying easterly of said line. Each of these wards so constituted shall have the same form of organization and the same representation in the city government and in the school

Ward divisions.

committee of Portland that the other wards in said city have at the time of the acceptance of this act, and warrants for the election of said officers shall be issued by the municipal officers of Portland, as provided hereafter, in due season for the municipal election first to be held in said city after the acceptance of this act.

Ward meetings, places of holding.

Section 3. The ward meetings of said ward ten shall be held in the basement of the Pleasantdale school house, and the meetings in said ward eleven shall be held at the South Portland hose house, until the city council shall otherwise provide.

Warrants for first meetings.

Section 4. The warrants for the first ward meetings in said wards ten and eleven shall be made returnable by the constable posting the same, to some voter in each of said wards, designated by the municipal officers of Portland, who shall call said ward meetings to order for the election by open ballot of a warden to preside at said meeting, and a ward clerk, and the warden and clerks so elected shall qualify and perform all the duties devolving upon the warden and ward clerk under the provisions of law. The necessary ballot and election clerks for wards ten and eleven shall be appointed according to law by the municipal officers of the city of Portland.

Voting lists for wards.

Section 5. From the lists of voters now registered in the several wards of South Portland, the board of registration of South Portland, upon the acceptance of this act, shall prepare two new lists, one to contain the names of all voters whose registered residence is within the limits of said ward ten, which list shall be the list of registered voters for said ward ten, and the other to contain the names of all voters whose registered residence is within the limits of said ward eleven, which list shall be the list of registered voters their records, to the board of registration of Portland at least twelve days prior to the municipal election next to be held after the acceptance of this act, and thereafter changes therein may be made as in the lists of registered voters in other Portland wards.

Property and obligations of South Portland, arrangements concerning.

Section 6. Upon the acceptance of this act, all the city property of South Portland together with all city moneys in the hands of the treasurer thereof, or under his control, becomes the property of the city of Portland, and the city of Portland shall assume all obligations of the city of South Portland then existing, and all indebtedness both temporary and bonded, and shall provide for the payment thereof according to the terms under which said indebtedness was contracted. Provided that the officials of said city of South Portland shall continue to manage and control the affairs in said city during the interval between the acceptance of this act and the inauguration of the mayor and city council elected to succeed them, as hereinafter provided, and during said term said officials may expend the available funds of the city in the regular course of business.

Section 7. Until the inauguration of the mayor and city council first to be elected, as hereinbefore provided, the present municipal officers, public officials, school committee and police of South Portland, shall continue in office for the purpose of performing the duties required of them by law, and by the terms of this act; but upon said inauguration the terms of all of them shall end.

Tenure of present city government.

Section 8. All persons upon whom taxes have been legally assessed by the city of South Portland and the old town of South Portland, and who have not paid the same, shall be required to make payment thereof to the treasurer of the city of Portland. Unpaid sidewalk, drain and sewer assessments, legally assessed by the city of South Portland shall be collected in the manner provided by the South Portland charter and ordinances, and the city of Portland shall have the same rights to enforce payment of said taxes, and sidewalk, sewer and drain assessments, as the city of South Portland would have had but for the passage of this act.

Unpaid taxes to whom to be paid.

Section 9. All rights, contracts, claims, immunities, privileges and franchises which might be exercised by the city of South Portland may be exercised and enforced by the city of Portland as its successor; and all privileges, exemptions and immunities granted by the city of South Portland shall remain binding upon the city of Portland. The passage of this act shall not affect any right accruing or accrued, or any suit, prosecution or other legal proceedings pending at the time when it shall take effect by acceptance as herein provided for, and no penalty or forfeiture previously incurred shall be affected thereby.

Rights, franchises, etc., pass with annexation.

—immunities, etc., remain upon Portland.

Section 10. Upon the day of the inauguration of the mayor and city council to be elected as hereinbefore provided, the control and superintendence of the present public schools of South Portland shall be vested in the school committee of Portland to the same extent and in the same manner as are other public schools of Portland, and the school facilities now furnished by the city of South Portland shall not be hereafter curtailed or abridged.

Schools.

Section 11. All official records and documents in the city of South Portland shall be transferred from the several departments to which they respectively belong to the corresponding department in the city of Portland, and the production, attestation or authentication of the same by the respective official custodian of the records of said several departments in the city of Portland

Records and documents.

shall have the same effect in any legal proceedings as if produced, attested or authenticated by the custodian of the records of the department in said South Portland from which the same were severally transferred.

Municipal court.

Section 12. The South Portland municipal court is hereby abolished, but for the purpose only of closing the business pending therein at the time of the approval of this act, the entire jurisdiction thereof, civil and criminal, shall be conferred upon the municipal court of the city of Portland, which court shall issue all executions or other process necessary to carry into effect any judgment, order or decree of said South Portland municipal court. All complaints, civil suits, recognizances, appeals in civil or criminal cases, and all other processes, civil or criminal, pending in said South Portland municipal court, shall be transferred forthwith to the municipal court for the city of Portland, to be entered on the docket thereof, and to be heard and disposed of as if originally entered in said municipal court for the city of Portland; and all writs, petitions, warrants and all processes whatever, returnable to said South Portland municipal court, shall be returnable to and be entered on the docket of said municipal court for the city of Portland as if originally entered therein. The judgments, decisions, orders and decrees of the supreme judicial court, at any law term, made in cases originating in said South Portland municipal court, shall be certified to the recorder of the municipal court for the city of Portland, to whose attestation of the same, or their contents, full faith shall be given.

Ward meetings for voting acceptance of this act.

Section 13. Ward meetings may be held at the usual place of meeting in said cities for the purpose of submitting the question of the acceptance of this act to the legal voters of said cities at any time within five years after the passage thereof, except in the months of September and November. At such meetings the polls shall be open from eight o'clock in the forenoon until five o'clock in the afternoon, and the vote shall be taken by written or printed ballots in answer to the question, "shall the act passed by the legislature in the year of our Lord one thousand nine hundred and three, entitled "An Enabling Act for the annexation of South Portland to Portland," be accepted?"

The regular ward officers shall preside at such meetings and use a check list to be prepared by the board of registration in the same manner as lists are prepared for municipal elections. The affirmative votes of a majority of the voters present and voting thereon shall be required for its acceptance.

—may be submitted to voters a second time.

If, at any meeting so held, this act shall fail to be thus accepted, it may, at the expiration of one year from any previous meeting, be again submitted for acceptance, provided it shall not be submitted more than three times in either city. Such meetings shall be called in each city upon the application of one hundred or more of the qualified voters of said cities, and the board of mayor and aldermen of said cities shall upon the application of said one hundred voters forthwith issue warrants for said meeting. The same proceedings shall be had respecting the sorting, counting, declaring and recording the returns of said votes as is provided for the election of mayors; and the board of mayor and aldermen of said cities shall within five days after said meeting, meet and compare the returns of the ward officers, if it appears that the majority of all the votes given in on said annexation in each city is in favor thereof, the mayors of said cities shall forthwith make proclamation of the fact and thereupon this act shall take effect and the city of South Portland shall thereafterwards be annexed to and become a part of the city of Portland.

Section 14. So much of this act as authorizes the submission of the question of its acceptance of the legal voters of the said cities shall take effect upon its passage, but it shall not take further effect unless accepted by the legal voters of both of said cities as herein prescribed, in which case all acts and parts of acts inconsistent with this act are hereby repealed.

When act shall take effect.

Approved March 28, 1903.

Chapter 404.

An Act to Incorporate the Piscataquis River Storage Company.

Be it enacted by the Senate and House of Representatives in Legislature assembled, as follows:

Section 1. William M. Currier, Frank H. Drummond, Charles C. Emerson, Henry Hudson, Henry Douglass, David R. Straw, Edward J. Mayo, Walter J. Mayo, Stephen O. Brown, Crowell C. Hall, their heirs, successors and assigns, are hereby created a body corporate under the name of the Piscataquis River Storage Company, for the purpose of making such improvements in Piscataquis river and its tributary waters as will enable them to store or hold water for the purpose of increasing and rendering more constant the power or energy of said Piscataquis river, and for that purpose may acquire existing dams by purchase or otherwise, or erect and maintain new dams at the outlets of any of the ponds or bogs or upon any of the streams tributary to said Piscataquis river, above the East Dover dam on said river, on lands which it may acquire, but in such

Corporators.

—corporate name.

—may acquire or erect dams.

598

CHAP. 404

—may flow lands.

manner as not to impair the usefulness of any existing dams without the consent of the owners of the same, and said corporation is hereby empowered to flow such lands by the erection of such new dams as may be necessary to carry out the provisions of this act. Said corporation shall be liable for all damages caused by such flowage to be ascertained and determined in the manner prescribed in chapter ninety-two of the revised statutes, and in said corporate name may sue and be sued, plead and be impleaded, and shall enjoy all the proper remedies at law and in equity to secure and protect them in the exercise and use of their rights and privileges and in the performance of their duties.

May hold real and personal estate.

Section 2. Said corporation is hereby authorized to purchase and hold any estate, real and personal, including the right to purchase and hold shares in the capital stock of any other corporation owning rights or privileges in or to the waters or powers of said Piscataquis river and its tributaries, and to make and adopt by-laws not repugnant to the constitution and laws of the state of Maine, but all dams and other structures authorized herein shall be so constructed as to facilitate and not to impede or interfere with the proper driving or floating of logs and wood.

Capital stock.

Section 3. The capital stock of said corporation shall be ten thousand dollars divided into shares of one hundred dollars each, with the right to increase said capital stock at any time by a majority vote of the shareholders to any amount not exceeding fifty thousand dollars.

—allotment of shares.

Section 4. Previous to the first meeting of said corporation one share of its capital stock may be subscribed but paid for in full as follows: One share by the owners of the power or privilege at Blanchard in the county of Piscataquis and state of Maine: one share to the owners of the power or privilege at Abbot, on the north branch of the Piscataquis river; one share by the owners of the power or privilege at Abbot village on the south branch of the Piscataquis river; one share by the owners of the power or privilege at Guilford in said county of Piscataquis; one share by the owners of each power or privilege at Foxcroft in said county; one share by the owners of each power or privilege at Dover village in said county; one share by the owners of the power or privilege at East Dover in said county; one share by the owners of the power or privilege at Howland. Said share allotted to the owners of each of said dams or privileges shall be divided among the owners of each dam or privilege according to their ownership, and a majority ownership in each dam or privilege shall determine how said dam or privilege shall be voted at all meetings of said corporation. If any of the dams or privileges hereinbefore enumerated are owned equally by two different persons or corporations, each shall be entitled to one-half vote of said share at any meeting of said corporation. No shares of said capital stock shall be at any time sold or owned by persons or corporations not owners in one of said powers or privileges enumerated or described above.

The first meeting of the corporation may be called by any two of the corporators named in this act, giving five days written notice by mail to each of the other corporators named in this act, stating time, place and purposes of such meeting, and at such meeting the necessary officers may be chosen, by-laws adopted and any other corporate business transacted. In choosing directors, one director shall be chosen from the owner or owners of each of the power or privileges hereinbefore enumerated which is represented by stock in the company.

After said first meeting stock may be issued as subscribed and paid for to the owners of said powers or privileges but only in such amounts as have been voted to be raised for the purpose of expenditure under this charter by a majority vote of the board of directors at a regular or special meeting. Owners of the described water powers and privileges shall at all times have the rights to subscribe equally for stock to be issued. Any transfer of ownership of any of the powers or privileges described or enumerated shall carry with it a transfer of the capital stock in this corporation then standing in the name of the owner or owners of said water power or privileges so transferred; but should the owners of any of the described water powers or privileges refuse or neglect for ten days after said meeting of board of directors, to subscribe for his or their proportional part as herein set forth, then said stock shall be equally divided among the owners of each of the water powers or privileges hereinbefore enumerated.

Section 5. Said corporation is authorized through and by its directors to regulate the volume and flow of water released from any of its storage reservoirs and the time for releasing the same, and may by its by-laws, provide for the charge and collection of rates or payments of money by users for power of any of its artificially stored and released water. If any users there be whose stockholdings are less in amount than their proportional part of the whole stock issued, according to the apportionment of interest which shall be determined by vote of the stockholders, and said charges may be recovered by said corporation before any justice of the supreme judicial court under proceedings in equity for the purposes brought against the owner or owners of the power or privilege so delinquent in stockholding, but said charges or rates shall be made only for the artificially stored and released water actually used for power pur-

600   PISCATAQUIS RIVER STORAGE COMPANY.

CHAP. 404

—proviso.

—exception.

poses, and not fully contributed to in stockholdings by said user or power owner, and shall in no case be at a rate greater than one dollar per additional horse power so furnished per month of two hundred and sixty hours, or at that rate for less time, provided, however, that the volume and flow of water from the storage reservoirs of the company shall be so regulated as to furnish as nearly as possible an equal continuous flow of water in the Piscataquis river, for the whole twenty-four hours of each and every day, except that the directors have the power to increase or decrease such equal daily flow to such extent and at such times and for such periods as may be assented to by all of the stockholders in this corporation, provided also, that said corporation through and by its directors shall not cause water to be held in any dams that it may construct or acquire on the north and south branches of said river, so as to interfere with the natural flow of water on said branches to the detriment of any of the existing water privileges on these branches.

Stockholders may vote in person or by proxy.

Section 6. Any corporation, any co-partnership and any individual who becomes the owner of any stock in this corporation in accordance with this act, is or are hereby empowered to take and hold such stock, and at any meeting of their corporation or on any other occasion, may be represented, vote and act, respectively, by such person or committee as may be chosen for the purpose.

Use of river for driving.

Section 7. From the twentieth day of March to the fifteenth day of June in each year, whoever has logs in the north and south branches of the Piscataquis river and in the Piscataquis river, shall be entitled without charge to all the necessary water to drive such logs. The directors of said corporation shall determine in each case the reservoir or reservoirs from which said water shall be taken.

Jurisdiction of court over corporation.

Section 8. The supreme judicial court has equitable jurisdiction over this corporation, its successors and assigns, and all parties interested, including driving of logs on said river and its tributaries, to regulate the use of the water stored in the lakes and reservoirs held under this charter, and the rights of the members between themselves.

Injury to dams, etc., punishment for.

Section 9. If any person wantonly or maliciously injure any of the dams or structures which may be constructed by said corporation, he shall on conviction thereof, be punished by a fine not exceeding five hundred dollars, or by imprisonment not exceeding one year, and shall be liable also to pay the triple damages to said corporation to be recovered in an action before any court of competent jurisdiction.

Section 10. This act shall take effect when approved.

Approved March 28, 1903.

Chapter 405.

An Act relating to prize logs on the Penobscot river and its tributaries.

Be it enacted by the Senate and House of Representatives in Legislature assembled, as follows:

Section 1. When logs or other lumber belonging to different owners become intermingled in driving upon any of the waters of the Penobscot river or any of the waters tributary to the Penobscot river above Penobscot boom, and any person or corporation desires to separate and detain his or its logs or other lumber at any sorting place or sorting boom or any place of sale or manufacture above said Penobscot boom, and in so separating and detaining his or its logs or other lumber, logs or other lumber without marks or means by which their ownership can be ascertained are also detained and held, said person or corporation shall keep an accurate account open to the inspection of all interested parties, of the number, kind, quality and quantity of such logs or other lumber, without marks or means by which their ownership can be ascertained, and when and where detained and held, and shall within a reasonable time thereafter pay to the Penobscot Lumbering Association at its office in Bangor, Maine, for all such logs or other lumber, without marks or means by which their ownership can be ascertained, so detained and held, such a price as a like kind and quality of logs or other lumber are worth, at the time when and place where they shall be so separated and held to be disposed of by said Penobscot Lumbering Association, as hereinafter provided. Such payment to be accompanied by a copy of said account.

Section 2. All logs or other lumber, without marks or means by which their ownership can be ascertained, which shall come into said Penobscot boom, shall as soon as practicable and within a reasonable time after the same shall have been rafted, be sold, or manufactured and sold, from time to time by said Penobscot Lumbering Association, and what remains of the proceeds of the same, after deducting boomage and all other reasonable expenses and charges, that is to say, the net proceeds of such sale or sales together with all moneys received under the provisions of section one of this act, shall constitute a fund, which shall yearly be divided ratably as nearly as practicable among all the known owners of logs or other lumber, that formed the drive or drives out of which said logs or other lumber without marks or means by which their ownership could be ascertained, came, to be ascertained by such owners submitting to said Penobscot Lumbering Association at Bangor, Maine, on or before Decem-

CHAP. 405

ber one, each year, by written statement, satisfactory evidence of the total quantity and value that they had in such drive or drives. In making such distribution said Penobscot boom scale or what is equivalent thereto shall be adopted as a basis of computation.

Association may have agents to measure prize logs.

Section 3. Said association shall have the privilege, if it deems the same desirable, to have its agents or servants at each and every place on any of said waters where any such logs or other lumber, without marks or means by which their ownership can be ascertained, are separated and held as aforesaid, whose duties shall be, if said association shall desire it, to take and keep accurate measurements of the length, and diameter at the top end of all such logs or other lumber, without marks or means by which their ownership can be ascertained, which are so separated and held, and whose duties shall also be to see that the accounts provided for in section one of this act are accurately kept and preserved; such agents or servants to be paid by said Penobscot Lumbering Association and the expense thereof deducted from the proceeds of such sales or receipts of money as above provided.

Account shall be kept.

Section 4. Said Penobscot Lumbering Association shall keep an accurate account of the number, kind, quality and amount of such logs or other lumber, without marks or means by which their ownership can be ascertained, which are rafted in their boom, and how the same shall have been disposed of, and the proceeds thereof, and also of the moneys received from all persons and corporations for such logs or other lumber so separated and held, which accounts shall be open to the inspection of all interested parties. And said Penobscot Lumbering Association shall be holden only to the exercise of reasonable judgment, care, diligence and management in relation to the powers and duties imposed upon it by this act.

Action of assumpsit for sums due.

Section 5. If any person or corporation shall not pay to said Penobscot Lumbering Association any money, which he or it is holden to pay in accordance with the provisions of this act, said Penobscot Lumbering Association may maintain an action of assumpsit against said person or corporation to recover the same, and the net amount of money so recovered in such action shall constitute a part of said fund to be distributed as above.

Inconsistent acts repealed

Section 6. All the provisions of said charter of the Penobscot Lumbering Association and amendments thereto relating to unmarked logs, sometimes called "prize logs," or to logs the ownership of which cannot be ascertained, inconsistent with this act, are hereby repealed.

And all the provisions of the charter or amendments thereto of any other corporation and all the provisions of any other private and special law, or other law, relating to unmarked logs, sometimes called "prizes," or logs or other lumber, the ownership of which cannot be ascertained, upon the waters of said Penobscot river or any of its tributaries above said Penobscot boom inconsistent with this act, are hereby repealed.

Section 7. Whoever, except as provided in this act, takes, carries away or otherwise converts to his own use any such logs or other lumber without marks or means by which their ownership can be ascertained, after they shall have become intermingled with the logs or other lumber of other owners for the purposes of driving as aforesaid, suitable to be manufactured into lumber or pulp, lying in said Penobscot river, or in any of the waters tributary to said Penobscot river, above said Penobscot boom, or on or near the bank or shore thereof, or puts any mark upon the same with intent to claim the same for himself or another, forfeits for every such log or stick twenty dollars, to be recovered on complaint of any person or by indictment. *Penalty for taking away prize logs.*

Section 8. The provisions of sections seven and eight of chapter forty-two of the revised statutes of eighteen hundred eighty-three, relating to logs and other lumber, carried by freshet on to lands, are not affected by this act. *Provisions not affected by this act.*

Section 9. This act shall take effect when approved.

Approved March 28, 1903.

Chapter 406.

An Act to prevent the throwing of sawdust and other mill waste into all tributaries of Seven Tree pond and Crawford pond in Union and Warren.

Be it enacted by the Senate and House of Representatives in Legislature assembled, as follows:

Section 1. No person or persons shall put, or allow the same to be done by any person within his employ, any sawdust, shavings, bark, or other mill waste, into any of the tributaries of Seven Tree pond, in Union, in the county of Knox, or in any of the tributaries of Crawford pond, in Union and Warren, in said Knox county, or place or deposit such mill waste, or other refuse, along the banks in such a manner that the same shall fall or be washed into said brooks or streams. *Throwing of refuse into Seven Tree pond or tributaries of Crawford pond, forbidden.*

Section 2. Any person violating the provisions of section one of this act, shall be subject to a penalty of not less than five dollars and not more than fifty dollars and costs for each offense. *Penalty for violation.*

Section 3. This act shall take effect January first, nineteen hundred and five.

Approved March 28, 1903.

CHAP. 407

Chapter 407.

An Act to consolidate and revise certain laws relating to closing certain lakes and ponds to ice fishing, and to close the tributaries to certain lakes and ponds, and restricting the number of fish that may be taken in one day in certain waters, and defining the manner of fishing in certain waters, and prohibiting the throwing of sawdust and other mill refuse into certain streams, and regulating the method of hunting ducks in certain waters, and regulating the taking of deer in certain counties.

Be it enacted by the Senate and House of Representatives in Legislature assembled, as follows:

All of the private and special laws relating to fishing through the ice.

Section 1. The provisions of the general law pertaining to fishing through the ice by residents of the state, during February, March and April of each year, shall not apply to any of the following named lakes and ponds, and it shall be unlawful to fish through the ice in the same for any kind of fish:

—arranged by counties.

IN ANDROSCOGGIN COUNTY: Allen pond, so called, in Greene, Lake Auburn in Auburn, Brettuns pond in Livermore, and Androscoggin pond situated partly in this county and partly in Kennebec county.

IN AROOSTOOK COUNTY: Number Nine lake in Township Nine, Range Three, and the close time on this lake shall be from October first to June first of the following year; Ross and Conroy lakes in Littleton and Monticello, and it shall be unlawful to fish in these last named lakes at any time before April twenty-two, nineteen hundred and six.

IN CUMBERLAND COUNTY: Sabbath Day pond in New Gloucester, Thomas pond in Raymond and Casco, Little Sebago pond, or lake, in Gray and Windham, and Great Watchic pond in Standish, in which last named pond the close time shall be from October first to May first of the following year.

IN FRANKLIN COUNTY: In all of the ponds and lakes situated wholly or partly in Franklin county, except Pease pond in Wilton, in which it shall be lawful to fish through the ice, as provided in the general law, on Saturdays of each week during the months of February, March and April of each year, and Indian pond, situated partly in Franklin and partly in Somerset county, in which last named pond it shall be lawful to fish through the ice as provided in the general law.

IN HANCOCK COUNTY: Noyes' pond in Bluehill, Eagle lake, Bubble pond sometimes called Turtle lake, Jordan pond and Long pond on Mt. Desert Island, Crocker pond and Pickerel pond in Township 32, Middle Division, Green lake, sometimes called Reed's pond, situated wholly or partly in Ellsworth, in which last named lake it shall be lawful to fish, as provided in the general law, on Fridays and Saturdays of each week, during the months of February, March and April, of each year, and First or Billings pond in the town of Bluehill, in which last named pond the close time shall be from October first to May first of the following year.

IN KENNEBEC COUNTY: Cobbosseecontee lake situated partly in Winthrop, Annabessacook lake and The Narrows pond situated in Winthrop, Lake Maranocook situated partly in Winthrop, Jimmy pond in Litchfield, Androscoggin pond situated partly in Wayne, Great, Long, East, North, Little, Ellis, McGraw and Snow ponds situated wholly or partly in this county, Flying pond in Vienna, and Three-Mile pond in China, Windsor and Vassalboro, in which last named pond it shall be lawful to fish for pickerel, as provided in the general law, on Saturdays of each week, for consumption in the family of the person taking the same.

IN KNOX COUNTY: Crystal in Washington, Grassy pond in Hope and Rockport; provided, further, that it shall be unlawful to fish for any kind of fish at any time in said Grassy pond before May first, nineteen hundred and four.

IN LINCOLN COUNTY: Dyer's pond in Jefferson.

IN OXFORD COUNTY: It shall be unlawful to fish through the ice for any kind of fish in the following named lakes and ponds in Oxford county: In all the lakes and ponds situated wholly or partly in this county, except North and Bird ponds in the town of Norway, the Five Kezar's, Moose, Bear, Long, Two Speck, Pappoose and McWain ponds in the town of Waterford, Kneeland, Burnt Land, Songo and Crooker ponds in the town of Albany, Proctor pond in the towns of Albany and Stoneham, Upper Stone and Horse Shoe ponds in Stoneham, Bradley, Farrington and Slab City ponds in the town of Lovell, Moose, Beaver, Long, Grandeur and Little ponds in Denmark, Lower Kezar, Lovewell's, Clay, Haley, Charles, Pleasant, Lower Kimball and Bog ponds situated wholly or partly in Fryeburg, Rattle Snake and Burnt Meadow ponds in Brownfield, Moose and Mud ponds in Paris, Round and Twitchell ponds in Greenwood, Hogan and Whitney ponds in Oxford, the two Clemons ponds, Middle, Barker and South East ponds in Hiram, Bungamuck pond in Hartford, Keyes and Stearns ponds in Sweden, Bickford, Long and Colcord ponds in Porter, Thompson pond situated partly in Oxford and partly in Cumberland county, North pond in Greenwood and Woodstock, in which ponds it shall be lawful to fish through the ice, as provided in the general law, during the months of February, March and April of each year; provided, however, that it shall be unlawful to fish for any kind of fish, at any time, in Indian pond in Greenwood before April first, nineteen hundred and six.

IN PENOBSCOT COUNTY: It shall be unlawful to fish through the ice for any kind of fish in Cold Stream pond in Enfield.

IN PISCATAQUIS COUNTY: It shall be unlawful to fish through the ice for any kind of fish in any of the lakes and ponds lying wholly or partly in Piscataquis county, except the following named lakes and ponds, in which it shall be lawful to fish through the ice as provided in the general law, to wit: Seboeis lake, Boyd lake, provided, further, that it shall be lawful to fish through the ice in Boyd lake for pickerel only during December and January of each year, Cedar lake, Ebemee pond, Schoodic lake, North and South Twin lakes, Pamadumcook lake, Ambejejus lake, Debsconeag lake, Nahmakanta lake, Chesuncook lake, Sebec lake, First Buttermilk pond, Big Benson pond, Big Huston pond, Center pond in Sangerville, Moosehead lake, Jo Mary lake, Caribou lake, Lobster lake, Chamberlain lake, Telos lake, Webster lake, Eagle lake, Allegash lake, Munsungan lake, Millinockett lake, Caucongomoc lake, Churchill lake, Chemquassabamticook lake, Grand lake, Second lake, Ragged lake, Pepper pond, Whetstone pond, and Large Greenwood pond in Elliottsville and Willimantic.

IN SOMERSET COUNTY: It shall be unlawful to fish through the ice for any kind of fish in any of the lakes and ponds lying wholly or partly in Somerset county, except the following named lakes and ponds, in which it shall be lawful to fish through the ice as provided in the general law, to wit: Moosehead lake, Palmer pond in Mayfield, Ellis, Round and Ten-Thousand-acre ponds, in Township One, Range Six, W. K. R., B. K. P., known as the Ten-Thousand-acre township, Rowell pond in Solon, Smith pond in Cornville, Oaks pond in Cornville, Pickerel pond in Flagstaff, Gilman pond in Lexington, Pierce pond in Township Two, Range Four, Sibley pond in Canaan, Fahi and Sandy ponds in Embden, Wyman and Weeks ponds in Brighton, Moose, Mud, Starbird and Stafford ponds in Hartland, Hancock pond in Embden, Indian pond in Saint Albans, Indian pond situated partly in Franklin and partly in Somerset county, White and Douglass ponds in Palmyra, Gammon pond situated partly in Somerset and partly in Franklin county, and Big Carry pond.

IN WASHINGTON COUNTY: It shall be unlawful to fish through the ice for any kind of fish in Narraguagus lake in Beddington; Grand Lake stream, the outlet of Grand lake, in Washington county, and so much of Grand lake as is one hundred yards above the dam at the outlet shall be closed to all fishing from October first to June first of the following year, and from said dam to a point one hundred yards below said dam on said stream it shall be unlawful to fish for any kind of fish at any time, and it shall be unlawful during open season on said stream and one hundred yards above the dam at the outlet of said lake, to fish for, take, catch or kill any fish by any other method than by the ordinary way of angling with rod and artificial flies.

IN YORK COUNTY: It shall be unlawful to fish through the ice for any kind of fish in the following named lakes and ponds in York county: Bonneg Beg pond in North Berwick and Sanford, "L" pond in Sanford and Wells, Messabesic pond, sometimes called Shaker pond, and Littlefield pond in Alfred, Middle Branch pond in Alfred and Waterboro, and Bunganeaut pond in Alfred and Lyman, in which last named pond the close time shall be from October first to May first of the following year.

Section 2. It shall be unlawful to fish for, take, catch or kill any fish at any time, except as herein provided, in any of the following named waters, to wit:

ANDROSCOGGIN COUNTY: The tributaries to Lake Auburn or Wilson pond, so called, and all that part of the waters of said Lake Auburn and Townsend brook, so called, that lie north of the road leading from the Turner road, so called, to North Auburn village and crossing said Townsend brook, shall be considered as tributary waters of said Lake Auburn, the tributaries to Taylor pond in the city of Auburn, the tributaries to Brettuns pond in Livermore, and the tributaries to Big Bear pond situated partly in Turner.

AROOSTOOK COUNTY: The tributaries to Madawaska lake, or in Ross and Conroy lakes, in Littleton or Monticello, before April twenty-second, nineteen hundred six.

CUMBERLAND COUNTY: The tributaries to Sabbath Day pond in New Gloucester, the tributaries to Sebago lake, except Crooked and North West rivers, the tributaries to Anonymous pond in the town of Harrison, the tributaries to Thomas pond in Raymond and Casco, the tributaries to Duck pond, or in Royal river from Sabbath Day pond to Jordan's Dam. Provided, further, that it shall be unlawful to fish in the tributaries to Great Watchic pond, in Standish, from October first to May first of the following year.

FRANKLIN COUNTY: The tributaries to Webb pond in Weld, except Alder brook down as far as the Mill Dam at Hildreth's Mills, the tributaries to Tufts and Dutton ponds in Kingfield and the outlet of the same from Dutton pond to Reed's falls, and from Tufts pond to Alder stream, the tributaries to Tim and Mid ponds in Township two, Range four,. W. B. K. P., the tributaries to Rangeley lake, the tributaries to Ross pond, or in Bemis stream a tributary to Mooselucmaguntic lake, or in Whetstone brook, which flows into Kennebago stream, from the foot of the boulders, so called, in said stream to the foot of the falls at the outlet of Kennebago lake, or in Metalluc and Mill brooks which flow into Upper Richardson lake, or in Coos brook, a tributary to Wilson lake in Wilton, from its entrance into said Wilson lake from the upper side of the Wilkins bridge over said Coos brook, and the Holland brook, a tributary to said Wilson lake, from its junction with Coos brook to the upper side of the Coos bridge over said Holland brook, or in the tributaries to Varnum and North ponds in Temple and Wilton, the tributaries to Clearwater pond in Farmington and Industry, the tributaries to Long pond and Sandy River pond lying wholly or in part in Sandy River plantation, or in Lufkin pond and its tributaries in the town of Phillips, the tributaries to Four ponds, so called, in Townships E and D, or in any of the tributaries to Webb's river above Goodwin Brothers' Mill Dam in Carthage, or in Sandy river or any of its tributaries above Small's Falls, so called, in Madrid, to Sandy River pond, before June first, nineteen hundred and five, or in the North Branch, called the Chandler Mill stream, or in the South Branch, called the Crossman stream, or in Bowen brook, or Saddleback stream that flows into Sandy river at Madrid village, or in the Ben Morrison brook which flows into Saddleback stream.

HANCOCK COUNTY: In the tributaries to Noyes' pond in Bluehill, or in the tributaries to Green lake in Dedham and Ellsworth, or in the tributaries to Eagle lake in Eden, or in the tributaries to Bubble pond or Turtle lake on the island of Mount Desert.

KENNEBEC COUNTY: In the tributaries to all of the lakes and ponds lying wholly or partly in the towns of Winthrop and Monmouth, or in the tributaries to Jimmy's pond in Litchfield, or in the tributaries to Three Mile pond in China, Windsor and Vassalboro, or in the tributaries to McGraw, Ellis, East, North, Great, Long, Little and Snow ponds situated partly in Oakland, Belgrade, Mount Vernon, Rome and Sidney.

KNOX COUNTY: In Branch and Meadow brooks, so called, in Thomaston and Rockland, before February ninth, nineteen hundred and four, and then it shall be lawful to fish in these brooks only during the month of June of each year; in the tributaries to Canaan lake, partly in Knox and partly in Waldo county, in the tributaries to Lermonds and Alfords ponds, the tributaries to Norton pond and the tributaries to Crystal lake in Washington. Grassy pond, in Knox county, is closed to all fishing until May first, nineteen hundred and four.

LINCOLN COUNTY: The tributaries of Dyer's pond in Jefferson.

OXFORD COUNTY: The tributaries to Anasagunticook lake in Canton and Hartford, the tributaries to Little Bear pond in Hartford and Turner, the tributaries to Howard's pond in Hanover, the tributaries to Lake Pennesseewassee and Little Pennesseewassee in Norway, the tributaries to Garland pond and Roxbury pond, Rapid river from the swing bridge at the Oxford Club house to Lake Umbagog, the tributaries to Songo pond in Albany, the tributaries to Sand and Pickerel ponds in Denmark, the tributaries to Bryant pond in Woodstock; Pleasant pond and its tributaries shall be closed to all fishing until March sixth, nineteen hundred four, and for five years thereafter it shall be lawful to fish therein only on Tuesdays, Thursdays and Saturdays of each week and but twenty-five fish shall be taken in any one day in these waters by any one person. It shall also be unlawful for any person to fish in any of the tributaries to Indian pond, South pond and Twitchell pond, in the town of Greenwood, or to fish for, take, catch or kill any fish at any time in Indian pond, above named, before April first, nineteen hundred and six. It shall also be unlawful to fish for, take, catch or kill at any time any kind of fish in Great brook or Cold brook, in Stoneham.

PENOBSCOT COUNTY: The tributaries to Dexter pond in Dexter.

PISCATAQUIS COUNTY: The tributaries to Lake Hebron or Hebron pond in Monson, the tributaries to Twin and Doughty ponds, known as Ship pond and Bear pond, in Elliottsville plantation, Ship pond stream above Buck's Falls, the brook that is the outlet of Garland pond in Sebec, the tributaries to Lake Onawa in Elliottsville plantation and Willimantic, the tributaries to Moosehead lake except Moose river, and the commissioners shall establish by metes and bounds the mouths of these tributaries, Davis stream in Willimantic, Monson pond stream, a tributary to Davis stream, Vaughan stream, a tributary to Long pond stream, Wilson stream, a tributary to Sebec lake, Lily pond, in Shirley, before February thirteenth, nineteen hundred and four; it shall also be unlawful to fish in Wilson river, between Wilson pond and Tobey falls, in Willimantic, except from May fifteenth to October first of each year; it shall also be unlawful to fish in Lower Wilson pond, Upper Wilson pond, Mountain pond, Rum pond and Horseshoe pond, being the upper waters of Wilson stream, and all the tributaries of Lower Wilson pond, Upper Wilson pond, Mountain pond, Rum pond and Horseshoe pond, except from July first to October first of each year, until April twenty-second, nineteen hundred and six.

SOMERSET COUNTY: The tributaries to Lake George in Canaan, Barret brook and its tributaries and Beaver brook in

Holeb, the brooks forming the outlet of Fish pond and Little Fish pond and Big Gulf stream and Little Gulf stream, Wood stream in Forsythe plantation above its entrance into Big Wood pond, the tributaries to Hayden lake in Madison, Mosquito stream, an inlet of Moxie pond, in The Forks plantation, East Moxie and Bald Mountain townships, to low water mark in said Moxie pond, the tributaries to Great Embden pond in Embden, Misery stream an inlet of Brassua lake, the tributaries to Moose pond, in Hartland and Harmony, except Main stream, Goodwin's brook and Higgins stream above the first dam on said Higgins stream, the west outlet of Moosehead lake, the tributaries to Parlin or Lang pond in township three, range seven, Lang stream and its tributaries, Parlin stream and its tributaries from Parlin pond to the mouth of Bean brook; provided, further, that it shall be unlawful to fish for, take, catch or kill any kind of fish in Morrill pond, in Hartland, before April first, nineteen hundred and five.

WALDO COUNTY: It shall be unlawful to fish for, take, catch or kill any fish in Sandy stream and its tributaries and the tributaries to Unity pond in Unity before April twenty-second, nineteen hundred and four, except that eels and suckers may be taken in their season in these streams.

WASHINGTON COUNTY: The tributaries to Lambert lake, situated partly in Lambert Lake plantation, and the tributaries to Lake Narraguagus in Beddington.

YORK COUNTY: The tributaries to Bonney Beg pond in Sanford and North Berwick.

Special provisions relating to number of fish that may be caught, and method of fishing, in certain waters.

—arranged by counties.

Section 3. ANDROSCOGGIN COUNTY: It shall be unlawful to take, catch and kill any black bass less than twelve inches in length in Sabattus pond, and no person shall take, catch or kill more than ten black bass in any one day in said pond.

CUMBERLAND COUNTY: It shall be unlawful to take, catch and kill any black bass less than twelve inches in length in Highland lake, in the northern part of Cumberland county, and no one person shall take, catch or kill more than ten bass in any one day in said lake.

FRANKLIN COUNTY: It shall be unlawful to fish for, take, catch or kill any kind of fish at any time in Rangeley stream from the lower wharf at the outlet of Rangeley lake down to the dead water at the upper end of the eddy, nor from the upper end of the eddy to the mouth of Kennebago stream from July first to May first. It shall be unlawful to fish for, take, catch or kill any kind of fish at any time in Kennebago stream between the foot of the first falls near its mouth to the upper falls at the outlet of the lake, from July first to May first. It shall be unlawful to fish in Cupsuptic river or its tributaries, above the foot of the

first falls near its mouth, except from May first to July first of
each year. It shall be unlawful to fish in South Bog stream
from its mouth up to the first quick water from July first to May
first. It shall be unlawful to fish for, take, catch or kill any fish
in Quimby pond, in Rangeley, except in the ordinary way of
angling with rod and artificial flies between sunrise and sunset
of each day from the fifteenth day of May to the first day of
October, and no person shall take, catch or kill or have in possession more than six fish in all in any one day from this pond. It
shall be unlawful to take, catch, or kill more than twenty-five
fish in any one day in Four ponds, so called, in townships E and
D. It shall be unlawful to fish in any manner except with artificial flies in South Bog stream and pool, so called, waters connected with Rangeley lake. It shall be unlawful to take more
than twenty-five trout from Tim and Mud ponds, in Township
Two, range four, W. B. K. P., or from Tufts or Dutton ponds,
in Kingfield, in any one day. It shall be unlawful to take from
the waters of Varnum or North pond, in Temple and Wilton,
and Clearwater pond, in the towns of Farmington and Industry,
more than three trout, togue and land-locked salmon in all in
any one day. It shall be unlawful to catch any trout in Tufts,
Dutton or Grindstone ponds, or their tributaries, in the town of
Kingfield, for sale, or sell any trout at any time taken from said
Tufts, Dutton or Grindstone ponds or their tributaries. It shall
be unlawful to fish for in any way, or catch any fish of any kind,
in the Seven ponds, so called, the Seven ponds stream, Little
Kennebago lake, so called, and the stream flowing out of Little
Kennebago lake to the dam at the head of Kennebago falls, or
in the stream flowing out of Kennebago lake commencing at a
point four rods above the Berlin Mills Company's bridge and
continuing down said stream to its junction with the stream flowing from Little Kennebago lake except in the ordinary method
of casting with artificial flies or fly fishing. It shall be unlawful
to take, catch or kill at any time any kind of fish in any of the
ponds lying on Saddleback mountain, or the outlet of the same
flowing into Dead River pond, or in any of the tributaries emptying into said outlet, or in Salmon lake or Gull pond in Dallas
plantation, except in open season and not in open season except
in the ordinary method of casting with artificial flies or fly fishing.
It shall be unlawful for any person to take, catch, kill or have
in possession in any one day more than twenty-five fish in all
taken in any of the streams lying wholly or partly in the towns
of Freeman, Salem and Strong, and it shall be unlawful for any
person to fish for, take, catch or kill any fish in any of these
streams except on Tuesdays, Thursdays and Saturdays of each

Chap. 407

week during open season. It shall be unlawful to fish for in any way or catch any fish of any kind in Kennebago lake, John's pond, Flat Iron pond, Blanchard pond, and all the streams flowing into the same, except in the ordinary method of casting with artificial flies or fly fishing. It shall also be unlawful to fish for, take, catch or kill in any one day, more than ten fish in all in Kennebago lake, Little Kennebago lake, John's pond, Flat Iron pond, Seven ponds, so called, or in any of the streams flowing into any of the above named lakes or ponds that are not closed to fishing, and in the stream flowing out of Little Kennebago lake to the dam at the head of Kennebago falls, and in the stream flowing out of Kennebago lake commencing four rods above the Berlin Mills Company's bridge and continuing down said stream to its junction with the stream flowing from Little Kennebago lake.

HANCOCK COUNTY: It shall be unlawful to fish for, take, catch or kill any trout in any of the waters lying wholly or partly in the county of Hancock for sale, or directly or indirectly sell any trout taken from any of these waters, or to take, catch, kill or have in possession in any one day more than twenty-five pounds of black bass from any of the waters lying wholly or partly in the towns of Eden, Mount Desert, Tremont, Hancock, Sullivan, Franklin, Eastbrook, Waltham, and townships number seven, number ten and number twenty-one, in the county of Hancock.

KENNEBEC COUNTY: It shall be unlawful to take, catch and kill any black bass less than twelve inches in length in Snow pond, or Messalonskee lake, Great pond, North pond, East pond, McGraw pond, Ellis pond, Lake Cobbosseecontee, Annabessacook lake, and Lake Maranocook, and no more than ten black bass shall be taken in any one day from either of the above named lakes or ponds, and it shall be unlawful for any person to sell or offer for sale any kind of fish, except eels, at any time, taken or caught in any of the above named lakes and ponds in this county, except Lakes Annabessacook, Maranocook and Cobbosseecontee.

OXFORD COUNTY: It shall be unlawful to take or catch any black bass, pickerel, or any other fish from the Lower Kezar pond or its tributaries for sale, or to sell the same, and no person shall take more than twenty pounds of fish in any one day from said Lower Kezar pond. It shall be unlawful to fish for, take or catch any fish in Ward's brook, Ward's pond, and Walker's pond, so called, except between the first day of May and August of each year, or to fish therein except with rod and single line and artificial flies or fly fishing. It is unlawful to fish for, take, or catch any fish in Ellis river or its tributaries, situated in Andover,

Andover West, North Surplus, and Roxbury, and Townships C and D, except on Tuesdays, Thursdays and Saturdays during the months of May, June and July, and to the fifteenth day of August of each year. It shall be unlawful to take, catch and kill any black bass less than twelve inches in length in Keoka lake, nor shall any one person take, catch or kill more than ten black bass in any one day in said lake. It shall be unlawful for any one person in any one day to take, catch or kill more than ten black bass in Upper Kezar pond, or to take any black bass from said pond less than twelve inches in length, or to take any smelts at any time in any of the tributaries of said pond. It shall be unlawful to fish for in any way, or catch any fish of any kind in the Magalloway river above Aziscohos Falls, or in any of the tributaries of said river north of said falls, or in Sunday pond, Long pond, Parmachenee lake, Wells pond, Otter pond, Rump pond, Billings ponds, Barker's pond, M. T. Abbey pond, Upper and Lower Black ponds, Cupsuptic pond and Lincoln pond except by the ordinary method of casting with artificial flies or fly fishing.

PISCATAQUIS COUNTY: It shall be unlawful to fish for, take, catch or kill any fish in Little Houston pond, in Katahdin Iron Works township, except with artificial flies.

SOMERSET COUNTY: It shall be unlawful to take, kill or carry away more than two fish of any kind, eels and suckers excepted, or ten pounds of fish, in any one day from Spring lake, so called, in Somerset county.

WASHINGTON COUNTY: It shall be unlawful during the open season on Grand Lake stream, and for one hundred yards above the dam at the outlet of Grand lake, to fish for, take, catch or kill any fish by any other method than by the ordinary way of angling with rod and artificial flies or fly fishing; it shall also be unlawful to fish for, take or kill any fish in said Grand Lake stream from the dam at the outlet of Grand lake to a point one hundred yards below said dam at any time.

Section 4. Whoever shall violate any of the provisions of sections one, two and three of this act shall be subject to the same penalty as is provided in the general law for illegal fishing and the illegal catching of fish.

Penalty for violation of sections 1, 2 and 3.

Section 5. No person shall put, or allow the same to be done by any person within his employ, into any of the streams, rivers or brooks lying wholly or in part in the towns of Naples, Casco and Raymond, in the county of Cumberland, or into any of the tributaries to any of the ponds or lakes lying wholly or partly in the towns of Vienna and Mt. Vernon or into McGraw, Ellis, East, North, Great, Long, Little or Snow ponds, or any of their

Throwing sawdust, etc., into certain waters, prohibited.

tributaries, in Kennebec and Somerset counties, or into Half-Moon stream or Sandy stream, or any of the tributaries to Unity pond, in the county of Waldo, or into the Saint Georges river, in Montville and Searsmont, in Waldo county, or into the tributaries to Seven-Tree pond or into the tributaries of Crawford pond, in Union and Warren, or into Ellis stream in Waldo, Brooks and Belfast, or into Norton, Brown or Heath brooks, or their tributaries, in Shapleigh and Limerick, any mill waste, slabs, edgings, sawdust or any other mill waste of a fibrous nature created in the manufacture of any sawn or planed lumber, or to place or deposit the same on the banks of any of these waters in such negligent or careless manner that the same shall fall or be washed into any of said waters, or with the intent that the same shall fall or be washed into any of said waters. Whoever shall violate any of the provisions of this section shall be subject to a penalty of not less than fifty dollars nor more than one hundred dollars and costs of prosecution for each offense. Trial justices, municipal and police courts shall have original and concurrent jurisdiction for offenses arising under this act, and all fines recovered shall be paid to the treasurer of the state for the benefit of the fund for the protection and propagation of fish.

Section 6. No person or persons shall cast or throw into the Ellis river or its tributaries any mill waste, slabs, edgings, bark, chips, shavings, sawdust, or any other mill waste of a fibrous nature created in the manufacture of any sawn or planed lumber, or shall place, pile or deposit on the banks of said Ellis river, or on the banks of any of its tributaries, any slabs, edgings, or any shavings or fibrous material created by the manufacturing of shingles, in such negligent or careless manner that the same shall fall or be washed into said river or said tributaries, or with the intent that the same shall fall or be washed into said river or said tributaries, whereby the navigation of said river may become impeded or injuriously affected, or which shall tend to impede or injuriously affect the navigation of, or fill up said river, or which shall fill up or obstruct, or tend to fill up or obstruct, the canal or wheel race of any woolen mill, cotton mill, flour mill, or other manufacturing establishment, or which shall damage or injuriously affect, or tend to damage or injuriously affect, the ice on said river, or on any of its tributaries, under a penalty for each offense, if the quantity shall not exceed five cords, of not less than five nor more than twenty dollars; if the quantity cast or thrown in, or that shall fall or be washed in as aforesaid, at one or different times, shall exceed five cords in all, under a penalty of not less than twenty nor more than five hundred dollars. All the penalties under the provisions of this section shall be recovered by complaint or indictment before any court having jurisdiction in like offenses.

Section 7. No person or persons shall cast or throw into the Aroostook river, or into any of its tributaries above the mouth of Beaver brook, in Sheridan plantation, in the county of Aroostook, from any steam or water power saw mill, any slabs, edgings, sawdust, chips, bark, mill waste, or any shavings or fibrous material created by the manufacturing of shingles, or shall place, pile or deposit on the banks of said Aroostook river, or its tributaries above the mouth of said brook, any slabs, edgings, sawdust, chips, bark, mill waste, or any shavings or fibrous material created by the manufacturing of shingles, in such negligent or careless manner that the same shall fall or be washed into said river, or its tributaries above the mouth of said brook, whereby the driving of logs or lumber down said river may become impeded or injuriously affected, or which shall tend to impede or injuriously affect the driving of logs or lumber down said river, or fill up or obstruct, or tend to fill up or obstruct the canal or wheel race of any manufacturing establishment upon said river, or any boom of logs upon said river above the mouth of said brook, or which shall damage or injuriously affect, or tend to damage or injuriously affect the booming of logs upon said river, under a penalty for each offense, if the quantity shall not exceed five cords, of not less than five nor more than twenty dollars. If the quantity cast or thrown in, or that fall or be washed in as aforesaid, at one or different times, shall exceed five cords in all, under a penalty of not less than twenty nor more than five hundred dollars; provided, however, that this act shall not apply to sawdust made by gang saws, main rotaries, nor up and down saws of any kind, in water mills now in use on said river above said dam. All the penalties under the provisions of this section shall be recovered by complaint or indictment before any court having jurisdiction in like offenses, or by action of debt before any court having competent jurisdiction, for the benefit of the county where the offense was committed. If the offense or offenses forbidden in this section shall be committed by any person or persons who may be in the employ of any mill owner or owners, mill occupant or occupants, such owner or owners, occupant or occupants, shall also be liable in the same penalties, recoverable in the same manner as hereinbefore provided.

Section 8. It shall be unlawful for any person at any time to use boats or launches of any kind propelled by steam, naphtha, gasolene, or electricity, or any other mode than the ordinary sail boat or row boat, in chasing, hunting, or gunning any sea birds,

Use of steam launches prohibited in taking ducks in Frenchman's bay or Upper Kezar pond.

KILLING OF GAME BIRDS AND DEER PROHIBITED.

CHAP. 407

duck or water fowl in any of the waters of Frenchman's bay, so called, on the coast of Maine, or in the waters of lower Kezar pond, in the county of Oxford, under a penalty of not less than twenty-five dollars nor more than one hundred dollars and costs of prosecution for each offense. For the purposes of this act Frenchman's bay is defined and bounded as follows: On the north by the towns of Hancock and Sullivan; on the east by the towns of Gouldsboro and Winter Harbor; on the south by Mount Desert island and a straight line from Schoodic point, so called, to Great Head, so called; on the west by Thompson's toll bridge.

Protection of deer in certain counties.

Section 9. No person shall in any manner hunt, take, catch or kill any deer in Kennebec, Knox, Waldo and Lincoln counties between December first and October fifteenth next following; and no person shall between October fifteenth and December first inclusive next following take, catch or kill more than two deer, not more than one of which shall be a doe or fawn; nor shall any person have in possession any deer or part thereof killed in violation of this section. It shall be unlawful for any person to hunt, chase, pursue, catch or kill any deer at any time in the towns of Eden, Mount Desert and Tremont, in Hancock county. It shall be unlawful to hunt, chase, catch or kill any deer or moose in the county of Sagadahoc until October first, nineteen hundred and five. No person shall take, catch, kill, chase or hunt any deer in the county of York, except during the month of October of each year, and no person shall during the open season in this county, take, catch, kill or have in possession more than two deer or parts thereof. The month of October is hereby made an open month for the hunting and killing of deer in the county of Androscoggin. It shall be unlawful to hunt, chase, catch or kill in any manner, any deer on any island within the limits of the town of Isle au Haut, in the county of Hancock, before October first, nineteen hundred and seven. It shall be unlawful to hunt, chase, catch or kill, in any manner, any deer within the limits of the town of Swan's Island, in the county of Hancock, before October first, nineteen hundred and six. Whoever shall violate any of the provisions of this section shall be subject to the same penalty as is provided in the general law of the state for the illegal hunting, chasing, catching, killing or having in possession any deer or part thereof.

Approved March 28, 1903.

Chapter 408.

An Act to incorporate the Munsungun Telephone Company.

Be it enacted by the Senate and House of Representatives in Legislature assembled, as follows:

Section 1. H. L. Dobson, H. M. Chapman, S. S. Thornton of Ashland, W. H. Rowe, C. E. Newcomb of Masardis, Miles D. Arbo and C. C. Libby of Oxbow Plantation or such of them as may vote to accept this charter, their associates and successors, are hereby created a corporation by the name of the Munsungun Telephone Company, with all the powers, rights and privileges, subject to all the duties and obligations of similar corporations under the general laws of this state. *Corporators.* *—corporate name.*

Section 2. Said corporation is hereby authorized to construct, own, maintain and operate telephone line or lines in the county of Aroostook and particularly between the town of Masardis and any sporting camp or lodge, situated on or near Munsungun stream in the county of Aroostook or county of Penobscot, having obtained consent of any municipality through which said line may be constructed, and said company shall have a right to locate and construct its lines upon and along any public highway or bridge in said counties, but in such a manner as not to incommode or endanger the customary public use thereof. *May construct telephone lines.*

Section 3. Said corporation is hereby authorized and empowered to connect its line or lines with those of any other telephone company or corporation on such terms as may be agreed upon, or to sell or lease its line or lines of telephone and property in whole or part, either before or after completion to any other telephone company or corporation, as provided by law upon such terms as may be agreed upon by contracting parties, which sale or lease shall be binding upon the parties; or may purchase or lease any other line or lines of telephone upon such terms and conditions as may be agreed upon by the parties thereto. *May connect with other lines.*

Section 4. If the land of any individual or corporation is taken under this act, and the parties cannot agree on the damages occasioned thereby, they shall be estimated, secured and paid in the manner provided in case of land taken for railroads. *Damages for land taken, how estimated.*

Section 5. The capital stock of said corporation shall be of such amount as said corporation may, from time to time determine to be necessary, but not exceeding the sum of fifty thousand dollars, for the sole purpose of owning, leasing, constructing, maintaining and operating the line or lines of telephone hereby authorized and contemplated. And the said corporation may purchase, hold, lease, sell and convey, all real estate and personal property necessary for the purposes contemplated in this charter. *Capital stock.* *—not to exceed $50,000.*

618 A. M. GODDARD—KITTERY AND YORK TELEPHONE COMPANY.

CHAP. 409
First meeting, how called.

Section 6. Any one of the incorporators named in this act may call the first meeting of the corporation by mailing a written notice signed by himself, postage paid, to each of the other corporators, seven days at least before the day of the meeting, naming the time, place and purposes of such meeting, and at such meeting a president, secretary, treasurer and directors may be chosen, by-laws adopted, present amount of capital stock fixed, and any corporate business transacted.

Section 7. This act shall take effect when approved.

Approved March 28, 1903.

Chapter 409.

An Act to authorize A. M. Goddard and others to build and maintain a movable sidewalk.

Be it enacted by the Senate and House of Representatives in Legislature assembled, as follows:

Movable sidewalk authorized.

Be it enacted that A. M. Goddard, Joseph Williamson, Lewis A. Burleigh and Willard L. McFadden are hereby authorized to build and maintain two lines of movable sidewalk or tramways in such location as may be approved by the municipal officers of Augusta, along Winthrop street in Augusta from a point opposite Dickman street to State street, and to operate the same by steam or electric power. Said associates are hereby authorized to charge and collect reasonable toll from each passenger carried upon said sidewalk or tramway.

Approved March 28, 1903.

Chapter 410.

An Act to incorporate the Kittery and York Telephone Company.

Be it enacted by the Senate and House of Representatives in Legislature assembled, as follows:

Corporators.

—corporate name.

Section 1. Edward S. Marshall, John C. Stewart, Horace Mitchell, J. Perley Putnam and Joseph P. Bragdon, and their associates, successors, assigns, are hereby created a body politic by the name of the Kittery and York Telephone Company, with all the rights, powers and privileges and subject to all the duties and obligations of similar corporations under the general laws of this state.

Section 2. Said corporation is hereby authorized to construct, own, maintain and operate a line or lines of telephone in and throughout the towns of Kittery, York and South Berwick, and within the limits aforesaid, to locate, construct and maintain its lines upon and along any public way, railroad, bridge, or private lands and across or under tide waters, but in such manner as not to discommode or endanger the customary public use of any such way, road or bridge, or to interrupt navigation, with the right to cut down trees and remove obstacles when necessary within the limits aforesaid, except ornamental, fruit or shade trees, and with power to establish and collect tolls on said lines. ^{May construct telephone lines.}

Section 3. If the land of any individual or corporation is taken under this act, and the parties cannot agree on the damages occasioned thereby, they shall be estimated, secured, determined and paid as in case of land taken for railroads. ^{Damages for taking land, how determined.}

Section 4. Said corporation is hereby authorized to connect its line or lines with those of any other company, or to sell or lease its lines, either before or after completion, to any other telephone or telegraph company, upon such terms as may be mutually agreed upon, which sale or lease shall be binding upon the parties, or to purchase or lease any other line or lines of telegraph or telephone, upon such terms and conditions as may be mutually agreed upon. ^{May connect with or sell to, other lines.}

Section 5. The capital stock of said corporation shall be of such amount as said corporation by vote of its stockholders may from time to time deem necessary, but not exceeding twenty thousand dollars, for the sole purpose of owning, leasing, constructing, maintaining and operating the line or lines of telephone hereby authorized. And said corporation may purchase, hold, lease, sell and convey real estate and personal property necessary and incidental to the purposes contemplated in this charter, and may issue its coupon or registered bonds as provided for telegraph and telephone companies organized under general law. ^{Capital stock.}

Section 6. Any one of the corporators named in this act may call the first meeting of this corporation, by mailing a written notice to each of the other corporators, seven days at least before the day of meeting, naming the time, place and purposes of such meeting; and at such meeting a president, secretary, treasurer, directors and other necessary officers may be chosen, by-laws adopted, and any corporate business transacted. ^{First meeting, how called.}

Section 7. This act shall take effect when approved.

Approved March 28, 1903.

Chapter 411.

An Act relating to the election of a Road Commissioner in the Town of Boothbay Harbor.

Be it enacted by the Senate and House of Representatives in Legislature assembled, as follows:

Tenure of road commissioner.

Section 1. The town of Boothbay Harbor is authorized at its next annual meeting, and thereafterwards, to fix the tenure of office of the road commissioner by it elected at not less than one nor more than five years. When the town fails to elect such officer and the selectmen have the power of appointment, as provided by general law, such appointment may be made for a term not exceeding five years as they may determine.

—selectmen may appoint when town fails to elect.

Section 2. This act shall take effect when approved.

Approved March 28, 1903.

Chapter 412.

An Act to incorporate the Tyler-Fogg Trust Company.

Be it enacted by the Senate and House of Representatives in Legislature assembled, as follows:

Corporators.

Section 1. Hiram H. Fogg, Linwood C. Tyler, Herbert A. Fogg, Frederick W. Hill, Charles H. Wood and Edward Wood, or such of them as may by vote accept this charter, with their associates, successors and assigns, are hereby made a body corporate and politic to be known as the Tyler-Fogg Trust Company, and as such shall be possessed of all the powers, privileges and immunities and subject to all the duties and obligations conferred on corporations by law.

—corporate name.

Location.

Section 2. The corporation hereby created shall be located at Bangor, Penobscot county, Maine; and may also establish a branch or agency in Brewer in said county.

Purposes.

Section 3. The purposes of said corporation, and the business which it may perform, are: first, to receive on deposit, money, coin, bank notes, evidences of debt, accounts of individuals, companies, corporations, municipalities and states, allowing interest thereon, if agreed, or as the by-laws of said corporation may provide; second, to borrow money, to loan money on credits, or real estate, or personal or collateral security, and to negotiate loans and sales for others; to guarantee the payment of the principal and interest of all obligations secured by mortgages of real estate running to said Tyler-Fogg Trust Company; third, to purchase, erect, own, maintain and operate safe deposit vaults,

—may own safe deposit boxes.

with boxes, safes and other facilities therein, to be rented to other parties for the safe keeping of moneys, securities, stocks, jewelry, plate, valuable papers and documents, and other property susceptible of being deposited therein, and to receive on deposit for safe keeping, property of any kind entrusted to it for that purpose; fourth, to hold and enjoy all such estate, real, personal and mixed, as may be obtained by the investment of its capital stock, or any other moneys and funds that may come into its possession in the course of its business and dealings, and the same sell, grant and dispose of; fifth, to act as agent for issuing, registering and countersigning certificates, bonds, stocks and all evidences of debt or ownership in property; sixth, to hold by grant, assignment, transfer, devise or bequest, any real or personal property or trusts duly created, and to execute trusts of every description; seventh, to act as executor, receiver, or assignee with the same powers and duties as are imposed by law upon natural persons acting in the same capacities, and subject to the same control of the court having jurisdiction of the same in all proceedings relating to the exercise of these powers; all papers may be signed and sworn to by any officer designated by the corporation for the purpose, and the officers shall be subject to citation and examination in the same manner and to the same extent as natural persons acting in the same capacities; no sureties shall be required upon the bond of the corporation when acting in said capacities unless the court or officer approving said bond shall require it; eighth, to hold for safe keeping all kinds of personal or mixed property, and to act as agents for the owners thereof, and of real estate for the collection of income on the same, and for the management and sale of the same; ninth, to do in general all the business that may lawfully be done by trust and banking companies.

—may execute trusts.

Section 4. The capital stock of said corporation shall not be less than fifty thousand dollars, divided into shares of one hundred dollars each, with the right to increase the said capital stock at any time, by vote of the shareholders, to any amount not exceeding five hundred thousand dollars. Said corporation shall not commence business as a trust or banking company, until stock to the amount of at least fifty thousand dollars shall have been subscribed and paid in, in cash.

Capital stock.

Section 5. Said corporation shall not make any loan or discount on the security of the shares of its own capital stock, nor be the purchaser or holder of any such shares unless necessary to prevent loss upon a debt previously contracted in good faith; and all stock so acquired shall, within six months from the time of its acquisition, be disposed of at public or private sale.

Shall not make loans on security of its own stock.

Board of directors.

Section 6. All the corporate powers of this corporation shall be exercised by a board of directors, who shall be residents of this state, whose number and term of office shall be determined by a vote of the shareholders at the first meeting held by the incorporators and at each annual meeting thereafter. The affairs and powers of the corporation may, at the option of the shareholders, be entrusted to an executive board of five members to be, by vote of the shareholders, elected from the full board of directors. The directors of said corporation shall be sworn to the proper discharge of their duties, and they shall hold office until others are elected and qualified in their stead. If a director dies, resigns, or becomes disqualified for any cause, the remaining directors may appoint a person to fill the vacancy until the next annual meeting of the corporation. The oath of office of such director shall be taken within thirty days of his election, or his office shall become vacant. The clerk of such corporation shall, within ten days, notify such directors of their election, and within thirty days shall publish the list of all persons who have taken the oath of office as directors.

—executive board.

Vacancies, how filled.

Board of Investment.

Section 7. The board of directors of said corporation shall constitute the board of investment of said corporation. Said directors shall keep in a separate book, specially provided for the purpose, a record of all loans, and investments of every description, made by said institution substantially in the order of time when such loans or investments are made, which shall show that such loans or investments have been made with the approval of the investment committee of said corporation, which shall indicate such particulars, respecting such loans or investments as the bank examiner shall direct. This book shall be submitted to the trustees or directors and to the bank examiner whenever requested. Such loans or investments shall be classified in the book as the bank examiner shall direct. No loan shall be made to any officer, or director of said banking or trust company except by the unanimous approval of the executive board in writing, and said corporation shall have no authority to hire money or to give notes unless by vote of the said board duly recorded.

—shall keep record of loans.

Director must own ten shares of stock.

Section 8. No person shall be eligible to the position of a director of said corporation who is not the actual owner of ten shares of the stock.

Reserve fund.

Section 9. Said corporation, after beginning to receive deposits, shall at all times, have on hand in lawful money, as a reserve, not less than fifteen per cent of the aggregate amount of its deposits which are subject to withdrawal on demand, provided, that in lieu of lawful money, two-thirds of said fifteen per cent may consist of balances, payable on demand, due from any national or state bank.

Section 10. All the property or money held in trust by this corporation shall constitute a special deposit and the accounts thereof and of said trust department shall be kept separate, and such funds and the investment or loans of them shall be specially appropriated to the security and payment of such deposits, and not be subject to any other liabilities of the corporation; and for the purpose of securing the observance of this proviso, said corporation shall have a trust department in which all business pertaining to such trust property shall be kept separate and distinct from its general business.

Trust funds shall constitute a special deposit.

Section 11. An administrator, executor, assignee, guardian or trustee, any court of law or equity, including courts of probate and insolvency, officers and treasurers of towns, cities, counties and savings banks of the state of Maine may deposit any moneys, bonds, stocks, evidences of debt or of ownership in property, or any personal property, with said corporation, and any of said courts may direct any person deriving authority from them to so deposit the same.

Administrators, etc., may deposit in.

Section 12. The shareholders of this corporation shall be individually responsible, equally and ratably, and not one for the other, for all contracts, debts and engagements of such corporation, to a sum equal to the amount of the par value of the shares owned by each in addition to the amount invested in said shares.

Responsibility of shareholders.

Section 13. Such corporation shall set apart as a guaranty fund not less than ten per cent of its net earnings in each and every year until such fund with the accumulated interest thereon, shall amount to one-fourth of the capital stock of said corporation.

Guaranty fund.

Section 14. The shares of said corporation shall be subject to taxation in the same manner and rate as are the shares of national banks.

Taxation.

Section 15. Said corporation shall be subject to examination by the bank examiner, who shall visit it at least once in every year, and as much oftener as he may deem expedient. At such visits he shall have free access to its vaults, books and papers, and shall thoroughly inspect and examine all the affairs of said corporation, and make such inquiries as may be necessary to ascertain its condition and ability to fulfill all its engagements. If upon examination of said corporation, the examiner is of the opinion that its investments are not in accordance with law, or said corporation is insolvent, or its condition is such as to render its further proceedings hazardous to the public or to those having funds in its custody, or is of the opinion that it has exceeded its powers or failed to comply with any of the rules or restrictions provided by law, he shall have such authority and take such

Shall be subject to examination by bank examiner.

action as is provided for in the case of savings banks by chapter forty-seven of the revised statutes. He shall preserve in a permanent form a full record of his proceedings, including a statement of the condition of said corporation. A copy of such statement shall be published by said corporation immediately after the annual examination of the same in some newspaper published where said corporation is established. If no paper is published in the town where said corporation is established, then it shall be published in a newspaper printed in the nearest city or town. The necessary expenses of the bank examiner while making such examination shall be paid by the corporation.

Section 16. Any five of the corporators named in this act may call the first meeting of the corporation by mailing a written notice, signed by all, postage paid, to each of the other corporators, seven days at least before the day of the meeting, naming the time, place and purpose of such meeting, and at such meeting the necessary officers may be chosen, by-laws adopted, and any other corporate business transacted.

Section 17. This act shall take effect when approved.

Approved March 28, 1903.

Chapter 413.

An Act to amend Section three of Chapter fifty of the Private and Special Laws of eighteen hundred and twenty-one as amended by Chapter one hundred and sixty-one of the Private and Special Laws of eighteen hundred and forty-eight, as amended by Chapter one hundred and seventy-one of the Private and Special Laws of eighteen hundred and sixty-two, relating to extending the time of controlling the water at the alewive fishery at Damariscotta Mills.

Be it enacted by the Senate and House of Representatives in Legislature assembled, as follows:

Section 1. Section three of chapter fifty of the private and special laws of eighteen hundred and twenty-one, as amended by chapter one hundred and sixty-one of the private and special laws of eighteen hundred and forty-eight, as amended by chapter one hundred and seventy-one of the private and special laws of eighteen hundred and sixty-two, is hereby further amended so that it shall be lawful for the joint fish committee of the towns of Nobleboro and Newcastle to control the water and sluiceways at the alewive fishery at Damariscotta Mills from the twentieth day of April to the fifteenth day of July in the years nineteen hundred and three and nineteen hundred and four; provided that said control in no way interferes with the rights which the Damariscotta Mills Water Power Company now have.

Section 2. This act shall take effect when approved.

Approved March 28, 1903.

Chapter 414.

An Act to enable the County of Sagadahoc to rebuild Merrymeeting Bay Bridge, accept Arrowsic Bridge, and to maintain both bridges free, to accept the Peoples' Ferry, and to acquire in conjunction with the County of Lincoln or town of Dresden the ferry between Richmond and Dresden, to operate the same and to reduce the tolls by at least one-half.

Be it enacted by the Senate and House of Representatives in Legislature assembled, as follows:

Section 1. Section five of chapter forty-two of the private and special laws of eighteen hundred and seventy-eight, is hereby repealed. *Section 5, chapter 42, private and special laws of 1878, repealed.*

Section 2. The county commissioners of Sagadahoc county are authorized and empowered to repair and rebuild the bridge over Merrymeeting Bay. *Repairs of Merrymeeting Bay bridge.*

Section 3. The town of Arrowsic may at any legal town meeting, called therefor by a majority vote, transfer and convey by gift to the county of Sagadahoc all the stock, franchises and property of the Arrowsic Bridge Company which shall thereupon vest in the county which is hereby authorized to accept and hold the same. *Arrowsic may transfer property of bridge company.*

Section 4. The city of Bath, through its city council, and the town of Woolwich at a legal town meeting called therefor, may by a majority vote transfer and convey by gift all its rights and interests in the franchises and property of the Peoples' Ferry Company with all the powers and privileges pertaining thereto subject to existing liabilities, to the county of Sagadahoc, the title to which shall thereupon vest in said county, and said county is hereby authorized to accept and hold the same for the purposes declared in the act of incorporation of said company. *Bath may transfer property of Peoples Ferry Co.*

Section 5. The county commissioners of Sagadahoc in conjunction with the town of Dresden or the county commissioners of the county of Lincoln may acquire possession of the ferry, between the town of Richmond and the town of Dresden on such terms as may be mutually agreed upon. *Acquisition of ferry by Sagadahoc and Lincoln counties.*

Section 6. From and after the acceptance of this act in the manner herein provided, the county of Sagadahoc is hereby authorized and empowered to maintain the Merrymeeting Bay bridge and the Arrowsic bridge free of tolls and the county commissioners of said county shall keep said bridges and approaches thereto in repair so that the same shall be safe and convenient for public travel. *Sagadahoc authorized to maintain bridges free of toll.*

Section 7. From and after the acceptance of this act in the manner herein provided, the county of Sagadahoc is hereby authorized and empowered to operate the Peoples' Ferry and to maintain the same and the property thereof in good condition, *Sagadahoc may operate Peoples' ferry.*

MERRYMEETING BAY BRIDGE.

CHAP. 414

and the county commissioners of said county are authorized and empowered to reduce the rate of tolls in force on the ferry aforesaid at the time of the passage of this act, by at least one-half.

Operation of ferry between Richmond and Dresden.

Section 8. The county of Sagadahoc is authorized and empowered to operate in conjunction with the county of Lincoln or the town of Dresden on such terms as may be mutually agreed upon and to maintain the same, the ferry between Richmond and Dresden, and to reduce the rate of tolls thereon in the same proportion as the rate herein established for the Peoples' ferry.

Sagadahoc may rebuild bridge, assume liabilities of Peoples ferry and part cost of ferry between Richmond and Dresden.

Section 9. The county commissioners of the county of Sagadahoc are authorized and empowered to defray the cost and outlay of repairing and rebuilding Merrymeeting Bay bridge, of assuming the ownership, interest and liabilities of Bath and Woolwich in the Peoples' ferry and of the cost apportioned to the county of Sagadahoc for the acquisition of the ferry between Richmond and Dresden in the manner herein provided for, by the issue of bonds of said county not exceeding the cost of executing the above specified purposes, made payable in not more than forty years from date, with annual interest not to exceed four per centum per annum, payable semi-annually, signed by the county treasurer and countersigned by said county commissioners, said bonds to be of such denominations as the county commissioners may deem advisable.

Maintenance of bridges and ferries provided for.

Section 10. From and after the acceptance of this act, as herein provided, the county commisisoners of the county of Sagadahoc shall include in their annual estimates of county taxes the sums necessary for the maintenance of the bridges aforesaid and for the operation and maintenance of the ferries aforesaid together with a sum equal to two per centum of the bonds issued in virtue of this act, which sum shall be set aside yearly, until with its past and prospective accretions, it shall be sufficient to provide for the payment of said bonds at maturity, and said sums and accretions shall constitute a sinking fund for the payment of said bonds, and shall be invested in such interest bearing securities as said commissioners shall approve or in such bonds, but shall not in any other manner be loaned to said county.

This act to be accepted by legal voters.

Section 11. No part of this act shall take effect unless and until it is accepted as a whole, by the legal voters of Sagadahoc county by a majority vote at meetings of the several towns and municipalities in said county, duly notified and warned, to be held on the first Monday in September next for the purpose of accepting or rejecting this act as a whole, at which meeting the vote shall be by ballot as follows: For rebuilding Merrymeeting Bay bridge, accepting the Arrowsic bridge and maintaining the two bridges free. Accepting the Peoples' Ferry and acquiring the ferry between Richmond and Dresden and maintaining and operating the same and reducing the tolls thereon by at least half, "yes," "no."

Section 12. The ballots shall be received, sorted and declared as votes for town officers are, and shall be recorded by the town and city clerks, and true copies thereof sealed and attested, shall be transmitted to the county commissioners of the county of Sagadahoc within six days. The commissioners shall open and declare the votes so returned by publishing the same in the Bath Independent and Enterprise in two issues of these papers. If errors appear in the returns they shall be corrected by the commissioners by proper evidence, and if a majority of the ballots returned have "ayes" upon them, it shall be deemed to be an acceptance of this act, and the same shall then be in force, but if there should be a majority of ballots with "no" thereon, it shall be deemed a rejection of the same.

Section 13. Before said meetings are called the county commissioners shall procure careful estimates by a competent and disinterested civil engineer of the entire cost of rebuilding Merrymeeting Bay bridge in a suitable manner, and of making the same and its approaches permanent and safe for public travel, and shall cause said estimates to be kept in their office at Bath open for public inspection for at least thirty days before the first Monday of September next.

Section 14. At a meeting in the city of Bath to be held under the provisions hereof, the check lists used at the March nineteen hundred and three municipal election, or copies thereof certified by the city clerk, shall be used. The board of registration shall be in session only on the day of said meeting, and any person legally qualified to vote at said meeting, whose name shall not be found upon said lists, may receive a certificate of his qualification from said board, and shall thereupon be permitted by the proper ward officers to cast his ballot as if his name were on said list. The vote in said city shall be by open ballot.

Section 15. If this act shall be accepted by the voters of Sagadahoc county as provided in section eleven, all acts and parts of acts inconsistent with this act shall thereby be repealed.

Section 16. This act shall take effect when approved.

Approved March 28, 1903.

Chapter 415.

An Act to annex certain Islands in Casco Bay to the County of Sagadahoc and the town of Phippsburg.

Be it enacted by the Senate and House of Representatives in Legislature assembled, as follows:

Islands annexed to Phippsburg.

Section 1. Bushy, Hen, Bear, Malaga, Burnt Coat, Blacksnake, Wood, Little Wood, Gooseberry, Flag, Mark, East Brown and Cow islands are hereby made and declared to be part of the county of Sagadahoc and of the town of Phippsburg therein.

Section 2. This act shall take effect when approved.

Approved March 28, 1903.

Chapter 416.

An Act for the assessment of a State Tax for the year one thousand nine hundred and three, amounting to the sum of nine hundred seventy thousand four hundred seventy-five dollars and seventy-seven cents.

Be it enacted by the Senate and House of Representatives in Legislature assembled, as follows:

Section 1. That each city, town, plantation, or any other place hereinafter named, within this state, shall be assessed and pay the several sums with which they respectively stand charged in the following lists; the same being in addition to the poll tax of one cent on each poll, a tax of two and three-fourths mills on the dollar of the present valuation for the current disbursements of the treasury, for the year nineteen hundred and three and for the school mill fund established by an act approved February twenty-seven, eighteen hundred and seventy-two.

State tax, 1903.

ANDROSCOGGIN COUNTY.

Auburn	Nineteen thousand seven hundred ten dollars and twenty cents	$19,710 20
Durham	Nine hundred seven dollars and forty-six cents	907 46
East Livermore	Two thousand six hundred twelve dollars and seventy-two cents	2,612 72
Greene	Eight hundred seven dollars and four cents	807 04
Leeds	Eight hundred forty-two dollars and ninety-three cents	842 93
Lewiston	Thirty-eight thousand six hundred twenty-five dollars and forty-three cents	38,625 43
Lisbon	Five thousand seven hundred twenty-four dollars and seventy-nine cents	5,724 79
Livermore	One thousand two hundred forty dollars and four cents	1,240 04
Mechanic Falls	Two thousand four hundred one dollars and ninety-seven cents	2,401 97
Minot	Nine hundred twenty-three dollars and fifty-two cents	923 52
Poland	Two thousand one hundred ninety-three dollars and forty-four cents	2,193 44
Turner	One thousand nine hundred one dollars and fifty-two cents	1,901 52
Wales	Five hundred thirty-five dollars and fifty-four cents	535 54
Webster	One thousand four hundred thirty-two dollars and four cents	1,432 04
Total	Seventy-nine thousand eight hundred fifty-eight dollars and sixty-four cents	$79,858 64

AROOSTOOK COUNTY.

Amity	One hundred eighty-five dollars and thirty-four cents	$185 34
Ashland	One thousand one hundred three dollars and thirty-six cents	1,103 36
Bancroft	One hundred fifty-two dollars and forty cents	152 40
Benedicta	One hundred fifty-nine dollars and forty-five cents	159 45
Blaine	Four hundred thirty-five dollars and twenty cents	435 20
Bridgewater	Eight hundred seventy-one dollars and eight cents	871 08

AROOSTOOK COUNTY—Continued.

Caribou	Three thousand eight hundred twenty dollars and thirty-seven cents	3,820 37
Crystal	Two hundred thirty-six dollars and two cents	236 02
Dyer Brook	Two hundred forty-one dollars and seventy-four cents	241 74
Easton	Seven hundred twenty-eight dollars and thirty cents	728 30
Fort Fairfield	Three thousand five hundred eighty-five dollars and forty-five cents	3,585 45
Fort Kent	Seven hundred thirty-six dollars and seventeen cents	736 17
Frenchville	Three hundred twenty-eight dollars and thirty-eight cents	328 38
Grand Isle	Three hundred thirty-nine dollars and eighty-six cents	339 86
Haynesville	One hundred eighty-three dollars and seventy-three cents	183 73
Hersey	One hundred sixty-two dollars and thirty cents	162 30
Hodgdon	Seven hundred twenty-nine dollars and forty-three cents	729 43
Houlton	Six thousand four hundred fifty-two dollars and two cents	6,452 02
Island Falls	Seven hundred four dollars and seventy-nine cents	704 79
Limestone	Nine hundred twenty-two dollars and thirty-four cents	922 34
Linneus	Six hundred seventy-seven dollars and sixty-three cents	677 63
Littleton	Eight hundred seventy-eight dollars and eleven cents	878 11
Ludlow	Three hundred thirty-four dollars and one cent	334 01
Madawaska	Five hundred forty-seven dollars and twenty-six cents	$547 26
Mapleton	Five hundred ninety-two dollars and ninety-five cents	592 95
Mars Hill	Seven hundred forty-four dollars and fourteen cents	744 14
Masardis	Three hundred one dollars and eighty-eight cents	301 88
Monticello	Nine hundred forty-four dollars and sixty-two cents	944 62
New Limerick	Four hundred eighty-eight dollars and eighty-three cents	488 83
New Sweden	Four hundred thirty-five dollars and twenty cents	435 20
Oakfield	Two hundred eighty-four dollars and fifty-two cents	284 52
Orient	One hundred thirty dollars and ninety-one cents	130 91
Perham	Three hundred thirty-one dollars and eighty-seven cents	331 87
Presque Isle	Three thousand nine hundred seventy-one dollars and thirty-eight cents	3,971 38

STATE TAX.

AROOSTOOK COUNTY—Concluded.

Saint Agatha	Two hundred seventy-one dollars and forty-seven cents	271 47
Sherman	Five hundred twenty-seven dollars and eighteen cents	527 18
Smyrna	Three hundred fourteen dollars and fifty-six cents	314 56
Van Buren	Seven hundred eight dollars and ninety cents	708 90
Washburn	Six hundred ninety-four dollars and nineteen cents	694 19
Weston	One hundred sixty-nine dollars and nineteen cents	169 19
Woodland	Five hundred thirty-five dollars and eighty-four cents	535 84
Cary Pl.	Eighty-four dollars and ninety-seven cents	84 97
Castle Hill Pl.	Two hundred ninety dollars and fifteen cents	290 15
Caswell Pl.	One hundred thirty-one dollars and eighty-four cents	131 84
Chapman Pl.	One hundred seventy-three dollars and fifty-five cents	173 55
Connor Pl.	One hundred fifty-three dollars and twenty-nine cents	153 29
Cyr Pl.	One hundred forty-seven dollars and nineteen cents	$147 19
Eagle Lake Pl.	One hundred thirty-one dollars and sixty-five cents	131 65
Hamlin Pl.	Two hundred eleven dollars and four cents	211 04
Macwahoc Pl.	One hundred nineteen dollars and sixty-five cents	119 65
Merrill Pl.	Two hundred fourteen dollars and eighty-four cents	214 84
Moro Pl.	One hundred thirty-seven dollars and seventy-eight cents	137 78
New Canada Pl.	Ninety-five dollars and ninety-six cents	95 96
Reed Pl.	Three hundred forty-six dollars and forty-two cents	346 42
St. Francis Pl.	One hundred thirty-seven dollars and four cents	137 04
St. John Pl.	One hundred sixteen dollars and eleven cents	116 11
Silver Ridge Pl.	One hundred ten dollars and forty-nine cents	110 49
Wade Pl.	One hundred sixty-one dollars and thirty-three cents	161 33
Wallagrass Pl.	One hundred thirty-eight dollars and eighty cents	138 80
Westfield Pl.	Two hundred forty-five dollars and sixty-four cents	245 64
Total	Thirty-nine thousand one hundred ten dollars and eleven cents	$39,110 11

Chap. 416

632

CHAP. 416

STATE TAX.

AROOSTOOK COUNTY WILD LANDS.

A, R. 2, W. E. L. S....	Eighty-six dollars and eleven cents......	$86 11
B, R. 2, W. E. L. S., Hammond	Two hundred forty-two dollars and forty-four cents	242 44
C, R. 2, W. E. L. S....	One hundred ninety-six dollars and ninety-eight cents	196 98
D, R. 2, W. E. L. S....	One hundred ninety-one dollars and ninety-five cents	191 95
E, R. 2, W. E. L. S....	One hundred twenty-two dollars and forty-five cents	122 45
No. 3, R. 2, W. E. L. S., Forkstown	Two hundred two dollars and thirteen cents	202 13
Cox Patent	Nine dollars and sixty-three cents.......	9 63
No. 2, R. 3, W. E. L. S., Glenwood	One hundred twenty-one dollars...........	121 00
No. 3, R. 3, W. E. L. S.	One hundred eighty-one dollars and eighty-three cents	181 83
No. 4, R. 3, W. E. L. S.	One hundred six dollars and five cents...	106 05
No. 7, R. 3, W. E. L. S., Dudley	One hundred ninety-six dollars and ninety-eight cents	196 98
No. 8, R. 3, W. E. L. S.	One hundred ninety-six dollars and ninety-eight cents	196 98
No. 9, R. 3, W. E. L. S.	Two hundred twelve dollars and fourteen cents	212 14
No. 10, R. 3, W. E. L. S.	Two hundred forty-two dollars and forty-four cents	242 44
No. 16, R. 3, W. E. L. S., Stockholm	Two hundred twenty dollars and forty cents	220 40
No. 17, R. 3, W. E. L. S., N. ½	Sixty-three dollars and sixty-two cents..	63 62
No. 17, R. 3, W. E. L. S., S. ½	Sixty-three dollars and sixty-two cents..	63 62
No. 1, R. 4, W. E. L. S. Yarmouth Academy.	One hundred seventy-four dollars and thirty-nine cents	174 39
No. 2, R. 4, W. E. L. S.	Two hundred twelve dollars and fourteen cents	212 14
No. 3, R. 4, W. E. L. S.	Two hundred twelve dollars and fourteen cents	212 14
No. 7, R. 4, W. E. L. S., Webbertown	Three hundred three dollars and five cents	303 05
No. 8, R. 4, W. E. L. S., St. Croix	One hundred ninety-six dollars and ninety-eight cents	196 98
No. 9, R. 4, W. E. L. S., Griswold	Two hundred twelve dollars and fourteen cents	212 14
No. 10, R. 4, W. E. L. S., N. E. ¼, Squawpan...	Thirty-seven dollars and eighty-eight cents	37 88
No. 10, R. 4, W. E. L. S., S. ½ & N. W. ¼. Squawpan	One hundred forty-seven dollars and seventy-three cents	147 73
No. 11, R. 4, W. E. L. S., S. W. ¼	Twenty-two dollars and seventy-three cents	22 73
No. 11, R. 4, W. E. L. S., N. ½ & S. E. ¼.......	One hundred twenty-five dollars..........	$125 00
No. 15, R. 4, W. E. L. S., Westmanland Pl.....	One hundred eighty-one dollars and eighty-three cents	181 83
No. 16, R. 4, W.E.L.S..	One hundred eighty-one dollars and eighty-three cents	181 83
No. 17, R. 4, W.E.L.S., N. ½	Twenty-two dollars and seventy-three cents	22 73
No. 17, R. 4, W.E.L.S., S. ½	Sixty-eight dollars and nineteen cents...	68 19
A, R. 5, N. part, W.E.L.S. Molunkus	Ninety-five dollars and four cents.........	95 04

STATE TAX. 633

CHAP. 416

AROOSTOOK COUNTY WILD LANDS—Continued.

A, R. 5, S. part, W.E.L.S., Molunkus	Sixty-two dollars and ninety-eight cents	62 98
No. 1, R. 5, W.E.L.S.	One hundred sixty-six dollars and sixty-eight cents	166 68
No. 7, R. 5, W.E.L.S.	One hundred ninety-six dollars and ninety-eight cents	196 98
No. 8, R. 5, W.E.L.S.	One hundred fifty-nine dollars and twelve cents	159 12
No. 9, R. 5, W.E.L.S.	One hundred twenty-one dollars and forty-four cents	121 44
No. 13, R. 5, W.E.L.S.	One hundred twenty-one dollars and twenty-two cents	121 22
No. 14, R. 5, W.E.L.S.	One hundred eighty-one dollars and eighty-three cents	181 83
No. 15, R. 5, W.E.L.S.	One hundred sixty-six dollars and sixty-eight cents	166 68
No. 16, R. 5, W.E.L.S.	Ninety dollars and ninety-one cents	90 91
No. 17, R. 5, W.E.L.S.	Eighty-two dollars and sixty cents	82 60
No. 9, R. 6, W.E.L.S., Oxbow	One hundred thirty-seven dollars and fifty cents	137 50
No. 10, R. 6, W.E.L.S., N. ½	Ninety-one dollars	91 00
No. 10, R. 6, W.E.L.S., S. ½	Sixty dollars and sixty-six cents	60 66
No. 11, R. 6, W.E.L.S., Garfield Pl.	Two hundred seven dollars and thirty-six cents	207 36
No. 12, R. 6, W.E.L.S., Nashville	One hundred eighty-one dollars and eighty-three cents	181 83
No. 13, R. 6, W.E.L.S., Portage Lake Pl.	One hundred thirty-six dollars and twelve cents	136 12
No. 14, R. 6, W.E.L.S.	One hundred sixty-six dollars and sixty-eight cents	166 68
No. 15, R. 6, W.E.L.S.	One hundred sixty-six dollars and sixty-eight cents	166 68
No. 16, R. 6, W.E.L.S.	Ninety-one dollars and eight cents	91 08
No. 9, R. 7, W.E.L.S.	One hundred eighty-two dollars and sixteen cents	182 16
No. 10, R. 7, W.E.L.S.	One hundred eighty-one dollars and eighty-three cents	181 83
No. 11, R. 7, W.E.L.S., E. ½	Eighty-three dollars and thirty-four cents	$83 34
No. 11, R. 7, W.E.L.S., W. ½	Eighty-three dollars and thirty-four cents	83 34
No. 12, R. 7, W.E.L.S.	One hundred sixty-six dollars and sixty-eight dollars	166 68
No. 13, R. 7, W.E.L.S., Pine & Spruce Timber	Ninety dollars and ninety-one cents	90 91
Land and other growth	Ninety dollars and ninety-one cents	90 91
No. 14, R. 7, W.E.L.S.	One hundred eighty-one dollars and eighty-three cents	181 83
No. 15, R. 7, W.E.L.S., Winterville	One hundred fifty-one dollars and eighty cents	151 80
No. 9, R. 8, W.E.L.S.	One hundred forty-nine dollars and thirteen cents	149 13
No. 10, R. 8, W.E.L.S.	One hundred eighty-six dollars and fifty-eight cents	186 58
No. 11, R. 8, W.E.L.S.	One hundred fifty-five dollars and ten cents	155 10
No. 12, R. 8, W.E.L.S.	One hundred fifty-five dollars and ninety-two cents	155 92
No. 13, R. 8, W.E.L.S.	One hundred fifty-five dollars and twenty-five cents	155 25
No. 14, R. 8, W.E.L.S.	One hundred fifty-one dollars and forty-eight cents	151 48
No. 15, R. 8, W.E.L.S., N. ½	Sixty-four dollars and forty-six cents	64 46
No. 15, R. 8, W.E.L.S., S. ½	Sixty-four dollars and forty-six cents	64 46

CHAP. 416

AROOSTOOK COUNTY WILD LANDS—Continued.

No. 10, R. 8, W.E.L.S..	One hundred thirty-eight dollars and eighty-nine cents	138 89
No. 11, R. 9, W.E.L.S..	One hundred seventy-four dollars and forty-four cents	174 44
No. 12, R. 9, W.E.L.S..	One hundred fifty-five dollars and thirty-nine cents	155 39
No. 13, R. 9, W.E.L.S..	One hundred fifty-two dollars and nine cents	152 09
No. 14, R. 9, W.E.L.S..	One hundred thirty-four dollars and sixty-six cents	134 66
No. 15, R. 9, W.E.L.S..	One hundred twenty-nine dollars and seventy-four cents	129 74
No. 16, R. 9, W.E.L.S..	One hundred fifty-three dollars and fifty-nine cents	153 59
No. 11, R. 10, W.E.L.S.	One hundred eighty-two dollars and sixty-seven cents	182 67
No. 12, R. 10, W.E.L.S.	One hundred twenty-nine dollars and ninety-eight cents	129 98
No. 13, R. 10, W.E.L.S.	One hundred forty-two dollars and twenty-eight cents	142 28
No. 14, R. 10, W.E.L.S.	One hundred forty dollars and five cents	140 05
No. 15, R. 10, W.E.L.S.	One hundred twenty-two dollars and thirteen cents	122 13
No. 16, R. 10, W.E.L.S.	Eighty-two dollars and thirty-one cents..	82 31
No. 17, R. 10, W.E.L.S.	Fifty dollars and eighty-two cents........	50 82
No. 18, R. 10, W.E.L.S.	One hundred twenty-two dollars and ninety-four cents	122 94
No. 11, R. 11, W.E.L.S.	One hundred sixty-seven dollars and five cents	167 05
No. 12, R. 11, W.E.L.S.	One hundred fifty-three dollars and nine cents	$153 09
No. 13, R. 11, W.E.L.S.	One hundred twenty-five dollars and sixteen cents	125 16
No. 14, R. 11, W.E.L.S., N. ½	Sixty-nine dollars and sixty-five cents...	69 65
No. 14, R. 11, W.E.L.S., S. ½	Sixty-one dollars and ninety-one cents...	61 91
No. 15, R. 11, W.E.L.S., N. ½	Fifty-two dollars and sixty-eight cents	52 68
No. 15, R. 11, W.E.L.S., S. ½	Fifty-two dollars and sixty-eight cents	52 68
No. 16, R. 11, W.E.L.S.	Eighty-eight dollars and ninety-eight cents	88 98
No. 17, R. 11, W.E.L.S.	One hundred five dollars and twenty-eight cents	105 28
No. 18, R. 11, W.E.L.S.	One hundred twenty-one dollars and seventy-six cents	121 76
No. 19, R. 11, W.E.L.S.	One hundred forty-five dollars and thirty-eight cents	145 38
No. 11, R. 12, W.E.L.S.	One hundred fifty-two dollars and seventy-three cents	152 73
No. 12, R. 12, W.E.L.S.	One hundred thirty-seven dollars and ninety-seven cents	137 97
No. 13, R. 12, W.E.L.S.	One hundred twenty-two dollars and thirty-eight cents	122 38
No. 14, R. 12, W.E.L.S.	One hundred twenty-two dollars.........	122 00
No. 15, R. 12, W.E.L.S.	One hundred thirty-two dollars and ninety-three cents	132 93
No. 16, R. 12, W.E.L.S.	Ninety dollars and forty-one cents	90 41
No. 17, R. 12, W.E.L.S.	One hundred twenty-one dollars and twenty cents	121 20
No. 18, R. 12, W.E.L.S., N. E. ¼	Thirty dollars and forty-three cents.....	30 43
No. 18, R. 12, W.E.L.S., W. ½	Sixty dollars and eighty-six cents........	60 86
No. 18, R. 12, W.E.L.S., S. E. ¼	Thirty dollars and forty-three cents.....	30 43
No. 19, R. 12, W.E.L.S.	One hundred forty-two dollars and eight cents	142 08
No. 20, R. 11 & 12, W. E. L. S..............	One hundred eighty-nine dollars and eighteen cents	189 18

STATE TAX.

AROOSTOOK COUNTY WILD LANDS—Concluded.

No. 11, R. 13, W.E.L.S.	One hundred fifty-two dollars and seventy-five cents	152 75
No. 12, R. 13, W.E.L.S.	One hundred twenty-one dollars and seventy-five cents	121 75
No. 13, R. 13, W.E.L.S.	One hundred thirty-seven dollars and fifty-two cents	137 52
No. 14, R. 13, W.E.L.S.	One hundred six dollars and thirty-four cents	106 34
No. 15, R. 13, W.E.L.S.	One hundred twenty-one dollars	121 00
No. 16, R. 13, W.E.L.S.	One hundred six dollars and six cents	106 06
No. 17, R. 13, W.E.L.S.	One hundred seven dollars and thirty-one cents	107 31
No. 18, R. 13, W.E.L.S.	One hundred ten dollars and twenty-eight cents	110 28
No. 11, R. 14, W.E.L.S.	One hundred fifty-one dollars and seventeen cents	$151 17
No. 12, R. 14, W.E.L.S., E. ½	Sixty-one dollars and eleven cents	61 11
No. 12, R. 14, W.E.L.S., W. ½	Sixty-one dollars and eleven cents	61 11
No. 13, R. 14, W.E.L.S.	One hundred twenty-three dollars and eighteen cents	123 18
No. 14, R. 14, W.E.L.S.	One hundred forty-nine dollars and fifty-four cents	149 54
No. 15, R. 14, W.E.L.S.	One hundred twenty dollars and seventy cents	120 70
No. 16, R. 14, W.E.L.S.	One hundred fifty-six dollars and eighty-five cents	156 85
No. 17, R. 14, W.E.L.S.	Seventy-two dollars and ninety-six cents	72 96
No. 11, R. 15, W.E.L.S., E. ½	Sixty-eight dollars and twenty-eight cents	68 28
No. 11, R. 15, W.E.L.S., W. ½	Sixty-eight dollars and twenty-nine cents	68 29
No. 12, R. 15, W.E.L.S.	One hundred six dollars and twenty-nine cents	106 29
No. 13, R. 15, W.E.L.S.	One hundred seven dollars and thirteen cents	107 13
No. 14, R. 15, W.E.L.S.	One hundred seventeen dollars and twenty-eight cents	117 28
No. 15, R. 15, W.E.L.S.	One hundred four dollars and two cents	104 02
No. 11, R. 16, W.E.L.S.	Ninety dollars and ninety-two cents	90 92
No. 12, R. 16, W.E.L.S.	Ninety dollars and ninety-one cents	90 91
No. 13, R. 16, W.E.L.S.	One hundred seventy dollars and ten cents	170 10
No. 14, R. 16, W.E.L.S.	Eighty-one dollars and eleven cents	81 11
No. 11, R. 17, W.E.L.S.	One hundred thirty-seven dollars and fifty cents	137 50
No. 12, R. 17, W.E.L.S.	Ninety-four dollars and seventy-five cents	94 75
Total	Seventeen thousand three hundred nineteen dollars and forty-nine cents	$17,319 49

AROOSTOOK COUNTY—TIMBER AND GRASS ON RESERVED LANDS.

A, R. 2, W. E. L. S.	Three dollars and seventy-one cents	$3 71
C, R. 2, W. E. L. S.	Seven dollars and fifty-six cents	7 56
D, R 2, W. E. L. S.	Seven dollars and ninety-seven cents	7 97
No. 3, R. 3, W.E.L.S.	Five dollars and eighty cents	5 80
No. 4, R. 3, W.E.L.S.	Three dollars and eight cents	3 08
No. 7, R. 3, W.E.L.S.	Seven dollars and twenty-six cents	7 26
No. 8, R. 3, W.E.L.S.	Seven dollars and twenty-six cents	7 26

CHAP. 416

AROOSTOOK COUNTY—TIMBER AND GRASS—Continued.

No. 9, R. 3, W.E.L.S..	Seven dollars and fifty-six cents............	7 56
No. 10, R. 3, W.E.L.S..	Nine dollars and sixty-three cents........	9 63
No. 17, R. 3, W.E.L.S..	Four dollars and eighty-one cents.........	4 81
No. 1, R. 4, W.E.L.S..	Six dollars and sixty cents.................	6 60
No. 2, R. 4, W.E.L.S..	Seven dollars and ninety-two cents........	7 92
No. 3, R. 4, W.E.L.S..	Eight dollars and twenty-five cents........	8 25
No. 7, R. 4, W.E.L.S..	Twelve dollars and thirty-eight cents....	12 38
No. 8, R. 4, W.E.L.S..	Seven dollars and fifty-six cents...........	7 56
No. 9, R. 4, W.E.L.S..	Eight dollars and twenty-five cents........	8 25
No. 10, R. 4, W.E.L.S..	Seven dollars and fifty-six cents...........	7 56
No. 11, R. 4, W.E.L.S..	Six dollars and eighty-seven cents.........	6 87
No. 16, R. 4, W.E.L.S..	Six dollars and eighty-seven cents.........	6 87
No. 17, R. 4, W.E.L.S..	Three dollars and nine cents................	3 09
No. 1, R. 5, W.E.L.S..	Six dollars and sixty cents..................	6 60
No. 7, R. 5, W.E.L.S..	Seven dollars and fifty-six cents...........	7 56
No. 8, R. 5, W.E.L.S..	Six dollars and nineteen cents..............	6 19
No. 9, R. 5, W.E.L.S..	Four dollars and thirteen cents............	4 13
No. 13, R. 5, W.E.L.S..	Four dollars and thirteen cents............	4 13
No. 14, R. 5, W.E.L.S..	Six dollars and eighty-eight cents.........	6 88
No. 15, R. 5, W.E.L.S..	Six dollars and nineteen cents..............	6 19
No. 16, R. 5, W.E.L.S..	Two dollars and seventy-five cents........	2 75
No. 17, R. 5, W.E.L.S..	Two dollars and seventy-five cents........	2 75
No. 10, R. 6, W.E.L.S..	Five dollars and fifty cents.................	5 50
No. 14, R. 6, W.E.L.S..	Six dollars and nineteen cents..............	6 19
No. 15, R. 6, W.E.L.S..	Six dollars and nineteen cents..............	6 19
No. 16, R. 6, W.E.L.S..	Two dollars and seventy-five cents........	2 75
No. 9, R. 7, W.E.L.S..	Six dollars and eighty-seven cents.........	6 87
No. 10, R. 7, W.E.L.S..	Six dollars and eighty-eight cents.........	6 88
No. 11, R. 7, W.E.L.S..	Six dollars and eighteen cents..............	6 18
No. 12, R. 7, W.E.L.S..	Six dollars and eighteen cents..............	6 18
No. 13, R. 7, W.E.L.S..	Two dollars and seventy-five cents........	2 75
No. 14, R. 7, W.E.L.S..	Six dollars and eighty|eight cents.........	6 88
No. 9, R. 8, W.E.L.S..	Five dollars and fifty cents.................	5 50
No. 10, R. 8, W.E.L.S..	Six dollars and eighty|eight cents.........	6 88
No. 11, R. 8, W.E.L.S..	Five dollars and fifty cents.................	5 50
No. 12, R. 8, W.E.L.S..	Five dollars and fifty cents.................	5 50
No. 13, R. 8, W.E.L.S..	Five dollars and fifty cents.................	5 50
No. 14, R. 8, W.E.L.S..	Five dollars and fifty cents.................	5 50
No. 15, R. 8, W.E.L.S..	Four dollars and eighty-one cents.........	4 81
No. 16, R. 8, W.E.L.S..	Four dollars and eighty-one cents.........	4 81
No. 11, R. 9, W.E.L.S..	Six dollars and nineteen cents..............	6 19
No. 12, R. 9, W.E.L.S..	Five dollars and fifty cents.................	5 50

STATE TAX.

CHAP. 416

AROOSTOOK COUNTY—TIMBER AND GRASS—Continued.

No. 13, R. 9, W.E.L.S.	Five dollars and fifty cents...............	5 50
No. 14, R. 9, W.E.L.S.	Four dollars and eighty-one cents........	4 81
No. 15, R. 9, W.E.L.S.	Four dollars and eighty-one cents........	4 81
No. 16, R. 9, W.E.L.S.	Four dollars and eighty-one cents........	4 81
No. 11, R. 10, W.E.L.S.	Six dollars and nineteen cents.............	6 19
No. 12, R. 10, W.E.L.S.	Four dollars and thirteen cents............	4 13
No. 13, R. 10, W.E.L.S.	Four dollars and eighty-one cents........	4 81
No. 14, R. 10, W.E.L.S.	Four dollars and eighty-one cents........	4 81
No. 15, R. 10, W.E.L.S.	Four dollars and thirteen cents............	4 13
No. 18, R. 10, W.E.L.S.	Five dollars and twenty cents.............	5 20
No. 11, R. 11, W.E.L.S.	Six dollars and nineteen cents.............	6 19
No. 12, R. 11, W.E.L.S.	Five dollars and fifty cents................	5 50
No. 13, R. 11, W.E.L.S.	One dollars and thirty-eight cents.........	1 38
No. 14, R. 11, W.E.L.S.	Four dollars and eighty-one cents........	4 81
No. 15, R. 11, W.E.L.S.	Three dollars and forty-three cents.......	3 43
No. 18, R. 11, W.E.L.S.	Four dollars and thirteen cents............	4 13
No. 19, R. 11, W.E.L.S.	Four dollars and thirteen cents............	4 13
No. 20, R. 11 & 12, W. E. L. S.	Five dollars and fifteen cents..............	5 15
No. 11, R. 12, W.E.L.S.	Five dollars and fifty cents................	5 50
No. 12, R. 12, W.E.L.S.	Four dollars and eighty-one cents.........	$4 81
No. 13, R. 12, W.E.L.S.	Four dollars and twelve cents.............	4 12
No. 14, R. 12, W.E.L.S.	Four dollars and twelve cents.............	4 12
No. 15, R. 12, W.E.L.S.	Four dollars and eighty-one cents.........	4 81
No. 16, R. 12, W.E.L.S.	Two dollars and seventy-five cents.......	.2 75
No. 17, R. 12, W.E.L.S.	Four dollars and twelve cents.............	4 12
No. 18, R. 12, W.E.L.S.	Four dollars and twelve cents.............	4 12
No. 19, R. 12, W.E.L.S.	Four dollars and thirteen cents............	4 13
No. 11, R. 13, W.E.L.S.	Five dollars and fifty cents................	5 50
No. 12, R. 13, W.E.L.S.	Four dollars and thirteen cents............	4 13
No. 13, R. 13, W.E.L.S.	Four dollars and eighty-one cents.........	4 81
No. 14, R. 13, W.E.L.S.	Three dollars and forty-four cents........	3 44
No. 15, R. 13, W.E.L.S.	Four dollars and thirteen cents............	4 13
No. 16, R. 13, W.E.L.S.	Three dollars and forty-four cents........	3 44
No. 17, R. 13, W.E.L.S.	Three dollars and forty-four cents........	3 44
No. 18, R. 13, W.E.L.S.	Four dollars and thirteen cents............	4 13
No. 11, R. 14, W.E.L.S.	Five dollars and fifty cents................	5 50
No. 12, R. 14, W.E.L.S.	Four dollars and thirteen cents............	4 13
No. 13, R. 14, W.E.L.S.	Four dollars and thirteen cents............	4 13
No. 14, R. 14, W.E.L.S.	Five dollars and fifty cents................	5 50
No. 15, R. 14, W.E.L.S.	Three dollars and seventy-nine cents.....	3 79
No. 16, R. 14, W.E.L.S.	Four dollars and thirteen cents............	4 13
No. 17, R. 14, W.E.L.S.	Three dollars and nine cents..............	3 09

AROOSTOOK COUNTY—TIMBER AND GRASS—Concluded.

No. 11, R. 15, W.E.L.S.	Four dollars and eighty-one cents.........	4 81
No. 12, R. 15, W.E.L.S.	Three dollars and forty-four cents........	3 44
No. 13, R. 15, W.E.L.S.	Three dollars and forty-four cents........	3 44
No. 14, R. 15, W.E.L.S.	Four dollars and thirteen cents............	4 13
No. 15, R. 15, W.E.L.S.	Three dollars and forty-four cents........	3 44
No. 11, R. 16, W.E.L.S.	Two dollars and seventy-five cents........	2 75
No. 12, R. 16, W.E.L.S.	Two dollars and seventy-five cents........	2 75
No. 13, R. 16, W.E.L.S.	Five dollars and sixteen cents.............	5 16
No. 14, R. 16, W.E.L.S.	Three dollars and sixty cents..............	3 60
No. 11, R. 17, W.E.L.S.	Four dollars and thirteen cents............	4 13
No. 12, R. 17, W.E.L.S.	Two dollars and seventy-five cents........	2 75
Total	Five hundred twenty-five dollars and thirty-two cents	$535 32

CUMBERLAND COUNTY.

Baldwin	Nine hundred seventy-seven dollars and eleven cents	$977 11
Bridgton	Three thousand seven hundred twenty-five dollars and eleven cents...............	3,725 11
Brunswick	Ten thousand nine hundred forty-one dollars and five cents	10,941 05
Cape Elizabeth	One thousand nine hundred fifteen dollars and forty-five cents	1,915 45
Casco	Seven hundred fifty-seven dollars and twenty-seven cents......................	757 27
Cumberland	Two thousand one hundred forty-one dollars and fifty-nine cents	2,141 59
Falmouth	Three thousand fifty-five dollars and twenty-four cents	3,055 24
Freeport	Three thousand two hundred twenty-nine dollars and six cents	3,229 06
Gorham	Four thousand ninety-six dollars and thirty-three cents	4,096 33
Gray	One thousand five hundred thirty-eight dollars and eighty-three cents............	1,538 83
Harpswell	One thousand nine hundred ninety-two dollars and fifty-nine cents.............	1,992 59
Harrison	One thousand one hundred thirty-one dollars and twenty-four cents............	1,131 24
Naples	Six hundred ninety-eight dollars and seventy-eight cents	698 78
New Gloucester	Two thousand nine hundred seventeen dollars and sixteen cents	2,917 16
North Yarmouth	Eight hundred ninety-five dollars and fifty-eight cents ....:	895 58
Otisfield	Six hundred forty-nine dollars and sixty-seven cents	649 67
Portland	One hundred thirty-five thousand two hundred two dollars and eighteen cents	135,202 18
Pownal	Seven hundred eight dollars and thirty-six cents	708 36

STATE TAX. CHAP. 416

CUMBERLAND COUNTY—Concluded.

Raymond	Five hundred fifty-two dollars and thirty cents	552 30
Scarborough	Two thousand six hundred eighty-three dollars and one cent	2,683 01
Sebago	Four hundred forty-one dollars and twenty-two cents	441 22
South Portland	Seven thousand one hundred forty-eight dollars and five cents	7,148 05
Standish	One thousand six hundred thirty-nine dollars and eighty-seven cents	$1,639 87
Westbrook	Ten thousand nine hundred ninety-nine dollars and sixty-two cents	10,999 62
Windham	Two thousand six hundred twenty-two dollars and ninety-four cents	2,622 94
Yarmouth	Three thousand six hundred thirty-nine dollars and eighty-two cents	3,639 82
Total	Two hundred six thousand two hundred ninety-nine dollars and forty-three cents	$206,299 43

FRANKLIN COUNTY.

Avon	Three hundred sixty-four dollars and seventy-seven cents	$364 77
Carthage	Three hundred forty-seven dollars and sixty-one cents	347 61
Chesterville	Six hundred eighty-one dollars and eighty-four cents	681 84
Eustis	Four hundred eleven dollars and thirty-nine cents	411 39
Farmington	Five thousand two hundred twenty-three dollars and ninety-three cents	5,223 93
Freeman	Two hundred sixty-eight dollars and fourteen cents	268 14
Industry	Two hundred eighty-three dollars and twenty-eight cents	283 28
Jay	Four thousand five hundred three dollars and twenty-five cents	4,503 25
Kingfield	Nine hundred ninety-three dollars and thirty-two cents	993 32
Madrid	Two hundred twenty-one dollars and seventy-four cents	221 74
New Sharon	One thousand fifteen dollars and ninety-five cents	1,015 95
New Vineyard	Four hundred forty-six dollars and fifty-four cents	446 54
Phillips	One thousand four hundred eighty-six dollars and eighty-two cents	1,486 82
Rangeley	One thousand twenty-one dollars and ninety-eight cents	1,021 98
Salem	One hundred thirty dollars and sixteen cents	130 16
Strong	Seven hundred ten dollars and fifty-nine cents	710 59
Temple	Three hundred forty-eight dollars and twenty-three cents	348 23
Weld	Five hundred sixty dollars and seventy-six cents	560 76
Wilton	Two thousand ninety-one dollars and sixty-eight cents	2,091 68
Total	Twenty-one thousand one hundred eleven dollars and ninety-eight cents	$21,111 98

FRANKLIN COUNTY WILD LANDS.

No. 4, Washington Pl..	Eleven dollars	$11 00
No. 2, R. 1, S. part Sandy River, W. B. K. P...	Ninety-two dollars and forty cents........	92 40
No. 2, R. 1, N. part Greenvale Pl., W. B. K. P.	Sixty-six dollars	66 00
No. 3, R. 1, Rangeley Pl., W. B. K. P.......	Five hundred thirty-nine dollars..........	539 00
No. 4, R. 1, B. K. P., "Elias Thomas Tract", Mt. Abram	Eighteen dollars and twenty-three cents..	18 23
No. 4, R. 1, B. K. P., N. E. part, "Mead Tract" Mt. Abram	Ninety-five dollars and fifty-four cents...	95 54
No. 4, R. 2, B. K. P., Crockertown	Two hundred forty-two dollars and forty-four cents	242 44
No. 4, R. 3, B. K. P., S. half, Wyman	One hundred seven dollars and sixty-one cents	107 61
D. R. 1..................	One hundred sixty-nine dollars and thirteen cents	169 13
No. 1, R. 2, W. B. K. P., Redington	Two hundred twelve dollars and fourteen cents	212 14
No. 2, R. 2, W. B. K. P., Dallas Pl.	Two hundred twelve dollars and fourteen cents	212 14
No. 1, R. 3, Coplin Pl., W. B. K. P.	One hundred eighty-one dollars and eighty-three cents	181 83
No. 2, R. 3, W. B. K. P., Lang Pl.	One hundred fifty-one dollars and fifty-two cents	151 52
No. 3, R. 3, W. B. K. P., Davis	Three hundred two dollars and fifty cents	302 50
No. 3, R. 2, B. K. P., Jerusalem	One hundred fifty-eight dollars and forty cents	158 40
No. 2, R. 4, W. B. K. P., Tim Pond	One hundred eighty-one dollars and eighty-three cents	181 83
No. 3, R. 4, W. B. K. P., Stetsontown	Two hundred thirteen dollars and seventy-seven cents	213 77
No. 1, R. 5, W. B. K. P., Jim Pond	Fifty-seven dollars and ninety-seven cents	57 97
No. 2, R. 5, W. B. K. P., Alder Stream	Two hundred twelve dollars and fourteen cents	212 14
No. 3, R. 5, W. B. K. P., Seven Ponds	Three hundred thirty-eight dollars and eighty cents	338 80
No. 1, R. 6, S. part W. B. K. P., Kibby	One hundred twenty-one dollars and twenty-two cents	121 22
No. 1, R. 6, N. part W. B. K. P., Kibby	One hundred eighty-two dollars and eighty-two cents	$182 82
No. 2, R. 6, W. B. K. P., Chain Pond	Two hundred six dollars and twenty-five cents	206 25
No. 3, R. 6, W. B. K. P., Mass. Gore	One hundred thirty dollars and forty-eight cents	130 48
No. 1, R. 7, W. B. K. P.	Two hundred twenty-two dollars and twenty cents	222 20
No. 2, R. 7, W. B. K. P., Merrill Strip	Seventy-six dollars and eighty-six cents...	76 86
No. 1, R. 8, W. B. K. P., Lowelltown	One hundred fifty dollars and eight cents	150 08

STATE TAX. 641

CHAP. 416

FRANKLIN COUNTY WILD LANDS—Concluded.

No. 2, R. 3, W. B. K. P., Beattie	One hundred fifty-four dollars	154 00
Gore north of Nos. 2 and 3, R. 6, Coburn	Ninety-six dollars and twenty-five cents	96 25
No. 6, N. of Weld & between Phillips and Byron, East part	One hundred twenty-eight dollars and twenty cents	128 20
No. 6, N. of Weld & between Phillips and Byron, West part	Seventy-five dollars and sixty-eight cents	75 68
Gore north of No. 1, R. 8	Seventy dollars and thirty-eight cents	70 38
Letter E	One hundred twenty dollars and twenty-six cents	120 26
Perkins	Forty-four dollars	44 00
Total	Five thousand three hundred forty-three dollars and seven cents	$5,343 07

FRANKLIN COUNTY—TIMBER AND GRASS ON RESERVED LANDS.

D., R. 1	Six dollars and sixty cents	$6 60
No. 1, R. 2, W. B. K. P.	Eight dollars and twenty-five cents	8 25
No 3, R. 3, W. B. K. P.	Thirteen dollars and twenty cents	13 20
No. 2, R. 4, W. B. K. P.	Six dollars and seventy-four cents	6 74
No. 3, R. 4, W. B. K. P.	Eight dollars and twenty-five cents	8 25
No. 1, R. 5, W. B. K. P.	One dollar and thirty-two cents	1 32
No. 2, R. 5, W. B. K. P.	Eight dollars and twenty-five cents	8 25
No. 3, R. 5, W. B. K. P.	Thirteen dollars and twenty cents	13 20
No. 1, R. 6, W. B. K. P.	Twelve dollars and eighty-three cents	12 83
No. 2, R. 6, W. B. K. P.	Six dollars and sixty cents	6 60
No. 3, R. 6, W. B. K. P.	Five dollars and thirty-nine cents	5 39
No 1, R. 7, W. B. K. P.	Nine dollars and sixty-two cents	9 62
No. 2, R. 7, W. B. K. P.	Two dollars and ninety-five cents	2 95
No 1, R. 8, W. B. K. P.	Five dollars and fifty cents	5 50
No 4, R. 1, B.P.W.K.R	Five dollars and twenty-eight cents	5 28
No. 3, R. 2, B.P.W.K.R.	Five dollars and twenty-eight cents	5 28
No. 4, R. 2, B.P.W.K.R.	Six dollars and sixty cents	6 60
No 4, R. 3, S. ½ B. P. W. K. R.	Four dollars and sixty-two cents	4 62
No. 6, North of Weld	Seven dollars and ninety-two cents	7 92
Tract north of No. 1, R. 3, W. B. K. P.	Two dollars and twelve cents	2 12
Total	One hundred forty dollars and fifty-two cents	$140 52

STATE TAX.

HANCOCK COUNTY.

Amherst	Two hundred twenty dollars and forty-eight cents	$220 48
Aurora	One hundred nine dollars and seven cents	109 07
Bluehill	One thousand five hundred thirteen dollars and seventy-eight cents	1,513 78
Brooklin	Five hundred eighteen dollars and thirty-eight cents	518 38
Brooksville	Six hundred thirty-two dollars and eighty-two cents	632 82
Bucksport	Two thousand six hundred seventy-four dollars and fifty-five cents	2,674 55
Castine	One thousand three hundred fifty-eight dollars and sixty cents	1,358 60
Cranberry Isles	Three hundred forty-eight dollars and ninety-seven cents	348 97
Deer Isle	One thousand thirty-nine dollars and sixty-eight cents	1,039 68
Dedham	Two hundred thirty-one dollars and thirty-one cents	231 31
Eastbrook	One hundred thirty-nine dollars and eighteen cents	139 18
Eden	Twelve thousand eight hundred sixty-seven dollars and fifty-six cents	12,867 56
Ellsworth	Five thousand two hundred thirty dollars and eighty-eight cents	5,230 88
Franklin	Nine hundred seven dollars and eighty-four cents	907 84
Gouldsboro	Eight hundred forty-nine dollars	849 00
Hancock	Eight hundred thirteen dollars and thirty-seven cents	813 37
Isle au Haut	One hundred ninety-five dollars and thirty-eight cents	195 38
Lamoine	Five hundred twelve dollars and twenty-eight cents	512 28
Mariaville	One hundred forty-one dollars and sixty-two cents	141 62
Mount Desert	Four thousand thirty-four dollars and twenty-one cents	4,034 21
Orland	Seven hundred forty dollars and ninety-three cents	740 93
Otis	Sixty-seven dollars and eighty-eight cents	67 88
Penobscot	Seven hundred thirty-eight dollars and seventy-seven cents	738 77
Sedgwick	Five hundred seventy-nine dollars and seventy cents	$579 70
Sorrento	Five hundred five dollars and forty-six cents	505 46
Stonington	Six hundred eighty-six dollars and ninety-four cents	686 94
Sullivan	Nine hundred twenty dollars and eleven cents	920 11
Surry	Four hundred sixty-eight dollars and ninety-five cents	468 95

STATE TAX. 643

CHAP. 416

HANCOCK COUNTY—Concluded.

Swan's Island	Three hundred eighty-six dollars and twenty-three cents	386 23
Tremont	One thousand four hundred eighty-six dollars and thirty-three cents	1,486 33
Trenton	Three hundred seventy-two dollars and seventy-six cents	372 76
Verona	One hundred seventy-nine dollars and ninety-five cents	179 95
Waltham	Two hundred two dollars and eighty-two cents	202 82
Winter Harbor	One thousand seven dollars and thirty-one cents	1,007 31
Long Island Pl.	Sixty one dollars and ninety-one cents	61 91
Total	Forty-two thousand seven hundred forty-five dollars and one cent	$42,745 01

HANCOCK COUNTY WILD LANDS.

No. 3, North Division	One hundred fifty-one dollars and fifty-three cents	$151 53
No. 4, North Division	One hundred fifty-one dollars and fifty-three cents	151 53
Strip N. of No. 3, N. Division	Fifty-three dollars and ninety-three cents	53 93
Strip N. of No. 4, N. Division	Fifty-three dollars and ninety-three cents	53 93
No. 7, South Div. N. part	Fifty-nine dollars and ninety-five cents	59 95
No. 7, South Div. S. part	Forty-five dollars and forty-six cents	45 46
No. 8, South Division	Thirty-nine dollars and sixty cents	39 60
No. 9, South Division	Nineteen dollars and eighty cents	19 80
No. 10	Ninety-four dollars and sixty-one cents	94 61
No. 16, Middle Division	Sixty dollars and sixty-one cents	60 61
No. 21, Middle Division Moose Hill	Sixty dollars and sixty-one cents	60 61
No. 22, Middle Division	Ninety dollars and ninety-two cents	90 92
No. 29, Middle Division	One hundred fifty-one dollars and fifty-two cents	151 52
No. 32, Middle Division	One hundred thirty-six dollars and thirty-seven cents	136 37
No. 33, Middle Division Great Pond	One hundred twenty-one dollars and twenty-two cents	121 22
No. 34, Middle Division	One hundred eighty-one dollars and eighty-three cents	181 83
No. 35, Middle Division	Seventy-five dollars and seventy-six cents	75 76
No. 39, Middle Division part of	One hundred five dollars and fifty-eight cents	105 58
No. 39, Middle Division "Black Tract, Tannery Lot"	Twenty-seven dollars and fifty cents	27 50
No. 40, Middle Division	One hundred fifty-one dollars and fifty-two cents	151 52
No. 41, Middle Division	Two hundred twelve dollars and fourteen cents	212 14
Butter Island	Seven dollars and seventy cents	7 70
Eagle Island	Thirteen dollars and seventy-five cents	13 75
Spruce Head & Bear Island	Two dollars and seventy-five cents	2 75

HANCOCK COUNTY WILD LANDS—Concluded.

Beach Island	One dollar and sixty-five cents	1 65
Hog Island	Four dollars and forty cents	4 40
Bradbury's Island	Three dollars and thirty cents	3 30
Pond, near Little Deer Isle	Fifty-five cents	55
Western Island	Fifty-five cents	55
Little Spruce Island	Sixty-nine cents	69
Marshall's Island	Thirteen dollars and seventy-five cents	13 75
Pickering's Island	Nine dollars and seven cents	9 07
Total	Two thousand one hundred four dollars and eight cents	$2,104 08

HANCOCK COUNTY--TIMBER AND GRASS ON RESERVED LANDS.

No. 3, North Division	Five dollars and twenty-eight cents	$5 28
No. 7, South Division	Forty-eight cents	48
No. 10	Two dollars and sixty-four cents	2 64
No. 16, Middle Division	One dollar and thirty-two cents	1 32
No. 22, Middle Division	Two dollars and sixty-four cents	2 64
No. 28, Middle Division	Five dollars and twenty-eight cents	5 28
No. 32, Middle Division	Four dollars and sixty-two cents	4 62
No. 34, Middle Division	Six dollars and sixty cents	6 60
No. 35, Middle Division	Two dollars and sixty-four cents	2 64
No. 39, Middle Division	Three dollars and thirty cents	3 30
No. 40, Middle Division	Five dollars and twenty-eight cents	5 28
No. 41, Middle Division	Seven dollars and ninety-two cents	7 92
Total	Forty-eight dollars	$48 00

KENNEBEC COUNTY.

Albion	One thousand twenty-four dollars and sixty-six cents	$1,024 66
Augusta	Twenty-one thousand nineteen dollars and eighty cents	21,019 80
Belgrade	One thousand one hundred ninety-eight dollars and ninety-three cents	1,198 93
Benton	One thousand two hundred thirty-eight dollars and twenty-one cents	1,238 21
Chelsea	Six hundred forty-two dollars and fifty-one cents	642 51
China	One thousand four hundred fifty-nine dollars and sixty-five cents	1,459 65
Clinton	One thousand six hundred twenty-seven dollars and ninety-eight cents	1,627 98
Farmingdale	One thousand six hundred two dollars and ten cents	1,602 10

STATE TAX.

KENNEBEC COUNTY—Concluded.

Fayette	Five hundred fifty-four dollars and ninety-eight cents	554 98
Gardiner	Nine thousand nine hundred thirty-one dollars and seventy-three cents	9,931 73
Hallowell	Four thousand one hundred twelve dollars and fifty-three cents	4,112 53
Litchfield	One thousand one dollars and forty-four cents	1,001 44
Manchester	Seven hundred nineteen dollars and twenty-one cents	719 21
Monmouth	One thousand eight hundred two dollars and fourteen cents	1,802 14
Mount Vernon	Eight hundred seventy-six dollars and forty-four cents	876 44
Oakland	Two thousand five hundred thirteen dollars and seventy-seven cents	2,513 77
Pittston	One thousand three hundred twenty dollars	1,320 00
Randolph	Eight hundred ninety-two dollars and four cents	892 04
Readfield	One thousand three hundred twenty-three dollars and fifty-three cents	1,323 53
Rome	Two hundred twenty-six dollars and ninety-one cents	226 91
Sidney	One thousand two hundred eight dollars and forty-two cents	1,208 42
Vassalborough	Two thousand six hundred forty-two dollars and twenty cents	2,642 20
Vienna	Three hundred thirty-eight dollars and fifty-two cents	338 52
Waterville	Sixteen thousand one hundred seventy-six dollars and fifty-six cents	16,176 56
Wayne	Six hundred dollars and eighty-three cents	600 83
West Gardiner	Eight hundred sixteen dollars and eighty-five cents	816 85
Windsor	Six hundred fifty dollars and thirty-nine cents	650 39
Winslow	Five thousand eight hundred thirty-nine dollars	5,839 00
Winthrop	Three thousand two hundred sixty-one dollars and five cents	3,261 05
Unity Pl.	Forty-seven dollars and twenty-eight cents	47 28
Total	Eighty-six thousand six hundred sixty-nine dollars and sixty-six cents	$86,669 66

KNOX COUNTY.

Appleton	Six hundred eighty-six dollars and twenty cents	$686 20
Camden	Six thousand two hundred ninety-one dollars and forty-eight cents	6,291 48
Cushing	Three hundred thirty-four dollars and fifty-five cents	334 55
Friendship	Six hundred six dollars	606 00

Chap. 416

KNOX COUNTY—Concluded.

Hope	Five hundred fifty-nine dollars and ninety cents	559 90
Hurricane Isle	One hundred thirty-eight dollars and seventy-three cents	138 73
North Haven	Six hundred sixty-one dollars and eighty-four cents	661 84
Rockland	Fifteen thousand one hundred fifty-seven dollars and eighty-nine cents	15,157 89
Rockport	Three thousand one hundred fifty-seven dollars and forty-four cents	3,157 44
So. Thomaston	One thousand twenty-eight dollars and forty-nine cents	1,028 49
St. George	One thousand one hundred thirty-three dollars and seventy-two cents	1,133 72
Thomaston	Three thousand five hundred ninety-nine dollars and ninety-two cents	3,599 92
Union	One thousand four hundred twenty-eight dollars and ninety-five cents	1,428 95
Vinalhaven	One thousand eight hundred nineteen dollars and seventy-one cents	1,819 71
Warren	Two thousand two hundred ninety-two dollars and sixty-nine cents	2,292 69
Washington	Seven hundred forty-four dollars and thirty-nine cents	744 39
Criehaven Pl.	Twenty-nine dollars and fifty-five cents	29 55
Matinicus Isle Pl.	One hundred three dollars and ninety-nine cents	103 99
Total	Thirty-nine thousand seven hundred seventy-five dollars and forty-four cents	$39,775 44

LINCOLN COUNTY.

Alna	Four hundred fifty-two dollars and forty-six cents	$452 46
Boothbay	One thousand five hundred forty-six dollars and thirty-five cents	1,546 35
Boothbay Harbor	Two thousand nine hundred nine dollars and six cents	2,909 06
Bremen	Three hundred eighty-two dollars and twenty-one cents	382 21
Bristol	Two thousand two hundred eighty-two dollars and forty-six cents	2,182 46
Damariscotta	One thousand two hundred fifty-eight dollars and three cents	1,258 03
Dresden	One thousand forty-one dollars and sixty-eight cents	1,041 68
Edgecomb	Four hundred ninety-two dollars and thirty-six cents	492 36
Jefferson	One thousand two hundred thirteen dollars and ninety-six cents	1,213 96
Newcastle	One thousand nine hundred one dollars and sixty-two cents	1,901 62
Nobleborough	Six hundred eighty-five dollars and forty-five cents	685 45

STATE TAX.

LINCOLN COUNTY—Concluded.

Somerville	One hundred forty dollars and forty-three cents	140 43
Southport	Eight hundred sixty-two dollars and thirty-two cents	862 32
Waldoboro	Two thousand five hundred forty dollars and sixty-two cents	2,540 62
Westport	Two hundred forty-four dollars and one cent	244 01
Whitefield	One thousand two hundred nineteen dollars and eighty-six cents	1,219 96
Wiscasset	One thousand three hundred eighteen dollars and sixty-seven cents	1,318 67
Monhegan Pl.	Ninety-four dollars and twenty-three cents	94 23
Total	Twenty thousand four hundred eighty-five dollars and seventy-eight cents	$20,485 78

OXFORD COUNTY.

Albany	Three hundred eighty-five dollars and eight cents	$385 08
Andover	Five hundred seventy-nine dollars and sixty-eight cents	579 68
Bethel	Two thousand three hundred fifty-nine dollars and twenty-six cents	2,359 26
Brownfield	Eight hundred fifty-five dollars and thirty-one cents	855 31
Buckfield	One thousand ninety-six dollars and fifty-seven cents	1,096 57
Byron	Two hundred forty-one dollars and ninety-seven cents	241 97
Canton	Nine hundred sixty-four dollars and eighty-seven cents	964 87
Denmark	Seven hundred ninety-two dollars and ninety-two cents	792 92
Dixfield	Nine hundred seventy-three dollars and ninety-four cents	973 94
Fryeburg	Two thousand two hundred thirty-seven dollars and twenty-one cents	2,237 21
Gilead	Three hundred sixty-one dollars and fifty-three cents	361 53
Grafton	One hundred sixty-two dollars and four cents	162 04
Greenwood	Four hundred sixty-three dollars and seventy-four cents	463 74
Hanover	Two hundred twenty dollars and seventy-two cents	220 72
Hartford	Seven hundred twenty dollars and twenty-four cents	720 24
Hebron	Six hundred twenty-five dollars and seventy-five cents	625 75
Hiram	Nine hundred sixty dollars and nine cents	960 09
Lovell	One thousand sixty-seven dollars and fifty-five cents	1,067 55

Chap. 416

OXFORD COUNTY—Concluded.

Mason	One hundred twenty-two dollars and fifty-one cents	122 51
Mexico	Nine hundred sixty dollars and fifty-seven cents	960 57
Newry	Three hundred twenty-seven dollars and forty-eight cents	327 48
Norway	Three thousand five hundred seventy dollars and eighty-nine cents	3,570 89
Oxford	One thousand two hundred thirty-five dollars and thirty-five cents	1,235 35
Paris	Three thousand seven hundred twenty-five dollars and thirty-three cents	3,725 33
Peru	Six hundred sixty-nine dollars and sixty cents	669 60
Porter	Six hundred fifty-two dollars and sixty-one cents	652 61
Roxbury	One hundred seventy-six dollars and fourteen cents	176 14
Rumford	Seven thousand five hundred eighty-one dollars and ninety-nine cents	7,581 99
Stoneham	Two hundred forty dollars and twenty-two cents	240 22
Stow	Three hundred thirty-seven dollars and nineteen cents	337 19
Sumner	Six hundred sixty-four dollars and fifty cents	664 50
Sweden	Four hundred eighteen dollars and eighty-seven cents	418 87
Upton	Two hundred eighty-six dollars and eighty-four cents	286 84
Waterford	Eight hundred six dollars and seven cents	806 07
Woodstock	Six hundred one dollars and forty-one cents	601 41
Milton Pl.	One hundred fifty-four dollars and forty-one cents	154 41
Total	Thirty-seven thousand six hundred dollars and forty-five cents	$37,600 45

OXFORD COUNTY WILD LANDS.

Fryeburg Acad. Grant	Forty-nine dollars and fifty cents	$49 50
A, 1, Riley Pl	Two hundred sixty nine dollars and fifty cents	269 50
Andover North Surplus	One hundred fifty-three dollars and sixty-two cents	153 62
Andover West Surplus	Sixty-four dollars and sixty-nine cents	64 69
C	Two hundred eighty-nine dollars and seventy-seven cents	289 77
C Surplus	One hundred fifty-one dollars and five cents	151 05
No. 4, R. 1, Richardsontown	Three hundred twenty-two dollars and eighty-five cents	322 85
No. 5, R. 1, Magalloway Pl.	Three hundred thirty-eight dollars and three cents	338 03

STATE TAX. 649

CHAP. 416

OXFORD COUNTY WILD LANDS—Concluded.

No. 4, R. 2, Adamstown	Six hundred seven dollars and twenty cents	607 20
No. 5, R. 2, Lincoln Pl.	Two hundred thirty-five dollars and ninety-eight cents	235 98
No. 4, R. 3, Lower Cupsuptic	Three hundred seventy-five dollars and thirty-seven cents	375 37
No. 5, R. 3, Parkertown	Two hundred thirty-four dollars and twenty-seven cents	234 27
No. 4, R. 4, Upper Cupsuptic	Two hundred seventy-three dollars and twenty-four cents	273 24
No. 5, R. 4, Lynchtown	Two hundred fifty-eight dollars and twenty-four cents	258 24
No. 4, R. 5, Oxbow	One hundred ninety-one dollars and four cents	191 04
No. 4, R. 6, Bowmantown	Two hundred dollars and forty-six cents	200 46
No. 5, R. 5, Parmachenee	Two hundred seven dollars and eighty-nine cents	207 59
Bachelder's Grant	One hundred thirty-seven dollars and fifty cents	137 50
Total	Four thousand three hundred sixty dollars and twenty cents	$4,360 20

OXFORD COUNTY—TIMBER AND GRASS ON RESERVED LANDS.

C. R. ., ... K. P.	Eleven dollars and eighty-eight cents	$11 88
No. 4, R. 1, W. B. K. P.	Eleven dollars and eighty-eight cents	11 88
No. 4, R. 2, W. B. K. P.	Twenty-three dollars and seventy-six cents	23 76
No. 4, R. 3, W. B. K. P.	Fifteen dollars and eighty-four cents	15 84
No. 5, R. 3, W. B. K. P.	Eight dollars and fifty-eight cents	8 58
No. 4, R. 4, W. B. K. P.	Ten dollars and fifty-six cents	10 56
No. 5, R. 4, W. B. K. P.	Nine dollars and twenty-four cents	9 24
No. 4, R. 5, W. B. K. P.	Seven dollars and ninety-two cents	7 92
No. 5, R. 5, W. B. K. P.	Seven dollars and ninety-two cents	7 92
No. 4, R. 6, W. B. K. P.	Eight dollars and twenty-five cents	8 25
Tract north of No. 4, R. 6, W. B. K. P.	Thirty-five cents	35
A, R. 1, (Riley)	Seven dollars and ninety-two cents	7 92
Andover, North Surplus	Three dollars and ninety-six cents	3 96
C. Surplus	Seven dollars and four cents	7 04
Total	One hundred thirty-five dollars and ten cents	$135 10

PENOBSCOT COUNTY.

Alton	Two hundred thirteen dollars and two cents	$213 02
Argyle	One hundred sixty one dollars and sixty-seven cents	161 67
Bangor	Forty-five thousand one hundred thirty-five dollars and twenty cents	45,135 20
Bradford	Six hundred ninety-two dollars and seventy-three cents	692 73
Bradley	Four hundred twenty dollars and seventeen cents	420 17
Brewer	Five thousand fifty-three dollars and thirty-two cents	5,053 32
Burlington	Three hundred ninety-three dollars and sixty-one cents	393 61
Carmel	Eight hundred six dollars and seventy-four cents	806 74
Carroll	Three hundred one dollars and seventy-five cents	301 75
Charleston	Eight hundred nineteen dollars and seventy-two cents	819 72
Chester	One hundred ninety-one dollars and ninety-one cents	191 91
Clinton	One hundred fifty-seven dollars and twenty-seven cents	157 27
Corinna	One thousand two hundred sixty-two dollars and fifty-three cents	1,262 53
Corinth	One thousand one hundred fifty-eight dollars and forty seven cents	1,158 47
Dexter	Three thousand three hundred two dollars and fifty-eight cents	3,302 58
Dixmont	Six hundred ninety-six dollars and six cents	696 06
Eddington	Four hundred thirty-five dollars and twenty-nine cents	435 29
Edinburg	Sixty-six dollars and five cents	66 05
Enfield	Six hundred forty-three dollars and forty-seven cents	643 47
Etna	Three hundred fifty-four dollars and eighty-one cents	354 81
Exeter	Nine hundred thirty-nine dollars and fifty-four cents	939 54
Garland	Eight hundred seventy dollars and forty-seven cents	870 47
Glenburn	Three hundred sixty-eight dollars and ninety-nine cents	365 99
Greenbush	Two hundred thirty dollars and fifty-seven cents	$230 57
Greenfield	One hundred fifteen dollars and twenty cents	115 20
Hampden	One thousand nine hundred sixteen dollars and forty-nine cents	1,916 49
Hermon	One thousand three dollars and twenty-three cents	1,003 23
Holden	Four hundred twenty-two dollars and fifteen cents	422 15

STATE TAX.

CHAP. 416

PENOBSCOT COUNTY Concluded.

Howland	Eight hundred forty-six dollars and seventy-four cents	846 74
Hudson	Two hundred ninety-three dollars and forty-nine cents	293 49
Levant	Four hundred sixty dollars and seventy cents	460 70
Lincoln	Four hundred sixty-four dollars and seventy-four cents	464 74
Lowell	Five hundred twenty-four dollars and eighty-three cents	524 83
Mattamiscontis	Three hundred fifty-eight dollars and thirty-one cents	358 31
Mattawamkeag	Six hundred seventy-four dollars and nineteen cents	674 19
Kenduskeag	One thousand three hundred forty-five dollars and thirty-five cents	1,345 35
Kingman	Two hundred dollars and twenty cents	200 20
Lagrange	Fifty-one dollars and ninety-six cents	51 96
Lee	Three hundred seventy-three dollars and forty-three cents	373 43
Maxfield	Seventy-one dollars and thirty-eight cents	71 38
Medway	One hundred seventy-three dollars and ninety-four cents	173 94
Milford	Eight hundred forty-seven dollars and ninety-four cents	847 94
Millinocket	One thousand nine hundred dollars and ninety-eight cents	1,900 98
Mount Chase	One hundred sixty seven dollars and seventy-six cents	167 76
Newburgh	Seven hundred thirteen dollars and ninety-three cents	713 93
Newport	One thousand six hundred forty-five dollars and seventeen cents	1,645 17
Old Town	Four thousand nine hundred twenty-two dollars and sixty-four cents	$4,922 64
Orono	Two thousand seven hundred ten dollars and twenty-five cents	2,710 25
Orrington	One thousand one hundred forty-five dollars and sixty-two cents	1,145 62
Passadumkeag	One hundred twenty-six dollars and seventy-two cents	126 72
Patten	One thousand three hundred fifty-three dollars and eighty-six cents	1,353 86
Plymouth	Four hundred sixty-eight dollars and eighty-five cents	468 85
Prentiss	Two hundred seven dollars and sixty-five cents	207 65
Springfield	Three hundred eighteen dollars and forty-seven cents	318 47
Stetson	Five hundred seventy-eight dollars and sixty-one cents	578 61
Veazie	Seven hundred eighteen dollars and seventy-two cents	718 72
Winn	Four hundred thirty seven dollars	437 00
Woodville	One hundred thirty-nine dollars and ten cents	139 10
Total	Ninety-two thousand three hundred seventy-five dollars and fifty-four cents	$92,375 54

652
CHAP. 416

STATE TAX.

PENOBSCOT COUNTY WILD LANDS.

No. 3, R. 1, N. B. P. P. East part	One hundred eighteen dollars and eighty cents	$118 80
No. 3, R. 1, N. B. P. P. West part	Fifty-eight dollars and eighty-five cents..	58 85
No. 4, R. 1, N. B. P. P. Lakeville Pl.	Two hundred fifty-four dollars any thirty-eight cents	254 38
No. 5, R. 1, N. B. P. P.	Sixty dollars and sixty-one cents	60 61
No. 6, R. 3, N. B. P. P. Webster Pl.	Eighty-six dollars and sixty-two cents	86 62
No. 7, R. 4, N. B. P. P. Drew Pl.	One hundred sixty-two dollars and eighty cents	162 80
No. 2, R. 8, N. W. P.	Two hundred seventy-seven dollars and forty-eight cents	277 48
No. 6, R. 8, N. W. P., E. half Seboeis Pl.	Eighty-three dollars and thirty-four cents	83 34
No. 3, R. 8, N. W. P., W. half Seboeis Pl.	Eighty-three dollars and thirty-four cents	83 34
No. 2, R. 9, N. W. P.	One hundred seventy-one dollars and twenty-seven cents	171 27
No. 3, R. 9, N. W. P., Eastern Division	Fifty-eight dollars and fifty-one cents	58 51
No. 3, R. 9, N. W. P., Middle Division	Sixty-eight dollars and eleven cents	68 11
No. 3, R. 9, N. W. P., Westerly part	Seventy dollars and ninety-seven cents	70 97
No. 1, R. 6, W. E. L. S.	One hundred twenty-one dollars	121 00
No. 2, R. 6, W. E. L. S., Hersey town	Two hundred eighty-five dollars and sixty-five cents	285 65
No. 3, R. 6, W. E. L. S., Stacyville Pl.	One hundred seventy-three dollars and twenty-five cents	173 25
No. 6, R. 6, W. E. L. S.	One hundred six dollars and seven cents	106 07
No. 7, R. 6, W. E. L. S.	One hundred eighteen dollars and ninety-one cents	118 91
No. 8, R. 6, W.E.L.S., N.½	Ninety one dollars and eight cents	91 08
No. 8, R. 6, W.E.L.S., S.½	Ninety-one dollars and eight cents	91 08
A. R. 7, W. E. L. S.	One hundred twenty-nine dollars and fifty-three cents	129 53
No. 1, R. 7, W. E. L. S.	Two hundred twenty-two dollars and thirty cents	222 30
No. 2, R. 7, W. E. L. S., Soldiertown	One hundred eighty-one dollars and eighty-three cents	181 83
No. 3, R. 7, W. E. L. S., S. part	Eighty-one dollars and seven cents	81 07
No. 3, R. 7, W. E. L. S., N. part	Sixty-nine dollars and seventy-six cents..	69 76
No. 4, R. 7, W. E. L. S., N. ½	Sixty dollars and sixty-one cents	$60 61
No. 4, R. 7, W. E. L. S., S. ½	Ninety dollars and ninety-one cents	90 91
No. 5, R. 7, W. E. L. S.	One hundred twenty-one dollars and twenty-two cents	121 22
No. 6, R. 7, W. E. L. S.	One hundred twenty-one dollars and twenty-two cents	121 22
No. 7, R. 7, W. E. L. S.	One hundred fifty-one dollars and fifty-two cents	151 52
No. 8, R. 7, W. E. L. S., N. half	Seventy-five dollars and seventy-six cents	75 76
No. 8, R. 7, W. E. L. S., S. W. ¼	Twenty-six dollars and fifty-one cents....	26 51

PENOBSCOT COUNTY WILD LANDS—Concluded.

No. 8, R. 7, W. E. L. S., S. E. ¼	Thirty-seven dollars and eighty-eight cents	37 88
East Hopkins Acad.	Thirty-eight dollars and twenty-two cents	38 22
West Hopkins Acad.	Forty-two dollars and five cents	42 05
No. 8, R. 8, W. E. L. S.	One hundred fifty-eight dollars and eighty-seven cents	158 87
A, R. 8 and 9, W.E.L.S., Long A	One hundred five dollars and fifty-three cents	105 53
A, R. 8 and 9, W.E.L.S., Veazie Gore	Six dollars and eighteen cents	6 18
No. 3, Indian purchase, W. E. L. S.	One hundred twenty-nine dollars and twenty-five cents	129 25
No. 4, Indian purchase, W. E. L. S.	One hundred forty-three dollars	143 00
No. 1, R. 8, W. E. L. S.	Ninety dollars and ninety-two cents	90 92
No. 2, R. 8, south half, W. E. L. S.	Eighty-three dollars and thirty-four cents	83 34
No. 2, R. 8, north half, W. E. L. S.	Eighty-three dollars and thirty-four cents	83 34
No. 3, R. 8, W. E. L. S.	One hundred fifty-one dollars and fifty-three cents	151 53
No. 4, R. 8, W. E. L. S.	Ninety dollars and ninety-two cents	90 92
No. 5, R. 8, W. E. L. S.	One hundred sixty-six dollars and sixty-eight cents	166 68
No. 6, R. 8, W. E. L. S., southeast quarter	Twenty-two dollars and seventy-three cents	22 73
No. 6, R. 8, W. E. L. S., west half	Sixty-eight dollars and nineteen cents	68 19
No. 6, R. 8, W. E. L. S., northeast quarter	Thirty-seven dollars and eighty-eight cents	37 88
No. 7, R. 8, W. E. L. S.	One hundred sixty-two dollars and fourteen cents	162 14
No. 1, North Division, Summit Pl.	One hundred twenty-one dollars and twenty-two cents	121 22
No. 2, North Division, Grand Falls Pl.	One hundred fifty-one dollars and fifty-three cents	151 53
Total	Five thousand seven hundred sixty-five dollars and seventy-six cents	$5,765 76

PENOBSCOT COUNTY—TIMBER AND GRASS ON RESERVED LANDS.

No. 1, R. 6, W. E. L. S.	Four dollars and thirteen cents	$4 13
No. 2, R. 6, W. E. L. S.	Eleven dollars	11 00
No. 6, R. 6, W. E. L. S.	Three dollars and forty-four cents	3 44
No. 7, R. 6, W. E. L. S.	Four dollars and twelve cents	4 12
No. 8, R. 6, W. E. L. S.	Six dollars and sixty cents	6 60
A, R. 7, W. E. L. S.	Four dollars and sixty-two cents	4 62
No. 1, R. 7, W. E. L. S.	Eight dollars and ninety-four cents	8 94
No. 2, R. 7, W. E. L. S.	Six dollars and sixty cents	6 60
No. 3, R. 7, W. E. L. S.	Five dollars and fifty cents	5 50
No. 4, R. 7, W. E. L. S.	Four dollars and thirteen cents	4 13
No. 5, R. 7, W. E. L. S.	Three dollars and ninety-two cents	3 92
No. 6, R. 7, W. E. L. S.	Four dollars and thirteen cents	4 13

PENOBSCOT COUNTY—TIMBER AND GRASS—Concluded.

No. 7, R. 7, W. E. L. S.	Five dollars and twenty-eight cents......	5 28
No. 8, R. 7, W. E. L. S.	Five dollars and fifty cents.............	5 50
A, R. 8 and 9, W.E.L.S.	Three dollars and forty-six cents........	3 46
No. 1, R. 8, W. E. L. S.	Four dollars and ninety-five cents........	4 95
No. 2, R. 8, W. E. L. S.	Five dollars and ninety-four cents........	5 94
No. 3, R. 8, W. E. L. S.	Five dollars and fifty cents..............	5 50
No. 4, R. 8, W. E. L. S.	Two dollars and seventy-five cents.......	2 75
No. 5, R. 8, W E L S.	Six dollars and nineteen cents............	6 19
No. 6, R. 8, W. E. L. S.	Four dollars and eighty-one cents........	4 81
No. 7, R. 8, W. E. L. S.	Six dollars and eighteen cents............	6 18
No. 8, R. 8, W. E. L. S.	Six dollars and eighteen cents............	6 18
No. 4, Indian Purchase, W. E. L. S.	Five dollars and fifty cents..............	5 50
No. 3, R. 1, N. B. P. P.	Five dollars and fifty cents..............	5 50
No. 5, R. 1, N. B. P. P.	One dollar and sixty-five cents...........	1 65
No. 2, R. 8, N. W. P...	Nine dollars and twenty-four cents........	9 24
No. 2, R. 9, N. W. P...	Four dollars and sixty-two cents.........	4 62
No. 3, R. 9, N. W. P...	Three dollars and ninety-six cents........	3 96
Hopkins Acad. Grant..	Two dollars and twenty cents.............	2 20
Total	One hundred fifty-six dollars and fifty-four cents	$156 54

PISCATAQUIS COUNTY.

Abbot	Four hundred seventy-one dollars and thirty-three cents	$471 33
Atkinson	Four hundred fourteen dollars and thirty-six cents	414 36
Blanchard	One hundred eighty-seven dollars and twelve cents	187 12
Brownville	One thousand two hundred eighteen dollars and eighty-one cents	1,218 81
Dover	Two thousand five hundred fifty-two dollars and sixty-six cents	2,552 66
Foxcroft	One thousand eight hundred twenty-eight dollars and fifty-nine cents........	1,828 59
Greenville	One thousand two hundred fifty-six dollars and twenty-six cents................	1,256 26
Guilford	One thousand six hundred fifty-two dollars and twenty-eight cents..............	1,652 28
Medford	One hundred ninety dollars and ninety-six cents	190 96
Milo	One thousand two hundred seventy-one dollars and forty-six cents...............	1,271 46
Monson	Six hundred seventy-two dollars and forty-nine cents	672 49
Orneville	Two hundred ninety dollars and fifty-nine cents	290 59
Parkman	Six hundred forty-nine dollars and nineteen cents	649 19

STATE TAX.

PISCATAQUIS COUNTY—Concluded.

Sangerville	One thousand four hundred fifty-nine dollars and fifty-six cents	1,459 56
Sebec	Four hundred fifty-three dollars and thirty-five cents	453 35
Shirley	Two hundred twenty-three dollars	223 00
Wellington	Two hundred sixty-five dollars and eighty-two cents	265 82
Williamsburg	One hundred seven dollars and twenty-two cents	107 22
Willimantic	Two hundred eighty-seven dollars and seventeen cents	287 17
Total	Fifteen thousand four hundred fifty-two dollars and twenty-two cents	$15,452 22

PISCATAQUIS COUNTY WILD LANDS.

No. 4, R. 8, N. W. P., south part Merrick Spool Co. Plant, Lakeview Pl.	One hundred sixty-five dollars	$165 00
No. 4, R. 8, N. W. P., E. ½ Lakeview Pl.	One hundred thirty-five dollars and forty-five cents	135 45
No. 4, R. 8, N. W. P., West part, Lakeview Pl.	Sixty-three dollars and thirteen cents	63 13
No. 6, R. 8, formerly Barnard Pl.	One hundred ten dollars and twenty-nine cents	110 29
No. 7, R. 8, formerly Bowerbank Pl.	Two hundred seventy-two dollars and seventy-four cents	272 74
No. 4, R. 9, N. W. P.	Two hundred twenty-seven dollars and twenty-nine cents	227 29
No. 5, R. 9, N. W. P.	Two hundred nine dollars and fifty-one cents	209 51
No. 6, R. 9, N. W. P., Katahdin Iron Works	Two hundred twenty-seven dollars and twenty-nine cents	227 29
No. 7, R. 9, N. W. P.	One hundred seventy dollars and thirty-nine cents	170 39
No. 8, R. 9, Elliottsville, N. W. P.	Two hundred sixty-one dollars and eleven cents	261 11
No. 1, R. 5, B.P.E.K.R., Little Squaw Town	Two hundred twelve dollars and fourteen cents	212 14
No. 1, R. 6, B.P.E.K.R., Big Squaw Town	Two hundred sixty-seven dollars and nine cents	267 09
No. 1, R. 9, W. E. L. S.	One hundred and twenty-one dollars and twenty-two cents	121 22
No. 2, R. 9, W. E. L. S.	One hundred fifty-one dollars and fifty-two cents	151 52
No. 3, R. 9, W. E. L. S., Mt. Katahdin	One hundred sixty-six dollars and sixty-eight cents	166 68
No. 4, R. 9, W. E. L. S.	Two hundred twenty-seven dollars and twenty-nine cents	227 29
No. 5, R. 9, W. E. L. S.	One hundred ninety-six dollars and seventy-seven cents	196 77
No. 6, R. 9, W. E. L. S., Trout Brook Town	Two hundred six dollars and thirteen cents	206 13
No. 7, R. 9, W. E. L. S., east half	Sixty dollars and forty-nine cents	60 49
No. 7, R. 9, W. E. L. S., west half	Seventy-five dollars and sixty-one cents	75 61

STATE TAX.

PISCATAQUIS COUNTY WILD LANDS—Continued.

No. 8, R. 9, W. E. L. S.	One hundred fifty-one dollars and twenty-three cents	151 23
No. 9, R. 9, W. E. L. S.	One hundred fifty-one dollars and three cents	151 03
No. 10, R. 9, W. E. L. S.	One hundred fifty-eight dollars and forty-five cents	158 45
A, R. 10, W. E. L. S.	One hundred fifty-one dollars and fifty-three cents	151 53
B, R. 10, W. E. L. S.	Ninety dollars and thirty-three cents	90 33
No. 1, R. 10, W. E. L. S.	One hundred fifty-one dollars and fifty-three cents	151 53
No. 2, R. 10, W. E. L. S.	One hundred fifty-one dollars and fifty-three cents	$151 53
No. 3, R. 10, W. E. L. S.	One hundred fifty-one dollars and fifty-three cents	151 53
No. 4, R. 10, W. E. L. S.	One hundred sixty-six dollars and sixty-eight cents	166 68
No. 5, R. 10, W. E. L. S., east half	Ninety-six dollars and sixty-three cents	96 63
No. 5, R. 10, N. W. fourth, W. E. L. S.	Fifty-five dollars and seventeen cents	55 17
No. 5, R. 10, S. W. fourth, W. E. L. S.	Thirty-two dollars and eighty-four cents	32 84
No. 6, R. 10, W. E. L. S.	One hundred seventy-one dollars and eighty-nine cents	171 89
No. 7, R. 10, W. E. L. S.	One hundred twenty-nine dollars and nineteen cents	129 19
No. 8, R. 10, W. E. L. S.	One hundred fifty-six dollars and forty-seven cents	156 47
No. 9, R. 10, W. E. L. S.	One hundred forty-two dollars and twenty-three cents	142 23
No. 10, R. 10, W. E. L. S.	One hundred eighty-four dollars and forty-seven cents	184 47
A, R. 11, W. E. L. S.	Two hundred twelve dollars and fourteen cents	212 14
B, R. 11, W. E. L. S.	Two hundred seventy-six dollars and fifty-nine cents	276 59
No. 1, R. 11, W. E. L. S.	One hundred eighty-one dollars and eighty-three cents	181 83
No. 2, R. 11, W. E. L. S., Rainbow Town	Two hundred twelve dollars and fourteen cents	212 14
No. 3, R. 11, W. E. L. S.	One hundred fifty-eight dollars and forty cents	158 40
No 4, R. 11, W. E. L. S.	One hundred eighty-three dollars and ninety-six cents	183 96
No. 5, R. 11, W. E. L. S.	Two hundred dollars and five cents	200 05
No. 6, R. 11, W. E. L. S.	One hundred fifty-one dollars and fifty-three cents	151 53
No. 7, R. 11, W. E. L. S.	One hundred fifty-six dollars and seventy-seven cents	156 77
No. 8, R. 11, W. E. L. S., N. E. ¼	Thirty-eight dollars and fifteen cents	38 15
No. 8, R. 11, W. E. L. S., W. ½ & S. E. ¼	One hundred thirty-seven dollars and thirty-two cents	137 32
No. 9, R. 11, W. E. L. S., N. ½	Ninety-one dollars and fifty-two cents	91 52
No. 9, R. 11, W. E. L. S., S. ½	Ninety-one dollars and fifty-two cents	91 52
No. 10, R. 11, W.E.L.S.	One hundred seventy-two dollars and twelve cents	172 12
No. 7, R. 10, N. W. P., Bowdoin College East	One hundred ninety-six dollars and ninety-eight cents	196 98
No. 8, R. 10, N. W. P., Bowdoin College West	Two hundred twelve dollars and fourteen cents	212 14
A, R. 12, W. E. L. S.	Two hundred thirty-seven dollars and thirty-three cents	237 33
No. 1, R. 12, W. E. L. S., N. two-thirds	One hundred sixteen dollars and sixteen cents	116 16
No. 1, R. 12, W. E. L. S., S. third	Sixty-three dollars and thirty-six cents	$63 36

STATE TAX. 657

CHAP. 416

PISCATAQUIS COUNTY WILD LANDS—Continued.

No. 2, R. 12, W.E.L.S.	One hundred ninety-six dollars and ninety-eight cents	196 98
No. 3, R. 12, W.E.L.S., E. half	Eighty-three dollars and thirty-four cents	83 34
No. 3, R. 12, W.E.L.S., W. half	Seventy-five dollars and seventy-six cents	75 76
No. 4, R. 12, W.E.L.S., E. half	One hundred six dollars and six cents....	106 06
No. 4, R. 12, W.E.L.S., W. half	Sixty-two dollars and fifty-seven cents...	62 57
No. 5, R. 12, W.E.L.S	One hundred ninety-two dollars and fifty-three cents	192 53
No. 6, R. 12, W.E.L.S.	One hundred seventy dollars and fifty-seven cents	170 57
No. 7, R. 12, W.E.L.S.	One hundred ninety-one dollars and forty-three cents	191 43
No. 8, R. 12, W.E.L.S.	Two hundred forty-three dollars and thirty-six cents	243 36
No. 9, R. 12, W.E.L.S., N. ½	Seventy-three dollars and fifty-one cents..	73 51
No. 9, R. 12, W.E.L.S., S. ½	Eighty eight dollars and twenty-one cents	88 21
No. 10, R. 12, W.E.L.S.	One hundred fifty-one dollars and eighteen cents	151 18
A, R. 13. W.E.L.S., Frenchtown	Three hundred ninety-three dollars and ninety-seven cents	393 97
A, 2, R. 13 and 14, W. E. L. S., Long "A"	One hundred sixty-five dollars and four cents	165 04
No. 1, R. 13, W.E.L.S.	Two hundred twenty-six dollars and thirty-eight cents	226 38
No. 2, R. 13, W.E.L.S.	One hundred fifty-six dollars and ninety-three cents	156 93
No. 3, R. 13, W.E.L.S.	One hundred sixty-four dollars and thirteen cents	164 13
No. 4, R. 13, W.E.L.S.	One hundred sixty-five dollars and thirty-one cents	165 31
No. 5, R. 13, W.E.L.S., Chesuncook	One hundred thirty-nine dollars and twenty-four cents	139 24
No. 6, R. 13, W.E.L.S.	Two hundred eleven dollars and six cents	211 06
No. 7, R. 13, W.E.L.S	Two hundred thirty-nine dollars and ninety-nine cents	239 99
No. 8, R. 13, W.E.L.S., Eagle Lake	One hundred eighty-eight dollars and thirty-nine cents	188 39
No. 9, R. 13, W.E.L.S.	Two hundred twelve dollars and sixteen cents	212 16
No. 10, R. 13, W.E.L.S.	One hundred sixty-eight dollars and twenty-eight cents	168 28
A, R. 14, W. E. L. S., Lily Bay	Three hundred twenty-four dollars and sixty-eight cents	324 68
No. 1, R. 14, W.E.L.S., North one-half, Spencer Bay	Eighty-eight dollars and thirty-seven cents	88 37
No. 1, R. 14, W.E.L.S., South one-half, Blake Town	Sixty-seven dollars and ninety-seven cents	$67 97
X, R. 14. W. E. L. S...	Forty-nine dollars and forty-one cents...	49 41
No. 3, R. 14 and 15, W. E. L. S., E. part......	One hundred forty-seven dollars and ninety-one cents	147 91
No. 3, R. 14 and 15, W. E. L. S., W. part......	Two hundred twenty-three dollars and sixty-five cents	223 65
No. 4, R. 14, W.E.L.S., S. E. ¼	Fifty-one dollars and twenty-seven cents	51 27

55

PISCATAQUIS COUNTY WILD LANDS—Concluded.

No. 4, R. 14, W.E.L.S., N. ½ & S. W. ¼	One hundred fifty-three dollars and seventy-nine cents	153 79
No. 5, R. 14, W.E.L.S.	One hundred ninety-four dollars and sixty cents	194 60
No. 6, R. 14, W.E.L.S.	Two hundred nineteen dollars and twenty-four cents	219 24
No. 7, R. 14, W.E.L.S., W. ½ & N. E. ¼	One hundred seventy-three dollars and ten cents	173 10
No. 7, R. 14, W.E.L.S., S. E. ¼	Fifty-three dollars and fifty-eight cents	53 58
No. 8, R. 14, W.E.L.S.	Two hundred three dollars and ninety-five cents	203 95
No. 9, R. 14, W.E.L.S.	One hundred seventy dollars and fifty-nine cents	170 59
No. 10, R. 14, W.E.L.S.	One hundred seventy-four dollars and eighty-seven cents	174 87
Sugar Island, W.E.L.S.	One hundred four dollars and fifty-six cents	104 56
Deer Island, W.E.L.S.	Forty-nine dollars and thirty-two cents	49 32
Middlesex Canal, W. E. L. S.	Two hundred twelve dollars and fourteen cents	212 14
Day's Acad. Grant, W. E. L. S.	One hundred forty-six dollars and ninety-eight cents	146 98
No. 4, R. 15, W.E.L.S.	One hundred sixty-eight dollars and eighty-four cents	168 84
No. 5, R. 15, W.E.L.S., N. W. ¼	Thirty-seven dollars and fifty-six cents	37 56
No. 5, R. 15, W.E.L.S., S. ½ & N. E. ¼	One hundred twelve dollars and sixty-seven cents	112 67
No. 6, R. 15, W.E.L.S.	One hundred eighty-six dollars and eighty-six cents	186 86
No. 7, R. 15, W.E.L.S., E. half	Ninety-seven dollars and twenty-five cents	97 25
No. 7, R. 15, W.E.L.S., W. half	Eighty-five dollars and ninety-seven cents	85 97
No. 8, R. 15, W.E.L.S.	One hundred seventy-one dollars and eighty-three cents	171 83
No. 9, R. 15, W.E.L.S.	One hundred seventy-three dollars and fifty-six cents	173 56
No. 10, R. 15, W.E.L.S.	One hundred fifty-three dollars and twenty-four cents	153 24
Moose Island	Six dollars and sixty cents	6 60
Kineo	Three hundred fifty-seven dollars and fifty cents	357 50
Farm Island, No. 3, R. 2, B.P.E.K.R.	Thirteen dollars and seventy-five cents	13 75
Kingsbury Pl.	Two hundred thirty-one dollars	231 00
Total	Seventeen thousand five hundred eighty-two dollars and ninety-seven cents	$17,582 97

PISCATAQUIS COUNTY—TIMBER AND GRASS ON RESERVED LANDS.

No. 2, R. 6, B.P.E.K.R.	Eleven dollars and eighty-eight cents	$11 88
No. 1, R. 9, W.E.L.S.	Six dollars and sixty cents	6 60
No. 2, R. 9, W.E.L.S.	Five dollars and fifty cents	5 50
No. 3, R. 9, W.E.L.S.	Six dollars and nineteen cents	6 19
No. 4, R. 9, W.E.L.S.	Eight dollars and ninety-four cents	8 94
No. 5, R. 9, W.E.L.S.	Seven dollars and fifty-six cents	7 56
No. 6, R. 9, W.E.L.S.	Seven dollars and fifty-six cents	7 56
No. 7, R. 9, W.E.L.S.	Four dollars and thirteen cents	4 13

STATE TAX.

CHAP. 416

PISCATAQUIS COUNTY—TIMBER AND GRASS—Continued.

No. 8, R. 9, W.E.L.S.,	Five dollars and fifty cents..................	5 50
No. 9, R. 9, W.E.L.S.,	Five dollars and fifty cents..................	5 50
No. 10, R. 9, W.E.L.S.	Five dollars and fifty cents..................	5 50
A, R. 10, W.E.L.S......	Five dollars and twenty-eight cents......	5 28
B, R. 10, W.E.L.S......	Three dollars and twelve cents............	3 12
No. 1, R. 10, W.E.L.S.	Five dollars and twenty-eight cents......	5 28
No. 2, R. 10, W.E.L.S.	Five dollars and twenty-eight cents......	5 28
No. 3, R. 10, W.E.L.S.	Five dollars and twenty-eight cents......	5 28
No. 4, R. 10, W.E.L.S.	Six dollars and nineteen cents............	6 19
No. 5, R. 10, W.E.L.S.	Eight dollars and twenty-five cents......	8 25
No. 6, R. 10, W.E.L.S.	Six dollars and nineteen cents............	6 19
No. 7, R. 10, W.E.L.S.	Four dollars and twelve cents............	4 12
No. 8, R. 10, W.E.L.S.	Five dollars and fifty cents..................	5 50
No. 9, R. 10, W.E.L.S.	Four dollars and eighty-one cents........	4 81
No. 10, R. 10, W.E.L.S.	Six dollars and nineteen cents............	6 19
A, R. 11, W.E.L.S......	Eight dollars and twenty-five cents......	8 25
B, R. 11, W.E.L.S......	Eight dollars and twenty-five cents......	8 25
No. 1, R. 11, W.E.L.S.	Six dollars and eighty-seven cents........	6 87
No. 2, R. 11, W.E.L.S.	Seven dollars and ninety-two cents......	7 92
No. 3, R. 11, W.E.L.S.	Five dollars and twenty-eight cents......	5 28
No. 4, R. 11, W.E.L.S.	Six dollars and nineteen cents............	6 19
No. 5, R. 11, W.E.L.S.	Seven dollars and fifty-six cents..........	7 56
No. 6, R. 11, W.E.L.S.	Five dollars and fifty cents..................	5 50
No. 7, R. 11, W.E.L.S.	Five dollars and fifty cents..................	5 50
No. 8, R. 11, W.E.L.S	Five dollars and fifty cents..................	5 50
No. 9, R. 11, W.E.L.S.	Six dollars and eighty-seven cents........	6 87
No. 10, R. 11, W.E.L.S.	Six dollars and eighteen cents............	6 18
A, R. 12, W.E.L.S......	Seven dollars and ninety-two cents........	7 92
No. 1, R. 12, W.E.L.S.	Five dollars and ninety-four cents........	5 94
No. 2, R. 12, W.E.L.S.	Seven dollars and twenty-six cents........	7 26
No. 3, R. 12, W.E.L.S.	Five dollars and twenty-eight cents......	5 28
No. 4, R. 12, W.E.L.S.	Four dollars and twelve cents............	4 12
No. 5, R. 12, W.E.L.S.	Six dollars and eighty-seven cents........	6 87
No. 6, R. 12, W.E.L.S.	Six dollars and nineteen cents............	6 19
No. 7, R. 12, W.E.L.S.	Six dollars and eighty-seven cents........	6 87
No. 8, R. 12, W.E.L.S.	Nine dollars and sixty-three cents........	9 63
No. 9, R. 12, W.E.L.S.	Five dollars and fifty cents	5 50
No. 10, R. 12, W.E.L.S.	Five dollars and fifty cents	5 50
1, R. 13, W.E.L.S......	Sixteen dollars and fifty cents............	16 50
A, 2, R. 13 & 14, W.E.L.S.	Six dollars and forty-two cents............	6 42
No. 1, R. 13, W.E.L.S.	Nine dollars and sixty-three cents..........	9 63
No. 2, R. 13, W.E.L.S.	Six dollars and eighty-seven cents........	6 87

CHAP. 416

PISCATAQUIS COUNTY—TIMBER AND GRASS—Concluded.

No. 2, R. 12, W.E.L.S.	Six dollars and eighty-seven cents..........	6 87
No. 4, R. 12, W.E.L.S.	Six dollars and eighty-seven cents..........	6 87
No. 5, R. 12, W.E.L.S.	Six dollars and nineteen cents.............	6 19
No. 6, R. 12, W.E.L.S.	Eight dollars and twenty-five cents.........	8 25
No. 7, R. 12, W.E.L.S.	Eight dollars and ninety-four cents.........	8 94
No. 8, R. 12, W.E.L.S.	Six dollars and eighty-eight cents..........	6 88
No. 9, R. 12, W.E.L.S.	Six dollars and eighty-eight cents..........	6 88
No. 10, R. 12, W.E.L.S.	Six dollars and nineteen cents.............	6 19
A. R. 14, W.E.L.S.......	Sixteen dollars and fifty cents..............	16 50
No. 1, R. 14, W.E.L.S.	Five dollars and twenty-eight cents........	5 28
No. 2, R. 14, W.E.L.S.	Two dollars and sixty-four cents............	2 64
No. 3, R. 14 & 15 W. E. L. S., east half........	Five dollars and ninety-one cents..........	5 91
No. 3, R. 14 & 15 W. E. L. S., west half........	Seven dollars and ninety-two cents.........	7 92
No. 4, R. 14, W.E.L.S.	Six dollars and eighty-eight cents..........	6 88
No. 5, R. 14, W.E.L.S.	Seven dollars and fifty-six cents............	7 56
No. 6, R. 14, W.E.L.S.	Eight dollars and twenty-five cents.........	8 25
No. 7, R. 14, W.E.L.S.	Seven dollars and fifty-six cents............	7 56
No. 8, R. 14, W.E.L.S.	Seven dollars and fifty-six cents............	7 56
No. 9, R. 14, W.E.L.S.	Six dollars and nineteen cents.............	6 19
No. 10, R. 14, W.E.L.S.	Six dollars and nineteen cents.............	6 19
X, R. 14, W.E.L.S......	One dollar and eighty-nine cents..........	1 89
Day's Academy, R. 15. W.E.L.S.	Three dollars and ninety-six cents........	3 96
No. 4, R. 15, W.E.L.S.	Six dollars and eighty-seven cents........	6 87
No. 5, R. 15, W.E.L.S.	Five dollars and fifty cents.................	5 50
No. 6, R. 15, W.E.L.S.	Six dollars and eighty-seven cents........	6 87
No. 7, R. 15, W.E.L.S.	Six dollars and eighty-seven cents........	6 87
No. 8, R. 15, W.E.L.S.	Six dollars and nineteen cents.............	6 19
No. 9, R. 15, W.E.L.S.	Six dollars and nineteen cents.............	6 19
No. 10, R. 15, W.E.L.S.	Five dollars and fifty cents.................	5 50
No. 4, R. 9, N. W. P.....	Eight dollars and fifty-eight cents.........	8 58
No. 5, R. 9, N. W. P.....	Eight dollars and fifty-eight cents.........	8 58
No. 6, R. 9, N. W. P.....	Eight dollars and fifty-eight cents.........	8 58
No. 7, R. 9, N. W. P.....	Six dollars and nineteen cents.............	6 19
No. 7, R. 10, Bowdoin College East. N. W. P.	Seven dollars and twenty-six cents........	7 26
No. 8, R. 10, Bowdoin College West, N.W.P.	Seven dollars and ninety-two cents.......	7 92
Total	Five hundred seventy-three dollars and eighteen cents	$573 18

STATE TAX.

CHAP. 416

SAGADAHOC COUNTY.

Arrowsic	One hundred eighty-four dollars and fourteen cents	$184 14
Bath	Eighteen thousand seventy-eight dollars and seventy cents	18,078 70
Bowdoin	Eight hundred six dollars and eighty-four cents	806 84
Bowdoinham	One thousand five hundred twenty-one dollars and fifty-seven cents	1,521 57
Georgetown	Six hundred twenty dollars and seventy-three cents	620 73
Perkins	One hundred twenty-one dollars and eighty cents	121 80
Phippsburg	One thousand one hundred forty dollars and seventy-five cents	1,140 75
Richmond	Two thousand nine hundred ninety-three dollars and twenty-two cents	2,993 22
Topsham	Two thousand seven hundred ninety-six dollars and forty cents	2,796 40
West Bath	Three hundred eighty-six dollars and sixty cents	386 60
Woolwich	Nine hundred fourteen dollars and thirty-seven cents	914 37
Total	Twenty-nine thousand five hundred sixty-five dollars and twelve cents	$29,565 12

SOMERSET COUNTY.

Anson	One thousand seven hundred sixty-two dollars and fifty-two cents	$1,762 52
Athens	Eight hundred fifty-nine dollars and eighty-eight cents	859 88
Bingham	Seven hundred twenty-five dollars and five cents	725 05
Cambridge	Three hundred fourteen dollars and ninety-one cents	314 91
Canaan	Eight hundred sixty-three dollars and fourteen cents	863 14
Concord	One hundred ninety-seven dollars and fifty-five cents	197 55
Cornville	Eight hundred forty-six dollars and eighty-seven cents	846 87
Detroit	Three hundred ninety-four dollars and five cents	394 05
Embden	Six hundred ninety-five dollars and ninety-three cents	695 93
Fairfield	Four thousand three hundred thirty-nine dollars and fifty-one cents	4,339 51
Harmony	Five hundred fifty-seven dollars and sixty-three cents	557 63
Hartland	One thousand two hundred sixty-four dollars and twenty-three cents	1,264 23
Madison	Four thousand nine hundred forty-four dollars and seventy-three cents	4,944 73
Mercer	Four hundred twenty-six dollars and sixty-three cents	426 63

SOMERSET COUNTY—Concluded.

Moscow	Two hundred eighty-six dollars and four cents	286 04
New Portland	Seven hundred sixty-one dollars and eighty cents	761 80
Norridgewock	One thousand six hundred sixteen dollars and fifty-eight cents	1,616 58
Palmyra	Nine hundred twenty-three dollars and thirty-three cents	923 33
Pittsfield	Three thousand seven hundred forty-two dollars and twenty-five cents	3,742 25
Ripley	Three hundred seventy-three dollars and seventy cents	373 70
St. Albans	One thousand seventy-one dollars and eighty-five cents	1,071 85
Skowhegan	Nine thousand five hundred eighty-five dollars and fifty-six cents	9,585 56
Smithfield	Three hundred eighty-five dollars and seventy-two cents	385 72
Solon	One thousand forty-eight dollars and twenty-three cents	1,048 23
Starks	Five hundred eighty-one dollars and sixty-four cents	581 64
Total	Thirty-eight thousand five hundred sixty-nine dollars and thirty-three cents	$38,569 33

SOMERSET COUNTY WILD LANDS.

No. 2, R. 1, B.P.W.K.R. Lexington Pl.	One hundred fifty-one dollars and fifty-three cents	$151 53
No. 1, R. 2, B.P.W.K.R. Pleasant Ridge Pl.	One hundred ten dollars and eighty-five cents	110 85
No. 2, R. 2, B.P.W.K.R. Highland Pl.	One hundred twenty-one dollars and twenty-two cents	121 22
No. 1, R. 3, B.P.W.K.R. Carrying Place Pl.	Sixty-one dollars and seven cents	61 07
No. 2, R. 3, B.P.W.K.R., East part, Carrying Place Town	One hundred twenty-six dollars and fifty-one cents	126 51
No. 2, R. 3, B.P.W.K.R., West part, mile strip, Carrying Place Town	Thirty-one dollars and sixty-eight cents	31 68
No. 3, R. 3, B.P.W.K.R. Dead River Pl.	One hundred twenty-one dollars and twenty-two cents	121 22
No. 4, R. 3, B.P.W.K.R., N. half, Bigelow Pl.	One hundred fifty-three dollars and twenty-three cents	153 23
No. 1, R. 4, B.P.W.K.R. Bowtown	One hundred sixty-three dollars and eighty-two cents	163 82
No. 2, R. 4, B.P.W.K.R., East half, Pierce Ponds	Eighty dollars and ten cents	80 10
West half, Pierce Ponds	One hundred nine dollars and fifty-two cents	109 52
No. 3, R. 4, B.P.W.K.R. No. ½	Ninety-nine dollars and seventeen cents	99 17
No. 3, R. 4, B.P.W.K.R. S. ½	Sixty-six dollars and eleven cents	66 11

STATE TAX. 663

CHAP. 416

SOMERSET COUNTY WILD LANDS—Continued.

No. 4, R. 4, B.P.W.K.R. Flag Staff Pl.	One hundred sixty-five dollars..............	165 00
No. 1, R. 5, B.P.W.K.R., East Can. Road. West Forks Pl.	Seventy dollars and ninety-one cents......	70 91
West Can. Road. West Forks Pl.	One hundred twenty-two dollars and eighty-one cents	122 81
No. 2, R. 5, B.P.W.K.R., East half, Lower Enchanted T'n..	Forty-four dollars and five cents..........	44 05
No. 2, R. 5, B.P.W.K.R., West half, Lower Enchanted T'n..	One hundred two dollars and eighty cents	102 80
No. 3, R. 5, B.P.W.K.R., Part, Pratt tract........	Two hundred twelve dollars and thirty-one cents	212 31
Part, Pray tract.........	Forty dollars and four cents................	40 04
8,000 acre tract............	Thirty-three dollars and thirteen cents....	33 13
No. 4, R. 5, B.P.W.K.R., West part No. 11......	Thirty-four dollars and forty cents......	34 40
East part, King Bartlett	Fifty-nine dollars and twenty-one cents	59 21
No. 1, R. 6, B.P.W.K.R., West part, 10,000 acre tract	Fifty-five dollars	55 00
East part Chase stream tract	Seventy dollars and sixty-two cents......	70 62
No. 2, R. 6, E.C.R., part Cold Stream	Seventy-one dollars and seventy-two cents	71 72
No. 2, R. 6, W.C.R., part Johnson Mountain...	One hundred three dollars and twelve cents	103 12
No. 2, R. 6, B.P.W.K.R. Upper Enchanted T'n, North ¼	One hundred twenty-one dollars and twenty-two cents	121 22
No. 3, R. 6, B.P.W.K.R. Upper Enchanted T'n, South ½	Ninety dollars and ninety-one cents......	90 91
No. 4, R. 6, B.P.W.K.R. Hobbstown	One hundred twenty-one dollars and twenty-two cents	121 22
No. 5, R. 6, B.P.W.K.R.	One hundred eighty-one dollars and eighty-three cents	181 83
Strip North of Nos. 1, 2, 3, R. 7, B.P.W.K.R.	Nineteen dollars and eighty cents..........	19 80
No. 1, R. 7, B.P.W.K.R. Sapling Township....	One hundred twenty-one dollars...........	121 00
No. 2, R. 7, B.P.W.K.R. Misery Township.....	Two hundred forty-one dollars and eighty-six cents	241 86
No. 3, R. 7, B.P.W.K.R. Parlin Pond	One hundred sixty dollars and sixty cents	160 60
No. 4, R. 7, B.P.W.K.R.	One hundred twenty-four dollars and ninety-four cents	124 94
No. 5, R. 7, B.P.W.K.R.	One hundred eight dollars and twenty-four cents	108 24
No. 6, R. 7, B.P.W.K.R. Appleton	One hundred thirty dollars and eighty-eight cents	130 88
No. 2, R. 1, B.P.E.K.R. Brighton Pl.	One hundred eighty-one dollars and eighty-three cents	181 83
No. 2, R. 2, B.P.E.K.R. Mayfield Pl.	One hundred seventy-three dollars and twenty-five cents	173 25

SOMERSET COUNTY WILD LANDS—Continued.

No. 1, R. 3, B.P.E.K.R. Caratunk Pl.	Three hundred twenty-five dollars and forty-nine cents	325 49
No. 2, R. 3, B.P.E.K.R. Bald Mountain	Two hundred twelve dollars and fourteen cents	212 14
No. 1, R. 4, B.P.E.K.R. The Forks Pl.	One hundred eighty-one dollars and eighty-three cents	181 83
No. 2, R. 4, B.P.E.K.R. East Moxie	One hundred fifty-two dollars and ninety-seven cents	$152 97
No. 1, R. 5, B.P.E.K.R. Moxie Gore	Two hundred thirty-five dollars and sixty-two cents	235 62
No. 2, R. 5, B.P.E.K.R. Square Town	One hundred ninety dollars and nineteen cents	190 19
No. 1, R. 6, B.P.E.K.R. Indian Stream Town	Seventy dollars and forty-seven cents	70 47
No. 1, R. 1, N.B.K.P., Taunton & Raynham Academy Grant	One hundred ten dollars and eighty-eight cents	110 88
No. 1, R. 1, N.B.K.P., Rockwood Strip	Thirty-one dollars and seventy-six cents	31 76
No. 2, R. 1, N.B.K.P., Sandwich Academy Grant	One hundred ninety dollars and eight cents	190 08
No. 2, R. 1, N.B.K.P., Rockwood Strip	Thirty-six dollars and eighty-seven cents	36 87
No. 3, R. 1, N.B.K.P., Long Pond	Two hundred twenty dollars and seventy-two cents	220 72
No. 4, R. 1, N.B.K.P., Jackman Pl.	Three hundred three dollars and five cents	303 05
No. 5, R. 1, N.B.K.P., Attean Pond	Two hundred seventy-two dollars and seventy-five cents	272 75
No. 6, R. 1, N.B.K.P., Holeb	One hundred thirty-four dollars and ninety-four cents	134 94
No. 1, R. 2, N.B.K.P., Tomhegan	Two hundred thirty-eight dollars and sixty-four cents	238 64
No. 2, R. 2, N.B.K.P., Brassua	One hundred sixty-five dollars and ninety-two cents	165 92
No. 3, R. 2, N.B.K.P., Thorndike	Two hundred forty-two dollars and forty-four cents	242 44
No. 4, R. 2, N.B.K.P., Mouse River Pl.	Two hundred fifty-three dollars and forty-four cents	253 44
No. 5, R. 2, N.B.K.P., Dennis	One hundred sixty-six dollars and sixty-eight cents	166 68
No. 6, R. 2, N.B.K.P., Forsyth	One hundred fifty-one dollars and twenty-five cents	151 25
Big W., N.B.K.P.	One hundred seven dollars and twenty-two cents	107 22
Little W., N.B.K.P.	Twenty-eight dollars and ten cents	28 10
No. 1, R. 3, N.B.K.P., part, Middlesex Grant	Ninety-eight dollars and fifty-two cents	98 52
No. 1, R. 3, N.B.K.P., part, Evans tract, Middlesex Grant	Twenty-two dollars and seventy cents	22 70
No. 2, R. 3, N.B.K.P., Soldier Town	One hundred sixty-one dollars and sixty-six cents	$161 66
No. 2, R. 3, N.B.K.P., E. half, Alder Brook	Ninety dollars and forty-two cents	90 42

SOMERSET COUNTY WILD LANDS—Continued.

No. 3, R. 3, N.B.K.P., W. half, Alder Brook	Ninety-six dollars and thirty-six cents....	96 36
No. 4, R. 3, N.B.K.P., Bald Mountain	One hundred sixty-six dollars and sixty-eight cents	166 68
No. 5, R. 3, N. B. K. P. Sandy Bay	One hundred sixty-four dollars and sixty-nine cents	164 69
Seboomook, N. B. K. P.	One hundred fifty-one dollars and fifty-three cents	151 53
No. 1, R. 4, N. B. K. P. Plymouth	One hundred thirty-six dollars and thirty-seven cents	136 37
No. 2, R. 4, N. B. K. P. Pittston Academy	Two hundred seven dollars and ninety-seven cents	207 97
No. 3, R. 4, N. B. K. P. Hammond	One hundred ninety-six dollars and ninety-eight cents	196 98
No. 4, R. 4, N. P. K. P.	One hundred thirty-three dollars and fifty-six cents	133 56
No. 5, R. 4, N. B. K. P.	Forty-nine dollars and fifty cents	49 50
No. 3, R. 5, N B. K. P. Dole Brook	One hundred fifty-one dollars and fifty-three cents	151 53
No. 4, R. 5, N. B. K. P.	Ninety-five dollars and eighty-six cents	95 86
No. 4, R. 16, W. E. L. S. Elm Stream	Eighty-two dollars and eighty-seven cents	82 87
No. 5, R. 16, W. E. L. S. E. half	Seventy-four dollars and forty-seven cents	74 47
No. 5, R. 16, W. E. L. S. W. half	Seventy-four dollars and forty-five cents	74 45
No. 6, R. 16, W. E. L. S.	One hundred forty-one dollars and sixty-five cents	141 65
No. 7, R. 16, W. E. L. S.	One hundred thirty dollars and sixty cents	130 60
No. 8, R. 16, W. E. L. S.	One hundred twenty-seven dollars and fifteen cents	127 15
No. 9, R. 16, W. E. L. S.	One hundred twenty-nine dollars and forty-eight cents	129 48
No. 10, R. 16, W. E. L. S.	One hundred fifty-three dollars and seventy-six cents.	153 76
No. 4, R. 17, W. E. L. S.	One hundred eighty-five dollars and thirty-four cents	185 34
No. 5, R. 17, W. E. L. S.	One hundred fifty-nine dollars and twenty-four cents	159 24
No. 6, R. 17, W. E. L. S.	One hundred fifty-four dollars and fifty-six cents	154 56
No. 7, R. 17, W. E. L. S.	One hundred forty-one dollars and forty-eight cents	141 48
No. 8, R. 17, W. E. L. S.	One hundred thirty-seven dollars and seventy-four cents	137 74
No. 9, R. 17, W. E. L. S.	One hundred twenty-eight dollars and thirteen cents	128 13
No. 10, R. 17, W. E. L. S. Big 10	One hundred seventy-seven dollars and ninety-six cents	$177 96
No. 4, R. 18, W. E. L. S.	One hundred ninety-nine dollars and forty-nine cents	199 49
No. 5, R. 18, W. E. L. S.	One hundred forty-six dollars and eighty-one cents	146 81
No. 6, R. 18, W. E. L. S.	One hundred seventy-one dollars and sixty cents	171 60
No. 7, R. 18, W. E. L. S.	One hundred five dollars and forty-eight cents	105 48
No. 8, R. 18, W. E. L. S	One hundred twenty-five dollars and eighty-six cents	125 86
No. 9, R. 18, W. E. L. S.	One hundred nine dollars and seventy-four cents	109 74
No. 5, R. 19, W. E. L. S.	One hundred nine dollars and eighty-two cents	109 82
No. 6, R. 19, W. E. L. S. Big 6	One hundred sixty dollars and thirteen cents	160 13

CHAP. 416

SOMERSET COUNTY WILD LANDS—Concluded.

No. 7, R. 19, W. E. L. S.	One hundred forty-three dollars and fifty-two cents	143 52
No. 8, R. 19, W. E. L. S.	Sixty-three dollars and sixty-nine cents	63 69
No. 5, R. 20, W. E. L. S.	One hundred twenty-three dollars and fifty cents	123 50
Total	Thirteen thousand seven hundred sixty-five dollars and three cents	$13,765 03

SOMERSET COUNTY—TIMBER AND GRASS ON RESERVED LANDS.

No. 2, R. 3, B.K.P.E.K.R.	Seven dollars and ninety-two cents	$7 92
No. 1, R. 4, B.K.P.E.K.R.	Five dollars and twenty-eight cents	5 28
No. 1, R. 5, B.K.P.E.K.R.	Eight dollars and fifty-eight cents	8 58
No. 2, R. 5, B.K.P.E.K.R.	Seven dollars and twenty-six cents	7 26
No. 1, R. 6, B.K.P.E.K.R.	Two dollars and seventy-four cents	2 74
No. 2, R. 3, B. K. P. W. K. R	Five dollars and twenty-eight cents	5 28
No. 1, R. 4, B. K. P. W. K. R	Six dollars and forty-four cents	6 44
No. 2, R. 4, B. K. P. W. K. R	Five dollars and twenty-eight cents	5 28
No. 3, R. 4, B. K. P. W. K. R	Six dollars and sixty cents	6 60
No. 2, R. 5, B. K. P. W. K. R	Three dollars and ninety-six cents	3 96
No. 3, R. 5, B. K. P. W. K. R	Ten dollars and fifty-six cents	10 56
No. 4, R. 5, B. K. P. W. K. R	Two dollars and sixty-four cents	2 64
No. 1, R. 6, B. K. P. W. K. R	Four dollars and twenty cents	4 20
No. 2, R. 6, B. K. P. W. K. R	Three dollars and ninety-six cents	3 96
No. 3, R. 6, B. K. P. W. K. R	Seven dollars and ninety-two cents	7 92
No. 4, R. 6, B. K. P. W. K. R	Three dollars and ninety-six cents	3 96
No. 5, R. 6, B. K. P. W. K. R	Three dollars and ninety-six cents	3 96
N 1. R. 7, B. K. P. W. K. R	Three dollars and seventy-six cents	3 76
No. 2, R. 7, B. K. P. W. K. R	Nine dollars and twenty-four cents	9 24
No. 3, R. 7, B. K. P. W. K. R	Nine dollars and sixty-eight cents	9 68
No. 4, R. 7, B. K. P. W. K. R	Four dollars and thirty-two cents	4 32
No. 5, R. 7, B. K. P. W. K. R	Three dollars and sixty cents	3 60
No. 6, R. 7, B. K. P. W. K. R	Five dollars and forty-four cents	5 44
No. 1, R. 1, N. B. K. P.	Five dollars and sixty-one cents	5 61
No. 2, R. 1, N. B. K. P.	Ten dollars and twenty-nine cents	10 29

STATE TAX. 667

CHAP 416

SOMERSET COUNTY—TIMBER AND GRASS—Concluded.

No. 3, R. 1, N. B. K. P.	Nine dollars and fourteen cents	$9 14
No. 5, R. 1, N. B. K. P.	Ten dollars and fifty-six cents	10 56
No. 6, R. 1, N. B. K. P.	Five dollars and fifty cents	5 50
No. 1, R. 2, N. B. K. P.	Eleven dollars	11 00
No. 2, R. 2, N. B. K. P.	Six dollars and nineteen cents	6 19
No. 3, R. 2, N. B. K. P.	Nine dollars and twenty-four cents	9 24
No. 6, R. 2, N. B. K. P.	Six dollars and nineteen cents	6 19
Little W., R. 2,N.B.K.P.	One dollar and twenty-three cents	1 23
Big W., R. 3,N. B. K. P.	Three dollars and ninety-six cents	3 96
No. 1, R. 3, N. B. K. P.	Three dollars and thirty cents	3 30
No. 2, R. 3, N. B. K. P.	Five dollars and twenty-eight cents	5 28
No. 3, R. 3, N. B. K. P.	Six dollars and sixty cents	6 60
No. 4, R. 3, N. B. K. P.	Five dollars and ninety-four cents	5 94
No. 5, R. 3, N. B. K. P.	Seven dollars and ninety-two cents	7 92
Seboomook, R. 4, N. B. K. P.	Five dollars and twenty-eight cents	5 28
No. 1, R. 4, N. B. K. P.	Four dollars and sixty-two cents	4 62
No. 2, R. 4, N. B. K. P.	Five dollars and ninety-four cents	5 94
No. 3, R. 4, N. B. K. P.	Seven dollars and twenty-six cents	7 26
No. 4, R. 4, N. B. K. P.	Four dollars and twelve cents	4 12
No. 5, R. 4, N. B. K. P.	One dollar and eighty cents	1 80
No. 3, R. 5, N. B. K. P.	Five dollars and fifty cents	5 50
No. 4, R. 5, N. B. K. P.	Three dollars and thirty-eight cents	3 38
No. 4, R. 15, W. E. L. S.	Three dollars and forty-four cents	4 44
No. 5, R. 16, W. E. L. S.	Five dollars and fifty cents	5 50
No. 6, R. 16, W. E. L. S.	Four dollars and eighty-one cents	4 81
No. 7, R. 16, W. E. L. S.	Four dollars and thirteen cents	4 13
No. 8, R. 16, W. E. L. S.	Four dollars and thirteen cents	4 13
No. 9, R. 16, W. E. L. S.	Four dollars and thirteen cents	4 13
No. 10, R. 16, W. E. L. S.	Five dollars and fifty cents	5 50
No. 4, R. 17, W. E. L. S.	Six dollars and eighty-eight cents	6 88
No. 5, R. 17, W. E. L. S.	Six dollars and nineteen cents	6 19
No. 6, R. 17, W. E. L. S.	Five dollars and fifty cents	5 50
No. 7, R. 17, W. E. L. S.	Four dollars and eighty-one cents	4 81
No. 8, R. 17, W. E. L. S.	Seven dollars and fifty-six cents	7 56
No. 9, R. 17, W. E. L. S.	Four dollars and thirteen cents	4 13
No. 10, R. 17, W. E. L. S.	Four dollars and thirteen cents	4 13
No. 4, R. 18, W. E. L. S.	Four dollars and eighty-one cents	4 81
No. 5, R. 18, W. E. L. S.	Five dollars and fifty cents	5 50
No. 6, R. 18, W. E. L. S.	Six dollars and nineteen cents	6 19
No. 7, R. 18, W. E. L. S.	Five dollars and fifty cents	5 50
No. 8, R. 18, W. E. L. S.	Four dollars and thirteen cents	4 13
No. 9, R. 18, W. E. L. S.	Two dollars and eighty-five cents	2 85
No. 5, R. 19, W. E. L. S.	Four dollars and five cents	4 05
No. 6, R. 19, W. E. L. S.	Four dollars and eighty-one cents	4 81
No. 7, R. 19, W. E. L. S.	Four dollars and eighty-one cents	4 81
No. 8, R. 19, W. E. L. S.	Two dollars and forty-one cents	2 41
Total	Three hundred ninety-four dollars and thirty-three cents	$394 33

WALDO COUNTY.

Belfast	Seven thousand seven hundred eleven dollars and thirty-four cents	$7,711 34
Belmont	Two hundred seventy-four dollars and fifty-seven cents	274 57
Brooks	Seven hundred two dollars	702 00
Burnham	Five hundred ninety-seven dollars and ninety-six cents	597 96
Frankfort	Six hundred seventy-five dollars and fifty-one cents	675 51
Freedom	Four hundred fifty-nine dollars and five cents	459 05
Islesborough	Two thousand seven dollars and forty-five cents	2,007 45
Jackson	Three hundred ninety-seven dollars and ninety-eight cents	397 98
Knox	Five hundred fifteen dollars and fifty-eight cents	515 58
Liberty	Six hundred dollars and thirty-five cents	600 35
Lincolnville	Eight hundred sixty-nine dollars and thirty-one cents	869 31
Monroe	Eight hundred dollars and thirteen cents	800 13
Montville	Eight hundred fifty-four dollars and nineteen cents	854 19
Morrill	Three hundred fifty-eight dollars and two cents	358 02
Northport	Eight hundred fifty-three dollars and forty-six cents	853 46
Palermo	Five hundred twenty-one dollars and eight cents	521 08
Prospect	Four hundred eighty-three dollars and twenty-seven cents	483 27
Searsport	One thousand seven hundred ninety-two dollars and sixty-eight cents	1,792 68
Searsmont	Nine hundred twenty-five dollars and twenty-eight cents	925 28
Stockton Springs	Seven hundred twenty-one dollars and eighty-nine cents	721 89
Swanville	Four hundred twenty-five dollars and eighty-three cents	425 83
Thorndike	Six hundred dollars and ninety-one cents	600 91
Troy	Seven hundred forty-seven dollars and ninety-nine cents	$747 99
Unity	Nine hundred sixty-two dollars and twenty-five cents	962 25
Waldo	Four hundred twenty-four dollars and ten cents	424 10
Winterport	One thousand five hundred forty-eight dollars and seven cents	1,548 07
Total	Twenty-six thousand eight hundred thirty dollars and twenty-five cents	$26,830 25

STATE TAX.

WASHINGTON COUNTY.

Addison	Five hundred fifty-nine dollars and seventy-five cents	$559 75
Alexander	One hundred sixty-two dollars and forty-one cents	162 41
Baileyville	Two hundred twelve dollars and sixty-six cents	212 66
Baring	Two hundred eleven dollars and twenty-three cents	211 23
Beddington	Ninety-one dollars and eighty-eight cents	91 88
Brookton	One hundred forty-four dollars and one cent	144 01
Calais	Seven thousand nine hundred thirty dollars and twenty cents	7,930 20
Centerville	One hundred thirty-six dollars and forty-five cents	136 45
Charlotte	Two hundred twenty-four dollars and nineteen cents	224 19
Cherryfield	One thousand four hundred forty-one dollars and twenty-nine cents	1,441 29
Columbia	Two hundred fifty-five dollars and twenty-three cents	255 23
Columbia Falls	Three hundred forty dollars and twenty-eight cents	340 28
Cooper	One hundred twenty-one dollars and eighty-nine cents	121 89
Crawford	Ninety-eight dollars and twenty-two cents	98 22
Cutler	Two hundred thirty-six dollars and ninety-seven cents	236 97
Danforth	Six hundred seventy-three dollars and sixty-five cents	673 65
Deblois	Fifty-nine dollars and twelve cents	59 12
Dennysville	Three hundred eighty-eight dollars and six cents	388 06
East Machias	One thousand one hundred thirty-eight dollars and twenty-four cents	1,138 24
Eastport	Five thousand six hundred seventy-eight dollars and eighty cents	5,678 80
Edmunds	Two hundred sixteen dollars and eighty-five cents	216 85
Forest City	Forty dollars and eighty-five cents	40 85
Harrington	Six hundred seventy-eight dollars and fifty-nine cents	$678 59
Jonesborough	Two hundred ninety-one dollars and forty-seven cents	291 47
Jonesport	One thousand two hundred fifty-seven dollars and seventy-three cents	1,257 73
Lubec	Two thousand three hundred twenty-one dollars and ninety-eight cents	2,321 98
Machias	Two thousand three hundred fifty-six dollars and eighty-three cents	2,356 83
Machiasport	Five hundred fifty-nine dollars and ninety cents	559 90

WASHINGTON COUNTY—Concluded.

Marion	Seventy-five dollars and five cents	75 05
Marshfield	One hundred fifty-three dollars and thirty-seven cents	153 37
Meddybemps	Seventy-seven dollars and thirty-eight cents	77 38
Milbridge	One thousand two hundred fifty-one dollars and fifty-two cents	1,251 52
Northfield	Ninety-seven dollars and fifty-three cents	97 53
Pembroke	Nine hundred twenty-eight dollars and ninety-five cents	928 95
Perry	Five hundred dollars and ninety-nine cents	500 99
Princeton	Six hundred eighty-five dollars and forty-nine cents	685 49
Robbinston	Four hundred fifty-nine dollars and fifty-five cents	459 55
Roque Bluffs	Sixty-eight dollars and ninety cents	68 90
Steuben	Four hundred eighty-eight dollars and ninety-four cents	488 94
Talmadge	One hundred sixty-one dollars and ninety-four cents	161 94
Topsfield	Two hundred thirteen dollars and sixty-five cents	213 65
Trescott	One hundred fifty dollars and eighty-five cents	150 85
Vanceboro	Four hundred twenty-one dollars and eighteen cents	421 18
Waite	Eighty dollars and seven cents	$80 07
Wesley	Ninety-nine dollars and fifty-four cents	99 54
Whiting	Two hundred thirty-nine dollars and fifteen cents	239 15
Whitneyville	One hundred sixty-two dollars and three cents	162 03
Total	Thirty-four thousand one hundred forty-four dollars and eighty cents	$34,144 80

WASHINGTON COUNTY WILD LANDS.

No. 18, East Division	Seventy-five dollars and seventy-six cents	$75 76
No. 19, East Division	Seventy-five dollars and seventy-six cents	75 76
No. 26, East Division	One hundred twenty-three dollars and seventy-five cents	123 75
No. 27, East Division	One hundred nineteen dollars and sixty-one cents	119 61
No. 18, Middle Division	Sixty dollars and sixty-one cents	60 61
No. 19, Middle Division S. E. quarter	Sixteen dollars and eighty-four cents	16 84
No. 19, Middle Division N. half & S.W. quarter	Thirty-seven dollars and ninety-two cents	37 92
No. 24, Middle Division	Ninety dollars and ninety-two cents	90 92

WASHINGTON COUNTY WILD LANDS—Concluded.

No. 25, Middle Division.	One hundred twenty-six dollars and fifty cents	126 50
No. 29, Middle Division.	One hundred thirty-six dollars and thirty-seven cents	136 37
No. 30, Middle Division.	One hundred sixty-six dollars and sixty-eight cents	166 68
No. 31, Middle Division.	One hundred sixty-six dollars and sixty-eight cents	166 68
No. 36, Middle Division.	Two hundred twenty-seven dollars and twenty-nine cents	227 29
No. 37, Middle Division.	One hundred sixty-six dollars and sixty-eight cents	166 68
No. 42, Middle Division	Two hundred twelve dollars and fourteen cents	212 14
No. 43, Middle Division E. half	Eighty-three dollars and thirty-four cents	83 34
No. 43, Middle Division W. half	Eighty-three dollars and thirty-four cents	83 34
No. 5, North Division N. half	Forty-one dollars and thirty-nine cents...	41 39
No. 5, North Division S. half	Seventy-five dollars and seventy-six cents	75 76
No. 6, North Division..	Ninety-four dollars and forty cents........	94 40
E. half, strip, N. of No. 6, N. Division	Thirty-one dollars and seventy-six cents..	31 76
W. half, strip, N. of No. 6, N. Division	Seventeen dollars and thirty-three cents..	17 33
Two mile strip, N. of No. 5	Thirty-three dollars	33 00
No. 1, R. 1, T. 8..........	Sixty-nine dollars and eighty-three cents..	69 83
No. 3, R. 1, T. S., Grand Lake Stream Plan	Two hundred twenty-five dollars and thirteen cents	225 13
No. 1, R. 2, T. S., Dyer.	Ninety dollars and ninety-two cents......	90 92
No. 1, R. 3, T. S. Lambert Lake Pl......	One hundred fifty-nine dollars and sixty-five cents	159 65
N. ½, R. 1, W. half, N. B. P. P.............	Ninety-one dollars and eight cents	$91 08
No. ½, R. 1, E. half, N. B. P. P.............	Ninety dollars and ninety-two cents	90 92
No. 7, R. 2, N. B. P. P. Kossuth Pl	One hundred seventy-seven dollars and ninety-five cents	177 95
No. 8, R. 3, N. B. P. P..	One hundred seventy-six dollars and fifty-eight cents	176 58
No. 10, R. 3, N. B. P. P. Forest	One hundred two dollars and thirty-four cents	102 34
No. 11, R. 3, N. B. P. P.	Forty-four dollars	44 00
No. 8, R. 4, N. B. P. P...	One hundred twenty-one dollars	121 00
East part Indian Township, strip, 1 mile wide.	Seventeen dollars and sixty cents	17 60
No. 9, R. 2, Codyville Pl., N. B. P. P.........	One hundred thirty-five dollars and eighty-one cents	135 81
No. 14, E. D. Pl..........	One hundred six dollars and twenty-six cents	106 26
No. 21, E. D. Pl..........	Ninety-one dollars and eight cents	91 08
Total	Three thousand nine hundred sixty-three dollars and ninety-eight cents	$3,963 98

WASHINGTON COUNTY—TIMBER AND GRASS ON RESERVED LANDS.

No. 19, East Division....	Two dollars and sixty-four cents	$2 64
No. 26, East Division....	Five dollars and twenty-eight cents	5 28
No. 5, North Division..	Five dollars and twenty-eight cents	5 28
No. 13, Middle Division.	One dollar and thirty-two cents	1 32
No. 19, Middle Division.	Three dollars and thirty cents	3 30
No. 24, Middle Division.	Two dollars and sixty-four cents	2 64
No. 25, Middle Division.	Three dollars and ninety-six cents........	3 96
No. 29, Middle Division.	Four dollars and sixty-two cents	4 62
No. 30, Middle Division.	Five dollars and ninety-four cents	5 94
No. 31, Middle Division.	Five dollars and ninety-four cents	5 94
No. 1, R. 1, Titcomb Survey	Two dollars and sixty-four cents	2 64
No. 1, R. 2, Titcomb Survey	Two dollars and seventy-five cents	2 75
No. 6, R. 1, N. B. P. P.	Six dollars and seventy-four cents	6 74
No. 8, R. 3, N. B. P. P.	Six dollars and sixty cents	6 60
No. 10, R. 3, N. B. P. P.	Two dollars and sixty-four cents	2 64
No. 11, R. 3, N. B. P. P.	One dollar and thirty-eight cents	1 38
No. 13, East Division....	One dollar and eighty-seven cents	1 87
No. 36, Middle Division.	Eight dollars and fifty-eight cents	8 58
No. 37, Middle Division.	Five dollars and ninety-four cents	5 94
No. 42, Middle Division.	Seven dollars and ninety-two cents	7 92
No. 43, Middle Division.	Six dollars and sixty cents	6 60
Total	Ninety-four dollars and fifty-eight cents..	$94 58

YORK COUNTY.

Acton	Seven hundred thirty-eight dollars and seventy-three cents	$738 73
Alfred	Nine hundred fifty-seven dollars and eighty-one cents	957 81
Berwick	Two thousand six hundred sixty-eight dollars and ninety-one cents	2,668 91
Biddeford	Twenty-two thousand two hundred thirty-three dollars and twelve cents	22,233 12
Buxton	One thousand eight hundred ninety-seven dollars and eighty-seven cents	1,897 87
Cornish	One thousand twenty-one dollars and nineteen cents	1,021 19
Dayton	Six hundred twelve dollars and eighty-seven cents	612 87
Eliot	One thousand two hundred sixty-seven dollars and sixty-six cents	1,267 66
Hollis	One thousand one hundred twenty-four dollars and forty cents	1,124 40
Kittery	One thousand nine hundred forty-seven dollars and seventy-eight cents	1,947 78

STATE TAX.

YORK COUNTY—Concluded.

Kennebunk	Six thousand ninety-three dollars and forty-eight cents	6,093 48
Kennebunkport	Three thousand six hundred ninety-eight dollars and sixty-nine cents	3,698 69
Lebanon	One thousand eighty-one dollars and seventy-six cents	1,081 76
Limington	Eight hundred sixty-seven dollars and fifty-two cents	867 52
Limerick	One thousand one hundred sixty-seven dollars and forty-three cents	1,167 43
Lyman	Nine hundred seventy-eight dollars and fourteen cents	978 14
Newfield	Six hundred forty-seven dollars and ninety-five cents	647 95
North Berwick	Two thousand fifty dollars and twenty-one cents	2,050 21
Old Orchard	Two thousand seven hundred thirty dollars and forty-four cents	2,730 44
Parsonsfield	One thousand two hundred twenty dollars and seventy-eight cents	1,220 78
Saco	Ten thousand nine hundred eighty-two dollars and eighty-eight cents	10,982 88
Sanford	Eight thousand thirty-five dollars and eighty-eight cents	8,035 88
Shapleigh	Six hundred sixty-seven dollars and forty-four cents	$667 44
South Berwick	Three thousand four hundred forty dollars and sixty cents	3,440 60
Waterboro	One thousand nineteen dollars and eighty-three cents	1,019 83
Wells	Two thousand three hundred ninety-six dollars and forty-seven cents	2,396 47
York	Six thousand sixty dollars and one cent	6,060 01
Total	Eighty-seven thousand six hundred nine dollars and eighty-five cents	$87,609 85

56

STATE TAX.

AP. 416

SUMMARY.

Androscoggin	Seventy-nine thousand eight hundred fifty-eight dollars and sixty-four cents..	$79,858 64
Aroostook	Fifty-six thousand nine hundred fifty-four dollars and ninety-two cents	56,954 92
Cumberland	Two hundred six thousand two hundred ninety-nine dollars and forty-three cents	206,299 43
Franklin	Twenty-six thousand five hundred ninety-five dollars and fifty-seven cents	26,595 57
Hancock	Forty-four thousand eight hundred ninety-seven dollars and nine cents	44,897 09
Kennebec	Eighty-six thousand six hundred sixty-nine dollars and sixty-six cents	86,669 66
Knox	Thirty-nine thousand seven hundred seventy-five dollars and forty-four cents	39,775 44
Lincoln	Twenty thousand four hundred eighty-five dollars and seventy-eight cents	20,485 78
Oxford	Forty-two thousand ninety-five dollars and seventy-five cents	42,095 75
Penobscot	Ninety-eight thousand two hundred ninety-seven dollars and eighty-four cents	98,297 84
Piscataquis	Thirty-three thousand six hundred eight dollars and thirty-seven cents	33,608 37
Sagadahoc	Twenty-nine thousand five hundred sixty-five dollars and thirteen cents	29,565 13
Somerset	Fifty-two thousand seven hundred twenty-eight dollars and sixty-nine cents	52,728 69
Waldo	Twenty-six thousand eight hundred thirty dollars and twenty-five cents	26,830 25
Washington	Thirty-eight thousand two hundred three dollars and thirty-six cents	38,203 36
York	Eighty-seven thousand six hundred nine dollars and eighty-five cents	87,609 85
Total	Nine hundred seventy thousand four hundred seventy-five dollars and seventy-seven cents	$970,475 77

Sect. 2. The treasurer of this state shall, in the month of April, in the year of our Lord one thousand nine hundred and three, send his warrant with a copy of this tax act, directed to the mayor and aldermen, selectmen or assessors of each city, town or plantation, taxed as aforesaid, requiring them respectively to assess, in dollars and cents, the sum so charged, according to the provisions of the law for the assessment of taxes and to add the amount of such tax to the amount of county and town taxes, to be by them assessed in each city, town and plantation or other place, respectively.

Sect. 3. The treasurer of state in his said warrant, shall require the said mayor and aldermen, selectmen or assessors, respectively, to pay or to issue their several warrant or warrants requiring the collectors of their several cities, towns and plantations, to collect and pay in to the treasurer of their respective cities, towns and plantations, the sum against said cities, towns and plantations, respectively, in this act contained, which said respective treasurer shall pay to the state treasurer on or before the first day of January, one thousand nine hundred and four, and said mayor, selectmen and assessors, respectively, shall return a certificate of the names of such collectors, with the sums which each collector may be required to collect, to said state treasurer, sometime before the first day of December, in the year of our Lord one thousand nine hundred and three.

Sect. 4. When the time for the payment of a state tax to the treasurer of state has expired, and it is unpaid, the treasurer of state shall give notice thereof to the municipal officers of any delinquent town, and unless such tax shall be paid within sixty days, the treasurer of state may issue his warrant to the sheriff of the county, requiring him to levy, by distress and sale, upon the real and personal property of any of the inhabitants of the town; and the sheriff or his deputy shall execute such warrants, observing the regulations provided for satisfying warrants against deficient collectors, as prescribed by chapter six of the revised statutes.

Sect. 5. When any state tax assessed upon any city or town remains unpaid, such city or town is precluded from drawing from the state treasurer the school funds set apart for such city or town, so long as such tax remains unpaid.

Sect. 6. This act shall take effect when approved.

Approved March 28, 1908.

Chapter 417.

An Act for the assessment of a State Tax for the year one thousand nine hundred and four, amounting to the sum of nine hundred seventy thousand four hundred seventy-five dollars and seventy-seven cents.

Be it enacted by the Senate and House of Representatives in Legislature assembled, as follows:

Section 1. That each city, town, plantation, or any other place hereinafter named, within this state, shall be assessed and pay the several sums with which they respectively stand charged in the following lists; the same being in addition to the poll tax of one cent on each poll, a tax of two and three-fourths mills on the dollar of the present valuation for the current disbursements of the treasury, for the year nineteen hundred and four and for the school mill fund established by an act approved February twenty-seven, eighteen hundred and seventy-two.

ANDROSCOGGIN COUNTY.

Auburn	Nineteen thousand seven hundred ten dollars and twenty cents	$19,710 20
Durham	Nine hundred seven dollars and forty-six cents	907 46
East Livermore	Two thousand six hundred twelve dollars and seventy-two cents	2,612 72
Greene	Eight hundred seven dollars and four cents	807 04
Leeds	Eight hundred forty-two dollars and ninety-three cents	842 93
Lewiston	Thirty-eight thousand six hundred twenty-five dollars and forty-three cents	38,625 43
Lisbon	Five thousand seven hundred twenty-four dollars and seventy-nine cents	5,724 79
Livermore	One thousand two hundred forty dollars and four cents	1,240 04
Mechanic Falls	Two thousand four hundred one dollars and ninety-seven cents	2,401 97
Minot	Nine hundred twenty-three dollars and fifty-two cents	923 52
Poland	Two thousand one hundred ninety-three dollars and forty-four cents	2,193 44
Turner	One thousand nine hundred one dollars and fifty-two cents	1,901 52
Wales	Five hundred thirty-five dollars and fifty-four cents	535 54
Webster	One thousand four hundred thirty-two dollars and four cents	1,432 04
Total	Seventy-nine thousand eight hundred fifty-eight dollars and sixty-four cents	$79,858 64

AROOSTOOK COUNTY.

Amity	One hundred eighty-five dollars and thirty-four cents	$185 34
Ashland	One thousand one hundred three dollars and thirty-six cents	1,103 36
Bancroft	One hundred fifty-two dollars and forty cents	152 40
Benedicta	One hundred fifty-nine dollars and forty-five cents	159 45
Blaine	Four hundred thirty-five dollars and twenty cents	435 20
Bridgewater	Eight hundred seventy-one dollars and eight cents	871 08

STATE TAX.

AROOSTOOK COUNTY—Continued.

Caribou	Three thousand eight hundred twenty dollars and thirty-seven cents............	3,820 37
Crystal	Two hundred thirty-six dollars and two cents	236 02
Dyer Brook	Two hundred forty-one dollars and seventy-four cents	241 74
Easton	Seven hundred twenty-eight dollars and thirty cents	728 30
Fort Fairfield	Three thousand five hundred eighty-five dollars and forty-five cents............	3,585 45
Fort Kent	Seven hundred thirty-six dollars and seventeen cents	736 17
Frenchville	Three hundred twenty-eight dollars and thirty-eight cents	328 38
Grand Isle	Three hundred thirty-nine dollars and eighty-six cents	339 86
Haynesville	One hundred eighty-three dollars and seventy-three cents	183 73
Hersey	One hundred sixty-two dollars and thirty cents	162 30
Hodgdon	Seven hundred twenty-nine dollars and forty-three cents	729 43
Houlton	Six thousand four hundred fifty-two dollars and two cents	6,452 02
Island Falls	Seven hundred four dollars and seventy-nine cents	704 79
Limestone	Nine hundred twenty-two dollars and thirty-four cents	922 34
Linneus	Six hundred seventy-seven dollars and sixty-three cents	677 63
Littleton	Eight hundred seventy-eight dollars and eleven cents	878 11
Ludlow	Three hundred thirty-four dollars and one cent	334 01
Madawaska	Five hundred forty-seven dollars and twenty-six cents	$547 26
Mapleton	Five hundred ninety-two dollars and ninety-five cents	592 95
Mars Hill	Seven hundred forty-four dollars and fourteen cents	744 14
Masardis	Three hundred one dollars and eighty-eight cents	301 88
Monticello	Nine hundred forty-four dollars and sixty-two cents	944 62
New Limerick	Four hundred eighty-eight dollars and eighty-three cents	488 83
New Sweden	Four hundred thirty-five dollars and twenty cents	435 20
Oakfield	Two hundred eighty-four dollars and fifty-two cents	284 52
Orient	One hundred thirty dollars and ninety-one cents	130 91
Perham	Three hundred thirty-one dollars and eighty-seven cents	331 87
Presque Isle	Three thousand nine hundred seventy-one dollars and thirty-eight cents............	3,971 38

STATE TAX.

AROOSTOOK COUNTY—Concluded.

Saint Agatha	Two hundred seventy-one dollars and forty-seven cents	271 47
Sherman	Five hundred twenty-seven dollars and eighteen cents	527 18
Smyrna	Three hundred fourteen dollars and fifty-six cents	314 56
Van Buren	Seven hundred eight dollars and ninety cents	708 90
Washburn	Six hundred ninety-four dollars and nineteen cents	694 19
Weston	One hundred sixty-nine dollars and nineteen cents	169 19
Woodland	Five hundred thirty-five dollars and eighty-four cents	535 84
Cary Pl.	Eighty-four dollars and ninety-seven cents	84 97
Castle Hill Pl.	Two hundred ninety dollars and fifteen cents	290 15
Caswell Pl.	One hundred thirty-one dollars and eighty-four cents	131 84
Chapman Pl.	One hundred seventy-three dollars and fifty-five cents	173 55
Connor Pl.	One hundred fifty-three dollars and twenty-nine cents	153 29
Cyr Pl.	One hundred forty-seven dollars and nineteen cents	$147 19
Eagle Lake Pl.	One hundred thirty-one dollars and sixty-five cents	131 65
Hamlin Pl.	Two hundred eleven dollars and four cents	211 04
Macwahoc Pl.	One hundred nineteen dollars and sixty-five cents	119 65
Merrill Pl.	Two hundred fourteen dollars and eighty-four cents	214 84
Moro Pl.	One hundred thirty-seven dollars and seventy-eight cents	137 78
New Canada Pl.	Ninety-five dollars and ninety-six cents	95 96
Reed Pl.	Three hundred forty-six dollars and forty-two cents	346 42
St. Francis Pl.	One hundred thirty-seven dollars and four cents	137 04
St. John Pl.	One hundred sixteen dollars and eleven cents	116 11
Silver Ridge Pl.	One hundred ten dollars and forty-nine cents	110 49
Wade Pl.	One hundred sixty-one dollars and thirty-three cents	161 33
Wallagrass Pl.	One hundred thirty-eight dollars and eighty cents	138 80
Westfield Pl.	Two hundred forty-five dollars and sixty-four cents	245 64
Total	Thirty-nine thousand one hundred ten dollars and eleven cents	$39,110 11

STATE TAX.

CHAP. 417

AROOSTOOK COUNTY WILD LANDS.

A, R. 2, W. E. L. S.	Eighty-six dollars and eleven cents	$86 11
B, R. 2, W. E. L. S., Hammond	Two hundred forty-two dollars and forty-four cents	242 44
C, R. 2, W. E. L. S.	One hundred ninety-six dollars and ninety-eight cents	196 98
D, R. 2, W. E. L. S.	One hundred ninety-one dollars and ninety-five cents	191 95
E, R. 2, W. E. L. S.	One hundred twenty-two dollars and forty-five cents	122 45
No. 3, R. 2, W. E. L. S., Forkstown	Two hundred two dollars and thirteen cents	202 13
Cox Patent	Nine dollars and sixty-three cents	9 63
No. 2, R. 3, W. E. L. S., Glenwood	One hundred twenty-one dollars	121 00
No. 3, R. 3, W. E. L. S.	One hundred eighty-one dollars and eighty-three cents	181 83
No. 4, R. 3, W. E. L. S.	One hundred six dollars and five cents	106 05
No. 7, R. 3, W. E. L. S., Dudley	One hundred ninety-six dollars and ninety-eight cents	196 98
No. 8, R. 3, W. E. L. S.	One hundred ninety-six dollars and ninety-eight cents	196 98
No. 9, R. 3, W. E. L. S.	Two hundred twelve dollars and fourteen cents	212 14
No. 10, R. 3, W. E. L. S.	Two hundred forty-two dollars and forty-four cents	242 44
No. 16, R. 3, W. E. L. S., Stockholm	Two hundred twenty dollars and forty cents	220 40
No. 17, R. 3, W. E. L. S., N. ½	Sixty-three dollars and sixty-two cents	63 62
No. 17, R. 3, W. E. L. S., S. ½	Sixty-three dollars and sixty-two cents	63 62
No. 1, R. 4, W. E. L. S., Yarmouth Academy	One hundred seventy-four dollars and thirty-nine cents	174 39
No. 2, R. 4, W. E. L. S.	Two hundred twelve dollars and fourteen cents	212 14
No. 3, R. 4, W. E. L. S.	Two hundred twelve dollars and fourteen cents	212 14
No. 7, R. 4, W. E. L. S., Webbertown	Three hundred three dollars and five cents	303 05
No. 8, R. 4, W. E. L. S., St. Croix	One hundred ninety-six dollars and ninety-eight cents	196 98
No. 9, R. 4, W. E. L. S., Griswold	Two hundred twelve dollars and fourteen cents	212 14
No. 10, R. 4, W. E. L. S., N. E. ¼, Squawpan	Thirty-seven dollars and eighty-eight cents	37 88
No. 10, R. 4, W. E. L. S., S. ½ & N. W. ¼ Squawpan	One hundred forty-seven dollars and seventy-three cents	147 73
No. 11, R. 4, W. E. L. S., S. W. ¼	Twenty-two dollars and seventy-three cents	22 73
No. 11, R. 4, W. E. L. S., N. ½ & S. E. ¼	One hundred twenty-five dollars	$125 00
No. 15, R. 4, W. E. L. S., Westmanland Pl.	One hundred eighty-one dollars and eighty-three cents	181 83
No. 16, R. 4, W.E.L.S.	One hundred eighty-one dollars and eighty-three cents	181 83
No. 17, R. 4, W.E.L.S., N. ½	Twenty-two dollars and seventy-three cents	22 73
No. 17, R. 4, W.E.L.S., S. ½	Sixty-eight dollars and nineteen cents	68 19
A, R. 5, N. part, W.E.L.S. Molunkus	Ninety-five dollars and four cents	95 04

AROOSTOOK COUNTY WILD LANDS—Continued.

A, R. 5, S. part, W.E.L.S., Molunkus	Sixty-two dollars and ninety-eight cents	62 98
No. 1, R. 5, W.E.L.S.	One hundred sixty-six dollars and sixty-eight cents	166 68
No. 7, R. 5, W.E.L.S.	One hundred ninety-six dollars and ninety-eight cents	196 98
No. 8, R. 5, W.E.L.S.	One hundred fifty-nine dollars and twelve cents	159 12
No. 9, R. 5, W.E.L.S.	One hundred twenty-one dollars and forty-four cents	121 44
No. 13, R. 5, W.E.L.S.	One hundred twenty-one dollars and twenty-two cents	121 22
No. 14, R. 5, W.E.L.S.	One hundred eighty-one dollars and eighty-three cents	181 83
No. 15, R. 5, W.E.L.S.	One hundred sixty-six dollars and sixty-eight cents	166 68
No. 16, R. 5, W.E.L.S.	Ninety dollars and ninety-one cents	90 91
No. 17, R. 5, W.E.L.S.	Eighty-two dollars and sixty cents	82 60
No. 9, R. 6, W.E.L.S., Oxbow	One hundred thirty-seven dollars and fifty cents	137 50
No. 10, R. 6, W.E.L.S., N. ½	Ninety-one dollars	91 00
No. 10, R. 6, W.E.L.S., S. ½	Sixty dollars and sixty-six cents	60 66
No. 11, R. 6, W.E.L.S., Garfield Pl.	Two hundred seven dollars and thirty-six cents	207 36
No. 12, R. 6, W.E.L.S., Nashville	One hundred eighty-one dollars and eighty-three cents	181 83
No. 13, R. 6, W.E.L.S., Portage Lake Pl.	One hundred thirty-six dollars and twelve cents	136 12
No. 14, R. 6, W.E.L.S.	One hundred sixty-six dollars and sixty-eight cents	166 68
No. 15, R. 6, W.E.L.S.	One hundred sixty-six dollars and sixty-eight cents	166 68
No. 16, R. 6, W.E.L.S.	Ninety-one dollars and eight cents	91 08
No. 9, R. 7, W.E.L.S.	One hundred eighty-two dollars and sixteen cents	182 16
No. 10, R. 7, W.E.L.S.	One hundred eighty-one dollars and eighty-three cents	181 83
No. 11, R. 7, W.E.L.S., E. ½	Eighty-three dollars and thirty-four cents	$83 34
No. 11, R. 7, W.E.L.S., W. ½	Eighty-three dollars and thirty-four cents	83 34
No. 12, R. 7, W.E.L.S.	One hundred sixty-six dollars and sixty-eight dollars	166 68
No. 13, R. 7, W.E.L.S., Pine & Spruce Timber	Ninety dollars and ninety-one cents	90 91
Land and other growth	Ninety dollars and ninety-one cents	90 91
No. 14, R. 7, W.E.L.S.	One hundred eighty-one dollars and eighty-three cents	181 83
No. 15, R. 7, W.E.L.S., Winterville	One hundred fifty-one dollars and eighty cents	151 80
No. 9, R. 8, W.E.L.S.	One hundred forty-nine dollars and thirteen cents	149 13
No. 10, R. 8, W.E.L.S.	One hundred eighty-six dollars and fifty-eight cents	186 58
No. 11, R. 8, W.E.L.S.	One hundred fifty-five dollars and ten cents	155 10
No. 12, R. 8, W.E.L.S.	One hundred fifty-five dollars and ninety-two cents	155 92
No. 13, R. 8, W.E.L.S.	One hundred fifty-five dollars and twenty-five cents	155 25
No. 14, R. 8, W.E.L.S.	One hundred fifty-one dollars and forty-eight cents	151 48
No. 15, R. 8, W.E.L.S., N. ½	Sixty-four dollars and forty-six cents	64 46
No. 15, R. 8, W.E.L.S., S. ½	Sixty-four dollars and forty-six cents	64 46

STATE TAX. 681

CHAP. 417

AROOSTOOK COUNTY WILD LANDS—Continued.

No. 16, R. 8, W.E.L.S..	One hundred thirty-eight dollars and eighty-nine cents	138 89
No. 11, R. 9, W.E.L.S..	One hundred seventy-four dollars and forty-four cents	174 44
No. 12, R. 9, W.E.L.S..	One hundred fifty-five dollars and thirty-nine cents	155 39
No. 13, R. 9, W.E.L.S..	One hundred fifty-two dollars and nine cents	152 09
No. 14, R. 9, W.E.L.S..	One hundred thirty-four dollars and sixty-six cents	134 66
No. 15, R. 9, W.E.L.S..	One hundred twenty-nine dollars and seventy-four cents	129 74
No. 16, R. 9, W.E.L.S..	One hundred fifty-three dollars and fifty-nine cents	153 59
No. 11, R. 10, W.E.L.S.	One hundred eighty-two dollars and sixty-seven cents	182 67
No. 12, R. 10, W.E.L.S.	One hundred twenty-nine dollars and ninety-eight cents	129 98
No. 13, R. 10, W.E.L.S.	One hundred forty-two dollars and twenty-eight cents	142 28
No. 14, R. 10, W.E.L.S.	One hundred forty dollars and five cents	140 05
No. 15, R. 10, W.E.L.S.	One hundred twenty-two dollars and thirteen cents	122 13
No. 16, R. 10, W.E.L.S.	Eighty-two dollars and thirty-one cents	82 31
No. 17, R. 10, W.E.L.S.	Fifty dollars and eighty-two cents........	50 82
No. 18, R. 10, W.E.L.S.	One hundred twenty-two dollars and ninety-four cents	122 94
No. 11, R. 11, W.E.L.S.	One hundred sixty-seven dollars and five cents	167 05
No. 12, R. 11, W.E.L.S.	One hundred fifty-three dollars and nine cents	$153 09
No. 13, R. 11, W.E.L.S.	One hundred twenty-five dollars and sixteen cents	125 16
No. 14, R. 11, W.E.L.S., N. ½	Sixty-nine dollars and sixty-five cents....	69 65
No. 14, R. 11, W.E.L.S., S. ½	Sixty-one dollars and ninety-one cents....	61 91
No. 15, R. 11, W.E.L.S., N. ½	Fifty-two dollars and sixty-eight cents	52 68
No. 15, R. 11, W.E.L.S., S. ½	Fifty-two dollars and sixty-eight cents	52 68
No. 16, R. 11, W.E.L.S.	Eighty-eight dollars and ninety-eight cents	88 98
No. 17, R. 11, W.E.L.S.	One hundred five dollars and twenty-eight cents	105 28
No. 18, R. 11, W.E.L.S.	One hundred twenty-one dollars and seventy-six cents	121 76
No. 19, R. 11, W.E.L.S.	One hundred forty-five dollars and thirty-eight cents	145 38
No. 11, R. 12, W.E.L.S.	One hundred fifty-two dollars and seventy-three cents	152 73
No. 12, R. 12, W.E.L.S.	One hundred thirty-seven dollars and ninety-seven cents	137 97
No. 13, R. 12, W.E.L.S.	One hundred twenty-two dollars and thirty-eight cents	122 38
No. 14, R. 12, W.E.L.S.	One hundred twenty-two dollars..........	122 00
No. 15, R. 12, W.E.L.S.	One hundred thirty-two dollars and ninety-three cents	132 93
No. 16, R. 12, W.E.L.S.	Ninety dollars and forty-one cents	90 41
No. 17, R. 12, W.E.L.S.	One hundred twenty-one dollars and twenty cents	121 20
No. 18, R. 12, W.E.L.S., N. E. ¼	Thirty dollars and forty-three cents......	30 43
No. 18, R. 12, W.E.L.S., W. ½	Sixty dollars and eighty-six cents........	60 86
No. 18, R. 12, W.E.L.S., S. E. ¼	Thirty dollars and forty-three cents......	30 43
No. 19, R. 12, W.E.L.S.	One hundred forty-two dollars and eight cents	142 08
No. 20, R. 11 & 12, W. E. L. S.	One hundred eighty-nine dollars and eighteen cents	189 18

CHAP. 417

AROOSTOOK COUNTY WILD LANDS—Concluded.

No. 11, R. 13, W.E.L.S.	One hundred fifty-two dollars and seventy-five cents	152 75
No. 12, R. 13, W.E.L.S.	One hundred twenty-one dollars and seventy-five cents	121 75
No. 13, R. 13, W.E.L.S.	One hundred thirty-seven dollars and fifty-two cents	137 52
No. 14, R. 13, W.E.L.S.	One hundred six dollars and thirty-four cents	106 34
No. 15, R. 13, W.E.L.S.	One hundred twenty-one dollars	121 00
No. 16, R. 13, W.E.L.S.	One hundred six dollars and six cents	106 06
No. 17, R. 13, W.E.L.S.	One hundred seven dollars and thirty-one cents	107 31
No. 18, R. 13, W.E.L.S.	One hundred ten dollars and twenty-eight cents	110 28
No. 11, R. 14, W.E.L.S.	One hundred fifty-one dollars and seventeen cents	$151 17
No. 12, R. 14, W.E.L.S., E. ½	Sixty-one dollars and eleven cents	61 11
No. 12, R. 14, W.E.L.S., W. ½	Sixty-one dollars and eleven cents	61 11
No. 13, R. 14, W.E.L.S.	One hundred twenty-three dollars and eighteen cents	123 18
No. 14, R. 14, W.E.L.S.	One hundred forty-nine dollars and fifty-four cents	149 54
No. 15, R. 14, W.E.L.S.	One hundred twenty dollars and seventy cents	120 70
No. 16, R. 14, W.E.L.S.	One hundred fifty-six dollars and eighty-five cents	156 85
No. 17, R. 14, W.E.L.S.	Seventy-two dollars and ninety-six cents	72 96
No. 11, R. 15, W.E.L.S., E. ½	Sixty-eight dollars and twenty-eight cents	68 28
No. 11, R. 15, W.E.L.S., W. ½	Sixty-eight dollars and twenty-nine cents	68 29
No. 12, R. 15, W.E.L.S.	One hundred six dollars and twenty-nine cents	106 29
No. 13, R. 15, W.E.L.S.	One hundred seven dollars and thirteen cents	107 13
No. 14, R. 15, W.E.L.S.	One hundred seventeen dollars and twenty-eight cents	117 28
No. 15, R. 15, W.E.L.S.	One hundred four dollars and two cents	104 02
No. 11, R. 16, W.E.L.S.	Ninety dollars and ninety-two cents	90 92
No. 12, R. 16, W.E.L.S.	Ninety dollars and ninety-one cents	90 91
No. 13, R. 16, W.E.L.S.	One hundred seventy dollars and ten cents	170 10
No. 14, R. 16, W.E.L.S.	Eighty-one dollars and eleven cents	81 11
No. 11, R. 17, W.E.L.S.	One hundred thirty-seven dollars and fifty cents	137 50
No. 12, R. 17, W.E.L.S.	Ninety-four dollars and seventy-five cents	94 75
Total	Seventeen thousand three hundred nineteen dollars and forty-nine cents	$17,319 49

AROOSTOOK COUNTY—TIMBER AND GRASS ON RESERVED LANDS.

A, R. 2, W. E. L. S.	Three dollars and seventy-one cents	$3 71
C, R. 2, W. E. L. S.	Seven dollars and fifty-six cents	7 56
D, R 2, W. E. L. S.	Seven dollars and ninety-seven cents	7 97
No. 3, R. 3, W.E.L.S.	Five dollars and eighty cents	5 80
No. 4, R. 3, W.E.L.S.	Three dollars and eight cents	3 08
No. 7, R. 3, W.E.L.S.	Seven dollars and twenty-six cents	7 26
No. 8, R. 3, W.E.L.S.	Seven dollars and twenty-six cents	7 26

STATE TAX. 683

CHAP. 417

AROOSTOOK COUNTY—TIMBER AND GRASS—Continued.

No. 9, R. 3, W.E.L.S..	Seven dollars and fifty-six cents............	7 56
No. 10, R. 3, W.E.L.S..	Nine dollars and sixty-three cents........	9 63
No. 17, R. 3, W.E.L.S..	Four dollars and eighty-one cents.........	4 81
No. 1, R. 4, W.E.L.S..	Six dollars and sixty cents..................	6 60
No. 2, R. 4, W.E.L.S..	Seven dollars and ninety-two cents.......	7 92
No. 3, R. 4, W.E.L.S..	Eight dollars and twenty-five cents.......	8 25
No. 7, R. 4, W.E.L.S..	Twelve dollars and thirty-eight cents....	12 38
No. 8, R. 4, W.E.L.S..	Seven dollars and fifty-six cents...........	7 56
No. 9, R. 4, W.E.L.S..	Eight dollars and twenty-five cents.......	8 25
No. 10, R. 4, W.E.L.S..	Seven dollars and fifty-six cents...........	7 56
No. 11, R. 4, W.E.L.S..	Six dollars and eighty-seven cents........	6 87
No. 16, R. 4, W.E.L.S..	Six dollars and eighty-seven cents........	6 87
No. 17, R. 4, W.E.L.S..	Three dollars and nine cents................	3 09
No. 1, R. 5, W.E.L.S..	Six dollars and sixty cents...................	6 60
No. 7, R. 5, W.E.L.S..	Seven dollars and fifty-six cents...........	7 56
No. 8, R. 5, W.E.L.S..	Six dollars and nineteen cents..............	6 19
No. 9, R. 5, W.E.L.S..	Four dollars and thirteen cents.............	4 13
No. 13, R. 5, W.E.L.S..	Four dollars and thirteen cents.............	4 13
No. 14, R. 5, W.E.L.S..	Six dollars and eighty-eight cents.........	6 88
No. 15, R. 5, W.E.L.S..	Six dollars and nineteen cents..............	6 19
No. 16, R. 5, W.E.L.S..	Two dollars and seventy-five cents........	2 75
No. 17, R. 5, W.E.L.S..	Two dollars and seventy-five cents........	2 75
No. 10, R. 6, W.E.L.S..	Five dollars and fifty cents...................	5 50
No. 14, R. 6, W.E.L.S..	Six dollars and nineteen cents..............	6 19
No. 15, R. 6, W.E.L.S..	Six dollars and nineteen cents..............	6 19
No. 16, R. 6, W.E.L.S..	Two dollars and seventy-five cents........	2 75
No. 9, R. 7, W.E.L.S..	Six dollars and eighty-seven cents........	6 87
No. 10, R. 7, W.E.L.S..	Six dollars and eighty-eight cents..........	$6 88
No. 11, R. 7, W.E.L.S..	Six dollars and eighteen cents...............	6 18
No. 12, R. 7, W.E.L.S..	Six dollars and eighteen cents...............	6 18
No. 13, R. 7, W.E.L.S..	Two dollars and seventy-five cents........	2 75
No. 14, R. 7, W.E.L.S..	Six dollars and eighty|eight cents..........	6 88
No. 9, R. 8, W.E.L.S..	Five dollars and fifty cents...................	5 50
No. 10, R. 8, W.E.L.S..	Six dollars and eighty|eight cents..........	6 88
No. 11, R. 8, W.E.L.S..	Five dollars and fifty cents...................	5 50
No. 12, R. 8, W.E.L.S..	Five dollars and fifty cents...................	5 50
No. 13, R. 8, W.E.L.S..	Five dollars and fifty cents...................	5 50
No. 14, R. 8, W.E.L.S..	Five dollars and fifty cents...................	5 50
No. 15, R. 8, W.E.L.S..	Four dollars and eighty-one cents.........	4 81
No. 16, R. 8, W.E.L.S..	Four dollars and eighty-one cents.........	4 81
No. 11, R. 9, W.E.L.S..	Six dollars and nineteen cents..............	6 19
No. 12, R. 9, W.E.L.S..	Five dollars and fifty cents...................	5 50

CHAP. 417

AROOSTOOK COUNTY—TIMBER AND GRASS—Continued.

No. 13, R. 9, W.E.L.S.	Five dollars and fifty cents..................	5 50
No. 14, R. 9, W.E.L.S.	Four dollars and eighty-one cents........	4 81
No. 15, R. 9, W.E.L.S.	Four dollars and eighty-one cents........	4 81
No. 16, R. 9, W.E.L.S.	Four dollars and eighty-one cents........	4 81
No. 11, R. 10, W.E.L.S.	Six dollars and nineteen cents..............	6 19
No. 12, R. 10, W.E.L.S.	Four dollars and thirteen cents............	4 13
No. 13, R. 10, W.E.L.S.	Four dollars and eighty-one cents........	4 81
No. 14, R. 10, W.E.L.S.	Four dollars and eighty-one cents........	4 81
No. 15, R. 10, W.E.L.S.	Four dollars and thirteen cents............	4 13
No. 18, R. 10, W.E.L.S.	Five dollars and twenty cents...............	5 20
No. 11, R. 11, W.E.L.S.	Six dollars and nineteen cents..............	6 19
No. 12, R. 11, W.E.L.S.	Five dollars and fifty cents..................	5 50
No. 13, R. 11, W.E.L.S.	One dollars and thirty-eight cents..........	1 38
No. 14, R. 11, W.E.L.S.	Four dollars and eighty-one cents........	4 81
No. 15, R. 11, W.E.L.S.	Three dollars and forty-three cents........	3 43
No. 18, R. 11, W.E.L.S.	Four dollars and thirteen cents............	4 13
No. 19, R. 11, W.E.L.S.	Four dollars and thirteen cents............	4 13
No. 20, R. 11 & 12, W. E. L. S.................	Five dollars and fifteen cents...............	5 15
No. 11, R. 12, W.E.L.S.	Five dollars and fifty cents..................	5 50
No. 12, R. 12, W.E.L.S.	Four dollars and eighty-one cents........	$4 81
No. 13, R. 12, W.E.L.S.	Four dollars and twelve cents..............	4 12
No. 14, R. 12, W.E.L.S.	Four dollars and twelve cents..............	4 12
No. 15, R. 12, W.E.L.S.	Four dollars and eighty-one cents........	4 81
No. 16, R. 12, W.E.L.S.	Two dollars and seventy-five cents........	2 75
No. 17, R. 12, W.E.L.S.	Four dollars and twelve cents..............	4 12
No. 18, R. 12, W.E.L.S.	Four dollars and twelve cents..............	4 12
No. 19, R. 12, W.E.L.S.	Four dollars and thirteen cents............	4 13
No. 11, R. 13, W.E.L.S.	Five dollars and fifty cents..................	5 50
No. 12, R. 13, W.E.L.S.	Four dollars and thirteen cents............	4 13
No. 13, R. 13, W.E.L.S.	Four dollars and eighty-one cents........	4 81
No. 14, R. 13, W.E.L.S.	Three dollars and forty-four cents........	3 44
No. 15, R. 13, W.E.L.S.	Four dollars and thirteen cents............	4 13
No. 16, R. 13, W.E.L.S.	Three dollars and forty-four cents........	3 44
No. 17, R. 13, W.E.L.S.	Three dollars and forty-four cents........	3 44
No. 18, R. 13, W.E.L.S.	Four dollars and thirteen cents............	4 13
No. 11, R. 14, W.E.L.S.	Five dollars and fifty cents..................	5 50
No. 12, R. 14, W.E.L.S.	Four dollars and thirteen cents............	4 13
No. 13, R. 14, W.E.L.S.	Four dollars and thirteen cents............	4 13
No. 14, R. 14, W.E.L.S.	Five dollars and fifty cents..................	5 50
No. 15, R. 14, W.E.L.S.	Three dollars and seventy-nine cents.....	3 79
No. 16, R. 14, W.E.L.S.	Four dollars and thirteen cents............	4 13
No. 17, R. 14, W.E.L.S.	Three dollars and nine cents................	3 09

STATE TAX.

AROOSTOOK COUNTY—TIMBER AND GRASS—Concluded.

No. 11, R. 15, W.E.L.S.	Four dollars and eighty-one cents.........	4 81
No. 12, R. 15, W.E.L.S.	Three dollars and forty-four cents.........	3 44
No. 13, R. 15, W.E.L.S.	Three dollars and forty-four cents.........	3 44
No. 14, R. 15, W.E.L.S.	Four dollars and thirteen cents............	4 13
No. 15, R. 15, W.E.L.S.	Three dollars and forty-four cents.........	3 44
No. 11, R. 16, W.E.L.S.	Two dollars and seventy-five cents........	2 75
No. 12, R. 16, W.E.L.S.	Two dollars and seventy-five cents........	2 75
No. 13, R. 16, W.E.L.S.	Five dollars and sixteen cents.............	5 16
No. 14, R. 16, W.E.L.S.	Three dollars and sixty cents..............	3 60
No. 11, R. 17, W.E.L.S.	Four dollars and thirteen cents............	4 13
No. 12, R. 17, W.E.L.S.	Two dollars and seventy-five cents........	2 75
Total	Five hundred twenty-five dollars and thirty-two cents	$525 32

CUMBERLAND COUNTY.

Baldwin	Nine hundred seventy-seven dollars and eleven cents	$977 11
Bridgton	Three thousand seven hundred twenty-five dollars and eleven cents.............	3,725 11
Brunswick	Ten thousand nine hundred forty-one dollars and five cents	10,941 05
Cape Elizabeth	One thousand nine hundred fifteen dollars and forty-five cents	1,915 45
Casco	Seven hundred fifty-seven dollars and twenty-seven cents	757 27
Cumberland	Two thousand one hundred forty-one dollars and fifty-nine cents	2,141 59
Falmouth	Three thousand fifty-five dollars and twenty-four cents	3,055 24
Freeport	Three thousand two hundred twenty-nine dollars and six cents	3,229 06
Gorham	Four thousand ninety-six dollars and thirty-three cents	4,096 33
Gray	One thousand five hundred thirty-eight dollars and eighty-three cents...........	1,538 83
Harpswell	One thousand nine hundred ninety-two dollars and fifty-nine cents................	1,992 59
Harrison	One thousand one hundred thirty-one dollars and twenty-four cents..............	1,131 24
Naples	Six hundred ninety-eight dollars and seventy-eight cents	698 78
New Gloucester	Two thousand nine hundred seventeen dollars and sixteen cents	2,917 16
North Yarmouth	Eight hundred ninety-five dollars and fifty-eight cents	895 58
Otisfield	Six hundred forty-nine dollars and sixty-seven cents	649 67
Portland	One hundred thirty-five thousand two hundred two dollars and eighteen cents	135,202 18
Pownal	Seven hundred eight dollars and thirty-six cents	708 36

STATE TAX.

CUMBERLAND COUNTY—Concluded.

Raymond	Five hundred fifty-two dollars and thirty cents	552 30
Scarborough	Two thousand six hundred eighty-three dollars and one cent	2,683 01
Sebago	Four hundred forty-one dollars and twenty-two cents	441 22
South Portland	Seven thousand one hundred forty-eight dollars and five cents	7,148 05
Standish	One thousand six hundred thirty-nine dollars and eighty-seven cents	1,639 87
Westbrook	Ten thousand nine hundred ninety-nine dollars and sixty-two cents	10,999 62
Windham	Two thousand six hundred twenty-two dollars and ninety-four cents	2,622 94
Yarmouth	Three thousand six hundred thirty-nine dollars and eighty-two cents	3,639 82
Total	Two hundred six thousand two hundred ninety-nine dollars and forty-three cents	$206,299 43

FRANKLIN COUNTY.

Avon	Three hundred sixty-four dollars and seventy-seven cents	$364 77
Carthage	Three hundred forty-seven dollars and sixty-one cents	347 61
Chesterville	Six hundred eighty-one dollars and eighty-four cents	681 84
Eustis	Four hundred eleven dollars and thirty-nine cents	411 39
Farmington	Five thousand two hundred twenty-three dollars and ninety-three cents	5,223 93
Freeman	Two hundred sixty-eight dollars and fourteen cents	268 14
Industry	Two hundred eighty-three dollars and twenty-eight cents	283 28
Jay	Four thousand five hundred three dollars and twenty-five cents	4,503 25
Kingfield	Nine hundred ninety-three dollars and thirty-two cents	993 32
Madrid	Two hundred twenty-one dollars and seventy-four cents	221 74
New Sharon	One thousand fifteen dollars and ninety-five cents	1,015 95
New Vineyard	Four hundred forty-six dollars and fifty-four cents	446 54
Phillips	One thousand four hundred eighty-six dollars and eighty-two cents	1,486 82
Rangeley	One thousand twenty-one dollars and ninety-eight cents	1,021 98
Salem	One hundred thirty dollars and sixteen cents	130 16
Strong	Seven hundred ten dollars and fifty-nine cents	710 59
Temple	Three hundred forty-eight dollars and twenty-three cents	348 23
Weld	Five hundred sixty dollars and seventy-six cents	560 76
Wilton	Two thousand ninety-one dollars and sixty-eight cents	2,091 68
Total	Twenty-one thousand one hundred eleven dollars and ninety-eight cents	$21,111 98

STATE TAX.

CHAP. 417

FRANKLIN COUNTY WILD LANDS.

No. 4, Washington Pl.	Eleven dollars	$11 00
No. 2, R. 1, S. part Sandy River, W. B. K. P.	Ninety-two dollars and forty cents	92 40
No. 2, R. 1, N. part Greenvale Pl., W. B. K. P.	Sixty-six dollars	66 00
No. 3, R. 1, Rangeley Pl., W. B. K. P.	Five hundred thirty-nine dollars	539 00
No. 4, R. 1, B. K. P., "Elias Thomas Tract" Mt. Abram	Eighteen dollars and twenty-three cents	18 23
No. 4, R. 1, B. K. P., N. E. part, "Mead Tract" Mt. Abram	Ninety-five dollars and fifty-four cents	95 54
No. 4, R. 2, B. K. P., Crockertown	Two hundred forty-two dollars and forty-four cents	242 44
No. 4, R. 3, B. K. P., S. half, Wyman	One hundred seven dollars and sixty-one cents	107 61
D, R. 1.	One hundred sixty-nine dollars and thirteen cents	169 13
No. 1, R. 2, W. B. K. P., Redington	Two hundred twelve dollars and fourteen cents	212 14
No. 2, R. 2, W. B. K. P., Dallas Pl.	Two hundred twelve dollars and fourteen cents	212 14
No. 1, R. 3, Coplin Pl., W. B. K. P.	One hundred eighty-one dollars and eighty-three cents	181 83
No. 2, R. 3, W. B. K. P., Lang Pl.	One hundred fifty-one dollars and fifty-two cents	151 52
No. 3, R. 3, W. B. K. P., Davis	Three hundred two dollars and fifty cents	302 50
No. 3, R. 2, B. K. P., Jerusalem	One hundred fifty-eight dollars and forty cents	158 40
No. 2, R. 4, W. B. K. P., Tim Pond	One hundred eighty-one dollars and eighty-three cents	181 83
No. 3, R. 4, W. B. K. P., Stetsontown	Two hundred thirteen dollars and seventy-seven cents	213 77
No. 1, R. 5, W. B. K. P., Jim Pond	Fifty-seven dollars and ninety-seven cents	57 97
No. 2, R. 5, W. B. K. P., Alder Stream	Two hundred twelve dollars and fourteen cents	212 14
No. 3, R. 5, W. B. K. P., Seven Ponds	Three hundred thirty-eight dollars and eighty cents	338 80
No. 1, R. 6, S. part W. B. K. P., Kibby	One hundred twenty-one dollars and twenty-two cents	121 22
No. 1, R. 6, N. part W. B. K. P., Kibby	One hundred eighty-two dollars and eighty-two cents	$182 82
No. 2, R. 6, W. B. K. P., Chain Pond	Two hundred six dollars and twenty-five cents	206 25
No. 3, R. 6, W. B. K. P., Mass. Gore	One hundred thirty dollars and forty-eight cents	130 48
No. 1, R. 7, W. B. K. P.	Two hundred twenty-two dollars and twenty cents	222 20
No. 2, R. 7, W. B. K. P., Merrill Strip	Seventy-six dollars and eighty-six cents	76 86
No. 1, R. 8, W. B. K. P., Lowelltown	One hundred fifty dollars and eight cents	150 08

FRANKLIN COUNTY WILD LANDS—Concluded.

No. 2, R. 2, W. B. K. P., Beattie	One hundred fifty-four dollars	154 00
Gore north of Nos. 2 and 3, R. 6, Coburn	Ninety-six dollars and twenty-five cents	96 25
No. 6, N. of Weld & between Phillips and Byron, East part	One hundred twenty-eight dollars and twenty cents	128 20
No. 6, N. of Weld & between Phillips and Byron, West part	Seventy-five dollars and sixty-eight cents	75 68
Gore north of No. 1, R. 8	Seventy dollars and thirty-eight cents	70 38
Letter E	One hundred twenty dollars and twenty-six cents	120 26
Perkins	Forty-four dollars	44 00
Total	Five thousand three hundred forty-three dollars and seven cents	$5,343 07

FRANKLIN COUNTY—TIMBER AND GRASS ON RESERVED LANDS.

D., R. 1	Six dollars and sixty cents	$6 60
No. 1, R. 2, W. B. K. P.	Eight dollars and twenty-five cents	8 25
No. 3, R. 3, W. B. K. P.	Thirteen dollars and twenty cents	13 20
No. 2, R. 4, W. B. K. P.	Six dollars and seventy-four cents	6 74
No. 3, R. 4, W. B. K. P.	Eight dollars and twenty-five cents	8 25
No. 1, R. 5, W. B. K. P.	One dollar and thirty-two cents	1 32
No. 2, R. 5, W. B. K. P.	Eight dollars and twenty-five cents	8 25
No. 3, R. 5, W. B. K. P.	Thirteen dollars and twenty cents	13 20
No. 1, R. 6, W. B. K. P.	Twelve dollars and eighty-three cents	12 83
No. 2, R. 6, W. B. K. P.	Six dollars and sixty cents	6 60
No. 3, R. 6, W. B. K. P.	Five dollars and thirty-nine cents	5 39
No. 1, R. 7, W. B. K. P.	Nine dollars and sixty-two cents	9 62
No. 2, R. 7, W. B. K. P.	Two dollars and ninety-five cents	2 95
No. 1, R. 8, W. B. K. P.	Five dollars and fifty cents	5 50
No. 4, R. 1, B.P.W.K.R.	Five dollars and twenty-eight cents	5 28
No. 3, R. 2, B.P.W.K.R.	Five dollars and twenty-eight cents	5 28
No. 4, R. 2, B.P.W.K.R.	Six dollars and sixty cents	6 60
No. 4, R. 2, & ½, B. P. W. K. R.	Four dollars and sixty-two cents	4 62
No. 6, North of Weld	Seven dollars and ninety-two cents	7 92
Tract north of No. 1, R. 2, W. B. K. P.	Two dollars and twelve cents	2 12
Total	One hundred forty dollars and fifty-two cents	$140 52

STATE TAX.

HANCOCK COUNTY.

Amherst	Two hundred twenty dollars and forty-eight cents	$220 48
Aurora	One hundred nine dollars and seven cents	109 07
Bluehill	One thousand five hundred thirteen dollars and seventy-eight cents	1,513 78
Brooklin	Five hundred eighteen dollars and thirty-eight cents	518 38
Brooksville	Six hundred thirty-two dollars and eighty-two cents	632 82
Bucksport	Two thousand six hundred seventy-four dollars and fifty-five cents	2,674 55
Castine	One thousand three hundred fifty-eight dollars and sixty cents	1,358 60
Cranberry Isles	Three hundred forty-eight dollars and ninety-seven cents	348 97
Deer Isle	One thousand thirty-nine dollars and sixty-eight cents	1,039 68
Dedham	Two hundred thirty-one dollars and thirty-one cents	231 31
Eastbrook	One hundred thirty-nine dollars and eighteen cents	139 18
Eden	Twelve thousand eight hundred sixty-seven dollars and fifty-six cents	12,867 56
Ellsworth	Five thousand two hundred thirty dollars and eighty-eight cents	5,230 88
Franklin	Nine hundred seven dollars and eighty-four cents	907 84
Gouldsboro	Eight hundred forty-nine dollars	849 00
Hancock	Eight hundred thirteen dollars and thirty-seven cents	813 37
Isle au Haut	One hundred ninety-five dollars and thirty-eight cents	195 38
Lamoine	Five hundred twelve dollars and twenty-eight cents	512 28
Mariaville	One hundred forty-one dollars and sixty-two cents	141 62
Mount Desert	Four thousand thirty-four dollars and twenty-one cents	4,034 21
Orland	Seven hundred forty dollars and ninety-three cents	740 93
Otis	Sixty-seven dollars and eighty-eight cents	67 88
Penobscot	Seven hundred thirty-eight dollars and seventy-seven cents	738 77
Sedgwick	Five hundred seventy-nine dollars and seventy cents	$579 70
Sorrento	Five hundred five dollars and forty-six cents	505 46
Stonington	Six hundred eighty-six dollars and ninety-four cents	686 94
Sullivan	Nine hundred twenty dollars and eleven cents	920 11
Surry	Four hundred sixty-eight dollars and ninety-five cents	468 95

HANCOCK COUNTY—Concluded.

Swan's Island	Three hundred eighty-six dollars and twenty-three cents	386 23
Tremont	One thousand four hundred eighty-six dollars and thirty-three cents	1,486 33
Trenton	Three hundred seventy-two dollars and seventy-six cents	372 76
Verona	One hundred seventy-nine dollars and ninety-five cents	179 95
Waltham	Two hundred two dollars and eighty-two cents	202 82
Winter Harbor	One thousand seven dollars and thirty-one cents	1,007 31
Long Island Pl.	Sixty one dollars and ninety-one cents	61 91
Total	Forty-two thousand seven hundred forty-five dollars and one cent	$42,745 01

HANCOCK COUNTY WILD LANDS.

No. 3, North Division	One hundred fifty-one dollars and fifty-three cents	$151 53
No. 4, North Division	One hundred fifty-one dollars and fifty-three cents	151 53
Strip N. of No. 3, N. Division	Fifty-three dollars and ninety-three cents	53 93
Strip N. of No. 4, N. Division	Fifty-three dollars and ninety-three cents	53 93
No. 7, South Div. N. part	Fifty-nine dollars and ninety-five cents	59 95
No. 7, South Div. S. part	Forty-five dollars and forty-six cents	45 46
No. 8, South Division	Thirty-nine dollars and sixty cents	39 60
No. 9, South Division	Nineteen dollars and eighty cents	19 80
No. 10	Ninety-four dollars and sixty-one cents	94 61
No. 16, Middle Division	Sixty dollars and sixty-one cents	60 61
No. 21, Middle Division Moose Hill	Sixty dollars and sixty-one cents	60 61
No. 22, Middle Division	Ninety dollars and ninety-two cents	90 92
No. 26, Middle Division	One hundred fifty-one dollars and fifty-two cents	151 52
No. 32, Middle Division	One hundred thirty-six dollars and thirty-seven cents	136 37
No. 33, Middle Division Great Pond	One hundred twenty-one dollars and twenty-two cents	121 22
No. 34, Middle Division	One hundred eighty-one dollars and eighty-three cents	181 83
No. 35, Middle Division	Seventy-five dollars and seventy-six cents	75 76
No. 39, Middle Division part of	One hundred five dollars and fifty-eight cents	105 58
No. 39, Middle Division "Black Tract, Tannery Lot"	Twenty-seven dollars and fifty cents	27 50
No. 40, Middle Division	One hundred fifty-one dollars and fifty-two cents	151 52
No. 41, Middle Division	Two hundred twelve dollars and fourteen cents	212 14
Butter Island	Seven dollars and seventy cents	7 70
Eagle Island	Thirteen dollars and seventy-five cents	13 75
Spruce Head & Bear Island	Two dollars and seventy-five cents	2 75

STATE TAX.

CHAP. 417

HANCOCK COUNTY WILD LANDS—Concluded.

Beach Island	One dollar and sixty-five cents	1 65
Hog Island	Four dollars and forty cents	4 40
Bradbury's Island	Three dollars and thirty cents	3 30
Pond, near Little Deer Isle	Fifty-five cents	55
Western Island	Fifty-five cents	55
Little Spruce Island	Sixty-nine cents	69
Marshall's Island	Thirteen dollars and seventy-five cents	13 75
Pickering's Island	Nine dollars and seven cents	9 07
Total	Two thousand one hundred four dollars and eight cents	$2,104 08

HANCOCK COUNTY—TIMBER AND GRASS ON RESERVED LANDS.

No. 3, North Division	Five dollars and twenty-eight cents	$5 28
No. 7, South Division	Forty-eight cents	48
No. 10	Two dollars and sixty-four cents	2 64
No. 16, Middle Division	One dollar and thirty-two cents	1 32
No. 22, Middle Division	Two dollars and sixty-four cents	2 64
No. 28, Middle Division	Five dollars and twenty-eight cents	5 28
No. 32, Middle Division	Four dollars and sixty-two cents	4 62
No. 34, Middle Division	Six dollars and sixty cents	6 60
No. 35, Middle Division	Two dollars and sixty-four cents	2 64
No. 39, Middle Division	Three dollars and thirty cents	3 30
No. 40, Middle Division	Five dollars and twenty-eight cents	5 28
No. 41, Middle Division	Seven dollars and ninety-two cents	7 92
Total	Forty-eight dollars	$48 00

KENNEBEC COUNTY.

Albion	One thousand twenty-four dollars and sixty-six cents	$1,024 66
Augusta	Twenty-one thousand nineteen dollars and eighty cents	21,019 80
Belgrade	One thousand one hundred ninety-eight dollars and ninety-three cents	1,198 93
Benton	One thousand two hundred thirty-eight dollars and twenty-one cents	1,238 21
Chelsea	Six hundred forty-two dollars and fifty-one cents	642 51
China	One thousand four hundred fifty-nine dollars and sixty-five cents	1,459 65
Clinton	One thousand six hundred twenty-seven dollars and ninety-eight cents	1,627 98
Farmingdale	One thousand six hundred two dollars and ten cents	1,602 10

KENNEBEC COUNTY—Concluded.

Fayette	Five hundred fifty-four dollars and ninety-eight cents	554 98
Gardiner	Nine thousand nine hundred thirty-one dollars and seventy-three cents	9,931 73
Hallowell	Four thousand one hundred twelve dollars and fifty-three cents	4,112 53
Litchfield	One thousand one dollars and forty-four cents	1,001 44
Manchester	Seven hundred nineteen dollars and twenty-one cents	719 21
Monmouth	One thousand eight hundred two dollars and fourteen cents	1,802 14
Mount Vernon	Eight hundred seventy-six dollars and forty-four cents	876 44
Oakland	Two thousand five hundred thirteen dollars and seventy-seven cents	2,513 77
Pittston	One thousand three hundred twenty dollars	1,320 00
Randolph	Eight hundred ninety-two dollars and four cents	892 04
Readfield	One thousand three hundred twenty-three dollars and fifty-three cents	1,323 53
Rome	Two hundred twenty-six dollars and ninety-one cents	226 91
Sidney	One thousand two hundred eight dollars and forty-two cents	1,208 42
Vassalborough	Two thousand six hundred forty-two dollars and twenty cents	2,642 20
Vienna	Three hundred thirty-eight dollars and fifty-two cents	338 52
Waterville	Sixteen thousand one hundred seventy-six dollars and fifty-six cents	16,176 56
Wayne	Six hundred dollars and eighty-three cents	600 83
West Gardiner	Eight hundred sixteen dollars and eighty-five cents	816 85
Windsor	Six hundred fifty dollars and thirty-nine cents	650 39
Winslow	Five thousand eight hundred thirty-nine dollars	5,839 00
Winthrop	Three thousand two hundred sixty-one dollars and five cents	3,261 05
Unity Pl.	Forty-seven dollars and twenty-eight cents	47 28
Total	Eighty-six thousand six hundred sixty-nine dollars and sixty-six cents	$86,669 66

KNOX COUNTY.

Appleton	Six hundred eighty-six dollars and twenty cents	$686 20
Camden	Six thousand two hundred ninety-one dollars and forty-eight cents	6,291 48
Cushing	Three hundred thirty-four dollars and fifty-five cents	334 55
Friendship	Six hundred six dollars	606 00

STATE TAX.

KNOX COUNTY—Concluded.

Hope	Five hundred fifty-nine dollars and ninety cents	559 90
Hurricane Isle	One hundred thirty-eight dollars and seventy-three cents	138 73
North Haven	Six hundred sixty-one dollars and eighty-four cents	661 84
Rockland	Fifteen thousand one hundred fifty-seven dollars and eighty-nine cents	15,157 89
Rockport	Three thousand one hundred fifty-seven dollars and forty-four cents	3,157 44
So. Thomaston	One thousand twenty-eight dollars and forty-nine cents	1,028 49
St. George	One thousand one hundred thirty-three dollars and seventy-two cents	1,133 72
Thomaston	Three thousand five hundred ninety-nine dollars and ninety-two cents	3,599 92
Union	One thousand four hundred twenty-eight dollars and ninety-five cents	1,428 95
Vinalhaven	One thousand eight hundred nineteen dollars and seventy-one cents	1,819 71
Warren	Two thousand two hundred ninety-two dollars and sixty-nine cents	2,292 69
Washington	Seven hundred forty-four dollars and thirty-nine cents	744 39
Criehaven Pl.	Twenty-nine dollars and fifty-five cents	29 55
Matinicus Isle Pl.	One hundred three dollars and ninety-nine cents	103 99
Total	Thirty-nine thousand seven hundred seventy-five dollars and forty-four cents	$39,775 44

LINCOLN COUNTY.

Alna	Four hundred fifty-two dollars and forty-six cents	$452 46
Boothbay	One thousand five hundred forty-six dollars and thirty-five cents	1,546 35
Boothbay Harbor	Two thousand nine hundred nine dollars and six cents	2,909 06
Bremen	Three hundred eighty-two dollars and twenty-one cents	382 21
Bristol	Two thousand one hundred eighty-two dollars and forty-six cents	2,182 46
Damariscotta	One thousand two hundred fifty-eight dollars and three cents	1,258 03
Dresden	One thousand forty-one dollars and sixty-eight cents	1,041 68
Edgecomb	Four hundred ninety-two dollars and thirty-six cents	492 36
Jefferson	One thousand two hundred thirteen dollars and ninety-six cents	1,213 96
Newcastle	One thousand nine hundred one dollars and sixty-two cents	1,901 62
Nobleborough	Six hundred eighty-five dollars and forty-five cents	685 45

LINCOLN COUNTY—Concluded.

Somerville	One hundred forty dollars and forty-three cents	140 43
Southport	Eight hundred sixty-two dollars and thirty-two cents	862 32
Waldoboro	Two thousand five hundred forty dollars and sixty-two cents	2,540 62
Westport	Two hundred forty-four dollars and one cent	244 01
Whitefield	One thousand two hundred nineteen dollars and eighty-six cents	1,219 86
Wiscasset	One thousand three hundred eighteen dollars and sixty-seven cents	1,318 67
Monhegan Pl.	Ninety-four dollars and twenty-three cents	94 23
Total	Twenty thousand four hundred eighty-five dollars and seventy-eight cents	$20,485 78

OXFORD COUNTY.

Albany	Three hundred eighty-five dollars and eight cents	$385 08
Andover	Five hundred seventy-nine dollars and sixty-eight cents	579 68
Bethel	Two thousand three hundred fifty-nine dollars and twenty-six cents	2,359 26
Brownfield	Eight hundred fifty-five dollars and thirty-one cents	855 31
Buckfield	One thousand ninety-six dollars and fifty-seven cents	1,096 57
Byron	Two hundred forty-one dollars and ninety-seven cents	241 97
Canton	Nine hundred sixty-four dollars and eighty-seven cents	964 87
Denmark	Seven hundred ninety-two dollars and ninety-two cents	792 92
Dixfield	Nine hundred seventy-three dollars and ninety-four cents	973 94
Fryeburg	Two thousand two hundred thirty-seven dollars and twenty-one cents	2,237 21
Gilead	Three hundred sixty-one dollars and fifty-three cents	361 53
Grafton	One hundred sixty-two dollars and four cents	162 04
Greenwood	Four hundred sixty-three dollars and seventy-four cents	463 74
Hanover	Two hundred twenty dollars and seventy-two cents	220 72
Hartford	Seven hundred twenty dollars and twenty-four cents	720 24
Hebron	Six hundred twenty-five dollars and seventy-five cents	625 75
Hiram	Nine hundred sixty dollars and nine cents	960 09
Lovell	One thousand sixty-seven dollars and fifty-five cents	1,067 55

STATE TAX.

CHAP. 417

OXFORD COUNTY—Concluded.

Mason	One hundred twenty-two dollars and fifty-one cents	122 51
Mexico	Nine hundred sixty dollars and fifty-seven cents	960 57
Newry	Three hundred twenty-seven dollars and forty-eight cents	327 48
Norway	Three thousand five hundred seventy dollars and eighty-nine cents	3,570 89
Oxford	One thousand two hundred thirty-five dollars and thirty-five cents	1,235 35
Paris	Three thousand seven hundred twenty-five dollars and thirty-three cents	3,725 33
Peru	Six hundred sixty-nine dollars and sixty cents	669 60
Porter	Six hundred fifty-two dollars and sixty-one cents	652 61
Roxbury	One hundred seventy-six dollars and fourteen cents	176 14
Rumford	Seven thousand five hundred eighty-one dollars and ninety-nine cents	7,581 99
Stoneham	Two hundred forty dollars and twenty-two cents	240 22
Stow	Three hundred thirty-seven dollars and nineteen cents	337 19
Sumner	Six hundred sixty-four dollars and fifty cents	664 50
Sweden	Four hundred eighteen dollars and eighty-seven cents	418 87
Upton	Two hundred eighty-six dollars and eighty-four cents	286 84
Waterford	Eight hundred six dollars and seven cents	806 07
Woodstock	Six hundred one dollars and forty-one cents	601 41
Milton Pl.	One hundred fifty-four dollars and forty-one cents	154 41
Total	Thirty-seven thousand six hundred dollars and forty-five cents	$37,600 45

OXFORD COUNTY WILD LANDS.

Fryeburg Acad. Grant	Forty-nine dollars and fifty cents	$49 50
A, 1, Riley Pl	Two hundred sixty-nine dollars and fifty cents	269 50
Andover North Surplus	One hundred fifty-three dollars and sixty-two cents	153 62
Andover West Surplus	Sixty-four dollars and sixty-nine cents	64 69
C	Two hundred eighty-nine dollars and seventy-seven cents	289 77
C Surplus	One hundred fifty-one dollars and five cents	151 05
No. 4, R. 1, Richardsontown	Three hundred twenty-two dollars and eighty-five cents	322 85
No. 5, R. 1, Magalloway Pl.	Three hundred thirty-eight dollars and three cents	338 03

CHAP. 417

STATE TAX.

OXFORD COUNTY WILD LANDS—Concluded.

No. 4, R. 2, Adamstown	Six hundred seven dollars and twenty cents	607 20
No. 5, R. 2, Lincoln Pl.	Two hundred thirty-five dollars and ninety-eight cents	235 98
No. 4, R. 3, Lower Cupsuptic	Three hundred seventy-five dollars and thirty-seven cents	375 37
No. 5, R. 3, Parkertown	Two hundred thirty-four dollars and twenty-seven cents	234 27
No. 4, R. 4, Upper Cupsuptic	Two hundred seventy-three dollars and twenty-four cents	273 24
No. 5, R. 4, Lynchtown	Two hundred fifty-eight dollars and twenty-four cents	258 24
No. 4, R. 5, Oxbow	One hundred ninety-one dollars and four cents	191 04
No. 4, R. 6, Bowmantown	Two hundred dollars and forty-six cents	200 46
No. 5, R. 5, Parmachenee	Two hundred seven dollars and eighty-nine cents	207 89
Bachelder's Grant	One hundred thirty-seven dollars and fifty cents	137 50
Total	Four thousand three hundred sixty dollars and twenty cents	$4,360 20

OXFORD COUNTY—TIMBER AND GRASS ON RESERVED LANDS.

C. R. 4, T. E. K. P.	Eleven dollars and eighty-eight cents	$11 88
No. 4, R. 1, W. B. K. P.	Eleven dollars and eighty-eight cents	11 88
No. 4, R. 2, W. B. K. P.	Twenty-three dollars and seventy-six cents	23 76
No. 4, R. 3, W. B. K. P.	Fifteen dollars and eighty-four cents	15 84
No. 5, R. 3, W. B. K. P.	Eight dollars and fifty-eight cents	8 58
No. 4, R. 4, W. B. K. P.	Ten dollars and fifty-six cents	10 56
No. 5, R. 4, W. B. K. P.	Nine dollars and twenty-four cents	9 24
No. 4, R. 5, W. B. K. P.	Seven dollars and ninety-two cents	7 92
No. 5, R. 5, W. B. K. P.	Seven dollars and ninety-two cents	7 92
No. 4, R. 6, W. B. K. P.	Eight dollars and twenty-five cents	8 25
Tract north of No. 4, R. 6, W. B. K. P.	Thirty-five cents	35
A, R. 1, (Riley)	Seven dollars and ninety-two cents	7 92
Andover, North Surplus	Three dollars and ninety-six cents	3 96
C. Surp'l	Seven dollars and four cents	7 04
Total	One hundred thirty-five dollars and ten cents	$135 10

STATE TAX.

PENOBSCOT COUNTY.

Alton	Two hundred thirteen dollars and two cents	$213 02
Argyle	One hundred sixty one dollars and sixty-seven cents	161 67
Bangor	Forty-five thousand one hundred thirty-five dollars and twenty cents	45,135 20
Bradford	Six hundred ninety-two dollars and seventy-three cents	692 73
Bradley	Four hundred twenty dollars and seventeen cents	420 17
Brewer	Five thousand fifty-three dollars and thirty-two cents	5,053 32
Burlington	Three hundred ninety-three dollars and sixty-one cents	393 61
Carmel	Eight hundred six dollars and seventy-four cents	806 74
Carroll	Three hundred one dollars and seventy-five cents	301 75
Charleston	Eight hundred nineteen dollars and seventy-two cents	819 72
Chester	One hundred ninety-one dollars and ninety-one cents	191 91
Clinton	One hundred fifty-seven dollars and twenty-seven cents	157 27
Corinna	One thousand two hundred sixty-two dollars and fifty-three cents	1,262 53
Corinth	One thousand one hundred fifty-eight dollars and forty-seven cents	1,158 47
Dexter	Three thousand three hundred two dollars and fifty-eight cents	3,302 58
Dixmont	Six hundred ninety-six dollars and six cents	696 06
Eddington	Four hundred thirty-five dollars and twenty-nine cents	435 29
Edinburg	Sixty-six dollars and five cents	66 05
Enfield	Six hundred forty-three dollars and forty-seven cents	643 47
Etna	Three hundred fifty-four dollars and eighty-one cents	354 81
Exeter	Nine hundred thirty-nine dollars and fifty-four cents	939 54
Garland	Eight hundred seventy dollars and forty-seven cents	870 47
Glenburn	Three hundred sixty-eight dollars and ninety-nine cents	365 99
Greenbush	Two hundred thirty dollars and fifty-seven cents	$230 57
Greenfield	One hundred fifteen dollars and twenty cents	115 20
Hampden	One thousand nine hundred sixteen dollars and forty-nine cents	1,916 49
Hermon	One thousand three dollars and twenty-three cents	1,003 23
Holden	Four hundred twenty-two dollars and fifteen cents	422 15

PENOBSCOT COUNTY Concluded.

Howland	Eight hundred forty-six dollars and seventy-four cents	846 74
Hudson	Two hundred ninety-three dollars and forty-nine cents	293 49
Levant	Four hundred sixty dollars and seventy cents	460 70
Lincoln	Four hundred sixty-four dollars and seventy-four cents	464 74
Lowell	Five hundred twenty-four dollars and eighty-three cents	524 83
Mattamiscontis	Three hundred fifty-eight dollars and thirty-one cents	358 31
Mattawamkeag	Six hundred seventy-four dollars and nineteen cents	674 19
Kenduskeag	One thousand three hundred forty-five dollars and thirty-five cents	1,345 35
Kingman	Two hundred dollars and twenty cents	200 20
Lagrange	Fifty-one dollars and ninety-six cents	51 96
Lee	Three hundred seventy-three dollars and forty-three cents	373 43
Maxfield	Seventy-one dollars and thirty-eight cents	71 38
Medway	One hundred seventy-three dollars and ninety-four cents	173 94
Milford	Eight hundred forty-seven dollars and ninety-four cents	847 94
Millinocket	One thousand nine hundred dollars and ninety-eight cents	1,900 98
Mount Chase	One hundred sixty seven dollars and seventy-six cents	167 76
Newburgh	Seven hundred thirteen dollars and ninety-three cents	713 93
Newport	One thousand six hundred forty-five dollars and seventeen cents	1,645 17
Old Town	Four thousand nine hundred twenty-two dollars and sixty-four cents	$4,922 64
Orono	Two thousand seven hundred ten dollars and twenty-five cents	2,710 25
Orrington	One thousand one hundred forty-five dollars and sixty-two cents	1,145 62
Passadumkeag	One hundred twenty-six dollars and seventy-two cents	126 72
Patten	One thousand three hundred fifty-three dollars and eighty-six cents	1,353 86
Plymouth	Four hundred sixty-eight dollars and eighty-five cents	468 85
Prentiss	Two hundred seven dollars and sixty-five cents	207 65
Springfield	Three hundred eighteen dollars and forty-seven cents	318 47
Stetson	Five hundred seventy-eight dollars and sixty-one cents	578 61
Veazie	Seven hundred eighteen dollars and seventy-two cents	718 72
Winn	Four hundred thirty seven dollars	437 00
Woodville	One hundred thirty-nine dollars and ten cents	139 10
Total	Ninety-two thousand three hundred seventy-five dollars and fifty-four cents	$92,375 54

STATE TAX. 699

CHAP. 417

PENOBSCOT COUNTY WILD LANDS.

No. 3, R. 1, N. B. P. P. East part	One hundred eighteen dollars and eighty cents	$118 80
No. 3, R. 1, N. B. P. P. West part	Fifty-eight dollars and eighty-five cents..	58 85
No. 4, R. 1, N. B. P. P. Lakeville Pl.	Two hundred fifty-four dollars any thirty-eight cents	254 38
No. 5, R. 1, N. B. P. P.	Sixty dollars and sixty-one cents	60 61
No. 6, R. 3, N. B. P. P. Webster Pl.	Eighty-six dollars and sixty-two cents....	86 62
No. 7, R. 4, N. B. P. P. Drew Pl	One hundred sixty-two dollars and eighty cents	162 80
No. 2, R. 8, N. W. P.	Two hundred seventy-seven dollars and forty-eight cents	277 48
No. 3, R. 8, N. W. P., E. half Seboeis Pl.	Eighty-three dollars and thirty-four cents	83 34
No. 3, R. 8, N. W. P., W. half Seboeis Pl.	Eighty-three dollars and thirty-four cents	83 34
No. 2, R. 9, N. W. P.	One hundred seventy-one dollars and twenty-seven cents	171 27
No. 3, R. 9, N. W. P., Eastern Division	Fifty-eight dollars and fifty-one cents....	58 51
No. 3, R. 9, N. W. P., Middle Division	Sixty-eight dollars and eleven cents	68 11
No. 3, R. 9, N. W. P., Westerly part	Seventy dollars and ninety-seven cents...	70 97
No. 1, R. 6, W. E. L. S.	One hundred twenty-one dollars	121 00
No. 2, R. 6, W. E. L. S., Hersey town	Two hundred eighty-five dollars and sixty-five cents	285 65
No. 3, R. 6, W. E. L. S., Stacyville Pl.	One hundred seventy-three dollars and twenty-five cents	173 25
No. 6, R. 6, W. E. L. S.	One hundred six dollars and seven cents..	106 07
No. 7, R. 6, W. E. L. S.	One hundred eighteen dollars and ninety-one cents	118 91
No. 8, R.6, W.E.L.S., N.½	Ninety one dollars and eight cents	91 08
No. 8, R.6, W.E.L.S., S.½	Ninety-one dollars and eight cents	91 08
A. R. 7, W. E. L. S.	One hundred twenty-nine dollars and fifty-three cents	129 53
No. 1, R. 7, W. E. L. S	Two hundred twenty-two dollars and thirty cents	222 30
No. 2, R. 7, W. E. L. S., Soldiertown	One hundred eighty-one dollars and eighty-three cents	181 83
No. 3, R. 7, W. E. L. S., S. part	Eighty-one dollars and seven cents	81 07
No. 3, R. 7, W. E. L. S., N. part	Sixty-nine dollars and seventy-six cents..	69 76
No. 4, R. 7, W. E. L. S., N. ½	Sixty dollars and sixty-one cents	$60 61
No. 4, R. 7, W. E. L. S., S. ½	Ninety dollars and ninety-one cents	90 91
No. 5, R. 7, W. E. L. S.	One hundred twenty-one dollars and twenty-two cents	121 22
No. 6, R. 7, W. E. L. S.	One hundred twenty-one dollars and twenty-two cents	121 22
No. 7, R. 7, W. E. L. S.	One hundred fifty-one dollars and fifty-two cents	151 52
No. 8, R. 7, W. E. L. S., N. half	Seventy-five dollars and seventy-six cents	75 76
No. 8, R. 7, W. E. L. S., S. W. ¼	Twenty-six dollars and fifty-one cents....	26 51

PENOBSCOT COUNTY WILD LANDS—Concluded.

No. 8, R. 7, W. E. L. S., S. E. ¼	Thirty-seven dollars and eighty-eight cents	37 88
East Hopkins Acad	Thirty-eight dollars and twenty-two cents	38 22
West Hopkins Acad	Forty-two dollars and five cents	42 05
No. 2, R. 8, W. E. L. S.	One hundred fifty-eight dollars and eighty-seven cents	158 87
A, R. 8 and 9, W.E.L.S., Long A	One hundred five dollars and fifty-three cents	105 53
A, R. 8 and 9, W.E.L.S., Veazie Gore	Six dollars and eighteen cents	6 18
No. 3, Indian purchase, W. E. L. S.		
No. 4, Indian purchase, W. E. L. S.	One hundred twenty-nine dollars and twenty-five cents	129 25
	One hundred forty-three dollars	143 00
No. 1, R. 8, W. E. L. S.	Ninety dollars and ninety-two cents	90 92
No. 2, R. 8, south half, W. E. L. S.	Eighty-three dollars and thirty-four cents	83 34
No. 2, R. 8, north half, W. E. L. S.	Eighty-three dollars and thirty-four cents	83 34
No. 3, R. 8, W. E. L. S.	One hundred fifty-one dollars and fifty-three cents	151 53
No. 4, R. 8, W. E. L. S.	Ninety dollars and ninety-two cents	90 92
No. 5, R. 8, W. E. L. S.	One hundred sixty-six dollars and sixty-eight cents	166 68
No. 6, R. 8, W. E. L. S., southeast quarter	Twenty-two dollars and seventy-three cents	22 73
No. 6, R. 8, W. E. L. S., west half	Sixty-eight dollars and nineteen cents	68 19
No. 6, R. 8, W. E. L. S., northeast quarter	Thirty-seven dollars and eighty-eight cents	37 88
No. 7, R. 8, W. E. L. S.	One hundred sixty-two dollars and fourteen cents	162 14
No. 1, North Division, Summit Pl.	One hundred twenty-one dollars and twenty-two cents	121 22
No. 2, North Division, Grand Falls Pl.	One hundred fifty-one dollars and fifty-three cents	151 53
Total	Five thousand seven hundred sixty-five dollars and seventy-six cents	$5,765 76

PENOBSCOT COUNTY—TIMBER AND GRASS ON RESERVED LANDS.

No. 1, R. 6, W. E. L. S.	Four dollars and thirteen cents	$4 13
No. 2, R. 6, W. E. L. S.	Eleven dollars	11 00
No. 6, R. 6, W. E. L. S.	Three dollars and forty-four cents	3 44
No. 7, R. 6, W. E. L. S.	Four dollars and twelve cents	4 12
No. 8, R. 6, W. E. L. S.	Six dollars and sixty cents	6 60
A, R. 7, W. E. L. S.	Four dollars and sixty-two cents	4 62
No. 1, R. 7, W. E. L. S.	Eight dollars and ninety-four cents	8 94
No. 2, R. 7, W. E. L. S.	Six dollars and sixty cents	6 60
No. 3, R. 7, W. E. L. S.	Five dollars and fifty cents	5 50
No. 4, R. 7, W. E. L. S.	Four dollars and thirteen cents	4 13
No. 5, R. 7, W. E. L. S.	Three dollars and ninety-two cents	3 92
No. 6, R. 7, W. E. L. S.	Four dollars and thirteen cents	4 13

STATE TAX. 701

CHAP. 417

PENOBSCOT COUNTY—TIMBER AND GRASS—Concluded.

No. 7, R. 7, W. E. L. S.	Five dollars and twenty-eight cents......	5 28
No. 8, R. 7, W. E. L. S.	Five dollars and fifty cents...............	5 50
A, R. 8 and 9, W.E.L.S.	Three dollars and forty-six cents..........	3 46
No. 1, R. 8, W. E. L. S.	Four dollars and ninety-five cents........	4 95
No. 2, R. 8, W. E. L. S.	Five dollars and ninety-four cents........	5 94
No. 3, R. 8, W. E. L. S.	Five dollars and fifty cents...............	5 50
No. 4, R. 8, W. E. L. S.	Two dollars and seventy-five cents.......	2 75
No. 5, R. 8, W E L. S.	Six dollars and nineteen cents.............	6 19
No. 6, R. 8, W. E. L. S.	Four dollars and eighty-one cents.........	4 81
No. 7, R. 8, W. E. L. S.	Six dollars and eighteen cents............	6 18
No. 8, R. 8, W. E. L. S.	Six dollars and eighteen cents............	6 18
No. 4, Indian Purchase, W. E. L. S.	Five dollars and fifty cents................	5 50
No. 3, R. 1, N. B. P. P.	Five dollars and fifty cents...............	5 50
No. 5, R. 1, N. B. P. P.	One dollar and sixty-five cents............	1 65
No. 2, R. 8, N. W. P...	Nine dollars and twenty-four cents........	9 24
No. 2, R. 9, N. W. P...	Four dollars and sixty-two cents..........	4 62
No. 3, R. 9, N. W. P...	Three dollars and ninety-six cents.........	3 96
Hopkins Acad. Grant..	Two dollars and twenty cents.............	2 20
Total	One hundred fifty-six dollars and fifty-four cents	$156 54

PISCATAQUIS COUNTY.

Abbot	Four hundred seventy-one dollars and thirty-three cents	$471 33
Atkinson	Four hundred fourteen dollars and thirty-six cents	414 36
Blanchard	One hundred eighty-seven dollars and twelve cents	187 12
Brownville	One thousand two hundred eighteen dollars and eighty-one cents	1,218 81
Dover	Two thousand five hundred fifty-two dollars and sixty-six cents	2,552 66
Foxcroft	One thousand eight hundred twenty-eight dollars and fifty-nine cents........	1,828 59
Greenville	One thousand two hundred fifty-six dollars and twenty-six cents................	1,256 26
Guilford	One thousand six hundred fifty-two dollars and twenty-eight cents...............	1,652 28
Medford	One hundred ninety dollars and ninety-six cents	190 96
Milo	One thousand two hundred seventy-one dollars and forty-six cents................	1,271 46
Monson	Six hundred seventy-two dollars and forty-nine cents	672 49
Orneville	Two hundred ninety dollars and fifty-nine cents	290 59
Parkman	Six hundred forty-nine dollars and nineteen cents	649 19

STATE TAX.

PISCATAQUIS COUNTY—Concluded.

Sangerville	One thousand four hundred fifty-nine dollars and fifty-six cents	1,459 56
Sebec	Four hundred fifty-three dollars and thirty-five cents	453 35
Shirley	Two hundred twenty-three dollars	223 00
Wellington	Two hundred sixty-five dollars and eighty-two cents	265 82
Williamsburg	One hundred seven dollars and twenty-two cents	107 22
Willimantic	Two hundred eighty-seven dollars and seventeen cents	287 17
Total	Fifteen thousand four hundred fifty-two dollars and twenty-two cents	$15,452 22

PISCATAQUIS COUNTY WILD LANDS.

No. 4, R. 8, N. W. P., south part Merrick Spool Co. Plant, Lakeview Pl.	One hundred sixty-five dollars	$165 00
No. 4, R. 8, N. W. P., E. ½, Lakeview Pl.	One hundred thirty-five dollars and forty-five cents	135 45
No. 4, R. 8, N. W. P., West part, Lakeview Pl.	Sixty-three dollars and thirteen cents	63 13
No. 6, R. 8, formerly Barnard Pl.	One hundred ten dollars and twenty-nine cents	110 29
No. 7, R. 8, formerly Bowerbank Pl.	Two hundred seventy-two dollars and seventy-four cents	272 74
No. 4, R. 9, N. W. P.	Two hundred twenty-seven dollars and twenty-nine cents	227 29
No. 5, R. 9, N. W. P.	Two hundred nine dollars and fifty-one cents	209 51
No. 6, R. 9, N. W. P., Katahdin Iron Works	Two hundred twenty-seven dollars and twenty-nine cents	227 29
No. 7, R. 9, N. W. P.	One hundred seventy dollars and thirty-nine cents	170 39
No. 8, R. 9, Elliottsville, N. W. P.	Two hundred sixty-one dollars and eleven cents	261 11
No. 3, R. 5, B.P.E.K.R., Little Squaw Town	Two hundred twelve dollars and fourteen cents	212 14
No. 2, R. 6, B.P.E.K.R., B'g Squaw Town	Two hundred sixty-seven dollars and nine cents	267 09
No. 1, R. 9, W. E. L. S.	One hundred and twenty-one dollars and twenty-two cents	121 22
No. 2, R. 9, W. E. L. S.	One hundred fifty-one dollars and fifty-two cents	151 52
No. 3, R. 9, W. E. L. S., Mt. Katahdin	One hundred sixty-six dollars and sixty-eight cents	166 68
No. 4, R. 9, W. E. L. S.	Two hundred twenty-seven dollars and twenty-nine cents	227 29
No. 5, R. 9, W. E. L. S.	One hundred ninety-six dollars and seventy-seven cents	196 77
No. 6, R. 9, W. E. L. S., Trout Brook Town	Two hundred six dollars and thirteen cents	206 13
No. 7, R. 9, W. E. L. S., east half	Sixty dollars and forty-nine cents	60 49
No. 7, R. 9, W. E. L. S., west half	Seventy-five dollars and sixty-one cents	75 61

STATE TAX. 703

CHAP. 417

PISCATAQUIS COUNTY WILD LANDS—CONTINUED.

No. 8, R. 9, W. E. L. S.	One hundred fifty-one dollars and twenty-three cents	151 23
No. 9, R. 9, W. E. L. S.	One hundred fifty-one dollars and three cents	151 03
No. 10, R. 9, W. E. L. S.	One hundred fifty-eight dollars and forty-five cents	158 45
A, R. 10, W. E. L. S.	One hundred fifty-one dollars and fifty-three cents	151 53
B, R. 10, W. E. L. S.	Ninety dollars and thirty-three cents	90 33
No. 1, R. 10, W. E. L. S.	One hundred fifty-one dollars and fifty-three cents	151 53
No. 2, R. 10, W. E. L. S.	One hundred fifty-one dollars and fifty-three cents	$151 53
No. 3, R. 10, W. E. L. S.	One hundred fifty-one dollars and fifty-three cents	151 53
No. 4, R. 10, W. E. L. S.	One hundred sixty-six dollars and sixty-eight cents	166 68
No. 5, R. 10, W. E. L. S., east half	Ninety-six dollars and sixty-three cents	96 63
No. 5, R. 10, N. W. fourth. W. E. L. S.	Fifty-five dollars and seventeen cents	55 17
No. 5, R. 10, S. W. fourth. W. E. L. S.	Thirty-two dollars and eighty-four cents	32 84
No. 6, R. 10, W. E. L. S.	One hundred seventy-one dollars and eighty-nine cents	171 89
No. 7, R. 10, W. E. L. S.	One hundred twenty-nine dollars and nineteen cents	129 19
No. 8, R. 10, W. E. L. S.	One hundred fifty-six dollars and forty-seven cents	156 47
No. 9, R. 10, W. E. L. S.	One hundred forty-two dollars and twenty-three cents	142 23
No. 10, R. 10, W. E. L. S.	One hundred eighty-four dollars and forty-seven cents	184 47
A, R. 11, W. E. L. S.	Two hundred twelve dollars and fourteen cents	212 14
B, R. 11, W. E. L. S.	Two hundred seventy-six dollars and fifty-nine cents	276 59
No. 1, R. 11, W. E. L. S.	One hundred eighty-one dollars and eighty-three cents	181 83
No. 2, R. 11, W. E. L. S., Rainbow Town	Two hundred twelve dollars and fourteen cents	212 14
No. 3, R. 11, W. E. L. S.	One hundred fifty-eight dollars and forty cents	158 40
No. 4, R. 11, W. E. L. S.	One hundred eighty-three dollars and ninety-six cents	183 96
No. 5, R. 11, W. E. L. S.	Two hundred dollars and five cents	200 05
No. 6, R. 11, W. E. L. S.	One hundred fifty-one dollars and fifty-three cents	151 53
No. 7, R. 11, W. E. L. S.	One hundred fifty-six dollars and seventy-seven cents	156 77
No. 8, R. 11, W. E. L. S., N. E. ¼	Thirty-eight dollars and fifteen cents	38 15
No. 8, R. 11, W. E. L. S., W. ½ & S. E. ¼	One hundred thirty-seven dollars and thirty-two cents	137 32
No. 9, R. 11, W. E. L. S., N. ½	Ninety-one dollars and fifty-two cents	91 52
No. 9, R. 11, W. E. L. S., S. ½	Ninety-one dollars and fifty-two cents	91 52
No. 10, R. 11, W.E.L.S.	One hundred seventy-two dollars and twelve cents	172 12
No. 7, R. 10, N. W. P., Bowdoin College East	One hundred ninety-six dollars and ninety-eight cents	196 98
No. 8, R. 10, N. W. P., Bowdoin College West	Two hundred twelve dollars and fourteen cents	212 14
A, R. 12, W. E. L. S.	Two hundred thirty-seven dollars and thirty-three cents	237 33
No. 1, R. 12, W. E. L. S., N. two-thirds	One hundred sixteen dollars and sixteen cents	116 16
No. 1, R. 12, W. E. L. S., S. third	Sixty-three dollars and thirty-six cents	$63 36

CHAP. 417

PISCATAQUIS COUNTY WILD LANDS—Continued.

No. 3, R. 12, W.E.L.S.	One hundred ninety-six dollars and ninety-eight cents	196 98
No. 3, R. 12, W.E.L.S., E. half	Eighty-three dollars and thirty-four cents	83 34
No. 3, R. 12, W.E.L.S., W. half	Seventy-five dollars and seventy-six cents	75 76
No. 4, R. 12, W.E.L.S., E. half	One hundred six dollars and six cents	106 06
No. 4, R. 12, W.E.L.S., W. half	Sixty-two dollars and fifty-seven cents	62 57
No. 5, R. 12, W.E.L.S.	One hundred ninety-two dollars and fifty-three cents	192 53
No. 6, R. 12, W.E.L.S.	One hundred seventy dollars and fifty-seven cents	170 57
No. 7, R. 12, W.E.L.S.	One hundred ninety-one dollars and forty-three cents	191 43
No. 8, R. 12, W.E.L.S.	Two hundred forty-three dollars and thirty-six cents	243 36
No. 9, R. 12, W.E.L.S., N. ½	Seventy-three dollars and fifty-one cents	73 51
No. 9, R. 12, W.E.L.S., S. ½	Eighty eight dollars and twenty-one cents	88 21
No. 10, R. 12, W.E.L.S.	One hundred fifty-one dollars and eighteen cents	151 18
A. R. 12, W.E.L.S., Frenchtown	Three hundred ninety-three dollars and ninety-seven cents	393 97
A. 2, R. 13 and 14, W. E. L. S. Long "A"	One hundred sixty-five dollars and four cents	165 04
No. 1, R. 13, W.E.L.S.	Two hundred twenty-six dollars and thirty-eight cents	226 38
No. 2, R. 13, W.E.L.S.	One hundred fifty-six dollars and ninety-three cents	156 93
No. 3, R. 13, W.E.L.S.	One hundred sixty-four dollars and thirteen cents	164 13
No. 4, R. 13, W.E.L.S.	One hundred sixty-five dollars and thirty-one cents	165 31
No. 5, R. 13, W.E.L.S. Chesuncook	One hundred thirty-nine dollars and twenty-four cents	139 24
No. 6, R. 13, W.E.L.S.	Two hundred eleven dollars and six cents	211 06
No. 7, R. 13, W.E.L.S.	Two hundred thirty-nine dollars and ninety-nine cents	239 99
No. 8, R. 13, W.E.L.S., Eagle Lake	One hundred eighty-eight dollars and thirty-nine cents	188 39
No. 9, R. 13, W.E.L.S.	Two hundred twelve dollars and sixteen cents	212 16
No. 10, R. 13, W.E.L.S.	One hundred sixty-eight dollars and twenty-eight cents	168 28
A. R. 14, W. E. L. S. Lily Bay	Three hundred twenty-four dollars and sixty-eight cents	324 68
No. 1, R. 14, W.E.L.S. North one-half, Spencer Bay	Eighty-eight dollars and thirty-seven cents	88 37
No. 1, R. 14, W.E.L.S. South one-half, Blake Town	Sixty-seven dollars and ninety-seven cents	67 97
X, R. 14, W. E. L. S.	Forty-nine dollars and forty-one cents	49 41
No. 3, R. 14 and 15, W. E. L. S., E. part	One hundred forty-seven dollars and ninety-one cents	147 91
No. 3, R. 14 and 15, W. E. L. S., W. part	Two hundred twenty-three dollars and sixty-five cents	223 65
No. 4, R. 14, W.E.L.S., S. E. ¼	Fifty-one dollars and twenty-seven cents	51 27

STATE TAX.

PISCATAQUIS COUNTY WILD LANDS—Concluded.

No. 4, R. 14, W.E.L.S., N. ½ & S. W. ¼	One hundred fifty-three dollars and seventy-nine cents	153 79
No. 5, R. 14, W.E.L.S.	One hundred ninety-four dollars and sixty cents	194 60
No. 6, R. 14, W.E.L.S.	Two hundred nineteen dollars and twenty-four cents	219 24
No. 7, R. 14, W.E.L.S., W. ½ & N. E. ¼	One hundred seventy-three dollars and ten cents	173 10
No. 7, R. 14, W.E.L.S., S. E. ¼	Fifty-three dollars and fifty-eight cents	53 58
No. 8, R. 14, W.E.L.S.	Two hundred three dollars and ninety-five cents	203 95
No. 9, R. 14, W.E.L.S.	One hundred seventy dollars and fifty-nine cents	170 59
No. 10, R. 14, W.E.L.S.	One hundred seventy-four dollars and eighty-seven cents	174 87
Sugar Island, W.E.L.S.	One hundred four dollars and fifty-six cents	104 56
Deer Island, W.E.L.S.	Forty-nine dollars and thirty-two cents	49 32
Middlesex Canal, W. E. L. S.	Two hundred twelve dollars and fourteen cents	212 14
Day's Acad. Grant, W. E. L. S.	One hundred forty-six dollars and ninety-eight cents	146 98
No. 4, R. 15, W.E.L.S.	One hundred sixty-eight dollars and eighty-four cents	168 84
No. 5, R. 15, W.E.L.S., N. W. ¼	Thirty-seven dollars and fifty-six cents	37 56
No. 5, R. 15, W.E.L.S., S. ½ & N. E. ¼	One hundred twelve dollars and sixty-seven cents	112 67
No. 6, R. 15, W.E.L.S.	One hundred eighty-six dollars and eighty-six cents	186 86
No. 7, R. 15, W.E.L.S., E. half	Ninety-seven dollars and twenty-five cents	97 25
No. 7, R. 15, W.E.L.S., W. half	Eighty-five dollars and ninety-seven cents	85 97
No. 8, R. 15, W.E.L.S.	One hundred seventy-one dollars and eighty-three cents	171 83
No. 9, R. 15, W.E.L.S.	One hundred seventy-three dollars and fifty-six cents	173 56
No. 10, R. 15, W.E.L.S.	One hundred fifty-three dollars and twenty-four cents	153 24
Moose Island	Six dollars and sixty cents	6 60
Kineo	Three hundred fifty-seven dollars and fifty cents	357 50
Farm Island	Thirteen dollars and seventy-five cents	13 75
No. 3, R. 2, B.P.E.K.R., Kingsbury Pl.	Two hundred thirty-one dollars	231 00
Total	Seventeen thousand five hundred eighty-two dollars and ninety-seven cents	$17,582 97

PISCATAQUIS COUNTY—TIMBER AND GRASS ON RESERVED LANDS.

No. 2, R. 6, B.P.E.K.R.	Eleven dollars and eighty-eight cents	$11 88
No. 1, R. 9, W.E.L.S.	Six dollars and sixty cents	6 60
No. 2, R. 9, W.E.L.S.	Five dollars and fifty cents	5 50
No. 3, R. 9, W.E.L.S.	Six dollars and nineteen cents	6 19
No. 4, R. 9, W.E.L.S.	Eight dollars and ninety-four cents	8 94
No. 5, R. 9, W.E.L.S.	Seven dollars and fifty-six cents	7 56
No. 6, R. 9, W.E.L.S.	Seven dollars and fifty-six cents	7 56
No. 7, R. 9, W.E.L.S.	Four dollars and thirteen cents	4 13

CHAP. 417

PISCATAQUIS COUNTY—TIMBER AND GRASS—Continued.

No. 8, R. 9, W.E.L.S.	Five dollars and fifty cents..................	5 50
No. 9, R. 9, W.E.L.S.	Five dollars and fifty cents..................	5 50
No. 10, R. 9, W.E.L.S.	Five dollars and fifty cents..................	5 50
A, R. 10, W.E.L.S......	Five dollars and twenty-eight cents......	5 28
B, R. 10, W.E.L.S......	Three dollars and twelve cents............	3 12
No. 1, R. 10, W.E.L.S.	Five dollars and twenty-eight cents......	5 28
No. 2, R. 10, W.E.L.S.	Five dollars and twenty-eight cents......	5 28
No. 3, R. 10, W.E.L.S.	Five dollars and twenty-eight cents......	5 28
No. 4, R. 10, W.E.L.S.	Six dollars and nineteen cents.............	6 19
No. 5, R. 10, W.E.L.S.	Eight dollars and twenty-five cents.......	8 25
No. 6, R. 10, W.E.L.S.	Six dollars and nineteen cents.............	6 19
No. 7, R. 10, W.E.L.S.	Four dollars and twelve cents..............	4 12
No. 8, R. 10, W.E.L.S.	Five dollars and fifty cents..................	5 50
No. 9, R. 10, W.E.L.S.	Four dollars and eighty-one cents.........	4 81
No. 10, R. 10, W.E.L.S.	Six dollars and nineteen cents.............	6 19
A, R. 11, W.E.L.S......	Eight dollars and twenty-five cents.......	8 25
B, R. 11, W.E.L.S......	Eight dollars and twenty-five cents.......	8 25
No. 1, R. 11, W.E.L.S.	Six dollars and eighty-seven cents.......	6 87
No. 2, R. 11, W.E.L.S.	Seven dollars and ninety-two cents.......	7 92
No. 3, R. 11, W.E.L.S.	Five dollars and twenty-eight cents......	5 28
No. 4, R. 11, W.E.L.S.	Six dollars and nineteen cents.............	6 19
No. 5, R. 11, W.E.L.S.	Seven dollars and fifty-six cents...........	7 56
No. 6, R. 11, W.E.L.S.	Five dollars and fifty cents..................	5 50
No. 7, R. 11, W.E.L.S.	Five dollars and fifty cents..................	5 50
No. 8, R. 11, W.E.L.S.	Five dollars and fifty cents..................	5 50
No. 9, R. 11, W.E.L.S.	Six dollars and eighty-seven cents.......	6 87
No. 10, R. 11, W.E.L.S.	Six dollars and eighteen cents.............	$6 18
A, R. 12, W.E.L.S......	Seven dollars and ninety-two cents.......	7 92
No. 1, R. 12, W.E.L.S.	Five dollars and ninety-four cents........	5 94
No. 2, R. 12, W.E.L.S.	Seven dollars and twenty-six cents.......	7 26
No. 3, R. 12, W.E.L.S.	Five dollars and twenty-eight cents......	5 28
No. 4, R. 12, W.E.L.S.	Four dollars and twelve cents..............	4 12
No. 5, R. 12, W.E.L.S.	Six dollars and eighty-seven cents.......	6 87
No. 6, R. 12, W.E.L.S.	Six dollars and nineteen cents.............	6 19
No. 7, R. 12, W.E.L.S.	Six dollars and eighty-seven cents.......	6 87
No. 8, R. 12, W.E.L.S.	Nine dollars and sixty-three cents.........	9 63
No. 9, R. 12, W.E.L.S.	Five dollars and fifty cents	5 50
No. 10, R. 12, W.E.L.S.	Five dollars and fifty cents	5 50
A, R. 13, W.E.L.S......	Sixteen dollars and fifty cents.............	16 50
A. 2, R. 13 & 14, W.E.L.S.	Six dollars and forty-two cents............	6 42
No. 1, R. 13, W.E.L.S.	Nine dollars and sixty-three cents.........	9 63
No. 2, R. 13, W.E.L.S.	Six dollars and eighty-seven cents.........	6 87

STATE TAX. 707

CHAP. 417

PISCATAQUIS COUNTY—TIMBER AND GRASS—Concluded.

No. 3, R. 13, W.E.L.S.	Six dollars and eighty-seven cents.........	6 87
No. 4, R. 13, W.E.L.S.	Six dollars and eighty-seven cents.........	6 87
No. 5, R. 13, W.E.L.S.	Six dollars and nineteen cents...............	6 19
No. 6, R. 13, W.E.L.S.	Eight dollars and twenty-five cents.........	8 25
No. 7, R. 13, W.E.L.S.	Eight dollars and ninety-four cents.........	8 94
No. 8, R. 13, W.E.L.S.	Six dollars and eighty-eight cents.........	6 88
No. 9, R. 13, W.E.L.S.	Six dollars and eighty-eight cents.........	6 88
No. 10, R. 13, W.E.L.S.	Six dollars and nineteen cents...............	6 19
A, R. 14, W.E.L.S......	Sixteen dollars and fifty cents...............	16 50
No. 1, R. 14, W.E.L.S.	Five dollars and twenty-eight cents.......	5 28
No. 2, R. 14, W.E.L.S.	Two dollars and sixty-four cents...........	2 64
No. 3, R. 14 & 15, W. E. L. S., east half........	Five dollars and ninety-one cents.........	5 91
No. 3, R. 14 & 15, W. E. L. S., west half........	Seven dollars and ninety-two cents.......	7 92
No. 4, R. 14, W.E.L.S.	Six dollars and eighty-eight cents.........	6 88
No. 5, R. 14, W.E.L.S.	Seven dollars and fifty-six cents.............	7 56
No. 6, R. 14, W.E.L.S.	Eight dollars and twenty-five cents.........	8 25
No. 7, R. 14, W.E.L.S.	Seven dollars and fifty-six cents.............	7 56
No. 8, R. 14, W.E.L.S.	Seven dollars and fifty-six cents.............	7 56
No. 9, R. 14, W.E.L.S.	Six dollars and nineteen cents...............	6 19
No. 10, R. 14, W.E.L.S.	Six dollars and nineteen cents...............	6 19
X, R. 14, W.E.L.S......	One dollar and eighty-nine cents.........	1 89
Day's Academy, R. 15, W.E.L.S.	Three dollars and ninety-six cents.......	3 96
No. 4, R. 15, W.E.L.S.	Six dollars and eighty-seven cents........	6 87
No. 5, R. 15, W.E.L.S.	Five dollars and fifty cents..................	5 50
No. 6, R. 15, W.E.L.S.	Six dollars and eighty-seven cents........	6 87
No. 7, R. 15, W.E.L.S.	Six dollars and eighty-seven cents........	6 87
No. 8, R. 15, W.E.L.S.	Six dollars and nineteen cents.............	6 19
No. 9, R. 15, W.E.L.S.	Six dollars and nineteen cents.............	6 19
No. 10, R. 15, W.E.L.S.	Five dollars and fifty cents..................	5 50
No. 4, R. 9, N. W. P.....	Eight dollars and fifty-eight cents........	8 58
No. 5, R. 9, N. W. P.....	Eight dollars and fifty-eight cents........	8 58
No. 6, R. 9, N. W. P.....	Eight dollars and fifty-eight cents........	8 58
No. 7, R. 9, N. W. P.....	Six dollars and nineteen cents.............	6 19
No. 7, R. 10, Bowdoin College East. N. W. P	Seven dollars and twenty-six cents.......	7 26
No. 8, R. 10, Bowdoin College West, N.W.P.	Seven dollars and ninety-two cents.......	7 92
Total	Five hundred seventy-three dollars and eighteen cents	$573 18

STATE TAX.

SAGADAHOC COUNTY.

Arrowsic	One hundred eighty-four dollars and fourteen cents	$184 14
Bath	Eighteen thousand seventy-eight dollars and seventy cents	18,078 70
Bowdoin	Eight hundred six dollars and eighty-four cents	806 84
Bowdoinham	One thousand five hundred twenty-one dollars and fifty-seven cents	1,521 57
Georgetown	Six hundred twenty dollars and seventy-three cents	620 73
Perkins	One hundred twenty-one dollars and eighty cents	121 80
Phippsburg	One thousand one hundred forty dollars and seventy-five cents	1,140 75
Richmond	Two thousand nine hundred ninety-three dollars and twenty-two cents	2,993 22
Topsham	Two thousand seven hundred ninety-six dollars and forty cents	2,796 40
West Bath	Three hundred eighty-six dollars and sixty cents	386 60
Woolwich	Nine hundred fourteen dollars and thirty-seven cents	914 37
Total	Twenty-nine thousand five hundred sixty-five dollars and twelve cents	$29,565 12

SOMERSET COUNTY.

Anson	One thousand seven hundred sixty-two dollars and fifty-two cents	$1,762 52
Athens	Eight hundred fifty-nine dollars and eighty-eight cents	859 88
Bingham	Seven hundred twenty-five dollars and five cents	725 05
Cambridge	Three hundred fourteen dollars and ninety-one cents	314 91
Canaan	Eight hundred sixty-three dollars and fourteen cents	863 14
Concord	One hundred ninety-seven dollars and fifty-five cents	197 55
Cornville	Eight hundred forty-six dollars and eighty-seven cents	846 87
Detroit	Three hundred ninety-four dollars and five cents	394 05
Embden	Six hundred ninety-five dollars and ninety-three cents	695 93
Fairfield	Four thousand three hundred thirty-nine dollars and fifty-one cents	4,339 51
Harmony	Five hundred fifty-seven dollars and sixty-three cents	557 63
Hartland	One thousand two hundred sixty-four dollars and twenty-three cents	1,264 23
Madison	Four thousand nine hundred forty-four dollars and seventy-three cents	4,944 73
Mercer	Four hundred twenty-six dollars and sixty-three cents	426 63

STATE TAX.

CHAP. 417

SOMERSET COUNTY—Concluded.

Moscow	Two hundred eighty-six dollars and four cents	286 04
New Portland	Seven hundred sixty-one dollars and eighty cents	761 80
Norridgewock	One thousand six hundred sixteen dollars and fifty-eight cents	1,616 58
Palmyra	Nine hundred twenty-three dollars and thirty-three cents	923 33
Pittsfield	Three thousand seven hundred forty-two dollars and twenty-five cents	3,742 25
Ripley	Three hundred seventy-three dollars and seventy cents	373 70
St. Albans	One thousand seventy-one dollars and eighty-five cents	1,071 85
Skowhegan	Nine thousand five hundred eighty-five dollars and fifty-six cents	9,585 56
Smithfield	Three hundred eighty-five dollars and seventy-two cents	385 72
Solon	One thousand forty-eight dollars and twenty-three cents	1,048 23
Starks	Five hundred eighty-one dollars and sixty-four cents	581 64
Total	Thirty-eight thousand five hundred sixty-nine dollars and thirty-three cents	$38,569 33

SOMERSET COUNTY WILD LANDS.

No. 2, R. 1, B.P.W.K.R. Lexington Pl.	One hundred fifty-one dollars and fifty-three cents	$151 53
No. 1, R. 2, B.P.W.K.R. Pleasant Ridge Pl.	One hundred ten dollars and eighty-five cents	110 85
No. 2, R. 2, B.P.W.K.R. Highland Pl.	One hundred twenty-one dollars and twenty-two cents	121 22
No. 1, R. 3, B.P.W.K.R. Carrying Place Pl.	Sixty-one dollars and seven cents	61 07
No. 2, R. 3, B.P.W.K.R., East part, Carrying Place Town	One hundred twenty-six dollars and fifty-one cents	126 51
No. 2, R. 3, B.P.W.K.R., West part, mile strip, Carrying Place Town	Thirty-one dollars and sixty-eight cents	31 68
No. 3, R. 3, B.P.W.K.R. Dead River Pl.	One hundred twenty-one dollars and twenty-two cents	121 22
No. 4, R. 3, B.P.W.K.R., N. half, Bigelow Pl.	One hundred fifty-three dollars and twenty-three cents	153 23
No. 1, R. 4, B.P.W.K.R. Bowtown	One hundred sixty-three dollars and eighty-two cents	163 82
No. 2, R. 4, B.P.W.K.R., East half, Pierce Ponds	Eighty dollars and ten cents	80 10
West half, Pierce Ponds	One hundred nine dollars and fifty-two cents	109 52
No. 3, R. 4, B.P.W.K.R. No. ½	Ninety-nine dollars and seventeen cents	99 17
No. 3, R. 4, B.P.W.K.R. S. ½	Sixty-six dollars and eleven cents	66 11

SOMERSET COUNTY WILD LANDS—Continued.

No. 4, R. 4, B.P.W.K.R. Flag Staff Pl.	One hundred sixty-five dollars	165 00
No. 1, R. 5, B.P.W.K.R., East Can. Road. West Forks Pl.	Seventy dollars and ninety-one cents	70 91
West Can. Road. West Forks Pl.	One hundred twenty-two dollars and eighty-one cents	122 81
No. 2, R. 5, B.P.W.K.R., East half, Lower Enchanted T'n.	Forty-four dollars and five cents	44 05
No. 2, R. 5, B.P.W.K.R., West half, Lower Enchanted T'n.	One hundred two dollars and eighty cents	102 80
No. 3, R. 5, B.P.W.K.R., Part, Pratt tract	Two hundred twelve dollars and thirty-one cents	212 31
Part, Pray tract	Forty dollars and four cents	40 04
8,000 acre tract	Thirty-three dollars and thirteen cents	33 13
No. 4, R. 5, B.P.W.K.R. West part No. 11	Thirty-four dollars and forty cents	$34 40
East part, King Bartlett	Fifty-nine dollars and twenty-one cents	59 21
No. 1, R. 6, B.P.W.K.R., West part, 10,000 acre tract	Fifty-five dollars	55 00
East part Chase stream tract	Seventy dollars and sixty-two cents	70 62
No. 2, R. 6, E.C.R., part Cold Stream	Seventy-one dollars and seventy-two cents	71 72
No. 2, R. 6, W.C.R., part Johnson Mountain	One hundred three dollars and twelve cents	103 12
No. 3, R. 6, B.P.W.K.R. Upper Enchanted T'n. North ½	One hundred twenty-one dollars and twenty-two cents	121 22
No. 3, R. 6, B.P.W.K.R. Upper Enchanted T'n. South ½	Ninety dollars and ninety-one cents	90 91
No. 4, R. 6, B.P.W.K.R. Hobbstown	One hundred twenty-one dollars and twenty-two cents	121 22
No. 5, R. 6, B.P.W.K.R.	One hundred eighty-one dollars and eighty-three cents	181 83
Strip North of Nos. 1, 2, 3, R. 7, B.P.W.K.R.	Nineteen dollars and eighty cents	19 80
No. 1, R. 7, B.P.W.K.R. Sapling Township	One hundred twenty-one dollars	121 00
No. 2, R. 7, B.P.W.K.R. Misery Township	Two hundred forty-one dollars and eighty-six cents	241 86
No. 3, R. 7, B.P.W.K.R. Parlin Pond	One hundred sixty dollars and sixty cents	160 60
No. 4, R. 7, B.P.W.K.R.	One hundred twenty-four dollars and ninety-four cents	124 94
No. 5, R. 7, B.P.W.K.R.	One hundred eight dollars and twenty-four cents	108 24
No. 6, R. 7, B.P.W.K.R. Appleton	One hundred thirty dollars and eighty-eight cents	130 88
No. 2, R. 1, B.P.E.K.R. Brighton Pl.	One hundred eighty-one dollars and eighty-three cents	181 83
No. 3, R. 1, B.P.E.K.R. Mayfield Pl.	One hundred seventy-three dollars and twenty-five cents	173 25

STATE TAX.

CHAP. 417

SOMERSET COUNTY WILD LANDS—Continued.

No. 1, R. 3, B.P.E.K.R. Caratunk Pl.	Three hundred twenty-five dollars and forty-nine cents	325 49
No. 2, R. 3, B.P.E.K.R. Bald Mountain	Two hundred twelve dollars and fourteen cents	212 14
No. 1, R. 4, B.P.E.K.R. The Forks Pl.	One hundred eighty-one dollars and eighty-three cents	181 83
No. 2, R. 4, B.P.E.K.R. East Moxie	One hundred fifty-two dollars and ninety-seven cents	$152 97
No. 1, R. 5, B.P.E.K.R. Moxie Gore	Two hundred thirty-five dollars and sixty-two cents	235 62
No. 2, R. 5, B.P.E.K.R. Square Town	One hundred ninety dollars and nineteen cents	190 19
No. 1, R. 6, B.P.E.K.R. Indian Stream Town	Seventy dollars and forty-seven cents	70 47
No. 1, R. 1, N.B.K.P., Taunton & Raynham Academy Grant	One hundred ten dollars and eighty-eight cents	110 88
No. 1, R. 1, N.B.K.P., Rockwood Strip	Thirty-one dollars and seventy-six cents	31 76
No. 2, R. 1, N.B.K.P., Sandwich Academy Grant	One hundred ninety dollars and eight cents	190 08
No. 2, R. 1, N.B.K.P., Rockwood Strip	Thirty-six dollars and eighty-seven cents	36 87
No. 3, R. 1, N.B.K.P., Long Pond	Two hundred twenty dollars and seventy-two cents	220 72
No. 4, R. 1, N.B.K.P., Jackman Pl.	Three hundred three dollars and five cents	303 05
No. 5, R. 1, N.B.K.P., Attean Pond	Two hundred seventy-two dollars and seventy-five cents	272 75
No. 6, R. 1, N.B.K.P., Holeb	One hundred thirty-four dollars and ninety-four cents	134 94
No. 1, R. 2, N.B.K.P., Tomhegan	Two hundred thirty-eight dollars and sixty-four cents	238 64
No. 2, R. 2, N.B.K.P., Brassua	One hundred sixty-five dollars and ninety-two cents	165 92
No. 3, R. 2, N.B.K.P., Thorndike	Two hundred forty-two dollars and forty-four cents	242 44
No. 4, R. 2, N.B.K.P., Mouse River Pl.	Two hundred fifty-three dollars and forty-four cents	253 44
No. 5, R. 2, N.B.K.P., Dennis	One hundred sixty-six dollars and sixty-eight cents	166 68
No. 6, R. 2, N.B.K.P., Forsyth	One hundred fifty-one dollars and twenty-five cents	151 25
Big W., N.B.K.P.	One hundred seven dollars and twenty-two cents	107 22
Little W., N.B.K.P.	Twenty-eight dollars and ten cents	28 10
No. 1, R. 3, N.B.K.P., part, Middlesex Grant	Ninety-eight dollars and fifty-two cents	98 52
No. 1, R. 3, N.B.K.P., part, Evans tract, Middlesex Grant	Twenty-two dollars and seventy cents	22 70
No. 2, R. 3, N.B.K.P., Soldier Town	One hundred sixty-one dollars and sixty-six cents	$161 66
No. 3, R. 3, N.B.K.P., E. half, Alder Brook	Ninety dollars and forty-two cents	90 42

SOMERSET COUNTY WILD LANDS—Continued.

No. 3, R. 3, N.B.K.P., W. half, Alder Brook	Ninety-six dollars and thirty-six cents	96 36
No. 4, R. 3, N.B.K.P., Bald Mountain	One hundred sixty-six dollars and sixty-eight cents	166 68
No. 5, R. 3, N. B. K. P. Sandy Bay	One hundred sixty-four dollars and sixty-nine cents	164 69
Seboomook, N. B. K. P.	One hundred fifty-one dollars and fifty-three cents	151 53
No. 1, R. 4, N. B. K. P. Plymouth	One hundred thirty-six dollars and thirty-seven cents	136 37
No. 2, R. 4, N. B. K. P. Pittston Academy	Two hundred seven dollars and ninety-seven cents	207 97
No. 3, R. 4, N. B. K. P. Hammond	One hundred ninety-six dollars and ninety-eight cents	196 98
No. 4, R. 4, N. P. K. P.	One hundred thirty-three dollars and fifty-six cents	133 56
No. 5, R. 4, N. B. K. P.	Forty-nine dollars and fifty cents	49 50
No. 3, R. 5, N B K P. Dole Brook	One hundred fifty-one dollars and fifty-three cents	151 53
No. 4, R. 5, N. B. K. P.	Ninety-five dollars and eighty-six cents	95 86
No. 4, R. 16, W. E. L. S. Elm Stream	Eighty-two dollars and eighty-seven cents	82 87
No. 5, R. 16, W. E. L. S. E. half	Seventy-four dollars and forty-seven cents	74 47
No. 5, R. 16, W. E. L. S. W. half	Seventy-four dollars and forty-five cents	74 45
No. 6, R. 16, W. E. L. S.	One hundred forty-one dollars and sixty-five cents	141 65
No. 7, R. 16, W. E. L. S.	One hundred thirty dollars and sixty cents	130 60
No. 8, R. 16, W. E. L. S.	One hundred twenty-seven dollars and fifteen cents	127 15
No. 9, R. 16, W. E. L. S.	One hundred twenty-nine dollars and forty-eight cents	129 48
No. 10, R. 16, W. E. L. S.	One hundred fifty-three dollars and seventy-six cents	153 76
No. 4, R. 17, W. E. L. S.	One hundred eighty-five dollars and thirty-four cents	185 34
No. 5, R. 17, W. E. L. S.	One hundred fifty-nine dollars and twenty-four cents	159 24
No. 6, R. 17, W. E. L. S.	One hundred fifty-four dollars and fifty-six cents	154 56
No. 7, R. 17, W. E. L. S.	One hundred forty-one dollars and forty-eight cents	141 48
No. 8, R. 17, W. E. L. S.	One hundred thirty-seven dollars and seventy-four cents	137 74
No. 9, R. 17, W. E. L. S.	One hundred twenty-eight dollars and thirteen cents	128 13
No. 10, R. 17, W. E. L. S. Big 10	One hundred seventy-seven dollars and ninety-six cents	$177 96
No. 4, R. 18, W. E. L. S.	One hundred ninety-nine dollars and forty-nine cents	199 49
No. 5, R. 18, W. E. L. S.	One hundred forty-six dollars and eighty-one cents	146 81
No. 6, R. 18, W. E. L. S.	One hundred seventy-one dollars and sixty cents	171 60
No. 7, R. 18, W. E. L. S.	One hundred five dollars and forty-eight cents	105 48
No. 8, R. 18, W. E. L. S	One hundred twenty-five dollars and eighty-six cents	125 86
No. 9, R. 18, W. E. L. S.	One hundred nine dollars and seventy-four cents	109 74
No. 5, R. 19, W. E. L. S.	One hundred nine dollars and eighty-two cents	109 82
No. 6, R. 19, W. E. L. S. Big 6	One hundred sixty dollars and thirteen cents	160 13

STATE TAX.   713

CHAP. 417

SOMERSET COUNTY WILD LANDS—CONCLUDED.

No. 7, R. 19, W. E. L. S.	One hundred forty-three dollars and fifty-two cents	143 52
No. 8, R. 19, W. E. L. S.	Sixty-three dollars and sixty-nine cents...	63 69
No. 5, R. 20, W. E. L. S.	One hundred twenty-three dollars and fifty cents	123 50
Total	Thirteen thousand seven hundred sixty-five dollars and three cents	$13,765 03

SOMERSET COUNTY—TIMBER AND GRASS ON RESERVED LANDS.

No. 3, R. 3, B.K.P.E.K.R.	Seven dollars and ninety-two cents	7 92
No. 3, R. 4, B.K.P.E.K.R.	Five dollars and twenty-eight cents	5 28
No. 1, R. 5, B.K.P.E.K.R.	Eight dollars and fifty-eight cents	8 58
No. 2, R. 5, B.K.P.E.K.R.	Seven dollars and twenty-six cents	7 26
No. 1, R. 6, B.K.P.E.K.R.	Two dollars and seventy-four cents	2 74
No. 2, R. 3, B. K. P. W. K. R	Five dollars and twenty-eight cents	5 28
No. 1, R. 4, B. K. P. W. K. R	Six dollars and forty-four cents	6 44
No. 2, R. 4, B. K. P. W. K. R	Five dollars and twenty-eight cents	5 28
No. 3, R. 4, B. K. P. W. K. R	Six dollars and sixty cents	6 60
No. 2, R. 5, B. K. P. W. K. R	Three dollars and ninety-six cents	3 96
No. 3, R. 5, B. K. P. W. K. R	Ten dollars and fifty-six cents	10 56
No. 4, R. 5, B. K. P. W. K. R	Two dollars and sixty-four cents	2 64
No. 1, R. 6, B. K. P. W. K. R	Four dollars and twenty cents	4 20
No. 2, R. 6, B. K. P. W. K. R	Three dollars and ninety-six cents	3 96
No. 3, R. 6, B. K. P. W. K. R	Seven dollars and ninety-two cents	7 92
No. 4, R. 6, B. K. P. W. K. R	Three dollars and ninety-six cents	3 96
No. 5, R. 6, B. K. P. W. K. R	Three dollars and ninety-six cents	3 96
N. 1, R. 7, B. K. P. W. K. R	Three dollars and seventy-six cents	3 76
No. 2, R. 7, B. K. P. W. K. R	Nine dollars and twenty-four cents	9 24
No. 3, R. 7, B. K. P. W. K. R	Nine dollars and sixty-eight cents	9 68
No. 4, R. 7, B. K. P. W. K. R	Four dollars and thirty-two cents	4 32
No. 5, R. 7, B. K. P. W. K. R	Three dollars and sixty cents	3 60
No. 6, R. 7, B. K. P. W. K. R	Five dollars and forty-four cents	5 44
No. 1, R. 1, N. B. K. P.	Five dollars and sixty-one cents	5 61
No. 2, R. 1, N. B. K. P.	Ten dollars and twenty-nine cents	10 29

SOMERSET COUNTY—TIMBER AND GRASS—Concluded.

No. 3, R. 1, N. B. K. P.	Nine dollars and fourteen cents	$9 14
No. 5, R. 1, N. B. K. P.	Ten dollars and fifty-six cents	10 56
No. 6, R. 1, N. B. K. P.	Five dollars and fifty cents	5 50
No. 1, R. 2, N. B. K. P.	Eleven dollars	11 00
No. 2, R. 2, N. B. K. P.	Six dollars and nineteen cents	6 19
No. 3, R. 2, N. B. K. P.	Nine dollars and twenty-four cents	9 24
No. 6, R. 2, N. B. K. P.	Six dollars and nineteen cents	6 19
Little W., R. 2.N.B.K.P.	One dollar and twenty-three cents	1 23
Big W., R. 2,N. B. K. P.	Three dollars and ninety-six cents	3 96
No. 1, R. 3, N. B. K. P.	Three dollars and thirty cents	3 30
No. 2, R. 3, N. B. K. P.	Five dollars and twenty-eight cents	5 28
No. 3, R. 3, N. B. K. P.	Six dollars and sixty cents	6 60
No. 4, R. 3, N. B. K. P.	Five dollars and ninety-four cents	5 94
No. 5, R. 3, N. B. K. P.	Seven dollars and ninety-two cents	7 92
Seboomook, R. 4, N. B. K. P.	Five dollars and twenty-eight cents	5 28
No. 1, R. 4, N. B. K. P.	Four dollars and sixty-two cents	4 62
No. 2, R. 4, N. B. K. P.	Five dollars and ninety-four cents	5 94
No. 3, R. 4, N. B. K. P.	Seven dollars and twenty-six cents	7 26
No. 4, R. 4, N. B. K. P.	Four dollars and twelve cents	4 12
No. 5, R. 4, N. B. K. P.	One dollar and eighty cents	1 80
No. 2, R. 5, N. B. K. P.	Five dollars and fifty cents	5 50
No. 4, R. 5, N. B. K. P.	Three dollars and thirty-eight cents	3 38
No. 4, R. 16, W. E. L. S.	Three dollars and forty-four cents	4 44
No. 5, R. 16, W. E. L. S.	Five dollars and fifty cents	5 50
No. 6, R. 16, W. E. L. S.	Four dollars and eighty-one cents	4 81
No. 7, R. 16, W. E. L. S.	Four dollars and thirteen cents	4 13
No. 8, R. 16, W. E. L. S.	Four dollars and thirteen cents	4 13
No. 9, R. 16, W. E. L. S.	Four dollars and thirteen cents	4 13
No. 10, R. 16, W. E. L. S.	Five dollars and fifty cents	5 50
No. 4, R. 17, W. E. L. S.	Six dollars and eighty-eight cents	6 88
No. 5, R. 17, W. E. L. S.	Six dollars and nineteen cents	6 19
No. 6, R. 17, W. E. L. S.	Five dollars and fifty cents	5 50
No. 7, R. 17, W. E. L. S.	Four dollars and eighty-one cents	4 81
No. 8, R. 17, W. E. L. S.	Seven dollars and fifty-six cents	7 56
No. 9, R. 17, W. E. L. S.	Four dollars and thirteen cents	$4 13
No. 10, R. 17, W. E. L. S.	Four dollars and thirteen cents	4 13
No. 4, R. 18, W. E. L. S.	Four dollars and eighty-one cents	4 81
No. 5, R. 18, W. E. L. S.	Five dollars and fifty cents	5 50
No. 6, R. 18, W. E. L. S.	Six dollars and nineteen cents	6 19
No. 7, R. 18, W. E. L. S.	Five dollars and fifty cents	5 50
No. 8, R. 18, W. E. L. S.	Four dollars and thirteen cents	4 13
No. 9, R. 18, W. E. L. S.	Two dollars and eighty-five cents	2 85
No. 5, R. 19, W. E. L. S.	Four dollars and five cents	4 05
No. 6, R. 19, W. E. L. S.	Four dollars and eighty-one cents	4 81
No. 7, R. 19, W. E. L. S.	Four dollars and eighty-one cents	4 81
No. 8, R. 19, W. E. L. S.	Two dollars and forty-one cents	2 41
Total	Three hundred ninety-four dollars and thirty-three cents	$394 33

STATE TAX.

WALDO COUNTY.

Belfast	Seven thousand seven hundred eleven dollars and thirty-four cents	$7,711 34
Belmont	Two hundred seventy-four dollars and fifty-seven cents	274 57
Brooks	Seven hundred two dollars	702 00
Burnham	Five hundred ninety-seven dollars and ninety-six cents	597 96
Frankfort	Six hundred seventy-five dollars and fifty-one cents	675 51
Freedom	Four hundred fifty-nine dollars and five cents	459 05
Islesborough	Two thousand seven dollars and forty-five cents	2,007 45
Jackson	Three hundred ninety-seven dollars and ninety-eight cents	397 98
Knox	Five hundred fifteen dollars and fifty-eight cents	515 58
Liberty	Six hundred dollars and thirty-five cents	600 35
Lincolnville	Eight hundred sixty-nine dollars and thirty-one cents	869 31
Monroe	Eight hundred dollars and thirteen cents	800 13
Montville	Eight hundred fifty-four dollars and nineteen cents	854 19
Morrill	Three hundred fifty-eight dollars and two cents	358 02
Northport	Eight hundred fifty-three dollars and forty-six cents	853 46
Palermo	Five hundred twenty-one dollars and eight cents	521 08
Prospect	Four hundred eighty-three dollars and twenty-seven cents	483 27
Searsport	One thousand seven hundred ninety-two dollars and sixty-eight cents	1,792 68
Searsmont	Nine hundred twenty-five dollars and twenty-eight cents	925 28
Stockton Springs	Seven hundred twenty-one dollars and eighty-nine cents	721 89
Swanville	Four hundred twenty-five dollars and eighty-three cents	425 83
Thorndike	Six hundred dollars and ninety-one cents	600 91
Troy	Seven hundred forty-seven dollars and ninety-nine cents	$747 99
Unity	Nine hundred sixty-two dollars and twenty-five cents	962 25
Waldo	Four hundred twenty-four dollars and ten cents	424 10
Winterport	One thousand five hundred forty-eight dollars and seven cents	1,548 07
Total	Twenty-six thousand eight hundred thirty dollars and twenty-five cents	$26,830 25

STATE TAX.

WASHINGTON COUNTY.

Addison	Five hundred fifty-nine dollars and seventy-five cents	$559 75
Alexander	One hundred sixty-two dollars and forty-one cents	162 41
Baileyville	Two hundred twelve dollars and sixty-six cents	212 66
Baring	Two hundred eleven dollars and twenty-three cents	211 23
Beddington	Ninety-one dollars and eighty-eight cents	91 88
Brookton	One hundred forty-four dollars and one cent	144 01
Calais	Seven thousand nine hundred thirty dollars and twenty cents	7,930 20
Centerville	One hundred thirty-six dollars and forty-five cents	136 45
Charlotte	Two hundred twenty-four dollars and nineteen cents	224 19
Cherryfield	One thousand four hundred forty-one dollars and twenty-nine cents	1,441 29
Columbia	Two hundred fifty-five dollars and twenty-three cents	255 23
Columbia Falls	Three hundred forty dollars and twenty-eight cents	340 28
Cooper	One hundred twenty-one dollars and eighty-nine cents	121 89
Crawford	Ninety-eight dollars and twenty-two cents	98 22
Cutler	Two hundred thirty-six dollars and ninety-seven cents	236 97
Danforth	Six hundred seventy-three dollars and sixty-five cents	673 65
Deblois	Fifty-nine dollars and twelve cents	59 12
Dennysville	Three hundred eighty-eight dollars and six cents	388 06
East Machias	One thousand one hundred thirty-eight dollars and twenty-four cents	1,138 24
Eastport	Five thousand six hundred seventy-eight dollars and eighty cents	5,678 80
Edmunds	Two hundred sixteen dollars and eighty-five cents	216 85
Forest City	Forty dollars and eighty-five cents	40 85
Harrington	Six hundred seventy-eight dollars and fifty-nine cents	$678 59
Jonesborough	Two hundred ninety-one dollars and forty-seven cents	291 47
Jonesport	One thousand two hundred fifty-seven dollars and seventy-three cents	1,257 73
Lubec	Two thousand three hundred twenty-one dollars and ninety-eight cents	2,321 98
Machias	Two thousand three hundred fifty-six dollars and eighty-three cents	2,356 83
Machiasport	Five hundred fifty-nine dollars and ninety cents	559 90

STATE TAX.

WASHINGTON COUNTY—Concluded.

Marion	Seventy-five dollars and five cents	75 05
Marshfield	One hundred fifty-three dollars and thirty-seven cents	153 37
Meddybemps	Seventy-seven dollars and thirty-eight cents	77 38
Milbridge	One thousand two hundred fifty-one dollars and fifty-two cents	1,251 52
Northfield	Ninety-seven dollars and fifty-three cents	97 53
Pembroke	Nine hundred twenty-eight dollars and ninety-five cents	928 95
Perry	Five hundred dollars and ninety-nine cents	500 99
Princeton	Six hundred eighty-five dollars and forty-nine cents	685 49
Robbinston	Four hundred fifty-nine dollars and fifty-five cents	459 55
Roque Bluffs	Sixty-eight dollars and ninety cents	68 90
Steuben	Four hundred eighty-eight dollars and ninety-four cents	488 94
Talmadge	One hundred sixty-one dollars and ninety-four cents	161 94
Topsfield	Two hundred thirteen dollars and sixty-five cents	213 65
Trescott	One hundred fifty dollars and eighty-five cents	150 85
Vanceboro	Four hundred twenty-one dollars and eighteen cents	421 18
Waite	Eighty dollars and seven cents	$80 07
Wesley	Ninety-nine dollars and fifty-four cents	99 54
Whiting	Two hundred thirty-nine dollars and fifteen cents	239 15
Whitneyville	One hundred sixty-two dollars and three cents	162 03
Total	Thirty-four thousand one hundred forty-four dollars and eighty cents	$34,144 80

WASHINGTON COUNTY WILD LANDS.

No. 18, East Division	Seventy-five dollars and seventy-six cents	$75 76
No. 19, East Division	Seventy-five dollars and seventy-six cents	75 76
No. 26, East Division	One hundred twenty-three dollars and seventy-five cents	123 75
No. 27, East Division	One hundred nineteen dollars and sixty-one cents	119 61
No. 18, Middle Division	Sixty dollars and sixty-one cents	60 61
No. 19, Middle Division S. E. quarter	Sixteen dollars and eighty-four cents	16 84
No. 19, Middle Division N. half & S.W. quarter	Thirty-seven dollars and ninety-two cents	37 92
No. 24, Middle Division	Ninety dollars and ninety-two cents	90 92

Chap. 417

717

WASHINGTON COUNTY WILD LANDS—Concluded.

No. 25, Middle Division.	One hundred twenty-six dollars and fifty cents	126 50
No. 29, Middle Division	One hundred thirty-six dollars and thirty-seven cents	136 37
No. 30, Middle Division.	One hundred sixty-six dollars and sixty-eight cents	166 68
No. 31, Middle Division.	One hundred sixty-six dollars and sixty-eight cents	166 68
No. 36, Middle Division.	Two hundred twenty-seven dollars and twenty-nine cents	227 29
No. 37, Middle Division.	One hundred sixty-six dollars and sixty-eight cents	166 68
No. 42, Middle Division	Two hundred twelve dollars and fourteen cents	212 14
No. 43, Middle Division E. half	Eighty-three dollars and thirty-four cents	83 34
No. 43, Middle Division W. half	Eighty-three dollars and thirty-four cents	83 34
No. 5, North Division N. half	Forty-one dollars and thirty-nine cents...	41 39
No. 5, North Division S. half	Seventy-five dollars and seventy-six cents	75 76
No. 6, North Division.	Ninety-four dollars and forty cents..........	94 40
E. half, strip, N. of No. 6, N. Division	Thirty-one dollars and seventy-six cents..	31 76
W half, strip, N. of No. 6, N. Division	Seventeen dollars and thirty-three cents..	17 33
Two mile strip, N. of No. 6	Thirty-three dollars	33 00
No. 1, R. 1, T. 8...........	Sixty-nine dollars and eighty-three cents..	69 83
No. 3, R. 1, T. 8., Grand Lake Stream Plan	Two hundred twenty-five dollars and thirteen cents	225 13
No. 1, R. 2, T. 8., Dyer.	Ninety dollars and ninety-two cents......	90 92
No. 1, R. 3, T. 8. Lambert Lake Pl......	One hundred fifty-nine dollars and sixty-five cents	159 65
N. 6, R. 1, W. half, N. B. P. P.............	Ninety-one dollars and eight cents	$91 08
No. 6, R. 1, E. half, N. B. P. P.............	Ninety dollars and ninety-two cents	90 92
No. 7, R. 2, N. B. P. P. Kossuth Pl	One hundred seventy-seven dollars and ninety-five cents	177 95
No. 8, R. 3, N. B. P. P..	One hundred seventy-six dollars and fifty-eight cents	176 58
No. 10. R. 3. N. B. P. P. Forest	One hundred two dollars and thirty-four cents	102 34
No. 11, R. 3, N. B. P. P.	Forty-four dollars	44 00
No. 8, R. 4, N. B. P. P...	One hundred twenty-one dollars	121 00
East part Indian Township, strip, 1 mile wide.	Seventeen dollars and sixty cents	17 60
No. 9, R. 2, Codyville Pl., N. B. P. P.........	One hundred thirty-five dollars and eighty-one cents	135 81
No. 14, E. D. Pl..........	One hundred six dollars and twenty-six cents	106 26
No. 21, E. D. Pl..........	Ninety-one dollars and eight cents	91 08
Total	Three thousand nine hundred sixty-three dollars and ninety-eight cents	$3,963 98

STATE TAX. CHAP. 417

WASHINGTON COUNTY—TIMBER AND GRASS ON RESERVED LANDS.

No. 19, East Division....	Two dollars and sixty-four cents	$2 64
No. 26, East Division....	Five dollars and twenty-eight cents	5 28
No. 5, North Division..	Five dollars and twenty-eight cents	5 28
No. 18, Middle Division.	One dollar and thirty-two cents	1 32
No. 19, Middle Division.	Three dollars and thirty cents	3 30
No. 24, Middle Division.	Two dollars and sixty-four cents	2 64
No. 25, Middle Division.	Three dollars and ninety-six cents........	3 96
No. 29, Middle Division.	Four dollars and sixty-two cents	4 62
No. 30, Middle Division.	Five dollars and ninety-four cents	5 94
No. 31, Middle Division.	Five dollars and ninety-four cents	5 94
No. 1, R. 1, Titcomb Survey	Two dollars and sixty-four cents	2 64
No. 1, R. 2, Titcomb Survey	Two dollars and seventy-five cents	2 75
No. 6, R. 1, N. B. P. P.	Six dollars and seventy-four cents	6 74
No. 8, R. 3, N. B. P. P.	Six dollars and sixty cents	6 60
No. 10, R. 3, N. B. P. P.	Two dollars and sixty-four cents	2 64
No. 11, R. 3, N. B. P. P.	One dollar and thirty-eight cents	1 38
No. 18, East Division....	One dollar and eighty-seven cents	1 87
No. 36, Middle Division.	Eight dollars and fifty-eight cents	8 58
No. 37, Middle Division.	Five dollars and ninety-four cents	5 94
No. 42, Middle Division.	Seven dollars and ninety-two cents	7 92
No. 43, Middle Division.	Six dollars and sixty cents	6 60
Total	Ninety-four dollars and fifty-eight cents..	$94 58

YORK COUNTY.

Acton	Seven hundred thirty-eight dollars and seventy-three cents	$738 73
Alfred	Nine hundred fifty-seven dollars and eighty-one cents	957 81
Berwick	Two thousand six hundred sixty-eight dollars and ninety-one cents	2,668 91
Biddeford	Twenty-two thousand two hundred thirty-three dollars and twelve cents	22,233 12
Buxton	One thousand eight hundred ninety-seven dollars and eighty-seven cents	1,897 87
Cornish	One thousand twenty-one dollars and nineteen cents	1,021 19
Dayton	Six hundred twelve dollars and eighty-seven cents	612 87
Eliot	One thousand two hundred sixty-seven dollars and sixty-six cents	1,267 66
Hollis	One thousand one hundred twenty-four dollars and forty cents	1,124 40
Kittery	One thousand nine hundred forty-seven dollars and seventy-eight cents	1,947 78

AP. 417

STATE TAX.

YORK COUNTY—Concluded.

Kennebunk	Six thousand ninety-three dollars and forty-eight cents	6,093 48
Kennebunkport	Three thousand six hundred ninety-eight dollars and sixty-nine cents	3,698 69
Lebanon	One thousand eighty-one dollars and seventy-six cents	1,081 76
Limington	Eight hundred sixty-seven dollars and fifty-two cents	867 52
Limerick	One thousand one hundred sixty-seven dollars and forty-three cents	1,167 43
Lyman	Nine hundred seventy-eight dollars and fourteen cents	978 14
Newfield	Six hundred forty-seven dollars and ninety-five cents	647 95
North Berwick	Two thousand fifty dollars and twenty-one cents	2,050 21
Old Orchard	Two thousand seven hundred thirty dollars and forty-four cents	2,730 44
Parsonsfield	One thousand two hundred twenty dollars and seventy-eight cents	1,220 78
Saco	Ten thousand nine hundred eighty-two dollars and eighty-eight cents	10,982 88
Sanford	Eight thousand thirty-five dollars and eighty-eight cents	8,035 88
Shapleigh	Six hundred sixty-seven dollars and forty-four cents	667 44
South Berwick	Three thousand four hundred forty dollars and sixty cents	3,440 60
Waterboro	One thousand nineteen dollars and eighty-three cents	1,019 83
Wells	Two thousand three hundred ninety-six dollars and forty-seven cents	2,396 47
York	Six thousand sixty dollars and one cent	6,060 01
Total	Eighty-seven thousand six hundred nine dollars and eighty-five cents	$87,609 85

STATE TAX.

SUMMARY.

Androscoggin	Seventy-nine thousand eight hundred fifty-eight dollars and sixty-four cents..	$79,858 64
Aroostook	Fifty-six thousand nine hundred fifty-four dollars and ninety-two cents	56,954 92
Cumberland	Two hundred six thousand two hundred ninety-nine dollars and forty-three cents	206,299 43
Franklin	Twenty-six thousand five hundred ninety-five dollars and fifty-seven cents	26,595 57
Hancock	Forty-four thousand eight hundred ninety-seven dollars and nine cents	44,897 09
Kennebec	Eighty-six thousand six hundred sixty-nine dollars and sixty-six cents	86,669 66
Knox	Thirty-nine thousand seven hundred seventy-five dollars and forty-four cents	39,775 44
Lincoln	Twenty thousand four hundred eighty-five dollars and seventy-eight cents	20,485 78
Oxford	Forty-two thousand ninety-five dollars and seventy-five cents	42,095 75
Penobscot	Ninety-eight thousand two hundred ninety-seven dollars and eighty-four cents	98,297 84
Piscataquis	Thirty-three thousand six hundred eight dollars and thirty-seven cents	33,608 37
Sagadahoc	Twenty-nine thousand five hundred sixty-five dollars and thirteen cents	29,565 13
Somerset	Fifty-two thousand seven hundred twenty-eight dollars and sixty-nine cents	52,728 69
Waldo	Twenty-six thousand eight hundred thirty dollars and twenty-five cents	26,830 25
Washington	Thirty-eight thousand two hundred three dollars and thirty-six cents	38,203 36
York	Eighty-seven thousand six hundred nine dollars and eighty-five cents	87,609 85
Total	Nine hundred seventy thousand four hundred seventy-five dollars and seventy-seven cents	$970,475 77

Sect. 2. The treasurer of this state shall, in the month of April, in the year of our Lord one thousand nine hundred and four, send his warrant with a copy of this tax act, directed to the mayor and aldermen, selectmen or assessors of each city, town or plantation, taxed as aforesaid, requiring them respectively to assess, in dollars and cents, the sum so charged, according to the provisions of the law for the assessment of taxes and to add the amount of such tax to the amount of county and town taxes, to be by them assessed in each city, town and plantation or other place, respectively.

Sect. 3. The treasurer of state in his said warrant, shall require the said mayor and aldermen, selectmen or assessors, respectively, to pay or to issue their several warrant or warrants requiring the collectors of their several cities, towns and plantations, to collect and pay in to the treasurer of their respective cities, towns and plantations, the sum against said cities, towns and plantations, respectively, in this act contained, which said respective treasurer shall pay to the state treasurer on or before the first day of January, one thousand nine hundred and five, and said mayor, selectmen and assessors, respectively, shall return a certificate of the names of such collectors, with the sums which each collector may be required to collect, to said state treasurer, sometime before the first day of December, in the year of our Lord one thousand nine hundred and four.

Sect. 4. When the time for the payment of a state tax to the treasurer of state has expired, and it is unpaid, the treasurer of state shall give notice thereof to the municipal officers of any delinquent town, and unless such tax shall be paid within sixty days, the treasurer of state may issue his warrant to the sheriff of the county, requiring him to levy, by distress and sale, upon the real and personal property of any of the inhabitants of the town; and the sheriff or his deputy shall execute such warrants, observing the regulations provided for satisfying warrants against deficient collectors, as prescribed by chapter six of the revised statutes.

Sect. 5. When any state tax assessed upon any city or town remains unpaid, such city or town is precluded from drawing from the state treasurer the school funds set apart for such city or town, so long as such tax remains unpaid.

Sect. 6. This act shall take effect when approved.

Approved March 28, 1903.

Chapter 418.

An Act to provide in part for the Expenditures of Government for the year nineteen hundred and three.

Be it enacted by the Senate and House of Representatives in Legislature assembled, as follows:

Section 1. In order to provide for the several acts and resolves of the legislature, requiring the payment of money from the treasury, and also to provide for the necessary expenditures of government for the current fiscal year of nineteen hundred and three, the following sums are hereby appropriated out of any moneys in the treasury, and the governor, with the advice and consent of the council, is authorized at any time prior to the first day of January next, to draw his warrant on the treasury for the same.

Expenditures of government, 1906.

School fund and mill tax due in nineteen hundred and two, two hundred eighty-nine dollars and twenty-six cents	$289 26
Temporary Home for Women and Children at Portland, two thousand five hundred dollars...	2,500 00
Children's Aid Society of Maine, one thousand two hundred fifty dollars	1,250 00
Inspectors of steamboats, deficiency, one thousand nine hundred seventy-nine dollars and forty-eight cents	1,979 48
King's Daughter's Union of Bangor, five hundred dollars	500 00
Preservation of regimental rolls, two thousand four hundred dollars	2,400 00
Soldiers' pensions, eighty-five thousand dollars..	85,000 00
Allagash road, five hundred dollars.............	500 00
Fish hatcheries and feeding stations, twenty-five thousand dollars	25,000 00
Improving and protecting dairy interests, three thousand dollars	3,000 00
Bath Military and Naval Orphan Asylum, nine thousand five hundred dollars...............	9,500 00
Extra pay of Maine volunteers in war with Spain, seven hundred ninety-two dollars............	792 00
State School for Boys, sixty-three thousand nine hundred dollars	63,900 00
Bernhard Pol, seventeen dollars and eighty-one cents	17 81
Maine State Year Book, one thousand three hundred dollars	1,300 00

Town of Sanford, eight hundred fifty-nine dollars and twenty-three cents.....................	859 23
City of Rockland, four hundred sixty-two dollars and eighty-seven cents	462 87
Society of the Sisters of Charity Hospital, nine thousand dollars	9,000 00
Women's Christian Temperance Union, five hundred dollars	500 00
Repairing elevator in State House, six hundred dollars	600 00
Maine School for the Deaf, twenty-three thousand five hundred dollars	23,500 00
Aroostook County Normal School, five thousand dollars	5,000 00
Central Maine General Hospital, twelve thousand five hundred dollars	12,500 00
Maine Eye and Ear Infirmary, five thousand dollars	5,000 00
Eastern Maine General Hospital, five thousand dollars	5,000 00
Augusta City Hospital, four thousand dollars....	4,000 00
Aid of soldiers in Aroostook war, three thousand dollars	3,000 00
Bounty on porcupines, five hundred dollars......	500 00
Schooling of children in unorganized townships, two thousand five hundred dollars...........	2,500 00
Bar Harbor Medical and Surgical Hospital, two thousand dollars	2,000 00
Maine Home for Friendless Boys, one thousand two hundred fifty dollars	1,250 00
Testimonials to soldiers in Spanish war, one thousand five hundred dollars................	1,500 00
Improvement of state roads, forty thousand dollars	40,000 00
Free high schools, three thousand dollars........	3,000 00
Fish hatchery at Rangeley lakes, six thousand dollars	6,000 00
Fish hatchery at Sebago lake, six thousand dollars	6,000 00
Maine Industrial School for Girls, for expenses, eleven thousand dollars.....................	11,000 00
Maine Industrial School for Girls, eleven thousand one hundred fifty dollars.....................	11,150 00
Roads and bridges in Indian township, eight hundred dollars	800 00
Passamaquoddy Indians, nine thousand two hundred fifty-five dollars	9,255 00

EXPENDITURES OF GOVERNMENT.

CHAP. 418

Penobscot Indians, eight thousand eight hundred nineteen dollars and seventy cents............	8,819 70
Clerks in adjutant general's office, one hundred dollars	100 00
Town of Trescott, one hundred fifty dollars....	150 00
Albert R. Buck, chairman, two hundred ninety-seven dollars and twenty-five cents..........	297 25
Young Women's Home of Lewiston, one thousand dollars	1,000 00
Society of the Sisters of Charity, for Healy Asylum, two thousand dollars...............	2,000 00
Lewiston contested election case, six hundred dollars and twenty-eight cents..................	600 28
Edmund C. Bryant, chairman, ninety-two dollars and twenty-nine cents	92 29
Preservation of Fort William Henry, one thousand two hundred fifty dollars.....................	1,250 00
Repairs of roads in Jerusalem Plantation, four hundred dollars	400 00
Repairs of road in town of Crystal, three hundred dollars	300 00
Maine General Hospital, seven thousand five hundred dollars	7,500 00
Saint Elizabeth's Roman Catholic Orphan Asylum, one thousand five hundred dollars............	1,500 00
Repairs of roads and bridges in Moscow, five hundred dollars	500 00
C. C. Libby, chairman, one hundred fifty-seven dollars and fifty cents......................	157 50
Town of Island Falls, one hundred fifteen dollars and fifty cents	115 50
Bangor Children's Home, one thousand dollars..	1,000 00
Passamaquoddy Indians, for church at Pleasant Point, one thousand dollars.................	1,000 00
Passamaquoddy Indians, for house occupied by Sisters of Mercy, one thousand dollars.......	1,000 00
Sea and shore fisheries, fifteen thousand dollars..	15,000 00
Knox County General Hospital, one thousand five hundred dollars	1,500 00
Madawaska Training School, one thousand two hundred fifty dollars......................	1,250 00
Repairs of road in Caratunk, five hundred dollars	500 00
Farmington State Normal School, two thousand dollars	2,000 00
Town of Houlton, four hundred twenty-three dollars and fourteen cents......................	423 14

CHAP. 418

Repairs in south wing of State Capitol, eight thousand dollars	8,000 00
Repairs on tomb of Governor Enoch Lincoln, one thousand dollars	1,000 00
Assistant messenger of the Senate, fifty dollars..	50 00
Topographic and geological survey, five thousand dollars	5,000 00
Emergency fund for prevention and extinguishment of forest fires, ten thousand dollars......	10,000 00
Public instruction in forestry, two thousand five hundred dollars	2,500 00
Pages of the Senate, fifty dollars..............	50 00
Reporter of Senate, two hundred dollars........	200 00
Postmaster of Senate, sixty dollars............	60 00
Transportation of mail, twenty-five dollars......	25 00
Repairs of highway in Upton, eight hundred dollars	800 00
Lyman E. Smith, five dollars and fifty-eight cents	5 58
Town of Cutler, two hundred fifty dollars......	250 00
Aid of navigation on Moosehead lake, seven hundred fifty dollars	750 00
Pay roll of the Senate, ten thousand four hundred seventy-one dollars	10,471 00
Pay roll of the House of Representatives, thirty-three thousand four hundred sixty-seven dollars	33,467 00
Legislative books, stationery and postage, five thousand five hundred dollars...............	5,500 00
Legislative printing, fourteen thousand dollars...	14,000 00
Norcross Transportation Company, two hundred dollars	200 00
York deeds, four thousand five hundred dollars..	4,500 00
Town of Mariaville, two hundred dollars........	200 00
Re-establishment of boundaries of public lots, one thousand dollars	1,000 00
Fred W. Lee, three hundred fifty dollars........	350 00
E. Parker Craig, fifty dollars..................	50 00
University of Maine for equipment, fifteen thousand dollars	15,000 00
Colby College, fifteen thousand dollars..........	15,000 00
Castine State Normal School, two thousand dollars	2,000 00
Town of Anson, five thousand dollars..........	5,000 00
J. Perley Dudley, three hundred fifty dollars......	350 00
John W. Mason, Secretary, four hundred dollars..	400 00
Town of Edmunds, one hundred fifty dollars.....	150 00

EXPENDITURES OF GOVERNMENT.

Rebuilding bridge across west branch Saint Croix river, two thousand dollars..................	2,000 00
Repairing Mattawamkeag bridge, two thousand dollars	2,000 00
Completing records of Clerk of Courts, Lincoln County, one thousand dollars................	1,000 00
City of Eastport, three hundred fifteen dollars and forty cents	315 40
City of Rockland, one hundred thirty-one dollars and fifty cents.............................	131 50
A. A. Burleigh, Chairman, one hundred eighty-seven dollars and sixty-six cents.............	187 66
Lee Normal Academy, one thousand dollars.....	1,000 00
Eastern Maine Insane Hospital, thirty thousand four hundred twenty-five dollars.............	30,425 00
Town of East Livermore, one thousand four hundred ninety-seven dollars and seventy-six cents,	1,497 76
Maine State Library, four thousand eight hundred sixty-two dollars	4,862 00
G. E. Morrison, chairman, one hundred dollars...	100 00
Pages of the House, fifty dollars...............	50 00
First assistant messenger of the House, twenty-five dollars	25 00
Board of cattle commissioners, one thousand dollars	1,000 00
Aid of navigation on Lewey, Long and Big Lakes, one hundred dollars.........................	100 00
Maine Insane Hospital, for stock barns, five thousand dollars	5,000 00
Repairing bridge in Drew Plantation, three hundred dollars	300 00
Clerk in State Library during legislative session, two hundred dollars........................	200 00
State House employees, four hundred seventy-five dollars	475 00
Repairing bridge in town of Milbridge, five hundred dollars	500 00
Bridge in town of Frenchville, five hundred dollars	500 00
Bridge in Wallagrass Plantation, three hundred dollars	300 00
Maine Children's Home Society, one thousand two hundred fifty dollars	1,250 00
Repairing bridge in New Sharon, one thousand five hundred dollars.......................	1,500 00
C. C. Libby, chairman, four hundred ten dollars..	410 00

CHAP. 418

George D. Gaddis, one hundred dollars..........	100 00
Stenographer and extra clerk hire in State Superintendent of School's office, five hundred dollars,	500 00
Western State Normal School at Gorham, ten thousand dollars...........................	10,000 00
J. Calvin Knapp, Secretary, fifteen dollars.......	15 00
R. E. Randall, Secretary, twenty dollars.........	20 00
State Committee of Young Men's Christian Association of Maine, three hundred twenty-seven dollars...................................	327 00
Town of Jackson, seventy-nine dollars and sixty cents......................................	79 60
Albion Oakes, Secretary, one hundred twenty-two dollars and eighty cents.....................	122 80
Preservation of town records, five hundred dollars,	500 00
Special epidemic or emergency fund, five thousand dollars...................................	5,000 00
Epidemic or emergency fund, eight thousand dollars......................................	8,000 00
Protection of lobsters with eggs attached, seven thousand five hundred dollars................	7,500 00
Burial expenses of soldiers' widows, five thousand dollars...................................	5,000 00
Bridge in Connor Plantation, two thousand dollars,	2,000 00
Rebuilding bridge in town of Mariaville, one thousand dollars	1,000 00
Bridges in town of Washburn, three thousand dollars..	3,000 00
Repairing bridge in Baileyville, two hundred fifty dollars.....................................	250 00
Town of Parkman, one hundred seventy-three dollars and eleven cents.....................	173 11
Commissioner to verify meridian lines, five hundred dollars...............................	500 00
Normal schools and training school, two thousand dollars.....................................	2,000 00
State laboratory, five thousand dollars..........	5,000 00
Analysis of concentrated commercial feeding stuffs, one thousand dollars..................	1,000 00
Contingent expenses of the legislature, fifteen thousand dollars	15,000 00
Express transportation for benefit of the legislature, one thousand sixty dollars..............	1,060 00
Contingent expenses of committees, one thousand seven hundred eighteen dollars and twenty-nine cents	1,718 29

EXPENDITURES OF GOVERNMENT.

CHAP. 418

Stenographers to officers of Senate and House, six hundred thirty-six dollars..................	636 00
Advertising laws, eight thousand five hundred dollars......................................	8,500 00
Lewy Mitchell, one hundred twenty dollars......	120 00
Joseph Mitchell, Jr., one hundred twenty dollars..	120 00
Revision of statutes, forty thousand dollars........	40,000 00
Revision of statutes, printing and binding, nine thousand five hundred dollars...............	9,500 00
Revision of statutes, printing and binding report, three thousand dollars......................	3,000 00
Revision of statutes, office supplies for committee, four hundred forty-six dollars and fifty cents..	446 50
Salary of public officers, one thousand dollars....	1,000 00
Salary of County Attorneys, twelve thousand five hundred dollars	12,500 00
Assistant librarian, one thousand two hundred dollars..	1,200 00
Analysis of commercial fertilizers, two thousand dollars	2,000 00
Board of registration of medicine, one thousand five hundred dollars.........................	1,500 00
Maine State Prison, twenty-nine thousand six hundred thirty-six dollars and sixteen cents......	29,636 16
Cecil John Rhodes scholarships, one hundred dollars	100 00
License fees of hawkers and peddlers, one thousand five hundred dollars....................	1,500 00
Maine Insane Hospital, forty-five thousand dollars,	45,000 00
Bounty on bears killed in Oxford county, five hundred dollars	500 00
Maine State Prison for electric lighting plant, two thousand six hundred dollars................	2,600 00
Preparing list of delinquent corporations of 1901, three hundred dollars......................	300 00
Wiscasset Bridge, ten thousand dollars.........	10,000 00
Amounting to the sum of eight hundred forty-two thousand two hundred forty-three dollars and sixty-seven cents	$842,243 67

Section 2. This act shall take effect when approved.

Approved March 28, 1903.

Chapter 419.

An Act to provide in part for the Expenditures of Government for the year nineteen hundred and four.

Be it enacted by the Senate and House of Representatives in Legislature assembled, as follows:

Expenditures of government, 1904.

Section 1. In order to provide for the several acts and resolves of the legislature, requiring the payment of money from the treasury, and also to provide for the necessary expeditures of government for the year nineteen hundred and four, the following sums are hereby appropriated out of any moneys in the treasury, and the governor, with the advice and consent of the council, is authorized, at any time between the first day of January, nineteen hundred and four, and the first day of January, nineteen hundred and five, to draw his warrant on the treasury for the same.

Clerks of law court, two thousand dollars........	$2,000 00
Temporary home for women and children at Portland, two thousand five hundred dollars.......	2,500 00
Children's aid society of Maine, one thousand two hundred fifty dollars.......................	1,250 00
King's Daughters' Union of Bangor, five hundred dollars	500 00
Preservation of regimental rolls, two thousand four hundred dollars.......................	2,400 00
Soldiers' pensions, eighty-five thousand dollars...	85,000 00
Fish hatcheries and feeding stations, twenty-five thousand dollars	25,000 00
Improving and protecting dairy interests, three thousand dollars	3,000 00
Bath Military and Naval Orphan Asylum, eight thousand five hundred dollars................	8,500 00
State School for Boys, sixty-one thousand four hundred dollars	61,400 00
Maine State Year Book, one thousand nine hundred dollars	1,900 00
Improvement of state roads, forty thousand dollars	40,000 00
Free high schools, three thousand dollars.......	3,000 00
Maine Industrial School for Girls, for expenses, eleven thousand dollars ....,............	11,000 00
Maine Industrial School for Girls, five hundred dollars	500 00
Roads and bridges in Indian township, six hundred dollars	600 00

EXPENDITURES OF GOVERNMENT.

CHAP. 419

Passamaquoddy Indians, eight thousand nine hundred twenty dollars	8,920 00
Penobscot Indians, eight thousand five hundred nineteen dollars and seventy cents	8,519 70
Penobscot Indians, shore rents, three thousand four hundred thirty-four dollars	3,434 00
Clerks in Adjutant General's office, one hundred dollars	100 00
Town of Trescott, one hundred fifty dollars	150 00
Young Women's Home of Lewiston, one thousand dollars	1,000 00
Society of the Sisters of Charity, for Healy Asylum, two thousand dollars	2,000 00
Society of the Sisters of Charity Hospital, nine thousand dollars	9,000 00
Women's Christian Temperance Union, five hundred dollars	500 00
Maine School for the Deaf, seventeen thousand five hundred dollars	17,500 00
Aroostook County Normal School, five thousand dollars	5,000 00
Central Maine General Hospital, twelve thousand five hundred dollars	12,500 00
Maine Eye and Ear Infirmary, five thousand dollars	5,000 00
Eastern Maine General Hospital, five thousand dollars	5,000 00
Augusta City Hospital, four thousand dollars	4,000 00
Aid of soldiers in Aroostook war, three thousand dollars	3,000 00
Bounty on porcupines, five hundred dollars	500 00
Schooling of children in unorganized townships, two thousand five hundred dollars	2,500 00
Maine soldiers' monument at Andersonville, five thousand dollars	5,000 00
Bar Harbor Medical and Surgical Hospital, two thousand dollars	2,000 00
Maine Home for Friendless Boys, one thousand two hundred fifty dollars	1,250 00
Preservation of Fort William Henry, one thousand two hundred fifty dollars	1,250 00
Maine General Hospital, seven thousand five hundred dollars	7,500 00
Saint Elizabeth's Roman Catholic Orphan Asylum, one thousand five hundred dollars	1,500 00

CHAP. 419

Repair of roads and bridges in Moscow, five hundred dollars	500 00
Bangor Children's Home, one thousand dollars..	1,000 00
Sea and shore fisheries, fifteen thousand dollars...	15,000 00
Knox County General Hospital, one thousand five hundred dollars	1,500 00
Madawaska Training School, one thousand two hundred fifty dollars.......................	1,250 00
Farmington State Normal School, two thousand dollars	2,000 00
Repairs in south wing of State Capitol, eight thousand dollars	8,000 00
Topographic and geological survey, five thousand dollars	5,000 00
Emergency fund for prevention and extinguishment of forest fires, ten thousand dollars.......	10,000 00
Public instruction in forestry, two thousand five hundred dollars	2,500 00
Transportation of mail, twenty-five dollars.......	25 00
School fund and mill tax, eighty-five thousand dollars	85,000 00
Temporary loan, three hundred thousand dollars,	300,000 00
Town of Cutler, two hundred fifty dollars.......	250 00
Aid of navigation on Moosehead Lake, seven hundred fifty dollars	750 00
Town of Mariaville, two hundred dollars........	200 00
Epidemic or emergency fund, eight thousand dollars	8,000 00
University of Maine, for equipment, twenty thousand dollars	20,000 00
Castine State Normal School, two thousand dollars	2,000 00
Lee Normal Academy, one thousand dollars.....	1,000 00
Eastern Maine Insane Hospital, thirty thousand four hundred twenty-five dollars.............	30,425 00
Maine State Library, four thousand eight hundred sixty-two dollars	4,862 00
Eastern Maine General Hospital, to pay outstanding debts, five thousand dollars..............	5,000 00
Bangor Children's Home, for new ward, two thousand dollars	2,000 00
Repairing bridge in town of Milbridge, five hundred dollars	500 00
Maine Children's Home Society, one thousand two hundred fifty dollars....................	1,250 00

Stenographer and extra clerk hire in Superintendent of Schools' office, five hundred dollars..	500 00
Western State Normal School at Gorham, ten thousand dollars	10,000 00
Preservation of town records, five hundred dollars,	500 00
Protection of lobsters with eggs attached, five thousand dollars	5,000 00
Agricultural societies, one thousand one hundred eighty-six dollars and seventeen cents.........	1,186 17
Burial expenses of soldiers' widows, five thousand dollars	5,000 00
Bridge in town of Bancroft, one thousand two hundred dollars	1,200 00
Commissioner to verify meridian lines, five hundred dollars	500 00
Normal schools and training school, nine thousand dollars	9,000 00
State laboratory, three thousand dollars.........	3,000 00
Analysis of concentrated commercial feeding stuffs, one thousand dollars.................	1,000 00
Analysis of commercial fertilizers, two thousand dollars	2,000 00
Board of registration of medicine, one thousand five hundred dollars.......................	1,500 00
Maine State Prison, seven thousand five hundred dollars	7,500 00
Cecil John Rhodes scholarship, one hundred dollars	100 00
Maine Insane Hospital, twenty thousand dollars,	20,000 00
Salary of County Attorneys, twelve thousand six hundred fifty dollars.......................	12,650 00
Assistant librarian, one thousand two hundred dollars	1,200 00
Salary of public officers, one thousand dollars....	1,000 00
Bounty on bears killed in Oxford county, five hundred dollars	500 00
Maine State Prison for electric lighting plant, five hundred dollars	500 00
Amounting to the sum of nine hundred forty-seven thousand five hundred twenty-one dollars and eighty-seven cents	$947,521 87

Section 2. This act shall take effect when approved.

Approved March 28, 1903.

Chapter 420.

An Act in regard to use of the Roads in town of Eden.

Be it enacted by the Senate and House of Representatives in Legislature assembled, as follows:

Certain roads may be closed to automobiles.

Section 1. The town of Eden in the county of Hancock, at any legal meeting of the voters thereof may close to the use of automobiles the following streets within its limits: Ocean Drive, Bay View Drive, from Duck Brook bridge to Hull's Cove bridge, the Eagle Lake roads as far as Eagle Lake and the Green Mountain drive. Any street so closed shall be marked at the entrance thereof by sign boards in large letters "No automobiles allowed on this road."

—term automobile defined.

The term "automobile" as used in this section applies to all motor vehicles propelled by power. For the violation of this act the town of Eden may vote at said meeting what punishment shall be inflicted for the violation thereof, but for the first offense,

—penalty.

not over twenty-five dollars and cost of prosecution; for the second offense, not over twenty-five dollars or thirty days' imprisonment, or both and cost of prosecution.

Section 2. This act shall take effect when approved.

Approved March 28, 1903.

Chapter 421.

An Act to maintain and operate a Draw Bridge at the outlet of Long Lake in the town of Naples.

Be it enacted by the Senate and House of Representatives in Legislature assembled, as follows:

Town of Naples authorized to maintain draw bridge.

Section 1. The town of Naples, in the county of Cumberland, is hereby authorized to maintain and operate the draw bridge at the outlet of Long lake, in said town, to allow the passage of steam and other boats through the same.

Keeper of toll bridge.

Section 2. The municipal officers of said town of Naples, on or before the first day of April annually, shall appoint a suitable person to act as keeper or tender of said bridge, and he or his duly qualified assistant shall have exclusive charge of the open-

—hours of attendance of keeper.

ing and closing of said bridge. Such keeper, or his assistant, shall be in constant attendance from the hour of seven o'clock in the morning until six o'clock at night during the months of June, July, August, and September, for the purpose of opening and closing said bridge to allow the passage of all boats and vessels through the bridge during said hours. And such drawtender, or his assistant, shall be in attendance to open and close such bridge for the passage of any boat at such additional time and hour as may be necessary, upon the request of any captain, agent or owner of said boat.

Section 3. Said bridge shall at all times be so opened and closed as not to unnecessarily hinder or obstruct navigation through, nor travel over it. *Opening and closing shall not obstruct travel or navigation.*

Section 4. Said municipal officers shall annually appoint a competent assistant to tend said bridge when the regular tender is unavoidably absent. *Keepers' assistant.*

Section 5. No person, unless the duly appointed drawtender or keeper or his qualified assistant, shall be allowed to open such bridge at any time, under a penalty of ten dollars for each offense, the same to be collected in an action of debt, in any competent court of jurisdiction. *Unauthorized persons shall not open draw.*

Section 6. This act shall take effect when approved.

Approved March 28, 1903.

Chapter 422.

An Act in relation to the salary of the Recorder of the Municipal Court of the City of Biddeford.

Be it enacted by the Senate and House of Representatives in Legislature assembled, as follows:

Chapter twenty-four of the private and special laws of eighteen hundred and ninety-nine is hereby amended as follows, namely: by striking out section two and inserting instead thereof the following: *Chapter 24, private and special laws of 1899, amended.*

'Section 2. For all services rendered, except when there is a vacancy in the office of judge, the recorder shall be paid from the county treasury the sum of three hundred dollars annually, payable on the first days of January, April, July and October, which shall be in full of all services rendered as such recorder.' *Salary of recorder*

Approved March 28, 1903.

RESOLVES

OF THE

STATE OF MAINE.

1903.

RESOLVES

OF THE

STATE OF MAINE.

1903

Chapter 1.

Resolves, protesting against the Hay-Bond Treaty.

Whereas, The fishing industry is one of the most important interests of this State, giving employment, as it does to twenty-five thousand men, having an invested capital of three million dollars, with an annual product valued at five million dollars; and

Whereas, Our own market takes by far the greater part of the catch of the New England fishing fleet, which alone makes it possible for that fleet to maintain its existence; and

Whereas, There is now pending in the Senate of the United States, with a view to obtaining the advice and consent of that body to its ratification, a convention between the governments of the United States and Great Britain for the improvement of commercial relations between the United States and His Brittanic Majesty's colony of Newfoundland, signed at Washington on the eighth day of November, 1902; and

Hay-Bond treaty, protesting against.

CHAP. 2

Whereas, Article 11 of said convention provides that certain produce of the Newfoundland fisheries shall be admitted into the United States, free of duty; Therefore,

Be it Resolved, by the Senate and House of Representatives of the State of Maine, in Legislature assembled, that the ratification of the aforesaid convention by the government of the United States will work irreparable injury to this great industry, by opening our home market to a competitor which, by reason of cheaper labor and smaller cost of building and maintaining its fleet, can land its product in the Atlantic ports of the United States at one-third less cost than the New England fleet is able to do; that it will render valueless many millions of capital now profitably employed in the fishing industry; that it will deprive many thousand men of employment in a business in which they are skilled; that it will deprive the naval and merchant vessels of the United States of a great training school for sailors; that the concessions granted by said convention, to importations from the United States are trifling in comparison, and wholly inadequate to compensate the people of the United States for the practical destruction of a great national industry.

And be it further Resolved, that this Legislature, in behalf of the people of this State, tenders its thanks to its Senators and Representatives in Congress for their steadfast and zealous opposition to the ratification of said treaty and that a copy of this joint resolution be transmitted to the Honorable William P. Frye, president pro tempore of the Senate of the United States, for presentation to the Senate in such manner as he may determine.

Approved January 11, 1903.

Chapter 2.

Resolve in aid of the Temporary Home for Women and Children at Portland.

Temporary Home for Women and Children, in aid of.

Resolved, That the sum of five thousand dollars be and hereby is appropriated for the use of the Temporary Home for Women and Children at Portland, of which two thousand five hundred dollars shall be paid to said institution during the year nineteen hundred and three, and two thousand five hundred dollars during the year nineteen hundred and four.

Approved February 13, 1903.

Chapter 3.

Resolve providing for a special epidemic or emergency fund.

Resolved, That the sum of five thousand dollars is hereby appropriated as a special epidemic or emergency fund, to be used, so far as may be necessary, by the state board of health, with the consent of the governor and council, in guarding against the importation of smallpox into the state and in preventing the spread from present infected places in the state and the governor is hereby authorized to draw his warrant for the same, or such part of the same as may be needed, out of any money in the treasury not otherwise appropriated, and this sum or such part of it as may be needed shall be available to the board when appropriated by the governor.

Approved February 18, 1903.

Chapter 4.

Resolve in favor of the Children's Aid Society of Maine.

Resolved, That the sum of two thousand five hundred dollars for the years nineteen hundred and three and nineteen hundred and four, be and hereby is appropriated from the treasury, for the use of the Children's Aid Society of Maine, to aid in maintaining the Home for Friendless and Destitute Girls at Belfast; said sum to be expended under the direction of the governor and council.

Approved February 18, 1903.

Chapter 5.

Resolve in favor of Nellie E. Flanders of Liberty.

Resolved, That a pension be allowed Nellie E. Flanders of Liberty, of eight dollars per month, from the first day of January, nineteen hundred three until such time as she shall receive a United States pension.

Approved February 19, 1903.

Chapter 6.

Resolve in favor of Benjamin Smith of Appleton in Knox County.

Benjamin Smith, in favor of.

Resolved, That Benjamin Smith of Appleton in the county of Knox, be paid the sum of ten dollars per month, commencing January one, nineteen hundred three, instead of the sum of eight dollars per month which he now receives.

Approved February 19, 1903.

Chapter 7.

Resolve providing for the compensation of Steamboat Inspectors for the years nineteen hundred, nineteen hundred and one, and nineteen hundred and two.

Steamboat inspectors, providing for compensation of.

Resolved, That the sum of one thousand eighty-seven dollars and thirty-two cents be and is hereby appropriated to pay John M. Taylor the compensation for the years nineteen hundred, nineteen hundred and one, and nineteen hundred and two, to which as steamboat inspector he is entitled, under chapter fifty-two, section twenty-three of the revised statutes; and that the further sum of eight hundred ninety-two dollars and sixteen cents be and is hereby appropriated to pay Horace Atwood the compensation for the years nineteen hundred, nineteen hundred and one, and nineteen hundred and two, to which as steamboat inspector he is entitled, under chapter fifty-two, section twenty-three of the revised statutes.

Approved February 20, 1903.

Chapter 8.

Resolve in favor of King's Daughters Union of Bangor.

King's Daughters Union, in favor of.

Resolved, That the sum of five hundred dollars for the year nineteen hundred and three, and five hundred dollars for the year nineteen hundred and four, be and is hereby appropriated for the purpose of assisting in maintaining the King's Daughters Union of Bangor.

Approved February 20, 1903.

Chapter 9.

Resolves providing for the preservation of Regimental Rolls in the Adjutant-General's office.

Resolved, That the adjutant-general is hereby authorized and directed under the advice and control of the governor and council to provide for the preservation of the enlistment, descriptive and muster rolls, and the monthly returns of the regiments and batteries in the war of the rebellion, now on file in the adjutant-general's office.

Resolved, That the sum of two thousand four hundred dollars for the year nineteen hundred and three, and two thousand four hundred dollars for the year nineteen hundred and four, is hereby appropriated for the preservation of said rolls.

Approved February 20, 1903.

Regimental rolls, preservation of, to provide for.

Chapter 10.

Resolve for State Pensions.

Resolved, That the sum of eighty-five thousand dollars be and is hereby appropriated to provide for state pensions for invalid soldiers and sailors, their widows and orphans, and the dependent children, parents and sisters of deceased soldiers and sailors eligible thereto under existing law, for the year nineteen hundred and three, and eighty-five thousand dollars for the year nineteen hundred and four.

Approved February 20, 1903.

State pensions, resolve for.

Chapter 11.

Resolve in favor of Mary C. Rankin, widow of Orlenzo K. Rankin, late of Company K, First New England Regiment, Mexican War.

Resolved, That a pension be allowed Mary C. Rankin of Liberty, of eight dollars per month, from the first day of January nineteen hundred and three.

Approved February 25, 1903.

Mary C. Rankin, in favor of.

Chapter 12.

Resolve in favor of the Bath Military and Naval Orphan Asylum.

Resolved, That there be and hereby is appropriated for the Bath Military and Naval Orphan Asylum the sum of eight thousand and five hundred dollars for the year nineteen hundred and three, and eight thousand and five hundred dollars for the year nineteen hundred and four; also the sum of one thousand dollars for repairs for the years nineteen hundred and three and nineteen hundred and four.

Approved February 25, 1903.

Chapter 13.

Resolve in favor of the dairying interests of the State of Maine.

Resolved, That there be, and hereby is appropriated, to be expended under the direction of the commissioner of agriculture, the sum of three thousand dollars for the year nineteen hundred and three, and three thousand dollars for nineteen hundred and four, for the purpose of improving and protecting the dairy interests of the state of Maine, by employing a dairy expert, and suitable assistants, and paying such expenses in connection therewith as the commissioner may approve.

Approved February 25, 1903.

Chapter 14.

Resolve for the purpose of operating the fish hatcheries and feeding stations for fish and for the protection of Fish.

Resolved, That the sum of twenty-five thousand dollars is hereby appropriated for the year nineteen hundred three and also twenty-five thousand dollars for the year nineteen hundred four to be expended by the commissioners of inland fisheries and game, under the direction of the governor and council, for the purpose of operating the fish hatcheries and feeding stations for fish in the state and for the protection of fish. Provided, also, that the commissioners of inland fisheries and game may purchase or lease real estate in the name of the state for the purpose of maintaining fish hatcheries and feeding stations for fish culture, and may also assist in maintaining fish hatcheries for fish culture owned and under the management of fish and game associations; provided, also, that the commissioners shall make a detailed statement in their report of all expenditures of money expended under this resolve.

Approved February 25, 1903.

Chapter 15.

Resolve in favor of Allegash Road.

Resolved, That there be and hereby is appropriated the sum of five hundred dollars to aid in repairing the Allegash road, extending from Ashland to the Allegash river in Aroostook county; provided, however, that said sum of five hundred dollars shall not be available unless there shall be provided by subscription or otherwise a like sum of five hundred dollars which shall be expended on said road in connection with the amount hereby appropriated, under the direction of an agent to be appointed for that purpose by the governor and council.

Approved February 25, 1903.

Chapter 16.

Resolves in relation to extra pay of Maine Volunteers in the War with Spain.

Resolved, That there be paid from the treasury of the state to the soldiers who were enlisted by the United States and sent to join the first regiment of infantry and battery A of the first heavy artillery under orders of the secretary of war, and who constituted a part of the quota of the state under the second call of the president for troops in the war with Spain, the same amount of extra pay that was received by the soldiers volunteering under the first call.

Resolved, That the governor and council shall audit all claims presented under the above resolve, and upon finding any claimant justly entitled to the extra pay under the same, the governor shall draw his warrant on the treasurer in favor of the paymaster general for the amount due.

Resolved, That the sum of seven hundred ninety-two dollars be and is hereby appropriated for extra pay of Maine volunteers in the war with Spain, to be expended under the direction and supervision of the governor and council.

Approved February 26, 1903.

Chapter 17.

Resolve in favor of the State Reform School.

State Reform School, in favor of.

Resolved, That there be and are hereby appropriated for and in behalf of the state reform school the following sums and for the following purposes, namely: For the year nineteen hundred and three, for current expenses, twenty thousand dollars; for ordinary repairs and improvements, two thousand dollars; for providing homes for boys and visiting boys out on probation, two hundred fifty dollars; for extra expense of coal, two thousand five hundred dollars; for one-half expense of erecting and furnishing two cottages, removing and rebuilding barn, remodeling, repairing and refurnishing main building and making survey and plan of farm, thirty-nine thousand one hundred fifty dollars. For the year nineteen hundred and four, for current expenses, twenty thousand dollars; for ordinary repairs and improvements, two thousand dollars; for providing homes for boys and visiting boys out on probation, two hundred fifty dollars; for one-half the expense of erecting and furnishing two cottages, removing and rebuilding barn, remodeling, repairing and refurnishing main building and making survey and plan of farm, thirty-nine thousand one hundred fifty dollars.

Approved February 26, 1903.

Chapter 18.

Resolve in favor of Bernhard Pol of Bangor, to re-imburse him for taxes paid through error.

Bernhard Pol, in favor of.

Resolved, That the sum of seventeen dollars and eighty-one cents be paid to Bernhard Pol of Bangor, to re-imburse him for taxes paid on township six, Range three, North Bingham's Kennebec Purchase, Somerset County, as said township is not in the state of Maine.

Approved March 4, 1903.

Chapter 19.

Resolve in favor of the purchase of the Maine State Year Book and Legislative Manual for the years nineteen hundred and three and nineteen hundred and four.

Resolved, That the secretary of state be authorized to contract for six hundred and fifty copies of the Maine State Year Book and Legislative Manual for nineteen hundred and three; also nine hundred and fifty copies of same for nineteen hundred and four, to be delivered on or before the first day of June of each year, at a cost not to exceed two dollars per copy. One hundred and fifty of said copies for each year to be delivered to the state librarian for the use of the state library, the remainder to be distributed in the usual manner.

Maine State Year Book, in favor of purchase of.

Approved March 4, 1903.

Chapter 20.

Resolve in favor of the town of Sanford.

Resolved, That there be paid out of the school fund for the year one thousand nine hundred and two, to the town of Sanford, the sum of eight hundred fifty-nine dollars and twenty-three cents, being the amount due said town, on account of its failure to make its annual return, by reason of sickness of its superintendent.

Sanford, in favor of town of.

Approved March 4, 1903.

Chapter 21.

Resolve providing for paying to the city of Rockland the amount deducted from its school fund for the year one thousand nine hundred and two, on account of imperfect school returns.

Resolved, That there be paid out of the school fund for the year one thousand nine hundred and three to the city of Rockland, the sum of four hundred sixty-two dollars and eighty-seven cents, being the amount deducted from said city's proportion of the school fund for the year one thousand nine hundred and two, on account of defect in its school returns.

Rockland, in favor of.

Approved March 4, 1903.

Chapter 22.

Resolves in relation to the completion of the fifth revision of the general and public laws, and appointing a Commissioner therefor.

Revision of public laws, in relation to.

Resolved, That John A. Morrill, of Auburn, be appointed a commissioner to complete the revision of the general and public laws of the state, incorporating the public laws of the present session, and to complete the index of the same, correcting the notes and marginal annotations of sections to correspond with the final draft of the revision; preparing marginal notes and references for new sections; adding references to all appropriate cases reported in the ninety-sixth volume of Maine reports and subsequent volumes and to all decisions interpreting the constitution of the United States and of the state of Maine which appear in the one hundred eighty-third volume of the reports of the supreme court of the United States and subsequent volumes; and carefully to superintend the printing of said revision and index, with such additions as may be made under the provisions of these resolves.

Resolved, That the foregoing work be performed by said commissioner under the supervision of Forrest Goodwin, George C. Wing, Howard Pierce, Beecher Putnam, Artemus Weatherbee, Henry W. Oakes, John W. Manson, Lincoln H. Newcomb, Natt T. Abbott and S. S. Thornton, members of the joint select committee of the present legislature on the revision of the statutes, who are hereby constituted a commission to sit during the recess of the legislature for that purpose, and to continue the work of said committee of the legislature for the completion of their work and the perfection of the revision.

Resolved, That the governor and council are hereby authorized to audit and cause to be paid, the services and expenses of said Morrill and said commissioners and of such clerks and other assistants as it may be necessary for said Morrill or said commissioners or committee to employ.

Resolved, That if said Morrill declines said duty, or becomes unable to perform it, the governor and council shall appoint some other suitable person to fill the vacancy, and do the duties herein prescribed for said Morrill.

Approved March 4, 1903.

Chapter 23.

Resolve to provide means for examination of claims for State Pensions.

Resolved, That the state pension clerk is hereby authorized to expend such sum, under the direction of the governor and council, not exceeding three hundred dollars yearly, as may be necessary to properly examine the claims presented to his office, the same to be paid out of the appropriation for state pensions for the years nineteen hundred and three and nineteen hundred and four, upon proper vouchers filed with the governor and council fully itemized as to dates, amounts and subject matter thereof.

Approved March 11, 1903.

Chapter 24.

Resolve in favor of establishing a Fish Hatchery and Feeding Station at the Rangeley Lakes.

Resolved, That the sum of six thousand dollars is hereby appropriated for the purpose of establishing a fish hatchery at one of the chain of Rangeley lakes or on the tributaries to the same to be located by the commissioners of inland fisheries and game and to be expended by said commissioners under the direction of the governor and council.

Approved March 11, 1903.

Chapter 25.

Resolve in favor of Roads in the Indian Township, Washington County.

Resolved, That the sum of eight hundred dollars be and is hereby appropriated to repair roads and bridges in the Indian Township, Washington county, for the year nineteen hundred three, and six hundred dollars for the year nineteen hundred four.

Said appropriations to be expended under the direction of the governor and council.

Approved March 11, 1903.

Chapter 26.

Resolve to provide for the expenses of the Maine Industrial School for Girls.

Resolved, That the sum of ten thousand five hundred dollars be and the same hereby is appropriated for the year nineteen hundred three and the same for the year nineteen hundred four. And for ordinary repairs and additional help on the farm the sum of five hundred dollars is hereby appropriated for the year nineteen hundred three and the same for the year nineteen hundred four. And for the expenses of the trustees of the said school the sum of five hundred dollars hereby is appropriated for the year nineteen hundred three and the same for the year nineteen hundred four.

Approved March 11, 1903.

Chapter 27.

Resolve in favor of establishing a modern Fish Hatchery and feeding station at Sebago Lake.

Resolved, That the sum of six thousand dollars is hereby appropriated for the purpose of establishing a fish hatchery and feeding station at Sebago lake, to be expended by the commissioners of inland fisheries and game, under the direction of the governor and council.

Approved March 11, 1903.

Chapter 28.

Resolve making appropriations for the Passamaquoddy tribe of Indians.

Resolved, That there be paid from the state treasury, to be expended under the direction of the governor and council, to the agent of the Passamaquoddy tribe of Indians, for the benefit of said tribe, for the years nineteen hundred and three and nineteen hundred and four, as follows: For May dividends, four hundred dollars each year; for November dividends, four hundred dollars each year; for distressed and contingent poor, four thousand dollars each year; for contingent purposes, two hundred dollars each year; for bounty on crops, two hundred dollars each year; for plowing, one hundred and fifty dollars each year; for salary of governor, one hundred dollars each year; for salary of lieutenant governor, forty dollars each year; for fertilizers, one hundred and fifty dollars each year; for salaries of priests, three hundred dollars each year; for agricultural purposes, six hundred dollars each year; for salary of agent, four hundred dollars each year; for educational purposes, eight hundred dollars each year; for basket ash, three hundred and fifty dollars each year; for wood for nineteen hundred and three, seven hundred and fifty dollars; for wood for nineteen hundred and four, six hundred and fifty dollars; for school books, thirty dollars each year; for police at Pleasant Point, fifty dollars each year; for seats for school room at Pleasant Point, for nineteen hundred and three only, one hundred and twenty-five dollars; for repairs of sisters' house at Peter Dana's Point, for nineteen hundred and three only, fifty dollars; for repairs of road at Peter Dana's Point, one hundred dollars each year; for painting school house and hall at Peter Dana's Point, for nineteen hundred and three only, sixty dollars.

Total for nineteen hundred and three, nine thousand two hundred and fifty-five dollars.

Total for nineteen hundred and four, eight thousand nine hundred and twenty dollars.

Approved March 11, 1903.

Chapter 29.

Resolves authorizing a Temporary Loan for the year nineteen hundred and three.

Resolved, That to provide for the wants of the treasury, the treasurer of state be, and is hereby authorized to procure on the faith of the state, if he shall deem it necessary, at any time during the year nineteen hundred and three, a temporary loan of three hundred thousand dollars, or so much thereof as may be needed.

Resolved, That the treasurer of state be, and hereby is authorized to give notes in behalf of the state, payable within two years from the date hereof, for such portions of the loan hereby authorized, as may be required.

Approved March 12, 1903.

Chapter 30.

Resolves authorizing a Temporary Loan for the year nineteen hundred and four.

Temporary loan for 1904, to authorize.

Resolved, That to provide for the wants of the treasury, the treasurer of state be, and is hereby authorized to procure on the faith of the state, if he shall deem it necessary, at any time during the year nineteen hundred and four, a temporary loan of three hundred thousand dollars, or so much thereof as may be needed.

Resolved, That the treasurer of state be, and hereby is authorized to give notes in behalf of the state, payable within three years from the date hereof, for such portions of the loan hereby authorized, as may be required.

Approved March 12, 1903.

Chapter 31.

Resolve making appropriation for Penobscot Tribe of Indians.

Penobscot tribe of Indians, in favor of.

Resolved, That there be paid from the state treasurer to the agent of the Penobscot tribe of Indians for the years nineteen hundred and three and nineteen hundred and four, to be applied for the benefit of said tribe, each year, as follows:

Interest on tribe's fund, each year, forty-four hundred and twenty-nine dollars and seventy cents; agricultural purposes, each year, eight hundred and fifty dollars; annuity, each year, seventeen hundred dollars; bounty on the crops, each year, two hundred dollars; schools, each year, six hundred and fifty dollars; salaries, each year, agent of tribe, four hundred dollars; governor of tribe, fifty dollars; lieutenant governor of tribe, forty dollars; constable, for police purposes, fifty dollars; Roman Catholic priest, one hundred dollars; superintendent of farming, fifty dollars; repair of convent foundations, nineteen hundred and three, one hundred and fifty dollars; furnace for school house, Old Town island, one hundred and fifty dollars; shore rentals, thirty-four hundred and thirty-four dollars, and that ten per cent of said shore rentals be appropriated and allowed to be used for municipal purposes.

Approved March 12, 1903.

Chapter 32.

Resolve waiving a forfeiture of the public lot in the southeast quarter of Township Number Four, Hancock County, North Division.

Resolved, That the forfeitures of the rights to the timber and grass on the public lot in the southeast quarter of township number four, Hancock county, north division, for alleged non-payment of taxes, are hereby waived and the owners thereof of record are restored to their rights therein as fully as if record of said forfeitures had not been made. Due record of this waiver shall be made in the offices of the state treasurer, the land agent and the board of state assessors.

Public lot, waiving of forfeiture of.

Approved March 18, 1903.

Chapter 33

Resolve authorizing the Land Agent to sell certain public lots in E plantation and Portage Lake plantation, in Aroostook county.

Resolved, That the land agent is hereby authorized to sell and convey to actual settlers thereon certain lands in E plantation and Portage Lake plantation, in Aroostook county, constituting part of the school lots of said plantations, if he deems advisable, for such price per acre and on such terms of payment as he may deem advantageous; provided, that in making sales of said lands the legal and equitable rights of persons claiming under said settlers shall be considered and preserved; and provided, also, that the proceeds of any sales made shall be added to the school funds of said plantations.

Sale of certain public lots, to authorize.

Approved March 18, 1903.

Chapter 34.

Resolve in favor of the Women's Christian Temperance Union.

Resolved, That there be and hereby is appropriated for the use of the Women's Christian Temperance Union, in aid of their work in behalf of homeless children, the sum of five hundred dollars for the year nineteen hundred three, and the sum of five hundred dollars for the year nineteen hundred four.

Women's Christian Temperance Union, in favor of.

Approved March 18, 1903.

CHAP. 35

Chapter 35.

Resolve in favor of the Society of the Sisters of Charity for the use of the Healy Asylum of Lewiston, Maine.

Society of Sisters of Charity, in favor of.

Resolved, That the sum of four thousand dollars be and is hereby appropriated to be paid to the Society of the Sisters of Charity for the use of the Healy asylum in Lewiston, of which two thousand dollars shall be paid during the year nineteen hundred and three and two thousand dollars during the year nineteen hundred and four.

Approved March 18, 1903.

Chapter 36.

Resolve in favor of the Young Women's Home of Lewiston.

Young Women's Home, in favor of.

Resolved, That there be and hereby is appropriated the sum of one thousand dollars, to be paid to the Young Women's Home of Lewiston, for the use of said institution for the year nineteen hundred and three, and one thousand dollars for the use of said institution for the year nineteen hundred and four.

Approved March 18, 1903.

Chapter 37.

Resolve in favor of Albert R. Buck, chairman of the committee on Maine State Prison.

Albert R. Buck, in favor of.

Resolved, That the sum of two hundred and twenty-nine dollars and thirty cents be paid to Albert R. Buck, chairman of the committee on Maine state prison, to defray expenses incurred by him on account of the visit of said committee to the Maine state prison at Thomaston during the present session in compliance with its official duties.

Approved March 18, 1903.

Chapter 38.

Resolve in favor of the committee on Revision of the Statutes.

Resolved, That the sum of four hundred and forty-six dollars and fifty cents be and is hereby appropriated for desks, typewriters and other necessary office supplies for the use of the committee on revision of the statutes; same to be expended by direction of the governor and council.

Revision of statutes, in favor of committee on.

Approved March 18, 1903.

Chapter 39.

Resolve in favor of the Town of Trescott.

Resolved, That the sum of three hundred dollars be and is hereby appropriated, to wit; one hundred and fifty dollars for the year nineteen hundred and three, and one hundred and fifty dollars for the year nineteen hundred and four, to the town of Trescott in maintaining its roads and bridges, said sums to be expended under the direction of the county commissioners of Washington county.

Town of Trescott, in favor of.

Approved March 18, 1903.

Chapter 40

Resolve in favor of the Maine School for the Deaf.

Resolved, That there be and hereby is appropriated for the Maine School for the Deaf, the sum of seventeen thousand five hundred dollars for the year nineteen hundred and three; also the sum of seventeen thousand five hundred dollars for the year nineteen hundred and four. Also the sum of six thousand dollars for the purchase of a building and lot to be used as a home for the pupils.

Maine School for the Deaf, in favor of.

Approved March 20, 1903.

Chapter 41.

Resolve in favor of repairing elevator in State House.

Resolved, That the sum of six hundred dollars be hereby appropriated for the purpose of repairing the elevator in the State House at Augusta, said appropriation to be expended under the direction of the superintendent of public buildings.

Elevator in State House, in favor of repair of.

Approved March 20, 1903.

Chapter 42.

Resolve in favor of the Augusta City Hospital.

Augusta City Hospital, in favor of.

Resolved, That there be and is hereby appropriated the sum of three thousand dollars to be paid to the Augusta City Hospital for the use of said institution for the year nineteen hundred and three, and three thousand dollars for the use of said institution for the year nineteen hundred and four, and that there be and is hereby appropriated the further sum of one thousand dollars, to be expended for repairs of said institution, for the year nineteen hundred and three, and one thousand dollars, to be expended for repairs of said institution, for the year nineteen hundred and four.

Approved March 22, 1903.

Chapter 43.

Resolve in favor of the Eastern Maine General Hospital.

Eastern Maine General Hospital, in favor of.

Resolved, That there be and is hereby appropriated the sum of five thousand dollars to be paid the Eastern Maine General Hospital for the use of said institution for the year nineteen hundred three, and five thousand dollars for the use of said institution for the year nineteen hundred four.

Approved March 23, 1903.

Chapter 44.

Resolve in favor of the Maine Eye and Ear Infirmary.

Eye and Ear Infirmary, in favor of.

Resolved, That there be and hereby is appropriated annually the sum of five thousand dollars to be paid to the treasurer of the Maine Eye and Ear Infirmary for the use of said institution, for the years nineteen hundred and three and nineteen hundred and four.

Approved March 22, 1903.

Chapter 45.

Resolve in favor of the Hospital of the Society of the Sisters of Charity of Lewiston, Maine.

Resolved, That there be and is appropriated the sum of five thousand dollars be paid to the Society of the Sisters of Charity of Lewiston, Maine, for the use of said society for the year nineteen hundred and three, and five thousand dollars for the year nineteen hundred and four. And that the further sum of four thousand dollars be and is hereby appropriated for the year nineteen hundred and three, and four thousand dollars for the year nineteen hundred and four, to be used to furnish and equip the new building recently erected.

Approved March 23, 1903.

Chapter 46.

Resolves in favor of the Central Maine General Hospital.

Resolved, That there be and hereby is appropriated the sum of five thousand dollars to be paid to the Central Maine General Hospital in Lewiston, for the use of said institution for the year nineteen hundred and three, and five thousand dollars for the use of said institution for the year nineteen hundred and four.

Resolved, That the further sum of seven thousand five hundred dollars be and hereby is appropriated to be paid to said Central Maine General Hospital to be and become a part of the building fund of said hospital for the year nineteen hundred and three, and seven thousand five hundred dollars for a like purpose for the year nineteen hundred and four.

Approved March 23, 1903.

Chapter 47.

Resolve in favor of a Maine Soldiers' Monument at the Andersonville, Georgia, National Cemetery.

Resolved, That the sum of five thousand dollars be and is hereby appropriated to be expended during the year one thousand nine hundred and four for the purpose of erecting a monument at the National Cemetery at Andersonville, Georgia, to perpetuate the memory of our patriotic Maine soldiers who gave their lives while confined therein as prisoners of war. The appropriation called for in this resolve shall be expended for the purpose named, under the direction and at the discretion of a commission to consist of the governor as chairman, ex-officio, and two other members, one of whom, at least, shall have been a prisoner of war at said Andersonville, said two commissioners to be appointed by the governor within two months after the passage of this resolve. . The reasonable expenses of said commission shall be allowed and paid out of the appropriation made by this resolve, and they shall complete their work and make their report thereon to the governor and council on or before the last day of December, nineteen hundred and four.

Approved March 24, 1903.

Chapter 48.

Resolve in favor of the Bar Harbor Medical and Surgical Hospital.

Resolved, That the sum of four thousand dollars is hereby appropriated to the Bar Harbor Medical and Surgical Hospital at Bar Harbor, Maine, two thousand dollars payable September first, nineteen hundred and three, and two thousand dollars payable September first, nineteen hundred and four.

Approved March 24, 1903.

Chapter 49.

Resolve in favor of the Maine Industrial School for Girls.

Resolved, That the sum of eleven thousand six hundred and fifty dollars be and hereby is appropriated for the use of the Maine Industrial School for Girls for the years nineteen hundred three and nineteen hundred four, for the following purposes: For the year nineteen hundred three; to provide for the deficit in erecting Erskine Hall, three thousand dollars; to fill the cellar and remove the debris of the former Erskine Hall which was burned and to grade the grounds, one thousand dollars; for farm buildings, four thousand five hundred dollars; for additional stock, farming tools and equipment, one thousand dollars; for an electric alarm system, two hundred fifty dollars; to wire the buildings and furnish fixtures for electric lighting, nine hundred dollars; for power for electric lighting, five hundred dollars. For the year nineteen hundred and four; for power for electric lighting, five hundred dollars.

Approved March 24, 1903.

Chapter 50.

Resolve in favor of the Maine Home for Friendless Boys.

Resolved, That there be and hereby is appropriated twenty-five hundred dollars for the use of the Maine Home for Friendless Boys at Portland, as follows: one thousand two hundred and fifty dollars for the year nineteen hundred and three, and one thousand two hundred and fifty dollars for the year nineteen hundred and four.

Approved March 24, 1903.

Maine Home for Friendless Boys, in favor of.

Chapter 51.

Resolve in favor of George B. Haskell, Jacob R. Little and Stephen J. Kelley, in payment of witnesses', magistrates' and officers' fees and disbursements made by them in the city of Lewiston contested election case.

Resolved, That the sum of six hundred dollars and twenty-eight cents is hereby appropriated, and that the state treasurer be and is hereby authorized and directed to pay said sum of six hundred dollars and twenty-eight cents to George B. Haskell, Jacob R. Little and Stephen J. Kelley, the sitting members, for witnesses', magistrates' and officers' fees and disbursements made by them in contesting their seats in the house of representatives, in the contested election case of the city of Lewiston.

Approved March 24, 1903.

George B. Haskell, Jacob R. Little and Stephen J. Kelley, in favor of.

Chapter 52.

Resolve in favor of Edmund C. Bryant, chairman of the committee on Reform School.

Resolved, That the sum of ninety-two dollars and twenty-nine cents be paid to Edmund C. Bryant, chairman of the committee on reform school, to defray expenses incurred by him on account of the visit of said committee to the reform school at South Portland during the present session in compliance with its official duties.

Approved March 24, 1903.

Edmund C. Bryant, in favor of.

Chapter 53.

Resolve for an appropriation for the preservation of the remains of Fort William Henry, now the property of the State of Maine.

Fort William Henry, in favor of preservation of remains of.

Resolved, That there be and hereby is appropriated the sum of twelve hundred and fifty dollars for the year one thousand nine hundred and three, and twelve hundred and fifty dollars for the year one thousand nine hundred and four, for the use of the Pemaquid commission, the same to be used for the preservation of the existing remains of Fort William Henry, now the property of the state of Maine, and for such other purposes connected with the care of the reservation as may, in their judgment, be necessary.

Approved March 24, 1903.

Chapter 54.

Resolve to aid in repairing roads in Jerusalem Plantation.

Jerusalem plantation, to aid in repairing roads of.

Resolved, That the sum of four hundred dollars be and the same hereby is appropriated for the year nineteen hundred and three to be expended under the direction of the county commissioners of Franklin county in repairing the roads of Jerusalem plantation in said Franklin county. But said money shall not be paid until said commissioners have produced satisfactory evidence to the governor and council that they have actually expended the sum of one thousand dollars on said roads.

Approved March 24, 1903.

Chapter 55.

Resolve in favor of the town of Crystal.

Crystal, town of, in favor of.

Resolved, That the sum of three hundred dollars be and the same hereby is appropriated for the year nineteen hundred and three to repair the road in the town of Crystal leading from Crystal station, on the Bangor and Aroostook Railroad, to the north line of Sherman, the same to be expended under the direction of the county commissioners of Aroostook county. But said money shall not be paid until said county commissioners have produced satisfactory evidence to the governor and council that an equal amount has been raised by the town of Crystal or other interested parties, and that there has actually been expended on said road the sum of six hundred dollars.

Approved March 24, 1903.

Chapter 56.

Resolve in favor of the Maine General Hospital.

Resolved, That there be and is hereby appropriated the sum of seven thousand five hundred dollars to be paid to the Maine General Hospital for the use of said institution for the year one thousand nine hundred and three, and seven thousand five hundred dollars to be paid to said institution for the year one thousand nine hundred and four.

Approved March 24, 1903.

Chapter 57.

Resolve in favor of the Saint Elizabeth's Roman Catholic Orphan Asylum of Portland.

Resolved, That there be and is hereby appropriated the sum of fifteen hundred dollars to be paid to the Saint Elizabeth's Roman Catholic Orphan Asylum of Portland for the use of said institution for the year nineteen hundred and three and fifteen hundred dollars for the use of said institution for the year nineteen hundred and four.

Approved March 24, 1903.

Chapter 58.

Resolve in favor of the town of Moscow.

Resolved, That the sum of five hundred dollars for the year nineteen hundred and three and five hundred dollars for the year nineteen hundred and four be and hereby is appropriated for the use and aid of the town of Moscow to partly reimburse said town for money expended and to be expended in making extraordinary repairs on the highways and bridges in said town, resulting from damages caused by the freshet of December, nineteen hundred and one. The same to be paid on certificate of the county commissioners of Somerset county that at least an equal amount has been expended by said town for said purpose.

Approved March 24, 1903.

Chapter 59.

Resolve in favor of the Committee on Maine State Prison.

Maine State Prison, in favor of committee on.

Resolved, That the sum of fifty-four dollars and twenty-five cents be paid to Albert R. Buck, chairman of the committee on Maine state prison, for expenses incurred by him in complying with an order of the legislature dated February six, nineteen hundred and three.

Approved March 24, 1903.

Chapter 60.

Resolve in favor of C. C. Libby, chairman of the Committee on Education.

C. C. Libby, in favor of.

Resolved, That the state treasurer be directed to pay to C. C. Libby, chairman of the committee on education, the sum of one hundred and fifty-seven dollars and fifty cents, the same being the expenses of the said committee on its recent visits to the various normal, training and industrial schools, and to Presque Isle to view the site of the proposed new normal school.

Approved March 24, 1903.

Chapter 61.

Resolve in favor of the town of Island Falls.

Island Falls, town of, in favor of.

Resolved, That the state treasurer is hereby authorized and directed to pay to the town of Island Falls the sum of one hundred and fifteen dollars and fifty cents, it being an abatement, in part, for taxes assessed by the state against the town of Island Falls for the years eighteen hundred and ninety-nine and nineteen hundred.

Approved March 24, 1903.

Chapter 62.

Resolve in favor of the Bangor Children's Home.

Resolved, That the sum of one thousand dollars per annum for the years nineteen hundred and three and nineteen hundred and four be and hereby is appropriated in aid of the current expenses of the Bangor Children's Home.

Approved March 24, 1903.

Bangor Children's Home, in favor of.

Chapter 63.

Resolve in favor of Passamaquoddy Tribe of Indians for the completion of a new church at Pleasant Point, in the Town of Perry.

Resolved, That the sum of one thousand dollars be and hereby is appropriated for the purpose of completing of the new church at Pleasant Point in the town of Perry. Said money to be paid from the fund, belonging to the Passamaquoddy tribe of Indians, now in the state treasury. Said fund being the money received by the state for stumpage and for land sold belonging to said tribe, and that said sum be expended under the direction of the governor and council.

Approved March 24, 1903.

Passamaquoddy tribe of Indians, in favor of completion of church.

Chapter 64.

Resolve in favor of rebuilding the house of the Sisters of Mercy at Peter Dana's Point, within the jurisdiction of the Passamaquoddy Tribe of Indians.

Resolved, That the sum of one thousand dollars be and hereby is appropriated for the purpose of rebuilding the house occupied by the Sisters of Mercy at Peter Dana's Point, within the jurisdiction of the Passamaquoddy tribe of Indians, said money to be paid from the fund belonging to the Passamaquoddy tribe of Indians, now in the state treasury, said fund being the money received by the state from stumpage and for land sold belonging to said tribe, and that said sum be expended under the direction of the governor and council.

Approved March 24, 1903.

Sisters of Mercy at Peter Dana's Point, in favor of rebuilding house of.

Chapter 65.

Resolve for an appropriation for the use of the Commissioner of Sea and Shore Fisheries.

Sea and shore fisheries, appropriation for.

Resolved, That the sum of fifteen thousand dollars be and is hereby appropriated for each of the years nineteen hundred and three and nineteen hundred and four, to be expended by the commissioner of sea and shore fisheries under direction of the governor and council.

Approved March 24, 1903.

Chapter 66.

Resolve in favor of Knox County General Hospital.

Knox County General Hospital, in favor of.

Resolved, That there be and hereby is appropriated the sum of fifteen hundred dollars to be paid to the Knox County General Hospital for the use of said institution, for the year nineteen hundred and three, and fifteen hundred dollars for the year nineteen hundred and four.

Approved March 24, 1903.

Chapter 67.

Resolve in favor of the Madawaska Training School.

Madawaska Training School, in favor of.

Resolved, That there be and is hereby appropriated the sum of twenty-five hundred dollars for the Madawaska Training School for repairs upon the training school buildings and school equipments, twelve hundred and fifty dollars being for the year nineteen hundred and three, and twelve hundred and fifty dollars for the year nineteen hundred and four, and that the same be expended under the direction of the trustees.

Approved March 25, 1903.

Chapter 68.

Resolve in aid of Carratunk for repairing road from Carratunk village to Pleasant pond in said plantation.

Resolved, That the sum of five hundred dollars be and hereby is appropriated for the use and aid of said plantation, to be expended on the road from Carratunk village to Pleasant pond in said plantation, for the purpose of making permanent improvements on said road and repairing extraordinary damage caused by the freshet of December, nineteen hundred and one, the same to be expended under the direction of the county commissioners of Somerset county, said amount to be paid when said commissioners shall certify that the improvements and repairs to that amount have been completed.

Carratunk Pl., in aid of repairing roads in.

Approved March 25, 1903.

Chapter 69.

Resolve in favor of the Farmington State Normal School.

Resolved, That there be and hereby is appropriated the sum of two thousand dollars for the year nineteen hundred and three, and two thousand dollars for the year nineteen hundred and four, to furnish and equip a chemical laboratory in the Farmington Normal School; to replace the old furniture; to grade the school grounds; to paint the outside wood work and to repair boiler condemned by the inspector.

Farmington State Normal School, in favor of.

Approved March 25, 1903.

Chapter 70.

Resolve in favor of the Town of Houlton.

Resolved, That the sum of four hundred and twenty-three dollars and fourteen cents be appropriated and paid to the town of Houlton, said sum being an abatement and refunding of a portion of the state taxes paid by said town for the year nineteen hundred and two.

Houlton, town of, in favor of.

Approved March 25, 1903.

CHAP. 71

Chapter 71.

Resolve authorizing the Land Agent to sell certain public lots in Dallas Plantation, in Franklin County.

Public lots in Dallas Pl., to authorize sale of.

Resolved, That the land agent is hereby authorized to sell and convey to actual settlers thereon, certain lands in Dallas plantation, in Franklin county, constituting part of the school lots of said plantation, if he deem advisable, for such price per acre and on such terms of payment as he may deem advantageous; provided, that in making sales of said lands, the equitable rights of persons claiming under said settlers shall be considered and preserved; and provided, also, that the proceeds of any sales made shall be added to the school funds of said plantation.

Approved March 25, 1903.

Chapter 72.

Resolve in favor of the Committee on Maine State Prison.

Maine State Prison, in favor of committee on.

Resolved, That the sum of thirteen dollars and seventy cents be paid to Albert R. Buck, chairman of the committee on Maine state prison, to defray expenses incurred by him on account of the visit of said committee to the Maine state prison at Thomaston during the present session in compliance with its official duties.

Approved March 25, 1903.

Chapter 73.

Resolve providing for completing the fireproofing and necessary repairs in the south wing of the State Capitol.

Repairs of south wing of state capitol, to provide for.

Resolved, That the sum of eight thousand dollars for the year nineteen hundred and three, and that the sum of eight thousand dollars for the year nineteen hundred and four, be and hereby is appropriated for the purpose of fireproofing, furnishing and completing the improvements in the south wing of the state capitol, which includes the rooms now occupied by the state assessors, the commissioner of industrial and labor statistics and the executive department, and that the sum be expended by the superintendent of public buildings under the direction of the governor and council.

Approved March 25, 1903.

Chapter 74.

Resolve providing for repairs to be made on the tomb of Governor Enoch Lincoln.

Resolved, That the sum of one thousand dollars be and is hereby appropriated for the purpose of improving the state grounds and making the necessary repairs on the tomb containing the remains of Governor Enoch Lincoln and others. The appropriation to be expended by the superintendent of public lands and buildings under the direction of the governor and council.

Governor Enoch Lincoln, to provide for repairs on tomb of.

Approved March 25, 1903.

Chapter 75.

Resolve providing for the Topographic and Geological Survey for the years nineteen hundred and three and nineteen hundred and four and for extending its work to include Hydrography.

Resolved, That the Topographic Survey Commission be and hereby is authorized to arrange with the director of the United States Geological Survey to enlarge the scope of its work and to include topography, hydrography and geology in its contract with the general government whereby the United States Geological Survey shall expend in the prosecution of the survey an amount equal to that expended by this state; that the chairman of said commission shall be paid an annual salary of three hundred dollars and the remaining members, each, two hundred dollars, and the chairman be designated state geologist; and that there be and hereby is appropriated for the work of said commission, including all expenses, the sum of five thousand dollars, for the year nineteen hundred and three and a like sum for the year nineteen hundred and four.

Topographical and geological survey, to provide for.

Approved March 26, 1903.

Chapter 76.

Resolve fixing the valuation of Reed Plantation in Aroostook County and Drew Plantation in Penobscot County.

Valuation of Reed Pl. and Drew Pl., to fix.

Resolved, That the present valuation of Reed plantation in Aroostook county be reduced by the sum of thirteen thousand seven hundred and twenty dollars, and that the valuation of Drew plantation in Penobscot county be increased in a like amount.

Approved March 27, 1903.

Chapter 77.

Resolve laying a Tax on Counties of the State for the years nineteen hundred and three and nineteen hundred and four.

Tax on counties, to lay.

Resolved, That the sum annexed to the counties in the following schedule is hereby granted as a tax on each county respectively to be appropriated, assessed, collected and applied to the purposes of paying the debts and necessary expenses of the same and for other purposes ordered by law:

For the year one thousand nine hundred and three:

Androscoggin, thirty-five thousand dollars; Aroostook, forty-five thousand dollars; Cumberland, ninety-four thousand five hundred and fifty dollars; Franklin, ten thousand dollars; Hancock, nineteen thousand eight hundred and fifty dollars; Kennebec, thirty thousand dollars; Knox, fifteen thousand dollars; Lincoln, nine thousand eight hundred and seventy-five dollars; Oxford, twenty-five thousand dollars; Penobscot, forty-five thousand dollars; Piscataquis, twenty-one thousand one hundred and sixty dollars; Sagadahoc, sixteen thousand two hundred dollars; Somerset, nineteen thousand nine hundred dollars; Waldo, ten thousand dollars; Washington, forty thousand dollars; York, forty thousand dollars.

And for the year one thousand nine hundred and four:

Androscoggin, thirty-five thousand dollars; Aroostook, forty-five thousand dollars; Cumberland, ninety-two thousand five hundred and fifty dollars; Franklin, ten thousand dollars; Hancock, nineteen thousand eight hundred and fifty dollars; Kennebec, thirty thousand dollars; Knox, fifteen thousand dollars; Lincoln, nine thousand eight hundred and seventy-five dollars; Oxford, twenty-five thousand dollars; Penobscot, forty-five thousand dollars; Piscataquis, twenty-one thousand one hundred and sixty dollars; Sagadahoc, fifteen thousand seven hundred dollars; Somerset, nineteen thousand nine hundred dollars; Waldo, ten thousand dollars; Washington, forty thousand dollars; York, forty thousand dollars.

Approved March 27, 1903.

Chapter 78.

Resolve for repairs of highway in Upton, Magalloway Plantation and township C, in the County of Oxford.

Resolved, That there shall be and is hereby appropriated the sum of eight hundred dollars to aid in repairing the county road known as the Carry road between Umbagog and Richardson lakes, situated in the town of Upton, Magalloway plantation, and township C, in Oxford county; and that the same be expended under the direction of the county commissioners of Oxford county.

Approved March 28, 1903.

Repairs of highway in Upton, Magalloway Pl., and township C.

Chapter 79

Resolve in favor of Lyman E. Smith of Brunswick, for attendance before Agricultural Committee, nineteen hundred and one.

Resolved, That the sum of five dollars and fifty-eight cents be paid Lyman E. Smith of Brunswick for attendance before agricultural committee of nineteen hundred and one.

Approved March 28, 1903.

Lyman E. Smith, in favor of.

Chapter 80.

Resolve in favor of the town of Cutler.

Resolved, That the sum of two hundred and fifty dollars for the year nineteen hundred and three, and two hundred and fifty dollars for the year nineteen hundred and four, be and hereby is appropriated to aid and assist the town of Cutler in the county of Washington, in repairing highways and bridges in said town. Said sum to be expended under the direction of an agent to be appointed by the governor and council. who are hereby authorized to appoint such agent.

Approved March 28, 1903.

Cutler, town of, in favor of.

CHAP. 81

Chapter 81.

Resolve in aid of navigation on Moosehead Lake.

Navigation of Moosehead lake, in aid of.

Resolved, That the sum of seven hundred and fifty dollars is hereby appropriated for the placing of buoys in Moosehead lake and the erection of lights in Moosehead lake and the maintenance of the same for the year nineteen hundred and three, and the sum of seven hundred and fifty dollars is hereby appropriated for the placing of buoys in Moosehead lake and the erection of lights in Moosehead lake and the maintenance of the same for the year nineteen hundred and four. Said buoys and lights shall be placed at such points in Moosehead lake as will best serve the needs of navigation thereon. All said moneys shall be expended under the direction of the state steamboat inspectors; any part of the money hereby appropriated for the placing of buoys and maintenance of lights which shall be unexpended at the end of the year nineteen hundred and four shall revert back to the state.

Approved March 28, 1903.

Chapter 82.

Resolve in favor of the Norcross Transportation Company.

Norcross Transportation Co., in favor of.

Resolved, That the sum of two hundred dollars be and the same hereby is appropriated out of the money in the treasury not otherwise appropriated to be paid to the Norcross Transportation Company to reimburse it in part for its expenditures in erecting buoys as guides to navigation in North Twin lake, North Twin thoroughfare, Pemaduncook lake, Pemaduncook thoroughfare and Ambegigus lake and thoroughfare. Said sum shall be paid to said company on the delivery to the governor and council of a certificate signed by one of the steamboat inspectors setting forth that said buoys have been erected at the places and in the manner approved by him.

Approved March 28, 1903.

Chapter 83.
Resolve in relation to the early York deeds.

Resolved, That the Maine Genealogical Society, agreeing to supervise the copying, attesting, editing, indexing and publishing of volumes twelve and thirteen of the public records of this state in the office of the register of deeds for York county, in the same manner as the eleven preceding volumes already published, except that, on account of their increased size, they are not required to be leaded, nor to have the tabular index, the governor and council shall purchase for the state four hundred and fifty copies of each volume at five dollars per volume; and the state librarian shall cause one copy of each volume to be placed in each registry of deeds in this state; the remaining copies to be distributed or exchanged at the discretion of said librarian.

Approved March 28, 1903.

Chapter 84.
Resolve in favor of the town of Mariaville.

Resolved, That the sum of two hundred dollars for the year nineteen hundred and three and two hundred dollars for the year nineteen hundred and four be and hereby is appropriated to aid in repairing and maintaining the roads and bridges in the town of Mariaville in the county of Hancock, said sums to be paid to the county commissioners of Hancock, the same to be expended under their direction.

Approved March 28, 1903.

Chapter 85.
Resolve in favor of the re-establishment, where necessary, of the boundaries of the lots reserved for public uses in the several plantations and unincorporated places.

Resolved, That the sum of one thousand dollars be and hereby is appropriated to be expended by the land agent in the re-establishment, where necessary, of the boundaries of the lots reserved for public uses in the several plantations and unincorporated places.

Approved March 28, 1903.

Chapter 86.

Resolve to pay for the printing and binding of the report of John A. Morrill, Commissioner for the Revision and Consolidation of the Public Laws.

Printing and binding revision report, to pay for.

Resolved, That the sum of three thousand dollars be and is hereby appropriated to pay for the printing and binding of the report of John A. Morrill, commissioner for the revision and consolidation of the public laws, made to the present legislature.

Approved March 28, 1903.

Chapter 87.

Resolve providing for an Epidemic or Emergency Fund.

Emergency fund, to provide for.

Resolved, That the governor and council are hereby instructed in times of unusual danger from infectious or epidemic diseases, to authorize the state board of health to expend such sums of money as the governor and council deem necessary for the public safety, any sums thus expended to be paid out of any unexpended balances that may be in the treasury for the years nineteen hundred and three and nineteen hundred and four, not exceeding eight thousand dollars each year.

Approved March 28, 1903.

Chapter 88.

Resolve in favor of the stenographers to the presiding and recording officers of the Senate and House.

Officers and stenographers of senate and house, in favor of.

Resolved, That the sum of three hundred dollars be and is hereby appropriated to be paid to Ethel Hodgkins of Ellsworth, for services as stenographer and typewriter operator to the president and secretary of the Senate, and twenty-one dollars for mileage; and three hundred dollars is hereby appropriated to be paid to Daisy B. Bartlett of Dixmont, for services as stenographer and typewriter operator to the speaker and clerk of the House, and fifteen dollars for mileage.

Approved March 28, 1903.

Chapter 89.

Resolve in favor of the Clerk and Stenographer, and the Messenger to the Judiciary Committee.

Resolved, That there be appropriated and paid to Fred W. Lee the sum of three hundred and fifty dollars for services as clerk and stenographer to the judiciary committee; and that there be appropriated and paid to E. Parker Craig the sum of fifty dollars for services as messenger to the same committee.

Approved March 28, 1903.

Chapter 90.

Resolve in favor of the Trustees of the University of Maine.

Resolved, That the trustees of the University of Maine are hereby authorized and directed to erect and equip at said university such machine, wood and iron working shops and laboratories as may be required for the use of the departments of mechanical and electrical engineering, and that there be, and hereby is, appropriated for this purpose the sum of thirty-five thousand dollars, of which sum fifteen thousand dollars shall be paid to said trustees during the current year and the balance during the year nineteen hundred and four.

Approved March 28, 1903.

Chapter 91.

Resolve in favor of Colby College.

Resolved, That there be and hereby is appropriated the sum of fifteen thousand dollars to be paid to Colby college for the use of said institution to enable it to rebuild and furnish its dormitory destroyed by fire in December last.

Approved March 28, 1903.

Chapter 92.

Resolve in favor of Castine State Normal School.

Castine State Normal School, in favor of.

Resolved, That there be and is hereby appropriated the sum of two thousand dollars for the year nineteen hundred and three, and two thousand dollars for the year nineteen hundred and four, for the purchase of land adjoining the normal school lot in Castine, and for putting in water into the school buildings, and for necessary repairs.

Approved March 28, 1903.

Chapter 93.

Resolve in favor of the Town of Anson.

Anson, town of, in favor of.

Resolved, That the sum of five thousand dollars be and is hereby appropriated to the inhabitants of the town of Anson, to aid them in the purchase of the Norridgewock falls bridge, which extends across the Kennebec river between the villages of Anson and Madison. Said sum is to be paid to the treasurer of the said town of Anson when the county commissioners of Somerset county shall certify that the inhabitants of said Anson and Madison have purchased said bridge of the proprietors thereof and have made it a bridge free for public travel.

Approved March 28, 1903.

Chapter 94.

Resolve in favor of the Clerk to the Committee on Revision of Statutes.

J. Perley Dudley, in favor of.

Resolved, That there be appropriated and paid to J. Perley Dudley the sum of three hundred and fifty dollars for services as clerk to the committee on revision of statutes.

Approved March 28, 1903.

Chapter 95.

Resolve in favor of John W. Manson, Secretary of the Committee on Legal Affairs.

Resolved, That there be appropriated and paid to John W. Manson, secretary of the committee on legal affairs, the sum of three hundred and fifty dollars for services of clerk and stenographer to the legal affairs committee; and that there be further appropriated and paid to John W. Manson the sum of fifty dollars, for services of messenger to same committee.

Approved March 28, 1903.

Chapter 96.

Resolve in favor of the Town of Edmunds.

Resolved, That the sum of one hundred and fifty dollars be and is hereby appropriated to aid said town of Edmunds in defraying extraordinary expenses incurred during the year nineteen hundred and two in maintaining roads and bridges and that said money be paid to the treasurer of said town, on or before May first, nineteen hundred and three.

Approved March 28, 1903.

Chapter 97.

Resolve in favor of re-building the bridge across the West Branch of the Saint Croix river connecting the town of Princeton with Indian Township.

Resolved, That the sum of two thousand dollars be and hereby is appropriated for the year nineteen hundred and three, for the purpose of building a steel bridge across the West Branch of the Saint Croix river connecting the town of Princeton with Indian Township. The same to be expended under the direction of the governor and council. Provided that the town of Princeton shall appropriate an equal amount for said purpose.

Approved March 28, 1903.

Chapter 98.

Resolve in favor of repairing Mattawamkeag Bridge.

Resolved, That there be and hereby is appropriated the sum of two thousand dollars to be expended in repairing the Mattawamkeag bridge, so called, situated in Mattawamkeag, Maine. Said appropriation to be expended by an agent to be appointed by the county commissioners of Penobscot county.

Approved March 28, 1903.

Chapter 99.

Resolve providing for a fund for completing the records of the Clerk of Courts of Lincoln County.

Resolved, That the sum of one thousand dollars be and hereby is appropriated for the purpose of defraying the expense to be incurred in making up and completing the records of the clerk of courts of Lincoln county from the April term, eighteen hundred and ninety-five, up to and including the October term, eighteen hundred and ninety-nine, the same to be paid by the state treasurer, under the direction of the governor and council, to the commissioner appointed pursuant to revised statutes, chapter seventy-nine, section thirteen, and upon receipt of certificates issued by any judge of the supreme judicial court of Lincoln county during term time or vacation.

Approved March 28, 1903.

Chapter 100.

Resolve in favor of the city of Eastport.

Resolved, That the sum of one thousand three hundred and fifteen dollars and forty cents be and hereby is appropriated from the treasury to be paid to the city of Eastport to reimburse said city for amount expended in the support and maintenance of one George Ketchell, an insane patient, properly a charge upon the state. The same to be paid when said claim shall be allowed by the governor and council.

Approved March 28, 1903.

Chapter 101.

Resolve in favor of the City of Rockland, on account of money paid the Hallowell Industrial School for the care of Mary Newell, a minor and member of the Passamaquoddy Tribe of Indians.

Resolved, That the sum of one hundred thirty-one dollars and fifty cents be and is hereby appropriated to be paid to the city of Rockland to reimburse said city for money paid out for care of Mary Newell at the Hallowell Industrial School.

Approved March 28, 1903.

Chapter 102.

Resolve favoring the establishment of a National Forest Reserve in the White Mountain Region.

Whereas, certain permanent and summer residents of this state have taken steps to memorialize Congress for the establishment of a national forest reserve in the White Mountain region; and

Whereas, the establishment of such a reserve would perpetuate valuable forest growths and forever preserve the headwaters of several important streams and thus benefit the commerce, industry and agriculture of all the New England states save one; and

Whereas, the White Mountain region is of increasing importance as a pleasure resort to fully one-quarter of the entire population of the country who reside within easy reach of it; therefore be it

Resolved by the Senate and House of Representatives in General Court convened:

That the legislature of Maine hereby expresses its approval of the proposition to establish a White Mountain national forest reserve.

That the consent of the state of Maine be and is hereby given to the acquisition by the United States by purchase, gift, or condemnation according to law, of such lands in this state as in the opinion of the federal government, may be needed for the establishment of a national forest reserve in the White Mountain region.

That power is hereby conferred upon Congress to pass such laws as it may deem necessary to the acquisition of lands in this state for the purposes of such a national forest reserve.

That power is hereby conferred upon Congress to pass such laws and to make, and provide for the making of, such rules and regulations, of both civil and criminal nature, and provide punishment for the violation thereof, as. in its judgment, may be necessary for the management. control and protection of such lands as may from time to time be acquired by the United States under the provisions of this joint resolution; provided, that the state of Maine shall retain a concurrent jurisdiction with the United States in and over such lands so far that civil process in all cases, and such criminal process as may issue under the authority of the state against any person charged with the commission of crime without or within said jurisdiction, may be executed thereon in like manner as if this joint resolution had not been passed.

That the senators and representatives in Congress from this state are hereby requested to urge upon Congress the importance of prompt and favorable action on behalf of the proposition to establish a White Mountain national forest reserve.

Approved March 28, 1903.

Chapter 103.

Resolve in favor of A. A. Burleigh, Chairman of the Committee on Interior Waters.

Resolved, That there be paid from the state treasury to A. A. Burleigh, chairman of the committee on interior waters, the sum of one hundred and eighty-seven dollars and sixty-six cents for expenses incurred by him on behalf of the committee, for reports of evidence and arguments in connection with hearing on Millinocket bill.

Approved March 28, 1903.

Chapter 104.

Resolve in favor of Lee Normal Academy.

Resolved, That the sum of one thousand dollars is hereby annually appropriated out of the school fund, for the term of two years, to Lee Normal Academy, an institution of learning located in the town of Lee, in the county of Penobscot; provided, however, that this appropriation is made on the express conditions that the trustees of said institution shall maintain and keep in operation a school equal in rank and grade of teaching with a first-class academy, and in which shall be given special and systematic instruction in the science and art of teaching;

that no part of this appropriation shall be devoted to other purposes than the payment of instructors in said institution; that the superintendent of public schools shall be, ex-officio, a member of the board of directors thereof; and that if, in the opinion of the governor and council, said institution at any time hereafter shall fail to fulfill the conditions contained in this resolve, they may, in their discretion, withhold the appropriation herein granted; and provided further, that said normal academy shall not be entitled to any aid from the state for the years nineteen hundred and three and nineteen hundred and four in addition to that carried by this resolve.

Approved March 28, 1903.

Chapter 105.

Resolve in favor of the Eastern Maine Insane Hospital.

Resolved, That the sum of thirty thousand four hundred and twenty-five dollars be and is hereby appropriated for and in behalf of the Eastern Maine Insane Hospital, at Bangor, for the year nineteen hundred and three, and thirty thousand four hundred and twenty-five dollars for said institution, for the year nineteen hundred and four, for the purpose of meeting current expenses and making repairs and improvements, said sums to be expended under the direction of the trustees of insane hospitals.

Approved March 28, 1903.

Chapter 106.

Resolve in favor of the town of East Livermore.

Resolved, That the state treasurer be and is hereby authorized and directed to pay to the town of East Livermore the sum of fourteen hundred and ninety-seven dollars and seventy-six cents, the same being to reimburse said town for expenses incurred in the relief of George W. Wing and his family, state paupers, the same to be paid when said claim shall be allowed by the governor and council: Provided also that said sum be accepted in full settlement of the claim of said town for state paupers to December thirty-one, eighteen hundred and ninety-nine.

Approved March 28, 1903.

CHAP. 107

Chapter 107.

Resolve in favor of the Maine State Library.

Maine State Library, in favor of.

Resolved, That the sum of four thousand and eight hundred and sixty-two dollars be and is hereby appropriated for the use of the Maine state library for the year nineteen hundred and three, and that a like sum be and is hereby appropriated for the year nineteen hundred and four, the same to be expended yearly for the following purposes: for current subscriptions, to works of history, biography, magazines, newspapers and to art, medical and scientific works, one thousand and five hundred dollars; for typewriting, telephone service, catalogue cards and contingent expenses, six hundred and twenty-five dollars; for purchase of digests and revised statutes, as issued, two hundred and fifty-three dollars; for the purchase of decisions of inferior courts and session laws, four hundred and eighty-four dollars; for text-books, advance sheets and reports, law magazines and odd numbers of Maine reports, one thousand dollars; to the purchase of new American reports, three hundred dollars; to the purchase of foreign reports, statutes and digests, seven hundred dollars.

Approved March 23, 1903.

Chapter 108.

Resolve in favor of G. E. Morrison, Chairman of the Committee on Salaries and of the Committee on Military Affairs.

G. E. Morrison, in favor of.

Resolved, That the state treasurer be authorized to pay G. E. Morrison, chairman of the committee on salaries and of the committee on military affairs, the sum of one hundred dollars, the same being for services of stenographer and clerical help employed during this session.

Approved March 23, 1903.

Chapter 109.

Resolve in favor of the Board of Cattle Commissioners of the State of Maine, for the prevention of the Foot and Mouth Disease among Cattle.

Resolved, That the governor and council are hereby authorized to pay out of any moneys not otherwise appropriated a sum not exceeding one thousand dollars, for necessary expenses incurred and liable to be incurred in guarding against the spread of foot and mouth disease among cattle.

Approved March 28, 1903.

Chapter 110.

Resolves providing for the collection of information in regard to the large Bridges within the State.

Resolved, That the state assessors be hereby authorized, empowered and directed to collect information from the municipal officers of the several towns within the state in regard to the bridges fifty feet or more in length, said information to be given upon blanks furnished by the state assessors, in the year nineteen hundred four, answer to the following inquiries:

First. Name of stream, river or other water crossed by the bridge.

Second. Length of each bridge between abutments.

Third. Length of approaches.

Fourth. Number of piers in each.

Fifth. Whether covered or open.

Sixth. The condition as to repair.

Seventh. When built.

Eighth. If state gave aid, the amount.

Ninth. Material, wood, iron or stone.

Tenth. Where situated, state road, law of nineteen hundred one, county road or town road.

Eleventh. Number of bridges in town less than fifty feet in length, and over ten feet.

Twelfth. Number of toll bridges in town.

Thirteenth. Amount raised by town for repair of bridges, year nineteen hundred three.

Fourteenth. Amount raised by town for repair of bridges, five years prior to March, nineteen hundred four.

Fifteenth. Amount raised by town for new bridges, nineteen hundred three.

Sixteenth. Amount raised by town for new bridges five years prior to March, nineteen hundred four.

Seventeenth. Amount expended by the town for the repair of iron bridges, nineteen hundred three.

Eighteenth. Amount expended by the town for the repair of iron bridges five years prior to March, nineteen hundred four.

Nineteenth. Amount expended by the town for the repair of wooden bridges five years prior to March, nineteen hundred four.

Twentieth. Estimated costs of new bridges to be built in the next two years.

Resolved, That the state assessors tabulate the above information in the order of the counties and send the same to the county commissioners of the several counties on or before September first, nineteen hundred four; that the county commissioners of the several counties are hereby authorized, empowered and directed to examine the same, and if said information is found incomplete that the county commissioners shall obtain the correct information necessary to complete and correct said returns, at the expense of the town in which deficiencies occur. Said expenses to be recovered in an action of debt against said town. The county commissioners shall certify to the correctness of said information and return the same to the state assessors by the first day of October, nineteen hundred four.

Resolved, That the state assessors shall have the same power to enforce the collection of the above information as in collecting returns for the state valuation and that said state assessors shall cause said information to be printed and report the same to the next legislature.

Resolved, That the state assessors send a copy of this resolve to the municipal officers of the several towns in the state within the month of April, nineteen hundred three.

Approved March 28, 1903.

Chapter 111.

Resolve in aid of Navigation on Lewey, Long and Big Lakes.

Resolved, That the sum of one hundred dollars is hereby appropriated for placing and maintaining buoys in Lewey lake and Long lake in Washington county. Said buoys shall be placed at such points on said waters as will best serve the needs of navigation thereof. All said money to be expended under the direction of the state steamboat inspectors.

Approved March 28, 1903.

Chapter 112.

Resolve in favor of the Maine Insane Hospital.

Resolved, That there be and hereby is appropriated for the Maine Insane Hospital the sum of five thousand dollars to be used for the following purposes: to remove, enlarge and renovate one of the stock barns to provide more room for the better classification of the herd of milch cows.

Approved March 28, 1903.

Chapter 113.

Resolve in favor of Drew Plantation.

Resolved, That the sum of three hundred dollars be and is hereby appropriated to aid Drew plantation, in the county of Penobscot, during the year nineteen hundred and three, in repairing the Mattawamkeag bridge.

Approved March 28, 1903.

Chapter 114.

Resolve providing for Clerk hire in State Library during legislative session of nineteen hundred and three.

Resolved, That the sum of two hundred dollars be and is hereby appropriated to pay W. F. Livingston or his services in the state library during the legislative session of nineteen hundred and three.

Approved March 28, 1903.

Chapter 115.

Resolve in favor of the Eastern Maine General Hospital.

Resolved, That the sum of five thousand dollars, be and hereby is appropriated for the year nineteen hundred four to be paid to said Eastern Maine General Hospital to assist in paying its indebtedness now outstanding and incurred for the purpose of completing, furnishing and equipping the new ward building at said institution, and to repay in part to said hospital the other indebtedness incurred by it for said purposes which it has paid; and for enlarging the grounds.

Approved March 28, 1903.

Chapter 116.

Resolve in favor of the Bangor Children's Home.

Bangor Children's Home, in favor of.

Resolved, That the sum of two thousand dollars be and hereby is appropriated for the year nineteen hundred and four in aid of the Bangor Children's Home, to be applied to the construction and furnishing of a ward for the reception and care of sick children in the same institution, to be paid by the state treasurer from any funds not otherwise appropriated.

Approved March 28, 1903.

Chapter 117.

Resolve in favor of State House employees.

State House employees, in favor of.

Resolved, That the sum of twenty-five dollars be paid to each of the State House employees, serving under the superintendent of public buildings, for extra services rendered during the session, as follows: W. L. Thompson, D. W. Pettengill, J. M. Libby, J. A. McDonald, J. A. Chase, Josiah Weymouth, W. L. Stevens, Peter Breen, Louis Butler, C. C. Richmond, O. I. Stone, O. O. Stetson, William George, Fred Brown, E. A. Weston, C. B. Pettengill, Dearborn Longfellow, A. B. Perkins and B. C. Friend. Nineteen in number, amounting to four hundred and seventy-five dollars.

Approved March 28, 1903.

Chapter 118.

Resolve in aid of repairing the bridge across the Narraguagus River in the town of Milbridge.

Bridge across Narraguagus river, in aid of.

Resolved, That the sum of five hundred dollars for the year nineteen hundred and three, and five hundred dollars for the year nineteen hundred and four, be and is hereby appropriated, to aid in repairing a bridge across the Narraguagus river in the town of Milbridge, said bridge to be repaired under the direction of the county commissioners of Washington county, and the amounts herein appropriated are to be paid annually when the governor and council are satisfied that the sum of one thousand dollars has been actually expended for repairs of said bridge by the town of Milbridge within the year for which payment is claimed.

Approved March 28, 1903.

Chapter 119.

Resolve to aid the town of Frenchville in building a Bridge across Gagnon Stream.

Resolved, That the sum of five hundred dollars be and hereby is appropriated to aid the town of Frenchville, in the county of Aroostook, in constructing and building a bridge across Gagnon stream, in said Frenchville. Said sum to be expended under the direction of the county commissioners.

Bridge across Gagnon stream, in aid of.

Approved March 28, 1903.

Chapter 120.

Resolve in favor of Wallagrass Plantation.

Resolved, That the sum of three hundred dollars be and hereby is appropriated for the year nineteen hundred three to assist in rebuilding a bridge across Wallagrass stream in Wallagrass plantation, and that the same be expended under the direction of the county commissioners of Aroostook county, and that the same be paid, when said commissioners shall certify to the governor and council that said bridge has been rebuilt at a cost of not less than five hundred dollars.

Wallagrass Pl., in favor of.

Approved March 28, 1903.

Chapter 121.

Resolve abating a part of the State Tax of the town of Bowdoinham for the years nineteen hundred and three and nineteen hundred and four.

Resolved, That, on account of the destruction of property by fire in Bowdoinham, December fourteenth, nineteen hundred and two, such a proportion of the state tax of said town for each of the years nineteen hundred and three and nineteen hundred and four as the sum of twenty thousand dollars bears to the entire assessed valuation for said town, be and is hereby abated.

Bowdoinham, part of state tax abated.

Approved March 28, 1903.

CHAP. 122

Chapter 122.

Resolve in favor of the town of New Sharon.

New Sharon, town of, in favor of.

Resolved, That the sum of fifteen hundred dollars be and hereby is appropriated for the year nineteen hundred and three, for the purpose of assisting to repair the highway bridge across the Sandy river in the town of New Sharon, and that the same be expended under the direction of the county commissioners of Franklin county. Said amount to be paid upon certificate of said commissioners to the governor and council that the repairs on said bridge have been completed at a cost of not less than three thousand dollars.

Approved March 28, 1903.

Chapter 123.

Resolve in favor of C. C. Libby, Chairman of the Committee on Education.

C. C. Libby, in favor of.

Resolved, That the sum of four hundred and ten dollars be paid from the state treasury to C. C. Libby to defray the expenses of committee on education and such members of the senate and house as joined, from Augusta to the University of Maine at Orono and return.

Approved March 28, 1903.

Chapter 124.

Resolve in favor of George D. Gaddis of East Machias.

George E. Gaddis, in favor of.

Resolved, That the sum of one hundred dollars is hereby appropriated, to be paid to George D. Gaddis of East Machias; the same being in full for services in taking care of state military property from December eighteen hundred and seventy-four to June in the year of our Lord nineteen hundred and two.

Approved March 28, 1903.

Chapter 125.

Resolve to provide for the services of a Stenographer and Typewriter, when needed, and for extra clerk hire in the office of the State Superintendent of Public Schools.

Resolved, That the sum of five hundred dollars be and the same hereby is appropriated, annually, to pay for the services of a stenographer and typewriter, when needed, and for extra clerk hire in the office of the state superintendent of schools.

Approved March 28, 1903.

Chapter 126.

Resolve in favor of the Western State Normal School at Gorham.

Resolved, That there be and hereby is appropriated the sum of ten thousand dollars for the year nineteen hundred and three and ten thousand dollars for the year nineteen hundred and four for the Western State Normal School at Gorham, the same to be expended by and under the direction of the trustees of the normal schools of the state.

Approved March 28, 1903.

Chapter 127.

Resolve in favor of J. Calvin Knapp, Secretary for the Committee on State Lands and State Roads.

Resolved, That the sum of fifteen dollars be paid to J. Calvin Knapp for cash paid out as secretary for the committee on state lands and state roads.

Approved March 28, 1903.

Chapter 128.

Resolve in favor of R. E. Randall, Secretary of the Committee on Education.

Resolved, That the sum of twenty dollars be paid to R. E. Randall for expenses paid as secretary of the committee on education.

Approved March 28, 1903.

Chapter 129.

Resolve in favor of the State Committee of the Young Men's Christian Association of Maine.

Resolved, That there be, and hereby is, appropriated the amount of three hundred twenty-seven dollars, to be paid the state committee of the Young Men's Christian Association, on account of expenses incurred by said committee for the benefit of the Maine soldiers during their encampment at Augusta during the Spanish-American war.

Approved March 28, 1903.

Chapter 130.

Resolve in favor of Joseph Mitchell, Jr., representative of the Penobscot Tribe of Indians.

Resolved, That the sum of one hundred and twenty dollars be and is hereby appropriated to pay Joseph Mitchell, Jr., representative of the Penobscot tribe of Indians, for his travel and attendance at this session of the legislature.

Approved March 28, 1903.

Chapter 131.

Resolve in favor of Lewy Mitchell, representative of the Passamaquoddy Tribe of Indians.

Resolved, That the sum of one hundred and twenty dollars be and is hereby appropriated to pay Lewy Mitchell, representative of the Passamaquoddy tribe of Indians, for his travel and attendance at this session of the legislature.

Approved March 28, 1903.

Chapter 132.

Resolve in favor of the Town of Jackson.

Resolved, That there be paid to the town of Jackson the sum of seventy-nine dollars and sixty cents, to reimburse the town for its loss of state school fund to that amount, on account of an error in the enumeration of persons between the ages of four and twenty-one on April one, nineteen hundred and one.

Approved March 28, 1903.

Chapter 133.

Resolve in favor of Albion Oakes, secretary of Committee on Ways and Bridges.

Resolved, That the sum of one hundred twenty-two dollars and eighty cents be paid Albion Oakes for disbursements and services as secretary of the Committee on Ways and Bridges.

Approved March 28, 1903.

Chapter 134.

Resolve in favor of Maine Children's Home Society, Augusta.

Resolved, That the sum of twenty-five hundred dollars be and hereby is appropriated for the use of the Maine Children's Home Society, twelve hundred and fifty dollars for the year nineteen hundred and three and twelve hundred and fifty dollars for the year nineteen hundred and four, to aid in maintaining the home of said society for friendless, destitute and needy children. No part of the above appropriation to be used to pay existing debts.

Approved March 28, 1903.

Chapter 135.

Resolve in favor of Connor Plantation.

Resolved, That the sum of two thousand dollars be and hereby is appropriated for the year nineteen hundred and three to aid in the construction of a steel bridge across the Little Madawaska river in Connor plantation. The same to be expended under the direction of the county commissioners of Aroostook county. Said amount to be paid upon certificate of said commissioners to the governor and council that said bridge has been completed at a cost of not less than six thousand dollars. Should the cost of constructing said bridge be less than six thousand dollars the amount to be paid under this resolve shall not exceed one-third of the total cost. And the county of Aroostook is hereby authorized to appropriate the sum of two thousand dollars to aid in the construction of said bridge.

Approved March 28, 1903.

Chapter 136.

Resolve in favor of the town of Mariaville, to assist in rebuilding Goodwin's bridge, in said town, which was carried away by an ice jam about two weeks ago.

Mariaville, town of, in favor of.

Resolved, That the sum of one thousand dollars be and is hereby appropriated to the town of Mariaville, during the year one thousand nine hundred and three to assist in rebuilding said Goodwin's bridge which was carried away by an ice jam.

Approved March 28, 1903.

Chapter 137.

Resolve waiving a forfeiture of the public lots in the north half of Township Number Four, Hancock county, north division.

Waiving forfeiture of public lots.

Resolved, That the forfeitures of the rights to the timber and grass on the public lots in the north half of Township Number Four, Hancock county, north division, for alleged non-payment of taxes, are hereby waived and the owners thereof of record are restored to their rights therein as fully as if record of said forfeiture had not been made. Due record of this waiver shall be made in the offices of the state treasurer, the land agent and the board of state assessors.

Approved March 28, 1903.

Chapter 138.

Resolve to aid the town of Washburn, in the county of Aroostook, in part payment of the cost and expense incurred by it in building a steel bridge across the Aroostook River.

Washburn, town of, in favor of.

Resolved, That the sum of three thousand dollars be and hereby is appropriated to aid the town of Washburn, in the county of Aroostook, in part payment of the cost and expense incurred by said town in building a steel bridge across the Aroostook river, in said town. Said sum shall be paid to the treasurer of said town, during the year nineteen hundred and three.

Approved March 28, 1903.

Chapter 139.

Resolve in favor of building a Bridge across the Mattawamkeag River in the Town of Bancroft.

Resolved, That the sum of twelve hundred dollars be and hereby is appropriated for the year nineteen hundred four, for the purpose of assisting in the construction of a steel bridge across the Mattawamkeag river in the town of Bancroft, and that the same be paid when the county commissioners of Aroostook county shall certify to the governor and council, that said bridge has been completed at a cost of not less than three thousand six hundred dollars. And the county of Aroostook is hereby authorized to appropriate the sum of twelve hundred dollars to aid in the construction of said bridge.

Approved March 28, 1903.

Chapter 140.

Resolve in favor of repairing the Bridge across the St. Croix River near Squirrel Point in Baileyville.

Resolved, That the sum of two hundred and fifty dollars be and hereby is appropriated for the year nineteen hundred and three, in aid of repairing the bridge across the St. Croix river at or near Squirrel Point in Baileyville and known as the Squirrel Point bridge, the same to be expended by an agent to be appointed by the county commissioners of Washington county, said amount to be paid upon the certificate of said commissioners, that said bridge has been thoroughly repaired at an expense of not less than five hundred dollars.

Approved March 28, 1903.

Chapter 141.

Resolve in favor of the Town of Parkman.

Resolved, That the sum of one hundred seventy-three dollars and eleven cents be and hereby is appropriated from the state treasury to reimburse the town of Parkman, for money expended in the commitment and support of Luella Harvey in the insane asylum at Augusta, Maine.

Approved March 28, 1903.

HAWKERS AND PEDDLERS.

Chapter 142.

Resolve in favor of paying the unexpired Licenses of Hawkers and Peddlers.

Licenses of peddlers, in favor of paying.

Resolved, That the treasurer of state be and hereby is authorized to pay to each and every person holding a state license as hawker and peddler, issued by the secretary of state prior to December nine, nineteen hundred and two, such an amount as the proportion of the unexpired time of such license subsequent to December nine, nineteen hundred and two, bears to the whole time for which said license was issued. And that the sum of fifteen hundred dollars be and hereby is appropriated out of any funds in the treasury, not otherwise appropriated, for the purpose of this resolve. Provided, however, that those receiving from the state any amount on account of unexpired licenses by virtue of special resolves finally passed and approved before the approval of this resolve, shall receive nothing in addition. Provided, further, that the treasurer of the state be and hereby is authorized to pay to each licensee who has paid for a state license since December nine, nineteen hundred and two, the amount paid by him not yet returned.

Approved March 28, 1903.

PAY ROLL OF THE SENATE.

PAY ROLL of the members and officers of the Senate of the Seventy-first Legislature, at the session held at Augusta, commencing on the seventh day of January, and closing on the twenty-eighth day of March, in the year of our Lord one thousand nine hundred and three.

DISTRICTS.	NAMES.	Amount for attendance.	Miles.	Mileage.	Total pay.
First......	George E. Morrison.....	150	80	$16	$166
	Freeman E. Rankin......	150	95	19	169
	Oliver C. Titcomb.......	150	125	25	175
Second....	Harry R. Virgin, President	300	65	13	313
	Thurston S. Burns	150	70	14	164
	Winburn M. Staples.....	150	115	23	173
	Charles H. Randall	150	65	13	163
Third.....	John M. Philbrook......	150	130	26	176
Fourth....	George C. Wing........	150	60	12	162
	Walter E. Plummer.....	150	40	8	158
Fifth	George M. Currier......	150	100	20	170
Sixth	John S. Hyde..........	150	40	8	158
Seventh...	Rutillus Alden..........	150	15	3	153
	Caleb C. Libby	150	15	3	153
	Joseph H. Manley	150	5	1	151
Eighth....	Edmund C. Bryant......	150	40	8	158
	Forrest Goodwin........	150	40	8	158
Ninth.....	Frank E. Guernsey......	150	80	16	166
Tenth.....	Isaiah K. Stetson	150	75	15	165
	Halbert P. Gardner......	150	185	37	187
	Amos W. Knowlton.....	150	75	15	165
Eleventh..	Luther Maddocks	150	85	17	167
Twelfth...	L. M. Staples	150	90	18	165
Thirteenth.	Lucius C. Morse	150	85	17	167
Fourteenth.	Albert R. Buck	150	115	23	173
	Edward S. Clark........	150	125	25	175
Fifteenth..	Emerson K. Wilson	150	135	27	177
	Bion M. Pike...........	150	220	44	194
Sixteenth..	Albert A. Burleigh......	150	220	44	194
	John W. Dudley........	150	270	54	204
	Howard Pierce	150	300	60	210

Total for attendance $4,800
Total for travel, 3,160 miles 632

$5,432

OFFICERS.

Office.	Names.	Amount for attendance.	Miles.	Mileage.	Total pay.
Secretary..	Kendall M. Dunbar......	$800	65	$13	$813
Ass't Sec'y.	Frank G. Farrington.....	300	5	1	300 301
Messenger..	Walter B. Clarke, at organization. Charles H. Lovejoy	150 150	75 20	15 4	300 165 154
Ass't Mess.	James F. Ashford.......	150	15	3	250 153
Folder	W. G. Fuller	150	45	9	150 159
Ass't Folder	John J. Dearborn	150	90	18	150 168
Postmaster	Hall C. Dearborn, at organization. Thomas A. Anderson	30 150	90 50	18 10	150 48 160
Door Keep'r	Stephen D. Lord........	150	110	22	150 172
Pages	Scott C. W. Simpson	75	65	13	150 88
	Albert W. Buck	75	115	23	75 98
	John D. Buck, at organization.	30	115	23	75 53
	Allen Clark, at organization.	30	70	14	44
Offic'l Rep'r	Edward K. Milliken	300	75	15	315 300

Total for attendance $4,740
Total for travel, 1,005 miles 201

$4,941

CHAPLAINS.

RESIDENCE.	NAMES.	Days.	Amount.
Augusta.......	Rev. Miss Atkinson	1	$2
	Rev. Mr. Colby	1	2
	Rev. Mr. Cudworth	2	4
	Rev. Mr. Degen	2	4
	Rev. Fr. Doherty	2	4
	Rev. Mr. Dunnack	2	4
	Rev. Mr. Gibson..............	2	4
	Rev. Mr. Hayden.............	2	4
	Rev. Mr. Hope................	2	4
	Rev. Mr. Livingston	7	14
	Rev. Mr. McKinnon...........	2	4
	Rev. Mr. Mosher	2	4
	Rev. Mr. Newbert	2	4
	Rev. Miss Wadsworth	1	2
Hallowell......	Rev. Mr. Canham.............	2	4
	Rev. Mr. Peckham	2	4
	Rev. Mr. Plummer	2	4
	Rev. Mr. Webber.............	2	4
	Rev. Mr. Wight	1	2
Gardiner	Rev. Mr. Bradeen.............	1	2
	Rev. Mr. Cashmore	2	4
	Rev. Mr. Clark	1	2
	Rev. Mr. Quimby.............	2	4
	Rev. Mr. Struthers............	2	4
	Rev. Mr. Tandberg	2	4
			$98

RECAPITULATION.

Members........................	$5,432
Officers........................	4,941
Chaplains	98
Total	$10,471

Chapter 143.

Resolve on the Pay Roll of the Senate.

Pay roll of the Senate.

Resolved, That there be paid out of the treasury of the state to the several persons named in the foregoing pay roll, the sum set against their names respectively, amounting to the sum of ten thousand four hundred and seventy-one dollars.

Approved March 28, 1903.

Chapter 144.

Resolve to provide for the expense of examination of candidates for the Cecil John Rhodes scholarships.

Cecil John Rhodes scholarships, examination for.

Resolved, That the sum of one hundred dollars be and the same is hereby appropriated, annually, to pay the expense of the examination of candidates for the Cecil John Rhodes scholarships, the same, or such part thereof as may be necessary, to be expended under the direction of the state superintendent of public schools.

Approved March 28, 1903.

Chapter 145.

Resolve in favor of Maine State Prison.

Maine State Prison, in favor of.

Resolved, That the sum of thirty-seven thousand one hundred and thirty-six dollars and sixteen cents be and hereby is appropriated for and in behalf of the Maine state prison to be expended under the direction and supervision of the governor and council. Six thousand six hundred and thirty-six dollars and sixteen cents deficiency in insane department; eight thousand dollars for sewer; two thousand dollars for repairs of buildings; two thousand five hundred dollars to pay for bills and notes outstanding and due; seven thousand five hundred dollars for current expenses; seven thousand five hundred dollars for current expenses for the year nineteen hundred and four.

Approved March 28, 1903.

PAY ROLL of the members and officers of the House of the Seventy-first Legislature, at the session held in Augusta, commencing on the seventh day of January, and ending on the twenty-eighth day of March in the year of our Lord one thousand nine hundred and three.

COUNTY OF ANDROSCOGGIN.

TOWNS.	NAMES.	Miles traveled.	Amount for attendance.	Amount for travel and attendance.
Auburn	Ansel Briggs	55	150	161
	Henry W. Oakes	55	150	161
East Livermore	Alphonso D. Cole	80	150	166
Greene	Henry H. Coburn	50	150	160
Lewiston	Michael A. Coyne	55	150	161
	Alonzo M. Garcelon	55	150	161
	Frank A. Morey	55	150	161
	George B. Haskell	55	150	161
	Stephen J. Kelley	55	150	161
	Jacob R. Little	55	150	161
	Patrick F. Tremblay	55	150	161
Lisbon	Winfield S. Hinckley	45	150	159
Mechanic Falls	Jesse M. Libby	70	150	164
Poland	Flavius B. Shackford	65	150	163
Turner	Rackley D. Leavitt	80	150	166
				2,427

COUNTY OF AROOSTOOK.

Ashland	S. S. Thornton	305	150	211
Caribou	George W. Irving	300	150	210
Dyer Brook	Harrison G. White	200	150	190
Easton	W. H. Dilling	265	150	203
Fort Fairfield	Joseph S. Hall	275	150	205
Fort Kent	John Sweeney	300	150	210
Hammond Pl	John W. Davidson	225	150	195
Houlton	Beecher Putnam	225	150	195
Linneus	Wendell C. Boyd	225	150	195
Madawaska	Theodule Albert	415	150	233
Presque Isle	George H. Smith	260	150	202
Van Buren	Henry A. Gagnon	305	150	211
Washburn	Alden E. Howes	270	150	204
				2,664

PAY ROLL OF THE HOUSE.

COUNTY OF CUMBERLAND.

TOWNS.	NAMES.	Miles traveled.	Amount for attendance.	Amount for travel and attendance.
Bridgton	James Carroll Mead	120	150	174
Brunswick	Barrett Potter	35	150	157
	Lemuel H. Stover	35	150	157
Casco	Gideon T. Cook	120	150	174
Falmouth	Frank B. Blanchard	55	150	161
Freeport	R. E. Randall	40	150	158
Gorham	Charles S. Purinton	80	150	166
Harpswell	Charles S. Thomas	90	150	168
New Gloucester	Charles H. Nelson	80	150	166
North Yarmouth	Isaac E. Hayes	65	150	163
Portland	George H. Allan	65	150	163
	Oakley C. Curtis	65	150	163
	Isaiah Daniels	65	150	163
	Morrill N. Drew	65	150	163
	Theodore A. Josselyn	65	150	163
	Robert B. Low	65	150	163
	Edward C. Swett	65	150	163
South Portland	J. Calvin Knapp	65	150	163
Standish	H. Herbert Sturgis	90	150	168
Westbrook	Albert A. Cordwell	70	150	168
	Almon N. Waterhouse	75	150	165
Windham	Fred S. Hawkes	80	150	166
				3,611

COUNTY OF FRANKLIN.

Farmington	H. Herbert Rice	100	150	170
Industry	Franklin W. Patterson	55	150	161
Rangeley	Harry A. Furbish	150	150	180
Wilton	Joseph W. Perkins	90	150	168
				679

COUNTY OF HANCOCK.

TOWNS.	NAMES.	Miles traveled.	Amount for attendance.	Amount for travel and attendance.
Brooksville	George H. Tapley	115	150	173
Bucksport	Oscar F. Fellows ...... Speaker.	105	300	321
Eden	Charles C. Morrison....	145	150	179
Ellsworth......	F. Carroll Burrill......	105	150	171
Hancock	Orlando W. Foss......	115	150	173
Sorrento	Sherman R. Downing ..	125	150	175
Stonington	Sumner P. Mills	200	150	190
Tremont	Alton E. Farnsworth...	150	150	180
				1,562

COUNTY OF KENNEBEC.

Augusta	Edwin C. Dudley......	5	150	151
	W. H. Gannett........	5	150	151
Chelsea	Charles H. Watson	10	150	152
China	William J. Thompson ..	30	150	156
Gardiner	Edgar E. Norton	10	150	152
Hallowell......	Joseph F. Bodwell.....	5	150	151
Oakland	Morrison Libby	25	150	155
Randolph	Bert E. Lamb.........	10	150	152
Sidney	Fred E. Blake	30	15	156
Waterville	Cyrus W. Davis........	20	150	154
	Fred Pooler	20	150	154
West Gardiner..	R. L. Snowe..........	15	150	153
Winslow	W. T. Reynolds.......	20	150	154
				1,991

COUNTY OF KNOX.

Camden	E. Frank Knowlton	100	150	170
Rockland	Sereno T. Kimball	95	150	169
	Arthur S. Littlefield ...	95	150	169
Rockport	Joseph H. Carleton	100	150	170
South Thomaston	Alden W. Butler	95	150	169
Thomaston	E. A. McNamara	85	150	167
Warren	Moses R. Spear	80	150	166
				1,180

COUNTY OF LINCOLN.

TOWNS.	NAMES.	Miles traveled.	Amount for attendance.	Amount for travel and attendance.
Nobleboro	Walter B. Clarke	75	150	165
Waldoboro	John W. Benner	80	150	166
Westport	Herman A. Greenleaf	75	150	165
Wiscasset	Richard H. T. Taylor	65	150	163
				659

COUNTY OF OXFORD.

Brownfield	Albert R. Hill	110	150	172
Canton	E. W. Howe	120	150	174
Oxford	G. J. Parrott	100	150	170
Paris	Hiram R. Hubbard	65	150	163
Rumford	Waldo Pettengill	120	150	174
Upton	Silas F. Peaslee	120	150	174
Waterford	Bertrand G. McIntire	100	150	170
				1,197

COUNTY OF PENOBSCOT.

Bangor	Lewis A. Barker	75	150	165
	George F. Cameron	75	150	165
	H. F. Ross	75	150	165
Bradford	William E. Bailey	110	150	172
Brewer	D. Allston Sargent	80	50	166
Carmel	John Ruggles	60	150	162
Corinna	Charles L. Jones	60	150	162
Dexter	E. A. Brewster	65	150	163
Dixmont	Lewis I. Bussey	60	150	162
Drew Pl	Alonzo R. Page	140	150	178
Enfield	John H. McGregor	115	150	173
Lincoln	A. Weatherbee	120	150	174
Milford	Albion Oakes	85	150	167
Millinocket	George W. Stearns	155	150	181
Old Town	Leslie A. Buzzell	85	150	167
Orono	George E. Thompson	85	150	167
Orrington	N. A. Nickerson	85	150	167
				2,856

PAY ROLL OF THE HOUSE.

COUNTY OF PISCATAQUIS.

TOWNS.	NAMES.	Miles traveled.	Amount for attendance.	Amount for travel and attendance.
Abbot	D. H. Buxton	100	150	170
Parkman	W. S. McKusick	105	150	171
Wellington	William Allen	100	150	170
Williamsburg	Robert J. Williams	125	150	175
				686

COUNTY OF SAGADAHOC.

Bath	Harold M. Sewall	40	150	158
	Albert H. Shaw	40	150	158
Georgetown	Warren C. Todd	55	150	161
Topsham	Eugene Thomas	35	150	157
				634

COUNTY OF SOMERSET.

Bingham	Mark Savage	65	150	163
Fairfield	George G. Weeks	25	150	155
Hartland	C. H. Smith	50	150	160
Madison	A. Ledyard Smith, Jr.	45	150	159
New Portland	John Knowlton	55	150	161
Pittsfield	J. W. Manson	40	150	158
Skowhegan	Edward P. Page	40	150	158
				1,114

COUNTY OF WALDO.

Belfast	Clarence O. Poor	70	150	164
Morrill	Elisha Merriam	75	150	165
Prospect	Elmer D. Clark	100	150	170
Troy	Mark T. Dodge	50	150	160
Winterport	Charles R. Hill	90	150	168
				827

PAY ROLL OF THE HOUSE.

COUNTY OF WASHINGTON.

TOWNS.	NAMES.	Miles traveled.	Amount for attendance.	Amount for travel and attendance.
Calais	George H. Eaton	215	150	193
Cherryfield	Fred I. Campbell	135	150	177
Cutler	F. W. Thurlow	250	150	200
Danforth	E. A. Putnam	165	150	183
Dennysville	Lyman K. Gardner	195	150	189
Eastport	Lincoln H. Newcomb	215	150	193
Harrington	Edward W. Shacktord	140	150	178
Lubec	Jacob C. Pike	220	150	194
Pembroke	A. S. Farnsworth	200	150	190
Machias	Alexander D. McFaul	175	150	185
				1,882

COUNTY OF YORK.

TOWNS.	NAMES.	Miles traveled.	Amount for attendance.	Amount for travel and attendance.
Biddeford	Kenneth W. Sutherland.	80	150	166
	J. B. E. Tartre	80	150	166
Buxton	Samuel A. Hill	80	150	166
Kennebunk	Lendall W. Nash	90	150	168
Kennebunkport	Palmer A. Twambly	95	150	169
Kittery	Charles L. Favour	125	150	175
Lebanon	W. B. Wentworth	110	150	172
Lyman	Ferdinand E. Tripp	85	150	167
Newfield	David W. Libby	140	150	178
Old Orchard	William J. Mewer	75	150	165
Saco	William J. Maybury	80	150	166
Sanford	Fred J. Allen	100	150	170
Shapleigh	Natt T. Abbott	115	150	173
Wells	Joseph D. Eaton	95	150	169
				2,370

OFFICERS.

OFFICE.	OFFICER.	Miles traveled.	Amount for attendance.	Amount for travel and attendance.
Clerk	W. S. Cotton	45	800	809
				300
Assistant Clerk	E. M. Thompson	5	300	301
				300
Messenger	George H. Fisher	90	150	168
				250
1st Ass't Mess.	William J. Smith	10	150	152
				150
2d Ass't Mess	W. H. Holmes	5	150	151
				150
1st Folder	J. F. Frederick	60	150	162
	Joseph H. Dixon	125	150	175
				150
2d Folder	Chapin Lydston	30	150	156
				150
3d Folder	L. E. Thornton	305	150	211
				150
	Louis J. Brann, at organization	55	40	51
Mail Carrier	Harry P. Hawes	15	150	153
				150
	Expenses			60
Ass't Mail Car'r.	Harry R. Coolidge	85	150	167
				150
	Isaac B. Clary, at organization	80	40	56
Door Keeper	R. C. Noyes	40	150	158
				150
Door Keeper	E. Parker Craig	195	150	189
				150
	Edward W. Delano	215	40	83
Pages	Charles Knowlton	105	75	96
				75
	Walter S. Cushing, at organization	40	30	38
	William B. Webb	40	75	83
				75
	Ernest L. McLean, at organization	55	30	41
Official Report's.	J. S. Estes	295	300	859
	A. H. Whitman	65	300	363

PAY ROLL OF THE HOUSE.

CHAPLAINS.

Residence.	Names.	Days.	Amount.
Augusta	Rev. Mr. Mosher	4	$8
	Rev. Mr. Dunnack	2	4
	Rev. Mr. Hayden	3	6
	Rev. Mr. Newbert	3	6
	Rev. Mr. Livingston	5	10
	Rev. Mr. Degen	2	4
	Rev. Mr. McKinnon	2	4
	Rev. Fr. Doherty	2	4
	Rev. Mr. Hope	3	6
	Rev. Mr. Cudworth	1	2
Hallowell	Rev. Mr. Wight	2	4
	Rev. Mr. Canham	3	6
	Rev. Mr. Webber	2	4
	Rev. Mr. Plummer	2	4
Gardiner	Rev. Mr. Cashmore	2	4
	Rev. Mr. Clark	2	4
	Rev. Mr. Quimby	2	4
	Rev. Mr. Struthers	2	4
	Rev. Mr. Bradeen	2	4
	Rev. Mr. Tandberg	2	4

RECAPITULATION.

Members of House.	$26,339
Officers of House	7,032
Chaplains of House	96
Total	$33,467

Chapter 146.

Resolve on the Pay Roll of the House.

Resolved, That there be paid out of the treasury of the state to the several persons named in the foregoing pay roll the sum set against their names respectively, amounting to the sum of thirty-three thousand four hundred and sixty-seven dollars.

Approved March 28, 1903.

Pay roll of the House.

Chapter 147.

Resolve in favor of an Electric Lighting Plant for the Maine State Prison.

Resolved, That the sum of three thousand one hundred dollars be and hereby is appropriated in behalf of an electric lighting plant for the Maine state prison, to be expended under the direction of the governor and council. One thousand dollars to install the plant; one thousand dollars to pay for wiring; five hundred dollars for fuel; five hundred dollars for fuel for the year nineteen hundred and four; one hundred dollars for inspection of plant; that the prison inspectors superintend the purchasing and installation of said plant, if they are able to contract with responsible parties to install a suitable plant within this appropriation, their services be paid for from the one hundred dollars this resolve carries for that purpose.

That such part of the seven thousand dollars appropriated for lights for the state prison, as may be unexpended, be available, if needed, to erect and carry on this plant.

Approved March 28, 1903.

Electric lighting plant for Maine State Prison, in favor of.

Chapter 148.

Resolves in relation to the publication and distribution of the Revised Statutes.

Resolved, That as soon as may be after the final enactment thereof, the governor and council cause four thousand copies of the revised statutes of the state with the constitution thereof, the constitution of the United States, the repealing act, and the index prepared by the commissioner for the revision and consolidation of the public laws, to be printed by the public printer and bound by the public binder, for the use of the state, at prices not exceed-

Publication and distribution of revised statutes.

ing those at which other work for the state is done by said officials. Said revised statutes shall be bound in one volume in such style as to size of page, width of margin, printing, paper and binding as may be approved by the governor and council.

Resolved, That the governor and council may also contract with some responsible person or persons for the publication of the revised statutes of the state with the constitution thereof, the constitution of the United States, the repealing act and the index aforesaid, upon such terms and conditions as they deem necessary for the interests of the state and shall have the right to reject any and all bids, provided that the retail price at which the statutes so published shall be sold within the state, shall not exceed the sum of three dollars and fifty cents a copy.

Resolved, That the secretary of state shall secure the copyright of said volume for the use of the state and that the title to the annotations and the index contained in said volume be and remain the property of the state.

Resolved, That the copies of said volume so printed and bound for the use of the state shall be deposited in the office of the librarian of the state library, who shall distribute the same as follows, namely: one copy to the governor and to each member of the executive council; one copy to each former governor of the state; one copy to each of the justices of the supreme judicial and superior courts and to the reporter of decisions; one copy to each former justice of the supreme judicial court; one copy to the judge of the circuit court of the United States, residing in the district of Maine; one copy to the judge of the district court of the United States for the district of Maine; to the following public officers, for the use of the respective offices they fill and the counties wherein they reside, one copy each, namely: the secretary of state, the treasurer of state, the adjutant general, the attorney general, the bank examiner, the insurance commissioner, the railroad commissioners, the state assessors, the state superintendent of public schools, the commissioners of inland fisheries and game, the commissioner of sea and shore fisheries, the state liquor commissioner, the land agent, the commissioner of industrial and labor statistics, the inspector of workshops, factories, mines and quarries, the commissioner of agriculture, the secretary of the state board of health, the cattle commissioners, the superintendent of the reform school, the superintendents of the insane hospitals, the superintendent of public buildings, the warden of the state prison, the principal of the Maine industrial school for girls, the public printer, the public binder; to each municipal or police court in the state, the clerks of courts, the county attorneys, sheriffs, judges of probate, registers of probate, registers of deeds, the court of county commissioners and the treasurers in each county; and to the several clerks of cities, towns and plantations, one copy each, for the use of their respective cities, towns and plantations; to each college and theological institution one copy, one copy to the Maine historical society, and one copy to each free public library in the state receiving state aid under the provisions of chapter one hundred and ten, of the public laws of eighteen hundred and ninety-five; one copy to the law library of each county in the state; one copy to the clerk of the United States courts for the district of Maine and one copy to the district attorney of the United States for the district of Maine; to the president of the United States one copy, to each senator and representative of the state in Congress one copy, to the secretary of state for the United States four copies; to the secretary of state of each state and to the secretary of each territory in the union, one copy each for the use of the library of such state or territory; to the library of congress two copies; to the librarian of the state library ten copies for the use of the library; to each member of the senate and house of representatives of the present legislature one copy; to the secretary of the senate one copy; to the clerk of the house of representatives one copy; to the commissioner for the revision and consolidation of the public laws one copy; the remainder of said copies so printed for the use of the state shall be deposited in the office of the librarian of the state library to be distributed from time to time as the legislature, or governor and council may direct. The several persons in the state furnished with the revised statutes as aforesaid, excepting the governor and ex-governors, the executive councilors, judges of the supreme judicial and superior courts, the former judges of the supreme judicial court, judges and officers of the United States court for the district of Maine, the senators and representatives in Congress, members and officers of the legislature and the commissioner for the revision and consolidation of the public laws, shall be responsible for the same and deliver it to his successor in office to be continually kept for the use of the office, and the copies so furnished for the use of such offices shall be marked as provided by section three of chapter one hundred fifty-one of the public laws of eighteen hundred and ninety-five and shall have a registered number conforming to the list to be kept by the librarian of the state library.

Approved March 28, 1903.

STATE OF MAINE.

OFFICE OF SECRETARY OF STATE,
AUGUSTA, May 12, 1903.

I hereby certify that the Acts and Resolves contained in this pamphlet have been carefully compared with the originals, and appear to be correctly printed.

BYRON BOYD,
Secretary of State.

NOTE—The Seventy-first Legislature of Maine convened on the seventh day of January and adjourned on the twenty-eighth day of March, 1903.

GOVERNOR HILL'S ADDRESS.

Gentlemen of the Seventy-First Legislature:

As representatives of the sovereign people, charged with the duty and responsibility of enacting such legislation as will best promote the common good, the obligation which you have accepted demands the most faithful and devoted service that you can render. Maine Legislatures have ever been composed of high-minded, patriotic men, who have had the best interest of the State at heart. They have been men well qualified by practical experience to direct and manage public affairs, and their unselfish labors for the general welfare have won the merited approbation of their fellow citizens. You will enter upon the laborious and exacting duties of the present session with the same just and generous measure of public confidence and support that has been accorded your predecessors. Into your hands the people of Maine have given the affairs of our State in the full faith that, recognizing the grave responsibility of the trust, you will administer it wisely and well. It is a pleasure and a privilege for me to welcome you to the Capitol and to assure you that I shall be ready at all times to heartily co-operate with you in every measure calculated to promote the best interests of the people whom we are honored to represent.

The future is full of promise, and the evidences of continued progress and development may be seen on every hand. Our various industries are as a rule successful and giving employment to more people than ever before, and every indication points to the continued growth and prosperity of the whole State.

There has been a substantial increase in our revenues, as a result of legislation enacted two years ago, which placed upon the corporate interests of the State a larger share of the public burdens. Not only has the entire temporary loan of $350,000 been paid, but $36,000 on account of the Eastern Maine Insane Hospital and $120,000 of the funded debt as well, while the amount of cash on hand December 31st was $240,013.67 greater than on the corresponding date two years ago.

This is a net gain of $746,013.67 in the last two years.

State Finances.

The total revenue of the State for the two years ending December 31st, 1902, was $4,430,105.52. The amount of cash on hand December 31st, 1900, was $198,879.01, making a total of $4,628,984.53. The amount disbursed during this period was $4,190,091.85, leaving a balance on hand December 31st, 1902, of $438,892.68. The greater portion of this sum will, however, be required to discharge obligations soon payable, and to meet promptly the regular and legitimate demands upon the Treasury, for it should be remembered that the State revenues during the first part of the year do not equal its necessary expenditures by several hundred thousand dollars.

The various State Departments and Institutions have been managed with care and economy. There was an unexpended balance of appropriations amounting to $32,769.67 reverting to the treasury at the close of 1901, and of $34,992.85 at the close of 1902.

From time to time an opportunity is offered for the purchase of State bonds of various maturities and I believe it would be sound business policy, and for the interest of the State, to give the Treasurer authority to buy such bonds whenever funds are available for the purpose. We should take advantage of these opportunities to more rapidly reduce our funded debt, which otherwise can only be paid as it matures.

Seventy thousand dollars becomes due and payable annually until 1912; then $78,000 each year until 1922, and after that $38,000 annually until 1929, when the last payment is made and the entire debt is discharged.

The net amount of State tax assessed during the past two years was $595,034.35, the total tax assessed against the cities, towns and organized plantations being $1,747,477.30, and the amount of the school fund and mill tax which they received from the State Treasury, $1,152,442.95; $805,451.42 was paid by the twenty cities of the State, $942,025.88 was paid by the towns and plantations, and $107,974.58 by the owners of wild lands. The twenty cities paid into the Treasury $426,320.82 more than they received from the school fund and 258 towns and plantations, or more than one-half, received from the school fund more than the State tax assessed against them. The average net State tax of the twenty cities of the State was 1.46 mills on each dollar of valuation, and for the towns and organized plantations, the average rate was one-half a mill on each dollar.

In addition to $1,791,570.32 received from the tax on cities, towns, plantations and wild lands during the past two years, the tax on Savings Banks has amounted to $1,038,191.43; on Trust and Banking Companies, $45,147.66; the tax on Railroads was $618,479.92; on Telegraph and Telephone Companies,

$36,809.91; on Express Companies, $17,320.32; on Insurance Companies, $152,208.26; on Collateral Inheritances, $78,828.43; on Corporations, $78,140.00; Organization of New Corporations, $131,485.00; other taxes and miscellaneous items, $441,924.27: making the total revenue from all sources $4,430,105.52.

The State Assessors report an increase of $8,880,227.00 during the past two years in the valuation of the cities, towns and plantations, their total valuation now being $325,948,121.00. Wild lands are valued at $25,528,930.00, an increase of $6,401,523.00, which together with an increase of $247,498.00 on timber, and grass on public lots, makes a total increase in valuation of $15,529,248.00. **State Valuation.**

The Assessors have labored earnestly and zealously to ascertain the true value of property in the State. The figures which they present have been carefully made, and show clearly and forcibly the prosperity of our people.

The depositors in our Savings Banks and Trust Companies and the shareholders in the Loan and Building Associations now number 237,740, equaling about a third of the entire population of the State. This is a gain of 23,760 during the past two years. **Savings Banks.**

On the 25th day of October, 1902, the total assets of all our State banking institutions were as follows: Savings Banks, $77,853,815.64; Trust Companies, $17,035,941.70; Loan and Building Associations, $2,854,626.60; a total of $97,744,383.94, as against $87,233,793.12 two years ago, being an average annual gain of over $5,000,000.00.

As a rule deposits are made in such small amounts that they could not be invested independently and often they are made by individuals who could not invest for themselves. When these accumulations are withdrawn, it is either to meet existing needs, or for use and investment in the business of the individual depositors. Through the influence of these institutions vast sums have been saved which have constantly contributed to the business enterprises of our State.

In the past two years these banks have paid to depositors $4,467,143.14 in dividends. This is the net income which they have returned to their patrons, after paying taxes, amounting to over $1,000,000.00, all the necessary expenses of their management, and setting aside a reasonable reserve. While the annual rate paid is small, it represents a material addition to the income of our people, and contributes largely to their present comfort and future welfare.

The fifty-one Savings Banks of Maine contribute nearly one-fourth of the total revenues of the State, having paid a tax of $537,720.51 during the past year.

In 1872, when the tax on Savings Banks was first established, the rate was one-half of one per cent. on the average deposits, and the banks then paid an average dividend to depositors of 6⅓ per cent. The tax now approximates three-fourths of one per cent., and the average dividend paid during the past year has been about 3¼ per cent. In other words, the State now receives about one-fifth of the net earnings of the banks. When it is remembered that more than three-fourths of all depositors have but $500 or less to their credit, and that a considerable portion of these deposits represent the small savings of the poor—pittances which have been slowly accumulated, oftentimes by the most rigid economy and self-denial, it is apparent that the State is exacting from the banks too large a proportion of their earnings.

The tax should be reduced to an average rate of not more than one-half of one per cent., and in order that this may be done without materially affecting the revenues of the State, I recommend a horizontal reduction of one-eighth of one per cent. to take effect the coming year, and a further reduction of one-eighth of one per cent. to take effect in 1904.

According to the estimates of the Bank Examiner, we may reasonably expect a yearly increase of about $3,000,000 in Savings Bank deposits. Thus in a few years the loss sustained by the Treasury on account of the reduction in the rate would be made good.

It should be remembered that these institutions are wholly mutual and no part of the profit goes to the management. The banks have made a splendid record for conservatism and to the highest degree enjoy the confidence of the public. They have encouraged the saving of millions of dollars which otherwise would have been wholly wasted or frittered away in needless expenditures.

Education. The State Superintendent of Public Schools reports that there were 213,526 persons of school age in the State on April 1st, 1902; 6,634 teachers were employed, of whom 1,481 were graduates of Normal Schools. There were 224 free High Schools, with 13,283 pupils enrolled.

It is gratifying to know that the parents of children who are in the schools, and citizens generally, are taking a greater interest in school work, and that much is constantly being done in the improvement of school grounds and buildings, and to make the schools in every possible way more attractive and efficient.

The State school fund and mill tax the past year amounted to $562,461. The school fund raised by the towns was $838,807, and the amount derived from various local resources $38,042, making the total amount available for the support of the common schools $1,439,310.

I recommend that the State school funds be apportioned on the basis of average attendance, instead of on the basis of the number of persons between four and twenty-one years of age, in the different towns and cities. It is only right that the State should so distribute these funds as to make the wisest use of them, and in a way that will accomplish the largest possible measure of practical good. For this reason the allotment should be based not upon the number of persons of school age, but rather upon the number actually attending our public schools and receiving instruction therein.

I believe that such change in the law would work to the benefit of our common schools, and I trust this matter will receive your early and careful consideration.

Our academies, seminaries, and institutes have the largest attendance in their history. The children in the rural and village communities at the present time show a more ardent desire for a higher education than was evinced by the boys and girls in the days when many of these institutions were founded, and when the men, whose subsequent distinguished careers did so much to give prestige to their State, were laying the foundations of future greatness.

The Normal Schools have increased their standards of admission, and as a result the students are better trained. These schools are in a most satisfactory condition in every way, and are making constant progress and improvement.

The Summer Training Schools are attended by a large proportion of our teachers, from which they derive many advantages. The Teachers' Institutes which have been largely attended, have afforded parents, teachers, students and school officials an opportunity to discuss the various questions relating to the work of the schools, and have been of inestimable value.

Under the provisions of the will of the late Cecil Rhodes, two students from this State may have the advantage of scholarships at Oxford University, England, and receive $1,500 each year during a residence there of three years.

A small appropriation may be necessary to enable the State to take advantage of the opportunity thus offered.

The general law providing for aid to academies, enacted by the legislature of 1901, appears to have fulfilled the expectations of its advocates, and has apparently proved an effective remedy for the evils previously existing, while at the same time giving aid to many worthy and deserving institutions which are doing splendid work in the various towns in which they are situated.

University of Maine. During the past year there has been a large increase in the number of students attending the State University. The condition of this institution seems entirely satisfactory from every point of view.

One hundred and sixty new students entered the University in the fall of 1902, every county in the State being now represented. There are twenty-three students from outside the State, nineteen being from Massachusetts, two from New Hampshire, one from New Jersey and one from Rhode Island. Of the freshman class, one hundred and one students entered upon technical courses, including Agriculture. The number of students in the institution pursuing technical studies is two hundred and sixty-seven. Twenty-nine new students entered the School of Law, making sixty in attendance in this department.

A large percentage of the students are seeking to obtain an education by their own efforts, and are wholly or partially self-supporting.

The building containing the drill-hall, chapel, gymnasium and administrative offices, which was built by the subscriptions of the alumni, has been completed and entirely paid for. It is a most excellent and serviceable building, and the work of the University would have been seriously crippled had it not been constructed.

It has been the policy of the institution to provide instruction in every line of practical work. Courses in Mining and Marine Engineering have been added, and special work in Forestry has been begun.

The trustees recommend the erection of a building which will serve as a mechanical laboratory, shops for iron and wood working, and a power plant. You will be asked for an appropriation for this purpose, and I am sure the needs of the University, which is doing excellent work in the education of our youth, will receive your most careful consideration.

Elections. Our present ballot law is manifestly defective in some important details. It should be simplified and made so clear and plain in all of its provisions that every citizen can understand it. It frequently happens that election officers, through a misunderstanding of the law, fail to count ballots which should be included in their returns. In every State election, hundreds of citizens lose their votes by reason of their failure to mark their ballots in accordance with the strict requirements of the law. This is not as it should be. No man should lose his ballot by reason of a mere technicality, when his intent is so clearly expressed as to be evident to all.

The right of suffrage, which is the highest privilege of citizenship, is the very foundation of our form of government. Justice demands that the law should be so modified that every man may exercise his franchise according to his own views and wishes, without endangering his ballot.

I commend this matter to your careful consideration and trust you will enact such changes in the law as will render it more easily understood, while preserving every essential feature of its present provisions.

Every safeguard of the general election should be placed about the caucus. Our present system is liable to grave abuse, and I earnestly recommend and urge the enactment of a direct primary law which will more completely preserve the purity of the ballot, and under severe penalties prevent the members of one party from participating in the caucuses of another. The necessity for some action is so apparent as to make comment on my part unnecessary. There have been so many instances of irregular practices in the primaries that some direct and controlling legislation is imperatively demanded. *Primary Elections.*

An awakened public sentiment among the people of Maine demands a more complete and vigorous enforcement of the prohibitory law. In nearly all our country towns the law is respected and obeyed. It is in the cities and larger villages that it has been most frequently and persistently violated. This condition of things is apparently due to the fact that in the larger places there has been wanting an active and healthy sentiment in support of the law, and indifference and opposition have made its enforcement more difficult. *The Prohibitory Law.*

Disrespect of one law breeds disrespect of all law, and there is a growing appreciation of the far-reaching demoralization that comes from the failure to honestly and fearlessly administer every law upon our statute books.

Officers whose duty it is to see that the law is observed have no option in the matter, if they respect their official obligation and are true to their official oath; but it is most important that every law should be sustained by an unquestioned public sentiment, for officials elected by popular suffrage seldom rise to higher conceptions of public duty than is represented by the prevailing sentiment of their constituents.

Good citizens may differ among themselves as to the best method of contending with the liquor evil, but they cannot afford to be otherwise than a unit in demanding the faithful, fearless, and impartial enforcement of every existing law, so long as it continues to be the law.

Among some of the most earnest and sincere friends of temperance in the State, there is a strong feeling that the prohibitory amendment should again be submitted to the people, that they may have an opportunity to declare themselves upon the question. They believe that such an expression of the popular will would give renewed strength to the law, and lead to more complete and thorough enforcement in those portions of the State where officials have failed to do their duty.

If you are satisfied that the people desire to express themselves upon this matter, it will be your duty to give them an opportunity to definitely pass upon the whole question at the polls.

Agriculture. The Commissioner of Agriculture reports that our agricultural interests are in a flourishing condition, and that there is a strong feeling of encouragement among the farmers of the State.

The Experiment Station and the State University are aiding much by teaching the science of agriculture. They are constantly bringing to light new truths and new methods, which have a marked effect in stimulating every line of farm work. The more general use of modern farm machinery and better scientific knowledge have served to stimulate production without a corresponding increase in cost. Crops, with the single exception of corn, have been abundant. Prices have been high, and farmers have found a ready market for their products.

The Commissioner further says that the condition of our farmers as a whole is constantly improving. Their indebtedness has largely been decreased, and many mortgages have been canceled. Farms are better equipped than ever before, and thrift and prosperity are everywhere noticeable. The usual number of Farmers' Institutes have been held, and have been well attended. Their work is of great educational value and is fully appreciated. The Commissioner has endeavored to secure the most practical and successful agriculturists in the country as instructors, and the corps of teachers at the University of Maine have aided greatly in promoting the success of these meetings.

Crop bulletins have been issued quarterly during the year. They are sent to between seven and eight thousand farmers of the State, going largely to those who have personally expressed a desire to receive them.

The Maine Dairymen's Association, which includes in its membership many of the most progressive dairymen in the State, advocates the employment of an instructor, whose duty it shall be to urge better methods in the production and handling of milk and cream, the work to be under the direction and control of the Commissioner of Agriculture.

Much can be done for the advancement of our dairy interests, if proper effort is made along the right lines and the value of these products can be largely increased.

A man thoroughly equipped for the work and competent to give instruction could greatly stimulate the growth of this industry by the introduction of the best methods.

It is unnecessary for me to urge the importance of encouraging in every possible way the interests of Agriculture, upon which so many of our people depend for employment and support. The prosperity of the farmer means the prosperity of the whole State, and his interests are the most important that are entrusted to our care.

Maine Cattle Commission. The Cattle Commissioners have condemned and destroyed more cattle and horses during the past two years than ever before in the same period. Owners of cattle are coming better to understand the dangers of tuberculosis, and the commissioners are called upon to make a larger number of investigations. As a result, many more cases are being discovered, and better protection is being afforded from the danger of infection.

The appropriation made by the last legislature has proved inadequate, and you will be asked to grant a still larger sum. It is unnecessary for me to point out the importance of continuing this work. I know you will willingly provide whatever amount may be needed to enable the Commissioners to pay promptly for all cattle and horses which they may find it necessary to destroy.

The National Guard. The total number of citizens of this State, between the ages of eighteen and forty-five, able to perform military duty, according to the last returns, is 104,268. Under the present law, the active militia is designated "The National Guard of the State of Maine." As now constituted, it consists of two Regiments of Infantry of twelve Companies each; a Naval Reserve; a Signal Corps; and an Ambulance Corps: a total of 1,318 men.

There has been great improvement in the work of these troops as a result of the active interest in the service which has been shown by both officers and men. The Spanish War has given us many veteran officers, whose services are of great value, and whose work has done much to improve the morale and increase the efficiency of the Guard. The annual encampment has been productive of good results, and both Regiments have made noticeable and praiseworthy advancement.

The Signal Corps and Ambulance Corps are worthy of special mention for the proficiency of their drill and the interest which their members manifest in the discharge of their duties.

The Naval Reserve, consisting of three officers and forty-six men, is most fortunate in being commanded by officers who have made themselves thoroughly familiar with their duties. The command would not suffer by comparison with any similar organization in the country. The practical experience which the men have gained as a result of their cruise each summer, has familiarized them with the service performed at sea, both officers and men being assigned to regular duty and treated in every way as if they were members of the United States Navy.

Insurance Department.
There was no supervision of Insurance in Maine prior to 1868, at which time the office of Bank and Insurance Examiner was created. In 1870 the office of Insurance Commissioner was established and a separate department was organized. Of sixty-eight foreign Fire and Marine Insurance Companies then doing business in the State, but twenty remained at the close of 1901. Of the forty-four old-line Life Insurance Companies, then under the supervision of the Department, only seventeen were licensed in 1901.

There is not a single Stock Fire Insurance Company organized under the laws of Maine, which is doing business in the State at the present time, our fire underwriting being largely done by foreign corporations. Nineteen companies, with capital aggregating $4,500,000, withdrew from the State in 1901, and it is now impossible to secure adequate insurance in licensed companies. It is unwise to impose upon these corporations unnecessary or burdensome restrictions, which must either force them to withdraw from the State, or charge increased premiums for insurance.

There has been a much smaller number of incendiary fires since the law was enacted giving the Commissioner authority to make investigations. During the past two years several persons have been convicted of incendiarism, and are now confined in the State Prison.

In 1901 the property loss by fire in this State was $2,170,024. The insurance loss on the same was $1,356,723, leaving a direct loss to property owners of more than $800,000 during a single year.

There has been a very large increase in the amount of business done in this State by the Life Insurance Companies during the last ten years. On December 31st, 1901, risks to the amount of $76,462,857 were in force, as against $31,726,436 on December 31st, 1891. There has also been a large increase in the membership of the fraternal beneficiary organizations, whose members are to be found in nearly every town in the State. Over no class of Insurance Corporations does the law give the Department so little control, and there are none whose operations should be more carefully guarded and protected.

The fees of this Department in 1870 amounted to $3,777, no tax being imposed at that time. In 1902 the fees collected by the Insurance Commissioner amounted to $16,694.50, the largest in the history of the Department; and the tax paid by the Companies was $79,127.78, making a total revenue from this source of $95,822.28.

The Forestry Commissioner, after a most careful and thorough investigation, reports that there is standing in Maine to-day over 21,000,000,000 feet of spruce timber, not less than 9 inches in diameter, at the height of 4 feet. The annual growth varies from 2 to 4 per cent., according to the character of the soil and other conditions, and the Commissioner believes it is safe to assume that when cut judiciously, it will make an average yearly growth of 3 per cent., or 630,000,000 feet. About 662,000,000 feet of spruce was cut in the State during the season of 1901-2; which is somewhat in excess of the average amount for the past few years. **Forestry.**

It is evident that the growth of our spruce forests is nearly keeping pace with the amount annually consumed. They are not likely to be exterminated by our industries, but their greatest danger is from fire.

It is estimated that there is also about 2,000,000,000 feet of spruce in the Androscoggin valley, in New Hampshire, for which the natural outlet is the pulp and saw mills of Maine. The new Fish River Railroad will turn a large part of the forest products of that section to Maine manufacturers, which formerly went down the St. John River to New Brunswick.

There is also a large growth of valuable hard woods of various kinds which will ultimately be a source of great wealth to the State and give employment to a large number of people.

The Forestry Commissioner, who has conducted his investigations with great care, has been aided in his work by the United States Department of Forestry, which during the past year sent an expert, accompanied by ten experienced foresters, to this State to study our forests. Nearly three months was spent in the work and the information thus obtained will be of great value.

There are about 80,000 acres of school or public lands under the care of the State Land Agent. These lands are located in eighty different plantations, situated in eleven counties. About $13,000 has been received during the past year from the timber on these lands, of which nearly $1,000 was collected in trespass cases. Frequent complaints of trespass upon public lands are received, and on account of the tracts being so widely scattered, much time and labor is required in making investigation and properly protecting the State's interest.

The Land Agent also has the care of Indian Township, so called, in Washington County. This town contains 22,400 acres. It is well located and is covered with young trees of different varieties which are making rapid growth. The soil is fertile and it is a valuable tract of land.

State Roads. One hundred and five towns have taken advantage of the act passed by the last legislature, which provided for the improvement of certain highways designated thereby as State Roads. I am convinced that these expenditures have on the whole been wisely and judiciously made, and I believe that the system thus established offers a practical and progressive plan of road improvement, free from many of the objections which have been urged against other methods.

This appropriation should be continued, and should be large enough so that every town which may desire to enjoy its benefits may be able to take advantage of its provisions. The amount which a town may receive should also be increased.

The St. Louis Exposition to Commemorate the Louisiana Purchase. The Legislature at its last session authorized the appointment of a Commission to have charge of the interests of the State at the St. Louis Exposition to Commemorate the Louisiana Purchase. This Exposition, which will be held at St. Louis in 1904, will be International in its character and bring together exhibits of every kind from all parts of the world. It is desirable that the resources of the State be creditably represented and particularly that we should take advantage of this opportunity to make more widely known the attractions which Maine presents to the summer visitor and sportsman.

A reasonable appropriation should be made for this purpose.

Inland Fisheries and Game. In twenty-five States of the Union, and throughout the Dominion of Canada, licenses must be secured before non-residents may hunt certain game, or hunt at all. In some sections of the United States the privilege of hunting is not extended to non-residents. The Commissioners of Inland Fisheries and Game in their annual report, which you will shortly receive, recommend the enactment of a license law to apply to non-resident hunters of large game. This would afford sufficient revenue to provide an efficient warden service and at the same time protect our game from being destroyed by a class of hunters who come to Maine in increasing numbers each year, leaving little if any money among our people, and apparently relying upon the sale of the game which they may secure to defray part or all of the expense of their vacations. Such visitors are not desirable. They are not a source of any revenue to our people, and I can personally see no reason why the State of Maine should maintain a game preserve for them free of cost. The property of all our people bears its part of the expense of maintaining this department, yet only a portion of our citizens participate directly in its benefits. Why, then, should not citizens of other States who come here to share these privileges bear some part of the cost of their maintenance?

As time goes on, a much larger number of people will come to Maine each year to spend their vacations and to hunt and fish. No other State in the Union presents so many attractions as ours, and we should see to it that everything possible is done to bring the desirable summer resident within our borders. Our game should be fully protected, and above all our lakes and streams should, wherever practicable, be stocked with the product of our fish hatcheries.

I know that you fully appreciate the great importance of the fish and game interests to the people of the State, and will take such action as is necessary to maintain our present advantageous position in these matters.

State Board of Health. It is the duty of the State and the municipality to protect the lives and health of its citizens. The State Board of Health, in co-operation with the local boards, constitutes a public health organization which is doing work of the greatest value and importance. We have come to rely upon its efforts to guard us from the danger of epidemics and I believe that our confidence in the efficiency of this department is fully warranted.

During the past two years, small-pox has been widely prevalent throughout the country, but our own State, although surrounded by the danger of infection, has suffered little, and the outbreaks of this disease have as a rule been promptly suppressed.

There has been a marked diminution of the death-rate from tuberculosis, as is shown by the reports of the Department of Vital Statistics. The decrease of the number of deaths from this cause in the last decade has been more than twenty-five per cent.

Sea and Shore Fisheries. The Sea and Shore Fisheries furnish business and employment to thousands of our citizens. We have no interest which requires more careful attention and protection, and none is more surely and certainly benefited by a wise and liberal policy on the part of the State. In no other employment or industry is it so easy for a poor man to earn an honest living, and none so quickly yields a reward to reasonable effort and gives support and an independent existence to so many citizens who might otherwise be dependent.

The capital required by the average fisherman who carries on business for himself is small, while his opportunity to live at home, supporting himself by his individual exertions, is only limited by the supply of the products of the sea, the abundance of which depends largely upon the vigilance of conscientious and competent officials in the protection of our fisheries from avoidable disaster and wilful destruction.

The Commissioner in charge of this Department fully appreciates the great importance of the interests entrusted to his care and can be relied upon to protect and foster them.

The so-called Hay-Bond treaty now under consideration in the Senate of the United States gives free entry into this country of the products of the Newfoundland fisheries. Its ratification would result in serious injury to our fishing interests by opening to the markets of this country the products of Newfoundland in competition with our own.

The welfare of the coast towns of Maine requires us to do everything in our power to prevent its acceptance.

Pensions.

Two thousand, two hundred and ninety-eight persons in 358 towns, cities and plantations receive State pensions. One thousand, two hundred and eighty-three are paid $2.00 per month, and only 174 receive over $4.00 per month. One thousand, two hundred and sixty-seven of these pensioners are invalids, and 926 are widows.

Though the amount paid to each is small, many a home is relieved from want and suffering thereby, and the recipients are thus enabled to maintain themselves without other public aid. This is but a slight recognition of our obligation to those valiant men who nobly fought for their country in its time of peril. I know it is unnecessary for me to urge the continuance of the appropriation required for their relief.

Railroads.

The total mileage of Steam Railroads in the State is 2,000.51, a gain of 81.53 miles during the past year. This gain is due to the construction of the Fish River Railroad from Ashland to Fort Kent, 52.50 miles; an extension of the Bangor & Aroostook Railroad from Van Buren two miles up the St. John River; an extension of the Rumford Falls & Rangeley Lakes Railroad north from Bemis, 12.66 miles; an extension of the Wiscasset,

Waterville & Farmington Railroad from Weeks Mills to Winslow, 14 miles; the construction of a branch of the York Harbor & Beach Railroad in Kittery, .34 of a mile, and a change in remeasurement of .03 of a mile.

There are 342.68 miles of Street Railways in the State, all but three miles being operated by electricity, a gain of 59.67 miles during the past year.

During the year ending June 30, 1902, the gross earnings of the Steam Railroads of Maine were $11,763,068.86, a gain over the previous year of $833,066.00, and an increase in the last ten years of $4,841,859.62. It will thus be seen that the receipts of our Steam Railroads have nearly doubled since 1892.

The number of tons of freight carried in 1902 was 8,868,303, a gain over the year 1892 of 5,173,369 tons, or about 150 per cent.

The gross earnings of the Street Railways for the year ending June 30, 1902, were $1,573,993.90. Eight thousand, four hundred and seventy-nine persons were employed upon both Steam and Street Railroads, who received during the year, wages amounting to $4,458,383.20.

Pemaquid Commission. The Commissioners in charge of Fort William Henry at Pemaquid will ask for an appropriation sufficient to properly preserve and care for the fort, as well as for the many valuable memorials which have been found there. Their report, which will soon be before you, is full of interest, and gives some account of the work which has already been done in this direction by citizens of Bristol and others. A small amount only would be required to preserve and to some degree restore this ancient fortification.

Public Buildings. Under the management and direction of our efficient Superintendent of Public Buildings, many needed improvements have been made in the State capitol. These changes, which have given our State House a much more creditable appearance, have been made at comparatively small cost and without the necessity of any large or unusual appropriations.

Bureau of Industrial and Labor Statistics. There is a growing interest in the reports of the Bureau of Industrial and Labor Statistics as the value of the work done by this Department becomes better known and understood. This is shown in a constantly increasing demand for these reports, and by the large number of inquiries received regarding the various industries and resources of the State, which has added materially to the work of this department.

State Library. The State Library has been greatly extended and developed during the past two years. The section of its work which is evidently of the greatest interest to the public is that connected with the traveling libraries. There are now eighty of these libraries in active use, or four thousand volumes, and the records returned to the State Librarian show that these books annually afford entertainment and instruction to over forty thousand readers. They are increasing in use in the small towns and neighborhoods, and even in the lumber camps. They are sought after by high schools, and prove very helpful to study clubs and granges. There are over one thousand institutions and organizations of various kinds in Maine, representing over fifty thousand readers, which have a right to demand the use of these libraries, or of any single volume that can safely be loaned from the State Library.

There can be little doubt that the number of these libraries must be doubled within the next few years, to meet the demand that now exists for them, unless the Legislature shall consider it wise and just to place some limitation upon the use of the State Library in educating the people, and shall restrict within more narrow limits the books that may be loaned.

Not only has this section of the library work been largely increased, but the exchange of public documents and reports has nearly doubled within the last three years, and it will be necessary to set apart for its use an increased number of each of these publications, if this system of exchange and distribution is to be maintained.

The Library has grown very rapidly through the acquisition of books and other works relating to historical studies, and in its legal section. During the past two years ten thousand books and pamphlets have been added. It now contains over 18,000 law reports, digests, and statutes, embracing decisions of every court in the United States, Canada, England, Ireland, and Scotland. There is not another library east of Boston so fully and completely equipped as this for the use of the student, the lawyer or the man of affairs. The librarian reports that every available inch of space where a book can be placed is now occupied; that every storeroom outside the library proper is crowded, and that there is urgent need of additional room in which to put the rapidly accumulating volumes, as well as to provide space for the accommodation of the people, for with all these valuable collections, there is not a single room where books may be consulted without inconvenience and interruption.

Maine Insane Hospital. There were six hundred and thirty-one patients in the Maine Insane Hospital, November 30th, 1902, three hundred and sixty-three of whom were men and two hundred and sixty-eight were women. This is an increase of thirty-one over the preceding year. There has been a slight increase in the death-rate due to the admission of an unusually large number of aged people, but the institution has been entirely free from infectious or contagious diseases of any kind.

The Asylum has been crowded in the woman's department, on account of the reconstruction of one entire wing. This work, which is now completed, is fireproof and contains many conveniences which will add greatly to the comfort of its occupants.

The work of reconstruction should be continued, and all the older portion of the Asylum should be thoroughly modernized. The Superintendent states that the remaining wings, properly arranged will provide for sixty-four additional patients and furnish accommodations much superior to those now existing. I recommend an appropriation for this purpose. This portion of the Hospital is greatly in need of repairs and in a condition not creditable to the State. A reasonable expenditure will not only put the institution in thoroughly first-class condition, but afford ample accommodations for such additional patients as may be admitted to the Asylum for some time to come.

The per capita cost of the board of the patients in this Institution during the past year has been $4.77¾ per week. This covers every expenditure in the management of the Institution.

Eastern Maine Insane Hospital.

The Eastern Maine Insane Hospital was opened July 3d, 1901, with one hundred and forty-seven patients who were transferred from the Asylum at Augusta. The number had increased to two hundred and nine on November 30th, 1902, of whom one hundred and fifteen were men and ninety-four were women. During the twelve months previous to this date, one hundred and eleven patients were admitted. Sixty-eight were discharged, thirty-seven having recovered and twenty-six being greatly improved.

Much has been done under the direction of the management to make the surroundings of this Hospital more attractive. Trees and shrubs have been planted, necessary roadways have been constructed, and the grounds have been graded and improved, so far as funds available would permit. Still more, however, must be accomplished to complete this work, and a considerable appropriation will be necessary to meet the requirements of the Institution in its various departments and to provide furnishings and equipment needed to maintain the Hospital at a proper standard.

A sufficient sum should also be provided to meet the deficiency in running expenses.

State Prison.

There are one hundred and eighty-three inmates of the State Prison, thirty-six of whom are under life sentence. Forty-seven have been admitted during the past year; fifty-two have been discharged, and four have died. On account of the advance in price of nearly all food products, there has been a considerable increase in the cost of maintaining the subsistence department, but on the whole the prison has made a fair showing and will not require so large an appropriation as two years ago.

Only four of these convicts are women, but I am convinced that this institution should have a matron, whose duty it shall be to take immediate charge of female prisoners. The State is not doing its whole duty in this respect, and I trust you will take some action to place this department of the prison on a right and proper basis.

Maine School for the Deaf.

During the past two years the attendance at the Maine School for the Deaf has largely increased, and the school has made most commendable progress and advancement in every way.

Ninety-two pupils are now in attendance, nearly every county in the State being represented. Nine teachers give instruction, and the course includes all the regular English branches. Industrial training is also given, the girls being taught sewing, cooking and the various duties of the household, while the boys are instructed in wood-working, glazing, painting, printing and cobbling.

This institution is well managed, and its needs should receive your careful consideration.

Bath Military and Naval Orphan Asylum.

There are sixty-eight children in the Bath Military and Naval Orphan Asylum, of whom thirty-seven are boys and thirty-one are girls. They are from four to fifteen years of age and all attend the public schools of the city.

This institution is doing good work, and its management is worthy of the highest commendation.

State Reform School.

A proper classification of the one hundred and forty-five boys in the State Reform School requires the building of two additional cottages modeled upon the same general plan as those already existing. Eighty-five of these boys live in the original building, which was erected about fifty years ago. This structure should be thoroughly remodeled to meet the present requirements of the institution. It is unfortunate that so many of these poor children should thus be congregated together, as it is practically impossible to separate those of vicious tendencies and criminal instincts, from those who have committed only trifling offences and who are simply the victims of poverty and misfortune.

It is neither right nor just that this institution should be termed a Reform School and that its inmates, who are only children, should be stigmatized as convicts. Nor should the time they spend here be termed imprisonment. The school should bear some more appropriate name. I trust that the needs of this school will receive your most careful consideration, and that you will grant a sufficient appropriation to meet its reasonable requirements.

There are one hundred and forty-eight girls under the care of **Maine Industrial School for Girls.** the Maine Industrial School for Girls. Of these sixty-nine are at the school, and the remainder have been placed in homes in different parts of the State. During the past year twenty-one girls have been admitted, fifteen have come of age, five have been permitted to marry, and ten have been discharged.

The trustees of the school ask that some provision be made for those who are feeble-minded, seven in all, our annual appropriation for the care of such children in the Massachusetts Home for the Feeble-Minded being insufficient for that purpose.

I am sure that an institution so worthy of public support will receive the most careful consideration at your hands, and that you will grant such appropriations as may be reasonably necessary for its support and maintenance.

I have endeavored briefly to present to you a comprehensive **Conclusion.** review of State affairs. The reports of the various departments and of the officers of the different State Institutions will give you in detail an account of their work. The sums set apart for their support have been ample for their requirements, as a rule, and I trust no new appropriation will be made unless you are fully satisfied, after the most thorough examination and careful consideration, that the best interests of the State require it. Not a dollar should be wasted or unnecessarily expended, but the same careful, prudent management, the same judicious economy which characterizes the administration of every successful private enterprise should be exercised in conducting the business of the State.

There should be no shadow of doubt as to the exact intent and meaning of every measure proposed for enactment. Every provision of the law should be absolutely plain and clear. The utmost care should also be exercised in scrutinizing the constitutionality of all contemplated legislation. It is always a source of trouble when a statute is found to be inconsistent with the organic law after the people have begun to act under it, and leads them to distrust and to question all new legislation.

As the trusted servants of the people, for a brief time having their interests in charge, let us see to it that they have no just cause to distrust our motives, or our desire to discharge our duties in a manner that will promote their welfare and merit their approbation.

The approval of our own judgment and conscience, the knowledge that our management of public matters receives the commendation of unprejudiced, fair-minded men, is the highest and best reward we can hope to receive for the time we devote to the public service. Resolutely and fearlessly let us determine to do our whole duty, unmoved by any consideration save a fixed purpose to labor devotedly for the upbuilding of every interest of our beloved State and for the permanent welfare of all its people.

COMMUNICATIONS.

STATE OF MAINE.
EXECUTIVE DEPARTMENT,
AUGUSTA, March 27, 1903.

To the Honorable House of Representatives:

I have examined the Resolve in favor of the town of Fort Kent, for the sum of $1,500. I return the same herewith without my approval and desire to submit for your consideration some facts and figures in relation to State finances.

The estimated income of the State for 1903 is about $2,100,000, and for 1904, approximately $2,000,000, a total of $4,100,000. Appropriations already made and pending aggregate over $4,650,000, an excess above probable income of $550,000, and an increase over the amount appropriated by the Seventieth Legislature for the years 1901 and 1902, of over $800,000.

The amount of cash in the treasury, available for the payment of current obligations, is less than $267,000, and nearly all will be required to meet necessary expenditures in excess of current revenues within the next three months. Of the above amount about $44,000 is due the present Legislature on pay roll.

It is evident that unless appropriations now under consideration are materially reduced, the State treasurer will be compelled to make a temporary loan, and since the constitution does not permit the creation of a State debt in excess of $300,000, except for war purposes, it seems to me most unwise to make any appropriations not absolutely required, which will result in the creation of a floating debt.

We should conduct the business of the State as we would our own affairs. The people demand and expect from us the same careful, prudent management which characterizes the administration of every successful private business, and that the promise of economy in public expenditures will be fulfilled.

Those who have been entrusted with the management of State matters will be held strictly responsible for any excessive or unwise appropriations. We can offer no excuse which will be considered a sufficient reason for a failure to do our whole duty in the fulfillment of the pledges which we have made, but the blame will rest upon us if we are faithless to our trust.

For the reasons here given, I submit this matter for your further consideration.

JOHN F. HILL.

STATE OF MAINE.

Executive Department,
Augusta, March 28, 1903.

To the President of the Senate and Speaker of the House of Representatives:

I transmit herewith a list of the acts and resolves passed during the present session of the Legislature and approved by me, numbering 663 acts and 148 resolves.

I have no further communication to make.

JOHN F. HILL.

Civil Government of the State of Maine

For the Political Years of 1903 and 1904.

GOVERNOR:
JOHN FREMONT HILL,
Augusta.

COUNCILORS.
CHARLES H. PRESCOTT, BIDDEFORD, *Chairman.*
CHARLES SUMNER COOK, PORTLAND.
SYLVESTER J. WALTON, SKOWHEGAN.
WILLIAM T. HAINES, WATERVILLE.
EDWARD E. CHASE, BLUEHILL.
NATHANIEL M. JONES, BANGOR.
GEORGE R. MURCHIE, CALAIS.

BYRON BOYD, AUGUSTA, *Secretary of State.*
A. I. BROWN, BELFAST, *Deputy Secretary of State.*
ORAMANDAL SMITH, LITCHFIELD, *Treasurer of State.*
AUGUSTUS B. FARNHAM, BANGOR, *Adjutant General.*
GEORGE M. SEIDERS, PORTLAND, *Attorney General.*
E. E. RING, ORONO, *Land Agent.*
W. W. STETSON, AUBURN, *State Superintendent of Schools.*
LEONARD D. CARVER, AUGUSTA, *State Librarian.*
STEPHEN W. CARR, BOWDOINHAM, *Insurance Commissioner.*
F. E. TIMBERLAKE, PHILLIPS, *Bank Examiner.*
A. W. GILMAN, FOXCROFT, *Commissioner of Agriculture.*
S. W. MATTHEWS, CARIBOU, *Labor Commissioner.*
NATHANIEL S. PURINTON, WEST BOWDOIN, *Private Secretary to Governor.*

SENATE.

HARRY R. VIRGIN, President.

1—York	George E. Morrison	Saco.
	Freeman E. Rankin	Wells.
	Oliver C. Titcomb	Acton.
2—Cumberland	Harry R. Virgin	Portland.
	Thurston S. Burns	Westbrook.
	Winburn M. Staples	Bridgton.
	Charles H. Randall	Portland.
3—Oxford	John M. Philbrook	Bethel.
4—Androscoggin	Geo. C. Wing	Auburn.
	Walter E. Plummer	Lisbon.
5—Franklin	George M. Currier	Farmington.
6—Sagadahoc	John S. Hyde	Bath.
7—Kennebec	Rutillus Alden	Winthrop.
	C. C. Libby	Pittston.
	Joseph H. Manley	Augusta.
8—Somerset	Edmund C. Bryant	Pittsfield.
	Forrest Goodwin	Skowhegan.
9—Piscataquis	Frank E. Guernsey	Dover.
10—Penobscot	Isaiah K. Stetson	Bangor.
	Halbert P. Gardner	Patten.
	Amos W. Knowlton	Newburg.
11—Lincoln	Luther Maddocks	Boothbay Harbor.
12—Knox	L. M. Staples (Dem.)	Washington.
13—Waldo	Lucius C. Morse	Liberty.
14—Hancock	Albert R. Buck	Orland.
	Edward S. Clark	Eden.
15—Washington	Emerson K. Wilson	Cherryfield.
	Bion M. Pike	Lubec.
16—Aroostook	Albert A. Burleigh	Houlton.
	J. W. Dudley	Castle Hill.
	Howard Pierce	Fort Kent.

Harry R. Virgin, President............Portland.
Kendall M. Dunbar, Secretary........Damariscotta.
Frank G. Farrington, Assistant Secretary..........................Augusta.
Charles H. Lovejoy, Messenger........Augusta, R. F. D. 4.
James F. Ashford, Assistant Messenger...Windsorville.
W. G. Fuller, Folder..................Unity.
John J. Dearborn, Assistant Folder.....Newburgh Village.
Thomas A. Anderson, Postmaster and Mail Carrier........................Hartland.
Stephen D. Lord, Doorkeeper..........East Lebanon.
Scott C. W. Simpson, Page............Portland.
Albert W. Buck, Page.................Orland.
Edward K. Milliken, Reporter.........Standish.

HOUSE OF REPRESENTATIVES.

OSCAR F. FELLOWS, Speaker.

ANDROSCOGGIN COUNTY.

Winfield S. Hinckley.....................Lisbon.
Flavius D. Shackford....................Poland.
Alphonso D. Cole........................East Livermore.
Rackley D. Leavitt......................Turner.
J. M. Libby.............................Mechanic Falls.
Henry H. Coburn.........................Greene.
Henry W. Oakes..........................Auburn.
Ansel Briggs............................Auburn.
Michael A. Coyne (Dem.).................Lewiston.
Frank A. Morey (Dem.)...................Lewiston.
Alonzo M. Garcelon (Dem.)...............Lewiston.
George B. Haskell.......................Lewiston.
Jacob R. Little.........................Lewiston.
Stephen J Kelley........................Lewiston.
Patrick F. Tremblay.....................Lewiston.

AROOSTOOK COUNTY.

George W. Irving........................Caribou.
Joseph S. Hall..........................Fort Fairfield.
John Sweeney............................Fort Kent.
S. S. Thornton..........................Ashland.
George H. Smith.........................Presque Isle.
Alden E. Howes..........................Washburn.
W. H. Dilling...........................Easton.
John W. Davidson........................Hammond Pl.
Beecher Putnam..........................Houlton.
Theodule Albert.........................Madawaska.
Wendell C. Boyd.........................Linneus.
Harrison G. White.......................Dyer Brook.
Henry A. Gagnon (Dem.)..................Van Buren.

CUMBERLAND COUNTY.

George H. Allan...........................Portland.
Isaiah Daniels.............................Portland.
Morrill N. Drew...........................Portland.
Theodore A. Josselyn.....................Portland.
Robert B. Low.............................Portland.
Edward C. Swett...........................Portland.
Oakley C. Curtis (Dem.)..................Portland.
Albert A. Cordwell.......................Westbrook.
Almon N. Waterhouse (Dem.)...............Westbrook.
Barrett Potter............................Brunswick.
Lemuel H. Stover (Dem.)..................Brunswick.
J. Calvin Knapp..........................South Portland.
James Carroll Mead........................Bridgton.
Charles S. Purinton........................Gorham.
Charles S. Thomas (Dem.).................Harpswell.
Isaac E. Hayes............................North Yarmouth.
Charles H. Nelson, (Dem.)................New Gloucester.
R. E. Randall.............................Freeport.
H. Herbert Sturgis........................Standish.
Fred S. Hawkes............................Windham.
Gideon T. Cook............................Casco.
Frank B. Blanchard (Dem.)................Falmouth.

FRANKLIN COUNTY.

H. Herbert Rice...........................Farmington.
Joseph W. Perkins.........................Wilton.
Harry A. Furbish..........................Rangeley.
Franklin W. Patterson....................Industry.

HANCOCK COUNTY.

F. Carroll Burrill........................Ellsworth.
Alton E. Farnsworth......................Tremont.
Orlando W. Foss...........................Hancock.
Oscar F. Fellows..........................Bucksport.
George H. Tapley..........................Brooksville.
Sherman R. Downing.......................Sorrento.
Charles C. Morrison......................Eden.
Sumner P. Mills...........................Stonington.

KENNEBEC COUNTY.

Edwin C. Dudley..........................Augusta.
William H. Gannett......................Augusta.
Cyrus W. Davis (Dem.)................Waterville.
Fred Pooler (Dem.)....................Waterville.
Edgar E. Norton........................Gardiner.
W. T. Reynolds.........................Winslow.
W. J. Thompson........................China.
Bert E. Lamb...........................Randolph.
Charles H. Watson.....................Chelsea.
Joseph F. Bodwell.....................Hallowell.
Reuben L. Snowe.......................West Gardiner.
Morrison Libby.........................Oakland.
Fred E. Blake..........................Sidney.

KNOX COUNTY.

Arthur S. Littlefield....................Rockland.
Sereno T. Kimball......................Rockland.
E. Frank Knowlton (Dem.).............Camden.
Joseph H. Carleton (Dem.)............Rockport.
Moses R. Spear (Dem.)................Warren.
E. A. McNamara (Dem.)...............Thomaston.
Alden W. Butler (Dem.)...............South Thomaston.

LINCOLN COUNTY.

John W. Benner (Dem.)................Waldoboro.
Walter B. Clarke.......................Nobleboro.
Richard H. T. Taylor (Dem.)..........Wiscasset.
Herman E. Greenleaf...................Westport.

OXFORD COUNTY.

Waldo Pettengill.......................Rumford.
George J. Parrott......................Oxford.
Hiram R. Hubbard......................Paris.
Albert R. Hill..........................Brownfield.
Elliott W. Howe........................Canton.
Silas F. Peaslee.......................Upton.
Bertrand G. McIntire (Dem.)..........Waterford.

PENOBSCOT COUNTY.

George F. Cameron...................Bangor.
Lewis A. Barker....................Bangor.
Harry F. Ross......................Bangor.
D. Allston Sargent.................Brewer.
Leslie A. Buzzell..................Old Town.
Alonzo R. Page.....................Drew Plantation.
Artemus Weatherbee.................Lincoln.
John H. McGregor...................Enfield.
Nathan A. Nickerson................Orrington.
William E. Bailey..................Bradford.
Albion Oakes.......................Milford.
John Ruggles.......................Carmel.
Charles L. Jones...................Corinna.
Louis I. Bussey....................Dixmont.
Elmer A. Brewster..................Dexter.
George W. Stearns..................Millinocket.
George E. Thompson (Dem.)..........Orono.

PISCATAQUIS COUNTY.

William S. McKusick................Parkman.
D. H. Buxton.......................Abbot.
Robert J. Williams.................Williamsburg.
William Allen......................Wellington.

SAGADAHOC COUNTY.

Albert H. Shaw.....................Bath.
Harold M. Sewall...................Bath.
Eugene Thomas......................Topsham.
Warren C. Todd.....................Georgetown.

SOMERSET COUNTY.

A. Ledyard Smith, Jr...............Madison.
John W. Manson.....................Pittsfield.
John Knowlton......................New Portland.
C. H. Smith........................Hartland.
Mark Savage........................Bingham.
Edward P. Page.....................Skowhegan.
George G. Weeks....................Fairfield.

WALDO COUNTY.

Clarence O. Poor..........................Belfast.
Charles R. Hill..........................Winterport.
Mark T. Dodge..........................Troy.
Elmer D. Clark..........................Prospect.
Elisha Merriam..........................Morrill.

WASHINGTON COUNTY.

Lincoln H. Newcomb.....................Eastport.
George H. Eaton..........................Calais.
Jacob C. Pike............................Lubec.
Frederick W. Thurlow (Dem.)............Cutler.
Edward W. Shackford....................Harrington.
Fred I. Campbell........................Cherryfield.
Alexander D. McFaul....................Machias.
Lyman K. Gardner.......................Dennysville.
Varney A. Putnam........................Danforth.
Albert S. Farnsworth (Dem.)............Pembroke.

YORK COUNTY.

Kenneth W. Sutherland...................Biddeford.
John B. E. Tartre........................Biddeford.
William J. Maybury......................Saco.
Fred J. Allen............................Sanford.
Natt T. Abbott..........................Shapleigh.
Joseph D. Eaton.........................Wells.
Lendall W. Nash.........................Kennebunk.
Charles L. Favour........................Kittery.
David W. Libby..........................Newfield.
William B. Wentworth...................Lebanon.
Samuel A. Hill..........................Buxton.
Ferdinand E. Tripp......................Lyman.
William J. Mewer........................Old Orchard.
Palmer A. Twambly......................Kennebunkport.

O. F. Fellows, Speaker.....................Bucksport.
W. S. Cotton, Clerk.......................Lisbon.
E. M. Thompson, Assistant Clerk...........Augusta.
George H. Fisher, Messenger...............Winterport.
William J. Smith, First Assistant Messenger...Gardiner.
W. H. Holmes, Second Assistant Messenger.....Augusta.
Harry P. Hawes, Mail Carrier..   ....Vassalboro.
Harry R. Coolidge, Assistant Mail Carrier......Livermore.
J. F. Frederic, First Folder..................Starks.
Chapin Lydston, Second Folder.............Litchfield.
Joseph H. Dixon, Third Folder..............Eliot.
R. C. Noyes, First Door Keeper..............Pittsfield.
E. Parker Craig, Second Door Keeper.......Island Falls.
Charles Knowlton, Page...................Ellsworth.
William B. Webb, Page....................Skowhegan.
J. S. Estes, Reporter........................Fort Fairfield.
A. H. Whitman, Reporter...................Portland.

INDEX.

A.

PUBLIC LAWS.

	PAGE
Abatement of tax on legacies to religious institutions..........	121
Abuttors on city streets, assessment of damages upon...........	129
Acknowledgment of deeds, relating to.......................	68
Actions against administrators and executors, defense of, relating to	136
Actions against administrators and executors, limitation of, relating to	165
Actions for libel or slander, relating to.......................	143
Acts and resolves, when same shall take effect.................	205
Adjutant General, clerk hire in office of, compensation for......	80
salary of	81
Administrators, actions against, defense of, relating to...........	136
and executors, relating to duties of..............	148
authorized to provide for care of burial lots.....	65
de bonis non, powers and duties of, relating to...	157
foreign, authorized to receive and dispose of personal property	184
limitation of actions against, relating to.........	165
shall testify in actions brought by them in certain cases	88
Admission of attorneys to practice law, relating to..............	110
Adulteration of feeding stuffs, penalty for.....................	193
Age of children required to attend school......................	107
Agents of schools in unincorporated places, appointment of.....	99
Agreement that building shall not be personal property not effectual in certain cases..	117
Agricultural societies, receipts exempt from attachment for three months	60
Agricultural societies, stipend to, relating to....................	177
Alleys, bowling, relating to......................................	54
Analysis of commercial feeding stuffs, to regulate...............	191
fertilizers, relating to...................	180
Androscoggin river, open season for shad and alewives in.......	7
Animals, estray, liability for damages by.....................	36
transportation of, relating to.......................	13
Appeals from magistrates in criminal cases.....................	135
Appointment of guardians for insane persons, relating to........	69
Appraisal of goods or beasts found, relating to.................	35
Appropriation for support of normal schools...................	181

INDEX.

	PAGE
Arms, repeal of certain sections relating to......................	45
Aroostook county commissioners, time of sessions of, changed...	122
sheriff, salary fixed..........................	53
Aroostook war, in aid of soldiers of...........................	97
Art, works of, to prevent injury to...........................	49
Assaults upon officers, relating to............................	117
Assessment and expenditure of permanent school fund in certain towns..	139
Assessment of damages upon abuttors on city streets, relating to,	129
state tax, duties of state treasurer in relation to..	46
Assessors, repeal of certain sections relating to returns made by,	46
Assistant librarian, to increase salary of........................	169
Associations, loan and building, relating to......................	61
Attachment of partnership property, relating to..................	65
property exempt from, relating to................	64
Attachments, dissolution of, by filing bond, relating to..........	67
Attested instruments, proof of, relating to.......................	93
Attorney, Hancock county, salary of, relating to.................	171
Kennebec county, salary fixed........................	48
York county, salary fixed............................	48
Attorneys at law, concerning.................................	17
examination of, relating to...........................	110
Augusta, close time for migratory fish between bridge and dam..	118
Automobiles on public ways, to regulate use of.................	200

PRIVATE AND SPECIAL LAWS.

Academy, Bridgton, amendment of corporation of trustees of....	478
Gorham, relating to..............................	269
Hebron, additional to incorporation of trustees of....	343
Acceptance of conveyance, Widow's island....................	570
Addison, to prohibit dumping of fish offal into waters of......	533
Aged Men, Portland, Home for, charter of amended..........	73
Agricultural Society, Androscoggin Valley, to incorporate......	231
Agriculture, students of, relating to...........................	169
Alewive fishery, Damariscotta Mills, control of water at.......	624
Androscoggin Log Driving Company, to incorporate..........	444
Valley Agricultural Society, to incorporate.........	231
Annexation, South Portland to Portland, enabling act for......	593
Anson, town of, authorized to buy bridge, with Madison.........	378
Appropriation for 1903, to provide in part for..................	12, 207
for 1904, to provide in part for..................	370
Aroostook county, to legalize acts of St. Francis plantation....	64
Valley R. R. Co. may acquire Presque Isle Electric Light Company	471
relating to approval of location...	469
Arrowsic bridge, acceptance of by Sagadahoc county, relating to,	625
Ashland Trust Company, to incorporate.......................	523
Assessment of State Tax, 1903...............................	629
1904	676
Assessors, Norway, doings of, made valid......................	346
Portland, election and tenure of, relating to..........	266
Athens, authorized to remove bodies of deceased persons......	267
Atlantic Shore Line Railway, consolidated with other lines....	284

	PAGE
Auburn and Turner Railroad Company, to incorporate........	33
Board of Public Works, charter amended............	210
city charter amended................................	206
Free Public Library, concerning.....................	216
lake, to protect waters of...........................	377
Mechanic Falls and Norway St. Ry., additional powers given	555
Municipal Court, jurisdiction of, relating to...........	375
Savings Bank, to construct safe deposit boxes........	6
Augusta, caucuses in, qualification for participation in..........	537
treasurer and collector of taxes, election of...........	353
Trust Company, amendment of charter of............	527
authorized to establish branch at Madison	527
change of name ratified..............	527
increase of capital stock authorized...	379
Water District, to incorporate.......................	509
Winthrop and Gardiner Ry. may supply electricity in certain towns	119
to amend charter of......	91

RESOLVES.

Academy, Lee Normal, in favor of...........................	42
Adjutant General's office, preservation of regimental rolls in....	7
Allagash road, in favor of.....................................	9
Andersonville, Maine Soldiers' Monument at..................	21
Anson, town of, in favor of...................................	38
Augusta City Hospital, in favor of...........................	20

B.

PUBLIC LAWS.

Bail in criminal prosecutions, to regulate taking of..............	96
Ballots, for state and city elections, to provide for printing of....	132
printing and distributing of...........................	8
Banks of discount, repeal of certain sections relating to.........	129
savings, investment of funds of, relating to...............	152
relating to duties of officers and corporators of...	45
Bastard children, relating to support of........................	27
Beans, standard weight of bushel of...........................	14
Bears, Oxford county, bounty on, to provide for................	197
Beasts, repeal of chapter relating to impounding of.............	41
estray, relating to.......................................	35
Beef, repeal of section relating to inspection of.................	41
Beet sugar, repeal of sections relating to bounties on...........	44
Big Carry pond, ice fishing in, prohibition repealed.............	126
Birds, game, close time on, relating to.........................	190
shore, protection of, act for...........................	200
Billiard rooms, may be permitted to remain open till midnight..	54
Births, marriages and deaths, prior to 1892, preservation of record of	168
Births, notification and record of.............................	141

INDEX.

	PAGE
Black bass, Highland lake, taking of, relating to................	70
Keoka lake, taking of, relating to.................	70
Black game, close time for.....................................	191
pond, ice fishing in, prohibition repealed................	126
Board of examiners of attorneys, relating to...............'......	110
of undertakers and embalmers, creation of,	75
Board of pharmacy, appointment of..........................	183
Bond for damages may be given for crossing lands for lumbering,	101
Bonds, collectors of taxes, relating to.........................	136
of treasurers of towns and plantations, relating to.....	125
Books in public places, to prevent injury to.....................	49
Bounties on beet sugar, repeal of sections relating to............	44
on silk, repeal of sections relating to..................	44
Bounty on bears, Oxford county, to provide for................	197
on porcupines, to establish.............................	204
Bowling alleys, may be permitted to be kept open till midnight...	54
Bridges and roads in unincorporated townships, relating to......	14
Brunswick, town, protection of shore birds in..................	200
Burial lots, provision for by executors, to provide for...........	65
of widows of soldiers, relating to......................	159
Burying grounds, relating to..................................	7
Bushel of beans, standard weight of...........................	14

PRIVATE AND SPECIAL LAWS.

Bagaduce river, relating to taking eels in.....................	91
Bait fishing, Blanchard pond, to prohibit......................	414
Magalloway river, Parmachenee, Barker's, Billings and Sunday ponds............................	412
Bangor and Aroostook Railroad, extensions authorized........	361
mortgage confirmed	24
purchase of Fish River R. R. authorized	24
yard tracks, extension of, in Houlton	70
Bangor and Brewer Steam Ferry Company, charter extended..	151
Bridge Company, time for tolls extended..............	506
Crosbyville Chapel, to legalize doings of...............	110
Loan and Trust Company, to amend and extend charter,	432
police force, pension to injured officers of.............	433
street railway, repeal of section relating to............	168
treasurer and collector, relating to.....................	571
to supply pure water to people of.....................	561
Trust Company, formerly Bangor Loan and Trust Co..	432
Banking and Trust Company, Bar Harbor, charter amended.....	438
Company, Boothbay Harbor, charter amended..........	462
Bar Harbor Banking and Trust Company, charter amended.....	438
Electric Light Company, extension of lines........	32
municipal court, to establish.......................	8
Barker's pond, to prohibit bait fishing in......................	412
Baskahegan Dam Company, charter amended.................	430
Bath, bridge over New Meadows river, authorized to build....	477
Military and Naval Orphan Asylum, relating to admissions to	479
municipal court, relating to appointment of recorder for..	505
street and sewer commission, to establish................	37

INDEX.

	PAGE
Bear island, annexed to Phippsburg.............................	628
Berwick, Eliot and York Street Railway, powers enlarged.....	25
Biddeford and Saco Water Company, bonds authorized........	43
Municipal Court, jurisdiction of, relating to..........	215
recorder of, relating to.............	735
Billing's Cove, seines and drag nets prohibited in................	351
pond, to prohibit ice fishing in...................	475
bait fishing in.......................	412
Birds, sea, hunting of, in launches prohibited...................	534
Black bass, Hancock county, taking of in waters of, to regulate..	549
Upper Kezar pond, taking of, to regulate..........	491
Snake island, annexed to Phippsburg....................	628
Blanchard pond, to prohibit bait fishing in....................	414
Bluehill and Bucksport Electric Railroad Company, charter extended	473
ice fishing in Billings pond, to prohibit................	475
Trust and Banking Company, to amend and extend charter	516
Water Company, to extend charter....................	242
Board of Public Works, Auburn, charter amended............	210
Bodies of deceased persons, Athens authorized to remove......	267
Monson authorized to remove.....	67
Bodwell Water Company authorized to generate electricity......	132
Bonds, Old Orchard Electric Light Company, to issue........	6
State of Maine, Treasurer of State to purchase........	8
Boom Company, Union, to incorporate.......................	428
Booms, Portage Lake Mill Co. authorized to maintain.........	564
Springer Lumber Co. to erect in Mattawamkeag river..	89
Boothbay Harbor, authorized to construct bridge..............	33
Banking Company, charter extended........	462
Electric Light and Power Company, to incorporate	336
road commissioner in, election of...........	620
roads in Isle of Springs....................	218
water supply of, relating to...............	341
Boothbay Railroad, time of construction of, to extend..........	528
Boston Excelsior Co., Sebec river, to erect piers and booms in..	414
Brewer School Board, to establish............................	352
Bridge, Boothbay Harbor authorized to construct..............	33
Company, Bangor, time for tolls on extended..........	506
Eliot, to ratify certain doings of............	69
Waterville and Winslow, to incorporate....	418
draw, Long Lake, to authorize........................	734
Eastport, to extend charter of........................	63
iron, Presumpscot river, relating to release of to county,	536
New Meadows river, to authorize....................	477
Norridgewock Falls, Anson and Madison authorized to purchase	378
sale of authorized................	339
Saint John River Toll, to incorporate..................	185
Ticonic Company, foot, stock of increased............	201
Wiscasset, made a public bridge......................	585
Bridgton Academy, incorporation of trustees of amended......	478
Water Company, to amend charter of...............	4
Brooks Village Corporation, to incorporate....................	529

	PAGE
Brownfield, treasurer and collector, relating to................	571
Brown or Heath brook, to prevent throwing sawdust into......	534
Brownville and Williamsburg Water Company, to incorporate..	333
Brunswick and Topsham Water District, to incorporate.......	245
Municipal Court, to establish......................	434
water supply, to defray expense of location of......	360
Bryant pond, close time on tributaries of.....................	476
Buckfield Water Power and Electric Light Company, to incorporate	422
Bucksport, fire wardens in, relating to........................	552
town of, authorized to refund debt.................	202
Buoys in West Branch Penobscot, Norcross Transportation Company to maintain	411
Burnt Coat Island annexed to Phippsburg.....................	628
Island, name changed................................	346
Bushby Island annexed to Phippsburg........................	628
Butler Spring Water Co. to consolidate with Sanford Light and Power Co.	295

RESOLVES.

Baileyville, in aid of bridge in................................	55
Bancroft, in aid of bridge in, across Mattawamkeag river.....	55
Bangor Children's Home, in favor of..........................	27
ward for sick in, in favor of........	48
Bar Harbor Medical and Surgical Hospital, in favor of.......	22
Bath Military and Naval Orphan Asylum, in favor of..........	8
Big Lake, in aid of navigation in..............................	46
Board of Cattle Commissioners, in favor of....................	45
Boundary of lots, re-establishment of.........................	35
Bowdoinham, to abate part of state tax of.....................	49
Bridge, Bancroft, Mattawamkeag river, in aid of..............	55
Connor plantation, in aid of............................	53
Gagnon stream, in favor of............................	49
Mariaville, in aid of...................................	54
Mattawamkeag, in favor of............................	40
Narraguagus river, in aid of...........................	48
New Sharon, in favor of...............................	50
St. Croix river, in aid of..............................	55
Wallagrass plantation, in aid of.......................	49
Washburn, in aid of...................................	54
West Branch St. Croix river, in favor of..............	39
Bridges, for information concerning...........................	45
Bryant, Edmund C., in favor of...............................	23
Buck, Albert R., in favor of..................................	18, 30
Burleigh, A. A., in favor of..................................	42

C.

PUBLIC LAWS.

Calais, close time for salmon, on portion of St. Croix river......	118
Calves, transportation of, in cars.............................	13
Capercailzie, close time for...................................	191
Cars for transportation of cattle, to have continuous passage....	13
spitting on floor of, prohibited..........................	106

INDEX.

	PAGE
Casks, lime, inspection of....................................	160
Cattle, estray, liability for damages by.......................	36
transportation of, in cars................................	13
Caucuses, political, manner of holding........................	174
Cemeteries, investment of trust funds for care of..............	7
Certificates of nomination, filing of..........................	132
Certification on deed considered as a record...................	5
state, of teachers, relating to..........................	47
Chesterville, town, ice fishing in certain ponds, permitted.....	126
Children, bastard, relating to support of......................	27
in unorganized townships, schooling of...................	98
of certain age, required to attend school...............	107
City elections, printing and distributing ballots for..........	8
Claims against estates of deceased persons, may be referred.....	102
Clerk hire, Adjutant General, compensation for.................	80
Clerks of court to be clerks of law court in certain counties...	19
Close season defined..	187
for game birds, relating to..............................	196
Coal sheds on railroads, locations for.........................	127
Collateral inheritance tax, religious institutions exempt from..	120
Collections by attorneys, relating to..........................	18
Collector of taxes and treasurer, may be same person...........	186
Collectors of taxes, bonds of..................................	136
relating to election of.................................	42
and treasurers, election of, made valid................	157
Commercial fertilizers, sale and analysis of...................	180
feeding stuffs, sale and analysis of....................	191
Commissioned officers, retirement of...........................	59
Commission for protection of forests, to create................	131
Commissioners, bail, powers and duties of......................	96
county, relating to duties of............................	56
pharmacy, appointment of.................................	183
Oxford county, compensation of...........................	5
Waldo county, compensation of............................	21
Committee of union of towns for employment of superintendent of schools..	34
Commitment by trial justices and judges of police courts.......	66
of insane persons..	3, 63
Common school funds, raising and expending of..................	128
schools, maintenance of..................................	139
Compensation of members of government..........................	202
of town officers...	87
Concentrated feeding stuffs, sale and analysis of..............	191
Consent for sale of mortgaged property shall be in writing.....	101
Construction of railways, municipal officers may direct manner of,	16
Contracts for water, gas and light, by municipalities..........	49
Conventions, county teachers', relating to.....................	47
Conveyance of scholars, relating to............................	51
Conveyances of real estate.....................................	5
record of	182
Co-partnership property, attachment on, relating to............	65
Cornville, town, ice fishing in Oaks pond permitted............	141
Corporations, relating to......................................	144, 199
Correction, relating to houses of..............................	37

	PAGE
Costs in taking lands for public uses, to regulate	89
of foreclosure, giving of lien to mortgagees	92
of magistrates for appeal and recognizance	147
separate executions for, by disclosure commissioners, abolished	158
County attorney, Hancock, salary of	171
Kennebec, salary of	48
Knox, salary of	198
Piscataquis, salary of	170
Sagadahoc, salary of	166
Somerset, salary of	170
Washington, salary of	167
York, salary of	48
County commissioners, Aroostook, time of sessions changed	122
Hancock, compensation of	120
Kennebec, compensation of	94
Oxford, compensation of	5
Waldo, compensation of	21
duties of, repeal of sections relating to	56
not eligible to certain other offices	94
County convention of teachers, relating to	47
County of Penobscot, register of probate, salary of	30
County of York, treasurer of, salary of	15
County treasurer's deed by tax sale, proof of title	33
County treasurers, duties of, repeal of sections relating to	42
County treasurer, York, salary of	15
Court, supreme judicial, clerks of, to be clerks of law court	19
Knox county, terms of	10
salary of justices of	16
Courts, authority of, over guardians ad litem or next friend	69
municipal, judges of, restricted in giving counsel	91
Criminal cases, appeal from magistrates in	135
Criminals, insane, examination of	112
Crossing lands for lumbering, no liability for trespass, if bond be given	101
Cumberland county, clerk of court shall be clerk of law term	19
protection of shore birds in	200

PRIVATE AND SPECIAL LAWS.

Calais, city of, ward and district lines in	345
Camden and Liberty Railway, to incorporate	123
city of, to incorporate	44
Trotting Park Association, additional rights given	202
Trust Company, charter extended	66
Campmeeting Association, Northport, to amend charter of	158
Caratunk Power Company authorized to erect dams, in Anson and Embden	338
Caribou authorized to hold stock in public building	551
Carrabasset river, dams across authorized	338
Stock Farms, to enlarge powers of	353
Castine Gas Company, to incorporate	375
Castle Hill, town of, to incorporate	130
Caucuses, Augusta, to fix qualification for participation in	537

INDEX.

	PAGE
Cemetery Association, Searsport Village, to incorporate........	472
Smith Family, Palermo, to incorporate..	192
Company, Mount Abram, to incorporate............	379
Central Trust Company, to incorporate......................	111
Chemical Fibre Co., Penobscot, authorized to generate electricity,	150
Cherryfield and Milbridge Street Railway, to incorporate........	466
Christian Association, Portland Young Women's, to hold real estate	269
Chapel, Crosbyville, to legalize doings of......................	110
Chipmunks and squirrels, Knox County, protection of..........	588
City, Auburn, charter amended................................	206
Brewer, school board established........................	352
Calais, ward and district lines in.......................	345
Camden, to incorporate................................	44
Dexter, time for acceptance of charter extended..........	380
Eastport, charter amended..............................	78
Marshal, duties and powers of..................	78
Gardiner, charter amended..............................	327
Lewiston, election of officers of........................	546
Old Town, charter amended............................	330
Portland, appointment of constables in.................	360
to amend charter of...........................	116
Rockland, to amend charter of..........................	587
Trust Company, Bangor, to incorporate..................	319
Westbrook, charter amended............................	142
date of elections changed.....................	119
Clams, Scarboro, to prevent taking of in......................	489
Clark, Clarence H., to extend wharf into Lubec Narrows......	564
Classical Institute, Coburn, to incorporate trustees of..........	156
Clinton Electric Light and Power Co. may supply light, heat, etc.,	185
Close time, Cupsuptic river...................................	523
Indian pond, and tributaries........................	476
lobsters, near Matinicus and Criehaven............	149
Coast Telephone Company, Maine, to incorporate..............	532
Cobbosseecontee, to prohibit ice fishing in.....................	405
Coburn Classical Institute, to incorporate trustees of............	156
Cochnewagon pond, to prohibit ice fishing in...................	404
Codfish, Frenchman's bay, taking of, relating to...............	323
Colby College, relating to president and trustees of............	229
Cold Spring Water Company, Winthrop, charter amended......	7
extended	268
Collector and treasurer, Bangor, relating to....................	571
Brownfield, relating to.................	571
Oakfield, relating to...................	572
Collector of Taxes, Augusta, election of, relating to............	353
Hallowell, election of, relating to..........	570
and treasurer, Waterville, relating to.......	571
Consolidation of inland fish and game laws.....................	604
Constables, Portland, to regulate appointment of...............	360
Conveyance of Widow's island, acceptance of...................	570
County building, Cumberland, erection authorized..............	350
commissioners, Cumberland, authorized to erect building,	350
Somerset, authorized to borrow money for court house......................	203
Piscataquis, authorized to make loan....................	131

	PAGE
Court, Auburn municipal, jurisdiction of, relating to............	375
Bar Harbor municipal, to establish.....................	8
Bath municipal, appointment of recorder for............	505
Biddeford, municipal, jurisdiction of, relating to........	215
recorder of, relating to...........	735
Brunswick, municipal, to establish.....................	434
Dover municipal, blanks for provided..................	227
charter amended	120
Eastport, to establish.................................	356
Ellsworth municipal, relating to.......................	453
house extension, Skowhegan, relating to, extension of....	203
Lewiston municipal, fees of clerk of....................	557
Old Town municipal, charter amended..................	231
Norway municipal, relating to jurisdiction of...........	580
Rockland, police, relating to..........................	177
Rumford Falls municipal, addition to charter of........	503
Westbrook municipal, charter amended................	188
West Hancock municipal, to amend charter of..........	161
Winthrop municipal, to establish......................	538
Cow island annexed to Phippsburg...........................	628
Crawford pond, to prevent throwing sawdust into tributaries of.	603
Criehaven, relating to taking lobsters near.....................	149
Crosbyville Chapel, to legalize doings of......................	110
Cumberland county commissioners to erect county building.....	350
deer in, open time on.....................	481
Illuminating Company, to incorporate..............	400
Trust Company, charter extended................	66
Cupsuptic pond, to prohibit bait fishing in.....................	413
river, close time for fishing in......................	523

RESOLVES.

Caratunk plantation, repair of road in, in favor of..............	29
Castine State Normal School, in favor of......................	38
Cattle Commissioners, in favor of............................	45
Central Maine General Hospital, in favor of....................	21
Children's Aid Society of Maine, in favor of...................	5
Home, Bangor, in favor of.....................	27
ward for sick in, in favor of........	48
Church at Pleasant Point, for completion of...................	27
Claims for state pensions, to provide for examination of........	13
Clerk hire, state library, during legislative session, to provide...	47
superintendent of schools, in office of...............	51
Clerk of committee on revision of statutes, in favor of..........	38
judiciary, in favor of..................	37
courts, Lincoln county, completion of records of......	40
Colby College, in favor of....................................	37
Commissioner for revision of statutes, appointment of.........	12
Committee on revision of statutes, in favor of..................	19
Compensation of steamboat inspectors, to provide for..........	6
Connor plantation, in aid of bridge in.........................	53
County tax for 1903 and 1904................................	32
Crystal, town, in favor of.....................................	24
Cutler, town, in favor of......................................	33

D.

PUBLIC LAWS.

	PAGE
Damages, assessment of upon abuttors upon city streets.........	129
by estray animals, liability for.......................	36
crossing lands for lumbering, bond to be given for....	101
done by dogs going at large........................	86
for taking land for street railroads..................	19, 30
Dealers in old junk, relating to................................	105
Deaths, notification and record of.............................	141
prior to 1892, preservation of record of.................	168
Debtors, insolvent court, discharge of, in pending cases.........	102
Deceased persons, claims against estates of.....................	102
Dedication of streets, relating to.............................	40
Deeds, acknowledgment of, relating to.........................	68
of release, record of..................................	182
real estate, relating to................................	5
fees of registers of..................................	95
Deer dogs, killing of authorized..............................	187
non-resident hunters for, license required...............	77
shipment of	78
Defacing of books, pictures, etc., in public places, to prohibit...	49
Defects in highways, damage by and notice of..................	85
Delinquent corporations, non-payment of tax forfeits charter....	199
Denny's river, fishing in regulated............................	118
Dentistry, practice of relating to.............................	72
Deposits, interest bearing, taxation of........................	137
unclaimed in savings banks, relating to..............	84
Descent of real estate..	122
Devises and bequests, acceptance of by cities and towns.......	149
Dexter pond, ice fishing in, prohibition repealed..............	105
Discharge of insolvent debtors, relating to...................	104
Disclosure commissioners, to abolish separate executions for costs,	158
Discount, banks of, repeal of sections relating to..............	129
Disorderly persons, relating to commitment of................	37
Dissolution of attachments by filing bond.....................	67
Divorce, relating to..	171
Divorces, in state, relating to................................	31
Dogs, licensing of..	81
going at large, relating to..............................	86
Drains and sewers, crossing railroad location.................	105
Duck, close time for...	190
protection of, act for.................................	200
Duties payable by public officers.............................	67

PRIVATE AND SPECIAL LAWS.

Damariscotta Mills, control of water at alewive fishery........	624
river, purse seines in, to prevent use of..........	549
smelts in tributaries of, to protect.........	538
tide wheel in, Frederick J. Merrill to construct	365

	PAGE
Dam Company, Baskahegan, to amend charter of..............	430
Duck Lake, to incorporate....................	487
Godfrey Falls, tolls for driving logs..........	592
Kibbie, to incorporate........................	544
Libby Meadow Brook, to incorporate..........	292
Sebec, to amend charter of....................	216
Saint John River, to incorporate..............	301
South Branch Moose River, to incorporate....	425
Wilson Stream, charter amended..............	81
Dam and piers, Hancock brook, erection of authorized..........	591
Improvement Company, Madunkeunk, to incorporate..	485
Sebasticook river, J. M. Jewell authorized to erect........	411
Dams, Caratunk Power Company authorized to erect...........	338
Dead River Log Driving Company, charter amended..........	378
Deceased persons, Athens authorized to remove bodies of......	267
Monson authorized to remove bodies of.....	67
Deer, Cumberland county, open time on.......................	481
Kennebec, Knox, Waldo and Lincoln counties, protection of	475
Mount Desert island, protection of......................	412
York county, better protection of.......................	532
Deposit boxes, Auburn Savings Bank to construct............	6
Dexter, city of, time for acceptance of charter extended.......	380
Dirigo Electric Light Company, to incorporate........	519
Water Company, charter extended....................	346
Dirigo Electric Light Company, Dexter, to incorporate........	519
Dover and Foxcroft Light and Heat Co., lease to ratified........	501
Village Fire Company, charter amended....	17
Dover Municipal Court, blanks provided for..................	227
charter amended	120
Drag nets, Billing's Cove, to prohibit use of, in................	351
Draw bridge, Long Lake, to authorize.......................	734
Drinking water, to supply people of Bangor with..............	561
Driving Company, West Branch Reservoir and Dam, to incorporate	277
Duck Lake Dam Company, to incorporate......................	487
Ducks, method of hunting for, relating to......................	604

RESOLVES.

Dairy interests, in favor of.....................................	8
Deeds, early York, in relation to..............................	35
Drew plantation, in favor of....................................	47
to fix valuation of...........................	32
Dudley, J. Perley, in favor of.................................	38

E.

PUBLIC LAWS.

Eastern Maine State Fair, receipts exempt from attachment for three months	60
stipend to	178
Education of youth, relating to.............................	53
Election of town superintendents............................	79

	PAGE
Elections of treasurers and collectors of taxes made valid	157
printing and distributing ballots for	8
voting at, to regulate	132
Electric lines, erection of posts for	194
posts and wires, erection of	102
Elliottsville, plantation, open ice fishing in Greenwood pond	119
Embalmers, registration of	74
Embalming bodies of persons who died of infectious diseases	74
Employment of superintendent of schools, relating to	34
Enlistments, relating to	57
Enumeration of school children in unorganized townships	98
Equity suits to quiet title	115
Erection of posts on electric lines, to regulate	194
Estates of deceased persons, claims against, relating to	102
trust, sale of may be authorized	71
Evidence by executors, may be given as to facts prior to appointment	88
Examination before judges of probate, relating to	72
of railroads	138
state, of teachers	47
Examiners for admission to practice as attorneys	110
of insane criminals, appointment of	112
of undertakers and embalmers, board of	75
Execution, property exempt from, relating to	64
Executors, actions against, defense of	136
and administrators, relating to duties of	148
limitation of actions against	165
Executors authorized to provide for care of burial lots	65
foreign, authorized to receive and dispose of personal property	184
Executors shall testify in actions brought by them in certain cases	88
Executions, separate, for costs, by disclosure commissioners, to abolish	158
Exemption of public property from taxation	43

PRIVATE AND SPECIAL LAWS.

Eagle Lake, navigation of by steam, authorized	401
East Branch Improvement Company, to incorporate	325
Brown island annexed to Phippsburg	628
Eastern Penobscot river, protection of fish in	552
East Pittston Village Corporation, relating to	567
East pond, to prohibit sale of fish taken from	489
Eastport Bridge, to extend charter of	63
city, charter amended	78
municipal court, to establish	356
Street Railway, to extend charter of	417
Eden, use of roads in	734
Eels, Bagaduce river, taking of, in, to regulate	91
Election of city officers, Lewiston, relating to	546
of road commissioners, Boothbay Harbor	620
of treasurer and collector of taxes, Hallowell	570
Elections, Portland, relating to	116
Electricity, Bodwell Water Co. authorized to generate	132

	PAGE
Electric Light Company, Bar Harbor, relating to...............	32
Buckfield, to incorporate...............	422
Dirigo, Dexter, to incorporate.........	519
Fryeburg, relating to..................	291
Kennebunk, authorized to issue bonds..	329
Old Orchard, to issue bonds..........	6
Electric Light and Power Company, Boothbay Harbor, to incorporate	336
Clinton, relating to........	185
Wells, to incorporate......	311
Wilton, charter extended..	157
Electric lighting plant, Kennebunk authorized to own..........	204
Railroad, Bluehill and Bucksport, charter extended....	473
Houlton and Danforth, to incorporate.......	572
Houlton and Woodstock, to incorporate.....	255
Milbridge and Cherryfield, relating to franchise of	456
Electric Railway Company, Lumberman's, to incorporate......	575
Winterport, Frankfort and Prospect, to incorporate	440
Eliot Bridge Company, to ratify certain doings of.............	69
Ellis pond, to prohibit sale of fish taken from.................	489
stream, to prohibit throwing sawdust into................	502
River Improvement Company, to incorporate..............	419
Ellsworth Municipal Court, relating to jurisdiction of.........	453
Street Railway Company, charter extended..........	167
Excelsior Company, to erect piers and booms in Sebec river....	414
Expenditures of government 1903, to provide in part for......12, 207, 723	
1904, to provide in part for........ 370, 730	
Extension of Bangor and Aroostook R. R. authorized..........	361

RESOLVES.

Early York deeds, in relation to............................	35
Eastern Maine General Hospital, in favor of....................	20
Insane Hospital, to assist in paying debt of......	47
East Livermore, town, in favor of............................	43
Eastport, city, in favor of....................................	40
Edmunds, town, in favor of..................................	39
Election case, Lewiston, in favor of contestants of.............	23
Electric Lighting plant for state prison, in favor of.............	69
Elevator in state house, for repair of..........................	19
Employees in state house, in favor of.........................	48
Enoch Lincoln, for repairs on tomb of........................	31
Epidemic or emergency fund, to provide......................	5. 36
Examination of candidates for Cecil John Rhodes scholarship...	60
in regard to state pensions, to provide for........	13
Eye and Ear Infirmary, in favor of............................	20

F.

PUBLIC LAWS.

	PAGE
Feeding stuffs, sale and analysis of, to regulate	191
Fees and costs of magistrates, relating to	147
analysis of commercial feeding stuffs	191
analysis of commercial fertilizers	180
bail commissioners	96
registers of deeds	95
undertakers and embalmers, for registration of	76
Fences unnecessarily high, a nuisance	119
Fencing of school house lots, relating to	108
Ferries, relating to	83
Fertilizers, commercial, sale and analysis of	180
Filing of nomination papers, relating to	132
Finding of money or goods, duties of finder	35
Fire arms, repeal of sections relating to	45
Fire wardens, forest, appointment of	131
Fisheries and game, inland, clerical errors and amendments	156
Fisheries, sea and shore, relating to	55, 186
Fish, Frenchman's bay, relating to taking of	21
Fishing, Denny's river regulated	118
Fishing, Goodwin's brook and Higgins stream, prohibition repealed	110
Squaw Pan lake, allowed in inlet of	100
through ice, Big Carry or West Carry pond, prohibition repealed	126
Black, Whittier and Perry ponds, prohibition repealed	126
Dexter pond, prohibition repealed	105
Indian pond, prohibition repealed	109
Large Greenwood pond, prohibition repealed	119
Oaks pond, prohibition repealed	141
Palmer pond, prohibition repealed	151
Fish, migratory, relating to	6, 93, 118
Foreclosure, lien for costs of, to mortgagees	92
on mortgage of personal property, notice of	169
Foreign executors, receipt and disposal of personal property by	184
Forest commission and fire wardens, to provide for	131
Forfeiture of charter of corporations when tax is not paid	199
Franklin county, close time on trout, etc., in	186
Free high schools, attendance at, relating to	53
Freeport, town, protection of shore birds in	200
Frenchman's bay, taking of fish in, relating to	21
Fuel yards, to enable establishment of	95
Funds of savings banks, investment of	152

PRIVATE AND SPECIAL LAWS.

Family Association, Pike, to incorporate	316
Farm, Carrabassett Stock, to enlarge powers of	353
Farmers' Telephone Company, to incorporate	579
Farmington Village Association, new charter granted	242

	PAGE
Farrell, William C., and Gagnon, Henry A., authorized to build dam in Hammond brook....................................	591
Female College, Maine Wesleyan Seminary, name changed.....	480
Ferguson Stream Improvement Company, to incorporate.......	427
Ferry Company, Bangor and Brewer, steam, charter extended...	151
Peoples', to incorporate.....................	200
Portland and Cape Elizabeth, to extend charter of	265
Fibre Company, Penobscot Chemical, authorized to generate electricity	150
Fire Company, Dover and Foxcroft, relating to................	17
Fire Insurance Company, Mutual, charter extended.............	152
wardens, Bucksport, relating to...........................	552
First pond, Bluehill, to prohibit ice fishing in..................	475
Fish and game, consolidation of laws relating to................	604
wardens, to provide temporarily for payment of..	590
destruction of, in East Penobscot river, relating to........	552
Frenchman's Bay, relating to taking certain kinds of......	323
offal, to prevent dumping of in waters of Jonesport and Addison	533
Fish River Improvement Company, to incorporate.............	438
Railroad, relating to mortgage of..................	105
relating to rights of way over public lots..	68
relating to width of location of..........	69
sale of authorized........................	24
to ratify lease of........................	24
to ratify mortgage of....................	23
Fish, shell, Georgetown, protection of.........................	118
to prohibit sale of from certain ponds in Kennebec and Somerset counties	489
Fishing, bait, Magalloway river, to prohibit....................	412
Otter pond, to prohibit...........................	412
consolidation of laws relating to......................	604
Cupsuptic river, close time for........................	523
ice, First or Billing's pond, to prohibit...............	475
Number Nine lake, to prohibit...................	474
Pease pond, relating to...........................	381
Thompson pond, relating to.......................	109
Weld pond, to prohibit...........................	535
in certain ponds in Kennebec county, relating to...	404
Kennebago lake, to regulate...........................	414
Little Sebago pond, open season for....................	491
Morrill pond, to prohibit.............................	490
Parlin stream, prohibition removed on part of..........	484
Quimby pond, to regulate.............................	413
Sebec lake, certain tributaries of opened for...........	479
Sebago lake, open season for.........................	403
Spring lake, limit on fish to be taken..................	484
Wilson lake, open season for.........................	550
in streams of Salem and Strong, to regulate..........	549
in tributaries of Wilson lake, to regulate.............	535
Flat Iron pond, to prohibit bait fishing in.....................	414
Flag Island, annexed to Phippsburg..........................	628
Foot Bridge Company, Ticonic, stock of increased..............	201

INDEX.

	PAGE
Forest Telegraph and Telephone Company, to incorporate	128
Fort Fairfield, town of, authorized to make loan	431
Kent Trust Company, to incorporate	153
Franklin Company, to reduce capital stock of	3
County, to regulate fishing in certain ponds of	414
Fraternity Temple Company, to incorporate	507
Free library, Rockland, to establish	157
public library, Auburn, concerning	216
Frenchman's Bay, hunting birds in boats propelled by steam, to prohibit	534
relating to taking certain kinds of fish in	323
Freeport branch of Lewiston Trust and Safe Deposit Co. authorized	499
deer in, open time on	481
Fryeburg Electric Light Company, relating to	291

RESOLVES.

Farmington State Normal School, in favor of	29
Feeding stations, appropriation for	8
Fish hatcheries, appropriation for	8
hatchery and feeding station, Sebago lake, in favor of	14
Rangeley lakes, in favor of	13
Flanders, Nellie E., in favor of	5
Foot and mouth disease, for prevention of	45
Forfeiture of public lots, waiver of	17
Forest Reserve, in favor of establishment of	41
Fort William Henry, for preservation of	24
Friendless Boys, Home for, in favor of	23
Frenchville, town, in aid of bridge in	49

G.

PUBLIC LAWS.

Game birds, close time for	190
Game, hunters for, license of, to provide for	77
Gas, contracts for by municipalities	49
Goods, lost, relating to disposition of	35
Goodwin brook, fishing on, prohibition repealed	110
Government, members of, compensation of	202
Greely brook, opened for fishing	187
Greenwood pond, ice fishing in, prohibition repealed	119
Guardians, ad litem, or next friend, authority of courts over	69
foreign, authorized to receive and dispose of personal property	184
for insane persons, relating to appointment of	69

PRIVATE AND SPECIAL LAWS.

Gagnon, Henry A., and Farrell, W. C., authorized to build dams	591
Game wardens, to provide temporarily for payment of	590
Gardiner, city charter amended	327
Water District, to incorporate	133
doubt removed	327

120   INDEX.

	PAGE
Gas and Power Company, Union River, relating to powers of...	16
Company, Castine, to incorporate..........................	375
Union, to incorporate............................	162
General Hospital, Knox County, to incorporate.................	160
Washington County, to incorporate..........	481
Georgetown, better protection of shell fish in.....................	118
Goddard, A. M., authorized to build movable sidewalk.........	618
Godfrey Falls Dam Company, relating to tolls charged by......	592
Gooseberry Island, annexed to Phippsburg....................	628
Gorham Academy, relating to.................................	269
Government, expenditures of, 1903, to provide in part for.....12, 207, 723	
1904, to provide in part for.......	370, 730
Grange, Huntoon, to incorporate executive committee of........	228
Granite Trust Company, charter extended......................	207
Great Northern Paper Co., authorized to erect piers, etc., in Kennebec river	183
Great pond, to prohibit sale of fish from........................	489
Greenville Water Company, to extend powers of................	313

RESOLVES.

Gaddis, George D., in favor of.................................	50
Gagnon stream, in aid of bridge across........................	49
Goodwin's bridge, in aid of rebuilding of......................	54
Gorham Normal School, appropriation for.....................	51

H.
PUBLIC LAWS.

Habeas corpus, bail commissioner may issue writ of............	96
Hancock county commissioners, salary of.....................	120
judge of probate, salary of.................	9
register of probate, salary of................	189
Harbors, placing of permanent moorings in....................	91
Hares, better protection of.......................................	173
Harpswell, town, protection of shore birds in..................	200
Health, public, relating to.......................................	185
Hearing, before commitment of insane persons.................	3
Heirship of real estate, relating to.............................	122
Herring, taking of with seines, to regulate.....................	6
Higgins stream, fishing in, prohibition repealed................	110
Highland lake, taking of black bass in, relating to..............	70
Highways, injuries on, relating to.............................	85
Hindering of officers, penalty for..............................	117
Home week, time set apart for.................................	33
Houses of correction, repeal of section relating to..............	37
Houses, work, establishment of.................................	39
Hunting deer with dogs, penalty for............................	187
Hunter's license, non-resident, providing for...................	77
Hygiene, laboratory of, to establish............................	185

PRIVATE AND SPECIAL LAWS.

Haddock, Frenchman's bay, taking of, relating to..............	319
Hake, Frenchman's bay, taking of, relating to..................	319

INDEX. 121

	PAGE
Half Moon stream, to prevent throwing sawdust into............	400
Hallowell, treasurer and collector, election of, relating to.......	570
Trust Company, to extend charter of................	317
Hammond brook, piers and dams in and improvement of........	591
Hancock County Railway Company, charter extended..........	167
taking black bass in waters of, to regulate....	549
trustees of public reservations, powers granted to	556
Hancock Water, Light and Power Company, to incorporate....	288
Hanscom, G. H., authorized to erect piers and booms in Mattawamkeag river	129
Hebron Academy, addition to charter of trustees of...........	343
Hen Island, annexed to Phippsburg.........................	628
Hill Plantation, formerly Winterville.........................	591
Hillside Water Company, to incorporate, (Frankfort).........	459
Hillside Water Company, to incorporate, (Winthrop)..........	341
Historical Society, Maine, may hold real estate to value of five hundred thousand dollars.........................	344
Home for Aged Men in Portland, to amend charter of..........	73
Horseshoe pond, to prohibit ice fishing in.....................	405
Hospital, Knox County General, to incorporate................	160
Maine General, charter amended.....................	36
Washington County General, to incorporate..........	481
Houlton and Danforth Electric Railroad Company, to incorporate	572
Woodstock Electric Railroad Company, to incorporate	255
to provide sewerage in...............................	217
to supply people of with water.......................	227
Hunting sea birds by use of launches, to prohibit...............	534
Huntoon Grange, to incorporate executive committee of........	228

RESOLVES.

Harvey, Luella, Parkman reimbursed for care of..............	55
Haskell, George B., in favor of...............................	23
Hay-Bond Treaty, protest against............................	3
Healey Asylum, in favor of...................................	18
Home for Friendless Boys, in favor of........................	23
Hospital, Augusta City, in favor of...........................	20
Bar Harbor, Medical and Surgical, in favor of........	22
Central Maine General, in favor of..................	21
Eastern Maine General, in favor of..................	20
Insane, in favor of...................	43
to assist in paying debt of....	47
Knox County General, in favor of...................	28
Maine General, in favor of.........................	25
Insane, to renovate barn......................	47
Sisters of Charity, Lewiston, in favor of............	21
House, in favor of officers of.................................	36
payroll of	69
Houlton, town, in favor of....................................	29
Hydrography, work of to be undertaken......................	31

I.

PUBLIC LAWS.

	PAGE
Ice fishing, Big Carry pond, prohibition repealed..............	126
Black, Whittier and Perry pond, prohibition repealed,	126
Dexter pond, prohibition repealed.................	105
Indian pond, prohibition repealed..................	109
Large Greenwood pond, prohibition repealed.......	119
Oaks pond, prohibition repealed..................	141
Palmer pond, prohibition repealed.................	151
Idle persons, relating to commitment of......................	37
Impounding beasts, repeal of chapter relating to..............	41
Improvement of state roads, relating to.......................	49
Incendiarism, inquests of, certain sections repealed...........	29
Indian pond, ice fishing in, prohibition repealed...............	109
Infectious diseases, embalming and transportation of bodies of persons dying from	74
Inheritance of real estate, relating to............................	122
tax, religious institutions exempt from...........	120
Injuries on highways, notice of and damages for..............	85
Inland fisheries and game, errors and amendments, relating to..	186
Inquests, suspected incendiarism, certain sections repealed......	29
Insane criminals, examination of, by physician................	112
persons, commitment of	3, 63
guardians for, appointment of..................	69
Insects, protection against, on trees and shrubs................	88
Insolvency courts, discharge of debtors in pending cases.......	104
Inspection of nails, pork, beef, pearl ashes, and potashes, repeal of sections relating to.......................................	41
Inspection of railroads, relating to.............................	138
Inspectors of lime casks, appointment of......................	160
Instruments, attested, attestation how proved..................	93
Intelligence offices, relating to...............................	90
Interest bearing deposits in trust and banking companies, taxation of	137
Intoxicating liquors, relating to...............................	133
Investment of trust funds for care of cemeteries...............	7

PRIVATE AND SPECIAL LAWS.

Ice Company, Maine Lake, authorized to increase capital stock..	193
fishing in certain ponds in Kennebec county, relating to.....	404
First or Billing's pond, to prohibit..................	475
Number Nine lake, to prohibit......................	474
Pease pond, relating to............................	381
Thompson pond, relating to.........................	109
Weld pond, to prohibit............................	535
Illuminating Company, Cumberland, to incorporate............	400
Improvement and Dam Company, Madunkeunk, to incorporate..	485
Company, East Branch, to incorporate...........	325
Ellis River, to incorporate................	419
Ferguson Stream, to incorporate........	427
Fish River, to incorporate.............	438
Round Pond, to incorporate...........	294
Sangerville, to ratify lease of..........	501

	PAGE
Indian pond, close time on, and on tributaries of...............	476
Insurance Company, Mutual Fire, charter extended............	152
International Trust and Banking Company, to incorporate......	101
Investment and Guarantee Company, to amend charter of........	507
Iron bridge over Presumpscot river, relating to................	536
Isle of Springs, relating to roads in...........................	218
Islands in Casco Bay, certain of acquired by annexation........	628

RESOLVES.

Indians, Passamaquoddy tribe, appropriation for................	14
for completion of church........	27
Penobscot tribe, appropriation for.....................	16
Indian township, in favor of roads in.........................	13
Industrial School for Girls, appropriation for 1904.............	22
to provide for expenses of.........	14
Island Falls, town, in favor of................................	26

J.
PUBLIC LAWS.

Judge of probate, Hancock, salary of..........................	9
Sagadahoc, salary of.......................	98
Washington, salary of......................	167
Judges of municipal courts, relating to giving counsel by.......	91
of police courts, commitments by, relating to..........	66
probate, examination before...........................	72
Junk, dealers in, relating to...................................	105
Justice of superior court, Cumberland, salary of................	181
Justices of supreme judicial court, salary of...................	16

PRIVATE AND SPECIAL LAWS.

Jenkin's Cove, Mattawamkeag river, piers in...................	171
Jewell, John M., authorized to build dam across Sebasticook river	411
Jimmy pond, to prohibit ice fishing in.........................	405
Johnson's Bay, Bion M. Pike authorized to extend wharf into..	567
John's pond, to prohibit bait fishing in.........................	414
Jonesport, to prohibit dumping of fish offal into waters of......	533
Railway Company, to incorporate....................	405
Jordan, Patrick Henry, pension to widow of...................	433

RESOLVES.

Jackson, town, in favor of.....................................	52
Jerusalem plantation, repair of roads in........................	24
Judiciary committee, in favor of officers of....................	37

K.

PUBLIC LAWS.

	PAGE
Keoka lake, taking of black bass in	70
Kennebec clerk of courts shall be clerk of law court	19
county attorney, salary of	48
close time in for trout, etc.	186
commissioners, salary of	94
Kennebec river, close time in for migratory fish between bridge and dam at Augusta	118*
Kennel license, provision for	82
Knox county attorney, salary of	198
protection of shore birds in	200
supreme judicial court, terms of, holden in	10

PRIVATE AND SPECIAL LAWS.

Katahdin Pulp and Paper Company, to extend powers of	68
Kennebago lake, to regulate fishing in	414
Kennebec county, protection of deer in, act for	475
Light and Heat Company, authorized to issue bonds,	23
Log Driving Company to maintain piers and booms in Kennebec river	403
river, Great Northern Paper Company may erect piers, etc., in	183
Samuel D. Warren authorized to erect piers and booms	473
Valley Railroad Company, to incorporate	251
Kennebunk Electric Light Company authorized to issue bonds	329
town of, authorized to own electric light plant	204
Kibby Dam Company, to incorporate	544
Kineo Trust Company, to incorporate	144
Kittery and York Telephone Company, to incorporate	618
Knox County General Hospital, to incorporate	160
protection of deer in, act for	475

RESOLVES.

Kelley, Stephen J., in favor of	23
King's Daughters Union, in favor of	6
Knapp, J. Calvin, in favor of	51
Knox County General Hospital, in favor of	28

L.

PUBLIC LAWS.

Laboratory of hygiene, establishment of	185
Land agent made forest commissioner	131
Lands or other property taken for railroads, relating to	30
taken for public uses, cost of, how determined	89
taking of by street railroads	28
Large Greenwood pond, ice fishing in, prohibition repealed	119
Laws, publication of, relating to	135
Legacies, devises and bequests, acceptance of by cities and towns,	149

	PAGE
Libellee residing in this state may have decree of divorce.........	31
Libel or slander, actions for..................................	143
Librarian, assistant, salary of.................................	169
License for hunting shore birds, relating to....................	200
of intelligence offices................................	90
non-resident hunters	77
Lien on estray animals for damage done by.....................	36
to mortgagees for costs of foreclosure....................	92
Light, contracts for, by municipalities.........................	59
Lime and lime casks, relating to...............................	160
Limitations of actions against executors and administrators....	165
Lincoln county, protection of shore birds in.....................	200
Lincoln's mill, fishing near, regulated..........................	118
Liquors, sale of, relating to	133
Loan and building associations, relating to.....................	61
Lobsters with eggs attached, protection of.....................	179
taking and sale of...................................	55
Location of railroads, recording of.............................	70
of railroads, width of.................................	27
of street railroads....................................	66
of streets	40
Lost goods, duties of finder....................................	35
Lots and grounds of schoolhouses, fencing of...................	108

PRIVATE AND SPECIAL LAWS.

Lake Auburn, to protect waters of............................	377
Webb, to prohibit ice fishing in..........................	535
Land Agent to convey rights of way to Fish River Railroad....	68
Lee Telephone Company, to incorporate.......................	442
Lewiston, Brunswick and Bath Street Railway, charter amended,	200
election of city officers..............................	546
Municipal court, relating to........................	557
Street department in, to provide for.................	415
Trust and Safe Deposit Company may establish branch at Freeport	499
Libby Meadow Brook Dam Company, to incorporate............	292
Liberty Water Company, to incorporate.......................	239
Library, Auburn, free public, acts and doings made valid........	216
Rockland free, may receive donations.................	157
Light and Heat Company, Kennebec, authorized to issue bonds..	23
Power Company, Boothbay Harbor, to incorporate...	336
Clinton, relating to....................	185
Hancock, to incorporate.............	288
Meduxnekeag, to incorporate.......	263
Newport, to increase powers of....	64
Sanford, to incorporate............	314
Wells, to incorporate..............	311
Wilton, electric, charter extended..	157
Light, Gas and Power Co., Union River, may issue bonds........	16
powers extended	558
Lilly Water Company, to incorporate..........................	163
Lincoln county, protection of deer in...........................	475
street railway, to confer additional powers on..	38
Electric Railway, additional powers given...............	110
pond, to prevent ice fishing in.........................	413

	PAGE
Lisbon, to supply town of, with pure water	393
Little pond, to prohibit sale of fish from	489
Sebago pond, to fix open season for fishing	491
Wood island annexed to Phippsburg	628
Livermore Falls Water Company, to incorporate	151
Loan, county of Piscataquis authorized to make	131
Fort Fairfield authorized to make	431
and Trust Co., Bangor, to amend and extend charter of,	432
Lobsters, relating to taking of near Matinicus and Criehaven	149
Lobster traps, Pigeon Bay, relating to	413
Location, Fish River Railroad, relating to width of	69
Log Driving Company, Androscoggin, to incorporate	444
Dead River, charter amended	378
Kennebec, to maintain piers, etc., in river,	403
Machias, charter amended	458
Moose river, charter amended	437
Passadumkeag, charter amended	170
Penobscot, charter amended	275
Logs, prize, Penobscot river, relating to	601
Long lake, Naples, draw bridge at outlet	734
pond to prevent sale of fish from	489
bait fishing in	412
Longwood, Real Estate Company, to construct wharf in Long Lake	527
Lubec and Machias Railway Company, to establish	408
Narrows, B. M. Pike authorized to build wharf into	567
C. H. Clark authorized to build wharf into	564
J. C. Pike authorized to build wharf into	564
Lubec, Smelts to prevent destruction of, in waters of	404
Trust and Banking Company, to incorporate	389
Water Company, to incorporate	364
Lumber Company, St. John River, may erect piers, etc	337
Lumbering Company, Penobscot, Charter amended	483
Lumberman's Electric Railway Company, to incorporate	575

RESOLVES.

Land Agent authorized to sell certain public lots	17
public lots in Dallas plantation	30
Lee Normal Academy, in favor of	42
Lewey and Long lakes, in aid of navigation of	46
Libby, C. C., in favor of	26, 50
Library, state, clerk hire in during legislative session	47
in favor of	44
License, peddlers', reimbursement for, part of	56
Lincoln county, for completion of records of clerk of courts	40
Enoch, Governor, repair of tomb of	31
Little, Jacob R., in favor of	23
Loan, temporary, 1903 and 1904	15

M.

PUBLIC LAWS.

	PAGE
Mackerel, taking of with seines, to regulate....................	6
Madawaska training school, relating to........................	181
Magistrates, fees and costs of, relating to.....................	147
Maine Mining Bureau, to create.............................	189
Maine State Agricultural Society, receipts exempt from attachment for three months....	60
stipend to	178
Maintenance of bastard children, relating to...................	27
Marriages and deaths, preservation of records of, prior to 1892..	168˙
Married women, relating to rights of..........................	57
Mayfield plantation, ice fishing in Palmer pond, permitted.....	151
Medicine, repeal of section relating to practice of..............	42
Members of the government, compensation of, relating to........	202
Menhaden, taking of with seines, relating to...................	6
Meridian lines and standard of length, relating to............	162
Merrymeeting bay, open season for shad and alewives in......	7
Metallurgical cabinet, to be established.......................	189
Migratory fish, in Mill river, relating to......................	118
not to be taken within 500 yards of dam, fishway or millrace	118
relating to	6
to correct error and repeal act relating to......	93
Militia, retirement of officers of, relating to....................	59
relating to enlistments in..............................	57
staff of commander-in-chief, relating to...............	173
Mill river, migratory fish in, relating to.......................	118
Mining bureau, to create......................................	189
Moorings, permanent, in harbors, placing of...................	91
Moose, non-residents to pay license for hunting of............	77
Moose, shipment of..	78˙
Mortgaged personal property, exchange or sale of regulated....	101
Mortgage of personal property, notice of foreclosure on, relating to	169
Mortgages, lien for costs of foreclosure on.....................	92
Motor vehicles on public streets, to regulate use of............	200
Municipal courts, judges of, counsel by, relating to............	91
officers may direct manner of construction of railroads	16
Municipalities authorized to contract for water, gas and light...	49
Musicians, enlistment of, by colonel of regiment...............	58
Mutilated lobsters, evidence that same are not of required length	55

PRIVATE AND SPECIAL LAWS.

Machias Log Driving Company, charter amended...............	458
Union Power Company, to incorporate.............	193
McGraw pond, to prohibit sale of fish taken from...............	489
Madison Branch of Augusta Trust Company, to authorize......	527
town of, authorized to purchase bridge with Anson.....	399
Madunkeunk Dam and Improvement Company, to incorporate..	485
Magalloway river, to prohibit bait fishing in...................	412
Maine and New Hampshire Railroad, to incorporate............	402
bonds, State Treasurer to purchase......................	8
Coast Telephone Company, to incorporate...............	532

INDEX.

	PAGE
Maine General Hospital, charter amended......................	36
Historical Society, authorized to hold real estate........	344
Investment and Guarantee Company, charter amended..	507
Lake Ice Company, authorized to increase capital stock..	193
Midland Railroad Company, to incorporate..............	211
Water and Electric Power Company, Dexter, charter extended...	470
Wesleyan Seminary and Female College, name changed,	480
Manchester and Winthrop, Augusta, Winthrop and Gardiner Railway authorized to furnish electricity to...................	119
Malaga island annexed to Phippsburg........................	628
Manufacturing Company, Matagamon, charter amended.........	80
Mattanawcook, charter extended......	80
Manufacturing and Power Company, Sebasticook, to incorporate,	429
Mapleton and Presque Isle Railroad Company, to incorporate...	122
Maranocook, to prohibit ice fishing in.........................	405
Mark island, annexed to Phippsburg.........................	628
Matagamon Manufacturing Company, charter amended........	80
Matinicus island, relating to taking lobsters near...............	149
Mattanawcook Manufacturing Company, charter extended.......	80
Mattawamkeag river, G. H. Hanscom authorized to erect piers in,	129
J. C. Patchell authorized to erect piers, etc., in	149
piers etc., in, at Jenkin's cove.............	171
Springer Lumber Co., to erect booms in..	89
Mayo, Edward J., wharf in Sebec Lake, authorized to maintain,	400
Meadow Brook Dam Company, Libby, to incorporate..........	292
Meduxnekeag Light and Power Company, to incorporate.......	263
Merchant's Trust Company, to incorporate....................	495
Merrill, F. J., authorized to construct tide wheel in Damariscotta river	365
Trust Company, to incorporate.......................	194
Merrymeeting Bay bridge, relating to rebuilding of............	625
Messalonskee lake, to prohibit ice fishing in...................	404
Midland Railroad Company, to incorporate....................	211
Milbridge and Cherryfield Electric Railway Company, relating to franchise of	456
Military and Naval Orphan Asylum, Bath, relating to..........	479
Millinocket Trust Company, to incorporate....................	258
Monson, town of, authorized to remove bodies of deceased persons	67
Moose River Log Driving Company, charter amended..........	437
South Branch Log Driving Company, to incorporate	425
Morrill pond, to prohibit fishing in...........................	490
Mortgage, Fish River Railroad, to ratify......................	105
Mount Abram Cemetery Company, to incorporate..............	379
Desert, protection of deer in...........................	412
Mousam River Railroad, consolidated with other lines..........	284
second channel authorized.....................	230
Movable sidewalk, A. M. Goddard and others to build.........	618
M. T. Alley pond, to prohibit bait fishing in...................	412
Municipal Court, Auburn, Jurisdiction of, relating to............	375
Bar Harbor, to establish......................	8
Bath, appointment of recorder for...........	505

INDEX.   129

	PAGE
Municipal Court, Biddeford, jurisdiction of, relating to	215
Biddeford, recorder of, relating to	735
Brunswick, to establish	434
Dover, charter amended	120
to provide blanks for	227
Eastport, to establish	356
Ellsworth, relating to	453
Lewiston, relating to	557
Norway, relating to	580
Old Town, relating to	231
Rumford Falls, additional to charter of	503
Westbrook, charter amended	188
West Hancock, charter amended	161
Winthrop, to establish	538
Munsungun Telephone Company, to incorporate	617
Mutual Fire Insurance Company, charter extended	152

RESOLVES.

Madawaska Training School, in favor of	28
Magalloway plantation, repair of road in	33
Maine Children's Home Society, in favor of	53
Eye and Ear Infirmary, in favor of	20
General Hospital, in favor of	25
Home for Friendless Boys, in favor of	23
Insane, to renovate barn	47
Industrial School for Girls, to provide for expenses of	14
appropriation for 1904	22
School for the Deaf, in favor of	19
state library, in favor of	44
state prison, appropriation for	60
electric lighting plant for	69
in favor of committee on	26, 30
year book, for purchase of	11
volunteers, in war with Spain, extra pay for	9
Manson, John W., in favor of	39
Mariaville, town, in favor of	54
aid of bridge in	35
Mattawamkeag bridge, in favor of	40
Messenger to judiciary committee, in favor of	37
Military and Naval Orphan Asylum, in favor of	8
Mitchell, Joseph, Jr., in favor of	52
Lewey, in favor of	52
Monument, Maine Soldiers, Andersonville, in favor of	21
Moosehead lake, in aid of navigation of	34
Morrill, John A., to pay for printing report of	36
Morrison, G. E., in favor of	44
Moscow, town, in favor of	25

N.

PUBLIC LAWS.

	PAGE
Nails, repeal of section relating to inspection of...............	41
National guard, officers in, retirement of......................	59
Naval reserve, established as part of the national guard........	72
Non-resident hunters on wild lands shall have guides..........	188
Normal schools, purposes and work of.......................	172
appropriation for	181
Notice of foreclosure of mortgage of personal property, relating to,	169
Nuisances, relating to...	119

PRIVATE AND SPECIAL LAWS.

Naples, drawbridge at outlet of Long Lake, to authorize.........	734
Water Company, to incorporate......................	517
Nashville Plantation, to legalize doings of.....................	536
Navigation, Eagle lake, by steam, to authorize.................	401
Range ponds, by steam or electricity, to authorize..	560
New Meadows river, bridge over to authorize..................	477
Newport Light and Power Company, to increase powers of.....	64
Norcross Transportation Co., to erect buoys in West Branch..	411
Normal School, Presque Isle, to establish......................	363
Norridgewock Falls Bridge, Anson and Madison authorized to purchase	378
sale of authorized.................	399
North pond, to prohibit sale of fish from.....................	489
Northport Wesleyan Grove Campmeeting Association, charter amended	158
Norton brook, to prohibit throwing sawdust into..............	534
Norway and Paris Street Railway may purchase Oxford Light Company	75
assessors of, doings of made valid....................	346
Municipal Court, relating to.........................	580
Number Nine lake, to prohibit ice fishing in..................	474

RESOLVES.

Narraguagus river, in aid of bridge across.....................	48
National Forest Reserve, in favor of..........................	41
Navigation, Lewey, Long and Big lakes, in aid of..............	46
Moosehead lake, in aid of.........................	34
Newell, Mary, in favor of Rockland for care of................	41
New Sharon, town, in aid of bridge in........................	50
Norcross Transportation Company, in favor of.................	34
Normal Academy, Lee, in favor of............................	42
School, Castine, in favor of........................	38
Farmington, in favor of........................	29
Western state, in favor of.....................	51
Number Four, waiver of forfeiture of public lots in.............	54

O.

PUBLIC LAWS.

Oaks pond, ice fishing in, prohibition repealed................	141
Obstructing officers, in discharge of duty, penalty for..........	117
Officers, obstructing or hindering of, penalty for..............	117
of savings banks, list of shall be published............	45
of ship's company, title and grade of..................	73
public, duties payable by............................	67
town, compensation of................................	87
truant, election of...................................	50
Old home week, time set apart for...........................	33
Old junk, dealers in, relating to.............................	105
Orange river, fishing in regulated............................	118
Oxford county, bounty on bears, to provide for................	197
commissioners, compensation of..............	5

PRIVATE AND SPECIAL LAWS.

Oakfield, treasurer and collector of relating to...................	572
Old Orchard Electric Light Company, to issue bonds...........	6
Trust and Banking Company, charter extended.....	223
Old Town, city charter amended............................	330
municipal court, relating to........................	231
Open season, Sebago lake, for fishing..........................	403
Wilson lake, for fishing.........................	550
Orland, destruction of fish in, relating to......................	552
Orono Pulp and Paper Co., authorized to generate electricity...	148
Orphan Asylum, Bath Military and Naval, relating to..........	479
Otter pond, to prohibit bait fishing in..........................	412
Overseers of Poor, Portland, election and tenure of.............	266
Oxford Light Company, authorized to sell its property..........	75

RESOLVES.

Oakes, Albion, in favor of......................................	53
Officers of Senate and House, in favor of.......................	36
Orphan Asylum, Bath, Military and Naval, in favor of..........	8
St. Elizabeth Roman Catholic, in favor of......	25

P.

PUBLIC LAWS.

Packing of paper, repeal of section relating to...................	148
sardines, to regulate..............................	139
Palmer pond, ice fishing in, prohibition repealed................	151
Paper, packing of, repeal of statute relating to.................	148
Pardons, repeal of certain sections relating to...................	58
Partnership property, relating to attachment of................	65
Partridge, close time for.......................................	190
Paupers having no legal settlement, relating to.................	114
Pawnbrokers, to regulate business of...........................	105
Pearl ashes, repeal of sections relating to inspection of..........	41
Pending cases in insolvency courts, discharge of debtors in.....	104

	PAGE
Penobscot, clerk of courts shall be clerk of law court..........	19
salary of register of probate......................	30
river, close time for migratory fish in portions of...	118
Permanent moorings in harbors, placing of....................	91
school fund, assessment and expenditure of in certain towns	139
Permit for erecting electric lines, from municipal officers......	194
Permits for erecting posts and wires, from municipal officers....	102
Perry pond, ice fishing in, prohibition repealed.................	126
Personal property, mortgaged, sale or exchange of regulated....	101
Persons, insane, appointment of guardians for..................	69
Pharmacy, appointment of commission of.......................	183
Pheasant, close time for..	191
Piscataquis county attorney, salary of.........................	170
Pictures in public places, to prevent injury to..................	49
Plans, recording of, to provide for.............................	51
Play grounds, fencing of, relating to...........................	108
Plover, close time for..	190
Political caucuses, relating to..................................	174
Pool rooms may be permitted to remain open till midnight.......	54
Porcupines, to establish bounty on.............................	204
Porgies, taking of with seines, to regulate.....................	6
Pork, to repeal certain section relating to inspection of..........	41
Posts and lines for electricity, erection of, to regulate...........	194
wires electric, municipal officers to control erection of.	102
Pot ashes, repeal of sections relating to inspection of..........	41
Pounds, repeal of chapter relating to...........................	41
Practice of dentistry, to regulate...............................	72
Probate, judge of, Hancock county, salary of..................	9
judges, relating to examination before................	72
Prohibitory law, enforcement of at fairs.......................	177
Proof of attested instruments, relating to......................	93
Property exempt from attachment and execution..............	64
taxation, relating to....................	43
title to when on leased land.........................	117
Prosecutions, criminal, taking of bail in.......................	96
Protection of forests, commission for, to create................	131
lobsters with eggs attached......................	179
shore birds, act for.............................	200
trees and shrubs from insects....................	88
Provisions of wills, waiving of by widows......................	59
Publication of list of officers of savings banks, required........	45
public laws, relating to.........................	135
Public drains and sewers, crossing of railroad locations by......	106
health, relating to.......................................	185
laws, publication of....................................	135
lots, "timber and grass" on, meaning of term............	197
officers, duties payable by..............................	67
schools, superintendent of, employment of.............	34
uses, costs in taking lands and property for.............	89
ways, to regulate use of automobiles on................	200
Purse and drag seines, to regulate use of......................	6

PRIVATE AND SPECIAL LAWS.

	PAGE
Palermo, Smith Cemetery Association, to incorporate...........	192
Park Association, Camden Trotting, relating to.................	202
Parlin stream, fishing in, prohibition in part removed............	484
Parmachenee lake, to prohibit bait fishing in.....................	412
Party caucuses, Augusta, qualification for participation in.......	537
Passadumkeag Log Driving Company, charter amended........	170
Patchell, Joseph C., to erect piers and booms in Mattawamkeag river	149
Patrons of Husbandry, Huntoon Grange, to incorporate.........	228
Patten, Tamarack Club, to incorporate........................	324
Telegraph and Telephone Company, to incorporate......	499
Trust Company, to incorporate........................	462
Peaks Island Water and Light Company, to incorporate........	565
Pease pond, ice fishing in, relating to..........................	381
Penobscot Chemical Fibre Company, may generate electricity...	150
Log Driving Company, charter amended............	275
Lumbering Company, charter amended..............	483
river, prize logs in, relating to......................	601
Pension to Widow of Patrick Henry Jordan...................	433
Peoples' Ferry, acceptance of by Sagadahoc County, relating to..	625
Company, to incorporate.......................	200
Pepperell Trust Company, to incorporate......................	98
Petit Menan Point, hunting on, relating to.....................	482
Phillips and Rangeley Railroad Company may purchase franchises of Madrid Railroad Company.......................	515
Trust Company, to incorporate........................	491
Phippsburg, annexation of certain islands to, act for............	628
Pickerel pond, to prohibit ice fishing in........................	405
Piers and booms, Kennebec river, Great Northern Paper Company to erect in.................	183
Log Driving Company, to erect in,	403
river, Sam'l D. Warren, to erect in,	473
Mattawamkeag river, G. H. Hanscom, to erect,	129
at Jenkin's cove.........	171
Joseph C. Patchell, to erect	149
Portage Lake Mill Company, to erect..........	564
St. John River Lumber Company, to erect at Van Buren	337
Sebec river, Boston Excelsior Co., to erect.....	414
Pigeon Hill bay, lobster traps in, relating to....................	413
Pike, Bion M., to extend wharf into Lubec Narrows............	567
Johnson's bay	567
Family Association, to incorporate......................	316
Jacob C., to extend wharf into Lubec Narrows...........	564
Piscataquis, County of, authorized to make loan.................	131
River Storage Company, to incorporate............	597
Pittsfield Trust Company, to incorporate.......................	85
Plantation, Saint Francis, to legalize acts of...................	64
Winterville, to change name of......................	591
Police Court, Rockland, relating to............................	177
force, Bangor, pension to injured members of............	433
Portland, to regulate............................	581

	PAGE
Pollock, Frenchman's bay, relating to taking of.................	323
Pollution of waters of Sebago lake, to prevent.................	156
Portage Lake Mill Company, maintain piers, etc., and operate steamboat	564
Portland and Brunswick Street Ry., additional powers given to..	76
Cape Elizabeth Ferry Co., to amend charter of...	265
Rumford Falls Railway, relating to powers of.....	365
to legalize doings of......	64
to regulate appointment of constables in..............	360
assessors, overseers and school committee of, election and tenure of.......................................	266
Central Trust Company, to incorporate..............	111
city, to amend charter of...........................	116
Home for Aged Men, to amend charter of...........	73
police force, to regulate.............................	581
school committee of, relating to......................	110
Widows' Wood Society, charter amended.............	198
Young Women's Christian Association, relating to....	269
Portsmouth, Kittery and York Street Railway, additional powers given	21
Power Company, Carrabasset, to erect dams in Anson and Embden	338
Maine Water and Electric, to extend charter of	470
Sanford, consolidated with other corporations	284
Sebasticook, reorganized with additional powers	10
Union River, in relation to powers of.......	16
to incorporate	193
Pownal, deer in, open time on...........................	481
Presque Isle Normal School, to establish.....................	363
Water Company, authorized to issue bonds.......	266
Presumpscot river, iron bridge over, relating to................	536
Prize logs on Penobscot river, relating to.....................	601
Proprietors of Union wharf, additional powers given to........	169
Protection of deer and moose in Sagadahoc county.............	532
Kennebec, Knox, Waldo and Lincoln counties,	475
squirrels and chipmunks in Knox county........	588
Prouts Neck Water Company, powers enlarged.................	270
Public building, Caribou authorized to hold stock in............	551
Library, Auburn, concerning..........................	216
Rockland, to establish.........................	157
Works, Auburn, charter amended.,...................	210
reservations, Hancock county, powers of trustees of....	556
Pulp and Paper Company, Katahdin, to extend powers of......	68
Orono, authorized to generate electricity	148
Pure water, Bangor, to supply people of, with.................	561
Houlton, to supply people of, with.................	227
Purse seines, Damariscotta river, to permit use of, in..........	549

RESOLVES.

	PAGE
Parkman, town, in favor of	55
Passamaquoddy Tribe of Indians, appropriation for	14
for completion of church	27
in favor of representative of	52
Pay roll of House	69
Senate	60
Peddlers' licenses, reimbursement in part of	56
Penobscot Tribe of Indians, appropriation for	16
in favor of representative of	52
Pensions, state, appropriation for	7
examination of claims for	13
Pol, Bernhard, in favor of	10
Portland, Temporary Home for Women and Children, in aid of	4
Preservation of Fort William Henry, in favor of	24
of regimental rolls	7
Prison, Maine state, appropriation for	60
electric lighting plant for	60
Protection of fish, appropriation for	8
Protection and distribution of Revised Statutes, relating to	69
Public lots, Dallas plantation, sale of authorized	30
Number Four, waiver of forfeiture of	54
re-establishment of boundaries of	35
waiving of forfeiture of	17

Q.

PUBLIC LAWS.

Quail, close time for	19c

PRIVATE AND SPECIAL LAWS.

Quimby pond, to regulate fishing in	413

R.

PUBLIC LAWS.

Rabbits, for better protection of	173
Railroad commissioners, additional powers over street railroads given	16
duties of, relating to	138
signals, protection of	18
surveys, relating to disturbance of marks of	167
Railroads, coal sheds, location of	127
land taken by, relating to	30
municipal officers may control location of	16
recording of location of	70
repeal of certain sections relating to	43
Railroads, street, extending statutes relating to	19
railroad commissioners given additional power over	16
location of, relating to	66

INDEX.

	PAGE
Railroads, street, taking of land by	28
ways across station grounds, relating to	61
width of location of	27
Raising and lowering of ways, damages for	43
Real estate, conveyances of, record of	5
descent of	122
Record of deeds of conveyance	5
deeds of release	182
locations of railroads	70
Recording of plans, to provide for	51
Reference table, of laws, preparation of by secretary of state	46
Reform school, name changed	109
amendment and extension of statute	22
Register of deeds, fees of	95
probate, Hancock county, salary of	189
Penobscot county, salary of	30
Sagadahoc county, salary of	170
Registered guides must accompany parties during certain months,	188
Release, deeds of, record of, relating to	182
Religious institutions, exemption of from collateral inheritance tax	120
Removal of snow from street railroads, municipal officers may direct	17
Repair of roads in unincorporated places, relating to	15
Reserve fund of savings banks, relating to	83
naval, to establish as part of National Guard	72
Retired list of officers of militia, relating to	59
Returns of assessors, repeal of certain sections relating to	46
savings banks, trust companies, etc., relating to	11
trust and banking companies, relating to	137
vital statistics, relating to	141
Roads and bridges in unincorporated townships, repair of	14
raising or lowering of, damages from	43
state, improvement of, statute for	49
Rogues, commitment of	37
Rules for descent of real estate	122

PRIVATE AND SPECIAL LAWS.

Railroad, Aroostook Valley Co. may purchase Presque Isle Electric Light Company	471
relating to	469
Auburn and Turner Co.	33
Bangor and Aroostook, may purchase Fish River R. R.,	24
extensions authorized	361
may extend yard tracks in Houlton	70
mortgage of confirmed	24
Bluehill and Bucksport, electric, charter extended	473
Boothbay, to extend time of construction of	528
Fish River, lease ratified	24
mortgage ratified	23
mortgage of, relating to	105
rights of way over public lands	68
sale of authorized	24
width of location of	69

INDEX.

	PAGE
Railroad, Houlton and Woodstock, electric, to incorporate	255
and Danforth, electric, to incorporate	572
Kennebec Valley, to incorporate	251
Maine and New Hampshire, to incorporate	402
Maine Midland, to incorporate	211
Milbridge and Cherryfield, electric, relating to franchise of	456
Mapleton and Presque Isle, to incorporate	122
Mousam River, consolidated with other lines	284
Phillips and Rangeley, authorized to purchase Madrid R. R.	515
Rumford Falls and Rangeley Lakes, to legalize doings of	67
Washington County, sale of, authorized	219
Wiscasset, Waterville and Farmington, franchise extended	74
Railway, Atlantic Shore Line, consolidated with other lines	284
Auburn, Mechanic Falls and Norway, additional powers given	555
Augusta, Winthrop and Gardiner, charter amended	91
to supply electricity, in Manchester and Winthrop	119
Bangor Street, repeal of section relating to	168
Berwick, Eliot and York, powers enlarged	25
Camden and Liberty, to incorporate	123
Cherryfield and Milbridge, to incorporate	466
Eastport, to extend charter of	417
Ellsworth, to extend charter of	167
Hancock County, to extend charter of	167
Jonesport, to incorporate	405
Lewiston, Brunswick and Bath, charter amended	200
Lincoln County, street, additional powers given	38
relating to	110
Lubec and Machias, to establish	408
Lumbermen's Electric, to incorporate	575
Norway and Paris, authorized to purchase Oxford Light Co.	75
Portland and Brunswick, additional powers given	76
and Rumford Falls, to legalize doings of	64
powers of, relating to	365
Portsmouth, Kittery and York, additional powers to	21
Rockland, Thomaston and Camden, charter amended	78
Sanford and Cape Porpoise, to consolidate with other lines	284
Skowhegan and Norridgewock, to extend line of	575
Waldo, to amend and extend charter of	71
Waterville and Oakland, additional powers given	82
Winterport, Frankfort and Prospect, to incorporate	440
Rangeley Trust Company, to incorporate	366
Water Company, to incorporate	106
Range ponds, navigation by steam or electricity, to authorize	560
Real Estate Co., Longwood, to construct wharf in Long Lake	527
Realty Company, Vickery, granted additional powers	111

INDEX.

	PAGE
Recorder, Bath municipal court, appointment of................	505
Biddeford municipal court, relating to.................	735
Reed plantation, to annex part of to Drew plantation..........	550
Reservoir Dam Company, West Branch, to incorporate..........	277
Reservations, public, Hancock, powers granted to trustees of...	556
Rights of way over public lands, to Fish River Railroad........	68
Road commissioners, Boothbay Harbor, election of, relating to..	620
Eden, relating to........................	734
Roads in Isle of Springs, relating to...........................	218
Rockland, city, to amend charter of...........................	587
free library, to establish...........................	157
police court, relating to...........................	177
Thomaston and Camden Street Ry., charter amended,	78
Round Pond Improvement Company, to incorporate............	294
Rumford Falls and Rangeley Lakes R. R. Co., to legalize doings of	67
municipal court, additional to charter of........	503
Village Corporation, limits of extended.........	106
Rump pond, to prohibit bait fishing in........................	412

RESOLVES.

Randall, E. E., in favor of..................................	51
Rangeley lake, in aid of fish hatchery at.....................	13
Rankin, Mary C., in favor of.................................	7
Records of clerk of courts, Lincoln county, completion of......	40
Reed plantation, to fix valuation of...........................	32
Reform School, in favor of.................................	10
Regimental rolls, preservation of, in adjutant general's office...	7
Repair, highway, Upton, in aid of.............................	33
south wing of Capitol, to provide for.................	30
tomb of Enoch Lincoln, to provide for................	31
Rhodes, Cecil John, scholarships, to provide for examination for,	60
Revised Statutes, publication and distribution of................	69
Revision of statutes, printing report of committee on..........	36
in favor of committee on................	19
in favor of clerk of committee on........	38
Revision of public laws, in relation to completion of............	12
Roads in Indian township, in aid of...........................	13
Rockland, city, reduction from school fund, to repay............	11
for care of Mary Newell, to repay for..........	41

S.

PUBLIC LAWS.

Sagadahoc county attorney, salary of.........................	166
judge of probate, salary of..................	98
protection of shore birds in..................	200
register of probate, salary of................	170
Saint Croix river, close time on trout, etc.....................	186
Salary, adjutant general.......................................	81
assistant librarian	169

INDEX.

	PAGE
Salary, county attorney, Hancock	171
Kennebec	48
Knox	198
Piscataquis	170
Salary, county attorney, Sagadahoc	166
Somerset	170
Washington	167
York	48
county commissioners, Kennebec	94
Waldo	21
judge of probate, Hancock	9
Sagadahoc	98
Washington	167
justice superior court, Cumberland	181
justices supreme judicial court	16
register of probate, Hancock	189
Penobscot	30
Sagadahoc	170
sheriff, Aroostook	53
county treasurer, York	15
Sale and analysis of commercial fertilizers	180
of mortgaged personal property, relating to	101
of trust property, authority for	71
Sales, tax, amendment of law relating to	32, 33
repeal of sections relating to	32
Salmon, close time for in portions of St. Croix river	118
landlocked, close time for	186
Sandpipers, close time for	190
Sardines, packing of, relating to	139
Savings banks, duties of officers and corporators of	45
investment of funds of	152
list of officers of to be published	45
reserve fund of	83
taxation of	11
unclaimed deposits in	84
Scholars, conveyance of	51
School agents in unorganized townships, appointment of	99
for boys, formerly reform school	109
children of certain age required to attend	107
committee, relating to powers and duties of	79
fund, permanent, expenditure of in certain towns	139
raising and expending of, relating to	128
tax from trust and banking companies, one half for	190
house lots, and grounds, relating to	108
Schooling of children in unorganized townships, relating to	98
Schools, normal and Madawaska training, appropriation for	181
superintendent of, to define powers of	147
appointment of	34
Sea and shore fisheries, statutes amended	55, 156
Sebago lake, close time in	187
Secretary of state, repeal of sections relating to duties of	45
to prepare tables of acts and resolves	46
Service in trustee suits, relating to	64
Sewers, public, crossing of railroad locations by	106
Shad, taking of with seines, to regulate	6

INDEX.

	PAGE
Shares of loan and building associations, maturity of............	61
Sheep, better protection of......................................	81
transportation of	13
Sheriff, Aroostook county, salary of............................	53
Ship's company, composition of................................	73
Shore birds, protection of, act for.............................	200
Short lobsters, relating to liberation of.........................	55
Signals, railroad, protection of................................	18
Silk, repeal of bounties on.....................................	44
Slander or libel, actions for, relating to.......................	143
Smelts, fishing for and sale of regulated.......................	156
Snipe, close time for	190
Snow, municipal officers may direct removal of from railroads..	17
Societies, agricultural, relating to exemption of receipts from attachment	60
Soldiers, Aroostook war, in aid of..............................	97
burial of widows of.............................	159
Somerset, county attorney, salary of...........................	170
Speed of automobiles on public ways, to regulate................	200
Spendthrift, appointment of guardian for.......................	70
Spitting on floors of street cars prohibited....................	106
Squaw Pan lake, fishing in allowed in inlet of..................	100
Staff of commander-in-chief of militia.........................	173
Standard of length and of meridian lines.......................	162
weight of beans, bushel of..........................	14
State and city elections, voting at, to regulate.................	132
elections, printing and distributing ballots for............	8
examination and certification of teachers.................	47
laboratory of hygiene, to establish......................	185
Station grounds, relating to ways across.......................	61
State of Maine, act to cede lands of to U. S...................	146
paupers, relating to...............................	114
reform school, relating to.............................	22
name changed	109
roads, improvement of................................	49
secretary of, repeal of sections relating to duties of........	45
treasurer, relating to duties of.........................	46
repeal of sections relating to duties of........	45
required to send warrants of assessment of state tax, to be assessed.............................	46
Statues in public places, to prevent injury to...................	49
Stickers, use of in voting.....................................	8
Stipend to agricultural societies...............................	177
Stray animals, liability for damages by........................	36
beasts, proceedings by finder of........................	35
Street cars, spitting on floors of, prohibited...................	106
railroads, extending of statutes relating to..............	19
locations of, relating to......................	66
commissioners given additional powers over....	16
taking of land by............................	28
Streets, abuttors on, assessment of damages upon..............	129
relating to dedication of.............................	40
Suits in equity, to quiet title..................................	115
trustee, relating to.......................................	63
Sunday, close time for hunting................................	187

INDEX.

	PAGE
Superintendent of schools, employment of.....................	34
powers of, to define................	147
town, election of...................	79
Superior court, Cumberland, salary of justice of..............	181
Support of bastard children...................................	27
Supreme judicial court, clerks of in certain counties shall be clerks of law courts................	19
Knox, times of holding terms of......	10
salary of justices of.................	16
Surgery, repeal of sections relating to practice of.............	42
Surveys of railroads, disturbance of marks of, to prohibit.....	167
Swine, transportation of, relating to..........................	13

PRIVATE AND SPECIAL LAWS.

Saco, Union Trust Company, to incorporate....................	138
Safety deposit boxes, Auburn Savings Bank to construct.......	6
Sagadahoc county, annexation of certain islands to, act for......	628
to rebuild Merrymeeting Bay bridge, etc....	625
protection of deer and moose in............	532
Saint Francis plantation, to legalize acts of.....................	64
Georges river, sawdust in, relating to....................	345
John River Dam Company, to incorporate..............	301
Lumber Company, to erect piers, etc., in Saint John river	337
River Toll Bridge Co., to incorporate........	185
Salem, to regulate fishing in streams in........................	549
Sandy stream, to prevent throwing sawdust into...............	400
Sanford and Cape Porpoise Ry. Co., consolidated with other lines,	284
Light and Power Company, to incorporate............	314
Light and Water Company, charter amended..........	295
may consolidate with other lines	295
Power Company, consolidated with other lines........	284
resolve in favor of amended........................	209
Trust Company, to amend charter of.................	118
Sangerville Improvement Company, to ratify lease of...........	501
Savings Bank, Auburn, to erect safe deposit boxes............	6
Sawdust, throwing into Norton, Brown or Heath brooks, to prevent	534
Ellis stream, to prevent.................	502
Half Moon stream, to prevent..........	400
St. Georges river, to prevent..........	345
Seven Tree and Crawford ponds, tributaries of	603
Scallop Island, former name Burnt Island.....................	346
Scarboro, to prohibit taking clams in..........................	489
School Board, Brewer, to establish.............................	352
Committee, Portland, female members of, election and tenure	266
election of, relating to...........	110
Skowhegan, election of, relating to........	351
Searsport, Village Cemetery Association, to incorporate.......	472
Water Company, to incorporate.....................	347
Sea birds, hunting of in launches prohibited..................	534

	PAGE
Sebago lake, open time for fishing in	403
to prevent pollution of waters of	156
Sebasticook Manufacturing and Power Company, to incorporate,	429
Power Company, legalized and additional powers given	10
river, J. M. Jewell to erect dam across	411
Sebec Dam Company, to amend charter of	216
lake, E. J. Mayo authorized to maintain wharf in	400
certain tributaries of opened for fishing	479
river, Boston Excelsior Company to locate piers and booms in	414
Second channel authorized in Mousam river	230
Security Trust Company, to incorporate	271
Seines, Billing's Cove, use of in prohibited	351
Damariscotta river, use of in prohibited	549
Selectmen, Waltham, to legalize doings of	476
Seven ponds, to regulate fishing in	414
Tree pond, to prevent throwing sawdust into tributaries of	603
Sewerage Company, Van Buren, to incorporate	297
Houlton, to provide in	217
Sewer Commission, Bath, to establish	37
Sewers, York, town of authorized to construct	548
Shell fish, Georgetown, better protection of, in	118
Sidewalk, movable, A. M. Goddard and others authorized to construct	618
Skowhegan and Norridgewock Railway and Power Co., authorized to extend line	575
extension of court house, relating to	203
school committee, election of	351
Smelts, Damariscotta river, to protect in spawning season	538
Lubec and Trescott, to protect	404
Upper Kezar pond, to protect in tributaries of	491
Steuben bay, to protect	490
Smith Cemetery Association, Palermo, to incorporate	192
Snow pond, to prevent sale of fish taken from	489
Soldiers in the war with Spain, testimonials to	209
Somerset county, authorized to secure loan for extension of court house	203
Trust Company, to incorporate	385
Sorrento, town of, charter amended	569
South Branch Moose River Dam Company, to incorporate	425
pond, close time on tributaries of	476
Portland, annexation of to Portland, enabling act for	593
Trust and Banking Company, charter extended,	131
West Harbor Trust Company, to incorporate	173
Spawning season, Damariscotta river, to protect smelts during	538
Springer Lumber Company, may erect piers, etc., in Mattawamkeag river	89
Spring lake, to limit number of fish to be taken from	484
Springvale Aqueduct Co., may consolidate with Sanford Light and Power Co.	295
Squirrel Island Village Corporation, to incorporate	93
Squirrels and chipmunks, Knox county, protection of	588
State Tax for 1903, assessment of	629
1904, assessment of	676

INDEX.

	PAGE
State Treasurer, may purchase bonds of State of Maine........	6
Steamboat, Portage Lake Mill Co. authorized to operate........	564
Steam Ferry Company, Bangor and Brewer, charter extended..	151
or electricity, navigation of Range ponds by, to authorize,	560
Steuben bay, to prevent destruction of smelts and tomcods in....	490
Stock Farms, Carrabassett, to enlarge powers of................	353
Storage Company, Piscataquis River, to incorporate............	597
Street Railroad, Auburn and Turner, to incorporate............	33
Houlton and Woodstock, to incorporate........	255
Railway, Auburn, Mechanic Falls and Norway, additional powers given	555
Augusta, Winthrop and Gardiner, charter amended	91
Bangor, repeal of section relating to...........	168
Berwick, Eliot and York, powers enlarged......	25
Boothbay, to extend time of construction of....	528
Camden and Liberty, to incorporate...........	123
Cherryfield and Milbridge, to incorporate......	466
Ellsworth, charter extended....................	167
Eastport, charter extended.....................	417
Hancock County, charter extended.............	167
Lincoln County, additional powers conferred...	38
Electric, relating to...................	110
Lewiston, Brunswick and Bath, charter amended,	200
Portland and Brunswick, additional powers granted	76
Portsmouth, Kittery and York, additional powers granted	21
Rockland, Thomaston and Camden, charter amended	78
Waldo, charter amended......................	71
Waterville and Oakland, additional powers granted	82
Street sewer improvement department, Lewiston, to provide for..	415
commission, Bath, to establish....................	37
Strong, to regulate fishing in streams of......................	549
Water Company, to extend charter of..................	292
Students of agriculture, relating to............................	169
Sullivan Harbor Water Company, to incorporate..............	449
town of, division of, amendment of..................	569
Sunday pond, to prohibit bait fishing in.......................	412
Superintendent of schools, Skowhegan, relating to election of....	351
Swan's Island Telephone and Telegraph Company, to incorporate,	83

RESOLVES.

Saint Elizabeth's Orphan Asylum, in favor of..................	25
Sale of public lots, in certain cases authorized..................	17
Dallas plantation, authorized...............	30
Sandy river, in aid of bridge across..........................	50
Sanford, town, in favor of....................................	11
School for the Deaf, in favor of..............................	19
Scholarships, Cecil John Rhodes, examination for, to provide for,	60
Sea and shore fisheries, appropriation for......................	28
Sebago lake, fish hatchery at.................................	14

	PAGE
Senate and House, in favor of officers of....................	36
pay roll of...	60
Sisters of Mercy, for rebuilding house of.....................	27
Smith, Benjamin, in favor of................................	6
Lyman C., in favor of...............................	33
Society of Sisters of Charity, in favor of....................	18
for hospital of..................	21
Soldiers' monument, Andersonville, for erection of............	21
State assessors, to collect information concerning bridges......	45
Capitol, to provide for repairs to south wing of..........	30
House, elevator, for repair of..........................	19
employees, in favor of.........................	48
library, in favor of......................................	44
clerk hire in during legislative session............	47
pensions, appropriation for.............................	7
examination of claims for......................	13
prison, appropriation for...............................	60
electric lighting plant for........................	69
in favor of committee on........................	26
reform school, in favor of.............................	10
tax, Bowdoinham, to abate part of.....................	49
Statutes, revision of, relating to..............................	36
Steamboat inspectors, compensation of, to provide for..........	6
Stenographer, committee on salaries, in favor of..............	44
judiciary committee, in favor of.................	37
superintendent of schools, to provide...........	51
Survey, topographic, geological and hydrographic, to provide for,	31

T.

PUBLIC LAWS.

Taxation of interest bearing deposits in trust and banking companies	137
exemption of property from.......................	43.
savings banks, relating to........................	11
Tax, collateral inheritance, religious institutions exempt from..	120
sales, repeal of sections relating to.......................	32
amendment of sections relating to..................	32, 33
Taxes, collectors of, bonds of...............................	136
election of	42
and treasurer, may be one and the same person	186
election of made valid......	157
from trust and banking companies, for school fund......	190
Teachers' county conventions, relating to......................	47
state examination and certification of................	47
Teal, protection of, act for.....................................	200
Telegraph and telephone companies, not to occupy route of other lines	108
Thibadeau's landing, relating to fishing above.................	100
Timber and grass, term defined..............................	197
Timber land, better protection of by bounty on porcupines......	204
Time when acts and resolves shall take effect..................	205

	PAGE
Title, suits in equity to quiet same............................	115
to personal property on leased land......................	117
Togue, close time for	186
Town officers, compensation of, relating to....................	87
records of marriages, etc., preservation of those prior to 1892..	168
superintendents of schools, election of..................	79
Training school, Madawaska, appropriation for................	181
Transportation, animals in cars..............................	13
bodies of persons who died of infectious diseases	74
game birds	191
game, regulations for	78
Treasurer, state, relating to duties of..........................	46
repeal of sections relating to duties of........	45
town, election of	42
York county, salary of............................	15
Treasurers and collectors of taxes, election of made valid......	157
may be the same persons...	186
county, repeal of sections relating to duties of......	42
towns and plantations, bonds of....................	125
Trees and shrubs, protection of, from insects and diseases......	88
Trespassers on wild lands	121
Trial justices, commitments by...............................	66
Trout, close time for...	186
Truants, relating to...	107
officers, election of	50
Trust and banking companies, one half of taxes from, appropriated for school fund..........	190
for school fund	190
taxation of interest bearing deposits in	137
Trust estates, judge of probate to authorize sale of.............	71
funds for care of cemeteries, investment of..............	7
Trustees, foreign, authorized to receive and dispose of personal property	184
process, service in	104
reform school, appointment of.......................	22
suits, service on trustee.............................	63

PRIVATE AND SPECIAL LAWS.

Tamarack Club, Patten, to incorporate........................	324
Tax, State, 1903, assessment of...............................	629
1904, assessment of.................................	676
Telegraph and Telephone Company, Forest, to incorporate......	128
Patten, to incorporate.....	499
Telephone and Telegraph Company, Swan's Island, to incorporate	83
Company, Farmers', to incorporate..................	579
Kittery and York, to incorporate..........	618
Lee, to incorporate...................	442
Maine Coast, to incorporate..............	532
Munsungun, to incorporate...............	617
Washington, to incorporate...............	457
Wells, to incorporate...........................	317

INDEX.

	PAGE
Temple Company, Fraternity, to incorporate...................	507
Testimonials to soldiers who served in the war with Spain......	209
Thompson pond, fishing through the ice, relating to...........	109
Three Mile pond, to prohibit fishing through ice...............	405
Ticonic Foot Bridge Company, increase of stock..............	201
Tide wheel, F. J. Merrill to construct in Damariscotta river......	365
Toll Bridge, St. John River Co., to incorporate................	185
Tolls, Bangor Bridge Company, time for taking of extended....	506
Tomcods, Steuben bay, to prevent destruction of................	490
Town, Bucksport, authorized to refund debt...................	202
Castle Hill, to incorporate.............................	130
Hall, Caribou, authorized to take stock in...............	551
Sanford, resolve in favor of amended....................	209
Waltham, to legalize doings of selectmen of.............	476
Williamsburg, to legalize doings of......................	166
Traps, lobster, Pigeon Hill bay, relating to.....................	413
Treasurer and collector, Bangor, relating to....................	571
Brownfield, relating to.................	571
Hallowell, relating to..................	570
Oakfield, relating to...................	572
Waterville, relating to.................	571
Treasurer, Augusta, relating to election of.....................	353
State, to purchase bonds of State of Maine.........	8
Trescott, to prevent destruction of smelts in waters of.........	404
Trotting Park Association, Camden, relating to................	202
Trust and Banking Company, Bluehill, to amend and extend charter of	516
International, to incorporate....	101
Lubec, to incorporate...........	389
Old Orchard, charter extended..	223
S. Portland, charter extended,	131
Van Buren, charter extended...	166
Trust and Safe Deposit Company, Lewiston, to have branch at Freeport	499
Trust Company, Ashland, to incorporate.......................	523
Augusta, capital stock, increase authorized.....	379
charter amended	527
Bangor City, to incorporate....................	319
Camden, charter extended......................	66
Central, to incorporate........................	111
Cumberland, charter extended..................	66
Fort Kent, to incorporate......................	153
Granite, charter extended......................	207
Hallowell, charter extended....................	317
Kineo, to incorporate.........................	144
Merchants, to incorporate.....................	495
Merrill, to incorporate........................	194
Millinocket, to incorporate....................	258
Patten, to incorporate........................	462
Pepperell, to incorporate.....................	98
Phillips, to incorporate.......................	491
Pittsfield, to incorporate......................	85
Rangeley, to incorporate......................	366
Saco, Union, to incorporate...................	138

INDEX.

	PAGE
Trust Company, Sanford, to amend charter	118
Security, to incorporate	271
Somerset, to incorporate	385
South West Harbor, to incorporate	173
Tyler-Fogg, to incorporate	628
Waldo, to extend and amend charter of	431
Wilton, to incorporate	381
Trustees, Bridgton Academy, incorporation of amended	478
Coburn Classical Institute, to incorporate	156
Hebron Academy, additional to charter	343
Public reservations, Hancock county, powers granted to	556
University of Maine, certain powers conferred on	581
Westbrook Seminary, relating to	177
Tuition of students of agriculture, University of Maine	169
Twitchell pond, close time on tributaries of	476
Tyler-Fogg Trust Company, to incorporate	628
Tyngstown Water Company, to incorporate	223

RESOLVES.

Tax on counties for 1903 and 1904	32
Temporary Home for Women and Children, in aid of	4
loans for 1903 and 1904, to authorize	15
Topographic survey, to provide for	31
Township C, in aid of repair of road in	33
Training School, Madawaska, in favor of	28
Transportation Company, Norcross, in favor of	34
Treaty, Hay-Bond, protest against	3
Trescott, town, in favor of	19
Trustees, University of Maine, in favor of	37

U.

PUBLIC LAWS.

Undertakers, registration of	74
Unincorporated townships, relating to roads and bridges in	14
Union of towns for employment of superintendent of schools	34
United States, act to cede jurisdiction of lands in Maine to	146
Unorganized townships, schooling of children in, relating to	98

PRIVATE AND SPECIAL LAWS.

Union Boom Company, to incorporate	428
Gas Company, to incorporate	162
Power Company, to incorporate	193
River Light, Gas and Power Company, in relation to powers of	16
to amend powers of	558
Water Storage Company, charter extended	333
Trust Company, of Saco, to incorporate	138
Wharf, additional powers conferred	169
Unity pond, to prevent throwing sawdust into tributaries of	400

	PAGE
University of Maine, students of agriculture at, relating to.....	169
Trustees of, certain powers conferred on...	581
Upper and Lower Black pond, to prohibit bait fishing in.......	413
Kezar pond, to regulate taking of black bass in.........	491
to prohibit taking smelts in tributaries of....	491

RESOLVES.

University of Maine, in favor of trustees of...................	37
Upton, town, in aid of repair of road in......................	33

V.

PUBLIC LAWS.

Vacancies, truant officer, how filled...........................	50
Vagabonds, relating to commitment of.........................	37
Vienna, town, ice fishing in certain ponds in, permitted........	126
Vital statistics, returns of, relating to........................	141
Voting, state and city elections, to regulate....................	132

PRIVATE AND SPECIAL LAWS.

Van Buren, St. John River Lumber Co., may erect piers and booms	337
Sewerage Company, to incorporate...............	297
Trust and Banking Company, charter extended...	166
name changed	166
Water Company, to increase stock and bonds of,	268
Vickery Realty Company, additional powers granted to.........	111
Village Cemetery Association, Searsport, to incorporate........	472
Corporation, Brooks, to incorporate.....................	529
East Pittston, relating to.................	567
Farmington, new charter granted.........	242
Rumford Falls, limits of extended........	106
Squirrel Island, to incorporate...........	93
Fire Company, Dover and Foxcroft, name changed and charter amended	17

RESOLVES.

Valuation of Drew and Reed plantations, to fix.................	32
Volunteers in war with Spain, extra pay for..................	9

W.

PUBLIC LAWS.

Waiving of provisions of will, relating to.......................	124
Waldo county, protection of shore birds in.....................	200
War, Aroostook, soldiers of, in aid of.........................	97
Washington county attorney, salary of, to establish............	167
judge of probate, salary of, to establish....	167
Watch and ward, repeal of sections relating to..................	44
Water, contracts for by municipalities.........................	49

INDEX.

	PAGE
Ways across lands for lumbering, bond may be given for damages,	101
across station grounds of railroads, relating to............	61
raising and lowering of, relating to damages from........	43
West Carry pond, ice fishing in, prohibition repealed............	126
White perch, close time on......................................	186
Whiting, town, fishing in Orange river, regulated..............	118
Whittier pond, ice fishing in, prohibition repealed..............	126
Widows of soldiers, burial of, relating to......................	159
waiving of provisions of wills by......................	59
Wild lands, trespassers on, relating to........................	121
Willimantic, town, Greenwood pond in, open for ice fishing....	119
Wills, waiving of provisions of, relating to....................	124
waiving of provisions of, by widows....................	59
Wilson pond, close time for trout in...........................	187
Wilton, town, close time for trout in...........................	187
Wires, electric, relating to......................................	102
Women appointed to solemnize marriages, etc., tenure and jurisdiction	82
married, relating to rights of...........................	57
Woodcock, close time for..	190
Work houses, new enactment, relating to......................	39
repeal of R. S. relating to......................	39
Works of art, to prevent injury to.............................	49

PRIVATE AND SPECIAL LAWS.

Waldo county, protection of deer in, act for....................	475
Street Railway Company, to amend and extend charter of,	71
Trust Company, to amend and extend charter of........	431
Waltham, to legalize doings of selectmen of....................	476
Wardens, to provide temporarily for payment of................	590
Ward lines, city of Calais, relating to..........................	345
Warren, Samuel D., authorized to erect piers and booms, Kennebec river	473
War with Spain, testimonials to soldiers who served in.........	209
Washington county, authorized to sell its railroad stock........	588
General Hospital, to incorporate...........	481
sale of railroad authorized................	219
Telephone Company, to incorporate...............	457
Water and Electric Power Company, Maine, charter extended..	470
Light Company, Peaks Island, to incorporate......	565
Power Company, Winn, charter amended..........	97
Bangor, to supply people of, with.......................	561
Damariscotta Mills, relating to control of..............	624
Houlton, to supply people of, with.....................	227
Lisbon, to supply people of, with......................	393
Water Company, Biddeford and Saco, authorized to issue bonds,	43
Bluehill, to extend charter of................	242
Bridgton, to amend charter of................	4
Brownville and Williamsburg, to incorporate..	333
Dexter, charter amended.....................	346
Greenville, to extend powers of..............	313
Hillside (Frankfort) to incorporate..........	459
Hillside (Winthrop) to incorporate..........	341
Hancock Light and Power, to incorporate....	288

INDEX.

	PAGE
Water Company, Liberty, to incorporate	239
Lilly, to incorporate	163
Livermore Falls, to incorporate	151
Lubec, to incorporate	364
Naples, to incorporate	517
Presque Isle, authorized to issue bonds	266
Prout's Neck, powers enlarged	270
Rangeley, to incorporate	106
Searsport, to incorporate	347
Strong, charter extended	292
Sullivan Harbor, to incorporate	449
Tyngstown, to incorporate	223
Van Buren, to increase stock and bonds of	268
Winthrop, Cold Spring, charter extended	268
to amend charter of	7
Wiscasset, charter amended	187
Water District, Augusta, to incorporate	509
Brunswick and Topsham, to incorporate	245
Gardiner, to incorporate	133
doubt removed	327
Water, Power and Electric Light Company, Buckfield, to incorporate	422
Company, Bodwell, authorized to generate electricity	132
Sebasticook, recognized	10
Waters, Lake Auburn, to protect	377
Water Storage Company, Union River, charter extended	333
supply, Boothbay Harbor, relative to	341
Brunswick, to defray expense of location of	360
Waterville and Oakland Street Railway, given additional powers,	82
Winslow Bridge Company, to incorporate	418
Treasurer and collector of taxes, relating to	517
Wayne pond, to prohibit ice fishing in	405
Weld pond, to prohibit ice fishing in	535
Wells Electric Light and Power Company, to incorporate	311
pond, to prohibit bait fishing in	412
Telephone Company, to incorporate	317
Wesleyan Grove Campmeeting Association, charter amended	158
Seminary and Female College, name changed	480
West Branch Driving and Reservoir Dam Company, to incorporate	277
Penobscot river, buoys in authorized	411
Westbrook, city of, charter amended	142
relating to	119
municipal court, charter amended	188
Seminary, trustees of, relating to	177
Western Hancock municipal court, charter amended	161
Wharf, Johnson's bay, B. M. Pike authorized to build into	567
Long lake, Longwood Real Estate Co., to construct into,	527
Lubec Narrows, B. M. Pike authorized to build into	567
C. J. Clark authorized to build into	564
J. C. Pike authorized to build into	564
Sebec lake, E. J. Mayo authorized to build into	400
Union, additional powers given	169

INDEX.

	PAGE
Widow's Island, acceptance of, relating to	570
Widows' Wood Society, Portland, charter amended	198
Williamsburg, to legalize acts of	166
Wilson Stream Dam Company, relating to	81
Wilton Electric Light and Power Company, charter extended	157
lake, to regulate fishing in tributaries of	535
open season for fishing in, relating to	550
Trust Company, to incorporate	381
Winn Water and Power Company, charter amended	97
Winterport, Frankfort and Prospect Electric Railway, to incorporate	440
Winterville Plantation, to change name of	591
Winthrop and Manchester, may receive electricity from Augusta, Winthrop and Gardiner Ry.	119
Cold Spring Water Co., relating to charter of	7, 268
municipal court, to establish	538
Wiscasset bridge made a public bridge	585
Water Company, charter amended	187
Waterville and Farmington Ry. Co., franchises extended	74
Wood Island annexed to Phippsburg	628
Society, Portland, Widows', charter amended	198

RESOLVES.

Waiving of forfeiture of public lots	17
Wallagrass plantation, in aid of bridge in	49
War with Spain, extra pay for soldiers in	9
Washburn, town, in aid of bridge in	54
West Branch, St. Croix river, in aid of bridge across	39
Western State Normal School, appropriation for	51
Woman's Christian Temperance Union, in favor of	17

Y.

PUBLIC LAWS.

Yards, fuel, to enable establishment of	95
York county attorney, salary established	48
treasurer, salary established	15
Youth, better education of, act for	53

PRIVATE AND SPECIAL LAWS.

Yard tracks, Bangor and Aroostook Railroad Company authorized to extend same in Houlton	70
York county, better protection of deer in	231
town of, authorized to construct sewers	548
Young Women's Christian Association, Portland, relating to	269

RESOLVES.

Year Book, in favor of purchase of	11
York deeds, in relation to	35
Young Men's Christian Associations, in favor of	52
Women's Home, in favor of	18

Lightning Source UK Ltd.
Milton Keynes UK
UKHW020019181218
334174UK00006B/136/P